D1561287

THE BLACKWELL COMPANION
TO LAW AND SOCIETY

BLACKWELL COMPANIONS TO SOCIOLOGY

The *Blackwell Companions to Sociology* provide introductions to emerging topics and theoretical orientations in sociology as well as presenting the scope and quality of the discipline as it is currently configured. Essays in the Companions tackle broad themes or central puzzles within the field and are authored by key scholars who have spent considerable time in research and reflection on the questions and controversies that have activated interest in their area. This authoritative series will interest those studying sociology at advanced undergraduate or graduate level as well as scholars in the social sciences and informed readers in applied disciplines.

Series List:

Forthcoming

The Blackwell Companion to Law and Society

Edited by

Austin Sarat

Blackwell
Publishing

© 2004 by Blackwell Publishing Ltd
except for editorial material and organization © 2004 by Austin Sarat

BLACKWELL PUBLISHING
350 Main Street, Malden, MA 02148-5020, USA
108 Cowley Road, Oxford OX4 1JF, UK
550 Swanston Street, Carlton, Victoria 3053, Australia

First published 2004 by Blackwell Publishing Ltd

Library of Congress Cataloging-in-Publication Data

The Blackwell companion to law and society / edited by Austin Sarat.
    p. cm. – (Blackwell companions to sociology ; 11)
Includes bibliographical references and index.
  ISBN 0-631-22896-9 (hardback : alk. paper)
1. Law–Social aspects. I. Sarat, Austin. II. Series.
K370.B554 2004
340′.115–dc22

                                                                2003019975

A catalogue record for this title is available from the British Library.

Set in 10/12pt Sabon
by Kolam Information Services Pvt. Ltd, Pondicherry, India
Printed and bound in the United Kingdom
by TJ International, Padstow, Cornwall

For further information on
Blackwell Publishing, visit our website:
http://www.blackwellpublishing.com

For my son Benjamin, my sweet prince.

Contents

Preface

The invitation to put together a one volume "companion" to a field as diverse as "law and society" was, as one could readily imagine, both exciting and daunting. Taking up this invitation provided a wonderful opportunity to survey the field, and to renew my acquaintance with the range of work being done in it and the wonderful scholars doing that work. Editing this volume was a re-education in itself. But the very range and diversity of scholarship posed a substantial challenge. What to include? What not to include? How to represent the breadth of theories, methods, and perspectives found in the law and society community?

These were formidable challenges. Despite the hard choices, inevitable omissions, and shades of emphasis, I am satisfied that *The Blackwell Companion to Law and Society* does a reasonable job in providing a guide to the field. Indeed the more than 30 essays in this volume may well constitute the best introduction to the field currently available. While working from a common template, all the authors interpreted their directions in their own ways. Readers will recognize a common format while also appreciating the various ways that format has been adapted. Taken together the essays collected here trace the evolution and history of the field, chart the present state of knowledge produced in law and society, and point to fruitful directions for further inquiry.

As surely as it highlights the diversity and fragmentation of the field of law and society scholarship, a compilation of research such as this inevitably tends toward "canonization" of a particular map of knowledge, a particular set of problems, and a particular set of texts. That is unavoidable and, to some extent, beneficial. Canonization helps us recognize what we share. It also provides a fruitful terrain of conflict and contestation. While having one's work canonized means having the pleasure of seeing one's name in lights, it carries with it the need to endure slings and arrows slung and shot by those seeking to advance new paradigms or just prove their academic mettle. A canon also might be thought of as a staple of shared knowledge, the things all of us must know if we are to be literate as law and society scholars, the things we need to read regardless of our particular subfield or research specialization.

While canons are about quality, they are also about work that defines who we are by identifying common concerns, concerns that go to the heart of problems and issues that recur in many, if not all, of the subfields that comprise law and society scholarship. Canons make demands on us as readers, requiring us to read beyond the limits of our most narrowly defined expertise, requiring us to remain familiar with theories and methods beyond those with which we are most comfortable.

As an advocate for disciplinization (a truly ugly word), I am drawn to Jack Balkin and Sanford Levinson's claim that "Every discipline, because it is a discipline, has a canon, a set of standard texts, approaches, problems, examples, or stories that its members repeatedly employ or invoke, and which help define the discipline as a discipline. If the study of law," they say, "is a discipline, it too must have its canons and its own sense of the canonical" (see ch. 3, p.31). For me a discipline is less a set of shared methods or theories (by that definition there would indeed be very few disciplines) than a set of shared conversations, or shared communities of readers. For each of us the canon establishes the minimum grammar with which we must be familiar if we are to talk law and society and to have our talk recognized by others. In this sense the canon provides one of the sets of horizontal linkages that define a discipline, setting off one set of intellectual inquiries from another. While the boundaries of the canon, like the boundaries of a grammar, are shifting, fluid, and contested, without a canon there can be little intelligible conversation.

But canons also provide a vertical or historical connection, a way for one generation to speak to another. Like the good parent who must – or so the books say – provide ways of being in the world for their children, both as a source of stability but also as the fuel of rebellion, so too a discipline that wants to take seriously its obligations to younger scholars must not shy away from the complex task of canonization. While having a hollow core may look like a way of being open, it is, I think, really a way of avoiding one generation's responsibility to another. If we cannot identify the faces that adorn our own Mount Rushmore, we cannot hope to earn the loyalties of those who will come after us, those who we would like to speak to us and about us in an unnamed future. Indeed, as Balkin and Levinson argue, "there is no better way to understand a discipline – its underlying assumptions, its current concerns and anxieties – than to study what its members think is canonical ... The study of canons and canonicity is the key to the secrets of the culture and its characteristic modes of thought."

Of course, canons and canonization also generate arguments about what is in and who is out. Listing the canon or candidates for canonization is always perilous, not only because it hurts the feelings of those not named and leads to blaming of the list makers, but because canons cannot be legislated or brought into being merely through naming and claiming. They exist as social facts, as empirical documentable phenomena in our syllabi, our footnotes, our stock of stories, the shared consciousness and taken-for-granted sense of who we are. But so too do the disagreements about the canon. Those disagreements are often healthy even when they are unpleasant.

What is honored by canonization may make us feel marginal if it seems distant from what we do or know. What is criticized as being unworthy of canonization may make us angry if it seems to embody the theories or methods that we deploy in our work. But contests over the canon keep the canon fresh; they renew it by requiring those who would defend this or that set of inclusions and exclusions to make explicit the questions or insights they see as defining the field. In so doing history becomes memory, the past becomes present. The taken-for-granted is renewed and reinvigorated as it is made explicit

The Blackwell Companion to Law and Society represents one document in the continuing articulation and contestation of the field called law and society. Because it is produced at a time of both a great vitality and great fragmentation in the field, what it canonizes will for some seem just right and, for others, will seem unduly tilted in this direction or that. However any reader receives it, I hope this book provides a way station, a temporary touchstone, honoring the contributions of law and society scholarship and fueling its further development.

I am grateful to the contributors for taking on the challenging work of field assessment. I am also grateful to Susan Rabinowitz, who proposed that I undertake this project and was very helpful in its earliest stages of development, and to Ken Provencher who saw it through to production. Thanks to Greg Call, Dean of the Faculty at Amherst College for his generous financial support and my colleagues in Amherst College's Department of Law, Jurisprudence, and Social Thought for providing a rich intellectual environment in which to work. Thanks especially to Stephanie, Lauren, Emily, and Benjamin for being the best of all companions.

Austin Sarat
July, 2003

Contributors

Gad Barzilai is professor in the political science department and also teaches in the law school. at Tel-Aviv University. He cofounded in 1996 the Law, Politics, and Society Program at Tel Aviv University, which is the first program in Israel in that field for graduate students. Since then he has been its codirector. In 1998 he cofounded the Israel Association of Law and Society, and later was its cochair (2000-1). He is active in several prestigious boards including the American Journal of Political Science, the American Association of Israel Studies, the Israel Association of Law and Society, and the International Committee of the Law and Society Association. He was a member of the Program Committee (2003) of the Law and Society Association. Among his books are *Communities and Law: Politics and Cultures of Legal Identities* (2003), *The Attorney General: Authority and Responsibility. Principles, Institutions in Comparative Perspective, Analysis and Recommendations for Reforms*, No. 6 (with David Nachmias, 1997), *Wars, Internal Conflicts, and Political Order* (1996), *The Israeli Supreme Court and the Israeli Public* (with Zeev Segal and Efraim Yaar, 1994), and *A Democracy in Wartime: Conflict and Consensus in Israel* (1992).

Jeannine Bell is Associate Professor of Law at Indiana University. She joined the faculty at Indiana in 1999, and is also an adjunct professor in the Department of Political Science. Her courses include Criminal Process, Seminars on the First Amendment, and Law and Society. Professor Bell is the author of *Policing Hatred: Law Enforcement, Civil Rights, and Hate Crime* (2002). She is a coauthor of another book, *Gaining Access to Research Sites*. She has written articles on the Family and Medical Leave Act, and on the legal response to hate crimes.

Susan B. Boyd is Professor of Law and holds the Chair in Feminist Legal Studies at the University of British Columbia, Canada. She is author of *Child Custody, Law, and Women's Work* (2003). Her edited collection *Challenging the Public/Private Divide: Feminism, Law, and Public Policy* was published in 1997.

Rosemary J. Coombe is a Tier One Canada Research Chair in Law, Communication, and Cultural Studies at York University in Toronto, where she teaches in the Communications and Culture Joint PhD/MA Program, and is cross-appointed to the Osgoode Hall Faculty of Law Graduate Program, and the Graduate Program in Social and Political Thought. Her work addresses the cultural, political, and social implications of intellectual property laws. Her book, *The Cultural Life of Intellectual Properties* is a legal ethnography of the ways in which intellectual property law shapes cultural politics in consumer societies. Recently, she has been working on two projects. With Andrew Herman she is engaged in a study of the ethics of property and propriety involved in the management of trademarks on the worldwide web and the ways in which digital environments enable consumers to interrupt and to contest the corporate assumption of goodwill.

Roger Cotterrell is Professor of Legal Theory at Queen Mary College, University of London. He is author of *The Sociology of Law* (2nd edn., 1992), *The Politics of Jurisprudence* (1989; US edn. 1992), *Law's Community* (1995), and *Emile Durkheim: Law In a Moral Domain* (1999), and editor of *Law, Democracy and Social Justice* (with B. Bercusson, 1988), *Law and Society* (1994), and *Sociological Perspectives on Law* (2001). In addition, he has published over 70 articles and essays related to his primary specialties, sociolegal theory and jurisprudence, as well as papers on public law, criminology, and the law of trusts. He is a member of the advisory boards of the *Journal of Law and Society*, *Sociologia del Diritto*, and the *Griffith Law Review*. He was Trustee of the Law and Society Association (USA) (1996–9), Chair of the LSA's Articles Prize Committee (1999–2000), and a member of the UK National Research Assessment Exercise Law Panel (1999–2001).

Eve Darian-Smith is Professor of Law and Society at the University of California, Santa Barbara. Her book *Bridging Divides: The Channel Tunnel and English Legal Identity* (1999) won the Law and Society Association's Best Book Prize. She is coeditor of *Laws of the Postcolonial* (1999) and author of the forthcoming *Culture, Custom, Power, Law: The Implications of Legal Anthropology for the Study of Law*. She is coeditor with Bill Felstiner of *Onati Proceedings*.

Lauren B. Edelman is Professor of Law and Sociology in the Jurisprudence and Social Policy Program at the University of California-Berkeley. She has published widely on the intersection of law and work, including empirical studies of organizational response to civil rights law, and of how human resource professionals interpret, implement, and transform civil rights law. She received a Guggenheim Fellowship in 2000, was President of the Law and Society Association in 2002–3, and was Fellow at the Center for Advanced Studies in the Social and Behavioral Sciences in 2003–4.

Lee Epstein is the Edward Mallinckrodt Distinguished University Professor of Political Science and Professor of Law at Washington University. She is the author or coauthor of over 70 articles and essays, as well as 12 books, including *The Supreme Court and Legal Change*, the *Constitutional Law for a Changing America Series* (moving into its 5th edition), *The Supreme Court Compendium* (now in its 3rd edition; winner of a Special Recognition Honor from the Law and Courts Section of the American Political Science Association and an Outstanding Academic Book Award from *Choice*), and *The Choices Justices Make* (winner of the Pritchett award for the Best Book on Law and Courts). She is a former chair of the Law and

Courts Section of the American Political Science Association and is currently the President of the Midwest Political Science Association.

Patricia Ewick is Professor of Sociology at Clark University. She is coeditor of *Studies in Law, Politics, and Society* and was associate editor of the *Law & Society Review*. Among her publications are "The Architecture of Authority: Law, Space and Science" (with Susan Silbey, in *The Place of Law*, Austin Sarat and Thomas Kearns, eds., 2003), "Mending Fences: Beyond the Epistemological Divide," *Law & Society Review* (2001), *Social Science, Social Policy, and the Law* (with Robert Kagan and Austin Sarat, 1999), and *The Common Place of Law: Stories from Everyday Life* (with Susan Silbey, 1998).

Laura E. Gómez is Professor of Law and Sociology at UCLA. She is the author of *Misconceiving Mothers: Legislators, Prosecutors, and the Politics of Prenatal Drug Exposure*. She is currently working on a book about law, race, and politics in nineteenth-century New Mexico. At UCLA she served as the codirector, with Professor Jerry Kang, of the School of Law's Concentration in Critical Race Studies, founded in 2000. She clerked for Judge Dorothy W. Nelson of the US Court of Appeals for the Ninth Circuit and worked in Congress as an aide to Senator Jeff Bingaman. She has served as an officer and member of the Board of Trustees of the Law and Society Association.

Lisa Hajjar teaches in the Law and Society Program at the University of California-Santa Barbara. She is the author of *Authority, Resistance and the Law: A Study of the Israeli Military Court System in the West Bank and Gaza* (forthcoming), "Law Against Order: Human Rights Organizations and the Palestinian Authority," *University of Miami Law Review* (2002), and "Sovereign Bodies, Sovereign States, and the Problem of Torture," *Studies in Law, Politics, and Society* (2002). She is a member of the Board of Trustees of the Law and Society Association.

Kathryn Hendley is Professor of Law and Political Science at the University of Wisconsin. She is a member of the Advisory Board, Central and East European Law Initiative of the American Bar Association and the Advisory Board on the Initiative in the Former Soviet Union, The John D. and Catherine T. MacArthur Foundation. Recent publications include "Which Mechanisms Support the Fulfillment of Sales Agreements? Asking Decision-makers in Firms," *Economic Letters* (with Peter Murrell, 2002), "Suing the State in Russia," *Post-Soviet Affairs* (2002), and "Punitive Damages for Contractual Breaches in Comparative Perspective: The Use of Penalties by Russian Enterprises, *Wisconsin Law Review* (with Peter Murrell and Randi Ryterman, 2001).

Valerie P. Hans is Professor of Criminal Justice and Psychology at the University of Delaware and holds a secondary appointment in the Legal Studies Program. In addition, she has been a visiting scholar at Stanford Law School, University of Pennsylvania Law School, the Wharton School of Business at the University of Pennsylvania, and the School of Law at the University of Cardiff in Wales. She served as Codirector of Research for the Special Committee on Gender of the District of Columbia Circuit's Task Force on Gender and Racial Bias, and is a member of the Delaware Task Force on Effective Use of Juries. She has participated in the grant review panel for the Law and Social Sciences Program of the National Science Foundation, and has been a member of the executive boards of the Law and

Society Association and the American Psychology-Law Society. Among her publications are *Judging the Jury* (with Neil Vidmar, 1986) and *Business on Trial: The Civil Jury and Corporate Responsibility* (2000).

Robert A. Kagan is Professor of Political Science and Law at the University of California, Berkeley, and director of the Center for the Study of Law and Society. His books include *Regulatory Justice; Going By the Book* (with E. Bardach), *Regulatory Encounters: Multinational Corporations and American Adversarial Legalism*, *Adversarial Legalism: The American Way of Law*, and *Shades of Green: Business, Regulation, and the Environment* (with N. Gunningham & D. Thornton).

Jack Knight is Sidney W. Sovers Professor of Government; Resident Fellow, Center in Political Economy; and Member, Committee on Social Thought and Analysis at Washington University. He has a BA and a JD from the University of North Carolina at Chapel Hill, and MA and PhD from the University of Chicago. His primary areas of interest are modern social and political theory, law and legal theory, political economy, and philosophy of social science. His publications include *Institutions and Social Conflict* (1992) and *Explaining Social Institutions* (with Itai Sened, 1995), and *The Choices Justices Make* (with Lee Epstein, 1997), as well as articles in various journals and edited volumes.

Nicola Lacey is Professor of Criminal Law at the London School of Economics and Adjunct Professor of Social and Political Theory at the Research School of Social Sciences of the Australian National University. She is the author of *State Punishment* (1988), *The Politics of Community* (with Elizabeth Frazer, 1993), *Unspeakable Subjects* (1998), and *Reconstructing Criminal Law* (with Celia Wells and Oliver Quick, 3rd edn., 2003). She is a Fellow of the British Academy and was in 2001 and 2003 visiting member of the Global Law Faculty at New York University.

Michael McCann is the Gordon Hirabayashi Professor for the Advancement of Citizenship at the University of Washington. He is author of *Rights at Work: Pay Equity Reform and the Politics of Legal Mobilization* (1994) and coauthor of *Distorting the Law: Politics, Mass Media, and the Litigation Crisis* (2004). He is currently working on a series of projects analyzing the political backlash against egalitarian civil rights and related social policies in the United States over the last 50 years.

Sally Engle Merry is Marion Butler McLean Professor in the History of Ideas and Professor of Anthropology at Wellesley College. She is also codirector of the Peace and Justice Studies Program. Her recent book, *Colonizing Hawai'i: The Cultural Power of Law* (2000), received the 2001 J. Willard Hurst Prize from the Law and Society Association. Her other books include *Law and Empire in the Pacific: Hawai'i and Fiji* (coedited with Donald Brenneis, forthcoming), *The Possibility of Popular Justice: A Case Study of American Community Mediation* (coedited with Neal Milner, 1993), *Getting Justice and Getting Even: Legal Consciousness among Working Class Americans* (1990), and *Urban Danger: Life in a Neighborhood of Strangers* (1981). She is past president of the Law and Society Association and the Association for Political and Legal Anthropology.

Elizabeth Mertz is Professor of Law at the University of Wisconsin and Senior Research Fellow at the American Bar Foundation. Recent publications include "The Perfidy of Gaze and the Pain of Uncertainty: Anthropological Theory and the

Search for Closure," in *Ethnography in Unstable Places: Everyday Lives in Contexts of Dramatic Political Change* (2002), *Ethnography in Unstable Places: Everyday Lives in Contexts of Dramatic Political Change* (edited with Carol Greenhouse and Kay Warren, 2002), and "Teaching Lawyers the Language of Law: Legal and Anthropological Translations," *John Marshall Law Review* (2001). Her current study, "The Language of Legal Education: A Sociolinguistic/Semiotic Study of the First-Year Law School Classroom," involves observational research in eight law schools across the country. This project was jointly funded by the American Bar Foundation and the Spencer Foundation. Her most recent project, conducted jointly with anthropologist Carol Greenhouse and sociologist Wamucii Njogu, will examine the careers of senior legal academics.

Leslie J. Moran is Head of Department of the Faculty of Law at Birkbeck College, University of London. He has written extensively on matters relating to gay issues in the law. He is one of a multidisciplinary team undertaking the largest study of lesbians, gay men, violence, and safety in the UK. The project is funded by the Economic and Social Research Council as part of an initiative on violence research. In 2000 he was visiting research fellow at Macquarie University undertaking research with Andrew Sharpe on violence against transgender people in Sydney. In December 2000 he organized a multidisciplinary seminar at Birkbeck on Critical Reflections on Hate Crime. He jointly organized "Law's Moving Image: A Conference on Law and Film," held at the Tate Gallery, Millbank in January 2001. He is currently editing a special edition of *Law and Critique* on "Critical Reflections on Hate Crime," and a volume of essays on law and film. He is completing a book provisionally entitled *Queer Violence*. He is a member of the editorial boards of *Law & Society Review*, *Law and Critique*, and *The Liverpool Law Review*.

Frank Munger is Professor of Law at New York Law School. A former editor of *Law & Society Review* and President of the Law and Society Association, his recent publications include *Laboring Below the Line: The New Ethnography of Poverty, Low-Wage Work, and Survival in the Global Economy* and *Rights of Inclusion: Law and Identity in the Lives of Americans with Disabilities* (with David Engel).

David Nelken is Distinguished Professor of Sociology and Legal Institutions and Social Change at the University of Macerata in Italy and Distinguished Research Professor of Law in Cardiff Law School, University of Wales. He previously taught law at Cambridge (1974–76), Edinburgh (1976–84), and University College, London (1984–90; Visiting Professor 1990–2000). He received a Distinguished Scholar award from the American Sociological Association (Criminology section) in 1985 and is currently a Trustee of the USA Law and Society Association and Vice President of the Research Committee on Law of the International Sociological Association. From 1992–2000 he was a member of the Secure Cities Committee of experts of the Emilia Romagna region of Italy. He has been Visiting Professor at Berkeley, Copenhagen, Florence, Jerusalem, New York, and Tel Aviv. He edits two series of criminology books and is on the editorial boards of 14 scientific journals. Recent books include *Comparing Legal Cultures*, *Contrasting Criminal Justice*, *Adapting Legal Cultures*, and *Law's New Boundaries*.

Laura Beth Nielsen is Research Associate at the American Bar Foundation. Recent publications include "Subtle, Pervasive, Harmful: Racist and Sexist Remarks in Public as Hate Speech," *Journal of Social Issues* (2002) and "Situating Legal

Consciousness: Experiences and Attitudes of Ordinary Citizens About Law and Street Harassment," *Law & Society Review* (2000). She is a member of the Board of Trustees, Law and Society Association and is coeditor of *Law & Social Inquiry*. She won the Dissertation Prize of the Law and Society Association in 2000.

Pat O'Malley is Canada Research Chair in Criminology and Criminal Justice, and Professor in the Departments of Sociology and Anthropology and of Law, at Carleton University, and was until recently Professor of Law and Deputy Dean of the Faculty of Law and Management, and Director of the National Centre for Socio-Legal Studies, at La Trobe University, Australia. He is the author and editor of many publications in the field of risk and security, and has been a member of various government bodies working in related areas of criminal justice, drug policy, and crime prevention. He is an editor of the Cambridge University Press "Law and Society" series, and serves on the editorial and advisory boards of many major international journals in the field. Much of his recent work has focused on the role of risk-based models in the government of social problems, including two edited collections: *Crime and the Risk Society* and *Crime Prevention in Australia*. Other recent published work has included field studies of drug dealing, analysis of the globalization of legal sanctions, and theoretical examination of contemporary governance. In 2000 he was awarded the Sellin–Gleuck Award by the American Society of Criminology for outstanding contributions to the discipline.

Tanina Rostain is Associate Professor of Law Codirector, Center for Professional Values and Practice at New York Law School. Her current research focuses on how lawyers and accountants interpret legal questions, a topic that has assumed great visibility after the collapse of energy giant Enron and the subsequent investigation of its accounting firm, Arthur Andersen. Among her publications are "Professional Commitments in a Changed World," *Fordham Law Review* (2002), "Educating Homo Economicus: Cautionary Notes on the New Behavioral Law and Economics Movement," *Law & Society Review* (2000), and "Ethics Lost: Limitations of Current Approaches to Lawyer Regulation," *Southern California Law Review* (1998).

Austin Sarat is William Nelson Cromwell Professor of Jurisprudence and Political Science and Professor of Law, Jurisprudence, and Social Thought at Amherst College. He is a past President of the Law and Society Association and the Association for the Study of Law, Culture, and the Humanities. He is the author or editor of more than 40 books, including *When the State Kills: Capital Punishment and the American Condition*, *Law's Violence* (with Thomas Kearns), *The Killing State*, *Pain, Death, and the Law*, and *Divorce Lawyers and Their Clients* (with William Felstiner). In 1997 he received The Harry Kalven Award given by the Law and Society Association for "distinguished research on law and society."

Stuart A. Scheingold is Professor Emeritus of Political Science at the University of Washington. Recent publications include *Cause Lawyering and the State in a Global Era* and *Cause Lawyering: Political Commitments and Professional Responsibilities* (both with Austin Sarat), and *Politics, Crime Control and Culture*. Previous publications include *The Politics of Rights: Lawyers, Public Policy and Political Change*, *The Politics of Law and Order: Street Crime and Public Policy*, and *The Politics of Street Crime: Criminal Process and Cultural Obsession*. He was a 1995 Research Fellow of the Japan Society for the Promotion of Science and in 1998–9 he held the

Walter S. Owen Visiting Chair in Law at the University of British Columbia. In 2001 he was awarded the Harry J. Kalven, Jr. Prize by the Law and Society Association.

Carroll Seron is Professor of Public Affairs and Sociology at Baruch College of the City University of New York. She is the author of *The Part-time Paradox: Time Norms, Professional Life, Family and Gender* (with Cynthia Fuchs Epstein, Bonnie Oglensky, and Robert Saute, 1999), *The Business of Practicing Law: The Work Lives of Solo and Small-Firm Attorneys* (1996), *Rationalizing Justice: The Political Economy of the Federal District Courts* (with Wolf Heydebrand, 1990), and *Court Reorganization: The Politics of Reform in the Federal Bankruptcy Court* (1978).

Richard K. Sherwin is Professor of Law at New York Law School. An expert on the use of visual representations and visual persuasion in litigation and litigants' public relations, he has written widely on the interrelationship between law and culture, including interdisciplinary works on law and rhetoric, discourse theory, political legitimacy, and the theoretical and practical dimensions of the relationship between law and film/television. A frequent public speaker both in the USA and abroad, he is a regular commentator for television, radio, and print media on the relationship between law, culture, and film, and has appeared on NBC's "Today Show," CourtTV, WNET, and National Public Radio. He is the author of *When Law Goes Pop: The Vanishing Line Between Law and Popular Culture* (2000).

Susan S. Silbey is Professor of Anthropology at MIT. She has written about the social organization of law in diverse institutional and informal settings including attorney generals' offices, courts, schools, private homes, and businesses; she has also studied alternative forms of dispute resolution including negotiation and mediation. She edited *Studies in Law, Politics, and Society* (1990–97) and *Law & Society Review* (1998–2000). In 1998, she published *The Common Place of Law: Stories from Everyday Life* (with Patricia Ewick) describing the ways in which Americans imagine, use, and construct the rule of law. Her current research looks at the roles and conceptions of law in scientific laboratories, comparing the place of law in expert communities and popular culture. She is supervising research on the development of new safety regimes in research labs, the effects of laboratory organization on gender hierarchies in science, and variations in engineering education. Professor Silbey is Past President of the Law and Society Association, and a fellow of the American Academy of Political and Social Science.

Jonathan Simon is Professor of Jurisprudence and Social Policy at the University of California, Berkeley. He obtained an AB in 1981, a JD in 1987, and a PhD in jurisprudence and social policy in 1991, all from the University of California at Berkeley. After law school he clerked for Judge William C. Canby, Jr., of the US Court of Appeals for the Ninth Circuit. He has written widely on criminal law and crime generally. In November 1999, he was awarded a Soros Senior Justice fellowship from the Open Society Institute to develop into a book his scholarship on the role of crime policy in transforming governance. Recent publications include *Cultural Analysis, Cultural Studies, and the Law: Moving Beyond Legal Realism* (with Austin Sarat, 2003) and *Embracing Risk: The Changing Culture of Insurance and Responsibility* (with Tom Baker, 2002).

Francis Snyder is Professor of European Law at the Université d'Aix-Marseille III, France, Centennial Visiting Professor at the London School of Economics, and

Professor of Law at the College of Europe (Bruges and Natolin). He is Codirector of the Academy of International Trade Law, Macao, China. His special interests are in European law, international trade law, and globalization and the law. The many honors, prizes, and research awards that he has received include Phi Beta Kappa, Charles Washburn Clark Prize, Wrexham Prize, Fulbright Fellowship, Ford Foundation Foreign Area Fellowship, Research Associate Award of the Canadian International Development Research Center, nomination for the Herskovits Prize, and Nuffield Foundation Social Science Personal Research Fellowship. He is the author or editor of approximately 20 books and the author of 160 articles. His books include *International Trade and Customs Law of the European Union* (1998), *Introduction to European Union Law* (in Chinese, 1996, 2nd edition in preparation), *New Directions in European Community Law* (1990), *Common Agricultural Policy of the European Community* (1990), and *Law of the Common Agricultural Policy* (1985). Among books he has edited are *The Europeanization of Law: The Legal Effects of European Integration* (2000), *Constitutional Dimensions of European Economic Integration* (1996), and *European Community Law* (1993).

Susan Sterett is Professor of Political Science at the University of Denver. She is the author of *Creating Constitutionalism?* (1997), *Public Pensions: Gender and Civic Service in the States, 1850–1937* (2003) and articles in journals including *Comparative Political Studies*, *Law and Social Inquiry*, *Studies in American Political Development*, and *Law & Society Review*.

Tom Tyler is Professor of Psychology and Law at New York University. He works in the areas of the dynamics of authority in groups, organizations, and societies; the psychology of justice; and law and regulation. Publications include *The Social Psychology of Procedural Justice* (with Allen Lind, 1980), "Public Trust and Confidence in Legal Authorities: What Do Majority and Minority Group Members Want From the Law and Legal Authorities?" *Behavioral Science and the Law* (2001); and *Why People Obey The Law: Procedural Justice, Legitimacy, and Compliance* (2000).

Francisco Valdes is Professor of Law at the University of Miami. He is a leading figure in the "LatCrit" movement and in gay rights scholarship. Professor Valdes is codirector of the Center for Hispanic and Caribbean Legal Studies and cochair of LatCrit, Inc. He teaches civil procedure, comparative law, critical race theory, law and sexuality, law and film, and US constitutional law. Recent publications include "Barely at the Margins: Looking for Latinas/os in the Law School Curriculum – A Survey With LatCritical Commentary,"*University of Florida Law Review* (2001), "Centering the Politics of Race in the Selection of George the Second: Scholars of Color Invoking the Traditions of Remembrance and Resistance," *Dickinson Law Review* (2001), and "Introduction, LatCrit at Five: Growing the Movement, Building the Institution, Incubating the Future," *Denver University Law Review* (with Elizabeth M. Iglesias, 2001).

Neil Vidmar is Russell M. Robinson II Professor of Law at Duke University. He has written numerous articles on criminal and civil juries and is coauthor of *Judging the Jury* (with Valerie Hans, 1986). In 1995 he published *Medical Malpractice and the American Jury: Confronting the Myths About Jury Incompetence, Deep Pockets and Outrageous Damage Awards*. A current jury project, supported by the National

Science Foundation, the State Justice Institute, and the American Bar Foundation, involved unprecedented access to the videotaped deliberations of 50 civil juries from the state of Arizona. Other research has involved the topics of alternative dispute resolution, procedural justice, battered woman syndrome and other forms of expert evidence, the Ontario Business Practices Act, mediation in domestic violence cases, and the death penalty. Two recent book chapters explore the social and psychological dynamic of retribution and revenge.

Jonathan Yovel is a senior lecturer of law and philosophy at the University of Haifa, Israel, as well as an author, lawyer, and civil rights activist. He was previously engaged in graduate studies of law, philosophy, and linguistics at Tel-Aviv, Oxford, Chicago and Northwestern. His diverse areas of research fall into two general categories: law and language; and theories of contract, commercial law, and related obligation. He has written and taught in the areas of contracts, ethics, political theory, jurisprudence, law and literature, and law and social sciences. Recent work appeared in *Northwestern University Law Review, Emory Law Journal, Cardozo Law Review, Cardozo Studies in Law and Literature, Stanford Agora, International Journal for the Semiotics of Law,* and elsewhere. He is a recipient of several research grants, and was a visitor at the University of Toronto Faculty of Law, Max Planck Institute, Heidelberg, Fordham University School of Law, and other academic institutions. His current interests center around legal polyphony, conceptions of tragedy, lay conceptions of justice, and relational and distributive approaches to contract law. His collection of short stories in Hebrew, *Trojan Horse,* has recently appeared.

1

Vitality Amidst Fragmentation: On the Emergence of Postrealist Law and Society Scholarship

Austin Sarat

In 1986 the Committee on Law and Social Science of the Social Science Research Council produced a volume entitled *Law and the Social Sciences*. This 740-page book, edited by two distinguished Yale Law Professors – Leon Lipson and Stanton Wheeler – was designed to be "a volume of assessment . . . not a collection of speculative essays and not a set of fresh research" (Lipson and Wheeler, 1986: 5). It contained 11 chapters, varied in the breadth of their coverage from the all-encompassing "Legal Systems of the World" and "Law and the Normative Order" to the more focused "Legislation" and "Lawyers." Each was written by a leading figure in the field who was instructed to survey available research in a designated subfield, highlighting the particular contributions of social science to our understanding of various legal phenomena. *Law and the Social Sciences* played an important role in the development of law and society research, appearing as it did in a period two decades into the life of the modern law and society movement in the United States. Rereading these essays one is struck by several things: their confidence about social science, their almost complete disinterest in issues of culture and identity, their association of law with the boundaries of nation-states, and their easy transition from description to prescription. Collectively the contributions were deemed by the editors to give "ample testimony to the vitality of sociolegal research as it has been practiced over the last quarter of a century" (Lipson and Wheeler, 1986: 10).

As they described the field, Lipson and Wheeler (1986: 2) highlighted two dimensions that gave it its shape and center of gravity. First, they said, is "the . . . perception that law is a social phenomenon and that legal doctrine and actors are integral parts of the social landscape." Second, they contended, is the view "that legal institutions not only are embedded in social life, but can be improved by drawing on the organized wisdom of social experience." At the time they wrote, law and society work was fully identified with the social scientific enterprise, and the social scientific enterprise was associated with a normative, reformist, policy orientation (Sarat and Silbey, 1988). Reflecting the continuing legacy of legal realism's optimism about the role of empirical research in the legal world (Schlegel, 1979) it was described, by the editors, as "the product of a generation of scholars – mostly social scientists and law professors – who believe that the perspectives, data, and methods of the social sciences are essential to a better understanding of law" (Lipson and Wheeler, 1986: 1).

FROM LEGAL REALISM TO LAW AND SOCIETY

The image of law and society as a field defined by the idea of enlisting social science to understand law and inform legal policy traces its lineage at least to the work of the early twentieth-century legal realists.[1] As is by now well known, realism emerged as part of the progressive response to the collapse of the nineteenth-century laissez-faire political economy. By attacking the classical conception of law with its assumptions about the independent and objective movement from preexisting rights to decisions in specific cases (Cohen, 1935; Llewellyn, 1931, 1960), realists opened the way for a vision of law as policy, a vision in which law could and should be guided by pragmatic and/or utilitarian considerations (Llewellyn, 1940).[2] Exposing the difference between law in the books and law in action, realists established the need to approach law making and adjudication strategically with an eye toward difficulties in implementation. Exploring the ways in which law in action, for example the law found in lower criminal courts, was often caught up in politics, realists provided the energy and urgency for reform designed to rescue the legal process and restore its integrity.[3] Realism attacked "all dogmas and devices that cannot be translated into terms of actual experience" (Cohen, 1935: 822); it criticized conceptualism and the attempt by traditional legal scholars to reduce law to a set of rules and principles which they insisted both guided and constrained judges in their decisions. The boldness of that assertion prompted Holmes (1881) to write that tools other than logic were needed to understand the law. Law was a matter of history and culture and could not be treated deductively.

Realists saw the start of the twentieth century as a period of knowledge explosion and knowledge transformation (Riesman, 1941). Some saw in both the natural and emerging social sciences the triumph of rationality over tradition, inquiry over faith, and the human mind over its environment (McDougal, 1941). They took as one of their many projects the task of opening law to this explosion and transformation. They argued that the law's rationality and efficacy were ultimately dependent upon an alliance with positivist science (see Schlegel, 1980). By using the questions and methods of science to assess the consequences of legal decisions, realists claimed that an understanding of what law *could* do would help in establishing what law *should* do (Llewellyn, 1931). As Yntema put it,

> Ultimately, the object of the more recent movements in legal science ... is to direct the constant efforts which are made to reform the legal system by objective analysis of its operation. Whether such analysis be in terms of a calculus of pleasures and pains, of the evaluation of interests, of pragmatic means and ends, of human behavior, is not so significant as that law is regarded in all these and like analyses as an instrumental procedure to achieve purposes beyond itself, defined by the conditions to which it is directed. This is the Copernican discovery of recent legal science. (1934: 209)

Legal realism initiated a dialogue between law and social science by staking a claim for the relevance of phenomena beyond legal categories (Cardozo, 1921; Pound, 1923; Llewellyn, 1940). Social science would help get at the positive, determinative realities, "the tangibles which can be got at beneath the words...[and would] check ideas, and rules and formulas by facts, to keep them close to facts" (Llewellyn, 1931: 1223). For law to be effective and legitimate, it had to confront such definite, tangible and observable facts; to ignore the facts of social life was folly. Social science could aid decision making by identifying the factors that limited the choices available to officials and, more importantly, by identifying the determinants of responses to those decisions. Aware of those determining conditions, the informed decision maker could and should adopt decisions to take account of what was or was not possible in a given situation.

The intellectual and institutional success of realism was enormous. After World War II, the behaviorist and functionalist orientations that had been urged by the scientific realists became conventional in mainstream social science, and in mainstream legal analyses and teaching. For social science, the unmasking of legal formalism and the opening of legal institutions to empirical inquiry offered, at one and the same time, fertile ground for research and the opportunity to be part of a fundamental remaking of legal thought. The possibility of influencing legal decisions and policies further allied social science and law. Rather than challenge basic norms or attempt to revise the legal structure, realism ultimately worked to increase confidence in the law (Brigham and Harrington, 1989) and to foster the belief that legal thinking informed by social knowledge could be enlisted to aid the pressing project of state intervention. Realism thus invited law and social science inquiry to speak to social policy, an invitation which many, though by no means all of its practitioners, took up.

The legacy of realism was realized in the last four decades of the twentieth century by the modern law and society movement (Garth and Sterling,1998; Tomlins, 2000). Indeed, the beginnings of the modern period of sociolegal research might be set with the formation of the Law and Society Association in 1964. While there is, and was, more to sociolegal research than can be encapsulated by the formation of that Association, its creation marked an important step forward for empirical studies of law. The Law and Society Association self-consciously articulated the value of empirical research for informing policy (see Schwartz, 1965).

The emergence of the law and society movement coincided with one of those episodes in American legal history in which law is regarded as a beneficial tool for social improvement; in which social problems appear susceptible to legal solutions; and in which there is, or appears to be, a rather unproblematic relationship between legal justice and social justice (Trubek and Galanter, 1974). Moreover, the rule of law served to distinguish the West from its adversaries in the Communist world, and hence the full and equal implementation of legal ideals was, to many reformers, essential. By the mid-1960s, liberal reformers seemed once again to be winning the battle to rebuild a troubled democracy; the political forces working, albeit modestly, to expand rights and redistribute wealth and power were in ascendancy. The national government was devoting itself to the use of state power and legal reform for the purpose of building a Great Society. The courts, especially the Supreme Court, were out front in expanding the definition and reach of legal rights. Because law was seen as an important vehicle for social change, those legal scholars who were critical of existing social practices believed they had an ally in the legal order.

Pragmatic social change was an explicit agenda of the state and an equally explicit part of the agenda of law and society research. Legality seemed a cure rather than a disease (Scheingold, 1974); the aspirations and purposes of law seemed unquestionably correct.

Thus, the modern law and society movement, like the realist movement before it, grew up in, and allied itself with, a period of optimism about law. "Social science provided a new professionalizing expertise that offered ways to manage the new social agenda" (Garth and Sterling, 1998: 412). The period was one in which "liberal legal scholars and their social science allies could identify with national administrations which seemed to be carrying out progressive welfare regulatory programs, expanding protection for basic constitutional rights and employing law for a wide range of goals that were widely shared in the liberal community and could even be read as inscribed in the legal tradition itself"(Trubek and Esser, 1987: 23). This period was, of course, also a period of extraordinary optimism in the social sciences, a period of triumph for the behavioral revolution, a period of growing sophistication in the application of quantitative methods in social inquiry (cf. Eulau, 1963).

The awareness of the utility of social science for policy can be seen clearly in the standard form of many law and society presentations which begin with a policy problem; locate it in a general theoretical context; present an empirical study to speak to that problem; and sometimes, though not always, conclude with recommendations, suggestions, or cautions. (For a discussion of this approach see Abel, 1973; Nelken, 1981; Sarat, 1985.) This standard form appears with striking clarity in some of the most widely respected, widely cited work in the field, though often social science serves legal policy by clarifying background conditions and making latent consequences manifest with little or no effort to recommend new or changed policies.

While *Law and the Social Sciences* (1986) appeared at the end of this period of optimism about social science and law, it and the field it sought to represent was still under the sway of the realist legacy, a legacy that gave the field a center of gravity and a sense of boundedness. *The Blackwell Companion to Law and Society* appears at a very different moment in the development of the field, a moment in which the basic logics of governance that provided the foundation for the marriage of social science and law are undergoing dramatic transformations, a moment in which "social science generally and law and society in particular [have] declined in relative prestige" (Garth and Sterling, 1998: 414). As a result, the hold of legal realism on the law and society imagination has loosened, relaxing the pull of the normative, reformist impulse in much of law and society research and the confident embrace of social science as the dominant paradigm for work that seeks to chart the social life of law.

DECLINE OF THE SOCIAL AND THE SEARCH FOR A POSTREALIST PARADIGM

The loosened hold of legal realism on the field of law and society scholarship coincides with, if it is not precipitated by, the decline of the social as central to the logic of governance throughout the societies of the West.[4] This decline comes after more than half a century that culminated in the "social liberal" state in the 1960s and 1970s. During that period the liberal rationality of government associated with laissez faire and methodological individualism was generally reordered around the social as a terrain for positive knowledge and for effective governmental intervention. Thus social liberalism produced a powerful fusion of law, social science, and government.

Traditionally law has had an important set of relationships to the state through the complex mechanisms of sovereignty, but in the twentieth century law became not just sovereign but governmental, and its path to government was through the social. The social sciences likewise established themselves as important adjuncts to governance, in part through the mediation of law (as well as medicine, to a lesser degree), including criminology, social work, and public health, and later with every aspect of economic and general policy (Shamir, 1995). Law and society scholarship never collapsed into pure policy studies, whatever the ambitions of some, but to a great extent its critical efficacy came from its relationships with governance (Sarat and Silbey, 1988).

However, after decades in which social problems set the agenda of government, the social has come to be defined as a problem to be solved by reconfiguring government (Rose, 1999; Simon, 2000). The general decline in confidence in virtually every institution and program of reform, or knowledge gathering, attached to the social is one of the most striking features of our present situation. Social work, social insurance, social policy, social justice, once expected to be engines of building a more rational and modern society, are today seen as ineffectual and incoherent. Socialism, once taken to be a very real competitor with liberalism as a program of modern governance, has virtually disappeared from the field of contemporary politics. The social sciences, and especially sociology (the most social), which had become court sciences at the highest levels in the 1960s and 1970s, are today largely absent from national government and are experiencing their own internal drift and discontent. Law and economics has become the hegemonic knowledge paradigm and has "provided much of the learning and legitimacy for the . . . turn away from social welfare and social activism" (Garth and Sterling, 1998: 414).

The United States clearly represents the extreme case of the problematization of the social. The most florid forms of the social – for example, social insurance, public transportation and housing, public health and social medicine, as well as socialism – were never as actively embraced by American state or federal governments as they were in comparably industrialized societies in Europe, Japan, Australia, and the Americas. Moreover, in no society was the political critique of the social as successful as it was in the United States under presidents like Ronald Reagan, George H. W. Bush, Bill Clinton, and George W. Bush. It is clear, however, that the crisis of the social is being experienced globally today, not only in the formerly welfarist Western nations, but in those states now industrializing.

Whether we like it or not, the practices of governance help set the agenda for legal scholarship, whether legal scholars imagine themselves as allies or critics of the policy apparatus (Ewick, Kagan, and Sarat, 1999). Although it would take a book of its own to describe transformations in the field of legal studies associated with the decline of the social as a nexus of governing, evidence abounds that the shifting engagement between law and society scholarship and government has altered the formation and deployment of legal knowledge at all levels. Likewise, the prestige of empirical research has been tied up with the access that social and legal scholars obtained as experimenters and expert consultants helping to administer a state engaged in interventions in problems like crime, gangs, and urban poverty. Even those discourses that have offered a more critical view of the enterprise of social policy and social research have often promoted both by exposing the gaps in action and imagination created by racism, patriarchy, and class privilege.

With the decline of the social as a logic of governance, law and society research has entered a period of freedom – freedom found in its increased alienation from, and irrelevance to, the governing ethos of the current era. Borrowing from Franklin Zimring (1993: 9), the field is experiencing the "liberating virtues of irrelevance" such that "scholars are now considering a wider and richer range of issues." This era of freedom is marked by great energy, vitality, and success for scholarship and, at the same time, disintegration and fragmentation of existing definitions and boundaries of law and society research.

INSTITUTIONALIZATION AND FRAGMENTATION OF LAW AND SOCIETY RESEARCH

As to institutionalization, since the appearance of *Law and the Social Sciences* in 1986 law and society has continued to be a lively and important terrain for scholars. At the start of the twenty-first century, the field is well institutionalized. Evidence for this is found in the numerous scholarly associations, or sections of associations, both in the United States and abroad, which bring together researchers to encourage work on the social lives of law. Some organizations have been formed to promote legal study within disciplines, for example, the Organized Section on Courts, Law, and the Judicial Process of the American Political Science Association, and American Psychology-Law Society/Division 41 of the American Psychological Association; others, such as the Research Committee on the Sociology of Law of the International Sociological Association, the Society for the Study of Political and Legal Philosophy, the American Society for Legal History, the Association for the Study of Law, Culture, and the Humanities, and the Law and Society Association, cross disciplinary lines.

Moreover, there are now numerous high quality journals, many with a truly international readership, through which law and society scholarship is disseminated, for example, *Law & Society Review, Law & Policy, Law & Social Inquiry, Law & History Review, Law & Critique, Studies in Law, Politics, & Society*, and *Social and Legal Studies: An International Journal*. Academic and trade publishers now recognize the vibrancy of the field, with lively law and society lists found at presses such as Oxford University Press, Cambridge University Press, and at the university presses of Michigan, Yale, Stanford, and Chicago, as well as Dartmouth/Ashgate and Hart Publishing.

In addition, a number of research institutes conduct interdisciplinary (but largely social science) research on law. Examples include the American Bar Foundation, the Rand Institute for Civil Justice, the Centre for Socio-Legal Studies at Oxford University, the Onati International Institute for the Sociology of Law. Since 1971, the National Science Foundation, through its Program in Law and Social Science, has also supported such research; funding for interdisciplinary work on law is also now regularly part of the activities of agencies like the National Endowment for the Humanities. These institutes and funding opportunities have invigorated the work of scholars studying the complex intersections of the legal and the social.

Providing further evidence of the institutionalization of the field are the interdisciplinary programs that now exist at more than 50 colleges and universities in the United States and a large number in the United Kingdom, continental Europe, and elsewhere. These programs introduce students to the fact that law is ubiquitous, that it pervades much of our lives, and provides a forum in which the distinctive temper of a culture may find expression. They introduce them to law's role in articulating values and dealing with conflict.

While all of this gives evidence of the range and vigor of law and society study, it barely evidences the veritable explosion and transformation of the field, since the publication of *Law and the Social Sciences*. Unlike the research of the 1970s and 1980s, today's postrealist law and society research is, to name just a few things, marked by:

1   New generations of scholars, many of whom continue to address venerable questions about law's social lives, while others strike out in new directions addressing important questions which were not recognized two decades ago;

2   The development of new interdisciplinary connections within the social sciences, as well as what Clifford Geertz referred to as the "blurring of genres" between the social sciences and humanities;

3   Disputes about what counts as social knowledge as well as new theorizations that have drained some of the optimism about the political utility of social knowledge;

4   Increasing abandonment of the reformist policy orientation of scholarship in favor of the description and analysis of the processes through which law performs in various social domains;

5   Globalization and internationalization of both legal phenomena and of law and society as a scholarly field.

From the mid-1960s through the early 1980s, when modern law and society scholarship began to take shape, there was a rough consensus about the methods and purposes of that research. Definitions and descriptions of the field abounded. Here are but a few: Lawrence Friedman (1986: 764) argued that "The law and society movement sits on a rather narrow ledge. It uses scientific method; its theories are, in principle, scientific theories; but what it studies is a loose, wriggling, changing subject matter, shot through and through with normative ideas. It is a science... about something thoroughly nonscientific." Frank Munger (1998: 24) suggested that law and society research is unified by "its dedication to testing ideas empirically rather than relying on logical derivations from premises." Felice Levine said that law and society work involves:

> the social study of law, legal processes, legal systems, normative ordering, law-related behaviors, and what is endemically legal in society. However broad in scope it is meant to embrace the study of law as a social phenomena, not the use of social science in or by law.... To see sociolegal work as science does not require a belief in a universal theory or universal laws or belief in the view that science is value free and not embedded in social life. Optimally, like other areas of social science inquiry law and society work must be both synthetic and flexible. (1990: 23)

These definitions suggest that there has never been a single style of law and society work or a litmus test for membership in the community, yet they highlight a rough consensus of the kind reflected in Lipson and Wheeler (1986), a consensus made possible by a widely shared view that law and society work was synonymous with law and social science with a gentle reformist edge often added. In the postrealist era that is emerging today, law and society research appears eclectic and noncumulative. It is neither organized around a single central insight nor an agreed-upon paradigm. "Law and society scholars," Robert Ellickson (1995: 118) contends, "have been handicapped because they do not agree on, and often don't show much interest in, developing basic theoretical building blocks."

Moreover, "social science" no longer occupies the virtually unchallenged position it once held, and social science itself no longer means what it once did. As demonstrated in the chapters that follow, in the postrealist era there is an abundant variety in the styles of research done under the rubric of law and society, and disagreement on what empirical means or whether law and society is synonymous with law and social science. While social science still is by far a predominant, and critically important, mode of inquiry, increasingly prevalent talk about interpretation, narrative, and identity seems suspiciously like the language of the humanities.

With particularity, multiplicity, and ambiguity as central virtues of postrealist law and society research, it should hardly come as a surprise when they precipitate a crisis of self-understanding in a community traditionally thought of in terms of its allegiance to social science. Just as a blurring of genres has occurred throughout the human sciences, so too feminism, studies of race and nationalism, and work in queer theory, to name just a few, have raised questions about the taken-for-granted identification of law and society with social science. The emergence of scholarship that emphasizes law's roles in shaping and responding to personal, group, and national identities has played a large part in opening up the boundaries of the field.

Where once legal doctrine would never be spoken about, today space is made for that work. Literary and humanistic perspectives have made some inroads. Work on the impact of the global and the postcolonial, as well as post-Marxist approaches and deconstruction, are found side by side with quantitative analysis. The traditions of law and society scholarship are, as they should be, up for grabs as new scholars redefine the field. With growth has come greater inclusiveness, but also fragmentation. With every gain in inclusiveness there will be an appropriate, though unsettling, increase in uncertainty about what law and society scholarship is and what law and society scholars do. One measure of the progress of this field is uneasiness about what its boundaries are, what is orthodox and what is heresy.

In addition, while realist legal studies almost always operate within a political body, usually the nation, with its exclusions made up not just of political borders but also of the nation's racial, cultural, and linguistic embodiments, the emerging postrealist law and society scholarship represented in this book increasingly confronts an array of breaches in this imaginary order in the form of globalization, identity politics, and/or the risk society for which the old realist paradigm seems inappropriate. Today then while law and society research and scholarship is vibrant and vital, the field is experiencing a period of pluralization and fragmentation. There is no longer a clear center of gravity nor a reasonably clear set of boundaries. Important scholarship proliferates under the banner of law and society even as that designation loses its distinctiveness. Evidence of both the vitality of the field and of its fragmentation is well represented in chapters of this book.

OVERVIEW OF BOOK

The work represented in *The Blackwell Companion to Law and Society* reflects the new facts of an emerging postrealist era. Whereas 15 years ago one could survey the field in 11 chapters, today it takes almost three times that number to even begin to do justice to the work being done under the law and society banner. And while then only three women and one international scholar were charged with the task of "canonizing" their subfield, in this book 19 women and nine international scholars are included as authors. The authors whose work is represented in this book represent different generations of law and society scholars as well as various theoretical, methodological, and political commitments – from positivism to interpretivism, from the new institutionalism to cultural studies.

The book is organized into six major sections. The first takes up and deepens the intellectual genealogy of the field begun in these pages. The second explores the complex connections of law and culture. The third examines the basic "subjects" of law and society, the institutional locations for doing what everyone would acknowledge to be legal work. The fourth moves from institutions to explore the domains of policy to which law and society scholarship has been addressed. The fifth examines the various ways in which law may be said to matter in social life. The sixth and last decenters the association of law and the nation-state, and it contains chapters that describe the past, present, and future of law in a global era.

While this organization provides but one idiosyncratic mapping of law and society scholarship, many themes recur from section to section and chapter to chapter. Among them several seem most important in marking the possibility of postrealist law and society scholarship, namely, law's constitutive role in shaping social life; the complexity of institutional processes, as well as the importance of law in everyday life; the ways legal institutions are transformed as well as the ways in which they resist change; the increased importance of global and international processes in national and local legality; the significance of new media and technologies in defining, portraying, and communicating about law; the intersections of law and identity; and law's role in both encouraging and responding to social consensus and social conflict.

A book like *The Blackwell Companion to Law and Society* demonstrates that it is hard to say with confidence just what constitutes or defines law and society research and, at the same time, particularly important to engage in that effort. Doing so will not in itself alleviate the confusion or uncertainty of the present moment, or chart the way forward toward a postrealist paradigm. Nor will doing so restore consensus in the face of fragmentation. But engagement with the diversity of styles of work reviewed in these pages should leave no doubt about the vitality and importance of law and society scholarship in this emerging postrealist era.

Notes

1   This argument is developed in Sarat and Silbey (1988).
2   Legal realism was by no means, however, a unified or singular intellectual movement. At one and the same time, the label legal realist has been applied to people like Felix Cohen

(1935), who took what Gary Peller (1985: 1222) later categorized as a deconstructive approach, a radical skepticism which challenged the claims of logical coherence and necessity in legal reasoning, and to others who embraced and believed in science and technique. Moreover, realism embodied three distinct political perspectives. It included a critical oppositional strand which sought to undermine the law's ability to provide legitimacy for political and economic elites by exposing the contradictions of classical legal formalism and the hypocrisy of legal authority. Realism also included a strand of scientific naturalism whose proponents attempted to advance a more enlightened, rational, and efficient social order by using the methods and insights of the empirical sciences to understand a wide range of human, political, and social phenomena. Among these scientific realists there were divisions between the pragmatic followers of Dewey and James and those realists who pursued a more positivistic version of empirical science. Finally, legal realism was a practical political effort which did not merely support or legitimate political elites but some of whose members were themselves the officials designing, making, and enforcing reform policies

3 Not all stands of realist inquiry were, however, equally confident that law could or should be rescued, or that its integrity could or should be restored. The deconstructivist strand, which came to be viewed, by mainstream legal scholars, as dangerously relativistic and nihilistic, tried to reorient legal thought by emphasizing its indeterminacy, contingency and contradiction. According to Peller, "This deconstructive, debunking strand of realism seemed inconsistent with any liberal notion of a rule of law distinct from politics, or indeed any mode of rational thought distinct from ideology... This approach emphasized contingency and open-ended possibilities as it exposed the exercises of social power behind what appeared to be the neutral work of reason" (Peller, 1985: 1223).

4 For an elaboration of the argument developed in this section see Sarat and Simon (2003).

References

Abel, Richard (1973) "Law books and books about law," *Stanford Law Review* 26: 175–228.
Brigham, John and Harrington, Christine (1989) "Realism and its consequences," *International Journal of the Sociology of Law* 17: 41–62.
Cardozo, Benjamin (1921) *The Nature of the Judicial Process.* New Haven, CT: Yale University Press.
Cohen, Felix (1935) "Transcendental nonsense and the functional approach," *Columbia Law Review* 34: 809–49.
Ellickson, Robert (1995) *Order Without Law: How Neighbors Settle Disputes.* Cambridge, MA: Harvard University Press.
Eulau, Heinz (1963) *The Behavioral Persuasion in Politics.* New York: Random House.
Ewick, Patricia, Kagan, Robert, and Sarat, Austin (1999) "Legacies of legal realism: Social science, social policy, and the law," in Patricia Ewick, Robert Kagan, and Austin Sarat (eds.), *Social Science, Social Policy, and the Law.* New York: Russell Sage, pp. 1–38.
Friedman, Lawrence (1986) "The law and society movement," *Stanford Law Review* 38: 763–80.
Garth, Bryant and Sterling, Joyce (1998) "From legal realism to law and society: Reshaping law for the last stages of the social activist state," *Law & Society Review* 32: 409–72
Holmes, O.W. (1881) *The Common Law.* Boston: Little Brown & Company.
Llewellyn, Karl (1931) "Some realism about realism," *Harvard Law Review* 44: 1222–64.
Llewellyn, Karl (1940) "On reading and using the newer jurisprudence," *Columbia Law Review* 40: 581–614.
Llewellyn, Karl (1960) *The Common Law Tradition: Deciding Appeals.* Boston: Little, Brown & Co.

Levine, Felice (1990) "Goose bumps and 'the search for signs of intelligent life' in sociolegal studies: After twenty-five years," *Law & Society Review* 24: 7–34.

Lipson, Leon and Wheeler, Stanton (eds.) (1986) *Law and the Social Sciences.* New York: Russell Sage Foundation.

McDougal, Myers (1941) "Fuller v. the American legal realists," *Yale Law Journal* 50: 827–40.

Munger, Frank (1998) "Mapping law and society," in Austin Sarat, Marianne Constable, David Engel, Valerie Hans, and Susan Lawrence (eds.), *Crossing Boundaries: Traditions and Transformations in Law and Society Research.* Evanston, IL: Northwestern University Press, pp. 21–80.

Nelken, David. (1981) "The 'gap problem' in the sociology of law," *Windsor Access to Justice Yearbook* 1: 35–61.

Peller, Gary (1985) "The metaphysics of American law," *California Law Review* 73: 1152–290.

Pound, Roscoe (1923) "The theory of judicial decision," *Harvard Law Review* 36: 641–62.

Riesman, David (1941) "Law and social science," *Yale Law Journal* 50: 636–53.

Rose, Nikolas (1999) *The Powers of Freedom.* Cambridge, UK: Cambridge University Press.

Sarat, Austin (1985) "Legal effectiveness and social studies of law: On the unfortunate persistence of a research tradition," *Legal Studies Forum* 9: 23–32.

Sarat, Austin and Silbey, Susan (1988) "The pull of the policy audience," *Law & Policy* 10: 97–166.

Sarat, Austin and Simon, Jonathan (2003) "Cultural analysis, cultural studies, and the situation of legal scholarship," in Austin Sarat and Jonathan Simon (eds.), *Cultural Analysis, Cultural Studies, and the Law.* Durham, NC: Duke University Press, pp. 1–34.

Scheingold, Stuart (1974) *The Politics of Rights.* New Haven, CT: Yale University Press.

Schlegel, John (1979) "American legal realism and empirical social science – I," *Buffalo Law Review* 28: 459–586

Schlegel, John (1980) "American legal realism and empirical social science – II," *Buffalo Law Review* 29: 195–324.

Schwartz, Richard (1965) "Introduction," Law and Society: Supplement to *Social Problems* 4: 1–7.

Shamir, Ronen (1995) *Managing Legal Uncertainty: Elite Lawyers in the New Deal.* Durham, NC: Duke University Press

Simon, Jonathan (2000) "Law after society," *Law & Social Inquiry* 24: 143–94.

Tomlins, Christopher (2000), "Framing the field of law's disciplinary encounters: A historical narrative," *Law & Society Review* 34: 911–72.

Trubek, David and Galanter, Marc (1974) "Scholars in self-estrangement," *Wisconsin Law Review* 1974: 1062–101.

Trubek, David and Esser, John (1987) "Critical empiricism in American legal studies: Paradox, program, or Pandora's box," *Law and Social Inquiry* 14: 3–52.

Yntema, H.E. (1934) "Legal science and reform," *Columbia Law Review* 34: 207–29.

Zimring, Franklin (1993) "On the liberating virtues of irrelevance," *Law & Society Review* 27: 9–18.

Part I

Perspectives on the History and Significance of Law and Society Research

2

Law in Social Theory and Social Theory in the Study of Law

ROGER COTTERRELL

What can social theory contribute to legal studies? And what place does law have as a concern of social theory? Three or four decades ago, when the field of "law and society" or sociolegal studies was first becoming a lively, popular focus for research, defining the relations of law and social theory meant mainly locating law's place in the theoretical traditions of the academic discipline of sociology, and asking what those traditions might offer the study of law. Now, however, social theory can no longer be considered the preserve of any particular academic discipline. It has to be defined in terms of its objectives rather than particular traditions that have shaped it.

LAW IN CLASSIC SOCIAL THEORY

Social theory is systematic, historically informed, and empirically oriented theory seeking to explain the nature of "the social." And the social can be taken to mean the general range of recurring forms or patterned features of interactions and relationships between people. The social is the ongoing life of human beings lived alongside and in relation to others; the compendium of institutions, patterns of interaction, networks, systems, and structures of collective life resulting from human coexistence. So it is the collective life of human groups and populations, but also the life of individuals in so far as this is shaped by their relation to those populations or groups. The social is a realm of solidarity, identity, and cooperation, but also of power, conflict, alienation, and isolation; of stable expectations, structures, systems, custom, trust, and confidence, but also of unpredictable action, unforeseen change, violence, disruption, and discontinuity.

Described in these expansive terms, the social seems bewilderingly general as an object or field of study. Debates about its nature and significance are fundamental today in assessing the significance of social theory itself. And the essence of the social has been seen in social theory in radically different ways. For example, in Max

Weber's (1978) work it appears as a limited number of distinct types of social action combined in innumerable ways to give rise to what we recognize as "capitalism," "bureaucracy," "domination," and all the other seemingly solid structures of the social world. Sometimes the social has been seen in terms of an evolution of human relations – for example in Marcel Mauss's (1990) famous analysis of the significance of gift relationships. Its essence has also been found in different types of cohesion of human populations (Durkheim, 1984) or sociality or bonding between the members of social groups (Gurvitch, 1947). Sometimes it has been understood as categories or institutional forms in terms of which individuals interrelate – for example, in Georg Simmel's (1971) analyses of "the stranger," "the metropolis," "fashion," "conflict," "exchange," and other phenomena.

The object that has served – implicitly or explicitly – as the primary focus for most social theory is "society," conceived as a unified totality in some sense, so that the study of how that totality exists could be distinct from, though related to, the study of politics, law, the economy or other more specific kinds of social action or experience. Society in this sense is "the sum of the bonds and relations between individuals and events – economic, moral, political – within a more or less bounded territory governed by its own laws" (Rose, 1996: 328). Even where social theory has not treated society directly as its object, its characterizations of the social assume that social phenomena cohere in some significant way: that social life forms a fabric of some kind; that it has continuity and scale and that particular exemplifications of the social relate to larger patterns, even if their exact limits or boundaries may be variable or hard to specify. The social includes class, race, gender, or specifically economic relations, for example, but social theory assumes it must treat all of these as components or examples of more general patterns or features of human interaction, and that its consistent focus must be on that generality. The social is always assumed to be in some sense intelligible as a unity.

In the classic social theory of the late nineteenth and early twentieth century, "society" was mainly typified by the politically organized and territorially bounded society of the modern Western nation-state. Given this position, it is not surprising that a strong sensitivity to law is found in the most ambitious and influential contributions to this theory – the work of Emile Durkheim, Weber, and Karl Marx. The reach of society could be seen as paralleling the jurisdictional reach of nation-state legal systems. As social theory examined the general social relations and structures comprising society, it encountered modern law as a society-wide system of definition and regulation of these relations and structures. In a sense, law and social theory competed in characterizing modern society, but law could be treated in social theory as exemplifying certain structures and patterns fundamental to this society.

So, for Durkheim, the substance of modern law (particularly contract, commercial, property, and criminal law) and its processes expressed the particular characteristics of modern social solidarity, by which he meant the manner in which modern society was integrated and given a sense of unity despite its increasing complexity, changeability, and diversity. A study of the development of law across the centuries could show how the structures of solidarity allowing modern society to cohere had gradually formed (Durkheim, 1984). His conclusion was that the only value system that could integrate modern societies – and so must be the moral foundation of all modern law – would be one requiring universal respect for the autonomy and human dignity of every individual citizen (Durkheim, 1975; Cotterrell, 1999: 103–47).

In a completely different way and using different methods, Weber also securely linked the study of law with the study of the social in its modern forms. Modern law exemplified a kind of rationality mirroring and running parallel with the rationalization of other aspects of life in the West. While formal legal rationality was a distinctive mode of thought and practice, it could be seen as part of a far wider rationalization of the modern world. The study of legal rationality's development and its interrelations with other varieties of rationality (especially in economic action, administration, and politics) could provide major insights into the nature of the social in the unique forms it had taken in the West (Weber, 1978: pt. 2, ch. 8).

Marx, seeking to analyze the nature and destiny of capitalism, saw law as in one sense superstructural, a support rather than an engine of capitalism's trajectory as a mode of production and as the overall structure of the social in the modern West. But he emphasized law's role in defining social relations, repressing class unrest, and helping to constitute the ways of thinking – above all in terms of property and contract – that serve as fundamental ideological supports of capitalist social relations (Cain and Hunt, 1979). Thus, like Durkheim and Weber, Marx saw a need to take account of the development of law to identify the way it produced particular ideas, ways of reasoning, or forms of practice at certain stages in history. So each of these writers saw law as essential in transforming the social – establishing foundations of modern society – however differently they might characterize this modernity in their work.

These brief comments may be enough to illustrate two points: that the concept of "modernity" has often, in practice, been inseparable from that of "society" in the vision of social theory, and that law was often treated in classic social theory as, in some way, a crucial marker, component, or agent of the coming into being of the modern world. More recent social theorists have often treated the emergence of a certain kind of legal system as crucial in this sense. Talcott Parsons, for example, saw the emergence of a "general legal system" – cutting across all traditional special statuses and providing a universal system of rights and obligations – as "the most important single hallmark of modern society" (Parsons, 1964: 353). But we shall see later that the concepts of "modernity" and "society," so central to social theory, are at the heart of debates surrounding it as an enterprise today.

Leaving aside these debates for the moment, what has social theory in its classic or traditional forms been able to offer legal studies? If social theory is abstract and broad in scope, law as a practice, and often as a field of study, has been said, by contrast, to be wedded to the "method of detail" (Twining, 1974), focused on particularity and immediate problem solving. Social theory in general has claimed that philosophical analyses, reflections on specific historical experience, and systematic empirical observations of social conditions can be combined to explain the nature of society. Social theorists' considerations of law are colored by this amalgam of philosophical, historical, and observational orientations. As a byproduct of its general concerns, social theory has often assessed law's capacities, limits, conditions of existence, and sources of authority and power. Its attraction for some legal scholars has been that its perspectives on law have been much wider than those the legal specialist alone could usually be expected to command. So social theory has been called on in sociolegal studies to escape the limits of law's method of detail as well as to counter narrow social scientific empiricism. The promise has always been to broaden social perspectives on law. The corresponding risk has always been that the broad perspective loses the richness and specificity of particular experiences or practices of the legal. The method of detail may need supplementing but has its value nonetheless.

Despite these claims for social theory's usefulness to legal studies and the promin-ent presence of law in the classics of social theory, the link between legal studies and social theory has usually been tenuous. That various changes in both law and social theory are bringing about a greater mutual dependence will be a main argument in later sections of this chapter. Nevertheless, until quite recently, the relationship could be characterized as predominantly one of disinterest or token acknowledgment.

Despite the example set by the classic writers, social theorists have often doubted whether law is important enough or sufficiently identifiable as a specific social phenomenon to deserve special consideration in any theory of the social. Could most of what needs to be analyzed be treated in terms of concepts such as adminis-trative action, state coercion, social norms, social control, ideology, reciprocity, conformity and deviance, bureaucratic norms, or custom? Law, as such, might not need theorizing: that could be left to jurists for their own purposes. The term "law" would remain for the social theorist only a commonsense label that might usefully designate clusters of phenomena to be explained theoretically without essential reference to it. In any event, law's identity and significance vary considerably between different societies. And general conceptions or definitions of law are dom-inated by juristic perceptions which most social theorists have not sought to upset.

For example, social theorists have rarely adopted the radical reformulations of the concept of law associated with what is now called social scientific legal pluralism (see e.g., Merry, 1988). Legal pluralism in this sense explicitly denies that juristic conceptions of law are universally adequate and adopts some wider conception of law that can embrace, for various analytical purposes, phenomena the lawyer would not recognize as legal – for example, private or "unofficial" norm systems of various kinds. Among major social theorists only Georges Gurvitch stands out as having radically rejected juristic conceptions of law in favor of an intricate, fully elaborated theory of legal pluralism integrated into his broader social theory. Significantly Gurvitch reached this position on the basis of his early sociolegal and philosophical inquiries (Gurvitch, 1935, 1947), rather than as a by-product of his later general sociological theory.

Indeed, in contrast to social theorists, it is those social scientists who see law as central to their research careers, and tend to refer to themselves as "law and society" or sociolegal scholars, who have most often embraced legal pluralist perspectives. But many sociolegal scholars have been content to follow social theory's general lead, paying homage to the broad insights about law to be found in classic social theory but otherwise mainly using "law" as a pragmatic umbrella term for clusters of social phenomena analyzed in terms of concepts familiar in their parent social science disciplines.

Just as social theory has tended to avoid law while considering its social manifest-ations, so lawyers and legal scholars have mainly avoided social theory. And cer-tainly, from a juristic standpoint the usefulness of a theory of the social may not seem obvious: the social might be viewed as what law itself creates as its own jurisdiction, the structure of the social being simply the regulatory structure that law provides. In this sense the social is the taken for granted locus and environment of legal practice. And, undoubtedly, from a juristic viewpoint, law seems endlessly resourceful in defining and adjusting its reach and the nature of the relations it regulates. The social is what law treats as such.

LAW AND CONTEMPORARY SOCIAL CHANGE

What is happening to change this typical relationship of disinterest? The relevant changes that have occurred in the situation of law and legal studies on the one hand, and of social theory on the other, have often been associated with the idea of the passing of modernity and its replacement with the "postmodern." "Post" implies that the new can only be understood as related to and, in some sense, a supplement or reaction to, what preceded it, but also that modernity's features can now be identified with finality, so that what follows is distinct from them.

According to Jean-François Lyotard's celebrated dictum, the most profound ex-emplification of postmodernity is a loss of faith in "grand narratives" (Lyotard, 1984: 37) in a fluid, rapidly changing, intensely self-questioning and uncertain (Western) world: the coming of "a new age of radical rootlessness and doubt" (Douzinas and Warrington, 1991: 9). This applies not only to comprehensive systems of thought such as Marxism and the great religions, but to general theories of "society" as a stable, integrated totality, to political ideologies of all kinds, and to the very idea of "science" as the progressive unveiling of truth. All are said to flounder on the rocks of patent social contingency and indeterminacy.

The result is a new privileging of "local knowledge" (Geertz, 1983) and a percep-tion of the failure or pointlessness of all attempts to generalize broadly about social change or social phenomena. The tendency in such circumstances might be to abandon social theory altogether. A new focus on the local and the specific, on the instability of social structures and institutions, and the exhilarating or frightening rootlessness of individual lives casts doubt on the usefulness of treating "society" as an object sufficiently solid to theorize (Rose, 1996; Bauman, 1992: 190). The dialectic of order/change and structure/agency in traditional sociological analyses of society does not seem to capture the sense of radical fluidity which postmodern thought associates with contemporary human coexistence in the most highly de-veloped nations of the world.

The idea that it is no longer useful to theorize society has sometimes led into more general but very opaque claims about "the death of the social" (Baudrillard, 1983: 2). The doomsday scenario here is that social theory loses its integrity having lost its object. It is replaced with a host of competing discourses – especially literary, feminist, psychoanalytic, economic, and cultural theory – that focus on human relations no longer considered in terms of any explicit overall conception of the social.

More concrete ideas bearing directly on the destiny of law can also be mentioned. The social is sometimes claimed to be disappearing as a specific primary field of government intervention, and enterprises organized around it (such as social work, social welfare, sociology, and socialism) are losing prestige (Simon, 1999: 144–7). A further claim is that the social as a field distinct from the political is atrophying. On one view, the social has become merely a population mass, silent and inert, no longer the active source of political energies but merely a passive recipient of governmental actions (Baudrillard, 1983: 19–25). A consequence would seem to be that legal interventions can hardly look for effective legitimation or direction from this source.

On another view, an individualization of lifestyles puts in issue the stability of many social institutions (e.g., traditional family, employment, and gender relations) but creates unprecedented opportunities for a radical remaking of the social through the spontaneous choices of individuals in relation to their own lives (Beck and Beck-Gernsheim, 2002; see also Beck, Giddens, and Lash, 1994). Thus politics is potentially transformed, its focus shifted toward the local and the personal but also, very importantly, toward the global (as in many environmental, security, and health concerns widely shared across national boundaries). Meanwhile, politics in nation-states becomes increasingly moribund in the traditional public sphere. Indeed, in a revitalized politics, lines between public and private, and national and global, might eventually become meaningless (Beck, 1992: ch. 8, 2000: ch. 2). The primary implication for legal studies would seem to be that the horizon and appropriate methods of regulation are changing in very fundamental ways.

The importance of this recent theorizing is certainly not to undermine the social as a category. Indeed, many theorists – including some, such as Jean Baudrillard, who have dramatically declared the social's demise – continue to refer to "society" without apparent embarrassment (Smart, 1993: 55–6). For legal studies, the importance of these writings is to show that the nature of the social cannot be assumed as unproblematic. Law may define the social as it regulates it, but it does so under conditions that the social itself provides. Law presupposes a conception of the social that defines not only its technical jurisdiction, but also the arena in which its interventions require rational integration, and the general source of its legitimation and cultural meanings. It follows that, as the identity, coherence, and shape of the social are questioned, assumptions about the nature and efficacy of law are also put in issue.

In contemporary social theory, Michel Foucault's work provides one of the most important vehicles for reconsidering the nature and scope of law in terms of fundamental long-term changes in the character of the social. It raises the question of whether law has failed to keep step with these changes and become marginalized as a result, increasingly giving way to other kinds of regulation and control. Foucault's works describe processes by which new kinds of knowledge and power have arisen, reinforcing each other to create what he calls disciplinary society (Foucault, 1977: 216). The prison, the asylum, the school, the medical clinic, and other particular institutional sites, have been primary foci for the gradual emergence of constellations of knowledge/power in which technical norms, expertise, training, and surveillance combine to regulate populations and define the place of individuals as autonomous, responsible subjects.

In lectures towards the end of his career, Foucault elaborated general implications for law of his earlier studies. He sharply contrasts the majesty of law with the "art of government" focused on administering social life (Foucault, 1991: 92). Law is, in his view, the expression of sovereign power: what is most important about it is that it demands obedience and requires that all affronts to the sovereignty it embodies be punished. The essence of law is, therefore, coercion. Foucault contrasts, with law's "occasional or discontinuous interventions in society," something he sees as very different: "a type of power that is disciplinary and continuously regulative and which pervasively, intimately and integrally inhabits society" (Fitzpatrick, 1992: 151). This is an autonomous, expert form of governing, focused specifically on regulating economy and population and relying on "multiform tactics" and a range of techniques, expertise, and information united only by a need for "wisdom and diligence" (Foucault, 1991: 95, 96).

Foucault calls this pervasive regulatory activity "governmentality" rather than government, to emphasize that it goes beyond and uses a far wider range of techniques than government in the usual political sense, and its sites of operation are not restricted to what is usually thought of as the public sphere but relate to all aspects of life. Nevertheless, the rise of governmentality marks a stage in the development of the state, from the "state of justice" and law, through the "administrative state" of regulation and discipline organized territorially, to the "governmental state" which aims at guaranteeing security and is "essentially defined no longer [exclusively] in terms of its territoriality... its surface area, but in terms of the mass of its population with its volume and density... " (Foucault, 1991: 104).

Significantly, law's destiny is left vague. Perhaps ultimately it is for jurists and sociolegal scholars to sort this out. The state's stages of development are cumulative so that eventually legal, administrative, and governmental state forms coexist. Some writers see Foucault as claiming that law is progressively replaced by technical and disciplinary norms, and charge him with propounding a narrow view of law, apparently ignoring its current scope and character (Hunt, 1993: ch. 12). Others argue that Foucault well recognizes law's nature and scope in contemporary society (Ewald, 1990) and sees only its old regulatory supremacy as undermined. His claim, undoubtedly, is that law has been reduced from its grandly sovereign status to a position alongside numerous other regulatory techniques, no more than a "tactic" of government to be used or not used, as appropriate (Foucault, 1991: 95).

From another point of view, the key debate around Foucault and law is about law's *potential*. In the newly recognized complexity and indeterminacy of society, does action through and on law provide an important means of navigating the social and the numerous decentered locations of power that Foucault's work emphasizes (e.g., Munro, 2001), or is it increasingly a distraction as a focus for solving or campaigning on important social issues (Smart, 1989), being tied to forms of state action and political projects that are increasingly remote from many regions of the social?

The ambiguous implications of Foucault's work show that social theory's changing images of the social destabilize established ideas of law, pointing in different directions toward new conceptualizations. A broad, loosened conception of law might see it metamorphosing into diverse regulatory strategies, forms, and tactics attempting to mirror the fluidity, contingency, and indeterminacy of the social (Rose and Valverde, 1998). Law might seem an indefinite aspect of a range of tactics of governance operating in sites – for example, schools, religious practices, rural traditions, campaigns to protect local industries (Cooper, 1998) – often distanced from the direct operation of state agencies.

In this context, new unifying principles arise, focused, for example, on the control of risk, so that risk emerges as a major category for making sense of the normative implications of contingency (Beck, 1992). Perceptions or calculations of risk can then be seen to operate as signals to alert or set in motion regulatory processes and provide their focus (e.g., Ericson and Haggerty, 1997). Equally, they can be rallying points for political and legal action (Franklin, 1998).

By contrast, conceptions of law that in some way emphasize its autonomy or distinct identity rather than its tactical flexibility might see it as in crisis, overburdened with regulatory tasks for which it is unsuitable (Teubner, 1987). Or they might emphasize as somewhat remarkable the fact that, in such conditions of complexity, the legal system copes; that it pours out rules and decisions despite the ever-increasing diversity of social life and the rapidity of social change.

Autopoiesis theory, developed as a form of social theory by the sociologist Niklas Luhmann (1995), can be seen in this context as a particularly inventive way of conceptualizing how law copes with changes in the nature of the social without losing its special identity in the process, and becoming – as Foucault seems to suggest – just part of a continuum of regulatory "tactics." Autopoiesis theory seeks to explain how law retains a distinctive character and stability in complex societies, at the same time as it addresses an ever-increasing range of problems thrown up by the fluidity and complexity of the social. The theory also suggests why legal interventions often produce unforeseen and unintended social consequences and why law often seems persistently unresponsive to demands emerging from the social.

In Luhmann's formulation, law is cognitively open but normatively closed, in so far as it has become an autopoietic (self-observing, self-producing, and self-reproducing) system of communication (Luhmann, 1992). This means that, like other social systems of communication (such as the economy, the polity, and science) law is necessarily open to information from its environment but, no less necessarily, it reads this information only in its own discursive terms. Law processes information solely for the purposes of applying its unique normative coding of legal/illegal in terms of which all its decisions must be made. Similarly, other systems interpret legal rules and decisions in terms of their own system codings, for example the criteria of efficient/inefficient in the case of the economy.

As social theory, autopoiesis theory clearly pictures law in the way it so often appears to jurists – as a self-founding discourse unfazed by circularity in its reasoning and invocations of authority. It shows how law can operate in this way and explains sociologically why it does. The theory claims that the increasing complexity of the social gives rise, in an evolutionary process, to the gradual differentiation of society into a number of specialized systems of communication, of which law is one. The legal system is thus not defined in terms of rules and institutions – as, for example, in Talcott Parsons' earlier theory of social differentiation as a response to complexity (Parsons, 1977: 174–6) – but by its distinctive discourse of legality and illegality.

Hence law can pervade the spaces of the social. As discourse it can exist anywhere and everywhere and the thematization of issues as legal (Luhmann, 1981) can occur in contexts not restricted to the formal legal institutions of the nation-state. Thus autopoiesis theory can accommodate the idea of an emerging "global law without a state" (Teubner, 1997), or of law's presence in the private realms that social theorists have identified as contemporary sites of a new politics and of the transformation of the social.

Nevertheless, the theory suffers, as many critics have pointed out, from an almost impenetrable abstraction. Attempts to use it in empirical sociolegal research have had limited success although it has provided a striking way of emphasizing, for example, legal discourse's perceived deafness or incomprehension when sometimes faced in court with the discourses of social welfare in cases involving children (King and Piper, 1995). Despite being among the most sophisticated and rigorous recent contributions to social theory and having had its legal implications extensively elaborated (e.g., Teubner, 1993; Pribán and Nelken, 2001), autopoiesis theory stands some way apart from many of the themes this chapter has stressed. It has not extensively examined the changing character of the social in concrete terms in relation to law, and it has not indicated how contemporary legal change can be interpreted in the light of social theory. It leaves relatively unexplored the details of the discursive character that it attributes to developed law. And the theory explains little about how autopoietic law will actually respond to what the social may throw up as regulatory problems. Its concern seems only to affirm that law will seek to address these matters always from its own point of view with its own discursive resources.

FOUNDATIONS OF LEGAL AUTHORITY

Autopoiesis theory attempts to bypass one question that has long been a major focus for social theory: what is the source and foundation of law's authority, the legitimacy that enables it to demand respect and command obedience? For Luhmann, the issue of law's legitimacy has been replaced by that of function: the question is simply about efficiency – whether law can effectively fulfill its social task of producing decisions according to its own criteria of legality/illegality. But one might still want to ask how functional success is to be judged and recognized. In fact, much recent social theoretical writing wrestles with questions about law's "grounds," its ultimate bases of authority or legitimacy.

Durkheim's classic social theory assumed that law and morality are inseparable and that morality is law's "soul." Since he understood morality as the normative structure of society, his social theory makes the strong claim that law finds all its meaning, authority, and effectiveness ultimately in this moral structure. Without such a grounding it becomes mere force or empty words (Cotterrell, 1999). In a sense, Weber's social theory turned these Durkheimian claims upside down. Modern law, having lost its "metaphysical dignity" with the discrediting of natural law theories, is revealed, in his view, as no more than "the product or the technical means of a compromise of interests" (Weber, 1978: 874–5). Law requires no moral authority. Instead, its rules and procedures, in their abstract formality, can themselves become a means of *giving* authority, as in the political authority of the rule of law as a legitimation of government. Weber's work is thus one of the clearest sources of the familiar idea of legitimacy through legality or procedure (Cotterrell, 1995: ch. 7).

Interestingly, the broad problems, if not the substance, of both Durkheim's and Weber's opposing positions are strongly present in recent writing on law in social theory and in invocations of social theory in legal studies. Postmodern ideas about the collapse of grand narratives might suggest that the authority or validity of all large-scale structures of knowledge has been put in question. But it could be argued that some kind of Weberian legitimacy through legality remains the only possibility of stable authority in the postmodern social environment. Contemporary law – explicitly constructed, particular, local in scope, and ever-changing – might seem the quintessentially postmodern form of knowledge or doctrine: not in any sense a grand narrative, but the perfect pragmatic embodiment of contingency, impermanence, artificiality, transience, and disposability; its doctrine continually adapted, amended, cancelled, supplemented, or reinterpreted to address new problems.

Hence postmodern writing on law has often emphasized law's simultaneous moral emptiness and social power in a world that has lost faith in other discourses (Goodrich, 1990). And autopoiesis theory's unconcerned recognition that the very essence of legal discourse is circular reasoning has some affinities with claims informed by postmodern perspectives: for example, that law's self-founded authority acts powerfully to disguise the incoherences of concepts such as "society" and "nation," even though legal thinking itself presupposes these concepts (Fitzpatrick, 2001).

Not unrelated to these lines of thought is a stress, in much recent sociolegal writing, on law's constitutive power (e.g., Brigham, 1996) – its ability actually to create the social (not just for immediate regulatory purposes but also in the wider consciousness of all who participate in social life) by shaping over time such general ideas as property, ownership, responsibility, contract, rights, fault, and guilt, as well as notions of interests, identity, and community. To be theoretically coherent, the idea of law as constitutive in this sense – with antecedents stretching back to Marx's views on law's ideological power – must ultimately either presuppose some notion of law as self-founding or recognize that law and the social are *mutually* constituting, that law gains its meaning and ultimate authority from the social at the same time as it shapes the social through its regulatory force. In other words, law is an aspect or field of social experience, not some mysteriously "external" force acting on it.

This last conclusion might reopen Durkheimian questions about the social bases of law's authority and imply that the social is more coherent, stable, and susceptible to theorization than many writings on postmodernity assume. This is what Jürgen Habermas's social theory claims. It presents an image of society as made up partly of systems (e.g., economic, political, and legal systems), such as Luhmann describes, and partly of what Habermas calls the "lifeworld." The lifeworld is the environment of everyday social experience in which customs, cultures, moral ideas, and popular understandings are formed and reproduced. The lifeworld provides experiential "background knowledge" (Habermas, 1996: 23) with the aid of which people interpret each other's conduct and communicative actions, and it is the source of solidarity and legitimations necessary to the maintenance of the various systems that make up society. Yet it is continually colonized, invaded, and transformed by these systems. So, for Habermas, the social exists in the interplay of system and lifeworld.

In contrast to all postmodern portrayals of contingency, indeterminacy, and moral vacuity as characteristics of contemporary life, Habermas pursues the Enlightenment project of the discovery of reason in law, society, and nature. He sees law not as self-grounding but as deriving its authority from reason – what he calls a communicative rationality, dependent for its adequate development on certain ideal conditions under which agreement between persons pursuing opposed or divergent interests becomes possible. Law, for Habermas, is the only medium that can link the lifeworld and the various systems of complex modern societies. Law, as a system itself, depends on the lifeworld for its authority and significance. The Durkheimian aspect of Habermas's thought is thus an insistence that law must be rooted in and express lifeworld sources of social solidarity. He sees law as having the main responsibility to coordinate contemporary societies, participating in both the instrumental rationality that pervades social systems and the consensus-oriented communicative rationality that the maintenance of lifeworld solidarity requires.

In his major work on legal theory (Habermas, 1996), he insists that law and morality are distinct, though both derive from the same ultimate founding principle of communicative rationality. The conditions for this rationality to flourish include certain specified basic rights that can only be secured through legal processes. These processes, in turn, both presuppose and must be designed to support democratic structures. Law and democracy are thus inseparably interwoven.

Habermas's ideas on law have been much discussed in sociolegal literature, perhaps mainly because they clearly affirm law's relation to reason and the possibility of law's rational justification in the face of postmodern doubts. But these ideas have significantly shifted location over time. From components of an empirically oriented social theory focused notably on conditions of legitimate government in capitalist societies (Habermas, 1975), they have turned into a more speculative legal philosophy. Interestingly, Habermas (1987: 249) has criticized Foucault's view of power as "utterly unsociological" but the same might be said of some of his own very abstract, general discussions of communicative rationality.

Perhaps the most thought-provoking feature of Habermas's recent work is the fact that law has come to assume a very central position in his picture of society. If law might seem in some images of postmodernity to be the epitome of contemporary valid knowledge, in Habermas's entirely different outlook it appears, potentially at least, to epitomize essential social processes of consensus formation through interpretive procedures that hold out possibilities for developing communicative rationality. Law's procedures are the devices by which rationally oriented communicative action becomes practically possible on a society-wide basis. From a certain standpoint, then, the significance of law for social theory is affirmed in the most unambiguous terms. Law is the foundation of central structures of social life; a set of processes and procedures on which society's very integrity depends.

LAW BEYOND NATION STATES

I suggested earlier that law had often been able to avoid entanglement with social theory because it could take the nature of the social for granted. Law constitutes in regulatory terms what it treats as the social but it has to *presuppose* an overall conception of the social in which its regulatory actions can make sense. For a long time Western legal thought was able to presuppose the political society of the modern nation-state as its overall conception of the social.

The growth of transnational regulation and regulatory aspirations (in human rights, commerce and finance, intellectual property, environmental protection, information technology, and many other areas) creates new incentives for legal studies to draw on the resources of social theory. This is because it potentially disturbs long-standing presuppositions about law's stable relation to the political society of the nation state. Social theory's efforts to understand the social as extending beyond the bounds of society in this sense, or as shaped by powerful transnational forces, are presently organized mainly around the portmanteau concept of globalization. But law does not figure prominently in theories of globalization, perhaps because it is usually seen as following rather than actively shaping the transnational extension of the social. Globalization is often described in terms of particular forms of this extension such as the harmonization of markets, the transformation of culture (understood, for example, as traditions, basic values, or beliefs), or the effects of new communication technologies. Law's role, even where seen as vital in these developments, is usually thought of as purely technical. Relatively few writers (cf. Teubner, 1997; Santos, 2002) see the need for theories of "global law" or legal transnationalization. Law in its traditional forms is widely assumed to be endlessly adaptable, capable of relating to the social wherever legal practice encounters it.

I think that some of the most important future relations of legal studies and social theory will, however, focus on the need to understand the changing character of law as it participates in developments currently associated with globalization. How far is

social theory, which so often assumed the political society of the nation state as
the social, helpful as law increasingly relates to a social realm demarcated in
other terms?

As has been seen, debates inspired by Foucault's work address the nature of
contemporary regulation (with its intricate, if somewhat indeterminate, links to
the law created by sovereign power) and the complexity of networks of power in
the social. These debates have great relevance for attempts to understand the nature
and social contexts of transnational regulation. It will surely be necessary to ask
whether, at some point, transnational regulatory forms can presuppose, to use
Foucault's terms, the "cutting off of the king's head" (cf. Foucault, 1979: 88–9) –
in other words, the freeing of regulatory strategies from the coercive demands of
national sovereign power. It will be necessary to consider how far transnational
social spaces can be created in which dispersed but pervasive power can be used not
merely to discipline individuals, but also to create possibilities for their autonomy –
the dual aspects of this power analyzed in Foucault's work. In related ways, Ulrich
Beck's writings (e.g., Beck, 1992, 2000) identify, in terms of individualization and
risk, new regulatory problems but also new foci of liberating political action that
can, as he stresses, relate as much to transnational as national arenas.

An engagement between legal studies and social theory beyond the nation state
focus does not depend entirely on posing new sociolegal questions. It can also be a
matter of presenting old ones in new contexts. Some of the most important old
questions are about the way law secures authority through responsiveness to the
experience or understandings of the population it regulates. Durkheim, always
concerned with these issues, offered an important theory of democracy that has
been largely unrecognized in sociolegal studies. He understood democracy, as an
ideal practice, to be less a matter of popular representation than of sensitive,
informed deliberation by means of which understandings, issues, and values rooted
in widespread everyday social experience can be recognized and translated into
effective regulation (Cotterrell, 1999: chs. 10 and 11).

Durkheim's concerns about the moral groundings of law have not become irrelevant. But they are much more difficult to address when the social can no longer
easily be thought of simply as a unified national political society. It has become hard
to assume or specify a basis of moral cohesion in such a society, given what social
theory has taught about the diversity, fluidity, and contingency of the social. And the
wider terrain of the social over which transnational regulation now operates might
seem even more obviously culturally diverse, variable, fragmented, and indefinite
in scope.

Communitarian writings have explored what moral bonds are possible and necessary in complex modern societies but, despite efforts to ground their analyses in the
traditions of social theory (Selznick, 1992), they tend to be vague about the extent of
existing moral consensus in these societies (Bauman, 1993: 44–5) and risk lapsing
into nostalgia for old forms of social solidarity or moralistic exhortations to recover
values. Some alternative approaches have sought a presocial "ethics of alterity" as a
basis of moral evaluation of the social (Bauman, 1989: ch. 7, 1993: 47–53) and, by
extension, a means of morally evaluating contemporary law (e.g., Cornell, 1992).

A different way forward might be to accept the concept of community as a
potentially useful replacement for or supplement to that of (national) society, and
to accept the need for solidarity in communities as the moral justification for
regulating them, but to see community as existing in radically different forms: in

instrumental relationships such as those that provide the basis of commerce; in affective relationships of friendship, love, or care; in relations based on shared beliefs or ultimate values; and in traditional relations based on shared environments or historical experiences. On such a view, the social is structured by the fluid, intricate interweaving of different types of community, whether this interweaving constitutes the society of the nation-state, or particular groups or patterns of human interaction in this society, or networks of interaction, interests, or concerns extending across nation-state borders. On this view, law is the regulation and expression of communities (Cotterrell, 1997).

Old questions about law's bases of authority or legitimacy remain very important as the social seems increasingly "globalized," unless a view such as Luhmann's is adopted, suggesting that law's successful functioning is all that matters. Even if function is everything, it is still necessary to ask what ultimate conditions can ensure that law's regulatory functions are fulfilled. Habermas writes (1996: 33) that coercive law "can preserve its socially integrating force only insofar as the addressees of legal norms can understand themselves, taken as a whole, as the rational *authors* of those norms" (emphasis in original). Whatever view is taken of his ideas about communicative rationality, this restatement of an old problem can be seen to have new urgency as law extends its reach beyond national frontiers, and national lawmaking is more generally seen as driven by transnational forces.

If democracy, as Habermas claims, can in some conditions provide a sense of popular authorship of law in the political societies of nation states, where is such a sense to be found in the social realms addressed by transnational regulation or by national law subject to transnational pressures? How is Durkheim's democratic deliberation about the social to be achieved transnationally to create regulation that promotes solidarity? Marxist writings in social theory have properly emphasized – sometimes in debate with Foucault (Poulantzas, 1978: 76–92) – law's sources in organized power and the nature of its coercive and persuasive force (Jessop, 1980). But questions about its moral authority remain. As the nature of the social changes, sociolegal research is challenged to consider these questions anew, perhaps long before they become dilemmas disrupting law's everyday practice of the "method of detail."

References

Baudrillard, J. (1983) *In the Shadow of the Silent Majorities or, The End of the Social and Other Essays*. New York: Semiotext(e).

Bauman, Z. (1989) *Modernity and the Holocaust*. Cambridge, UK: Polity.

Bauman, Z. (1992) *Intimations of Postmodernity*. London: Routledge.

Bauman, Z. (1993) *Postmodern Ethics*. Oxford: Blackwell.

Beck, U. (1992) *Risk Society: Towards a New Modernity*. London: Sage.

Beck, U. (2000) *What is Globalization?* Cambridge, UK: Polity.

Beck, U. and Beck-Gernsheim, E. (2002) *Individualization: Institutionalized Individualism and its Social and Political Consequences*. London: Sage.

Beck, U., Giddens, A., and Lash, S. (1994) *Reflexive Modernization: Politics, Tradition and Aesthetics in the Modern Social Order*. Stanford, CA: Stanford University Press.

Brigham, J. (1996) *The Constitution of Interests: Beyond the Politics of Rights*. New York: New York University Press.

Cain, M. and Hunt, A. (eds.) (1979) *Marx and Engels on Law*. New York: Academic Press.

Cooper, D. (1998) *Governing Out of Order: Space, Law and the Politics of Belonging.* London: Rivers Oram Press.

Cornell, D. (1992) *The Philosophy of the Limit.* New York: Routledge.

Cotterrell, R. (1995) *Law's Community: Legal Theory in Sociological Perspective.* Oxford: Oxford University Press.

Cotterrell, R. (1997) "A legal concept of community," *Canadian Journal of Law and Society* 12: 75–91.

Cotterrell, R. (1999) *Emile Durkheim: Law in a Moral Domain.* Stanford, CA: Stanford University Press.

Douzinas, C. and Warrington, R. (1991) *Postmodern Jurisprudence: The Law of Texts in the Texts of Law.* London: Routledge.

Durkheim, E. (1975) "Individualism and the intellectuals," in W. S. F. Pickering (ed.), *Durkheim on Religion: A Selection of Readings with Bibliographies.* London: Routledge & Kegan Paul, pp. 59–73.

Durkheim, E. (1984) *The Division of Labour in Society.* London: Macmillan.

Ericson, R. and Haggerty, K. (1997) *Policing the Risk Society.* Toronto: University of Toronto Press.

Ewald, F. (1990) "Norms, discipline, and the law," *Representations* 30: 138–61.

Fitzpatrick, P. (1992) *The Mythology of Modern Law.* London: Routledge.

Fitzpatrick, P. (2001) *Modernism and the Grounds of Law.* Cambridge, UK: Cambridge University Press.

Foucault, M. (1977) *Discipline and Punish: The Birth of the Prison.* New York: Pantheon.

Foucault, M. (1979) *The History of Sexuality*, vol. 1. London: Allen Lane.

Foucault, M. (1991) "Governmentality," in G. Burchell, C. Gordon, and P. Miller (eds.), *The Foucault Effect: Studies in Governmentality with Two Lectures by and an Interview with Michel Foucault.* London: Harvester Wheatsheaf, pp. 87–104.

Franklin, J. (1998) *The Politics of Risk Society.* Cambridge, UK: Polity.

Geertz, C. (1983) *Local Knowledge: Further Essays in Interpretive Anthropology.* New York: Basic Books.

Goodrich, P. (1990) *Languages of Law: From Logics of Memory to Nomadic Masks.* London: Weidenfeld and Nicolson.

Gurvitch, G. (1935) *L'expérience juridique et la philosophie pluraliste du droit.* [*Legal Experience and Pluralist Philosophy of Law*] Paris: Pedone.

Gurvitch, G. (1947) *Sociology of Law.* London: Routledge & Kegan Paul.

Habermas, J. (1975) *Legitimation Crisis.* Boston: Beacon Press.

Habermas, J. (1987) *The Philosophical Discourse of Modernity: Twelve Lectures.* Cambridge, UK: Polity.

Habermas, J. (1996) *Between Facts and Norms: Contributions to a Discourse Theory of Law and Democracy.* Cambridge, UK: Polity.

Hunt, A. (1993) *Explorations in Law and Society: Toward a Constitutive Theory of Law.* New York: Routledge.

Jessop, B. (1980) "On recent Marxist theories of law, the state, and juridico-political ideology," *International Journal of the Sociology of Law* 8: 339–68.

King, M. and Piper, C. (1995) *How the Law Thinks About Children*, 2nd edn. Aldershot, UK: Gower.

Luhmann, N. (1981) "Communication about law in action systems," in K. Knorr-Cetina and A. Cicourel (eds.), *Advances in Social Theory and Methodology.* London: Routledge and Kegan Paul, pp. 234–56.

Luhmann, N. (1992) "Operational closure and structural coupling: The differentiation of the legal system," *Cardozo Law Review* 13: 1419–41.

Luhmann, N. (1995) *Social Systems.* Stanford, CA: Stanford University Press.

Lyotard, J.-F. (1984) *The Postmodern Condition: A Report on Knowledge.* Minneapolis: University of Minnesota Press.

Mauss, M. (1990) *The Gift: The Form and Reason for Exchange in Archaic Societies.* London: Routledge.

Merry, S. (1988) "Legal pluralism," *Law & Society Review* 22: 869–96.

Munro, V. (2001) "Legal feminism and Foucault: A critique of the expulsion of law," *Journal of Law and Society* 28: 546–67.

Parsons, T. (1964) "Evolutionary universals in society," *American Sociological Review* 29: 339–57.

Parsons, T. (1977) *The Evolution of Societies.* Englewood Cliffs, NJ: Prentice-Hall.

Poulantzas, N. (1978) *State, Power, Socialism.* London: New Left Books.

Pribán, J. and Nelken, D. (eds.) (2001) *Law's New Boundaries: The Consequences of Legal Autopoiesis.* Aldershot, UK: Ashgate.

Rose, N. (1996) "The death of the social? Re-figuring the territory of government," *Economy and Society* 25: 327–56.

Rose, N. and Valverde, M. (1998) "Governed by law?" *Social and Legal Studies* 7: 541–51.

Santos, B. de S. (2002) *Toward a New Legal Common Sense: Law, Globalization and Emancipation,* 2nd edn. London: Butterworth, 2002.

Selznick, P. (1992) *The Moral Commonwealth: Social Theory and the Promise of Community.* Berkeley: University of California Press.

Simmel, G. (1971) *On Individuality and Social Forms: Selected Writings.* Chicago: University of Chicago Press.

Simon, J. (1999) "Law after society," *Law and Social Inquiry* 24: 143–94.

Smart, B. (1993) *Postmodernity.* London: Routledge.

Smart, C. (1989) *Feminism and the Power of Law.* London: Routledge.

Teubner, G. (ed.) (1987) *Juridification of Social Spheres: A Comparative Analysis in the Areas of Labor, Corporate, Antitrust and Social Welfare Law.* Berlin: de Gruyter.

Teubner, G. (1993) *Law as an Autopoietic System.* Oxford: Blackwell.

Teubner, G. (ed.) (1997) *Global Law Without a State.* Aldershot, UK: Dartmouth.

Twining, W. (1974) "Law and social science: The method of detail," *New Society* June 27: 758–61.

Weber, M. (1978) *Economy and Society: An Outline of Interpretive Sociology.* Berkeley: University of California Press.

Further Reading

Cotterrell, R. (ed.) (2001) *Sociological Perspectives on Law. Volume 1: Classical Foundations. Volume 2: Contemporary Debates.* Aldershot, UK: Ashgate.

Febbrajo, A. and Teubner, G. (eds.) (1992) *State, Law, Economy as Autopoietic Systems.* Milan: Giuffrè.

Hunt, A. and Wickham, G. (1994) *Foucault and Law: Towards a Sociology of Law as Governance.* London: Pluto.

Rosenfeld, M. and Arato, A. (eds.) (1998) *Habermas on Law and Democracy: Critical Exchanges.* Berkeley: University of California Press.

Tie, W. (1999) *Legal Pluralism: Toward a Multicultural Conception of Law.* Aldershot, UK: Ashgate.

Wickham, G. and Pavlich, G. (eds.) (2001) *Rethinking Law, Society and Governance: Foucault's Bequest.* Oxford: Hart.

3

Profession, Science, and Culture: An Emergent Canon of Law and Society Research

CARROLL SERON AND SUSAN S. SILBEY

A recurring conversation over several decades among scholars from a variety of disciplines about a specific site for investigation – the law – has produced a set of perspectives that exemplifies some of the most important contemporary insights in many social science fields: that is, the "site" of social action matters to the meaning and organization of that action. Over the last decade or so, across the social sciences there has been a turn away from large-scale theory development and abstract modeling to more situated and contextualized analyses of sites of social action. While a concern for the close analysis of the sites of social action has long been a part of American social science (see e.g., Becker, Strauss, Hughes, and Greer, 1961; Gusfield, 1963), of late it has enjoyed a more widespread acceptance in the mainstream of the disciplines. Contemporary social scientists are finding ways to bridge the epistemological and theoretical paradigms that fuel their knowledge production while simultaneously creating deep chasms within each discipline. Thus the move to cultural analysis in many fields signals an effort to synthesize behavioral and structural as well as micro and macro perspectives. In its push to look closely at various formal and informal settings where legal activity – in all its guises – may unfold, the discipline of law and society is unusually well poised to make a major contribution to the theoretical development of a sociology of culture.

Tracing the canon of law and society research across a wide variety of formal and informal sites demonstrates that scholars have long documented that legality is not what it claims to be: it is both less and more; it is also raced, gendered, and unequal. What, from the standpoint of formal law and legal institutions, may be aberrant practice, is, when viewed from the ground up, routine and normal. Legality is situated and contingent on the particularities of time and place. In studying the formal institutions of law – courts, lawyers, policing, or administrative agencies, law and society scholars captured the importance of nuance, context, contingency, time, and place. But a review of the classics demonstrates, as well, that this insight goes further. For in also studying sites beyond the formal institutions of legality, these scholars revealed that the activities of doing law occur before the law begins; that is, law is *in* society, or laced through, between, and in society's culture. These themes emerge from a review of the classical canon of law and society research and are remarkably contemporary. They demonstrate that social theory and the concepts that guide its unfolding must be anchored by an appreciation for the contingent, the local, the culturally embedded, and the margins of social action. By researching the gap between the claims of law and its practices, and importantly the space within that gap, law and society scholars have moved closer to the mainstream of contemporary scientific and humanistic inquiry.

To demonstrate our argument that law and society is currently poised to make a substantial contribution to contemporary social theory, this essay is divided into two sections. The first section maps the intellectual background and professionalization of law and society research. Briefly, this map demonstrates that early law and society scholars used the newly minted methodologies of social science to answer the legal realists' question – does law deliver on its promise; is the law on the books the same as the law in action? The contemporary discipline of law and society takes up and expands this question to look at the constitution of legal action, not merely its instrumental forms. The research develops in a more professionalized setting, that is, with the trappings of associations, journals, funded support, and academic programs. Yet upon closer scrutiny this history also shows that the professionalization of law and society has not been quite as robust as its more mainstream counterparts, in part, we argue, because of the absence of a core theoretical frame to anchor an early body of research, or explicit connection to the central theoretical problems pursued by the more central social science disciplines.

The second section offers a brief tour through the classics of law and society, our construction of a law and society canon, including the work on courts, disputing, lawyers, juries, policing, and administrative enforcement and regulation. Every discipline, to the extent it is a discipline, develops a canon, a set of standard texts, approaches, problems, examples, and stories that its members repeatedly employ or invoke, that help define the discipline. A canon is what one reads as a rite of passage into an intellectual and professional community of scholars, and what one shares as part of the experience of membership. If the study of law (and here we add the crucial supplement) *and society* is a discipline, it too must have its canons and its own sense of the canonical (Balkin and Levinson, 1996; also see Sarat, 1998). A mature discipline generates a mature canon, classic research that defines the field, provides the point of departure for interactions of the moment, referenced for support or differentiation. In this sense, a canon of texts is both the objectification of a social process and a discursive engagement that "mutates continuously" in the frictional spaces of institutional reproduction (Guillory, 1987: 498). As the moment's residue of unceasing enterprise, a canon provides, therefore, a foundation for connection and contestation across generations and across subfields, promoting new questions and new research (Sarat, 1998). Any particular work is canonical or classical to the extent that it is part of the ongoing historically sedimented yet immanently unstable referential process.

In the law and society canon we can discover the major, timely, and important contributions of this research. Law and society scholars anticipated by many decades the importance of time and context to explain social action, in this case legality. By focusing so closely on the gap between the law on the books and the law in action, it turns out that law and society scholars opened the way for a cultural analysis of law, exploring with a variety of methodological and theoretical tools – from the social sciences and humanities – how that gap provides the space for the social construction of law and legality.[1]

TRACING THE ORIGINS OF THE CANON: ANTECEDENTS AND INTELLECTUAL CURRENTS

The discipline of law and society has diverse intellectual roots. While the relationship between law and society was central to the work of Marx, Weber, and Durkheim, in the United States law and society took its initial questions from legal realism. Housed in law schools, the American legal realists began with the premise that it is not sufficient to understand the meaning and role of law only as it appears on the "books"; rather, one must study the law "in action" using the techniques of social science. American social science developed, in contrast to its European parentage, with a rigorous attention to methodology. Law and society scholarship, specifically, sought to answer the questions posed by legal realism using the pragmatic, sometimes positivist, methods of American social science. In this forging of question and method, law and society scholarship paid much less attention to the development of a social theory of law and its role in modernization and social change, the paradigmatic questions of all the social sciences (Ross, 1991).

Law and modernization

From different analytical points of departure, Marx, Weber, and Durkheim set out to explain the processes of modernization or the transition from traditional to industrial society. Each pursued the analysis of social phenomena at the broadest level, seeing law as part of the transformation of social, political, and economic institutions. Emile Durkheim, for example, argued that law had become an embodiment of the "collective conscience" in societies with advanced divisions of labor, where interdependence and reciprocity prevailed. For Durkheim, "law is the example par excellence of the social fact. It is a visible symbol of all that is essentially social" (Hunt, 1978: 65). For Weber (1947, 1954), the forms of social organization that are characteristically modern are premised upon formal legal rationality and bureaucratic administration. These particularly legal features of modern society generate pronounced, and seemingly insoluble, tensions with which most modern societies struggle: contradictions between demands for predictability and equally valued demands for substantive justice. Marx deals with law somewhat less explicitly than Weber or Durkheim, and more critically. In contributing the concept of ideology, and its relationship to both material conditions of production and state power, Marx makes a major contribution to the study of modernization. In this context, both the law as it is written and the law as it is lived or experienced may be examined as a "hybrid phenomenon of politics and ideology, or a politico-ideological artifact" (Sumner, 1979: 266). While law is only one among many ideological "weapons," it contributes to the concealment or distortion in the formation and transformation of class relations. Thus, the study of law, it may be inferred, provides a lens for understanding how exploitative, unequal class relations are disguised and mystified.

For Durkheim, Marx, and Weber, law was the central site for mediating state and civil society, as well as the engine of modernization and social change.

The empirical study of law-in-action

In the passage from Europe to the United States, and in the development from social theory to sociological profession and practice, the understanding of the relationship between law, society, and modernity met new frontiers. The impact shaped the substantive agenda and methods of research. The social study of law became largely the province of the law school rather than the arts and science disciplines. In keeping with the interests of the legal academy and profession, law was defined primarily in terms of processes of creating and enforcing formal law, as machine rather than as a system of meaning. In this conceptual transformation, what law tells us about society is less important than what law does to society.

By adopting the lawyer's definition of their subject, social scientists limited their foci and topics of research to those of interest to the profession (Schlegel, 1995). At that moment, the question of law and modernization posed, if in different ways, by Durkheim, Weber, and Marx, was eclipsed. In the 1920s the American legal realists made the close exploration of a gap between the formal law and the law in action the central focus of their research. Thus, for example, studies of banking transactions and parking patterns were pursued with vigor to demonstrate whether law was following custom or whether practice conformed to law (Schlegel, 1995). Although scholars often produced findings about the law in action that challenged the most fundamental premises of the legal scholar, the research was not motivated by an overarching question grounded in social theory; they rarely pursued the relationship of these legal practices to the macro transformations of modern society.

To the traditional legal scholars' claim that law can be explained through the close reading of texts, its own printed materials, the turn of the century law and society scholar responded that law must be understood and explained empirically, as it is practiced and implemented in various formal and informal institutional settings ("law in action"). Thus in response to the legal formalists' claim that law is a science of close reading, social scientists offered a science of close observation. The policy and professional questions posed by the realists could be answered by their colleagues across campus with their newly minted training in social scientific methods. Each of the disciplines (sociology, psychology, anthropology, political science, economics) spawned a distinct set of research methods (and sometimes unquestioned middle level theories and assumptions) that nonetheless, at bottom, shared a fundamental commitment to the key tenets of scientific method: empirical, objective, and systematic observation of human behavior. From its earliest days, social scientists used both qualitative and quantitative techniques to record observation, but in either case they emphasized the scientific foundation of the enterprise.[2]

If the overarching topic of the social sciences was and remains the question of modernity (Ross, 1991: 8), scholars in the United States quickly developed a tidy division of labor to ensure more pragmatic (if fragmented) handles on this big question. The legal realists' questions animated much of the research, while the social scientists' methods – both quantitative and qualitative – provided the discipline of law and society. This division of labor led to specialization by field and methods of inquiry, so that, for example, jury studies eventually became the activity of social psychologists who had been trained in small group research and simulation, while judicial decision making became an activity of political scientists using statistical modeling techniques. Sometimes this division of labor reproduced narrow disciplinary and technical questions focused on operationalization, reliability, and validity, in which the virtues of the conceptual marriage between law and social science could be lost. Often, however, the persistent conversations across disciplinary boundaries invigorated the law and society scholarship so that the understanding of the constitutive role of law in society and culture came to predominate within law and society research. This move to a cultural/constitutive perspective developed earlier, we suggest, than in the traditional social science disciplines because of the challenge each disciplinary perspective offered to each other and because the diverse disciplinary perspectives were nonetheless all focused on the same relationship: law and society.

Professionalization of law and society

Intellectual currents are necessary but not sufficient for the development of a discipline. A discipline, as a distinct field of instruction and learning, also requires a professional home, or an institutional arrangement that ensures control over conditions of work and the development of a distinct body of knowledge. "The most strategic distinction" between professionals and other occupational incumbents "lies in legitimate, organized autonomy" (Freidson, 1970: 71) to legitimate the discretionary judgment derived from a body of abstract theories and concepts (Freidson, 2001). The prized autonomy to exercise discretionary judgment derives in large part from a distinct and protected knowledge base achieved through (1) a process of educational credentialing attached to a university, (2) the certification through licensing, and (3) the formation of a professional association that represents the interests and values of the discipline (but see Freidson, 2001).[3] The relationship between the modern university and professional authority cannot be overestimated: the university legitimates both credentialing and, through research, new theory, concepts, and methods.

Echoing the professional projects of science and social science, law and society has negotiated a place in the academy, albeit at the margins, securing professional autonomy through the formation of an association, the introduction of peer review journals, sources of support for research, and academic training. As an interdisciplinary field, however, law and society never secures the same level of autonomy and status as disciplinary fields, particularly in the social sciences (see e.g., Garth and Sterling, 1998; Schlegel, 1995; Tomlins, 2000). Nonetheless, if specialization is an indicator of professional advancement, the proliferation of associations, journals, research support, and training programs document the increasing maturity of the discipline.[4]

But specialization is only one piece of the professional picture. The theoretical foundation of knowledge is more fundamental for the development of an autonomous profession (Freidson, 2001) and, in this regard, law and society is on much less firm ground. Law and society as a discipline begins with the practical observation that law is made on the streets or "in action" and, as we document below, sets out to demonstrate whether and to what extent the law lives up to its promise in all its formal (courts, regulatory agencies) or informal (dispute processing, policing) homes. Thus, at its core, law and society research is motivated by a pragmatic, perhaps unabashed ideological concern. Is it what it claims to be? Until this question is itself made the subject of critical analysis, we suggest, law and society cannot move from the margins to the central problems addressed by the social sciences. Marx, Weber, and Durkheim grappled with law in the story of emerging modernity. But, unlike other areas of social research (e.g., organizational theory, social stratification, political sociology), their theoretical questions and the debates that derive from them did not drive the American empirical project to explain the role of law in modernization. To the extent that law and society research is not motivated by these, or other, central, organizing theoretical questions where empirical research may contribute to further development of theory and concepts, the profession grows from a less robust foundation than other specializations within the social sciences and, hence, enjoys less autonomy. As one indicator, most law and society scholars reside in various social science departments, such as political science, sociology, anthropology, or psychology rather than in departments of law and society. But, insofar as law and society scholarship can build on its canon, reframing to address the central questions (e.g., about social change and modernity, as well as power and inequality), it has the capacity to contribute important and durable insights to contemporary social theory.

THE CLASSICS OF LAW AND SOCIETY

Intellectual roots and professional organization provide the grounds for developing a canon. In canonical shorthand, the discipline of law and society studies that terrain we have already identified as the "law in action."[5] Law in action unfolds in courtrooms between judges and lawyers, among lawyers in their private offices, behind closed doors when juries make decisions, in negotiations among bureaucrats in regulatory agencies, on the street where police officers meet citizens, or in the actions and minds of citizens themselves when they make demands of the law, or contemplate and decide that this is not a matter for law.

Law in action is imagined in opposition to law on the books, that is, the traditional doctrinal stuff of law (cases, statutes, constitutions) conventionally regarded as the lawyer's particular and professional terrain. Staking its unique claim on the opposition between law-on-the-books and law-in-action, law and society scholarship reproduced, in the terminology and topics relevant to law, a host of morally colored dualisms that characterized Western philosophy and scholarship, oppositions between ideals and practices, words and actions, concept and phenomenon, force and norm, rationality and convention/tradition. By working outside the boundaries of law's official reality, law and society scholarship identified for itself a capacious ground. At the same time, it may have – for a long while – limited its conceptual imagination. Students of law and society have historically pursued the study of law-in-action in (1) courts, (2) lawyers' offices, (3) juries, (4) regulatory agencies, (5) police work, and (6) citizens' interactions with those legal actors and agencies. We will use these categories to organize our presentation of the classics in law and society because they were often developed, presented, and interpreted through these terms and what became subfields of the discipline. Over time, however, as the discourse and exchange developed, law and society scholars began to deconstruct their own categories and terminology and began to seek out the traces of legality in spaces further removed from formal or official law, for example, in theaters, homes, and hospitals. What began as a response to legal formalism sometimes became a narrow self-referential, disciplinary scientism. As often, or perhaps more often – this is a point of lively contestation – law and society developed by supplementing disciplinary questions, whether they derived from the legal academy or the social sciences. The continuing engagement led, we argue, to the cultural study of law that now characterizes a large part of the contemporaneously emerging law and society canon.

Reading the canon of law and society research, we noted several common themes. First, the practices and resources of law are unequally distributed and highly stratified. Studies show that social background and organizational capacity matter for access to law and the quality of legal services delivered and received. Second, what may seem aberrant malfeasance, extralegal and idiosyncratic from the standpoint of law on the books is, in practice, "normal" (Sudnow, 1965). Third, legal activities are situated and contingent on the particularities of specific times and places; for example, lawyers, much research shows, are not of one profession, one "brotherhood" (Goode, 1957); rather, lawyers' work and identities depend on who their clients are (Heinz and Lauman, 1982), where they went to school (e.g., Landinsky, 1963), or whether they work in the city or the country (e.g., Handler, 1967; Landon, 1990). Fourth, as both institutionalized and discursive practice, law consists of historically and culturally developed activities regulating and legitimating the use of force in social groups. It is simultaneously word and deed. Its legitimacy is inseparable from its activity, including the possibility of material violence (what Habermas, 1999, refers to as its factiticity).

Interestingly, and importantly, the sum of these themes is more than their individual parts. In the late twentieth century, across the mainstream social science disciplines there has been an important intellectual turn toward a more modest set of claims about the degree to which empirical findings may contribute to a general theory and set of concepts to guide understanding of modern society. It is now commonplace to couch theory and concept in time and place and to recognize the degree to which social patterns are contingent, local, culturally embedded, and emerge from negotiating the boundaries of professional and nonprofessional transactions (see e.g., Lamont and Fournier, 1992). Ironically, given its intimate contact with the legal academy and profession, the discipline of law and society stands poised to make a major contribution to this larger turn in social science theory precisely because the discipline has been discovering this point (the contingency of cultural locations and practices) for generations across multiple sites of legal encounter. What may have begun as a professional weakness (a sidestepping of the role of theory qua theory) for the discipline of law and society in the mid-twentieth century may prove to be its most important contribution to the social sciences more generally at the beginning of the twenty-first century.

Courts

Whereas legal scholars study judges' appellate decisions to identify the legal rules in force at any particular moment, students of law and society began by studying judges' backgrounds and patterns of decision making. Other law and society scholars reacted to what they saw as an overly behaviorist model and studied day-to-day interactions with lawyers, plaintiffs, defendants, and other court personnel to describe the courts. In both studies of judicial behavior and local courts, this field of law and society inquiry began by addressing questions that plagued jurisprudential and constitutional scholars for centuries: how consistent and predictable is judicial decision making and how can we justify nonelected powerful decision makers in a representative democracy? The field developed, however, to produce complex organizational and cultural accounts of the work of courts in the constitution of communities and the role of the judiciary in governance.

Growing out of a behavioral approach that takes "the behavior of individuals or groups of individuals as the primary unit of analysis" (Ulmer, 1961: 1), a large body of research developed early in the 1950s and 1960s that explained judicial activity at the appellate level as a function of judges' background and political ideology (Peltason, 1955; Schubert, 1965; Schmidhauser, 1960). The groundwork for the behavioral model of courts that later developed into richly textured analyses of court organization and culture was laid in several classic studies by C. Herman Pritchett on the Roosevelt (1948) and Vinson courts ([1954] 1966), and in Walter Murphy's synthetic statement in *Elements of Judicial Strategy* (1964). In effect, Pritchett and Murphy brought legal realism to political science. In the formalist account, judges mechanically decide cases by following the precedents of prior cases, *stare decisis* (but see Levi, 1949: 4–5). By following precedent, justices eschew their own policy preferences and honor the rule of law. By studying dissenting opinions, Pritchett showed that the willingness of justices to sublimate policy preferences varied historically. Over the decades, scholars of judicial decision making have generally confirmed Pritchett's hypothesis that justices were "motivated by their own preferences," rather than by transparent law (Pritchett, 1948: xiii). In *The Elements of Judicial Strategy*, Murphy elaborated and extended Pritchett's insight and suggested that the Supreme Court operates in a context not unlike that of elected officials, where justices strategically negotiate their positions on what cases to hear, which opinions to join, and what arguments to make in light of their expectations of what other justices and institutions would do.

The next generation of law and society students reacted to these studies of judicial decision making by turning their attention to the work of local courts. Blumberg's (1967) "The Practice of Law as a Confidence Game: Organizational Cooptation of a Profession," a study of criminal case decision making in a local court, is emblematic of a movement out of appellate courts to examinations of litigation in trial courts. In turning to the local level, Blumberg shows that the overwhelming majority of criminal cases are plea bargained, rather than tried; further, the work of the local court is more about efficiency and speed than about fairness and due process of law (also see Packer, 1968). In mapping his argument, Blumberg describes the organizational structure of the local court and the way in which this "organization" in fact encompasses the work of the judge as well as that of the local prosecutor, the clerk's office, probation, and defendant's counsel to form a bureaucratic "sieve" for the expeditious disposition of cases through negotiated pleas. He concludes that the day-to-day work of local courts is more akin to a rational, efficient bureaucratic system than it is to a procedurally fair, if slow, model of deliberative (judicial-like) decision making guided by doctrinal rules and procedural constraints. To study only the lofty reaches of appellate decision making, Blumberg implicitly claims, is to miss the main event in local courts where most of the work of law takes place.

In *The Process is the Punishment*, Feeley (1977) followed Blumberg's lead with close observation in the lower court trenches, but challenged the claim that these courts are bureaucratically organized, open systems where court players seek to ensure efficient outcomes. Feeley displayed the ways in which efforts to do "good," that is, to ensure substantive justice, are regularly compromised. This supposedly transparent and open system is fraught with politics, especially through elections and patronage appointments. Despite strong impulses for flexibility and commitments to substantive justice, pretrial costs shape the entire process, such that the process is the punishment (p. 291). Capturing a central tenet of much law and society research, Feeley intones Hand's observation, "Thou shalt not ration justice" (cited p. 291), only to report that in the most numerous courts in the nation, handling the major share of all legal business, in fact, one finds systematically rationed justice.

Jacob's (1965) work dispels similar myths about local civil courts. He demonstrates, for example, that the quality of justice depends on the quality of legal services and its availability to the public, that the quality of legal services available to a citizen is a function of that citizen's wealth and his or her ability to pay, that the American Bar Association (while willing to promulgate rules of ethics) is equally if not more concerned with protecting its members' interests, and finally that solo lawyers who work on the margins of the profession often engage in unethical practices (1965: 66; also see Carlin, 1962).

Galanter's seminal article, "Why the 'Haves' Come out Ahead: Speculation on the Limits of Legal Change" (1974), synthesized the work on civil courts up to the early 1970s and pushed it an important step further. Galanter developed a model of the cumulative effects of disadvantage between those he terms "one-shot" and "repeat" players in the civil courts. The sources of disadvantage are familiar from earlier studies; differences in knowledge of the system, experience, resources, and social access will impact the kind and quality of justice. The "repeaters," the large organizational clients of the civil courts, will come out ahead of the lone, individual "one-shot" players, Galanter hypothesizes. Galanter's hypothesis lays the foundation for a large body of research on courts and disputing, including the Civil Litigation Research Project (CLRP, Trubek, Sarat, Felstiner, Kritzer, and Grossman, 1983; see *Law & Society Review*, 1980–81) and the longitudinal study of case outcomes in the United States, in other countries, and comparatively across nation states (*Law & Society Review*, 1994).

Contemporary studies of courts remain largely the province of political science, even within law and society. While a much more elaborated and sophisticated model of judicial decision making continues to inform some scholars (Lee Epstein, 1998; Epstein, Segal, Spaeth, and Walker, 1996), others have built on the study of court cultures to understand the construction of constituencies (Eisenstein, Flemming, and Nardulli, 1988; Flemming, Nardulli, and Eisenstein, 1992; Nardulli, Eisenstein, and Flemming, 1988). Nonetheless, the contributions of this research go beyond political science; as we shall demonstrate below, findings from the study of courts complement findings from studies of other legal institutions and challenge the claims of the legal academy to special expertise and authority. Courts are, these findings make clear, highly stratified institutions – the kind of civil or criminal justice that you receive depends on what you have and the kind of lawyer you can get (Casper, 1972). Moreover, the court studies demonstrate that the "haves" come out ahead, not because of malfeasance or incompetence, but because courts are complex social institutions embedded in networks of relationships which both enable and constrain the courts' work. What may, at first glance, seem a social aberration from the standpoint of appellate case law is in fact normal practice: efficiency trumps effectiveness, administration of justice trumps adjudication, these findings show

PROFESSION, SCIENCE, AND CULTURE

(Heydebrand and Seron, 1990). Courts are not only, or even mainly, about abstract legal precedent or reasoned judgment (Levi, 1949).

Across a wide body of research at various tiers, law and society studies show that the work of courts is locally shaped and culturally entwined in place and setting. Idiosyncratic and particularistic practices develop among teams or work groups and between and among judges, lawyers, and court personnel to shape the disposition of legal matters, the constitution of subjects and communities, as well as the quality of justice and the meaning of the rule of law (Jacob and Eisenstein, 1991). By closely observing the intersection of actors, organization, and history, the research on courts moved beyond more narrow disciplinary interests in sharpening methodological tools and honing concepts through those tools to study, for example, the contemporary work of constitutional courts to shape individual subjectivities as well as societies. At the same time, by consistently focusing on litigation and the work of courts, this research developed an appreciation for particularity and local variation within what might seem like general organizational and representational practices.

Disputing

The body of work that gave distinctive shape and substance to the field of law and society began by looking outside of courts, or any other formal institution of law. In a truly groundbreaking study, *The Cheyenne Way* (1941), Llewellyn and Hoebel claimed that the place to begin research is the "trouble case," places where the taken for granted modes of social interaction break down. Building on the concept of the "trouble case", disputing establishes a central premise of the discipline of law and society: studying law must begin *before* law, or legal norms, emerge. In *The Cheyenne Way*, Hoebel and Llewellyn threw out the lawyer's understanding of law as organized social control and violence and replaced it with a notion of law as a system of normative regulation with four basic functions: disposition of "trouble cases"; preventive channeling, orientation, and expectations to avoid conflict; allocation of authority; and "net drive" providing incentive, direction, and harmonization of activity. In effect, Llewellyn and Hoebel collected under the rubric of law several, but not all, basic social functions. This way of viewing law challenged a claim for the preeminence of courts as the central site for legal production and organization. Also, in articulating this "discovery" of *law in society*, the discipline of law *and* society began to develop parallel sites for research that were not limited to the legal realist's agenda.

Laura Nader, trained in anthropology and one of the group who organized the Law and Society Association and journal, built on the work of Llewellyn and Hoebel as well as post-World War II anthropologists such as Gulliver, Evans-Pritchard, Gibbs, Radcliffe Brown, and Bohannon, to champion the concept of dispute as the building block for a sociocultural study of law. Through the lens of the dispute process it is possible, she argued, to develop a social theory that explains the relationship between social control and social change. Equally, Nader (1978) argued for contextualized ethnographies of courts, if appropriate, but where disputing remained the organizing construct. This body of work begins, then, with the premise that disputes are windows on society, openings in the social fabric, or moments of exploration in which the collectivity is challenged, transformed, or repaired.

Anthropologists were not, however, alone in noticing that much law-like activity took place outside of the formal institutions of law, or in noting the virtue of studying trouble and dispute. In the second most widely cited paper in the law and society canon, Stewart Macaulay, a professor of law at the University of Wisconsin, published in the *American Sociological Review* (1963) a study of the "noncontractual" relations among automobile manufacturers and their franchisees. Although the relationships between manufacturers and dealers are entirely legalized, Macaulay observed that disagreements and disputes between them were handled through informal discussion and negotiation, rather than by invoking the provisions and remedies of the contracts that legally obligated the parties. Macaulay also discovered that the binding business agreements were frequently made without knowledge of the relevant rules of contract law and that, in many cases, the contracts might be invalid according to those rules, were they challenged in court. But they were rarely challenged because businessmen routinely sought to avoid the law, lawyers, and the courts in conducting their affairs. The desire to continue relationships and norms of decency underwrote a panoply of informal, "man-to-man" discussions in lieu of professional hermeneutical readings of contractual language, a set of findings that supported Merton's (1968) middle-range theory of norms and their role in social relations.

In the 1970s a series of papers further developed the notion of dispute and disputing (Felstiner, 1974, 1975; Abel, 1973; Danzig and Lowy, 1975). The claim that disputes, and their resolution, do not occur only in courts of law, or even in the close "shadow of the law" (Mnookin and Kornhauser, 1979) laid the foundation for this large-scale, systematic survey of citizens' disputing experience, where respondents were asked about their reliance on a range of formal and informal institutions associated with disputing. The Civil Litigation Research Project (CLRP), a collaboration organized out of the University of Wisconsin, and funded by the US Department of Justice, began with the assumption that it is possible to use "disputes as a link between [the study of] law and society" (Trubek, 1980–81: 496). Important findings and resilient models emerged from this research, perhaps the largest and most ambitious attempt to use the concept of dispute to organize empirical work on law. First, despite popular representations to the contrary, results supported Macaulay's qualitative findings of two decades earlier. Even when citizens have grievances and complaints, they prefer to avoid the law or the use of third parties to resolve the dispute. Most Americans do not pursue grievance through law; they "lump" their losses rather than litigate (Felstiner, Abel, and Sarat, 1980–81). Second, and importantly, the subject of disputes (i.e., whether it is a commercial, family, or civil rights issue) matters and is modeled by a distinctly shaped pyramid (Miller and Sarat, 1980–81). Third, despite some important challenges to the dispute processing paradigm (Engel, 1980; Kidder, 1980–81), a "life history perspective" of disputing proved fruitful in redefining the concept of dispute and formulating the disputing pyramid as the model of how citizens "mobilize" the law.

Thus a large body of law and society literature has looked at the genesis of legal action from a variety of perspectives and with a range of methods: from studies of the legal needs of the general public (Curran, 1977), to variations in legal use by social class and race (Carlin, 1962; Black and Reiss, 1967; Silberman, 1985; Caplowitz, 1974), and community organization (Merry, 1990; Yngvesson, 1993). What was sometimes begun as part of a policy agenda, to make more law more accessible, to determine whether equal justice prevailed, led to fundamental rethinking of the law in action paradigm, including significant internal struggles about method and politics (Silbey and Sarat, 1987; Sarat and Silbey, 1988; *Legal Studies*

Forum, 1985; Trubek and Esser, 1989). What started out as no more than "a general set of orientiations" crystallized into a major perspective and direction for research, analogous one might say to the physicists' search for elementary particles through ambitious experiments and giant, international collaborations.

The project and the dispute concept was not, however, without active criticism and revision; its ambition seemed to direct attention to its limitations. Some anthropologists, for example, argued that the focus on trouble and the management of trouble was distracting attention from the far more general pattern of acquiescence and normative integration in social life. They worried that the dispute perspective condemned social science, again as the legal profession had traditionally done, to studying the tip of the iceberg; as a result, the claim of social science knowledge to challenge or enhance knowledge within the legal field would be limited. Other scholars criticized the concept for its boundless quality. They worried that following the life history of disputes, if taken to its logical extent, would undermine social scientific aspirations by dissolving law into all of social relations (Kidder, 1980–81), at the same time farther and farther away from the institutions of the official law. Law and society would no longer have a subject, and thus no particular or distinctive professional claim.

As sociolegal scholarship has moved to include a wider range of methods and approaches, such as those associated with the humanities, this same worry is repeated. We see this, however, not as a loss of focus on the legal but rather as an opportunity to connect with and contribute to contemporary social theory. The disputing research, like much contemporary scholarship, sought to model and test theories connecting micro and macro social phenomenon. Joining anthropological theory and methods to legal concerns enabled the observations of the systematic construction of the material that becomes the stuff of official law; at the same time, this happy marriage encouraged anthropologists to see how much of everday life and normativity was saturated with law, providing additional concepts with which to understand cultural and social phenomenon. We now turn to the actors who perform central roles in the transformation of disputes from normative conflicts to legal cases.

Lawyers

The legal scholar begins with the premises that all attorneys are part of a common and shared professional enterprise and that the role of the academic community is to serve the profession by first educating each generation of lawyers concerning the technical rules of legal doctrine and procedure, and second by developing a common set of ethical standards for professional practice. Early law and society scholars borrowed concepts from a long-standing sociological tradition to explain the factors that distinguish a profession such as law from other occupations. Parsons (1949) had posited that the growth of the professions is one of the most important characteristics of the twentieth century and, further, that a profession may be distinguished from other occupations by its commitment to serve the public interest, by its organization into small collegial communities, and by its commitment to the self-regulation of entry, education, and retention of members.

Two early classics pursued these Parsonian questions by looking at how the profession of law is practiced in solo settings (Carlin, 1962) and in large firms (Smigel, 1969). Carlin's study, *Lawyers on their Own*, paints a portrait of the solo practitioner that is far removed from the lofty reaches of legal scholars' claims to universalistic value orientations. The solo lawyer's calling to serve individual clients is not a rewarding or professionally gratifying one, Carlin found. For example, he shows that solo lawyers are forced to engage in quite aggressive tactics to get clients in the door – practices that may be marginal, if not unethical (see Carlin, 1962). Solo lawyers may find themselves in competition with others for an individual client's various needs such as a house closing, simple will, or contract. For the solo lawyer, Carlin claimed, the norm of collegiality may be more myth than practice as they report lonely, isolated work lives. Indeed, a solo lawyer's lot may be so precarious that he (and it was all men) is forced to supplement his legal practice with other forms of work in order to make a living. Finally, Carlin demonstrated, solo lawyers tended to be the sons of immigrants, many of whom worked their way through proprietary night law schools.[6]

Smigel's (1969) study of the legal elite, *Wall Street Lawyers*, paints a very different picture of legal practice. Wall Street lawyers worked in large firms and served institutional clients. Yet all firms are not the same. Smigel identified two tiers among Wall Street firms, the "white shoe" (WASP) firms that tend to handle corporate securities, and the ethnic firms composed of newly arrived, upwardly mobile and Ivy League educated Catholics and Jews that tended to do corporate litigation. Wall Street lawyers go to school together, but there is an ethno-religious division of labor in their work lives, Smigel finds. Complementing the Parsonian paradigm, Smigel also reported that, despite the size of the Wall Street firms, they were by no means Weberian bureaucracies with rules, hierarchies, and specializations. Rather, his findings showed that the organization of the Wall Street firm of the late 1950s echoed the profession's ideal of collegiality: lawyers are generalists, educated in all facets of the law; associates, almost all male, are mentored by partners who, in turn, make decisions collectively about matters of policy and candidacy for partnership.

If one allows the gender question to be raised one may ask: is law a variation on a male fraternity, that is, a closed company of men? In her pioneering study, Cynthia Fuchs Epstein (1998) examined the work lives of those women who achieved the pedigrees of elite legal education and sought to break into Smigel's Wall Street firms. Deviants from the gender norms of their generation, these women used the legal language of fairness and equality to gain entry to the fraternity, but tended to find themselves relegated to specialties that are stereotypically feminine, such as trusts and wills and estates.[7]

In their classic study, *Chicago Lawyers*, Heinz and Laumann (1982) build on these in-depth ethnographies of various domains of practice to explain the stratification and network within the profession at large. Beginning with the classic question in social stratification (to what degree does background impact upward mobility?), Heinz and Laumann explain the organization and social networks of the legal profession in a large city (also see Landinsky, 1963). Based on a survey of a random sample of Chicago lawyers, they conclude that the legal profession may be best understood as two "hemispheres" organized around client bases of one-shot individuals or repeat player organizations (Galanter, 1974). If one knows whether an attorney serves individuals or organizational clients, Heinz and Laumann argue, one may predict the social background of the incumbent's father, where the incumbent went to law school, the incumbent's social network for getting more clients, and the social status of the incumbent in the eyes of his peers.[8] In many respects, Heinz and

Laumann's larger, more systematic, and quantitative study of the profession lends support to Carlin's picture of the precarious solo practitioner, Smigel's portrait of the comforts enjoyed by the elite men of the profession, and Cynthia Fuchs Epstein's description of the ways in which women are often all but ignored or required to work in stereotypically feminine areas of specialization.[9]

Despite the law and society scholar's ambition to challenge the normative claims of the legal scholar, there was a more fundamental tendency to leave the institutional pillars of the profession unexamined. As the social sciences in the United States took a more critical, neo-Marxist turn in the late 1960s, the sociology of professions developed new conceptual models to explain the relationship between social class and the "professional project" (Larson, 1977) as well as the deprofessionalization or proletarianization of professional labor (Haug, 1973, 1975; Oppenheimer, 1973).[10] This sociological work, particularly that of Larson (1977), laid the foundation for a large-scale, comparative study of the legal profession (Abel and Lewis, 1989) that, in many respects, returns the study of lawyers to the intellectual roots of the social sciences, or the role of lawyers in modernization. Together, this body of work documents the ways in which the profession is laced with structural inequalities, the ways in which the legal scholar's claim to what would be idiosyncratic is found to be normal practice, and the ways in which a professional's background (gender, geographical location, father's occupation) shapes opportunities and outcomes for mobility.

Building on the early twentieth-century Chicago School of sociology, Everett Hughes and his students, particularly Freidson (1970), Becker, Strauss, Hughes, and Greer (1961), and Strauss (1961) had offered an important methodological challenge to large-scale survey research, such as Heinz and Laumann's study through the use of a close, systematic, and inductive method to study professionals at work. Through their grounded examination of professional labor, they demonstrate the ways in which a legitimate autonomy to exercise discretionary judgment unfolds in practice. While much of this research examines the medical profession and the relationship between doctors and a support team of nurses and other staff, these scholars document the ways in which hierarchy, status, and position are constituted and interpreted in and through practice (also see Abbott, 1981). Recent law and society studies of the legal profession take as their starting point the blending of the traditional and the interpretive bent; that is, there is a recognition of the need to anchor the interpretation of lawyers' practice in the context of the rules, work settings, and institutional constraints that are specific to the profession of law. To take but one contemporary example, Mather, McEwen, and Maiman (2001) document the ways in which socialization, identity, and communities of practice create spaces for divorce lawyers to shape a culture of professional labor.

Juries

Variously described as the bulwark of true democracy (DeTocqueville, 1938) or as a vestigial organ of the body politic (Griswold, 1973), juries are seldom used in American courts.[11] Nonetheless, Llewellyn (1969) argued in his introductory lectures for first year law students that the imagining or assumption of decision making by a jury of lay people lies at the heart of the legal process, animating and explaining the rules of evidence and the entire trial process. Because of its central, yet ambiguous, role, the civil and criminal jury has long been a subject of debate concerning its ability to provide competent, fair, and equitable decisions. This age-old debate within jurisprudence has turned on questions of fundamental values and normative judgment, the relationship between law and democratic participation.

The student of law and society expands the normative and philosophical questions about the jury to inquire about how juries actually behave. For example, confronted with a similar case or fact pattern, do juries behave differently from judges? What is the process of decision making within a jury? And, further, in that process do gender and social background matter? Does size make a difference? Echoing studies of courts and lawyers, the student of law and society examines the jury empirically.

In 1952, researchers at the University of Chicago Law School began the first systematic study of the American jury system with a grant from the Ford Foundation. The research became known as the Chicago Jury Project, and it marked one of the first postrealist efforts to study empirically the legal system. The Chicago Jury Project produced three books: *The American Jury* (Kalven and Zeisel, 1966), *Delay in Court* (Zeisel, Kalven, and Bucholz, 1959) and *The Jury and the Defense of Insanity* (Simon, 1967).

Kalven and Zeisel (1966) examined whether and to what extent juries depart from judges in deciding criminal cases where the fact patterns of the cases are the same. They enlisted 55 judges to complete questionnaires about their proposed verdict in a criminal trial prior to learning the jury's verdict. After comparing the judges' verdicts to the decisions reached by juries, the authors found that there is a small proportion of criminal cases where the judge's and jury's decision depart, and that "there is no category [of criminal cases] in which the jury is totally at war with the law" (p. 76). Also, their findings revealed that as a general rule juries are competent and do understand the facts. Thus their findings lend support to the claim that a jury of one's peers may understand the facts of a case and, on balance, come to decisions that are in conformity with legal precedent. If jurors do understand the facts as presented, why do juries reach different conclusions from judges in some instances? At a general level their findings suggest that jurors' decisions rest on a somewhat closer, more individualistic evaluation of the circumstances surrounding a particular case. For example, in contrast to a judge, jurors may be willing to acquit if they find police or prosecutorial practices highly improper (p. 319).

Simon (1967) examined the jury's ability to weigh the insanity defense, and specifically the Durham rule adopted in the District of Columbia in 1954. At its core, the Durham rule establishes that a criminal defendant may be excused from prosecution if his or her act was the result of mental disease or defect. In the aftermath of the adoption of this rule, findings suggest that more criminal defendants are acquitted than before, but that jurors feel somewhat constrained by the black or white framework of the legal rules. Her findings show that jurors would prefer to find defendants guilty and to commit them to an institution that both punishes and treats – an option that is not available to them under the rule. Simon brings a strong sociological eye to her study and also examines the impact of social status and gender on jury decision making: while she finds some evidence that jurors of lower social status are somewhat more likely to favor the defendant than their higher status counterparts, that "housewives" are somewhat more likely to be punitive than other members of the jury, and that the foreman is somewhat more likely to be a person of higher social status, there is "no consistent evidence that the opinions of jurors in higher socioeconomic statuses carried more weight than the opinions of lower status jurors" (p. 118).[12]

Despite their groundbreaking results, Kalven and Zeisel were concerned that perhaps they had, like much legal research before them, studied the wrong thing, the tip of the jury iceberg, that is, the cases where juries and judges disagree. Perhaps they should have focused on the more than three-fourths of all jury activity where there was agreement between the professional and lay judgment; perhaps they should study the deliberation process rather than the outcome. Thus, in 1954, with support of judges in Wichita, Kansas, participating attorneys, and strict control over the process and anonymity of the participants, Kalven and Zeisel made audio recordings of six jury deliberations. Public notice eventually brought Congressional notice and in 1955 the Subcommittee on Internal Security of the Senate Committee on the Judiciary held hearings on researchers' access to jury deliberations. Because the project observed actual jury deliberations, Congress decided that it had infringed privacy rights and the sanctity of the jury. In 1964, Congress passed legislation prohibiting recording of federal jury deliberations, and most states followed suit.

From the mid-1950s, when the data were collected, until the late 1990s, only two jury deliberations have been recorded since Kalven and Zeisel's initial attempt (Hans and Vidmar, 1991). Thus the extensive body of jury research that developed following this early project was conducted largely by social psychologists interested in small group dynamics who could draw upon their discipline's tradition of experimental simulations as well as surveys (posttrial and judicial). The themes to emerge from this research are by now familiar. Research on jury deliberations has focused on leadership roles, discussion content, participation, and to the extent possible in simulations, the structure of deliberations including the role of social status, gender, and sequence of participation. The research has served well the social scientists' interests in developing methodological sophistication and a program of normal, iterative scientific study. Pursuing the legal profession's agenda, the studies have also shown that juries – perhaps the most democratic pillar of the law – perform their duties in a manner that complements the more fundamental claims of the law: jurors take their responsibilities for rational deliberation seriously; they consider issues of social circumstance as well as legal doctrine, and do so in a manner that is fair and reasonable.

Currently, there is a study underway in Arizona that will allow scholars once again to study actual jury deliberations. With the opportunity to study 50 actual transcripts of jury deliberations in cases that raise a variety of legal issues at a range of monetary stakes, this groundbreaking work may push the boundaries of research on juries, providing a foundation to join research on juries to a wider range of literature in law, as well as culture. With the ability to observe and transcribe the jury deliberations, it may be possible to analyze how juror's processes of "reading" and "making" facts as well as their legal consciousness and understandings of the law shape deliberation and outcome (Diamond et al., 2003).

Policing

Whereas the modern legal profession and its various off-shoots developed its own research agenda in the academy, policing did not participate in this core project of professionalization (Bittner, 1990: 311–13). Police were studied as part of general sociological and criminological inquiry about deviance, crime, and social control. Social movements of the 1960s, particularly the civil rights movement, laid the foundation for research on policing. As Bittner (1990) explains, the civil rights

movement exposed middle-class college students to something they had never experienced, the surveillance practices of the police; equally, the civil rights movement
gave people "from the wrong side of the track" a voice to demand examination of
surveillance by police that had long been a part of their daily routines. In the 1960s
the police became a centerpiece of "embattled" public debate (Bittner, 1990: 312);
with abundant resources for social science investigation (p. 313), an agenda of
critical study emerged, though one that was not designed or launched by the police
themselves.

Skolnick (1966), Reiss (Reiss, 1971; Black and Reiss, 1967), and Bittner (1970,
1990) conducted seminal studies of policing and, in the process, laid the foundation
for an important line of law and society research. Policing, these scholars demonstrate, operates in a context of enormous social and cultural ambiguity. In the
popular imagination, police work is "tainted" because, in the eyes of citizens, its
fundamental charge is to ensure social control and social order, to do society's dirty
work in areas that most would prefer to forget is a problem – among racial and
ethnic minorities, the young, and the poor (Bittner, 1970). Tainted police work was,
however, frequently subject to judicial review and oversight as courts stepped into
the fray through decisions that sought to define the boundaries of appropriate police
practices. When the courts discovered the police's use of a heavy hand to ensure
social order, a large gap between constitutional rights and police practices, decisions
followed – especially in the wake of 1960s protest – to establish "legal restraints" by
protecting civil liberties and to insure consistency between the law on the books and
law in action (Skolnick, 1966).[13]

Beyond the more abstracted social ambiguities about the public's expectations of
officers' roles and responsibilities, and the ambiguity between what the law books
required and the police delivered, there are very particular ambiguities for police "on-
the-street," when an officer is called to the scene. As Black and Reiss (1967) explain, a
call comes in and a curtain is raised on a "social stage for face-to-face encounters." But
each dimension of that stage is "ambiguous," from the setting to the social status of
the actors to the plot that will unfold (p. 8). Will it be a plot that involves "family
trouble," "a man with a complaint," or a "B & E [breaking and entering] report"?
Each of these encounters has the potential to raise "matters involving subtle human
conflicts and profound legal and moral questions" (Bittner, 1970: 9).

Against this backdrop, police develop their own informal norms or "hidden
principles" (Skolnick, 1966) of work. For example, officers operate in a potentially
dangerous environment but, unlike the soldier in battle, the danger is highly episodic
(Black and Reiss, 1967) and may, in fact, take only about a third of any officer's time
(Bittner, 1970). Or, in doing the work to control society's nuisances – the prostitute
or even the traffic violator – police see such activities as "affronts" to their competence (Skolnick, 1966: 111). The police are, however, also called on to perform like
social workers or "problem solvers" (Bittner, 1970) and carry, as well, a certain
authority, not unlike a community's schoolteacher (Skolnick, 1966). Thus, when
confronted with the citizen who does not take that authority seriously, "policemen
seem more hostile or authoritarian, or more likely to ridicule citizens of both races
when the citizens are agitated than when they are calm or detached" (Black and
Reiss, 1967: 35).

At the end of the day and on the street alone or with a partner, as each of
these students of policing demonstrates, in perhaps their most important actions –
encounters with citizens – police officers' work takes place on a stage "where

departmental control is minimal" and sometimes nonexistent (Black and Reiss, 1967: 10), and where law seems quite distant. Although proceeding from different vantage points, these authors demonstrate that, like their counterparts carrying out administrative regulation (see next subsection below), at its core, police enjoy enormous discretion. While rules can be placed "on the books" to limit and guide police action "on the street," "no matter how far we descend on the hierarchy of more and more detailed formal instructions, there will always remain a step further down to go, and no measure of effort will ever succeed in eliminating, or even in meaningfully curtailing, the area of discretionary freedom of the agent whose duty is to fit rules to cases" (Bittner, 1970: 4).

Studies of policing share themes with other arenas of law and society research, yet also bring new and important insights about society's relationship to law. Policing, like judging, is anchored by a cultural expectation that a commitment to social order is balanced by a commitment to legality. Like other aspects of legal practice, this commitment to legality is something other than literal fidelity to law on the books because here, like elsewhere, there is a persistent gap. Even though the most important *"role of the police"* is to serve *"as a mechanism for the distribution of non-negotiable coercive force employed in accordance with the dictates of an intuitive grasp of situational exigencies"* (Bittner, 1970: 46; italics in original), these officers of the law are nonetheless called to balance this responsibility with that of "legality." But the social context of this balancing act by police is anchored by paradoxical, and perhaps unique, social dynamics. Policing takes place "on the street" where it is seen by the public, yet largely unobserved or unsupervised by other legal actors. For citizens, their most typical encounter with the law is through the police (Skogan, 1994). Yet for legal elites, authorities, writers, and commentators on the law, police are remote, overlooked, and sometimes embarrassing stepchildren of the legal system. They do the dirty work of the legal system, cleaning up social messes, deploying situated force, dispensing the violence inherent in all law, yet they are routinely regarded as outside the law. The discretionary authority of policing coupled with the impact of the "situational exigencies" of the moment, including the highly differential experiences of policing by race and ethnicity, renders policing a much less idealized activity of law than judging or, perhaps, lawyering. It is against this discretionary backdrop of "situational exigencies" that internal cultural norms and socially situated orientations among the police unfold. Police see themselves as good "craftsmen," engaged in discretionary routines to ensure social order; thus there is little tolerance for those who they believe misunderstand the police, seek to limit their discretion – including courts – or undervalue the day-to-day dangers of their work lives (Skolnick, 1966). Perhaps because of the overwhelming situatedness of policing, and the essential connection between policing and legal authority, as well as the very marked features of the subculture of policing, research on the police has produced some of the most enduring insights about the importance of contingency and context for legal culture.

Administrative law and regulation

Echoing findings from policing, discretion emerges as the centerpiece for understanding administration law enforcement and regulation. Since the 1880s, a good part of American law has been devoted to the regulation of routine business practice. From some perspectives, this type of regulation is an extension of the public order, policing functions that are a central feature of any state and that were deployed in the early republic to create the normative framework and capital for both commerce and the state (Hurst, 1964). With the establishment of the Interstate Commerce Commission in 1881, created to regulate the monopolistic policies of the railroad industry, the United States invented a form of quasi-executive-legislative-judicial agency that would simultaneously develop expertise to oversee, through investigation and quasi-judicial deliberation, matters relevant to congressionally regulated aspects of social life. This hybrid legal form has taken on special significance in American history, politics, and law, however, because this late nineteenth-century regulation came about as part of a continuing contest about the prerogatives of capital and the possibilities as well as the shape of the modern (welfare) state.

A good part of the early law and society scholarship focused directly on the work of the various administrative agencies that emerged at the end of the nineteenth and beginning of the twentieth centuries as part of the attempt to describe the relationship between the law-on-the-books and the law-in-action. Taking the moral aspirations of the rule of law quite seriously (as effort to limit official power by a system of rules, Dicey, 1915), a desire to reduce the arbitrariness of power (Selznick, 1969), and accountability for the use of force (Davis, 1972a), observers declared the regulation of business for the common good to be a failure. A consensus developed among scholars that things never quite work as they ought when legislation is translated into administrative action. Much effort was devoted to understanding how agencies mandated to serve the public become ineffective and indolent (Bernstein, 1955; Edelman, 1964; Shapiro, 1968; Kolko, 1965; Orren, 1974).

Various explanations were suggested to explain why public regulatory agencies seem to serve the interests they were designed to regulate and control. The explanations ranged from analyses of the symbolic nature of the legislative process that produces inconsistent mandates (Edelman, 1964), to analyses of the segmented structure of a system that encourages a division of the commonweal among interested parties to the exclusion of the unorganized public (Lowi, 1969).

Taking a closer look inside the agencies, researchers demonstrated that discretion is unavoidable and necessary to meet statutory goals (Davis, 1972a; Kadish and Kadish, 1973; Lipsky, 1980). Although statutes set theoretical limits to official action, they cannot determine how things are done within those limits. By choosing among courses of action and inaction (Davis, 1972b: 91), individual law enforcement officers become agents of clarification and elaboration of their own authorizing mandates (Jowell, 1975: 14). Bureaucrats – public and private administrators – become lawmakers "freely" creating what Ross (1970) referred to as a third aspect of law beyond written rules or courtroom practices. This law in action arises in the course of applying the formal rules of law in both private settings and public bureaucracies. It is the working out of authorizing norms through organizational settings. In the process of working out mandates, organizations modify the goals they were designed to serve. Members of organizations temper internal and environmental pressures to ensure the survival of the organization and, implicitly, the survival of the organization's goals. Public bureaucracies implement policy within special constraints, and often fail to provide mandated services. Agents in "street level" bureaucracies are expected to interact with clients regularly, but their work environments are pressured and stressful. Resources are limited. Mandates are too frequently ambiguous or conflicting. The clients are the lifeblood of the organization, but they are not the primary reference group for decision making or accountability. As a result, it is difficult to assess or reward job performance. Agents cope with these stresses by developing routines and simplifications that economize on resources. They invent definitions of effectiveness that their procedures are able to meet (Silbey, 1980–81: 851). They mobilize whatever legal rule, statute, or procedure will accomplish the substantive goal, even if it is not part of the agency's authorizing mandate (Silbey and Bittner, 1982). In so doing, they may alter the concept of their job, redefine their clientele, and effectively displace the organization's stated mandate.

In response to the discovery of discretion, policy analysts argued for more formal control through rulemaking to confine, structure, and review administrative and law enforcement discretion. But, here again, law and society scholars observed unintended consequences. Kagan suggested that with demands for greater control of discretion came changes in the style of government regulators. In *Going by the Book*, Bardach and Kagan described this shift "away from a traditional enforcement style that relied heavily on persuasion, warnings, and informal negotiations, and towards a legalistic style that stresses strict application of legal regulations and prompt impositions of heavier legal sanctions for all detected violations" (Bardach and Kagan, 1980: 1). The new legalistic style, Bardach and Kagan described, was not adopted uniformly across all agencies or jurisdictions; indeed, administrative law enforcement has been notably pluralistic, with scholarship on regulation since these early classical studies being occupied in tracking the relationship between styles of regulation and outcomes.

The progeny of these early efforts is enormous, but the focus has, with several notable exceptions, been influenced by the policy agenda, that is, keeping organizational routines consistent with formal legal mandates (Sarat and Silbey, 1988). Defining, measuring, and assessing the forms and degrees of compliance with regulatory mandates has become a research industry in itself and over the decades this activity has become more and more technical and, some suggest, accurate and effective. In this regard, law and society research pursued the legal academy's agenda, allying itself with the instrumental agenda of policy and legal elites. Nonetheless, some research in this field has, like other subfields of law and society research, also devoted attention to issues of inequality and power, tracing the ways in which routine administration privileges repeat players and organizational actors, by documenting the salience of professional and situational constraints (Silbey, 1980–81; Ewick, 1985).

Recently, however, researchers from diverse perspectives seem to have reached consensus that organizational culture is a key variable influencing the dynamics of compliance and the probability of sustainable improvement in administrative regulation.[14] Several terms, such as "regulatory culture," "regulatory style," "governing style," or "regulatory context," are currently used to refer to characteristic features of politics, science, and the law that purportedly describe or explain – it is not clear which – variations among jurisdictions, agencies, and even nations (Epp, 2001; Vogel, 1986). Although these terms are often deployed within a traditional policy framework, this move in studies of regulatory enforcement and administration invites us to look inside the corporate subjects of regulation rather than simply at their outputs and thus to introduce a more cultural and constitutive perspective to studies of regulatory administration. At this point, the traditional studies of administrative regulation join with research pursued from a more critical, Foucauldian perspective, to look at the law from the vantage point of the subjects rather than the agents of law enforcement.

Thus, in the field of administrative law and regulation, the jurisprudential interest in questions of discretion married with theoretical interests in power to forge a more complex analysis of the modern state. Moving beyond narrow interests in compliance by the regulated, or control of administrative regulation, contemporary law and society scholars are also observing ways in which aspects of law – not merely its promulgation and rule making but its distinctively interpretive activities – are resources in the process in state building.

CONCLUSION

Reflecting developments in the social sciences at large, law and society research is at a crossroads. Based on our review of the "canon-in-progress," we see three competing paradigms at work in law and society scholarship that seem to be of a piece with the central debates in the social sciences over the course of the twentieth century: (1) research that uses scientific methods for public policy as in the realist tradition, (2) the development of a general theory of law with testable hypotheses, and (3) a closely textured sociological understanding of culture.

First, in each of the subfields of law and society, some researchers build on a tradition to study the "gap" between law on the books and law in action. To be sure, methods and conceptual lenses have become much more sophisticated; nonetheless, the themes and frameworks build from a legal realist foundation. As we suggest, there is a healthy debate among students of the courts that continues to study the role of judging building on a behaviorist model; or, as we also demonstrate, there are those who continue to examine whether incentives for compliance and effective regulation deliver on their promise.

Second, the discipline of law and society, like the social sciences more generally, continues to develop grand theories of society and processes of modernization and, based on theory, derive testable hypotheses. In the discipline of law and society, Donald Black's *The Behavior of Law* (1976) exemplifies this paradigm. Black contends that it is time to abandon the normative underpinning of much law and society research (including, one presumes, some of his own work on policing) to develop a "theory of law." Black begins with the premise that "it is possible to formulate propositions that explain the quantity and style of law in every setting" (p. 6). Conceptualizing social control as the "normative aspect of social life" that may take the form of law or, possibly, other variables of social life, such as "etiquette, custom, ethics, bureaucracy and the treatment of mental illness" (p. 105) Black argues, for example, "social control is a quantifiable variable" (p. 105). If social control has multiple indicators and is quantifiable, then, it follows, *"law varies inversely with other social control"* (p. 107). Black's work represents an important attempt to develop a theory of law, and one that has been tested empirically by many of his students and collaborators (Morrill, 1995; Baumgartner, 1988; Cooney, 1998; Tucker, 1999).

Third, the law and society literature has discovered law everywhere, not only in courtrooms, prisons, and law offices, but in hospitals, bedrooms, schoolrooms, in theaters, and films and novels, and certainly on the streets and in police stations and paddy wagons. And there are times when the law and society scholar maps the places where law ought to be but is not. For law and society scholarship, then, "the law is all over" (Sarat, 1990). By relying on this insight – that the law is where it does not appear to be – law and society scholarship has been exploring the cultural life of law through an entirely different set of concepts and themes than those that organized the generative studies of the gap between law on the books and law in action. Rather than focus on what law does, it has moved on to study what law means by studying law, for example, as consciousness, representational and discursive practices, or as part of the constitution of identity, gender, and govern-mentality.

Upon closer examination, this "discovery" of a sociology of legal culture in fact stands on the shoulders of Philip Selznick's seminal work. The turn toward a neo-institutional, cultural lens was at the core of Selznick's research on organ-izations, law, and industrial sociology. In focusing on the institution, Selznick develops a lens and a bridge between ideals and values (Kagan, Kryger, and Winston, 2002): a focus on institution encompasses a place for theoretical frame, methodological direction, and normative reflection. Law, and legality, is a par-ticularly apt institution for social science inquiry because it embodies a "mainstay of cultural identity" as well as "the bridge between justice and community" (Selznick, 1992: 435). For the student of law or legality, the task then is to "explore the meaning of legality itself…the quality of legality and the gradations within it" in all its many obvious, hidden, and emerging sites (Selznick, 1959: 124; 1961).

Today, a sociology of culture focuses on the relations of identity and conscious-ness, social construction and constitutive labyrinths, an indeterminancy marked by historicity, and the unfolding of power in its myriad forms and sites. These themes complement research in law and society that uncovered the hierarchies of a law that was expected to be equal, the normalcy of what should have been unexpected, the ways in which legality is contingent on time and place, and yet the recurring power of law as an institution of society. The emergence of a canon indebted to Selznick's close intellectual, theoretical, and political reading of the institutions of law marks both a longstanding conversation and a new beginning.

Notes

1 Following Ewick and Silbey (1998), we use the word legality to refer to the meanings, sources of authority, and cultural practices that are recognized as legal, regardless of who employs them or for what ends. Legality is an analytic term rather than a socially approved state of affairs. In this rendering, people may invoke and enact legality in ways neither approved nor acknowledged by law.

2 Scientific studies of social life emerged with diverse forms of observation and interpret-ation. Nonetheless, an aspiration for a science of society, beginning with the work of Auguste Comte in the 1830s and 1840s, shared with legal scholarship of the late eighteenth to nineteenth centuries a positivistic bent. In law, as in social science generally, positivism refers to a philosophical position that maintains that valid knowledge consists solely of replicable observations of empirical phenomena; speculations about deep causes, meanings, or essences is not part of scientific knowledge. In this positivist view, we can know only what we can observe, and what we can observe is all that exists. In Western legal systems and jurisprudence of the last two hundred years, legal positivism

has been the dominant orientation of the profession and academy. From the positivist perspective, law consists only of the rules promulgated by official authorities empowered to make binding rules (e.g., legislatures, regulatory agencies, judges).

> These rules of law... constitute the law, the data which it is the lawyer's task to analyze and order. In this sense law is a "given" – part of the data of experience. If it can be recognized as existing according to certain observational tests it can be analyzed. The tests by which legal positivism recognizes the existence of law or particular laws are thus analogous to those by which a scientist might recognize the presence of a particular chemical. (Cotterrell, 1992: 10)

The positivist conception enacts modern rationalism that in the law culminates in efforts to create comprehensive systems of logically ordered and conceptually coherent doctrines, celebrated as legal reasoning and critiqued as legalistic reasoning.

In social science, however, positivism was never the entire methodological orientation. For example, much of the Chicago School of sociology used qualitative methodologies of observation or techniques developed in anthropology for which the observer's interpretive skills and the subjective meanings of the actors remained central commitments. Nonetheless, these qualitative, interpretive social scientists also couched their work in the commitment to systematic, scientific observation (see e.g., Dorothy Ross's discussion of W. I. Thomas's work in Ross, 1991: 347–57). After World War II, with more sophisticated statistical techniques in place and the first inklings of the role that modern computers could play, the push toward large-scale and more positivistic research was given new emphasis (Converse, 1987). Social scientific research required large teams of scholars and expensive data-gathering techniques. The emergence of nonprofit organizations and foundations during the Progressive Era played an important role in the development of these new scientific studies of society.

3   The classic professions are the law, medicine, university teaching, and ministry. These professions were, however, refashioned in light of the rise of modern science and, with it, the modern university, particularly in the United States (Larson, 1977). In this turn, the ministry becomes a less central player in the contemporary story of professional powers (also see Freidson, 1986).

4   In addition to the Law and Society Association, there are such specialized sociolegal studies associations as the American Psychology–Law Society (APLS), the American Society for Legal History (ASLH), the American Society of Criminology (ASC), the American Sociology Association Section on the Sociology of Law, the Association for Political and Legal Anthropology (PoLAR), the Australian and New Zealand Society of Criminology (ANZSOC), the Australian and New Zealand Law and History Society, the Canadian Law and Society Association, the Commission on Folk Law and Legal Pluralism, the European Community Studies Association (ECSA), the International Political Science Association Research Committee on Comparative Judicial Studies, the International Sociological Association Research Committee on Sociology of Law (RCSL), the Israeli Association for Law and Society (ILSA), Réseau Européen Droit et Société (European Network on Law and Society), the Research Committee on Comparative Judicial Studies of the International Political Science Association, the Socio-Legal Studies Association (SLSA), the Society for the Study of Social Problems (SSSP), the Vereniging voor de Sociaal-wetenschappelijke bestudering van het Rech (VSR; Dutch and Belgian Law and Society Association), and Vereinigung für Rechtssoziologie. In the area of publications, scholars may submit their work to *Law & Society Review*, or a variety of other peer review journals, including *Law and Social Inquiry*, etc. While Russell Sage no longer supports sociolegal research, that mantle has been taken up by the National Science Foundation, the American Bar Foundation, and the Soros Foundation, among others. Today, there are PhD programs at the University of California, Irvine, University

of California, Berkeley, New York University, and Arizona State University. Thus notable institutional steps have been taken to ensure the professional autonomy of law and society as a discipline.

5   Importantly, shorthand terms and jargon are important building blocks of professional communities: those who "know" are distinguished from the unschooled. Learning the terms of a discipline is an important part of a young professional's socialization or rite of passage into the discipline (Becker, Strauss, Hughes, and Greer, 1961). Our discussion of the professional development of the discipline of law and society in this section empha-sizes the formal, structural constraints required to build a modern, scholarly community. Informal rituals of socialization, including the learning of jargon, to distinguish insiders from outsiders is equally important. For a study of the socialization of law students, see Stover (1989).

6   Carlin's study was replicated by Handler (1967) in a small, mid-western city. Handler does not find as precarious a professional existence for lawyers as does Carlin in urban settings. More recently, portions of Carlin's study was replicated by Van Hoy (1997), also in Chicago.

7   Of course, the world of large firm practice is quite different today. See, e.g., Hagan and Kay (1995) and Epstein, Seron, Oglensky, and Saute (1999).

8   Four percent of the respondents to the first study of Chicago lawyers were women; the authors did not examine the career trajectory of these respondents.

9   For a replication of the Heinz and Laumann study in a rural setting, see Landon (1990).

10 Beginning in the late 1960s there was a discovery, or a rediscovery, of the work of Marx in the United States that was in large measure fueled by the political activism of the day. Beginning in the late 1970s, the questions posed by Critical Theory and the Frankfurt School shaped a new generation of legal scholars and led to the Critical Legal Studies (CLS) movement (Munger and Seron, 1984; Trubek and Esser, 1989). A long, contested, and interesting debate ensued; it is, perhaps, ultimately impossible to sort out the timing and directionality of the influence. The point is that Marxian social theory became central to the discipline of law and society, but again it was reintroduced in large measure through hot debates in law schools.

11 Less than 10% of cases go to trial and of those few are heard before juries.

12 Across many studies, women, people of low status occupations, and minorities have been found to participate less than their white, male, high status counterparts (Strodtbeck and Mann, 1956; Strodtbeck, James, and Hawkins, 1957; James, 1959; Hawkins, 1961; Nemeth, Endicott, and Wachtler, 1976; Kirchmeyer, 1993).

13 For example, *Miranda v. Arizona* (1961), *Mapp v. Ohio* (1966). In a hallowed tradition of looking beyond the "law on the books," research demonstrates even in the wake of Supreme Court decisions, policing is "situational" and contextual: race, ethnicity and age matter in one's experience of the police (Bittner, 1970; also see Decker, 1981; Huang and Vaughn, 1996; Tuch and Weitzer, 1997).

14 This neo-institutionalist framework represents a return to the work of Selznick, a point we take up in the conclusion.

References

Abbott, Andrew (1981) *The System of Professions: An Essay on the Division of Expert Labor.* Chicago: University of Chicago Press.

Abel, Richard (1973) "A comparative theory of dispute institutions in society," *Law & Society Review* 8: 217–347.

Abel, Richard and Lewis, Philip (eds.) (1989) *Lawyers in Society.* Berkeley: University of California Press.

Balkin, Jack M. and Levinson, Sanford (1996) "How to win cites and influence people," *Chicago Kent Law Review* 71: 843.

Bardach, Eugene and Kagan, Robert (1980) *Going by the Book*. Philadelphia: Temple University Press.

Baumgartner, M.P. (1988) *The Moral Order of a Suburb*. New York: Oxford University Press.

Becker, Howard, Strauss, Anselm, Hughes, Everett, and Greer, Blanche (1961) *Boys in White: Student Culture in Medical School*. Chicago: University of Chicago Press.

Bernstein, Marver (1955) *Regulating Business by Independent Commission*. Princeton, NJ: Princeton University Press.

Bittner, Egon (1970) *The Functions of the Police in Modern Society*. Washington, DC: Government Printing Office.

Bittner, Egon (1990) *Aspects of Police Work*. Boston: Northeastern University Press.

Black, Donald (1971) "Social organization of arrest," *Stanford University Law Review* 23: 1087–111.

Black, Donald (1976) *The Behavior of Law*. New Haven, CT: Yale University Press.

Black, Donald and Reiss, Albert, Jr. (1967) *Studies in Crime and Law Enforcement in Major Metropolitan Areas*. Washington, DC: Supt. of Docs, US Government Printing Office.

Blumberg, Abraham (1967) "The practice of law as a confidence game: Organizational cooptation of a profession," *Law & Society Review* 1(2): 15–39.

Caplowitz, D. (1974) *Consumers in Trouble: A Study of Debtors in Default*. New York: Free Press.

Carlin, J.E. (1962) *Lawyers on their Own: A Study of Individual Practitioners in Chicago*. New Brunswick, NJ: Rutgers University Press.

Carlin, J.E. and Howard, J. (1965) "Legal representation and class justice," *UCLA Law Review* 12: 381–437.

Casper, Jay (1972) *American Criminal Justice: The Defendant's Perspective*. Washington, DC: US Government Printing Office.

Converse, Jean M. (1987) *Survey Research in the United States: Roots and Emergence*. Berkeley, CA.: University of California Press.

Cooney, Mark (1998) *Warriors and Peacemakers: How Third Parties Shape Violence*. New York: NYU Press.

Cotterrell, Roger (1992). *The Sociology of Law*. London: Butterworths.

Curran, Barbara A. (1977) *Legal Needs of the Public*. Chicago: American Bar Foundation.

Danzig, Richard and Lowy, J. (1975) "Everyday disputes and mediation in the United States: A reply to Professor Felstiner," *Law & Society Review* 9: 675–94.

Davis, Kenneth Culp (1972a) *Discretionary Justice*. Baton Rouge: Louisiana State University Press.

Davis, Kenneth Culp (1972b) *Administrative Law Text*. St. Paul, MN: West Publishing Company.

DeTocqueville, Alexis (1938) *Democracy in America*. New York: Allard & Saunders.

Decker, S.H. (1981) "Citizen attitudes toward the police: A review of past findings and suggestions for future policy." *Journal of Police Science and Administration* 9(1): 80–7.

Diamond, S.S., Vidmar, N., Rose, M., Ellis, L., and Murphy, B. (2003) "Juror discussions during civil trials: A study of Arizona's Rule 39(f) Innovation," *Arizona Law Review*, 45: 1–81.

Dicey, A.V. (1915) *The Law of the Constitution*. London: Macmillan Co.

Edelman, Murray (1964) *The Symbolic Uses of Politics*. Urbana: University of Illinois Press.

Eisenstein, James, Flemming, Roy B., Nardulli, Peter (1988) *Contours of Justice*. Boston: Little Brown and Company.

Engel, David (1980) "Legal pluralism in an American community: Perspectives on civil trial court," *American Bar Foundation Research Journal*, 3: 425.

Epp, Astrid (2001) "Contested cultures of regulation: The conflict over GM Food in Germany and in the United States," Paper presented at the Law and Society Association meeting in Budapest, Hungary.

Epstein, Cynthia Fuchs (1998) *Women in Law,* 2nd edn. Urbana and Chicago: University of Illinois Press.

Epstein, Cynthia Fuchs, Seron, Carroll, Oglensky, Bonnie, and Saute, Robert (1999) *The Part-time Paradox: Time Norms, Professional Life, Family and Gender.* New York: Routledge.

Epstein, Lee (1998) *Choices Judges Make.* Washington, DC: Congressional Quarterly Press.

Epstein, Lee, Segal, Jeffrey A., Spaeth, Harold J., and Walker, Thomas G. (1996) *Supreme Court Compendium: Data, Decisions, Developments.* Washington, DC: Congressional Quarterly Press.

Ewick, Patricia (1985) "Redundant regulation: Sanctioning broker-dealers" *Law & Policy* 7(4): 421–45.

Ewick, Patricia and Silbey, Susan (1998) *The Common Place of Law: Stories from Everyday Life.* Chicago: University of Chicago Press.

Feeley, Malcolm (1977) *The Process is the Punishment.* New York: Russell Sage Foundation.

Felstiner, William L.F. (1974) "Influences of social organization on dispute processing," *Law & Society Review* 9: 63–94.

Felstiner, William L.F. (1975) "Avoidance as dispute processing: An elaboration," *Law & Society Review* 9: 695–706.

Felstiner, William, Abel, Richard, and Sarat, Austin (1980–81) "The emergence and transformation of disputes: Naming, blaming, claiming...," *Law & Society Review* 15 (3–4): 631–54.

Flemming, Roy B., Nardulli, Peter, and Eisenstein, James (1992) *The Craft of Justice: Politics and work in Criminal Court Communities.* Philadelphia: University of Pennsylvania Press.

Freidson, Elliott (1970) *The Profession of Medicine: A Study of the Sociology of Applied Knowledge.* New York: Dodd, Mead.

Freidson, Eliot (1986) *Professional Powers: A Study of the Institutionalization of Formal Knowledge.* Chicago: University of Chicago Press.

Freidson, Elliott (2001) *Professionalism: The Third Logic.* Chicago: University of Chicago Press.

Galanter, Marc (1974) "Why the 'haves' come out ahead: Speculations on the limits of legal change," *Law & Society Review* 9(1): 95–160.

Garth, Bryant and Sterling, Joyce (1998) "From legal realism to law and society: Reshaping law for the last stages of the activist state," *Law & Society Review* 32(2): 409–72.

Goode, William (1957) "A community within a community: The professions," *American Sociological Review* 22: 194–200.

Griswold, Erwin (1973) *The Judicial Process* (Benjamin Cardozo Lectures). New York: Association of the Bar of the City of New York.

Guilllory. J. (1987) "Canonical and non-canonical literary canon: A critique of the current debate," *English Literary History* 54(3): 483–527.

Gusfield, Joseph (1963) *Symbolic Crusade: Status Politics and the American Temperance Movement.* Urbana: University of Illinois Press.

Habermas, Jürgen (1999) *Between Facts and Norms.* Cambridge, MA: MIT Press.

Hagan, John and Kay, Fiona (1995) *Gender in Practice.* New York: Oxford University Press.

Handler, Joel (1967) *The Lawyer and His Community: The Practicing Bar in a Middle-Sized City.* Madison: University of Wisconsin Press.

Hans, Valerie and Vidmar, Neil (1991) "American jury at twenty five years," *Law and Social Inquiry* 16(2): 323–52.

Haug, Marie (1973) "Deprofessionalization: An alternative hypothesis for the future," *Sociological Review Monograph* 20: 195–211.

Haug, Marie (1975) "The deprofessionalization of everyone?" *Sociological Focus* August: 197–213.

Hawkins, Charles (1961) "Interaction and coalition realignments in consensus-seeking groups: A study of experimental jury deliberations," Doctoral dissertation, University of Chicago, Department of Sociology.

Heinz, Jack and Laumann, Edward (1982) *Chicago Lawyers: The Social Strucutre of the Bar.* New York: Russell Sage Foundation; Chicago: American Bar Foundation.

Heydebrand, Wolf and Seron, Carroll (1990) *Rationalizing Justice: The Political Economy of the Federal District Courts.* New York: SUNY Press.

Huang, W.S.W., and Vaughn, M.S. (1996) "Support and confidence: Public attitudes toward the police," in Timothy J. Flanagan and Dennis R. Longmire (eds.), *Americans View Crime and Justice: A National Public Opinion Survey.* Thousand Oaks, CA: Sage, pp 31–45.

Hunt, Alan (1978) *The Sociological Movement in Law.* London: Macmillan Press.

Hurst, Willard (1964) *Law and Economic Growth: The Legal History of the Lumber Industry in Wisconsin, 1836–1915.* Cambridge, MA: Harvard University Press.

Jacob, Herbert (1965) *Justice in America: Courts, Lawyers and the Judicial Process.* Boston: Little Brown and Company.

Jacob, Herbert and Eisenstein, James (1991) *Felony Justice: Organizational Analysis of Criminal Courts.* Lanham, MD: University Press of American.

James, Rita M. (1959) "Status and competence of jurors," *American Journal of Sociology* 64: 563–70.

Jowell, Jeffrey (1975) *Law and Bureaucracy: Administrative Discretion and the Limits of Legal Action.* Port Washington, NY: Dunellen Publications, Kennikat Press.

Kadish, Mortimer H. and Kadish, Sanford (1973) *Discretion to Disobey.* Palo Alto, CA: Stanford University Press.

Kagan, Robert A., Kryger, Martin, and Winston, Kenneth (2002) *Legality and Community: Essays in Honor of Philip Selznick.* Berkeley: University of California Press.

Kalven, Harry Jr. and Zeisel, Hans (1966) *The American Jury.* Boston: Little, Brown and Company.

Kidder, Robert (1980–81) "The end of the road: Problems in the analysis of disputes," *Law & Society Review* 15(3–4): 717–26.

Kirchmeyer, Catherine (1993) "Multicultural task groups: An account of the low contribution level of minorities," *Small Group Research* 24: 127–48.

Kolko, Gabriel (1965) *Railroads and Regulation.* Princeton, NJ: Princeton University Press.

Lamont, Michele and Fournier, Marcel (1992) *Cultivating Differences: Symbolic Boundaries and the Making of Inequality.* Chicago: University of Chicago Press.

Landinsky, Jack (1963) "Careers of lawyers: Law practice and legal institutions," *American Sociologial Review* 28: 47–54.

Landon, Donald D. (1990) *Country Lawyers: The Impact of Context on Professional Practice.* New York: Prager.

Larson, Magali Safarti (1977) *The Rise of Professionalism: A Sociological Analysis.* Berkeley: University of California Press.

Law & Society Review (1980–81) Special Issue on Dispute Processing and Civil Litigation 15 (3–4): 389–920.

Law & Society Review (1994) Special Issue on Law and Society in Southeast Asia 28 (3): 409–720.

Legal Studies Forum (1985) Special Issue on Law, Ideology and Social Research, IX (1).

Levi, Edward (1949) *An Introduction to Legal Reasoning.* Chicago: University of Chicago Press.

Lipsky, Michael (1980) *Street-level Bureaucracy.* New York: Russell Sage Foundation.

Llewellyn, Karl (1969) *The Bramble Bush.* Dobbs Ferry, NY: Oceana Publishers.

Llewellyn, Karl and Hoebel, E. Adamson (1941) *The Cheyenne Way.* Norman: University of Oklahoma Press.

Lowi, Theodore (1969) *The End of Liberalism.* New York: W.W. Norton & Co.

Macaulay, Stewart (1963) "Non-contractual relations in business: A preliminary study," *American Sociological Review* 28: 55–67.

Mather, Lynn, McEwen, Craig, and Maiman, Richard (2001) *Divorce Lawyers.* New York: Oxford University Press.

Mapp v. Ohio (1961) 367 U.S. 643.

Merry, Sally E. (1990) *Getting Justice and Getting Even*. Chicago: University of Chicago Press.

Merton, Robert K. (1968) *Social Theory and Social Structure*. New York: Free Press.

Miller, Richard and Sarat, Austin (1980–81) "Grievances, claims and disputes: Assessing the adversary culture," *Law & Society Review* 15(3–4): 525–66.

Miranda v. Arizona (1966) 384 U.S. 436.

Mnookin, Robert and Kornhauser, Lewis (1979) "Bargaining the shadow of the law: The case of divorce," *Yale Law Journal* 88: 950.

Morrill, Calvin (1995) *The Executive Way*. Chicago: University of Chicago Press.

Munger, Frank and Seron, Carroll (1984) "Critical legal theory versus critical legal method: A comment on method," *Law and Policy* 6: 257–99.

Murphy, Walter (1964) *Elements of Judicial Strategy*. Chicago: University of Chicago Press.

Nader, Laura. (1978) *The Disputing Process: Law in Ten Societies*. New York: Columbia University Press.

Nardulli, Peter F., Eisenstein, James, and Flemming, Roy B. (1988) *The Tenor of Justice: Criminal Courts and the Guilty Plea Process*. Champaign-Urbana, IL: University of Illinois Press.

Nemeth, Charlan, Endicott, Jeffrey, and Wachtler, Joel (1976) "From the 50s to the 70s: Women in jury deliberations." *Sociometry* 39(4): 293–304.

Oppenheimer, Martin (1973) "The proletarianization of the professional," *Sociological Review Monograph* 20: 213–27.

Orren, Karen (1974) *Corporate Power and Social Change*. Baltimore: Johns Hopkins Press.

Packer, Herbert (1968) *The Limits of the Criminal Sanction*. Stanford, CA: Stanford University Press.

Parsons, Talcott (1949) " The professions and social structure," in Talcott Parsons (ed.), *Essays in Sociological Theory*. New York: Free Press, pp. 34–50.

Peltason, Jack (1955) *Federal Courts in the Political Process*. Garden City, NY: Doubleday Books.

Pritchett, C. Herman (1948) *The Roosevelt Court: A Study in Judicial Politics and Values*. New York: Macmillan.

Pritchett, C. Herman ([1954] 1966) *Civil Liberties and the Vinson Court*. Chicago: University of Chicago Press.

Reiss, Albert J. (1971) *The Police and the Public*. New Haven, CT: Yale University Press.

Ross, Dorothy (1991) *The Origins of American Social Science*. Cambridge, UK: Cambridge University Press.

Ross, H. Lawrence (1970) *Settled Out of Court*. Chicago: Aldine Press.

Sarat, Austin (1990) "'... the law is all over': Power, resistance and the legal consciousness of the welfare poor," *Yale Journal of Law and the Humanities* 2(2): 343–79.

Sarat, Austin (1998) "President's column," *Law & Society Association Newsletter*, October.

Sarat, Austin and Silbey, Susan S. (1988) "Pull of the policy audience," *Law & Policy* 10(2,3): 97–166.

Schlegel, John Henry (1995) *American Legal Realism and Empirical Social Science*. Chapel Hill: University of North Carolina Press.

Schmidhauser, John R. (1960) *The Supreme Court: Its Politics, Personalities, and Procedures*. New York: Holt, Rinehart and Winston.

Schubert, Glendon (1965) *Judicial Policy-making: Political Role of Courts*. Chicago: Scott Foresman.

Selznick, Philip (1959) "The sociology of law," in Robert K. Merton, Leonard Broom, and Leonard S. Cottrell, Jr. (eds.), *Sociology Today*, New York: Basic Books, pp. 115–27.

Selznick, Philip (1961) "Sociology and natural law," *Natural Law Forum* 6: 84–108.

Selznick, Philip (1969) *Law, Society, and Industrial Justice*. New York: Russell Sage Foundation.

Selznick, Philip (1992) *The Moral Commonwealth: Social Theory and the Promise of Community*. Berkeley and Los Angeles: University of California Press.

Shapiro, Martin (1968) *The Supreme Court and Administrative Agencies*. New York: Free Press.

Silberman, Mathew (1985) *The Civil Process*. Orlando, FL: Academic Press.

Silbey, Susan S. (1980–81) "Case processing in an attorney general's office," *Law & Society Review* 15(3–4): 849–910.

Silbey, Susan S. and Bittner, Egon (1982) "The availability of law," *Law & Policy* 4(4): 399–434.

Silbey, Susan S. and Sarat, Austin (1987) "Critical traditions in law and society research," *Law & Society Review*, 21(1): 165–74.

Silbey, Susan S. and Sarat, Austin (1989) "Dispute processing in law and legal scholarship: From institutional critique to the reconstruction of the juridical subject," *Denver Law Review* 66(3): 437–98.

Simon, Rita (1967) *The Jury and the Defense of Insanity*. Boston: Little, Brown and Co.

Skogan, W.G. (1994). *Contacts Between Police and Public: Findings from the 1992 British Crime Survey*. London: HMSO Books.

Skolnick, Jerome (1966) *Justice Without Trial*. New York: John Wiley & Sons.

Smigel, E.O. (1969) *The Wall Street Lawyer: Professional Organization Man*. Bloomington, IN: Indiana University Press.

Stover, Robert V. (1989) *Making it and Breaking it: The Fate of Public Interest Commitment During Law School*. Champaign-Urbana: University of Illinois Press.

Strauss, Anselm (1961) *Images of the American City*. New York: Free Press of Glencoe.

Strodtbeck, Fred L., James, Rita M., and Hawkins, Charles (1957) "Social status and jury deliberations," *American Sociological Review* 22: 713–19.

Strodtbeck, Fred L. and Mann, Richard D. (1956) "Sex-role differentiation in jury deliberations," *Sociometry* 19: 3–11.

Sudnow, David (1965) "Normal crimes: Sociological features of the penal code in a public defender's office," *Social Problems* 12(3): 253–76.

Sumner, Colin (1979) *Reading Ideologies: An Investigation into the Marxist Theory of Ideology and Law*. London: Academic Press.

Tomlins, Christopher (2000) "Framing the field of law's disciplinary encounters: A historical narrative," *Law & Society Review* 34(4): 911–72.

Trubek, David (1980–81) "Studying courts in context," *Law & Society Review* 15(3–4): 485–502.

Trubek, David M. and Esser, John (1989) "Critical empiricism in American legal studies: Paradox, program or Pandora's box," *Law and Social Inquiry* 14(1): 3–52

Trubek, David, Sarat, Austin, Felstiner, William L.F., Kritzer, Herbert, and Grossman, Joel (1983) "The costs of ordinary litigation," *UCLA Law Review* 31: 72–127.

Tuch, S.A. and Weitzer, R. (1997) "The polls – trends: Racial differences in attitudes toward the police," *Public Opinion Quarterly* 61: 642–63.

Tucker, James (1999) *Therapeutic Corporation*. Oxford: Oxford University Press.

Ulmer, Sidney (1961) *Introductory Readings in Political Behavior*. Chicago: Rand McNally & Company.

Van Hoy, Jerry (1997) *Franchise Law Firms and the Transformation of Personal Practice*. Westport, CT: Quorum.

Vogel, David (1986) *National Styles of Regulation: Environmental Policy in Great Britain and the United States*. Ithaca, NY: Cornell University Press.

Weber, Max (1947) *The Theory of Social and Economic Organization*, trans. A. M. Henderson and Talcott Parsons. New York: Free Press.

Weber, Max (1954) *Max Weber on Law in Economy and Society*, ed. Max Rheinstein and Edward Shills. New York: Simon and Schuster.

Yngvesson, Barbara (1993) *Virtuous Citizens, Disruptive Subjects: Order and Complaint in a New England Court*. New York: Routledge.

Zeisel, Hans, Kalven, Harry Jr., and Bucholz, Bernard (1959) *Delay in Court*. Westport, CT: Greenwood Press.

Part II
The Cultural Life of Law

4

The Work of Rights and the Work Rights Do: A Critical Empirical Approach

Laura Beth Nielsen

Introduction

The connection between social justice and legal rights motivates scholarly research in several disciplines. A "right" is not merely a claim of ownership; it is a claim about justice, legitimacy, and power (or resistance to power). Rights protect individuals from the illegitimate exercise of state authority, they are a mechanism by which individuals protect and assert themselves within organizations, and they often are fundamental to strategies for social reform.

Political theorists long have debated the individual's relationship to the state and the role of rights in regulating this relationship. It is only recently, however, that theoretical and political debates have led to efforts to examine the processes by and through which ordinary citizens think about, invoke, and fail to invoke their rights. What is the practical effect of a right? Why do some right-holders assert their rights while others do not? Why do some right-claims succeed while others fail?

Scholars debate whether rights are conferred by state action or are possessed simply by virtue of being human and then recognized or respected by local, national, and international governing bodies. Governments can confer or recognize rights by constitution, statute, or judicial action. Rights pertain to substantive matters – from holding property to political participation to freedom of expression to privacy to due process to a clean environment to nondiscrimination in employment, to name just a few. (See, e.g., The Universal Declaration of Human Rights adopted on December 10, 1948, by the General Assembly of the United Nations.)

Legal rights are important for protecting individual autonomy and resisting the arbitrary or tyrannical imposition of state power, but they also are important tools in the struggle for equality. Rights are one vehicle by which groups can challenge structural barriers to advance substantive legal, political, social, and economic equality. One may assert legal rights to vindicate an individual claim or as part of a larger movement for social reform or both (Hull, 2001). Often the two are connected in important ways, but these agendas may be at odds. Social movements often are propelled by litigation and rights claims, but the individual desire to settle a lawsuit to end personal difficulties associated with it can make rights-oriented strategies for social reform difficult (Albiston, 1999). Although settlement may vindicate the individual's rights, it removes the matter from public discourse, thereby eliminating potential broad-based social change that adjudication might accomplish.

In this essay, I argue that we cannot understand even the most basic functions of rights unless we can explain when individuals believe they enjoy a right and when they will seek to vindicate it. Without empirically grounded theories of rights consciousness and rights-claiming behavior, we cannot understand how rights can or should operate in a social system. This essay selectively examines existing empirical scholarship about rights: specifically, who uses them, in what contexts, and with what success? I begin with a discussion of political theorists and the fundamental questions they ask about rights. Arguing that both political theorists and social reformers will benefit from an empirical understanding of how rights work, I identify some important empirical questions unanswered by political theory. And, although there have been efforts to bring together rights theorists with other academic disciplines (Sarat and Kearns, 1996), my purpose is to demonstrate that empirical social scientists have made great strides toward understanding how rights operate in the social world.

POLITICAL THEORISTS ON RIGHTS

It is important to preface a discussion of critical and social scientific analyses of rights with a brief overview of political theories of rights. The history of the discourse of rights is itself part of the context for empirical research on rights because social scientists sometimes look to political theory to inform empirical analyses.

Political theorists have long debated the rights individuals should enjoy as humans and as citizens of a state. The earliest rights theorists thought rights served to protect us as individuals from one another (the right to self-preservation; Hobbes, 1909) and from the potentially abusive power of the state (Locke, 1967). Theoretical debates about rights are important because they pose alternative visions of the ideal relationship between individuals and the state. Thus rights theory tends to focus on government accountability and individual rights. Theories of rights can be roughly categorized into succeeding "generations," each of which benefits from and critiques the generation that precedes it (for more on the "generations of rights" see also Marshall, 1950).

The first generation of rights primarily concerns rights to freedom and autonomy traditionally associated with liberal democratic societies, such as the freedom of religion, speech, and citizenship. These "negative rights" guarantee individuals freedom from state action rather than any positive assistance, although first generation rights also include some positive rights such as the rights to political participation and fair treatment.

Second generation rights focus on economic, social, and well-being rights such as the right to be "free from hunger," the right to an adequate standard of living, a basic education, just working conditions and basic health care. They are similar to first generation rights in that they are individualistic, but differ because in order to be realized they require the redistribution of limited resources. Second generation rights theorists ask what it means to enjoy a right or liberty without the material conditions necessary to exercise that right (Waldron, 1995) and claim that these socioeconomic rights are crucial for those who wish to exercise their political rights (Waldron, 1996). For example, is there any significance to the "right" to abortion for poor women who cannot afford the procedure (MacKinnon, 1989)? Theoretical debates about second generation rights emphasize (re)distributive justice and the process by which rights are invoked, and examine material barriers to exercising individual rights (Nozick, 1974: 238).

Third generation rights concern "group" or "solidarity" rights including the right to a healthy environment, to peace, to sharing a common heritage and cultural practices. These theorists claim a "positive duty on the part of the state to protect the cultural conditions which allow for autonomous choice... Respect for the autonomy of members of minority cultures requires respect for their cultural structure" (Kymlicka, 1989: 903). Third generation rights theories inspire debate about privileging individual rights over group rights. These theories take into account that rights often are the product of liberal or social democratic societies and may not be relevant to those outside that context. In other words, the political rights advanced by Western Liberalism may be far less important to those living in hunger and poverty in economically disadvantaged countries.

Debates over what rights citizens should enjoy lead to other theoretical questions. For example, to what extent do rights confer duties (Dworkin, 1977)? And can the rule of law prevail when procedural rights are guaranteed, but without substantive justice (Dworkin, 1977, 1985)? Implicit in these theoretical analyses are a host of empirical questions relating to how rights work in different social, legal, political, geographic, and socioeconomic contexts. As political theorists struggled with these important questions, a critique of rights emerged from scholars associated with the Critical Legal Studies movements.

The Critique of Rights

As a result of several landmark cases, such as *Brown v. Board of Education* and *Roe v. Wade*, there was broad consensus that legal rights led rather directly to social change. The language of rights – in these cases the right to equal protection and the right to privacy – provided the rationale by which individual plaintiffs prevailed. These individual victories were said to generate social change. Yet both empirical social scientists and theoretically minded critical legal studies scholars began to reconsider the effect of rights-based litigation on social change. Sociolegal scholars long have observed that many people who believed they had legal claims were not pursuing those claims (simply coping or "lumping it") and that this varied according to the nature of the claim/right at stake and the relationship of the parties involved (Curran, 1977; Felstiner, Abel, and Sarat, 1980; Macaulay, 1963). Scholars associated with critical legal studies challenged the taken-for-granted notion of the power of rights. These scholars argued that rights are socially constructed (Scheingold, 1974), vacuous (Tushnet, 1984), reified (Aron, 1989; Gabel, 1981), and overutilized (Glendon, 1991). Some feminists argued that rights embody male norms and therefore will not ultimately aid women (Olsen, 1984) or at least will do so only problematically (MacKinnon, 1989). Like their political theory counterparts, critical scholars criticized the notion of rights as appearing formally neutral but being unequally enjoyed by individuals.

At the same time that the political left was developing this critique of rights, a critique of rights strategies emerged from the political right as well. From the right, critics argued that rights, particularly judicially enforced rights, amount to an illegitimate introduction of political agendas into judicial proceedings and the legal profession. In response to seemingly successful litigation-oriented strategies for social reform on the left, conservative critics adopted a market-based model of public interest law, in which public interest representation should be nonpolitical and limited to providing access to the legal marketplace for poor individuals (Johnson, 1991). This critique led to action on the part of the political right who viewed public interest lawyers as inappropriately using the courts for their social agendas (Johnson, 1991), and they led the movement to cut government funding for the Legal Services Corporation and to challenge the standing of public interest organizations to sue (Aron, 1989).

These critiques of rights sparked two distinct but related responses. The first largely was theoretical and focused on the utility of rights. The second was a renewed interest in the empirical study of rights.

THE CRITIQUE OF THE CRITIQUE OF RIGHTS

Critical race and feminist theorists, among others, developed their own critique of the "critique of rights." Clinging to the idea that rights are something more than "myths" (Scheingold, 1974), critical race and feminist theorists responded to the critique of rights by arguing that rights serve as a significant source of power for members of traditionally disadvantaged groups precisely *because* of the characteristics inherent in the social construction of a legal right. "Rights" are said to apply equally to everyone, they are "neutral," and are backed by the legitimate authority of law and the state. While this may not be true in practice, this ideal may serve as a source of power for the disadvantaged.

In *The Alchemy of Race and Rights*, Patricia Williams (1991) makes this argument persuasively as she recounts the story of searching for and renting an apartment at a time when her colleague and friend, Peter Gabel, was doing the same. For Williams, "still engaged in a struggle to set up transactions at arm's length, as legitimately commercial, and to portray [her]self as a bargainer of separate worth, distinct power, [and] sufficient rights to manipulate commerce," good faith and trustworthiness were shown in her rush to sign a detailed lease. Gabel, on the other hand demonstrated his good faith and trustworthiness to his future landlord by exchanging a cash deposit for no more than a friendly handshake (Williams, 1991: 147–8). By looking to formal law, Williams gained important legitimacy as well as protective distance from her landlords.

Williams's story illuminates that "one's sense of empowerment defines one's relation to the law in terms of . . . rights/no-rights" (Williams, 1991: 148). Gabel, privileged in many ways, established his trustworthiness by ignoring law; he did not need it. Williams, on the other hand, found the "establishment of identity and the formulation of an autonomous social self" by becoming a leasor in the formal legal sense of the word. Williams looked to law to regulate the relationship in a predictable way because of a well-grounded fear that without that regulation the dynamics of race and gender hierarchy would work to her disadvantage. Her perspective about the benefits of rights was informed by her history and the history of her ancestors as slaves. She chose to allow the language of legal rights to define herself and the relationship.

Rights may be more or less important for individuals depending on their circumstances and social location, as well as their understanding of the law and the way law works. For members of traditionally disadvantaged groups, the language of legal rights provides a common ground for discourse, establishing community norms, and membership (Milner, 1989; Minow, 1987). For those who enjoy the benefits of various systems of unearned privilege defined by race, social class, and gender, rights may be less important for ensuring one's needs than they are for those who do not.

Williams is not the only legal theorist to point out that legal rights, indeed law itself, work differently for those differently situated (Bumiller, 1988; Delgado, 1993; Ewick and Silbey, 1992, 1998; MacKinnon, 1987, 1989; McGuire, 1995; Nielsen, 2000; Yngvesson, 1988; Young, 1990), but this theoretical insight has spurred a new interest in the empirical study of rights, rights-claimers, and the effects of organizational setting on the utility of rights. Because rights are necessarily embedded in law, these insights led scholars to study the relationship between individuals and the law. These theoretical debates raise important empirical questions – how do those differently situated with respect to the law think about, use, or fail to invoke their legal rights?

EMPIRICAL TESTS OF RIGHTS DEBATES: CONTEXT MATTERS IN THE WORK RIGHTS DO

Many social scientists are turning to a view of the social role of law and the role of rights in it that takes account of the variable functions and effects of rights in different contexts. This interpretive framework extends a fundamental insight gained by social scientists when they ask ordinary citizens about exercising their rights: the exercise of legal rights is conditioned by and often is less important than community norms and social relationships. Empirical data continually demonstrate that people in ongoing relationships are far less likely to exercise their legal rights with respect to these relationships. This principle holds for those in business (Macaulay, 1963), in families, in communities (Yngvesson, 1985), and in employment relationships (Albiston, 2001a, 2001b; Edelman and Chambliss, 1999; Edelman, Erlanger, and Abraham, 1992; Edelman and Suchman, 1997).

In this section, I will discuss how the interpretive turn in sociolegal research has aided our understanding of rights. Building on that foundation, I return to the primary question that motivates this essay: how do rights work? I will briefly survey empirical work on this question by looking at the use of rights in four distinct, but related contexts: (1) by individuals, (2) within organizations, (3) for social movements, and (4) in the context of globalization (Albiston, 2001a).

The interpretive turn

The empirical study of rights has been part of and is influenced by the interpretive turn in sociolegal research. As with sociolegal studies more generally (Suchman and Edelman, 1996), the study of rights has become less concerned with instrumental effects – inquiring whether rights produce social change – and more concerned with attention to the constitutive character of rights, inquiring how rights work. This has led to a flood of empirical work about what types of individuals are likely to invoke their rights, not just in legal settings, but also in their everyday lives and struggles.

Interpretive sociolegal scholars reject the notion that law and society are separate. Rather, they presume that meanings, ideologies, rights, conceptions of rights, law, and social relationships are not static categories, but are continually being constructed, negotiated, altered, and resisted (Ewick and Silbey, 1992, 1998; Harrington and Yngvesson, 1990). Thus they share the theoretical orientation of many modern theorists that practice, structure, and ideology are interrelated (Bourdieu, 1977). The critical empirical approach (Harrington and Yngvesson, 1990) embraces the complexity of law and legal rights as locations of power. In this view, law is as much constituted by society as law constitutes society.

Interpretive scholars look to the utility of rights in a variety of social settings to examine who invokes rights, when are rights claims made, and when are they successful, looking for both intended and unintended consequences of rights. This literature teaches us that legal rights are affected by the organizational settings in which they are applied, the nature of the competing claims being made to the rights claims, and according to the different social locations of the individual rights claims (Merry, 1990; Nielsen, 2000; Sarat, 1990; Sarat and Kearns, 1995; Yngvesson, 1985).

Individuals and rights

Rights are often thought of as naturally inhering in persons. As such, it is useful to begin a review of empirical analyses of rights with a discussion of individuals and rights. Pursuing legal rights requires a willing plaintiff who first must "name, blame, and claim" (Felstiner et al., 1980). In other words, individuals must name the problem, blame someone for it, and claim their legal remedy. Whether or not individuals identify problems as legal ones (or as breaches of their rights) is complex. How individuals understand their day-to-day problems is affected not just by the law itself, but also by how the problems are defined by court actors such as judges (Merry, 1990), court clerks (Yngvesson, 1988), friends and neighbors (Albiston, 2001b; Ewick and Silbey, 1998; Nielsen, 2000, Nielsen, forthcoming), and past experiences with law and legal actors (Macaulay, 1963; Merry, 1990; Nielsen, 2000; Sarat and Kearns, 1995).

There is important variation among individuals in their willingness to pursue a legal claim. For example, individuals may not know the law or may eschew the category of victim; individuals often prefer to maintain relationships rather than assert legal rights; and individuals exist in socioeconomic, race, and gender hierarchies that affect their ability and willingness to pursue legal claims.

Perfect legal knowledge does not automatically spring into the minds of individuals; individuals often do not know what rights they enjoy and when they have been breached (Ewick and Silbey, 1998). As a corollary, ideology about rights is important because people may have an inflated idea of what their rights are, turning everything into a discussion of "rights" where none truly exist (Glendon, 1991). It is not just "law" that constitutes decisions about when and where to look for assistance when one has been wronged, but also competing ideologies about law, self-sufficiency, and gender roles to name just a few (Nielsen, 2000).

The internal processes through which people identify themselves as victimized runs contrary to what psychologists know about coping behavior. The "right" to experience a discrimination-free workplace, for example, often is not vindicated because individuals do not know that what happened to them is legally actionable (failure to "name") or because those who know they are victims may be reluctant to turn to the law for redress for a variety of reasons (Bumiller, 1988).

Even when individuals understand that they have a legal right that has been breached and they know who is responsible, they may not choose to pursue it for a variety of reasons. They may fear retaliation (Ewick and Silbey, 1998); they may have become accustomed, due to their social location, to being harmed without redress (Sarat, 1990); or they may not believe that legal actors will believe their claims or be responsive to them (Taub and Schneider, 1998). Individuals come to the law (and the law often comes to them) with a body of knowledge, assumptions, ideology, and experience with the law and legal actors that affects whether or not they will assert their legal rights.

Rights in organizations

How does the organizational setting in which one operates affect how rights work, if at all? Recent trends in the study of claiming behavior and rights explores the fundamental tension between rights claims/claims to legitimate legal or political authority versus the institutions, norms, organizations, and social systems that compete. Organizations used to be considered arenas in which implementing "due process" guarantees would ensure movement toward substantive justice within the organization (Selznick, 1969). More recently, however, scholars of organizations are less optimistic about the success of law and law-like structures in organizations (Edelman and Chambliss, 1999; Edelman et al., 1992; Edelman and Suchman, 1997). Organizational structures can obscure responsibility, making it difficult for those who suffer a deprivation of some right to identify the deprivation or know who or what is responsible for it (Nelson and Bridges, 1999). Finally, organizations have their own set of actors responding to the organization's imperatives which can be in competition with rights.

Scholars of organizations used to suggest that the implementation of law in organizations held with it the possibility of imbuing the organization with other values (Selznick, 1969). More recently, scholars of the "new institutionalism" are less optimistic about the possibility for law translating into better substantive outcomes in organizations. Although organizations can be a good source for information about the law, new institutionalists suggest that law in organizations such as workplaces results in a bureaucratization of law whereby legal aims (in this case to protect the right of employees not to be discriminated against on the grounds of race and/or gender) become coopted, translated into business goals rather than legal mandates, limiting their effectiveness. Finally, this limitation translates back into affirmative protection for the company by establishing the standard practices by which a firm will be evaluated (Edelman and Chambliss, 1999; Edelman and Suchman, 1997).

In her study of the Family and Medical Leave Act, Catherine Albiston examines what happens in the workplace when legal rights (in this case the recently provided statutory right to family and medical leave) are asserted and are in opposition to institutionalized ideas regarding what it means to be a satisfactory worker, notions about the social organization of the family and gender roles therein, as well as the institution of work itself (Albiston, 2000, 2001b). Legal claims hardly trump competing claims. Rather, legal claims are filtered, transformed, and contested in the workplace. Albiston's respondents report legitimate rights claims being countered by claims about the inability of the company to function without replacing the worker requesting the leave – it is "just business." Even more insidiously, legitimate requests for leave are met with resistance because the reason given does not comport with traditional gender/family roles (e.g., when a man requests leave to be home when a baby is born or adopted) (Albiston, 2001b). Nevertheless, Albiston also finds that workers sometimes successfully employ the norms embodied in the new law to contest institutionalized ideas about work in their negotiations over leave (Albiston, 2001a, 2001b).

The hospital is the setting for a study of decisions about the treatment of severely premature infants that is instructive about rights in an organizational context (Heimer and Staffen, 1998). Although not explicitly framed as a study of rights, in *For the Sake of the Children*, Heimer and Staffen explore what happens when legal claims confront moral and professional claims. Parents enjoy the legal right to make medical decisions for their children – a right that is bolstered by the patients' rights movement. The infants, however, enjoy certain rights which become the obligation of the professionals to ensure. Doctors, nurses, social workers, and lawyers must balance the rights of the child and the parent at times. And mere law is not enough to determine outcome (Heimer, 1996). The confluence of professional knowledge and institutional power can be determinative when mounted against some parents (poor, uneducated, perceived as "uncaring") while other parents are able to resist, often invoking their rights. Clearly, rights are not determinative. Rather, they are mediated through the organization and the professionals operating within it.

These are but two examples of studies of rights in organizations, but they demonstrate how organizational prerogatives can compete with, filter, distort, or amplify rights claims.

Movements

A prominent focus in the debate on the effects of rights is the basic question: can courts bring about social change? Following in the tradition of empirical examination of rights in particular social contexts, the 1990s saw the publication of two important empirical works on the question of the utility of rights, Gerald Rosenberg's *The Hollow Hope* (1991) and Michael McCann's *Rights at Work* (1994). McCann and Rosenberg come to very different conclusions about the role of rights in America, yet both books are deeply empirical, in the sense that they marshal and analyze much empirical data about legal rights and their effects on the social world.

Although his inquiry is not specifically about legal rights per se, in his study of the Supreme Court, Rosenberg uses three case studies to examine the United States Supreme Court's ability to produce social change. Based on his study of

Roe v. Wade, Brown v. Board of Education, and a variety of environmental cases, Rosenberg ultimately concludes that courts do not have the requisite institutional capacity to produce social change. He argues that the legal rights guaranteed by the cases he examines are products of the social movements in which they are embedded. Rosenberg's three case studies led him to conclude that the court has little or no capacity for social change (except in very circumscribed circumstances). In fact, the important "successes" of the civil rights movement, the prochoice movement, and the environmental movement were accomplished through political action, and court action lagged behind. In his view, rights (at least judicially enforced ones) do not matter or they matter very little in promoting social change. Indeed, Rosenberg argues that the lure of litigation serves to drain important resources from other, potentially more meaningful, avenues for social reform.

Rosenberg's thesis drew heavy criticism from other social scientists, who criticized Rosenberg for using questionable data (McCann, 1993) and for developing an instrumental model of rights and their relationship to social change. Several scholars developed new empirical evidence demonstrating the utility of law and rights, especially in the struggle for civil rights in the United States (Donohue and Heckman, 1997; McCann, 1994; Smith and Welch, 1997).

McCann's book is a study of pay equity reform in the workplace and his question is slightly different than Rosenberg's. Rather than inquiring if rights work to bring about social change, McCann examines *how* rights work at multiple phases of a reform movement. This difference allows him to be attentive to the subtle and unintended consequences of rights, not just for social change, but also for people's consciousness; the role rights discourses play in arguments; and the role of rights in mobilizing individual actors who are part of social movements. He examines the influence of rights and law generally in four phases of legal mobilization: movement building, the struggle to compel formal changes in official policy, the struggle for control over actual policy reform, and the transformative legacy of legal action. In each phase and for each player in the movement, legal rights hold different promises, pitfalls, and power. McCann's respondents indicate that legal rights "raise expectations" (McCann, 1994: 64), provide a legal language in which to claim harms (p. 65), and thus serve to catalyze a social movement. McCann recognizes that legal reform movements will be more or less successful given a variety of structural and material supports. Variation in supports (such as perceptions of political opportunity and organizational resources) helps to explain variation in the effectiveness of social movements.

McCann concludes that rights are very important for social movements, not just for legal successes, but also for individual actors in those movements. If an individual is motivated to take some action by the idea that they have a "right" to something (in this case equal pay), rights have effects. The action may be as small as challenging someone in an argument or as large as organizing a labor union, but the concept of rights reinforces their claims in the face of powerful opposing forces. McCann's examination of the subtle, but cumulative, effects of rights on individuals' consciousness and actions is a telling example of how the study of formal legal rights only in legal settings misses a lot of the work rights do – in the minds of individuals, in private conversations, and in larger social movements.

Rosenberg's and McCann's empirical studies each teach us important things, even though they ultimately represent opposing perspectives on the utility of rights for social change. Because rights are claims that often are vindicated in court, Rosenberg makes an important contribution by demonstrating the institutionally imposed difficulties that courts face in attempting to bring about social change. McCann, in contrast, makes an important contribution by showing how rights work to shape action in legal and nonlegal settings, such as the workplace, in union organizing, or in social movement activity. While Rosenberg and McCann reach different conclusions, they advance the understanding of rights by illuminating the mechanisms through which rights claims relate to the social world.

More recently, scholars of social movements have begun to combine these analyses to examine the mediating influences of culture, institutions, and ideologies on right's utility in social movements. Jonathan Goldberg-Hiller's case study of same-sex marriage convincingly argues that the effectiveness of rights-based social movements has privileged the "structural consequences" of rights at the expense of the social, cultural, and institutional contexts in which rights operate (Goldberg-Hiller, 2002).

The McCann–Rosenberg debate over the question of the utility of rights for social change raises a broader question about the role of rights in a social movement. The study of social movements primarily addresses the political opportunities that give rise to social movements, the mobilizing structures through which social movements organize, and the framing processes through which organizers define their movement and its goals (McAdam, McCarthy, and Zald, 1996). Those who think of rights as important engines for social change may believe that rights embody promise for accomplishing social change (a political opportunity), that rights are an effective way to capitalize on this promise (mobilizing structure), or that the law is an effective way to "frame" a particular problem. The extent to which a movement should invest in law (as opposed to other avenues for change) can be the source of significant controversy among participants in social movements. This was the case when the NAACP Inc. Fund proposed and ultimately undertook the litigation strategy that led to *Brown v. Board of Education* (Cruse, 1987). Moreover, scholars of rights demonstrate that pursuing a rights strategy can factionalize an interest group. Setting an agenda in terms of rights can normalize some members of the community (those who favor gay marriage, for example), effectively excluding the more radical fringe of a movement (Warner, 2000), making the decision about the utility of a rights strategy all the more difficult.

Another way to consider the utility of rights in a social movement is to understand the role of lawyers and litigation-based strategies in efforts at social change. A strong material base is important for the success of any social movement. For those that employ a litigation or rights-oriented strategy, this means lawyers. A thriving area of research in this vein is the literature on cause lawyering (Sarat and Scheingold, 2001, 1997). Cause lawyers are those ideologically dedicated to their political cause, who pursue it despite financial and professional impediments to doing so. Empirical work on cause lawyers helps us understand the ideological motivation of lawyers committed to social change through legal strategies (Menkel-Meadow, 1998; Polikoff, 1996), the institutional and organizational contexts in which they operate, and how this varies cross-nationally (Dotan, 1998; Hajjar, 1997), as well as how it varies according to political ideology (Heinz, Paik, and Southworth, 2003; Southworth, 2000).

The literature on cause lawyering, which details both successes and failures, demonstrates the importance of the study of rights in social movements. These studies demonstrate that the social organization of lawyers is another variable that mediates the relationship between rights and social change.

Comparative and transnational studies of rights

The comparative and transnational study of rights embodies two areas of related research. Comparative studies of rights focus on the domestic political affairs of various countries and the work rights can do in those contexts. Transnational research in the field of rights examines the effort by the global community to advance or resist rights – most notably human rights – around the world.

Much of the empirical scholarship on the "rights explosion" focuses (perhaps disproportionately) on the United States, and even more specifically on the civil rights movement in the United States. However, comparative research about the "rights explosion" demonstrates that it is not a uniquely American phenomenon; legal rights are used to advance social causes in many countries (Epp, 1998; Feldman, 2000; Heyer, 2000, 2001; Sarat and Scheingold, 2001), even in countries in which cultural and legal norms are less adversarial than in the United States (Epp, 1998; Feldman, 2000; Ginsburg, 2002).

The comparative perspective on the use of rights in social movements also suggests that the success of such movements is dependent on a number of factors beyond the strength of the rights claim itself. Moreover, this literature reveals that rights transform when they are imported into difference cultural and sociopolitical settings (Ginsburg, 2002; Heyer, 2000, 2001).

In addition to understanding the use of rights in domestic politics cross-nationally, scholars of transnational rights movements study rights in an international context. Scholars of international rights movements entertain differing opinions about the utility of rights in the global context. Pressure can be brought to bear by the international community on governments or transnational actors such as corporations to advance social causes including human rights, the environment, and women's rights. A variety of international organizations are involved in global rights movements. The World Bank and the International Monetary Fund often use their influence to protect and define property rights on the international stage. Other nongovernmental organizations (NGOs) such as Amnesty International and the individual activists in such organizations pursue rights strategies via campaigns that put pressure on sovereign states to improve conditions within their borders. This global activist community, focused on myriad substantive rights, has become more powerful in the last two decades because of cheaper air travel, improved communication technologies, and stronger international networks (Keck and Sikkink, 1998: 14).

Globalization theorists disagree, however, on the promise for influencing conditions within nation-states when pressure is brought to bear by the global community. Some argue that global cultural forces constitute state action and form (Meyer, Boli, Thomas, and Ramirez, 1997; Meyer and Hannan, 1979) and can quite significantly affect domestic politics. Other globalization scholars see transnational civil society as "an arena of struggle, a fragmented and contested area" (Keck and Sikkink, 1998: 199). Actors in this arena nonetheless ultimately employ networks of transnational actors to transmit enlightened ideals to international actors including governments (Sikkink, 1993). These lawyers and activists are determined to "use law as an instrument to promote the rights and advancement of disadvantaged populations and to further social justice" (Golub and McClymont, 2000: 1).

Others are less optimistic about the positive influence of international law and accompanying rights claims due to a variety of structural forces that can diminish the influence of transnational actors (Dezalay and Garth, 2001). Some argue that the decline in sovereignty renders citizenship problematic in this new era (Sassen, 1996). They worry about the hegemonic expansion of Western legal and cultural ideals on cultures and nations with very different practices (Hardt and Negri, 2000). Moreover, the success of particular transnational rights movements ultimately seems dependent on ties with the United States and therefore should be viewed with some skepticism (Dezalay and Garth, 2001). Pressure for international law or global human rights is, like other areas of transnational law, "reorganization and reshuffling of hierarchies of positions, modes of legitimate authority, and structures of power," between and among international organizations, NGOs, and sovereign states which means that rights have limited utility for social change in the face of other powerful forces (Dezalay and Garth, 1996: 11). When systems of rights are imported as mechanisms by which individuals can seek access to material benefits, these systems displace existing systems of entitlement claims that may be effective (Kagan, Garth, and Sarat, 2002).

The global context provides a compelling arena in which scholars can examine the production of rights. Rights are socially constructed, the product of sociopolitical struggle and compromise among powerful elites, making the history of the emergence of particular rights important for understanding power, compromise, and authority in context. Like the other arenas in which rights are invoked, context matters for the meaning of rights in the global context. International discourses, concerned as they often are with human rights, emphasize the idealized form of rights as somehow universal. Yet empirical studies of rights in the transnational environment show the relativity of rights in action. In a global context, rights can be used to speak law to power but are themselves embedded in and even created by power structures and relations. Thus, even though the power structures in which rights conflicts are embedded in the transnational context can bolster the claim to a right, the transnational contexts often make abundantly clear that there is seldom consensus on what constitutes a right or how rights should be implemented.

Although I have delineated these four different contexts for the empirical study of rights, it must be understood that these four contexts are inextricably linked. Obviously, individuals live and work in organizations that are governed by political bodies that are operating in a global economy.

CONCLUSION

Scholars of law and society must continue to study the work of rights and the work rights do. To do so, we should continue to analyze rights in social context(s), not just in formal legal institutions. Scholars of rights must continue to go to these social settings to examine the competing formal and informal systems, institutions, and claims that define rights and produce or minimize their social effects. Scholars should continue systematic documentation of the successes and failures to exercise rights by rights-holders with careful attention to how social location (race, class, and gender, to name just a few) affects these dynamics.

Empirical examination of the social world already has shown that rights work differently for different people in different contexts. Rights may be important legal constructs that allow the powerless to challenge or resist the more powerful, but the empirical scholarship demonstrates that the most powerless and the systematically disadvantaged are less likely to know they enjoy rights, are less likely to pursue their rights, and are less likely to be successful when they do (Galanter, 1974). Moreover, when rights are conferred on individuals in organizations, the organizational context serves as a filter to reinterpret, render subordinate to managerial prerogatives (and perhaps render meaningless) legal rights enjoyed by individuals. In social movements, rights may be diverting resources from more fruitful avenues of social reform. Finally, in the global context, legal rights are said by some to be the exportation of American hegemony to cultures with other models of dispute resolution, different values, and different power relationships. But these characterizations represent only one side of the debate about the role of rights in social systems.

Rights also function as tools in social reform movements: they present strategies to pursue in a litigation context; and they have the capacity to affect consciousness and feelings of entitlement. Thus they have significant effects for individuals. Rights are a mechanism by which individuals in organizations may override competing organizational prerogatives. The notion that one enjoys a legal right may be the incentive for an individual to join or even form a coalition of like-minded individuals to pursue social change. Moreover, once a social movement has begun, legal rights may be a powerful way to affect social change. Finally, in a global context rights may be a very useful way for the international community to influence government actors on issues of social justice, environmental quality, and democratic participation.

It is the complex and contradictory character of the role of rights in social processes that is the great challenge and promise of critical empirical studies of rights. The empirical understanding of rights is crucial because rights are inextricably linked with substantive justice and equality. Neither political theorists nor sociolegal scholars can afford to ignore this connection.

Note

With special thanks to the people who provided helpful comments including Catherine (KT) Albiston, Bryant Garth, Tom Ginsburg, Katharina Heyer, Bonnie Honig, Kay Levine, Ann Lucas, Tracey Meares, Robert Nelson, Austin Sarat, and Ben Steiner. Adriene Hill provided excellent research assistance.

References

Albiston, C.R. (1999) "The rule of law and the litigation process: The paradox of losing by winning," *Law & Society Review* 33(4): 869–910.

Albiston, C.R. (2000) "Legal consciousness and the mobilization of civil rights: Negotiating family and medical leave rights in the workplace," Paper presented at the Law and Society Association Annual Meeting, Miami, FL, May 2000.

Albiston, C.R. (2001a) "The institutional context of civil rights: Mobilizing the family and medical leave act in the courts and in the workplace," dissertation, University of California, Berkeley.

Albiston, C.R. (2001b) "The struggle to care: Negotiating family and medical leave in the workplace," Working Paper #26, Center for Working Families, University of California, Berkeley.

Aron, N. (1989) *Liberty and Justice For All: Public Interest Law in the 1980s and Beyond.* Boulder, CO: Westview Press.

Bourdieu, P. (1977) *Outline of a Theory of Practice.* Cambridge, UK: Cambridge University Press.

Brown v. Board of Education (1954) 347 U.S. 483.

Bumiller, K. (1988) *The Civil Rights Society: The Social Construction of Victims.* Baltimore: John Hopkins University Press.

Cruse, H. (1987) *Plural but Equal: A Critical Study of Blacks and Minorities and America's Plural Society.* New York: William Morrow.

Curran, B.A. (1977) *The Legal Needs of the Public: The Final Report of a National Survey.* Chicago: American Bar Foundation.

Delgado, R. (1993) "Words that wound: A tort action for racial insults, epithets, and name calling," in C.R.L. Mari, J. Matsuda, Richard Delgado, and Kimberle W. Crenshaw (eds.), *Words That Wound: Critical Race Theory. Assaultive Speech, and the First Amendment.* Boulder, CO: Westview Press, pp. 89–110.

Dezalay, Y. and Garth, B.G. (1996) *Dealing in Virtue: International Commercial Arbitration and the Construction of a Transnational Legal Order.* Chicago: University of Chicago Press.

Dezalay, Y. and Garth, B.G. (2001) "Constructing law out of power: Investing in human rights as an alternative political strategy," in A. Sarat and S. Scheingold (eds.), *Cause Lawyering and the State in a Global Era.* New York: Oxford University Press, pp. 354–81.

Donohue, J.J. and Heckman, J. (1997) "Continuous versus episodic change: The impact of civil rights policy on the economic status of blacks," in John J. Donohue III (ed.), *Foundations of Employment Discrimination Law.* New York: Foundation Press, pp. 225–42.

Dotan, Y. (1998) "The global language of human rights: Patterns of cooperation between state and civil rights lawyers in Israel," in A. Sarat and S. Scheingold (eds.), *Cause Lawyering: Political Commitments and Professional Responsibilities.* New York: Oxford University Press, pp. 244–63.

Dworkin, R. (ed.) (1977) *Taking Rights Seriously.* Cambridge, MA: Harvard University Press.

Dworkin, R. (ed.) (1985) *A Matter of Principle.* Cambridge, MA: Harvard University Press.

Edelman, L.B. and Chambliss, E. (1999) "Sociological perspectives on equal employment law," Paper presented at the Conference on the New Frontiers in Law's Engagement with the Social Sciences, Chicago, May 1999.

Edelman, L.B., Erlanger, H.S., and Abraham, S.E. (1992) "Professional construction of law: The inflated threat of wrongful discharge," *Law and Society Review* 26(1): 47–83.

Edelman, L.B. and Suchman, M.C. (1997) "The legal environments of organizations," *Annual Review of Sociology* 23: 479.

Epp, C.R. (1998) *The Rights Revolution: Lawyers, Activists, and Supreme Courts in Comparative Perspective.* Chicago: University of Chicago Press.

Ewick, P. and Silbey, S. (1992) "Conformity, contestation, and resistance: An account of legal consciousness," *New England Law Review* 26: 731–49.

Ewick, P. and Silbey, S.S. (1998) *The Common Place of Law: Stories From Everyday Life.* Chicago: University of Chicago Press.

Feldman, E.A. (2000) *The Ritual of Rights in Japan: Law, Society, and Health Policy.* Cambridge, UK: Cambridge University Press.

Felstiner, W., Abel, R., and Sarat, A. (1980) "The emergence and transformation of disputes: Naming, blaming, and claiming," *Law and Society Review* 15: 631–55.

Gabel, P. (1981) "Reification in legal reasoning," *Research in Law and Sociology* 3: 25–52.

Galanter, M. (1974) "Why the 'haves' come out ahead: Speculations on the limits of legal change," *Law and Society Review* 9(1): 95–160.

Ginsburg, T. (2002) "Confucian constitutionalism? The emergence of judicial review in Korea and Taiwan," *Law and Social Inquiry* 27(4): 763–800.

Glendon, M.A. (1991) *Rights Talk: The Impoverishment of Political Discourse.* New York: The Free Press.

Goldberg-Hiller, J. (2002) *The Limits to Union: Same-sex Marriage and the Politics of Civil Rights*. Ann Arbor: University of Michigan Press.

Golub, S. and McClymont, M. (2000) "Introduction: A guide to this volume," in S. Golub and M. McClymont (eds.), *Many Roads to Justice: The Law-Related Work of the Ford Foundation*. The Ford Foundation, pp. 1–20.

Hajjar, L. (1997) "Cause lawyering in transnational perspective: National conflict and human rights in Israel/Palestine," *Law and Society Review* 31(3): 473–504.

Hardt, M. and Negri, A. (2000) *Empire*. Cambridge, MA: Harvard University Press.

Harrington, C.B. and Yngvesson, B. (1990) "Interpretive sociolegal research," *Law and Social Inquiry* 15(1): 135–48.

Heimer, C.A. (1996) "Explaining variation in the impact of law: Organizations, institutions, and professions," *Studies in Law, Politics and Society* 15: 29–59.

Heimer, C.A. and Staffen, L.R. (1998) *For the Sake of the Children: The Social Organization of Responsibility in the Hospital and Home*. Chicago: University of Chicago Press.

Heinz, J.P., Paik, A., and Southworth, A. (2001) "Lawyers for conservative causes: Clients, ideologies, and social proximities," *Law and Society Review* 37(1): 5–50.

Heyer, K. (2000) "From special needs to equal rights: Japanese disability law," *Asia-Pacific Law and Policy Journal* 1(1); 6–24.

Heyer, K. (2001) "Rights on the road: Disability politics in Japan and Germany," PhD dissertation, University of Hawai'i at Honolulu.

Hobbes, T. (1909) *Hobbe's Leviathan: Reprinted from the Edition of 1651 with an Essay by the Late W.G. Pogson Smith*. Oxford: Clarendon Press.

Hull, K. (2001) *Wedding Rites/Marriage Rights: The Cultural Politics of Same Sex Marriage*. Evanston, IL: Northwestern University.

Johnson, L.H. (1991) "The new public interest law: From old theories to a new agenda," *Boston University Public Interest Law Journal* 1(1): 169–91.

Kagan, R.A., Garth, B., and Sarat, A. (2002) "Facilitating and domesticating change: Democracy, capitalism, and law's double role in the twentieth century," In A. Sarat, B. Garth, and R.A. Kagan (eds.), *Looking Back at Law's Century*. Ithaca, NY: Cornell University Press, pp. 1–31.

Keck, M.E. and Sikkink, K. (1998) *Activists Beyond Borders: Advocacy Networks in International Politics*. Ithaca, NY: Cornell University Press.

Kymlicka, W. (1989) "Liberal individualism and liberal neutrality," *Ethics* 99: 883–98.

Locke, J. (1967) *Two Treatises of Government: A Critical Edition with an Introduction by Peter Laslett*, 2nd edn. London: Cambridge University Press.

Macaulay, S. (1963) "Non-contractual relations in business: A preliminary study," *American Sociological Review* 28: 55.

MacKinnon, C. (1987) *Feminism Unmodified: Discourses on Life and Law*. Cambridge, MA: Harvard University Press.

MacKinnon, C. (1989) *Toward a Feminist Theory of the State*. Cambridge, MA: Harvard University Press.

Marshall, T.H. (1950) *Citizenship and Social Class and Other Essays*. Cambridge, UK: Cambridge University Press.

McAdam, D., McCarthy, J.D., and Zald, M.N. (eds.) (1996) *Comparative Perspectives on Social Movements : Political Opportunities, Mobilizing Structures, and Cultural Framings*. New York: Cambridge University Press.

McCann, M.W. (1993) "Reform litigation on trial," *Law and Social Inquiry* 17: 715–43.

McCann, M.W. (1994) *Rights at Work: Pay Equity Reform and the Politics of Legal Mobilizations*. Chicago: University of Chicago Press.

McGuire, K.T. (1995) "Repeat players in Supreme Court: The role of experienced lawyers in litigation," *The Journal of Politics* 57(1): 187–96.

Menkel-Meadow, C. (1998) "The causes of cause lawyering: Toward an understanding of the motivation and commitment of social justice lawyers," in A. Sarat and S. Scheingold (eds.),

Cause Lawyering: Political Commitments and Professional Responsibilities. New York: Oxford University Press, pp. 31–68.

Merry, S.E. (1990) *Getting Justice and Getting Even: Legal Consciousness Among Working-Class Americans.* Chicago: University of Chicago Press.

Meyer, J., Boli, J., Thomas, G.M., and Ramirez, F.O. (1997) "World society and the nation-state," *American Journal of Sociology* 103(1): 144–81.

Meyer, J.W. and Hannan, M.T. (eds.) (1979) *National Development and the World System.* Chicago: University of Chicago Press.

Milner, N. (1989) "The denigration of rights and the persistence of rights talk: A cultural portrait," *Law and Social Inquiry* 14(4): 631–75.

Minow, M. (1987) "Interpreting rights: An essay for Robert Cover," *Yale Law Journal* 96: 1860–1915.

Nelson, R.L. and Bridges, W.P. (1999) *Legalizing Gender Inequality: Courts, Markets, and Unequal Pay for Women in America.* Cambridge, UK: Cambridge University Press.

Nielsen, L.B. (2000) "Situating legal consciousness: Experiences and attitudes of ordinary citizens about law and street harassment," *Law and Society Review* 34: 201–36.

Nielsen, L.B. (forthcoming) *License to Harass: Law, Hierarchy, and Offensive Public Speech.* Princeton, NJ: Princeton University Press.

Nozick, R. (1974) *Anarchy, State, and Utopia.* New York: Basic Books.

Olsen, F. (1984) "Statutory rape: A feminist critique of rights analysis," *Texas Law Review* 63: 387–432.

Polikoff, N. (1996) "Am I my client? The role confusion of a lawyer activist," *Harvard Civil Rights-Civil Liberties Law Review* 31: 458.

Roe v. Wade (1973) 410 U.S. 113.

Rosenberg, G.N. (1991) *The Hollow Hope: Can Courts Bring About Social Change?* Chicago: University of Chicago Press.

Sarat, A. (1990) "'The law is all over': Power, resistance, and the legal consciousness of the welfare poor," *Yale Journal of Law and Humanities* 2(2): 343–79.

Sarat, A. and Kearns, T.R. (1995) *Law in Everyday Life.* Ann Arbor: University of Michigan Press.

Sarat, A. and Kearns, T.R. (eds.) (1996). *Legal Rights: Historical and Philosophical Perspectives.* Ann Arbor: University of Michigan Press.

Sarat, A. and Scheingold, S. (eds.) (2001) *Cause Lawyering and the State in a Global Era.* New York: Oxford University Press.

Sarat, A. and Scheingold, S. (eds.) (1997) *Cause Lawyering: Political Commitments and Professional Responsibilities.* New York: Oxford University Press.

Sassen, S. (1996) *Losing Control? Sovereignty in an Age of Globalization.* New York: Columbia University Press.

Scheingold, S. (1974) *The Politics of Rights: Lawyers, Public Policy, and Political Change.* New Haven, CT: Yale University Press.

Selznick, P. (1969) *Law, Society, and Industrial Justice.* New York: Russell Sage Foundation.

Sikkink, K. (1993) "Human rights, principled issue-networks, and sovereignty in Latin America," *International Organization* 47: 411–41.

Smith, J.P. and Welch, F.R. (1997) "Black economic progress after Myrdal," in John J. Donohue III (ed.), *Foundations of Employment Discrimination Law.* New York: Foundation Press, pp. 215–24.

Southworth, A. (2000) "Review essay: The rights revolution and support structures for rights advocacy," *Law & Society Review* 34(4): 1203–19.

Suchman, M.C. and Edelman, L.B. (1996) "Legal rational myths: The new institutionalism and the law and society tradition," *Law and Social Inquiry* 21: 903.

Taub, N. and Schneider, E. (1998) "Women's subordination and the role of law," in D. Kairys (ed.), *The Politics of Law: A Progressive Critique*, 3rd edn. New York: Basic Books, pp. 328–55.

Tushnet, M. (1984) "An essay on rights," *Texas Law Review* 62: 1363.

Waldron, J. (1995) "Rights," in R.E. Goodin and P. Pettit (eds.), *A Companion to Contemporary Political Philosophy*. Oxford: Blackwell, pp. 575–85.

Waldron, J. (1996) "Rights and needs: The myth of disjunction," in A. Sarat and T. R. Kearns (eds.), *Legal Rights: Historical and Philosophical Perspectives*. Ann Arbor: University of Michigan Press, pp. 87–112.

Warner, M. (2000) *The Trouble with Normal: Sex, Politics, and the Ethics of Queer Life*. Cambridge, MA: Harvard University Press.

Williams, P.J. (1991) *The Alchemy of Race and Rights*. Cambridge, MA: Harvard University Press.

Yngvesson, B. (1985) "Law, private governance, and continuing relationships," *Wisconsin Law Review*, 1985: 623–46.

Yngvesson, B. (1988) "Making law at the doorway: The clerk, the court, and the construction of community in a New England town," *Law and Society Review* 22(3): 409–48.

Young, I.M. (1990) *Justice and the Politics of Difference*. Princeton, NJ: Princeton University Press.

5

Consciousness and Ideology

PATRICIA EWICK

From their roots in nineteenth-century social theory, consciousness and ideology have had an uneasy relationship. As initially conceived, consciousness and ideology were opposed to one another. Whereas ideology represented the concealment of power, consciousness entailed its unmasking. In this classical tradition, both concepts were ideational. Ideology was associated with systems of beliefs that naturalized inequality. Consciousness, by contrast, was the awareness, held by individual subjects, that these beliefs were distorted, partial, and interested. So perfect was this opposition that the phrase "*false* consciousness" came to be synonymous with ideology, a conceptual inversion that created identity.

As the concepts have developed during the twentieth century, ideology and consciousness are no longer understood to be necessarily opposed to one another. As with so many other conceptual couplets (structure/agency or power/resistance), elements that were initially conceived of as distinctive and opposed have been construed as internal components of a larger process of social construction. For instance, while there is still much that is contested about the nature and meaning of ideology, there is an emerging consensus over what it is *not*. Few contemporary sociolegal scholars would claim that ideology is a grand set of ideas that in its seamless coherence imposes belief. It is not, in other words, a system of ideas that strictly determines what people think, that is, their consciousness, false or otherwise. In fact, the most promising reformulations of ideology propose that it is not a body of abstracted ideas at all (static, coherent, or otherwise). Rather, ideology is a complex process "by which meaning is produced, challenged, reproduced, [and] transformed" (Barrett, 1980; 97; see also Bahktin, 1987; Billig, 1991; Steinberg, 1991, 1999). Construed as a process, ideology shapes social life, not because it prevents thinking (by programming or deceiving people into a state of resignation or complacency), but because ideology actively invites thinking. In order to remain viable, ideology has to be lived, worked out, and worked on. It has to be expressed and applied and challenged. People have to use it to make sense of their lives and the world around them. In order to be a source of meaning and sense making, ideology must be polysemic, open, varied, and complex. Without these qualities, it would be useless and wither; or it would become a source of derision, fear, or ridicule. It would, in short, cease to be ideological.

Consciousness likewise figures prominently in this process of social construction. First, it too has been expanded to denote more than ideas that individual knowers have about power and inequality. Consciousness represents participation in the production of the very social structures that generate the degree and types of inequality existing in a society (Ewick and Silbey, 1997). In this sense, legal consciousness entails both thinking and acting: telling stories, complaining, lumping grievances, working, marrying, divorcing, suing a neighbor, or refusing to call the police. Through the circuitry of social practice, the boundary between structure and agency is blurred. With this blurring, consciousness is dislodged from the mind of an individual knower insofar as knowing always entails the invocation of cultural schemas and deployment of differentially available resources. It, in other words, emerges out of, even as it shapes, social structures.

Presented in this way, ideology and consciousness appear as similar, if not the same. Both are dynamic, cultural productions that have no virtual existence outside or apart from the words, deeds, and interactions that constitute social life. However, there remains a single crucial difference between consciousness and ideology. That difference is power. Ideology articulates power insofar as it embodies what Dorothy Smith has called procedures for "not knowing." This conceptualization of ideology actually retains an element of concealment. But, emerging out of a constitutive theory of law, this understanding of ideology deftly avoids making any claims about a foundational truth that can be opposed to ideology. Ideology, it is proposed, inheres in the *processes* or form of concealment, rather than in the *content* of that which is concealed.

In this essay, I will explore recent empirical research on consciousness and ideology in order to examine the various "procedures for not knowing" that comprise legal ideologies and assess the utility of these conceptual reformulations for sociolegal studies.

CLASSICAL AND CONTEMPORARY FORMULATIONS OF IDEOLOGY AND CONSCIOUSNESS

The starting point for most discussions of ideology and consciousness is typically the Marxist formulation of the terms. In the *German Ideology* (1970), Marx and Engels characterize ideology as a form of cognitive distortion, a false or illusory representation of the real. In this rendering, ideology is equated with the realm of the ideal. Ideologies operate to explain history according to philosophy and religious systems. Accordingly, they disguise the material interests embedded in the operation of society. Ideology thus operates to prevent men and women from perceiving the real conditions of existence, or their own "real" interests as they might find expression in those conditions.

Overcoming the ideological, for Marx, required a "study of actuality," or the empirical examination of the practical relations of everyday life. Such a study would explode the illusion of the ideal, revealing the embedded material interests that obscured the so-called actual. From the point of view of historical subjects of such ideologies, this would lead to class consciousness, or an appreciation and realization of these interests. Laboring under the illusions offered by religion and philosophy was, by contrast, to have false consciousness. Thus, for Marx, consciousness either sustained (false) or penetrated (class) ideology.

In contemporary sociolegal research, ideology and consciousness remain robust and central concepts. Indeed, given the focus of sociolegal scholars on power, culture, language, and ideas, the concepts are indispensable. And, although there are few strict adherents to classical Marxist formulation of the terms, aspects of this view of ideology and consciousness appear in many contemporary sociolegal accounts. Some contemporary Marxist structuralism, for instance, treats ideas, including cultural symbols and narratives, as a superstructural residue of material conditions that serves the interests of the elites.

Following from this perspective, law and legal consciousness are considered epiphenomena insofar as a particular social and economic structure is understood to produce a corresponding or appropriate legal order, including legal subjects. Work in this tradition often describes how the needs of capitalist production and reproduction mold legal behavior and consciousness. Studies focus on the production and practice of law, its accommodation to class interests, and the inequities that result.

For instance, Chambliss (1964) links the emergence, dormancy, and reemergence of the law of vagrancy to the changing needs of a ruling class. He describes how a decline in labor supply and the consequent pressure for increasing wages following the Black Death was opposed by the landed gentry through the passage of laws against vagrancy. These laws prohibited travel from one community to another, thus tying laborers to the land. As feudalism broke down, such laws were no longer needed and remained largely unenforced for the following century. Eventually, in the sixteenth century during a period of expanding trade, vagrancy laws were resurrected and revised to function as vehicles for policing and regulating the public roads where commercial traffic in goods and persons had become common. Whereas initially the focus of the statutes was on the "idle" and "those refusing labor," in the sixteenth century their emphasis was on "vagabonds" and "rogues." As the needs of the economic system and the material interests of the ruling class changed, so too did the law of vagrancy.

Late twentieth-century sociolegal scholars largely rejected this version of ideology as merely an epiphenomenal expression of underlying class domination, identifying a number of problems with the concept. Perhaps most troublesome has been the Marxist legacy of ideology as illusion or as a form of "false consciousness" (Hunt, 1985). The main reason for contemporary unease with the idea of false consciousness has been the rejection or questioning of the existence of an underlying truth, in an Enlightenment sense of an objective reality. Indeed, many of the dualities that characterized the ideological critiques of the nineteenth and early twentieth century (science/ideology, real/ideal, subject/object) have been disputed or rejected by contemporary scholars. Most significantly, they have rejected the possibility of a system of ideas and symbolic forms that misrepresents a social reality that exists prior to or independently from those ideas (Thompson, 1990).

A corollary of this criticism, insofar as it questions the notion of distortion or concealment, is the charge that ideology as false consciousness misrepresents or underestimates the degree to which subjects see through prevailing power relations. Subjects are instead reconceived of as being conscious of the power relations that suffuse their everyday social interactions. This insight has led sociolegal scholars to examine the consciousness of legal subjects as a terrain of struggle, contestation, inventiveness and resistance, rather than as a repository of ideological representations received from above. Legal subjects are seen as being much more actively engaged in ideological processes of both reproduction and resistance. In interactions with legal authorities as well as with one another, individuals invoke, comment upon, reject, and revise the symbolic meanings that comprise the ideological. In doing so, they creatively constitute – sometimes knowingly and sometimes unknowingly – the situated power relations within which they act (Bumiller, 1988; Ewick and Silbey, 1995, 1997; Sarat, 1990; Scott, 1985, 1990).

Finally, scholars have reconsidered the relationship of ideology to dominant classes. Empirical analysis of law creation, interpretation and enforcement has demonstrated that ideology is not aligned in an a priori way with a particular or single set of dominant interests and imposed downward upon the masses. This is to say, no particular set of ideas is ideological, per se. According to Hunt (1985: 16), "The class dimension of ideology is not an intrinsic property of words or concepts, but instead arises from the way in which ideological elements are combined and interrelated. Ideologies are not to be treated 'as if they were political number plates worn by social classes on their backs' (Poulantzas, 1975)."

One solution to the problems associated with the concept of ideology as epiphenomenal illusion has been to abandon the notion of ideology as "ruling idea," and simply equate it with "idea," or to be more precise, contested idea. Ideology loses it pejorative connotation and assumes a more neutral and descriptive bent. In this formulation, ideology becomes synonymous with "system of ideas," "system of symbols," or "system of beliefs." Ideology is seen as animating social action, but it is not aligned with any *particular* type of action, political project, or set interests. Ideology, here, assumes a pluralist and democratic quality. What is achieved by democratizing ideology is a recasting of subjects as conscious actors who are active in the process of making sense of the world and their experiences. For instance, Sally Merry has characterized ideology as a

> set of symbols and meanings by which individuals make sense of their world and their experience, suggesting that it is neither false nor true, but one of a range of ways of making the world coherent. Cultures provide multiple and competing sets of symbolic forms and meanings from which individuals choose. These symbolic systems are subject to redefinition through experience and changes in the social system itself. (Merry 1985: 61)

While this move avoids some of the pitfalls associated with earlier uses of the ideology, it falls headlong into a number of others. Most notably, this approach to ideology neutralizes the term by severing its connection to power and subordination. Unfortunately, stripping ideology of its negative aspects leaves unanswered many of the problems that it was initially formulated to draw attention to, questions such as domination, inequality, and social reproduction. For instance, in her critique of this approach, Silbey (1998) observes that focusing on the freely choosing subjects fails to take into account the ways in which power and privilege are embedded in institutions and language: "Unfortunately, the emphasis on the choosing subjects selecting from tool kits of available symbols, metaphors, and strategies elides the actions of collectivities seeking to privilege their vision of the world as reality, and the efforts of others in turn to find the means to resist such attempts" (p. 282).

Adopting a definition of ideology that equates it with a "system of beliefs" relieves many of the tensions that inhere in the classical concept of ideology. But the solution comes at a high price. Ideology loses most of its critical capacity, and thus its usefulness as a social scientific concept.

More recently, efforts have been made to salvage the critical capacity of the term and not abdicate its association with power. These reformulations retain the idea that ideologies legitimate and reproduce social inequality, without making any explicit assertion that (1) there is a real underlying truth that is being obscured, (2) subjects' consciousness is passively and automatically reflective of ruling ideologies, or (3) ideologies are necessarily aligned with the interests of one class. The most promising of these formulations have conceived of ideologies as operating not by concealing or masking the truth, but through the artful *production* of truth.

IDEOLOGY AND DISCOURSE: THE ARTFUL PRODUCTION OF TRUTH

Reformulating ideology in such a way as to recognize it as a creative and constitutive process parallels Foucault's reconceptualization of power (1977). Whereas Foucault asks us to consider power as a productive capacity, a similar claim has been made about ideology. Rather than focus on it as a *camera obscura*, it is increasingly understood to be a lens, providing not just an (inverted) vision of the real but actually producing the real. This claim grows out of the social constructivist or constitutive theory of social life. Within this framework, consciousness and ideology are understood to be part of a reciprocal process in which the meanings given by individuals to their world become patterned, stabilized, and objectified. These meanings, once institutionalized, become part of the material and discursive systems that limit and constrain future meaning making.

This view of ideology recognizes that it does not simply operate alongside domination; it is not simply a tool to be used to hide or create a distraction from the real. Rather the social meanings that we define as ideological are constitutive of domination. We can thus define ideology as "the ways in which meaning serves, in particular circumstances, to establish and sustain relations of power which are systematically asymmetrical" (Thompson, 1990: 7).

It is important to note that, in this definition, ideology is not defined by its content. It can only be recognized within particular sociohistorical contexts and, more specifically, by its operation within those contexts. In short, ideologies are known in terms of their effects. A particular set of meanings can only be said to be ideological insofar as it "serves" power (Thompson, 1990). The emphasis is thus on the active verb *serve*, reminding us that ideological analysis can only take place by examining the particular situational contexts in which struggles over meaning occur and paying attention to how those struggles contingently stabilize power.

Focusing on ideology as a process of meaning making necessarily implicates an examination of discourse, or "the process and product of socially situated and institutionally ordered ways people communicate their representations of lived and imagined realities" (Steinberg, 1999: 743). Generated through discourse, ideology is interactive and embedded in particular social contexts (see Bakhtin, 1987; Umphreys, 1999). Being interactive suggests that the meanings produced through this process are never singular or fixed, but are continually available for interpretive innovation, or deployment in new settings or for unanticipated purposes. Being socially situated, however, suggests that the possibilities for meaning making are, while open, also constrained. In part, the constraints reflect past discursive practices that have become institutionalized. Rules of evidence and cross-examination in a criminal trial illustrate such institutionalized constraints. Constraints may also reflect the sedimentation of meaning that is imported into any given setting. As Bakhtin observed:

> The living utterance, having taken meaning and shape at a particular historical moment in a socially specific environment, cannot fail to brush up against thousands of living dialogic threads, woven by socio-ideologic consciousness around the object of the utterance, it cannot fail to become an active participant in social dialogue. And not all words for just anyone submit equally easily to appropriation... many words stubbornly resist, other remain alien. (Bakhtin, 1987: 276)

The fact that some words resist appropriation, or remain alien, suggests that past struggles over the word have privileged some meanings and suppressed others Observing that discourse is principally organized around practices of exclusion, Mills writes, "Whilst what it is possible to say seems self-evident and natural, this naturalness is a result of what has been excluded, that which is almost unsayable" (1997: 12). It is generally recognized that, while the particular content of ideology cannot be specified ahead of time, its effects will be to make that which is arbitrary appear inevitable and natural. In this way, the contingency of power and hierarchy are stabilized through the processes of "not knowing," an essential part of the artful production of truth.

Law is, of course, an ideological discourse par excellent in that it is in the business of meaning making. As many scholars have noted, the law shapes our lives in ways that are rarely recognized. It invests us with identities and subjectivities, it shapes the physical and material world we live in, and it explicitly establishes rules and practices of other institutions. Finally, law is deliberately designed to operate as a "terrain of struggle." Much of the law – its organizations, professional practices, and rules of procedure – operates as an arena in which the dialogic conflicts are fought. Most importantly, however, presenting itself as a "referee" in these struggles, the legal system denies that it is an active or interested participant in the struggles. Thus, legal decisions and meanings are ideological precisely because they *appear* to be nonideological.

MODES OF LEGAL IDEOLOGY

The reformulation of ideology as a process of meaning making that serves power has had significant empirical consequences and conceptual ramifications. It has led to a body of sociolegal research that considers the "ideological effects" of certain practices and discourses. The phrase "ideological effects" is a somewhat cumbersome locution, but one that usefully emphasizes and makes explicit the contingent and transactional nature of ideology. Moreover, an attention to ideological effects has directed attention away from content of ideology toward a specification of techniques and forms through which meaning is made and deployed in the service of power. What Ronen Shamir wrote generally of law and society research, we might say of law and ideology: "an important achievement of recent sociolegal scholarship on law. . . is that it portrays the form of law, rather than its specific content, as the deeper layer of its mode of operation" (1996: 235).

John Thompson (1990) has identified five modes through which legal ideology operates and has linked each of these with typical forms of symbolic constructions, although he acknowledges that these forms of symbolic constructions may be associated with any or all of the various modes. Still, without making a claim about the exhaustivity or exclusivity of this catalog of forms, I would argue for the utility of such a typology. The analytic purchase of defining the form of ideology consists of its ability to specify *how* ideology artfully generates truth and creates ways of "not knowing" by suppressing alternative meanings, without reference to the content, or *what*, of ideology. This approach thus avoids some of the recurring problems of the concept, without sacrificing its critical role in explaining systematic asymmetries. Furthermore, by asking *how* ideology works we are denoting a process or a technique. Focusing on the various ideological forms invites us to examine the operation and effects of these techniques. It requires that we understand ideology and consciousness as ongoing participatory activities that over time constitute particular social and historical worlds.

Legitimation

Prominent, and most familiar, among the ideological modes of operation is legitimation. Legal ideologies and corresponding legal consciousness are ways in which social organizations produce the means of authorizing, sustaining, and reproducing themselves. By focusing on the legitimating effects of law, research describes the ways in which law helps people see their worlds, private and public, as both natural and right. In short, ideologies legitimate systematic asymmetries by depicting situations as worthy of support.

A principle strategy of legitimation, at least since the last century, is *rationalization*, or the application of logic and a positivist epistemology such that the resulting relations of power appear inevitable, and thus inarguable. For example, in their examination of a moral panic over mugging that occurred in England during the 1970s, Hall, Critcher, Jefferson, Clarke, and Roberts attach considerable significance to the use of statistics by politicians and journalists: "Statistics – whether crime rates or opinion polls – have an ideological function: they appear to *ground* free floating and controversial impressions in the hard, incontrovertible soil of numbers. Both the media and the public have enormous respect for 'the fact' – *hard facts*. And there is no fact so 'hard' as a number. . ." (Hall et al., 1978: 9; italics in original). Similarly, Jonathan Simon (1988) has written of the ideological effects of "actuarial practices" whereby the collection of data and use of seemingly neutral statistical techniques create categories of persons who then become the object of social control. Thus women, by virtue of their longer life expectancy compared to men, become a category for setting insurance premiums; or high rate offenders give rise to a typical profile, which becomes the basis for criminal justice policy. Moreover, because these techniques create subpopulations based on statistical features of a population, rather than on interactive communities, these practices disable traditional forms of resistance and collective protest. Most significantly, these techniques are politically powerful, in part, because they seem to be unconnected to political projects, and are lodged squarely in rational analysis of data. Simon observes:

Actuarial techniques play a central role in a proliferating set of social practices. They are at the same time a regime of truth, a way of exercising power, and a method of ordering social life. Actuarial practices have not seemed very important nor attracted much interest from social observers in part because they are already so familiar, and in part because they fit so unobtrusively into various substantive projects (e.g. educating, hiring, premium setting) in which they are subordinated as a means to an end. Yet this unobtrusiveness is precisely why they have become so important; they make power more effective and efficient by diminishing its political and moral fallout. (1988: 772)

Appeals to legitimacy are also couched in claims to *universalization*, whereby situations that benefit a class of individuals or groups are depicted as benefiting or as available to all. Whereas actuarial practices create distinctions that seem inevitable and thus legitimate, *universalization* achieves a similar outcome by denying difference. Balbus, for example, argues that certain features of liberal law, such as the highly prized claims to formal equality and procedural justice, serve to buttress and legitimate the inequality of the existing economic order. The formal equality instantiated in due process rights provides "a stable and apparently neutral framework from which bourgeois class interests in accumulation and profit maximization can flourish"; but due process and formal equality also help convince the "propertyless that they have the legal right and, hence, the real opportunity of rising into the bourgeoisie" (Balbus, 1973: 6).

Narrative is also a powerful technique of legitimation. By presenting events in the form of a story, depictions of the world are embedded in plots that unfold in a particular and inevitable chain of events leading to a moral claim about meaning. Research in a variety of settings has demonstrated the ideology effects of narrative by illustrating how stories can contribute to the reproduction of existing structures of meaning and power.

It is the narrative form, rather than the content of any particular story, that constitutes the principle means through which narratives operate ideologically. First, the ideological effects of narrative inhere in narratives' ability to colonize consciousness. Well-plotted stories cohere by relating various (selectively appropriated) events and details into a temporally organized whole. The coherent whole, the configuration of events and characters arranged in believable plots, preempts alternative stories. The events seem to speak for themselves. Narratives also sustain power relations to the extent that they conceal the social organization of their production and plausibility. Narratives embody general understandings of the world that by their deployment and repetition come to constitute and sustain the lifeworld. Yet because narratives depict specific persons existing in particular social, physical, and historical locations, those general understandings often remain unacknowledged. By failing to make these manifest, narratives draw on unexamined assumptions and causal claims without displaying these assumptions and claims or laying them open to challenge or testing.

Dissimulation

Power is not only served through legitimation. It may also be served through deception. Thompson's use of deception as a mode of ideological operation appears to replicate the false consciousness misstep of earlier formulations. Yet, as he persuasively points out, so intent were social theorists on severing the connection between ideology with falsity that they may have ignored the fact that, although not a defining characteristic, deception can be mobilized to sustain domination and relationships of power. Dissimulation represents the techniques of concealment and distortion that may be used to this end. Through such discursive strategies as euphemism, displacement, and trope, meaning is deployed to distort or obscure an alternative truth.

In her analysis of language and ideology in South Africa and the United States, Mertz (1988) illustrates the operation of dissimulation in the official account of the system of South African apartheid. Paying close attention to the words, phrases, and texts used to describe the unjust history of white supremacy and black disenfranchisement, Mertz observes that "complex and ambiguous situations are glossed authoritatively in single words; difficult political decisions and situations are expressed as simple and straightforward. Problems are not even acknowledged; instead, declarative and assertive language is used to describe the setting as the government wishes it to be seen" (1998: 671). She illustrates this by citing a government publication.

> The Government of the RSA (Republic of South Africa) is intensely aware of the special problems that are created by an historical heritage that has placed the White nation in a position of trusteeship over various underdeveloped Bantu people. In an artificially integrated unified state, the Bantu would, as a result of their enormous backlog in comparison with the Whites, be doomed to become a backward proletariat...However, by creating for each Bantu people the opportunity to grow into an independent nation in a geopolitically acknowledged sphere of influence...the possibility that the divergent interests of the groups concerned will lead to a continual political struggle for power is obviated. (Mertz, 1988: 670).

The parallels to Israeli depictions of Bedouin settlements in the Negev are striking. In his analysis of Bedouins under the law of Israel, Shamir (1996) cites a judicial opinion denying the petitioners' claims that a historical injustice had been committed. The opinion ends with an account of the situation that denies injustice in the present by alluding to a history of primitiveness and backwardness and offers aid, indeed salvation, through the promise of law's order.

> Under the circumstances, and with an overall perspective of the historical developments that the Bedouins in this area experience, it is difficult not to sympathize with these people and to feel a desire to help them in their distress, and it seems that this is also the sentiment of the authorities...But this sentiment cannot drive us to allow the existence of constructions that were illegally constructed or to order the authorities not to implement the law. (1996: 251)

In each example, a history of oppression is glossed over with phrases like "white political *leadership*," or "the historical *developments* that the Bedouins experience." In each example, systematic government policies designed to disenfranchise South African Blacks or Bedouin nomads, are presented in the language of *trusteeship* or a *desire to help*. In each example, the order imposed by the law is offered as an alternative to chaos or *continual struggle*.

Displacement is another discursive strategy designed to dissimulate, without necessarily deceiving. The strategy of displacement consists of invoking meaning associated with one object, or developed in one context, to another object or context. Referring again to Hall et al.'s history of moral panic in *Policing the Crisis*, the authors assign paramount importance to the transplantation of the idea of mugging from its American context. The imported term carried a host of additional associations and references that generated an abundance of meaning. Without the supplement of associations – including the ideas of general social crisis and rising crime rate of the United States – the panic, and the ensuing government campaign, might never have occurred.

It is crucial to reiterate the point that euphemism or displacement, as well as other rhetorical devices such as trope, do not represent the falsification or covering up of truth. In other words, they are ideological, not because they destroy or conceal truth, but because they generate meaning. Through the creation of meaning they come to constitute the situations and relationships they depict. Subjugated, Bantu remain in "underdeveloped" homelands. Denied their ownership claims, Bedouin remain "uprooted." Framed within the American example, a cluster of petty crimes generates moral and social panic. Ideologies, Greenhouse (1988) wrote, are thus self-fulfilling. Therein lies their capacity to serve power.

Unification and fragmentation

Although Thompson presents unification and fragmentation as separate, they can be arguably collapsed into a single category or mode. In one way or another, the processes denoted by unification and fragmentation entail the symbolic construction of social entities through the drawing of boundaries. Those boundaries, once drawn, create the effect of within-group homogeneity and between-group difference. In particular instances, the creation of groups and persons that result from this process inhibit the possibilities of discursive challenge that might otherwise develop across groups. In other instances, the boundaries enhance conflict and dispute between the constructed groups, deflecting efforts to resist power-holders. Finally, when the groups are arranged in a hierarchy of value, the resulting categories come to legitimate differential treatment that preserves inequality.

We can see both fragmentation and unification operating simultaneously in the discursive struggle over the meaning of welfare. According to Williams (1998), with the passage of the 1996 Personal Responsibility and Work Opportunity Reconciliation Act the federal entitlement to cash assistance for poor single-parent families was eliminated. Central to this political outcome was the rhetorical association of "entitlement" with the right of poor people to receive governmental benefits. Using the term entitlement to describe the transfer of benefits to the poor strongly implied that these payments were a legal innovation and distinct from the multitude of other entitlements guaranteed to all citizens by our legal system. Much of private law, contract, and tort law, for instance, is based on the legal concept of entitlement. The state, by establishing these seemingly neutral, market-structuring background rules, effectively creates and preserves inequality even as it denies doing so. Characterizing welfare "entitlements" as an aberration in American legal culture discursively produced an outgroup of welfare recipients whose dependency upon the state seemed to distinguish them from "hardworking" Americans (Williams, 1998: 579).

It is important to note that an extreme, or limiting, case of fragmentation is achieved when social action is understood in entirely individual and nonrelational terms. The individuation that underwrites capitalist economy in general, for instance, protects the resulting inequality and asymmetries in power by impeding the development of challenging groups such as labor unions. Thus by characterizing wage earners as "independent" and "autonomous" (in a sense, constructing a boundary around the individual worker as the only real or authentic social entity) the law deflects attention from the structural inequities produced by the market. Following this line of reasoning, critical legal theorists have focused on the ideological effects of rights discourse in this regard. Observing that the recognition of legal rights is premised on such a radical individuation, they contend that liberal legal celebration of rights actually disempowers the individual. As Gordon notes,

> [T]he rhetoric of rights can be dangerously double-edged, as the black civil rights movement has discovered. Floored entitlements can be turned into ceiling. Formal rights without practical enforceable content are easily substituted for real benefits. Anyway, the powerful can always assert counterrights (to vested property, to differential treatment according to "merit,"...) to the rights of the disadvantaged. (Gordon, 1998: 657)

Reification

A final mode of ideology that I would like to discuss in this essay is reification. In its various guises reification always involves the denial of "a social and historical character of social-historical phenomena" (Thompson, 1990: 65). Rather than perceive law and legality as a constellation of related actors and actions, objectified in particular material forms and enacted by historical subjects, it is perceived as existing "out of history." It is detached from human action and consciousness. A reified world provides a dehumanized vision. In such a vision, law may find expression in human action and intention; it may be "expressed" or "reflected" in a judge's pronouncement, a jury's verdict, or a jailer's keys, but it is only incidentally related to such enactments. The observable, discrete, and particular world of human social interaction becomes a vessel or container for the legal, which is understood to exist independently from these forms.

Reification is achieved through abstractions that aggregate concrete historical actors and actions into a transcendent entity detached from the original. The process is complete when the abstraction itself is concretized, endowed with the ontological independence of a thing that exists separately from the empirical manifestations that gave rise to it.

In his history of "the most famous tort case of modern times" (*Palsgraf v. Long Island Railroad Company*), John Noonan (1976) traces the processes of reification that shaped the selection of "facts" that led up to (i.e., "determined") the judicial decision. The appellate decision denied Mrs Palsgraf recovery for the injury she suffered when a scale toppled over and struck her on the platform of Long Island Railroad on a hot August morning in 1924. As the case was rendered in both judicial opinion and in subsequent commentary, no mention is ever made of Mrs Palsgraf's age, marital status, or occupation, of the extent of her injury, of its effect on her children, of the financial burden she suffered, of the defendant, its assets, of the legal ordeal Mrs Paltsgraf endured, of the various counsel involved, or of the person of the judge (Benjamin Cardozo).

Instead, through the various decisions, arguments, and opinions that we call the legal process, an underlying rule was distilled from these events. "Many a common law suit can be lifted from meanness up to dignity," Cardozo wrote, "if the great judge is by to see what is within." The "rule" that was distilled from the messy events of that August morning assumed the following form as it appeared in *Restatement of Torts* as an Illustration of Clause b of the rule:

> A, a passenger of the X and Y Railway Company, is attempting to board a train while encumbered with a number of obviously fragile parcels. B, a trainman of the company, in assisting A does so in such a manner as to make it probable that A will drop one or more of the parcels. A drops a parcel which contains fireworks, although nothing in its appearance indicates this. The fireworks explode, injuring A's eyes. The railway company is not liable to A. (Noonan, 1976: 150)

As this example illustrates, much of the transformation involved in reification is achieved through textualization, or writing, inscription and other modes of encoding communication that permits its extraction, preservation, and retrieval separated from ongoing interaction. As Dorothy Smith observed, "texts speak in the absence of speakers" (Smith, 1990: 210). And it is this capacity that imparts to texts the power to transcend time, place, and social interaction, and, in so transcending, to seem to determine the actions of historical actors who are necessarily caught in place and time.

Textuality, for instance, confers authority to the judge's printed opinion through the system of precedents. To bind current decisions by prior decisions, and to distinguish later precedents from earlier precedents, requires a record and the valorization of the record. "Lawyers are trained not even to think of the reality of the case and therefore, to pay attention to only the printed version of what occurred. As a result, over time, it has been forgotten that the printed opinion is only a representation of reality" (Katsh, 1989: 36).

Textuality also defines the grounds of participation in the modern trial. The texuality of law demands that "the trial's result must endure the way a written text endures," James Clifford observes in his account of the Mashpee Indian land claim trial. Plaintiffs "represent themselves through scripted exchanges with attorneys, in statements for the record," depositions become the grounds for interrogating and perhaps discrediting persons in proceedings witnessed. The law has come to reflect the "logic of literacy of the historical archive rather than of changing collective memory" (Clifford, 1988: 329).

This feature of law has consequences for the distribution of social power, or ideological effects. Strategically entering the law's text is problematic for those with few resources and little power. In his account of the Mashpee Indian trial, Clifford observes the contradiction that led to the denial of their land claim. Without an uninterrupted history of *documented* cultural practice, the Mashpee claim was rejected. Yet this rejection, premised as it was upon a highly textualized view of culture, was willfully blind to a century or more of adaptations and appropriations that were necessitated by their subordination within dominant white culture. The very cultural subordination that led to selectively abandoning aspects of their cultural practice and adopting white culture (i.e., speaking English, dressing in nontribal clothes, etc), disqualified the legitimacy of the Mashpee's claim of cultural integrity. Of course, had they been in a position to present their culture as a well-preserved museum archive, they would no doubt have had sufficient power to retain the lands they now claimed.

CONCLUSION: REGAINING CONSCIOUSNESS

In the last few pages I have written a great deal about ideology and little about consciousness. In concluding, then, I will be explicit about the role of consciousness in the processes I have just outlined. Recall that in the classic understanding of consciousness and ideology, the concepts stood in a profound relation of tension to one another. Within a social world in which ideology prevailed, one lacked consciousness, or was falsely conscious. By contrast, developing class consciousness entailed overcoming ideology. Beginning with Marx himself, that simplistic view of the relationship has been abandoned. In contemporary usages, ideology is an effect, a contingent outcome of particular symbolic practices that generate meaning.

The emphasis in this conceptualization on the active production of meaning shifts our attention back to consciousness. Consciousness denotes participation in that process. The need to constantly remake the world derives from the fact that meanings are not fixed but are always dynamic. According to Steinberg (1991) the dynamism derives from two sources: first, meaning is never wholly fixed by the signs used to convey it. Because signs are polyphonic, when they are embedded in a new context, what they mean can be challenged and changed. Second, the meaning produced by signs is a result of their relationship to the larger discourse of which they are a part. They never float free of their history, or of future objectives.

Thus consciousness can neither overcome nor be colonized by ideology. Consciousness, construed as an active process of meaning making, produces, reproduces, or challenges ideology. Moreover, which of those various contingencies are realized can never be theoretically stated. The relationship between ideology, consciousness, and social structure is ultimately a result of particular social historical transactions and can only be known and understood empirically. South Africa is no longer under white rule. The Mashpee are once again in court. Reading John Noonan's account of Palsgraf v. Long Island Railroad generations of lawyers and judges know of details of Mrs Palsgraf's plight that were submerged in the judicial record. In short, defined as a form of sense making that serves power, ideology is lived, worked out, and worked on. It must be constantly invoked and applied and that means it is open to challenge and contest. People use ideological forms to make sense of their lives. And it is through that sense making that people produce not only those lives but also the specific structures within which they live.

References

Bahktin, M.M. (1987) *The Dialogic Imagination: Four Essays*. Austin, TX: University of Texas Press.

Balbus, I.D. (1973) "The concept of interest in pluralist and Marxian analysis," *Politics and Society* 1: 151–77.

Barrett, M. (1980) *Women's Oppression Today: Problems in Marxist Feminist Analysis*. London: Verso.

Billig, M. (1991) *Ideology and Opinions: Studies in Rhetorical Psychology*. London: Sage Publications.

Bumiller, K. (1988) *The Civil Rights Society: The Social Construction of Victims*. Baltimore: Johns Hopkins University Press.

Chambliss, W. (1964) "A sociological analysis of the law of vagrancy," *Social Problems* 12: 67–77.

Clifford, J. (1988) *The Predicament of Culture: Twentieth-Century Ethnography, Literature, and Art*. Cambridge, MA: Harvard University Press.

Ewick, P. and Silbey, S. (1995) "Subversive stories and hegemonic tales: Toward a sociology of narrative," *Law & Society Review* 29: 197–226.

Ewick, P. and Silbey, S. (1997) *The Commonplace of Law: Stories from Everyday Life*. Chicago: University of Chicago Press.

Foucault, M. (1977) *Discipline and Punish: The Birth of the Prison*. New York: Vintage.

Gordon, R.W. (1998) "Some critical theories of law and their critics," in David Kairys (ed.), *The Politics of Law*. New York: Basic Books, pp. 641–61.

Greenhouse, C. (1988) "Courting difference: Issues of interpretation and comparison in the study of legal ideologies," *Law & Society Review* 22: 687–798.

Hall, S., Critcher, C., Jefferson, T., Clarke, J., and Roberts, B. (1978) *Policing the Crisis: Mugging, the State and Law and Order*. New York: Macmillan.

Hunt, A. (1985) "Ideology of law: Advances and problems in recent applications of the concept of ideology to the analysis of law," *Law & Society Review* 19: 11–37.

Katsh, Ethan M. (1989) *Electronic Media and the Transformation of Law*. New York: Oxford University Press.

Marx, K. and Engels, F. (1970) *The German Ideology*, ed. C.J. Arthur. London: Lawrence and Wishart.

Merry, Sally E. (1985) "Concepts of law and justice among Americans: Ideology as culture," *Legal Studies Forum* 9: 59–70.

Mertz, E. (1988) "The uses of history: Language, ideology and law in the United States and South Africa," *Law & Society Review* 22: 661–85.

Mills, Sara (1997) *Discourse*. London: Routledge.

Noonan, J. (1976) *Persons and Masks of the Law*. New York: Farrar, Straus & Giroux.

Poulantzas, N. (1975) *Political Power and Social Classes*. London: New Left Books.

Sarat, A. (1990) " 'The law is all over…': Power, resistance and the legal consciousness of the welfare poor," *Yale Journal of Law and Humanities* 2: 343–79.

Scott, J.C. (1985) *Weapons of the Weak*. New Haven, CT: Yale University Press.

Scott, J.C. (1990) *Domination and the Arts of Resistance: Hidden Transcripts*. New Haven, CT: Yale University Press.

Shamir, R. (1996) "Suspended in space: Bedouins under the law of Israel," *Law & Society Review* 30: 231–57.

Silbey, S. (1998) "Ideology, power, and justice," in Bryant Garth and Austin Sarat (eds.), *Power and Justice in Law and Society Research*. Evanston, IL: Northwestern University Press, pp. 272–308.

Simon, J. (1988) "Ideological effects of actuarial practices," *Law & Society Review* 22: 771–800.

Smith, D. (1987) *The Everyday World as Problematic: A Feminist Sociology*. Boston: North-eastern University Press.

Smith, D. (1990) *Texts, Facts and Femininity: Exploring the Relations of Ruling*. London: Routledge.

Steinberg, M (1991) "Talkin' class: Discourse, ideology, and their roles in class conflicts," in Scott G. McNall, Rhonda Levin, and Rick Fantasia (eds.), *Bringing Class Back in: Contemporary and Historical Perspective*. Boulder, CO: Westview Press, pp. 261–84.

Steinberg, M. (1999) "The talk and back talk of collective action: A dialogic analysis of repertoires of discourse among nineteenth-century English cotton spinners," *American Journal of Sociology* 105: 736–80.

Thompson, J. B. (1990) *Ideology and Modern Culture*. Stanford, CA: Stanford University Press.

Umphreys, M.M. (1999) "The dialogics of legal meaning: Spectacular trials, the unwritten law and narratives of criminal responsibility," *Law & Society Review* 33: 393–423.

Williams, L.A. (1998) "Welfare and legal entitlements: The social roots of poverty," in David Kairys (ed.), *The Politics of Law*. New York: Basic Books, pp. 569–90.

6

Law in Popular Culture

Richard K. Sherwin

A culture may be defined by the hold it has on us, how it holds us together in association.
(John Rajchman, *Le Savoir-Faire Avec L'Inconscient: Ethique et psychanalyse*)

Introduction: What is Popular Legal Studies?

Law embodies forms of communication, commemoration, and advocacy with a singular institutional authority: its meanings are backed by the power of the state. But law's power, like its meanings, is all over: not only in formal venues, such as courtrooms, legislatures, and government agencies, but also in everyday social practices (Sarat, 1990). People absorb a broad array of stories and images about the law, lawyers, and the legal system from books, newspapers, television news programs, documentaries, docudramas, and feature films. We carry these stories and images in our heads wherever we go, including voting booths and jury rooms, where legal meanings – popular, formal, and mixtures of the two – take effect.

There is a two-way traffic between law and popular culture. Real legal issues and controversies give rise to popular legal representations just as popular legal representations help to inform and shape real legal issues and case outcomes (Sherwin, 2000). Dramatic reenactments of notorious trials reach the screen at breakneck speed. Consider the case of Erik and Lyle Menendez. Two major docudramas about the case were produced, including reenactments of the crime, while the brothers were still on trial for the murder of their parents. Both movies aired after an initial mistrial, and *prior* to the brothers' second jury trial. Cognizant of the impact that the docudramas might have on prospective jurors, defense lawyer Leslie Abramson threatened to air a live interview with Erik Menendez on a competing network directly opposite one documentary's broadcast unless the producers incorporated details more favorable to the defense. As Lisa Scottoline has written, "the wall between fiction and reality has become porous as a cell membrane. With reality passing through it to fiction, and fiction flowing back...into reality" (Scottoline, 2000: 656). Consider actress Julia Roberts's portrayal of Erin Brockovich, fierce champion of small-town victims of the toxic effects of polluted ground water in a tort suit against a greedy and indifferent corporate defendant. No sooner is the film breaking records at the box office than the *real* Erin Brockovich shows up in television ads seeking to defeat corporate sponsored tort reform proposals that would place limits on tort damages.

But the blurring of Hollywood fictions and legal reality is occurring not only in movie theaters and on TV screens at home. It is also taking place inside the courtroom. Consider the prosecutors in real homicide cases who compare the accused to film characters from Francis Ford Coppola's *The Godfather* or Oliver Stone's *Natural Born Killers*. Or the state's attorney who establishes a "knowing and voluntary" waiver of *Miranda* rights based on the defendant's familiarity with a popular TV show (Kemple, 1995).

Of course, in one sense, the intermingling of truth and fiction in legal discourse is nothing new. To paraphrase contemporary American novelist Don DeLillo, law cases, like novels and theater, are all about reliving things. Lawyers are storytellers, and the best, most compelling stories are the ones that adapt familiar narrative forms featuring recognizable character types driven by ordinary feelings, motives, and desires. Advocates who can integrate their case theory into an effective story form, and play it out in court within evidentiary constraints, consistent with the applicable law, are more likely to be persuasive before a jury than those who merely present facts and recite black letter rules. The crime and the motive, the negligent act and the pain and suffering that it allegedly caused, the broken promise and the lost profits that resulted – none of these things exists, as a matter of law, unless and until they have been proven, which is to say, until the decision maker, whether judge or juror, believes them to be so. To succeed in this effort reliance upon the strength of deductive and inductive logic alone will not do. Stories must be told, characters evoked, states of mind laid bare. And that requires the fictional method, the imaginary ground plot, the apt image – fruits of the advocate's facility with the raw materials out of which meanings are made, and made to stick in the decision maker's mind. In short, it requires familiarity with the resources of popular culture.

An important part of the advocate's craft, therefore, is to be able to identify, as well as present, the best available story under the circumstances. Perhaps it will be a clue-building whodunit, like the one prosecutor Marcia Clark told during her summation in the O.J. Simpson double murder trial. As she rattled off each clue, there on a looming screen jurors saw yet another fragment of Simpson's face click into place: his opportunity to kill (click), his motive (click), the victim's blood on his socks and glove (click), the blood trail that he left at the scene (click). Until there it is: the familiar face of O.J. Simpson. The mystery has been solved. Or perhaps the sober, logical rhetoric of the state's detective story will yield to a more animated telling. Perhaps the story will become a hero's tale in which systemic racism and abuse of power will have to be resisted by an impassioned jury. This was the narrative strategy of Johnnie Cochran in defense of O.J. Simpson. Cochran launched the jurors on a heroic quest against "genocidal racism." "If you don't stop it [i.e., the state's cover-up] then who? Do you think the police department is going to do it? ... You police the police through your verdict," he proclaimed. Or it might be a transcendent narrative, a mythic tale of the founding of the American polity, like the story told by defense lawyer Gerry Spence. Spence cast jurors along with his client Randy Weaver as heroic defenders of Jeffersonian liberty against the tyranny of the state in a case arising from the shooting of a federal marshal who came onto Weaver's property to arrest him for illegally manufacturing and selling a firearm. "Go back to 1775 and the Continental Congress," Spence told the jurors, "Jefferson was there, Adams was there ... They were just local guys doing their job, like you are local people doing your job . . . and they did something permanent and magnificent and lasting, and that is what you will do with your verdict" (Sherwin, 2000: 57).

Popular conceptions, categories, emotions, and beliefs about law, truth, and justice enter into the legal system in a variety of ways. They enter the law when jurors substitute their own commonsense beliefs for confusing rules of law quickly read by judges in jury instructions that go beyond the ordinary lay person's ability to absorb (Smith, 1991). Popular legal representations also enter the law when the mass media obsessively stoke a community's desire for revenge, as occurred in 1994, when Californians, incensed by the sexual abuse and murder of 12-year-old Polly Klaas, voted in favor of the nation's toughest mandatory sentencing rules, subsequently known as the "three-strikes-and-you're-out law. Law may even change as the result of a film, like *The Thin Blue Line*, Errol Morris's so-called "documentary" exposé of the frame-up of an innocent man on death row in a real capital murder case. As the judge, lawyers, eyewitnesses, defendant, and defendant's companion at the time of the murder speak in turn before Morris's camera their prejudices, lies, and pathologies come into view. The film's indictment of the way in which the defendant's conviction and sentence to death in the electric chair were obtained was so compelling that it prompted a review of the case. That review led to the condemned man's release from prison. The fact that Morris's "documentary" used actors to stage dramatic reenactments of key events, or that Morris incorporated visual overlays from grade "B" detective dramas to critically or humorously comment on a particular witness's testimony, all backed by Philip Glass's hypnotic score, seem to have gone unnoticed, in deference to the filmmaker's self-professed search for the truth (Sherwin, 1994: 53, n. 52).

In the age of images, legal reality can no longer be properly understood, or assessed, apart from what appears on the screen. The visual mass media, especially television, have become the major source of worldly knowledge and common sense (Pfau, Mullen, Deidrich, and Garrow, 1995). To paraphrase Robert Ferguson (1994: 40), we can only tell the stories we know – *and know how to tell within the parameters of a given medium*. As Marshall McLuhan famously put it in 1964, "the medium is the message" (McLuhan, 1994). The advent of television in particular has changed the way journalism and politics are practiced. From Ronald Reagan's classic campaign film "A New Beginning" in 1984, to Bill Clinton's 1992 campaign feature "A Man from Hope," politics, like journalism, has gone visual. The visual mass media today – from film to TV to the Internet – are similarly changing the practice and consumption of law.

Today, electronic monitors pervade modern American courtrooms. On the screen jurors and judges watch video depositions, distant witnesses, day-in-the-life videos documenting personal injuries, as well as all manner of evidentiary exhibits – from projected images of physical and documentary evidence, to computerized graphics, digital animations, and simulated crimes and accidents. Jurors even watch movies made for closing argument (*Standard Chartered PLC*, 1989). And, of course, people watch at home, sometimes obsessively. At such times the extraordinary case, like the double murder trial of O.J. Simpson, acquires an amplified cultural significance. Larger social issues, like race and the cult of celebrity, unfurl on a national, even global, stage. In the aftermath, laws change and new policies develop. And here, too, the medium matters. The notoriety of a trial has only partly to do with the legal issues that it raises. Its popularity also depends on the extent to which the trial's story and character types meet or clash with the aesthetic protocols of the medium itself.

Take the Courtroom Television Network, or Court TV, which has billed itself as a "window" on the American justice system. The trials it shows plainly belie such a claim. The frequent depiction of interpersonal, often sexual, violence that these trials offer is highly unrepresentative of the vast majority of real trials. And when a more typical nonviolent civil dispute does make an appearance – a contract dispute, say – odds are it will feature a celebrity, like the lawsuit starring actress Pamela Anderson and the producers of the popular television series *Bay Watch*. To advertise its coverage of this case Court TV showed scenes of a bikini-clad Anderson happily romping on a *Bay Watch* beach. Sex, violence, and the cult of celebrity: this is, of course, the familiar formula for successful commercial TV fare. It is what viewers have come to expect (and, judging from the ratings, most like to see). Successful law shows mimic these desires and expectations. If they do not, it is unlikely that they will show up in the first place, much less remain on the air.

But what if similar expectations and production values were to shape and inform legal storytelling inside the courtroom? What if law and entertainment merged? If popular cultural visual techniques were to make their way into the courtroom, would we protest – assuming we notice? Should we distinguish between the persuasive effects of verbal as compared with *visual* metaphors? Does a change in the technology of communication make a difference in content? Do changes in dominant storytelling practices change the minds and culture of storytellers and audiences alike? And if they do, what sort of legal difference does that make? How do these changes affect the search for truth, the authority of law, and the struggle for justice in society? Raising and finding answers to these sorts of questions are critical goals of popular legal studies. Along this path of inquiry we begin to see that the interpenetration of law and popular culture is as much an aesthetic phenomenon, and a technological one (in McLuhan's sense), as it is a matter of substantive law.

The academic study of law in popular culture is of relatively recent vintage, but the interpenetration of the one by the other is as old as Western law itself. As classicist Kathy Eden (1986: 7–8) points out, the average Athenian citizen participated "very directly and very regularly" both as spectator and as judge in the tragic and legal performance. Indeed, the dramatic discourse of ancient Greek tragedy informed the public's understanding of law just as legal discourse helped to shape and inform the discourse of ancient Greek tragedy. The Greek experience is hardly unique. Two thousand years later, in Elizabethan England, Philip Sidney noted that the practical task of demonstrating legal and factual truths depends upon the fictional method (Duncan-Jones, 1989). How else can one reconstruct reality in the courtroom (Bennett and Feldman, 1981)? How else, but through the fictional devices of narration and drama, can one breathe life into the corpus of naked fact? Without the compelling force of drama, in conjunction with (though at times even in defiance of) the formal demands of law, advocates cannot activate belief and compel judgment by those whose duty it is to respond to the demands of truth and justice.

But today we face new issues and new challenges associated with the rise of digital communication and the proliferation of visual mass media. On the one hand, digital technology makes it possible to depict objects and events with previously unimaginable clarity. Images offer an immediacy of access to trained as well as untrained eyes. With the help of visual images, previously hidden physical details may be brought into plain sight: the way chemicals seeped into nearby ground water, the way a defective tail wing caused an airplane to crash, or how ammonia molecules were deliberately used by cigarette manufacturers to more effectively deliver nicotine.

Yet, precisely because of their ease of access and credibility ("seeing is believing"), visual images introduce new challenges – as the unwary prosecutor in the Rodney King case would have done well to note. Locked into his own literalist take on George Holliday's amateur video of police officers surrounding and beating King, the prosecutor never paused to consider how the defense team's digital reconstruction changed the visual narrative. By isolating visual frames and altering their flow, the defense reversed causation: instead of a story of racially prejudiced white cops beating an unarmed black motorist jurors saw a series of images in which police officers carefully "escalated and de-escalated" levels of force in direct response to King's aggressive resistance of arrest.

Of central concern here is the peculiar efficacy of *visual* persuasion. There are three factors to consider. First, because photograph, film, and video images appear to *resemble reality* they tend to arouse cognitive and especially emotional responses similar to those aroused by the real thing depicted. Movies, television, and other image-based entertainments have overwhelmed text-based media in popularity largely because they seem to simulate reality more thoroughly, engulfing the spectator (or, in the case of interactive computer and video games and immersive virtual environments, the participant) in vivid, lifelike sensations. To the extent that persuasion works through emotion as well as reason, images persuade more effectively than words alone. Second, because images appear to offer a *direct, unmediated* view of the reality they depict, they tend to be taken as *credible representations* of that reality. Unlike words, which are obviously constructed by the speaker and thus are understood to be at one remove from the reality they describe, photograph, film, and video images (whether analog or digital) appear to be *caused by* the external world, without the same degree of human mediation and hence interpretation; images thus seem to be *better evidence* for what they purport to depict (Kassin and Dunn, 1997). Third, when images are used to communicate propositional claims at least some of their meaning always remains *implicit*. Images cannot be reduced to explicit propositions. In this respect, images are well-suited to leaving intended meanings unspoken, as would-be persuaders may prefer to do – especially when evidentiary rules forbid making a given claim explicitly (Messaris, 1997).

Images, therefore, do not simply "add" to the persuasive force of words; they *transform* argument and, in so doing, have the capacity to persuade all the more powerfully. Unlike words, which compose linear messages that must be taken in sequentially, at least some of the meaning of images can be grasped all at once. This rapid intelligibility permits visual messages to be greatly condensed (it takes a lot less time to see a picture than to read a thousand words), and allows the image creator to communicate one meaning after another in quick succession. Such immediacy of comprehension enhances persuasion. When we think we've got the whole message at once we are *disinclined* from pursuing the matter further. And increasingly rapid image sequences *disable* critical thinking because the viewer is too busy attending to the present image to reflect on the last one. For both reasons, the visual message generates less counterargument, and is therefore more likely to retain our belief. Images, moreover, convey meaning through an *associational* logic which operates in large part subconsciously, and through its appeal to viewers' emotions. Finally, images readily lend themselves to intertextual references that link the communication to other works and other genres, enabling arguments to draw on the audience's presumed familiarity with those other works and genres and thus to appropriate meaning from the culture at large. An audience's pleasure in the familiar, their belief that they are perceiving reality, combined with quick and easy comprehension, make it more fun to watch than to read. And because viewers are occupied and entertained, they are both less able and less willing to respond critically to the persuasive visual message. Hence the message is more likely to be accepted.

The logic of new communication technologies cannot be kept outside the law, nor has it been. The modern (print-based, rule-oriented, linear-causal, objective proof-driven) explanatory style has not passed away, but that style's ascendancy over truth and law is at an end. Today, viewers absorb a postmodern mindset from their everyday screen practices, in which images image other images and the simulated attains parity with lived experience. Consider: ours is a time when an American president's video deposition, in the early stages of impeachment, was reviewed on the front page of *The New York Times* by the newspaper's film and television critic. (In her review, the critic dutifully noted the tape's "unlikely resemblance to Louis Malle's film *My Dinner With Andre*.") We live in a time when the American public can name TV judges but not real ones, and when real judges are expected to behave in court like the judges people see on TV (Podlas, 2001). Sometimes, judges even comply. Sometimes, so do police officers and lawyers.

Notably, these concerns are not confined to American legal institutions and culture alone. Growing tensions associated with the globalization (and homogenization) of culture as a result of reconfigured international trade patterns extend beyond market competition for produce and manufactured goods. Globalization has also sped the importation to other countries of American popular culture and its representations of law. Consider, in this regard, the Canadian nationals who insist on their *Miranda* rights when stopped by Canadian police. Having been virtually "naturalized" by an inundation of American law films and TV shows they apparently feel entitled to the same rights and privileges as "other" US citizens. Or consider German jurists who rise in court to contest rulings from the bench or who dramatically cross-examine witnesses on the stand. The habitual consumption of American popular legal culture, together with the adversarial norms that they embody, seems to have led them to forget the inquisitorial (nonadversarial, dossier-oriented) character of their own continental legal tradition (Machura and Ulbrich, 2001). These developments lead one to speculate whether the transnational appeal of adversarial legal melodrama, a genre prominently featured within Anglo-American popular culture (Clover, 2000), might be reconstituting global common sense (Herman and McChesney, 1997).

A basic premise of popular legal studies holds that the study and critique of law must now take into account new developments in popular culture and communication technology and the socioeconomic conditions under which popular legal representations are produced. Building on critical insights into the construction of legal consciousness in society (Ewick and Silbey, 1998), the study of law in popular culture offers a multidisciplinary approach to the reciprocal process of institutional and individual legal meaning making.

In pursuit of this goal, the study of law in popular culture brings together a theory, a practice, a field, a pedagogy, and an ethos. The theory builds upon constructivist insights which tell us that the particular form of expression – the discourse, the metaphor, the image that is used – is essential to the kind of truth that may be expressed. It uses a multidisciplinary approach (including cognitive and cultural psychology, anthropology, linguistics, and rhetoric; and media, film, and communication studies) to understand how legal meanings are made and transmitted in society. The practice engages microanalytic studies in which specific legal behavior is examined and assessed using a variety of analytical tools, including empirical as well as broader interpretive studies. The field ranges from formal sites and practices of legal meaning making (the courtroom, the legislature, the governmental agency) to everyday sites and practices (where people give voice to legal meanings in social discourse and absorb popular legal meanings from a variety of cultural artifacts including images on the screen). The pedagogy is eclectic, relying on diverse perspectives to build up, not necessarily in linear fashion, a mosaic of insights that may be brought to bear upon new and concrete fields of legal action. In this respect, the pedagogy of popular legal studies resembles the practice of the classical rhetor who would draw upon accumulated topics (i.e., discrete areas of substantive knowledge and aesthetic forms) as the particular situation required. Finally, the ethos that emerges from this multidisciplinary, constructivist approach takes shape in response to two central queries: who is responsible for assigning meaning to public symbols, and how is that responsibility being carried out? (Ober, 1989: 339). These questions lead, in due course, to a renewed encounter with the role and distribution of power under color of law in a democratic society.

In what follows I shall attempt to shed further light on each of these aspects of the study of law in popular culture while also fleshing out the parameters of this still emerging field.

THE INTERPENETRATION OF LAW AND POPULAR CULTURE

Heightened awareness of the culture-shaping role of law in the United States can be traced to the writings of French historian Alexis de Tocqueville. It was Tocqueville who famously observed of American society in the 1830s that "[t]here is hardly a political question in the United States which does not sooner or later turn into a judicial one." "The spirit of law," Tocqueville wrote, "infiltrates through society right down to the lowest ranks, till finally the whole people have contracted some of the ways and tastes of a magistrate" (Tocqueville, 1969: 270). What Tocqueville failed to note, however, is that the flow works both ways: popular legal meanings also infiltrate *upward* into the highest echelons of legal power. Being part of a community means that we interpret events in overlapping ways using shared cognitive and cultural meaning-making tools. Many of the meaning-making tools that legal officials use enter into the domain of popular legal consciousness through popular cultural representations. But popular culture also produces its own tools and methods. It generates its own images, signs, stories, characters, and metaphors in the course of making sense of legal reality. In this way, official and unofficial legal meanings, sometimes unmixed, others times intermingled, routinely circulate through the mass media of popular culture.

As John Denvir succinctly puts it, "we can learn a great deal about law from watching movies" (Denvir, 1996: xi). And as Paul Joseph (2000: 257) observes, "popular culture reflects the already existing perception of law even as it helps to mold and reinforce it." Through law films we confront the great moral dilemmas of the day, whether it is the intractable racism depicted in *To Kill A Mockingbird* (1962), the effects of homophobia dramatized in *Philadelphia* (1993), or the legitimacy of capital punishment in films like *Dead Man Walking* (1995) and *The Green Mile* (1999) (Greenfield, Osborn, and Robson, 2001). Popular movies such as *King of the Pecos* (1936) and *The Man Who Shot Liberty Valance* (1962) confront viewers with troubling questions about the relationship between violence and the rule of law (Ryan, 1996; Nevins, 1996). Through a comparative analysis of law films one can also discern significant shifts in the objectives of popular legal representations. For example, one may contrast the Weimar law film genre during the late 1920s and the early 1930s, in which the social conflicts and political upheavals of the time were clearly in evidence, with the films that emerged after the Nazi takeover (in 1933) of the German film industry. During the Nazi period, German films used the law "to demonstrate the 'humane' and 'benevolent' character of the political system,... or to propagate the efficiency and security of the law system, thus glossing over the actually existing perversion of the law" (Drexler, 2001: 71). A comparative analysis of law films also reveals significant shifts in social norms and expectations regarding lawyers and the legal system. Consider in this regard the profound disillusionment with law's capacity to accommodate the demands of justice reflected in Martin Scorsese's *Cape Fear* (1991) as compared with J. Lee Thompson's more optimistic 1962 original (Sherwin, 1996). In a similar vein, one might also contrast the highpoint of heroic lawyer movies, such as *Young Mr. Lincoln* (1939) with the ensuing decade's "cycle of cynical and stylistically expressionistic films" (Rafter, 2001) such as *Stranger on the Third Floor* (1940) and *The Lady From Shanghai* (1948), films that Norman Rosenberg has deftly called "law noirs" (Rosenberg, 1996).

It has also been noted that law films often get the rules wrong (Asimow and Bergman, 1996). This is surely at least partly the result of the different needs and demands of cinematic and televisual storytelling as opposed to written and oral legal narratives. Competition for market share, in conjunction with extant formulas and expectations regarding what a good film or TV show looks like, also play a role in actively shaping the public's perception of litigation, trial lawyers, and the legal system as a whole. As Ray Surrette has written, "The crimes that dominate the public consciousness and policy debates are not common crimes but the rarest ones. Whether in entertainment or news, the crimes that define criminality are the acts of predator criminals" (Surrette, 1994: 131).

The media's preference for emotionally stimulating and visually compelling stories is matched by its aversion to complexity. Multiple causes and systematic wrongs are considerably more difficult to narrate visually than straightforward melodramas featuring easily identifiable good guys and bad guys (Feigenson, 1999–2000). At the same time, the power and efficacy of new forms of visual storytelling have not been lost on advocates, whether in litigation practices or in litigation public relations and other forms of legal and political advertising. As Lawrence Friedman notes, "The media spread slogans like 'three strikes and you're out' or 'old enough to do the crime, old enough to do the time.' Criminal policy is made by Polly Klaas and... tort policy is made by the hot coffee at McDonald's, and various other urban legends" (Friedman, 2000: 557).

Popular legal representations in films and on television not only help to shape and inform public perceptions; they also serve as cultural barometers. They can tell us about shifting public beliefs and opinions regarding law, lawyers, and the legal system generally. As Suzanne Shale writes, "Unless we pay attention to how the mass entertainment industry represents law and the legal system, we cannot hope to know what relationship subsists between law and its subjects" (Shale, 1996: 992). We may look to popular legal representations as a fruitful source of insight into popular disenchantment with, and criticism of, lawyers and the system of justice. For example, from the 1970s on, film depictions of lawyers have been almost uniformly negative. Over the same period, polls have consistently shown that the public's regard for lawyers in the United States has undergone a prodigious decline. Since 1977, the number of Americans who believed lawyers had "very great prestige" has slipped from 36 percent to 19 percent (Asimow, 2000).

Just as the emergence of a popular vengeance film genre (such as the highly successful Charlie Bronson vigilante films of the 1970s) may betoken broad public dissatisfaction with law's inability to resolve outbreaks of criminal violence, a similar phenomenon may also be noted with respect to the notorious case. In these compelling public dramas clearly more is at stake than the fates of the particular parties in court. These trials are vastly overdetermined with social, political, cultural, and psychological meanings for the nation at large. They are sites of law where the deepest, most intractable conflicts of the day play out. For example, in 1991, the O.J. Simpson double murder trial enacted the clash between state racism and the cult of celebrity. In 1907, the trial of Harry Thaw for the murder of Stanford White, New York's most renowned architect, evoked nostalgia for natural law justice in the face of modern disenchantment and uncertainty. And in 1859, the trial of John Brown following his failed attempt to provoke a slave uprising by attacking a federal armory at Harper's Ferry (where few slaves were to be found) dramatized the clash between pointless violence and the heroic melodrama that was generated by leading transcendentalist thinkers such as Ralph Waldo Emerson and Henry David Thoreau (Sherwin, 2000). Whether unconsciously simmering or explicitly confronted, symbolic legal conflicts will either be successfully worked through at trial, or meet with further irresolution or repression, thus ensuring some future restaging.

On this view, then, the transmission and reception of notorious trials and popular legal representations alike may offer opportunities for resistance and critique as well as for broad affirmation or reinterpretation of inherited legal meanings. Indeed, popular culture's reactions to, and reflections of, legal reality may provide the public with aspirational, perhaps even utopian, yearnings. As Austin Sarat (2000: 429) writes, "Film is not simply a mirror reflecting distorted legal and social realities. Rather, film always projects alternative realities which are made different by their filmic invention, or the editing and framing on which film always depends." For example, at one extreme, one may point to the subversive impact on law (and on the norms that constitute the Western liberal tradition) deriving from the skeptical, acausal, postmodern visual narratives of Quentin Tarantino and David Lynch, among others (Sherwin, 2000). At the other end of the postmodern spectrum, however, we also encounter a strongly affirmative paradigm in which acausality, constructivist epistemology, and ethical renewal acquire new and highly potent forms of expression. This may be seen, for example, in the brilliant filmmaking of Krzysztof Kieslowski, among others (Sherwin, 2001).

The reality effects of popular legal representations suggest what is missing from Tocqueville's early insight into the relationship between American law and culture. Tocqueville may have been right when he noted that "the spirit of law infiltrates through society right down to the lowest ranks," but this insight, on its own, leaves an important component out of the equation, namely: how popular cultural representations help to provide the meaning-making tools and topics that constitute law, from everyday legal practices to the highest ranks of judicial decision making. Let us consider in further detail how this may be so.

LEGAL MEANING-MAKING TOOLS AND TOPICS

It is now widely accepted that our sense of history, like our sense of memory and self-identity, is in large measure the result of arranging and telling stories. And just as it is through stories that we construct the meaning of individual and collective experience so also it is through stories that we are moved to blame (or exonerate) others (Pennington and Hastie, 1993). Legal scholars, however, have been less quick than their counterparts in other academic fields to heed the implications attending the cultural shift to visual literacy. For if reality today is increasingly being perceived as the effect of the sign, and if visual images have come to be seen as more real than the real (Baudrillard, 1990), then that is what we should expect to see in journalism, advertising, politics, and law. And, indeed, that is precisely what is taking place. It is the play of signs relating to signs and of images invoking other images that we see when lawyers visually reconstruct reality in the courtroom.

The principal source of stories and storytelling styles in our time is television and film. The parameters that these media set increasingly serve as the measure of reality as most people know it. What we think about and the cognitive tools we use to think with lie, in large measure, within the province of the visual mass media. Increasingly, lawyers are realizing that effective persuasion requires not only tapping into the reality that people carry in their heads, but also emulating the habits of perception and the styles of thought that extensive exposure to mass-mediated popular culture has produced. Advocates today know, and are putting to use, what advertisers and politicians have known and practiced for quite some time: how to get the message out; how to tailor content to medium; and how to spin the image, edit the bite, and seize the moment on the screen and in the mind of the viewer. Courtroom videos have emulated TV news shows, game shows, and commercials. They also have directly incorporated feature film images. In at least one instance, blurring the line between film and reality constituted a key trial strategy. According to Jeremiah Donovan, lead defense attorney in a complex organized crime trial, the state's evidence was so extreme (like the board with a hundred human bones attached to it), that it caused jurors to experience a loss of reality. Pieces of evidence seemed like "props in a drama." This insight inspired Donovan to turn his summation "into a story...that sounded like a movie plot" (Sherwin, 2000: 31).

This aestheticization of the real in actual legal practices also coincides with the rapid development of litigation public relations and high-priced media campaigns for law reform. Legal battles are now being waged not only inside the courtroom, but also before television cameras on the courthouse steps, on popular TV talk shows, and in paid legal advertisements. As one Chicago-based personal injury lawyer put it, "Publicity is an issue in civil and criminal cases all the time." And once the image spinning begins, it is hard not to respond. As one corporate spokesman put it, "If we allow the imagery that the attorneys and the spokesmen for our competitors have laid out for the news media to absorb and to linger, we would be paying many kinds of costs in correcting that damage in the perception of the general public" (not to mention the perceptions of prospective jurors) (Sherwin, 2000: 148). Publicity via mass media communication, it turns out, is but one more tool in the contemporary advocate's toolbox. Even Justices of the United States Supreme Court have acted with an eye to the efficacy, and manipulability, of mass media images (Sherwin, 2000).

The deliberate deployment of popular legal representations, both inside and outside the courtroom, for the sake of advancing the interests of a particular client or a preferred legal position, implicates a broad array of topics, including media literacy, cultural and cognitive heuristics, and, of course, legal ethics. This development makes it imperative for law teachers and legal scholars to study the various ways, both conscious and unconscious, in which we construct, perpetuate, modify, or abandon legal meanings. In order to adequately assess this meaning-making process legal scholars need to acquire greater familiarity with the full range of meaning-making tools and competencies of lawyers, judges, jurors, and the lay public, as well as those of public relations agents and other communication experts. What kinds of stories and storytelling styles, what story elements and character types, what popular metaphors and legal categories, what communication technologies and associated forms of logic are available, and under what conditions, and with what effect upon feeling, belief, and judgment?

This is, of course, another way of stating the pivotal query that guides Aristotle's approach to rhetoric, namely: what are the available means of persuasion in the face of a given legal conflict or controversy (Aristotle, 1954: 24)? A more expansive restatement of rhetoric's goals along similar lines today would incorporate insights into the meaning-making process from a variety of scholarly domains, including cognitive psychology, cultural anthropology, sociology, linguistics, media studies, film studies, and advertising. This continuing effort to breach the walls that have traditionally balkanized legal studies, unduly limiting its field of research as well as its theory base, practice, pedagogy, and range of analytical tools, brings us face to face with the constitutive elements of popular legal studies, a subject to which we now turn.

THE LAW/CULTURE MATRIX: CONSTITUTING POPULAR LEGAL STUDIES

The genre of cultural studies has been providing scholars with interdisciplinary tools since the late 1970s (Hall, Critcher, Jefferson, Clarke, and Roberts, 1978; Williams, 1980). Cultural studies focuses on the production, circulation, and assimilation of symbolic forms. It is largely concerned with how institutions and local practices generate social meanings (Turner, 1993). This eclectic approach has been somewhat belatedly adopted by a number of legal scholars who have sought to go beyond appellate caselaw, statutory interpretation, and social policy, the dominant topics of law teaching and academic writing, in order to more broadly encompass legal meaning-making practices throughout society (Sherwin, 1992). As Barbara Yngvesson has written, "[t]he spirit of law isn't just invented at the top, but is transformed, challenged and reinvented in local practices that produce a plural legal culture in contemporary America" (Yngvesson, 1989: 1689). Whether it is starting rumor campaigns to contest corporate control over cultural symbols (Coombe, 1998), getting a court clerk to recognize a story of abuse as a legal claim (Yngvesson, 1989), or resisting mediators who construct images of problems in therapeutic as opposed to legal terms (Silbey and Merry, 1986), these practices at the local level constitute the "microphysics of power" (to use a Foucauldian phrase). Here we find highly contextualized forms of cultural dominance and resistance.

Legal cultural scholars such as Jerome Bruner, Anthony Amsterdam, and Neal Feigenson similarly offer a microanalysis of local practices that isolates a broad range of linguistic, narrative, and rhetorical elements. Whether it is decoding a Supreme Court opinion as a "combat myth" or a "demon lover adultery tale" (Bruner and Amsterdam, 2000) or a personal injury lawyer's summation as a melodrama of personal blame (as opposed to systemic responsibility) (Feigenson, 2000), these scholars ask, what are the popular cultural codes, the familiar schemas and scripts, the common vocabularies of motive and intentionality, and the hierarchy of beliefs and values, that are in play within a given site of cultural production? In search of the constitutive elements of legal consciousness, which is to say the popular cultural materials out of which legal meanings are shaped, disseminated, and absorbed, cultural legal studies has branched out to the quotidian world of film, television, and the Internet, among other sources.

If the guiding insight that informs popular legal studies is that law is not autonomous, that the boundary between law and culture is quite porous, its scholarly method follows suit. This emphatically practical, multidisciplinary approach to cultural analysis forces critical theory to touch down by bringing to bear a broad array of analytical tools within specific, concrete contexts. At the same time, however, popular legal studies also remains sensitive to the dangers of excessive critique and pervasive disenchantment (Sherwin, 2000). Familiar postmodern gestures of irony and playful skepticism fail to do justice to the ongoing need for empirical discovery, interpretive insight, and normative commitment. To further this more affirmative goal, the search for new sites of law, and for the social ramifications of its power, must continue to expand.

The pedagogy of this form of study is eclectic, participatory, and pragmatic. As our stories and storytelling technologies and practices change so too do our forms of belief and judgment and our expectations about what constitutes proof and effective persuasion. With the ascendancy of electronic monitors inside the courtroom, students of law must be able to account for the everyday associations that jurors bring to the screen. They must also accommodate the familiar programs and information schemas that viewers absorb from computers at home and in the office. By the same token, they may need to come to grips with jurors' increased expectations about being allowed to surf screen data for themselves. As computer users internalize the thinking tools provided by software in conjunction with Internet-bred habits of data search (or "surfing") via free association, concomitant adjustments may be needed in legal communication and advocacy. Accordingly, legal education must adapt to the contingencies of technology and the emerging vernacular of the digital mind (Lessig, 1999; Rohl and Ulbrich, 2000).

Finally, popular legal studies also points to new ethical issues and challenges. For example, as more people, practiced in the techniques of digital production, come to realize the manifold ways in which perceived realities may be constructed or changed, a new skepticism may emerge. How will legal advocates reassert the authority of truth claims? Conversely, how will law in the age of digital images cope with the mind's default capacity for acceptance and belief (Gilbert, 1991; Gerrig, 1993)? Will new levels of media literacy meet the challenge of critically confronting persuasive images on the screen? Or will the engineering of belief and judgment tighten its grip on the mind (Ewen, 1996)? We should also consider whether the power that attaches to legal meanings will stream down from an elite, self-appointed group of culture producers, or will it percolate up from the authentic needs, desires, and imaginings of indigenous communities? The story of Marcus Arnold, the 15-year-old who became the Internet's highest-rated legal advice giver, provides an intriguing, albeit inconclusive indicator. Marcus believed that he had learned enough law from watching TV to give legal advice without conducting actual research. Notably, when his age and *modus operandi* became known this had no dampening effect on his popularity (Lewis, 2001). Is this a tribute to Marcus's communicative skills (as well as a slap at the profession's communicative failings)? Does it portend the ascendancy of a populist legal culture which operates to the detriment of counterintuitive legal expertise? As we learn more about the law/culture matrix, basic questions about the continued vitality of democratic principles are bound to emerge with new vigor. Once we ask who assigns meaning to legal symbols in society, how, and with what effect, we directly confront the political and ethical dimensions of popular legal studies. Ethics, in this context, is a matter of taking responsibility for meanings. And it is with this challenge in mind that we turn to the scholarly program, and global implications, of studying law in popular culture.

FUTURE PROSPECTS

A major objective of popular legal studies is to explore how legal meanings are brought "on and off line" or are kept more or less permanently suppressed. Concomitant with this research is the effort to examine the social, political, and psychological processes that may account for how and why this meaning selection process occurs. Empirical research can help to uncover the social scripts, stock stories, stereotypes, myths, metaphors, and other cognitive or linguistic representations that people use, under what circumstances and with what effect, in constructing beliefs and judgments about particular legal outcomes as well as more general legal issues. This empirical inquiry is of particular interest in light of the increased use of visual technology inside the courtroom as well as growing reliance upon techniques of visual persuasion in the domain of popular mass media (such as litigation public relations). To date, an empirical analysis of the actual effects of computer animation, movies depicting a day in the life of accident victims, video arguments, digitally reenacted crimes and accidents, and legal advertising has barely begun. As social psychology researchers Neal Feigenson and Meghan Dunn (2003) note:

> Without useful empirical research, advisory committees and legislatures are not yet in a position to draft, recommend, and enact evidentiary rules to address the uses of modern methods of visual communication . . . Without a reliable understanding of the effects of visual technologies, both on the jury and on the trial process itself, judges are unable to estimate accurately the probative or prejudicial effects of visual evidence . . . It is particularly important that the research be grounded in and elucidate psychological theory concerning perception and social judgment. If the mechanisms by which current visual technologies influence trial participants can be identified and understood, the benefits and risks of emerging technologies can be more readily and accurately evaluated.
> Feigenson and Dunn, 2003: 110–11

In addition to new empirical studies, aiding in both the production and evaluation of new visual strategies of persuasion, legal scholarship should also continue to pursue interpretive studies of popular legal representations. Analyzing images from film, television, and the Internet may not only expose how public expectations and beliefs are being shaped and informed by these media, they also may offer new insights into the cognitive tools and cultural content that people bring with them to court and elsewhere where legal meanings are elicited, debated, and perhaps transformed. These cultural sources also may be mined for normative content, whether as sites of popular resistance to legal authority, mass cultural manipulation, or as exemplars of new forms of affirmation and utopian striving (Sherwin, 2001).

Bringing popular cultural studies into the classroom means that visual representations may be imported for multiple uses. Providing insights into the law/culture matrix promises to enhance knowledge of what lawyers do, what law consists of (and where it may be found), as well as how it enables the enactment of particular models of self, other, and normative worlds, or suppresses them (Cover, 1983). Notably, this study crosses national boundaries. As numerous commentators have noted, the United States is the dominant exporter of popular culture, including popular legal culture. What impact does this have on importing nations? This inquiry brings new importance to issues surrounding the ownership and control of the means and content of mass communication (Herman and McChesney, 1997). Is the global convergence of media control a precursor to a transnational popular legal culture? Explorations of the possible nexus between transnational corporate marketing strategies and Americocentric ideologies, technologies, and institutions may benefit from taking popular legal representations into account. The postcolonial impact of new technologies and new market conditions on indigenous cultural patterns of legal meaning making warrants further analysis.

As a related matter, one might also consider a subfield of popular legal studies that takes as its focus law and media ecology. Douglas Reed has noted a powerful confluence of legal and judicial proceedings on the one hand, and the power of the mass media, including the use of television experts and a sophisticated polling capacity, on the other. According to Reed, this has generated an extraconstitutional mechanism significantly affecting the policy-making and governing process. He calls it the juridico-entertainment complex. This complex "transforms legal proceedings and legal conflict into consumable commodities that purport to educate and enlighten, but simultaneously titillate, amuse, and otherwise entertain a mass audience" (Reed, 1999). The global exportation and consumption of American popular legal representations in conjunction with shifting trade practices and the proliferation of new mass communication technologies, raises the possibility that the juridico-entertainment complex may become a transnational phenomenon (Machura and Ulbrich, 2001). As a concomitant of the commodification of, and global trade in, popular legal representations, issues concerning media literacy, Internet access, intellectual property, software design, privacy, antitrust enforcement, and international trade regulations assume a particularly pressing importance within the field of popular legal studies.

In this regard, it is also important to bear in mind the tension between mass (commodified) culture and popular (indigenous) culture and the concomitant strain between the imposition of consumerist forms of identity and the struggle to create more authentic or more meaningful forms of identity. As an agency of cultural production, and a cultural product in its own right, law mediates (at times repressively, at other times creatively) between competing ways of life. To be sure, the relationship between culture and identity is complex. The colonization of individual self-consciousness by hegemonic cultural forces, such as the dominance of mass-mediated popular representations, is never total. The reality of lived experience remains, and constitutes itself anew in local cultural forms of expression (Ewing, 1997: 18–19; Turner, 1993: 427). Maintaining a sense of the multiplicity of discursive possibilities and practices aids cultural analysis, even if it entails contradictory relations with others and among incommensurable fragments of self-identity. On this view, the study of indigenous popular legal representations around the globe may provide a rich source of descriptive and critical cultural insights regarding resistance, affirmation, and transformation in the face of new forms of state or private manipulation and control of legal consciousness.

Conclusion

Law adds the force of the state to cultural norms. But how are those norms constructed, commemorated, transmitted, and imposed? There is a two-way traffic between law and popular culture, and it behooves us to understand how the one helps to shape and inform the other. How else can we discern whose norms the law encodes or excludes? Popular legal studies reflects a broader scholarly move to elucidate how meanings are made and conveyed in society. It accounts for the communicative and persuasive elements of legal practice as well as the quotidian practices of popular legal meaning making by members of the public at large. Changes in dominant storytelling practices portend changes of mind and culture. Today, our stories are increasingly visual. Understanding the complex and ubiquitous process of legal meaning making requires that legal scholars come to grips with these developments.

The study of law in popular culture embraces a multidisciplinary analysis of the manifold ways in which the interpenetration of law and popular culture constitutes legal consciousness. Along the way, it uncovers sites of resistance and creative affirmation. It also encounters new forms of dominance. We may see this, for example, where legal persuasion and commercial entertainment values merge, leaving heightened sensory gratification as the benchmark for popular judgment and belief. Whether this standard or some other will ultimately prevail remains to be seen. In the meantime, the study of law in popular culture may help us to monitor and assess who gets to assign meaning to the public symbols of law, and with what legal and political effect. Taking responsibility for the production and effects of legal consciousness is one (perhaps the most crucial) way in which we take responsibility for the kind of society in which we live.

References

Aristotle (1954) *The Rhetoric*. New York: The Modern Library.
Asimow, Michael (2000) "Bad lawyers in the movies," *Nova Law Review* 24: 531–91.
Asimow, Michael and Bergman, Paul (1996) *Reel Justice: The Courtroom Goes to the Movies*. Kansas City: Andrews and McMeel.
Baudrillard, Jean (1990) *Fatal Strategies*. New York: Semiotext(e).
Bennett, W. Lance and Feldman, Martha S. (1981) *Reconstructing Reality in the Courtroom*. New Brunswick, NJ: Rutgers University Press.

Bruner, Jerome and Amsterdam, Anthony (2000) *Minding the Law*. Cambridge, MA: Harvard University Press.

Clover, Carol (2000) "Law and the order of popular culture," in Austin Sarat and Thomas R. Kearns (eds.), *Law in the Domains of Culture*. Ann Arbor, University of Michigan Press, pp. 97–119.

Coombe, Rosemary J. (1998) *The Cultural Life of Intellectual Properties*. Durham, NC: Duke University Press.

Cover, Robert (1983) "The Supreme Court, 1982 term – Foreword: Nomos and narrative," *Harvard Law Review* 97: 4–68.

Denvir, John (1996) *Legal Reelism: Movies as Legal Texts*. Urbana: University of Illinois Press.

Drexler, Peter (2001) "The German courtroom film during the Nazi period: Ideology, aesthetics, historical context", in Stefan Machura and Peter Robson (eds.), *Law and Film*. Oxford: Blackwell, pp. 64–78.

Duncan-Jones, Katherine (ed.) (1989) *Sir Philip Sidney*. Oxford: Oxford University Press.

Eden, Kathy (1986) *Poetic and Legal Fiction in the Aristotelian Tradition*. Princeton, NJ: Princeton University Press.

Ewen, Stuart (1996) *PR! A Social History of Spin*. New York: Basic Books.

Ewick, Patricia and Silbey, Susan (1998) *The Common Place of Law: Stories from Everyday Life*. Chicago: University of Chicago Press.

Ewing, Katherine Pratt (1997) *Arguing Sainthood*. Durham, NC: Duke University Press.

Feigenson, Neal (1999–2000) "Accidents as melodrama," *New York Law School Law Review* 43: 741–810.

Feigenson, Neal (2000) *Legal Blame: How Jurors Think and Talk About Accidents*. Washington, DC: American Psychological Association.

Feigenson, Neal and Dunn, Meghan A. (2003) "New visual technologies in court: Directions for research," *Law and Human Behavior* 27: 109–26.

Ferguson, Robert (1994) "Story and transcription in the trial of John Brown," *Yale Journal of Law and the Humanities* 6: 343–79.

Friedman, Lawrence (2000) "Lexitainment: Legal process as theater," *DePaul Law Review* 50: 539–58.

Gerrig, Richard (1993) *Experiencing Narrative Worlds*. New Haven, CT: Yale University Press.

Gilbert, Daniel (1991) "How mental systems believe," *American Psychologist* 46: 107–19.

Greenfield, Steve, Osborn, Guy, and Robson, Peter (2001) *Film and the Law*. London: Cavendish Publishing.

Hall, Stuart, Critcher, Charles, Jefferson, Tony, Clarke, John, and Roberts, Brian (1978) *Policing the Crisis: Mugging, the State, and Law and Order*. New York: Holmes and Meier Publishers.

Herman, Edward S. and McChesney, Robert W. (1997) *The Global Media*. London: Cassell.

Joseph, Paul (2000) "Introduction: Law and popular culture," *Nova Law Review* 24: 527–29.

Kassin, S. and Dunn, M. (1997) "Computer-animated displays and the jury: Facilitative and prejudicial effects," *Law and Human Behavior* 21: 269–81.

Kemple, Thomas M. (1995) "Litigating illiteracy: The media, the law, and *The People of the State of New York v. Adelbert Ward*," *Canadian Journal of Law and Society* 1: 73–97.

Lessig, Lawrence (1999) *Code*. New York: Basic Books.

Lewis, Michael (2001) *Next: The Future Just Happened*. New York: W.W. Norton & Co.

Machura, Stefan and Ulbrich, Stefan (2001) "Law in film: Globalizing the Hollywood courtroom drama," *Journal of Law and Society* 28: 1117–32.

McLuhan, Marshall (1994) *Understanding Media: The Extensions of Man*. Cambridge, MA: MIT Press.

Messaris, Paul (1997) *Visual Persuasion: The Role of Images In Advertising*. Thousand Oaks, CA: Sage.

Nevins, Francis M. (1996) "Through the Great Depression on horseback," in John Denvir (ed.), *Legal Reelism: Movies as Legal Texts*. Urbana: University of Illinois Press, pp. 44–69.

Ober, Josiah (1989) *Mass and Elite in Democratic Athens: Rhetoric, Ideology, and the Power of the People*. Princeton, NJ: Princeton University Press.

Pennington, Nancy and Hastie, Reid (1993) "Explanation-based decision making," *Cognition* 49: 123–63.

Pfau, Michael, Mullen, Lawrence J., Deidrich, Tracy, and Garrow, Kirsten (1995) "Television viewing and public perceptions of attorneys," *Human Communications Research* 21: 307–30.

Podlas, Kimberlianne (2001) "Please adjust your signal: How television's syndicated courtrooms bias our juror citizenry," *American Business Law Journal* 39: 1–24.

Rafter, Nicole (2001) "American criminal trial films", in Stefan Machura and Peter Robson (eds.), *Law and Film*. Oxford: Blackwell, pp. 9–24.

Reed, Douglas S. (1999) "A new constitutional regime: The juridico-entertainment complex." Unpublished paper presented at the annual meeting of the Law and Society Association, May 1999, Chicago.

Rohl, Klaus F. and Ulbrich, Stefan (2000) "Visuelle rechtskommunikation," *Zeitschift für Rechtssoziologie*, 21(2).

Rosenberg, Norman (1996) "Law noir," in John Denvir (ed.), *Legal Reelism: Movies as Legal Texts*. Urbana: University of Illinois Press, pp. 280–302.

Ryan, Cheyney (1996) "Print the legend: Violence and recognition in *The Man Who Shot Liberty Valance*", in John Denvir (ed.), *Legal Reelism: Movies as Legal Texts*. Urbana: University of Illinois Press, pp. 23–43.

Sarat, Austin (1990) "'The law is all over': Power, resistance, and the legal consciousness of the welfare poor," *Yale Journal of Law and the Humanities* 2: 343–79.

Sarat, Austin (2000) "Exploring the hidden dimension of civil justice: 'Naming, blaming, and claiming'," *DePaul Law Review* 50: 425–52.

Scottoline, Lisa (2000) "Get off the screen," *Nova Law Review* 24: 653–72.

Shale, Suzanne (1996) "The conflicts of law and the character of men," *University of San Francisco Law Review* 30: 991–1022.

Sherwin, Richard K. (1992) "Lawering theory: An overview – what we talk about when we talk about law," *New York Law School Law Review* 37: 9–53.

Sherwin, Richard K. (1994) "Law frames: Historical truth and narrative necessity in a criminal case," *Stanford Law Review* 47: 39–83.

Sherwin, Richard K. (1996) "Picturing justice symposium: Images of law and lawyers in the visual media," *University of San Francisco Law Review* 30: 991–1022.

Sherwin, Richard K. (2000) *When Law Goes Pop: The Vanishing Line Between Law and Popular Culture*. Chicago: University of Chicago Press.

Sherwin, Richard K. (2001) "Nomos and cinema," *UCLA Law Review* 48: 1519–43.

Silbey Susan S. and Merry, Sally E. (1986) "Mediator settlement strategies," *Law and Policy* 8: 7–32.

Smith, Vicki (1991) "Prototypes in the courtroom: Law representations of legal concepts," *Journal of Personality and Social Psychology* 61: 857–72.

Standard Chartered PLC v. Price Waterhouse (1989) CV 88–34414 (Super. Ct., Maricopa Co., Ariz. 1989).

Surrette, Ray (1994) "Predator criminals as media icons," in Gregg Barak (ed.), *Media, Process, and the Social Construction of Crime*. New York: Garland Publishing, pp. 131–58.

Tocqueville, Alexis de (1969) *Democracy in America*. New York: Doubleday/Anchor.

Turner, Terence (1993) "Anthropology and multiculturalism: What is anthropology that multiculturalists should be mindful of it?" *Cultural Anthropology* 8(4): 411–29.

Williams, Raymond (1980) *Problems in Materialism and Culture*. London: Verso.

Yngvesson, Barbara (1989) "Inventing law in local settings: Rethinking popular legal culture," *Yale Law Journal* 98: 1689–1709.

Further Reading

Chase, Anthony (1986) "Toward a legal theory of popular culture," *Wisconsin Law Review* 1986: 527–69.

Friedman, Lawrence (1989) "Law, lawyers, and popular culture," *Yale Law Journal* 98: 1579–1606.

Merry, Sally (1990) *Getting Justice and Getting Even*. Chicago: University of Chicago Press.

Rentschler, Eric (1996) *The Ministry of Illusion: Nazi Cinema and its After Life*. Cambridge, MA: Harvard University Press.

Sherwin, Richard K. (1995) "Law and the myth of the self in mass media representations," *International Journal for the Semiotics of Law/Revue Internationale de Semiotique Juridique* 8: 299–326.

Sherwin, Richard K. (1996) "Framed," in John Denvir (ed.), *Legal Reelism: Movies as Legal Texts*. Urbana: University of Illinois Press, pp. 70–94.

Sherwin, Richard K. (1999–2000) "'Foreword' to symposium law/media/culture: Legal meaning in the age of images," *New York Law School Law Review* 43: 653–9

Stachenfeld, Avi and Nicholson, Peter (1996) "Blurred boundaries: An analysis of the close relationship between popular culture and the practice of law," *University of San Francisco Law Review* 30: 903–16.

Yngvesson, Barbara (1988) "Making law at the doorway," *Law & Society Review* 22: 409–48.

Yngvesson, Barbara (1993) *Virtuous Citizens, Disruptive Subjects*. New York: Routledge.

7

Comparing Legal Cultures

David Nelken

This chapter will tackle some theoretical and methodological problems in under-standing legal cultures in a comparative framework. I shall first discuss what is meant by legal culture and whether this is a useful concept. Secondly, I shall consider the different ways in which legal culture can be studied comparatively. For each of these (interrelated) topics I shall offer a brief overview of some of the relevant academic debates. I shall also illustrate my own preferred approach to these issues by making specific reference to an ongoing case study of the problem of legal delay in Italy.

In one sense legal delay is just one of the many aspects of legal culture that can be brought to life by adopting a comparative perspective. But it also has some claim to being of fundamental importance. Delay in the courts was the subject of the first major postwar empirical sociolegal studies in the USA, and cross-national research into legal culture could do worse than take legal delay as a key topic for future enquiry. Concern about delay – an undue degree of waiting – must be defined in terms of expectations. So research on this topic – as my case study will suggest – can provide a litmus test of the extent to which supernational standard ideas about what is the appropriate length (and therefore kind) of legal process are spreading or being imposed.

The Italian situation is also a particularly interesting one because the extreme delays (up to 10 years or more in many civil cases) embedded in an otherwise thriving capitalist economy challenges any residual credibility scholars might want to afford to Weber's claims about the interdependence of law and capitalism. Put another way, legal delay can also be seen as a measure of the lack of centrality of legal expectations and remedies in Italy as compared to other forms of governance. To understand difficulties in reducing court delays (in Italy or elsewhere) we there-fore need to treat them not merely as a problem of court management but as aspects of attitudes and behavior that can take us to the heart of the relations between legal culture and the wider society.

Those who set out to study other legal cultures, however, should be under no illusions about the difficulties (and even studies of one's own legal culture are implicitly comparative). It is no longer (if it ever was) sufficient to describe legal doctrines, procedure, and institutions – even with an eye to the "law in action" – as if given settings each have their own characteristic ways of doing law which can be collected and classified. Comparativists must now take account of a variety of radical objections to their enterprise and adapt their methods of investigation to take into account the intellectual and social developments that lie behind such challenges. Like all other basic conceptual building blocks of social science the idea of "culture" is itself highly problematic. Within anthropology the process of producing accounts of other cultures is highly contested; emphasis has increasingly come to be placed on the "teller" and the "telling" as opposed to what is being told (Clifford and Marcus, 1986).

Culture is also a term that is much abused outside the academy, as in talk of "culture wars" (Kuper, 1999) or the concern for "Asian values" which some politicians allege to be at risk from the spread of Western legal practices. Comparison as such is no longer seen as an easy panacea for parochialism. It can easily be corrupted by the opposing vices of "occidentalism" or "orientalism," whereby we either assume that other cultures are bound to be inherently like us – or else, using them as a foil, we transform them into something intrinsically "other" (Cain, 2000). Apart from stereotyping, there is also the danger of treating societies as if they were static; "all totalizing accounts of society, tradition and culture," it is said, "are exclusionary and enact a social violence by suppressing continuing and continually emergent differences" (Coombe, 2000: 31).

The "unit" of legal culture does not have to be restricted to national legal systems (Nelken, 1995). But there are those who question whether it even makes sense to seek to identify patterns in national legal cultures at a time when these are allegedly being fragmented and reconstituted by wider developments. For many scholars it is the ongoing process of globalization that is undermining the existence of distinct legal cultures. As national cultures are influenced by global flows and trends their purported uniformity, coherence, or stability will often be no more than an ideological projection or rhetorical device – manipulated by elements within the culture concerned or by outside observers. This chapter will be particularly concerned with this crucial issue, which will be discussed both theoretically and with the help of the running case study of court delay.

Contrary to the claims put forward by Lawrence Friedman (Friedman, 1994), however, there is no necessary connection between globalization and the assumption of inevitable convergence (Nelken, 1997b). This means that there is no substitute for case studies that allow us to see how globalization actually interacts with persisting and sometimes rediscovered national, regional, and local differences. Nor should globalization be treated as somehow the bearer of universal reason but rather seen as the expression of some temporarily homogenous local practice and standard. In this respect, there is a pressing need to give more attention to the way past and present work in the sociology of law assumes and mobilizes a (local) vision of legal culture even (or even especially) where the problem of legal culture is left unexplicated rather than being squarely addressed.

THE MEANINGS OF LEGAL CULTURE

The study of the role law plays in other societies provides an opportunity to investigate some of the most interesting and often puzzling features of the law–society relationship. Why do the UK and Denmark, the countries that complain most about the imposition of EU law, turn out to be those that have the best records of obedience? Conversely, why does Italy, whose public opinion is most in favor of Europe, have such a high rate of noncompliance? Why does Holland, otherwise so allegedly similar, have such a low litigation rate compared to neighboring Germany? Why in the United States and the UK does it often takes a sex scandal to create official interest in doing something about corruption whereas in Latin countries it takes a major corruption scandal to excite interest in marital unfaithfulness? Such questions lead us (or should lead us) to reconsider broader theoretical issues in the study of law and society. How does the importance of enforcement as an aspect of law vary in different societies? What do we gain – and what do we lose – when we define "law" only in terms of litigation rates? How does culture condition the boundaries of law and in what ways does law help shape those selfsame boundaries?

But the intellectual promise of comparing legal cultures is often betrayed. A common form of collective comparative work proceeds on the basis of what we might describe as comparison "by juxtaposition": "this is how we do it in Denmark, how do you do it in your country?" Usually this is policy-driven research on the lookout for new ideas. Almost always it fails to get to grip with the questions of comparability which should be the object of any comparative exercise. What are we trying to understand? Why are *these* societies being compared? Are we comparing like with like? To do better than this does not require taking in a larger number of countries: if anything the opposite is true. An in-depth study of even one foreign society can furnish important findings if examined with reference to a theoretical problem. Haley, for example, in a classic study examines "law as a window on Japan and Japan as a window on law," so as to describe what happens when a society tries to subordinate law to the maintenance of existing social consensus (Haley, 1991: 4).

The type of comparative study that tries to explain the way law is embedded in larger frameworks of social structure and culture takes some clues from the work of comparative lawyers but tries to go further. It will study the extent to which law is party- or state-directed (bottom-up or top-down). It will examine the number, role, and power of courts and legal professions; the role and importance of the judiciary; the nature of legal education and legal training. It will concern itself with ideas of what is meant by "law" (and what law is "for"), of where and how it is to be found (types of legal reasoning, the role of case law and precedent, of general clauses as compared to detailed drafting, of the place of law and fact). It will also look for "functional equivalents" to law, as in the way comparative lawyers recommend the heuristic strategy of assuming that foreign societies meet similar social problems by using unfamiliar types of law and legal techniques (Zweigert and Kotz, 1987).

But social scientists will also want to consider the role of other legal and nonlegal institutions, and alternatives to law, including not only arbitration and mediation, but also the many "infrastructural" ways of discouraging or resolving disputes

(Blankenburg, 1997). In addition, they would argue the need to take account of competing professional expertises, and even other forms of governance within civil society such as the family or patron–client networks. Differences in legal culture will also be sought in approaches to regulation, administration, and dispute resolution. Attention will be given to the role of religious or ethical norms and the ambit of the informal. They will also want to understand the contrasting attitudes to the role of law, formal and substantive ideas of legitimacy, and the need for or acceptability of public participation, which often accompany such differences.

Having said this, there is little agreement on how best to grasp legal culture – nor should we expect there to be. For different purposes, and in line with competing approaches to social theory, legal culture will be seen as manifested through institutional behavior, or as a factor shaping and shaped by differences in individual legal consciousness, as a pattern of ideas that lie behind behavior, or as another name for politicolegal discourse itself. Sometimes legal culture is identified independently from political culture; at other times it is identified as an inseparable aspect of political culture (see Brants and Field, 2000). It may be sought in "high culture" and "low culture." When treated as constitutive of cultural consciousness generally this may be examined through structured interviews about the sense of justice (Hamilton and Sanders, 1992), contextualized as part of everyday narratives, as in the work of the Amherst school, or distilled from the ideology behind legal doctrine, as in the writings of American critical legal scholars.

There are even disputes over whether such a protean concept is really useful. Roger Cotterrell (Cotterrell, 1997) criticizes Friedman's broad brush use of the concept, claiming that it is too vague and impressionistic. He argues instead for the study of the way professionally managed legal ideology shapes wider consciousness. But, for Friedman, even a vague concept can subsume other less vague and more measurable categories. Legal culture determines when, why and where people turn for help to law, or to other institutions, or just decide to "lump it." For example, he suggests, it would be a finding about legal culture if French but not Italian women were reluctant to call police to complain about sexual harassment (Friedman, 1997). Friedman also introduced an influential distinction between the "internal legal culture" of legal professionals and academics and the "external legal culture" representing the opinions and pressures brought to bear by wider social groups.

The comparative study of legal delay certainly can be helped by making resort to some idea of legal culture. Different levels of tolerance for court delay would seem a clear instance of the existence of measurable subcategories of behaviors and attitudes which Friedman suggests are usefully encompassed by the concept of legal culture. Court delays also represent a good example of the need to give attention to the presence or absence of "infrastructural" alternatives to litigation as recommended by Blankenburg (Blankenburg, 1997). But the concept of legal culture is especially valuable when it allows us to get beyond the search for "functional equivalents," the assumption that societies at similar levels of development use law or its alternatives so as to resolve similar problems. It may help us appreciate that the culture may simply not provide an obvious "solution" – especially if the "problem" is conceived in different terms or even not seen as such. The power of culture includes the capacity to produce relatively circular definitions of what is worth fighting for and against, and institutions and practices may express genuinely different histories and distinct priorities.

In the case of legal delay it is particularly interesting to ask who defines delay (which is, by definition, unjustified waiting) as a problem – and when and why. Undue haste can also be a problem! We also need to explore how Italian law, jurisprudence, and practice itself defines delay and how it allocates its scarce resources – with different rules for penal and civil cases, such as the special urgent procedures for labor cases, as compared to the priority given to business cases in the New York courts described in Kalven and Zeisel's classic account of delay in those courts (Kalven and Zeisel, 1959).

Writing about legal culture presupposes a working definition of what is meant by culture and how legal culture relates to general culture. Some cultures are more legalistic, others more pragmatic. Under the influence of religious traditions or philosophical idealism law may sometimes be treated as more of an aspiration than a blueprint for guiding behavior (as in some civil law countries); other societies may model their law more closely after what is already considered reasonable behavior by the wider culture (as in some common law jurisdictions). Distance between law and other norms may reflect previous foreign domination, the crumbling of empires, or the imposition of foreign models of law.

In many societies there is a wide gulf between legal culture and general culture, as where the criminal law purports to maintain principles of impersonal equality before the law in societies where clientilistic and other particularistic practices are widespread. We should be wary of treating the slowness of court processes in Italy as simply a reflection of general culture. In its private sector Italian firms provide fierce international competition on delivery dates and service; the delay of the courts seems to be part and parcel of the more general differences between the "public" sector and the "private" sector.

A vexed question is when an explanation is rightly described as "cultural" rather than "structural." Do we need to resort to culture to explain legal delay in Italy? Perhaps it can be explained by the interests of government and business? There has been considerable debate, for example, about whether the low use of courts in Japan should be explained in terms of a specifically widely felt Japanese (and more generally Asian) dislike of going to law, or whether it is more a result of a deliberate set of government-created disincentives to litigation. Certainly any comprehensive account of the persistence of legal delay in Italy must relate (if not reduce) descriptions of cultural specificities to aspects of social structure and economic and political interests. More than in other developed economies the court system in Italy seems to provide the world of business with little more than a highly inefficient "default " system if all else fails.

Delay usually favors debtors – who are likely to be weaker parties, but "repeat players" also find ways to avoid or even exploit delay. Some of the richer business-people find alternatives to civil courts by using the same judges in privately paid judicial arbitration. They also stand to gain from delay in the criminal courts where business and political activity is illegal. The less powerful, without recourse to speedy justice, are forced to rely on their personal and group affiliations in civil society. And, in large part, these extended social, political, and kinship group networks ultimately involve dependence on the powerful in their role as guarantors of reliability, brokers of resources, and mediators of disputes.

STUDYING LEGAL CULTURE COMPARATIVELY

It is one thing to describe legal culture, another to use the concept in the course of explaining the connection between variables. Cotterrell has complained that the concept of legal culture seeks to explain too much, indeed that it can lead to confusion between what needs to be explained and what constitutes the explanation (Cotterrell, 1997). Friedman replies that our accounts of legal culture can serve to capture an essential intervening variable in influencing the type of legal changes that follow on large social transformations such as those following technological break-throughs (Friedman, 1997: 34). In fact there seems no reason in principle why legal culture cannot, on different occasions, represent what is explained and what does the explaining. This is still more true for a single ingredient of legal culture such as the relative level of court delay. Patterns of delay help constitute what we mean when we speak of legal culture, but they also are explained (and help explain) the other features that make up internal and external legal culture.

There is, nonetheless, an important divide between those scholars who look for "indicators" of legal culture in the activity of courts and other legal institutions, and those who insist instead on the need to interpret cultural meaning. The first approach makes use of the concept of culture (or deliberately simplified aspects of it) to explain variation in levels and types of litigation or social control; the second approach seeks to use legally related behavior by institutions and individuals as itself an "index" of culture. On the first approach the strategy will be to translate local terms into scientific Esperanto; we should set out to measure, for example, variations in official "decision making" rather than talk about the elusive concept of "discretion" across different cultures. On the second approach our aim is to provide "thick descriptions of law" as "local knowledge" (Geertz, 1973, 1983). So we should be precisely concerned with cultural packaging, with the difficulties of faithfully translating another system's ideas of fairness and justice and of making proper sense of its web of meanings.

Among those following the first approach some authors have drawn a contrast, in some ways related to Friedman's typology, between the factors conditioning the "supply side" of law as embodied in the availability and activities of legal and paralegal institutions, and the "demand" side representing attitudes to law and the use of legal institutions (Blankenburg, 1997). In a well-known so-called "natural experiment" Blankenburg seeks to explain why Germany has one of the highest rates of litigation in Europe and Holland one of the lowest, when both countries are socially and culturally so similar and economically interdependent. He argues that it would be implausible in this case to attribute differences in litigation to differences in "folk" or general culture. Rather, the larger supply of alternatives in Holland is determinate in accounting for their avoidance of litigation. This, in his view, proves that the "supply side" of legal culture, and in particular the institutional shape of legal infrastructure, is more likely to yield a satisfactory explanation than "demand-side" factors in explaining patterns of legal behavior.

Blankenburg's argument is not free from the ambiguities identified by Cotterrell. It is not always clear whether his aim is to find a way of characterizing differences in (national) legal cultures or instead to use the concept of legal culture itself as a tool for explaining the behavior of legal institutions. Sometimes legal culture seems to be the explanation of the filters and alternatives that Blankenburg sees as characterizing

Dutch "law in action"; at other times it seems to be the name we give to such patterns of litigation and avoidance (in which case it would be tautologous to use this as part of any explanation). Criticism can also be levelled at the viability of any net distinction between supply and demand; it is difficult to decide, for example, whether lawyers' strategies are one or the other.

Blankenburg's analysis also shows the serious limits to approaches to culture that focus on behavioral patterns at the expense of the exploration of meaning (Nelken, 1997a). All comparative work involves the exploration of similarities and differences: the problem is how to find cross-cultural criteria for isolating and identifying such variables for the purpose of demonstrating similarities or differences in legal culture. This is not merely a technical question. Variations in the rates of crime, litigation, or court delay are already the product of (unknown) cultural processes which need to be understood before they can be used to explain cultural differences. Blankenburg assumes, for instance, that the level of demand for courts can be treated as a constant as between Germany and Holland. But the assumption of functional equivalence across cultures (whatever institution is concerned) is always questionable; what counts as alternatives or "supplements" is itself culturally contingent. We could just as well say that it is the different function of the courts in Holland that means that the availability of lawyers and welfare legislation leads to less litigation. In another society (including Germany) the alternatives that Blankenburg uses to explain the low rate of litigation in Holland could easily merely lead to greater litigation.

Interpretative approaches, by contrast, try to grasp the secrets of legal culture by focusing on key local terms (sometimes admitted to be almost but not quite untranslatable). Blankenburg himself explores the meaning of the term *beleid* in Holland, which refers to the often explicit policy guidelines followed by government, criminal justice personnel, and complex (public) organizations in general (Blankenburg and Bruinsma, 1994). Other scholars have examined the idea of the state in common law and Continental countries and have sought to understand, for example, why litigation is seen as essentially democratic in the USA and as antidemocratic in France. In this endeavor they will seek to bring out contrasts in the meaning and use of crucial ideas and ideals. What is meant by the "rule of law" when this is conjured up as the *Rechtsstaat* or the *stato di diritto*? How does the Italian term *garantismo* relate to the Anglo-American notion of "due process"? What are the differences between "law and order" and what the Germans call *innere sicherheit*? Why is *lokale justiz* not the same as "community crime control" (Zedner, 1995)? These enquiries presuppose that concepts both reflect and constitute culture. They show the changes undergone by the meaning of "contract" in a society where the individual is seen as necessarily embodied in wider relationships (Winn, 1994), or the way that the Japanese ideogram for the new concept of "rights" came to be a sign associated with "self-interest" rather than morality (Feldman, 1997).

The problem faced by all interpretative approaches, however, is deciding whose ideas we should be trying to understand (Nelken, 1995, 2003). For different purposes we may be interested in the views and behavior of politicians, legal officials, legal and other professionals, or legal scholars – in the powerful or the powerless. Though we will always want to know what the natives think it does not follow that we actually want to think like a native. We may want to know more or less than they do – and for certain purposes we may even come to know more. But if we do not and cannot always look to them for corroboration of our ideas we then risk sometimes imposing our own erroneous interpretations. This is all the more likely because, however much they may tell us about what is being observed, the outsider's views always owe a great deal to where the observer is coming from. Likewise, what is described, and how much the account is found convincing, will depend on what his or her home audience is likely to find plausible (Nelken, 2000). The scholar's small contribution to the ultimately quixotic project of encompassing "the enormous interplay of interpretations in and about a culture" (J. Friedman, 1994: 73) may then itself join the flux of communications through which cultures reinvent themselves.

In examining the problem of court delays in Italy both the positivist and interpretative approaches have something to offer. Certainly much can be explained in terms of the supply of litigation possibilities not keeping pace with demand. Since the last world war there has been a sevenfold increase in the number of civil cases filed – as well as a large increase in the number of private lawyers, yet the number of judges has increased much less (Cassese, 2001). Access to courts is relatively cheap, especially as compared to the UK and the USA, and there is a relative paucity of what Blankenburg called "infrastructural alternatives"– only the very rich can afford judicial arbitration and there are still few mediation schemes set up by local chambers of commerce.

But why does the pressure of unfulfilled demand not lead to change? Surely the lack of alternatives must itself be explained? The relatively low proportion of cases that lawyers settle before trial must have much to do with the level of court delay. Lawyers and judges in Italy will tell you there is "no culture of compromise." There is also very little sign of managerialism in the running of Italian courts; the heads of judicial sections are never chosen for managerial ability and often lack it. The court administration (or *cancelleria)* struggles to cope while relying on antiquated information technology; and at least some of the generally poorly paid employees work with the leisurely ethos that characterizes much public employment in Italy. By comparison with Anglo-American legal cultures lay participation in judicial matters is highly restricted: even those recruited into the recently introduced system of honorary Justices of the Peace to deal with low-level civil cases are required to have law degrees.

More generally, Italian legal culture is one that pursues high ideals, especially in the sphere of procedural protections, in a context of scarce resources. The complexity of procedural safeguards has grown at the same time as court loads have been increasing. On the criminal side, for example, since the introduction of the new code of criminal procedure in 1989, the system now seeks to combine guarantees that belong to both the accusatorial and the inquisitorial approaches. It seeks to incorporate the forensic heat of the adversarial trial together with double checking by different judges and high possibilities of reversibility (all cases can be retried *on the facts* on appeal). The judge's role in civil trials is central as it is in France, but in Italy they are expected to write much longer "motivations" of their decisions. (And judges explain that they can only get round to thinking about the case and writing their sentences once all the facts have come in.)

BEYOND NATIONAL LEGAL CULTURE

Whatever the influence of globalization, the effort to explain or interpret legal culture at the level of the nation-state continues to be an important ambition of comparative sociology of law (Gessner, Hoeland, and Varga, 1996). Scholars typic-ally still write about what they call "the Japanese approach to law," "Dutch legal culture," "French criminal justice," and so on. Even those who try to unsettle stereotypes concerning which nations are supposedly most or least litigious (Feldman, 2000) take it for granted that legal culture is an aspect of the nation state. How far can this be justified?

On the one hand, national authorities do continue to use law to impose insti-tutional and procedural similarities for all sorts of political and legal reasons. Jurisdictions may also mobilize or reflect wider social and cultural similarities between legal culture and general culture which roughly coincide with their political boundaries. While it is true that there will often be considerable differences within the nation-state this may not cancel out significant differences among nations. In Italy, for example, legal delay is much greater in the south of the country, but all its courts have delays well above the European average.

On the other hand, limiting our focus to the level of the national state will not always be appropriate. At the microlevel it may be more productive for some purposes to study the culture of the local courthouse; different social groups, interests, or professional associations; or the roles and relationships of individuals in engaging or avoiding disputes. At the macrolevel, nation-states are becoming more interdependent (though not necessarily more similar). Different legal systems participate in world or regional bodies and in common projects or trends such as the attempt to construct a "Fortress Europe" or combat political corruption or money laundering. Each respond in their own way to Europeanization, Americanization, and globalization, and each is affected by the culture of modernity (or postmodern-ity). As Coombe rightly argues, law is found not only in national legal cultures but also in the practices of international armed forces, arbitration, refugee camps and enterprise zones (Coombe, 2000: 44). To some extent it is also true, as she claims, that individuals inhabit a "deterritorialized world" (2000: 42); we can participate via the media in the communities of others with whom have no geographical proximity or common history, and can live partly imagined lives via the mass media.

Studies of legal culture do sometimes go beyond the nation-state to explore wider cultural entities; not only by speaking of the civil law and common law (or "Anglo-American") legal worlds long identified by comparative lawyers (Varga, 1992), but also by using more idiosyncratic categories such as "Latin legal culture" (Garapon, 1995), or even "modern legal culture" (L. Friedman, 1994). Increasingly, attention is also being given to the so-called "third cultures" of international trade, communi-cation networks, and other transnational processes (see, e.g., Dezalay and Garth, 1996; Snyder, 1999 and chapter 33 in this volume; Teubner, 1997). The boundaries between units of legal culture(s) are fluid and they intersect at the macro and micro level in ways that are often far from harmonious. But this untidiness, as well as the not infrequent attempts to conceal or resolve it, are all part of the phenomenon of living legal cultures.

Legal culture also has a dynamic aspect. Students of comparative legal culture will also want to get to grips with the increasing pace of legal transfer (Nelken, 2001a, 2001b, 2001c; Teubner, 1998). Of special interest for wider theorizing in law and society is the way such transfers are geared to the difficult process of attempting to bring about an imagined future – using foreign law to *change* existing society and culture. The hope is that law may be a means of resolving current problems by transforming their society into one more like the source of such borrowed law; legal transfer becomes part of the effort to become more democratic, more economically successful, more secular – or more religious. In what is almost a species of sympathetic magic, borrowed law is deemed capable of bringing about the same conditions of a flourishing economy or a healthy civil society that are found in the social context from which the borrowed law has been taken. Hence ex-communist countries try to become more like selected examples of the more successful market societies, or South Africa models its new constitution on the best that Western regimes have to offer rather than on constitutional arrangements found in its nearer neighbors in Africa.

The search for dissimilar legal models is perhaps most likely where the legal transfer is imposed by third parties as part of a colonial project, and/or insisted on as a condition of trade, aid, alliance, or diplomatic recognition. It also characterizes the efforts of international organizations, such as the International Monetary Fund, when they seek to reshape societies according to a supposedly universal pattern of political and financial integrity. And it may be requested or accepted mainly as a symbolic way of marking willingness to accept the "rules of the game" of the wider global economy. This explains the adhesion to intellectual property or antitrust provisions of the World Trade Organization by countries who have few ways of enforcing such rules – or little need to do so.

Past legal transfers were sought by elites concerned to "modernize" their society or otherwise bring it into the wider family of "civilized" nations. Japan and Turkey are the most obvious examples. There is much discussion of whether or not such transfers can succeed. But even when they do succeed for all apparent purposes this may be at a high price. There is, for example, continuing controversy in Japan about the significance of the 1890 reception of Western law. Some indigenous scholars say Japan has an underlying culture that is incompatible with modern Western law; others reject this argument, alleging that it is an invention of the power elite by which the people are led to believe in their nonlitigiousness (and lack of interest in rights) so as to leave power holders undisturbed (Tanase, 2001: 195). But, more important, because Japan achieved its incredible modernization not by Western law but through bureaucratic authoritarianism, there are some who feel that Japan has not yet achieved the modern.

Having achieved modernization without "the modern" they were told was necessary, Tanase argues, Japanese have a sense of unease and engage in a compulsive search for the modern that only leaves them frustrated. As examples of the consequent ambivalent approach to law, he points to the stigma attached to using legal remedies among neighbors as well as to a special concern with deciding what other than law can make something count as legal. Interestingly, however, his conclusion is not that Japanese culture is irreducibly different but that postmodern law will increasingly comes to resemble the Japanese approach, treating law as having a hollow core inside which can be negotiated flexibly in relation to others in the course of improvising workable ad hoc arrangements (Tanase, 2001: 197). This attempt at a phenomenological approach to legal culture, fascinating as it is, also reminds us of the difficulty of all such interpretative exercises. How many Japanese fit the portrait Tanase is painting? Are we – and should we be – concerned with elites or with everyman and everywoman? Should we give Tanase's account more or less credibility because he is part of the culture he is describing?

While many of those engaged on missions of legal transfer are willing to leave the issue of whether the requested law is appropriate to be resolved by the host countries, some scholars return all the more convinced that law only makes sense in terms of its own (national) environment. Thus one leading constitutional scholar reports that his experience in China confirmed him in the view that the type of administrative law used in the USA would not be currently workable there. It is too interdependent with wider features of its host society, above all the presence of a litigious culture and the presumption that party involvement by numerous interest groups can be counted on to comment on and improve bureaucratic regulations. Recommendations for change must therefore rather draw on identifiable features of existing Chinese society:

> [B]y a sort of double reflection, the characterization of American law that China's distance illuminates, becomes a way of perceiving what the underlying characterisation of a Chinese law would be. That law draws upon the hierarchy, centralization and governmental prestige in the Chinese system. It would create governmental supervisory agencies, independent of other agencies, but possessing the full power and prestige of government, to enforce statutorily required procedures. (Rubin, 2000: 108)

One of the most important tasks for those currently studying comparative legal culture is to try to capture how far the globalization of law is actually leading to the imposition of one local (especially Anglo-American) model of legal culture on other societies (Heydebrand, 2001; Santos, 1995). A deep-lying assumption of this type of legal culture is what has been described as "pragmatic legal instrumentalism." This is the idea that law is something which does or should "work" for those in civil society who set it in motion, together with the claim that this is something which can or should be assessed in ways which are separable from wider political debates. This can have revolutionary effects – for good or bad – when introduced into legal cultures where it is said of official law that in the past it instituted without regulating (Lopez-Ayllon, 1995).

With the advance of globalization some have argued that the preeminence of the positive law of the nation state in the modern period can be seen as no more than a temporal fusion of law's globalizing and localizing elements. If so it is only through carefully considered case studies in different settings that we will be able to assess how the current balance is shifting. Criticism of the length of court procedures in Italy is certainly at least in part a result of the growing influence of "pragmatic instrumentalism" as well as by other developments outside its national boundaries that are linked to Europeanization or globalization. The very definition of delay is reflexively determined as Italy is forced to compare itself to other allegedly similar societies (or economic competitors). Most important, as we shall see, is the role of a higher court – the Strasbourg Court – which is not even in Italy but which enforces the convention of Human Rights to which Italy has signed up.

Internal and external pressures for change can interact, sometimes in surprising ways. To date there have been a number of internal reforms in Italy, both of penal and civil procedure, which have attempted to speed up court processes, often borrowing (selectively) ideas from legal systems abroad – most notably from the Anglo-American types of legal culture. For example, in 1989 a new code of criminal procedure famously introduced many elements of the adversarial approach to penal procedure as basic modifications of the previous Continental inquisitorial system. But although the code included a version of plea bargaining and a variety of other measures that could have reduced court delays – and were intended to do so – there has been relatively little use of these possibilities. The introduction of so many adversarial elements may even have added to delays because stringent interpretation of the requirement that those involved in deciding on the strength of the prosecution case can play no role in deciding the case itself now means that as many as seven or eight judges may handle a case. The most recent proposals for "a just process" include much discussion of the right to speedier trials. But the likelihood of this coming about (and the real commitment to such an aim) is made suspect by the continuing and even increasing emphasis on multiplying points and methods of procedural rights and controls (indeed the goal of more efficiency in dispatching cases is treated as yet another such right).

In theory pressures to reduce delays could come from any of the following: the economic sphere (from business or other trading partners), the political domain (from larger political associations and international agreements), and the cultural environment (through communication and media connections). Surprisingly perhaps, the requirements of economic convergence (L. Friedman, 1994) seem to have had little effect on legal processes so far. Political pressures from the moves to greater harmonization within the Europe Union are of greater importance. Legal delay regularly comes to public notice in the form of horror stories of individuals suffering from legal/administrative inefficiency. But the elite newspapers in Italy have also given considerable space over recent years to the very high level of convictions of the Italian state at the European Court of Human Rights in Strasbourg for its failure to guarantee trials within a reasonable period. But what the Strasbourg court considers unreasonable delay – at around five years – is not much longer than the average time *first* hearing civil cases take in many courts in Italy. Of the roughly 40 signatories of the Human Rights Convention, including countries from the former Soviet Union, ex-Yugoslavia, and Turkey, Italy manages to receive roughly half of all convictions for this sort of breach. Dealing with cases from Italy is even adding to the delays of the European Court itself!

Research on a large sample of cases discussed by the Court reveals that delays range from four to 18 years (Nelken, 2001d). Most cases are on the civil side, but no more than a seventh involve anything like commercial disputes. The "problem" as it is perceived in Italy is not so much the cost in damages awarded to complainants – an average of four thousand pounds (around $6,000) for "moral damages." This is relatively modest as compared to the costs of speeding up the justice system. Rather the main concern is with loss of face; Italy has been placed under special surveillance by the European Council of Ministers for five years for its systematic violation of this article of the convention and (in theory) risks being excluded from the convention. This potential exclusion is then linked to the (strange but often voiced) elite fear of being considered "behind" by more advanced European states and, as such, of not being considered really part of "Europe."

It could be objected that since Italy was a willing signatory to the European convention we should consider the European Court no more than a higher level court of appeal of the *same* legal culture. But, for the ordinary trial lawyers I have been interviewing, the average time taken for court cases in Italy is experienced as something normal; exceptional cases are seen as ones that overrun the Italian norm. The Council of Ministers and the Strasbourg court are therefore engaged here in something like an attempt to "normalize" a deviant approach to legal procedure and court practice rather than merely the provision of appeal for exceptional cases of extreme breaches of the convention. According to one "human rights" lawyer who specializes in taking cases to Strasbourg, "...the European Court, the Court is almost a 'Court of Miracles' because it seems to be an organization which is outside time and space. You can go there to punish the powerful. Because that is what it is all about we could say that what it offers is revolutionary, even anarchic justice." (He did go on to add, however, that the actual damages that the court awards to someone "crushed by the national legal system" are far too low to compensate for what can have been lost.)

The resort to the Strasbourg court by Italian citizens shows how law can be both agent and object of Europeanization and globalization. It also demonstrates how such trends can be either progressive or destructive forces – or both together. The spread of human rights can be a boon, but it may also threaten rival conceptions of justice and social solidarity (Man and Wai, 1999). It may be a blessing for law to help resolve local or international social problems but it depends on what terms, and on whose terms. Undoubtedly many individual Italians suffer misery and loss as a result of existing court delays – and various groups including businesspeople lack an effective form of state-sponsored dispute processing. But the effect of imposing Strasbourg standard time (as well as of the increasing influence of Anglo-American forms of civil and criminal procedure) in the Italian context could easily be to reduce existing protections to accused persons. In general in both criminal and civil cases it could lead to greater party control of legal processes and to more "shallow case processing" especially where weaker parties are involved. Making court processes more "rational" and timely would also undermine – for better or worse – the role of the mediators who presently channel and resolve potential social conflicts.

But it would be premature to conclude that European harmonization of court delay is round the corner in Italy (and other case studies will likely turn up similar dialectics between change and resistance). What has now been decided is to create a new level of national appeal (at the adjoining district court of appeal) where parties must first go to seek damages for undue delay, thereby delaying recourse to Strasbourg as well as giving parties an incentive to seek remedies that do not place Italy in a bad light internationally. Decisions there are supposed to be provided within four months. Judges who are found responsible for breaching bureaucratic time limits for dealing with cases also now risk having to pay damages and not, as previously, only risk criticism as a result of internal disciplinary hearings by the Supreme Judicial Council. But these are "remedies" that are unlikely to do much to change the average speed of trials. Reproducing much of the same pattern and logic of the national legal culture that has led to delay, they are likely only to add to it.

References

Blankenburg, E. (1997) "Civil litigation rates as indicators for legal culture," in D. Nelken (ed.), *Comparing Legal Cultures*, Aldershot, UK: Dartmouth, pp. 41–68.

Blankenburg, E. and Bruinsma, F. (1994) *Dutch Legal Culture*, 2nd edn. Deventer, Netherlands: Kluwer.

Brants, C. and Field, S. (2000) "Legal cultures, political cultures and procedural traditions," in D. Nelken (ed.), *Contrasting Criminal Justice*. Aldershot, UK: Dartmouth, pp. 77–116.

Cain, M. (2000) "Orientalism, occidentalism and the sociology of crime," *British Journal of Criminology* 40: 239–60.

Cassese, S. (2001) " L'esplosione del diritto. Il sistema giuridico Italiano dal 1975 al 2000," *Sociologia Del Diritto* 28(1): 55–66.

Clifford J. and Marcus G. (1986) *Writing Culture: The Poetics and Politics of Ethnography*. Berkeley: University of California Press.

Coombe, R.J. (2000) "Contingent articulations: A critical cultural studies of law," in A. Sarat and T. Kearns (eds.), *Law in the Domains of Culture*. Ann Arbor: University of Michigan Press, pp. 21–64.

Cotterrell, R. (1997) "The concept of legal culture," in D. Nelken (ed.), *Comparing Legal Cultures*. Aldershot, UK: Dartmouth, pp. 13–32.

Dezalay, Y. and Garth, B. (1996) *Dealing in Virtue*. Chicago: University of Chicago Press.

Feldman, E. (1997) "Patients' rights, citizen movements and Japanese legal culture," in D. Nelken (ed.), *Comparing Legal Cultures*: Aldershot, UK: Dartmouth, pp. 215–36.

Feldman, E. (2000) "Blood justice, courts, conflict and compensation in Japan, France and the United States," *Law & Society Review* 34(3): 651–702.

Friedman, J. (1994) *Cultural Identity and Global Process*. London: Sage.

Friedman, L. (1994) "Is there a modern legal culture?" *Ratio Juris* 1994: 117.

Friedman, L. (1997) "The concept of legal culture: A reply," in D. Nelken (ed.), *Comparing Legal Cultures*, Aldershot, UK: Dartmouth, pp. 33–40.

Garapon, Antoine (1995) "French legal culture and the shock of 'globalization'," *Social and Legal Studies*, Special issue on legal culture, diversity and globalization 4(4): 493–506.

Geertz, C. (1973) "Thick description: Towards an interpretive theory of culture," in C. Geertz, *The Interpretation of Culture*. London: Fontana, pp. 3–32.

Geertz, C. (1983) *Local Knowledge: Further Essays in Interpretive Anthropology*. New York: Basic Books.

Gessner, V., Hoeland, A., and Varga, C. (eds.) (1996) *European Legal Cultures*. Aldershot, UK: Dartmouth.

Haley, J. (1991) *Authority without Power: Law and the Japanese Paradox*. New York: Oxford University Press.

Hamilton, V. and Sanders, J. (1992) *Everyday Justice: Responsibility and the Individual in Japan and the United States*. New Haven, CT: Yale University Press.

Heyderbrand, W. (2001) "Globalization and the rule of law at the end of the 20th century," in A. Febbrajo, D. Nelken, and V. Olgiati (eds.), *Social Processes and Patterns of Legal Control: European Yearbook of Sociology of Law 2000*. Milan: Giuffrè, pp. 25–127.

Kalven, S. and Zeisel, H. (1959) *Delay in the Courts*. New York: Little Brown.

Kuper, A. (1999) *Culture: The Anthropologists Account*. Cambridge, MA: Harvard University Press.

Lopez-Ayllon, S. (1995) "Notes on Mexican legal culture," *Social and Legal Studies*, Special issue on legal culture, diversity and globalization 4(4): 477–92.

Man, S.W. and Wai, C.Y. (1999) "Whose rule of law? Rethinking (post) colonial legal culture in Hong Kong," *Social and Legal Studies* 8: 147–70.

Nelken, D. (1995) "Understanding/invoking legal culture," in *Social and Legal Studies*, Special issue on legal culture, diversity and globalization 4(4): 435–52.

Nelken, D. (1997a) " Puzzling out legal culture: A comment on Blankenburg," in D. Nelken (ed.), *Comparing Legal Cultures*, Aldershot, UK: Dartmouth, pp. 58–88.

Nelken, D. (1997b) "The globalization of crime and criminal justice: prospects and problems," in M. Freeman (ed.), *Law and Opinion at the end of the 20th Century*. Oxford: Oxford University Press, pp. 251–79.

Nelken, D. (2000) "Telling difference: Of crime and criminal justice in Italy," in D. Nelken (ed.), *Contrasting Criminal Justice*. Aldershot, UK: Dartmouth, pp. 233–64.

Nelken, D. (2001a) "The meaning of success in transnational legal transfers," *Windsor Yearbook of Access to Justice* 19: 349–66.

Nelken, D. (2001b) "Towards a sociology of legal adaptation," in D. Nelken and J. Feest (eds.), *Adapting Legal Cultures*. Oxford: Hart Publishing, pp. 4–55.

Nelken, D. (2001c) "Beyond the metaphor of legal transplants? Consequences of autopoietic theory for the study of cross-cultural legal adaptation," in J. Priban and D. Nelken (eds.),

Law's New Boundaries: The Consequences of Legal Autopoiesis. Aldershot, UK: Dartmouth, pp. 265–302.

Nelken, D. (2001d) "Legal culture, globalization and court delay in Italy," Paper presented and distributed at the Law and Society/RCSL conference, Budapest, July 2001.

Nelken, D. (2003) "Comparativists and transfers," in P. Legrand and R. Munday (eds.), *Comparative Legal Studies: Traditions and Transitions.* Cambridge, UK: Cambridge University Press.

Rubin, E. (2000) "Administrative law and the complexity of culture," in A. Seidman, R. Seidman, and J. Payne (eds.), *Legislative Drafting for Market Reform: Some Lessons from China.* Basingstoke, UK: Macmillan, pp. 88–108.

Santos, B. de Sousa (1995) *Towards a New Common Sense.* London: Routledge.

Snyder, F. (1999) "Governing economic globalization: Global legal pluralism and European law," *European Law Journal* 5: 334–74.

Tanase, T. (2001) "The empty space of the modern in Japanese law discourse," in D. Nelken and J. Feest (eds.), *Adapting Legal Cultures.* Oxford, Hart Publishing, pp. 187–98.

Teubner, G. (1997) "Global Bukowina: Legal pluralism in the world society," in G. Teubner (ed.), *Global Law without a State.* Aldershot, UK: Dartmouth, pp. 3–38.

Teubner, G. (1998) "Legal irritants: Good faith in British law, or how unifying law ends up in new divergences," *Modern Law Review* 61(1): 11–32.

Varga, C. (ed.) (1992) *Comparative Legal Cultures.* Aldershot, UK: Dartmouth.

Winn, J.K. (1994) "Relational practices and the marginalization of law: Informal practices of small businesses in Taiwan," *Law & Society Review* 28(2): 193–232.

Zedner, L. (1995) "In pursuit of the vernacular; comparing law and order discourse in Britain and Germany," *Social and Legal Studies* 4: 517–34.

Zweigert, K. and Kotz, H. (1987) *An Introduction to Comparative Law.* Oxford: Oxford University Press.

Further Reading

Kagan, R.A. (2001) *Adversarial Legalism: The American Way of Law.* Cambridge, MA: Harvard University Press.

Nelken, D. (ed.) (1997) *Comparing Legal Cultures.* Aldershot, UK: Dartmouth.

Nelken, D. (ed.) (2000) *Contrasting Criminal Justice.* Aldershot, UK: Dartmouth.

Nelken, D. (2003) "Beyond compare? Criticizing 'the American way of law'," *Law and Social Enquiry* 28(3): 181–213.

Nelken, D. and Feest, J. (eds.) (2001) *Adapting Legal Cultures.* Oxford: Hart Publishing.

Part III

Institutions and Actors

8

The Police and Policing

JEANNINE BELL

In its barest sense, "policing" requires that individuals have the ability to use force to regulate behavior and control public order. While those who engage in policing may not need to use physical force to control behavior in most cases, they have the ability to do so. Around the world, there are many groups of individuals who do not fit traditional notions of what we consider to be "police," but nonetheless may use force to control public order – Immigration and Nationalization Service officers in the United States, private security guards, vigilantes, and samurai warriors in Japan. Though this chapter briefly explores private nonstate policing and alternative policing, most of the discussion concerns public police whose authority stems from the state. To focus this discussion of the police, a traditional definition is used. In this chapter, "the police" include those individuals authorized by the group of which they are members to use physical force in order to regulate relations among group members (Bayley, 1985: 7).

After a brief description of the organization and structural function of police power as it has been defined around the world, this chapter will examine three enduring issues of interest to sociolegal scholars who study the police and policing power in a variety of national contexts. In the first section, the tension between two functions with which police are charged, order maintenance and law enforcement, will be analyzed. The second section will address police–citizen relations, with special emphasis on the difficult relationship between minorities and the police. Methods of increasing police accountability are described in the third section.

The organizational structure of police agencies is an important feature when comparing police forces around the globe. Scholars have characterized nations as having either single or multiple police forces with either centralized or decentralized command structures (Reichel, 1994; Bayley, 1985). Singular police forces have only one police force to supervise. Multiple systems are characterized by several different types of police agencies at different levels of government, for example at the federal, state, or local level. National, centralized, singular police forces – such as those in

Denmark, Nigeria, and Saudi Arabia – are organized to enforce the law as if the entire country were a single jurisdiction under one set of laws. Decentralized systems of policing, like those that exist in the United States, Germany, Britain, and Canada concentrate police powers in a variety of state and federal locations, allowing each of these centers the authority to craft responses to local problems (Reichel, 1994).

Research collected from countries around the world shows that citizens of different nations have different expectations of their police forces. One researcher comparing police forces around the world theorizes that part of this has to do with the public demand for police services and willingness of citizens to seek out the police (Bayley, 1985: 130). As a society becomes less able to maintain social discipline through informal social processes, both the volume and the character of situations to which the police in different countries must respond will increase. A comparison of several countries demonstrates that variance in nations' expectations can be attributed to differences in the countries' technological capabilities and population size. For example, police in more developed countries and cities are required to spend less of their time controlling crime than those located in undeveloped countries and rural areas. With the exception of the United States, where police spend more time processing crime and less time on service than police in similar countries, police in developed countries tend to spend more time engaged in attending to noncrime matters and providing service, such a settling disputes (Bayley, 1985).

ORDER MAINTENANCE VS. LAW AND ORDER

One of the primary functions of the police all over the world is to maintain order. In democratic societies police are required to maintain order under the rule of law. The duty to maintain order under the rule of law places a further burden on the police. The principle of accountability to the rule of law requires that police officers serve a variety of functions – as rule enforcers, social servants, moralists, and street fighters – to name several important roles that police officers must fill. In diverse situations, officers must themselves decide which situations require them to play which roles (Skolnick, 1966: 17).

In a country like the United States, where procedural protections for suspects regulate police officers' investigative power, the police are charged with enforcing the law in a way that conforms to procedural dictates. On the face of it, maintaining order seems to demand that all known violators of the law be arrested. Procedural protections, however, set limits on manner in which violators may be apprehended. For instance, in the United States, even if the police have a suspicion that someone has committed a crime they are prevented from detaining that person until they have a strong belief that the suspect has engaged in criminal activity. Viewed in this manner maintaining order can sometimes be at odds with enforcing the law (Goldstein, 1960).

Police officers' jobs are complicated not only by task-oriented ambiguity, but also by ambiguity in the text of the law that the police are required to enforce. Some ambiguities appear in the form of overbroad provisions that seem to prohibit a range of conduct. Other ambiguity may stem from the fact that some laws on the books are in conflict with social mores or expectations. Examples of such laws include obsolete laws, laws that remain on the books because of legislative inaction, and laws that proscribe adultery (LaFave, 1962). Enforcing these type of laws would violate public expectations.

The tension between maintaining order and enforcing the law also complicates democratic oversight of the police. Society's difficulty overseeing the police is compounded by the invisibility of much of police behavior, and the large role that discretion plays in police officers' jobs. For instance, in the United States a patrol officer's decision to not invoke the law, for example when he or she decides not to write a traffic citation, because of the structure of the appeals and review process, is largely invisible (Goldstein, 1960). Thus, even when the law unambiguously governs a situation, police may use their discretion not to enforce the law.

Numerous sociolegal scholars have explored how police cope with the tension between maintaining order and enforcing the law, and how police do decide to enforce the law (Goldstein, 1960; Skolnick, 1966; Worden, 1989; Lundman, 1994; Boyd, Hamner, and Berk, 1996; Bell, 2002). Much of the sociolegal work in the area of policing involves observational studies of the police. In these studies, trained researchers often spend several months observing police officers at work and take notes on their behavior. The data that researchers collect is then coded and analyzed. Such studies of the police have revealed that because of conflicting organizational goals, diverse situations, and the demands of the different communities that the police serve, officers do not behave in a ministerial way, strictly enforcing the law (Smith and Visher, 1981). Scholars have found that instead of enforcing the law uniformly, police enforce the law selectively, sometimes neglecting to apply the law in situations that the text of the law defines as violations.

Researchers who study the police have identified several factors on which police base their decisions to apply the law. Police officers' decision making has been attributed mainly to two types of factors, situational – based on the characteristics of the situation at hand, and attitudinal factors – linked to the officer's beliefs and attitudes. One of the most studied police decisions is the decision to arrest a suspect. In exploring whether an individual police officer is likely to engage in formal action – to arrest the suspect – researchers note that police may base their decision to arrest on the severity of the offense; on characteristics of the suspect (sex, race, social, social class, demeanor, sobriety); on the characteristics of the victim; or on the relationship between the victim and the suspect (Worden, 1989: 669).

Research highlighting situational factors reveals that the police selectively enforce the law in minority communities, and against minority violators (LaFave, 1962; Wilson, 1973; Smith and Visher, 1981; Harris, 1999). Several early studies of the selective application of the law by the police reveal the nonenforcement of the law in minority communities because of police officers' assumptions that lawbreaking was accepted behavior in the black community (Wilson, 1973; LaFave, 1962). More recent studies show that police use their discretion to more frequently stop, question, and search racial minorities, and also are more likely to apply formal sanctions against minorities than whites (Harris, 1999; Russell, 1998).

Police officers also have the discretion to decide whether they will use physical force. Though the ability to use force is an important factor in policing, as this chapter suggests, much of police control occurs without physical force being used. Studies show that police rarely use physical force. For example, one study of use of force by the International Association of Chiefs of Police indicated that police in the United States use force in less than one half of 1 percent of all calls for police service (Adams, 1999: 3). When the police do use force, it typically occurs in the context of trying to make an arrest. The study also found that the force used by police is most likely to consist of shoving or pushing a suspect rather that discharging the officer's firearm (ibid.).

Two important approaches to policing adopted in many cities take different perspectives on the use of force by the police. Community policing, the first approach, emphasizes community and police cooperation in the maintenance of order. Community policing strives to make citizen and police coproducers of public order in part by increasing police accountability in all areas, including the use of force (Adams, 1999: 2). The other approach, aggressive policing, sometimes called the "broken windows" approach, seeks to reduce crime by increasing enforcement in the area of "quality of life" crimes – public drinking, vandalism, and other order maintenance offenses. The emphasis on increased attention to crime and heightened enforcement may make regimes implementing aggressive policing more likely to use or abuse force (Adams, 1999: 2).

The role that weapons play is inextricably linked to the context in which policing takes place, especially the nature of state citizenship, the relationship between the police and the military, and in some sense to the degree of resistance to state authority (Waddington, 1999: 152). For instance, the institutionalization of arms in cities in Ireland, and other former colonies of the British Empire, can be contrasted strongly with that of the Metropolitan Police in London and forces in other cities throughout England and Wales. In Irish cities, contemporary police carry firearms. This originates from the British government's arming the police to impose colonial rule and preparing them to quell potential rebellions. Residents of London, by contrast, a city where most police do not carry firearms, were free citizens when policing developed.

Attitudinal factors in law enforcement

In addition to situational factors, attitudinal factors have served as important explanations for the use of police discretion. An important attitudinal factor that scholars have found to influence police decisions to apply the law is the officer's feeling about the seriousness of the violation. Police are less likely to enforce the law when they believe that the violation is not a serious one, and therefore less deserving of their energy. In such cases, they use their discretion to impose a lesser sanction, such as issuing a warning.

When police attitudes about the seriousness of the law determine whether or not it is enforced, police have the ability to nullify the law's effect through inaction or through misapplication. This is particularly true in cases in which law and/or procedure has changed in an attempt to alter police behavior. In circumstances in which police behavior is dictated by organizational norms, in order to be effective, changes in procedures must address preexisting police norms. For example, police officers in many cities in the United States have remained reluctant to respond to female spouse abuse calls, even in the face of changes designed to increase officer responsiveness, such as additional training and specialized domestic violence units. Studies of police officers responding to domestic violence calls show officers' responses to spousal abuse are determined in part by the fact that they do not consider such incidents to be serious violations of the law (Hirschel and Hutchinson, 1992). Officers' behavior in domestic violence cases may also be motivated by the fact that they sympathize with the perpetrator, or that they do not believe the violence committed by husbands against their wives is a crime (Walker, 1993).

Hate crime is another area in which police department norms may heavily influence the ways in which officers enforce the law. State hate crime statutes attach additional penalties to crimes motivated by bias or prejudice on the basis of race, religion, and sexual orientation. The requirement that officers determine the crime's motivation requires that police departments place special emphasis on hate crimes – even if they are low-level crimes – a category of crime which is frequently not investigated by the police. Studies have shown that police officers are reluctant to properly enforce hate crime laws unless procedures are implemented that address preexisting police norms regarding crime severity. (Boyd et al., 1996; Bell, 2002).

Changes in police procedures that require police to behave in ways at odds with preexisting organizational norms may nonetheless be successful. One study of how police in a specialized unit enforce hate crime law in a large city in the United States, "Center City," revealed that detectives enforce the hate crime law in spite of a departmental institutional culture that rejected the enforcement of low-level crimes. Police officers enforcing hate crime law may face additional disincentives, when, as in Center City, the community is mobilized against its enforcement. In Center City, incorporating the detectives into a specialized, racially mixed unit, provided the support and institutional space for norm changes needed to enforce hate crime law (Bell, 2002).

Perhaps because police forces contain so few minority officers and white women officers, many accounts of police behavior do little to examine differences among officers based on identity. More recently, police studies have attempted to explore the relationship between racial and gender identity and police officers' behavior (Martin, 1994; Oberweis and Musheno, 1999; Bell, 2002; Miller, 1999). Such works generally compare the experiences of white women and racial and ethnic minority officers with those of their white male counterparts. These studies show, as in other contexts, that the work experiences of minority and female officers are frequently marked by sexism, racism, or some combination of the two. As a result, collegiality among minority and white male officers is clearly affected.

In interviews minority and white female officers, similar to white male officers, often raise the importance of their identity as police officers (Martin, 1994; Oberweis and Musheno, 1999). Despite the importance of the "cop" identity, being women and people of color gives officers perspectives that allow them to view situations from a different vantage point. Though more research is needed to isolate the precise effect of officers' racial and gendered identities on their behavior, the existing social-legal research in the area suggests that given officers' power and proclivity to invoke the law strategically, minority and female officers' added perspective may increase their sensitivity to diverse populations and therefore their decision to invoke the law. (Bell, 2002; Oberweis and Musheno, 1999)

POLICE–CITIZEN ENCOUNTERS

Around the world situations that the police handle can be broken into the following large categories: responding to crime, crime investigation, crime prevention, mediating disputes and quarrels, dealing with noncrime situations and traffic control

(Bayley, 1985: 150). Researchers have attributed the tendency of citizens in richer and more developed countries to encounter the police in noncrime situations, or in the context of citizen-generated service calls, to two main factors (Bayley, 1985: 149). First, in rural and less developed areas, other social groups may provide support in noncrime-related situations. Second, the absence of communication technology may also make it more difficult for citizens to summon the police. Thus citizens in less developed areas rely less on the police (Bayley, 1985).

In the United States, one survey of police–citizen contacts shows that roughly one fifth of the population had face-to-face contact with the police in the 12 months prior to the survey. Nearly half of the respondents who had had encounters with police officers had called or otherwise contacted the police. Common situations in which citizens encountered the police include: requesting assistance from the police, providing information about their own victimization, and giving information about a crime they had witnessed. The survey revealed an important racial difference in citizen–police contact. Though whites were more likely than minorities to have had contact with the police during the previous 12 months, minorities represented a relatively large percentage of those handcuffed during their encounter. A larger percentage of blacks and Hispanics reported being subject to force by the police – including being choked, hit, threatened with a gun or having some other type of force used on them – than whites (Greenfield, Langan, and Smith, 1997).

Recently sociolegal research on how citizens perceived the police has addressed racialized differences in perception of the police. Data from a number of surveys show that African Americans are more likely than whites to believe that the police treat African Americans more harshly than whites (Russell, 1998; Weitzer, 2000). A recent study, based on interviews with residents of three Washington DC neighborhoods, described residents' perceptions of police behavior and analyzed the relationship between racial background and perceptions of the police. Two of the neighborhoods studied were middle-class, the other disadvantaged. The study revealed that race is an important predictor of citizens' attitudes toward the police. Black and white respondents agreed that the police treated blacks differently than whites. Whites, however, believed that police officers' actions were justified, while blacks ascribed officers' discriminatory behavior to invidious motives. The study also examined the provision of police services, finding class differences among the black respondents. The majority of disadvantaged residents believed that their neighborhood received inferior treatment by the police, while only a minority of middle-class residents found this to be the case (Weitzer, 2000).

In the United States, minorities' perceptions of the police – particularly the perceptions of African Americans and Latinos – are very much affected by how they view themselves as being treated by the police. One form that discriminatory treatment has taken is the use of racial profiling – when the police target individuals for investigation because the officer believes that persons of their race are more likely to engage in criminal behavior. Many of the complaints about racial profiling occur in the context of the investigation of traffic offenses. Minorities have argued that they are more likely than whites to be stopped by the police for speeding, more likely to be ticketed, and more likely to be searched for drugs. The prevalence of such practices and their wide distribution among the African American population have led many to call racial profiling in this context, DWB – "driving while black." Police officers deny that they are engaged in racial profiling. They insist higher arrest statistics for minorities justify the targeting of blacks and other minorities

(Harris, 1999: 267). Scholars have noted the circularity of this argument and questioned its empirical basis (Harris, 1999; Skolnick and Caplovitz, 2001).

Studies of police procedures in Ohio, Maryland, and New Jersey, analyzing the proportion of drivers stopped by race, show that a disproportionate numbers of African American drivers received tickets (Harris, 1999; Knowles, Persico, and Todd, 1999). Several studies of police behavior and racial profiling compare the race of drivers on the road with police data describing the rate at which blacks are stopped, ticketed, and arrested on a particular section of road. In one study of stops on the New Jersey Turnpike the race of drivers on the road was ascertained by counting cars on the road. This study also noted by race whether drivers were driving at the speed limit. In this study, though there was no statistical difference between the speed at which black and white drivers drove, 73.2 percent of those stopped and arrested on the turnpike were black, while only 13.5 percent of cars had a black driver or passenger (Harris, 1999).

Scholars have identified a number of possible negative consequences that may stem from police officers engaging in racial profiling. When the police treat law-abiding minorities as if they are criminal suspects solely because of their race, fear and distrust is bred in these communities (Harris, 1999). Distrust and fear of the police may lead to a failure of community–police crime fighting initiatives and in extreme cases, incendiary violence (Skolnick and Caplovitz, 2001). In addition to the effect on minority–police relations, there is also the effect of this strategy on law enforcement. Stopping minorities, irrespective of other markers of criminal activity, is not an effective method of criminal law enforcement (Skolnick and Caplovitz, 2001).

Community policing

Implemented in a variety of countries around the globe, including China, Israel, Japan, the United Kingdom, Hong Kong, and the United States, community policing involves the implementation of mechanisms designed to strengthen ties between communities and the police. Community policing places a focus on returning police to the community. Greater contact between citizens and the police is intended to decrease suspicion and distrust of the police, making citizens more likely to report crimes and leading to the increase of citizens' satisfaction with the police. One of the aims of community policing is for the public to play a more active and coordinated role in fighting crime, and thus help the police (Skolnick and Bayley, 1988; Miller, 1999). When residents share crime-fighting responsibility with the police, the "successes" or blame for increases and decreases in the city's crime rate is shared as well (Miller, 1999).

Community policing is designed to be a significant departure from the so-called reactive style of policing in which police officers spend most of their time in centralized locations, responding to citizens' calls for assistance. Both the language and action involved in community policing is different. One study of community policing found that in order to get citizens committed to community policing, the "talk" is a friendly departure from normal authoritarian police discourse. Residents are described as "customers 'invested' in the joint production of community stability" (Miller, 1999: 194). Community policing also involves actual programmatic changes. Research on community policing programs on four continents reveals that adopting community policing involves four separate areas of programmatic change:

(1) organizing community-based crime prevention; (2) reorienting patrol activities to emphasize the provision of services in nonemergencies; (3) increasing accountability to local communities; and (4) decentralizing command (Skolnick and Bayley, 1988).

Engaging the community in crime prevention is one of the best-known hallmarks of community policing programs. Extensive community-based crime prevention, or "Neighborhood Watch" programs exist in the United States, Great Britain, Japan, and Singapore. In London, for example, Neighborhood Watch involves bolstering security by having the police conduct safety education and sessions where the police supply material for marking residents' property, and by the police urging neighborhood residents to act as the "eyes and ears" of the police. Though lectures on safety and security, community safety meetings, and coordinated media campaigns, Neighborhood Watch programs like those in London provide information about security and crime prevention (Skolnick and Bayley, 1988).

Communities that have had fractured relationships with the police may be reluctant to maintain the level of cooperation with the police required for community crime prevention. In such communities, in order for community policing to work, police departments must take measures to demonstrate to citizens that the police are accountable to the community. One common mechanism designed to increase police accountability is the creation of "liaison officers." In the United States, departments committed to community policing frequently create liaison officers for ethnic and racial minorities and gays and lesbians. The purpose of these officers is to develop relationships with individuals in the community, to build trust between the communities and the police, and to respond to these communities' unique needs. Another method of increasing police accountability includes programs that allow citizens to observe the police. For instance, in both Britain and Sweden citizens may inspect police stations (Skolnick and Bayley, 1988).

In addition to involving the community and building trust with the community, community policing typically requires some type of structural change in police departments' response to crime. Many departments implementing community policing have chosen to reorient patrol activities. Reorienting patrol activities requires most police departments to change from a model of crime fighting in which patrol officers primarily respond to service calls issued by radio dispatch to one in which patrol officers engage in random motorized patrols. A predicted benefit of changing the police role is that police will become more attentive and responsive to citizens (Miller, 1999). In several cities in the United States, and in Japan, Australia, and Norway, reorienting patrol activities has involved moving the police from larger centralized locations to smaller police stations locted in residential and commercial neighborhoods. Officers in these stations are encouraged to get to know the community in many ways. For instance in the ministations in Japan (*koban*) and Singapore's Neighborhood Police Posts, officers patrol, make security surveys, promote crime prevention, serve as a sounding board for residents' complaints, and go door to door offering services and soliciting suggestions on police-related issues. In other cities, in an attempt to reorient patrol activities, police departments have reinstituted foot and bicycle patrols (Skolnick and Bayley, 1988).

Reorienting patrol activities is not the only structural change made by police departments making the transition to community policing. Often the structure of decision making must change as well, with a decentralization of command. When this type of reorganization of the authority to make decisions about police priorities occurs, power is taken from centralized decision makers and given to those responsible for policing the community. In many cases, this involves redrawing command areas and enhancing decision making throughout the command structure (Skolnick and Bayley, 1988). Decentralizing command is more easily attainable for police organizations with a tradition of decentralized decision making. In departments that rely heavily on centralized command structures, effective management, accountability, and control of the rank and file may be lost, and a breakdown of professional standards of behavior may result when community policing is implemented (Mawby, 1999).

Studying community policing as it is implemented, scholars have questioned both its logic and its goals. The goal of community policing – to change the focus of traditional policing and to provide greater community involvement – is ambitious. In the attempt to implement community policing, many police departments have encountered obstacles that prevent them from effectively making the transition from more traditional forms of policing. One of the most significant obstacles that community policing programs encounter is from officers, whose support is needed to move from reactive policing. Studies of several police department have revealed that many officers are not receptive to community policing (Lyons, 1999; Rosenbaum and Lurigio, 1994; Scheingold, 1991; Miller, 1999). Some police officers who, as a result of community policing, have been forced to make rather dramatic changes in their job function have felt threatened, and have acted as obstacles to the successful implementation of such programs (Rosenbaum and Lurigio, 1994; Lurigio and Skogan, 1994). The emphasis on performing nonemergency work and interacting with citizens has also led to disaffection as officers referred to duties performed in connection with community policing as "social work" or "not real police work" (Miller, 1999: 103; Rosenbaum and Lurigio, 1994: 306).

If community policing is to be successfully implemented, research suggests that specific conditions must be met to overcome these types of structural obstacles to its acceptance. Resentment can occur when officers are forced to make changes that they feel have been thrust on them by "desk cops" unfamiliar with policing realities. In one city this was avoided when higher-ups employed participatory management (Miller, 1999: 198). In the end it may be easier to implement community policing if the changes involved do not represent such a dramatic departure from previous policing styles. In Holland, Sweden, and Canada, community policing has been embraced, most likely because community policing is consistent with the traditional forms of police organization in those countries (Mawby, 1999).

The reorientation of patrol activities and efforts to jump-start community crime prevention are sometime packaged and sold to communities as attempts to empower communities and to dramatically change the structure of authority in crime fighting. This requires, of course, that the community wants to have more contact with the police. This is not always the case, particularly in cities where minorities have been subject to police harassment and brutality. In these neighborhoods, community leaders are reluctant to support measures like community policing which are specifically designed to increase the number of police in the community and therefore citizen's contact with the police (Lyons, 1999; Rosenbaum and Lurigio, 1994).

One study of community policing in Seattle, Washington indicates that the implementation of community policing may only constitute a modest break from traditional law enforcement practices (Lyons, 1999). In reality, community policing may empower the police more than it empowers the communities in which it is implemented (Lyons, 1999). Analysis of the stories told by police officials, community activists, and city officials revealed that community policing uses stories to encourage deference to the state and deflect critical scrutiny from the city's shift to an emphasis on law and order. Stories about policing as professional fear reduction through problem-solving partnerships thus helped to limit the scope of law (Lyons, 1999: 172).

In a similar vein, scholars who draw on the work of the French philosopher Michel Foucault criticize community policing for the myriad ways it enhances disciplinary surveillance, allowing police to penetrate, and ultimately to dominate, the community. Behavior in which the police are more involved with youth – providing youth centers, for example – and more involved with residents in their homes blurs the line between state and society (Scheingold, 1991: 189). In this way, state power becomes projected into and through "a community mobilized against criminal behavior and incipient criminality, such as graffiti, disorderly conduct and the like" (ibid.).

Nonstate policing

As mentioned earlier, nonstate actors are also responsible for policing. In the latter part of the twentieth century, around the world there has been a significant increase in the number of policing functions performed by nonstate or private actors, or private policing. Individuals engaged in private policing – security guards, private investigators, bouncers – may be performing similar activities to the public police, like investigation of crime, providing property and personal protection, surveillance activity, and order maintenance. The rapid growth in private police has been attributed to a variety of factors including socioeconomic changes, the increase of corporate involvement in public life, and an increase in the number of large private spaces, such as shopping centers, to be policed (Reichman, 1987).

Though the activities in which they engage are similar, private police can be distinguished from public police in two main ways. First, private police generally operate almost entirely in the private sphere, maintaining order and minimizing disruption within private spaces. Second, in the vast majority of cases their role enforcing the criminal law is restricted to seeking the assistance of state-oriented police (Reiss, 1987: 26). Operating in the private sphere, without the authority to enforce criminal law, deprives private police of the legitimacy for their action that public police possess (ibid.).

Some situations involving policing by private citizens have their roots in a state authority having relinquished policing power. In other words, private policing sometimes originates from the state having turned over policing functions to private individuals or institutions. This has certainly been the case with the policing of inmate populations in a number of countries – Great Britain, the United States, and Australia – where private prisons have been created. In the United States, large increases in the prison population, and desires for reduced cost, has resulted in the widespread creation of private prisons. Frequently, for-profit private prisons operated in the United States are built and run by private companies. States and the federal government then contract with private prisons to provide for the incarceration of inmates. In Great Britain, the privatization of policing has led to "civilianization" of police posts in which jobs normally performed by sworn personnel are instead carried out by less expensive civilian officers (Johnston, 1992: 55).

"Alternative policing" which involves community residents is another form of nonstate policing. Though citizens are doing the policing, alternative policing can be distinguished from community policing in that in alternative policing, the community plays a much greater role in criminal law enforcement. For example, in most community policing regimes, the citizens' main role is an advisory one. Citizens may provide information about lawbreakers, but do little if any actual policing. Alternative policing, by contrast, involves actual policing of part of the community or policing of particular types of conflicts by nonstate actors, frequently communities and interest groups. Alternative policing styles have been identified in rural Alaska, the Philippines, Peru, Italy, China, Brazil, South Africa, and Indonesia.

Alternative styles of policing need not originate from state inaction. Rather, communities and interest groups may themselves create alternate policing options because they view the state as ill equipped to provide services. Alternate policing styles may also develop because citizens question the state's legitimacy to intervene in the community. Developing countries where the duty to maintain order is spread through the wider community, rather than being only the duty of the states, are particularly amenable to alternate policing styles (Findlay and Zvekić, 1993). Alternative policing styles involving residents of two developing countries, China and Indonesia, are described below.

In Indonesia, the neighborhood policing system is called a "self-motivated" or "self-willed" safety system in order to highlight the active role that the community should take in policing. One of the main components of the neighborhood policing system is the neighborhood patrol, which is made up of men (usually heads of households) between 18 and 50 years old. The men take turns patrolling urban neighborhoods between 9 p.m. and 4 a.m. These patrols, which received official recognition by the Indonesian police system in the early 1980s, draw on traditions established when the country was a Dutch colony which empowered village chiefs to form patrols in which all village residents were required to participate (Reksodiputro and Purnianti, 1993).

Though participation in the patrols in now noncompulsory, in more cohesive rural areas there is social pressure to participate in the common defense of the neighborhood. This is less true in the cities themselves, where the patrols exist, but hired individuals take the place of residents. The patrol groups are supported by an administrative organization that collects money to defray the expenses of patrols, including the purchasing of batteries for searchlights, and coffee and cigarettes (Reksodiputo and Purnianti, 1993).

In the Philippines, the *barangay*, a settlement of 30 to 100 families, is the country's smallest territorial unit. Though barangays operate at the local level, they provide services that in other countries are provided by the national government, including agricultural support services, health and social welfare services, and the maintenance of the justice system. In Quezon City, located in the metropolitan area around Manila, alternative policing has developed which gives policing authority to groups composed entirely of civilian volunteers as part of the Barangay Ronda System (Leones, 1993).

Though the Barangay Ronda system is not the only police power in the barangays – there are professional police affiliated with the state that also have responsibility to police the barangays – the power given to citizens in these groups is far greater than even the most ambitious attempt to "empower" citizens under community policing regimes. The Barangay Ronda's duties are similar to that of uniformed law enforcement officers. In addition to reporting suspicious-looking characters and monitoring of the areas like citizens who do "neighborhood watch," citizens working as part of the rondas also receive and investigate citizen complaints, provide physical security to local officials, and coordinate evacuations in emergencies (Leones, 1993).

CONTROLLING THE POLICE

One method of holding the police accountable is through public appeals to political leaders who hold some supervisory duties over the police. The system for holding the police accountable by using political means is related in part to how the police are organized. National police systems, like that in France, are frequently supervised by an agency or minister of the national government, and may be held accountable at the national political level (Loveday, 1999: 132). In systems that are more fragmented, with police at many levels, control of the police is more roundabout. In the United States, if the police serve under an elected sheriff, or if the head of the police is appointed by the city's mayor, it may be possible for voters to hold those officials accountable for police misbehavior (Loveday, 1999).

In the United States, attempts to hold police accountable for their actions have included the use of criminal process against officers, civil rights suits seeking damages for violations of individual rights, and suits seeking injunctive relief. In 1991 the acquittal of several Los Angeles police officers for the beating of Rodney King is a prominent example of the ways in which the criminal process can fail to hold police officers accountable for misconduct. Suits requesting money damages may also fail to serve as a deterrent for large police department, even if the plaintiff wins. For instance, members of Los Angeles Police Department have told researchers that they view damages awards as a reasonable price to pay to use violent actions that deter crime (Skolnick and Fyfe, 1993). The assumption is that given Los Angeles' size, paying out damage awards costs the city less than increasing the number of police officers to an adequate number (Skolnick and Fyfe, 1993).

Attempts to hold the police accountable for their actions can also occur when criminal defendants challenge police behavior. These defendants often argue that an individual police officer violated one of their rights under the United States Constitution. Defendants' rights under the Fourth, Fifth, and Sixth Amendments restrict many aspects of the investigative process including police searches of persons and property, the arrest and detention of individuals, and the interrogation of suspects. Violation of defendants' Constitutional rights has important implications for law enforcement. For instance, the Fourth Amendment to the United States Constitution prohibits unreasonable searches and seizures. If the police wish to search a suspect's home, in most cases the prohibition against unreasonable searches and seizures requires that they obtain a search warrant. If in the collection of evidence the police are found to have violated a defendant's Constitutional rights under the Fourth Amendment then under the exclusionary rule, a rule established by the United States Supreme Court, the evidence cannot be used at the defendant's trial.

In the context of perhaps one of the most famous cases in American criminal procedure, *Miranda v. Arizona*, scholars have long debated whether the announcement of constitutional principles has any affect on police behavior (see Leo and

Thomas, 1998). In 1966 in *Miranda*, the Supreme Court announced procedures designed to make police interrogation less coercive. The Court based its decision in part on the coercive nature of the current practices described in police interrogation manuals. The Court found that custodial interrogations subject the suspect to an inherently coercive environment with many psychological pressures. Therefore, the Court placed the burden on the government to inform suspects of their rights to silence, to inform suspects that anything thay say can be used against them, and to inform suspects of their rights to counsel.

Since the *Miranda* decision, sociolegal scholars have evaluated empirically police interrogation procedures. One of the most detailed of these studies was based on one researcher's observation of 122 interrogations conducted by 45 different police detectives who were part of a large, urban police department (Leo, 1996). The law requires that before commencing interrogation the interrogating officer must recite the familiar *Miranda* warnings. If the suspect invokes either the right to counsel or the right to silence, the interrogation is to cease. In the vast majority of interrogations in the study, the defendants waived their rights and the interrogation proceeded. In 4 percent of interrogations observed, the detectives continued questioning the defendant despite the suspect's invocation. Though any evidence that the defendant provided could not be used in the prosecution's case-in-chief, by speaking the defendant could provide damaging information. The detectives who continued to question defendants were aware of this fact, but neglected to reveal to the defendants that if they chose to testify, anything they said could be used against them on cross-examination (Leo, 1996: 276).

In the years since the *Miranda* decision, several scholars have argued that the procedures mandated by the Court have handcuffed the police, preventing them from gathering evidence needed to convict criminal defendants. The study of police interrogations describe above suggests otherwise. In most cases, 64 percent of interrogations observed, the detectives were successful – the suspect provided detectives with incriminating information. The study also revealed that detectives use a number of tactics to get the suspect to confess. The most successful of these tactics involved appealing to the suspect's conscience, identifying contradictions in the suspect's story, and praising or flattering the suspect (Leo, 1996: 278). The study concludes that the tactics that the Court frowned on in *Miranda* are exceedingly common, a finding that suggests that the courts have limited power to create rules that actually change police behavior.

CONCLUSION

Much of the recent research on the police has explored the effectiveness and operation of recent innovations and policing regimes, such as community policing or order maintenance policies. There remain a number of important areas for further research. More observational studies of the police that explore and analyze officers' actions are needed. In this regard, such research might examine the relationship between police officers' role and their behavior, and the relationship between police norms and rule making.

One area of particular interest to law and society scholars is police officers' approach to the law. There is much room for research on the relationship between the dictates of the law and the views of those responsible for enforcing it. Research is needed that further explores police officers' guidelines for enforcing the law and their knowledge and understanding of legal rules and principles.

Finally, there is a need for more comparative studies of policing systems – examination of policing systems cross-nationally. This involves in part studying policing regimes that have been little studied – such as regimes in Africa and in the recently democratized countries of Eastern Europe. Particular attention should be paid to alternative policing regimes and nonstate policing in other countries as well. In each area, special attention should be paid to the structure, function, and utility of recent innovations. Research in each of these areas will greatly increase the breadth, depth, and comprehensiveness of research on police and policing.

References

Adams, Kenneth (1999) "What we know about police use of force," in *Use of Force by the Police*. Washington, DC: National Institute of Justice, pp. 1–14.

Bayley, David H. (1985) *Patterns of Policing: A Comparative International Analysis*. New Brunswick, NJ: Rutgers University Press.

Bell, Jeannine (2002) *Policing Hatred: Law Enforcement, Civil Rights and Hate Crime*. New York: New York University Press.

Boyd, Elizabeth, Hamner, Karl M., and Berk, Richard (1996) "Motivated by hatred or prejudice: Categorization of hate-motivated crimes in two police divisions," *Law & Society Review* 30: 819–50.

Findlay, Mark and Zvekić, Uglieša (eds.) (1993) *Alternate Policing Styles, Cross Cultural Perspectives*. Boston: Kluwer Law and Taxation Publishers.

Goldstein, Joseph A. (1960) "Police discretion not to invoke the criminal process: Low-visibility decisions in the administration of justice," *Yale Law Journal* 69: 543–94.

Greenfeld, Lawrence A., Langan, Patrick A., and Smith, Steven K. (1997) *Police Use of Force: Collection of National Data*. Washington, DC: US Department of Justice, National Institute of Justice.

Harris, David A. (1999) "The stories, the statistics, and the law: Why 'driving while black' matters," *Minnesota Law Review* 84: 265.

Hirschel, J. David and Hutchinson, Ira W. III (1992) "Female spouse abuse and the police response: The Charlotte, North Carolina experiment," *Journal of Criminal Law and Criminology*, 83: 73–119.

Johnston, Les (1992) *The Rebirth of Private Policing*. London: Routledge.

Knowles, John, Persico, Nicola, and Todd, Petra (1999) "Racial bias in motor vehicle searches: Theory and evidence," *Journal of Political Economy* 109: 203–29.

LaFave, Wayne R. (1962) "The police and non enforcement of the law – Part II," *Wisconsin Law Review* 1962: 179–239.

Leo, Richard A. (1996) "Inside the interrogation room," *The Journal of Criminal Law and Criminology* 86: 266–303.

Leo, Richard A. and Thomas, George C. III (eds.) (1998) *The Miranda Debate: Law, Justice, and Policing*. Boston: Northeastern University Press.

Leones, Celia S. (1993) "Alternative policing in the Philippines," in Mark Findlay and Uglieša Zvekić (eds.), *Alternate Policing Styles, Cross Cultural Perspectives*. Boston: Kluwer Law and Taxation Publishers, pp. 101–8.

Loveday, B. (1999) "Government accountability and the police," in in R.I. Mawby (ed.), *Policing Across the World: Issues for the 21st Century*. London: UCL Press, pp. 132–50.

Lundman, Richard J. (1994) "Demeanor or crime? The midwest city police-citizen encounters study," *Criminology* 32: 631–56.

Lurigio, Arthur J. and Skogan, Wesley G. (1994) "Winning the hearts and minds of police officers: An assessment of staff perceptions of community policing in Chicago," *Crime and Delinquency* 40: 315–30.

Lyons, William (1999) *The Politics of Community Policing: Rearranging the Power to Punish*. Ann Arbor: University of Michigan Press.

Martin, Susan E. (1994) "Outsider within the station house: The impact of race and gender on black women police," *Social Problems* 41(3): 383–400.

Mawby, Rob (1999) "Approaches to comparative analysis: The impossibility of becoming an expert on everywhere," in in R.I. Mawby (ed.), *Policing Across the World: Issue for the 21st Century*. London: UCL Press, pp. 187–203.

Miller, Susan L. (1999) *Gender and Community Policing: Walking the Talk*. Boston: Northeastern University Press.

Oberweis, Trish and Musheno, Michael (1999) "Policing identities: Cop decision making and the constitution of citizens," *Law and Social Inquiry* 24: 897–923.

Reichel, Phillip L. (1994) *Comparative Criminal Justice Systems*. Englewood Cliffs, NJ: Prentice Hall.

Reichman, Nancy (1987) "The widening web of surveillance: Private policing unraveling deception claims," in Clifford D. Shearing and Philip C. Stenning (eds.), *Private Policing*. Newbury Park, CA: Sage, pp. 247–65.

Reiss, Albert J. (1987) "The legitimacy of intrusion into private space," in Clifford D. Shearing and Philip C. Stenning (eds.), *Private Policing*. Newbury Park, CA: Sage, pp. 19–44.

Reksodiputro, Mardjono and Purnianti, Yanti (1993) "Community oriented policing in urban Indonesia," in Mark Findlay and Uglieša Zvekić (eds.), *Alternate Policing Styles, Cross Cultural Perspectives*. Boston: Kluwer Law and Taxation Publishers, pp. 91–100.

Rosenbaum, Dennis P. and Lurigio, Arthur J. (1994) "An inside look at community policing reform: Definitions, organizational changes, and evaluation findings," *Crime and Delinquency* 40: 299–314.

Russell, Kathryn (1998) *The Color of Crime*. New York: New York University Press.

Scheingold, Stuart (1991) *The Politics of Street Crime*. Philadelphia: Temple University Press.

Skolnick, Jerome H. (1996) *Justice Without Trial: Law Enforcement in Democratic Society*. New York: Wiley.

Skolnick, Jerome H. and Bayley, David H. (1988) *Community Policing: Issues and Practices Around the World*. Washington, DC: National Institute of Justice.

Skolnick, Jerome H. and Caplovitz, Abigail (2001) "Guns, drugs and profiling: Ways to target guns and minimize racial profiling," *Arizona Law Review* 43: 413–37.

Skolnick, Jerome H. and Fyfe, James (1993) *Above the Law: Police and the Excessive Use of Force*. New York: The Free Press.

Smith, Douglas A. and Visher, Christy A. (1981) "Street-level justice: Situational determinants of police arrest decisions," *Social Problems* 29: 167–7.

Waddington, P.A.J. (1999) "Armed and unarmed policing," in in R.I. Mawby (ed.), *Policing Across the World: Issues for the 21st Century*. London: UCL Press, pp. 151–66.

Walker, Samuel (1993) *Taming the System: The Control of Discretion in Criminal Justice, 1950–1990*. New York: Oxford University Press.

Weitzer, Ronald (2000) "Racialized policing: Residents' perceptions in three neighborhoods," *Law and Society Review* 34: 129–55.

Wilson, James Q. (1973) *Varieties of Police Behavior: The Management of Law and Order in Eight Communities*. New York: Atheneum.

Worden, Robert E. (1989) "Situational and attitudinal explanations of police behaviors: A theoretical reappraisal and empirical assessment." *Law & Society Review* 23: 667–711.

9

Professional Power: Lawyers and the Constitution of Professional Authority

Tanina Rostain

Until the 1970s, American sociolegal research on the legal profession was in the grip of a functionalist framework, which assumed that professions arose organically to address the problem of order in modern society (Durkheim, 1957; Parsons, 1954). According to functionalist accounts, the role of professions was to mediate between individual interests, on the one hand, and state institutions, on the other. Presupposing this view, sociolegal studies of lawyers typically focused on whether lawyers complied with accepted professional norms, which presumably articulated the appropriate role of lawyers in modern society, without questioning the genesis, function, or legitimacy of the norms themselves. Thus some studies examined whether lawyers served as independent counselors, whose function was to mediate between clients' interests and societal values (Smigel, 1964), or as zealous partisans, whose job within the adversary system was to advocate single-mindedly on behalf of clients (Blumberg, 1967; Macaulay, 1979). Other studies investigated the underlying bases for lawyers' failures to adhere to codes of ethics, which supposedly reflected the norms governing lawyers' roles (Carlin, 1966; Handler, 1967). In focusing on the divergence between the profession's normative expectations and the realities of everyday practice, this early sociolegal scholarship engaged in its own variation of the "gap studies" then prevalent within sociolegal scholarship, which focused on the failures of the state to deliver on the promises of liberal democracy (Abel, 1980; Garth and Sarat, 1998).

In the 1970s, new theories emerged that rejected functionalist approaches in favor of accounts that viewed the institutions of professionalism as the result of a collective mobility project undertaken to attain economic rewards and prestige (Abbott, 1988; Freidson, 1986, 1973; Larson, 1977). The new paradigm represented a shift from theories of structure to theories of action (MacDonald, 1995) and gave rise to empirical questions as to how people " 'make' or 'accomplish' professions by their activities" (Freidson, 1983: 27). Whereas the construction and deployment of professional power had remained largely invisible within functionalist theories, which had taken lawyers' status and legitimacy in society for granted, the changed focus on professionals as social actors brought the problem of power to the foreground.

This theoretical reorientation ignited an explosion of sociolegal research on the legal profession. During the last 30 years, empirical research seized on questions of how power is produced, amassed, legitimated, and deployed by lawyers, and contested by competitors, clients, and others, to investigate the many varied sites of organized and day-to-day professional activity. Recent sociolegal investigations of lawyers have focused variously on the interactions among professionals' market activities, their deployment of expert knowledge in their work, and the different – and often conflicting – ideologies they invoke to justify their protected status in the market, the value of their services to clients, and the importance of their role in society at large. While these studies all share a fundamental preoccupation with the problem of professional power, they differ about its constitution and exercise. Many studies, drawing on Marxist and Weberian thought, investigate how the institutions of professionalism advance the material and status interests of lawyers (e.g., Abel, 1989; Heinz and Laumann, 1982; Nelson, 1988) Pursuing insights from the work of Foucault and Bourdieu (e.g., Bourdieu, 1987), other studies focus on the social construction of power to examine how professional authority itself is constituted in the ideological claims and discourse of lawyers (Sarat and Felstiner, 1995; Shamir, 1995). Read together, these studies illuminate the multiple dimensions of professional power.

This chapter describes sociolegal investigations of lawyers and the legal profession since the 1970s. Consistent with the emphasis found in sociolegal research in the United States, I concentrate on studies of American lawyers, bringing in relevant comparative and international studies when available. Because the professional project is typically defined around activities involving the provision of legal services to clients, I focus on studies of practicing lawyers. I do not address studies of judges, lawmakers, or legal academics, though the activities of these groups of lawyers undoubtedly play important legitimating functions in the construction of lawyers' professional authority (e.g., Halliday, 1987; Shamir, 1995).[1]

Sociolegal research on the legal profession can be organized along several lines, including theoretical, methodological, and historical lines. This chapter organizes this research to offer multiple views of the spheres in which lawyers work. Lawyers exercise professional power in various arenas, including in their public organized bar activities and their day-to-day work (Nelson and Trubeck, 1992). The first section of this chapter describes sociohistorical studies of the American legal profession, which have focused principally on the organized bar's efforts to coalesce around and effectively press a shared economic and ideological agenda. Scholars adopting a historical lens have debated whether the goal of creating and controlling the market for lawyers' services adequately accounted for lawyers' professional activities or whether ideological interests also played a role (Abel, 1989; Halliday, 1987; Shamir, 1995).

Although the most visible arena, organized activities are but one of many in which lawyers construct and deploy power. This chapter next turns to sociolegal studies of specific practice settings, where lawyers enact conceptions of professionalism in their day-to-day representation of clients. Research has established a dramatic divide in the American private bar between lawyers who represent corporations, and who enjoy greater economic rewards and social standing, and those who represent individuals, who are at the lower end of the economic and social hierarchy of the bar (Heinz and Laumann, 1982 Heinz, Nelson, Laumann, and Michelson, 1998). The two "hemispheres" of private practice provide a useful map to organize the wealth of sociolegal research in this area. In particular, this frame highlights important differences between the corporate and individual sphere in the specific tasks lawyers perform for their clients, the expert and ideological claims they make, and the organizational structures of their work. Within each sphere, too, sociolegal studies have exposed significant variations in the way lawyers construct professional power, and in particular how they accede to, resist, or reframe market incentives in advancing their professional agendas.

While the vast majority of lawyers represent private clients, many are also found in government or public interest law (Carson, 1999: 24). Public interest or "cause" lawyering has drawn significant attention from sociolegal scholars as an alternative sphere in which professional power is constructed and deployed. Studies of cause lawyering have primarily focused on liberal/left lawyering. This research illuminates lawyers' efforts to bridge the gap between the egalitarian premises underlying law's authority in a liberal democracy, which hold that everyone has equal access to law, and the exercise of professional authority, which posits that access is mediated through special expertise. In contrast to cause lawyers, government lawyers have not been the subject of sustained empirical investigation. The dearth of studies in this area make it difficult to explore questions of how lawyers in government practice might seek to appropriate, contain, or transform the power that the state places at their disposal.

THE ORGANIZED BAR

Sociohistorical investigations of the American legal profession have concentrated on the workings of the organized bar and its elite members, a visible locus of lawyers' collective efforts to demarcate markets and advance political and ideological agendas. Such research has considered the legal profession's collective influence on lawmaking in areas involving regulation of lawyers and competitors – where lawyers seek to exercise direct control of the market for their services – and in areas more broadly affecting the material and ideological interests of lawyers and their clients. This scholarship debates whether lawyers' organized activities should be understood as attempts to create and protect a monopoly over the market for their services – the market control thesis – or also reflect the pursuit of social status or independent ideological commitments.

Abel's study of the American legal profession from the late nineteenth century through the 1960s makes a strong case for the market control hypothesis. As described by Abel, the American bar's growing power depended on obtaining a monopoly over the market for legal services, by asserting control over the "production of producers" and over the "production by producers." In the early years, the organized bar gained control over the supply and training of new lawyers by introducing and formalizing educational requirements and bar standards, excluding immigrants and their sons, and reinforcing barriers already in place for women and minorities. In subsequent decades, the American bar obtained control over the "production by producers." It established restrictions on competition from out-

siders, and despite populist opposition, by 1930 had secured an expansive monopoly, which extended well beyond advocacy in court to such matters as giving legal
advice, drafting instruments, and transferring deeds (Abel, 1989: 26, 113). During
the same period, the bar sought through prohibitions on advertising and other
measures to dampen competition from within, particularly from the lower stratum
of the bar (Abel, 1989: 115–22). Comparative studies of legal professions around
the world reveal parallel historical trajectories in common law countries. In contrast,
the history of legal professions in civil code countries does not conform to the
market control thesis, exhibiting different types of relations among the lawyers,
the state, universities, and the market. In particular, these studies demonstrate a
much more central role for the state in the creation of law-related occupations and
little evidence of a collective project actively undertaken by lawyers as a whole (Abel
and Lewis, 1988a, 1988b, 1989; Abel, 1988; Rueschemeyer, 1973).

Abel treats professional ideology primarily as an instrument to advance market
control. Other sociohistorical scholars maintain that lawyers often pursue ideological interests independent of their function in furthering collective market interests (Halliday, 1987; Gordon, 1983, 1984; Shamir, 1995). Gordon has argued that
the specific content of lawyers' ideologies – their own explanations and justifications
for the positions they espouse – has behavioral and social consequences (Gordon,
1983, 1984). According to Gordon, lawyers view themselves as having obligations
to a universal legal order – a set of rules and procedures for the regulation of social
relations consistent with prevailing political understandings of the good. Consequently, they should be understood as "struggling to work out a relationship between their beliefs and their practices – between the ideal and the actual – with
which they could live in comfort" (Gordon, 1984: 53). Halliday argues that during
significant periods of its history, the American legal profession has devoted collective
effort to advancing civic professionalism, more specifically to creating and safe-
guarding an autonomous legal realm not subject to the vagaries of politics (Halliday,
1987; cf. Powell, 1988). Historical studies of lawyers in Europe and the United
States suggest that they have been active participants in the rise of Western political
liberalism – a role not adequately explained by market control (Halliday and
Karpik, 1997).

Through a study of the American bar during the 1930s, Shamir argues that the
market control thesis does not explain the response of elite lawyers to the creation of
an administrative arena under the New Deal. Instead of seizing on the new administrative regime to expand the market for legal services – as market control theory
would predict – the organized bar devoted considerable energy to criticizing the
creation of administrative mechanisms on the ground that they violated fundamental principles of due process. Shamir argues that lawyers resisted the pluralist
conception of law advanced by the administration in favor of a specific understanding of law that maintained and reinforced their privileged status. The organized bar
opposed new administrative sources of law, because they "threatened to compromise
the asserted distinct professional identity of lawyers and to subvert the hierarchical
organization of the field around the centrality of the courts" (Shamir, 1995: 124).

Halliday and Shamir differ as to whether professional ideology is best understood
as reflecting normative commitments to the values of liberal democracy, which
requires consideration of lawyers' motivations (Halliday, 1999) or should be assimilated into a larger account of status enhancement (Shamir, 1995), which stresses the
effects of their conduct. But this theoretical difference may be less significant than it

first appears. On the one hand, an analysis based on motivations, such as Halliday's, must take into account that lawyers' conceptions of law's "ideals" are socially constructed. Lawyers' motivations are shaped by their location in a social field in which their status as guardians of the legal order is reinforced and legitimated (cf. Shamir, 1995: 129; Bourdieu, 1987). On the other hand, any normative claim can arguably be explained by its function in enhancing its producer's authority; the concept of status enhancement, consequently, may add little explanatory value.

During most of the twentieth century, the American bar was able to control the market for their services. Since the late 1970s, American lawyers' power to limit competition from outsiders has begun to erode. With the application of antitrust prohibitions to lawyers' collective activities, the organized bar has been increasingly impeded in its efforts to enlist the state to police the unauthorized practice of law, particularly when such practice is engaged in by other professionals such as account-ants (Wolfram, 2000; Abel, 1989: 229). As a consequence, American lawyers have been forced to confront increasing and direct competitive pressures from alternative service providers in both the corporate and personal legal services sectors. At the same time, the bar has not been able to assert control over the number of new entrants into the profession, which has expanded as a result of greater access to higher education, increased demand for legal service, and the elimination of discrim-inatory barriers (Abel, 1989). In the United States, the ratio of lawyers to general population has more than doubled between 1970 and 1988 (Sander and Williams, 1989: 433).[2] This extraordinary growth has resulted in intensified competition within the profession.

Lawyers have taken refuge in specialization, which has made it more difficult for lawyers as a group to identify common economic or ideological interests as a basis for a collective agenda (Abel, 1989: 237; Heinz and Laumann, 1982; Heinz et al., 1998: 762). The growing fragmentation of the bar has been attributed to lawyers' own entrepreneurial ingenuity. As Nelson and Trubek observe, "the key to the economic and political success of American lawyers as a group has been their adaptiveness. But the cost has been the erosion of a distinctive professional tradition and the absence of centralized power within the profession capable of enforcing a particular vision of professional ideals" (1992: 13).

Sociolegal research on specific practice settings offers a detailed mapping of the divergent ideological, epistemic, and organizational paths taken by lawyers in pursuit of clients during the last several decades. The next two sections of this chapter organize these studies around the divide in the private bar between lawyers who represent corporations and those who represent individuals, a divide that was already well entrenched by the mid-1970s (Heinz and Laumann, 1982). Corporate and personal services lawyers differ along a number of variables including: social background (personal lawyers come from less prestigious social backgrounds); educational background (corporate lawyers come from elite national law schools whereas personal services lawyers are from local schools); substantive areas of specialization (corporate and personal services lawyers each practice in areas rele-vant to their respective clients' needs); practice setting (corporate lawyers work in large firms whereas personal services lawyers work in small or solo firms); prestige associated with practice (corporate practice is accorded significantly greater prestige than personal legal services); and income (the income of corporate lawyers far outpaces that of personal services lawyers, though successful personal injury lawyers represent a notable exception) (Heinz and Laumann, 1982; Heinz et al., 1998;

Sander and Williams, 1989; Auerbach, 1976; Carlin, 1966). Each sphere of practice has given rise to distinct ideologies. Within each sphere, too, lawyers have generated varying local ideologies, areas of expertise, and workplace organizations to reinforce their professional authority and obtain clients.

THE CORPORATE BAR

During the twentieth century, lawyers in corporate firms were, by all economic and social measures, the elite of the bar. Sociolegal research has investigated the inter-relations among corporate lawyers' elevated social and economic standing, their construction and deployment of varying professional ideologies, and the organiza-tional structures within which they practice. Scholars have tied the ascendancy of this segment of the bar to the corporate law firm, which reached its heyday "circa 1960" (Galanter and Palay, 1991). They have also traced the recent decline of the professional power of lawyers in corporate firms – vis-à-vis clients and other pro-viders of corporate legal services – as they have faced intensified market pressures, their work has become highly specialized, and their firms have grown larger and more bureaucratic.

The "business lawyer" first appeared on the scene around the turn of the nine-teenth century, soon displacing the solo trial lawyer as the paradigm of professional-ism. In contrast to courtroom advocates – general practitioners who represented a range of clients – this new type of lawyer specialized in addressing the ongoing legal needs of corporate enterprises and business entrepreneurs (Galanter and Palay, 1991). As these lawyers expanded their work to include planning, counseling, negotiating, document drafting, and representation in other forums, their practice shifted from "the courtroom to the law office and the conference room" (Gordon, 1984: 59; Hobson, 1986; Lipartito, 1990). Law offices, which had been loose affiliations among lawyers who occasionally shared staff or clients, now took on a more formal structure. Under this new system, traditionally associated with Paul D. Cravath, clients "belonged" to the whole firm; lawyers worked in teams; proceeds and costs were shared among partners according to a predetermined formula; and associates were recruited from law school and progressed, under the tutelage of senior lawyers, toward partnership (Galanter and Palay, 1991: ch. 2). The training of associates built on the education they had received at a handful of elite schools, all of which employed the curriculum and pedagogic methods instituted by Christopher Langdell at Harvard in the late nineteenth century (LaPiana, 1994; Stevens, 1983). From the outset, business lawyers were criticized as captive to a narrow set of client interests (Berle, 1933; Hobson, 1986). Nevertheless, over the first half of the twen-tieth century, the locus of prestige and power shifted to the large corporate law firm. Galanter and Palay note that by 1960 "the traditional badges of the profession – an independent general practice rendering personal services to all sorts of people – were no longer the marks by which the truly 'professional' lawyer was identified. Instead it was large firm lawyers who embodied the professional ideal" (1991: 32).

With the advent of the corporate law firm, an ideology that tied claims of normative authority and practical expertise to the firm context emerged to legitimate the prerogatives of power enjoyed by corporate lawyers. In its stronger version, this ideology conceived of corporate practice as a "public calling" and anchored corpor-ate lawyers' authority in their role of mediating between their clients' interests and the societal values reflected in law (Brandeis, [1914] 1996; Gordon, 1988, 1990; Luban, 1988; Kronman, 1993). The weaker version of this ideology posited lawyers in corporate firms as ideally suited to counsel corporations to forego short-term benefits and act in their long-term interests. This version portrayed lawyers in elite firms as generalists, who had mastered the various aspects of corporate practice and could advise clients on all aspects of their business (Gordon, 1988, 1990; Kronman, 1993).

Just as the earlier paradigm of professionalism extolled the virtues of solo general practice, both versions of corporate professional ideology stressed the epistemic and motivational benefits of firm practice, which traditionally permitted lawyers to enjoy long-standing relationships with clients while maintaining independence from any single client. Stable relationships with corporate clients, formalized through broad retainer agreements, provided lawyers with detailed and wide-ranging knowledge of their clients' business operations, as well as the security to provide advice that clients might not want to hear, or so it was claimed. Independence from any one client played a parallel function. A large corporate clientele enhanced lawyers' expertise by exposing them to diverse areas of corporate law. A broad client base also supposedly empowered them to give unwelcome counsel and even to resist clients' directives to pursue goals deemed unwise (Gordon, 1988, 1990; Smigel, 1964). These attributes were enhanced by a loosely organized firm structure, which maximized lawyers' autonomy to determine the workplace conditions best suited to furthering their role (Smigel, 1964).

What is the evidence that corporate lawyers in representing clients ever acted on this ideology – particularly in its strong, socially constructive version? Data about lawyers' conversations with their clients, which are traditionally shrouded in confidentiality, are difficult to obtain. Gordon has argued that lawyers were historically sufficiently independent from their clients to act consistently with a socially constructive view of their role (Gordon, 1988, 1990; see also Carruthers and Halliday, 1998: 526–39). The contrary position has held that at least since the New Deal corporate lawyers were subordinate to their clients and single-mindedly pursued corporate interests so long as it inured to their – the lawyers' – benefit (Auerbach, 1976; Felstiner, 1998; see also Shamir, 1995).

The powerful socializing processes of large firm practice, and in particular its narrow focus on corporate representation, raises doubt as to whether corporate lawyers, even if they wanted to act as independent counselors, could ever maintain a perspective independent from their clients. A survey study of corporate practitioners in Chicago in the 1980s found that corporate lawyers strongly identified with client interests in the substantive areas in which they practiced (Nelson, 1988; see also Kagen and Rosen, 1985). Moreover, even though corporate lawyers adhered in the abstract to an independent counselor ideology, they reported that they rarely if ever disagreed with a client's proposed course of conduct (Nelson, 1988). (Research suggests that this socialization process begins even before entering corporate practice in law school: Granfield, 1992.)

Scholars have debated whether corporate lawyers have historically acted consistent with an independent counselor ideology. They agree that by the late twentieth century, the underlying conditions upon which the independent counselor ideology had been premised no longer existed. By the turn of the century, corporate law firms had grown exponentially in size and undergone significant bureaucratization. Whereas in the 1950s the largest firms numbered around 100 lawyers and few firms exceeded 50, 35 years later, the largest firms could count upward of one thousand lawyers and many employed several hundred lawyers (Galanter and Palay, 1991: 47; Thomas, Schwab, and Hansen, 2001). Scholars have ascribed this extraordinary growth to the interaction of various market factors, including the dramatic increase in the demand for corporate legal services (Nelson, 1988; Galanter and Palay, 1991; Thomas et al., 2001), the need to provide a greater range of specializations (Nelson, 1988; Flood, 1988; Spangler, 1986: 37), as well as growth dynamics internal to firms (Galanter and Palay, 1991).[3]

During this same period, firms' relationships to clients underwent a fundamental transformation. Corporations expanded their corporate law departments and moved their routine legal work in-house. Inside counsel became much more active in overseeing the work of outside firms, imposing budgetary limits, and shopping among different firms. Rather than entering into comprehensive long-term retainer agreements, corporations at the turn of the twentieth century employed firms in isolated and out of the ordinary transactions requiring highly specialized expertise. As a consequence, the balance of work done by corporate law firms shifted toward litigation and unique high-stakes transactions, a change that mirrored a substantial upsurge in corporate litigation, which had also become more complex and pro-tracted (Galanter and Palay, 1991). As the nature of outside corporate legal services shifted, technical expertise in narrow subspecialties grew at the expense of broad knowledge of corporate law and the business affairs of clients, which had been prerequisites to fulfilling an independent counselor function.

With these changes, an adversarial ideology that emphasized single-minded pur-suit of client interests became more pronounced. As noted by participants, by the 1990s corporate litigation was marked by a hyperadversarial orientation shaped by client expectations of "scorched earth/ take no prisoners" tactics and the absence of formal constraints imposed through judicial supervision or informal constraints anchored in a cohesive firm culture (ABA, 1998). This adversarial ethos has been successfully exported off-shore. As Dezalay and Garth show in a detailed study of international arbitration, American firms have marketed their technical expertise to transform international commercial arbitration into another arena of litigation "American-style" (1996: ch. 3; compare Boon and Flood, 1999).

Consistent with corporate firms' intensified focus on the business aspects of practice, a similarly aggressive partisan ethos took hold in transactional work. Historically, corporate lawyers were always active in identifying and developing commercial opportunities for their clients (Hobson, 1986; Lipartito, 1990), but their visibility in deal making and "creative legal engineering" reached unprecedented heights at the end of the twentieth century (McBarnet, 1992: 257). Prompted by the intensified focus on profit and competition within the business world, corporate lawyers took advantage of receptive political and regulatory climates to engage in a range of innovative private lawmaking, including such pioneering new legal devices as antitakeover mechanisms or "poison pills" (Powell, 1993), developing a global distressed debt market (Flood, 1995), and devising new tax avoidance instruments (McBarnet, 1992). Lawyers were energetic participants in the enactment of bank-ruptcy reforms in the United States that increased the earning potential and trans-formed the status of a once-derogated type of practice into a prestigious corporate specialization (Carruthers and Halliday, 1998: 444–9, 526–39). Demonstrating a similar entrepreneurial spirit, Silicon Valley lawyers embraced risk-sharing strategies during the technology boom of the 1980s and 1990s to absorb the uncertainty of new start-ups (Friedman, Gordon, Pirie, and Whatley, 1989; Suchman and Cahill, 1996).[4] The combination of firm growth, intensified business ethos and hyperpartisanship has resulted in intricate "tangled loyalties," which law firms have been required to address through increasingly complex formal and informal conflict-checking systems (Shapiro, 2002). Scholars have begun to document comparable practice trends in countries that do not share an Anglo-American legal tradition – even in such places as reputedly lawyer-phobic as Japan (Milhaupt and West, 2002). As entrepreneurial corporate legal services proliferated, the ideology of corporate practice shifted. If corporate firm lawyers in the 1960s tended to premise their professional authority on claims of broad legal and business expertise and independence from particular clients, corporate lawyers at the end of the century were more likely to emphasize their highly specialized knowledge, aggressive business attitude, and enthusiastically partisan orientation.[5]

The shift from independent counselor to single-minded partisan may signal the beginning of a decline of corporate lawyers' professional power. Under the logic of the former ideology, corporate lawyers were to be accorded professional autonomy because, it was claimed, they were able to resist economic pressures exerted by their clients and gave socially constructive advice (or, at the very least, counseled clients in accordance with their long-term interests). Whether corporate lawyers will be able to vest their professional authority in a more purely partisan construction of their role is unclear. As skepticism has grown in the United States that corporate lawyers are willing to – or can – control their clients' unlawful conduct, the state has begun to exert control over aspects of practice traditionally left to self-regulation. (One indication that corporate lawyers' discretionary authority has been curtailed in the wake of recent corporate scandals is the enactment in 2002 of the Sarbanes Oxley Act, which requires up-the-ladder reporting of potential securities law violations.) Meanwhile, corporate lawyers themselves appear increasingly eager to divest themselves of a distinct professional persona. Large law firms are beginning to imitate the structure of professional service firms and adopt the rubric of consultancy. Hoping to emulate the success of large accounting firms, some large American firms were, at the turn of the twenty-first century, marketing their services in the economistic idiom of "value added" and shifting from selling legal services to "products" (Rosen, 2003; cf. Thomas et al., 2001). These trends are also apparent to in the international sphere (Dezalay and Sugarman, 1995).

The ideology of inside counsel has followed a parallel trajectory as that of corporate lawyers in corporate firms. Inside counsel, who as recently as the early 1980s were widely perceived as second-class citizens of the corporate bar (Spangler, 1986: ch. 3; Heinz and Laumann, 1982), seized on the decline of the corporate law firm to assert that the locus of professional power and prestige had moved in-house to corporate law departments. During the time that these departments expanded and the legal matters they handled grew in number and complexity, an inside counsel "movement" emerged that extolled general counsel's autonomy and decision-making authority within the corporate structure (Chayes and Chayes, 1985; Rosen, 1989).

This construction of professionalism appears to have been short-lived. Because in-house lawyers have a single client, the structural conditions that might enable them to resist managerial directives have been absent. A study of corporate counsel in the late twentieth century found that even though they typically ascribed to traditional characterizations of their role as "cops" or "counselors," in practice they overwhelmingly deferred to managers. The study further identified an emerging entrepreneurial conception of the inside counsel's role that incorporated a managerial focus on short-term profits. These entrepreneurial corporate counsel, who identified themselves as business people, viewed law as a source of profit, to be marketed within the corporation and deployed aggressively in outside corporate dealings (Nelson and Nielson, 2000; cf. Gunz and Gunz, 2002).

Despite broad changes in firms and general counsel departments, corporate practice continued at the end of the twentieth century to command great prestige within the bar as a whole (Heinz and Laumann, 1982; Heinz et al., 1998; Sandefur, 2001). Heinz and Laumann argue that corporate lawyers derive a great part of their status from the power of the clients who hire them rather than from some independent capacity to amass and exercise professional power. Although some aspects of the status bestowed on corporate lawyers derive from claims of professional expertise (and specifically the legal complexity of the fields in which they practice), this complexity is itself the product of the economic strength of corporate clients, who have always been able to devote much greater financial resources to hiring lawyers to work at length on their problems (Sandefur, 2001). The glory of corporate practice is, in larger part, the refracted glory of working for the most powerful private institutions in the world (Heinz and Laumann, 1982). As corporations have grown even bigger and expanded globally, the glory of representing them can only have increased.

In addition to exploring the ways in which the structures and ideologies of corporate practice have incorporated, reflected, and recast market incentives, socio-legal scholarship has investigated the extent to which the construction of professional power relates to the continuing exclusion of women and minorities, particularly as partners. Following the elimination of discriminatory barriers in law school and bar admissions, the numbers of women and minorities joining the American legal profession have steadily increased since the 1970s. By the late 1990s, women represented 45 percent and minorities 20 percent of new entrants (Chambliss, 2000). Despite this increase, both are significantly underrepresented among the ranks of corporate lawyers, controlling for age, educational background, and other relevant variables (Rhode, 2000; Chambliss 2000: 9; Wilkins and Gulati, 1996). Gender and racial disparities reflect structural and ideological factors that reinforce one another. At the most basic level, women and minorities continue to report persistent bias and discriminatory treatment (Hensler and Resnik, 2000; ABA, 2001; Rhode, 2000: 39). In addition, women and minorities have suffered from the operation of informal "old boy" networks and the absence of representation in positions of power (Rhode, 2000, 2001; Chambliss and Uggen, 2000). For women, the extraordinary time demands of elite practice are inconsistent with bearing primary child care responsibilities – a role they are still by and large expected to assume (Chambers, 1989; Rhode, 1996; Hagan and Kay, 1995). The absence of minority lawyers to some extent reflects the exclusion of minorities from corporate boardrooms. In addition, law firms' recruitment and training practices have been shown systematically to disadvantage minority lawyers (Wilkins and Gulati, 1996).

Political commitments and professional ideology also play a part in the relative absence of women and blacks in corporate practice. Studies suggest that women and minority law students tend to have more liberal political values than their classmates and so are more likely to eschew corporate practice from the outset (Abel, 1989: 96).

Critiquing adversarial ideology, feminist scholars have further argued that the expectation that lawyers be combative is in tension with gendered socialization processes, which encourage women to be conciliatory and conflict adverse (Menkel-Meadow, 1985, 1994; Pierce, 1995; Rhode, 2000). More broadly, Wilkins has argued that the dominant ideology of the American bar is one of "bleached-out" professionalism, in which a lawyer' race, gender, religion, or ethnicity is irrelevant to his or her professional self-definition (1998a, 1998b).

PERSONAL LEGAL SERVICES

In the late twentieth century, lawyers who represented individuals – the other hemisphere of private practice in Heinz and Laumann's topography – came from less privileged backgrounds and enjoyed much less prestige than corporate lawyers. They also suffered from a significant income disparity, which grew during the 1980s and 1990s (Heinz and Laumann, 1982; Sander and Williams, 1989). Although the percentage of personal legal services lawyers was on the decline, they still comprised the majority of lawyers in private practice in the United States and nearly half the lawyers overall (Heinz et al., 1998; Sander and Williams, 1989; Carson, 1999). Lawyers who provided personal legal services, practicing in such areas as divorce, personal injury, residential real estate, and estate planning, were concentrated in solo or small firm practices of 10 lawyers or fewer (Heinz and Laumann, 1982: 442–3).

The personal services bar varies in clientele, market approach, degree of specialization, ideology, and organization of practice. These lawyers share a broad commitment to helping their clients navigate the legal system, but this commitment takes on very different forms in different practice settings. Studies of solo and small firm practitioners (Seron, 1996), franchise law firms (Van Hoy, 1997), divorce lawyers (Sarat and Felstiner, 1995; Mather, McEwen, and Maiman, 2001), personal injury lawyers (Kritzer, 1998a, 2001; Baker, 2001) and country lawyers (Landon, 1990) have illuminated the different constructions of professional power and authority deployed in this sphere and the varying organizational structures that underlie them.

With some exceptions, personal services lawyers do not lay claim to highly technical or formal expertise. As they report, the substantive areas of law in which they practice are not particularly complex; nor do they spend significant amounts of time engaged in legal research. (Cain, 1979; Seron, 1996; Van Hoy, 1997; Kritzer, 1990) The specific legal tasks they are called upon to perform – drafting divorce or personal injury complaints, closing documents and wills – are routine (and often delegated to paralegals or secretaries in their offices) (Seron, 1996; Van Hoy, 1997; Kritzer, 1990; cf. Landon, 1990: 90–1). The straightforward aspect of personal legal services work has given rise to two divergent trends in the style and organization of practice. Traditional forms of practice, typically found among solo and small firm lawyers, emphasize the human, problem-solving element of the work. Entrepreneurial forms, in contrast, focus on lowering costs and increasing efficiency through increased field specialization and the adoption of mass production and marketing technologies. Resisting the portrayal of personal services work as involving little legal knowledge, a third form of practice, which commands higher fees and greater status, marries a problem-solving orientation to technical substantive or procedural expertise (often imported from the arena of corporate civil litigation) (Seron, 1996;

Mather et al., 2001; Van Hoy; 1997). These personal legal services specialists, which include high-end divorce and white-collar defense lawyers, may occupy departments within larger corporate firms or work in small or mid-size "boutique" firms (Mather et al., 2001; Mann, 1985). This distinction among traditional, entrepreneurial, and specialized approaches to lawyering, while oversimplified, offers a useful topography of personal legal services practice (Seron, 1996; Mather et al., 2001).

Traditional personal services lawyers portray their goal as humanizing law and legal processes for their clients in their dealings with the legal system (Seron, 1996; Mather et al., 2001; Landon, 1990). Even if – as is typically the case – they have seen the same problem many times before, they claim to treat each client as an individual. According to traditional practitioners, the particulars of a client's life circumstances, rather than technical legal issues, provide the basis for intellectual challenge and professional engagement (Seron, 1996; Van Hoy, 1997; Schön, 1983). Divorce lawyers, for instance, have described their goal as that of assisting clients to shift from the immediate crisis precipitated by divorce to adjusting to the resulting long-term economic, social, and other life changes (Mather et al., 2001). Although traditional practitioners identified good listening and communication skills as their most important professional assets, they did not see their job as that of providing emotional or psychological support, and typically they referred their clients to outside counseling (Seron, 1996; Mather et al., 2001; Sarat and Felstiner, 1995). Instead they claimed to use these skills in the service of eliciting information and developing client rapport (Mather et al., 2001; Sarat and Felstiner, 1995). To the extent that legal knowledge was important, it was framed in terms of the ability to predict how a client's case will turn out – a form of inside or local knowledge of the workings of the legal system, developed through day-to-day experience, not formalized study (Seron, 1996; Sarat and Felstiner, 1995; Kritzer, 1998b). As Seron noted in her study of small firm and solo lawyers in New York, traditional lawyers spent many hours of their working day talking with clients on the phone and face to face and giving them emotional support.

In a study of divorce practice in Maine and New Hampshire, traditional lawyers described their role as that of the "reasonable" attorney (Mather et al., 2001). The reasonable attorney knew divorce law, and in particular the expected range of outcomes, remained "objective" – that is avoided overidentification with clients – and was honest and fair minded in dealings with opposing counsel and in court. With the advent of no-fault divorce and statutorily determined property division and nonnegotiable child support guidelines, the legal system in Maine and New Hampshire left few opportunities for undiluted advocacy (Mather et al., 2001: 117). Subjects of the study saw themselves as Brandeisian "counselors for the situation"; rather than fight for every last advantage sought by a client, they devoted their energies to transforming clients' expectations so that they were, in their lawyers' opinion, reasonable and practical.

By contrasting their reasonableness, objectivity and experience with a client's emotional volatility and vulnerability, divorce lawyers were able to negotiate the tension between affirming their own professional authority and respecting client autonomy (Mather et al., 2001: 92). This tension is implicit throughout law practice. In lawyers' assertions of professional authority, they invite deference to their expertise in an autonomous realm of knowledge. But the sphere of knowledge to which they lay claim includes normative considerations that overlap and intersect with interests, goals, and values that clients, under basic liberal democratic tenets, are supposed to define and choose for themselves (Halliday, 1987). This tension between the ideals of expert and client authority is particularly acute in the sphere of personal legal services, where, with the exception of a subgroup of specialists, practitioners do not lay claim to sophisticated or esoteric legal knowledge but instead base their professional authority on experiential knowledge of local legal institutions and the human consequences – social and economic – of participating in legal processes (Mather et al., 2001; Sarat and Felstiner, 1995).

This tension emerges in the various methods to which divorce lawyers resorted to get their clients to be "reasonable." Most common were "cooling-out" techniques – ranging from stalling the case to persuasion – which lawyers applied to assist clients to get beyond their immediate emotional reactions and view their situation "pragmatically" (though, occasionally, divorce lawyers characterized their job as educating overly passive or acquiescent clients about their legal rights in order to motivate them to seek settlement terms to which they were entitled). The lawyers interviewed contended that the level of emotional intensity of divorce justified their efforts to influence clients' perspectives so that they engaged in "rational" decision making (Mather et al., 2001: 92). But even in other areas of ordinary litigation lawyers expended considerable energies to shape the frame within which clients view their case (Kritzer, 1998a; Rosenthal, 1974). Thus a study of plaintiff personal injury lawyers found that they imposed on their clients their moral valuations of the different sources of potential money awards, convincing them of the rationality of relinquishing monetary claims above amounts covered by insurance (Baker, 2001). One apparent exception to this tendency was rural practice, which exhibited strong convergence between the social, political, and economic values of lawyers and their clients (Landon, 1990: ch. 7).

As Sarat and Felstiner (1995) have shown, the conflict between professional and client authority inevitably gives rise to power contests over the construction and meaning of clients' interactions with law that emerge in lawyer–client conversations. Offering a micro-analysis of client–lawyer interactions in divorce cases, Sarat and Felstiner have exposed the struggles between lawyers and clients to define the meaning of the divorce process in a client's life. As Sarat and Felstiner observed, in seeking to account for the failure of their marriages and their spouses' actions, clients invoked the language of excuse, responsibility, and fault. Their lawyers resisted such personalized terms, which were irrelevant to no-fault divorce, and sought to emphasize situational explanations, based on the workings of the legal system. In this process, "the lawyer's construction of meaning works to justify his authority and invites client dependence" (Sarat and Felstiner, 1995: 51). Sarat and Felstiner further showed how clients, rather than passively acquiescing in lawyers' accounts, engage in a struggle over the construction of the events, insisting on more individualized portrayals of social relationships (1995; see also Griffiths, 1986: 155). Ultimately, lawyers "win" this struggle, because they control access to the legal system and the benefits it bestows. In this sense, personal services lawyers of necessity dominate their clients (Abel, 1989; Sarat and Felstiner, 1995). But, as Sarat and Felstiner note, in conversation, clients "resist their lawyers' efforts to limit the scope of social life relevant to their interaction. As a result, they insure both the fragility of power in lawyer–client relations and the elusiveness of the meaning-making process" (Sarat and Felstiner, 1995: 52).[6]

Whereas traditional personal services lawyers here emphasized individualized attention, entrepreneurial personal services lawyers characterized their work differently. According to entrepreneurs, clients want legal services that are low-cost and efficient. They therefore organize their practices to standardize the services they sell. Entrepreneurial strategies are reflected in large-volume law firms, which specialize in personal injury (Kritzer, 2001), workers' compensation (Seron, 1996), and other personal legal services, and in franchise law firms – Jacoby and Meyers and Hyatt Legal Services are the biggest and best known – which offer a menu of basic legal services, including divorce, wills, real estate closings, and personal injury.

As the entrepreneurial lawyers interviewed by Seron in her study of solo and small firm practitioners described themselves, they were "business people first and lawyers second." They brought a strong commercial ethos to their practice (occasionally supplemented by a commitment to providing affordable legal services). Entrepreneurial lawyers placed great emphasis on marketing and on organizing their practices so that they could handle a large volume of similar cases. To market their services, they pioneered the use of large targeted advertising campaigns in electronic and print media and organized their practices around selling prepackaged "one size fits all" legal services. The business model adopted by entrepreneurial personal services lawyers typically involved a significant division of labor within the firm, a hierarchical reporting system, and standard operating procedures to which all employees – support staff and lawyers alike – were required to adhere (Seron, 1996: 90; Van Hoy, 1997).

Entrepreneurial personal services lawyers placed a heavy reliance on specialized support staff, who significantly outnumbered the lawyers employed and enjoyed a quasi-professional status (Seron, 1996). In his ethnographic study of franchise law firms in the early 1990s, Van Hoy observed that whatever discretionary decision making occurred in this type of practice was delegated to secretaries. Secretaries made the initial contact with clients, screened their cases to determine whether they were appropriate for the firm, and even occasionally dispensed basic legal advice to induce clients to make appointments. As Van Hoy further observed, secretaries were the ones who wrote letters to clients and drafted legal documents using boilerplate forms available on the firm's computer system. Lawyer employees, in contrast, were confined to selling the services of the firm and "processing law." (Their drafting work was limited to filling out selection modules for cases so that secretaries knew which form to print.) Even as entrepreneurial lawyers insisted that clients' primary concern was cost and speed of services, they also acknowledged that clients still expected some level of personalized service. Lawyers sought to accommodate this expectation by fostering relationships between clients and the firm as a whole, which functioned as a collective alter ego for its named partners (Seron, 1996) and resorted to subterfuge to make clients believe they were receiving individualized attention (Van Hoy, 1997).

Both traditional and entrepreneurial personal services lawyers have been vulnerable to competition from paraprofessionals. The threat of low-cost competition is not only a problem for entrepreneurial lawyers, but also for traditional lawyers, who construct their expertise around experientially gained knowledge rather than technical expertise. In the area of advocacy, where lawyering skills and know-how have long been assumed to be at a premium, paraprofessionals may be as effective and certainly less expensive than lawyers in handling routine personal civil litigation cases (Kritzer 1990: 170–6; see also Rhode, 1981). Comparing the performance of lawyers and nonlawyers in unemployment compensation, state tax, social security, and labor grievance cases, Kritzer (1998b) concluded that the requisite expertise for competent advocacy is knowledge of the processes of the specific forum rather than general legal training. According to Kritzer, personal legal services have entered a postprofessional era. As these services have become more narrowly specialized, they have also become more routinized and require a more limited expertise, attainable with training short of a full-fledged legal education (Kritzer, 1998b). If, at the turn of the twentieth century, traditional and entrepreneurial styles of practice coexisted and vied for the same stratum of clients (Seron, 1996), in the long run, both forms of practice may be supplanted by less costly services provided by nonlawyer parapro-fessionals (Seron, 1996; Kritzer, 1998b) or do-it-yourself products, which have proliferated with the availability of information technology and growth of the Internet.

In contrast to traditional practitioners and entrepreneurs, who discount the im-portance of formal legal knowledge, a third group of personal legal services pro-viders upgrade their practices through a broad substantive specialization strategy. White-collar criminal defense lawyers, for example, integrate sophisticated know-ledge of federal white collar criminal law and "insider" knowledge of prosecutorial priorities and strategies (often garnered from prior prosecutorial experience) to offer aggressive representation of well-off individuals and corporations. Unlike street crime defense, this work typically focuses on the pretrial and even preindictment stages of a prosecution, and its success often turns on the ability to exploit ambigu-ities in broadly worded statutes and complex documentary evidence (Mann, 1985). Similarly, within the matrimonial bar, a subgroup of specialists describe their ex-pertise to include, not only divorce law, but also tax, trust and estates law, finance, and psychology. In contrast to the informal information exchanges used by general practitioners, these divorce specialists, who cater to a more affluent clientele, employ more expensive formal discovery techniques adapted from large firm civil litigation practice (Mather et al., 2001). As Mather and her coinvestigators found, divorce specialists included a large proportion of women who were motivated by political values to seek to enhance the stature of divorce practice consistent with political commitments to empowering women economically and socially (Mather et al., 2001: 85–6). In these niches within personal legal services practice, as in corporate practice, the availability of financial resources permits the development and deploy-ment of sophisticated substantive and procedural legal expertise and information management strategies. Mass tort and plaintiff securities lawyers represent very successful hybrids of entrepreneurial and specialist orientations. Often pooling financial resources, expertise, and clients among firms, these lawyers, who typically take cases based on a contingency fee, pursue high volume practices in areas requir-ing substantive specialization in law, the health sciences, and other areas (Resnik, Curtis, and Hensler, 1996).

CAUSE LAWYERING

As sociolegal research has shown, lawyers in private practice deploy ideologies that vary in response to the different markets for their services. At a more abstract level, however, these ideologies all embrace an instrumental conception of lawyers' services tied to the logic of the market. In this conception, lawyers offer their expertise for sale to clients without necessarily espousing their goals. In contrast, cause lawyers eschew constructions of professional authority rooted in the sale of purportedly neutral technical expertise. A "morally activist lawyer shares and aims to share with her client responsibility for the ends she is promoting in her representation" (Luban, 1988: xxii) Cause lawyers are not agnostic as to the objectives of representation. Rather, their ambition is to use legal mechanisms and processes to challenge dominant power relations – in other words to "speak law to power" (Abel, 1998). As noted above, the professional ideologies deployed by lawyers to legitimate the collective authority of the bar and their authority in day-to-day representation of clients incorporate, if partially and uneasily, such alternative conceptions of lawyers' roles. In contrast to the "hired gun" view, these accounts recognize that law is a public good, by its own terms accessible to all, and embodies varying – if often conflicting – substantive accounts of the collective good (Halliday, 1987). Cause lawyers, whether on the left or the right of the political spectrum, seek to "reconnect law and morality and make tangible the idea that lawyering is a 'public profession,' one whose contribution goes beyond the aggregation, assembling, and deployment of technical skills" (Sarat and Scheingold, 1998a: 3). At the same time, in embracing overtly political goals, cause lawyering provides a critique of the prevailing neutral account of lawyering and exposes the dominant economic and political interests it serves (Sarat and Scheingold, 1998b; Cain and Harrington, 1994).

Most sociolegal studies of cause lawyering have focused on lawyers who endorse liberal/progressive values. As this research has shown, lawyers on the left must negotiate a tension between the prerogatives of professional power and the substantive goals of justice and equality that they embrace (Sarat and Scheingold, 1998b). This tension, noted in the context of personal legal services, emerges sharply in liberal/progressive cause lawyering, which is self-consciously committed to challenging power asymmetries. Sociolegal studies have investigated the various ideological and organizational approaches adopted by cause lawyers to negotiate the conflict between the exclusionary premises of the professional project, which – whether undertaken for cause or profit – is animated by the idea of limited access to specialized knowledge, and moral commitments to the values of inclusiveness, equality, and client empowerment. At one end of the liberal/progressive cause lawyering continuum, lawyers deploy traditional conceptions of professional expertise to make meaningful law's promise of equal access for disadvantaged persons (Scheingold, 1994) These lawyering practices are not always clearly distinguishable from traditional personal legal services. At the other end of the spectrum, cause lawyers invoke law's promise of justice to pursue client and community empowerment strategies that destabilize the concept of professional authority as a whole (Sarat and Scheingold, 1998b: 7; Wexler, 1970). Scholars have noted the recent emergence of "critical lawyering," which incorporates post-structural commitments to addressing domination at microsites of power within legal services provided on a fee basis (Trubek and Kransberger, 1998). Critical lawyers affirm their commitments to social justice by practicing in substantive areas where there are perceived community needs and engaging in community organizing, legislative lobbying, and other overtly political activities. Within their practices, they attempt to integrate insights from feminist and other critical theoretical perspectives, focusing on resisting the reduction of client narratives to legal categories, collaborating with clients in all aspects of decision making, and organizing their workplaces nonhierarchically (Trubek and Kransberger, 1998; see also Alfieri, 1991; Lopez, 1992)

Just as liberal/progressive cause lawyers must confront the tension between professional authority and client autonomy, so must they negotiate the boundaries between law and politics. Cause lawyers seek to dissolve this line by exposing how law, despite its claim of politically neutrality, advances specific political and material interests. By resorting to legal institutions, legal rights, and "law talk," however, cause lawyering recreates this same boundary (Garth, 1987; Sarat and Scheingold, 1998b). Critics have argued that the law-based strategies on which liberal/progressive cause lawyers rely practically and imaginatively constrain the transformative possibilities available and even turn cause lawyers into unwitting apologists for the established order. Sociolegal scholarship has exposed these tendencies in the retreat of cause lawyers to defensive postures vis-à-vis civil rights gains in liberal democracies (Garth, 1987), and in the demise of left-activist lawyer communities, whose members have abandoned larger scale political mobilization in favor of individual client service (Scheingold, 1998). In contrast, other research has highlighted liberal/progressive lawyers' capacity to mobilize the transformative possibilities reflected in legal norms. Historical studies have investigated the conditions underlying the success of legal advocacy as a strategy in the American civil rights movement (Carle, 2001, 2002). Other research suggests that even in advanced liberal democracies, lawyers can be effective in activating the dignitary values reflected in procedural claims in ways that publicize the plight of disempowered groups (Sterett, 1998).

Cause lawyers face parallel challenges as they navigate the currents of globalization and democratization in the international arena. As research has shown, lawyers have succeeded in some instances in deploying rule of law values to contravene abuses of power by repressive regimes in the Third World (Abel, 1995; Lev, 1998). Scholars have argued that the impact of globalization is ambiguous. Insofar as international networks provide economic and political leverage for advocacy groups to work for social change, they are often tied to funding sources committed to the expansion of free market ideals; as a consequence they privilege a neoliberal agenda over the goal of improving material and social welfare. Such networks may also impede the development of indigenous social movements to deal with the most pressing local threats (White, 2001; Scheingold, 2001). While acknowledging these risks, other scholars argue that they are overblown. Although Third World cause lawyering borrows from Western legal traditions, some research suggests that it seeks to articulate an alternate critical perspective grounded in local concerns. A study of 22 public interest law organizations in Asia, Africa, and Latin America concludes that worries that international human rights advocacy has been coopted by Western neo-liberal values, "understate the original and substantial contribution to the world's human rights culture being made by Third World cause lawyers" (Ellmann, 1998: 356).

However one reads the record of progressive cause lawyering – as one of success or failure, advance or retreat, challenge or cooptation – the proliferation of liberal/progressive cause lawyering practices itself reveals an important dimension of law's power at the end of the twentieth century (Sarat and Scheingold, 1998b, 2001). To advance their agendas, liberal/left cause lawyers often forego material rewards, undergo professional and social marginalization, and frequently put their lives at risk (Abel, 1995). Whether they follow more narrowly defined legal avenues or engage more broadly in politics, these activists pursue transformative ideals whose source they locate in the law itself. In mobilizing legal symbols and resources, they thus deploy the power of law, which is grounded in its aspiration to justice, to challenge state and corporate power (cf. Silbey, 1998).

Conclusion: Directions for Future Research

Theories of the professions that emerged in the late 1970s framed professionalism as a collective project to obtain economic, social, and political power. In particular, these new theories sought to draw attention to the intersections between professionals' market activities and their deployment of expert and ideological claims. On the heels of these new conceptualizations, sociolegal research began to investigate lawyers' organized activities and daily practices with a view to understanding the many dimensions of professional power. These studies illuminate the varied ideological and organizational strategies lawyers in private practice pursue to control and compete in markets for their services and, in the case of cause lawyers, to mobilize legal virtues to advance justice claims. Further sociolegal research is important to explore what accoutrements of professional power – anchored in ideological claims of specialized expertise, client service, or public commitment – are likely to survive into the twenty-first century. In addition, with the rise of globalization, continued research is critical to investigate lawyers' complex engagements in the creation of international legal regimes, institutions, and markets – areas that have only begun to be studied.

Recent sociolinguistic and psycholinguistic scholarship has sought to expose the power of legal language. As has been noted, law is at the end of the day "a profession of words" (Constable, 1998). Drawing on this insight, research has begun to investigate how lawyers establish professional authority in their formal discourse and informal "law talk" (Conley and O'Barr, 1998; Sarat and Felstiner, 1995, Mertz, 1996). Future microinvestigations of legal practice can shed light on how lawyers' ideological and expert claims interact to generate professional power and reveal the interdependencies between the power(s) of lawyers and the power(s) of law.

Notes

Elizabeth Chambliss, Denny Curtis, Stephen Ellmann, Frank Munger, Judith Resnik, Austin Sarat, and Susan Silbey provided helpful comments on an earlier draft. The author also thanks Amy Garzon, Christine Harrington, and Monica Lima for their excellent research assistance.

1 This chapter also omits extended discussion of a growing law and economics literature that uses game-theoretic, efficiency-based, and other economic models to investigate lawyers' work.
2 Carson (1999: 1) reports somewhat lower but still dramatic rates of growth.
3 For an assessment of the empirical evidence explaining law firm growth, see Sander and Williams (1992).
4 Scholars have pointed to these various facilitative activities to argue that lawyers, rather than functioning as a drain on the economy – as prevailing wisdom in the 1980s held – further economic development by reducing uncertainty and other transaction costs (though such activities often serve to enrich individual clients at the expense of the public at large) (Gilson, 1984; Suchman and Cahill, 1996; Friedman et al., 1989)
5 This is not to imply that foreign lawyers, have not, for their part, appropriated American legal expertise to fight their own local "palace wars" (Dezalay and Garth, 2002: ch. 12).
6 In highlighting the conflict between lawyers and clients and particularly lawyers' efforts to manipulate and dominate their clients, Sarat and Felstiner offer a characterization of divorce practitioners that is sharply at odds with the more positive portrayal evoked by

Mather and her coresearchers. Differences in methodologies and samples may, at least partially, account for this contrast. Whereas Mather and her coauthors based their analysis primarily on interviews with divorce lawyers, Sarat and Felstiner had the additional benefit of observing lawyer–client interactions. On the other hand, Sarat and Felstiner's sample reflected a less elite segment of the divorce bar, while Mather's study drew from a broader and more diverse sample (Sarat and Felstiner, 1995: 10)

References

ABA Commission on Women in the Legal Profession (2001) *The Unfinished Agenda: Women in the Legal Profession*. Chicago: ABA.

ABA Ethics Beyond the Rules Task Force (1998) *Report: Ethics Beyond the Rules*. Chicago: ABA. Reprinted in *Fordham Law Review* 67: 691–895.

Abbott, A. (1988) *The System of Professions: An Essay on the Division of Expert Labor*. Chicago: University of Chicago Press.

Abel, R.L. (1980) "Taking stock," *Law & Society Review* 14: 429–33.

Abel, R.L. (1988) *The Legal Profession in England and Wales*. Oxford: Blackwell.

Abel, R.L. (1989) *American Lawyers*. New York: Oxford University Press.

Abel, R.L. (1995) *Politics By Other Means: Law in the Struggle Against Apartheid, 1980–1994*. New York: Routledge.

Abel, R.L. (1998) "Speaking law to power: Occasions for cause lawyering," in A. Sarat and S. Scheingold (eds.), *Cause Lawyering: Political Commitments and Professional Responsibilities*. Oxford: Oxford University Press, pp. 69–117.

Abel, R.L. and Lewis, P.C. (1988a) *Lawyers in Society, Vol. 1, The Common Law World*. Berkeley: University of California Press.

Abel, R.L. and Lewis, P.C. (1988b) *Lawyers in Society, Vol. 2, The Civil Law World*. Berkeley: University of California Press.

Abel, R.L. and Lewis, P.C. (1989) *Lawyers in Society, Vol. 3, Comparative Theories*. Berkeley: University of California Press.

Alfieri, A.V. (1991) "Reconstructive poverty law practice: Learning lessons of client narrative," *Yale Law Journal* 100: 2107–47.

Auerbach, J.S. (1976) *Unequal Justice: Lawyers and Social Change in Modern America*. New York: Oxford University Press.

Baker, T. (2001) "Blood money, new money, and the moral economy of tort law in action," *Law & Society Review*, 35: 275–320.

Berle, A.A. (1933) "Modern legal profession," *Encyclopedia of the Social Sciences* 5: 340–5.

Blumberg, A.S. (1967) "The practice of law as a confidence game: Organizational cooptation of a profession," *Law & Society Review* 1: 15–39.

Boon, A. and Flood, J. (1999) "Trials of strength: The reconfiguration of litigation as a contested terrain," *Law & Society Review* 33: 595–636.

Bourdieu, P. (1987) "The force of law: Toward a sociology of the juridical field," *Hastings Law Journal* 38: 814–53.

Brandeis, L.D. ([1914] 1996) *Business: A Profession*. Boston: Small, Maynard & Co.

Cain, M. (1979) "The general practice lawyer and the client: Towards a radical conception," *International Journal of the Sociology of Law* 7: 331–54.

Cain, M. and Harrington, C.B. (eds.) (1994) *Lawyers in a PostModern World: Translation and Transgression*. New York: New York University Press.

Carle, S.D. (2002) "Race, class, and legal ethics in the early NAACP (1910–1920)," *Law & History Review*, 20: 97–146.

Carle, S.D. (2001) "From Buchanan to Button: Legal ethics and the NAACP (Part II)," *University of Chicago Law School Roundtable* 8: 281–307.

Carlin, J. (1966) *Lawyers on Their Own?* New Brunswick, NJ: Rutgers University Press.

Carruthers, B.G. and Halliday, T.C. (1998) *Rescuing Business: The Making of Corporate Bankruptcy Law in England and the United States*. Oxford: Clarendon Press.

Carson, C.N. (1999) *The Lawyer Statistical Report: The U.S. Legal Profession in 1995*. Chicago: American Bar Foundation.

Chambers, D.L. (1989) "Accommodation and satisfaction: Women and men lawyers and the balance of work and family," *Law & Social Inquiry* 14: 251–87.

Chambliss, E. (2000) *Miles to Go 2000: Progress of Minorities in the Legal Profession*, American Bar Association Commission on Racial and Ethnic Diversity in the Profession. Chicago: American Bar Association.

Chambliss, E. and Uggen, C. (2000) "Men and women of elite law firms: Reevaluating Kanter's legacy," *Law & Social Inquiry* 25: 41–68.

Chayes, A. and Chayes, A. (1985) "Corporate counsel and the elite law firm," *Stanford Law Review* 37: 277–300.

Conley, J.M. and O'Barr, M.O. (1998) *Just Words: Law, Language, and Power*. Chicago: University of Chicago Press.

Constable, M. (1998) "Reflections on law as a profession of words," in B.G. Garth and A. Sarat (eds.), *Justice and Power in Sociolegal Studies*. Evanston, IL: Northwestern University Press, pp. 19–35.

Dezalay, Y. and Garth, B.G. (1996) *Dealing in Virtue: International Commercial Arbitration and the Construction of a Transnational Legal Order*. Chicago: University of Chicago Press.

Dezalay, Y. and Garth, B.G. (2002) *The Internationalization of the Palace Wars: Lawyers Economists and the Contest to Transform Latin American States*. Chicago: University of Chicago Press.

Dezalay, Y. and Sugarman, D. (eds.) (1995) *Professional Competititon and Professional Power: Lawyers, Accountants and the Social Construction of Markets*. London: Routledge.

Durkheim, E. (1957) *Professional Ethics and Civic Morals*. New York: The Free Press.

Ellmann, S. (1998) "Cause lawyering in the third world," in A. Sarat and S. Scheingold (eds.), *Cause Lawyering: Political Commitments and Professional Responsibilities*. Oxford: Oxford University Press, pp. 349–430.

Felstiner, W.L.F. (1998) "Justice, power, and lawyers," in B.G. Garth and A. Sarat (eds.), *Justice and Power in Sociolegal Studies*. Evanston, IL: Northwestern University Press, pp. 55–79.

Flood, J. (1988) *Anatomy of Lawyering: An Ethnography of a Corporate Law Firm*. Ann Arbor, MI: University Microfilms International.

Flood, J. (1995) "The cultures of globalization: Professional restructuring for the international market," in Y. Dezalay and D. Sugarman (eds.), *Professional Competition and Professional Power: Lawyers, Accountants and the Social Construction of Markets*. New York: Routledge, pp. 139–69.

Freidson, E. (1973) *Professions and Their Prospects*. New York: Sage.

Freidson, E. (1983) "The theory of the professions: The state of the art," in R. Dingwall and P. Lewis (eds.), *The Sociology of the Professions*. London: Macmillan, pp. 19–37.

Freidson, E. (1986) *Professional Powers: A Study of the Institutionalization of Formal Knowledge*. Chicago: University of Chicago Press.

Friedman, L.M., Gordon, R.W., Pirie, S. and Whatley, E. (1989) "Law, lawyers, and legal practice in Silicon Valley: A preliminary report," *Indiana Law Journal* 64: 555–67.

Galanter, M. and Palay, T. (1991) "The transformation of the big law firm," in R.L. Nelson, D.M. Trubek, and R.L. Solomon (eds.), *Lawyers' Ideals, Lawyers' Practices: Transformations in the American Legal Profession*. Ithaca, NY: Cornell University Press, pp. 31–62.

Garth, B.G. (1987) "Independent professional power and the search for a legal ideology with a progressive bite," *Indiana Law Journal* 62: 183–214.

Garth, B.G. and Sarat, A. (1998) "Justice and power in law and society research on the contested careers of core concepts," in B.G. Garth and A. Sarat (eds.), *Justice and Power in Sociolegal Studies*. Evanston, IL: Northwestern University Press, pp. 1–18.

Gilson, R.J. (1984) "Value creation by business lawyers: Legal skills and asset pricing," *Yale Law Journal* 94: 239–313.

Gordon, R.W. (1983) "Legal thought and legal practice in the age of American enterprise," in G.L. Geison (ed.), *Professions and Professional Ideologies in America*. Chapel Hill: University of North Carolina Press, pp. 70–110.

Gordon, R.W. (1984) "The ideal and the actual in the law: fantasies and practices of New York City lawyers," in G.W. Gawalt (ed.), *The New High Priests: Lawyers in Post Civil War America*. Westport, CT: Greenwood Press, pp. 51–74.

Gordon, R.W. (1988) "The independence of lawyers," *Boston University Law Review* 68: 1–83.

Gordon, R.W. (1990) "Corporate law practice as a public calling," *Maryland Law Review* 49: 255–92.

Granfield, R. (1992) *Making Elite Lawyers*. New York: Routledge.

Griffiths, J. (1986) "What do Dutch lawyers actually do in divorce cases?" *Law & Society Review* 20: 135–75.

Gunz, H.P. and Gunz, S.P. (2002) "The lawyer's response to organizational professional conflict: An empirical study of the ethical decision making of in-house counsel," *American Business Law Journal* 39: 241–87.

Hagan, J. and Kay, F. (1995) *Gender in Practice: A Study of Lawyers' Lives*. New York: Oxford University Press.

Handler, J. (1967) *The Lawyer and His Community*. Madison: University of Wisconsin Press.

Halliday, T.C. (1987) *Beyond Monopoly: Lawyers, State Crises, and Professional Empowerment*. Chicago: University of Chicago Press.

Halliday, T.C. (1999) "Politics and civic professionalism: Legal elites and cause lawyers," *Law & Social Inquiry* 24:1013–43.

Halliday, T.C. and Karpik, L. (eds.) (1997) *Lawyers and the Rise of Western Political Liberalism: Europe and North America from the Eighteenth to Twentieth Centuries*. Oxford: Clarendon Press.

Heinz, J.P. and Laumann, E.O. (1982) *Chicago Lawyers: The Social Structure of the Bar*. Chicago: American Bar Foundation.

Heinz, J.P., Nelson, R.L., Laumann, E.O., and Michelson, E. (1998) "The changing character of lawyers' work: Chicago in 1975 and 1995," *Law & Society Review* 32: 751–75.

Hensler, D. and Resnik, J. (2000) "Contested identities: Task forces on gender, race, and ethnic bias and the obligations of the legal profession," in D.L. Rhode (ed.), *Ethics in Practice*. New York: Oxford University Press, pp. 240–63.

Hobson, W.K. (1986) *The American Legal Profession and the Organizational Society, 1890–1930*. New York: Garland Publishing.

Kagan, R.A. and Rosen, R.E. (1985) "On the social significance of large law firm practice," *Stanford Law Review* 37: 399–443.

Kritzer, H.M. (1990) *The Justice Broker: Lawyers and Ordinary Litigation*. New York: Oxford University Press.

Kritzer, H.M. (1998a) "Contingent fee lawyers and their clients: Settlement expectations, settlement realities, and issues of control in the lawyer–client relationship," *Law & Social Inquiry* 23: 795–821.

Kritzer, H.M. (1998b) *Legal Advocacy: Lawyers and Nonlawyers at Work*. Ann Arbor: University of Michigan Press.

Kritzer, H.M. (2001) "From litigators of ordinary cases to litigators of extraordinary cases: Stratification of the plaintiffs' bar in the twenty-first century," *DePaul Law Review* 51: 219–40.

Kronman, A.T. (1993) *The Lost Lawyer: Failing Ideals of the Legal Profession*. Cambridge, MA: The Belknap Press of Harvard University Press.

Landon, D.D. (1990) *Country Lawyers: The Impact of Context on Professional Practice*. New York: Praeger.

LaPiana, W.P. (1994) *Logic and Experience*. Oxford: Oxford University Press.

Larson, M. S. (1977) *The Rise of Professionalism: A Sociological Analysis*. Berkeley: University of California Press.

Lev, D. (1998) "Lawyers' causes in Indonesia and Malaysia," in A. Sarat and S. Scheingold (eds.), *Cause Lawyering: Political Commitments and Professional Responsibilities*. Oxford: Oxford University Press, pp. 431–52.

Lipartito, K. (1990) "What have lawyers done for American business? The case of Baker and Botts of Houston," *Business History Review*, September: 489.

Lopez, G.P. (1992) *Rebellious Lawyering: One Chicano's Vision of Progressive Law Practice*. Boulder, CO: Westview Press.

Luban, D. (1988) "The noblesse oblige tradition in the practice of law," *Vanderbilt Law Review* 41: 717–40.

Macaulay, S. (1979) "Lawyers and consumer protection laws," *Law & Society Review* 14: 115–71.

MacDonald, K.M. (1995) *The Sociology of the Professions*. London: Sage.

Mann, K. (1985) *Defending White-Collar Crime: A Portrait of Attorneys at Work*. New Haven, CT: Yale University Press.

Mather, L., McEwen, C.A., and Maiman, R.J. (2001) *Divorce Lawyers at Work: Varieties of Professionalism in Practice*. Oxford: Oxford University Press.

McBarnet, D. (1992) "It's not what you do but the way you do it: Tax evasion, tax avoidance, and the boundaries of deviance," in David Downes (ed.), *Unravelling Criminal Justice: Eleven British Studies*. London: Macmillan, pp. 247–67.

Menkel-Meadow, C. (1985) "Portia in a different voice: Speculations on a women's lawyering process," *Berkeley Women's Law Journal* 1: 39–63.

Menkel-Meadow, C. (1994) "Portia redux: Another look at gender, feminism, and legal ethics," *Virginia Journal of Social Policy & the Law* 2: 75–114.

Mertz, E. (1996) "Recontextualization as socialization: Text and pragmatics in the law school classroom," in Michael Silverstein and Greg Urban (eds.), *Natural Histories of Discourse*. Chicago: University of Chicago Press, p. 229.

Milhaupt, C.J. and West, M.D. (2002) "Law's dominion and the market for legal elites in Japan," The Center for Law and Economic Studies Working Paper no. 206, Columbia Law School.

Nelson, R.L. (1988) *Partners with Power: The Social Transformation of the Large Law Firm*. Berkeley: University of California Press.

Nelson, R.L. and Nielson, L.B. (2000) "Cops, counsel, and the entrepreneurs: constructing the role of inside counsel in large corporations," *Law & Society Review* 34: 457–94.

Nelson, R.L. and Trubek, D.M. (1992) "Introduction: New problems and new paradigms in studies of the legal profession," in R.L. Nelson, D.M. Trubek, and R.L. Solomon (eds.), *Lawyers' Ideals, Lawyers' Practices: Transformation in the American Legal Profession*. Ithaca, NY: Cornell University Press, pp.1–30.

Parsons, T. (1954) *Essays in Sociological Theory*. Glencoe, IL: The Free Press.

Pierce, J.L. (1995) *Gender Trials: Emotional Lives in Contemporary Law Firms*. Berkeley: University of California Press.

Powell, M.J. (1988) *From Patrician to Professional Elite: The Transformation of the New York City Bar Association*. New York: Russell Sage Foundation.

Powell, M.J. (1993) "Professional innovation: Corporate lawyers and private law making," *Law & Social Inquiry* 18: 423–52.

Resnik, J., Curtis, D.E., and Hensler, D.R. (1996) "Individuals within the aggregate: relationships, representation, and fees," *New York University Law Review* 71: 296–401.

Rhode, D.L. (1981) "Policing the professional monopoly: A constitutional and empirical analysis of unauthorized practice prohibitions," *Stanford Law Review* 34: 1–112.

Rhode, D.L. (1996) "Myths of meritocracy," *Fordham Law Review* 65: 585–94.

Rhode, D.L. (2000) *In the Interests of Justice: Reforming the Legal Profession*. New York: Oxford University Press.

Rhode, D.L. (2001) *The Unfinished Agenda: A Report on the Status of Women in the Legal Profession*. Chicago: American Bar Association.

Rosen, R.E. (1989) "The inside counsel movement, professional judgment and organizational representation," *Indiana Law Journal* 64: 479–553.

Rosen, R.E. (2003) "We're all consultants now: How change in client organizational strategies influences change in the organization of corporate legal services," *Arizona Law Review* 44: 637–83.

Rosenthal, D. (1974) *Lawyer and Client: Who's in Charge?* New York: Russell Sage Foundation.

Rueschemeyer, D. (1973) *Lawyers and Their Society: A Comparative Study of the Legal Profession in Germany and the United States*. Cambridge, MA: Harvard University Press.

Sandefur, R.L. (2001) "Work and honor in the law: Prestige and the division of lawyers' labor," *American Sociological Review* 66: 382–403.

Sander, R.H. and Williams, E.D. (1989) "Why are there so many lawyers? Perspectives on a turbulent market," *Law & Social Inquiry* 14: 431–79.

Sander, R.H. and Williams, E.D. (1992) "A little theorizing about the big law firm: Galanter, Palay, and the economics of growth," *Law & Social Inquiry* 17: 391–414.

Sarat A. and Felstiner, W.L.F. (1995) *Divorce Lawyers and Their Clients: Power and Meaning in the Legal Process*. New York: Oxford University Press.

Sarat A. and Scheingold, S. (eds.) (1998a) *Cause Lawyering: Political Commitments and Professional Responsibilities*. Oxford: Oxford University Press.

Sarat A. and Scheingold, S. (1998b) "Cause lawyering and the reproduction of professional authority: An introduction," in A. Sarat and S. Scheingold (eds.), *Cause Lawyering: Political Commitments and Professional Responsibilities*. Oxford: Oxford University Press, pp. 3–28.

Sarat A. and Scheingold, S. (eds.) (2001) *Cause Lawyering and the State in a Global Era*. Oxford: Oxford University Press.

Scheingold, S. (1994) "The contradictions of radical law practice," in M. Cain and C.B. Harrington (eds.), *Lawyers in a Post-Modern World*. New York: New York University Press, pp. 265–85.

Scheingold, S. (1998) "The struggle to politicize legal practice: A case study of left-activist lawyering in Seattle," in A. Sarat and S. Scheingold (eds.), *Cause Lawyering: Political Commitments and Professional Responsibilities*. Oxford: Oxford University Press, pp. 118–48.

Scheingold, S. (2001) "Cause lawyering and democracy in transnational perspective," in A. Sarat and S. Scheingold (eds.), *Cause Lawyering and the State in a Global Era*. Oxford: Oxford University Press, pp. 382–405.

Schön, D.A. (1983) *The Reflective Practitioner: How Professionals Think in Action*. New York: Basic Books.

Seron, C. (1996) *The Business of Practicing Law: The Work Lives of Solo and Small-Firm Attorneys*. Philadelphia: Temple University Press.

Shamir, R. (1995) *Managing Legal Uncertainty: Elite Lawyers in the New Deal*. Durham, NC: Duke University Press.

Shapiro, S.P (2002) *Tangled Loyalties: Conflict of Interest in Legal Practice*. Ann Arbor: Michigan Press.

Silbey, S.S. (1998) "Ideology, power, and justice," in B.G. Garth and A. Sarat (eds.), *Justice and Power in Sociolegal Studies*. Evanston, IL: Northwestern University Press, pp. 272–308.

Smigel, E. (1964) *The Wall Street Lawyer: Professional Organization Man?* New York: Macmillan.

Spangler, E. (1986) *Lawyers for Hire: Salaried Professionals at Work*. New Haven, CT: Yale University Press.

Sterett, S. (1998) "Caring about individual cases: Immigration lawyering in Britain," in A. Sarat and S. Scheingold (eds.), *Cause Lawerying: Political Commitments and Professional Responsibilities*. Oxford: Oxford University Press, pp. 293–316.

Stevens, R. (1983) *Law School: Legal Education in America From the 1850's to the 1980's*. Chapel Hill: University of North Carolina Press.

Suchman, M.C. and Cahill, M.L. (1996) "The hired gun as facilitator: lawyers and the suppression of business disputes in Silicon Valley," *Law & Social Inquiry* 21: 679–712.

Thomas, R.S., Schwab, S.J. and Hansen, R.G. (2001) "Megafirms," *North Carolina Law Review* 80: 115–98.

Trubek, L. and Kransberger, M. E. (1998) "Critical lawyers: Social justice and the structures of private practice," in A. Sarat and S. Scheingold (eds.), *Cause Lawyering: Political Commitments and Professional Responsibilities*. Oxford: Oxford University Press, pp. 201–26.

Van Hoy, J. (1997) *Franchise Law Firms and the Transformation of Personal Legal Services*. Westport, CT: Quorum Books.

Wexler, Stephen (1970) "Practicing law for poor people," *Yale Law Journal* 79: 1049–67.

White, L. (2001) "Two worlds of Ghanian cause lawyers," in A. Sarat and S. Scheingold (eds.), *Cause Lawyering and the State in a Global Era*. Oxford: Oxford University Press, pp. 35–67.

Wilkins, D.B. (1998a) "Identities and roles: Race, recognition, and professional responsibility," *Maryland Law Review* 57: 1502–94.

Wilkins, D.B. (1998b) "Fragmenting professionalism: Racial identity and the ideology of bleached out lawyering," *International Journal of the Legal Profession* 5: 141–73.

Wilkins, D.B. and Gulati, G.M. (1996) "Why are there so few black lawyers in corporate law firms? An institutional analysis," *California Law Review* 84: 501–614.

Wolfram, C.W. (2000) "The ABA and MDP's: Context, history, and process," *Minnesota Law Review* 84: 1625–54.

10

Courts and Judges

LEE EPSTEIN AND JACK KNIGHT

If there is one word that characterizes the study of courts and judges it is diversity – diversity in the kinds of questions scholars raise, the theories they invoke, and the methodologies they use to assess the expectations their theories generate.

Given this mix, it would be, on the one hand, a near-daunting task to cover all the research developments in a single essay; that would necessitate a much larger volume, perhaps even two or three. And it would require not just two scholars who work primarily as political scientists and legal academics but rather many, hailing from the disciplines of anthropology, economics, psychology, and sociology. These social sciences, and various pockets in the humanities as well, have produced mounds of research on the subject of courts and judges – at least some of which has, for all the usual reasons, failed to join the piles already on our desks.

On the other hand, despite the multiplicity of specific research questions, theories, and methodologies, analysts of courts and judges have coalesced around a similar set of general substantive concerns. We can group these under four headings: judicial selection and retention, accessing judicial power, limitations on judicial power, and judicial decision making.

In what follows, we devote space to each of these topics. But, out of the belief that any attempt to cover all the questions specialists have raised about them and the results their inquiries have yielded would be superficial at best and misleading at worst, we explore one key debate within each. What these explorations reveal is that, over the past decade or so, scholars have made great strides in their quest to understand the various phenomena associated with courts and judges but still have some distance to travel. While the gaps in our understanding may be narrowing, they nonetheless remain wide.

An Overview of Questions, Theories, and Methodology

Before turning to the four substantive topics, we take a brief detour. In this section we consider the three building blocks of most research programs – questions, theory, and methodology – and offer some observations about their use in studies of judges and courts.

Substantive research questions

Since we dedicate the bulk of this essay to exploring four substantive topics, we need not say too much here about the kinds of substantive questions scholars ask. But one point bears some emphasis: over the past two decades – perhaps even longer – the types of questions engaging analysts have not changed all that much. So, for example, in his classic treatment of judicial selection and tenure, Haynes (1944: 44) pointed to the immense scholarly and public interest in the subject. In the "United States alone," he noted, "whole shelves could be filled with the speeches, debates, books and articles that have been produced . . . dealing with the choice and tenure of judges." Writing nearly 40 years later, Dubois (1986: 31) claimed that "It is fairly certain that no single subject has consumed as many pages in law reviews and law-related publications over the past 50 years as the subject of judicial selection."

What has changed – actually expanded – are the empirical targets of questions regarding courts and judges. While scholars writing just a decade ago may have framed their questions in general terms, they almost invariably studied them in the context of the US Supreme Court. That has changed, almost remarkably so. Today, when we pick up a study on judicial selection, it is just as likely to explore practices in the US states or as they pertain to lower federal court judges as it is to consider US Supreme Court nominations. When we read a scholarly essay on judicial decision making, it might still focus on US Supreme Court justices but some nontrivial probability exists that it is about lower appellate and trial judges – both in the states and in the federal ladder.

Perhaps more intriguing, research is beginning – though just beginning – to branch out beyond the American context altogether, to consider courts and judges throughout the world, in Europe (e.g., Stone, 1994), Latin America (e.g., Helmke, 1999), Asia (e.g., Ramseyer, 1994), and even Africa (e.g., Widner, 2001). Important comparative studies on virtually all the topics we cover in this chapter, from judicial selection and tenure to judicial decisions, are now appearing both in disciplinary journals as well as in the more specialized ones.

In what follows we are attentive to what *may be* this sea-change in the study of courts and judges – the expansion of the targets of our inquiries – discussing and exploring specific research findings (with the caveat that because much of the literature on courts and judges continues to focus on the US Supreme Court, our essay must, to some extent, follow suit). For now, and assuming that this potential development is as exciting and self-evidently important to readers as it is to us, it seems worthy to consider, first, why it seems to be occurring and, in turn, what steps the law and society community might take to ensure that it does.

Of course we are only speculating here but one factor contributing to the new emphasis on US judges other than "the Supremes" is simple observation. We live in a day and age when lower appellate court decisions – such as those over affirmative action, which have divided circuits all over the country but into which the US Supreme Court seems reluctant to tread – and even those of trial courts (think Microsoft) seem to be making more news than virtually any the Supreme Court has issued in the last few years (save *Bush v. Gore*, 2000). The old wisdom, that trial courts simply "adjudicate" and courts of appeals merely rubberstamp the "adjudications" of their lower court colleagues seems just that – old and even more to the point, wrong (Mather, 1995). We also live in a day and age when we, as citizens, are bombarded with press reports of courts throughout the world generating major policies. Tribunals in Hungary and South Africa have ruled the death penalty unconstitutional; those in India and Germany have rendered constitutional "positive discrimination" programs for discriminated-against minorities; and courts in Germany and Ireland have upheld the rights of fetuses to life. These issues strike at the heart of democratic policy making, and yet the final word came from courts. Which means, as more and more scholars are acknowledging, we ignore the growing importance and power of courts abroad at our own peril.

But there is more – at least in the US context. Over the past decade or so, we have seen the production of several multiuser public databases on courts and their decisions. We think here of Harold J. Spaeth's US Supreme Court Data Base, which contains scores of attributes of Court decisions, handed down since 1953, ranging from the date of the oral argument to the identities of the parties to the litigation to how the justices voted; and Donald R. Songer's US Court of Appeals Data, which houses information on cases decided in the courts of appeals between 1925 and 1996.

To be sure, these databases are not panaceas; they cannot directly answer every question scholars may have on courts and judges. On the other hand, users can adapt them to suit many purposes, thereby answering a range of perennial ones. That scholars are now doing so seems evident, for, at least in our estimation, the existence of these multiuser databases has contributed enormously to the expansion of our empirical reference points. To see this, we only need consider the growth of research on the US Courts of Appeals. Just a few years ago, prior to the appearance of Songer's data set, circuit courts received only limited scholarly attention at conferences and in the journals; today, entire panels are devoted to courts of appeals and articles about them are no longer a rarity.

This makes the lack of an equivalent to the US Court of Appeals or US Supreme Court Data Base for courts outside America's borders all the more unfortunate. Several efforts are in progress – we think here of the project C. Neal Tate and his colleagues have undertaken to collect information on decisions of several high courts abroad. But, again assuming agreement over the desirability of efforts focusing in part or in full on courts elsewhere, we would encourage the community to develop more of these critical resources. Some, such as the Tate project, might mirror the existing US Supreme Court and US Court of Appeals databases to the extent that they would focus on court decisions. But we could imagine others that would be more institutionally based, containing data on factors such as the formal rules and norms governing the selection of judges elsewhere and those pertaining to jurisdiction and standing, as well as data on workloads. As anyone who has tried to collect such information on a large-scale basis can attest, this will be no easy task. But it is one that would provide an important and perhaps even necessary – if the Court of Appeals project is any indication – inducement for more research on courts abroad.

Theory

If there has been a growth industry in the study of courts and judges it is in the realm of theory – "a reasoned and precise speculation about the answer to a research question" (King, Keohane, and Verba, 1994: 19). Just a little over 50 years ago, the vast majority of studies lacked any; many were simply doctrinal analyses of the products of judicial deliberations – that is, decisions and opinions – that were heavy on the doctrine, short on analysis, and devoid of theoretical underpinnings. But, as Thomas Walker (1994: 4) has written, all that changed in the late 1950s and early 1960s: "Theoretical innovation exploded. Attitude theory, social background theory, role theory, fact pattern analysis, and others were used in attempts to explain judicial decision making." To Walker's list, we – writing in 2001 – could add dozens more that scholars now invoke to guide their work on courts and judges (and not just research on judicial decision making), ranging from theories that are simple, small, or tailored to fit particular circumstances to those that are grander in scope, seeking to provide insight into a wide range of phenomena.

This is not to say that atheoretical work on courts and judges no longer sees the light of day. But these days scholars working in the traditional academic disciplines, along with their counterparts in the law schools, are acknowledging, in increasing numbers, the value of using theory to develop "observable implications" (i.e., things that we would expect to detect in the real world if our theory is right) that they can then assess against "data" (more on this below). Eskridge's (1991a, 1991b, 1994) seminal work on statutory interpretation, which invokes positive political theory (PPT) to understand how justices interpret statutes, serves to make the point. Under his use of PPT, justices have goals, which, according to Eskridge, amount to seeing their policy preferences written into law, but realize that they cannot achieve them without taking into account the preferences and likely actions of other relevant actors – including congressional gatekeepers (such as chairs of relevant committees and party leaders), other members of Congress, and the President – and the institutional context in which they work.

To develop observable implications from this account, Eskridge employs pictures of the sort we display in Figures 10.1a and b. In each, we depict a hypothetical set of preferences over a particular policy, say, a civil rights statute. The horizontal lines represent the (civil rights) policy space, here, ordered from left (most "liberal") to right (most "conservative"); the vertical lines show the preferences (the "most preferred positions") of the relevant actors: the President, the median member of the Court, of Congress, and of the key committees and other gatekeepers in Congress that make the decision over whether to propose civil rights legislation to their respective houses. Note we also identify the committees' indifference point "where the Court can set policy which the committee likes no more and no less than the opposite policy that could be chosen by the full chamber" (Eskridge, 1991a: 378).

Now suppose that the Court has accepted a case that calls for it to interpret the civil rights statute. How would the Court proceed? From Eskridge's theory the following observable implication emerges: given the distribution of the most preferred positions of the actors, the 10.1a Court would not be willing to take the risk and interpret the statute in line with its most preferred position. It would see that Congress could easily override that position and that the President would support Congress. Rather, under Eskridge's theory, the best choice for justices interested in seeing the law reflect their policy preferences is to interpret the statute near the

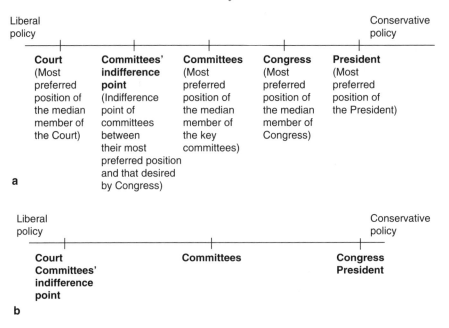

Figure 10.1 a Observable implication 1: Policy is set on the commitee's indifference point. **b** Observable implication 2: Policy is set on the commitee's indifference point/Courts' most preferred position.

committees' indifference point. The reason is simple: since the committees are indifferent between that point and the position preferred by the median legislator, they would have no incentive to introduce legislation to overturn a policy set at their indifference point. Thus, the Court would end up with a policy close to, but not exactly on, its ideal point without risking a congressional backlash. The distribution of preferences in Figure 10.1b points to a different observable implication: the Court would set policy in a way that reflects its sincerely held preferences. For if it votes its preferences (which are comparatively liberal) and sets the policy at its most preferred position, the relevant congressional committees would have no incentive to override the Court: since their indifference point is the same as the Court's most preferred position, they would be indifferent to the policy preferred by the Court. Note that for both implications the theory suggests the main explanatory variables – the preferences of the key actors relative to one another and the dependent variable – of the Court's interpretation of a statute.

Positive political theory is not the only or necessarily best tool (though we believe it is) for analyzing statutory interpretation. But the broader point of the Eskridge example should not be missed – and happily, at least these days, it is not – the importance of starting with theory, and "good" theory ("good" to the extent that it is capable of generating observable implications about the phenomenon it seeks to describe or explain) to guide *empirical* research.

Methodology

We emphasize "empirical" to acknowledge that our discussion thus far has, in fact, focused primarily on empirical research – research based on observations of the world (i.e., on data or facts about the world). We do so for a simple reason: even though *purely* normative or theoretical work on courts and judges exists, the vast majority of studies in this field, including the many articles whose main purpose is normative, are empirical. This is not to suggest, however, that all research on courts and judges, at least in terms of its methodology, is similar. Quite the opposite: it differs on at least two dimensions – the types of data invoked and tools used to analyze data.

On both, the range is large. "Data" on courts and judges come in quantitative (numerical) and qualitative (nonnumerical) forms; they are in some studies historical and, in others, contemporary; they may be based on legislation or case law, the results of interviews or survey research, or the outcomes of secondary archival research or primary data collection. Some data that scholars in this field use are quite precise, relatively certain, or both; others are vague or very uncertain. They have been directly observed or indirect proxies, and they have been anthropological, sociological, economic, legal, and political. In other words, if the word "empirical" denotes evidence about the world based on observation or experience, then that evidence, in research on courts and judges, comes in just about every conceivable form, from just about any conceivable source.

Ditto for the types of tools scholars invoke to analyze their data. These days analytic strategies range from simple categorization to complex multivariate models. In other words, methodological diversity abounds, as does methodological innovation. That is (at least in part) because specialists in methodology (though not necessarily in things judicial) have come to see that the unique sorts of data scholars have amassed on courts and judges can provide useful fodder for the development and assessment of innovative analytic strategies (e.g., Caldeira, Wright, and Zorn, 1999; Caldeira and Zorn, 1998; Martin, 2001). We think here of work making use of Bayesian hierarchical (Martin and Quinn, 2001) and event count (Spriggs and Hansford, 2001) models, to name just two.

What results have these and the multitude of other procedures yielded? In the next sections, we address this question via an exploration of four substantive topics that have long intrigued scholars of courts and judges.

JUDICIAL SELECTION AND RETENTION

Of all the difficult choices confronting societies when they go about designing legal systems, among the most controversial are those pertaining to judicial selection and retention: how ought a nation to select its judges and for how long should those jurists serve? Indeed, some of the most fervent constitutional debates – whether they transpired in Philadelphia in 1787 (Farber and Sherry, 1990) or in Moscow in 1993–4 (Hausmaninger, 1995) – over the institutional design of the judicial branch implicate not its power or competencies; they involve who would select and retain its members.

It is thus hardly surprising to find an immense amount of scholarship on questions pertaining to judicial selection and retention, ranging from the primarily normative (Garrow, 2000; Oliver, 1986) to the mainly empirical (Segal, Cameron, and Cover, 1992), to work falling between the two (Hall, 2001). In this section, we focus on one that has generated considerable debate in recent years: what effect(s) do rules governing selection and retention have on the types of men and women who will serve and, in turn, the choices they, as judges, will make? This is a question that strikes at the heart of many debates over the constitutional design of the judicial branch but it is one that yields mixed responses from scholars.

Let us begin with the extent to which the rules affect who becomes judges. At least at the US federal level, where Article II of the Constitution mandates that judges attain their positions through presidential nomination and Senate confirmation, the answer appears to be a good deal. For, depending on the level of the position (trial, circuit, or supreme court), the president enjoys some latitude on who to nominate and, thus, at least according to Sheldon Goldman (1997), are relatively free to advance one or some combination of motivations: the personal (using the nominating power to please a friend or associate), partisan (viewing nominations as vehicles for shoring up electoral support for their party or for themselves within their party or policy), and policy (attempting, via nominations, to enhance the substantive policy objectives of an administration).

Undoubtedly, then, because the formal rules embedded in Article II of the Constitution bestow on the President the power of nomination, presidents have been able to pursue distinct objectives, leading to the nomination of different kinds of people to the bench. But – and this is a big but – because the rules also specify that presidents must obtain the Senate's approval of their nominees, the rules may constrain their ability to achieve their goals (whatever they may be). And, indeed, research has shown that presidents understand this constraint and act accordingly (Moraski and Shipan, 1999). So when the President and the Senate share preferences over the future direction of the judiciary the President is relatively free to appoint a nominee of his choice; but when they are distant, the President must move toward the Senate if he wants to see his nominee confirmed. Seen in this way, the formal rules governing judicial selection not only seem to have an impact on the actors charged with appointing judges but, and more relevant here, they have an effect on who will and will not attain seats on the nation's judiciary. Robert Bork, though clearly a favorite of the Reagan administration, was simply untenable, ideologically speaking, from the Senate's point of view; Anthony Kennedy, though perhaps not Reagan's ideal appointment, was acceptable.

Do we find the same impact of rules at the state level? Surely if it were the case that if most governors operated under the same institutional context as presidents, we might find similar, if not identical, effects. But most do not. These days, election (whether by partisan or nonpartisan ballot) is the principal method of selection of appellate judges in 22 states; the legislatures elects the judges in two states; and the so-called merit plan operates in 22 states. Only in four states does the executive (with the approval of elected bodies in New Jersey and New Hampshire) appoint judges.

Whether these different procedures yield different kinds of judges is an interesting question, and, after years of debate, some consensus appears in the offing. At the very least, it appears clear that the various mechanisms fail to yield judges with "markedly different or superior judicial credentials" (Glick and Emmert, 1987: 232). Slightly more controversial is whether the mechanisms produce a more diverse bench. But even here researchers are converging – with the vast majority now agreeing with Flango and Ducat (1979: 31): "it appears that neither educational, legal, local, prior experience, sex, race, nor role characteristics clearly distinguish among judges appointed under each of the five types of selection systems" (see, e.g., Alozie, 1990; Berg, Green, Schmidhauser, and Schneider, 1975; Canon, 1972; Champagne, 1986; Dubois, 1983; Glick, 1978; Glick and Emmert, 1987; Watson and Downing, 1969; but see also Graham, 1990; Scheb, 1988; Tokarz, 1986; Uhlmann, 1977.)

But these findings do not speak to the second part of the question (and, perhaps the more consequential one at that) that we asked at the onset of this section: what effect(s) do rules governing selection and retention have on the choices that the actors appointed under those systems – judges – make? Do different methods of selection recruit judges with distinct outlooks toward their roles, substantive issues of public policy, or both?

While attempts to address these questions have generated scores of scholarly papers, unfortunately little agreement exists. Some commentators contend that judges who are elected are not likely to behave any differently from those who are appointed (Canon and Jaros, 1970; Flango and Ducat, 1979; Lee, 1970). And it has been strongly argued that accountability to the people, the reason for electing judges, does not occur, because voters are usually unaware and uninformed about the activities of judges. So judges in these electoral states are just as free as their appointed counterparts to ignore the whims of the public and political officials when making their decisions. Other scholars disagree. Hall (2001) shows that judicial elections are as competitive as those for Congress. Given that more than 90 percent of congressional incumbents who stand for re-election win, this figure is not dramatic, but it may mean that elected judges cannot afford to ignore public sentiment when making their decisions.

And there is mounting evidence that they do not. Academics have demonstrated that popularly elected justices are more likely to suppress dissent (Brace and Hall, 1993; Vines, 1962; Watson and Downing, 1969) and reach decisions that reflect popular sentiment (Croly, 1995; Gryski, Main, and Dixon, 1986; Hall 1987a, 1987b; Pinello, 1995; Tabarrok and Helland, 1999).

Though these findings are intriguing, far more scholars ought to weigh in before we can answer conclusively questions about the effect of judicial selection and retention systems on judicial choices. That work could (continue to) commence at the state level, where variation in formal mechanisms abounds. But, to us, the most promising avenues for future study lie beyond the borders of the United States. Indeed, as readers will undoubtedly notice, notably missing from our discussion thus far are analyses of judicial selection and retention abroad. That is because such analyses are notably missing from the literature, even though the variation abroad makes for the stuff of truly comparative analyses. For, while many nations, typically those using the civil law system, have developed similar methods for training and "choosing" ordinary judges, they depart from one another rather dramatically when it comes to the selection of constitutional court justices. In Germany, for example, justices are selected by Parliament, though six of the 16 must be chosen from among professional judges. In Bulgaria, one-third of the justices are selected by Parliament, one-third by the President, and one-third by judges sitting on other courts. Moreover, in some countries with centralized judicial review, justices serve for a limited period of time. In South Africa, for instance, they hold office for a single 12-year term, in Italy a single nine-year term. In others, including the Czech and Korean Republics, justices serve for a set, albeit renewable, term.

Variation is even present in societies that grew out of similar legal traditions and created their court structures at roughly the same historical moment. Table 10.1, which depicts the formal institutions governing the selection of constitutional court judges in the former republics of the Soviet Union, makes this clear: The republics

Table 10.1   Selection systems used in the former republics of the Soviet Union

Country	Selection system	Tenure
Armenia	Parity in appointment: Parliament and President.	Life tenure
Azerbaijan	Nominated by President. Appointed by Parliament.	10-year renewable terms[a]
Belorussia	Parity in appointment: President and upper Chamber of Parliament	11-year renewable terms
Estonia	Nominated by the Chief Justice of Supreme Court. Appointed by Parliament	Life tenure
Georgia	Parity in appointment: President, Parliament, Supreme Court	Nonrenewable 10-year term
Kazakhstan	Parity in appointment: President, Chairs of Upper and Lower Houses	Nonrenewable 6-year term but half members must be renewed every 3 years.
Latvia	3 nominated by Parliament; two each by the Cabinet of Ministers and Supreme Court. Appointed by Parliament.	Nonrenewable 10-year term
Lithuania	Parity in nomination: President, the Chairs of Parliament and Supreme Court. Appointed by Parliament.	Nonrenewable 9-year term
Kyrgyzstan	Nominated by President. Appointed by Parliament.	Nonrenewable 5-year term
Moldova	Parity in appointment: Parliament, the President, and Magistracy	6-year renewable terms[a]
Russia	Nominated by President. Appointed by upper chamber of Parliament.	Was life tenure; changed to nonrenewable 12-year term.
Tajikistan	Nominated by President. Appointed by Parliament.	Nonrenewable 5-year term
Turkmenistan	Nominated and appointed by President.	5-year term but President can remove before completion
Ukraine	Nominated by President. Appointed by Parliament.	Nonrenewable 5-year term
Uzbekistan	Nominated by President. Appointed by Parliament.	Nonrenewable 5-year term

Notes: [a] Different procedures may be used for nomination and appointment of the Chief Justice.

took at least five different approaches: (1) executive/legislative parity (each able to appoint a specified number of judges; (2) executive/judicial (along with, in some instances, legislative) parity; (3) executive nomination (usually) with legislative confirmation; (4) executive/legislative/judicial parity in nomination with parliamentary confirmation; (5) judicial appointment.

We ought to exploit this variation to address some of the perennial concerns in this area of inquiry – for example, those we have considered in this section – as well as to open some new avenues. While so much of the literature has focused on the effects of judicial selection, and we have followed suit, future work ought to consider questions that scholars have devoted almost no time answering – those associated with institutional choice: why do societies choose particular selection and retention institutions? Why do they formally alter those choices? Comparative analyses, again owing to variation among countries, present an extremely fruitful way to gain leverage on these sorts of important but heretofore unaddressed questions.

ACCESS TO COURTS

Just as institutions governing judicial selection vary from country to country, so too do those pertaining to access to courts. But, as a general matter, judges can only decide issues when they come to court in accordance with the jurisdictional rules that the constitutional text or the legislature has prescribed. Yet even then, the judicial process does not automatically go into operation. Judges, in the United States and throughout the world, have imposed a series of informal barriers or developed norms that act as barriers to their courtrooms.

The use of formal and informal norms has given rise to many questions, ranging from whether those norms work to the advantage of particular litigants, to what effect they (and other forces) may have on the agendas of courts. Here we explore yet another – what factors, whether norms or others, influence how judges serving on discretionary courts make decisions over which disputes to hear and resolve and which to reject, that is, how do they go about setting their agendas? This question has fascinated generations of judicial specialists (e.g., Boucher and Segal, 1995; Caldeira and Wright, 1988; Schubert, 1959; Tanenhaus, Schick, Muraskin, and Rosen, 1963; Ulmer, 1972) – as well it should. After all, agenda setting is one of the most important activities undertaken by justices, or any political actors for that matter (see Cobb and Elder, 1983; Kingdon, 1984; Riker, 1993). And it is made even more so in the case of courts, given that the workloads in some are truly monumental – the US Supreme Court receives roughly 7,000 requests for review, the Russian Constitutional Court about 8,000 – and their discretion seemingly equally as high – these days, Supreme Court justices typically hear and decide fewer than 100 cases per term, Russian justices roughly 40. Even courts with fewer cases on their dockets, such as the Canadian Supreme Court, which receives about 450 requests for leave each year, may exercise a substantial degree of discretion; indeed, the Canadian Court decides only about 80 per year.

And, yet, despite all the literature on this topic, scholars have not come to agreement on an answer. Some offer *legal or jurisprudential* models to explain the agenda-setting process (Provine, 1980); others see it as a clear example of *sincere* voting to further policy goals (Krol and Brenner, 1990); still a third set suggest that it is laden with *strategic* calculations (Caldeira, Wright, and Zorn, 1999); finally there are those who point to the *litigants* themselves (Ulmer, 1978). This disagreement, we should stress, is not just a matter of emphasis; it is fundamental and it is an impediment to the development of an understanding of a crucial part of the judges' work – the establishment of their institutional agenda. We return to this point later in the section. For now, let us consider the four basic perspectives with the acknowledgement that while all are dominant, no one dominates.

Scholars adhering to a legal or jurisprudential account hold that judges seek to reach principled decisions at the agenda-setting stage – those based largely on the impartial dictates of various rules governing their review process. In the United

States, that would be Rule 10, which specifies that the justices will accept cases over which conflict exists in the state and federal courts or with Supreme Court precedent; in Canada, the key institution is Section 40(1) of a 1975 amendment of the Supreme Court Act, which places emphasis on the "public importance" of issues raised by counsel (Flemming, Krutz, and Schwank, 1999). When judges follow these sorts of rules, so the argument goes, they are engaging in principled agenda setting because the rules themselves are impartial as to the type of possible result over a particular petition. If judges looked only at whether conflict existed or not or whether the dispute was of public importance their agenda-setting decisions would not reflect their own policy preferences over the substantive consequences of a case but, rather, those of the dictates of the rule itself.

Certainly, there is some support that judges do, in fact, behave in this way. Based on interviews with US Supreme Court justices and their clerks, Perry (1991: 127) concludes that: "Without a doubt, one of the most important things to all the justices is when there is a conflict in the circuits. All of them are disposed to resolve conflicts when they exist and want to know if a particular case poses a conflict." Flemming et al.'s (1999) research reinforces this general conclusion from beyond the borders of the United States. Based on a painstakingly detailed analysis of the Canadian Supreme Court's agenda-setting decisions, they conclude that "jurisprudential factors that reflect the 'public importance' rule" (1999: 21) are the most significant predictors of review.

While virtually all scholars who study agenda setting believe that the legal approach has some merit, many would take issue with the view that it provides *the* key to explaining agenda setting, at least in the US Supreme Court. As Caldeira and Wright (1988: 1114) write, Rule 10 is not all that helpful in understanding "how the Court makes gatekeeping decisions." During the 1989 term, for example, the justices declined to review more than 200 petitions that in one way or another met the criteria stated in its rule (Baum, 2001); and, of the 184 cases it agreed to decide during its 1981 term, only 47 (25%) possessed real conflict (O'Brien, 2000).

Seen in this way, the legal considerations listed in various court rules may act as constraints on the justices' behavior (e.g., the American Supreme Court might reject petitions lacking genuine conflict) but they do not necessarily further our understanding of what occurs in cases meeting the criteria. That is why scholars have looked elsewhere, with one set urging for the adoption of the *sincere policy model* (also called an error-correction or reversal approach). On this account, judges have policy goals at the review stage – that is, they would like to see the final opinion of their court reflect their preferred position – and they achieve them by voting sincerely. In operational terms, judges will vote to grant those cases in which they disagree with the lower court outcome. For example, a right-of-center judge will vote to hear cases in which the lower court reached a liberal decision; a left-of-center justice would prefer to review those decided conservatively below.

Because in many countries constitutional tribunals are not part of the ordinary court system, this hypothesis is quite difficult to assess outside the context of American-styled judiciaries. Nonetheless, at least within the United States, a good deal of support exists for it. In a study that considered the effect of policy preferences while holding constant other factors that may affect the agenda-setting decision, Caldeira and Wright (1988: 1120), for example, conclude that "justices' ideological predilections affect their decisions in much the same way that other elite political actors are motivated by their personal ideological agendas." Providing some confirmation of these results, albeit of agenda setting of a somewhat different form, is George's (1999) study of the determinants of the decision to grant en banc review by US Courts of Appeals. Her data show that "extremely conservative courts of appeals ... are far more likely to rehear a liberal decision en banc than a conservative one" (1999: 256).

In light of these sorts of findings, many scholars have come to accept the view that judges are policy-oriented and actively make choices to advance that goal at the review stage or, for that matter, at all others (see, e.g., Caldeira, Wright, and Zorn, 1999; Epstein and Knight, 1998; Eskridge, 1991b; Gely and Spiller, 1990; Maltzman, Spriggs, and Wahlbeck, 2000; Spiller and Gely, 1992). Where questions arise is over whether they pursue their policy goals in a vacuum (i.e., they always vote on the basis of their sincere preferences) or they pursue them with some consideration of the preferences and likely actions of their colleagues. On the *strategic policy account*, they do the latter: in deciding whether or not to review a case, judges take into account the likelihood of their ability to win at the merits stage. After all, proponents of this account ask, why would policy-oriented justices vote to review a case if they did not think their side could muster sufficient support at the merits stage?

Does the evidence support this view? Yes but it is not monolithic. As early as 1959, Schubert relied on inferences from patterns of data (rather than actual certiorari votes) to argue that during the 1940s, liberals on the US Supreme Court chose to grant FELA cases in which the lower court had decided against the worker *and* in which the worker would have a good chance of winning at the merits stage. In other words, justices "defensively deny" (when they decline to review cases that they would like to hear because they believe they will not prevail at the merits stage) but they do not "aggressively grant" (when they take a case that "may not warrant review because they have calculated that it has certain characteristics that would make it particularly good for developing a doctrine in a certain way, and the characteristics make it more likely to win on their merits..." Perry, 1991: 208). But Boucher and Segal (1995) claim that justices pay attention to probable outcomes when they wish to affirm (an aggressive grant strategy) but not when they desire the Court to reverse, while Caldeira and his colleagues (1999) find evidence of both aggressive grants and defensive denials.

Yet a fourth perspective on agenda setting asserts that the status of particular parties, whether "repeat players" or "one-shotters," "upperdogs" or "underdogs" explains review decisions. McGuire and Caldeira (1993), for example, show that the US Supreme Court is more likely to grant review when an experienced attorney represents the appellant; Ulmer (1978) demonstrates that upperdogs, under certain conditions, have a clear advantage in the American high court; and Flemming and his colleagues (1999: 23) assert that "the status of parties and kinds of lawyers who represent them influence the odds of leave" in the Canadian Supreme Court – though with the caveat that "they take a backseat" to those factors designed to capture the "public importance" rule. Finally, along similar lines, numerous studies have indicated that when the federal government is a petitioner to a suit, the US Supreme Court is more likely to grant review (Armstrong and Johnson, 1982; Caldeira and Wright, 1988; Tanenhaus et al., 1963; Ulmer, 1984).

Why the United States (which is represented by the Solicitor General in the Supreme Court) is so successful is open to speculation. What we do know, and what we hope readers can gather from even this short review, is that it is easy to understand why some scholars have concluded that the agenda-setting literature is a "mess" (Boucher and Segal, 1995). Even those who agree on the basic motivation of judges at the review stage – the pursuit of policy – disagree over whether judges advance that goal by always voting sincerely or by making strategic calculations about the eventual outcome at the merits stage.

It is also worth stressing that this "mess" is a nontrivial one. To the contrary: it has a major effect on our ability to reach a precise understanding of the agenda-setting process, to generate clear-cut predictions. Compounding matters even further is the existence of other plausible explanations that scholars have yet to consider in any serious fashion. For example, it is possible that judges do engage in strategic agenda setting but not with regard to one another; rather they may be attentive to the preferences and likely actions of other relevant actors – such as executives and parliaments – when they go about their agenda-setting task. Consider this comment, from a justice on the Russian Constitutional Court:

> When in December 1995, before the [parliamentary] elections and in the very heat of the electoral campaign, we received a petition signed by a group of deputies concerning the constitutional validity of the five percent barrier for party lists. We refused to consider it. I opposed considering this request, because I believe that the Court should not be itching for a political fight... The Court must avoid getting involved in current political affairs, such as partisan struggles. (Nikitinsky, 1997: 85)

Though this does not provide proof positive of the existence of yet another explanation of agenda-setting decisions, it is suggestive: The field may be even messier than many scholars think.

What then could be done to clean up this "mess"? Several things come to mind. First, scholars ought to refrain from taking certain "short cuts" when they conduct their studies – short cuts that are potentially problematic and may explain the mixed findings in this area. One that comes readily to mind is selection on the dependent variable: in a nontrivial fraction of published studies (e.g., Brenner, 1979; Krol and Brenner, 1990; Palmer, 1982; Provine, 1980) the authors analyze only those cases to which the court in question granted review rather than the full set of petitions – grants and denials. We understand why scholars invoke this strategy – they may lack the time, resources, or both to take another route. But we also must acknowledge that it is replete with potential pitfalls, the most important one being the introduction of bias: since we know (at least in the US context) that cases granted review are not representative of the universe of petitions – in fact, a great deal of research has demonstrated that they vary systematically from nongranted cases – it may be difficult to reach high quality inferences about the way in which justices select cases to review by considering only those petitions they grant. Second, as scholars eliminate this and other shortcuts, they could make an important addition. Just as with the case for judicial selection and retention, they ought to increase the reach of their studies to include discretionary courts abroad. As the author of one of the few comparative analyses in this area (Flemming, 1997: 1) put it: "Very little is known about agenda setting by courts of final appeal in countries other than the United States. As a consequence, we do not know if the large and well-developed American literature on this topic can be generalized beyond the U.S. Supreme Court." Having just undertaken an extensive review of the relevant literature, we could not agree more.

LIMITATIONS ON JUDICIAL POWER

In the last section we examined research exploring how judges on discretionary courts make decisions that, in effect, limit access to their tribunals; this section considers scholarship investigating the limitations imposed on judges by their political and institutional settings. Just as the other bodies of literature we have thus far considered are vast, so too is the research in this area – with previous work suggesting that judges must be (or need not be) attentive to the preferences and likely actions of a wide range of actors, from members of the executive and legislative branches (e.g., Eskridge, 1991a, 1991b; Spiller and Gely, 1992) to judges on higher courts (Segal, 1995; Songer, Segal, and Cameron, 1994) to citizens (Mishler and Sheehan, 1993, 1996; Stimson, MacKuen, and Erikson, 1995).

In what follows, we have chosen to focus on literature exploring the limits that elected political actors may (or may not) impose on judges. We do so for several reasons, chief among them is this: while questions concerning the effect of elected actors are not new – scholars have been raising them for nearly a half century, maybe longer – today's researchers have invoked new theories and methodologies, as well as expanded their substantive concerns to incorporate courts abroad and to explore them. Accordingly, this line of inquiry has a very contemporary feel to it and one worthy of consideration here.

The central question within this recent spate of literature is a simple one: to what extent do members of legislatures and executives constrain the behavior of judges? Developing clear responses, though, is far from simple. To begin with there is the matter of why we even pose this question, at least as it pertains to judges who need not face re-election or attain approval from elected actors to retain their jobs; in other words, why would we even expect judges with, say, life tenure, to pay heed to the preferences and likely actions of elected actors? Some scholars say we should not. Segal and Spaeth (1993), for example, claim that, under certain institutional conditions – including the existence of life tenure, the lack of superiors in the judicial hierarchy, and the dearth of political ambition – judges on high or constitutional courts will be free to ignore the desires of elected actors. Under these conditions, the judges will simply behave in ways that accord with their own policy preferences.

But others say that even judges who meet Segal and Spaeth's conditions must take into account the preferences and likely actions of legislatures (Epstein and Knight, 1998; Epstein, Knight, and Martin, 2001; Murphy, 1964; Rosenberg, 1992). They make this claim on a number of grounds: key among them is that even if judges are "single-minded seekers of legal policy" (George and Epstein, 1992: 325) as Segal and Spaeth contend, why would those judges not care about the ultimate state of that policy? To rephrase the question: why would justices who are policy-preference maximizers take a position they know the legislature would overturn? To argue that justices would do this – merely vote their attitudes – is to argue that courts are full of myopic thinkers, who consider only the shape of policy in the short term. Such an argument does not square with much important writing about how American-style courts interpret statutes – including Eskridge's (1994, 1991a, 1991b), which we discussed earlier. It also does not seem to sit comfortably with an emerging body of literature on constitutional adjudication. While legislatures and executives cannot typically pass legislation to overturn decisions reached by courts on constitutional grounds, they can take many other steps to punish "errant" courts, thereby making it difficult for them not just to achieve policy goals but to develop or maintain some level of legitimacy, as well. Rosenberg (1992) outlines a few of these steps, all of which the US Congress, the President, or both have attempted to take:

> (1) [U]sing the Senate's confirmation power to select certain types of judges; (2) enacting constitutional amendments to reverse decisions or change Court structure or procedure; (3) impeachment; (4) withdrawing Court jurisdiction over certain subjects; (5) altering the selection and removal process; (6) requiring extraordinary majorities for declarations of unconstitutionality; (7) allowing appeal from the Supreme Court to a more 'representative' tribunal; (8) removing the power of judicial review; (9) slashing the budget; (10) altering the size of the Court. (Rosenberg, 1992: 377)

Rosenberg's list of weapons pertains directly to the American context. Even more radical steps have been taken abroad. In Russia, for example, President Boris Yeltsin, angry at its ability to check his power, suspended his nation's constitutional court in 1993. The justices were not able to resume their work until nearly two years later, when Russia adopted a new constitutional text.

It is these sorts of weapons, scholars argue, that lead judges to pay attention to the preferences and likely actions of those in a position to deploy them. But is such behavior on the part of justices wide-scale and wide-ranging? Given the state of existing literature, it is hard to tell.

Which takes us to a second complication: even if we believe that judges feel constrained by legislatures and executives, documenting that is extremely difficult. The chief problem is this: when judges rule in favor of, say, the existing regime, they may do so because they share the preferences of that regime, not because they are attempting to appease that regime. And distinguishing these forms of behavior – sincerely and sophisticated, respectively – turns out to be no easy task.

This is not to say that scholars have not tried. Quite the opposite: they have produced interesting analyses of the relationship between executives and legislatures and courts in Argentina (Helmke, 1999), Russia (Epstein, Knight, and Shvetsova, 2001), Germany (Vanberg, 1999), and, of course, the United States (Spiller and Gely, 1992). But the results have been somewhat mixed and the literature insufficiently developed to reach any firm conclusions yet.

What this suggests is that we still have a long distance to travel before we fully understand the effect elected actors may have on courts. We could say the same about the flipside – the constraint courts may place on legislatures and executives, which is, as some scholars have recognized, a topic ripe for further systematic analysis (Martin, 2001; Stone, 1994, 1995; Sweet, 2000) as well as about the many other actors with whom courts, directly or indirectly, interact. These include, as we mentioned at the onset, the public and other judges in the hierarchy. We are making substantial progress on these fronts but both deserve even more sustained attention given the potentially important role they may play developing a fuller appreciation of the role of courts in their societies.

JUDICIAL DECISION MAKING

It seems that we have started each new section with the claim that "this area has generated an immense amount of research." This is certainly true with regard to the other areas but it is doubly so for judicial decision making. Over the past five decades, members of the law and society community have produced mounds of paper attempting to explain judicial decisions – be they decisions that involve fact finding, using precedent, or interpreting laws or constitutional texts. The result is a vast literature that approaches the subject from normative and positivist perspectives, with theories adopted and adapted from the social sciences and humanities, and with data that are qualitative and quantitative.

Once again no one chapter, much less a section of one chapter, could consider all this scholarship. And we will not try. Rather, our intent is to highlight an area that has attracted considerable attention from scholars studying judges in common law (and now even civil law) systems: what role does precedent play in court decisions? Research has supplied three distinct answers: a lot, some, or none.

When it comes to lower tribunals, there is little disagreement among scholars that precedent probably matters a lot – though they disagree on why that may be so. To some, the explanation lies in the hierarchy of justice (Segal, 1995; Songer, Segal, and Cameron 1994): because lower court judges do not want to be reversed by their "superiors," they abide by precedent established by those superiors. Take trial court judges: although their superiors – jurists on intermediate appellate courts – give a certain presumption to their judgments, reversals of lower courts' rulings do occur. By the same token, tribunals of last resort may have the opportunity to review decisions made by intermediate appellate courts; and they, too, have not hesitated to reverse their colleagues on lower courts. Rehnquist once explained why the US Supreme Court had, in the early 1980s, reversed 27 of 28 rulings by the Court of Appeals for the Ninth Circuit: "When all is said and done, some panels of the Ninth Circuit have a hard time saying no to any litigant with a hard luck story." Such extensive monitoring of one particular circuit may be exceptional; but, as Segal and his colleagues have demonstrated (Segal, 1995; Songer, Segal, and Cameron, 1994), the mere threat of review by the Supreme Court may induce judges of intermediate appellate courts to follow the commands of their superiors.

To others, the explanation lies not in the desire of judges to avoid reversal but in their interest in following "their professional obligations," in reaching principled decisions. Research adopting this view, as Kahn (1999) puts it,

> assumes that justices make decisions in an institutional context which informs the choices they make. It assumes that the Court's institutional norms and commitments are important for the maintenance of constitutional principles and Court decision-making. Moreover, justices must be principled in their decision-making process if they are to have the continued respect of their colleagues, the wider interpretive community, citizens, and leaders. Justices must not only convince us that a specific case decision is wise, but also that the principles upon which they base their decision, and upon which future cases are based, are appropriate. (Kahn, 1999: 176)

This perspective informs not just the use of precedent by lower court judges but, quite pointedly, by courts of last resort as well. And it is this part of the explanation – along with many others suggesting that precedent matters a lot for jurists serving on their nation's highest courts – that is the source of substantial disagreement. While Kahn and other adherents of his brand of "historical institutionalism" suggest that justices will follow principles, such as *stare decisis*, even when the principles are at odds with their preferences, others respond "poppycock": when judges do not have superiors, when they have life tenure, they need not be constrained by precedent just as they need not be attentive to the preferences of legislatures and excutives; they can vote in accord with their own policy preferences (Segal and Spaeth, 1993, 1996; Spaeth and Segal, 1999).

There is yet a third response – one that lies between these two extremes: precedent neither is completely determinant or indeterminate of judicial outcomes; rather, it can serve as a constraint on justices acting on their personal preferences (Epstein and Knight, 1998; Knight and Epstein, 1996). On this account, judges have a preferred rule that they would like to establish in the case before them, but they strategically modify their position to take account of a normative constraint – a norm favoring precedent – in order to produce a decision as close as is possible to their preferred outcome.

Why would they do so? At least two reasons come to mind. First, there are prudential reasons to suggest that judges might follow precedent rather than their own policy preferences. *Stare decisis* is one way in which courts respect the established expectations of a community. To the extent that the members of a community base their future expectations on the belief that others in that community will follow existing laws, courts have an interest in minimizing the disruptive effects of overturning existing rules of behavior. If courts seek to radically change existing rules, then the changes may be more than that to which the members of the community can adapt, resulting in decisions that do not produce rules that will be efficacious. Second, there are normative reasons why justices may follow precedent as opposed to their own preferences. If a community has a fundamental belief that the "rule of law" requires courts to be constrained by precedent, then judges can be constrained by precedent even if they personally do not accept that fundamental belief. The constraint follows from the effect of the community's belief in its willingness to accept and comply with the decisions of their courts. If the members of the community believe that the legitimate judicial function involves the following of precedent, then they will reject as normatively illegitimate the decisions of any court that regularly and systematically violate precedent. To the extent that judges are concerned with establishing rules that will engender the compliance of the community, they will take account of the fact that they must establish rules that are legitimate in the eyes of that community. In this way a norm of *stare decisis* can constrain the actions of even those judges who do not share the view that they should be constrained by past decisions.

Just as all three responses to questions about the importance of precedent have their logical merit, so too do they have empirical support. As for the view that precedent has a major effect on court decisions, we already have mentioned a study by Segal and his colleagues substantiating as much at the intermediate appellate court level. At the highest rungs of judicial systems the effect too has been documented both in studies relying on historical and qualitative evidence (e.g., Kahn, 1999) and on contemporary and quantitative data (e.g., George and Epstein, 1992).

But there are equally as many studies that dispute these findings, that claim precedent has an almost negligible effect on decisions – even in those produced by lower courts. Research by Cross and Tiller (1998) suggests that judges of US Court of Appeals are less than faithful followers of precedents they do not like. When there is a "whistleblower" on the court – that is, a judge "whose policy preferences differ from the majority's" (Cross and Tiller, 1998: 2155) and who will expose the majority's failure to apply relevant precedents – the majority will follow *stare decisis*. But when a whistleblower is not present, according to Cross and Tiller, the court will attempt to manipulate precedents to conform to its political values. Segal and Spaeth (1996), focusing on the US Supreme Court, invoke a clever research design to arrive at a similar conclusion. They hypothesize that if precedent matters, it ought to affect the subsequent decisions of members of the Court. If a justice dissented from a decision establishing a particular precedent, the same justice would not dissent from a subsequent application of the precedent. But that was not the case. Of the 18 justices included in their study, only two occasionally subjugated their preferences to precedent (see also Spaeth and Segal, 1999).

Finally, in a critique of Segal and Spaeth's work, we (Knight and Epstein, 1996) offered widespread evidence of behavior that is consistent with the existence of a norm of respect for precedent and that is inconsistent with the lack of such a norm. That evidence ranged from the use of precedent in attorneys' briefs, to appeals to precedent made by Supreme Court justices in their private conferences, to citations to precedent in court decisions.

Undoubtedly, this debate will continue as all sides muster more and more support for their positions. Some of that support will inevitably come from research that maintains a focus on US courts at all levels, but we think researchers would be well advised to gather evidence from other tribunals. Work that systematically looks at the correlates of judicial decisions in other common law systems certainly exists (for a view, see Tate and Haynie, 2001) but much of it is dated or considers just a few (with precedent often not among them). At least to us, scholars of different minds on the importance (or lack thereof) of precedent should find it nearly irresistible to turn to courts abroad to develop and assess more and more observable implications of their theories. We could of course say the same about virtually every topic we explored herein.

DISCUSSION

If anything, this brief essay has lived up to a promise we made at the onset: we could only skim the surface (and now have). We did not cover many strains of research in the areas we did cover; we left uncovered many areas altogether. Within the latter, we are particularly regretful that we lacked space to discuss the impact of courts and judges – a subject that is of considerable interest to law and society scholars and one that has generated deep debate in recent years, or at least since publication of Rosenberg's (1991) *The Hollow Hope*. In that path-breaking book, Rosenberg argued that *Brown v. Board of Education* (1954) produced little integration in public schools in the South until Congress, at the insistent urging of the President, the Department of Justice, the US Commission on Civil Rights, and the broader civil rights movement, had enacted various pieces of civil rights legislation. This specific finding, along with Rosenberg's more general claim – that only under a very particular set of circumstances can courts generate significant social change – has its share of supporters and detractors. Standing out among the latter is McCann (1994) who documents how various groups and attorneys used litigation to extract from reticent employers compliance with statutes and appellate decisions promoting the cause of equal pay for women.

And, yet, even with this (and other) glaring omission(s), we see the emergence of several themes. Some concern the role rules play in structuring the choices judges make; others implicate the generalizability of findings across judges working at different levels in their legal systems and in different societies. But at least one takes us back to our starting point: while scholars have traveled some distance in their quest to understand various features of judicial processes as they pertain to courts and judges, substantial gaps remain in our knowledge. Assuming a continued emphasis on the development of theory, the expansion of our empirical targets, and the application of cutting-edge technology, however, judicial specialists will fill these gaps and fill them soon enough to make the task of those who write chapters on "Courts and Judges" for future volumes even more daunting than the one we faced.

References

Alozie, Nicholas A. (1990) "Distribution of women and minority judges: The effects of judicial selection methods," *Social Science Quarterly* 71: 315.

Armstrong, Virginia and Johnson, Charles A. (1982) "Certiorari decisions by the Warren and Burger courts: Is cue theory time bound?" *Polity* 15: 141–50.

Baum, Lawrence (2001) *The Supreme Court*, 7th edn. Washington, DC: CQ Press.

Berg, Larry L., Green, Justin J., Schmidhauser, John P., and Schneider, Ronald S. (1975) "The consequences of judicial reform: A comparative analysis of California and Iowa appellate systems," *Western Political Quarterly* 28: 263.

Boucher, Robert L., Jr. and Segal, Jeffrey A. (1995) "Supreme Court justices as strategic decision makers: Aggressive grants and defensive denials," *Journal of Politics* 57: 824–37.

Brace, Paul and Hall, Melinda Gann (1993) "Integrated models of dissent," *Journal of Politics* 55: 919–35.

Brenner, Saul (1979) "The new certiorari game," *Journal of Politics* 41: 649–55.

Brown v. Board of Education (1954) 347 U.S. 483

Caldeira, Gregory A. and Wright, John R. (1988) "Organized interests and agenda setting in the U.S. Supreme Court," *American Political Science Review* 82: 1109–28.

Caldeira, Gregory A., Wright, John R. and Zorn, Christopher J. (1999) "Sophisticated voting and gate-keeping in the Supreme Court," *Journal of Law, Economics, & Organization* 15: 549–77.

Caldeira, Gregory A. and Zorn, Christopher J. (1998) "Of time and consensual norms in the Supreme Court," *American Journal of Political Science* 42: 874–902.

Canon, Bradley C. (1972) "The impact of formal selection process on the characteristics of judges – reconsidered," *Law and Society Review* 6: 579–93.

Canon, Bradley C. and Jaros, Dean (1970) "External variables, institutional structure and dissent on state Supreme Courts," *Polity* 3: 175–200.

Champagne, Anthony (1986) "The selection and retention of judges in Texas," *Southwestern Law Journal* 40: 53–117.

Cobb, Roger W. and Elder, Charles D. (1983) *Participation in America: The Dynamics of Agenda Building*. Baltimore: Johns Hopkins University Press.

Croly, Steven P. (1995) "The majoritarian difficulty: Elective judiciaries and the rule of law," *University of Chicago Law Review* 62: 689–791.

Cross, Frank B. and Tiller, Emerson H. (1998) "Judicial partisanship and obedience to legal doctrine: Whistleblowing on the Federal Courts of Appeals," *Yale Law Journal* 107: 2155–76.

Dubois, Philip L. (1983) "The influence of selection system and region on the characteristics of a trial court bench: The case of California," *Justice System Journal* 8: 59–87.

Dubois, Philip (1986) "Accountability, independence, and the selection of state judges: The role of popular judicial elections," *Southwestern Law Journal* 40: 31–52.

Epstein, Lee and Knight, Jack (1998) *The Choices Justices Make*. Washington, DC: CQ Press.

Epstein, Lee, Knight, Jack, and Martin, Andrew D. (2001) "The Supreme Court as a *strategic* national policy maker," *Emory Law Journal* 50: 101–29.

Epstein, Lee, Knight, Jack, and Shvetsova, Olga (2001) "The role of constitutional courts in the establishment and maintenance of democratic systems of government," *Law & Society Review* 35: 117–64.

Eskridge, William N. Jr. (1991a) "Overriding Supreme Court statutory interpretation decisions," *Yale Law Journal* 101: 331–417.

Eskridge, William N. Jr. (1991b) "Reneging on history?: Playing the court/congress/president civil rights game," *California Law Review* 79: 613–84.

Eskridge, William N. Jr. (1994) *Dynamic Statutory Interpretation.* Cambridge, MA: Harvard University Press.

Farber, Daniel A. and Sherry, Suzanna (1990) *A History of the American Constitution.* St. Paul, MN: West.

Flango, Victor Eugene and Ducat, Craig R. (1979) "What difference does method of judicial selection make? Selection procedures in state courts of last resort," *Justice System Journal* 5: 25–44.

Flemming, Roy B. (1997) "Deciding to decide in Canada's Supreme Court," Paper presented at the Conference Group on the Scientific Study of Judicial Politics, Atlanta, GA.

Flemming, Roy B., Krutz, Glen S., and Schwank, Jennifer Renee (1999) "Agenda setting on the Supreme Court of Canada," Paper presented at the Conference on the Scientific Study of Judicial Politics, College Station, Texas.

Garrow, David J. (2000) "Mental decreptitude on the U.S. Supreme Court: The historical case for a 28th amendment," *University of Chicago Law Review* 67: 995.

Gely, Rafael and Spiller, Pablo T. (1990) "A rational choice theory of Supreme Court decision making with applications to the *State Farm* and *Grove City* cases," *Journal of Law, Economics, & Organization* 6: 263–300.

George, Tracey E. (1999) "The dynamics and determinants of the decision to grant en banc review," *Washington Law Review* 74: 213–74.

George, Tracey E. and Epstein, Lee (1992) "On the nature of Supreme Court decision making," *American Political Science Review* 86: 323–37.

Glick, Henry R. (1978) "The promise and performance of the Missouri Plan: Judicial selection in the fifty states," *University of Miami Law Review* 32: 509–41.

Glick, Henry R. and Emmert, Craig F. (1987) "Selection systems and judicial characteristics: The recruitment of state Supreme Court judges," *Judicature* 70: 228–35.

Goldman, Sheldon (1997) *Picking Federal Judges.* New Haven, CT: Yale University Press.

Graham, Barbara Luck (1990) "Judicial recruitment and racial diversity on state courts: An overview," *Judicature* 74: 28.

Gryski, Gerard S., Main, Eleanor C., and Dixon, William J. (1986) "Models of state high court decision making in sex discrimination cases," *Journal of Politics* 48: 143–55.

Hall, Melinda Gann (1987a) "Constituent influence in state Supreme Court: Conceptual notes and a case study," *Journal of Politics* 49: 1117–24.

Hall, Melinda Gann (1987b) "An examination of voting behavior in the Louisiana Supreme Court," *Judicature* 71: 40–6.

Hall, Melinda Gann (2001) "State Supreme Court in American democracy: Probing the myths of judicial reform," *American Political Science Review* 95: 315–30.

Hausmaninger, Herbert (1995) "Towards a 'new' Russian constitutional court," *Cornell International Law Journal* 28: 349.

Haynes, Evan (1944) *The Selection and Tenure of Judges.* Newark, NJ: National Conference of Judicial Councils.

Helmke, Gretchen (1999) "Ruling against the rulers: Insecure tenure and judicial independence in Argentina, 1976–1995," Working paper, University of Chicago.

Kahn, Ronald (1999) "Institutional norms and Supreme Court decision making: The Rehnquist Court on privacy and religion," in Cornell W. Clayton and Howard Gillman (eds.), *Supreme Court Decision-Making.* Chicago: University of Chicago Press, pp. 175–98.

King, Gary, Keohane, Robert O., and Verba, Sidney (1994) *Designing Social Inquiry: Scientific Inference in Qualitative Research*. Princeton, NJ: Princeton University Press.

Kingdon, John W. (1984) *Agendas, Alternatives, and Public Policies*. Boston: Little, Brown.

Knight, Jack and Epstein, Lee (1996) "The norm of *stare decisis*," *American Journal of Political Science* 40: 1018–35.

Krol, John F. and Brenner, Saul (1990) "Strategies in certiorari voting on the United States Supreme Court," *Western Political Quarterly* 43: 335–42.

Lee, Francis G. (1970) "An explanatory variable of judicial behavior on bi-partisan state Supreme Courts," PhD thesis, University of Pennsylvania.

Maltzman, Forrest, Spriggs, James F. II , and Wahlbeck, Paul J. (2000) *Crafting Law on the Supreme Court*. Cambridge, UK: Cambridge University Press.

Martin, Andrew D. (2001) "Congressional decision making and the separation of powers," *American Political Science Review* 95: 361–78.

Martin, Andrew D. and Quinn, Kevin M. (2001) "Bayesian learning about ideal points on the Supreme Court, 1953–1999," Paper presented at the Political Methodology Society, Atlanta, GA.

Mather, Lynn (1995) "The fired football coach," in Lee Epstein (ed.), *Contemplating Courts*. Washington, DC: CQ Press, pp. 170–202.

McCann, Michael W. (1994) *Rights at Work*. Chicago: University of Chicago Press.

McGuire, Kevin T. (1995) "Repeat players in the Supreme Court: The role of experienced lawyers in litigation success," *Journal of Politics* 57: 187–96.

McGuire, Kevin T. and Caldeira, Gregory A. (1993) "Lawyers, organized interests, and the law of obscenity: Agenda-setting in the Supreme Court." *American Political Science Review* 87: 717–28.

Mishler, William and Sheehan, Reginald (1993) "The Supreme Court as a countermajoritarian institution? The impact of public opinion on Supreme Court decisions," *American Political Science Review* 87: 716–24.

Mishler, William and Sheehan, Reginald (1996) "Public opinion, the attitudinal model, and Supreme Court decision making: A micro-analytic perspective," *Journal of Politics* 56: 169–200.

Moraski, Brian J. and Shipan, Charles R. (1999) "The politics of Supreme Court nominations: A theory of institutional choice and constraints," *American Journal of Political Science* 43: 1069.

Murphy, Walter F. (1964) *Elements of Judicial Strategy*. Chicago: University of Chicago Press.

Nikitinsky, Leonid (1997) "Interview with Boris Ebzeev, Justice of the Constitutional Court of the Russian Federation," *Eastern European Constitutional Review* Winter: 83–8.

O'Brien, David M. (2000) *Storm Center: The Supreme Court in American Politics*, 5th edn. New York: W.W. Norton & Co.

Oliver, Philip D. (1986) "Systematic justice: A proposed constitutional amendment to establish fixed, staggered terms for members of the United States Supreme Court." *Ohio State Law Review* 47: 799.

Palmer, Jan (1982) "An econometric analysis of the U.S. Supreme Court's certiorari decisions," *Public Choice* 39: 387–98.

Perry, H.W. (1991) *Deciding to Decide: Agenda Setting in the United States Supreme Court*. Cambridge, MA: Harvard University Press.

Pinello, Daniel R. (1995) *The Impact of Judicial Selection Method on State-Supreme-Court Policy*. Westport, CT: Greenwood.

Provine, Doris Marie (1980) *Case Selection in the United States Supreme Court*. Chicago: University of Chicago Press.

Ramseyer, J. Mark (1994) "The puzzling (in)dependence of courts: A comparative approach," *Journal of Legal Studies* 23: 721.

Riker, William H. (ed.) (1993) *Agenda Formation*. Ann Arbor: University of Michigan Press.

Rosenberg, Gerald N. (1991) *The Hollow Hope*. Chicago: University of Chicago Press.

Rosenberg, Gerald N. (1992) "Judicial independence and the reality of political power," *Review of Politics* 54: 369–98.

Scheb, John M. (1988) "State appellate judges' attitudes toward judicial merit selection and retention: Results of a national survey," *Judicature* 72: 170–4.

Schubert, Glendon (1959) "The certiorari game," in Glendon Schubert (ed.), *Quantitative Analysis of Judicial Behavior*. New York: Free Press, pp. 210–55.

Segal, Jeffrey A. (1995) "Decision making on the U.S. Courts of Appeals," in Lee Epstein (ed.), *Contemplating Courts*. Washington, DC: CQ Press, pp. 227–46.

Segal, Jeffrey A., Cameron, Charles M., and Cover, Albert D. (1992) "A spatial model of roll call voting: Senators, constituents, presidents, and interest groups in Supreme Court confirmations," *American Journal of Political Science* 36: 96–121.

Segal, Jeffrey A and Spaeth, Harold J. (1993) *The Supreme Court and the Attitudinal Model*. New York: Cambridge University Press.

Segal, Jeffrey A and Spaeth, Harold J. (1996) "The influence of stare decisis on the vote of United States Supreme Court justices," *American Journal of Political Science* 40: 971–1003.

Songer, Donald R., Segal, Jeffrey A., and Cameron, Charles M. (1994) "The hierarchy of justice: Testing a principal-agent theory of Supreme Court-Circuit Court interactions," *Journal of Politics* 38: 673.

Spaeth, Harold J. and Segal, Jeffrey A. (1999) *Majority Rule or Minority Will : Adherence to Precedent on the U.S. Supreme Court*. New York: Cambridge University Press.

Spiller, Pablo T. and Gely, Rafael (1992) "Congressional control of judicial independence: The determinants of U.S. Supreme Court labor-relations decisions, 1949–1988." *RAND Journal of Economics* 23: 463–92.

Spriggs, James F. II and Hansford, Thomas G. (2001) "Explaining the overruling of U.S. Supreme Court precedent," *Journal of Politics* 63: 1091–111.

Stimson, James A., MacKuen, Michael B., and Erikson, Robert S. (1995) "Dynamic representation," *American Political Science Review* 89: 543–65.

Stone, Alec (1994) *The Birth of Judicial Politics in France*. New York: Oxford University Press, 1994.

Stone, Alec (1995) "Complex coordinate construction in France and Germany," in C. Neal Tate and Torbjörn Vallinder (eds.), *The Global Expansion of Judicial Power*. New York: New York University Press, pp. 205–30.

Sweet, Alec Stone (2000) *Governing with Judges: Constitutional Politics in Europe*. New York: Oxford University Press.

Tabarrok, Alexander and Helland, Eric (1999) "Court politics: The political economy of tort awards," *Journal of Law & Economics* 42: 157–87.

Tanenhaus, Joseph, Schick, Marvin, Muraskin, Matthew, and Rosen, Daniel (1963) "The Supreme Court's certiorari jurisdiction: Cue theory," in Glendon Schubert (ed.), *Judicial Decision Making*. New York: Free Press, pp. 111–32.

Tate, C. Neal and Haynie, Stacia L. (2001) "Comparative judicial politics: Intellectual history and bibliography," Paper presented at the American Political Science Association, San Francisco, CA.

Tokarz, Karen L. (1986) "Women judges and merit selection under the Missouri Plan," *Washington University Law Quarterly* 64: 903–51.

Uhlmann, Thomas M. (1977) "Race, recruitment, representation: Background differences between black and white trial court judges," *Western Political Quarterly* 30: 457–70.

Ulmer, S. Sidney (1972) "The decisions to grant certiorari as an indicator to decision 'on the merits'," *Polity* 4: 429–47.

Ulmer, S. Sidney (1978) "Selecting cases for Supreme Court review: An underdog model," *American Political Science Review* 72: 902–10.

Ulmer, S. Sidney (1984) "The Supreme Court's certiorari decisions: Conflict as a predictive variable," *American Political Science Review* 78: 901–11.

Vanberg, Georg Stephan (1999) "The politics of constitutional review: Constitutional court and parliament in Germany." PhD thesis, University of Rochester.

Vines, Kenneth N. (1962) "Political functions on a State Supreme Court," in Kenneth N. Vines and Herbert Jacob (eds.), *Tulane Studies in Political Science: Studies in Judicial Politics*. New Orleans: Tulane University, pp. 51–77.

Walker, Thomas G. (1994) "The development of the field," Paper presented at the Columbus Conference on the State of the Field of Judicial Politics, Columbus, OH.

Watson, Richard A. and Downing, Rondal G. (1969) *The Politics of Bench and Bar: Judicial Selection under the Missouri Nonpartisan Court Plan*. New York: Wiley.

Widner, Jennifer A. (2001) *Building the Rule of Law*. New York: Norton.

Further Reading

Baum, Lawrence (1997) *The Puzzle of Judicial Behavior, Analytical Perspectives on Politics*. Ann Arbor: University of Michigan Press.

Benesh, Sara C. (2002) *The U.S. Courts of Appeals and the Law of Confessions: Perspectives on the Hierarchy of Justice*. New York: LFB Scholarly Publishing.

Brace, Paul and Hall, Melinda Gann (1997) "The interplay of preferences, case facts, context, and rules in the politics of judicial choice," *Journal of Politics* 59: 1206.

Brenner, Saul (1989) "Fluidity on the United States Supreme Court: A reexamination," in Sheldon Goldman and Austin Sarat (eds.), *American Court Systems*. New York: Longman, pp. 479–85.

Brenner, Saul and Krol, John F. (1989) "Strategies in certiorari voting on the United States Supreme Court," *Journal of Politics* 51: 828–40.

Burbank, Stephen B. and Friedman, Barry (eds.) (2002) *Judicial Independence at the Cross-roads*. Thousand Oaks, CA: Sage Publications and the American Academy of Political and Social Science.

Caldeira, Gregory A. (1987) "Public opinion and the U.S. Supreme Court: FDR's court-packing plan," *American Political Science Review* 81(4): 1139–53.

Caldeira, Gregory A. and Gibson, James L. (1992) "The etiology of public support for the Supreme Court," *American Journal of Political Science* 36: 635–64.

Caldeira, Gregory A. and Gibson, James L. (1995) "The legitimacy of the Court of Justice in the European Union: Models of institutional support," *American Political Science Review* 89: 356–76.

Cameron, Charles M., Cover, Albert D., and Segal, Jeffrey A. (1990) "Senate voting on Supreme Court nominees: A neoinstitutional model," *American Political Science Review* 84: 525–34.

Cameron, Charles M., Segal, Jeffrey A., and Songer, Donald R. (2000) "Strategic auditing in a political hierarchy: An informational model of the Supreme Court's certiorari decisions," *American Political Science Review* 94: 101–16.

Caminker, Evan H. (1994) "Why must inferior courts obey superior court precedent?" *Stanford Law Review* 46: 817–73.

Canon, Bradley C. and Johnson, Charles A. (1998) *Judicial Policies: Implementation and Impact*, 2nd edn. Washington, D.C.: CQ Press.

Carter, Stephen L. (1994) *The Confirmation Mess: Cleaning up the Federal Appointments Process*. New York: Basic Books.

Clayton, Cornell W. and Gillman, Howard (eds.) (1999) *Supreme Court Decision-Making*. Chicago: University of Chicago Press.

Cook, Beverly Blair (1977) "Public opinion and federal judicial policy," *American Journal of Political Science* 21: 567–600.

Cook, Beverly Blair (1982) "Women as Supreme Court candidates: From Florence Allen to Sandra Day O'Connor," *Judicature* 65: 314–26.

Cross, Frank B. (1997) "Political science and the new legal realism: A case of unfortunate interdisciplinary ignorance," *Northwestern University Law Review* 92: 251–326.

Dahl, Robert A. (1957) "Decision-making in a democracy: The Supreme Court as a national policymaker," *Journal of Public Law* 6: 279–95.

Epstein, Lee (1995) *Contemplating Courts*. Washington, DC: CQ Press.

Epstein, Lee and Knight, Jack (2000) "Toward a strategic revolution in judicial politics: A look back, a look ahead," *Political Research Quarterly* 53: 625–61.

Ferejohn, John and Weingast, Barry (1992a) "Limitation of statutes: Strategic statutory interpretation," *Georgetown Law Review* 80: 565–82.

Ferejohn, John and Weingast, Barry (1992b) "A positive theory of statutory interpretation," *International Review of Law and Economics* 12: 263–79.

Gates, John B. and Johnson, Charles A. (eds.) (1991) *The American Courts: A Critical Assessment*. Washington, DC: CQ Press.

Gibson, James L. (1978) "Judges' role orientations, attitudes, and decisions: An interactive model," *American Political Science Review* 72: 911–24.

Gibson, James L., Caldeira, Gregory A., and Baird, Vanessa A. (1998) "On the legitimacy of high courts," *American Political Science Review* 92(2): 343–58.

Gillman, Howard (2001) *The Votes that Counted*. Chicago: University of Chicago Press.

Howard, J. Woodford (1968) "On the fluidity of judicial choice," *American Political Science Review* 62: 43–56.

Howard, J. Woodford (1977) "Role perceptions and behavior in three U.S. courts of appeals," *Journal of Politics* 39: 916–38.

Kornhauser, Lewis A. (1992a) "Modeling collegial courts I: Path dependence," *International Review of Law and Economics* 12: 169–85.

Kornhauser, Lewis A. (1992b) "Modeling collegial courts II. Legal doctrine," *Journal of Law, Economics, & Organization* 8: 441–70.

Lim, Youngsik (2000) "An empirical analysis of Supreme Court justices' decision making," *Journal of Legal Studies* 29: 721–51.

McNollgast (1995) "Politics and courts: A positive theory of judicial doctrine and the rule of law," *Southern California Law Review* 68: 1631–83.

Murphy, Walter F. (1959) "Lower court checks on Supreme Court power," *American Political Science Review* 53: 1017–31.

Murphy, Walter F. (1962) *Congress and the Court*. Chicago: University of Chicago Press.

Murphy, Walter F., Pritchett, C. Herman, and Epstein, Lee (2001) *Courts, Judges, and Politics*, 5th edn. New York: McGraw-Hill.

Murphy, Walter F. and Tanenhaus, Joseph (1990) "Publicity, public opinion and the court," *Northwestern University Law Review* 84: 983–1036.

Peretti, Terri (1999) *In Defense of a Political Court*. Princeton, NJ: Princeton University Press.

Posner, Richard A (1985) *The Federal Courts*. Cambridge, MA: Harvard University Press.

Posner, Richard A (1993) "What do judges and justices maximize? (the same thing everybody else does)," *Supreme Court Economic Review* 33: 1–26.

Priest, George L. and Klein, Benjamin (1984) "The selection of disputes for litigation," *Journal of Legal Studies* 13–55.

Pritchett, C. Herman (1948) *The Roosevelt Court*. New York: Macmillan.

Pritchett, C. Herman (1961) *Congress against the Supreme Court*. Minneapolis, MN: University of Minnesota Press.

Revesz, Richard L. (1997) "Environmental regulation, ideology, and the D.C. circuit," *Virginia Law Review* 83: 1717–72.

Rohde, David W. and Spaeth, Harold J. (1976) *Supreme Court Decision Making*. San Francisco: W. H. Freeman.

Rosenberg, Gerald N. (2000) "Across the great divide (between law & political science)," *The Greenbag* 3: 267–72.

Rowland, C.K., and Robert A. Carp (1996) *Politics & Judgment in Federal District Courts.* Lawrence: University Press of Kansas.

Sakolar, Rebecca Mae (1992) *The Solicitor General: The Politics of Law.* Philadelphia: Temple University Press.

Schneider, Daniel M. (2001) "Empirical research on judicial reasoning: Statutory interpretation in federal tax cases," *New Mexico Law Review* 31: 325–52.

Schubert, Glendon (1965) *The Judicial Mind: The Attitudes and Ideologies of Supreme Court Justices, 1946–1963.* Evanston, IL: Northwestern University Press.

Schwartz, Herman (2000) *The Struggle for Constitutional Justice in Post-Communist Europe.* Chicago: University of Chicago Press.

Scigliano, Robert G. (1971) *The Supreme Court and the Presidency, The Supreme Court in American Life.* New York: Free Press.

Segal, Jeffrey A. (1984) "Predicting Supreme Court decisions probabilistically: The search and seizure cases," *American Political Science Review* 78: 891–900.

Segal, Jeffrey A. (1997) "Separation-of-powers games in the positive theory of law and courts," *American Political Science Review* 91: 28–44.

Segal, Jeffrey A. and Cover, Albert D. (1989) "Ideological values and the votes of U.S. Supreme Court justices," *American Political Science Review* 83: 557–65.

Segal, Jeffrey A., Timpone, Richard J., and Howard, Robert M. (2000) "Buyer beware? Presidential success through Supreme Court appointments," *Political Research Quarterly* 53: 557–95.

Sheldon, Charles H. and Lovrich, Nicholas P. Jr. (1991) "State judicial recruitment," in John B. Gates and Charles A. Johnson (eds.), *The American Courts: A Critical Assessment.* Washington, DC: CQ Press, pp. 161–88.

Sheldon, Charles H. and Maule, Linda S. (1997) *Choosing Justice: The Recruitment of State and Federal Judges.* Pullman: Washington State University Press.

Sisk, Gregory C., Heise, Michael, and Morriss, Andrew P. (1998) "Charting the influences on the judicial mind: An empirical study of judicial reasoning," *New York University Law Review* 73: 1377–1500.

Spriggs, James F. II. (1996) "The Supreme Court and federal agencies: A resource-based theory and analysis of judicial impact," *American Journal of Political Science* 40: 1122–51.

Stearns, Maxwell L. (1999) *Constitutional Process: A Social Choice Analysis of Supreme Court Decision Making.* Ann Arbor: University of Michigan Press.

Tate, C. Neal. (1981) "Personal attribute models of voting behavior of U.S. Supreme Court justices," *American Political Science Review* 75: 355–67.

Tate, C. Neal and Handberg, Roger (1991) "Time binding and theory building in personal attribute models of Supreme Court voting behavior, 1916–88," *American Journal of Political Science* 35: 460–80.

Tate, C. Neal and Vallinder, Torbjörn (1995) "The global expansion of judicial power: The judicialization of politics," in C. Neal Tate and Torbjörn Vallinder (eds.), *The Global Expansion of Judicial Power.* New York: New York University Press, pp. 1–10.

Vines, Kenneth N. (1964) "Federal District Court judges and race relations cases in the south," *Journal of Politics* 26: 338–57.

Whittington, Keith E. (2000) "Once more unto the breach: Post-behavioralist approaches to judicial politics," *Law and Social Inquiry* 25: 601–34.

11

Jurors and Juries

VALERIE P. HANS AND NEIL VIDMAR

Many countries employ some form of lay participation, including the jury, in their legal systems. Lay participation in legal decision making is justified on a number of grounds. For example, supporters of the jury system claim that it improves decision making and reduces the impact of biased or corrupt judges. The lay jury more fully represents the community than elite law-trained judges. Jury service is said to educate the public about the rules and responsibilities of citizenship. Jury decisions better reflect contemporary community values and are thus more likely to be seen as legitimate. This chapter surveys the theoretical ideas, empirical studies, and political context surrounding the use of the jury in criminal and civil trials.

The enthusiasm for lay participation in the form of the jury has waxed and waned over the centuries, and in recent times has again become increasingly controversial. Some opponents maintain that although laypersons may once have been appropriate as legal decision makers, today's criminal and civil disputes are often too complex on evidentiary and legal grounds for lay jurors to fully understand. The jury is also charged with being soft on crime, racist, and holding other prejudices. Business leaders chime in with complaints about the anticorporate bias and unpredictability of civil jury decisions. Criticisms over incompetence and bias have stimulated political and legal efforts to reduce the jury's scope.

The political controversy over the jury has encouraged a good deal of scholarly work about the jury as an institution. In the tradition of law and society scholarship, some researchers have examined the historical, social, and political factors that encourage or discourage the use of the jury and other forms of lay participation in legal decision making.

Other scholarship has focused more specifically on how the jury fulfills its multiple functions. Models of juror and jury decision making and empirical studies of the impact of evidence, legal instructions, individual attitudes, and personal characteristics have provided new insights into how jurors undertake their task. Additional work has addressed the criticisms that jurors are incompetent and biased. Results from that work have largely acquitted the jury, although areas of vulnerability have been identified. Jury reforms based on this empirical research have been implemented.

The chapter provides an overview of these developments and concludes with a consideration of new directions in jury use and scholarship. We also reflect on the jury's functions as a democratic institution.

A HISTORICAL AND COMPARATIVE PICTURE OF THE JURY

Historians of law have identified rudimentary forms of the jury as far back as thirteenth century England (Green, 1985). These early jurors, predominantly white male property owners, were more like witnesses than fact finders. Prominent residents from the local community were sworn to testify about their knowledge of a civil or criminal dispute. The jury was gradually shifted from witnessing to fact-finding over the next few centuries. Yet even so the jury was often under the control of the judge, who had the power to overturn its verdict and even punish the jurors for what he considered an improper verdict.

A jury *de mediatate linguae*, or mixed jury, heard some early English cases, in which two communities contributed equal numbers of jurors to deliberate together and reach a verdict (Constable, 1994). The use of the mixed jury reflected the view that in some disputes between parties from different communities, a fair and legitimate resolution necessitated the involvement of people from both communities. Mixed juries drew on the legal traditions and different orientations of both communities in arriving at their verdicts. A few juries *de mediatate linguae* were used in the early history of the United States, and employed in New Zealand up to the middle of the twentieth century when crimes involved whites and Maori aboriginals.

As the institution of the jury evolved over several centuries, it came to have more power and independence, although judges still continued to dominate trial proceedings and to comment upon the evidence for the jury (Beattie, 1986). Despite the fact that early juries were composed of land-owning men with high community standing, they often acquitted defendants of the charges against them even though the facts strongly suggested guilt. In line with the sentiments of their communities, the jury served the function of mitigating harsh laws that mandated hanging and extreme punishments for minor offenses. The extent to which jury verdicts reflect leniency, deeper appreciation of the context, or nullification of the law continues to intrigue historians of law and scholars of contemporary jury systems.

A critical point in the jury's development was reached in *Bushell's case* in 1670. Quakers William Penn and William Mead faced charges of seditious assembly for preaching Quaker religious doctrine in the London streets. The judge instructed the jury to convict upon the law and evidence, but the jurors resisted and ultimately acquitted the Quaker defendants. The judge then convicted the jurors of returning a false verdict, fined them and sent them to prison along with the defendants! The juror Edward Bushell appealed the punishment, which was overturned. Bushell's case is lauded as a key one for jury autonomy. Henceforth jurors could not be punished for what a judge considered to be a wrongful verdict.

A second important milestone in jury independence was the *Seven Bishops case*. James II, King of Great Britain from 1685 to 1688, converted to Catholicism, in spite of the fact that the Anglican Church was the official state religion. In 1688 he reissued a Declaration of Indulgence that lifted many restrictions on Catholics. He ordered it to be read in the churches. Seven bishops protested that order on the ground that it was contrary to the rulings of Parliament. James put them on trial for seditious libel. A jury acquitted the bishops, creating a political defeat for James's government. The jury verdict in the Seven Bishops case is seen as a decision that helped establish the power of Parliament and an independent judiciary over the king. The jury rejected the king's policy and the views of the king's judges by a verdict that was based on questions of intent and libel, thereby laying the groundwork for later legal opinions establishing the jury's ability, if not its right, to nullify the law (Green, 1985).

British imperialism facilitated global dissemination of the jury (Vogler, 2001). As an essential component of English law, the jury was transported to the American colonies, took root, and flourished there. As the Empire expanded to other parts of the world in the eighteenth century, British colonists established the right of Englishmen to be tried by jury, although they often denied extending that right to indigenous people in the colonies. Jury systems were established in Africa, parts of India, Australia, New Zealand, and in some Caribbean and South American countries. European legal theorists became enamored of English legal procedures, including the right to trial by jury, and as a result a number of European countries adopted the jury for a time.

North America, in both its colonial and postcolonial phases, proved to be fertile ground for the institution of the jury. Local juries were potent vehicles for resisting British rule in the American colonies (Alschuler and Deiss, 1994). Protecting the right to jury trial was a priority for the framers of the United States Constitution, who mentioned the criminal jury in the Constitution and enshrined the right to criminal and civil juries in the Constitution's Sixth and Seventh Amendments. Both criminal and civil juries continue to decide cases in the United States today, although most disputes are resolved by other means such as settlements and plea agreements.

Use of the criminal jury for resolving charges of serious crimes survives in many other countries, including Australia, Canada, Ireland, Northern Ireland, New Zealand, Scotland, and more than 40 other nations. As a practical matter, the civil jury is nearly extinct outside of the United States, two provinces of Canada, and very occasionally in Australia (Vidmar, 2000). Some countries incorporate lay decision making into the justice system through different methods. Lay judges sit in mixed tribunals with law-trained judges to decide cases in Germany, Croatia, and elsewhere (Ivković, 1999). Other countries employ lay assessors to assist the judge (Vidmar, 2002; Vogler, 2001).

Now that recent research has established the extent of the jury and other forms of lay participation worldwide (see Vidmar, 2000, 2002; Thaman, 2001), sociolegal scholars are starting to analyze how social, political, and other factors shape lay participation in legal systems over time and place. That work is still at an early stage, but some patterns are apparent. In many countries formerly under British rule, the jury did not survive after independence because it was seen as an instrument of colonial oppression, particularly when it had been restricted to English colonists, or when it was associated with unfair verdicts against native residents. Rejection of the jury systems occurred even when other aspects of the legal system were retained. In other instances, when colonial rule lifted, indigenous law, having no history of the jury, re-emerged and took hold.

The increasing professionalism of the bar and the judiciary has been a major factor in reducing reliance on the jury. Some legal systems, such as those in the Netherlands and France, strongly emphasize the role of the professional judge in investigating and developing evidence. The English-style jury is seen as incompatible with that emphasis.

Over time, as law and legal training expanded in the common law countries, the perceived value of the untutored members of the jury began to decrease, and restrictions on what the jury could do were put into place. For example, in earlier times juries were charged with interpreting and applying both the law and the facts. In England a division between the function of the judge as the law giver and the jury as the fact finder began to emerge in the 1700s. But in the United States, it was not until the end of the nineteenth century that the roles of judge and jury became more sharply delineated. Judges became the experts on the law, and juries were limited to deciding the facts (Alschuler and Deiss, 1994).

Other reasons for a decline in the use of the jury lie outside the institution itself. For example, in the United States, criminal cases are overwhelmingly resolved by plea bargain rather than trial. Sentencing guidelines and mandatory minimum sentences have further increased the power of prosecutors in getting defendants to agree to plead guilty. In civil cases in the United States, alternative forms of dispute resolution have been promulgated, diverting many cases from the jury. All these factors have produced a situation in which juries are coming to play a largely symbolic, but nevertheless very important, role in the justice system. In the United States today, it is estimated that juries decide somewhere between 5 and 10 percent of criminal cases, while in the United Kingdom the estimate is even lower at 1 percent of criminal cases (Auld, 2001).

Despite the declining numbers, scholars and other commentators point to the continuing significance of trial by jury. Alexis de Toqueville was an early observer of the educational benefits of jury service. Writing in the 1800s about the United States, he maintained that participation on juries was a prime method of educating the public about the justice system and instilling in citizens a keen sense of justice. Marc Galanter (1993) has noted that juries cast a long shadow, having an impact far beyond their decisions in specific cases. Their verdicts send messages to potential wrongdoers and victims, to negligent corporations, to lawyers and judges, about likely outcomes in criminal and civil cases. These jury shadows enhance the effect of the jury even if juries decide relatively few cases as they do today. Political efforts to restrict or eliminate the jury only underscore the continuing power of the institution.

CURRENT DEBATES OVER THE INSTITUTION OF THE JURY

Over its history, the jury has been praised as a bulwark against tyranny and a palladium of liberty on the one hand and a bastion of prejudice and incompetence on the other. The debate has intensified in recent years, in both political and legal arenas. Adding to the factors of increasing professionalism and alternatives to jury trial described above, there have been specific efforts to channel and limit the scope and power of the jury.

In England, the birthplace of the jury, where it was once heralded as a key component of a just society, Lloyd-Bostock and Thomas write that a negative view of the jury has gained ground; it is seen as "a costly, somewhat incompetent anachronism that merely creates opportunities for exploitation by 'professional' criminals at great public expense" (Lloyd-Bostock and Thomas, 2000: 53). These views have accompanied the virtual elimination of the British civil jury, and a substantial decline in the number of crimes deemed eligible for jury trial (Auld, 2001).

In the United States, over the last three decades a number of social and political issues thrust the jury's fairness and competence front and center. In contrast to the vast majority of countries worldwide, the United States still retains the death penalty, and the jury's role in capital cases has proven to be problematic. The 1972 case of *Furman v. Georgia* overturned all death penalty statutes because of evidence of inequity and capriciousness in capital jury trials and death sentences. However, a few years later the Supreme Court ruled that because states had corrected the procedural deficiencies, capital punishment was constitutional. Much recent empirical research on death penalty juries strongly suggests that those procedural corrections have severe inadequacies (Bowers and Steiner, 1998). The jury's role in deciding guilt as well as punishment in capital cases remains very controversial.

Fairness issues emerged on other fronts. American juries were found to over-represent white men to the exclusion of racial and ethnic minorities and women, requiring new approaches to selection of jury pools (Fukurai, Butler, and Krooth, 1993; *Taylor v. Louisiana*, 1975). Juries in the south were accused of practicing jury nullification, ignoring the letter of the law to acquit people charged with civil rights violations. Political trials during the civil rights and Vietnam War era stimulated the development of social science techniques for jury selection. On efficiency grounds, many jurisdictions changed jury size and decision rule, often without much prior study, raising concerns about the reliability of jury verdicts.

The American civil jury as an institution was also thrust into the spotlight. In the United States, legal decisions dating from the 1960s expanded tort liability, particularly in business and industry. Juries now decided cases that formerly would have been tossed out of court or decided by judges. Business leaders vehemently argued that a group of uninformed citizens was unlikely to be fair, competent, and impartial in deciding increasingly complicated disputes. They asserted that juries are tempted to play Robin Hood, granting plaintiffs generous awards from the deep pockets of business corporations. These twin concerns about the jury's supposed proplaintiff bias and incompetence fueled sharp attacks on the American civil jury. Business and insurance companies lobbied state legislatures to place new restrictions on the civil jury, in many cases successfully (Hans, 2000; Vidmar, 1995).

The work juries do also guarantees the jury's role as a storm center. Jury decisions often have political, social, and economic consequences that go beyond the parties in a particular case. Criminal jury trials may involve charges of the most serious kind. Civil jury cases can involve billions of dollars and place a doctor's or a large corporation's reputation at stake. Juries decide high profile and other cases because the parties have come to loggerheads and cannot agree on a settlement or plea bargain. The adversarial battle of jury trial can be bitter and protracted. Juries throughout history have arrived at verdicts that shocked the public, the litigants, and legal commentators. Whether it's the Salem witch trials of colonial New England, the celebrity murder trial of football star O. J. Simpson, or the English fraud case against Kevin and Ian Maxwell, the sons of wealthy British press baron Robert Maxwell, jury trials make headlines with their verdicts. And not all observers will agree that the jury got it right.

RESEARCHING THE JURY: EARLY DEVELOPMENTS

One striking consequence of the legal and political debates over the jury's performance has been to encourage scholarly work on the jury as an institution. The field of
jury studies received a major impetus from such debates. For instance, the earliest
systematic research on the jury was developed to address growing criticism that the
American jury was an outmoded and inefficient method of dispute resolution
(Kalven and Zeisel, 1966: 5–9). As debates over the jury's continuing role intensified,
scholars responded by testing the claims in the debates, examining jury behavior,
and measuring the impact of proposed or enacted reforms.

The contemporary field of jury studies can be traced to the 1950s when Harry
Kalven, Jr. and Hans Zeisel of the University of Chicago Law School directed a novel
research program designed to examine the American jury (Hans and Vidmar, 1991).
In the postwar United States, there were heated debates about whether the jury had
outlived its usefulness. At the University of Chicago Kalven and Zeisel initiated a
collaborative research project to study the jury's operations. Drawing on their
diverse perspectives from the fields of law and social science, their group of researchers generated a new multidisciplinary research model that served as a paradigm for
future sociolegal projects (Simon and Lynch, 1989).

The Chicago Jury Project was not just the first systematic study of the jury. It
remains one of the best. The research team employed multiple methods to examine
the jury, including analysis of jury trial statistics, post-trial interviews, experimental
jury simulations, and courtroom observations. The best-known part of the project
was a judicial questionnaire that was sent to judges presiding over jury trials in state
courts throughout the United States. Hundreds of judges participated in this path-
breaking research, providing their views and descriptions of the case, the jury's
verdict, and the hypothetical verdict the judge would have reached in a bench
trial. The results were presented in an influential book, Kalven and Zeisel's *The
American Jury* (1966).

A central finding of the research was that in both criminal and civil cases, juries
and judges agreed on the verdict most of the time. In 78 percent of the cases, the
judge's hypothetical verdict and the jury's actual decision were the same. When they
disagreed in criminal cases, the jury tended to be more lenient. Disagreements were
linked primarily to the distinctive values that juries bring to their task, including the
jury's more generous interpretation of reasonable doubt, jury sentiments toward
the defendant, and disagreements with the law. In civil cases the disagreements
between judge and jury were about evenly split between plaintiffs and defendants.

Notably, the difficulty of the evidence did *not* produce higher rates of judge–jury
disagreement. One would have expected more disagreements if juries had trouble
understanding complicated evidence. This was a critically important finding, as even
in the 1950s commentators were questioning the wisdom of relying on lay decision
makers in an increasingly complex legal world. Kalven and Zeisel concluded that
juries were generally competent fact finders. Their overall message about jury
competence and performance was quite positive, and was frequently cited in scholarly books and articles and legal opinions (Hans and Vidmar, 1991). The impact of
their research on political debate is difficult to trace, yet it probably protected the
institution of the American jury in the decades that followed. Although the research
was conducted in the 1950s, the basic finding of relatively high agreement between

judge and jury has been replicated in more recent projects (Hannaford, Hans, and Munsterman, 2000; Heuer and Penrod, 1994).

Empirical research on the jury in other countries occurred much later. Like the Chicago Jury Project, research in countries such as Great Britain, Canada, Australia, and New Zealand was stimulated by concerns about whether the jury was still a suitable decision maker for contemporary disputes. However, a major impediment to research in these common law countries is that jurors are either expressly forbidden or strongly discouraged from discussing their jury deliberations. There are other hurdles. The British researchers Baldwin and McConville (1979) proposed replicating Kalven and Zeisel's judge–jury agreement study, but English judges would not cooperate.

British research undertook alternative approaches to studying the jury, including shadow juries and mock jury studies, to answer questions about the English jury that could not be addressed with actual juries (McCabe and Purves, 1974). As part of an overview of the Canadian jury system, the Law Reform Commission of Canada (1980) commissioned several studies, including public opinion and juror surveys and mock jury research. With increasing concern about jury performance in New Zealand and Australia, law commissions in those two countries recently obtained exceptions to the law prohibiting jurors to discuss their experiences so that researchers could undertake jury interviews (Young, Cameron, and Potter, 1999; Chesterman, Chan, and Hampton, 2001).

JURY SIMULATION METHODOLOGY

Although analysis of judge–jury disagreement was the central focus of *The American Jury*, scholars associated with the project, notably Fred Strodtbeck and Rita James Simon, undertook experimental studies of mock juries to answer current legal questions about the jury. Perhaps because the study designs were developed within the Chicago Jury Project's collaborative law–social science framework, these original jury simulations presented realistic trial materials to subjects drawn from jury pools, and were designed to address questions central to legal debates about the jury. For example, Simon's work tested the effect of different legal definitions of the insanity defense (Simon, 1967).

Subsequent generations of jury researchers enthusiastically adopted jury simulation methodology. Psychologists in particular leapt at the opportunity to test psychological theories using the engaging vehicle of the jury trial. A number of theoretical developments within psychology – social perception and cognition, attribution theory, prejudice, and group process – could be examined by studying jury decision making. However, in contrast to the Chicago Jury Project's collaborative interdisciplinary model, some of the psychologists who employed the jury simulation paradigm did not have lawyer collaborators, learned law on their own, and were much more interested in psychological questions than in legal ones. From a legal perspective, many early jury simulations were poorly conceptualized (Vidmar, 1979).

A case in point is a 1969 article published in a highly respected American psychology journal. Psychologists David Landy and Elliott Aronson used jury simulation methodology to test a social psychological theory of attraction. College students read brief written descriptions of cases that included information that would not be allowed in actual courtrooms, making individual sentencing recommendations instead of verdicts. Concluding that the character of the victim and the defendant affected sentencing, Landy and Aronson commented on their study's relevance to actual juries, invoking Kalven and Zeisel's findings on the impact of character (Landy and Aronson, 1969). A focus on answering psychological rather than legal questions, minimal and often inappropriate legal materials, and unwarranted generalizations to the legal realm characterized this and some other early jury simulation studies, lessening their value for the field of jury studies (Vidmar, 1979; Weiten and Diamond, 1979).

The courts have also debated the validity and generalizability of jury simulation studies. In the United States, some Supreme Court cases have cited jury research. *Ballew v. Georgia* (1978) dealt with the constitutionality of five-person juries. The Supreme Court drew on jury simulation research contrasting six-person versus twelve-person juries to reach its decision that jury size was an important factor and that six people at a minimum were needed to protect important jury functions. In contrast, *Lockhart v. McCree* (1986) evaluated a challenge to the death penalty based on jury simulation findings that death-qualified juries were conviction-prone. The *McCree* majority concluded that the jury simulation research was flawed and could not be generalized to real juries. Social scientists, though, pointed out that the opinions in both *Ballew* and *McCree* made errors in their assessments or applicability of the jury simulations. Just as psychologists were sometimes naïve about the law, so too were the judges found lacking in the fine points of assessing research methodology and empirical data.

The expansion of empirical scholarship on juries

Despite critical assessments, and a chilly reception in the legal arena, jury simulation as a method of research, and the jury as an object of scholarly study, continued to expand in the United States and elsewhere, for example, Honess, Levi, and Charman (1998) and Lloyd-Bostock (2000) in England and in Canada, Schuller and Hastings (1996). Part of the impetus was the social and political debate over the continuing validity of the institution. Developments in various scholarly fields encouraged interdisciplinary and collaborative research, enabling professors trained in social science disciplines to undertake more legally sophisticated research. Although unrealistic jury simulations still find their way into the journal literature, contemporary research on juries includes many jury simulations of high verisimilitude (e.g., Hastie, Penrod, and Pennington, 1983; Horowitz and Bordens, 1990; Cowan, Thompson, and Ellsworth, 1984; Honess, Levi, and Charman, 1998) as well as studies of real-world jurors (Bowers and Steiner, 1998; Hannaford, Hans, and Munsterman, 2000; Diamond, Vidmar, Rose, Ellis, and Murphy, 2003).

SCHOLARLY RESEARCH FINDINGS

Using a variety of increasingly sophisticated methods, jury scholars have developed a substantial body of knowledge about the jury. We have already noted some of that work, but it is worthwhile to sketch out other findings from the field of jury studies. Some projects ask theoretical questions about how attitudes and characteristics influence individual judgments about legal issues, models of legal decision making, and group processes. Other research is more applied in nature, addressed to jury performance and jury reform.

Individual characteristics of jurors

One set of questions explores the impact of attitudes and personal characteristics on how individual jurors perceive evidence and legal issues. This is linked to a central legal concern, jury selection. The importance of individual characteristics is a long-standing interest of psychologists, so it is not surprising that many psychology-trained jury scholars have examined whether demographic and attitudinal factors play a role in evidence evaluation and verdict preference. With a few notable exceptions, characteristics such as a person's age, gender, education, income, and racial or ethnic identity have only modest or inconsistent impact on verdicts in mock juror studies (Diamond, 1990).

Specific attitudes toward crime and justice are linked to juror decision making. For instance, death penalty support is associated with conviction-proneness and a crime-control orientation, attitudes that shape the evaluation of evidence, verdict preferences, and evaluation of aggravating and mitigating circumstances (Butler and Moran, 2002; Fitzgerald and Ellsworth, 1984). White men, in contrast to racial and ethnic minorities and women, are more likely to support capital punishment. On the civil justice side, beliefs in a civil litigation crisis are linked to more hostile assessments of the plaintiff's case (Hans, 2000). Case-specific attitudes tend to have the strongest relationship to judgments, such as attitudes toward the crime of rape as predictors of mock juror evaluations of sexual assault evidence, or attitudes toward police in cases involving police evidence. A common finding is that attitudes have more impact when the evidence is ambiguous and could support either verdict.

Jury selection consultants

Using insights from the jury studies field, and conducting their own polls and focus groups, a cadre of professional experts serve as jury selection consultants in criminal and civil trials in the United States. The origins of a systematic, research-based approach to jury selection date to the political trials of the early 1970s, when social scientists used techniques like public opinion polling and observation of nonverbal behavior to assist lawyers defending politically unpopular clients such as Vietnam War protesters. Jury selection consultants have developed and expanded different methods, which now typically include mock juror focus groups, survey research, case analysis, pretrial investigation of potential jurors, and in-court observation of voir dire. These methods are used to develop profiles of "ideal" jurors who favor the client's side. For example, in the controversial O. J. Simpson double-murder trial, the defendant's jury selection consultant determined that less educated jurors were more desirable as her research showed that they tended to be more skeptical of DNA evidence, a central piece of evidence linking the defendant to the murders.

The practice of jury consulting remains controversial even as it expands. Some jury scholars assert that the methods used, particularly the cheaper and popular mock juror focus group, are ineffective, and that jury consultants promise too much. Others express unease about the ethical implications of "stacking" the jury: does it promote or undermine justice? Wealthy parties use it most, creating equity concerns. Controversial or not, lawyers in many major criminal and civil trials in the United States employ jury consultants, and the major professional organization, the American Society of Trial Consultants, which began in the early 1980s with a handful of participants, now boasts over 400 members (Kressel and Kressel, 2002).

Models of juror decision making

The development of models of juror decision making constitutes an important theoretical contribution to jury research. The question is: how do jurors take the different pieces of evidence presented in a legal case and put them together to arrive at a legal judgment? The most commonly accepted theoretical model is the "story model" (Bennett and Feldman, 1981; Pennington and Hastie, 1986). This model posits that jurors arrange evidence into a narrative account or story, which includes important events, circumstances, states of mind, motives, and character evaluations. To arrive at a verdict, jurors find the best fit between the story they've developed and the available verdict alternatives. Psychologists Pennington and Hastie (1986) and others have tested the story model. They found that mock jurors represent the evidence in the form of a story, and that evidence presented in story order is more compelling.

Although the story model has gained wide support, diverse psychological models have been applied to the task of juror decision making, including information integration theory (Anderson, 1981) and Bayesian approaches (Schum and Martin, 1982). Other researchers have studied how psychological phenomena such as reliance on prototypes (Smith, 1991) and the hindsight bias (Casper, Benedict, and Perry, 1989) affect juror decision making. There are numerous studies showing that jurors sometimes have difficulty understanding the judge's legal instructions. Drawing on psycholinguistic theory, scholars have proposed revising instructions to promote better comprehension and application (Elwork, Sales, and Alfini, 1982).

GROUP DECISION PROCESSES ON THE JURY

A third theoretical concern is how juries combine their diverse individual perspectives into a group decision. How significant is jury deliberation? What group processes operate to facilitate or hamper the reaching of a verdict?

Decades ago, Kalven and Zeisel offered an analogy between jury deliberation and the development of already-exposed film: "It brings out the picture, but the outcome is predetermined" (Kalven and Zeisel, 1966: 489). Drawing on a line of Chicago Jury Project data in which actual jurors were asked to provide their first-ballot votes, Kalven and Zeisel found that majorities ruled. When a substantial majority favored one side or another, the jury almost always decided along with its majority preference. Many mock jury studies have replicated that basic result, finding that as the initial majority increases in size the likelihood of a congruent verdict also increases (Kerr, 1993). In some studies, though, a leniency bias has been discovered. Jurors in the numerical minority arguing for acquittal have greater impact than a comparable minority arguing for conviction. Apparently, it is easier to raise a reasonable doubt than to convince those with doubts (MacCoun and Kerr, 1988).

Researchers have developed some interesting insights about how jurors move from one verdict preference to another and finally to unanimity during the course of deliberation. As the deliberation goes on, jurors generally move in the direction of the current majority view. There is a significant momentum effect. If one side gains a new member, then it is more likely to gain additional members. These social transition phenomena can be explained by normative and informational factors. As the majority increases, the social pressures on the minority increase and the jury deliberation includes a larger number of arguments that support the majority position.

Research using mock juries has analyzed the way that such groups begin the deliberation process, and has discovered that how the jury begins is linked to the overall nature of the deliberation. Juries that take a public vote right away are more "verdict-driven"; they form subgroups with other jurors who have similar views and present arguments and evidence that support their position. In contrast, "evidence-driven" juries delay voting, instead beginning with a general review and assessment of the evidence in the case. The evidence-driven jurors try to develop a joint account of the events before taking a vote later on in deliberation (Hastie, Penrod, and Pennington, 1983).

But does it make any difference? According to Kalven and Zeisel, the deliberation process is basically no more significant than film developer. Yet even if verdict outcomes fit the majority rule model, deliberation serves a number of functions that in our view enhance the reliability and legitimacy of jury decision making. Deliberation allows the collective pooling of information, corrects mistaken recollections or conclusions, and clarifies and solidifies positions (Hans and Vidmar, 1986). Furthermore, in an empirical study of the relationship between first votes and final verdicts, Sandys and Dillehay (1995) found that there is often substantial discussion prior to a first vote, so first votes probably already reflect group process effects.

Deliberation may be quite important in civil jury trials, especially for damage awards. In one study with civil jurors, most jurors reported that although they knew who should win the case, they did not have a specific dollar figure in mind (Mott, Hans, and Simpson, 2000). The specific amounts are generated during jury deliberation, as jurors propose, justify, and adjust different levels of compensation for plaintiffs. An intriguing polarization of awards has been found in some mock jury studies in which individual award preferences are taken at the beginning of the deliberation and contrasted with the final mock jury award (Diamond and Casper, 1992).

Finally, researchers have examined how jury size and decision rule affect group deliberations, jury verdicts, and jury damage awards (Hans, 2001; Hastie, Penrod, and Pennington, 1983; Saks and Marti, 1997). Smaller juries are less likely to represent all segments of the community. Majority decision rule juries tend to have shorter and more verdict-driven deliberations, and to pay less attention to those expressing minority views. Juries have somewhat more trouble reaching a unanimous as opposed to a majority verdict, however.

JURY REFORM

Whether justified or not, critiques of the jury have led to regular demands for jury reform. From its inception centuries ago, the institution of the jury has continually been in the process of change and modification. But the jury reforms have intensified in recent years. These include overhauling jury selection procedures so that more representative juries hear cases, changing the jury's size and decision rule, modifying trial practices to promote better jury decision making, improving jury instructions, and channeling and restricting the jury's role (Munsterman, Hannaford, and Whitehead, 1997). Jury scholars have advocated some of these reforms, and have critiqued or tested the impact of others.

Researchers have undertaken comparative demographic analyses of communities and jury pools, identifying instances in which the jury pool underrepresents particular demographic groups in the local population. These analyses have been presented within the context of legal challenges to the jury pool in particular cases (see, e.g., Fukarai, Butler, and Krooth, 1993). The challenges have led in some instances to improvements in the selection of jury pools. However, other scholars point to continuing problems in the representativeness of juries. For example, Baldus and his colleagues have discovered that the jury selection process in capital cases, including the lawyers' peremptory challenges, functions to exclude racial and ethnic minorities (Baldus, Woodworth, Zuckerman, Weiner, and Broffitt, 2001). This work points toward the necessity of additional reform.

Other reforms have modified the trial process to take into account the findings of jury research. B. Michael Dann (1993), then an Arizona trial judge, wrote a significant article in the *Indiana Law Journal*, arguing that trial practice should be changed to take into account the documented tendency of jurors to take an active approach in their decision making. He observed that current adversary trial practice reinforces juror passivity, although jury research has found that jurors actively evaluate evidence and generate stories from the beginning of the trial. Dann chaired an influential jury reform committee in Arizona, which proposed sweeping reforms of its jury system, including allowing jurors to ask questions of witnesses, take notes during trial (in some jurisdictions that is still forbidden), and permitting civil jurors to discuss the evidence as the case proceeds rather than waiting until the start of jury deliberations as is the standard practice in the United States. Strikingly, though, Australia, New Zealand, and England have no case law forbidding jurors to discuss the evidence together during trial, as long as it is not discussed with nonjurors. Canadian jury instructions specifically instruct the jurors that they may discuss evidence among themselves while the trial is going on. Many of the Arizona committee's jury reform proposals were adopted in Arizona, and have been reviewed and in some instances adopted in other US jurisdictions as well.

Jury scholars have studied the impact of these trial practice reforms. Heuer and Penrod (1996) conducted two field experiments in the United States using actual jury trials to study the effect of allowing jurors to ask questions of witnesses. In the experiments, half of the jury trials were randomly assigned to a condition in which the jurors were instructed that they could ask questions, while in the other half of the jury trials, jurors were not given this instruction. The researchers then compared what occurred in the two sets of trials. Heuer and Penrod discovered that jurors who were allowed to ask questions did so, but not excessively. On average they asked one question per two hours of testimony. The question asking had no discernible impact on verdicts overall, but jurors who were allowed to ask questions reported that they felt better informed and had enough information to reach a verdict. After their research was released, the American Judicature Society distributed the results of the project along with suggestions for implementation. By all accounts, the once rare practice of allowing jurors to ask questions of witnesses has now become more frequent (Munsterman et al., 1997).

The highly controversial Arizona reform, allowing civil jurors to talk among themselves during the trial, was evaluated in two field experiments (Diamond et al., 2003; Hannaford, Hans, and Munsterman, 2000). In each study, some jury trials were randomly assigned to a condition in which civil jurors were given the instruction that they could talk about the case prior to deliberation, while in the remaining jury trials they were prohibited to engage in such discussion. Hannaford et al. found that about a third of the juries allowed to discuss the evidence did not take advantage of the opportunity, because of a lack of breaks in short trials, or because some jurors were uncomfortable with the idea. Although it was difficult to measure, Hannaford et al. found no strong evidence that jurors who engaged in discussion prejudged the evidence. Instead, many jurors reported that they changed their minds frequently as the evidence developed. Jurors who discussed the evidence said they found it quite helpful; however, no impact on verdicts was observed. Jurors who discussed the evidence did say their jury experienced more conflict.

The Diamond et al. (2003) field experiment was unique in that the trials, jury discussions, and jury deliberations were videotaped, with the knowledge and consent of all parties including the jurors. They found that in complex cases, midtrial discussions improved comprehension. With some possible minor exceptions, discussion did not appear to foster premature judgment of the verdict, as many critics had feared.

The Future of the Jury and Jury Research

In England in particular, there is much evidence that the criminal jury may be on the way to near extinction. A small minority of Canadian judges would like to see it disappear as well, even though the right to jury trial is enshrined in the Canadian constitution. Changes in Canada's criminal code have reduced the defendant's right to opt for jury trial. There are some grumbles about juries in New Zealand and Australia, and it is possible that in the future some restrictions on the right to judgment by one's peers will appear in those countries. Due to their constitutional status, criminal and civil juries are not likely to disappear in the United States, but there are signs that the percentage of both civil and criminal cases tried by juries is declining. Moreover, tort reform movements in the US produced legislative changes such as limits on the amounts of pain and suffering and punitive damages that juries can award. Cross-cutting these trends, in criminal cases a few recent US Supreme Court decisions (*Apprendi v. New Jersey*, 2000; *Ring v. Arizona*, 2002) have expanded the issues that juries are required to decide.

Pressures to reduce the right to criminal juries arise out a number of factors, chief among them the professional aggrandizement of judge power, the economic costs of jury trials, and empirically unsupported assertions about jury bias and incompetence. There are also concerns about the tainting of jurors in a mass media age. Community opinions can be shaped in advance of trial, precluding a fair evaluation of the case. In civil cases, as noted above, there are claims of jury bias against corporate and other deep pocket defendants, incompetence, and the unreliability of decisions, that is alleged to cause chaos by the uncertain predictive shadow that they cast on the rest of the tort system, thereby stifling innovation in products and affecting American competitiveness.

Most of the negative claims about the criminal and civil jury systems have not stood up to careful empirical tests. One important role for jury research is to continue to expand the number of empirical studies of the jury, particularly field studies that will have greater weight with judges and legislators. New studies based on a better understanding of individual and group decision-making processes may assist in developing procedural changes to assist jurors.

The complicated issue of scholarly objectivity arises in these research endeavors. Many jury researchers have a positive view of the jury to begin with. Perhaps this is due to their knowledge of the fact that prior studies have usually exonerated the jury, but there is also some indication of ideological commitment to the jury system. Some jury research is funded by organizations with specific interest in reform movements. Conducting research in an environment in which the institution one studies is regularly subject to political attack, and when the findings are used to promote a particular agenda, whether one agrees with that agenda or not, challenges traditional notions of scientific objectivity.

Moving beyond the performance assessment that has characterized much jury research to date, there is another important role for sociolegal research on the jury, one that has been somewhat neglected. That goal is to assess the democratic and other symbolic functions served by the jury. Lay participation in legal systems is close to ubiquitous. Even though a few European countries such as Denmark and Belgium have limited forms of the jury system, most do not. Instead, most other European countries utilize laypersons in adjudicating serious criminal charges by means of mixed tribunals of judges and laypersons. Countries in Africa, Asia, the Caribbean, and Brazil in South America also inject laypersons into their criminal legal systems.

The recent revival of juries in Spain and Russia (Thaman, 1999), and the dissatisfaction with the exclusively judge-based system in Japan (Lempert, 1992), raise identical questions. Why is lay participation so omnipresent? Do laypersons simply provide a necessary patina of legitimacy to the legal process? Or do they contribute in some substantive way as well, perhaps keeping the professionals in touch with contemporary norms and social attitudes? Furthermore, how do different methods of lay participation, including juries, lay assessors, and lay judges, compare in their ability to inject commonsense judgment into the legal systems? These are profound but difficult questions to which at this point there can only be speculation. They pose a theoretical and empirical challenge to sociolegal scholars from a number of academic disciplines, including sociologists, historians, political scientists, lawyers, and social psychologists. The goal of understanding the prevalence and variation in lay participation in law is a significant one. It promises to remain an intriguing topic of sociolegal research in the years to come.

References

Alschuler, A.W. and Deiss, A.G. (1994) "A brief history of the criminal jury in the United States," *University of Chicago Law Review* 61: 867–928.

Anderson, N.H. (1981) *Foundations of Information Integration Theory.* New York: Academic Press.

Apprendi v. New Jersey (2000) 503 U.S. 466.

Auld, L.J. (2001) *A Review of the Criminal Courts of England and Wales* (2001). Available online at <http://www.criminal-courts-review.org.uk/>.

Baldus, D.C., Woodworth, G., Zuckerman, D., Weiner, N.A., and Broffitt, B. (2001) "The use of peremptory challenges in capital murder trials: A legal and empirical analysis," *University of Pennsylvania Journal of Constitutional Law* 3: 3–169.

Baldwin, J. and McConville, M. (1979) *Jury Trials.* London: Oxford University Press.

Ballew v. Georgia (1978) 435 U.S. 223.

Beattie, J.M. (1986) Crime and the Courts in England 1660–1800. Princeton, NJ: Princeton University Press.

Bennett, W.L. and Feldman, M. (1981) Reconstructing Reality in the Courtroom. New Brunswick, NJ: Rutgers University Press.

Bowers, W.J. and Steiner, B.D. (1998) "Choosing life or death: Sentencing dynamics in capital cases," in J.R. Acker, R.M. Bohm, and C.S. Lanier (eds.), America's Experiment with Capital Punishment: Reflections on the Past, Present, and Future of the Ultimate Penal Sanction. Durham, NC: Carolina Academic Press, pp. 309–49.

Butler, B.M. and Moran, G. (2002) "The role of death qualification in venirepersons' evaluations of aggravating and mitigating circumstances in capital trials," Law and Human Behavior 26: 175–84.

Casper, J.D., Benedict, K., and Perry, J.L. (1989) "Juror decision making, attitudes, and the hindsight bias," Law and Human Behavior 13: 291–310.

Chesterman, M., Chan, J., and Hampton, S. (2001) Managing Prejudicial Publicity. Sydney: Law and Justice Foundation of New South Wales.

Constable, M. (1994) The Law of the Other: The Mixed Jury and Changing Conceptions of Citizenship, Law, and Knowledge. Chicago: University of Chicago Press.

Cowan, C.L., Thompson W.C., and Ellsworth, P.C. (1984) "The effects of death qualification on jurors' predisposition to convict and on the quality of deliberation," Law and Human Behavior 8: 53–79.

Dann, B.M. (1993) "'Learning lessons' and 'speaking rights': Creating educated and democratic juries," Indiana Law Journal 68: 1229–79.

Diamond, S.S. (1990) "Scientific jury selection: What social scientists know and do not know," Judicature 79: 178–83.

Diamond, S.S. and Casper, J.D. (1992) "Blindfolding the jury to verdict consequences: Damages, experts, and the civil jury," Law & Society Review 26: 513–63.

Diamond, S.S., Vidmar, N., Rose, M., Ellis, L., and Murphy, B. (2003) "Juror discussions during civil trials: A study of Arizona's Rule 39(f) Innovation," Arizona Law Review 45:1–81. Available at <http://www.law.duke.edu/pub/vidmar/ArizonaCivilDiscussions.pdf> and at <http://www.law.northwestern.edu/faculty/fulltime/diamond/papers/arizona_civil_discussions.pdf>.

Elwork, A., Sales, B.D., and Alfini, J.J. (1982) Making Jury Instructions Understandable. Charlottesville, VA: Michie.

Fitzgerald, R. and Ellsworth, P.C. (1984) "Due process vs. crime control: Death qualification and jury attitudes," Law and Human Behavior 8: 31–51.

Fukurai, H., Butler, E.W., and Krooth, R. (1993) Race and the Jury: Racial Disenfranchisement and the Search for Justice. New York: Plenum.

Furman v. Georgia (1972) 408 U.S. 238.

Galanter, M. (1993) "The regulatory function of the civil jury," in R. Litan (ed.), Verdict: Assessing the Civil Jury System. Washington, DC: Brookings Institution, pp. 61–102.

Green, T. (1985) Verdict According to Conscience. Chicago: University of Chicago Press.

Hannaford, P.L., Hans, V.P., and Munsterman, G.T. (2000) "Permitting jury discussions during trial: Impact of the Arizona reform," Law and Human Behavior 24: 359–82.

Hans, V.P. (2000) Business on Trial: The Civil Jury and Corporate Responsibility. New Haven, CT: Yale University Press.

Hans, V.P. (2001) "The power of twelve: The impact of jury size and unanimity on civil jury decision making," Delaware Law Review 4: 1–31.

Hans, V.P. and Vidmar, N. (1986) Judging the Jury. New York: Plenum.

Hans, V.P. and Vidmar, N. (1991) "The American Jury at twenty-five years," Law & Social Inquiry 16: 323–51.

Hastie, R., Penrod, S.D., and Pennington, N. (1983) Inside the Jury. Cambridge, MA: Harvard University Press.

Heuer, L. and Penrod, S. (1994) "Juror notetaking and question asking during trials: A national field experiment," *Law and Human Behavior* 18: 121–50.

Heuer, L. and Penrod, S. (1996) "Increasing juror participation in trials through note taking and question asking," *Judicature* 79: 256–62.

Honess, T.M., Levi, M., and Charman, E.A. (1998) "Juror competence in processing complex information: Implications from a simulation of the Maxwell trial," *Criminal Law Review* 1998: 763–73.

Horowitz, I.A. and Bordens, K.S. (1990) "An experimental investigation of procedural issues in complex tort trials," *Law and Human Behavior* 14: 269–85.

Ivković, S.K. (1999) *Lay Participation in Criminal Trials: The Case of Croatia*. Lanham, NY: Austin & Winfield.

Kalven, H., Jr. and Zeisel, H. (1966) *The American Jury*. Boston: Little, Brown.

Kerr, N.L. (1993) "Stochastic models of juror decision making," in R. Hastie (ed.), *Inside the Juror*. New York: Cambridge University Press, pp. 116–35.

Kressel, N.J. and Kressel, D.F. (2002) *Stack and Sway: The New Science of Jury Consulting*. Boulder, CO: Westview Press.

Landy, D. and Aronson, E. (1969) "The influence of the character of the criminal and his victim on the decisions of simulated jurors," *Journal of Experimental Social Psychology* 5: 141–52.

Law Reform Commission of Canada (1980) *The Jury in Criminal Trials*. Ottawa: Minister of Supply and Services Canada.

Lempert, R. (1992) "A jury for Japan?" *American Journal of Comparative Law* 40: 37–71.

Lloyd-Bostock, S. (2000) "The effects on juries of hearing about the defendant's previous criminal record: A simulation study," *Criminal Law Review* 2000: 734–55.

Lloyd-Bostock, S. and Thomas, C. (2000) "The continuing decline of the English jury," in N. Vidmar (ed.), *World Jury Systems*. Oxford: Oxford University Press, pp. 53–91.

Lockhart v. McCree (1986) 476 U.S. 162.

MacCoun, R.J. and Kerr, N.L. (1988) "Asymmetric influence in mock deliberation: Jurors' bias for leniency," *Journal of Personality and Social Psychology* 54: 21–33.

McCabe, S. and Purves, R. (1974) *The Shadow Jury at Work*. Oxford: Blackwell.

Mott, N.L., Hans, V.P., and Simpson, L. (2000) "What's half a lung worth? Civil jurors' accounts of their award decision making," *Law and Human Behavior* 24: 401–19.

Munsterman, G.T., Hannaford, P., and Whitehead, G.M. (eds.) (1997) *Jury Trial Innovations*. Williamsburg, VA: National Center for State Courts.

Pennington, N. and Hastie, R. (1986) "Evidence evaluation in complex decision making," *Journal of Personality and Social Psychology* 51: 242–58.

Ring v. Arizona (2002) 122 S.Ct. 2428.

Saks, M.J. and Marti, M.W. (1997) "A meta-analysis of the effects of jury size," *Law and Human Behavior* 21: 451–67.

Sandys, M. and Dillehay, R.C. (1995) "First-ballot votes, predeliberation dispositions, and final verdicts in jury trials," *Law and Human Behavior* 19: 175–95.

Schuller, R.A. and Hastings, P.A. (1996) "Trials of battered women who kill: The impact of alternative forms of expert evidence," *Law and Human Behavior* 20: 167–87.

Schum, D.A. and Martin, A.W. (1982) "Formal and empirical research on cascaded inference in jurisprudence," *Law & Society Review* 17: 105–51.

Simon, R.J. (1967) *The Jury and the Defense of Insanity*. Boston: Little, Brown.

Simon, R.J. and Lynch, J.P. (1989) "The sociology of law: Where we have been and where we might be going," *Law & Society Review* 23: 825–47.

Smith, V.L. (1991) "Prototypes in the courtroom: Lay representations of legal concepts," *Journal of Personality and Social Psychology* 61: 857–72.

Taylor v. Louisiana (1975) 419 U.S. 522.

Thaman, S.C. (1999) "Europe's new jury systems: The cases of Spain and Russia," *Law and Contemporary Problems* 62: 233–59.

Thaman, S.C. (2001) "The idea of the conference," *International Review of Penal Law* 72: 19–23.

Vidmar, N. (1979) "The other issues in jury simulation research: A commentary with particular reference to defendant character studies," *Law and Human Behavior* 3: 95–106.

Vidmar, N. (1995) *Medical Malpractice and the American Jury.* Ann Arbor: University of Michigan Press.

Vidmar, N. (ed.) (2000) *World Jury Systems.* Oxford: Oxford University Press.

Vidmar, N. (2002) "Juries and lay assessors in the Commonwealth of Nations: A contemporary survey," *Criminal Law Forum* 13: 385–407.

Vogler, R. (2001) "The international development of the jury: The role of the British Empire," *International Review of Penal Law* 72: 525–51.

Weiten, W. and Diamond, S.S. (1979) "A critical review of the jury simulation paradigm: The case of defendant characteristics," *Law and Human Behavior* 3: 71–93.

Young, W., Cameron, I., and Potter, S. (1999) *Juries Survey: Report of Findings.* Wellington, New Zealand, Law Reform Commission.

Further Reading

Abramson, J. (2000) *We the Jury: The Jury System and the Ideal of Democracy.* Cambridge, MA: Harvard University Press.

Daniels, S. and Martin, J. (1995) *Civil Juries and the Politics of Reform.* Evanston, IL: Northwestern University.

Feigenson, N. (2000) *Legal Blame: How Jurors Think and Talk about Accidents.* Washington, DC: APA Books.

King, N.J. (1999) "The American criminal jury," *Law and Contemporary Problems* 62: 41–67.

Litan, R.E. (ed.) (1993) *Verdict: Assessing the Civil Jury System.* Washington, DC: Brookings Institution.

12

Regulators and Regulatory Processes

Robert A. Kagan

The ever-proliferating rules and enforcement agents of the regulatory state have become very important components of contemporary legal systems. Every day, at least in economically advanced democracies, scores of governmental inspectors fan out across the community – a white-collar police force enforcing regulations concerned with workplace safety, air and water pollution, fire prevention, quality of care in nursing homes, cleanliness in food processing plants, the proper maintenance of airliners, elevators, school buses, and railroad tracks, and many more other potential hazards. Still more regulatory officials scrutinize applications seeking permits for factory expansions, new construction projects, new pharmaceuticals, and new stock issues. The tightening web of regulatory obligations demands much attention and money from business firms and other organizations. Regulatory officials, agencies, and rules quite often are enmeshed in political and legal conflict. And that conflict has attracted the attention of sociolegal scholars. This essay seeks to summarize certain aspects of what they have learned about regulators and regulatory processes, primarily in economically advanced democracies, for these have been the major focus of research.

VARIETIES OF REGULATION

All branches of law – criminal law, contract law, tort law, traffic law, and so on – have a regulatory function, for they are designed to deter behaviors that have been politically defined as harmful or antisocial, and to encourage socially responsible behavior. Conventionally, however, the term "regulation" is reserved for bodies of law that are elaborated through the promulgation of administrative rules and enforced by specialized government agencies. And typically, the term "regulation" is reserved for bodies of law that seek to control the behavior of business firms, other large organizations, and professional service providers. Whereas criminal and civil law typically are enforced via legal actions against alleged violators after the fact of harm, regulation is prophylactic in purpose, seeking to prevent harmful activities before they occur. While the initial costs of civil law enforcement are borne by injured parties who must gather evidence and hire lawyers, in regulatory programs (as in the enforcement of criminal law by police departments) the government shoulders these costs, free of charge to complainants.

Programs of governmental regulation often are superimposed on pre-existing systems of private regulation aimed at the same set of hazards. For in most societies, the first line of defense against dangerous products and unfair practices is the incentive system created by private markets; the threat of developing a bad reputation and losing business motivates most enterprises to establish quality control systems of various kinds. It was not government regulation that induced the manufacturers of motor vehicles to develop meaningful braking systems. Contract and tort law provide a second line of defense; by enabling victims of broken promises or negligent behavior to threaten enterprises with legal penalties, they create incentives for responsible behavior, inducing many companies and trade organizations to create systems of "self-regulation" (Rees, 1994; Gunningham and Rees, 1997). Professional societies and engineering organizations have established countless private codes and standards – such as "generally accepted accounting practices," hospital accreditation regimes, and standards for appropriate insulation and wiring for electrical appliances (Cheit, 1990). The demand for legally binding *governmental* regulation (the subject of this essay) often arises when markets and liability law fail to generate a politically acceptable level of self-regulation and protection against particular kinds of harms and injustices – although such "market failures" are not the sole reason for regulatory enactments.

Protective regulation

There is nothing new about governmental regulation, for there are many circumstances in which "market failures" do occur. For centuries, governments have enacted and enforced regulations to control land use, prevent misleading or dangerous commercial practices, and coordinate cooperative activities. A colonial Massachusetts law required each town to appoint a "gager or packer" to ensure that "the best be not left out" in sealed packages of beef and pork (Hughes, 1975: 133). As far back as the eighteenth century, Dutch *Waterschappen* enforced regulations requiring owners of ditches and canals to maintain their waterways in certain ways (Huppes and Kagan, 1989: 221).

Massachusetts required public inspection of sealed packages because of an "information failure" – consumers confronted with opaque packages were unable to protect themselves in advance by boycotting merchants who sold lower quality packets, and hence merchants had incentives to leave out the best parts. Government inspection provides an early warning system when consumers can't detect product defects, or may be unable to trace injuries or illnesses to a particular vendor. Hence most governments regulate what additives may be included in packaged foods and beverages, and government inspectors enforce sanitation-related regulations in food and pharmaceutical manufacturing factories. Similarly, securities laws and regulators, seeking to ensure that "the worst" not be hidden from investors, require companies offering stock to the public to disclose their true financial status. Government regulations require the providers of many services, from health care to ship operation and construction engineering, to meet educational and other licensure requirements because their clients cannot easily determine whether practitioners know what they are talking about. Governments regulate and inspect the facilities, staffing, and procedures of nursing homes because elderly, unwell patients often lack the ability to detect or complain about deficiencies themselves. And governments impose "safety and soundness" regulations on banks, limiting the quantity and nature of their loans, for depositors cannot easily assess a bank's vulnerability to failure.

The *Waterschappen* dealt with a different brand of market failure, commonly labeled a "collective action" or "free rider" problem (Olson, 1968). For the Dutch, flood control systems were a "collective good" – but individual farmers, who would benefit even if they didn't do their share, were tempted to shirk in maintaining them. Regulatory obligations, strictly enforced by the collectivity, solved the problem. To use slightly different terminology, a lazy Dutch farmer's canal-maintenance failures were an "externality," imposing on others costs that did not show up on the lazy farmer's books. Yet the purchaser of the farmer's produce neither knew nor cared. No single diligent farmer had sufficient incentive to bring legal action against the lazy one, and in any event, the collective need was to deal *in advance* with the weak link in the chain of canal maintainers.

Much contemporary environmental law is designed to deal with similar market failures. Fisheries regulations impose catch limitations on individual boats, which otherwise can precipitate a "tragedy of the commons" (Hardin, 1968) that will destroy the fishery as a whole. Air and water pollution regulations seek to force manufacturers and municipalities to "internalize" the costs that their emissions impose on ecosystems, which are powerless to organize boycotts or bring lawsuits to help themselves. Late twentieth-century Dutch *Waterschappen*, seeking to protect water quality from agricultural run-off, enforced regulations that limit how much manure farmers can spread on their soil (Huppes and Kagan, 1989).

Economic regulation

The examples discussed above are all instances of what often is referred to as "protective regulation" or "social regulation" – designed to prevent physical harms, dangerous deficiencies, and injustices that are not deterred by competitive pressures and the threat of lawsuits. Another category of regulation, however, often known as "economic regulation," seeks a rather different set of goals – to control the misuse of economic power, or to stabilize markets and employment in the face of the "creative destruction" of competition. One common example is governmental regulation of prices charged by "natural monopolies" such as public utilities, ferries, railroads, water supply systems, and electrical power plants (Anderson, 1981). Antitrust regulations or competition policies seek to control the abuse of market power by blocking mergers, interlocking directorates, or cartel-like agreements that large businesses establish to shield themselves from competition.

Even absent clear market failure or abuse of market power, governments from time to time have imposed "price control" regulations on entire industries (such as rental housing) to slow inflation (Ulman and Flanagan, 1971; Kagan, 1978) or simply to respond to consumers' political discontent. Similarly, governments often have enacted regulations in order to stabilize employment in times of recession or to foster the growth or stability of particular firms or industries. Among the latter are regulatory regimes that limit the number or type of firms that can enter a market, such as air transport (Caves, 1962; Levine, 1965). Many nations have restricted the opening of large discount chain stores in order to protect the markets of small family-owned stores. Prolabor governments often have sought to offset employers' market power by enforcing minimum wage statutes, requiring employers to provide paid holidays and other benefits, and imposing restrictions on dismissals (Freeman, 1994). For many years, Japan's Ministry of Finance used its regulatory authority over financial institutions to prevent the most efficient firms from driving less efficient ones out of business (Milhaupt and Miller, 2000).

In the last two decades, political pressures for greater economic efficiency and "deregulation" have induced many governments to eliminate or substantially modify many programs of economic regulation, such as those that had stabilized markets (and restrained competition) in banking, transportation, and telecommunications (Derthick and Quirk, 1985). Ironically, the elimination of monopolies and regulated cartels in those markets spawns increases in *protective* regulation, as consumers complain about the externalities generated by a larger number of more competitive firms that seek to cut costs or reduce service to less profitable customers (Vogel, 1996).

Economic analysis and new directions in protective regulation

In addition to eliminating some economic regulation, economic analysis and political pressures for economic efficiency have resulted in changes in many programs of protective regulation. Protective regulations, too, have an economic dimension (Leone, 1986). When regulations insist that advocacy services in court may be provided only by persons who have obtained a law degree and have passed a demanding examination, that regulatory regime restricts the number of legal practitioners, which means higher fees for clients. So too, protective regulations of all kinds, from those dealing with water pollution to those regulating child care centers, generally benefit the (typically larger) providers who are better able to afford to comply and limit market entry by "cut rate" competitors. Braithwaite (1994) found that US regulations concerning nursing home safety are so costly to comply with that only very large – and thus more impersonal – facilities were able to survive. Not surprisingly, therefore, scholars have traced particular regulatory rules, such as certain US air pollution standards, to particular firms and labor unions who ally with environmental groups to seek regulations that will bolster their competitive position (Ackerman and Hassler, 1986; Vogel, 1995)

In response to these tendencies, as well as to pressures for economic efficiency stimulated by the intensification of competition in an increasingly open and globalized world market, many governments have created bodies that "regulate the regulators," subjecting existing and proposed regulations to cost-benefit analysis and requiring agencies to adopt the most cost-effective alternatives in seeking their objectives (Morgan, 1999). Further, some governments have sought alternatives to traditional "command and control" methods of protective regulation which prescribe the same precautions or performance standards for all firms – a method that often is quite inefficient and wasteful (Weber, 1998). Instead, some governments have imposed taxes on polluting emissions or pollution-generating raw materials, which gives regulated enterprises more flexibility in determining which reduction measures are most cost-efficient (Huppes and Kagan, 1989). The US Environmental

Protection Agency initiated a "bubble program," under which a manufacturing plant could modify the restrictions imposed by detailed source-by-source air pollution permits as long as it could find ways of ensuring that its overall emissions (into an imaginary plant-wide bubble) did not increase (Levin, 1982). In addition, the federal government instituted two successful emissions quota trading programs, which in effect establish a restrictive "bubble" over an entire industry, thus giving competitors an incentive to mutually find the most cost-effective ways of cutting harmful pollutants. One of these programs accelerated (and made more efficient) the phasing out of lead additives in gasoline (Nussbaum, 1992). The second, mandated by the Clean Air Act Amendments of 1990, successfully encouraged electricity generating companies to devise their own plans for cutting sulfur dioxide emissions, a major source of acid rain (Stewart, 2001: 103–12).

As another alternative to command and control regulation, governments have simply required enterprises to report or publicize the risks associated with their products or processes, thus providing consumers and communities with information relevant to self-protection. For example, the Toxic Release Inventory (TRI) mandated by the US Emergency Planning and Community Right-to-Know Act, enacted in 1986, requires companies simply to measure and publicly disclose the levels of toxic chemicals in their air and water emissions of toxic chemicals; that alone stimulated manufacturers to reduce on-site inventories and releases of hazardous materials (Konar and Cohen, 1997). Additionally, governments increasingly have encouraged self-regulatory programs by industries and particular firms. One technique has been to grant enterprises greater flexibility with respect to command and control regulation if the regulated enterprises can demonstrate the ability to go "beyond compliance" through innovative self-regulation (Gunningham and Grabosky, 1998; Hazard and Orts, 2000; Coglianese and Nash, 2001; Rees, 1988).

POLITICS AND REGULATION

Politics and the growth of regulation

Although government regulation has existed for centuries, the number and reach of regulatory laws and programs have grown exponentially in capitalist countries since the late nineteenth century. At one level of analysis, regulation has grown because the urbanization, rapid technological change, impersonality, and environmental degradation associated with modernization have generated countless *new risks* of harm and injustice. Similarly, the growth of science has stimulated regulation by providing more *knowledge about risks*, particularly invisible ones, ranging from the late nineteenth century discovery of the relationship between insanitary conditions and disease to the discovery of the carcinogenic effects of certain chemicals and tobacco products in the latter part of the twentieth century (Bardach and Kagan, 1982: 7–25).

But knowledge of risk does not automatically spawn new regulations. From this perspective, regulation is the product of *intensifying political demands for regulation* together with *governmental responsiveness* to those demands. The growth of regulation, however, also consequently reflects two important political factors. On the demand side, Lawrence Friedman (1985) has argued, richer and better educated societies have become increasingly *intolerant* of harms, injustices, and risks that previously had been fatalistically accepted or regarded as tolerable. On the responsiveness side, the key development appears to have been the deepening and the increasing competitiveness of electoral democracy, which has made competing political parties eager to satisfy voters' desire for more protection from harm, mistreatment, and economic insecurity (Bardach and Kagan, 1982). Bursts of new regulatory statutes often have stemmed from powerful political movements, such as (to refer only to examples from the United States) the labor movement during the Great Depression, the civil rights movement of the 1960s, and the environmental and womens' movements of the late 1960s and early 1970s.

It also is increasingly clear that the acceleration of globalization – that is, the increasing integration of the world's economic, financial, and communications systems – contributes to the growth of regulation (Shapiro, 1993). Far from driving national legal systems toward ever-greater reduction in the regulatory burdens on business, Vogel (1995) and others have shown that at least in the field of protective regulation, nations with less stringent regulations face powerful political pressures to emulate the laws of nations with tougher regulations. The pressures stem from more rapid international information flows about risks and solutions, from international agreements and European Union directives, and most importantly, from "Baptist–bootlegger" political alliances; the latter occur when nongovernmental organizations that want tougher regulations team up with multinational corporations that are accustomed to complying with stringent regulations and want other governments to impose those same stringent standards on their less sophisticated competitors (Vogel, 1995). Thus financial systems around the world are gravitating toward stringent American bank safety standards (Kapstein, 1989) and the stringent disclosure requirements of American securities laws, while the USA followed Germany and Scandinavian countries in enacting more stringent standards for emissions of dioxin in wastewater from pulp and paper mills.

Politics and regulatory effectiveness

Most proregulatory political movements also stimulate a political counter-reaction, as regulated enterprises organize to limit the stringency of regulatory rules and the aggressiveness of regulatory enforcement. Some scholars, in fact, have argued that the political advantages of regulated businesses almost inevitably undermine the effectiveness of regulation in actually shaping behavior. Edelman (1964) viewed the enactment of regulatory laws as little more than "symbolic politics," since politicians typically have been more eager to announce new regulatory programs than to fund them adequately. Because regulated enterprises are a key source of information to regulatory agencies (and also often seek the appointment of "proindustry" regulatory officials), some scholars advanced the "capture theory," which holds that regulatory agencies usually adopt rules and procedures that favor the interests not of the public but of the dominant firms in the regulated industry (Bernstein, 1955). And in the early days of "Chicago School" economics, conservative scholars saw regulation as a mechanism whereby private interests – from dairy farmers to shipping companies, labor unions, and minority advocacy groups seeking "affirmative action" regulations – capture "monopoly rents," using law to dampen competition or shift resources into their own constituents' pockets (Stigler, 1975).

Later researchers, however, have cast doubt on such theories. The "capture theory," it emerged, is far from an iron law of regulation (Quirk, 1981; Wilson, 1980), particularly with respect to the highly visible programs of protective regulation (environmental protection, workplace safety, antidiscrimination) that were enacted in the latter part of the twentieth century. One important antidote to "capture by the regulated" has been the rise (especially in rich democracies) of nonprofit advocacy organizations that have been empowered to participate in policy-making processes on behalf of the constituencies who in principle are supposed to benefit from regulation (McCann, 1986). Similarly, while rent-seeking is indeed an important aspect of regulatory politics, here too the degree to which the rent seekers succeed *varies*, depending in large part on the degree to which opposing interests are able to participate in the regulatory decision-making process and to publicize economically inefficient regulatory policies and practices.

In addition, while many governmental programs reflect "symbolic politics" to some extent, the notion that political machinations usually reduce regulatory legislation to ineffectiveness is far from true. Many agencies, of course, do lack the resources and political backing to enforce their rules adequately (Gunningham, 1987), and few of them have enough resources to do what advocates of regulation consider an optimal job (what government agency does?). The collapse of many important fisheries is sad testimony to the repeated failures of regimes that seek to restrict the number of fishing boats and the size of the catch (Stone, 1997). Partly due to political pressures, American officials charged with regulating the savings and loan industry failed to prevent disastrously large numbers of overly risky loans in the 1980s, leading to the collapse of many lenders (Rubin, 2000).

But many other regulatory regimes receive enough ongoing political backing to bring about remarkable changes in behavior. To mention just a few examples, regulation has markedly improved the safety of banking, dairy products, electrical systems in housing, pharmaceuticals, and motor vehicles. Regulation has sharply reduced death rates in coal mines (Braithwaite, 1985; Lewis-Beck and Alford, 1980). Regulation has compelled manufacturers and municipalities to spend billions of dollars on emissions controls and wastewater treatment, diminishing many forms of air and water pollution (Scruggs, 1999), even in an era of rapid industrial and population growth (Easterbrook, 1999). In the United States, regulation has banished cigarette smoking from thousands of workplaces and restaurants (Kagan and Skolnick, 1993), and, partly by supplementing public with private enforcement, has increased employment opportunities and earnings for African Americans (Burstein and Edwards, 1994). Sociolegal scholars have devoted more attention to the analysis of regulatory processes than to forging theories of when regulation is effective in changing behavior and when less so. It seems clear, however, that political factors – including the levels of political organization of both supporters and opponents of regulation – are of crucial importance.

Partisan electoral politics, too, has been shown to affect regulatory policies and enforcement methods. As the costs imposed by the regulatory state have grown, conservative political parties often promise to reduce regulatory burdens on the business sector, while left-of-center parties typically promise to make regulation more stringent and effective. Once elected, political party leaders affect agencies' policies and enforcement methods in many ways – by appointing or influencing the appointment of top agency officials; by expanding or contracting agency staffing and resources through the budget process; by legislative oversight hearings; and sometimes by telling regulatory officials how they would like regulatory issues of urgent political concern to be handled (Kagan, 1993: 401). Scholz and Wei (1986), after controlling for interstate differences in the agencies' "task environment," found that workplace safety officials in states with Democratic governors and Democrat-controlled legislatures imposed more and larger penalties than those in Republican states. Fines imposed by OSHA, the US federal workplace safety agency, declined in the early 1980s after President Reagan, newly elected following a campaign denouncing "excessive government regulation," appointed a new agency head (ibid). Conversely, in 1982 and 1983, aggressive oversight hearings by congressional Democrats forced President Reagan's administration to reverse course: after an initial decline, federal environmental clean-up orders and criminal prosecutions for regulatory offenses increased to levels that exceeded those that prevailed during the preceding Democratic administration (Wood, 1988; Wood and Waterman, 1991).

Sociolegal studies in Western Europe also have found that regulatory administration is affected by political party dominance and political leaders' concerns. Hutter (1988), for example, found that British environmental control officers who worked under an elected local council dominated by the Labour Party prosecuted violators more often than officers in Conservative Party districts. Niemeijer (1989) found Dutch municipal regulators sometimes relaxed time-consuming procedural rules concerning land use plans and building permits when top municipal officials believed the planned project was important to the community's economic health – although that depended on whether bending the rules was likely to stimulate political protest or legal appeals by project opponents.

Indeed, in many democracies, political protest and legal action by citizen groups have become almost as important as electoral politics in shaping regulatory agency activity, and sometimes more so. In the 1980s, after dramatic protests by AIDS activists, the US Food and Drug Administration relaxed regulations that had prevented distribution of experimental AIDs drugs before they were fully tested for safety and efficacy (*Regulation*, 1988). In both Germany and the United States, systematic litigation by opponents of nuclear power, challenging licensing decisions by regulatory authorities, effectively halted the construction of new power plants (Boyle, 1998). In the United States, litigation by environmental groups often delays and redesigns construction projects, from ports to highways and garbage disposal sites, that had been approved by regulators (Welles and Engel, 2000; Kagan, 2001). That dynamic has increased in the UK, France, and Germany as well (Sellers, 1995). Conversely, where local complainants lack the capability for sustained political organization and pressure, regulatory implementation is more vulnerable to the political influence of local regulated enterprises (Morag-Levine, 1994).

NATIONAL STYLES OF REGULATION

Regulatory agencies employ the coercive powers of the state. They make rules that not only constrain private behavior but that often – as in the case of environmental and safety regulations – compel business firms to invest large sums of money to prevent or reduce potential hazards. Regulatory officials demand entry into factories and company offices, pore through their records, and require firms to conduct studies, compile reports, and disclose information to the public. Regulatory officials often exercise substantial discretionary powers to halt operations they deem hazardous, to forbid the shipment and sale of products, and to delay progress on expensive and urgent projects. These substantial and intrusive powers raise the perennial questions: who shall guard against abuse of authority by the guardians, and how?

And how can the regulators' authority be constrained without unduly curtailing *their* ability to control the powerful economic entities whose activities they are assigned to regulate? Much regulatory law reflects governmental and judicial efforts to answer those questions.

Many sociolegal scholars have conducted detailed studies of how regulatory law is formulated and implemented. Others have examined how political systems, regulated enterprises, and proregulation advocacy groups seek to hold regulatory officials accountable for the coercive powers they exercise. Some of the most striking findings concern the distinctiveness of the United States's "regulatory style." Compared with other economically advanced democracies, it repeatedly is found, American laws and regulations are more detailed, prescriptive, and complex (Kagan, 2000). Second, American regulatory regimes more often employ a legalistic enforcement style. That is, when American regulators encounter rule violations, rather than negotiating with regulated enterprises about how to solve the problem, they are more likely than their counterparts in other countries to issue formal legal citations, and to impose legal penalties for violations, and their legal sanctions tend to be much more severe (Braithwaite, 1994, 1985; Kelman, 1981; Aoki and Cioffi, 1999). Moreover, in the United States, governmental enforcement much more often is supplemented by enforcement via private lawsuits, particularly in the fields of antitrust, securities, workplace discrimination, and environmental regulation. Third, relationships between regulators and regulated entities in the United States much more often are *adversarial* (Wallace, 1995); legal contestation of regulatory rules and agency decisions is far more common, both by regulated entities and by citizen advocates of stricter regulation (Brickman, Jasanoff, and Ilgen, 1985; Church and Nakamura, 1994). Fourth, regulatory rules and methods in the United States more often are enmeshed in political controversy and conflict, as rival interests and politicians battle over regulatory appointments and strive to lock their policy preferences into law (Vogel, 1986).

These differences in regulatory style and processes reflect different national approaches to the problem of administrative accountability. In most democratic countries, the principal methods by which officials are held accountable are administrative supervision and political oversight. Opposition political parties and the news media play an additional watchdog role. But far more than other democracies, the United States also employs litigation (and the threat of litigation) as an additional accountability mechanism. Because of the unusually broad American rules concerning "standing to sue," a wide range of interested parties – including public interest lawyers, acting as self-appointed "private attorneys general" – can bring lawsuits against alleged violations of public law by governmental bodies. And American regulatory statutes more often authorize and encourage private litigation directly against regulatory violators, rather than reserving regulatory enforcement to governmental bodies (Kagan, 2001).

Behind these distinctively American regulatory processes lie distinctive political traditions and structures. Regulatory processes tend to be far less legalistic and adversarial in neocorporatist polities in which strong, nationwide industrial associations have the authority to negotiate with regulators and commit their membership to agreed-upon regulatory standards (Badarraco, 1985, Wallace, 1995). In parliamentary systems that have cohesive political parties, the government in power can quickly override regulatory decisions that displease it, and hence it does not need to write detailed laws or authorize citizen suits to constrain the regulatory bureaucracy

(Moe, 1990; Kelemen, 1998). In the United States, in contrast, the dominant political culture reinforces suspicion of concentrated authority, by both the political left and the political right. Hence political and economic power both are fragmented. Because the United States lacks a large, highly professional, and trusted national bureaucracy and strong national business associations, detailed laws, heavy penalties, and ready access to judicial review are the preferred mode of controlling both government and industry (Kagan, 2001).

THE DILEMMAS OF REGULATORY ENFORCEMENT

Two contrasting mental models of governmental regulation dominate discussion of the enforcement or implementation process. The first model pictures regulation as a *legal process*. It conceives of regulations as authoritative legal norms whose violation demands punishment. The other model pictures regulation as a *social process*. It emphasizes cooperative government–business problem solving and a remedial response to violations. In every democracy, some advocacy groups and politicians insist that governments should zealously pursue a legalistic approach, while business groups and many regulatory officials insist that a more cooperative approach is more desirable and effective, overall.

The legalistic model reflects the historical weight of criminal law in shaping society's response to deviant behavior. But it is no accident that the task of enforcing regulatory statutes generally is entrusted to specialized administrative agencies rather than to traditional criminal law enforcement bodies. In contrast to traditional criminal law, the standards articulated and enforced by regulatory programs often are not well-established norms, embodying long-accepted standards of wrongful behavior. The regulatory goal is usually not to prohibit all pollution, but only pollution above levels that are demonstrably harmful to human health or ecosystems; not all sources of danger in the workplace, but only "unreasonable hazards." Typically, however, determining what is "harmful" or "unreasonable" requires case-by-case judgments about particular activities in a wide variety of contexts, difficult to specify in legal rules. Moreover, as Philip Selznick (1969: 14–16) has put it, the primary social function of administration is not to determine "the legal coordinates of a situation" in light of pre-established legal rules, but "to get the work of society done," to refashion "human or other resources so that a particular outcome will be achieved." Effective regulation, in this perspective, requires whatever blend of rules and exhortation, threat and education, toughness and compromise, will best induce particular regulated enterprises to cooperate.

On the other hand, some regulatory violations do transgress long-established norms of criminal law; among these are intentional fraud, lying to law enforcement and other governmental officials, and reckless disregard for the health and safety of others. And even for run-of-the-mill regulatory violators, it is by no means clear that a cooperation-seeking approach always improves regulatory effectiveness. In the hands of gullible, overly busy, or politically vulnerable regulatory officials, a problem-solving enforcement style can degenerate into death-dealing laxity (Gunningham, 1987). Thus regulatory advocacy groups and some enforcement officials, particularly in the United States, argue that in order to deter opportunism on the part of regulated business, serious or willful violations of regulatory requirements must regularly be met by strict enforcement and severe punishment.

Yet for several reasons, criminal prosecution of regulatory violations is relatively infrequent (Hawkins, 1984; Spence, 2001). While there are some entrepreneurs who make systematic evasion of regulatory law the heart of their business strategy, most regulatory rule violations – in contrast to embezzlement, bribery, and most other white-collar crimes – are not committed as ends in themselves, but occur as side-effects of legitimate, socially valuable business operations. Research on specific regulatory programs in contemporary democracies repeatedly finds that the vast majority of regulated firms are committed to regulatory compliance, mostly for good business reasons (Gunningham, Kagan, and Thornton, 2003; Mehta and Hawkins, 1998; Bardach and Kagan, 1982: 64–6; Ayres and Braithwaite, 1992) Yet regulatory rules, by their very nature, tend to be overinclusive: promulgated in response to accidents, deceptions, and environmental offenses of the worst kind, regulations mandate precautionary measures that also apply to a wide variety of less dangerous conditions and to basically honest enterprises (Bardach and Kagan, 1982: 66–71). Hence to regulators, most regulatory violations and most violators do not appear to deserve serious legal punishment.

Similarly, many regulatory violations involve failure to file timely and fully accurate reports, or failure to take certain precautionary measures. Those violations, unlike most traditional crimes, usually do not result in any immediate, tangible harm to others. In those and other cases that appear to involve only "technical violations," regulators, judges, and regulated businesses often think it unfair to subject a businessperson or firm to the moral obloquy and harsh sanctions of the criminal law. In practical terms, moreover, criminal prosecution, with its high burden of proof, ties up agency officials in extended labor-intensive investigations and court hearings, while always entailing a significant possibility of a legal defeat (Hawkins, 1989; Coffee, 1981: 400–7).

For all these reasons, most regulatory agencies claim that they strive for a flexible enforcement style: legalistic and punitive when needed, but accommodative and helpful in others, depending on the reliability of the regulated enterprise and the seriousness of the risks or harms created by particular violations (Hawkins, 1984). Academic analyses by scholars who have studied regulatory enforcement generally support this approach. John Scholz (1984) models the regulatory enforcement as an iterative prisoner's dilemma. If the regulator seeks punitive legal sanctions for every detected violation, the regulated company might be expected to mount as strong a legal defense as possible – resulting in long legal delays and frustrating the goal of immediate reduction in the risks that the rules were designed to deal with. On the other hand, if the regulator withholds prosecution in return for the regulated firm's promise to cure the violation promptly, the firm might just keep stalling, since the legal threat has diminished. Scholz concludes that the best outcome for society, over time, results from a negotiated compromise whereby regulators withhold penal action and even agree to accept "substantial compliance" rather than demand literal compliance with all legal rules – as long as the regulated firm provides credible commitments to remedy the most serious violations quickly. At the same time, however, the regulator must develop a reputation for imposing prompt and costly legal sanctions whenever the regulated entity prevaricates or delays. Scholz labels this the "tit for tat" enforcement strategy; that means meeting noncooperation with punishment, while meeting cooperation with forbearance (see also Bardach and Kagan, 1982; Hawkins, 1984).

Ayres and Braithwaite (1992) agree that cooperation is cheaper and better than punishment, as long as the threat of punishment lies behind the invitation to cooperate. Yet they also find that in order to make that threat credible, regulators must have at their disposal legal sanctions that are less severe, quicker, and cheaper than criminal prosecution, and hence more likely to be used. The most effective regulators can plausibly threaten to meet a regulated enterprise's noncooperation by successively moving up a "pyramid of sanctions" – beginning with legal citation or warning letter, then intensified surveillance, then administratively imposed fines, then larger court-imposed civil penalties, and only then to criminal penalty or delicensure. When an agency enjoys such a range of options, Ayres and Braithwaite point out, most regulatory work gets done expeditiously and effectively at the bottom layers of the pyramid. It is perhaps for that reason that nonlegalistic regulatory regimes in Japan (Aoki and Cioffi, 1999; Wokutch and Vansandt, 2000) and Western Europe (Verweij, 2000; Scruggs, 1999; Dwyer, Brooks, and Marco, 2000) often are equally or even more effective than their legalistic counterparts in the United States.

For some sociolegal scholars, a salient question has been why some regulatory agencies and individual regulators turn to legalistic rule application and legal sanctions more often than others (May and Winter, 2000; Kagan, 1993). Often, the law on the books helps explain the regulators' choices. For example, when statutes impose a very high and difficult-to-meet standard of proof on the prosecutors, or authorize only very small penalties, regulators are more likely to resort to "bargain and bluff" enforcement styles (Hawkins, 1984; Kitamura, 2000). Sometimes, however, the agency's enforcement style is shaped not by law but by the costs and incentives faced by the regulated population. Agencies are more likely to employ a cooperative approach, researchers have found, when they deal with larger enterprises that have professional compliance staffs and a reputational stake in being seen as good corporate citizens. Conversely, regulators seem to feel more compelled to adopt a more legalistic, deterrence-oriented approach when dealing with smaller firms which are less visible to inspectors, less familiar with the rules, more financially hard-pressed, and hence more tempted to evade the law (Shover et al, 1984).

Similarly, regulators face more pressures to adopt an aggressive, sanction-oriented enforcement style when the regulations call for very large and costly changes in behavior, and hence evoke resistance from regulated entities – although the risk of a political backlash in those circumstances may also induce regulatory officials to bend the rules and be more accommodative (Kagan, 1993). In addition, as noted earlier, political factors, including the political ideology of the government in power, have been shown to influence regulatory enforcement style. Finally, as discussed briefly in the following section, enforcement style often is influenced by the degree of discretion granted front-line regulatory bureaucrats, which in turn depends in significant measure on those officials' level of professionalization.

REGULATORY OFFICIALS

In 1981, following the inauguration of Ronald Reagan, an avowedly antiregulation president, the US Environmental Protection Agency *increased* the frequency with which it issued pollution abatement orders (Wood, 1988). Regulatory officials, we are thus reminded, often have their own agendas and commitments, notwithstanding the political signals and statutory standards they are expected to heed. Most sociolegal research on this subject, however, has focused on the United States, where regulatory bureaucracies generally are less well buffered against overt political pressures than are bureaucracies in Western Europe and Japan (Wilson, 1989: 295–312; Harris and Milkis, 1996; Landy, Roberts, and Thomas, 1993).

Among high agency officials in American regulatory agencies, James Q. Wilson (1980: 374–82) points out, some are "careerists," seemingly motivated above all by the desire to avoid political controversy and protect agency budgets. Others, whom he labels "politicians," see their tenure as a stepping-stone to greater political visibility or electoral office; they are more likely to court publicity-generating battles with regulated enterprises. Still other agency chiefs, in Wilson's typology, are "professionals," who try to adhere to analytically supported policies regardless of external political influences. Because regulatory agency chiefs in the USA often come from outside the career civil service, occasionally they reshape agency policy dramatically. In the late 1970s and early 1980s, academic economists Alfred Kahn and Darius Gaskins led the Civil Aviation Board and the Interstate Commerce Commission, respectively, in a radical deregulatory direction (Derthick and Quirk, 1985). Law professor William Baxter, appointed to the Reagan Adminstration Department of Justice, shifted the intellectual basis and direction of antitrust law enforcement toward policies favored by free market economists. In the 1970s, the leaders of California's air pollution control board helped organize and finance environmental advocacy groups, hoping thereby to strengthen their own political constituency (Sabatier, 1975). But the political activism of some agency heads in the United States, together with the frequency of elections, also means that regulatory policy can shift dramatically over relatively short periods of time. Moreover, there often is substantial turnover in regulatory personnel in the American civil service. Hence regulated enterprises often experience regulatory policy in the United States as more malleable and uncertain than in other economically advanced democracies (Kagan, 2000)

As in the case of regulatory agency leaders, the political attitudes and professional commitments of rank and file agency officials often have an impact on regulatory policy and enforcement style (Hawkins, 1984; Hutter, 1997; Hedge, Menzel, and Williams, 1988), as do their day-to-day working conditions and level of supervision. Regulatory bureaucrats tend to be less legalistic when they regularly meet face to face with regulated businesspeople, rather than simply deal with files and records (Kagan, 1978: 152–4). Regulators more often are legalistic when they lack adequate information and are under strong organizational pressures to process cases quickly or meet performance quotas (ibid: 127–43). According to some studies of American agencies, staff lawyers tend to push for more legalistic enforcement strategies than those preferred by agency engineers, scientists, or economists (Melnick, 1983: 259–60; Katzmann, 1980; Weaver, 1980; Mashaw and Harfst, 1991).

In Germany, regulatory officials concerned with bank safety and soundness are career government employees, subjected to much more extensive education and training than their counterparts at the US Federal Reserve Board. One consequence is that the highly professional German officials are trusted to make programmatically sensible judgments, whereas the American regulators are bound by an immensely voluminous, complex, and detailed body of legal rules (Rubin, 1997). More generally, when regulatory officials are ill-paid and poorly educated, there is a greater risk that they will be corrupted or captured, or abuse their power.

Under these conditions, legislators and top agency officials are more likely to restrict front-line officials' discretion through detailed rules and checklists – which tends to produce a more legalistic or mechanical enforcement style (Bardach and Kagan, 1982). The maturation of government regulation, therefore, would seem to require greater societal investment in the professionalization of regulatory personnel, much as has occurred with respect to police departments in recent decades. But amid many competing demands on governmental resources, it is not clear that all nations can generate the political will to follow that course.

DIRECTIONS FOR FUTURE RESEARCH

When compared to the level and depth of sociolegal research on the enforcement of traditional criminal law, criminal behavior, policing, and criminal procedure, sociolegal research on regulatory programs, procedures, and compliance has been minimal and small-scale. Like clearings in a rainforest, existing studies cover but a small part of the terrain, and are always at risk of being rendered obsolete by the flow of events. Three especially urgent priorities stand out, however. The first is the need for more sociolegal research on regulatory processes and implementation in less developed countries. The second is the need for more direct comparisons of regulatory processes across economically advanced democracies, particularly in terms of (1) examining the conditions under which globalization does or does not induce national regulatory systems to converge toward common norms and regulatory methods (Vogel and Kagan, 2002; Unger and van Waarden, 1995; Kagan, 1997), and (2) determining the relationship between different implementation methods and on-the-ground outcomes. The third is the need for sociolegal research on the process of professionalization of regulatory personnel, emphasizing how variation in education, training, support, and organizational philosophy shapes the effectiveness and flexibility of regulatory processes.

References

Ackerman, Bruce and Hassler, William (1986) *Clean Coal/Dirty Air.* New Haven, CT: Yale University Press.

Anderson, Douglas (1981) *Regulatory Politics and Electrical Utilities.* Boston: Auburn House.

Aoki, Kazumasu and Cioffi, John (1999) "Poles apart: Industrial waste management regulation and enforcement in the United States and Japan," *Law & Policy* 21: 213–45.

Ayres, Ian and Braithwaite, John (1992) *Responsive Regulation.* New York: Oxford University Press.

Badaracco, Joseph L.(1985) *Loading The Dice: A Five Country Study of Vinyl Chloride Regulation.* Boston: Harvard Business School Press.

Bardach, Eugene and Kagan, Robert A. (1982) *Going by the Book: The Problem of Regulatory Unreasonableness.* Philadelphia: Temple University Press.

Bernstein, Marver (1955) *Regulating Business by Independent Commission.* Princeton, NJ: Princeton University Press.

Boyle, Elizabeth Heger (1998) "Political frames and legal activity: The case of nuclear power in four countries," *Law & Society Review* 32: 141–74.

Braithwaite, John (1985) *To Punish or Persuade: Enforcement of Coal Mine Safety.* Albany, NY: SUNY Press.

Braithwaite, John (1994) "The nursing home industry," in Michael Tonry and Albert J. Reiss, Jr. (eds.), *Beyond the Law: Crime in Complex Organizations.* Chicago: University of Chicago Press, pp. 11–54.

Brickman, Ronald, Jasanoff, Sheila, and Ilgen, Thomas (1985) *Controlling Chemicals: The Politics of Regulation in Europe and the United States.* Ithaca, NY: Cornell University Press.

Burstein, Paul and Edwards, Mark (1994) "The impact of employment discrimination litigation on racial disparity in earnings: Evidence and unresolved issues," *Law & Society Review* 28: 79–108.

Caves, Richard (1962) *Air Transport and its Regulators.* Cambridge, MA: Harvard University Press.

Cheit, Ross E. (1990) *Setting Safety Standards: Regulation in the Public and Private Sectors.* Berkeley: University of California Press.

Church, Thomas W. and Nakamura, Robert (1994) "Beyond superfund: Hazardous waste cleanup in Europe and the United States," *Georgetown International Environmental Law Review* 7: 15–76.

Coffee, John C. Jr. (1981) "No soul to damn, no body to kick: An unscandalized inquiry into the problem of corporate punishment," *Michigan Law Review* 74: 386–459.

Coglianese, Cary and Nash, Jennifer (2001) *Regulating from the Inside: Can Environmental Management Systems Achieve Policy Goals?* Washington, DC: Resources for the Future.

Derthick, Martha and Quirk, Paul (1985) *The Politics of Deregulation.* Washington, DC: The Brookings Institution.

Dwyer, John Richard Brooks and Marco, Alan (2000) "The air pollution permit process for U.S. and German automobile assembly plants," in Robert A. Kagan and Lee Axelrad (eds.), *Regulatory Encounters: Multinational Corporations and American Adversarial Legalism.* Berkeley: University of California Press, pp. 173–221.

Easterbrook, Greg (1999) "America the O.K.," *The New Republic*, January 4 and 11, pp. 19, 22.

Edelman, Murray (1964) *The Symbolic Uses of Politics.* Urbana: University of Illinois Press.

Freeman, Richard (1994) "How labor fares in advanced economies," in R. Freeman (ed.), *Working Under Different Rules.* New York: Russell Sage Foundation, pp. 1–28.

Friedman, Lawrence M. (1985) *Total Justice.* New York: Russell Sage Foundation.

Gunningham, Neil (1987) "Negotiated non-compliance: A case study of regulatory failure," *Law & Policy* 9(1): 69–93.

Gunningham, Neil and Grabosky, Peter (1998) *Smart Regulation.* Oxford: Clarendon Press.

Gunningham, Neil, Kagan, Robert A., and Thornton, Dorothy (2003) *Shades of Green: Business, Regulation, and Environment.* Stanford CA: Stanford University Press.

Gunningham, Neil and Rees, Joseph (1997) "Industry self-regulation," *Law & Policy* 19(4): 363–414.

Hardin, Garrett (1968) "The tragedy of the commons," *Science* 162: 1243–8.

Harris, Richard and Milkis, Sidney (eds.) (1996) *The Politics of Regulatory Change: A Tale of Two Agencies*, 2nd edn. New York: Oxford University Press.

Hawkins, Keith (1984) *Environment and Enforcement: Regulation and the Social Definition of Deviance.* Oxford: Oxford University Press.

Hawkins, Keith (1989) " 'FATCATS' and prosecution in a regulatory agency: A footnote on the social construction of risk," *Law & Policy* 11: 370–91.

Hazard, Geoffrey C. Jr. and Orts, Eric W. (2000) "Environmental contracts in the United States,' in Karl Detekelaere and Orts, Eric W. (eds.), *A Comparative Approach to Regulatory Innovation in the United States and Europe.* New York: Kluwer Law International, pp. 71–92.

Hedge, David, Menzel, Donald, and Williams, George (1988) "Regulatory attitudes and behavior: The case of surface mining regulation," *Western Political Quarterly* 41: 323–40.

Hughes, Jonathan (1975) *Social Control in the Colonial Economy.* Charlottesville: University of Virginia Press.

Huppes, Gjalt and Kagan, Robert A. (1989) "Market-oriented regulation of environmental problems in The Netherlands," *Law & Policy* 11: 215–39.

Hutter, Bridget (1988) *The Reasonable Arm of the Law? The Law Enforcement Procedures of Environmental Health Officials.* Oxford: Clarendon Press.

Hutter, Bridget (1997) *Compliance: Regulation and Environment.* Oxford: Clarendon Press.

Kagan, Robert A. (1978) *Regulatory Justice: Implementing A Wage Price Freeze.* New York: Russell Sage Foundation.

Kagan, Robert A. (1993) "Regulatory enforcement," in D. Rosenbloom and R. Schwartz (eds.), *Handbook of Regulation and Administrative Law.* New York: Marcel Dekker, pp. 383–42.

Kagan, Robert A. (1997) "Should Europe worry about adversarial legalism?" *Oxford Journal of Legal Studies* 17: 165–83.

Kagan, Robert A. (2000) "The consequences of adversarial legalism," in Robert A. Kagan and Lee Axelrad (eds.), *Regulatory Encounters: Multinational Corporations and American Adversarial Legalism.* Berkeley: University of California Press, pp. 372–413.

Kagan, Robert A. (2001) *Adversarial Legalism: The American Way of Law.* Cambridge, MA: Harvard University Press.

Kagan, Robert A. and Skolnick, Jerome (1993) "Banning smoking: Compliance without enforcement," in Robert Rabin and Stephen Sugarman (eds.), *Smoking Policy: Law, Politics and Culture.* New York: Oxford University Press, pp. 69–94.

Kapstein, Ethan (1989) "Resolving the regulators' dilemma: International coordination of banking regulations," *International Organizations* 43: 323–47.

Katzmann, Robert (1980) *Regulatory Bureaucracy: The Federal Trade Commission and Antitrust Policy.* Washington: Brookings Institution.

Kelemen, R. Daniel (1998) "Regulatory federalism: The European Union in comparative perspective," unpublished PhD dissertation, Stanford University.

Kelman, Steven (1981) *Regulating America, Regulating Sweden: A Comparative Study of Occupational Safety and Health Policy.* Cambridge, MA: MIT Press.

Kitamura, Yoshinobu (2000) "Regulatory enforcement in local government in Japan," *Law & Policy* 22: 305–18.

Konar, Shameek and Cohen, Mark (1997) "Information as regulation: The effect of community right-to-know laws on toxic emissions," *Journal of Environmental Economics and Management* 32: 109–24.

Landy, Marc, Roberts, Marc, and Thomas, Stephen (1993) *The Environmental Protection Agency: Asking the Wrong Questions,* expanded edn. New York: Oxford University Press.

Leone, Robert (1986) *Who Profits? Winners, Losers and Government Regulation.* New York: Basic Books.

Levin, Michael H. (1982) "Getting there: Implementing the 'bubble' policy," in Eugene Bardach and Robert A. Kagan (eds.), *Social Regulation: Strategies for Reform.* San Francisco: Institute of Independent Studies Press, pp. 59–92.

Levine, Martin (1965) "Is regulation necessary? California air transportation and national regulatory policy," *Yale Law Journal* 74: 1416.

Lewis-Beck, Michael and John Alford (1980) "Can government regulate safety? The coal mine example," *American Political Science Review* 74: 745–55.

Mashaw, Jerry L. and Harfst, Daniel (1991) *The Struggle for Auto Safety.* Cambridge, MA: Harvard University Press.

May, Peter and Winter, Soeren (2000) "Reconsidering styles of regulatory enforcement: Patterns in Danish agro-environmental inspection." *Law & Policy* 22: 145–73.

McCann, Michael (1986) *Taking Reform Seriously: Perspectives on Public Interest Liberalism*. Ithaca, NY: Cornell University Press.

Mehta, Alex and Hawkins, Keith (1998) "Integrated pollution control and its impact: Perspectives from industry," *Journal of Environmental Law* 10: 61–78.

Melnick, R. Shep (1983) *Regulation and The Courts: The Case of The Clean Air Act*. Washington, DC: The Brookings Institution.

Milhaupt, Curtis and Miller, Geoffrey (2000) "Regulatory failure and the collapse of Japan's home mortgage lending industry: A legal and economic analysis," *Law & Policy* 22: 245–90.

Moe, Terry M. (1990) "Political institutions: The Neglected side of the story" *Journal of Law, Economics, and Organization* 6: 213–53.

Morag-Levine, Noga (1994) "Between choice and sacrifice: Constructions of community consent in reactive air pollution regulation," *Law & Society Review* 28: 1035–77.

Morgan, Bronwen (1999) "Regulating the regulators: Meta-regulation as a strategy for reinventing government in Australia" *Public Management* 1: 49–65.

Niemeijer, Bert (1989) "Urban land-use and building control in The Netherlands: Flexible decisions in a rigid system," *Law & Policy* 11: 121–52.

Nussbaum, B. (1992) "Phasing down lead in gasoline in the U.S.: Mandates, incentives, trading, and banking," OECD Workshop on Reducing Greenhouse Gas Emissions, June, Paris.

Olson, Mancur, Jr. (1968) *The Logic of Collective Action*. New York: Schocken Books.

Quirk, Paul (1981) *Industry Influence in Federal Regulatory Agencies*. Princeton, NJ: Princeton University Press.

Rees, Joseph (1988) *Reforming the Workplace: A Study of Self-Regulation in Occupational Safety*. Philadelphia: University of Pennsylvania Press.

Rees, Joseph (1994) *Hostages of Each Other: The Transformation of Nuclear Safety Since Three Mile Island*. Chicago: University of Chicago Press.

Regulation (1998) "Dying for drugs," 3: 9–11.

Rubin, Edward L. (1997) "Discretion and its discontents," *Chicago Kent Law Review* 72: 1299–1336.

Rubin, Edward L. (2000) "Communing with disaster: What we can learn from the Jusen and Savings and Loan crises," *Law & Policy* 22: 291–303.

Sabatier, Paul (1975) "Social movements and regulatory agencies: Toward a more adequate – and less pessimistic – theory of 'clientele capture'," *Policy Sciences* 6: 301–42.

Scholz, John T. (1984) "Cooperation, deterrence and the ecology of regulatory enforcement," *Law & Society Review* 18: 601–46.

Scholz, John T. and Wei, Feng H. (1986) "Regulatory enforcement in a federalist system," *American Political Science Review* 80: 1249–70.

Scruggs, Lyle A. (1999) "Institutions and environmental performance in seventeen Western democracies," *British Journal of Political Science* 29(1): 1–31.

Sellers, Jeffery M. (1995) "Litigation as a local political resource: Courts in controversies over land use in France, Germany and the United States," *Law and Society Review* 29: 475–517.

Selznick, Philip (1969) *Law, Society and Industrial Justice*. New York: Russell Sage Foundation.

Shapiro, Martin (1993) "The globalization of law," *Indiana Journal of Global Legal Studies* 1: 37–64.

Shover, Neil, Lynxwiler, John, Groce, Stephen, and Clelland, Donald (1984) "Regional variation in regulatory law enforcement: The Surface Mining Control and Reclamation Act of 1997," in Keith Hawkins and John Thomas (eds.), *Enforcing Regulation*. Boston: Kluwer-Nijhoff, pp. 121–46.

Spence, David B. (2001) "The shadow of the rational polluter: Rethinking the role of rational actor models in environmental law," *California Law Review* 89: 917–98.

Stewart, Richard B. (2001) "A new generation of environmental regulation?" *Capital University Law Review* 29(21): 28–182.

Stigler, George (1975) *The Citizen and the State.* Chicago: University of Chicago Press.

Stone, Christopher (1997) "Too many fishing boats, too few fish," *Ecology Law Quarterly* 24: 504–44.

Ulman, Lloyd and Flanagan, Robert (1971) *Wage Restraint: A Study of Incomes Policies in Western Europe.* Berkeley, CA: University of California Press.

Unger, Brigitte and Waarden, Frans van (1995) *Convergence or Diversity? Internationalization and Economic Policy Response.* Aldershot, UK: Avebury.

Verweij, Marco (2000) "Why is the River Rhine cleaner than the Great Lakes (despite looser regulation)?" *Law & Society Review* 34: 1007–54.

Vogel, David (1986) *National Styles of Regulation: Environmental Policy in Great Britain and the United States.* Ithaca, NY: Cornell University Press.

Vogel, David (1995) *Trading Up: Consumer and Environmental Regulation in a Global Economy.* Cambridge, MA: Harvard University Press.

Vogel, David and Kagan, Robert A. (eds.) (2002) *Dynamics of Regulatory Change: How Globalization Affects National Regulatory Policies.* Berkeley, CA: University of California Press/University of California International and Area Studies Digital Collection. Available at <http://repositories.cdlib.org/uciaspubs/editedvolumes/1>.

Vogel, Steven (1996) *Freer Markets, More Rules: Regulatory Reform in Advanced Industrial Countries.* Ithaca, NY: Cornell University Press.

Wallace, David (1995) *Environmental Policy and Industrial Innovation: Strategies in Europe, the U.S., and Japan.* London: Royal Institute of International Affairs/Earthscan Publications, Ltd.

Weaver, Suzanne (1980) "Antitrust division of the Department of Justice," in James Q. Wilson (ed.), *The Politics of Regulation.* New York: Basic Books, pp. 123–51.

Weber, Edward (1998) *Pluralism by the Rules: Conflict and Cooperation in Environmental Regulation.* Washington, DC: Georgetown University Press.

Welles, Holly and Engel, Kirsten (2000) "A comparative study of solid waste landfill regulation: Case studies from the United States, the United Kingdom, and the Netherlands," in Robert A. Kagan and Lee Axelrad (eds.), *Regulatory Encounters: Multinational Corporations and American Adversarial Legalism.* University of California Press, pp. 122–72.

Wilson, James Q. (1980) *The Politics of Regulation.* New York: Basic Books.

Wilson, James Q. (1989) *Bureaucracy.* New York: Basic Books.

Wokutch, Richard and Vansandt, Craig (2000) "National styles of worker protection in the United States and Japan: The case of the automotive industry" *Law & Policy* 22: 369–84.

Wood, B. Dan (1988) "Principals, agents, and responsiveness in clean air enforcement," *American Political Science Review* 82: 213–34.

Wood, B. Dan and Waterman, Richard (1991) "The dynamics of political control of the bureaucracy," *American Political Science Review* 85: 801–28.

Further Reading

Aalders, Marius and Wilthagen, Ton (1997) "Moving beyond command-and-control: Reflexivity in the regulation of occupational safety and health and the environment," *Law & Policy* 19: 415–43.

Beierle, Thomas C. and Cayford, Jerry (2002) *Democracy in Practice: Public Participation in Environmental Decisions.* Washington, DC: Resources for the Future.

Black, Julia (1997) *Rules and Regulators.* Oxford: Clarendon Press.

Braithwaite, John (2002) *Restorative Justice and Responsive Regulation.* Oxford and New York: Oxford University Press.

Braithwaite, John and Drahos, Peter (2000) *Global Business Regulation*. Cambridge, UK: Cambridge University Press.

Fischbeck, Paul S. and Farrow, R. Scott (eds.) (2002) *Improving Regulation: Cases in Environment, Health, and Safety*. Washington, DC: Resources for the Future.

Haufler, Virginia (2002). *A Public Role for the Private Sector: Industry Self-Regulation in a Global Economy*. Washington, DC: Carnegie Endowment for International Peace.

Hawkins, Keith (2002) *Law as Last Resort: Prosecution Decision-Making in a Regulatory Agency*. Oxford: Oxford University Press

Kunreuther H.C., McNulty, P.J., and Kang, Y. (2002) "Third-party inspection as an alternative to command and control regulation. Risk analysis." *Risk Analysis* 22: 309–18.

Majone, Giandomenico (ed.) (1996) *Regulating Europe*. London: Routledge.

McBarnet, Doreen and Whelan, Christopher (1991) "The elusive spirit of the law, formalism and the struggle for legal control," *Modern Law Review* 54: 847–73.

McCubbins, Matthew, Roger Noll, Barry Weingast (1989) "Structure and process: Politics and policy: administrative arrangements and the political control of agencies," *Virginia Law Review* 75: 431–82.

Parker, Christine (2002) *The Open Corporation: Effective Self-Regulation and Democracy*. Cambridge, UK: Cambridge University Press.

Power, Michael (1997). *The Audit Society: Rituals of Verification*. Oxford: Oxford University Press.

Sunstein, Cass R. (1990) "Paradoxes of the regulatory state," *University Chicago Law Review* 57: 407–40.

Viscusi, Kip (2002) *Regulation Through Litigation*. Washington, DC: Brookings Institution Press.

13

The Legal Lives of Private Organizations

Lauren B. Edelman

The Nexus of Law and Organizations

This essay draws on developments in organization theory and in sociolegal studies, particularly the recent literature that explicitly addresses the intersection of law and organizations, to offer a portrait of law within and around private organizations. The legal lives of private organizations may be understood as a complex web of rules, norms, customs, ritual, and ideology. This web provides the infrastructure for the exchange of normative ideas between the legal and organizational realms. Moreover, it allows organizations to be at once responsive to and constitutive of law in broader society.

The legal lives of private organizations interact with the broader legal environments through a vast array of formal legal rules and informal social norms. Statutes at the local, state, national, and sometimes international levels regulate key elements of organizational life, including trade, mergers, product design, employee governance, employee health and safety. And organizations operate within a web of regulation that extends beyond the formal law to professional certification and licensing rules, union contracts, and business customs. The direction of social control is not only from society to organizations; both laws and norms tend to arise out of the problems that characterize everyday organizational transactions, and more broadly out of the practices and ideologies of industrial capitalism.

A second point of interaction relates to the legal and law-related tools and routines that organizations use in their everyday operations. Law provides for the organization of economic exchange through contracts and for the accumulation of capital through property law. Organizational growth occurs through the legal machinery of transactions, mergers, and joint ventures. Organizational transformation takes place within the realms of bankruptcy law, antitrust law, and the law of mergers and acquisitions. Even organizational birth and death are accomplished through the legal acts of incorporation and dissolution, respectively. In all of these realms, lawsuits and the threat of lawsuits also constitute a normal part of organizational toolkits as they negotiate with their suppliers, customers, competitors, regulators, and employees. These legal rubrics matter even in their absence, by providing a set of norms, threats, and language that constitute the less formal realm of economic exchange and social action (e.g., Macaulay, 1963).

Law is also bound up with the very existence of organizations in that many elements of organizational life are legal in form. The legal regimes of various states and countries may motivate (or discourage) the creation of organizations; for example, US multinationals may form in response to the more lax labor laws of Third World countries. The form of organizations is responsive to law; for example, whether an organization is created as a partnership or a corporation is often driven by tax policy. At a more fundamental level, notions of property, contract, and employment shape the boundaries, roles, legitimate and illegitimate forms, and behaviors of organizations. But at the same time, the evolving practices of organizations shape our understandings of the meaning of law and of compliance.

The following sections explore the interaction between law and organizations in more detail. The first section provides an overview of theories of organizations and law from classical social theory through contemporary neoinstitutional perspectives. The second section elaborates multiple facets of the legal environments of organizations and explores the implications of a metatheoretical debate between materialist and cultural perspectives on organizational environments. The third section proposes and outlines a theory of law as endogenous, that is, as generated within the social context it seeks to regulate. Finally, the conclusion suggests a number of unresolved questions that warrant future research about the interaction of legal and organizational environments.

THEORETICAL FRAMES

The complex interplay between law and organizations is a central theme in classical social theory. Emile Durkheim (1964) emphasized the role of law in preserving social organization and the division of labor in modern society. Karl Marx saw legal forms as critical in the ideological and actual reproduction of the organization of production and, more fundamentally, in the preservation of class hierarchies (Marx and Engels, 1978; Cain and Hunt, 1979). Max Weber (1947) offered the most comprehensive theorization of the link between legal and organization life, contending that legal-rational organizational structures and rationally organized legal structures embodied kindred tensions between efficacy, predictability, and domination. Yet despite the linkages between law and organizations in classical social theory, scholarship in the sociology of law and organization theory, until relatively recently, proceeded quite independently.

Organization theory from the 1940s through the 1970s drew on the Weberian legacy by exploring the rational, purposive, and coordinated activities of bureaucracy. Yet law is absent from these analyses, largely because scholars were interested in the internal structures and behaviors of organizations as opposed to the environments of organizations. More recent organization theory adopts a more "open systems" approach, looking to the interrelations of organizations and their environments rather than at individual organizations (Scott, 1998). Open systems perspectives on organizations brought the law into organization theory, albeit in a rather tangential way: law is of interest less in its own right than as a source of uncertainty that organizations sought to tame or as a mechanism for creating a more favorable environment (Pfeffer and Salancik, 1978; Stigler, 1971; Zald, 1970; Scott, 1998). These accounts generally portray organizations as rational actors seeking to maximize profits through rational means (Edelman and Suchman, 1997).

Neoinstitutional organization theory developed in the late 1970s, and gave law a more central place in organizational analysis. In contrast to the materialist approaches that emphasize organizations' strategic response to and use of law, neoinstitutional accounts emphasize the cultural aspects of law (Edelman and Suchman, 1997). Drawing on Berger and Luckmann's (1967) work on the social construction of reality, neoinstitutional theory highlights the role of taken-for-granted cultural rules, models, and myths in structuring organizations. Seminal works by Meyer and Rowan (1977), DiMaggio and Powell (1983), and Meyer and Scott (1983) suggest that organizations exist within *"organizational fields,"* which are defined as "organizations that, in the aggregate, constitute a recognized area of institutional life: key suppliers, resource and product consumers, regulatory agencies, and other organizations that produce similar services or products" (DiMaggio and Powell, 1983: 148). Organizations within those fields tend to incorporate institutionalized models, not only because of rational analysis of their costs and benefits but also because certain actions, forms, or rituals come to be understood as proper and natural.

By emphasizing the cultural aspects of organizational life, neoinstitutional theory served as a natural vehicle for theorizing the intersection of law and organizations. However, early institutional theory generally portrayed law as stable, exogenous, and coercive. In these accounts, the direction of causation was generally *from* law *to* organizations (e.g., Meyer and Rowan, 1977; DiMaggio and Powell, 1983; Fligstein, 1990).

Law and society scholarship, which developed in the 1960s, paints a very different portrait of law. Far from the exogenous and coercive vision of law in organization theory, the law and society tradition holds that law itself is a culturally and structurally embedded social institution. While very little law and society scholarship considered the intersection of law and organizations (Selznick, 1969 and Macaulay, 1963 are notable exceptions), this perspective was a natural fit with the more cultural conception of organizations developed in neoinstitutional organization theory.

The neoinstitutional perspective on law and organizations, which has evolved over the past dozen or so years, combines organizational scholars' insights on the institutional nature of organizations with sociolegal scholars' insights on the institutional nature of law. Edelman (1990, 1992) argues that organizations are highly responsive to their "legal environments" or the law-related aspects of organizational fields. Legal environments include formal law and its associated sanctions; informal practices and norms regarding the use, nonuse, and circumvention of law; ideas about the meaning of law and compliance with law; and the broad set of principles, ideas, rituals, and norms that may evolve out of law (Edelman, 1990, 1992; Edelman and Suchman, 1997; Cahill, 2001). In the next section, I discuss recent scholarship on the intersection of law and organizations within legal environments.

THE LEGAL ENVIRONMENTS OF ORGANIZATIONS

Legal environments generate at least three sites of intersection between law and organizations. In particular, legal environments operate as a set of *facilitative* tools that allow organizations to structure their relations with other parts of their environments; as a set of *regulatory* edicts that actively impose societal authority on various aspects of organizational life; and as a set of *constitutive* constructs that subtly influence organizational form and structure (Edelman and Suchman, 1997).

These three facets of legal environments can further be understood via two dominant modes of interaction: those suggested by the materialist account, and those suggested by the cultural perspective. Materialist perspectives conceptualize organizations as rational purpose entities that use, manipulate, and maneuver around the law. Cultural perspectives, on the other hand, conceptualize organizations as institutionalized entities that are highly responsive to the normative ideals, symbolic rituals, and scripted roles associated with law (see Edelman and Suchman, 1997, for an extensive review of the three facets of legal environments and two metatheoretical perspectives).

The facilitative environment

The facilitative legal environment comprises a set of passive procedural vehicles and forums that organizations may mobilize to resolve disputes, to structure their relations with other organizations, to govern their employees, to influence the behavior of regulatory agencies, and to gather information. Materialist perspectives on the facilitative environment stress how organizations strategically use legal tools to influence other actors in their environments and to control the market. In contrast, cultural perspectives are more likely to highlight the role of norms in shaping the use of both law and extralegal tools.

Materialist perspectives emphasize the strategic use of law and the increasing relevance of litigation to organizational life, emphasizing the rise in business's use of civil litigation (Cheit, 1991; Galanter and Rogers, 1991) and a concomitant rise in the number and status of both inhouse counsel and independent corporate law firms (Galanter and Rogers, 1991). The increase in litigation itself results in increased insurance use (Cheit, 1991), elevated bankruptcy rates (Delaney, 1989), and less willingness to undertake high-risk innovation (Cheit, 1991).

Studies of informal dispute resolution portray a mix of cultural and materialist perspectives. For example, Macaulay's (1963) seminal study of contract disputes showed that businessmen preferred to handle exchange relationships informally and to resolve disputes according to the norms of the business community rather than through lawsuits. Although business *culture* is central to Macaulay's analysis, the businessmen in his study saw informal dispute resolution as more *efficient* than litigation. More recent work shows a rise in the use of alternative dispute resolution techniques such as mediation and arbitration to handle interbusiness disputes (Lande, 1998; Morrill, 1995) as well as a dramatic rise in the use of internal grievance procedures and various informal dispute resolution techniques for handling intraorganizational conflict (Edelman, Erlanger, and Lande, 1993; Edelman and Cahill, 1998; Edelman, Uggen, and Erlanger, 1999; Edelman and Suchman, 1999). Other work focuses on differences in disputing norms across organizations (Cahill,

2001) and nations (Gibson and Caldeira, 1996; Kagan and Axelrad, 2000; Kagan, 2001; Cahill, 2001; Saguy, 2000).

Organizations also engage the facilitative environment when they seek constraints on the market or regulation of competitive industries. Here again the literature reflects a mix of materialist and cultural perspectives. Industries use law strategically to secure direct government subsidies, rules that limit entry into the industry, rules that hinder competitors or otherwise provide an advantage against competitors, and rules that allow the management of competition (Stigler, 1971; Gable, 1953; Pfeffer, 1974; Zhou, 1993). Industries and organizations also seek favorable rule-making outcomes from administrative agencies (Posner, 1974; Clune, 1983; Hawkins, 1984; Blumrosen, 1993). Sometimes alignments between industries and regulators come about through political and cultural processes. In the case of property insurance, for example, rate regulation was enacted over industry opposition but produced institutions and political settlement that protected insurance companies and agents from price competition (Schneiberg, 1999; Schneiberg and Bartley, 2001).

The notion of a facilitative legal environment, then, calls attention both to legal strategies for structuring economic interaction and to norms of interaction that influence and arise out of organizational life.

The regulatory environment

The regulatory legal environment consists of substantive rules that actively impose societal authority on various aspects of organizational life. Laws that regulate organizations (such as antidiscrimination laws, health and safety laws, and antitrust laws), the administrative regulations of enforcement agencies (such as the Equal Employment Opportunity Commission and Occupational Safety and Health Administration), and the substantive decisions of courts (both interpreting statutes and articulating common law doctrines) all constitute the regulatory environment. The regulatory environment also includes informal norms that have lawlike functions, such as norms about consistent treatment of employees or about diversity. Materialist perspectives see law as a set of externally imposed constraints on organizations, accompanied by incentives and penalties. In contrast, cultural accounts portray organizations as inhabiting highly structured organizational fields in which legal rules and social norms generate structures and rituals that become institutionalized elements of organizational life.

In the materialist view, organizations calculate the relative value of compliance and noncompliance and alter their behavior accordingly (Diver, 1980; Paternoster and Simpson, 1996; Braithwaite and Makkai, 1991; Genn, 1993). The sanctions associated with noncompliance are often insufficient to deter illegal behavior because the risk of legal judgments or administrative fines will often seem minimal in comparison to market-related risks such as product failure. In other words, legal sanctions are usually too small and too slow to affect rational organizational planning (Stone, 1975; Jowell, 1975). Organizational decentralization, moreover, tends to obscure the locus of negligent decision making and to foster interdepartmental competition that subordinates legal compliance to market performance.

Cultural theorists challenge the notion that organizations rationally calculate the costs and benefits of compliance, suggesting instead that because much law regulating organizations is ambiguous, the meaning of compliance is socially constructed over time. The regulatory environment takes form gradually through organizational mimicry, the diffusion of professional norms, and the normative influence of state rules (Edelman, 1990, 1992; Sutton, Dobbin, Meyer, and Scott, 1994; Dobbin, Sutton, Meyer, and Scott, 1993; Dobbin and Sutton, 1998; Edelman and Petterson, 1999; Edelman et al., 1999; Heimer, 1999; Kelly and Dobbin, 1998; Edelman, 2002). Law is thus filtered through managerial traditions and prerogatives and through the lenses of professionals within organizations who manage organizational responses to law. Organizations with the most linkages to the public sector tend to take a prominent role in defining compliance – often creating internal procedures, offices, and rules meant to demonstrate attention to law. These internal legal structures, which often mirror public legal institutions in form more than substance, often come to be understood as necessary (and sometimes sufficient) elements of compliance (Edelman, 1992). And over time, these structural symbols of compliance acquire increasing legitimacy and rationality in the eyes of other organizations, employees, regulators, and even courts (Edelman, 1990, 1992; Edelman et al., 1999).

Scholars in both the materialist and cultural camps call attention to various forms of regulatory "capture," in which organizational power leads regulators to overlook or even to facilitate the legally questionable practices of regulatory organizations (Blumrosen, 1965, 1993; Wirt, 1970; Ackerman, Ackerman, Sawyer, and Henderson, 1974; Conklin, 1977; Cranston, 1979; Diver, 1980; Clune, 1983; Vaughan, 1983; Hawkins, 1984; but see Levine, 1981; Horowitz, 1987; Luchansky and Gerber, 1993). Industry exercises significant power over regulators because public agencies tend to rely on industry for expertise, information, and personnel to staff their agencies (Bardach, 1989; Breyer, 1982; Makkai and Braithwaite, 1992).

Although regulatory capture may result from strategic action on the part of industry, cultural theorists emphasize the role that organizational institutions and politics play in shaping regulatory policy. European scholarship sees regulation as the product of political contests, social policy, the economic practices of major social institutions (e.g., banks), and broad cultural schema (Lange and Regini, 1989; Regini, 1995; Majone, 1994). Similarly, economic sociologists call attention to the role of cultural ideas, industrial practices, science, and political struggles in shaping regulation (Dobbin, 1994; Stryker, 1989, 1990, 2000; Pedriana and Stryker, 1997; Yeager, 1990).

The regulatory environment, then, is both the realm in which legal rules exert control over organizations and the realm in which organizations strive to shape the rules that govern them. There is considerable debate in the literature, however, over whether law operates primarily as a set of incentives and disincentives to which organizations strategically respond or as a set of normative ideals that are gradually incorporated into organizational life.

The constitutive environment

The constitutive legal environment is more subtle than the facilitative and regulatory environments, but it is equally important. It consists of a set of concepts, definitional categories, labels, and ideas that play a subtle and often invisible role in how organizations come into existence, how they organize their activities and relationships, and how they arrange their governance functions. Legal labels such as the "corporate person" help to define which activities are legitimate and which are not. Key conceptual dichotomies such as public/private, procedure/substance, employer/

employee, exempt/nonexempt, and full-time/part-time, as well as concepts such as labor pool, applicant, qualified, merit, and disability also derive meaning and impact in part from the constitutive legal environment. Law generates understandings of what is and is not a corporation, of who is and is not an employee, and of what constitutes a binding agreement between employer and employee (or between organizations), as well as more fundamental constructs such as fairness, efficiency, and rationality. Law causes certain organizational routines (including procedures for hiring, firing, and promotion and rules regarding leave, dress, language, or accent) to appear natural and normal.

Because it is where culture does its work, the constitutive environment receives far more attention among cultural than among materialist scholars. Studies have addressed the ways in which contract law delineates symbols and rituals for forming binding agreements (Suchman, 1995), how property law shapes ideas about organizations' control over resources and ideas (Campbell and Lindberg, 1990), and how bankruptcy law affects organizations' commitments to their various stakeholders (Delaney, 1989). Other studies show that law generates particular organizational features, such as affirmative action policies (Edelman and Petterson, 1999) or the "poison pill" takeover defense (Powell, 1993; Davis, 1991). And other research suggests that law codifies ground rules for entire organizational forms. For example, law helped to construct the modern limited-liability corporation (Coleman, 1974, 1990; Seavoy, 1982; Roy, 1990; Creighton, 1990; Klein and Majewski, 1992) and to shape the boundaries between and forms of private firms, public agencies, collective enterprises, and nonprofit organizations (Nee, 1992; Hansmann, 1996; Campbell and Lindberg, 1990).

At a still more fundamental level, law offers basic logics that seep into the culture and infrastructure of social interaction within organizations. As Weber (1947) observed, modern organizations and modern law both embrace the logic of "legal-rationality" or the importance of general and distinctively legal rules. Legal-rationality is not entirely the product of law; rather law and organizations resonate in a way that reinforces the logic of legal-rationality within both institutions, generating lawlike ideas of citizenship (Selznick, 1969) and fairness (Edelman, 1990) within organizations.

Although materialist work tends to downplay the constitutive elements of organizational environments, law and economics scholarship implicitly incorporates elements of the constitutive environment. For example, it notes that law may affect the relative appeal of market contracting vis-à-vis hierarchical organization through its impact on "transaction costs" or the costs of bargaining (Williamson, 1975, 1981, 1985, 1991; Posner, 1972; Masten, 1990). Further, by establishing property relations and other rules that affect the balance of power among economic actors, law in many ways constitutes both the market and the economy (Campbell and Lindberg, 1990).

Organizations are not only the *objects* of the law as a constitutive environment; they also help to *shape* legal rules that in turn affect the market. This occurs both directly, through lobbying and litigating, and indirectly, as organizations devise new strategies to circumvent, evade, or exploit laws, which in turn affect legal rules (Powell, 1993; Gilson, 1984; Suchman, 1995).

The constitutive environment of organizations, then, is a realm where law does its subtle work. Rather than providing procedural tools or substantive rules, law provides cognitive possibilities and values that influence the structure, form, and strategies of organizations. Whereas the literature on the facilitative and substantive legal environments portrays organizations as both producers and receivers of law, the literature on the constitutive environment tends to see the law as the primary domain of action and organizations mostly as the receivers of legal thought.

THE ENDOGENEITY OF LAW

Most accounts of law and organizations assume that law is *exogenous*, or determined outside of and prior to entering the realm of organizations. In most treatments of law and organizations, then, the direction of law is downward – from government to organizations.

To the extent that scholarship does focus on the effect of organizations on law, moreover, it does so primarily in the context of the facilitative and regulatory legal environments. Scholars recognize that both organizational strategy and organizational norms may influence the uses of law and the content of regulation. But there has been less attention to how organizational institutions provide cognitive categories and rationales that become part of legal environments – in other words, to how organizations act as producers (as well as receivers) of the constitutive legal environment.

In the remainder of this essay, I propose and outline a theory of law as *endogenous* – that is, as generated within the social realm that it seeks to regulate. Legal environments play a key role in legal endogeneity theory, not just as the arenas in which organizations make sense of the law, but rather as the portals of interaction between legal and organizational fields.

Legal endogeneity is made possible largely by the overlap between two key social spheres – *organizational fields* and *legal fields*. Organizational fields, or the immediate environments of organizations, are sites where common notions of management, efficiency, fairness, legality, and rationality take form. Within organizational fields, certain ways of doing things come to be seen as successful and tend to diffuse quickly across broad categories of organizations, so much so that they are often justified as rational and even as necessary for organizational success (e.g., Tolbert and Zucker, 1983; Fligstein, 1985; Edelman, 1990; DiMaggio, 1991).

Legal fields, which I define as the social sphere that is centered around legal institutions and actors, are the legal analog to the organizational fields. Just as ideas about business practices flow through organizational fields, ideas about law, justice, compliance, negotiation, and governance are exchanged among legal actors and through the everyday actions and thoughts of citizens vis-à-vis their legal orders. Legal fields comprise not only the formal law but also informal legal practices and norms and patterns of negotiation "in the shadow of law" (Mnookin and Kornhauser, 1979).

Organizational and legal fields are far from empirically distinct since they share common organizations, actors, and processes. Nonetheless, organizational and legal fields may be conceptually distinguished by their institutional logics. Organizational fields are characterized by capitalist/managerial logics, in which the financial bottom line generally trumps concerns about legality, fairness, or social norms. Ideals of legality are generally secondary to the ideal of rationality, and concerns about law tend to be subsumed by concerns about maximizing market shares, preserving business relationships, maintaining traditional lines of authority, and of course, increasing productivity and profit.

Legal fields, in contrast, are characterized by a formal rights-based (or liberal legal) logic, which celebrates the notion of a universal and general system of legal rules adjudicated by an impartial and passive judiciary. Liberal legal logic holds that individual rights-holders will recognize rights violations and will mobilize their legal rights. Advocacy of these rights by partisan adversaries will ultimately produce justice independent of any political or social constituency.

Law and society scholarship points out, of course, that other less formal logics coexist (and sometimes compete) with liberal legal logic within legal fields. These alternative logics often emphasize the value of community norms and dispute resolution outside of formal law; here rights matter but are tempered by other social norms (Macaulay, 1963; Ellickson, 1991). Thus the logic of legal fields is really a mix of liberal legal logic and a set of informal procedures that provide alternative mechanisms for achieving justice. In both its formal and informal manifestations, however, the logic of legal fields emphasizes rights and justice over efficiency and rationality.

Although legal and organizational fields are formed around fundamentally different logics, there is substantial overlap between them. The legal environments of organizations are at once the law-related elements of organizational fields and the organization-related elements of legal fields. The overlap between organizational and legal fields allows for a blurring of organizational and legal logics. As organizations encounter and respond to law, legal ideas flow into organizational fields, infusing concepts of efficient management with notions of rights and justice. Similarly, as legal actors and institutions negotiate the boundaries of organizations, managerial ideas flow into legal fields, infusing the law with ideas that originate in the effort for efficiency and profit.

The exchange of ideas within the social space at the intersection of organizational and legal fields is facilitated by a key group of *compliance professionals* – that is, lawyers, managers, consultants, and other specialists both within and outside of organizations whose work involves managing the law for organizations. Compliance professionals within organizations include human resource professionals who handle legal requirements or design organizational policy in light of law; in-house counsel who handle compliance or legal issues either as a major or minor component of their work; compliance specialists, such as affirmative action or safety officers; and general administrators whose roles include the administration of legal requirements. Compliance professionals outside of organizations include lawyers who advise organizations on legal issues or how to handle legal problems, and various management consultants who provide similar sorts of advice. Attorneys who represent either organizations or parties who have complaints against organizations also act as compliance professionals. In some cases, external compliance professionals work closely with organizations, as in the case of lawyers on retainer or regular management consultants; in other cases, compliance professionals have more fleeting interactions with organizations, as in the case of consultants who provide one-shot advice or who maintain websites that offer advice.

Compliance professionals act as social filters through whom legal ideas must pass on their way to organizations and through whom organizational constructions of law must pass on their way back to the legal realm. In the process of advising clients, making policy, resolving problems, or seeking change, these compliance professionals have multiple opportunities to shape both organizations and law.

Compliance professionals influence the path of law at multiple stages during its journey through organizational fields. These stages are: (1) the construction of law and the legal environment by compliance professionals, (2) the construction and diffusion of symbolic forms of compliance, (3) the managerialization of law within organizations, (4) the framing of legal issues, and (5) judicial deference to organizational institutions. I discuss each briefly below.

The construction of law and the legal environment by compliance professionals

Top managers in organizations generally learn about the law not from reading statutes or cases or administrative regulations but rather through the compliance professionals in and around their organizations. Laws become relevant parts of organizational fields only when they are made known to organizational actors. Compliance professionals are the first-line interpreters of law; they communicate to organizational administrators what laws are relevant, how they are relevant, and how much threat they pose.

Different compliance professions are likely to present somewhat different visions of the legal environment, reflecting the logics of the fields within which they work. Persons within a given profession often have similar forms of education (and sometimes social backgrounds), and because they tend to be connected through professional networks, they interact at conferences, write for and read their professional journals, participate in online forums and workshops, and exchange views at work or in the context of professional transactions. Thus certain ideas about law tend to become institutionalized within particular professions.

There is in fact a complex relation – to some extent a hierarchy – among the professions, which promotes a systematic transformation of legal information as it enters organizational fields. Lawyers from elite law firms often stand at the apex of this hierarchy, providing initial admonitions about changes in law or new threats posed by patterns of litigation. These elite lawyers write for websites and professional journals; they lead workshops for other lawyers and for managers; they serve as consultants to more general lawyers and, especially, to in-house counsel for organizations. Elite lawyers may be likely to emphasize or even to exaggerate the threatening aspects of legal environments both because they see that role as necessary to protect their organizational clients and because they stand to gain a larger market for their services by emphasizing their capacity to insulate organizations from environmental threats (cf. Bisom-Rapp, 1999).

The construction and diffusion of symbolic forms of compliance

Armed with a vision of law and legal threats provided by compliance professionals, organizations seek rational solutions to those threats. Here again, the role of compliance professionals is critical – once these professionals have identified legal threats, they gain organizational power by offering solutions to those threats (Edelman, Abraham, and Erlanger, 1992).

Public governance serves as a ready source of legitimized models for private governance, and therefore as a source of solutions to laws that challenge organizational governance. The early phases of compliance with laws related to organizational governance, then, tend to involve the creation of structures that mimic public legal institutions at least in form. For example, in response to the ambiguous civil rights mandates of the 1960s and 1970s, employers created rules and policies that look like statutes, offices that look like administrative agencies, compliance officers who look like administrative officers or even police, and grievance procedures that look like courts (Edelman et al., 1999). These antidiscrimination rules, civil rights offices, grievance procedures, and other legal structures served as visible symbols of attention to law.

Early adopters of symbolic forms of compliance tend to be organizations with considerable visibility – either because they are industry leaders or because they have connections to the public sector. The forms of compliance adopted by these organizations, in turn, serve as ready models of legitimate compliance for other organizations (Edelman, 1992). Networks of compliance professionals help to diffuse these forms of compliance. As certain forms of compliance become increasingly prevalent, the rationality of those solutions becomes "mythical" or taken for granted (Meyer and Rowan, 1977; Edelman, 1990, 1992).

The managerialization of law

The rapid diffusion of symbolic forms of compliance among organizational populations does not necessarily mean that these forms result in substantive change. Because it is generally the form rather than the substance of compliance that attains an institutionalized status, there is variation in how enthusiastically management, as well as the personnel who staff compliance structures, embrace legal ideals. In some cases, compliance structures are created primarily as symbolic gestures, with little intent that the structures change organizational policies or practices. Organizations can maximize both legitimacy and rationality while minimizing the substantive impact of those structures by creating formal governance structures that appear legitimate while simultaneously decoupling deviant organizational practices from those structures (Edelman, 1992). In other cases, top management actively encourages attention to legal ideals.

Once in place, however, compliance structures tend to evolve independently of the intentions of organizational strategists because they serve as vehicles for the making of legal meaning. Legal meaning may derive in part from the actions of those who staff compliance structures and from those who interact with these structures, but it is inescapable that legal meaning will incorporate to some extent the logic of the organizational fields within which organizational actors operate. Thus, although compliance structures have law-like forms, their existence within organizational fields means that the logic of efficiency and rationality will often trump the logic of rights and justice.

Managers make sense of law within the context of organizational constraints and objectives. However concerned they are with legal compliance, that concern is inevitably secondary to their interest in efficient production or provision of services. Thus, as organizations interpret legal requirements, process legal paperwork, and attempt to resolve law-related problems, the law is increasingly filtered through managerial norms and tempered by managerial concerns. Organizations may become increasingly legalized or influenced by legal values and rules, but at the same time, legal ideals tend to become infused with traditional managerial ways of thinking, thus producing a *managerialization of law* (Edelman, Fuller, and Mara-Drita, 2001).

The managerialization of law takes a variety of forms. First, organizational policy makers may managerialize the law as they promulgate rules to effectuate law within the organization (e.g., rules banning sexual harassment). But this *internal legislation* does not ensure replication of public law or recognition of legal ideals. Rather, in an effort to combine legal and managerial goals, managers are likely to build discretion into rules, to replace legal standards (such as disparate treatment) with managerial standards (such as consistency), or even to circumvent legal standards. For example, when courts began to articulate a theory under which terminated employees could sue employers for violation of an "implied contract," employers quickly began to revise their personnel policies and employment contracts to avoid legal risk by explicitly specifying that their employees worked "at will" and thus could be fired without reason (Edelman et al., 1992). Internal legislation, therefore, may essentially legislate away some or all of the thrust of legal ideals (Edelman and Suchman, 1999).

Second, compliance structures may managerialize the law through *internal adjudication* of law-related complaints. Various forms of internal complaint handling are becoming increasingly common in organizations. The creation of internal dispute resolution gives organizational personnel a significant role in determining what constitutes a problem, whether the problem is one that is legal in nature, whether the problem can or should be resolved, whether and how legal standards might affect the resolution of the problem, and how the problem ought to be resolved. Edelman et al. (1993) find that internal complaint handlers tend to recast discrimination complaints as typical managerial problems, such as poor management or interpersonal difficulties, and to resolve them in those terms. Poor management may be remedied by training or through pragmatic solutions such as transferring the employee; interpersonal difficulties are handled with therapeutic solutions, such as counseling, employee assistance programs, or mediation-like exchanges. While these remedies serve the organization's purpose in ensuring smooth employment relations and often resolve the employees' complaints, they tend to discourage attention to legal rights. In so doing, these remedies depoliticize and delegalize issues, potentially affecting not only the particular dispute but also both employee and employer reactions to future disputes (Edelman et al., 1993; Edelman and Cahill, 1998; Edelman and Suchman, 1999).

Third, managerial rhetoric and managerial trends may managerialize the law by *reframing legal ideas*. Rhetoric about "managing diversity" and "valuing diversity," for example, subtly yet powerfully shapes the meaning of equal employment opportunity. Formal EEO law creates rights to nondiscrimination on the basis of race, color, sex, religion, and national origin. These attributes are not random, but rather embrace the moral ideal that historical disenfranchisement creates an entitlement to special protection against any further discrimination. Although managerial rhetoric on diversity appears to buttress EEO law and to draw on the same moral ideal, the shift from equal opportunity to diversity language is much more than a change in packaging. Rather, diversity rhetoric dilutes the focus on historical disenfranchisement by placing diversity on the basis of cultural differences, geographical differences, lifestyle differences, and even matters such as communication style, dress style, and taste in food on a par with diversity on the basis of legally protected categories. Further, managerial rhetoric about diversity tends to portray antidiscrimination law in a negative light, asserting that while law imposes inefficient rules on organizations, diversity management promotes creativity, harmony, and profit. Thus managerial rhetoric about diversity tends to reframe legal values in terms of traditional managerial goals (Edelman et al., 2001).

Fourth, organizations managerialize the law by *internalizing the practice of law*. In recent years, organizations have built increasingly large and sophisticated internal legal staffs. In large firms, these lawyers not only handle complaints and litigation but also screen corporate documents for possible exposure to liability and manage the distribution of work to outside counsel (Rosen, 1989; Galanter and Rogers, 1991; Nelson and Nielsen, 2000; Nelson, 1994). Internal legal staffs are both more likely and more able than outside lawyers to interpret and implement the law in ways that subordinate legal values to managerial values like profitability, efficiency, and hierarchical authority (Edelman and Suchman, 1999).

Finally, organizations may managerialize the law even through their responses to mandatory reporting requirements such as filling out mandatory forms detailing workforce statistics for the EEOC. Although seemingly routine, reporting workforce statistics involves legal meaning making: issues such as which employees are classified as underrepresented minorities, who is "employed" at the time of the count, and how various positions are classified can both depend on and influence the character of compliance within a firm.

These examples illustrate but do not exhaust the ways in which law becomes managerialized within organizational fields. The managerialization of law may hasten the legalization of organizations in that legal values recast in managerial terms may be more easily assimilated into organizational governance. However, the managerialization of law may also weaken, de-emphasize, and depoliticize legal ideals by subsuming them within managerial goals.

The framing of legal issues

Organizations are powerful engines of socialization. The internal legal cultures of organizations condition how individuals within and around organizations view the ideals of law, the reach of law, the threat of law, and the fairness and legality of employers' law-related actions and structures (Fuller, Edelman, and Matusik, 2000; cf. Bumiller, 1987, 1988; Felstiner, Abel, and Sarat, 1981; Ewick and Silbey, 1998).

The managerialization of law, then, powerfully affects which actions or policies appear proper and which are injurious; it promotes certain types of claims and certain framing of legal issues and discourages others. To the extent that organizational culture recasts discrimination problems as interpersonal or managerial problems, or diversity along extralegal dimensions is understood to be as important as race and gender diversity, promotion decisions that favor white males or the lack of women or minorities in a workplace are less likely to be seen as legally problematic.

The extent to which organizational actions are seen as legally problematic, in turn, has critical implications for both whether and how these actions are framed in the legal realm. For example, employees, employers, and their lawyers all play a role in framing legal issues. The role of employers is obvious; they are the promulgators of managerialized conceptions of law. Employees play a role through their visions of which managerial actions are legally injurious and which are legitimate.

Lawyers for both employees (generally plaintiffs) and employers (generally defendants) lawyers, in different ways, help to reinforce and legitimate managerialized models of compliance. Employees' lawyers act as critical gatekeepers to the legal realm, in that they are less likely to pursue actions where employers meet the institutionalized ideals of compliance. Even where employees have good reason to avoid an internal grievance procedure, for example, plaintiffs' lawyers are less likely to pursue a case where employees failed to use those procedures. Employers' lawyers act as conduits of managerialized logic to the court by framing their law-related procedures and policies *as compliance* and by defending their actions in terms of legitimized rationales such as market rates and business necessity. To the extent that managerialized conceptions of law seep into the emergence and framing of disputes by employers, employees, and lawyers, those conceptions also shape both the logic and the lexicon of disputing in the legal realm.

Judicial deference to organizational constructions of law

Whereas traditional top-down perspectives on law suggest that courts ought to serve as a corrective to organizational constructions of compliance that deviate from legal purposes, the idea of legal endogeneity suggests instead that courts tend to be influenced by compliance practices that become institutionalized in organizational fields.

Just as employers tend to take their cues from norms and practices in their legal environments, judges tend to take their cues from norms and practices that become institutionalized in organizations. Because organizational and legal fields overlap, institutionalized ideas about law and compliance flow unobtrusively into the judicial realm. Thus courts often accept employers' symbolic indicia of compliance without recognizing the extent to which employers' legal structures fail to protect legal rights, and in some cases even thwart those rights. In this way, institutionalized – and managerialized – organizational practices tend to be (re)incorporated into judicial standards for EEO compliance. When courts incorporate ideas from the organizational realm into new case decisions, law becomes endogenous (Edelman et al., 1999).

The endogeneity of law is perhaps clearest with respect to employers' internal grievance procedures. The personnel profession promoted the legal value of grievance procedures during the 1970s and early 1980s even though there were no statutes mandating grievance procedures, and even though – at the time – courts tended to reject the idea that such procedures could constitute evidence of EEO compliance. Personnel professionals claimed, nonetheless, that grievance procedures would be viewed by judges as evidence of fair treatment, and that employers therefore would be well served by creating them.

In the mid-1980s, courts began to do precisely what the personnel professionals had been suggesting. In 1986, the Supreme Court in *Meritor Savings Bank v. Vinson* suggested that an effective grievance procedure might protect an employer from liability for sexual harassment. Shortly thereafter, a federal circuit court of appeals adopted a similar standard in race harassment cases (*Hunter v. Allis-Chalmers*, 1986). And in 1998, the Supreme Court declared that an employee's failure to use an employer's internal grievance procedure might protect an employer from liability for harassment by its supervisory employees (*Faragher v. City of Boca Raton*). When courts proclaimed that internal grievance procedures could help employers avoid liability, they reinforced the legitimacy and rationality of grievance procedures as a form of compliance with law (even though those grievance procedures may in fact do little to ensure equal employment opportunity).

Law regulating organizations is endogenous, then, because its meaning is formed in part through the actions of organizations and the models of organizational action that become institutionalized in organizational fields. Legal ambiguity encourages organizations to create internal legal structures designed to symbolize attention to law. Once in place, those structures engender struggles over the meaning of law as professionals and other officials seek to implement law within organizations. Because of their training, experience, and professional purview, organizational actors tend to construct law in ways that are consistent with traditional managerial prerogatives and goals. Over time, as these constructions of law become institution-alized, they subtly and gradually affect how other social actors – including judges – understand the meaning of law, and of rational compliance with law.

CONCLUSION

Scholarship about the legal lives of private organizations has benefited significantly from the recent rapprochement of organizational and sociolegal scholarship. Socio-legal scholars have begun to move from an overly simplistic view of organizations as goal-oriented rational actors toward an understanding of the less formal and less rational elements of organizational life. At the same time, organization theorists have begun to question the idea of law as a coercive and determinative force, becoming attentive to the study of law in its social context (Suchman and Edelman, 1996). The result is an increasingly nuanced understanding of how the legal lives of organizations are critically intertwined with the legal life of society.

Despite significant progress in understanding the complex interplay of law and organizations, however, a number of gaps deserve attention in future scholarship. First, scholars should attend to the contradictions (or apparent contradictions) between the materialist and cultural perspectives. In explaining the legal lives of organizations, how can we reconcile the materialist emphasis on rational strategy with the cultural emphasis on institutionalized ideas and rituals? Are there funda-mental contradictions in these metatheoretical perspectives, or is the character of organizations' legal lives both rational and normative?

Second, scholarship should pursue the ways in which the facilitative, regulatory, and constitutive legal environments of organizations are simultaneously arenas for organizations to shape understandings of law (Edelman and Suchman, 1997). The state may create tools to facilitate interaction, but organizations shape the law as they mobilize those tools in ways that create new legal issues and possibilities or when they develop organizational mechanisms to evade legal obstacles (e.g., when cartels escape antitrust constraints or when creative accounting circumvents corpor-ate reporting requirements). The state may create rules to constrain organizational behavior but organizations negotiate and reshape those constraints as they shape the meaning of compliance. And the state may help to constitute organizations through legal definitions of corporations, of shareholders, and of employees. But the consti-tutive environment is shaped more by organizational institutions than by the pens of legislators.

And most importantly, more attention should be paid to the endogeneity of law and to the role of organizations in shaping the form and content of law. In any given situation, law may appear exogenous to particular organizational actions or struc-tures and organizations may be seen as either complying or resisting the force of law. But attention to the *process* of legal construction is likely to reveal that the legal environments of organizations – which lie at the interstices of organizational and legal fields – are a fertile ground of legal *and* of organizational construction. It is in these spaces that boundary-spanning professionals such as lawyers, managerial consultants, personnel officers, compliance officers, and others interpret and ultimately *define* the law.

While I have provided an initial sketch of a theory of the endogeneity of law in the employment context (Edelman et al., 1999), similar processes are almost certainly at work in other social arenas. Healthcare, antitrust, bankruptcy, the environment, and crime are among the arenas in which attention to the endogeneity of law is likely to prove fruitful. In these and other areas, law and society scholarship should seek to delineate the social fields in which understandings of law develop, the social actors that span the boundaries of social fields, and the processes of social interaction and institutionalization that generate both legal and social change.

Cross-national analyses of legal endogeneity are also important. Differences in the roles of courts and training of judges between civil and common law nations may affect the extent to which institutionalized organizational practices may seep into judicial decision making. And national culture is likely to interact with organizational culture and individual legal consciousness in ways that alter the extent and process of legal endogeneity (cf. Cahill, 2001).

The policy implications of legal endogeneity, moreover, are critical. To the extent that law is endogenous, or shaped within the organizational fields that it seeks to regulate, the social control *of* organizations is in a very real sense social control *by* organizations – not overtly, but rather through the influence of institutionalized models of governance.

Note

I would like to thank Catherine T. Albiston, Hamsa Murthy, Austin Sarat, Willow Tracy, and Kay Levine for comments on an earlier version. One section of this essay ("The Legal Environments of Organizations") draws heavily on prior collaborative work with Mark Suchman (Edelman and Suchman, 1997).

References

Ackerman, B.A., Ackerman, S.R., Sawyer, J.W. Jr., and Henderson, D.W. (1974) *The Uncertain Search for Environmental Quality*. New York: Free Press.

Bardach, E. (1989) "Social regulation as a generic policy instrument," in L.M. Salamon (ed.), *Beyond Privatization: The Tools of Government Action*. Washington, DC: Urban Institute, pp. 197–230.

Berger, P.L. and Luckmann, T. (1967) *The Social Construction of Reality*. New York: Doubleday.

Bisom-Rapp, S. (1999) "Bulletproofing the workplace: Symbol and substance in employment discrimination law practice," *Florida State University Law Review* 26(4): 959–1038.

Blumrosen, A.W. (1965) "Anti-discrimination laws in action in New Jersey: A law-sociology study," *Rutgers Law Review* 19: 187–287.

Blumrosen, A.W. (1993) *Modern Law: The Law Transmission System and Equal Employment Opportunity*. Madison: University of Wisconsin Press.

Braithwaite, J. and Makkai, T. (1991) "Testing and expected utility model of corporate deterrence," *Law & Society Review*, 25(1): 7–40.

Breyer, S. (1982) *Regulation and its Reform*. Cambridge, MA: Harvard University Press.

Bumiller, K. (1987) "Victims in the shadow of the law: A critique of the model of legal protection," *Signs* 12: 421–34.

Bumiller, K. (1988) *The Civil Rights Society: The Social Construction of Victims*. Baltimore: Johns Hopkins University Press.

Cahill, M.L. (2001) *The Social Construction of Sexual Harassment Law: The Role of the National, Organizational, and Individual Context*. Burlington, VA: Dartmouth.

Cain, M. and Hunt, A. (eds.) (1979) *Marx and Engels on Law*. New York: Academic Press.

Campbell, J.L. and Lindberg, L.N. (1990) "Property rights and the organization of economic activities by the state," *American Sociological Review*, 55: 634–47.

Cheit, R.E. (1991) "Corporate ambulance chasers: The charmed life of business litigation," *Studies in Law, Politics, and Society* 11: 191–240.

Clune, W.H. (1983) "A political model of implementation and the implications of the model for public policy, research, and the changing role of lawyers," *Iowa Law Review* 69: 47–125.

Coleman, J.S. (1974) *Power and the Structure of Society*. New York: Norton.

Coleman, J.S. (1990) *Foundations of Social Theory*. Cambridge, MA: Belknap Press of Harvard University.

Conklin, J.E. (1997) *Illegal But Not Criminal: Business Crime in America*. Englewood Cliffs, NJ: Prentice-Hall.

Cranston, R. (1979) *Regulating Business: Law and Consumer Agencies*. London: Macmillan.

Creighton, A.L. (1990) "The emergence of incorporation as a legal form for organizations," unpublished PhD dissertation, Department of Sociology, Stanford University.

Davis, G.F. (1991) "Agents without principles? The spread of the poison pill through the intercorporate network," *Administrative Science Quarterly* 36: 583–613.

Delaney, K.J. (1989) "Power, intercorporate networks, and 'strategic bankruptcy'," *Law and Society Review* 23: 643–66.

DiMaggio, P.J. (1991) "Constructing an organizational field as a professional project: U.S. art museums, 1920–1940," in Walter W. Powell and Paul J. DiMaggio (eds.), *The New Institutionalism in Organizational Analysis*. Chicago: University of Chicago Press, pp. 267–92.

DiMaggio, P.J. and Powell, W.W. (1983) "The iron cage revisited: Institutional isomorphism and collective rationality in organizational fields," *American Sociological Review* 48: 147–60.

Diver, C. (1980) "A theory of regulatory enforcement," *Public Policy* 28: 257–99.

Dobbin, F. (1994) *Forging Industrial Policy: The United States, Britain, and France in the Railway Age*. New York: Cambridge University Press.

Dobbin, F. and Sutton, J.R. (1998) "The strength of a weak state: The rights revolution and the rise of human resource management divisions," *American Journal of Sociology* 104: 441–76.

Dobbin, F., Sutton, J.R., Meyer, J.W., and Scott, W.R. (1993) "Equal employment opportunity law and the construction of internal labor markets," *American Journal of Sociology* 99: 396–427.

Durkheim, E. (1964) *The Division of Labor in Society*; trans.George Simpson. New York: Free Press.

Edelman, L.B. (1990) "Legal environments and organizational governance: The expansion of due process in the workplace," *American Journal of Sociology* 95(6): 1401–40.

Edelman, L.B. (1992) "Legal ambiguity and symbolic structures: Organizational mediation of civil rights law," *American Journal of Sociology* 97(6): 1531–76.

Edelman, L.B. (2002) "Legality and the endogeneity of law," in Robert Kagan, Martin Krygier, and Kenneth Winston (eds.), *Legality and Community: On the Intellectual Legacy of Philip Selznick*. Lanham, MD: Rowman & Littlefield, pp. 187–202.

Edelman, L.B., Abraham, S.E., and Erlanger, H.S (1992) "Professional construction of law: The inflated threat of wrongful discharge doctrine," *Law & Society Review* 26(1): 47–83.

Edelman, L.B. and Cahill, M. (1998) "How law matters in disputing and dispute processing (or, the contingency of legal matter in alternative dispute resolution)," in Bryant Garth and Austin Sarat (eds.) *How Law Matters*. Evanston, IL: Northwestern University Press, pp. 15–44.

Edelman, L.B., Erlanger, H.S., and Lande, J. (1993) "Internal dispute resolution: The transformation of civil rights in the workplace," *Law & Society Review* 27(3): 497–534.

Edelman, L.B., Fuller, S. Riggs, and Mara-Drita, I. (2001) "Diversity rhetoric and the managerialization of law," *American Journal of Sociology* 106(6): 1589–641.

Edelman, L.B. and Petterson, S. (1999) "Symbols and substance in organizational response to civil rights law," *Research in Social Stratification and Mobility* 17: 107–35.

Edelman, L.B. and Suchman, M.C. (1997) "The legal environments of organizations," *Annual Review of Sociology* 23: 479–515.

Edelman, L.B. and Suchman, M.C. (1999) "When the haves hold court: Speculations on the organizational internalization of law," *Law & Society Review* 33(4): 941–91.

Edelman, L.B., Uggen, C., and Erlanger, H.S. (1999) "The endogeneity of legal regulation: Grievance procedures as rational myth," *American Journal of Sociology* 105: 406–54.

Ellickson, R. (1991) *Order Without Law: How Neighbors Settle Disputes*. Cambridge, MA: Harvard University Press.

Ewick, P. and Silbey, S.S. (1998) *The Common Place of Law: Stories from Everyday Life*. Chicago: University of Chicago Press.

Faragher v. City of Boca Raton (1998) 118 S.Ct. 1115.

Felstiner, W., Abel, R.L., and Sarat, A. (1981) "The emergence and transformation of disputes: Naming, blaming, claiming . . . ", *Law & Society Review* 15(3–4): 631–54.

Fligstein, N. (1985) "The spread of the multidivisional form among large firms 1919–1979," *American Sociological Review* 50(3): 77–91.

Fligstein, N. (1990) "The structural transformation of American industry: An institutional account of the causes of diversification in the largest firms, 1919–1979," in Walter W. Powell and Paul J. DiMaggio (eds.), *The New Institutionalism in Organizational Analysis*. Chicago: University of Chicago Press, pp. 311–36.

Fuller, S.R., Edelman, L.B., and Matusik, S.F. (2000) "Legal readings: Employee interpretation and mobilization of law," *The Academy of Management Review* 25(1): 200–16.

Gable, R.W. (1953) "NAM: Influential lobby or kiss of death?" *Journal of Politics* 15: 254–73.

Galanter, M. and Rogers, J. (1991) "Transformation of American business disputing? Some preliminary observations," Working Paper. Madison, WI: Institute of Legal Studies.

Genn, H. (1993) "Business responses to the regulation of health and safety in England," *Law and Policy* 15(3): 219–33.

Gibson, J.L. and Caldeira, G.A. (1996) "The legal cultures of Europe," *Law & Society Review* 30(1): 55–85.

Gilson, R.J. (1984) "Value creation by business lawyers: Legal skills and asset pricing," *Yale Law Journal*, 94(2): 239–313.

Hansmann, H. (1996) *The Ownership of Enterprise*. Cambridge, MA: Belknap.

Hawkins, K. (1984) *Environment and Enforcement: Regulation and the Social Definition of Pollution*. Oxford: Clarendon Press.

Heimer, C. (1999) "Competing institutions: Law, medicine, and family in neonatal intensive care," *Law & Society Review* 33: 17–67.

Horowitz, M.J. (1987) "Understanding deregulation," *Theory and Society* 15: 139–74.

Hunter v. Allis-Chalmers (1986) 797 F.2d 1417.

Jowell, J.L. (1975) *Law and Bureaucracy: Administrative Discretion and the Limits of Legal Action*. Port Washington, NY: Kennikat.

Kagan, R.A. (2001) *Adversarial Legalism: The American Way of Law.* Cambridge, MA: Harvard University Press.

Kagan, R.A. and Axelrad, L. (eds) (2000) *Regulatory Encounters: Multinational Corporations and American Adversarial Legalism.* Berkeley: University of California Press.

Kelly, E. and Dobbin, F. (1998) "How affirmative action became diversity management: Employer response to antidiscrimination law, 1961–1996," *American Behavioral Scientist* 41: 960–84.

Klein, D.B. and Majewski, J. (1992) "Economy, community, and law: The turnpike movement in New York, 1797–1845," *Law & Society Review* 26(3): 469–512.

Lande, J. (1998) "Failing faith in litigation? A survey of business lawyers' and executives' opinions," *Harvard Negotiation Law Review* 3: 1–70.

Lange, P. and Regini, M. (1989) *State, Market and Social Regulation: New Perspectives on Italy.* Cambridge, UK: Cambridge University Press.

Levine, M. (1981) "Revisionism revised? Airline deregulation and the public interest," *Law and Contemporary Problems* 44: 179–95.

Luchansky, B. and Gerber, J. (1993) "Constructing state autonomy: The Federal Trade Commission and the Celler-Kefauver Act," *Sociological Perspectives* 36(3): 217–40.

Macaulay, S. (1963) "Non-contractual relations in business: A preliminary study," *American Sociological Review* 28: 55–70.

Majone, G. (1994) "The rise of the regulatory state in Europe," *West European Politics* 17: 77–101.

Makkai, T. and Braithwaite, J. (1992) "In and out of the revolving door: Making sense of regulatory capture," *Journal of Public Policy* 12: 61–78.

Marx, K. and Engels, F. (1978) *The Marx–Engels Reader,* ed. Robert Tucker. New York: W.W. Norton.

Masten, S.E. (1990) "A legal basis for the firm," in O.E. Williamson and S.G. Winter (eds.), *The Nature of the Firm: Origins, Evolution and Development.* New York: Oxford University Press, pp. 196–212.

Meritor Savings Bank v. Vinson (1986) 106 S. Ct. 2399.

Meyer, J.W. and Rowan, B. (1977) "Institutionalized organizations: Formal structure as myth and ceremony," *American Journal of Sociology* 83: 340–63.

Meyer, J.W. and Scott, W.R. (1983) *Organizational Environments: Ritual and Rationality.* Beverly Hills, CA: Sage Publications.

Mnookin, R.H. and Kornhauser, L. (1979) "Bargaining in the shadow of the law: The case of divorce," *Yale Law Journal* 88: 950.

Morrill, C. (1995) *The Executive Way: Conflict Management in Corporations.* Chicago: University of Chicago Press.

Nee, V. (1992) "Organizational dynamics of market transition: Hybrid forms, property rights, and mixed economy in China," *Administrative Science Quarterly* 37: 1–27.

Nelson, R.L. (1994) The future of American lawyers: A demographic profile of a changing profession in a changing society," *Case Western Reserve Law Review* 44: 345–406.

Nelson, R.L. and Nielsen, L.B. (2000) "Cops, counsel, or entrepreneurs: The shifting roles of lawyers in large business corporations," *Law & Society Review* 34: 457–94.

Paternoster, R. and Simpson, S. (1996) "Sanction threats and appeals to morality: Testing a rational choice model of corporate crime," *Law & Society Review* 30: 549–83.

Pedriana, N. and Stryker, R. (1997) "Political culture wars 1960s style: Equal employment opportunity – affirmative action law and the Philadelphia Plan," *American Journal of Sociology* 99: 847–910.

Pfeffer, J. (1974) "Administrative regulation and licensing: Social problem or solution?" *Social Problems* 21: 468–79.

Pfeffer, J. and Salancik, G.R. (1978) *The External Control of Organizations.* New York: Harper and Row.

Posner, R.A. (1972) *Economic Analysis of Law.* Boston: Little, Brown.

Posner, R.A. (1974) "Theories of economic regulation," *Bell Journal of Economic and Management Science* 5: 335–58.

Powell, M.J. (1993) "Professional innovation: Corporate lawyers and private lawmaking," *Law and Social Inquiry* 18(3): 423–52.

Regini, M. (1995) *Uncertain Boundaries: The Social and Political Construction of European Economies.* Cambridge, UK: Cambridge University Press.

Rosen, R.E. (1989) "The inside counsel movement, professional judgement, and organizational respresentation," *Indiana Law Journal* 64: 479–553.

Roy, W. (1990) "Functional and historical logics in explaining the rise of the American industrial corporation," *Comparative Social Research* 12: 19–44.

Saguy, A.C. (2000) "Employment discrimination or sexual violence?: Defining sexual harassment in American and French law," *Law & Society Review* 34(4): 1091–128.

Schneiberg, M. (1999) "Political and institutional conditions for governance by association: Private order and price controls in American fire insurance," *Politics & Society* 27(1): 67–103.

Schneiberg, M. and Bartley, T. (2001) "Regulating American industries: Markets, politics and the institutional determinants of fire insurance regulation," *American Journal of Sociology* 107: 101–46.

Scott, W.R. (1998) *Organizations: Rational, Natural, and Open Systems,* 4th edn. Englewood Cliffs, NJ: Prentice-Hall.

Seavoy, R.E. (1982) *The Origins of the American Business Corporation, 1784–1855: Broadening the Concept of Public Service During Industrialization.* Westport, CT: Greenwood Press.

Selznick, P. (1969) *Law, Society, and Industrial Justice.* New York: Russell Sage.

Stigler, G.J. (1971) "The theory of economic regulation," *Bell Journal of Economics and Management Science* 2(Spring): 3–21.

Stone, C.D. (1975) *Where the Law Ends: The Social Control of Corporate Behavior.* New York: Harper & Row.

Stryker, R. (1989) "Limits on technocratization of the law: The elimination of the National Labor Relations Board's Division of Economic Research," *American Sociological Review* 54: 341–58.

Stryker, R. (1990) "A tale of two agencies: Class, political-institutional and organizational factors affecting state reliance on social science," *Politics & Society* 18: 101–41.

Stryker, R. (2000) "Legitimacy processes as institutional politics: Implications for theory and research in the sociology of organizations," *Research in the Sociology of Organizations* 17: 179–223.

Suchman, M.C. (1995) "Localism and globalism in institutional analysis: The emergence of contractual norms in venture finance," in W.R. Scott and S. Christensen (eds.), *The Institutional Construction of Organizations.* Thousand Oaks, CA: Sage Publications, pp. 39–63.

Suchman, M.C. and Edelman, L.B. (1996) "Legal-rational myths: The new institutionalism and the Law & Society tradition," *Law & Social Inquiry* 21(4): 903–41.

Sutton, J.R., Dobbin, F., Meyer, J.W., and Scott, W.R. (1994) "Legalization of the workplace," *American Journal of Sociology* 99(4): 944–71.

Tolbert, P.S. and Zucker, L.G. (1983) "Institutional sources of change in the formal structure of organizations: The diffusion of Civil Service reform, 1880–1935," *Administrative Science Quarterly* 28: 22–39.

Vaughan, D. (1983) *Controlling Unlawful Organizational Behavior: Social Structure and Corporate Misconduct.* Chicago: University of Chicago Press.

Weber, M. (1947) *The Theory of Social and Economic Organization,* trans. A.M. Henderson and T. Parsons. New York: Oxford University Press.

Williamson, O.E. (1975) *Markets and Hierarchies: Analysis and Antitrust Implications.* New York: The Free Press.

Williamson, O.E. (1981) "The economics of organization: The transactions cost approach," *American Journal of Sociology* 87: 548–77.

Williamson, O.E. (1985) *The Economic Institutions of Capitalism.* New York: Free Press.

Williamson, O.E. (1991) "Comparative economic organization: The analysis of discrete structural alternatives," *Administrative Science Quarterly* 36: 269–96.

Wirt, F. (1970) *The Politics of Southern Equality: Law and Social Change in a Mississippi County.* Chicago: Aldine.

Yeager, P. (1990) *The Limits of Law: The Public Regulation of Private Pollution.* Cambridge, UK: Cambridge University Press.

Zald, M.N. (1970) "Political economy: A framework for comparative analysis," in Mayer N. Zald (ed.), *Power in Organizations.* Nashville, TN: Vanderbilt University Press, pp. 221–61.

Zhou, X. (1993) "Occupational power, state capacities and the diffusion of licensing in the American states: 1890 to 1950," *American Sociological Review* 58(4): 536–52.

Further Reading

Baer, X., March, J.G., and Saetren, X. (1998) "Implementation and ambiguity," in J. March (ed.), *Decisions and Organizations.* Oxford: Blackwell, pp. 150–164.

Baron, J.N. and Bielby, W.T. (1980) "Bringing the firms back in: Stratification, segmentation, and the organization of work," *American Sociological Review* 45: 737–65.

Baron, J.N. and Bielby, W.T. (1985) "Organizational barriers to gender equality: Sex segregation of jobs and opportunities," in Alice S. Rossi (ed.), *Gender and the Life Course.* New York: Aldine, pp. 233–51.

Baron, J.N., Mittman, B.S., and Newman, A.E. (1991) "Targets of opportunity: Organizational and environmental determinants of gender integration within the California civil service, 1979–1985," *American Journal of Sociology* 96: 1362–402.

Bielby, W.T. and Baron, J.N. (1984) "A woman's place is with other women: Sex segregation within organizations," in B.F. Reskin (ed.), *Sex Segregation in the Workplace: Trends, Explanations, Remedies.* Washington, DC: National Academy Press, pp. 27–55.

Blau, P.M. and Schoenherr, R.A. (1971) *The Structure of Organizations.* New York: Basic Books.

Coase, R.H. (1937) "The nature of the firm," *Economica* 16: 386–405

Collins, H. (1982) *Marxism and Law.* New York: Oxford University Press.

Dill, W.R. (1958) "Environment as influence on managerial autonomy," *Administrative Science Quarterly* 2: 409–43.

Donahue, J.J. III (1986) "Is Title VII efficient?" *University of Pennsylvania Law Review* 134(6): 1411–31.

Edwards, R. (1979) *Contested Terrain: The Transformation of the Workplace in the Twentieth Century.* New York: Basic Books.

Gordon, D.M., Edwards, R., and Reich, M. (1982) *Segmented Work, Divided Workers: The Historical Transformation of Labor in the United States.* Cambridge, UK: Cambridge University Press.

Hall, R. (1963) "The concept of bureaucracy: An empirical assessment," *American Journal of Sociology* 69: 32–40.

Hoffmann, E. A. (2001) "Confrontations and compromise: Dispute resolution at a worker cooperative coal mine," *Law and Social Inquiry* 26: 555–96.

Kanter, R. (1977) *Men and Women of the Corporation.* New York: Basic Books.

Laumann, E.O. and Knoke, D. (1987) *The Organizational State: Social Change in National Policy Domains.* Madison: University of Wisconsin Press.

Powell, W.W. and DiMaggio, P.J. (eds.) (1991) *The New Institutionalism in Organizational Analysis.* Chicago: University of Chicago Press.

Pugh, D.S., Hickson, D.J., Hinings, C.R., and Turner, C. (1968) "Dimensions of organization structure," *Administrative Science Quarterly* 13: 65–91.

Scott, W.R. (2001) *Institutions and Organizations*. Thousand Oaks, CA: Sage.

Selznick, P. (1948) "Foundations of the theory of organization," *American Sociological Review* 13: 25–35.

Selznick, P. (1949) *TVA and the Grass Roots*. Berkeley: University of California Press.

Selznick, P. (1957) *Leadership in Administration: A Sociological Interpretation*. New York: Harper & Row.

Simon, H.A. (1964) "On the concept of organizational goal," *Administrative Science Quarterly* 9: 1–22.

Simon, H.A. (1966) *The New Science of Management Decision*. New York: Harper.

Stigler, G.J. (1968) *The Organization of Industry*. Homewood, IL: RD Irwin.

Suchman, M.C. (2001) "Organizations and the law," in N. J. Smelser and Paul B. Baltes (eds), *International Encyclopedia of the Social and Behavioral Sciences*. Oxford: Elsevier, pp. 10948–54.

Udy, S.H., Jr. (1959) *Organization of Work*. New Haven, CT: Human Relations Area Files.

Udy, S.H., Jr. (1962) "Administrative rationality, social setting, and organizational development," *American Journal of Sociology* 68: 299–308.

Weick, K.E. (1979) *The Social Psychology of Organizing*, 2nd edn. Reading, MA: Addison-Wesley.

Wholey, D.R. and Sanchez, S.M. (1991) "The effects of regulatory tools on organizational populations," *Academy of Management Review* 16: 743–67.

Part IV

Domains
of Policy

14

Legal Regulation of Families in Changing Societies

Susan B. Boyd

Approaches and Methods

Over the past two decades, law and society approaches to family relations and law have emerged as a serious field of study and become increasingly diverse in terms of theory, methodology, and scope. Whereas *Law and the Social Sciences* (Lipson and Wheeler, 1987) offered no chapter on family law, to overlook this topic in any review of law and society scholarship would now be a serious omission. In the mid-1980s, a burgeoning sociolegal literature emerged on family law, much of it emanating from England (e.g., Eekelaar, 1984; Eekelaar and Maclean, 1986; Freeman, 1984; Smart, 1984). Sociolegal journals that had not paid much attention to family law offered special issues on law and family. As Herbert Jacob said in his introduction to the "Special Section on Law and the Family" of the *Law & Society Review* (1989: 539): "Family policy has suddenly attained a prominent place on the political agenda and family law has become a livelier field of academic scholarship."

Sociolegal scholars were well-equipped to enter this field because it is virtually impossible to examine laws on the family in a positivist or exclusively doctrinal framework. Since the 1970s, many changes have occurred in relation to the socio-legal regulation of the family, reflecting shifts in family relations, gender relations, and employment patterns of women. These changes have also embodied challenges to heteronormative definitions of family. By the 1980s, most legal systems had moved toward no-fault divorce, typically ascribing reciprocal "gender-neutral" financial obligations between husbands and wives, rather than assuming female dependency and male economic obligation. Children's rights and welfare were becoming more central to discussions of law and social policy. By the 1990s, attention had turned to legal regulation of same-sex relationships. Family law has provided a terrain for social struggles over the concept of "family" itself, the roles of "husbands" and "wives" and "mothers" and "fathers," and the centrality of marriage to regulation of the family by the state.

Sociological, historical, and theoretical approaches brought insights to the changing dynamics of family law and challenged notions that the family was – or could be – an unregulated private sphere (O'Donovan, 1985; Olsen, 1983; Rose, 1987). They also cracked open the very concept of family law, showing that law regulates and constructs families in numerous ways not confined to laws on marriage breakdown (Graycar, 2000). These works often drew on literature that addressed the "politics of the family" (e.g., Barrett and McIntosh, 1982; Zaretsky, 1976). It was increasingly clear that simply calling for more or less state intervention into the family to address problems missed the complex relationship between state, market, and family. Despite the existence of powerful ideologies regarding the privacy of family life, the history of legal regulation of family relations challenges any rigid notion of the public/private divide emanating from liberalism. Even when law purports to stay outside the family, effects can be identified, notably the reinforcing of gendered power relations and violence within it. Moreover, the conditions under which law regulates – or abdicates – the "private" sphere of family typically reflect and often reinforce unequal social relations along the lines of gender, race, class, sexual orientation, and disability (Boyd, 1997; Fineman, 2000; O'Donovan, 1985; Olsen, 1983; Ursel, 1992).

Generally, with the growing invocation of rights discourse in relation to family issues, especially in jurisdictions with bills of rights, family law increasingly has a clear public aspect (Harvison Young, 2001) as a wider range of issues related to "family" are considered by courts and legislatures. However, this trend toward public debate about family relations does not necessarily mean that families and familial responsibilities are supported through public funds (Fineman, 2000). Many current debates reflect struggles over the extent to which there should be regulation of, and public support for, familial relations. Answers typically reflect varying theoretical perspectives, as well as which social groups writers place at the center of their analysis.

Researchers who direct attention to disempowered groups (e.g., single mothers, aboriginal people) have interrogated the ways in which laws on families interact with and/or embody social relations of power along lines such as gender, race, class, and sexuality. As a result, topics formerly considered as outside family law, such as abortion, reproduction, and social welfare, are now often included within sociolegal analyses of family relations. Sociolegal scholars have questioned the traditional norm of "family," exposing the ways in which dominant familial ideologies influence and are reinforced by various types of law. This approach permits a more complex approach to legal analysis, with attention paid not only to legal results but also to discursive patterns in legal decision making. Early analyses identified clearly patriarchal elements in the way that family law regulated relationships and their breakdown (Smart, 1984). Such authors typically suggested that law reinforces dominant ideologies and existing power relations in society. The ideology of motherhood has been explored in depth (e.g., Boyd, 2003; Fineman, 1995; Kline, 1993) and more recently, the representation of fatherhood in law has been investigated, with links to the underlying heterosexual norm of family law (Collier, 1999, 2001).

Other works complicated the picture by focusing on race and poverty. They explored how single and African American mothers were demonized in poverty discourse and in child welfare discourse, the solution often being a patriarchal one of locating absent fathers and returning them to the family, particularly in terms of financial contribution (Fineman, 1995; Roberts, 1997). The processes through which aboriginal children are brought into the Canadian child "welfare" system were linked to the history of colonialist legal regulation and control of aboriginal families (Kline, 1992). Also, familial ideology based on a nuclear model with stay-at-home mother and breadwinner father provided a filter for negative evaluation of parenting by aboriginal mothers (Kline, 1993). This type of work illustrated how a legal principle such as "best interests of the child" – already established as indeterminate (Mnookin, 1975) – had a disparate impact depending on which families it was applied to. Cultures that assign responsibility for children to those outside the nuclear family, for instance to extended family members or members of a community, do not fit well into liberal legal frameworks premised on a nuclear family model of ideal parenting.

Scholars influenced by post-structuralism have examined law's constitutive role in relation to society, raising conceptual questions about the precise relationship between family law and ideology. Many authors now emphasize the mutually constitutive roles of law and society, rather than assuming that law shapes social relations, or social relations shape law, in a one-way relationship (e.g., Mahoney, 1991). Some have drawn on autopoietic theories to analyze how law gives meaning to social concepts such as "children" (King and Piper, 1990). Most recently, authors have highlighted the need to study the role of individual agency, within material and ideological constraints, in relation to discursive constructions within law (Fegan, 2002). It has also been shown that law constitutes a site of struggle that can provide opportunities for challenges to meanings and definitions. The extent to which law's normative definitions have been challenged in recent years cannot be underestimated, notably by those seeking recognition of those living outside a heterosexual or marriage model of family (Gavigan, 1999; Goldberg-Hiller, 1999). That said, critical thinkers have shown that while the legal system has provided openings to inject new meanings of family into law and society, legal liberalism has constrained the shape of these new meanings.

Increasingly diverse methods have been used to explore the operation of family laws. Some researchers have examined case results, court files, or divorce rates and other statistics. Others have surveyed divorced women and men, conducted observations of courts or lawyer/client interactions, or interviewed parents, lawyers, women who have made choices about abortion, counselors, and judges. Legislative debates have also been analyzed. Fathers' rights groups have been interviewed or observed and their submissions to law reform bodies investigated. Some authors have employed narratives to highlight individual experiences of the legal system that had previously been overlooked. In some jurisdictions, particular efforts have been made to measure the impact of laws on family relations, often by research centers such as the Oxford Centre for Socio-Legal Studies and the Leeds Centre for Research on Family, Kinship and Childhood in England; the Australian Institute of Family Studies, the Family Law Research Unit of Griffith University, and the Justice Research Centre of Sydney in Australia; and the Canadian Research Institute on Law and the Family. Researchers with the Australian Family Court have also produced important empirical work.

Recent studies suggest that modern family law is characterized by complexity, fragmentation, and a variety of processes. It is therefore increasingly difficult to state at any level of generality the nature and effects of family law. Some studies have shifted the focus from analysis of final judicial decisions towards both the process of decision making (e.g., judicial discretion) and interim decisions, which effectively constitute final decisions for many parties (Dewar and Parker, 1999: 109; Rhoades, Graycar, and Harrison, 2000). The adequacy of "grand theories," for example those addressing the public/private divide, has been questioned, in part due to their excessive focus on a unitary notion of law (Rose, 1987). An alternative approach is to explore the relationship between social relations, social knowledge, and law in its full diversity, including how law absorbs or colonizes other forms of expert knowledge and regulatory processes (e.g., King and Piper, 1990).

Significantly, some scholars producing empirically based knowledge have developed methodologies by reference to theoretical questions raised by those studying law's constitutive role and its complex, often contradictory role in social change. The strongest work reflects the exploration both of family law's operation in the "real world," in a variety of settings, and its role in relation to ideological and material struggles (e.g., Rhoades, 2000; Sarat and Felstiner, 1995). To the extent that law has been employed in an effort to engineer changes "from above" in the nature of postdivorce family life (Smart and Neale, 1999), it is important to identify its role in shaping beliefs as well as to assess its impact, including both intended and unintended consequences. It is also important to identify ways in which traditional norms, for instance an ideology of heterosexuality (Collier, 1999) or a breadwinner/homemaker ideology (Didick, 1999), continue to permeate even the "new" family law.

The rest of this chapter uses four themes to illustrate key insights of the vast literature offering sociolegal approaches to family law: (1) gender, equality, and family; (2) constituting and redefining family; (3) redefining legal parenthood; and (4) privatization and the new family law: the discursive and the material. These themes correspond roughly to the chronological order in which they emerged within sociolegal approaches in Canada, Australia, England, and the United States, although in practice they interact and overlap. The contradictory implications of trends toward sex equality arise in several contexts. The impact of increasing recognition of same-sex relationships is key, as is cultural and racial diversity.

GENDER, EQUALITY, AND FAMILY

Alongside the new interest in family law during the 1980s came the rising influence of feminist approaches, heightening awareness of the gendered consequences of family relations, breakdown, and law reform, and offering new theoretical approaches to equality, the public/private divide, and power. Researchers too numerous to list began to inquire seriously into the relationship between the new gender-neutral family law norms and women's continuing economic disadvantage (e.g., Fineman, 1991; Weitzman and Maclean, 1992). Despite women's increased (though not equal) participation in the labor force, studies showed that their standard of living tended to plummet upon divorce, whereas men's tended to rise. Women's continuing socially constructed responsibility for childcare and households was identified as a significant impediment to any simplistic imposition of formalistic views of equality. However, this knowledge sat uneasily alongside statistics indicating the increase in women's labor force participation. Although some judges were willing to recognize the contributions of longtime homemakers to families and spouses through property division and/or support awards, studies revealed that they were less willing to provide support for younger women separating from their spouses in the middle of ongoing caregiving responsibilities for children. Although employed women still assumed greater responsibility for domestic labor than their male partners, judges and legislators struggled with which policy norms to prioritize: the self-reliance, independence, and "clean break" associated with liberal individualism, or compensation to address financial disadvantage and need resulting from continuing unequal gender relations rooted in structures of state, market, and family.

In addition to a focus on substantive law norms, serious concerns emerged in the literature about process issues for disadvantaged groups. Due to their relative economic disadvantage, women encounter particular impediments in gaining access to the legal process and to legal advice. Funding for legal aid for family issues tends to be less than adequate, if not nonexistent, which in turn has a gendered impact on women (Mossman, 1994). Violence against women was also identified as a key factor generating substantive inequality for women in family law disputes with male partners (e.g., Sheehan and Smyth, 2000). The prevalence of violence against women in intact families, and also at or after separation, was contrasted to the construction of domestic abuse as rare or exceptional in family litigation (Mahoney, 1991). It was shown that abused women encounter the legal system from a position of disadvantage in terms of bargaining power with their ex-partners and that abusive men often use legal processes to seek power and control over women who have left them. Women's position of disadvantage in this context is exacerbated by the increasing emphasis on paternal contact with children and declining funding for legal aid.

Critical analyses of the trend toward informal processes of dispute resolution, especially family mediation, questioned the ability of mediators to maintain a neutral stance or to screen adequately for woman abuse (e.g., Astor, 1994), or even to deliver on its promises of offering a more humane, relational mode of dispute resolution (Grillo, 1991). Others suggested the trend toward mediation obscured the complex process of resolving issues on family breakdown and its gendered dynamics, and connected the rise of mediation to the new shared parenting norms, which enhanced fathers' rights claims (Fineman, 1991). Although some scholars pointed out the problems of mediation when used in relation to spouses with a power imbalance, particularly when domestic abuse was involved, others noted that only a small percentage of the divorcing population resolve disputes with legal representation (Pearson, 1993). Newer studies point to the failure of most dispute resolution processes, including negotiation, mediation, and litigation, to take abuse seriously (Neilson, 2002). And studies based on analysis of actual mediations suggest that mediators marginalize domestic violence even when disputants raise it (Greatbatch and Dingwall, 1999). This tendency is likely to aggravate any inequality of bargaining power already existing between the parties and may prejudice the ability of women to obtain fair economic settlements.

The focus of this research on the rules and processes regulating family breakdown, a moment that reveals the vulnerability – economic and otherwise – of individual family members, did not overlook the life of intact families. Rather, it studied the way that the normative order of intact families interacted with the legal system once the taken-for-granted interdependence of family members ended. Other literature, discussed next, focused more particularly on how families were normatively constituted and regulated by law and, as well, at how families were being redefined within law and society.

CONSTITUTING AND REDEFINING FAMILY

Alongside the study of the effects of laws on family breakdown, which vary according to factors such as gender and class, came more profound challenges to the meaning of "family" and legal definitions such as "spouse," "parent," and "child." These challenges have been central to both legal changes and scholarly debates over the past two decades. A major transformation in family law has been the decentering of marriage as the key determinant of family connections. During the late 1970s and the 1980s, many legal systems began to legally recognize the relationships of unmarried cohabitants, imposing certain rights and obligations on them in the event of separation. The legal concept of the legitimacy of children, determined by reference to marriage ties, correspondingly diminished in importance. The functional similarity of marriage and cohabitation, and the biological and relational bonds between parent and child, were increasingly emphasized rather than the traditional family based on marriage between a man and a woman.

Scholars working on lesbian and gay family forms most clearly deconstructed the heterosexual norm in family law, drawing on the growing social visibility of same-sex relationships. The fact that children were being raised, and conceived, within same-sex relationships was contrasted to the normative assumption within most laws that a child has two parents of the opposite sex (Polikoff, 1990). Legal systems that already recognized opposite-sex cohabitation were challenged to expand these laws to include same-sex cohabitants, notably in Western Europe through the use of registered domestic partnerships (Bailey, 2000) and in Canada, as opposite-sex definitions of "spouse" were challenged using constitutional equality rights (Gavigan, 1999). In jurisdictions such as the United States, where unmarried opposite-sex cohabitants were not recognized by statute to the same extent, the debate centered more clearly on whether to open the legal institution of marriage to same-sex partners. Scholars investigated the use of domestic partnerships at local levels as an alternative that bestowed status recognition based on contractual undertakings (Goldberg-Hiller, 1999). Domestic partnership legislation often forms a paradox, being portrayed as a political compromise that preserves the status of traditional marriage while providing a parallel legal regime for same-sex partners. A debate arose concerning the mode through which same-sex relationships should be recognized, with some scholars – particularly feminists – questioning the centrality of the quest for marriage rights by lesbians and gay men. These authors paid more attention to the role that marriage (and the nuclear family norm) has played in social histories of disadvantaged groups (Polikoff, 1993; Robson, 1994). Despite this debate, most scholars are now grappling not with whether to legally constitute same-sex relationships, but rather with which mechanism should be used to do so.

Apart from challenges to heteronormativity, the literature suggests that the normative primacy of the nuclear family has been challenged to an extent, as laws on adoption and child welfare have cautiously accommodated a wider definition of "family." For example, trends toward "open adoption" allow some birth mothers, or even birth families, to stay involved in children's lives after adoption, whereas once most countries rigorously protected the integrity of the new adoptive nuclear family. In North America, extended family members and aboriginal communities are recognized in some legal procedures concerning child protection and adoption. These trends have generated scholarly debates about the relevance that cultural background and racial identity ought to have, particularly in relation to child protection and mixed-race adoption, and about the role that community and identity ought to play in legal processes concerning the severing of original family ties and the construction of new ties (Kline, 1992; Perry, 1993–4). The boundaries around "family" have to some degree been fragmented both in legal practice and in sociolegal discourse.

Alongside the redefinition of family, and especially the diminished focus on marriage as the central organizing feature of family law, came a new social and scholarly focus on parent–child ties, particularly father–child ties. Indeed, other than the same-sex marriage debate, the question of legal definitions of parenthood is the most controversial in modern family law, raising questions about when biological ties as opposed to social or functional ties should determine legal relationships, rights, and responsibilities.

REDEFINING LEGAL PARENTHOOD

The legal system and scholarly literature have increasingly grappled with the question of what constitutes a legal parent (Bainham, Day Sclater, and Richards, 1999), canvassing determinants ranging from legal presumptions (mainly of paternity), to biological and genetic links, to intention, to social or functional definitions of parenting. The elimination of illegitimacy as a legal concept in many jurisdictions has diminished the former primacy of the marriage tie between husband and wife in determining legal paternity, and generated an emphasis on biological fatherhood (Smart and Neale, 1999). This emphasis has arisen in custody disputes over children a mother places for adoption and also in relation to child support (Sheldon, 2001). The new emphasis on paternal biological ties is surprising given the modern cross-jurisdictional emphasis on best interests of the child, which need not rest on biology. It has a tendency to impose culturally specific values on indigenous communities. Recognition of the role of the social parent in same-sex households has generated comment on the fact that attendant legal rights and duties in relation to children might potentially accrue to several parties, not always based on biology. Child support obligations imposed on stepparents who act in the place of a parent raise similar questions. Complex questions arise in situations involving use of reproductive technologies such as insemination of donated sperm or implantation into a woman of a fertilized egg created from donated genetic material. Several potential parents can be identified in surrogacy arrangements based on both social and biological referents, with the question being who should be recognized and for what purposes.

The legal regulation of parenting after separation or divorce has generated a huge literature, also raising issues of rights based on genetic parenthood versus social responsibility. Carbone identifies "the largest practical disagreement underlying modern family law disputes" as "the issue of whether the law should promote the continued involvement of both parents in their children's upbringing or whether it should place greater priority on securing support for those providing the care" (Carbone, 2000: 228). Much of the literature invokes social science studies or assesses the impact on children and parents of various types of legal orders. Many social scientists make law reform recommendations, and legally trained scholars invoke social science studies in their arguments for and against legal changes.

This area of sociolegal studies offers a cautionary tale about objectivity and the politics of research: the social scientific studies are often pervaded by the same ideologies and biases that influence law. Equally inevitably, their results differ. Moreover, in this, as in all fields of research, some research is held out as undisputed and objective/scientific (e.g., Galatzer-Levy and Kraus, 1999), while other knowledge (especially that emanating from feminist or minority voices) is viewed as tainted and less than authoritative (Moloney, 2001; for critique, see Boyd, 2003; Rhoades, Graycar, and Harrison, 2001: 74–5).

This literature is also striking for the extent to which the "truths" that it offers have changed over time. The early work of Goldstein, Freud, and Solnit (1973) suggested that children benefit from continuity of caregiving and support for a primary parent's autonomy that may result from sole custody awards. An emphasis on primary caregiving in child custody determinations emerged in some literature as a result, and to redress the increased indeterminacy of decision making resulting from the demise of the tender years doctrine and the emergence of the best interests of the child standard (Mnookin, 1975). Analyses of the gendered nature of responsibility for children showed that the emphasis on caregiving responsibility was rooted in the reality of children's lives (e.g., Fineman, 1995). Studies of contested and uncontested cases showed that, in practice, mothers had custodial responsibility of (especially younger) children more often than fathers, although fathers gained custody more often when they defended their cases (e.g., Bordow, 1994). The child's residence before the decision was an influential factor, and parents who decided the issue themselves mainly chose the mother as custodial parent.

By the late 1980s and the 1990s, a new "truth" emerged: that children fared better when they had ongoing relationships with both parents. Fathers' rights groups used research bolstering this "truth" to argue for joint custody norms or presumptions (Bertoia and Drakich, 1993; Kay and Tolmie, 1998). In fact, studies indicate that there are no simple answers (Kelly, 1993) and that contact between children and nonresidential parents (usually fathers) is not necessarily positive for children, especially if conflict between parents exists. Nor does custody status in and of itself significantly predict the postdivorce adjustment of children (Kline Pruett and Santangelo, 1999). Nevertheless, some form of shared custody was increasingly accepted as the best scenario. Many jurisdictions introduced legislative reforms intended to enhance maximum contact between nonresidential parents and children, including joint custody preferences. Research shows that joint legal custody awards have increased considerably (Maccoby and Mnookin, 1992; Melli, Brown, and Cancian, 1997), yet the majority of children subject to these awards reside with their mothers. A gendered division of labor thus continues after parents separate, but more authority is accorded to the nonresidential parent (Boyd, 2003). More recently, a new wave of legislative reforms, for example in Australia and England, has eschewed the language of "custody" and "access" in favor of parenting regimes that presume a continuation of each parent's responsibility/authority in a child's life. Such reforms were typically undertaken in response to political calls for change rather than actual problems in the law (Rhoades, 2000; Smart and Neale, 1999). Denial of access is not the widespread problem it is often thought to be, nor are false allegations of sexual abuse during custody disputes (Pearson, 1993). Yet the status of biological fathers has been legally enhanced through an invocation of children's "best interests." In practice, a presumption that contact is in a child's best interests has arisen, rendering other concerns about children's well-being, including abuse, less significant (Bailey-Harris, Barron, and Pearce, 1999; Rhoades et al., 2000). Attempts to build in safeguards against the worst abuses of the system against women and children have tended to take a back seat to provisions that encourage contact.

These new legal regimes arguably are rewriting "the code of family responsibility... in terms of the only ties left – the ones to children" (Carbone, 2000: xiii), with decreased emphasis on a father's relationship to the mother when determining his parental status, rights, and responsibilities. In terms of law's constitutive role, one might argue that men are being awakened into a new kind of fatherhood within a redefined masculinity. However, the consequences of these new legal regimes are contradictory and gendered, reflecting the necessity of considering law's discursive role in relation to material constraints on human conduct. The new regimes create parental ties and responsibilities between parents – based largely on biology – that are enforceable in a way that older ties were not, sometimes even when parents have not cohabited. Mothers are legally constituted in a way that obliges them to ensure that their children build relationships with biological fathers, often compromising their own autonomy. The next section discusses ways of understanding these often contradictory trends.

PRIVATIZATION AND THE NEW FAMILY LAW: THE DISCURSIVE AND THE MATERIAL

Sociolegal scholars have attempted to explain the apparent paradox of modern family law identified in the previous section. On the one hand, family law increasingly supports the diversity of families, liberal divorce, and serial monogamy. On the other hand, it enforces ongoing financial and psychosocial obligations between spouses and between parents and children.

Finding legal fathers for children, both for financial support and psychological well-being, is thought to be crucial to preserve children from harm (Fineman, 1995; Kaganas, 1999), despite mixed social science findings. Some authors suggest that this trend is linked to child support, which has become a key focus of family law, often accompanied by legislated guidelines and enhanced enforcement. The notion of a "clean break" between adults once they cease to be spouses is illusory for adults with joint parental obligations – whether caregiving or financial – to children. The new emphasis in child custody law on coparenting has been linked to the (re)privatization of economic responsibilities: "While, ostensibly, the new model of family life is driven by the welfare discourse alone, it is clear that less altruistic considerations also come into play. These include the treasury-led assumption that if biological fathers continue to see their children then they will carry on paying for them" (Smart and Neale, 1999: 38). Although in law, child support and custody/access are separate issues, in practice the two appear connected (Pearson, 1993). Certainly, at the political level, fathers' rights advocates have argued for enhanced custodial rights to accompany (or obviate) their financial obligations.

Studying the contradictions of family law requires a consideration of law's discursive effects *and* their operation within material constraints, whether economic or psychological. The apparent contradictions in the "new" family law have been explored by reference to the role of family law in liberal democracies that rely heavily on privatized, often familial, responsibility for the economic well-being of individuals. Authors who interrogate the historical role of the state and law in regulating gender and family relations have revealed an overall trend to privatize the costs associated with social reproduction (the production of human life through procreation, socialization, and daily maintenance) within the family (Ursel, 1992). In intact relationships, women's unpaid responsibility for domestic labor has allevi-ated the need for broader public responsibility for the social costs of reproduction. Once relationships are severed, the limits of this system and the resulting financial consequences are revealed, both in terms of women and children's diminished standard of living and in terms of the difficulty of meeting the financial needs of two households. Nevertheless, legal responses to relationship breakdown also rely on privatization of the costs of social reproduction, assuming that the financially more secure adult (often male) will continue to support his former partner and his children. Historical research reveals that this system relies on gender-based norms. During the emergence of the social welfare state, support obligations were imposed on husbands who deserted "deserving" wives (Chunn, 1992). Thus the legal system operated at both material and discursive levels: as it enforced privatized economic responsibility, it reinforced behavior viewed as appropriate to the heterosexual roles of husband and wife.

Research on contemporary trends reveals that, despite its ostensible liberalization and gender neutrality, modern family law is embedded within the trend toward fiscal conservatism and economic retrenchment, including privatization, that accelerated during the 1980s. Carbone suggests that the bottom line of modern family law in the United States is the treasury rather than marital ties:

> In the new era, women may engage in sex for the same reasons as men – with no promise to marry needed or implied. The state, however, still demands a guarantor. The obligation not to impose the consequences of the sexual act on the public fisc is, in these cases, subject only to the father's ability to pay, and the state's ability to make him. (Carbone, 2000: 162)

A (re)privatization of economic responsibility has been identified in relation to support law, including the extension of responsibilities to stepfathers and same-sex partners (Cossman, 2000). Judges and legislators tend to be more sympathetic to legal claims that reflect privatized responsibility – even as between same-sex partners – than those that cast responsibility upon the state or society in general.

These trends do not have a neutral impact. The advantage to the state of privatiz-ing the costs of social reproduction, and the corresponding detrimental impact on women, has been revealed. For instance, the introduction of child support guidelines and stepped up enforcement of child support obligations (Mossman, 1997) are often touted by governments as addressing the economic disadvantage of women and children. However, the capacity of family law to address women and children's poverty has been seriously questioned (Eichler, 1990; Pulkingham, 1994). The private sphere of family is already overburdened and when the social safety net is cut back, women and children tend to fall through the cracks (Mossman and Maclean, 1997), in particular black women and single mothers (Beller and Graham, 1993). Ironically, efforts to reinforce private child support obligations have had limited success. These legal changes fail to address the impossibility of supporting two households with income barely adequate to handle one (Pearson, 1993: 296). Authors increasingly recommend that broader changes to family and economic policies are necessary in addition to changes to family law per se, pointing to the need for collective action by state and society to provide adequate economic safety nets for those in economic need. The links between family law and social welfare law are highlighted in this literature.

The promotion of private ordering, the diminution of publicly funded legal aid, and general fragmentation of family law processes can also be viewed as a form of "re-privatization" of family law in the sense that the role of the public sphere in monitoring the fairness of outcomes is diminished (Neave, 1994). Inequalities in bargaining power may be overlooked and therefore entrenched, much as they once were when families were ostensibly unregulated by law. Access to justice may be unequal, as may substantive outcomes, and both the process and the results may be gendered, as the terms of bargaining are altered in favor of those who are more powerful (Dewar, 2000). While earlier systems were flawed in their ability to deliver fair process or equal outcomes, recent trends arguably render power differentials less visible and therefore exacerbate them. Ironically, claims that family law is less and less a "private" field (Harvison Young, 2001) emerge alongside arguments that family law trends reinforce a privatized family form that is built on gendered, racialized, and class-based social relations. Both claims may be accurate, as public regulation of families tends to rely on and reinforce privatized responsibilities (Boyd, 1997). The overall lesson for sociolegal scholars is the need to pay attention to material relations when examining the operation and impact of norms within family law.

FOR THE FUTURE: THE LIMITS OF LAW

Precisely because laws on the family have changed so radically since the 1970s, and because the ways in which law regulates family transcend disciplinary boundaries within law itself, family law offers a perfect terrain for sociolegal studies. This field of research offers general lessons for sociolegal scholars. Although Foucault's work suggests that law has been displaced by social science and psydiscourses as a technique of governance, work in this area shows it is the *relationship* between legal and social knowledge rather than displacement of one by the other that is key.

Sociolegal scholarship on the family has identified the differential impact of laws, depending on the social location of family members based on gender, race, class, and/or sexual identity, all of which affect access to legal services. These insights raise questions about an old chestnut: the extent to which parties bargain in the shadow of the law (Mnookin and Kornhauser, 1979). The impact of a judge's potential decision on bargaining is a top-down metaphor that assumes that parties pay attention to legal norms and attend to law in the same way. This assumption may not reflect the current complexity of family law processes, nor the extent to which law's shadow is mediated by many other factors. These include social location as well as legally related factors such as legal aid policies, court procedures, professional styles (Dewar and Parker, 1999) or communities of legal practice (Mather, McEwen, and Maiman, 2001). As Dewar points out (2000: 74), "the very meaning given to legal rules may vary according to where in the system they are being applied," whether in private ordering or litigation, whether with or without legal advice. Bargaining power of parties varies widely depending on various factors such as gender and also on whether a party is legally aided, privately funded, or unrepresented (Hunter, Genovese, Melville, and Chrzanowski, 2000).

Studies on family law show that law's impact within society in any particular instance is difficult to predict and there is no necessary causal relationship between legislative change and social, or even legal, outcomes. Sending positive messages by encouraging processes such as mediation or using new legal terminology such as "joint custody" or "parental responsibility" has not succeeded in changing behavior or making parents share responsibilities. Despite the intent of parenting law reformers to reduce conflict and enhance shared parental responsibilities, conflict and litigation have increased and most children still reside primarily with their mothers (Dunne, Wren Hudgins, and Babcock, 2000; Rhoades et al., 2000). Drawing on this lesson, Dewar and Parker (1999) suggest that legislative messages regarding parental responsibilities are heard differently by different audiences. Thus legislative provisions can acquire different meanings in different parts of the system, and for various participants in the system. This "principle of variable reception" means that, in the context of the new wave parenting laws, settlement-promoting messages are more apt to be heard by those who already are more likely to make a consensual agreement about postdivorce parenting.

A related important insight, at a more systemic level, is that family law's capacity to deal with deeply rooted social problems such as the sexual division of labor, or child poverty (which is usually closely related to parental poverty) is limited unless it is integrated with accompanying social policy changes. Studies suggest that male participation in childcare would be encouraged more effectively by adequate public policy on and support for familial responsibilities outside a patriarchal framework than by legally enacting shared parenting norms in relation to postseparation parenting. There is a growing sense that family law has been asked to solve too many deeply rooted economic and social problems, when it is only a microcosm of a much more complex social system that influences familial relations.

Another lesson gleaned from examination of legal regulation of family issues is that withdrawal of law from a social field may require the study of effects or constraints as they emerge in other areas. For instance, the trends in some jurisdictions to decriminalize abortion and protect women's reproductive choice from veto by male partners did not eliminate the difficulties that women experience in exercising meaningful choice concerning abortion. Power has shifted to another terrain, that of the medical profession, requiring attention to different areas of law (Sheldon, 1997). As the criminal law has withdrawn, more power has been accorded to doctors, meaning that health law comes further into focus (Lessard, 1993). Well-entrenched obstacles persist in relation to women's reproductive choice, including for young women, those living in remote communities, and ethnic minorities. These obstacles point to the need for researchers to attend to material and ideological constraints on individual autonomy as well as the limits of law in resolving social problems.

The best law and society scholarship places law and law reform in a context that explores its contradictions, limits, and possibilities, as well as its relationship to power. As we have seen, numerous contradictions arise within modern family law, for example, between the new emphasis on biological parenthood, especially paternity, for the purposes of assigning child support obligations, and the new emphasis on social parenting evidenced, for instance, in the so-called "second mother" adoptions. Such contradictions raise the question of whether one family law can accommodate the variety of familial forms now existing, both within and outside the traditional, heterosexual, nuclear definition of family. Some authors have suggested that various legal constructs are needed to deal with various aspects of parenthood:

parentage (genetic parentage), parenthood (ongoing legal status as a parent involving responsibility for raising a child), and parental responsibility (legal power and duties associated with raising a child (Bainham et al., 1999). These trends challenge sociolegal scholars to confront fragmentation and contradiction in family law, while keeping in mind the social relations of power. Although many calls have been made to place children at the center of analysis, the purported new focus of family law and policy on the welfare of children must be read with a critical eye: "the deployment of the welfare discourse in divorce is linked as much to adult moral, emotional and political agendas as to the welfare of children" (Day Sclater and Piper, 1999: 20). The challenge for twenty-first century scholars is to assess what the role of family law can be within a less clearly status-based system, but one that rests on various social hierarchies still related to persistent, if shifting, power relations of gender, race, class, and sexuality.

Note

Thanks to Reg Graycar, Rosemary Hunter, Mary Jane Mossman, and Helen Rhoades for their comments on a draft of this chapter.

References

Astor, H. (1994) "Violence and family mediation: Policy," *Australian Journal of Family Law* 8: 3–21.

Bailey, M. (ed.) (2000) "Symposium: Domestic partnerships," *Canadian Journal of Family Law* 17(1).

Bailey-Harris, R., Barron, J., and Pearce, J. (1999) "From utility to rights? The presumption of contact in practice," *International Journal of Law, Policy and the Family* 13: 111–31.

Bainham, A., Day Sclater, S., and Richards, M. (eds.) (1999) *What is a Parent? A Socio-Legal Analysis*. Oxford: Hart Publishing.

Barrett, M. and McIntosh, M. (1982) *The Anti-social Family*. London: Verso.

Beller, A.H. and Graham, J.W. (1993) *Small Change: The Economics of Child Support*. New Haven, CT and London: Yale University Press.

Bertoia, C. and Drakich, J. (1993) "The fathers' rights movement: Contradictions in rhetoric and practice," *Journal of Family Issues* 14: 592–615.

Bordow, S. (1994) "Defended custody cases in the Family Court of Australia: Factors influencing the outcome," *Australian Journal of Family Law* 8: 252–63.

Boyd, S.B. (ed.) (1997) *Challenging the Public/Private Divide: Feminism, Law, and Public Policy*. Toronto: University of Toronto Press.

Boyd, S.B. (2003) *Child Custody, Law, and Women's Work*. Toronto: Oxford University Press.

Carbone, J. (2000) *From Partners to Parents: The Second Revolution in Family Law*. New York: Columbia University Press.

Chunn, D.E. (1992) *From Punishment to Doing Good: Family Courts and Socialized Justice in Ontario 1880–1940*. Toronto: University of Toronto Press.

Collier, R. (1999) "From women's emancipation to sex war? Men, heterosexuality and the politics of divorce," in S. Day Sclater and C. Piper (eds.), *Undercurrents of Divorce*. Aldershot, UK: Ashgate, pp. 123–44.

Collier, R. (2001) "In search of the 'good father': Law, family practices and the normative reconstruction of parenthood," *Studies in Law, Politics and Society* 22: 133–69.

Cossman, B. (2000) "Developments in family law: The 1998–99 term," *Supreme Court Law Review* 11(2): 433–81.

Day Sclater, S. and Piper, C. (1999) *Undercurrents of Divorce*. Aldershot, UK: Ashgate.

Dewar, J. (2000) "Family law and its discontents," *International Journal of Law, Policy and the Family* 14: 59–85.

Dewar, J. and Parker, S. (1999) "The impact of the new Part VII Family Law Act 1975," *Australian Journal of Family Law* 13: 96–116.

Didick, A. (1999) "Dividing the family assets," in S. Day Sclater and C. Piper (eds.), *Undercurrents of Divorce*. Aldershot, UK: Ashgate, pp. 209–30.

Dunne, J.E., Wren Hudgins, E. and Babcock, J. (2000) "Can changing the divorce law affect post-divorce adjustment?" *Journal of Divorce and Remarriage* 33(3–4): 35–54.

Eekelaar, J. (1984) *Family Law and Social Policy*, 2nd edn. London: Weidenfeld and Nicholson.

Eekelaar, J. and Maclean, M. (1986) *Maintenance After Divorce*. Oxford: Clarendon Press.

Eichler, M. (1990) "The limits of family law reform or, the privatization of female and child poverty," *Canadian Family Law Quarterly* 7: 59–84.

Fegan, E. (2002) "Recovering women: Intimate images and legal strategies," *Social and Legal Studies* 11: 155–84.

Fineman, M.A. (1991) *The Illusion of Equality: The Rhetoric and Reality of Divorce Reform*. Chicago and London: University of Chicago Press.

Fineman, M.A. (1995) *The Neutered Mother, The Sexual Family, and Other Twentieth-Century Tragedies*. New York: Routledge.

Fineman, M.A. (2000) "Cracking the foundational myths: Independence, autonomy, and self-sufficiency," *Journal of Gender, Social Policy and Law* 13: 13–29.

Freeman, M.D.A. (ed.) (1984) *State, Law, and the Family: Critical Perspectives*. London: Tavistock.

Galatzer-Levy, R. and Kraus, L. (eds.) (1999) *The Scientific Basis of Child Custody Decisions*. New York: John Wiley & Sons.

Gavigan, S.A.M. (1999) "Legal forms and family norms: What is a spouse?" *Canadian Journal of Law and Society* 14: 127–57.

Goldberg-Hiller, J. (1999) "The status of status: Domestic partnership and the politics of same-sex marriage," *Studies in Law, Politics and Society* 19: 3–38.

Goldstein, J., Freud, A., and Solnit, A. (1973) *Beyond the Best Interests of the Child*. New York: Free Press.

Graycar, R. (2000) "Law reform by frozen chook: Family law reform for the new millennium?" *Melbourne University Law Review* 24: 737–55.

Greatbatch, D. and Dingwall, R. (1999) "The marginalization of domestic violence in divorce mediation," *International Journal of Law, Policy and the Family* 13: 174–90.

Grillo, T. (1991) "The mediation alternative: Process dangers for women," *Yale Law Journal* 100: 1545–610.

Harvison Young, A. (2001) "The changing family, rights discourse and the Supreme Court of Canada," *Canadian Bar Review* 80: 750–92.

Hunter, R., with Genovese, A., Melville, A., and Chrzanowski, A. (2000) *Legal Services in Family Law*. Sydney: Justice Research Centre.

Jacob, H. (1989) "From the special section editor," *Law and Society Review* 23(4): 539–41.

Kaganas, F. (1999) "Contact, conflict and risk," in S. Day Sclater and C. Piper (eds.), *Undercurrents of Divorce*. Aldershot, UK: Ashgate, pp. 99–120.

Kay, M. and Tolmie, J. (1998) "Fathers' rights groups in Australia and their engagement with issues in family law," *Australian Journal of Family Law* 12: 19–68.

Kelly, J.B. (1993) "Current research on children's postdivorce adjustment: No simple answers," *Family and Conciliation Courts Review* 31: 29–49.

King, M. and Piper, C. (1990) *How the Law Thinks About Children*. Aldershot, UK: Gower.

Kline, Marlee (1992) "Child welfare law, 'best interests of the child' ideology, and First Nations," *Osgoode Hall Law Journal* 30: 375–425.

Kline, Marlee (1993) "Complicating the ideology of motherhood: Child welfare law and First Nations women," *Queen's Law Journal* 18: 306–42.

Kline Pruett, M. and Santangelo, C. (1999) "Joint custody and empirical knowledge: The estranged bedfellows of divorce," in R.M. Galatzer-Levy and L. Kraus (eds.), *The Scientific Basis of Child Custody Decisions*. New York: John Wiley & Sons, pp. 389–424.

Lessard, H. (1993) "The construction of health care and the ideology of the private in Canadian constitutional law," *Annals of Health Law* 2: 121–59.

Lipson, L. and Wheeler, S. (eds.) (1987) *Law and the Social Sciences*. New York: Russell Sage Foundation.

Maccoby, E.E. and Mnookin, R.H. (1992) *Dividing the Child: Social and Legal Dilemmas of Custody*. Cambridge, MA: Harvard University Press.

Mahoney, M. (1991) "Legal images of battered women: Redefining the issue of separation," *Michigan Law Review* 90: 1–94.

Mather, L., McEwen C.A., and Maiman, R.J. (2001) *Divorce Lawyers at Work*. New York: Oxford University Press.

Melli, M.S., Brown, P.R., and Cancian, M. (1997) "Child custody in a changing world: A study of postdivorce arrangements in Wisconsin," *University of Illinois Law Review* 1997: 773–800.

Mnookin, R.H. (1975) "Child-custody adjudication: Judicial functions in the face of indeterminacy," *Law and Contemporary Problems* 39: 226–92.

Mnookin, R.H. and Kornhauser, L. (1979) "Bargaining in the shadow of the law: The case of divorce," *Yale Law Journal* 88: 950–97.

Moloney, L. (2001) "Researching the Family Law Reform Act: A case of selective attention?" *Family Matters* 59: 64–73.

Mossman, M.J. (1994) "Gender equality, family law and access to justice," *International Journal of Law and the Family* 8: 357–73.

Mossman, M.J. (1997) "Child support or support for children? Re-thinking 'public' and 'private' in family law," *University of New Brunswick Law Journal* 46: 63–85.

Mossman, M.J. and Maclean, M. (1997) "Family law and social assistance programs: Re-thinking equality," in P.M. Evans and G.R. Wekerle (eds.), *Women and the Canadian Welfare State*. Toronto: University of Toronto Press, pp. 117–41.

Neave, M. (1994) "Resolving the dilemma of difference: A critique of 'The role of private ordering in family law'," *University of Toronto Law Journal* 44: 97–131.

Neilson, L.C. (2002) "Comparative analysis of law in theory and law in action in partner abuse cases: What do the data tell us?" *Studies in Law, Politics and Society* 26: 141–87.

O'Donovan, K. (1985) *Sexual Divisions in Law*. London: Weidenfeld and Nicholson.

Olsen, F.E. (1983) "The family and the market: A study of ideology and legal reform," *Harvard Law Review* 96: 1497–578.

Pearson, Jessica (1993) "Ten myths about family law," *Family Law Quarterly* 27: 279–99.

Perry, T.L. (1993–4) "The transracial adoption controversy: An analysis of discourse and subordination," *N.Y.U. Review of Law and Social Change* 21: 33–108.

Polikoff, N. (1990) " 'This child does have two mothers': Redefining parenthood to meet the needs of children in lesbian-mother and other nontraditional families," *Georgetown Law Journal* 78: 459–576.

Polikoff, N. (1993) "We will get what we ask for: Why legalizing gay and lesbian marriage will not dismantle the legal structure of gender in every marriage," *Virginia Law Review* 79: 1535–50.

Pulkingham, J. (1994) "Private troubles, private solutions: Poverty among divorced women and the politics of support enforcement and child custody determination," *Canadian Journal of Law and Society* 9: 73–97.

Rhoades, H. (2000) "Posing as reform: The case of the Family Law Reform Act," *Australian Journal of Family Law* 14: 142–59.

Rhoades, H., Graycar, R., and Harrison, M. (2000) *The Family Law Reform Act 1995: The First Three Years*. University of Sydney and Family Court of Australia, available at <http://www.familycourt.gov.au/papers/html/fla1.html>.

Rhoades, H., Graycar, R., and Harrison, M. (2001) "Researching family law reform: The authors respond," *Family Matters* 59: 68–75.

Roberts, D. (1997) *Killing the Black Body: Race, Reproduction, and the Meaning of Liberty*. New York: Pantheon.

Robson, R. (1994) "Resisting the family: Repositioning lesbians in legal theory," *Signs* 19: 975–96.

Rose, N. (1987) "Beyond the public/private division: Law, power and the family," *Journal of Law and Society* 14: 61–76.

Sarat, A. and Felstiner, W. (1995) *Divorce Lawyers and Their Clients: Power and Meaning in the Legal Process*. New York: Oxford University Press.

Sheehan, G. and Smyth, B. (2000) "Spousal violence and post-separation financial outcomes," *Australian Journal of Family Law* 14: 102–18.

Sheldon, S. (1997) *Beyond Control: Medical Power and Abortion Law*. London: Pluto Press.

Sheldon, S. (2001) " 'Sperm bandits,' birth control fraud and the battle of the sexes," *Legal Studies* 21(3): 460–80.

Smart, C. (1984) *The Ties That Bind: Law, Marriage and the Reproduction of Patriarchal Relations*. London: Routledge & Kegan Paul.

Smart, C. and Neale, B. (1999) *Family Fragments?* Cambridge, UK: Polity Press.

Ursel, J. (1992) *Private Lives, Public Policy: 100 Years of State Intervention in the Family*. Toronto: Women's Press.

Weitzman, L. and Maclean, M. (eds.) (1992) *Economic Consequences of Divorce: An International Perspective*. Cambridge, MA: Harvard University Press.

Zaretsky, E. (1976) *Capitalism, The Family, and Personal Life*. New York: Harper and Row.

15

Culture, *"Kulturkampf,"* and Beyond: The Antidiscrimination Principle under the Jurisprudence of Backlash

Francisco Valdes

Introduction

The arc of history is long, as Martin Luther King, Jr. once observed, and it does not fall on any one generation to see its hopes fulfilled. But history has no necessary valence; it is a complex site of multiple contestations. Nor is history's arc linear; it is multifaceted, full of contradictions and interruptions, a fitful unfolding always contingent, constantly in flux. The "arc" of history is not preordained fate, but rather the momentary sum of social experience – plus a sense of trajectory context-ualized by intergenerational perspective. During the past two or so centuries, the arc of history has unfolded toward a slow and difficult national shift from formal subordination to formal equality, culminating in the formal embrace of the anti-discrimination principle during the middle-to-latter decades of the twentieth century under the liberal conception of "equal opportunity." Against this historic back-ground, perhaps the most notable development in "equality" and "antidiscrimina-tion" law (in the United States) in recent years has been the twin emergence of "outsider" and "backlash" jurisprudence from the legal academy, both in reaction and follow-up to liberalism's sociolegal legacies: many other lively and incisive formations also have arisen during this time, both within and beyond the legal academy, but these two represent the most sharply contrasting descriptions of liberalism, and prescriptions for a jurisprudential follow-up to its social and legal antidiscrimination legacies.

While it would be a terrible oversimplification to view either backlash or outsider jurisprudence as a monolithic formation, these two contemporary camps do repre-sent recognized discourses on law, policy, and politics – and on their substantive relationship to society and culture – that bracket the jurisprudential landscape; in effect, outsiders and backlashers present to the nation a policy crossroads in the present phase of the historic and fitful national march from slavery to segregation to antidiscrimination and, perhaps, beyond. From today's vantage point, it is not hyperbole to observe the two jurisprudential formations locked in a resolute struggle over the direction of history's arc in the national (and international) articulation of the values that have come to be known as the antidiscrimination principle (Brest, 1976). However, the two camps are very differently situated in structural and political terms: in the past two decades, backlash scholarship has sprung from its origins in the nation's legal academy and now occupies the federal courts, from where its preferences are inscribed into law. The latter, meanwhile, remains chiefly in the academy, from which it continues to elaborate the insights, methods, and principles that may guide equality's legal revival some time in the future.

The basic question on which both camps pivot is whether the historic national march must continue, or be rolled back. For backlashers, the imperative is a return to "tradition" while for outsiders the need is for "antisubordination" social change. For normative grounding and doctrinal guidance, the former looks to the past while the latter looks to the bottom. These twin jurisprudential developments thereby represent a simultaneous and conflicted process of theoretical expansion and doctrinal contraction that reflects a larger and volatile sociopolitical phenomenon.

This larger phenomenon – termed *kulturkampf* by Antonin Scalia in his dissent from the Supreme Court's ruling in *Romer v. Evans* (1996) – has been described more widely and commonly as the "culture wars" of the past quarter century (Hunter, 1991). The culture wars, as outlined below, are conducted with a manifest recognition that culture always involves power, and so is partly responsible for the differences in individuals' and groups' abilities to define and meet their needs. These "culture" wars professedly are about the "soul" of the nation – as represented by the distribution of rights and their social effect on the allocation of goods across and among "different" groups: the culture wars, including their jurisprudential dimension, represent a cultural counter-revolution to reassert "traditional values" disturbed during liberal reforms that accommodated and facilitated social change in the latter half of the twentieth century and to reassert the right to dominance of "traditional values" in cultural, economic, and political terms. The culture wars are aptly named: they are about culture and its construction of power in law and society; the culture wars are about shaping and reshaping social life by law.

In large part, therefore, the antidiscrimination principle – its past, present, and future – has been the site for many of the culture wars' themes and battles. In the form of backlash jurisprudence, the culture wars depict the use of law and policy not only to construct social culture but also to achieve the supremacy of a particular normative conception of "culture" using constitutional rhetoric. The politics underlying the culture wars are, in some basic ways, therefore akin to the politics of cultural fundamentalism: a "return" to "tradition" that valorizes colonial and neocolonial arrangements. The antidiscrimination principle, or rather its social potential, stands in the way of these "traditional" politics and their sociolegal hierarchies.

This larger phenomenon has generated a fresh layer of sociolegal experience from which to draw new insight, especially relating to antidiscrimination areas of study, because the chosen principal means of antidiscrimination rollbacks pursued via cultural warfare is law and policy. These culture wars thus provide a current phenomenon upon which to apply the basic postulates of cultural studies about law – including its constitutive social roles (Coombe, 1998). These culture wars represent, in some basic ways, law *as* society.

Thus, while many lenses may be used to help understand recent developments in the law, policy, and jurisprudence of antidiscrimination, the culture wars provide a social frame with much explanatory power. They contextualize the emergence and evolution of both jurisprudential camps – and their common point of departure: liberalism's legacies. Indeed, these culture wars frame all contemporary jurisprudence – whether backlash, outsider, or in-between. They have much explanatory power because contemporary jurisprudence generally – and the backlash and outsider genres in particular – are part and parcel of these culture wars.

Against this historical backdrop and in contemporary context, the current jurisprudential status quo, in the most general terms, may be described as the coexistence of three basic conceptions of "equality" – or of a socially just society – through "antidiscrimination" law and policy: (1) the "formal equality" conception of liberal jurisprudence, which triumphed in the 1930s–70s to affirm the repudiation of *de jure* discrimination and remains generally, but increasingly less, embedded in the fabric of law; (2) the neocolonialist or traditionalist conception of backlash jurisprudence, which arose in the 1970s and 1980s to "roll back" the perceived and actual social effects of liberalism's formal triumphs, and today increasingly succeeds in repealing or undermining liberalism's antidiscrimination legacy and in checking its social effects; and (3) the "antisubordination" conception of critical outsider jurisprudence, which emerged in the 1980s and seeks to build on liberalism's gains to transcend its limitations socially and materially, while resisting the rise of backlash and its contraction of the law to reverse social antidiscrimination progress. With the culture wars as context, this chapter outlines and describes the status quo, focusing on these three chief "schools" of antidiscrimination thought in the United States as reflected in the recent literature.

LIBERALISMS AND LEGACIES: EQUAL OPPORTUNITY, AFFIRMATIVE ACTION, AND . . . ?

The background for today's antidiscrimination status quo is set by the coincidence of a fairly constant "liberal" sway over the federal Congress, Executive, and Supreme Court during the 1930s to 1960s and a period of national ferment that witnessed "liberation" movements like the labor movement, civil rights movement, women's rights movement, student antiwar movement, gay-lesbian-bisexual liberation movement, and environmental movement. That historical coincidence produced the so-called "second reconstruction" – a body of federal legislation, executive orders, and constitutional precedents that collectively represented the most recent formal repudiation of federal legal support for neocolonial structures of systemic subordination. That repudiation focused largely on "race, color, creed, national origin, and sex" – some of the main identity axes that, throughout the nation's history, had been deployed legally and culturally to elevate over the remainder of contemporary society those categories of persons and groups identified with some of the "original" immigrants who colonized North America and surrounding continents. But the labors necessary to bring about that national, incremental, and still-unfinished repudiation has spawned a new and broader awareness of "identity" and "difference" in relationship to law and equality, an awareness that helps to account for both outsider and backlash jurisprudence.

Those antidiscrimination enactments achieved significant social effects: empirical studies report, and no one really doubts, that some improvements in the social and material conditions of traditionally subordinated communities have taken place due to formal civil rights reforms. But formal equality never disturbed the basic neocolonial color and character of the pre-existing socioeconomic hierarchy in the United States. Its success was in loosening the exclusive grip of "traditional" elites over the resources of the country, and in allowing a few from "traditionally" marginalized groups access to long-denied knowledge and power. Over time, social experience with formal equality showed how liberal antidiscrimination reforms were limited in everyday life.

For example, the formal and normative focus on equal opportunity as the objective of liberal legal reform effectively bifurcated theoretical "opportunity" from social reality, allowing dominant groups to salve the nation's conscience without requiring material disgorgement of ill-gotten gains. Similarly, the doctrinal and jurisprudential embrace of "color blindness" as the ideal response to generations of *de jure* subordination blinded the law to inbred inequalities and actual social realities, thus creating a yawning gap between the legal fictions of formal equality and the lived experience of real persons in everyday circumstances. Under these circumstances, a disjunction arose between law on the books and law in society: the formal color blindness of the law did not permit it to "see" the color consciousness of social life. As a result, legal reformation failed to generate social transformation. Instead, "equal opportunity" in employment, education, and other areas became a legally required and well-intentioned intonation of institutions everywhere, both public and private, even as positions of social status and assets of economic value remained concentrated throughout society and the economy largely along "traditional" lines of color, nationality, sex, and other axes of sociolegal identity. In jurisprudential context, then, the brief federal experiment with "affirmative action" – especially the momentary flirtation with "quotas" during the 1970s ended by *Regents of University of California v. Bakke* (1998) – marked both the crest and limits of liberal progress in the nation's incremental progression from slavery to antidiscrimination (Jones, 1988), and represented a peak in efforts to make "equal opportunity" socially meaningful. But at that historical moment, as "affirmative action" became a follow-up concept to implement formal equality socially, the rise of traditionalist backlash had begun to take hold via the culture wars.

Liberalism's jurisprudential and policy losses have been aided by many factors, but one especially relevant to the antidiscrimination principle's vitality has been its conflicted anxiety over accusations – perceptions or realities – of "political" elements in liberal or neo/postliberal jurisprudence or scholarship. These accusations can be traced to the "judicial activism" rhetoric similarly leveled against liberal judges during liberalism's twentieth century heyday. Then and now, these accusations are leveled as such mostly by backlash-identified scholars, activists, politicians, and judges to denigrate the legitimacy of "liberal values" enacted into law during the New Deal and since. These accusations resonate both with the acculturated public, as well as with mainstream liberalisms, precisely because they evoke, literally, the norms and ideals embodied in the values of "formal equality" under the antidiscrimination principle, which have been predominant since the middle decades of the last century: blindness to all except the "merit" of the individual. But the fact –

clearly understood and acted upon both by backlashers and outsiders – is that all jurisprudence and scholarship is necessarily "political" in a highly legalistic society such as the United States. While the former deny it and the latter proclaim it, this mutual recognition is amply evident in the social focus and outcome orientation of both. Only "mainstream" liberalisms remain ambivalent on the question, striving to be apolitical, and sometimes thereby encountering dilution and disorientation.

Confirming the salience of liberal-identified concerns over the law/politics distinction, legal and social mainstream academics in the late 1980s formed an "attitudinal" model for the statistical analysis of judicial decision-making behaviors, measuring the political ideology of judges' rulings against their known or perceived political orientation prior to appointment based on media reports and similar "independent" indicia of personal ideology. This attitudinal model "holds that the Supreme Court decides disputes in light of the facts of the case vis-à-vis the ideological attitudes and values of the judges" (Segal and Spaeth, 1993: 65). It therefore rejects the traditional "legal model" that posits "impartial" judges "objectively" applying "neutral" principles to assure the "principled" reign of the "rule of law" – meaning dispassionate judges, using "reasoned judgment" to apply "fair" principles consistently in their adjudication of private disputes and public issues, regardless of their personal politics or ideological preferences. While various liberal scholars have noted institutional and other reasons to explain these high correlations, including judicial internalization of the "legal model's" precepts, this empirical correlation strikes at the conceptual crux of the law/politics distinction and thus threatens idealized "rule of law" perceptions and aspirations *within* the United States – a concern underscored by the *Bush v. Gore* (2000) intervention of some current appointees to the Supreme Court bench, and in particular the 5–4 order to halt all vote counting in the 2000 presidential election.

This uncertainty over the law/politics distinction was manifest in the "internal" splits within liberal jurisprudence of the 1970s and 1980s, which sharpened existing variations of liberalisms and equality. This split divided, on the one hand, the various "mainstream" centrisms focused on cohering and reconciling legal doctrine through "process" theories and like means of upholding the "legal model" of judicial operations to help preserve and/or comply with the law/politics distinction from, on the other hand, the liberal-identified "crits" who "trashed" conventional accounts of legal doctrine and showed its socially hypocritical inconsistencies. Heir to the socially focused skepticism of the realists and their "hunch" during the earlier part of the same century, though not necessarily to their empiricism, "critical legal studies" emerged in the late 1970s and early 1980s as liberalism's "radical" edge to expose how the law's "indeterminacy" was manipulated for political and ideological ends. This camp trained critical attention on socioeconomic stratification – the construction of class – despite the formal "equality of opportunity" promised to all under liberal law. Focusing on their deconstruction of texts and realities, critical legal scholars dismissed the integrity of formal equality rights, and more generally of law's principled character. Under this critique, "rights" effectively meant nothing because elite-identified judges manipulate "indeterminacy" in accordance with their personal cultural politics. Rather than being a tool of progressive reform, law was a tool of economic privilege, of social control. For these reasons, critical legal studies were labeled cynical, nihilistic, Marxist. Yet critical legal studies have more than stood their ground – today, most observers acknowledge the basic point that judges make "law and policy" in the inevitable junctures of indeterminacy that punctuate adjudication (Kennedy, 1997). This basic stance blurs the law/politics distinction because it postulates that politics motivate law, including specifically juridical acts. This point is the thrust not only of critical legal studies but also of the literature produced in the scholarship that investigates the attitudinal model of adjudication. This basic stance, as we'll see next below, also was the point of departure for certain key strains of outsider jurisprudence. The law/politics distinction, in sum, is central to understanding the ways of today's jurisprudential camps and their approaches to antidiscrimination analysis and policy in the context of cultural warfare.

During this time, other formations, both "internal" and "external" to the legal academy – law and society, law and social sciences, law and culture, law and literature, therapeutic jurisprudence, even liberal strains of law and economics – continued to elaborate the basic liberal values of the twentieth century. Scholars associated with these various genres of scholarship have mapped how discrimination is organized socially, structurally, and economically. They have explored the transnational and cross-cultural dimensions of law. They have threaded interdisciplinary insights and shown how discrimination is organized around ingroups as well as around outgroups – how some practices focus on ingroup privilege and others on outgroup exclusion, thereby not only keeping some groups "out" but additionally keeping specific groups "in." Some of these formations are more "critical" than others, some more color-and-identity conscious than others, some more aware and frank about their cultural politics than others. But as a group, they subscribe to the basic legacy of the antidiscrimination principle bequeathed by the New Deal/civil rights eras. Even as the substance of that subscription is under attack, liberalisms therefore continue unfolding in various shades and strands in antidiscrimination scholarship and jurisprudence. Alongside them, outsiders and backlashers have prescribed sharply contrasting alternatives to influence the immediate and long-term valence of history's arc.

OUTSIDER JURISPRUDENCE: SOCIAL TRANSFORMATION, ANTISUBORDINATION, AND THE "OUTCRITS"

In the early to mid-1980s, outsider scholars were drawn to critical legal studies conferences and related postliberal "networks" to explore the continuing socio-economic stratification of American society despite decades of legal reformation. However, the focus of critical legal studies on "class" did not easily accommodate the study of "intersections" – the interaction of multiple axes of sociolegal positioning that, in tandem, produce complicated patterns of privilege or subordination based on "identity," including the interaction of identities based on class, race, gender, and sexual orientation. The "recognition" of identity-based differentials in social analyses of law's consequences became impracticable in the "critical networks" of those times. Moreover, "rights" mattered more to outsiders: though they shared the crits' view that formal rights often function as a manipulated palliative for a guilty nation's collective conscience, outsiders concluded that "having rights" was better than not. Consequently, in the mid-to-late 1980s a "rupture" occurred between critical legal studies and crit-identified outsider scholars, mostly women and racial/ethnic minorities, who then pioneered the field known today as outsider jurisprudence through the creation of new academic venues focused on the critical study of particular "identities" and their relationship to the social status quo established historically by law (Symposium, 1987).

Thus, in the early to mid-1980s feminist scholars focused critical attention on social and legal discrimination based specifically on sex and gender, while scholars of color inaugurated the critical race theory summer workshops in 1989 to reclaim momentum for racial justice in the wake of formal equality's limited social effects; in this evolution, critical race feminism was spearheaded by women of color to examine multiplicities of identity and discrimination based on race and gender (Crenshaw, 1991; Harris, 1990; Matsuda, 1996). During these times, regional conferences as well as local programs threaded the jurisprudential networks and antidiscrimination discourses of outsiders, including the Asian American legal scholarship conferences. By the mid-1990s, these developments were joined by the initiation of the annual LatCrit conferences, devoted to the study of social and legal issues especially germane to Latina/os communities, and the organization of periodic gatherings for sexual minority scholars engaged in Queer legal studies. Most recently, OutCrits identified with various of these formations have focused on bridging the "domestic" and "international" to help "bring rights home" based, indirectly or directly, on international developments – a focus that generally but critically seeks incorporation of the international to augment domestic understandings of the antidiscrimination principle. The term "OutCrit" consequently signifies both the social position – outsider – and analytical stance – critical – of these multiply diverse formations vis-à-vis law and culture. Yet each genre or strain of outsider jurisprudence came into existence in its own way through series of varied, sometimes overlapping, meetings and conferences, some of which continue and some of which presently do not. The origins of outsider jurisprudence, though traceable to specific events, were relatively spontaneous and disorganized.

But, even in the late 1980s, as outsider jurisprudence stirred, two-thirds of all law faculties had one or less member of color: 30 percent of all law schools had no teachers of color and another 34 percent listed only one. A widely noted survey by the Society of American Law Teachers that studied racial and gender patterns in the hiring, retention, and firing of law faculty in the United States reported in 1988 – perhaps the precise historical moment marking the formation of outsider jurisprudence – that a "typical law school faculty had thirty one members, including those teaching in classrooms and clinics, or holding positions as head librarians or academic deans. Of these thirty one people . . . one was black, Hispanic or other minority [and] five were women," thus creating the "societies of one" that characterized nonwhite faculty representation in the "typical" institutional scenario of the mid-to-late 1980s (Chused, 1988: 538). By the mid-1990s, law faculties averaged 3.4 professors of color per school and 16.7 women per school. Despite the mid-century's equality mandates, the lived experience of traditionally subordinated groups in the closing decades of the twentieth century, as reflected both in outsiders' legal narratives and in the statistical portraits of governmental and other studies, still remained mired in the legacies of the eighteenth and nineteenth centuries. Given these social and professional facts, it is little wonder that narrative as an early technique took hold, for social and intellectual reasons, among outsider pioneers who were in the process of naming and documenting a denied social *and* personal reality: the persistence of discrimination despite decades of formal equality, and despite much social fuss and institutional fanfare about it all.

While their forms of "legal storytelling" began with personal, professional, and social anecdotes, outsider scholars appreciated the structural and systemic nature and dimensions of the social scripts evidenced in those anecdotes. They noted that antidiscrimination commitments generated by a convergence of social interests between minority outgroups and majority ingroups are limited, fragmentary, temporary, unreliable. To substantiate their critical analysis of liberalism's social limits, and to provide normative anchoring for socially relevant reform, outsiders turned "to the bottom" – the search for substantive policy-making insight in the wells of human disempowerment created and supported, in part, through or despite law, including or despite antidiscrimination law. In doing so, they realized that social transformation requires coalition building within and between groups, and that these coalitional efforts must be anchored not in strategic moments of interest convergence, not in the coincidence of "essentialized" identities, but in substantive antisubordination principles collectively generated and mutually practiced. They concluded that coalitional enterprise therefore requires self-critical, as well as critical, consistencies or continuities in analysis and praxis. And they have come to understand that antisubordination theory and praxis entail not only "intersectional" but "multidimensional" frames of analysis and action – frames that account for the "multiplicity" of structures and systems of identity relations that interlock to produce the socioeconomic currents that sweep some along, and Others aside. Seeking to resist the substantive retrenchment of domestic law under the prevailing regimes of backlash jurisprudence and the culture wars, outsider scholars also have begun to mine international sources and comparative frameworks for antidiscrimination and antisubordination potential. While not all outsider scholarship is "critical" in nature, these have been among the basic characteristics of outsider – and especially "OutCrit" – interventions in the legal discourse of the United States since the emergence of outsider jurisprudence in the 1980s.

As a set, these methods have been activated to induce recognition of outgroup claims to social equity not vindicated by liberalism's legacies. Most recently, therefore, outsider discourse has gone beyond "affirmative action" and toward reparations to reinvigorate antidiscrimination policy: while necessarily taking different forms in different contexts, the basic concept of reparations is to help "level the playing field" not by "affirmative action" programs that can be dismissed as a handout to the needy but through repayment of "the debt" due a creditor for labor and other social goods previously rendered but never compensated. Birthed during the onset of the culture wars, outsider jurisprudence has been and remains conscious of position and politics, of circumstances and consequences, as they define and delimit formal versus substantive equality in ever-changing scenarios.

Not surprisingly, each OutCrit genre of legal scholarship has been subjected to the same critique as other "crits" in the legal academy: outsiders have been criticized for turning to narrative rather than empiricism, to deconstruction rather than legal reform, to politics rather than objectivity. As in the case of critical legal scholars, these critiques are cogent to some extent: crits, including outsider crits, openly profess and apply these methods and markers of "postmodern" scholarship. But these criticisms therefore fail to address, much less dislodge, the principal claims staked by outsiders: that color blindness remains a legal fiction that occludes contrary social facts; that formal equality has not eliminated identity-based forms of social discrimination instilled by law; that racism, patriarchy, and other forms of supremacy have been normalized socially and "institutionalized" structurally through generations of *de jure* enforcement and social acculturation; and that the constitutional command of "equal protection" would remain in default until the nation mustered the will to undertake structural transformation (Valdes, Culp, and Harris, 2002). As a whole, then, and apart from controversies over method, this body of "OutCrit" scholarship reflects a collective substantive reaction to and critique of the continuing exclusion and marginalization of women, people of color, sexual minorities, and other "outsiders" from the economic and cultural mainstreams of society, as well as from the legal academy and policy-making venues of the United States, despite the formal legal advances of the civil rights era under liberalism's tutelage.

As this summary indicates, the rise of outsider jurisprudence coincided with the limited increase in the flow of scholars (and students) into the legal academy from groups traditionally excluded on the basis of race, ethnicity, sex, and sexual orientation – an increase allowed and aided, in great part, by liberalism's very reforms: outsider jurisprudence, like all other contemporary formations, flows from liberalism's many and varied legacies. But in historical and substantive perspective perhaps the most significant aspect of this emergence is that it signaled the coalescence for the first time ever of an outsider-identified intelligentsia within the legal academy of the United States, and one devoted to antisubordination imperatives rather than to antidiscrimination promises (Delgado, 1992). The distinction between the two is significant: the antidiscrimination principle is formally color-blind, focused on abstract opportunity. It therefore cannot see, much less target, substantive or structural sources of inequality. The antisubordination mandate, on the other hand, is focused on "substantive" equality: on actual social transformation, which by definition entails ingroups' relinquishment of domination's now-familiar comforts. Under the antisubordination principle, positive recognition of formal rights is a step toward, not the goal nor end of, equality. The distinction between "antidiscrimination" and "antisubordination" represents a shift in foundational principles and purposes for the formulation of law and policy – one to which backlash jurisprudence is diametrically opposed.

BACKLASH JURISPRUDENCE: THE POLITICS OF RETRENCHMENT AND REPLACEMENT

In the most basic of substantive terms, backlash jurisprudence seeks to arrest the redistributive impact and potential of the antidiscrimination principle without formally repudiating formal equality. It seeks not only to prevent further social gains under the antidiscrimination principle but also to reverse the social change already accrued under formal equality during the past several decades in the name of that very principle. Like outsider jurisprudence and critical legal studies, it represents a politically conscious and socially sensitive reaction to liberalism's many legacies – a directly opposed reaction. And as with the crits and outsiders, the emergence of backlash scholarship and jurisprudence in the legal academy of the United States is traceable to specific events in the early to mid-1980s. Today, however, backlash jurisprudence represents more than a strain of legal scholarship. In the wake of the culture wars, it represents the juridical portion of the culture wars. Though it is not, like other jurisprudential formations, a monolithic phenomenon, backlash scholarship and jurisprudence do have a relatively centralized history of origins, development, and action; backlashers seem to have succeeded more than the "crits" in organizing "networks" for the cultivation and dissemination of their ideas.

Formally established in 1982, the "Federalist Society" has served as a central point of incubation for backlash jurisprudence. The Society is organized around various divisions, including one that consists of student organizations at law schools around the country, which serve as "chapters" that have helped to establish "law and policy" student journals, which effectively form a network of periodicals that construct a "discourse" for the dissemination of backlash ideas. Since its founding, the Federalist

Society has become not only the intellectual center for the promulgation and incul-
cation of these ideas in the form of backlash jurisprudence, but also a primary site in
which to train cultural warriors and funnel them into the legal professions for the
purpose of implementing backlash as "law and policy." In particular, the Society has
become a startlingly direct pipeline into the federal judiciary and other law-and-
policymaking apparatuses of the federal government (Landay, 2000).

The Society accounts for one-third of the current Supreme Court: Antonin Scalia,
Clarence Thomas, and the Chief Justice, William Rehnquist, generally are regarded
to be members – although membership is a closely held secret of the otherwise
publicity-oriented group. Generally understood patterns show that those three tap
for prestigious clerkships only or chiefly students within the tightly knit networks of
the Society. One of those three – Antonin Scalia – established one of the Society's
founding local chapters at the University of Chicago Law School while a faculty
member there. That strategic leap was followed with a similar attempt to install in
the Supreme Court another former law professor and backlash scholar who likewise
had spearheaded the establishment of an early local chapter – Robert Bork at Yale.
Though that nomination failed, it forms part of the record in which the Federalist
Society has become the crucible of backlash.

Through this Society, backlash academics set out in the 1980s to establish the legal
framework of social retrenchment, using techniques sometimes described now as "law
and economics" to generate theories about "public choice" that would provide a
justification for the roll back of formal antidiscrimination law and other reforms
initiated during and since the New Deal. To create a professedly "principled" rather
than unabashedly "political" platform for this agenda, backlash scholars and judges
have argued that constitutional interpretation and law should prioritize "original
intent" and "history" or "tradition" to assure that judges are exercising judicial
powers on bases other than personal politics, values, or ideology; this methodology,
backlash jurisprudence explains, assures a "principled" application of "neutral" legal
principles that will legitimize law and distinguish it from politics (Scalia, 1989; Berger,
1997; Bork, 1971). The backlash stance, then, is one of professed formalism based on
the apolitical judge or scholar who objectively and impersonally decides cases through
the consistent and circumspect application of certain and neutral legal rules as
opposed to the politicized analyses and motivations of everyone else – liberals, crits,
outsiders. This stance includes, moreover, explicit attacks on outsider scholarship that
appear calculated to subvert its intellectual integrity and methodologies (Rosen, 1996;
Farber and Sherry, 1995). The rhetorical strategies of backlash jurisprudence therefore work to deny the holdings and findings of the attitudinal model as applied to
backlashing judges and situate backlashers to accuse other jurisprudential formations
of mere "politics" – but the record produced by the texts and acts of backlash
jurisprudes confirms that political ideology is their primary organizing principle.

In retrospect, the 1986 pronouncements of five justices on behalf of the Supreme
Court in *Bowers v. Hardwick* provided an early glimpse of the coming future.
Having recited erroneous "history" to assert "tradition" as a barrier to equal
recognition of same-and-cross intimacy (Goldstein, 1988), the five-judge majority
intoned that: "The Court is most vulnerable and comes nearest to illegitimacy when
it deals with judge made constitutional law having little or no roots in the language
or design of the constitution." This casual reliance on both tradition and federalism
to draw that doctrinal line was portentous. Since then, the repeated yet strategic
invocation of history, tradition, and federalism has become talismanic, dictating

ever-stricter limitations in the doctrinal reformulation of antidiscrimination and other civil rights under both the federal Constitution and other sources of law. Indeed, as widely noted, the reinterpretative process of backlash jurisprudence has effectively inverted antidiscrimination law to license and legitimate "traditional" patterns of discrimination and their stratifying social effects (Aoki, 1996; Crenshaw, 1988; Wildman, 1984). Three years later, in the 1989 term, it became clear that Bowers was to be part of a much larger calculation.

Three of those 1989 rulings – *Atonio v. Wards Cove Packing Co., Inc., City of Richmond v. J.A. Croson, Co.*, and *Patterson v. McLean Credit Union* – exemplify backlash jurisprudence, and its social hostility to civil rights while paying formal lip service to the antidiscrimination principle. The first two focus on race in antidiscrimination employment contexts, both under the constitution and federal legislation, while the latter focuses on race and the Fourteenth Amendment in affirmative action nonfederal set-aside programs. In each case, the majority claimed adherence to the antidiscrimination principle and its remedial mandates. Since this trio of rulings, and with the arguable exception of *Grutter v. Bollinger* (2003), only white people have prevailed before the Supreme Court under the federal Constitution's Equal Protection Clause and in each instance to roll back "affirmative action" programs designed primarily to interrupt self-perpetuating patterns instilled over time by law and implement societally the "opportunity" promised under formal equality. This stunning reversal in the social application of the antidiscrimination principle was accomplished through repeated reversals of direct precedent and ongoing trends that have formed the arc of recent history both domestically and internationally. As Justice Marshall said shortly afterward, "the Court's approach to civil rights cases has changed markedly... It is difficult to characterize last term's decisions as a product of anything other than a deliberate retrenching of the civil rights agenda" (Marshall, 1990: 166–7). Thus by the close of the 1980s, as critical legal studies struggled and outsider jurisprudence emerged, backlash scholarship was becoming backlash jurisprudence: "liberal" precedents were increasingly being overturned, doctrinal revision was intensifying, and the politics of retrenchment and replacement were taking hold. Since then, every single member of the Supreme Court – other than the five forming the current backlash bloc – has done the same as Justice Marshall: since 1989, every court member other than the current backlash majority has dissented vigorously against recently asserted juxtapositions of "civil rights" against "federalism" to dismantle both areas of law as they incrementally have been put into place since the Civil War amendments, through the New Deal, and up to the civil rights era (Leuchtenberg, 1966).

To engineer this sweeping restructuring, the cases since 1995 – another turning-point term, with rulings such as *Adarand Constructors, Inc. v. Pena* and *United States v. Lopez* – have focused on, but certainly not been limited to, four constitutional provisions and their interaction in or with civil rights law. The first, Congressional power under the Commerce Clause of Article I, is the only one of the four found in the body of the original document. The other three are found in the amendments to the original: the Tenth Amendment, the Eleventh Amendment, and Section 5 of the Fourteenth Amendment, which contains its enforcement provisions. The Commerce Clause and Section 5 have proven over history to be the main sources of federal legislative authority over civil rights law and policy – over federal authority to legislate the antidiscrimination principle into law, and to enforce the Equal Protection Clause of the Fourteenth Amendment in relatively proactive ways, as illustrated by the landmark cases of *Heart of Atlanta Motel v. United States*

(1964) and *Katzenbach v. McClung* (1964). Using the Tenth and Eleventh Amendments, by the mid-1990s these five judges were prepared to halt that history: in the cases that followed, the five current backlash judges single-handedly have sidelined the main constitutional tools used historically by Congress to enact into law federal antidiscrimination policy, thus turning back the hands of time to the 1930s, when a similarly activist group of judges on the Supreme Court used that tribunal to block federal power to legislate social or formal reform.

As this sketch indicates, the factual details and doctrinal crannies of backlash jurisprudence are myriad, but the overarching pattern of substantive and social results is not. In *Bowers v Hardwick* (1986) and *United States v. Lopez* (1995), for example, the judges invoked federalism to reduce drastically the role of both judicial and political branches of the federal government in protecting individual constitutional rights under the Fourteenth Amendment and the Commerce Clause. In *City of Richmond v. J.A. Croson, Co.* (1989) and *Adarand Constructors, Inc. v. Pena* (1995) the judges demanded that affirmative action remedies be equated with invidious discrimination and thus be subjected to strict – or "fatal" – judicial scrutiny. In *Atonio v. Wards Cove Packing Co., Inc.* (1989) and *Patterson v. McLean Credit Union* (1989), they eagerly reversed precedent to hike evidentiary standards for civil rights claimants and narrow antidiscrimination remedies available under federal civil rights statutes. In other cases, both before and since the examples noted here, backlash judges have commanded or blessed similar acts that, in effect if not intent, compound vulnerabilities imposed historically by law and society on traditionally marginalized groups or persons (Cross, 1999; Eskridge, 1997; Estreicher and Lemos, 2000; Getches, 2001; Goldsmith, 2000; Hunter, 2000; Jackson, 1998; Post, 2000; Redish, 1993; Siegel, 1997; Ziegler, 1996).

In other culture war cases, for instance, backlash judges have substantially narrowed the reproductive rights of women to make "choice" little more than a legal formality for less-privileged women; severely curtailed the Voting Rights Act to undercut minority electoral strength, as well as local and federal power to act on behalf of minorities under the statute; drastically reduced the constitutional protection of individuals' rights against the state's accusation of criminality; and repeatedly undermined indigenous cultural rights and constricted tribal self-governance for American Indians. Using doctrinal as well as procedural devices, the substantive and social bottom line of these and similar backlash rulings is the social and economic reconsolidation of "traditional" hierarchies in which groups, persons, or interests identified with Anglo, white, Christian, and heterosexual "traditions" are elevated systematically and culturally over sectors or aspects of society associated with non-Anglo, nonwhite, nonheterosexual, non-Christian traditions. The pattern of substantive and social results formed over time by the "traditional" form of identity politics manifest in backlash jurisprudence is consistent when tracked along the fault lines of the culture wars: when state power is used on behalf of "traditional" outgroups, or to uphold the "liberal" legacy of the twentieth century somehow, the use of state power is judicially invalidated or narrowed, either directly through substantive pronouncements or indirectly through procedural and similar roadblocks; when, on the other hand, state power is used on behalf of "traditional" – or neocolonial – ingroups, or to retrench the "liberal" legacy somehow, the use of state power is judicially accommodated, congratulated, and validated. As we see next below, backlash jurisprudence therefore is integral to the success of cultural warfare against "traditional" outgroups and on behalf of "traditional" ingroups.

THE CULTURE WARS: LEGAL REFORM, NEOCOLONIAL REACTION, SOCIAL CONFLICT

As with backlash and outsider jurisprudence, the stirrings of today's culture wars go back to the 1970s and 1980s, to the times when the liberal antidiscrimination initiatives of earlier decades were increasingly contested from all sides. But the moment of its official declaration occurred in 1992, from the podium of the Republican National Convention, when presidential contender Patrick Buchanan explicitly declared "cultural war" for the "soul of America." Since then, the invocation of "cultural war" to explain and motivate social, legal, and political action has taken place repeatedly and increasingly: in 1980, the year of Reagan's election, the term was used in public newspapers, magazines, and related media only four times, in 1990 it was used 76 times, and in 1992 – the year of formal declaration – 575 times. By the turn of the century, in the year 2000, the term had been used 1,902 times, including in the tense context of resolving the November 2000 presidential election: at that time, as the postelection voting issues remained in contest, a backlash-identified talk show host based in the nation's capital declared, "This is culture war – two mutually exclusive world views continue to fight for preeminence in our culture" (Kuhnhenn and Hutcheson, 2001). And the term's use in published court opinions is not limited to Scalia's invocation of *kulturkampf* in his *Romer v. Evans* (1996) and *Lawrence v. Texas* (2003) dissents: the term appears in several other opinions in which the judges describe the cases as exemplars of the culture wars, or refer to the culture wars as the social context for those controversies. The culture wars, then, are not a theoretical construct, but rather an increasingly documentable phenomenon that is concrete both in legal and social dimensions and discourses. As described below, the culture wars' three fronts, or "prongs," of attack, concentrate on interrelated levers of sociolegal control – majoritarian politics, judicial review, and public spending – to mount a "take back" campaign focused on the antidiscrimination principle and its liberal legacies.

The first of these fronts or prongs, the targeted use of majoritarian politics to repeal or undermine "liberal" legislation or precedent, is primary because it sets the stage for the second and third prongs or fronts. This first prong has taken two principal forms. The first, as indicated by the historical notes above, has been the capture and domestication of the "representative" branches of the federal and state governments. But when these conventional sorts of electoral politics have fallen short, as they sometimes do, majoritarian cultural warriors have turned this first line of attack toward "popular" referenda to commandeer policy making when elected officials hesitate to play backlash politics. At both the federal and state levels, this principal prong of the culture wars has been trained on antidiscrimination targets.

At the state level, this "direct" form of electoral attack has produced Prop. 187, and then Prop. 209, in the bellwether state of California. In formal terms, these two propositions generally mandated the exclusion of "undocumented" (and mostly nonwhite) persons from state programs or services and the dismantlement of affirmative action based on race, ethnicity, and sex. In social effect, these two propositions materially and symbolically have made pariahs of undocumented residents and resegregated state educational institutions. This form of attack also is aptly illustrated by the "popular" campaigns to overturn judicial antidiscrimination rulings under the state constitutions of Hawaii and Alaska in same-sex marriage cases through a direct amendment of those states' fundamental charters. In both states, the judiciary had determined that equality provisions in those state constitutions prohibited *de jure* discrimination in marriage laws on the basis of sex or sexual orientation, but "popular" reaction restored the reign of formal inequality. Quite explicitly by the 1990s, this primary front or prong of the culture war had been mobilized in the name of the "angry white male" bent on taking back what he still imagines naturally his. This "front" of the culture wars, then, exploits the numerical, structural, economic, and social capital that historically has benefited earlier immigrants from the European colonial era on the American continents and their successors as recognized and recognizable social groups.

This prong is not simply majoritarian politics-as-usual, wherein self-interested "factions" are expected to jockey for social and economic goods, but rather a concerted multipronged campaign for the "soul" of the nation in which the "enemy" consistently is a historically marginalized and now-vulnerable social group. In effect, this targeting amounts to a kind of "cultural cleansing" that in the course of events will leave the purified society looking and feeling like the 1780s as much as politically and physically possible. This repeated resort to "direct democracy" to circumvent the processes and outcomes of "deliberative democracy" and impose instead a fixed conception of culture as a matter of substantive law has raised questions about the meaning of "democracy" in a society putatively devoted not only to republican self-government for its own sake, but as a means toward a foundational yet long-postponed aspiration that still adorns the portico of the nation's Supreme Court: "Equal Justice for All."

At the federal level, this core effort is proximately traceable to the politics of Richard Nixon and his assertion of a "silent majority" seething quietly against the social effects of the preceding legal progress in domestic civil rights, but the watershed moment was the 1980 election of Ronald Reagan and the occupation of the White House by his savvy coterie of handlers, who especially in the second term used every institutional means available to arm backlashers for the culture wars. However, perhaps the pivotal moment of triumph in the steady escalation of culture war through majoritarian electoral politics came in the 1994 congressional elections, which put into legislative office the standard bearers of the "Contract with America" and its agenda of reactionary traditionalism and sociolegal retrenchment. That "contract" called for sweeping overhauls of immigration, welfare, civil rights, and similar areas of law designed to cut back individual rights and public funds in each instance. And when some of these welfare and immigration "reforms" were enacted into law during the mid-1990s, they combined with prior and ongoing efforts in backlash lawmaking (and jurisprudence) to reduce antidiscrimination protections and minimize public lifelines to vulnerable individuals and communities.

The cumulative results of this first prong or front has been twofold: first, as summarized above, "direct" democracy has been orchestrated to gut the civil rights laws "deliberative" democracy, thereby steadily (re)normalizing a social environment increasingly hostile to immigrants, sexual minorities, racial and ethnic minorities, women, the poor, the disabled, and other Others; and second, as described below, the use of this electoral clout has helped launch the second prong or front of the culture wars, thereby shielding and coddling first-prong efforts. This second prong, the installation into lifetime federal judgeships of persons who will use federal judicial powers to reinforce the gains made under the culture wars' first prong or front, is a strategic move made both to protect backlash legislation as well as to clip back "liberal" or inconvenient precedent. Hence, the interactive, synergistic nature of the culture wars' various prongs or fronts.

The second line or prong of attack amounts to court packing, pure and simple, but on a massive and increasingly organized scale. The electoral tides generated under the first prong have enabled a restocking of the national judiciary on the basis of race, gender, class and – especially – ideology to restore the dominance of selected "traditions" and those they favor in law and society: by way of example, it is no simple coincidence that approximately two-thirds of all federal judges remained white, Anglo and male in the year 2002; that most recently, during the seven years between 1995 and 2002, the net increase in federal judges of color was a mere three – from 134 in 1995 to 137 (of 862) – despite the increasing multiculturalism of the nation's population (Alliance for Justice, 2002; Federal Judicial Center, 2002). It is no simple coincidence – nor mere reflection of "individual merit" – that so many of these new backlash judges have been drawn from the ranks of the Federalist Society.

At bottom, the principal twin purposes of this second line or prong have been, first, to neutralize the federal judiciary as a check on backlash lawmaking under prong one and, second, to reverse the New Deal-to-civil rights legacy of liberalism – including a bright-line rejection of international developments or standards in domestic law, at least when they might have the effect of invigorating antidiscrimination rights. This recomposition campaign has ensconced backlash scholarship as law: the jurisprudential results, and the categorical consistency of the social "winners" and "losers" under those results perhaps are most crisply exemplified by the Supreme Court itself, as discussed earlier. In those cases, as noted above, backlash judges maneuver to produce substantive and social results that minimize both individual rights as well as state and federal power to legislate and enforce civil rights; in those cases, doctrinal and technical devices are interposed strategically to revise or upset precedent and engineer a general regression of the antidiscrimination principle both in law and society. The apparent and growing divergence between word and deed under formal equality has prompted serious skepticism about the present efficacy of the "rule of law" within the United States in the wake of backlash lawmaking and jurisprudence.

The third line or prong of attack is the targeted control of the federal spending power to fund or defund particular programs or policies, as the case may be, in order to accomplish de facto roll-backs that cannot be effectuated wholesale, or directly. This third prong perhaps is best illustrated by the funding battles over abortion, legal aid for the poor, and social services for immigrants and so-called "welfare mothers," but it also is shown in the campaign, under the Solomon amendments, to withhold federal funds – including financial aid to students – from universities that do not permit military recruiters and ROTC programs to bring discrimination onto their campuses due to military policies of discrimination on the basis of sex, gender, and sexual orientation. Once again, these examples illustrate the culture wars' focus on the antidiscrimination principle in both formal and social terms: each of these examples, once again, represents a moment of regression in the formal and social life of the antidiscrimination principle under the "traditional" identity politics of backlash law and policy. Again, in this third prong or line of attack, the targets of backlash via the culture wars remain constant: social outgroups made historically marginal and currently vulnerable in cultural, electoral and/or material terms by law's intergenerational enforcement of various formal supremacies.

This prong of the culture wars also works in tandem with the others, as illustrated by *Rust v. Sullivan* (1991), in which the Supreme Court rubberstamped the selective federal defunding of programs that provide abortion-related information to thwart in practice, as much as possible, women's right to informed and unfettered reproductive choice. In this particular case, the Supreme Court approved the federal government's exceedingly lopsided use of its institutional clout to override, as much as possible through this means, all proreproductive views, messages, and choices on a social issue; and it did so in sweeping terms that implicated "values" or concerns for "states' rights" that often are invoked in backlash jurisprudence to disapprove precisely this type of situation. In this particular case, the first prong of the culture wars produced the national legislature with the will and animus to target women's rights for systematic and strategic retrenchment, the second produced the "supreme" tribunal that would undermine reproductive rights jurisprudentially and shield discriminatory or abusive legislation from effective challenges, and the third line of attack – in conjunction with the first and second – produced and protected the federal defunding statute when other jurisprudential and legislative efforts to erase abortion altogether continued to falter despite intensifying traditionalist fire. Under this third line of attack, working in tandem with the prior two prongs of the culture wars, public programs and policies that serve as lifelines to vulnerable communities and groups – including college students who need federal loans to secure an education – effectively are threatened or cut, even though backlashers may not have been able to muster the power to effectuate a direct, substantive take-back of the "right" or "benefit" under assault.

As the preceding discussion notes, the cultural politics of this warfare – including backlash jurisprudence – represent a combination of supremacist Eurocentric ideologies exported globally via European conquest and its attendant kinds of commerce. This combination historically and currently favors the white European male who is propertied, heterosexual, and Christian. It favors European-identified cultures and images – customs, languages, religions, and phenotypes. It disfavors racial/ethnic minorities, non-Christian sects, women, indigenous people, sexual minorities, immigrants (especially non-European ones), the disabled, and other traditionally disempowered groups. It combines, in sum, Europe's predominant strains of racism, nativism, androsexism, heterosexism, and cultural chauvinism, which in the centuries of colonialism were exported globally and, more recently, are being reinforced through the social, economic, cultural, legal, and political processes of corporate globablization. The organizing principle and ideology of backlash politics and jurisprudence thus may fairly be described as a Euroheteropatriarchy – the combination of biases and prejudices that, in backlash hands, reinforces neocolonialism by law in the name of the antidiscrimination principle. As the new millennium begins, history's arc finds the liberal legacy of the antidiscrimination principle poised at a crossroads between the backlash effort to re-establish Euroheteropatriarchy by force of law and the OutCrit effort to infuse it with transformative social effect based on antisubordination imperatives.

CONCLUSION

The domestic ascendancy of liberalism during the postwar period also shaped the design of global human rights, which came to be described in "generational" terms that reflect the liberal conception of "civil rights" and formal equality. Nonetheless, this increasingly international effort has not been entirely delimited by Western taste; the combined effect of the three generations, which include group rights, positive rights, and social-economic rights, go beyond liberalism's promise of "equal opportunity" for atomized individuals. Against the backdrop of the culture wars, this effort has produced an international human rights regime that, in relative terms, stands out against the increasingly cramped premises and contours of individual rights dictated in recent years by backlash jurisprudence in the United States. In this global scheme, Western influence has been projected to the international, but not vice versa; under backlash jurisprudence, which adamantly opposes integration, at least with respect to antidiscrimination law, this status quo is unlikely to change.

As with the domestic situation, international antidiscrimination-related "progress" is neither linear nor neat; the formal and the social are nowhere congruent. But in many, though not entirely consistent, respects, the international flux continues to point toward a formal expansion of these rights globally beyond their liberal Western origins, as illustrated in the country-by-country "Listing of Rights by Category" that tracks the three-generation model internationally of the Human and Constitutional Rights Resource (2002). Their Comparative Constitutional Rights Chart displays how the *formal* rights expansion is taking place around the world in substantive policy terms, again, at least on a formal plane – and in contrast to the *formal* rights contraction underway in the United States. This disjunction of trajectories in domestic and international settings – coupled with the divergent visions of backlash on the one hand, and of critical legal studies and outsider jurisprudence on the other – sets the stage for the pending policy issues that will define the next phase of the historical march from formal inequality, to formal equality, to substantive equality: whither equality's revival?

References

Adarand Constructors, Inc. v. Pena (1995) 515 U.S. 200.

Alliance for Justice (2002) "Status of the judiciary: April 2002 summary update," retrieved from <http://www.afj.org/jsp/notes.html>.

Aoki, Keith (1996) "The scholarship of reconstruction and the politics of backlash," *Iowa Law Review*, 81: 1467–88.

Atonio v. Wards Cove Packing Co., Inc. (1989) 493 U.S. 802.

Berger, Raoul (1997) *Government by Judiciary: The Transformation of the Fourteenth Amendment*. Indianapolis: Liberty Fund.

Bork, Robert (1971) "Neutral principles and some First Amendment problems," *Indiana Law Journal* 47: 1–35.

Bowers v. Hardwick (1986) 478 U.S. 186.

Brest, Paul (1976) "Foreword: In defense of the anti-discrimination principle," *Harvard Law Review* 90: 1–54.

Bush v. Gore (2000) 531 U.S. 98.

Chused, Richard H. (1988) "The hiring and retention of minorities and women on American law school faculties," *University of Pennsylvania Law Review* 137: 537–69.

City of Richmond v. J.A. Croson Co. (1989) 488 U.S. 469.

Coombe, Rosemary (1998) "Critical cultural legal studies," *Yale Journal of Law and the Humanities* 10: 463–86.

Crenshaw, Kimberle (1988) "Race, reform, and retrenchment: Transformation and legitimation in anti-discrimination law," *Harvard Law Review* 101: 1331–87.

Crenshaw, Kimberle Williams (1991) "Mapping the margins: Intersectionality, identity politics, and violence against women of color," *Stanford Law Review* 43: 1241–99.

Cross, Frank B. (1999) "Realism about federalism," *New York University Law Review* 74:
1304–35.

Delgado, Richard (1992) "The imperial scholar revisited: How to marginalize outsider
writing ten years later," *University of Pennsylvania Law Review* 140: 1349–72.

Eskridge, William N. Jr. (1997) "A jurisprudence of 'coming out': Religion, homosexuality,
and collisions of liberty and equality in American public law," *Yale Law Journal* 101:
2411–74.

Estreicher, Samuel and Lemos, Margaret H. (2000) "The section 5 mystique, Morrison,
and the future of federal anti-discrimination law," *The Supreme Court Review* 2000:
109–73.

Farber, Daniel A. and Sherry, Suzanna (1995) "Is the critique of merit anti-semitic?," *California Law Review* 83: 853–84.

Federal Judicial Center (2002) "The federal judges biographical database," retrieved from
<http://air.fjc.gov/history/judges_frm.html>.

Getches, David H. (2001) "Beyond Indian law: The Rehnquist court's pursuit of states' rights,
color-blind justice and mainstream values," *Minnesota Law Review* 86: 267–362.

Goldsmith, Jack (2000) "Statutory foreign affairs preemption," *The Supreme Court Review*
2000: 173–222.

Goldstein, Anne (1988) "History, homosexuality, and political values: Searching for the
hidden determinants of Bowers v. Hardwick," *Yale Law Journal* 97: 1073–1103.

Grutter v. Bollinger (2003) 539 U.S. ——.

Harris, Angela P. (1990) "Race and essentialism in feminist legal theory," *Stanford Law
Review* 42: 581–616.

Heart of Atlanta Motel v. United States (1964) 379 U.S. 241.

Human and Constitutional Rights Resource (2002) "Human and constitutional rights,"
retrieved from <www.hrcr.org.chart/categories.html>.

Hunter, James Davison (1991) *Culture Wars: The Struggle to Define America*. New York:
Basic Books.

Hunter, Nan D. (2000) "Expressive identity: Recuperating dissent for equality," *Harvard Civil
Rights-Civil Liberties Law Review* 35: 1–55.

Jackson, Vicki C. (1998) "Federalism and the uses and limits of the law: Printz and principle?"
Harvard Law Review 111: 2180–59.

Jones, Jr., James E. (1988) "Origins of affirmative action," *University of California-Davis Law
Review* 21: 383–420.

Katzenbach v. McClung (1964) 379 U.S. 294.

Kennedy, Duncan (1997) *A Critique of Adjudication: Fin de Siecle*. Cambridge, MA: Harvard
University Press.

Kuhnhenn, James and Hutcheson, Ron (2001) "Ashcroft is next political flash point; partisan
lines are clearly drawn," *Miami Herald*, January 11, Section 1A.

Landay, Jerry (2000) "The conservative cabal that's transforming American law, the Federalist
Society," *Washington Monthly* 32: 19–23.

Lawrence v. Texas (2003) 539 U.S. ——.

Leuchtenberg, William E. (1966) "The origins of Franklin D. Roosevelt's court packing plan,"
Supreme Court Review 1966: 347–400.

Marshall, Hon. Thurgood (1990) "Transcription of remarks, annual judicial conference,
second circuit of the United States," *Federal Rules Decisions* 130: 166–9.

Matsuda, Mari (1996) *Where Is Your Body? And Other Essays on Race, Gender and Law*.
Boston: Beacon Press.

Patterson v. McLean Credit Union (1989) 484 U.S. 814.

Post, Robert C. and Siegel, Reva B. (2000) "Equal protection by law: Federal antidiscrimina-
tory legislation after Morrison and Kimmel," *Yale Law Journal* 110: 441–526.

Redish, Michael H. (1993) "Taking a stroll through Jurassic park: Neutral principles and the originalist-minimalist fallacy in constitutional interpretation," *Northwestern University Law Review* 88: 165–74.

Regents of University of California v. Bakke (1998) 438 U.S. 265.

Romer v. Evans (1996) 517 U.S. 620.

Rosen, Jeffrey (1996) "The bloods and the crits: O.J. Simpson, critical race theory, the law and the triumph of color in America," *New Republic* 27: 27.

Rust v. Sullivan (1991) 500 U.S. 173.

Scalia, Antonin (1989) "Originalism: The lesser evil," *University of Cincinnati Law Review* 57: 849–65.

Segal, Jeffrey A. and Spaeth, Harold J. (1993) *The Supreme Court and the Attitudinal Model.* New York: Cambridge University Press.

Siegel, Reva (1997) "Why equal protection no longer protects: The evolving forms of status-enforcing state action," *Stanford Law Review* 49: 1111–48.

Symposium (1987) "Minority critiques of the critical legal studies movement," *Harvard Civil Rights-Civil Liberties Law Review* 22: 297–446.

United States v. Lopez (1995) 514 U.S. 549.

Valdes, Francisco, Culp, Jerome, and Harris, Angela (eds.) (2002) *Histories, Crossroads and a New Critical Race Theory.* Philadelphia: Temple University Press.

Wildman, Stephanie M. (1984) "The legitimation of sex discrimination: A critical response to supreme court jurisprudence," *Oregon Law Review* 63: 265–307.

Zeigler, H. (1996) "The new activist court," *American University Law Review* 45: 1367–401.

Further Reading

Abrams, Kathyrn (1991) "Hearing the call of stories," *California Law Review* 79: 971–1052.

Altman, Andrew (1993) *Critical Legal Studies: A Liberal Critique.* Princeton, NJ: Princeton University Press.

Amar, Vikram David and Estreicher, Samuel (2001) "Conduct unbecoming a coordinate branch," *Green Bag* 4: 351–6.

Barnes, David W. and Stout, Lynn A. (1992) *The Economics of Constitutional Law and Public Choice.* St. Paul, MN: West Publishing.

Baron, Jane B. (1994) "Resistance to stories," *Southern California Law Review* 67: 255–86.

Berger, Raoul (1997) "Reflections on constitutional interpretation," *Brigham Young University Law Review* 1987: 517–36.

Blasi, Vincent (1990) *Law and Liberalism in the 1980s.* New York: Columbia University Press.

Bork, Robert (1985) "Styles in constitutional theory," *South Texas Law Journal* 26: 383–96.

Brisbin, Richard A. (1997) *Justice Antonin Scalia and the Conservative Revival.* Baltimore, MD: The Johns Hopkins Press.

Calmore, John O. (1997) "Exploring Michael Omi's 'messy' real world of race: An essay for 'naked' people longing to swim free," *Law & Inequality Journal* 15: 25–82.

Carter, Stephen (1991) *Reflections of an Affirmative Action Baby.* New York: Basic Books.

Chang, David (1991) "Discriminatory impact, affirmative action, and innocent victims: Judicial conservatism or conservative justices?" *Columbia Law Review* 91: 790–844.

Chang, Robert S. (1993) "Toward an Asian American legal scholarship: Critical race theory, post-structuralism, and narrative space," *California Law Review* 81: 1241–1324.

Colker, Ruth (1986) "Anti-subordination above all: Sex, race, and equal protection," *New York University Law Review* 61: 1003–66.

Culp, Jerome McCristal Jr. (1994) "Colorblind remedies and the intersectionality of oppression: Policy arguments masquerading as moral claims," *New York University Law Review* 69: 162–96.

Delgado, Richard and Stefancic, Jean (2001) *Critical Race Theory*. New York and London: New York University Press.

Dong, Selena (1995) "Too many Asians: The challenge of fighting discrimination against Asian Americans and preserving affirmative action," *Stanford Law Review* 47: 1027–57.

Epstein, Richard (1987) "The proper scope of the commerce power," *Virginia Law Review* 73: 1387–1456.

Farber, Daniel and Frickey, Phil (1987) "The jurisprudence of public choice," *Texas Law Review* 65: 873–928.

Fineman, Martha (1995) *The Neutered Mother, The Sexual Family and Other 20th Century Tragedies*. New York: Routledge.

Freshman, Clark (1991) "Beyond atomized discrimination: Use of acts of discrimination against 'other' minorities to prove discriminatory motivation under federal employment," *Stanford Law Review* 43: 241–73.

Gelfand, M. David and Werhan, Keith (1990) "Federalism and separation of powers on a 'conservative' court: Currents and cross-currents from Justices O'Connor and Scalia," *Tulane Law Review* 64: 1443–76.

Gould, William B. IV (1990) "The Supreme Court and employment discrimination law in 1989: Judicial retreat and congressional response," *Tulane Law Review* 64: 1485–1514.

Harris, Cheryl L. (1993) "Whiteness as property," *Harvard Law Review* 106: 1707–91.

Iglesias, Elizabeth M. (1996) "Rape, race and representation: The power of discourse, discourses of power, and the reconstruction of heterosexuality," *Vanderbilt Law Review* 49: 869–992.

Iglesias, Elizabeth M. and Valdes, Francisco (2001) "LatCrit at five: Institutionalizing a postsubordination future," *University of Denver Law Review* 78: 1261–1345.

Jaffa, Harry V. (1994) *Original Intent and the Framers of the Constitution: A Disputed Question*. Washington DC: Regnery Gateway.

Kairys, David (ed.) (1982) *The Politics of Law: A Progressive Critique*. New York: Pantheon Books.

Kairys, David (1993) *With Liberty and Justice for Some: A Critique of the Conservative Supreme Court*. New York: The New Press.

Karst, Kenneth L. (1991) "Religion, sex, and politics: Cultural counterrevolution in constitutional Perspective," *University of California at Davis Law Review* 24: 677–734.

Kelman, Mark (1988) "On democracy-bashing: A skeptical look at the theoretical and 'empirical' practice of the public choice movement," *Virginia Law Review* 74: 199–274.

Kennedy, David (2000) "When renewal repeats: Thinking against the box," *New York University Journal of International Law and Politics* 32: 335–500.

Klarman, Michael J. (1991) "The puzzling resistance to process-based theories," *Virginia Law Review* 77: 747–832.

Kramer, Larry D. (1998) "But when exactly was judicially-enforced federalism 'born' in the first place?" *Harvard Journal of Law & Public Policy* 22: 123–38.

Levit, Nancy (1989) "The caseload conundrum, constitutional restraint and the manipulation of jurisdiction," *Notre Dame Law Review* 64: 321–66.

MacKinnon, Catharine (1991) "Reflections on sex equality under law," *Yale Law Journal* 100: 1281–1328.

Menkel-Meadow, Carrie (1988) "Feminist legal theory, critical legal studies, and legal education or 'the Fem-Crits go to law school'," *Journal of Legal Education* 38: 61–86.

Mezey, Naomi (2001) "Approaches to the cultural study of law," *Yale Journal of Law and the Humanities* 13: 35–67.

Minow, Martha (1990) *Making All The Difference*. New York: Basic Books.

Posner, Richard (1998) "Against constitutional theory," *New York University Law Review* 73: 1–22.

Rawls, John (1993) *Political Liberalism*. New York: Columbia University Press.

Rhode, Deborah (1989) *Justice and Gender: Sex Discrimination and the Law*. Cambridge, MA: Harvard University Press.

Rubenfeld, Jed (2002) "The Anti-antidiscrimination agenda," *The Yale Law Journal* 111: 1141–78.

Scales, Ann C. (1986) "The emergence of feminist jurisprudence: An essay," *Yale Law Journal* 95: 1373–1403.

Scalia, Antonin (1997) *A Matter of Interpretation: Federal Courts and the Law*. Princeton, NJ: Princeton University Press.

Schlag, Pierre (1997) "The empty circles of liberal justification," *Michigan Law Review* 96: 1–46.

Schwartz, Bernard (1990) *The New Right and the Constitution: Turning Back the Legal Clock*. Cambridge, MA: Harvard University Press.

Spellman, Elizabeth V. (1988) *Inessential Woman: Problems of Exclusion in Feminist Thought*. Boston: Beacon Press.

Steiner, Henry J. and Alston, Philip (1996) *International Human Rights in Context: Law, Politics, Morals*. Oxford: Clarendon Press.

Strum, Susan and Lani, Guinier (1996) "The future of affirmative action: Reclaiming the innovative ideal," *California Law Review* 84: 953–1036.

Sunder, Madhavi (2001) "Cultural dissent," *Stanford Law Review* 54: 495–567.

Sunstein, Cass R. (1996) "Foreword: Leaving things undecided," *Harvard Law Review* 11: 4–101.

Thomas, Clarence (1987) "Toward a 'plain reading' of the constitution – the declaration of independence in constitutional interpretation," *Howard Law Journal* 30: 983–95.

Thomas, Kendall (1992) "Beyond the privacy principle," *Columbia Law Review* 92: 1431–516.

Tushnet, Mark (1985) "Conservative constitutional theory," *Tulane Law Review* 59: 910–27.

Valdes, Francisco (1996) "Unpacking hetero-patriarchy: Tracing the conflation of sex, gender and sexual orientation to its origins," *Yale Journal of Law and Humanities* 8: 161–211.

West, Robin (1994) *Progressive Constitutionalism*. Durham, NC: Duke University Press.

Westley, Robert (1998) "Many billions gone: Is it time to reconsider the case for black reparations?" *Boston College Law Review* 40: 429–76.

Williams, Joan (1991) "Dissolving the sameness/difference debate: A post-modern path beyond essentialism and critical race theory," *Duke Law Journal* 40: 296–323.

Williams Jr., Robert A. (1989) "Documents of barbarism: The contemporary legacy of European racism and colonialism in the narrative traditions of federal Indian law," *Arizona Law Review* 31: 237–78.

Winter, Steven L. (1980) "Indeterminacy and incommensurability in constitutional law," *California Law Review* 78: 1441–1542.

16

The Government of Risks

Pat O'Malley

Twenty years ago, a trawl through the annals of law and society research, including sociological criminology, would have uncovered the merest handful of discussions of risk. Most of these would have taken the form of studies of risk taking among youthful offenders; almost no one studied risk as a *technique* deployed by law and government. Beginning in the mid-1980s, a growing wave of sociolegal research and theory has focused on the rise of risk as a framework in terms of which government is oriented. Commencing with works by Douglas and Wildavsky (1983), Shearing and Stenning (1985), Reichmann (1986), and Simon (1987, 1988), risk has now become one of the central organizing foci of sociological theory, and increasingly of law and society research. There has been some research of this sort carried out in traditional law and society areas – with the bulk being focused on criminal justice, and to a lesser extent insurance law. But for the most part the main wave has focused far less on law than on practices of everyday governance of the self; on the operation of institutions such as environmental agencies; and on the work of professionals in such areas as psychiatry, health, education, and employment. In part, this may reflect the influence of Foucauldian scholarship in the area, which has tended to direct attention toward the "dispersal of government" (Rose, 1996). In part it may also be because other major strands of thought (e.g., Beck, 1992) suggest that risk politics have now escaped the major social institutions and are to be found in the "sub-political" domain that is associated with mass individualization. Whatever the reason, the time is clearly overdue for the analysis of risk and government to extend into many traditional areas of law and society work. This chapter will outline the current shape of the risk and governance field, indicate how it has been developed in the field of criminal justice, and how areas of law largely untouched by the approach – such as torts – provide an almost tailor-made opportunity for law and society scholars to extend its reach.

There is general agreement that the rise of risk research reflects an increase in the extent to which governments, police, the professions, commercial enterprises, and private individuals manage their tasks through intellectual frameworks and practical techniques of risk management. This claimed pervasiveness of risk, and the "risk consciousness" to which it is linked by some writers, gives rise to the term "The Risk Society" (Simon, 1987; Beck, 1992, 1997; Ericson and Haggerty, 1997). Certainly governmental organizations now are extensively involved in such practices, examples including: identifying and managing people "at risk" of offending (Simon, 1998; Hebenton and Thomas, 1996); assessing risks to self and others presented by psychiatric patients (Rose, 1996, 2002); sponsoring and operating risk-screening and preventative programs for pathological diseases (Petersen and Lupton, 1996; Weir, 1996); actively assessing, researching, and managing environmental risks (Douglas, 1992; Douglas and Wildavsky, 1983) and so on. Simultaneously, individuals, families, and communities are being advised on, trained in, and made responsible for the management of risks. Fitness and health is one of the most obvious areas where new risk-bearing profiles and behaviors are constantly being identified and linked with a plethora of techniques from dietary and exercise regimes to prophylactic surgery. Even in financial security and risk management matters, individuals increasingly are advised to make personal provision for risks by the purchase of financial advice, insurance, share market investments, and superannuation. For the middle class at least these have become a part of everyday life.

Such developments are taken to indicate an emerging society based on risk consciousness and risk management. While there are substantial disagreements over the scope, scale, novelty, and causes at issue, a substantial literature exists identifying the array of emerging techniques of governing through risk.

KEY CHARACTERISTICS OF RISK-BASED GOVERNMENT

Risk-based government is most clearly contrasted with disciplinary governance. Disciplinary or "normalizing" institutions and practices of government typically are organized around five elements: establishing an ideal or norm (of health, education, physique, etc); examination to create a unique individual case record; comparison of the individual case with the norm in order to diagnose the problem; bringing the individual into compliance with the norm; using the accumulated evidence to further develop knowledge for use in examination, diagnosis, and intervention. As Foucault (1977) points out, hospitals, schools, courts, prisons, factories, bureaucracies, and universities are all founded on this model. Risk-based government is argued to differ from this "disciplinary" model in certain key respects.

First, government through risk focuses on individuals or cases primarily as members of statistical distributions (risk categories) rather than as unique cases. In risk techniques, individuals are assigned to risk categories, and governed according to this "membership" status. Membership of a motor vehicle insurance risk category is a classic example. Accordingly, the unique case record of the individual becomes less important, except as an aid to such assignment. One frequent consequence is a focus on governing subjects' behaviors rather than their intentions or motivations. Thus strict liability or no-fault techniques may displace civil law negligence or criminal law intent. Likewise, behavioral regulation may also displace rehabilitative reform and its focus on motives and mind states. In line with this, government focuses more on manipulation of distributions than of cases. In "designing-out crime" – for example the speed bump – individuals disappear completely from examination and the frequency of behaviors alone is targeted. These models often assume universal abstract "rational choice" actors (e.g., rational drivers will slow down or suffer automatic penalties in the form of discomfort and/or damaged vehicles). As this suggests, professional diagnosis and treatment of individual cases is downgraded in favor of highly routinized classification of cases against risk indicators linked with preventative measures. Probation, medical, psychiatric, and police reports have all been subject to such shifts in various jurisdictions. Frequently this has been in response to critiques of the inaccuracy of professional diagnoses compared with decisions based on statistical data (Glaser, 1985; Cohen, 1985).

Second, risk-based government governs the future, through prediction. Consequently, much government disperses from institutions to "the community." This occurs because risk factors and the "at risk" individuals to be targeted are still located in their normal environment – as intervention is required before the predicted harms occur. Intervention may take universal forms (e.g., anticrime streetscape design and CCTV) or targeted forms such as special diets for people "at risk" of heart disease, and "self-esteem" programs for "at risk" young "predelinquents." Indeed, being "at risk" or "a risk" becomes a trigger for government intervention. As a corollary, disciplinary institutions and expertises take on risk-based functions with respect to these new "predicted deviants". Teachers become responsible for assessing student educational, health, violence, and other risks; nurses are enlisted to identify people with "at risk" alcohol consumption; police are required to notify the community about the presence of high risk subjects. Another corollary is netwidening, as problem categories are broadened to include members of high risk categories. Such interventions may effect significant and coercive restrictions on the "at risk" individual. For example the British Crime and Disorder Act 1998 created "Sex Offender Orders." This is a new civil order which can be applied for by the police against any former sex offender whose behavior in the community gives the police "reasonable cause for concern that an order is necessary to protect the public from serious harm from him." There is no test of seriousness with respect to the actual behavior, which has to be considered only in terms of its relevance to the risk of future offending.

As this indicates, while statistical and actuarial data are usually held to be critical to the government of risks, other techniques are also deployed. In areas such as medical diagnosis (Weir, 1996), social work (Parton, 1998), and criminal justice assessments (Kemshall, 1998), statistical data may not be available nor be regarded as adequate to the task. This clinical assessment and professional judgment about risk may play a much more central role than statistical prediction in sentencing parole and probation – even though many argue that the rise of risk reflects disenchantment with such modes (Kemshall, 1998; cf. Feeley and Simon, 1992). Nevertheless, what remains critical is that the orientation shifts away from the individual and disciplinary mode toward the categorical and predictive.

Third, risk-based government is claimed to appear "amoral" because it is less focused on, or concerned with, moral order than is usual. This follows partly from the fact that risks are identified by scientific research or actuarial calculation rather than as emerging out of moral prescriptions. Thereby risks appear as "realities" that it would be irrational to deny, ignore, or resist. In addition, a focus on the prevention or minimization of harms, rather than on normative conformity, means that particular values and moral requirements are subordinated to abstract principles of risk reduction. Thus harm minimization drug strategies such as needle and syringe exchanges may tolerate certain kinds of illegal and morally condemned activities in the name of overall harm reduction (O'Malley, 1999). Such "toleration" has been seen as a critical resource of risk government, allowing it to extend its reach and exercise power at low cost, because of low levels of resistance produced (Simon, 1988). Ironically, while government can appear morally neutral in this process, the individual's failure to govern risks becomes morally reprehensible or irrational. Risk is often a gateway to blame (Douglas and Wildavsky, 1983). Thus what once may have been thought of as chance or accident is now thought of as statistically predictable and thus governable. "Accidents," in this sense of *unpredictable harms*, are becoming a marginal and even a questionable category (Green, 1997).

Despite these appearances of technical objectivity, most critical writers argue that risks are cultural or governmental creations (Douglas and Wildavsky, 1983). First, they are ways of apprehending and dealing with things rather than real things in themselves (Ewald, 1991). For example, while pregnancy remains the same empirical condition as ever, in much medical practice it is being transformed from being akin to an illness, to being a risk-bearing condition. And whatever arguments are made about apparent moral neutrality, the value implications here are frequently near the surface, as with the moral (and sometimes legal) governance of those pregnant women deemed to expose their fetuses to risks. Second, risk is not a real state of things, but a value-laden way of thinking of them and dealing with them. To characterize something as a risk means that it has been judged as an unwanted condition to be mitigated or averted. Focus on the technologies of prediction often leads us to ignore the moral dimension of evaluation that has occurred in the process of their design and operation. Thus, for example, many members of "handicapped" minorities (e.g., people with Down's syndrome) have objected that pre-emptive abortions based on risk identification amounts to a form of eugenics that effectively discriminates against them and denies the value of the lives of those who are "other." To categorize the risk-identification techniques per se as technically neutral is thus to miss the point that they are designed for a moral and political purpose.

While these general features are used to describe the nature of the government of risk, in specific fields its forms are many and varied. Two areas of particular relevance to law and society – criminal justice and tort law – will be explored in more detail.

CRIMINAL JUSTICE AND RISK

No doubt the greatest volume of research into risk-based legal governance has been carried out in relation to criminal justice, broadly conceived. Most especially this has been with respect to crime prevention, actuarial justice, risk-based sanctions, and risk-based policing.

Crime prevention

While crime prevention dates back beyond the formation of Peel's police in the early nineteenth century, recently it both has changed focus and become more central in many countries. Through to the 1980s, crime prevention in Britain and Australia, for example, was primarily a minor aspect of police work, largely focused on routine security matters affecting commercial property; or it was regarded as a matter for broader social planning, addressing the social conditions that generate crime. In this latter respect, nevertheless, it was a marginal issue reflected in short-term and poorly funded projects adjunct to urban planning. However, in both countries, beginning with "safer communities" developments of the mid-1980s, and marked by multimillion dollar initiatives, governments in the mid-1990s have focused on crime prevention as a central component of their crime control strategies. In Australia, even though criminal justice overwhelmingly is a state government concern, the high profile work of the Federal Justice Office and now of the federal government's "National Crime Prevention" project, reflect the priority given to this strategy.

Both separately and in tandem with these developments, police have focused increasingly on crime prevention, developing and incorporating new preventative initiatives. Familiar examples include "partnerships in policing," community policing, Neighbourhood Watch, and Police–Community Crime Committees (O'Malley, 1997). In the mid-1990s Victoria Police estimated that there were 300 identifiable crime prevention programs in that Australian state alone. As these developments suggest, there was a change from the idea of crime prevention as the sole responsibility of police. Since the 1980s and 1990s crime prevention has distinctively focused on risk management and community/individual responsibility. Situational crime prevention and "target hardening" have become more central, moving away from a focus on offenders and the social causes of crime toward dealing with "criminogenic" situations and opportunity structures. Considerable emphasis is placed on the responsibility of potential victims to reduce their "at risk" status. This has been carried out through skilling, awareness, and information programs aimed at increasing accurate recognition of risks, and teaching techniques for risk management and reduction. The British Home Office for example, has run major programs on this, including several focused on women's exposure to crime risks (Stanko, 1996). Residential "communities" are enjoined to become responsible for risk reduction in their neighbourhoods. As well, some nonspatially based associations – such as "the small business community" and the "gay community" – are sometimes enlisted into parallel programs.

"Actuarial justice"

Until the 1980s, it was still the case that individual justice, tailored to the individual offender's needs, was the preferred model in most jurisdictions. Over the past decade other models have begun to displace this. Especially in the USA, and more recently in the UK, Australia, and Canada, sentencing decisions may now be based on the risk profile of the offender. In such processes, very little need be known about the offense or the offender other than the membership of the case in high risk pools. Frequently the sentence is tariff-based and linked to actuarial tables predicting reoffending. Normally these are based on predictors related to offense history. The "three strikes and you're out" models, extensively applied in the USA and to a lesser extent in Australia (see, e.g., Crimes [Serious and Repeat Offenders] Act 1992 [WA]) and in the UK (Hood, 1996) are at least ostensibly based on evidence of the risks of recidivism for such offenders.

By focusing on predictive factors for reoffending, risk-based sentencing may rupture the judicial value placed on proportionality between offence seriousness and severity of sanction. Equally it challenges traditional visions both of individual justice and of just desserts. Nevertheless, actuarial sentencing has been defended as technically "objective," as deterrence-based, and as limiting the scope for judicial bias. It also has been represented as "protecting the public" and thus has an "actuarial" moral and governmental justification in its own right. In the United States, arguments indicting the poor predictive power of professional judgments by judges, psychiatrists, and probation officers have been used to favor sentencing from actuarial tables. It has been suggested that the elected nature of American judges has made them more likely to cooperate with such trends. Declining faith in the social sciences may also be relevant. But equally important may be shifts toward a "victim focus" and toward "accountability" and "efficiency" in justice (Feeley and Simon, 1992, 1994; Glaser, 1985).

Risk-based sanctions

Not only sentencing methods and rationales, but also the nature of sanctions are argued to be increasingly risk-oriented. In particular such orientations are witnessed in the displacement of therapeutic sanctions by those focused more on security. With respect to imprisonment, incapacitation has emerged as a major goal, most explicitly in the USA but also in Britain and elsewhere. This emerges primarily in the explicit role of prisons in "warehousing" offenders who have been consigned to life or long-term incarceration on the basis of their risk of reoffending. The prison in this capacity manages crime risks to the public. Incapacitation is also reflected in emphasis on the cost-effectiveness of imprisonment. Whereas the opposite was argued in the welfare era, recent analyses claim to demonstrate that by taking in the costs both of the crime and crime control measures forestalled by imprisonment, general incapacitation is economically advantageous compared to having high risk offenders at large.

Alongside this shift, all manner of new sanctions have emerged (or been re-invented) that effect risk reduction through incapacitation. These include: curfews for selected offenders, sometimes based on custodial contracts with parents; electronic monitoring of offenders, to restrict movement out of or into high risk zones; intensive correction orders to monitor the risk behaviors of offenders; and detention in hostels focused on risk management (O'Malley, 1992). By only a little extension of this principle, the risk-based, preventative approach has spilled over beyond the array of offenders to govern "at risk" persons or situations – who in a sense become subject to "quasi sanctions." These include the use of curfews keeping all teenagers at home after dark or prohibiting them from certain places such as shopping malls. But most prominent are "Megan's Laws" in the USA and their parallel in the UK, that require community notification of the presence of ex-offenders in order to facilitate risk awareness among residents (Simon, 1998). This clearly raises the vexed question of whether this constitutes an indefinite and cruel extension of sanctions for past offences, especially where – as in some jurisdictions – the person concerned is required to post notices on their domicile. Equally significantly, all future sentencing for such offences thereby bears with it what can be regarded as a punitive postrelease condition. (For a discussion of these juridical disputes, see Levi, 2000.) Such examples indicate a blurring of what it is to be "an offender." While those merely "at risk" usually cannot legally be punished, having committed no crime, risk-reducing interventions (e.g., curfews, reporting requirements, restrictions on movement) may be identical with legal sanctions, and in almost all cases represent a restriction on legal rights. As is also illustrated by the example of blood alcohol content offences, the status of being "at risk" (i.e., having a BAC above a certain level) readily drifts into a new offence in its own right. Extending such preventative logic still further, there are now proposals in the UK to incarcerate persons whose personality disorders represent high risks but who have not previously offended.

Risk-based policing

As noted, police are already involved in crime prevention operations to an unprecedented scale and extent. On top of this, major research in Canada indicates that police have become information brokers in the field of security, primarily operating as gatherers of risk-relevant data and functioning as a clearing house for such knowledge (Ericson and Haggerty, 1997). Such evidence suggests that many aspects of policing are being transformed into risk management, for example by restructuring all incident and other police report forms around risk (e.g., "safety" and "security") dimensions. Police also play an important role in providing information relating to building codes and local government design specifications relevant to crime risk management. In particular this change has been effected through the expanding influence of the insurance industry, the primary risk-based institution in modern societies, which itself has been a major proponent of and participant in the growth of crime prevention.

RISK AND TORT LAW

The emergence of tort law, which largely governed the field of accidental harms, is argued to reflect the ethos of early nineteenth-century liberal capitalism. The development of the central, disciplinary, doctrine of negligence required that legal subjects bore responsibility for harms they inflicted carelessly, and in a sense torts legislated risk awareness. Yet the doctrine of privity of contract reduced risk liability basically to relationships between contracting parties. In the case of workplace accidents this was narrowed still further by doctrines such as *volenti* (positing the employee's voluntary assumption of many risks) and the fellow servant rule (relieving the employer of liability where harm could be traced to negligence of other employees). As a result, harms were largely left to lie where they fell, and little early tort law could be considered "risk management." However, between 1890 and 1940 much of this changed in the direction of insurance-based or actuarial governance. The earliest developments were in the displacement of much "industrial" tort law to workers' compensation schemes in Britain and elsewhere. Responding to difficulties of redress for injury under tort law, a form of social insurance was established, administered by tribunals largely on amoral, actuarial, and no-fault bases (Cane, 1993).

In the following years – for example through *Donoghue v. Stevenson* (1932) in the UK and *McPherson v. Buick Motor Co.* (1916) in the USA – the legal duty of care was greatly expanded as legal subjects' liability for risk was extended to protect all parties foreseeably affected by their actions. By massively increasing their exposure to legal liability, not only did this force risk consciousness on all major parties (employers, manufacturers, transport operators, etc), but effectively it required them to take out some form of insurance coverage. Indeed, as the century progressed, mechanisms such as product and public liability insurance became compulsory for businesses and governments in most jurisdictions. In turn, as the cost of this insurance was built into the price of commodities and services paid for by the populace, much of tort law effectively became a form of social insurance. About the same time, compulsory third party motor insurance emerged to extend the reach of insurance-based risk management still further into the fabric of tort law (Simon, 1997).

The functional impact of these changes led to major debates over the *total* substitution of tort law by social insurances. Criticisms focused on a series of perceived disadvantages of law that could be eliminated or reduced by simpler insurance mechanisms. These included: the enormous transaction costs created by tort law (10 times those of administrative tribunals), the lengthy delays created by legal procedure, prohibitive expense, intimidating atmosphere, the often unpredictable and unjust outcome of trials when compared with insurance procedures, problems associated with the "once and for all" rule in tort damage awards compared with pension schemes available under insurance, and many other criticisms. Most radically, changes were effected in New Zealand during the 1970s, which removed virtually the whole field of accident compensation from the courts to a social insurance fund – a model closely considered and partially adopted elsewhere (in the UK and Australia) in following years. Even in jurisdictions where such fundamental shifts did not occur, explicit risk-managerial thinking further altered the law of torts. For example, under the "deep pockets" principle in the USA, the courts trace liability not to the most immediate source but to that party best able to bear the financial burden of risk – it being more critical to distribute loss in a socially effective fashion than (in a disciplinary fashion) to sheet consequences home to those at fault. One consequence, it is argued, is that the deterrent effect of high insurance premiums which follow from this acts as a further risk-minimizing mechanism by driving out high risk industries and products (Priest, 1990). Or again, the development of class actions acts as a "social" risk-spreading mechanism. For example, in many instances successful actions provide compensation in the form of funds to be accessed not only by those already injured, but also by those suffering harms as yet undetected (e.g., relating to the Exxon Valdez and the Bhopal disasters). As a roll-on effect, many jurisdictions now require high risk industries to contribute to a fund held in reserve to cover the risk of future mass accidents (Abraham, 1986). Linked with this, associated strategies, such as the market share model for allocating damages in joint actions (i.e., where the specific producer of a generic commodity cannot be identified, and damages are shared among the various producers according to their market share) provide close parallels to actuarial sentencing in criminal law. Here, the relevant probability is not that of reoffending, but the probability that the specific producers were responsible for the injury at issue. More recently, there are signs that "preventative" or "anticipatory" damages are being considered and even awarded where recovery is based on the cost of neutralizing risks (Fleming, 1997)

Of course, many of these risk-based changes in tort law long predated the current period usually understood as the era of the risk society. But as this makes clear, the first 60 years of the twentieth century witnessed the rise of systematic government of risk through social insurance technologies. Welfare state unemployment, health, old age and sickness pensions, all operated to spread risk and insure harms through taxation, by redistributing incomes across time and social space. A key question thus becomes whether the techniques of risk are themselves the definitive issue in relation to the current ascendancy of government through risk. Has the past 30 years simply witnessed the continuation, reformation, and growth in the form of long-term processes of risk governance? Or is the contemporary government of risk a novel reflection of much grander changes in the current social and world order? We now turn to consider these theoretical questions.

EXPLANATIONS FOR THE RISE OF THE RISK SOCIETY

Many explanations have been provided for these changes, and a summary paper cannot review all of them. The two outlined here are currently the most influential approaches, and exist more or less at polar ends of a spectrum of generalization – although some have tried to combine the two (Ericson and Haggerty, 1997).

The "risk society" thesis

The work of Ulrich Beck and his followers (e.g., Beck, 1992, 1997; Lash et al., 1994) suggests that the current prominence of risk reflects fundamental contradictions in the industrial-scientific nature of modern society. The past half century has been marked by the development and recognition of global risks created by science and technology. These include environmental pollution and destruction, nuclear contamination from industry and weaponry, and the impact of mass global transportation on the spread of disease. The novel feature of these "modernization risks" is not just their global and undiscriminating impact, but also and especially that they are unavoidable by-products of science and industry. They cannot be eliminated without eliminating the core features of modernity itself. Each new advance thus brings with it new risks. "Progress," the core value of modern societies, thereby is brought into question. As consciousness of harms becomes more pressing and prominent, science is directed by governments and markets to identify and measure them. This scientific work only serves to heighten the sense of insecurity, as more and more as yet unseen and unknown risks are identified. Also, as risk measurement becomes more sensitive, nothing appears as risk free. "Risk consciousness" becomes central, and class consciousness declines. Government and culture become oriented toward the identification and management of risks, and problems previously governed by other means are reframed in risk terms.

Nevertheless, for this approach the techniques of risk per se are not the critical issue – this role is given to consciousness of modernization risks which drives the further development of risk techniques. Thus Beck has no qualms agreeing that the welfare state was "the insurance state" (1992) and relied on risk and actuarial techniques. Nevertheless he claims that the risk society postdates this. He argues that the key characteristic of the welfare state is that its risk management governed the class consciousness and legitimation crises created by the unequal distribution of "goods" (both in the sense of moral benefits and material wealth). This differentiates it fundamentally, in his eyes, from a state where risk consciousness is central, and legitimacy problems arise from the distribution of "bads" (harms). In the risk society, it is stressed, many governmental claims made about the ability to predict, manage, and reduce harms are bogus, especially those relating to global harms.

These risks – for example the effects of global warming and the likelihood of nuclear weapon strikes – are argued, rather, to be uninsurable, either because unpredictable (despite claims by governmental science), because of their scale, or because the harms cannot be rectified with money. In consequence, government through risk appears often as little more than a series of ideological attempts to increase security and downplay the legitimation crisis of modernization risks.

The main strength of the thesis is that it is consistent with the wide spectrum of shifts in science, medicine, and in government, as well as in everyday life. However, the grandiose claims made about global crises generating a universal risk consciousness which displaces or restructures class, race, and gender consciousness are also the source of its main weaknesses. In part this is because little evidence is adduced to demonstrate such a fundamental shift. Overwhelmingly, generalized risk consciousness is asserted rather than documented. Linked with this, the account is pitched at such an abstract level that it is rarely the case that any but the most extended link can be made between the theorized global change and specific changes alleged to be effects or instances of it. The corollary is that the roles of more immediate factors – the impact of business concerns to minimize harm rather than enforce morals, or the fiscal strength of the insurance industry – are either ignored or reduced to a mere effect of global risk consciousness. Also, because of its all-encompassing claims, counterevidence or evidence of other trends is discounted, usually being regarded merely as evidence of "noise" or incomplete transition to the risk society. Consequently the impact of cross-cutting developments in government strategies and techniques – such as a turn toward more punitive and moralistic criminal justice (Garland, 1996) – is not considered. Further, the account deals poorly with the fact that exposure to risk has also come to be regarded as a *positive* force in contemporary consciousness, particularly with respect to risk-taking economic activity. Examples include share market participation, entrepreneurialism, innovativeness, and self-fulfillment (e.g., high risk sports). Here, the risk-aversive consciousness claimed to be dominant is repudiated in contemporary rationalities of neoliberal governance (Simon, 2002).

Despite these many problems, a key strength of the approach is that it is linked by Beck (1992, 1997) to a politics that does recognize positive contributions of risk in major areas (e.g., some medicine). It focuses on the attempt to differentiate such socially positive and beneficial techniques from negative "ideological" interventions, in order that global risks can be dealt with at the root source of modernization.

Governmentality

The governmental approach suggests that large-scale risk management is not a new technique of government, being characteristic of government-based social insurances and similar schemes in the welfare state. It makes no claims about the universality of risk consciousness, or about its social role. Rather, it argues that risk is a variable technique of government, and that the current era is distinguished by the ascendancy of new forms over the "social" forms of the welfare era. Neoliberalism is displacing "social" risk techniques – to which it is hostile – with complex techniques of risk management based on market models, private insurance, and increased individual responsibility for risk management (O'Malley, 1992). Part of this shift is the exposure of subjects and institutions to market risks and the generalized spread of modes of consciousness and techniques of governance seen as indigenous to the business sector (Shearing and Stenning, 1985). This contrasts with welfare social governance, regarded by neoliberals as creating a "no-risk" society and inactive, overly risk-averse, and dependent subjects. Accordingly risk taking (enterprise, innovation, competition) is regarded as being just as important to neoliberal governments as is risk reduction: the key task for government and individual is to know when and how to employ each to maximum advantage.

In this configuration, the role of the state is to promote autonomous risk management by individuals and private sector entities. This is reflected in a number of distinctive features of contemporary risk-based government. One is "empowerment" – the attitudinal and "knowledgable" reformation of individuals. This includes providing carrot and stick techniques for increasing a certain kind of personal autonomy in risk (e.g., restricting access to public health and providing tax incentives to enter private health insurance; providing tax incentives to convert fixed benefit retirement policies into share-based individual retirement accounts). The state also provides basic information on the basis of which "informed choices" may be made about personal governance of risk. This may be seen, for example, with respect to public information programs on crime risks, health hazards, industrial accidents, drug harm minimization, and so forth. In turn, those responsible for creating risks for others (violent offenders, psychiatric patients, drunk drivers, etc) become the target for coercive risk minimization. The extension of the market model also includes constituting crime victims as customers of justice, and places emphasis on shifting the burden of risk from victims to offenders – accounting for the rise of incapacitating penalties in criminal law, risk-based sentencing, and so on.

In general advocates of this approach eschew both the generalization of risk to a characteristic of a whole "risk society," preferring to associate it only with the ascendancy of certain techniques of government. Despite this, and while no claims are made about generalizing risk consciousness, it is argued that broader cultural effects do flow on – for example, the rise of "extreme sports" is understood as an effect of neoliberalism's emphasis on the value of risk taking and self-fulfillment (Simon, 2002).

The approach accounts well for the salient redistribution of risk managerial roles between government and individuals in the past 20 years, and for the distinctive forms recently being taken by many risk-based government and commercial programs. It also makes more direct and empirically mappable links between particular initiatives and the broader processes generating risk-based government. However, its heavy emphasis on the political dimensions of risk places a number of limitations on its utility and plausibility. It underestimates the extent to which the ascendancy of risk management reflects the increased capacity of science and medicine both to identify and deal with risks, and the positive model this has provided for intervention more generally. Likewise, its (implicitly hostile) reduction of risk to a reflex of political ideology compromises the model's capacity to evaluate the benefits of different risk-based approaches. Furthermore, most analyses take for granted that neoliberalism is politically unrivaled, and create an overdrawn picture of consistent neoliberal risk management. The approach thus frequently is accused of assuming the success of the neoliberal project and blinkering itself to the consideration of alternative developments (Frankel, 1997).

The Future of Risk

Taking these principal positions together, it can be argued that each is too one-dimensional. Related research has tended to accumulate convenient examples for illustrating and exploring the novelty and prevalence of contemporary risk-based government. One result is that the spread and reach of risk-based government may be exaggerated. Another, perhaps more critical, is that there are many key issues about which little is known. For example, there has been little exploration focusing on the variety of technologies and models of risk management deployed (e.g., actuarial, clinical, or experiential; probabilistic and nonprobabilistic; individually or collective in focus etc). The combinations and distributions of these have not been charted or built into much theory. Also, the models developed have focused on the novelty of risk-based government, and have generally failed to consider key questions. These include how risk interacts with other modes of government, in which fields risk develops most or least readily, what hybrids form and how they are managed, and what are the conditions that restrict the application and growth of risk-based government.

Despite occasional lapses, neither of the major approaches would propose that risk-based government necessarily will continue to expand or intensify, nor that the nature and directions of any such growth can be readily predicted. A salutary lesson in these terms is to be learned from the field of drug regulation. Risk-based programs in harm minimization (needle and syringe exchanges, safe injecting facilities, provision of bleach sachets, and a score of other measures), which are almost taken for granted in much of Europe and Australasia, have been frustrated or simply ruled out of court in the USA under the "War on Drugs" (Broadhead, 1991). On the other hand, such risk-based tactics as workplace drug testing – even where these contribute little or nothing to workplace safety – have become commonplace in the USA but are infrequently met with elsewhere (O'Malley and Mugford, 1992). Risk is not politically consistent, it is simply a variable technique, and it may be deployed in different forms to quite distinct ends by parties with divergent and even diametrically opposed ends. When this is linked to the open-ended and innovative nature of politics and policy, exercises in prediction about the future of risk rapidly come unhinged. This caution is vital to observe.

In the first place, the politics of legal governance are often volatile – as is readily witnessed in criminal justice. Currently, an enormously diverse array of strategies and philosophies can be seen at work alongside and in competition with incapacitation regimes. These include punitive models (e.g., just deserts sentencing, the revival of chain gangs and expansion of the death penalty); disciplinary models as in intensive corrections and boot camps; reintegrative justice conferences; and even "enterprising prisoner" models (where prisoners are progressively given increasing responsibility for governing their own lives and programs). None of the latter can readily be understood as "risk-driven." Yet with which does the future lie? Even the future of crime prevention is hardly assured. Evidence in support of the cost-effectiveness of risk-based techniques in this area is equivocal, and there is no guarantee that these will continue to gain or sustain support (Brandon, 1999). Moreover, there have been sustained attacks on risk-based models on the grounds that they are discriminatory. For example, arguments that women should become more skilled in minimizing the risk of crime victimization has been assailed as victim blaming and as ignoring the social determinants and real sources of women's criminal victimization (Stanko, 1996).

There has also been considerable resistance to the introduction and spread of risk-based models in the field of sentencing. The judiciary has long been a source of resistance in this respect, and their concerns with the violation of principles such as the proportionality of offence and sanctions are pervasive and often effective (Freiberg, 2000). In this respect it should also be stressed that notions of individual justice resonate strongly with liberal and neoliberal politics and may work against the proliferation of risk. Which themes come to the fore in the politics of any liberal government is rarely certain. Considerable resistance has also surfaced in criminal justice bureaucracies. Recent research indicates that administrators and state lawyers' recognition of the potential for risk-based sentencing to swamp the courts and the prisons has been among an array of factors that has made "three strikes and you're out" policies in the USA frequently inoperative in practice (Austin, Clark, Hardyman, and Henry, 1999).

Much the same can be said about civil law and justice. Thus proponents of the "governmentality" model could – in terms of the rise of neoliberal politics – account readily for the fact that the expected "death of torts" and its displacement by socialized accident insurance has not occurred. This certainly makes sense of developments in Britain and Australia during the 1970s, where the New Zealand scheme was considered but rejected. It also makes sense of the New Zealand situation itself, in which the scheme has been progressively reined in over the past 20 years (Palmer, 1998). But is it so easy to predict what forms tort law will take in the future? Even if we accept the ongoing ascendancy of neoliberalism, and the place of risk in this formation, will the future take the form of mass first party, all-risks insurance and the associated demise of torts (Atiyah, 1998)? Or will it take the form of a revitalized tort law based on individual deterrence as proposed by the Chicago School, and only by imaginative overreach seen to be risk-related? Either would appear to be consistent with neoliberal concerns.

An alternative proposition is that, contrary to assumptions of macro forces leading the government of risk, there is little reason to assume that the properties of current techniques of the "risk society" are necessarily fixed and its growth inevitable. This would suggest that just how government through risk will develop is likely to depend very much on the ways in which risk techniques and mentalities are deployed. Risk, as has been seen already, may certainly be used oppressively. But in some cases, risk-based models may be (and are being) used to deliver resources to poor and oppressed people, and arguments that they provide better protection for victims than offender-focused correctionalism cannot be dismissed out of hand. If this "political" interpretation of risk's future is accepted, then it becomes vital to understand the strengths and limitations, benefits and dangers of specific techniques and practices, and to develop a politics of risk to which theory and research can provide some guidance.

CONCLUSIONS: A SOCIOLEGAL AGENDA FOR RISK RESEARCH

While the two areas selected as illustrations of risk-based governance in this chapter are drawn from mainstream areas of law, it is clear from the discussion that law is just one of many sites in which risk has moved to become a major *telos* of government. Yet, as noted, with the exception of criminal justice, law has been perhaps the least examined field of all. This may be surprising, as many of the risk-related issues raised above with respect to tort law would be familiar to critical tort law scholars. Yet the fact of the matter remains that even these clearly relevant and already well developed debates have not yet been drawn into the mainstream discussion of risk. Probably the most important conclusion to be drawn, in consequence, is that a large, significant, and promising research agenda exists for sociolegal scholars concerned to explore key issues in the risk society literature. Much of this may involve basic but vital questions such as those intimated in the previous section, concerning the extent and nature of any shift toward risk in diverse areas of law. This, perhaps, may be seen simply as "applying" this risk model rather than developing it. But critical theoretical questions are perhaps *best* addressed in the law and society field.

To begin with, the overwhelming emphasis in risk research has been on negative models of risk: risk avoidance, risk reduction, and risk spreading. But with respect to the corporate sector risk has been valorized by neoliberals as the source of wealth and public good. While it is not necessary to agree with these claims, they represent a series of theoretical challenges. If risk has primarily been examined as a technique for mitigating harm, how should we proceed in considering its governmentally envisaged role in creating benefits? In the risk society literature, little or no research has examined the development of contract law as a technique for creating a stable environment in which entrepreneurs proceed to exploit risk (O'Malley, 2000). Likewise risk research has failed to explore recent changes in contract law in response to various neoliberal emphases on the centrality of markets, competition, and increased innovativeness. The same applies to corporate and "competition" law, which clearly have been extensively remodeled to promote "responsible risk taking" (Wilson, 2000). What are the changes occurring in these areas and how extensive are they? How should the "risk society" literature respond in trying to understand such techniques' "positive" risk – that is, what can we say about the ways in which risk is imagined to create maximize wealth creation through manipulation of legal technique?

Even if we consider only the mainstream concerns with risk as a defensive technology, it is surprising how little research has appeared on recent changes in such key areas as insurance law. In Australia, for example, the definitive requirement that parties to an insurance contract must have an "insurable (i.e., fiscal) interest" in that which is insured, has recently been abandoned. Yet from its introduction in the "Gaming Act" of 1774 (14 Geo III c.48) this requirement has been a principal means of distinguishing between insurance and gambling. Is this linked with the reinvention of gambling as a "leisure industry"? What implications has it for legal and social conceptions of both risk and insurance in the light of the momentous debates over the morality of insurance that characterized the nineteenth century (e.g., Zelizer, 1979)? Does it, in its turn, signal a reconceptualization of insurance as a positive rather than simply defensive technique of risk?

The list is almost endless, for no matter where we turn with respect to law, current issues of risk surface. And by implication alone, all law has been subsumed under the generalizations of risk society theorists. That these generalizations are often overblown, and in consequence in need of considerable refinement, is not in doubt. The agenda for law and society research thus is very clear.

References

Abraham, K. (1986) *Distributing Risk. Insurance, Legal Theory and Public Policy*. London: Yale University Press.

Atiyah, P. (1998) *The Damages Lottery*. Oxford: Hart.

Austin, J., Clark, J., Hardyman, P., and Henry, D. (1999) "The impact of 'three strikes and you're out'," *Punishment and Society* 1: 131–62.

Beck, U. (1992) *Risk Society: Toward a New Modernity*. New York: Sage.

Beck, U. (1997) *World Risk Society*. Cambridge, UK: Polity Press.

Brandon, C. (1999) "Value for money? A review of the costs and benefits of situational crime prevention," *British Journal of Criminology* 39: 345–69.

Broadhead, R. (1991) "Social constructions of bleach in combatting aids among injecting drug users," *The Journal of Drug Issues* 21: 713–37.

Cane, P. (1993) *Accidents, Compensation and the Law*, 5th edn. London: Butterworths.

Cohen, S. (1985) *Visions of Social Control*. Cambridge, UK: Polity Press.

Donoghue v. Stevenson (1932) AC 562.

Douglas, M. (1992) *Risk and Blame. Essays in Cultural Theory*. London: Routledge.

Douglas, M. and Wildavsky, A. (1983) *Risk and Culture*. Berkeley: University of California Press.

Ericson, R. and Haggerty, K. (1997) *Policing the Risk Society*. Oxford: Clarendon Press.

Ewald, F. (1991) "Insurance and risks," in G. Burchell, C. Gordon, and P. Miller (eds.), *The Foucault Effect: Studies in Governmentality*. London: Harvester/Wheatsheaf, pp. 197–210.

Feeley, M. and Simon, J. (1992) "The new penology. Notes on the emerging strategy of corrections and its implications," *Criminology* 30: 449–74.

Feeley, M. and Simon, J. (1994) "Actuarial justice. The emerging new criminal law," in D. Nelken (ed.), *The Futures of Criminology*. New York: Sage, pp. 43–62.

Fleming, J. (1997) "Preventative damages," in N. Mullaney (ed.), *Torts in the Nineties*. North Ryde, New South Wales: Law Book Co, 56–71.

Foucault, M. (1977) *Discipline and Punish*. London: Peregrine Books.

Frankel, B. (1997) "Confronting neoliberal regimes. The post-Marxist embrace of populism and realpolitik," *New Left Review* 226: 57–92.

Freiberg, A (2000) "Guerillas in our midst? Judicial responses to governing the dangerous," in M. Brown and J. Pratt (eds.), *Dangerous Offenders. Punishment and Social Order*. London: Routledge.

Garland, D. (1996) "The limits of the sovereign state," *British Journal of Criminology* 36: 445–71.

Glaser, D. (1985) "Who gets probation or parole? Case study versus actuarial decision making," *Crime and Delinquency* 31: 367–78.

Green, J. (1997) *Risk and Misfortune. A Social Construction of Accidents*. London: UCL Press.

Hebenton, B. and Thomas, T. (1996) "Sexual offenders in the community: Reflections of problems of law, community and risk management in the USA, England and Wales," *International Journal of the Sociology of Law* 24: 427–43.

Hood, R. (1996) "Protecting the public. Automatic life sentences, parole and high risk offenders," *Criminal Law Review* 1996: 788–800.

Kemshall, H. (1998) *Risk in Probation Practice*. Aldershot, UK: Dartmouth.

Lash, S., Beck, U., and Giddens, A. (eds.) (1994) *Reflexive Modernization*. Cambridge, UK: Polity Press.

Levi, R. (2000) "The mutual constitution of risk and community," *Economy and Society* 29: 512–29.

McPherson v. Buick Motor Co. (1916) 111 NE 1050.

O'Malley, P. (1992) "Risk, power and crime prevention," *Economy Society* 21: 252–75.

O'Malley, P. (1997) "Policing, politics and postmodernity," *Social and Legal Studies* 6: 363–81.

O'Malley, P. (1999) "Consuming risks. Harm minimisation and the government of 'drug users'," in R. Smandych (ed.), *Governable Places. Readings in Governmentality and Crime Control.* Advances in Criminology Series, Aldershot, UK: Dartmouth, pp. 179–96.

O'Malley, P. (2000) "Uncertain subjects. Risks, liberalism and contract," *Economy and Society* 29: 460–84

O'Malley, P. and Mugford, S. (1992) "Moral technology. The political agenda of random drug testing," *Social Justice* 18: 122–46.

Palmer, G. (1998) "New Zealand's accident compensation scheme: Twenty years on," *University of Toronto Law Journal* 44: 223–85.

Parton, N. (1998) "Risk, advanced liberalism and child welfare: The need to discover uncertainty and ambiguity," *British Journal of Social Work* 28: 5–27.

Petersen, A. and Lupton, D. (1996) *The New Public Health. Health and Self in the Age of Risk.* Sydney: Allen and Unwin.

Priest, T. (1990) "The new legal structure of risk control," *Daedalus* 119: 207–20.

Reichman, N. (1986) "Managing crime risks: Toward an insurance based model of social control," *Research in Law and Social Control* 8: 151–72.

Rose, N. (1996) "Psychiatry as a political science. Advanced liberalism and the administration of risk," *History of the Human Sciences* 9: 1–23.

Rose, N. (2002) "Risk of madness," in T. Baker and J. Simon (eds.), *Embracing* Risk. Chicago: Chicago University Press, pp. 209–37.

Shearing, S. and Stenning, P. (1985) "From Panopticon to Disneyland: The development of discipline," in A. Doob and E. Greenspan (eds.), *Perspectives in Criminal Law.* Toronto: Canada Law Book Co, pp. 335–49.

Simon, J. (1987) "The emergence of a risk society: Insurance, law, and the state," *Socialist Review* 95: 61–89.

Simon, J. (1988) "The ideological effects of actuarial practices," *Law and Society Review* 22: 772–800.

Simon, J. (1997) "Driving governmentality: Automobile accidents, insurance and the challenge to social order in the inter-war years, 1919–1941," *Connecticut Insurance Law Journal* 4: 522–88.

Simon, J. (1998) "Managing the monstrous. Sex offenders and the new penology," *Psychology, Public Policy and Law* 4: 453–67.

Simon, J. (2002) "Taking risks: Extreme sports and the embrace of risk in advanced liberal societies," in T. Baker and J. Simon (eds.), *Embracing Risk.* Chicago: Chicago University Press, pp. 177–208.

Stanko, E. (1996) "Warnings to women. Police advice and women's safety in Britain," *Violence Against Women* 2 (1996), 5–24.

Weir, L. (1996) "Recent developments in the government of pregnancy," *Economy and Society* 23: 372–92.

Wilson, G. (2000) "Business, state and community: 'Responsible risk takers,' New Labour and the governance of corporate business," *Journal of Law and Society* 27: 151–77.

Zelizer, V. (1979) *Morals and Markets. The Development of Life Insurance in the United States.* New York: Columbia University Press.

Further Reading

Baldwyn, R. (1997) *Law and Uncertainty. Risks and Legal Processes.* London: Kluwer.

Economy and Society (2000) Special issue on "Configurations of Risk" 29(4).

Green, J. (1997) *Risk and Misfortune. A Social Construction of Accidents.* London: UCL Press.

Hood, C. and Jones, D. (1996) *Accident and Design. Contemporary Debates in Risk Management*. London: UCL Press.

Lupton, D. (1999) *Risk*. London: Routledge.

O'Malley, P. (ed.) (1998) *Crime and the Risk Society*. Aldershot, UK: Dartmouth.

Krimsky, S. and Golding, D. (eds.) (1992) *Social Theories of Risk*. New York: Praeger.

Stenson, K. and Sullivan, B. (eds.) (2000) *Crime, Risk and Justice*. London: Willan.

17

Thinking About Criminal Justice: Sociolegal Expertise and the Modernization of American Criminal Justice

JONATHAN SIMON

INTRODUCTION: CRIMINAL JUSTICE AS A PROBLEM OF POST WORLD WAR II GOVERNANCE

Under tremendous pressure from the pent-up demands of societies constrained by nearly a generation of depression and war, postwar governments, especially in North America and Australia, turned with new interests to the "social problems" that had been apparent during the last boom years of the 1920s – crime, urban decay, racial and ethnic violence, corruption of municipal services. The particular focus of post-war politicians was on modernizing the state agencies that addressed these social problems, and criminal justice agencies loomed large from the very start. In the United States this played out as a problem of federalism, how should the federal government (greatly expanded by its role in fighting both depression and war) modernize state and local criminal justice agencies? To answer that question a new kind of knowledge was needed that was neither criminal law nor a science of legislation nor a science of criminal motivation. Rather it was a social science of criminal justice agencies. This new discourse was distinctive for three themes.

First and foremost, sociolegal studies involved empirical examination of legal conduct by criminal justice actors, prosecutors, police officers, public defenders, judges, and so forth. This differentiated law and society criminal justice from the bulk of academic criminal law scholarship within law schools, most of which remained normative and theoretical. It also distinguished law and society from a great deal of contemporary criminology in the 1950s that was still dominated by the problem of explaining the motivation of criminal deviants, leaving both law and the administrative performance of institutions to the unstudied horizon.

Second, law and society research was linked quite self-consciously with efforts at the highest levels (generally the Supreme Court) to reform the performance of the legal system at the local level. Decisions like *Gideon v. Wainright* (1963), *Mapp v. Ohio* (1961), and *Miranda v. Arizona* (1966) expressed an almost empirical vision of the criminal justice system.[1] On the other end these decisions all mandated potentially far-reaching changes in the practice of the criminal justice system. They also carried more or less explicit ambitions about how legal change would benefit traditionally disadvantaged groups in the legal system. In this sense they led to a series of natural quasi-experiments; a striking before and after.

Third, sociolegal scholarship on criminal justice was highly focused on the legal profession both as a subject of research and as an audience for publications. Decisions like the ones cited above raised the salience of lawyers in the criminal justice system, and they raised the stake of the organized legal profession in the performance of the criminal justice system. Sociolegal scholarship worked into this escalating cycle of expectations. It maintained that lawyers in the system often performed less like the idea of adversarial advocates than that of bureaucrats. It also portrayed the penetration of legal norms into criminal justice systems as critical to reform. This would require greater involvement yet by the courts and the bar.

This sociolegal framework, with its emphasis on criminal justice, would prove highly successful. Starting with the Ford Foundation investment in the American Bar Foundation's Survey of Administration of Criminal Justice in the United States (ABF Survey hereinafter), a great deal of money and effort went into a host of law and society research on criminal justice. The influence of this vision reached its apotheosis in President Johnson's Commission on Crime and the Administration of Justice appointed to forge a Great Society agenda for criminal justice reform in 1965.

By the early 1970s the commitment by the federal government to modernizing state and local criminal justice was expanding but reoriented toward fighting a "war on crime." The modernization of criminal justice institutions was deemed more essential then ever, but the deeply critical view of current institutions in the law and society framework was eliminated.

THE BIRTH OF A SOCIOLEGAL DISCOURSE ON CRIMINAL JUSTICE 1953–75

The ABF Survey

The take-off of a sociolegal approach to criminal law and criminal justice took place in the span of a little over a decade and a half between 1953 and 1965. The beginning date is when a committee of the American Bar Association, headed by Justice Robert Jackson, issued a call for a major new survey of the administration of justice from policing to the finality of conviction (Jackson, 1953: 743). The end date is when the first volume written based on the study appeared in print.

Justice Jackson's "preliminary statement" (Jackson Statement hereinafter) published in the American Bar Association Journal in August of 1953, is a curious document in some respects. It begins by speaking in unreserved terms about a crisis in American criminal justice.

Our criminal procedure, as exhibited in many of our most publicized trials, is not creditable to our people or to our profession, and in less noticed day-to-day routine operation it is even less so. There is widespread doubt that existing criminal procedures can be relied upon either adequately to protect society or to protect the individual accused. (Jackson 1953: 743)

"Nearly everyone agrees" according to the Statement, "that our law enforcement process is sadly deficient."

It is tempting to read into Justice Jackson's alarming terms our long-running concern with high crime levels as the cause of this crisis, but the date is 1953 – well before the disturbing take-off in violent crimes reported to the police in the 1960s. Instead, Justice Jackson's statement reflects the concerns shared by elite members of the legal profession in both the federal government and the very top corporate law firms: concerns with the administration of law as a function of government, and in particular the potentially embarrassing spectacle of the world's dominant democracy depicted through the lens of southern courtrooms in the mid-1950s where equal treatment remained not even a pretense in many cases. Jackson was, above all, the pre-eminent example of the American jurist who had seen deeply into the nature of the Nazi legal system when he conducted prosecutions for the United States as part of the Nuremberg trials in 1945–9, including trials of Nazi judges.[2]

Justice Jackson identified twin evils that bedevil the system. Too many crimes are never reported or subjected to legal process and the ones that do begin too often end with the dismissal of serious charges. Too many individuals are at risk of wrongful conviction because of interrogation techniques and other problems in the criminal process. Meanwhile judicial decisions attempting to alleviate either problem move in the absence of any real knowledge about what is being done in practice and why, and thus risk doing as much damage as good.

The projected survey pushed into and opened a new space for knowing and acting on the crime problem. For much of the twentieth century the battle between law and the social sciences had created a rough bifurcation between the legal determination of guilt and the penocorrectional treatment (or punishment) of the causes of crime. While deferentially suggesting no intent to trespass on either preserve, the Jackson Statement in fact worked a reterritorialization of the crime problem. With its emphasis on the performance of the criminal process, presumably from policing right through to corrections, the Statement suggested another kind of expertise altogether concerned neither with culpability or the determinants of crime, but with the practices, mentalities, and discourses of the criminal process itself and its professionals.

The survey, originally envisioned to be a pilot project for a "more general investigation" (Unsigned, 1969: 351) was conducted in three states: Kansas, Michigan, and Wisconsin. The strategy essentially was to carry out parallel surveys of doctrine and practice in the criminal process from arrest through conviction and sentencing. Fieldwork commenced in 1956 and ended in 1957. Observers were sent to observe the work of police officers, prosecutors, and trial courts and to ask questions. By the end of 1957, over 2,000 field reports averaging 10 pages of notes had been collated by subject matter into seven mimeographed volumes. These volumes constituted in a strict sense the ABF Survey called for by Jackson, at least what could be considered a reasonable field test of such a national survey.

On the basis of these volumes, a number of scholars set to work producing detailed monographic studies of each stage of the process (LaFave, 1965; Newman, 1965; Tiffany, McIntyre, and Rotenberg, 1967; Dawson, 1969; Miller, 1969). Although the final volumes took nearly 15 years after the Jackson statement to appear, the field notes reproduced in one hundred sets circulated widely among criminal law experts starting in December of 1957, merely four years after the Statement. This circulation led to a wave of scholarship that commented on the Survey results, mainly in law review articles analyzing particular doctrines. In addition to providing considerable grist for courts, these articles launched many major figures in academic criminal law into research agendas shaped by the Survey concerns.

The other side of deviance: Police and the exercise of police power

It may have been an accident that Wayne LaFave's volume on police powers of search and seizure was the first in the series to be published. In any event it was a salient accident because no part of the criminal justice enterprise better exemplified the governmental and epistemological innovations of law and society discourse than the police. The 500-page monograph offered an exhaustive description of police procedure, as it had existed in the late 1950s, just before the revolution in criminal procedure that was already well under way in 1965.

Earlier national studies of criminal justice had reported ominously on the persistence of violence and lawlessness by the police, for example the Wickersham Commission Report (1931), but until the 1950s no serious effort by either lawyers or social scientists was made to make policing a subject of knowledge collection.[3] The central finding of the LaFave book was the relative autonomy of the police in making all the crucial legal judgments leading up to an arrest. While considerable space for judicial and prosecutorial influence on arrest could be found in the law of all three studied states, in none were judges and prosecutors of practical importance. LaFave criticized the courts for clinging to reassuring but groundless beliefs about their own ultimate authority over the power to arrest. Yet, in examining alternative sources of regulation, including courts, prosecutors, and legislatures, LaFave consistently came to the conclusion that it was a better strategy to recognize the appropriateness of police discretion and to focus on uplifting the exercise of that discretion. The centrality of discretion meant that courts and other policy makers could not rely on the case law of a jurisdiction to know how the criminal law was actually enforced. To bring police discretion under a legal sway, empirical knowledge on an ongoing basis would be required (LaFave, 1965: 82).

Within a year of *Arrest*, a second major book on policing and the rule of law was published, Jerome Skolnick's *Justice Without Trial: Law Enforcement in Democratic Society* (Skolnick, [1965] 1975). Like LaFave, Skolnick was primarily interested in the initial stages of police–citizen encounters and the police power to arrest, along with its collateral search and seizure opportunities. Both scholars were also interested precisely in how the web of police decision making intersected with and related to the growing web of judicially announced law of criminal procedure. The primary and decisive difference between the two projects was in the depth of their sociological analysis.[4] While *Arrest* remains self-consciously descriptive in its account of police practices, Skolnick brought the strong suits of American sociological theory to his interpretation.

The problem of judicially constructed reforms, especially the exclusionary rule and with it a whole set of demands for restraint in the performance of searches and seizures, is not just a problem of reforming a system that is invisible. The now visible system is one that has its own very structural resistance to legal reform. The police officer as craftsman, as democratic bureaucrat, builds a career around initiative in pursing the substantive goals of the organization. A law bent on assuring the due process of criminal defendants was bound to affront that vocational mandate.

Like LaFave, Skolnick saw police discretion as a key to the new law and society knowledge. Through his sociological analysis of police culture, Skolnick moved police discretion from the simple absence of rules to the resistance of an affirmative police culture with its own substantive ethic of police work. In this context police discretion was not analogous to the discretion given administrative agencies created as specialized functionaries. Police departments were long-standing and very insular organizations with their own values, ethnic biases, and forms of expertise (Skolnick, [1965]1975: 82).

Skolnick's analysis seemed like bad news for the proponents of the due process revolution. He offered the first systematic observations on how the police were responding to the exclusionary rule and suggested strong reasons why the sanction was not likely to produce change by itself in the short term. Yet ultimately the battle between craft-oriented occupational culture and the rule of law was a pragmatic challenge to political leadership rather than a reason to abandon the due process revolution. Skolnick was touching directly on the antinomies that Herbert Packer (1968) would help frame for a generation as the battle between due process and crime control.

Criminal justice

Policing was far from the only criminal justice topic that interested the first phase of the modern law and society movement. The major developments in both law and society that were stimulating the new wave of empirical research and policy reform in policing were also relevant to topics like punishment, juvenile justice, bail, and the role of lawyers in the criminal process. Reform of the bail system, and of the provision of defense lawyers for the poor, were two of the most active issues in the early 1960s. A more traditional area, the sociology of punishment and correc-tions, moved in a distinctly sociolegal direction starting in the late 1950s and early 1960s, influenced in part by the same intellectual trends that were influencing the study of police.

Court reform

The triangle of research, reform, and rights affecting policing was also taking shape around the same time period in a broad range of criminal justice practices and fields. Two of the most important areas of reform dealt with the parts of the criminal process that were directly downstream from policing: bail, or as it came to be called by reformers, conditions set for pretrial release, and the appointment of defense lawyers.

The common law practice of releasing criminal defendants pending trial on the basis of a cash bond had come in the course of the 1950s to seem a glaring example of inequality. Clearly cash bail as a condition for release favored those with resources. It was also widely acknowledged that judges used bail to detain those they thought dangerous as well as to assure attendance at future legal proceedings. In the 1950s and early 1960s it was only too evident how both factors played into the efforts of a white supremacist power structure in the south to use criminal justice institutions to maintain control. The power of judges to preventively detain arrested suspects who might commit future crimes if left free in the community was not at this point seen as a countervailing benefit to bail administration.

The first sustained critique of the bail system was a law review article published by Caleb Foote (1965). Foote argued that cash bail, at least as to the indigent, violated the 8th Amendment's prohibition against "excessive bail" as well as the equal protection clause of the 14th Amendment. Reform of the bail system never came before the Supreme Court in the 1960s, when it might have taken up Foote's constitutional challenge. His criticisms, however, were taken up by reformers in the executive and legislative branches of government at both the federal and local level (Goldkamp and Gottfredson, 1995).[5] The key to the wave of bail reforms that followed was the kind of research-based, foundation-funded project that the ABF surveys had modeled. The Vera Institute of Justice conducted a series of empirical studies designed to validate a methodology for identifying suspects with a low risk of becoming fugitives. The Vera approach became widely influential during the 1960s and 1970s, including the Federal Bail Reform Act of 1966. The new model built research into the administration of justice by having researchers interview all arrestees, and produce an audit of their flight risk for the use of the judge in setting conditions of release.

The apparatus of legal rights that the Supreme Court constructed around criminal suspects and defendants starting in the 1950s presupposed that those exposed to criminal trial be represented by counsel capable of making pretrial motions to exclude evidence collected in improper searches and seizures, or coerced confessions. It was not until 1963, in *Gideon v. Wainright*, that the Supreme Court finally held that all defendants facing felony charges must be provided with a lawyer if they could not afford one (Lewis, 1964). *Gideon*, and its unfolding expansion through to the present, may constitute the most significant and enduring legacy of the ABF survey and the discourse that arose from it emphasizing law as a key player in modernizing criminal justice. You cannot have law, in the American legal system at any rate, without lawyers. But as soon as they were ushered in to do the legal work required by the due process revolution, lawyers also became a focus of empirical research. The sociolegal strategy required the researcher to treat the players in the legal field as subject to their own career incentives. The resulting portrait invariably problematized the role of lawyers. Abraham Blumberg's (1967) examination of how public defenders related to their clients and to other court personnel suggested that notwithstanding their ethical obligation to zealously advocate on the behalf of their clients, lawyers for the poor were likely to favor their everyday colleagues in the courtroom work group.

Imprisonment

By the turn of the twentieth century, the new disciplines of sociology, psychology, and social work were already establishing multiple and overlapping links with the criminal courts and the prison system. For example, Illinois created an official position within its prison bureau for a state prison actuary responsible for conducting statistical studies of parole revocation and its correlates. By the 1950s, the goal of scientific rehabilitation was an official state policy in most parts of the United States. A juvenile entering the New York City juvenile justice system for skipping school might expect to be interviewed, surveyed, and probed by a wide range of quasi-professionals employing a variety of social science methods (Simon, 1998). As the 1960s began, this penocorrectional establishment seemed quite solid, although by the end of that decade it would be in shambles.

Rehabilitation remained in the background as the reason for many social science observers to get inside prisons, but the research increasingly cast the prison as a window into the capacity of a social order to be governed by the rule of law (Clemmer, [1940] 1958; Sykes, 1958). During the 1960s a host of empirical studies explored this problematic from a number of different vantage points. Did prisons create a distinct culture associated with their unique custodial features, or is any particular prison culture an ever-changing mix of that which was brought into the prison from the outside? (See the essays in Cloward, Cressey, Grosser et al., 1960.) Does prison culture vary with the style of social organization favored by the prison (Studt, Messinger, and Wilson, 1968)? Is the culture found in prisons a product of the prison or of criminal subcultures to which the inmate belonged before imprisonment?

Law and Society Scholarship and the War on Crime, 1975–99

By 1967 the sociolegal framework had succeeded in raising the salience of criminal justice agencies at the highest levels of government. Through President Johnson's Commission on the Administration of Justice (1967), law and society entered into the major effort to integrate the crime issue into the administration's Great Society domestic programs. The Report and the legislative recommendations that came out of it in 1967 shared the emphasis on modernizing criminal justice for a democratic racially integrated society as a priority just as great as more effective crime control. Research would operate as a wedge of national reform to uproot the power of traditional local knowledge over the administration of justice. A year later, however, when the adoption of the Omnibus Crime Control and Safe Streets Act of 1968,[6] legislated a major federal financial commitment to improving state and local criminal justice, it was clear that a very different kind of governmental program was being mobilized. Unlike the sociolegal discourse on criminal justice, this new framework made crime itself – the rising levels of violent crime in America – the central problem. It was not the social order with its racisms and parochialisms reproduced in the police that needed to be changed by government, but protected against the threat of violent crime and fear of crime.

The war on crime

Loyal opposition: studying the war on crime

In many respects the Johnson administration's effort to launch a war on crime as a final drive to modernize and legalize criminal justice was the high point for the triangle of research, reform, and rights. By 1968, however, it was law and order and not modernization and legalization that were the dominant focus. Skolnick opened the first chapter of *Justice Without Trial* with comments pointed directly at this gathering political storm: "[T]he common juxtaposition of 'law and order' is an oversimplification. Law is not merely an instrument of order, but may frequently be its adversary" (Skolnick, [1966] 1975: 8).

Just a few years later, writing in late 1968 or 1969, the unsigned author of the "Epilogue to the Survey" published in the last volume of the ABF series in 1969 was blunt in his skepticism that the new war on crime could be won.

> We know that the system cannot be comprehended in a formula – "law and order" or otherwise – nor reconstituted in a stroke. We thus can infer, for example, that a fresh "war on crime" will be a failure: a campaign to control crime conceived on the model of a war effort will lack the durability, subtlety, and pervasiveness required to do the job. This is a truth that we are reluctant to acknowledge in these days of extremity, but one which must be faced. (Unsigned, 1969: 352)

Sociolegal discourse on criminal justice was not over by any means, but it was increasingly located in opposition. Although federal funding for research would continue to grow, scholars identified with the law and society movement and deploying variations on the criminal justice framework forged by the ABF Survey and influential parallel work like Jerome Skolnick's, would, with some exceptions, remain outside the mainstream of research funded directly for the war on crime by the Law Enforcement Assistance Administration (LEAA) and its successors.

Instead of competing with other research experts for the research components of federal funding, many scholars influenced by the sociolegal research paradigm turned to studying the effects of the war on crime itself (and implicitly or explicitly the prime threat to a social order constituted on due process of law) (Feeley and Sarat, 1980; Scheingold, 1984). Their conclusions were overall devastating to the positive goals of the law: research had not helped to effectively combat crime and the political dynamic it was creating could not be expected to lead to real reforms in the long run. In 1975 the Justice Department itself asked the National Academy of Sciences to assemble a study team to evaluate the research progress of the war on crime. The Report, coauthored by sociolegal scholars, Susan White and Samuel Krislov (1977) was scathing in its assessment of the LEAA effort. Writing in summary they described the overall quality of the funded research product as "not high, and much has been mediocre" (1977: 17)[7]

But if the research associated with the war on crime was increasingly technocratic (Heydebrand and Seron, 1990) in orientation, a new programmatic vision for combining research and reform was emerging. Perhaps no single book better exemplified this new program than James Q. Wilson's influential *Thinking About Crime* (1975). Outlining what would become an all purpose neoconservative critique of the failures of the Great Society programs of the Kennedy and Johnson administrations (based in many respects on the research, reform, rights triangle), Wilson called for an end to fighting crime by reforming society and for a renewed focus on deterring and incapacitating the willful offender. The book and subsequent work by Wilson (Wilson and Kelling, 1982) has influenced a generation of politicians and policy makers. It was reprinted in a revised edition in 1983 to accompany President Ronald Reagan's ramping up of the war on crime.[8]

Crime, law, and hegemony: the history of criminal justice

The triangle of research, reform, and rights was bound to invest the sociology of law and its promise of producing new pathways of knowledge and action as the most influential sociolegal strand in the 1950s and 1960s. The war on crime and the new focus on crime control closed the door to much of the empirical sociology of criminal justice agencies, as sociologists were now considered at best to be suspect allies in the war on crime. Perhaps this closure and the resulting intellectual gap, helps explain the importance of historical scholarship in launching a new and more critical study of criminal justice institutions in the 1970s (Thompson, 1975; Hay, Linebaugh, Rule et al., 1975; Rothman, 1971, 1980; Foucault, 1977; Ignatieff, 1978; Hindus, 1980). Historians were not as dependent on the sensitivities of those who controlled access to gather data. The historical view also permitted a comparative study of anticrime initiatives by governments and the role of such initiatives in struggles to stabilize political hierarchies.

One influential source was the research on British criminal justice in the seventeenth and eighteenth centuries being conducted by E. P. Thompson and his students and colleagues at Warwick University in England (Thompson, 1975; Hay et al., 1975). Thompson's study of the Black Act, for example, dealt with a piece of legislation that introduced scores of new capital offenses but whose effects at the gallows were far more subtle. In a sense it raised the same sociological questions as the Omnibus Crime Control and Safe Streets Act of 1968. A second influential body of historical research focused on prison and its rise as the dominant tool of modern punishment. David Rothman's 1971 book, *The Discovery of the Asylum: Social Order and Disorder in the New Republic* offered a critical functionalist alternative to the traditional view that the prison reflected the growing humanity of enlightened society. Rothman saw the prison and its equivalent, the asylum, less as a means of humane treatment, and more as technologies for recapturing the sense of secure order that had been destroyed by the revolution. A similar revisionist effort that became even more influential was Michel Foucault's *Discipline and Punish* (1975, published in English 1977), a study of the "birth of the prison." Foucault argued that the emergence of the prison as a normal punishment for serious crime reflected the rise of a new technology of power based on surveillance, disciplinary training of individuals, and normalizing expertise. As the reformist narrative of American criminal justice turned toward repression and vengeance, Foucault's analysis was a powerful reminder that the relationship between knowledge and power in penality was not fixed or predictable (Garland, 1985, 1990; Cohen 1985; Simon, 1993; Beckett, 1997).

Criminal justice reform and sociolegal scholarship in the era of the war on crime

The war on crime ultimately promoted its own modernization agenda for state and local criminal justice institutions. The objective of creating safety for the public was the dominant consideration of this modernization. In Herb Packer's (1968) sense, crime control had triumphed over due process.

Sentencing

No body of work is as representative of the possibilities and aspirations of sociolegal scholars in this era as policing was for the 1950s and 1960s. Perhaps the strongest case can be made for sentencing research as the best analog for the period running from the mid-1970s until the turn of the twenty-first century. In an important sense, sentencing as a subject of sociolegal studies did not exist in the first half of our study period, 1953–75. Only after penal correctionalism began to lose its dominance could sentencing as such break itself off from the theory of punishment and become a field of legal and sociolegal analysis.

While a great deal of the most influential writing, including the American Friends Service Committee's *Struggle for Justice* (1971) and Andrew Von Hirsch's (1976) *Doing Justice*, were more overtly normative and even moralistic, it was moral reasoning about processes and actors whose behavior in an empirical sense was a direct referent. This work appeared to have considerable influence on four or five state legislatures that in the mid and late 1970s formulated new sentencing systems (Tonry, 1996). Under the general slogan of "just desserts" or the "justice model" these states replaced the indeterminate sentence with "determinate sentencing" along a variety of lines including legislatively drawn presumptive sentences, judicially created "voluntary" guidelines, and sentencing grids drawn by specially appointed sentencing commissions (Tonry, 1996: 27).

A second wave of research beginning in the late 1970s and growing throughout the 1980s involved empirical research aimed at testing the practicality of different strategies for utilizing imprisonment (and the threat of imprisonment) to diminish crime rates. Within this second wave, the first focus was on deterrence that had been the traditional logic of sentencing in the nineteenth century, in the era before the rise of treatment and indeterminacy. Deterrence theory benefited from its association with law and economics then enjoying its own renaissance of interest in elite law schools like the University of Chicago and Yale (Zimring and Hawkins, 1982). The resurrection of the American death penalty after 1972 also put the death penalty back into play as a research issue although with no clear winners (Van den Haag, 1975).

At virtually the same time, incapacitation began its rise as a justification for the increasingly long prison terms being turned out by legislatures in the absence of any good empirical evidence that deterrence worked. Incapacitation, once referred to as prevention, arose first at the end of the nineteenth century as a eugenic purpose to imprisonment and the death penalty, as both served to remove the convicted prisoner from the gene pool. In the 1970s incapacitation returned, focused purely on preventing crimes that might otherwise be committed by a convicted criminal were they to remain free or be released earlier (Blumstein, Cohen, and Nagin, 1978; Zimring and Hawkins, 1995). Much of this research was purely deductive; working from assumptions about the average rate of offending by criminals when they were free in the community (which came to be known as *lambda* for the Latin letter used in equations), economists sought to calculate the incapacitative effect of various sentencing schemes. Disappointment with even these speculative results followed quickly. Mass incarceration was too expensive to be justified by realistic assessments of *lambda*. This led to a variation known as "selective incapacitation" in which empirical work on self-reported rates of offending by already imprisoned robbers and burglars was used to see if predictive factors could be identified with sufficient power to make incapacitation effects worth the cost of long-term imprisonment (Greenwood, 1982).

A third wave of scholarship began to concern itself with the growth of mass incarceration itself. This responsive scholarship took two forms. One was an effort to expand alternatives to incarceration by discovering and creating new forms of "intermediate sanction." Like the crime warriors, the intermediate sanctions scholars tended to presume that probation or parole were too focused on services and did not operate as effective deterrents or by providing incapacitation. Most of the new ideas centered on ways to make community sanctions more punitive and more control-oriented, so they could compete with imprisonment as serious sanctions for crime (Davies, 1993).

The dramatic shifts in penal justifications and the incarceration rate have combined sentencing analysis with considerations raised by the history of criminal justice scholars in the 1970s and the sociology of imprisonment in the 1960s. The dramatic rise in American incarceration rates in the 1980s and continuing unbroken for nearly two decades to the year 2000 seemed to suggest that something fundamental had shifted in the logic of American criminal justice. Sociolegal scholars have attributed the rise to racialized politics (Miller, 1996; Beckett, 1997), a crisis of American governance (Scheingold, 1991; Simon, 1997), and a "culture of control" (Garland, 2001).

Perhaps the most important example of the integration of research and reform in this period was the United States Sentencing Commission appointed as a result of the Crime Control Act of 1984. A statistical study of judicial sentencing in the federal courts was undertaken to provide a descriptive baseline. The commission developed guidelines that would reshape these patterns to achieve greater uniformity and greater crime control. In contrast to earlier commissions in the states that were more influenced by just desserts considerations, the United States Sentencing Commission was open to deterrence and incapacitation as well and consciously decided to increase the level of imprisonment (tripling the size of the federal prison population within a decade) (Tonry, 1996: 58). Many federal judges perceive the guidelines as having removed any significant role for judicial judgment (Stith and Cabranes, 1998).

Death penalty

The death penalty seemed a waning part of American criminal justice during the first period of our survey. While death sentences continued to be handed down in the 1950s, and executions took place, by the 1960s with public opinion turning against executions, the abolition of the death penalty seemed likely in the near future. The most important contribution of sociolegal scholars to this topic may have been the historical research on the use of the death penalty undertaken as part of the President's Commission in 1966. The research which showed that the penalty had been employed in a racially discriminatory manner helped influence the Supreme Court's decision in 1972 to strike down existing death penalties in *Furman v. Georgia* (1972) (Meltsner, 1973). The Supreme Court's decision, however, helped instead to resurrect the death penalty, with over 30 states re-enacting the death penalty within three years of the decision. Public support quickly returned to mid-century highs and the states began a long march back toward regular use of the death penalty (joined by the federal government starting in the 1990s).

This resurrection has become an intense subject of sociolegal scholarship. In a sense this was the triangle in reverse. An assertion of rights and research had let to a dramatic regression rather than reform, and more research followed. First socio-legal scholars turned to the question of what the public understood about the death penalty and how that affected its support (Sarat and Vidmar, 1976), a topic that has continued to be frequently re-examimed (Ellsworth and Gross, 1994). Second, sociolegal scholars have sought to explore the changes in American political and legal culture that could account for this historic shift in the direction of change on the death penalty (Zimring and Hawkins, 1986; Sarat, 2001; Banner, 2002). Third, sociolegal scholars have continued to track the political demography of the death penalty exposing the endurance of racism and most recently the frequency of error (Baldus, Woodworth, and Pulaski, 1990; Liebman, Fagan, Gelman, West, Davies, and Kiss, 2002). Unlike the 1960s, however, the contemporary Supreme Court has remained wary of accepting sociolegal knowledge in assessing the death penalty. The Baldus et al. study, for example, showed that despite controlling for hundreds of sentencing relevant variables, the race of the victim still dramatically influenced the chances of receiving a death penalty in Georgia. The Supreme Court dismissed the power of such statistics to prove discrimination in *McCleskey v. Kemp* (1987)

Bail and pretrial release

By the end of the 1960s, the pretrial release question was being seen through an entirely different lens. Rather than being concerned with indigent arrestees losing effective access to rights by being held in custody pending trial, the new discourse raised the issue of the arrestee who returns to predatory crime upon returning to the community. Even if that person is not a flight risk they may pose a risk of crime. This approach of preventively detaining "dangerous" arrestees, based on a hearing and individualized assessment by a judge, was affirmed by the Supreme Court in *United States v. Salerno* (1987), which rejected any right to pretrial release as advocated earlier by Foote. In 1984, the federal government endorsed the focus on public safety in the Bail Reform Act of 1984. By 1978, 23 states and the District of Columbia had redrafted laws to reflect public safety as a primary concern (Goldkamp and Gottfredson, 1995: 41). By 1984, when the US Supreme Court upheld such prevent-ive detention laws, an additional 11 states and the Federal Government had followed suit.

In the 1980s this concern with protecting the public from potentially dangerous arrestees combined with the earlier concerns about arbitrariness coalesced in experi-mentation and policy innovation with voluntary guidelines for bail decisions. Socio-legal scholars John S. Goldkamp and Michael R. Gottfredson developed an influential model through a program of research and collaboration with judges in the Philadelphia courts (Goldkamp and Gottfredson, 1995).

Lawyers and the limits of the adversary process

Sociolegal scholars since the mid-1970s have continued to produce critical studies of the actual practice of the criminal courts that suggest the incompleteness of the due process revolution launched back in the 1950s. Despite the triumph of the right to counsel for all criminal defendants facing jail or prison time, research shows that many defendants, even in capital cases, lack competent counsel. In the 1980s the Supreme Court adopted a standard of competent representation in *Strickland v. Washington* (1984) that discourages lower courts from closely scrutinizing the effectiveness of lawyers' conduct, leaving broad margins for "strategic judgment." This standard, like many adopted by the Court since the 1970s, seems to shut the law off from empirical study, leaving it to judges to make singular decisions with little ability to make systematic comparisons (Scheck, Neufeld, and Dwyer, 2000).

The period since the 1970s has witnessed an extraordinary expansion of the power of prosecutors in the criminal process. Decisions once left largely to judges, for example, whether a juvenile charged with a serious crime should be tried in adult court, are now made by prosecutors. Long sentences for many crimes and the abolition of parole also means that prosecutorial decisions about charging cannot be effectively checked by judges or parole boards. Prosecution was surprisingly little studied prior to the 1980s (MacDonald, 1979). After 1980, the adoption of new tough-on-crime measures became an impetus for sociolegal scholars to study how prosecutors responded (McCoy, 1993). The extraordinary political power of prosecutors today creates few incentives to invite close scrutiny by social scientists.

Policing

The war on crime took pressure off police to modernize organizationally (although some of that pressure continued from other sources including the civil liability system and political accountability). Since then, policing has taken research inside in ways that draw on the social sciences as well as engineering. Under the rubric of "community-based policing" and "problem-solving policing," police managers have used surveys of citizens and close analysis of crime report rates to shift police deployment and tactics. Community policing can trace its roots to sociolegal research on the limits of then normal modern police strategy of rapid response to crime reports with a priority on serious crimes (Goldstein, 1976; Skogan and Hartnett, 1997; Skolnick and Bayley, 1986), but the popularity of community policing has not opened a new era of collaboration between police managers and sociolegal studies.

Gender and race discrimination in criminal justice

The role of criminal justice institutions in promoting racial discrimination was one of the main concerns of sociolegal studies in the 1950s and 1960s and the triangle of research, reform, and rights that followed. The old research, reform, and rights triangle has remained vital in criminal sentencing in one important respect, the issue of discrimination. The presumption that the heavy indeterminate style of sentencing systems, standard in the 1960s, were used discriminatorily against African Americans and other racial and ethnic minorities while being exercised in favor of certain female and white-collar defendants was one of the major criticisms that led to its abandonment. Police use of deadly force has been shown to be influenced by the race of the suspect (Skolnick and Fyfe, 1993) and police in the 1990s were documented to be using racial profiling in selecting drivers to be stopped as suspected drug couriers (Cole, 1999).

Even as the war on crime has pushed crime repression to the forefront of policy and other factors into the rear, the question of discrimination has remained important. Where race seems to be a determinative factor in decision making the Supreme Court has continued to expand constitutional rights otherwise in retreat (e.g., *Tennessee v. Garner*, 1985; *Batson v. Kentucky*, 1986; but see *McCleskey v. Kemp*, 1987).

Since 1980 the issue of gender discrimination has emerged as a major focus of research and policy innovation. Two of the most important were rape (Estrich, 1987) and domestic violence (Berk and Loseke, 1981; Dobash and Dobash, 1992). Both were striking examples of how both legal doctrine and criminal justice practice were deeply and visibly gendered. Like evidence of race discrimination in criminal justice, the treatment of rape and domestic violence suggested that criminal justice institutions were not only failing to prevent the use of criminal force for promoting gender domination but were collaborating in that use. Rape inside marriage was not even a crime in most states in 1960. Police noncriminal treatment of domestic violence cases was one of the first most enduring findings of the law and society study of the police.

Because the victimization of women had been so totally ignored by the criminal justice system, this was one area where the war on crime was compatible with a real effort to reshape and modernize the social organization of criminal justice institutions themselves. Police and prosecutors have become major consumers of sociolegal research on gender discrimination in law enforcement. This alliance has pushed some sociolegal scholars into a tighter alliance with proponents of the war on crime than they might otherwise have had. At the same time because women victims and their advocates have had real reasons to doubt the good faith of law enforcement they bring critical evaluation to bear that is generally lacking within the war on crime.

CONCLUSION

As the criminal justice system emerges in the early twenty-first century as a major site for recasting the governance of liberal societies it is more vital than ever to construct flows of knowledge about how that system works beyond the law. The war on crime and the consequent enhancement of the power of criminal justice agencies have created a sociolegal paradox. At the moment when criminal justice agencies are becoming extraordinarily influential on the shape of law and governance generally, they are becoming ever less amenable to close empirical research that is not completely controlled by the agencies themselves. A vast industry of research expertise exists for criminal justice fed by the steady investment of federal dollars in such research since the Omnibus Crime Control and Safe Streets Act of 1968. This research typically remains within the narrow confines of evaluating particular programs and affords little opportunity to study how criminal justice agencies know and act on their targets. It has a family link to sociolegal studies, but it lacks the critical analysis of criminal justice categories. Continuing that tradition without the access that the old triangle of research, reform, and rights had is the most pressing issue for current scholars. Sociolegal scholars have turned to new ways to access knowledge including litigation. They have also shifted their attention to the cultural constellations that surround the criminal justice system.

Notes

1 Justice White's concurrence in *Duncan v. Louisiana* (1967) is one of the most programmatic statements of this empirical constitutionalism.

2 In a series of criminal procedure opinions, Jackson invoked the specter of totalitarianism in warning against the excesses of law enforcement. See *Harris v. United States* (1947), *Brinegar v. United States* (1949), and *Elkins v. United States* (1960).

3 William Westley (1953) is often cited as the first serious sociological study of American policing (e.g., Skolnick 1975: 45 n. 4).

4 LaFave was a young scholar of legal doctrine set to work at an early stage of his career on the largest mass of observational data about the police ever assembled. Skolnick was a young sociologist exposed to the influence of one of the handful of elite law schools that was beginning to invest in the law and social science intersection in new ways at the beginning of the 1960s.

5 The Justice Department, under Attorney General Robert Kennedy, early on identified bail reform as a crucial pathway to address inequality. Local administrators also saw bail as crucial to a less celebrated but crucial problem, jail overcrowding, which only grew worse as the arrest rate went up in the 1960s.

6 Pub. L. No. 90–351, Subsection, 201–406, 82 Stat. 197 (1968)

7 Two other important surveys of American opinion on criminal law enforcement were conducted in the late 1970s by scholars with a sociolegal bent. See Stinchcombe, Adams, Heimer et. al. (1980); Jacob, Lineberry, et. al. (1983).

8 In many respects Wilson and Skolnick paralleled each other. Both brought first class 1950s social science methods to the study of the police for the first time in the 1960s. Both were interested in the problem of law and the capacity of the liberal state to regulate effectively. Both were sharply affected by the rise of radical student movements at American universities. Skolnick at Berkeley supported the students while Wilson at Harvard was outraged. (For the rest of his career Wilson would continue to blame most of the nation's social problems on those students and their pernicious moral influence.) While Skolnick became one of the most important liberal public intellectuals (see Skolnick, 1969), Wilson became the leading rightist public intellectual. While Skolnick never wrote a book-length rejoinder to Wilson, it is noteworthy that the first book in the 1980s to offer a law and society response to what had become the Wilsonian orthodoxy of crime policy and to receive considerable public discussion was written by Skolnick's student Elliot Currie (1987).

References

American Friends Service Committee (1971) *Struggle for Justice: A Report on Crime and Punishment in America*. New York: Hill & Wang.

Baldus, David, Woodworth, George, and Pulaski, Charles A. Jr. (1990) *Equal Justice and the Death Penalty: A Legal and Empirical Analysis*. Boston: Northeastern University Press.

Banner, Stuart (2002) *The Death Penalty: An American History*. Cambridge, MA: Harvard University Press.

Batson v. Kentucky (1986) 476 U.S. 79.

Beckett, Katherine (1997) *Making Crime Pay*. New York: Oxford University Press.

Bell v. Wolfish (1979) 441 U.S. 520.

Berk, Sarah Fenstermaker and Loseke, Donileen R. (1981) "Handling family violence: Situational determinants of police arrest in domestic disturbances," *Law & Society Review* 15: 317–36.

Blumberg, Abraham S. (1967) "The practice of law as a confidence game: Organizational cooptation of a profession," *Law & Society Review* 1: 15–39.

Blumstein, Alfred, Cohen, Jacqueline, and Nagin, Daniel (eds.) (1978) *Panel on Research on Deterrent and Incapacitative Effects, Committee on Research on Law Enforcement and Criminal Justice, Assembly of Behavioral and Social Sciences, National Research Council.* Washington, DC: National Academy of Sciences.

Brinegar v. United States (1949) 338 U.S. 160.

Clemmer, Donald ([1940]1958) *The Prison Community*, 2nd edn. New York: Holt, Rinehart & Winston.

Cloward, Richard A., Cressey, Donald R., Grosser, George H., et al., (1960) *Theoretical Studies in Social Organization of the Prison.* New York: Social Science Research Council.

Cole, David (1999) *No Equal Justice: Race and Class in the American Criminal Justice System.* New York: New Press.

Cohen, Stanley (1985) *Visions of Social Control.* London: Polity Press.

Currie, Elliot (1987) *Confronting Crime.* New York: Pantheon.

Davies, Malcolm (1993) *Punishing Criminals: Developing Community-based Intermediate Sanctions.* Westport, CT: Greenwood Press.

Dawson, Robert O. (1969) *Sentencing.* Boston: Little, Brown.

Dobash, R. Emerson and Dobash, Russell P. (1992) *Women, Violence and Social Change.* London: Routledge.

Duncan v. Louisiana (1967) 391 U.S. 145.

Elkins v. United States (1960) 364 U.S. 206

Ellsworth, Phoebe and Gross, Samuel (1994) "Hardening of the attitudes: Americans' views on the death penalty," *Journal of Social Issues* 50: 19–52.

Estrich, Susan (1987) *Real Rape.* Cambridge, MA: Harvard University Press.

Feeley, Malcolm M. and Sarat, Austin (1980) *The Policy Dilemma: Federal Crime Policy and the Law Enforcement Assistance Adminisatration, 1968–1978.* Minneapolis: University of Minnesota Press.

Foote, Caleb (19654) "The coming constitutional crisis in bail," *University of Pennsylvania Law Review* 113: 959–99, 1125–85.

Foucault, Michel (1977) *Discipline and Punish: The Birth of the Prison*, trans. Alan Sheridan. New York: Pantheon.

Furman v. Georgia (1972) 408 U.S. 238.

Garland, David (1985) *Punishment and Welfare.* Brookfield, VT.: Gower.

Garland, David (1990) *Punishment and Modern Society.* Chicago: University of Chicago Press.

Garland, David (2001) *The Culture of Control: Crime and Social Order in a Contemporary Society.* Chicago: University of Chicago Press.

Gideon v. Wainright (1963) 372 U.S. 335.

Goldkamp, John and Gottfredson, Michael (1995) *Personal Liberty and Community Safety : Pretrial Release in the Criminal Court.* New York: Plenum Press.

Goldstein, Hermann (1976) *Policing a Free Society.* Cambridge, MA : Ballinger Pub. Co.

Greenwood, Peter (1982) *Selective Incapacitation.* Santa Monica: RAND Corporation.

Harris v. United States (1947) 331 U.S. 145.

Hay, Douglas, Linebaugh, Peter, Rule, John G., et. al. (1975) *Albion's Fatal Tree.* New York: Pantheon.

Heydebrand, Wolf and Seron, Carroll (1990) *Rationalizing Justice: The Political Economy of Federal District Courts.* Albany: State University of New York Press.

Hindus, Michael (1980) *Prison and Plantation: Crime, Justice, and Authority in Massachusetts and South Carolina, 1767–1878.* Chapel Hill: University of North Carolina Press.

Ignatieff, Michael (1978) *A Just Measure of Pain: The Penitentiary in the Industrial Revolution.* London: Penguin.

Jackson, Robert (1953) "Criminal justice: The vital problem of the future," *American Bar Association Journal* 39: 743–6.

Jacob, Herbert and Lineberry, Robert L., with Heinz, Anne M., Beecher, Janice A., Moran, Jack, and Smith, Duanne H. (1983) *Governmental Responses to Crime: Crime on Urban Agendas*. Washington, DC: National Institute of Justice.

LaFave, Wayne (1965) *Arrest: The Decision to Take a Suspect into Custody*. Boston: Little Brown and Company.

Lewis, Anthony (1964) *Gideon's Trumpet*. New York, Random House.

Liebman, James, Fagan, Jeffrey, Gelman, Andrew, West, Valerie, Davies, Garth, and Kiss, Alexander (2000) *A Broken System, Part II: Why There is so Much Error in Capital Cases, and What Can Be Done About It*. New York: Columbia Law School.

McDonald, William F. (1979) *The Prosecutor*. Beverly Hills, CA: Sage Publications.

Mapp v. Ohio (1961) 367 U.S. 643.

McCleskey v. Kemp (1987) 481 U.S. 279.

McCoy, Candace (1993) *Politics and Plea Bargaining: Victims' Rights in California*. Philadelphia: University of Pennsylvania Press.

Meltsner, Michael (1973) *Cruel and Unusual Punishment: The Supreme Court and Capital Punishment*. New York: Random House.

Miller, Frank W. (1969) *Prosecution: The Decision to Charge a Suspect with a Crime*. Boston: Little, Brown.

Miller, Jerome G. (1996) *Search and Destroy: African-American Males and the Criminal Justice System*. Cambridge, UK: Cambridge University Press.

Miranda v. Arizona (1966) 384 U.S. 436.

Newman, Donald J. (1965) *Conviction: The Determination of Guilt or Innocence Without Trial*. Boston: Little, Brown.

Packer, Herbert (1968) *The Limits of the Criminal Sanction*. Stanford, CA: Stanford University Press.

President's Commission on Law Enforcement and the Administration of Justice (1967) *The Challenge of Crime in a Free Society: A Report*. Washington: US Government Printing Office.

Rothman, David J. (1971) *The Discovery of the Asylum: Social Order and Disorder in the New Republic*. Toronto: Little, Brown.

Rothman, David J. (1980) *Conscience and Convenience: The Asylum and its Alternatives in Progressive America*. Boston: Little, Brown.

Sarat, Austin (2001) *When the State Kills: Capital Punishment and the American Condition*. Princeton, NJ: Princeton University Press.

Sarat, Austin and Vidmar, Neil (1976) "Public opinion, the death penalty, and the Eighth Amendment: Testing the Marshall hypothesis," *Wisconsin Law Review* 1976: 171–97.

Scheck, Barry, Neufeld, Peter, and Dwyer, James (2000) *Actual Innocence: Five Days to Execution and other Dispatches from the Wrongly Convicted*. New York: Doubleday.

Scheingold, Stuart (1984) *The Politics of Law and Order: Street Crime and Public Policy*. New York: Longman.

Scheingold, Stuart (1991) *The Politics of Street Crime: Criminal Process and Cultural Obsession*. Philadelphia: Temple University Press.

Simon, Jonathan (1993) *Poor Discipline: Parole and the Social Control of the Underclass 1890–1990*. Chicago: University of Chicago Press.

Simon, Jonathan (1997) "Governing through crime," in George Fisher and Lawrence Friedman (eds.), *The Crime Conundrum: Essays on Criminal Justice*. Boulder, CO: Westview Press, pp. 171–90.

Simon, Jonathan (1998) "Ghosts of the disciplinary machine: Lee Harvey Oswald, life-history, and the truth of crime," *Yale Journal of Law and the Humanities* 10: 75–113.

Skogan, Wesley G. and Hartnett, Susan M. (1997) *Community Policing, Chicago Style*. New York: Oxford University Press.

Skolnick, Jerome ([1966] 1975) *Justice Without Trial: Law Enforcement in Democratic Society*, revised edn. New York: John Wiley & Son.

Skolnick, Jerome (1969) *The Politics of Protest: A Taskforce Report Submitted to the National Commission on the Causes and Prevention of Violence*. New York: Simon and Schuster.

Skolnick, Jerome and Bayley, David (1986) *The New Blue Line: Police Innovation in Six American Cities*. New York: Free Press/London: Collier Macmillan.

Skolnick, Jerome and Fyfe, James (1993) *Above the Law: Police and the Excessive Use of Force*. New York: Free Press.

Stinchcombe, Arthur, Adams, Rebecca, Heimer, Carol A., et al. (1980) *Crime and Punishment – Changing Attitudes in America*. San Francisco: Jossey-Bass Publishers.

Stith, Kate and Cabranes, Jose A. (1998) *Fear of Judging: Sentencing Guidelines in the Federal Courts*. Chicago: University of Chicago Press.

Strickland v. Washington (1984) 466 U.S. 668.

Studt, Elliot, Messinger, Sheldon and Wilson, T. P. (1968) *C-Unit: Search for Community in Prison*. New York: Sage.

Sykes, Gresham M. (1958) *The Society of Captives*. Princeton, NJ: Princeton University Press.

Tennessee v. Garner (1985) 471 U.S. 1 (1985).

Thompson, E.P. (1975) *Whigs and Hunters: The Black Act*. New York: Pantheon.

Tiffany, Lawrence, McIntyre, Donald Jr., and Rotenberg, Daniel L. (1967) *Detection of Crime: Stopping and Questioning, Search and Seizure, Encouragement and Entrapment*. Boston: Little, Brown.

Tonry, Michael H. (1996) *Sentencing Matters*. New York: Oxford University Press.

United States v. Salerno (1987) 107 S.Ct. 2045.

Unsigned (1969) "Epilogue to the Survey of the Administration of Criminal Justice," in *Prosecution: The Decision to Charge a Suspect with a Crime*. Boston: Little, Brown, pp. 351–7.

Van den Haag, Ernst (1975) *Punishing Criminals: Concerning a Very Old and Painful Question*. New York: Basic Books.

Von Hirsch, Andrew (1976) *Doing Justice: The Choice of Punishments*. New York: Hill and Wang.

Westley, William (1953) "Violence and the police," *American Journal of Sociology* 59: 34–41.

White, Susan O. and Krislov, Samuel (eds.) (1977) *Understanding Crime: An Evaluation of the National Institute of Law Enforcement and Criminal Justice*. Washington, DC: National Academy of Sciences.

Wickersham Commission (1931) *Reports of the United States Commission on Law Enforcement and Observance*. Washington, DC: Government Printing Office.

Wilson, James Q. ([1975] 1983) *Thinking About Crime*, 2nd edn. New York: Basic Books.

Wilson, James Q. and Kelling, George L. (1982) "Broken windows: The police and neighborhood safety," *Atlantic Monthly* March: 29.

Zimring, Franklin and Hawkins, Gordon (1982) *Deterrence*. Chicago: University of Chicago Press.

Zimring, Franklin and Hawkins, Gordon (1986) *Capital Punishment and the American Agenda*. Cambridge, UK and New York: Cambridge University Press.

Zimring, Franklin and Hawkins, Gordon (1995) *Incapacitation: Penal Confinement and the Restraint of Crime*. New York: Oxford University Press.

Further Reading

Bail – pretrial release

Davis, Kenneth Culp (1969) *Discretionary Justice: A Preliminary Inquiry*. Urbana: University of Illinois Press.

Feeley, Malcolm (1979) *The Process is the Punishment: Handling Cases in a Lower Criminal Court*. New York: Russell Sage Foundation.

Flemming, Roy B (1982) *Punishment Before Trial: An Organizational Perspective of Felony Bail Processes.* New York: Longman.

Goldfarb, Ronald L (1965) *Ransom: A Critique of the American Bail System.* New York: Harper & Row.

Goldkamp, John S. (1979) *Two Classes of Accused: A Study of Bail and Detention in American Justice.* Cambridge, MA: Ballinger.

Schall v. Martin (1984) 467 U.S. 253.

Gender and race discrimination in criminal justice

Daly, Kathleen (1994) *Gender, Crime, and Punishment.* New Haven, CT: Yale University Press.

Hanmer, Jalna Jill Radford and Stanko, Elizabeth A. (1989) *Women, Policing, and Male Violence: International Perspectives.* London and New York: Routledge.

Kennedy, Randall (1997) *Race, Crime, and the Law.* New York: Pantheon.

Ogletree, Charles (1995) *Beyond the Rodney King Story: An Investigation of Police Conduct in Minority Communities.* Boston: Beacon Press.

History of criminal justice

Chambliss, William J. (1964) "A sociological analysis of the law of vagrancy," *Social Problems* 12: 67–77.

Friedman, Lawrence M. (1993) *Crime and Punishment in American History.* New York: Basic Books.

Green, Thomas (1995) "Freedom and criminal responsibility in the age of Pound: An essay on criminal justice," *Michigan Law Review* 93: 1915–2053.

Lichtenstein, Alex (1996) *Twice the Work of Free Labor: The Political Economy of Convict Labor in the South.* London: Verso.

Marion, Nancy E. (1994) *A History of Federal CrimeControl Initiatives, 1960–1993.* Westport, CT: Praeger.

Monkkonen, Eric H. (ed.) (1991) *Courts and Criminal Procedure.* Westport, CT: Meckler.

Rusche, George and Kirchheimer, Otto (1939) *Punishment and Social Structure.* New York: Columbia University Press.

Walker, Samuel (1993) *Taming the System: The Control of Discretion in Criminal Justice, 1950–1990.* New York: Oxford University Press.

Juvenile justice

Cohen, Stanley (1967) "Mods, rockers, and the rest," *The Howard Journal* 12: 121–30.

Lefstein, Norman, Stapleton, Vaughn, and Teitelbaum, Lee (1969) "In search of juvenile justice: Gault and its implementation," *Law & Society Review* 3: 491–562.

Platt, Anthony (1977) *The Child Savers: The Invention of Delinquency,* 2nd edn. Chicago: University of Chicago Press.

Schlossman, Steven L. (1977) *Love and the American Delinquent: The Theory and Practice of Progressive Juvenile Justice, 1825–1920.* Chicago: University of Chicago Press.

Lawyers and criminal justice

Mann, Kenneth (1985) *Defending White-Collar Crime: A Portrait of Attorneys at Work.* New Haven, CT: Yale University Press.

McDonald, William F. (1979) *The Defense Counsel.* Beverly Hills, CA: Sage Publications.

Paulsen, Monrad G. (1961) *The Problem of Assistance to the Indigent Accused.* Philadelphia: American Law Institute.

Penology and sentencing

Andenaes, Johannes (1971) "Deterrence and specific offenses," *University of Chicago Law Review* 38: 537–80.

Ashworth, Andrew (2000) *Sentencing and Criminal Justice*, 3rd edn. London: Butterworth.

Bortner, M.A., Zatz, Marjorie S., and Hawkins, Darnell (2000) "Race and transfer: Empirical research and social context," in Jeffrey Fagan and Franklin E. Zimring (eds.), *The Changing Borders of Juvenile Justice*. Chicago: University of Chicago Press, pp. 277–320.

Bottoms, Anthony (1994) "The philosophy and politics of punishment and sentencing," in Chris Clarkson and Rod Morgan (eds.), *The Politics of Sentencing Reform*. New York: Oxford University Press, pp. 17–50.

Braithwaite, John (1989) *Crime, Shame and Reintegration*. New York: Cambridge University Press.

Bright, Charles (1994) *The Powers that Punish: Prison and Politics in the Era of the "Big House," 1920–1955*. Ann Arbor: University of Michigan Press.

Carroll, Leo (1974) *Hacks, Blacks, and Cons*. Lexington, MA: Lexington Books.

Christie, Nils (2000) *Crime Control as Industry: Toward Gulags, Western Style*. London: Routledge.

Cummins, Eric (1994) *The Rise and Fall of California's Radical Prison Movement*. Stanford, CA: Stanford University Press.

DiIulio, John J., Jr. (1987) *Governing Prisons: A Comparative Study of Correctional Management*. New York: Free Press.

Dumm, Thomas (1987) *Democracy and Punishment: Disciplinary Origins of the United States*. Madison: University of Wisconsin Press.

Emerson, Robert (1969) *Judging Delinquents: Contexts and Process in Juvenile Court*. Chicago: Aldine.

Feeley, Malcolm M. and Rubin, Edward L. (1998) *Judicial Policy Making in the Modern State: How the Courts Reformed America's Prisons*. Cambridge, UK and New York: Cambridge University Press.

Feeley, Malcolm and Simon, Jonathan (1992) "The new penology: Notes on the emerging strategy of corrections and its implications," *Criminology* 30: 449–74.

Foucault, Michel ([1978] 2000) "About the concept of the 'dangerous individual' in nineteenth-century legal psychiatry," in *Essential Works of Michel Foucault, 1954–1984, Vol. 3, Power*, ed. James Faubion. New York: New Press, pp. 176–200.

Giallombardo, R. (1966) *A Study of Women's Prison*. New York: Wiley.

Goffman, Ervin (1961) *Asylums*. New York: Doubleday.

Greenberg, David F. and Stender, Fay (1972) "The prison as a lawless agency," *Buffalo Law Review* 21: 799–838.

Hawkins, Gordon (1976) *The Prison: Policy and Practice*. Chicago: University of Chicago Press.

Irwin, John (1980) *Prisons in Turmoil*. Boston: Little, Brown.

Irwin, John and Cressey, Donald R. (1962) "Thieves, convicts, and the inmate culture," *Social Problems* 10: 142–55.

Jacobs, James B. (1977) *Stateville: The Penitentiary in Mass Society*. Chicago: University of Chicago Press.

Mauer, Marc (1999) *Race to Incarcerate*. New York: The New Press.

Morris, Norval (1974) *The Future of Imprisonment*. Chicago, University of Chicago Press.

Morris, Norval and Tonry, Michael (1990) *Between Prison and Probation: Intermediate Punishments in a Rational Sentencing System*. New York: Oxford University Press.

Rhine, Edward E. (1990) "The rule of law, disciplinary practices, and Rahway State Prison: A case study in judicial intervention and social control," in John J. DiIulio, Jr. (ed.) *Courts, Corrections, and the Constitution: The Impact of Judicial Intervention on Prisons and Jails*. New York: Oxford University Press, pp. 173–222.

Roberts, Julian V. (1997) "The role of criminal record in the sentencing process," in Michael Tonry (ed.) *Crime and Justice: A Review of Research*, vol. 2. Chicago: University of Chicago Press, pp. 303–62.

Ross, H. Laurence, Campbell, Donald T., and Glass, Gene V. (1970) "Determining the social effects of a legal reform: The British 'breathalyser' crackdown of 1967," *American Behavioral Scientist* 13: 493–509.

Rusche, George and Kirchheimer, Otto (1939) *Punishment and Social Structure*. New York: Columbia University Press.

Sparks, Richard and Bottoms, A.E. (1995) "Legitimacy and order in prisons," *British Journal of Criminology* 46: 45–52.

Sykes, Gresham M. and Matza, David (1957) "Techniques of neutralization: A theory of delinquency," *American Sociological Review* 22: 664–70.

Sykes, Gresham M. and Messinger, Sheldon L. (1960) "The inmate social system," in R.A. Cloward et al. (eds.), *Theoretical Studies in Social Organization of the Prison*. New York: Social Science Research Council, pp. 11–13.

Tittle, Charles R. and Logan, Charles H. (1973) "Sanctions and deviance: Evidence and remaining questions," *Law & Society Review* 3: 371–82.

Tonry, Michael and Zimring, Franklin E. (eds.) (1984) *Reform and Punishment: Essays on Criminal Sentencing*. Chicago: University of Chicago Press.

Useem, Bert and Kimball, Peter (1989) *States of Seige: U.S. Prison Riots, 1971–1986*. New York: Oxford University Press.

Wheeler, Stanley (1969) "Socialization in correctional institutions," in David A. Goslin (ed.), *Handbook of Socialization Theory and Research*. New York: Rand McNally &. Co., pp. 1005–23.

Wolfgang, Marvin E. and Riedel, Marc (1973) "Race, judicial discretion, and the death penalty," *Annals of the American Academy of Political and Social Science* 407: 119–33.

Wright, Erik O. (1973) *The Politics of Punishment*. New York: Harper & Row.

Zimring, Franklin E. (1991) *The Scale of Imprisonment*. Chicago: University of Chicago Press.

Police

Bittner, Egon (1967) "The police on skid-row: A study of peace keeping," *American Sociological Review* 32: 699–715.

Bordua, David J. (1967) *The Police*. New York: John Wiley & Sons.

Chambliss, William J. and Seidman, Robert B. (1971) *Law, Order, and Power*. Reading, MA: Addison-Wesley.

Ericson, Richard V. and Haggerty, Kevin (1997) *Policing the Risk Society*. Toronto: University of Toronto Press.

Foote, Caleb (1956) "Vagrancy-type law and its administration," *University of Pennsylvania Law Review* 104: 603–50.

Fyfe, James (1982) "Blind justice: Police shootings in Memphis," *Journal of Criminal Law & Criminology* 73: 707–22.

Goldstein, Herman (1976) *Policing a Free Society*. Cambridge, MA: Ballinger,

Piliavin, Irving and Briar, Scott (1964) "Police encounters with juveniles," *American Journal of Sociology* 70: 206–14.

Remington, Frank J. (1965) "Editor's foreword," in *Arrest: The Decision to Take a Suspect into Custody*. Boston: Little Brown and Company.

Report by the Commission to Investigate Allegations of Police Corruption in New York City (1972), Whitman Knapp, Chairman, August 3. New York: Bar Press.

Wilson, James Q. (1968) *Varieties of Police Behavior: The Management of Law and Order in Eight Communities*. Cambridge, MA: Harvard University Press.

18

Rights in the Shadow of Class: Poverty, Welfare, and the Law

Frank Munger

Persistent poverty is a source of conspicuous failure in developed economies such as the United States, which boasts of its affluence and vigorously advocates free labor markets, laissez faire capitalism, and law around the globe. To many, it seems self-evident that the extremes of wealth and power created by a capitalist economy and free labor market will result in unequal justice for rich and poor. Documenting and explaining the legal inequities experienced by poor people has appealed to the critical impulse of sociolegal scholars who perceive the treatment of those who live in poverty as an important example of flaws in the law's promise of equal justice.

Sociolegal research on the legal experiences of the poor reflects an understanding of the close connection between economic inequality and law. Yet economic inequality has always created a dilemma for sociolegal scholars. Early sociolegal research was embedded in the values of liberal legalism and the perspectives of American social science. Although sociolegal scholarship is often critical of liberal legalism, it has been strongly influenced by it. Liberal legalism accepts the legitimacy of economic inequality and simultaneously maintains that equal justice is achievable. Because economic inequality is morally acceptable there is a presumption that legal inequities are transient, that law can be insulated from social differences, and, at the same time, that many policies creating or preserving economic differences are legitimate. As a result, injustice caused by morally condemned extremes of poverty has been an easier target for sociolegal scholars than class inequalities sustaining the economic core of capitalism.

Further, American social science was shaped from its early stages by the pragmatism of the Chicago School, which turned away from European social theories of class according to which poverty and class conflict are inevitable by-products of unregulated capitalism (Simon, 1999). Chicago School sociology embraced a perspective more consistent with the faith that America is a "classless" society, conceiving of poverty as a product of transient social disorganization, dysfunction, and individual failure, while the forces of the market were considered an inevitable,

indeed foundational, aspect of American society. Alice O'Connor's (2001) percep-
tive history identifies this perspective as a problem at the core of "poverty knowledge." Poverty scholars have persistently focused on the capacities and
competitiveness of the poor. When they have also considered the political and
institutional sources of poverty they have failed to develop an effective counter-
perspective to the popular political discourse about the poor's moral failure and
individual accountability; to the contrary they have reinforced that perspective by
the amount of time and attention they have devoted to it, making it more complex
and nuanced, but never effectively contesting its legitimacy.

If sociolegal studies have been swept along by the tide of development in American social science (Sarat and Simon, 2001; Simon, 1999), they have also kept alive a
critical perspective, growing from legal realism's critique of liberal legalism's claims
and strengthened by the contributions of the critical legal studies movement. Research blends different, sometimes inconsistent, explanations of the relationship
between poverty and law. Some scholars, like O'Connor, perceive that poverty
springs from the relationship between those who benefit from a competitive labor
market and a capitalist economy and those who inevitably suffer (see Wright, 1994).
According to this *relational* perspective, poverty arises from systemic sources, and
poverty relief inevitably creates conflict between groups with different economic and
political interests. Few sociolegal studies actually pursue the implications of this
perspective. More frequently, a second perspective prevails, which focuses on differences between the poor and the mainstream. This approach emphasizes how law
matters to poor *individuals* – how poor persons' perceptions of law, legal capacities,
and experiences of law and legal culture are different from those of other persons.
While research from an individual perspective may illuminate the shortcomings of
liberal legalism, research must adopt a relational perspective to explore the law's
role in poverty's persistence, welfare's failure, and the promise of rights.

This chapter describes three approaches to research on poverty and law that blend
these contrasting perspectives. During the civil rights era of the 1960s and 1970s,
sociolegal research on poverty focused on the failure of law's promise of equal justice
for the poor. A second type of research, evolving out of the first, examines how law
matters from the perspective of the poor. This research has studied, in particular, the
"legal consciousness" of poor persons that illuminates practices of legal domination
and resistance in everyday life. Contemporary scholars increasingly pursue a
third approach that examines welfare state politics and administration. Through
this approach, scholars are examining whether law assists in the realization of
power and privilege for some through welfare state institutions that create poverty
and dependency for others.

Critical examination of the relationship between law, poverty, and the welfare
state has had little effect on policy makers. Why should that concern us? Some have
suggested that sociolegal studies should ignore the "pull of the policy audience"
(Sarat and Silbey, 1988). But many poverty scholars believe that turning away from
power holders defeats what they believe to be a central purpose of their work (see
Ewick, Kagan, and Sarat, 1999; Handler, 1992; Gilliom, 2001). Scholars face the
challenge of conducting research that will deepen the understanding of citizens and
policy makers without allowing the myths, stereotypes, and misconceptions created
by the politics of public discourse on the poor to narrow their vision. This chapter
concludes by describing two difficult issues confronting scholars who hope to change
policies that oppress and exclude poor persons – race and political power. Race,

intertwined with class and gender, so deeply divides American society that it has become an element of governance. Scholars must not only illuminate the disastrous relationship between race and welfare but discover means by which rights can be mobilized to achieve a different conception of democracy.

POVERTY RESEARCH IN THE ERA OF CIVIL RIGHTS

Poverty came to the attention of sociolegal scholars who followed in the path of poverty rights lawyers during the founding years of the law and society movement in the United States. President Kennedy moved poverty to the national agenda in the early 1960s. Fueled by continuing racial disparities underscored by the civil rights movements, urban riots, and the Kerner Commission's condemnation of the flawed opportunities for poor minorities, poverty programs became a high priority for most of the next decade. Office of Economic Opportunity (OEO) legal services was created in 1965, and, as program after program was adopted by Congress, federally funded community organizers and lawyers ensured that poverty rights would have an impact. The prestigious legal services unit led by Ed Sparer at Mobilization for Youth began its systematic attempt to constitutionalize a right to subsistence, building on, among other authorities, the pathbreaking scholarship of Charles Alan Reich (1964, 1965) who maintained that citizens' nearly universal dependence on a wide variety of government benefits had created property rights that deserved constitutional protection.

Liberal legalism and the powerful example of the civil rights movement drew sociolegal scholars' attention initially to the impact of legal process and new legal rights for the poor. These studies of law and poverty provide a starting point for later research, not only by showing that poverty undermines equal justice, but also by examining how formal legal process is "captured" by the social organization of its context (Black, 1976; Macaulay, 1984).

Two studies of law and poverty published in the first volume of the *Law & Society Review* are among the early classics of the field. Carlin, Howard, and Messenger (1966) offered a broad-ranging study of the disadvantages of the poor in the civil justice system. Abraham Blumberg (1967) described the practice of criminal defense law as a "confidence game" which served the goals of professional insiders who must depend on each other's goodwill more than on the goodwill of their clients.

Their research took the form of an impact or "gap" study (see Abel, 1980), which examined the difference between formal law's claims and its achievements. Abel's pejorative term "gap study" does not capture the nuanced interpretations of scholars who employed this framework in the 1960s and 1970s when the impact of law on the poor emerged as a relevant and important aspect of civil rights, or contemporary scholars who conduct impact research with the benefit of more sophisticated historical and contextual methods to guide interpretation. Carlin et al. chose law and poverty "because this area seems to us most likely to call into question conventional assumptions about the structure, conditions, and consequences of legal administration" (Carlin et al., 1966: 9). However, their findings were not limited to the failure of the formal conventions and rules of the legal system, but included fundamental and continuing flaws in politics, governmental administration, the training and professional culture of lawyers, and the institutions that socialize the poor in ways that leave them at a disadvantage.

Blumberg, similarly, explains his research by drawing into question the impact of recent legal decisions that protected the rights of criminal defendants. Yet the insight he derives from his study of defenders' interactions with prosecutors and judges is not limited to the formal defects in implementation of legal norms. He describes in some detail the process by which interactions with other participants coopt the role of defense attorneys and influence their relationships with clients.

Both studies contain the seeds of future trends in sociolegal research on the "legal consciousness" of poor persons, the influence of context, and the social interests that compete with the law's formal assumptions about the goals of legal process. Both bring into focus the importance of the participants themselves – the competence, resources, and dispositions they bring to the process. With respect to the latter, Carlin et al. offered an extended analysis of the "legal competence" of the poor litigant.

Levine and Preston (1970) surveyed poor persons concerning their "resource orientation" – the likelihood that they would make use of an attorney to resolve a dispute. The survey showed overwhelmingly that the poor lacked knowledge of their rights and of the availability of legal services lawyers. Those poor who had knowledge often believed they would lose, a belief that discouraged them from contacting a lawyer. Likewise, Felstiner's (1974) analysis of dispute behavior concluded that the poor are far more likely to "lump" than litigate their grievances. Levine and Preston also showed that there was considerable variation in knowledge, but a "positive" resource orientation was concentrated among younger, white, poor persons.

Studies on which Carlin et al. drew in their analysis viewed the poor as a particularly unfortunate and vulnerable group that was frequently victimized (see Caplovitz, 1963 who studied unethical dealing with poor consumers; Wald, 1965 reporting oppressive treatment of welfare recipients by creditors in the automobile market; Note, 1965 describing lax code enforcement in low-rent housing). Victimization followed from the poor's lack of market alternatives, lack of political power, consignment to less rights-oriented legal forums, and lack of knowledge and resources to contest wrongful treatment. In each of these ways, the poor were depicted as different from the mainstream and unable to protect themselves. The failure of law to protect the poor drew both legal and sociolegal scholars to examine the roles played by attorneys who represented the poor (see Carlin, 1962; Carlin and Howard, 1965; O'Gorman, 1963; Katz, 1978; Abel, 1979; Handler, Hollingsworth, and Erlanger, 1978).

Some of O'Connor's criticisms of American poverty research apply to these civil rights era studies of poverty and law. Carlin and his coauthors studied only the poor; for them, the term "class" has no particularly political or relational meaning. Blumberg made no comparisons between rich and poor (still less between social classes), though the ability of defense attorneys to conduct a "confidence game" may have depended in significant part on the class differences among the participants he describes (e.g., clients versus attorneys, public defenders versus attorneys in white-collar civil or criminal matters). The inevitable link between poor clients and criminal justice is too obvious for comment. Although civil rights era research did more than document the limits of liberal legal justice, it seldom explored the origins of poverty, the politics underlying policies, or whether the economic inequality was *created* or *sustained* by law.

The studies ignored an important tradition of research on African American poverty that probed the sources of poverty and placed lives in context, including interactions with authorities (DuBois, 1899; Frazier, 1939; Liebow, 1967; Stack, 1976; Ladner, 1971). Further, scholars emphasized the unique characteristics of poor individuals, not the causes of their social circumstances. Criminal justice scholars, who studied the legal processes most involved with the poor, seldom gave critical attention to individuals' poverty or class (contrast Chambliss, 1964 and Hagan, 1994). Conceptualizing poverty in relational terms might have led to different questions: whether the disadvantages experienced by some are sustained by benefits they confer on others, and, in particular, who is advantaged by the particular kind of competence required by the legal system?

Finally, this research offered a limited view of legal process. Reich's arguments about the importance of entitlements were widely discussed but little sociolegal research pursued their implications for the poor. Poor persons encounter administrative decision makers relatively more frequently (Mayhew and Reiss, 1969) and are more likely to face informal but coercive administrative decision making than wealthier citizens (Lipsky, 1984). When poverty programs moved off the scene in the 1970s and 1980s, sociolegal poverty research all but disappeared.

Galanter's (1974) seminal essay, "Why the 'haves' come out ahead" took stock of the critique of liberal legalism's promise to "have nots." The overwhelming evidence of bias against "have nots" showed that the capacity of the law to bring about social change was limited by the very social factors that formal changes in the law were intended to neutralize. Galanter's synthesis is powerful because the legal system's bias was not limited to subordinate persons such as the incompetent poor but worked against other individuals as well whose lack of experience and resources disadvantage them. But Galanter's synthesis focused, like much mainstream poverty research, on the competitive disadvantages of individuals. Differences in litigants' legal competence, together with the legal system's inherent inability to alter the effects of this social inequality, create legal bias. Because his essay focuses on legal process rather than social relationships, Galanter did not explore the legal bases for class privilege or power, but limited his discussion to the process by which those with power use law to their advantage.

"Haves" is a summation but also a turning point that can be readily marked in research on poverty. Scholars were already moving away from a self-contained view of legal process. Legal process was not passive and reactive. Law and its context were *interactive*, and law helped to *constitute* the social relations that led to legal inequality. Increasingly sophisticated studies showed the varieties of legal experience of individuals in different social roles, contexts, and backgrounds, problematizing the very concept of legal equality (Mayhew and Reiss, 1969; Moore, 1974; and Felstiner, Abel, and Sarat, 1980). These trends suggested to many scholars that analysis of the relationship between social hierarchy and legal inequality should be studied from a more subjective perspective and in the varied contexts of everyday experience.

How Law Matters for the Poor – Legal Consciousness, Domination, Resistance

Poverty research of the civil rights era was transformed by the collapse of the War on Poverty. A conservative backlash against civil rights and poverty rights, termination or cutback of many poverty programs, and racial politics made the work of progessive and critical poverty scholars unwelcome among policy makers and discouraged new research projects. Since the 1970s, government-sponsored poverty research has been carefully limited to program evaluation and impact studies, narrowly focused on incremental program goals (Katz, 1989).

For scholars outside the narrowing mainstream of government-sponsored poverty research, a critical perspective on poverty was maintained within an evolving field of sociolegal research. An important shift in perspective marked this evolution. The new trope – law in context – focused on the disjunction between formal law and law's role in context – law in everyday life. Greater attention was given to the law's noninstrumental roles in everyday life – symbolic, contested, and constitutive. The new perspective made the interpretations of ordinary persons central to understanding the meaning and effects of law. Ordinary persons interpreted and gave meaning to law at sites of everyday interaction and contention such as families, neighborhoods, and workplaces as well as in lawyers' offices and courts.

Studying law in everyday life provided an important new window on inequality and domination, and "legal consciousness" became a focus of such studies. The poor, women, African Americans, were no longer simply categories of litigants. Law shaped their consciousness as individuals and citizens and thus influenced their routines and interactions in everyday life. The poor and oppressed, as legal actors, acquired agency both as individuals and as actors within systems of culture and meaning through the development of their legal consciousness. Indeed, the emphasis on agency became a defining element of critical research on law, which claimed to give voice to the "other" – a voice that had previously been lost in the larger picture of liberal legalism and legal process (Silbey and Sarat, 1987).

Three influential studies illustrate this pursuit. Ewick and Silbey (1992) describe the legal consciousness of "Millie," a poor black domestic housekeeper charged with a hit and run accident involving her uninsured car while it was being driven by a friend of a relative without her permission. Austin Sarat describes the legal consciousness of the "welfare poor," who seek assistance from legal services attorneys, concluding that it is "substantially different from other groups in society for whom law is a less immediate and visible presence" (1990: 344). Lucie White (1990) studies the welfare hearing of "Mrs. G.," examining the culture and history that shapes subordination. She suggests that the law seamlessly reinforces the inequalities experienced by her client throughout her life and creates a consciousness of humiliation – as a morally stigmatized recipient, intimidation – because her voice is silenced in welfare proceedings, and objectification – displacement of her true needs by bureaucratic definitions of "needs" and "entitlements."

The concept of legal consciousness has had an important influence on studies of law and poverty, for example, research on legal process (Mahoney, 1991; Alfieri, 1993), the attorney–client relationship (Alfieri, 1991, 2001; Davis, 1993; Harris, 1999; Lopez, 1992; Trubek, 1994; White, 1988; Sarat and Felstiner, 1995; for critique see Simon, 1996), and the impact of specific welfare laws (see below).

Perhaps the most profound and controversial influence, however, has been on the way scholars perceive the distributive impact of law, for above all these studies suggest that the subtle influence of legal consciousness on legal process and legal rights explains – one more time – why the "haves" come out ahead. Engel (1998) criticizes these studies for conceptualizing the legal consciousness of the poor categorically. Legal consciousness, he argues, is treated as a collective mindset reproduced by law rather than the end product of an interactive and intersubjective process that shapes each individual's consciousness. For Ewick and Silbey, Sarat, and White, the agency of subordinate persons in such settings *is* resistance and "tactical." Engel also suggests that legal consciousness research has overlooked insights long established in the sociolegal field – potential variation in legal consciousness over different substantive areas of law, the multicentered relationship between law and society, and the mediation of unofficial systems of rules and meanings.

The problem of agency

At stake in the analysis of the law's role in power and resistance is the capacity of the poor for self-help and for political struggle. Critics McCann and March (1996) argue that scholars have been too quick to declare poor persons independent and autonomous actors on the basis of isolated acts of disobedience or circumvention of the law. Progressive scholars believe change from the bottom up is necessary for lasting democratic and egalitarian reform, and they resist the image of subordinate persons as passive, apathetic, or possessing false beliefs in the legitimacy of oppressive authority. But misjudging the autonomy of the poor can have negative consequences, Handler (2002) argues, because the image of the poor as willful and capable accords well with the arguments of conservatives and the moral politics of welfare that blame the poor for their poverty.

McCann and March find that three justifications for the significance of such "little events" are suggested by the studies themselves. The first is that the studies map "oppositional consciousness," debunking the theory that subordinate persons possess a false consciousness of the "myth of rights." These findings are similar to those of a long line of Marxist social historians (Hay, 1975; Thompson, 1975; Genovese, 1976).

Second, small acts of resistance may be "significant in a psychological, or existential sense" because they affirm "basic dignity, autonomy, and personhood" (McCann and March, 1996: 226). But McCann and March are deeply skeptical about such claims, concluding that "many of these works could be read as sorry accounts of experiences that only deepen the sense of what John Gaventa (1980) calls 'powerlessness' among marginalized citizens" (McCann and March, 1996: 227; cf. Roberts, 2000), and studies confirm his conclusion (White, 1993; Soss, 1999).

Handler (1996, 2002) argues that isolated acts of resistance can be empowering only as part of a developmental process, such as that described in White's (2002, and in preparation) study of mothers in a Head Start program. Similarly, Gilliom's (2001) interviews with poor Appalachian women about welfare surveillance suggested to him that everyday acts of resistance could "work as forms of politics" where particular conditions were met – tangible improvements, sharing and collaboration among participants, and "ethical grounding or ideology within which to frame resistant practices" (Gilliom, 2001: 103). Gilliom found the women countered control by embracing an ethic of care that elevated commitments to others over compliance with welfare regulations.

A third justification for studying everyday acts of resistance is their potential for political escalation. Yet most studies of law and everyday resistance have focused on the actions of isolated individuals, with little examination of their relationships to group identity or support, making them unlikely candidates for collective political action. Context is critical for the political potential of law. Understanding the politics of power and resistance requires a frame of reference that indicates what is at stake and what is gained or lost in particular encounters between dominant and subordinate persons, that is, a relational framework of understanding. Moreover, resistance with the potential to escalate politically is about broad struggles – against racism, economic exploitation, or patriarchal control – and not merely tactical maneuvering against judges, clerks, administrators or other officials (McCann and March, 1996: 220; cf. Handler, 1992). In brief, scholars studying the legal consciousness of poor persons must pay more attention to the social organization and institutional context underlying domination and resistance.

WELFARE STATE ADMINISTRATION – DEPENDENCY BY LAW

Contemporary scholars recognize the continuing but contingent role of state power in creating and maintaining poverty, and many are also interested in reconstituting the welfare state – a search for an *affirmative* and more democratic welfare state (Garland, 2001; Sarat and Simon, 2001; Handler and Hasenfeld, 1997). The American welfare state's long history of stigmatizing and inadequate assistance for the poor might well make us doubt whether truly affirmative programs will be adopted without substantial political change. Both civil rights era impact research and studies of legal consciousness suggest that the poor will often be among the most oppressed and the least capable of politically altering this familiar pattern.

Sociolegal scholars have been energized not only by frustration with their declining influence in an era of "cultural politics" (Simon, 1999; Garth and Sterling, 1998), but also by concern about the effects of welfare state retrenchment on minorities, immigrants, workers, women, and the poor. Global crises connecting First and Third World economies have always enhanced the critical understanding of sociolegal scholars, and some poverty scholars have explored this connection in their research (e.g., Handler, 2003; Coombe, 1995; Santos, 1995; White, 1998; Nightingale, 2002).

Critical scholarship – race, gender, class, in the welfare state

If, as McCann and March claim, research on legal consciousness of the poor requires a relational and political perspective, critical race and critical feminist scholars have played an important role not only by developing a relational perspective on poor women and minorities, but also by addressing the issue of political voice. Critical feminist and critical race scholars were among the first to place legal domination of poor women and minorities in historical and institutional context and, in this context, to explore the role of emancipatory practices capable of undermining legal domination.

Critical histories of the evolution of poverty and welfare set the stage for sociolegal research on contemporary welfare state policy and its administration. Although a generation of progressive scholars of working-class conflict examined the role of law in class domination and politics (Piven and Cloward, 1971; Hay, 1975; Thompson, 1975), Gordon (1988b) criticized them for ignoring the evolving nature of poverty, in particular its concentration among minorities and women, groups never assimilated into the primary labor market and unlikely to participate in the class struggles envisioned by nineteenth-century theorists (see also Quadagno, 1992). Critical feminist and critical race historians (Gordon, 1988a, 1994; Quadagno, 1994; Sterett,

1997; Skocpol, 1992) have transformed our understanding by showing that patri-archy and racism have molded the character of the American system of public relief. Fraser and Gordon (1994) trace the cultural shifts in the concept of "dependency" that prefigured (and were reinforced by) these welfare policies. Dependency carries taken-for-granted connotations that limit the discourse about welfare, especially assumptions about "human nature, gender roles, the causes of poverty, the nature of citizenship, the sources of entitlement, and what counts as work and as a contribution to society" (Fraser and Gordon, 1994: 311).

Significantly, critical race and feminist scholars place the identities and conscious-ness of poor persons in a concrete historical and *relational* context. They have demonstrated that a relational view of inequality was essential – inequality continues because of the support for institutions that maintain patriarchy and white privilege.

Further, critical scholars emphasize the importance of variations in context and perspective in determining the role that rights play in the lives of weak and powerless persons. While rights often constituted domination of the oppressed, historical examples showed that they could also be turned to the advantage of subordinate persons under circumstances that permitted their movements to gain power (Crenshaw, 1988; Schneider, 1986; see also Piven and Cloward, 1977). The role of rights, they argued, also depended on voice and perspective. Minow's (1990) analy-sis of contemporary and historical examples showed that the law may promote inclusion and full citizenship when the experiences of those who have experienced poverty and oppression influence legislative, administrative, or judicial processes. Conversely, she traces the counterintuitive stigmatizing effects of many civil rights laws to their origin in the consciousness of legislators, judges, and professionals who lack a complete understanding of the ways that society creates the disadvantages encountered by the oppressed.

Finally, critical scholars' sensitivity to voice has caused them to raise important questions about studies of domination and oppression – how can scholars "know" the experiences of socially oppressed groups and interpret or "give voice" to their concerns (see Minow, 1990: 195–8; cf. Sarat, 1990; White, 1990)? The importance of the poor's own voice in the realization of rights suggests to some scholars that the poor must play a central role in the research enterprise itself, shaping issues, gathering and interpreting data, and discovering ways to deploy rights for change (Ansley, 2002).

Critical scholarship on poverty and the welfare state, like studies of legal con-sciousness and law in everyday life, have strengthened the growing perception among poverty scholars that the poor are active rather than apathetic and have experiences and values as varied as the mainstream. Scholars have begun to shift their attention to understanding how the poor "navigate the welfare state from below" (Katz, personal communication, 1997). The question is, what have scholars learned about the welfare state and how does that enrich their research on poverty and law?

Moral citizenship

Critical history of poverty law shows that fundamental economic conflicts that divide society along lines of class, gender, and race underlie welfare state policies: the desire of employers and the well-to-do to preserve the advantages they derive from the market versus the desire of workers, working poor, unemployed caretakers and others unable to obtain a living wage job for greater economic security (Katz, 1986, 1989; Handler and Hasenfeld, 1991; Fraser and Gordon, 1994). Why do these economic conflicts rarely emerge in public discourse?

The history of Anglo-American welfare policy shows that economic interests of groups divided by class, race, and gender have been expressed in a discourse of moral identity and social citizenship (Gordon, 1994; Handler and Hasenfeld, 1991). Eligibility for social provision has never been a universal right, but rather a residual for those deserving poor who cannot support themselves. Sociolegal poverty scholars, among others, have described the important distinction drawn between the *deserving* poor, who merit social insurance and protection against the hardships of the free labor market, and the *undeserving* poor, who merit help only in times of severe hardship and under conditions intended to reform their flawed moral character (Katz, 1986, 1989; Handler and Hasenfeld, 1991; Fraser and Gordon, 1994). In this respect, social rights resemble a contract rather than a universal citizenship entitlement (cf. Mead, 1986). Individuals are obligated to make themselves self-sufficient by fulfilling the roles – as wage earner, as wife of a wage earner, as a married parent – that society envisions for them. Those who do not conform are undeserving of welfare (Pearce, 1990; Mink, 1990).

Welfare law plays a different role in other cultures that associate different identities with dependency. Anglo-American culture is representative of societies that Esping-Anderson terms "liberal" welfare regimes," that place "unbounded faith in market sovereignty" (1990, 1999: 81) and offer low level, means-tested welfare benefits designed to reinforce labor market participation (others are Australia, New Zealand, and Canada). Most European countries – such as Austria, France, Germany, and Italy – together with Japan have "conservative" welfare regimes that emphasize preservation of family and social status, for example by providing family benefits sufficient to allow women to remain at home in traditional nonworking roles. Scandinavian countries have "social democratic" welfare regimes that decommodify labor through universal, nonmeans-tested benefits. In theory, the implications of differences between these regimes for the moral identity of welfare recipients are great. Handler (2002) has argued that the regimes are converging in practice due to the growing strength of conservative ideology and to inevitable similarities of bureaucratic behavior. But whether or not there are additional points of similarity or difference, the strong association between historical development, moral discourse, and social provision seems beyond question.

The moral content of the discourse of social citizenship has provided a powerful tool for explaining the details of welfare policy (Gordon, 1988b; Skocpol, 1992; Sterett, 1997), the evolution and impact of social movements for poverty rights (Piven and Cloward, 1977; Handler, 1978), and the role of gender and race in the relationship between poverty lawyers and their clients (Davis, 1993; Lopez, 1992; Alfieri, 1991). Fraser and Gordon (1994) trace the relationship between the changing moral stigma of "dependency" and welfare in the twentieth century. Early programs stigmatized particular women – poor, immigrant, unmarried – but not others, for example the white widow. With the increasing enrollment of unmarried African American women in Aid to Families with Dependent Children (AFDC) in the 1960s, the image of deviant dependency was again a mirror image of white, middle-class normality – now the unmarried female head of an African American household. Disturbed by rising rates of employment among mothers in white families, increasing divorce and declining marriage rates, Americans experienced a "moral panic about dependency" in the 1980s (Fraser and Gordon, 1994). Welfare reform in the 1990s reflects the latest politically inspired image – generations of African American teenage mothers trapped by welfare in a cycle of helpless dependency (see P. Williams, 1991; Roberts, 1997b, 1999).

Above all, Garland (2001) argues, the emphasis of the market on voluntary choice grounds the moral identity assigned to persons. The poor, the unemployed, the unmarried, the underqualified, the discriminated against, the abused who cannot work or cannot earn enough for themselves and their families to survive are presumed to have chosen not to work and to rely on welfare. They are subjected to discipline in exchange for benefits under conditions designed to make them seek work and behave in other ways deemed appropriate for citizenship by achieving self-sufficiency through work or marriage and by discouraging the "moral hazard" of unnecessary reliance on benefits.

A substantial body of scholarship describes policies reflecting welfare mothers' moral identity and ignoring their actual behavior and experiences (Fraser and Gordon, 1994; see also Fineman, 1999; J.A. White, 2000; Roberts, 1997b; McKinnon, 1993; Karst, 1989). Studies of poor women examine the origins and effects of morally stigmatizing welfare policies that inhibit rather than help poor women in performing the labor that society tacitly demands – responsibly caring for families (Gordon, 1994; Edin and Lein, 1997; McClain, 1996; Raphael, 1996; Gilliom, 2001). Some welfare policies, particularly those affecting reproductive rights, have been applied with a marked racial bias and reflect stereotypes that prevailed in the welfare reform discourse of the 1990s about the unfitness of young black women for parenting (Roberts, 1997a). Similarly, state officials have continued to remove a disproportionate number of black children from their mothers and place them in foster care (Roberts, 1999). Scholars describe a mismatch between the images of welfare recipients and their actual lives that turns the public face of assistance and rehabilitation into a less visible reality of inappropriate and punitive effects (L. Williams, 1992).

Myth and ceremony in administration

One of the most provocative observations in Galanter's (1974) massive mapping of legal process appears almost as an afterthought in a long aside on "appended" dispute resolution systems, including administrative adjudication, mediation, negotiation, and nonlegal dispute resolution. He suggested that resort to appended systems was less about rights and more about restoring relationships, but his characterization ignored precisely the problem of "class" justice. Because the rapidly increasing importance of welfare state entitlements shifted rights disputes from courts to bureaucracies for many citizens but for poor citizens in particular, for the poor, this exception threatened to swallow his paradigm. The relatively poor and powerless, far more than the affluent and powerful, encounter layers of informal administrative decision making respecting important rights.

Because welfare policies are based on moral identity as well as on the needs of the poor, Handler and Hasenfeld (1991) argue that there has always been a wide gap between the rhetoric of poverty policies and the practical administration of welfare. They refer to the gap as the "myth and ceremony" of welfare policy – "myth" because of the discourse of policy making and legislation that relies on stereotypical and contradictory images of the poor, and "ceremony" because difficulties in administering policies that bear little relation to the real needs of poor people typically result in token enforcement for a few recipients and widespread, unacknowledged administrative default for the rest. Policies requiring welfare recipients to work have historically been impossible to enforce because they have ignored the real problems that the labor market creates for those who are poor. For example, in the early 1960s, the law required social services for recipients but in reality agencies lacked the capacity and had little incentive to provide such services (Handler, 1990). Rising welfare roles due in part to an aggressive welfare rights movement eventually ended ceremonial compliance as formal emphasis shifted to eligibility determination (W. Simon, 1983).

Research suggests that recent welfare reforms will repeat the pattern. Welfare reform has tightened work requirements, imposed lifetime time limits, and added other restrictions that require close supervision and enforcement (Kost and Munger, 1996). Women who are particularly creative in acquiring support from others in a resource-poor environment are more successful in maintaining employment (Henly, 2002) and raising children (Edin and Lein, 1997), but they often must violate specific mandates of the welfare law in order to maintain their families (Gilliom, 2001). Those with multiple barriers to employment – such as lack of education or transportation – or who have a disability (up to 40 percent of the deeply impoverished) cannot work (Danziger et al., 1999). Welfare administrators offer meager assistance in coping with these problems, and yet all recipients face mandatory time limits on welfare. The new law encourages sanctioning recipients for their "voluntary" failure to comply by reducing or ending welfare support without respect to need. Reviewing these and other studies, Handler and Hasenfeld (1997) conclude that the moral images that influence welfare legislation will lead to more myth and ceremony.

The myth that a formal declaration of entitlement to welfare will guarantee benefits has long been discredited by studies showing that administrative practices impeding recipients' efforts to become eligible result in "bureaucratic disentitlement" (Lipsky, 1984; see also Bennett, 1995). Caseworkers, like legislators, are influenced by their "moral typification" of recipients (Hasenfeld, 1983; Brodkin, 1997). The myth that formal policies and due process will guarantee individual autonomy and empowerment has been thoroughly examined and criticized by Simon (1983) and by Handler (1986, 1990).

Empowerment of welfare recipients may be even more difficult in the new era of entrepreneurial government and management by objective. Under the new system, welfare caseworkers are given even more discretion to achieve the goals set by supervisors, but Diller (2000) suggests that top-down control continues to be exercised in ways that limit the range of outcomes of client–caseworker interaction, if not the means by which they may be achieved. Serious questions arise about whether liberal legalism can insure that discretion is exercised without arbitrariness or discrimination. How much discretion entrepreneurial government creates in practice, how such discretion will be used, and whether there are effective means of checking abuses are important issues for further research (see, e.g., a rare study of racial bias in welfare by Gooden, 1998).

Welfare as "private government"

Macaulay's (1986) insightful analysis of "private government" reminds us that social networks, neighborhoods, associations, corporations, contracts and other private relations that "govern" individuals often mediate the effects of public policy and law.

He reminds us that the law's attempts to set terms for relationships within organizations or between contracting parties rarely counters existing imbalances in power. Macaulay's analysis also encourages looking beyond welfare administration to its impact on the social relationships in the private world of welfare recipients which welfare law ultimately attempts to govern.

Sociolegal scholarship suggests that his insight is particularly applicable to postreform welfare administration where multiple layers of public and private organization interact and mediate in carrying out federal and state mandates. Two concepts laden with market ideology – devolution and privatization – have legitimated giving more control of welfare to state and local governments and permitting private service providers to assume responsibilities for welfare previously assumed by public servants (Katz, 2001). Both concepts suggest that greater efficiency will be achieved – more effective welfare at lower cost. In truth the system of welfare in the USA has always been highly decentralized. States and their subdivisions have administered federally funded welfare since the program's inception and private providers have always played an important role.

States have responded to the devolution of new responsibilities by giving local administrators even more control and by contracting out core welfare administration as well as more specialized services. State and local politics control the level of welfare spending as well as the symbolic emphasis placed on work and supporting services (Cashin, 1999). Reliance on private entrepreneurs to provide administration of welfare depends on a contracting process controlled by administrators beholden to the same political constitutencies who resist spending and restrict welfare (Bezdek, 2001).

Gilliom (2001) has shown that increasingly intrusive welfare surveillance and control of recipients harms welfare recipients' relationships with others and their self-images. The myth of welfare reform is that strict accountability will ultimately strengthen poor women's social capital, but the reality is that such intrusive administration often undermines existing social relationships and impedes investment in new social capital (Edin and Lein, 1997; Stack, 1976). Gilliom's interviewees found that evasion and circumvention of welfare law were necessary for survival of their families but in turn this often unavoidable behavior had harmful effects on their self-image as moral citizens (Gilliom, 2001; contrast Rothstein, 2001).

Thus there is a risk that decentralization will simply disguise the process of domination of welfare recipients who will not be helped to achieve self-sufficiency and whose failure will confirm the myth of their dependency. Welfare recipients will have become even more dependent *by law* (Munger, 2002). While some have argued for revival of a stronger welfare state (Lowi, 1998; Karst, 1997), others point to research suggesting that the outcome of devolution and privatization is indeterminate. Handler (1996), for example, describes case studies that show that empowerment can be achieved when the administrative priorities of the powerful are contested politically and also through "empowerment by invitation" when administration creates opportunities for development of self-confidence and participatory competence. He suggests that the latter form of empowerment is possible only when power holders gain something from participation by dependent people, such as stability, profitability, or legitimacy, and when such opportunities continue long enough to allow a sense of efficacy and trust in participation to develop (Handler, 2002). Lucie White's (2002) analysis of mothers' empowerment through participation in a Head Start program illustrates his argument.

Sociolegal research on the administration of welfare in the welfare state is poised to break new ground by focusing on the complexity of organizational and institutional structures and processes that shape the law's symbolic and constitutive impact. State, local, and private compliance with statutory (and constitutional) welfare law requirements; the spread of welfare program innovations among the states (see, e.g., Soule and Zylan, 1997); symbolic compliance at the institutional level; the "capture" of local programs by their social, political, and economic context – all seem ripe for study. In turn, sociolegal poverty scholars exploring the cultural and symbolic roles of law in the welfare state can benefit from available literatures on the new institutionalism and organizational theory (Suchman and Edelman, 1996; see also Smith, 1988) that address these and similar processes of organizational change and development.

GOVERNING THROUGH POVERTY – TWO CHALLENGES FOR RESEARCH

The Russell Sage Foundation (Farley, Danziger, and Holzer, 2000) began its analysis of the relationship between race and poverty in Detroit by asking why blacks and whites live in segregated communities 50 years after racial covenants were declared unconstitutional and 30 years after the Fair Housing Act outlawed racial discrimination in the housing market. The Foundation's sociologists find an answer in public attitudes toward race. They do not comment, as they should, that the law's role has been shaped by the same racial divide, notwithstanding seemingly benign actions of the Supreme Court and Congress (cf. Freeman, 1998). Sociolegal scholars have much to contribute to an understanding of law's complex role in maintaining the welfare state's institutions that divide social classes and exclude many from equal opportunity.

The problem of race

Lee Rainwater (1970) and Herbert Gans (1969), in separate essays, tried to explain why oppressive poverty policies *seemed* different and difficult to attack politically. Rainwater guessed that the wretched conditions and insecurity of the poor were threatening to the mainstream, whose security and affluence similarly depend on the contingencies of the labor market. The cognitive dissonance between the mainstream's sense of security and these "betrayers of the American dream" (Murphy, 1987: 116–17; see also Wuthnow, 1996) was relieved by creating an identity for the poor that makes them different – self-indulgent, foolish, improvident, pleasure-seeking, or corrupt. Today, in a world of increasingly insecure labor conditions, these characterizations of the mainstream and the poor are no longer merely unself-conscious underpinnings of identity but appear at the forefront of poverty politics that keep an insecure working class allied with employers who are hostile to public and private welfare. Gans always claimed the sources of punitive attitudes toward the poor were much more concrete and visible. The existence of the poor benefits more affluent citizens, taxpayers at large, and government administrators. Stereotypical thinking about the underclass makes it easier to go on enjoying these benefits.

Jonathan Simon (1997) has brought to our attention the increasing importance of the image of the "other" in American governance. Simon has demonstrated that the growing divisions among racial groups and between rich and poor have greatly altered our expectations for and practices of governance. The fact that such divisions are marked by differences in culture and political perspective makes consensus, negotiation, and reconciliation of conflicts among the interests of these groups difficult. Simon argues that an image of the criminal "other"– a person of color, poor, predatory, and urban – drives a wide range of public policies of containment, separation, statistically based crime prevention, and punishment that affect not only criminal justice but also land use, transportation, public funding of schools, national electoral politics, and other major institutional arenas.

Poverty, like crime, is also a means of governance. Welfare recipients, like criminals, are stereotyped, reinforcing an image of an "other" whose morally undeserving behavior explains and motivates policies of redistribution and regulation. Welfare dependency is perceived to be a pervasive moral threat, a fear legitimated by the stereotypical identities attached to welfare mothers. Patricia Williams (1991) asks what could possibly justify the shocking murder of a welfare mother in her apartment by fully armed police for "resisting eviction?" Roberts (1997a) describes "genocide" through family planning programs whose racially disparate practices have a significant impact on reproduction among poor black women. Images of the unmarried teenage black woman render the public unsympathetic to welfare recipients and favorable to punitive conditions and harsh sanctions (L. Williams, 1995). Like crime, welfare – and the racial stereotypes that sustain it – help constitute the relationship between social hierarchy and social order.

To conduct more relevant and effective research on poverty, scholars must acknowledge the deep racial fault line in American society and its effects on the identity, self-concept, and behavior of the poor. Race is nearly invisible in mainstream policy research on poverty, and this despite an incontrovertible reality: not only are the experiences of persons of color who are poor different, but different at least in part because persons of color are perceived and treated differently. Martin Gilens (1999) observes a fundamental premise – unexamined in most research on poverty – of the public perception of welfare in the United States: welfare (much like crime) is a province populated by African Americans.

Scholars who want to understand poverty and the public policy debates that surround it must grapple with race-coded discourse. Euphemisms such as "the underclass," "welfare poor," and "cycle of poverty" may sanitize language, but they cannot mask our racialized perceptions of poverty. Nor can they mask the continuing processes of cultural and institutional separation that isolate African Americans from the mainstream. Our race-coded discourse about poverty divides the poor and working classes into two groups: whites who suffer the effects of declining wages, benefits, and job security and therefore are deserving; and blacks who a priori are stigmatized as potential welfare recipients and therefore are undeserving. Until this divide is bridged, Gilens suggests, little will change in the symbolic politics of poverty.

Our concerns about the deep divide between blacks and whites in America, as well as the persistence of patriarchal values, should lead us to a more profound understanding of the stakes in the economic order that fuel them (see insightful criticism by J. Williams, 1999; Roberts, 1997b). The division created by race is ultimately part of a larger and more complex story of race, gender, and class, as Jonathan Simon suggests, which greatly complicates the identities of the poor but also creates a broader potential for political change.

The problem of politics

Underlying the moral politics, welfare in all its forms has served dominant economic interests, especially their interest in stabilizing the supply of labor. Katz (2001) describes the relationship among the American welfare state's three sectors – public, independent (not-for-profit), and private. The private sector consists primarily of employee pension and medical care, together with mixed public–private welfare such as unemployment and workers compensation programs. One reason that the stigma attaching to public welfare programs has remained difficult to change is the political split between segments of the working class created by the mix of public and private welfare – workers dependent upon private, contributory welfare are opposed to being taxed a second time to support public welfare for still poorer, and typically minority, unemployed persons (see Noble, 1997). Some political movements by poor people have been sufficiently destabilizing in domestic politics to influence the passage of more favorable legislation (Piven and Cloward, 1971). More often, carefully limited liberalization of public welfare, for example during the New Deal, has been supported by larger employers interested in labor market stability.

Contemporary welfare reform is just one of many related changes in public and private governance that is supported by stereotyping groups that dominant economic interests want to control (Garland, 2001). The attack on "dependency" has included downsizing workers compensation, reducing worker security and representation, restricting consumer access to bankruptcy, limiting relief to unemployed and displaced workers, and contention over health insurance reform (see McCluskey, 1999; Katz, 2001). Workers' benefits not related to the bottom line are characterized as a form of economic fat, privilege, and immoral dependency, the mirror image of efficient, market-driven, and, therefore, "fair" labor policy. All of these active interventions by the state to *re*regulate the labor market enable employers to pursue low wage and flexible labor strategies to increase profitability.

The assault on dependency thus creates a potential basis for broad political coalition. Still more broadly, as Gilliom (2001) has suggested, the common experience of welfare state surveillance and control of citizens may provide an even wider source of shared understanding and political action.

When law fails in its promise to become an effective enabling force for protecting equal rights in the welfare state, we are left with "the long walk home . . . to politics" (Simon, 1992). The question is how to think about welfare politics. This final task for law and society scholars has already been begun by examining the mutually constitutive role of identity, welfare policies, and the practices of governance. Recent law and society studies examine the effects of enacted law on everyday lives of marginal and excluded persons (Engel and Munger, forthcoming; Munger, 2002; L. White, study of Head Start mothers, in preparation), while others document processes of constituency building, media imaging, and administration (Davis, 1993; Diamond, 2000; Piven and Cloward, 1977; McCann, 1994; L. Williams, 1995; Edelman, Erlanger, and Lande, 1993; Handler, 1996; Seron, Van Ryzin, Frankel, and Kovath, 2001). But few have examined the process of political change suggested by feminist histories (Minow, 1990; Schneider, 2000): how a cycle initiated through reinterpretation of identities, movement building, and enactment of law might lead to change for the poor.

CONCLUSION

O'Connor has faulted mainstream poverty scholars for allowing themselves to be coopted by the moral framework of conservatives and failing to create an effective alternative understanding of the institutional sources of poverty. Yet many sociolegal scholars who study law and poverty believe they are on a different course. Their research has been motivated by a desire to expose injustice, tell the stories of those oppressed by law, explain why such inequality persists in the welfare state, and thereby create openings for change. Three qualities of recent law and society poverty research suggest the importance of this commitment.

First, for most sociolegal scholars studying poverty the issue is now inequality, not whether the poor have legal experiences that are different from the mainstream. Critical histories of the origins of poverty programs and studies that relate poverty to governance of the morally undeserving – the poor, unmarried mothers, minorities, criminals, and the "underclass" – demonstrate that they are kept isolated and poor in part because of benefits that others derive from law.

Second, researchers are no longer "seeing like a state" (Scott, 1998). Most researchers have rejected the conceptualization of the poor that informs poverty policy and administration and discourages research on race, the causes of poverty, and the labor market. Ethnography, interpretive sociology, and cultural studies have created sightlines for understanding poverty that are different from the state's own. Government-sponsored research, conducted according to a more limited vision, plays an important role in legitimating welfare policy making but must now be read in the context of research by sociolegal scholars and others that speaks directly to the value of such policies from another perspective.

Third, scholars suggest many roles for themselves in bringing about social change. Impact research and detailed case studies that describe processes underlying poverty and injustice speak explicitly to the impulse toward (and faith in) reform. Studies of voices of the oppressed, legal consciousness and resistance, and the poor's political capacity attempt to share the scholar's power to create knowledge with those who have the most direct need for it and the greatest interest in change. The latter are "participatory" in spirit – speaking with the oppressed so that scholars can accurately represent their cause. Some scholars are self-consciously participatory in method as well. Increasingly, scholarship suggests strategies for the activist scholar or the scholar in collaboration with the political allies and subjects of poverty research. Strategies include exploration of genuinely participatory methods for research, debates about more egalitarian and mutually empowering relationships with clients, mapping the opportunities for broader democratic participation in resistance, rights-related movements, and a more inclusive moral discourse.

Scholarship on the relationships between poverty, inequality, and governance still leaves many questions unanswered. Fortunately, sociolegal research suggests places to begin answering the questions that poverty scholars find most compelling. Scholars pursue a better understanding of who controls the market and how law helps or hinders them. Scholars want to know more about how moral identity is formed and changed. Research may eventually suggest how to "democratize" poverty by making the identity of poor persons more visible and less alien to a large proportion of the citizenry in modern, economically developed societies. Further, power and change are often mediated by local social organization and politics, a vast uncharted terrain concerning the relationships between local empowerment and laws that guide "devolution," "decentralization," and "marketization."

Finally, there is an emerging consensus that social change through rights will frequently depend on politics. Politics may include the micropolitics of individual resistance, but more significantly will require organizing movements in the public arena. Scholars have suggested that there are openings for political escalation of poverty issues. Movements may successfully deploy new rights, but have often failed in their attempts to do so. Thus, scholars' most ambitious project is understanding how the poor's experiences – including their experiences of subordination and stigmatizing moral identity – can merge with the political interests of other citizens in movements for rights that will enable reconstruction of a more democratic and egalitarian affirmative state.

References

Abel, R. (1979) "Socializing the legal profession: Can redistributing lawyers' services achieve social justice?" *Law and Policy Quarterly* 1: 5–52.

Abel, R. (1980) "Taking stock," *Law & Society Review*, 14: 429–43.

Alfieri, A. (1991) "Reconstructive poverty law practice: Learning lessons of client narrative," *Yale Law Journal* 100: 2107–47.

Alfieri, A. (1993) "Impoverished practices," *Georgetown Law Journal* 81: 2567–663.

Alfieri, A. (2001) "Race prosecutors, race defenders." *Georgetown Law Journal* 89: 2227–77.

Ansley, F. (2002) "Who counts? The case for participatory research," in F. Munger (ed.), *Laboring Below the Line: The New Ethnography of Poverty, Low-wage Work, and Survival in the Global Economy*. New York: Russell Sage Foundation, pp. 245–70.

Bennett, S. (1995) "'No relief but upon the terms of coming into the house' – controlled spaces, invisible disentitlements, and homelessness in an urban shelter system," *Yale Law Journal* 104: 2157–211.

Bezdek, B. (2001) "Contractual welfare: Non-accountability and diminished democracy in local government contracts for welfare-to-work services," *Fordham Urban Law Journal* 28: 1559–608.

Black, D. (1976) *The Behavior of Law*. New York: Academic Press.

Blumberg, A.S. (1967) "The practice of law as a confidence game: Organizational cooptation of a profession," *Law & Society Review* 1(2): 15–39.

Brodkin, E.Z. (1997) "Inside the welfare contract: Discretion and accountability in state welfare administration," *Social Service Review* 71: 1–33.

Caplovitz, D. (1963) *The Poor Pay More: Consumer Practices of Low-Income Families*. New York: Free Press.

Carlin, J. (1962) *Lawyers on Their Own: A Study of Individual Practitioners in Chicago*. New Brunswick, NJ: Rutgers University Press.

Carlin, J. and Howard, J. (1965) "Legal representation and class justice," *University of California Law Review* 12: 381–437.

Carlin, J., Howard, J., and Messenger, S. (1966) "Civil justice and the poor," *Law & Society Review* 1(1): 9–90.

Cashin, S.D. (1999) "Federalism, welfare reform, and the minority poor: Accounting for the tyranny of state majorities," *Columbia Law Review* 99: 552–627.

Chambliss, W. (1964) "A sociological analysis of the law of vagrancy," *Social Problems* 12: 67–77.

Coombe, R. (1995) "The cultural life of things: Anthropological approaches to law and society conditions of globalization," *American University Journal of International Law and Policy* 10: 791–835.

Crenshaw, K. (1988) "Race, reform, and retrenchment: Transformation and legitimation in antidiscrimination law," *Harvard Law Review* 101: 1331–87.

Danziger, S., et al. (1999) "Barriers to work among welfare recipients," *Focus* 20: 31–5.

Davis, M. (1993) *Brutal Need: Lawyers and the Welfare Rights Movement, 1960–1973*. New Haven, CT: Yale University Press.

Diamond, M. (2000) "Community lawyers: Revisiting the old neighborhood," *Columbia Human Rights Law Review* 32: 67–131.

Diller, M. (2000) "The revolution in welfare administration: Rules, discretion, and entrepreneurial government," *New York University Law Review* 75: 1121–220.

DuBois, W.E.B. (1899) *The Philadelphia Negro*. Philadelphia: University of Pennsylvania Press.

Edelman, E.B., Erlanger, H.S., and Lande, J. (1993) "Internal dispute resolution: The transformation of civil rights in the workplace," *Law & Society Review* 27: 497–533.

Edin, K. and Lein, L. (1997) *Making Ends Meet: How Single Mothers Survive Welfare and Low-Wage Work*. New York: Russell Sage Foundation.

Engel, D. (1998) "How does law matter in the constitution of legal consciousness?" in B. Garth and A. Sarat (eds.), *How Does Law Matter?* Evanston, IL: Northwestern University Press, pp.109–44.

Engel, D. and Munger, F. (forthcoming) *Rights of Inclusion: Law and Identity in the Life Stories of Americans with Disabilities*. Chicago: University of Chicago Press.

Esping-Anderson, G. (1990) *The Three Worlds of Welfare Capitalism*. Cambridge, UK: Polity Press.

Esping-Anderson, G. (1999) *Social Foundations of Postindustrial Economies*. New York: Oxford University Press.

Ewick. P. and Silbey S. (1992) "Conformity, contestation, and resistance: An account of legal consciousness," *New England Law Review* 26: 731–49.

Ewick, P., Kagan, R., and Sarat, A. (1999) "Legacies of legal realism: Social science, social policy, and the law," in P. Ewick, R. Kagan, and A. Sarat (eds.), *Social Science, Social Policy, and the Law*. New York: Russell Sage Foundation, pp. 1–38.

Farley, R, Danziger, S., and Holzer, H.J. (2000) *Detroit Divided*. New York: Russell Sage Foundation.

Felstiner, L.F. (1974) Influences of social organization on dispute processing," *Law & Society Review* 9: 63– 94.

Felstiner, W., Abel, R., and Sarat, A. (1980) "The emergence and transformation of disputes: Naming, blaming, and claiming," *Law & Society Review* 15: 631–55.

Fineman, M.A. (1999) "Cracking the foundational myths: Independence, autonomy, and self-sufficiency," *American University Journal of Gender and Social Policy* 8: 13–29.

Fraser, N. and Gordon, L. (1994) "A genealogy of *dependency*: Tracing a keyword of the US welfare state," *Signs* 19: 309–36.

Frazier, E.F. (1939) *The Negro Family in the United States*. Chicago: University of Chicago Press.

Freeman, A. (1998) "Antidiscrimnation law from 1954 to 1989: Uncertainty, contradiction, rationalization, denial," in D. Kairys (ed.), *The Politics of Law: A Progressive Critique*, 3rd edn. New York: Basic Books, pp. 285–311.

Galanter, M (1974) "Why the 'haves' come out ahead: Speculations on the limits of legal change," *Law & Society Review* 9: 95–160.

Gans, H. (1969) "Culture and class in the study of poverty: An approach to anti-poverty research," in D.P. Moynihan (ed.), *On Understanding Poverty: Perspectives From the Social Sciences*. New York: Basic Books, pp. 201–28.

Garland, D. (2001) *The Culture of Control: Crime and Social Order in Contemporary Society*. Chicago: University of Chicago Press.

Garth, B. and Sterling, J. (1998) "From legal realism to law and society: Reshaping law for the last stages of the social activist state," *Law & Society Review* 32: 409– 71.

Gaventa, J. (1980) *Power and Powerlessness: Quiescence and Rebellion in an Appalachian Valley.* Urbana: University of Illinois Press.

Genovese, E. (1976) *Roll, Jordan, Roll.* New York: Pantheon Books.

Gilens, M. (1999) *Why Americans Hate Welfare: Race, Media, and the Politics of Antipoverty Policy.* Chicago: University of Chicago Press.

Gilliom, J. (2001) *Overseers of the Poor: Surveillance, Resistance, and the Limits of Privacy.* Chicago: University of Chicago Press.

Gooden, S. (1998) "All things not being equal: Differences in caseworkers' support toward black and white welfare clients,"*Harvard Journal of African-American Public Policy* 4: 23–33.

Gordon, L. (1988a) *Heroes of Their Own Lives: The Politics and History of Family Violence, Boston 1880–1960.* New York: Penguin.

Gordon, L. (1988b) "What does welfare regulate?" *Social Research* 55: 611–30.

Gordon, L. (1994) *Pitied But Not Entitled: Single Mothers and the History of Welfare, 1890–1935.* New York: Academic Press.

Hagan, J. (1994) *Crime and Disrepute.* Thousand Oaks, CA: Pine Forge Press.

Handler, J.F. (1978) *Social Movements and the Legal System: A Theory of Law Reform and Social Change.* New York, Academic Press.

Handler, J.F. (1986) *The Conditions of Discretion: Autonomy, Community, Bureaucracy.* New York: Russell Sage Foundation.

Handler, J.F. (1990) *Law and the Search for Community.* Philadelphia: The University of Pennsylvania Press.

Handler, J.F. (1992) "Postmodernism, protest, and the new social movements," *Law & Society Review* 27: 697–731.

Handler, J.F. (1996) *Down from Bureaucracy: The Ambiguity of Privatization and Empowerment.* Princeton, NJ: Princeton University Press.

Handler, J.F. (2002) "Quiescence: the Scylla and Charybdis of empowerment," in F. Munger (ed.), *Laboring Below the Line: The New Ethnography of Poverty, Low-wage Work, and Survival in the Global Economy.* New York: Russell Sage Foundation, pp. 271–80.

Handler, J.F. (2003) *Social Citizenship and Workfare in the United States and Western Europe: The Paradox of Inclusion.* Cambridge, UK: Cambridge University Press.

Handler, J.F. and Hasenfeld, Y. (1991) *Moral Construction of Poverty: Welfare Reform in America.* Newbury Park, CA: Sage Publications.

Handler, J.F. and Hasenfeld, Y. (1997) *We the Poor People: Work, Poverty, and Welfare.* New Haven, CT: Yale University Press.

Handler, J.F., Hollingsworth, E.J., and Erlanger, H.S. (1978) *Lawyers and the Pursuit of Legal Rights.* New York: Academic Press.

Harris, B. (1999) "Representing homeless families: Repeat player implementation strategies" *Law & Society Review* 33: 911–39.

Hasenfeld, Y. (1983) *Human Service Organizations.* Englewood Cliffs, NJ: Prentice Hall.

Hay, D. (1975) "Property, authority, and criminal law," in D. Hay, P. Linebaugh, J. G. Rule, E.P. Thompson, and C. Winslow (eds), *Albion's Fatal Tree: Crime and Society in Eighteenth-century England.* New York: Pantheon Books, pp. 17– 63.

Henly, J. (2002) "Informal support networks and the maintenance of low-wage jobs," in F. Munger (ed.), *Laboring Below the Line: The New Ethnography of Poverty, Low-wage Work, and Survival in the Global Economy.* New York: Russell Sage Foundation, pp. 179–203.

Karst, K. (1989) *Belonging in America: Equal Citizenship and the Constitution.* New Haven, CT: Yale University Press.

Karst, K. (1997) "The coming crisis of work in constitutional perspective," *Cornell Law Review* 82: 523–71.

Katz, J. (1978) "Lawyers for the poor in transition: Involvement, reform, and the turnover problem in the legal services program," *Law & Society Review* 12: 275–300.

Katz, M.B. (1986) *In the Shadow of the Poorhouse: A Social History of Welfare in America*. New York: Basic Books.

Katz, M.B. (1989) *The Undeserving Poor: From the War on Poverty to the War on Welfare*. New York: Pantheon.

Katz, M.B. (2001) *The Price of Citizenship: Redefining the American Welfare State*. New York: Metropolitan Books.

Kost, K. and Munger, F. (1996) "Fooling all of the people some of the time: 1990s welfare reform and the exploitation of American values," *Virginia Journal of Social Policy & the Law* 4: 3–126.

Ladner, J. (1971) *Tomorrow's Tomorrow: The Black Woman*. Lincoln: University of Nebraska Press.

Levine, F. and Preston, E. (1970) "Community resource orientation among low income groups," *Wisconsin Law Review* 1970: 80–113.

Liebow, E. (1967) *Tally's Corner: A Study of Negro Streetcorner Men*. Boston: Little, Brown.

Lipsky, M. (1984) "Bureaucratic disentitlement in social welfare programs," *Social Services Review* 58: 3–27.

Lopez, G. (1992) *Rebellious Lawyering: One Chicano's Vision of Progressive Law Practice*. Boulder, CO: Westview.

Lowi, Theodore (1998) "Think globally, lose locally," *Boston Review*, online at <http://bostonreview.net/ BR23.2/lowi.html>

Macaulay, S. (1984) "...Is there any 'there' there" *Journal of Law and Policy* 6: 149–87.

Macaulay, S. (1986) "Private government," in L. Lipson and S. Wheeler (eds.), *Law and the Social Sciences*. New York: Russell Sage Foundation, pp. 445–518.

Mahoney, M. (1991) "Legal images of battered women: Redefining the issue of separation," *Michigan Law Review* 90: 1–94.

Mayhew, L. and Reiss, A.J. (1969) "The social organization of legal contacts," *American Sociological Review* 34: 309–18.

McCann, M.W. (1994) *Rights at Work: Pay Equity Reform and the Politics of Legal Mobilizations*. Chicago: University of Chicago Press.

McCann, M. and March, T. (1996) Law and everyday forms of resistance: A socio-political assessment," *Studies in Law, Politics, and Society* 15: 207–36.

McClain, L. (1996) "'Irresponsible' reproduction," *Hastings Law Journal* 47: 339–453.

McCluskey, M. (1999) "Subsidized lives and the ideology of efficiency," *American University Journal Gender Social Policy & Law* 8: 115–52.

McKinnon, C.A. (1993) "Reflections on law in the everyday life of women," in A. Sarat and T. Kearns (eds.), *Law in Everyday Life*. Ann Arbor, MI: University of Michigan Press, pp.109–22.

Mead, L. (1986) *Beyond Entitlement: The Social Obligations of Citizenship*. New York: Free Press.

Mink, G. (1990) "The lady and the tramp: Gender, race, and the origins of the American welfare state," in L. Gordon (ed.), *Women, the State, and Welfare*. Madison, WI: The University of Wisconsin Press, pp. 92–122.

Minow, M. (1990) *Making all the Difference: Inclusion, Exclusion, and American Law*. Ithaca, NY: Cornell University Press.

Moore, S.F. (1974) "The semi-autonomous social field as an appropriate subject of study," *Law & Society Review* 7: 719–46.

Munger, F. (2002) "Dependency by law: Welfare and identity in the lives of poor women," in A. Sarat, L. Douglas, and M.M. Umphrey (eds.), *Lives in the Law*. Ann Arbor: University of Michigan Press.

Murphy, R. (1987) *The Body Silent*. New York: Holt.

Nightingale, C. (2002) "Looking for stories of inner city politics: From the personal to the global," in F. Munger (ed.), *Laboring Below the Line: The New Ethnography of Poverty,*

Low-wage Work, and Survival in the Global Economy. New York: Russell Sage Foundation, pp. 111–21.

Noble, C. (1997) *Welfare as We Knew It: A Political History of the American Welfare State.* New York: Oxford University Press.

Note (1965) "Enforcement of municipal housing codes," *Harvard Law Review* 78: 801–60.

O'Connor, A. (2001) *Poverty Knowledge: Social Science, Social Policy, and the Poor in Twentieth Century U.S. History.* Princeton, NJ: Princeton University Press.

O'Gorman, H. (1963) *Lawyers and Matrimonial Cases: A Study of Informal Pressures.* New York: Free Press.

Pearce, D. (1990) "Welfare is not for women: Why the war on poverty cannot conquer the feminization of poverty," in L. Gordon (ed.), *Women, the State, and Welfare.* Madison, WI: The University of Wisconsin Press, pp. 265–79.

Piven, F. and Cloward, R. (1971) *Regulating the Poor: The Functions of Public Welfare.* New York: Pantheon Books.

Piven, F. and Cloward, R. (1977) *Poor Peoples' Movements: Why They Succeed, How They Fail.* New York, Pantheon Books.

Quadagno, J. (1992) "Social movements and state transformations: Labor unions and racial conflict in the war on poverty," *American Sociological Review* 57: 616–34.

Quadagno, J. (1994) *The Color of Welfare: How Racism Undermined the War on Poverty.* New York: Oxford University Press.

Rainwater, L. (1970) "Neutralizing the disinherited: Some psychological aspects of understanding the poor," in V.L. Allen (ed.), *Psychological Factors in Poverty.* Chicago: Markham Press, pp. 9–27.

Raphael, J. (1996) "Domestic violence and welfare receipt: Toward a new feminist theory of welfare dependency," *Harvard Women's Law Journal* 19: 201–25.

Reich, C.A. (1964) "The new property," *Yale Law Journal* 73: 733–87.

Reich, C.A. (1965) "Individual rights and social welfare: Emerging legal issues," *Yale Law Journal* 74: 1245–57.

Roberts, D. (1997a) *Killing the Black Body: Race, Reproduction, and the Meaning of Liberty.* New York: Pantheon.

Roberts, D. (1997b) "Spiritual and menial housework," *Yale Journal of Law & Feminism* 9: 51–79.

Roberts, D. (1999) "Poverty, race, and new directions in child welfare policy," *Washington University Journal of Law and Policy* 1: 63–76.

Roberts, D. (2000) "The paradox of silence: Some questions about silence as resistance," *Michigan Journal of Race and the Law* 5: 927–41.

Rothstein, B. (2001) "Social capital in the social democratic welfare state," *Politics and Society* 29: 207–41.

Santos, B. de S. (1995) "Three metaphors for a new conception of law: The frontier, the baroque, and the south," *Law & Society Review* 29: 569–84.

Sarat, A. (1990) "'...The law is all over': Power, resistance and the legal consciousness of the welfare poor," *Yale Journal of Law & the Humanities* 2: 343–79.

Sarat, A. and Felstiner, W. (1995) *Divorce Lawyers and their Clients: Power and Meaning in the Legal Process.* New York: Oxford University Press.

Sarat, A. and Silbey, S. (1988) "The pull of the policy audience," *Law & Policy* 10: 97–165.

Sarat, A. and Simon, J. (2001) "Beyond legal realism?: Cultural analysis, cultural studies, and the situation of legal scholarship," *Yale Journal of Law & Humanities* 13: 3–32.

Schneider, E. (1986) "The dialectic of rights and politics: Perspectives from the women's movement," *New York University Law Review* 61: 589–652.

Schneider, E. (2000) *Battered Women and Feminist Lawmaking.* New Haven, CT: Yale University Press.

Scott, J. (1998) *Seeing Like a State: How Certain Schemes to Improve the Human Condition Have Failed*. New Haven, CT: Yale University Press.

Seron, C., Van Ryzin, G., Frankel, M., and Kovath, J. (2001) "The impact of legal counsel on outcomes for poor tenants in New York city's housing court: Results of a randomized experiment," *Law & Society Review* 35: 419–34.

Silbey, S. and Sarat, A. (1987) "Critical traditions in law and society research," *Law & Society Review* 21: 165–74.

Simon, J. (1992) "'The long walk home' to politics," *Law & Society Review* 26: 923–41.

Simon, J. (1997) "Governing through crime," in L. Friedman and G. Fisher (eds.), *The Crime Conundrum: Essays on Criminal Justice*. Bridgeport, CT: Westview, pp. 171–89.

Simon, J. (1999) "Law after society," *Law and Social Inquiry* 24: 143–94.

Simon, W. (1983) "Legality, bureaucracy, and class in the welfare system," *Yale Law Journal* 92: 1198–269.

Simon, W. (1996) "The dark secret of community based lawyering: A comment on poverty law scholarship in the post-modern, post-Reagan era," *University of Miami Law Review* 48: 1099–114.

Skocpol, T. (1992) *Protecting Soldiers and Mothers: The Political Origins of Social Policy in the United States*. Cambridge, MA: The Belnap Press of Harvard University.

Smith, R. (1988) "Political jurisprudence: The new institutionalism and the future of public law," *American Political Science Review* 82: 89–108.

Soule, S.A. and Zylan, Y. (1997) "Runaway train? The diffusion of state-level reform in ADC/AFDC requirements, 1950–1967," *American Journal of Sociology* 103: 733–62.

Soss, J. (1999) "Lessons of welfare policy design, political learning, and political action." *American Political Science Review* 93: 363–80.

Stack, C. (1976) *All Our Kin: Strategies for Survival in a Black Community*. New York: Basic Books.

Sterett, S. (1997) "Serving the states: Constitutionalism and social spending 1860s–1920s," *Law and Social Inquiry* 22: 311–56.

Suchman, M. and Edelman, L. (1996) "Legal rational myths: The new institutionalism and the law and society tradition," *Law and Social Inquiry* 21: 903–41.

Thompson, E.P. (1975) *Whigs and Hunters: The Origins of the Black Act*. New York: Pantheon.

Trubek, L. (1994) "Lawyering for poor people: Revisionist scholarship and practice," *Miami Law Review* 48: 983–97.

Wald, P. (1965) *Law and Poverty*. Washington, DC: US GPO.

White, J.A. (2000) *Democracy, Justice and the Welfare State: Reconstructing Public Care*. University Park, PA: The Pennsylvania State University.

White, L. (1988) "To learn and teach: Lessons from Driefontein on lawyering and power," *Wisconsin Law Review* 1988: 699–769.

White, L. (1990) "Subordination, rhetorical survival skills, and Sunday shoes: Notes on the hearing of Mrs. G.," *Buffalo Law Review* 38: 1–58.

White, L. (1993) "No exit: Rethinking welfare dependency from a different ground," *Georgetown Law Journal* 81: 1961–2002.

White, L. (1998) "Facing south: Lawyering for poor communities in the twenty-first century," *Fordham Urban Law Review* 25: 813–29.

White, L. (2002) "Care at work," in F. Munger (ed.), *Laboring Below the Line: The New Ethnography of Poverty, Low-wage Work, and Survival in the Global Economy*. New York: Russell Sage Foundation, pp. 213–44.

Williams, J. (1999) "Implementing antiessentialism: How gender wars turn into race and class conflict," *Harvard BlackLetter Law Journal* 15: 41–81.

Williams, L.A. (1992) "The ideology of division: Behavior modification welfare reform proposals," *Yale Law Journal* 102: 719–46.

Williams, L.A. (1995) "Race, rat bites, and unfit mothers: How media discourse informs welfare legislation debate," *Fordham Urban Law Journal* 22: 1159–96.

Williams, P. (1991) *The Alchemy of Race and Rights*. Cambridge, MA: Harvard University Press.

Wright, E.O. (1994) *Interrogating Inequality: Essays on Class Analysis, Socialism and Marxism*. London: Verso.

Wuthnow, R. (1996) *Poor Richard's Principle: Recovering the American Dream Through the Moral Dimensions of Work, Business, and Money*. Princeton, NJ: Princeton University Press.

19

Immigration

SUSAN STERETT

If the physicality, the brute force of law is ever clearly implicated outside of criminal law, it is in immigration. People die in the desert crossing from Mexico, among other places, to the United States. They die because the United States Immigration and Naturalization Service has increased enforcement efforts along the geographically more hospitable parts of the border (Thompson, 2001). They also suffocate in shipping containers, trying to get past immigration officials (Lavery, 2001). People sometimes die or disappear when they have been denied refugee status in a European state and are returned to their home state (Harlow, 1994, War, 1994). Some people languish in prison while they have an ambiguous legal status: immigrants convicted of crimes are often subject to deportation after having served their sentence. Law facilitates choices about movement as well as restricts them. Families form across national boundaries through pregnancy, adoption, and marriage, sometimes in order to comply with immigration laws. Children and spouses of those legally settled are often entitled to settle, though sometimes after intrusive evaluations of family relationships (Ihenacho, 1991).

Law is integral to immigration; without law applicable within and across national state boundaries, what we call immigration would only be the movement of people, with no legal consequences (Coutin, 2000). Migration despite states' efforts to stop it has led to questions concerning the sovereignty of states and their effectiveness. Since law includes as well as excludes, and is both supranational as well as domestic, focusing on "effectiveness" does not wholly capture the meaning of law. Furthermore, the marginal lives people lead when undocumented, the disappearance of those who cannot gain refugee status, and the formation of families across national boundaries demonstrate states' ongoing power to govern population. That power often works through bureaucratic governance in which officials and advocates contest meanings of broad mandates. States, sovereignty, and international obligations are made through myriad daily decisions and negotiations.

CATEGORIZING IMMIGRATION

Formal immigration policy often divides immigration into three types. People can be admitted for reasons of labor demands in the host country, because they have family connections in the host country, or as refugees. In addition, people accumulate time in a country sometimes in violation of their conditions of entry, and can gain permission to stay on humanitarian grounds (see e.g., Coutin, 2000). People can (and do) strategize across categories, and state officials try to police that (Coutin, 2000; Salyer, 1994; Sterett, 1997a). For example, a state might be eager to admit a veterinarian and less eager to grant refugee status. A lawyer would do well to recommend to clients with the right job skills that they apply for a residence permit on the basis of work skills rather than asylum, even if they entered the country fleeing persecution. Migrants may or may not get that advice and migrants can always find bad advisors eager to take their money.

The demand for labor and the difference in wages between the West and poor countries have also meant that people settle without any legal status. Undocumented workers clean houses, pick fruit and vegetables, and work in restaurants. Particularly before the 1970s, states have also met demands for inexpensive labor by creating temporary worker status, in which people are welcome as long as the host state determines it needs the laborers. Both European states and the United States found that people stay or try to when granted a temporary work permit, making temporary work permits not as temporary and simple a solution to employment demands as employers and states had hoped (Calavita, 1994; Wayne, 2001). In the United States the employment of low-wage workers from other countries, whether on work permits, or as undocumented workers, has depressed wages and seems to have discouraged native workers from moving to places with high rates of immigration (Jencks, 2001). While native workers with high skills have not as strongly opposed the immigration of those who do not compete with them for jobs, they have opposed the temporary work visas granted to those with competing skills (Wayne, 2001). When workers are not in a country legally they are especially vulnerable to employers and their decisions concerning work conditions, even if they legally are entitled to the same work protections as documented workers. Where they are not, employers have every reason to prefer workers who are not settled legally; undocumented workers today sometimes occupy the most low-paid positions in which they are vulnerable to abuses, such as not getting wages owed them (Calavita, 1998). In the United States, many employers in low-wage sectors prefer recent immigrants, documented or not, to native employees, particularly African Americans (Lichter and Waldinger, 2001; Lee, 2001). Immigrants who gain work permits because they have particularly valuable skills are in a different position.

Becoming legal can require documentation that is not always easy to muster. The regulatory apparatus of the late modern state depends on papers (Ewick and Silbey, 1998; Torpey, 1999; Coutin, 2000). In many European countries and in the United States, one can gain permanent residence permits by documenting continuous residence (Coutin, 2000; Groenendijk, Guild, and Dogan, 1998). That sounds easier than it is: when people live with relatives or friends, their names may never appear on any utility bills or rent receipts or leases. People may work without a work permit, thereby not accumulating legal time that would allow them to gain a permanent residency permit (Calavita, 1998). Susan Coutin has argued that immigration law creates "spaces of nonexistence," in which people are not legally resident in a country because they cannot document their presence. Without documenting their residence, they are legally not there, which makes much of what they do illegal. Yet they are physically present, absent from their home: they have, as legally documented persons, disappeared (Coutin, 2000; for the impossibility of complying with Spanish immigration laws, see Calavita, 1998). As Hannah Arendt put it in 1951, "The stateless person, without right to residence and without the right to work, had of course constantly to transgress the law" (Arendt, 1951: 286).

Legal or not, immigrants, asylum seekers, and refugees have become increasingly mistrusted and subject to exclusion through national policies and supranational agreements. Nativism has colored political debates, particularly from the mid-1970s, throughout Western countries. Nativism has arisen not only from economic self-interest; popular debate has assumed that immigration will cause receiving countries to lose their character, and that such a loss would be significant (see e.g., Perea, 1997; on earlier exclusions in the United States, see Calavita, 2000; Haney-Lopez, 1996). Such a claim depends on a belief in racial difference: Europe, for example, is opening its internal borders while reaching supranational agreements to facilitate excluding others.

STATE MAKING AND INTERNATIONAL OBLIGATIONS

Immigration management is a state-making project: it enacts who belongs and who does not belong inside the borders, a question usually precedent to citizenship (Brubaker, 1992; Constable, 1993; Maurer, 1997; Torpey, 1999). States claim the ability to exclude and include as a prerogative of sovereignty, which implies autonomy and control. The minutiae of paperwork required for legal residence is the ordinary practice of making a state (Sayer, 1994: 371; Roseberry, 1994), engaged in by administrative officials in local offices as much as prime ministers in national capitals. Without officials to follow through on rules, the claims to being able to exclude mean little. Only by attending to how officials decide can we begin to understand how a state works, even if by attending to the details of decision making, states become no longer easy to distinguish from the social forces they manage and that shape them (see e.g., Calavita, 1992, 2000; Gilboy, 1991).

States' claims to autonomy and control immediately raise questions about the place of international obligations and how states interpret them. First, the Geneva Convention on Refugees, drafted in 1951 in response to the terrible problems of statelessness during World War II, defines a refugee as "a person who has a well-founded fear of persecution for reasons of race, religion, nationality, membership of a particular social group or political opinion" (as cited in Cohen and Joly, 1989: 8). Accompanying the Convention is the principle of *nonrefoulement*: asylum seekers cannot be returned to a country in which they are in danger. Both have been incorporated in the European Union into the Treaty of Amsterdam, the fundamental agreement now governing the European Union (Goodwin-Gill, 2001). Next, the European Convention on Human Rights (ECHR), also a post-World War II document, provides for a right against torture, relevant when people are subject to deportation, and a right to effective internal remedies to pursue European rights. The European Court of Human Rights has interpreted the right against torture to provide wider protection than the Geneva Convention by protecting against non-state violence (Blake, 2001: 112). The ECHR also guarantees a right to a family life. Immigrants who have long been settled in a country can find themselves subject to deportation orders; one way of challenging such an order is via the ECHR, demon-strating that deportation would destroy an existing family life. Finally, under the Treaty of Amsterdam, the European Court of Justice also enforces the right of free movement of labor, under which national restrictive regulations have been chal-lenged (see e.g., Bhabha, 1998). Each of these instruments raises questions relevant to law and society scholarship: how have states understood what they require? What are the networks of knowledge and institutions that have defined what constitutes a well-founded fear of persecution, or what constitutes a family life? Ties among countries, the international conferences that promote sharing information (Riles, 2000), and the reports that collect that information (e.g., Groenendijk, Guild, and Dogan, 1998; Guild, 1999; Guild and Harlow, 2001) all deserve attention in understanding how immigration control has developed into a loosely coupled inter-national regulatory regime.

In Europe, in addition to these international agreements and institutions, less formal agreements govern immigration. European states have tried to harmonize their immigration controls, facilitating movement within signatory states while making it easier to exclude those outside (Guild, 2001). The Dublin Convention, signed by the member states of the European Union in 1990, provides that the first state in which an asylum seeker lands will be the one to determine refugee status. If the asylum seeker landed in one member state before the one in which he or she applies for asylum, the state may return the asylum seeker to what states call the "safe third country." The point is to discourage forum shopping and to share refugees (Neuman, 1993; Joly, 1996). However, officials in the border states that are most accessible to poor states torn apart by war worry that they will find themselves accepting the most immigrants and asylum seekers. In addition, as one immigration barrister in the United Kingdom pointed out, the Convention discour-ages taking anything into account that could ease the assimilation of asylum seekers: for example, people might seek asylum in one country because it has historic ties with the country of origin or because the asylum seeker has family members in that country (Blake, 2001).

The Schengen Convention, also signed in 1990 but by fewer states, duplicates provisions for asylum seeking in the Dublin Convention. It reaches beyond Dublin in coupling the regulation of asylum seeking with the loosening of regulation of the movement of those who are citizens of the member states. In coupling the two, it poses most starkly the distinction between those who belong and those who do not, and regional choices to differentiate them (Bhabha, 1998, 1999). Excluding people becomes particularly important as the European Council has extended its commit-ment to equal rights by declaring at the Tampere meeting in 1999 that the rights of legal immigrants should be like those of member states' citizens (Groenendijk, 2001: 232–5). After September 11, 2001, the European Union has committed itself to further harmonization of immigration procedures to try to exclude people likely to commit terrorist acts.

Constituting families is also regulated by the Hague Convention on Intercountry Adoption, signed in 1993. Each signatory country chooses how to implement it domestically, including the United States and many European countries (see e.g., Duncan, 2000). Intercountry adoption has grown internationally. The United States has received the most children, though countries throughout Western Europe are receiving countries (Selman, 2000: 20). South Korea was once the predominant sending country; China has replaced it, with Russia not that far behind. Each year receiving countries accept about 30,000 children, about equal to the number of people granted refugee status in the European Union, and about half the number of people granted either refugee status or discretionary leave to stay in the countries to which they have fled (Duncan, 2000; UNHCR, 2001: 10). The different rates of intercountry adoption across national states result in part from law: some states make it easy to adopt internationally while others do not.

Do international agreements make for a loss of control, or a loss of sovereignty for national states (e.g., Sassen, 1996)? Some scholarship on the social welfare rights within national states and the international obligations for human rights have concluded that national membership is losing its significance (Aleinikoff, 2000; Soysal, 1994; Jacobson, 1996). For the great numbers of those excluded from ever entering the regulatory regime, or denied residency status after having entered, however, states still have force (Bhabha, 1998; Brubaker, 1994). Enforcing international obligations requires domestic mobilization, and immigration law sometimes governs outsiders who can find it difficult to mobilize resources. Finally, states that have committed to international obligations represent themselves as *liberal* states, or states that are committed to human equality and rights. To live up to those obligations hardly impairs their sovereignty; it enacts it (Joppke, 1998). However, state officials are not always eager to implement rights. Officials hurry to exclude people before they can invoke their rights. In Britain, Home Office officials try to deport before someone can ask for an attorney. In 1993, Joy Gardner's struggle with Home Office officials led to her death; she rapidly became a symbol for activists of the violence of immigration control (Harlow, 1994). In the United States airlines put people on planes back home before they can ask for an exclusion hearing (Gilboy, 1997). Most notoriously in the United States, those trying to reach the country to apply for asylum from Haiti were prevented from entering in 1991 and 1992 to keep them out of the asylum system (see e.g., Neuman, 1993).

Administrative officials manage immigration in much greater detail than legislatures do. Governments find flexibility when they can change policy without debating it beforehand, which is often more likely when the control is through an executive (Calavita, 1992). In Britain, the executive branch acceded to a decision from the European Court of Justice and decisions from their own courts that made it more difficult to implement a public policy that was hostile to marriages between citizens of the United Kingdom and those who lived abroad, enforced against those from the Indian subcontinent (Sterett, 1999). The British government has no obligation to publish rules, and indeed they only announced this policy in response to a written question in Parliament. In the United States the Immigration and Naturalization Service announced that it would provide "S visas" and assistance in gaining citizenship for all those who helped catch those responsible for the attacks of September 11, 2001. The American bracero program, which operated from World War II until the 1960s, was legislatively authorized but depended on executive control. In Spain, the constitutional regulation of the rights of immigrants is broad and vague; the precarious legal existence immigrants experience is based in complex and often contradictory administrative regulation (Calavita, 1998).

Particular decisions granting or denying residence or refugee status cumulate into patterns that vary cross-nationally. To take refugees as a prominent example, in

2000, the United States granted the largest number of people refugee status, followed by Canada, Germany, and the United Kingdom. The United Kingdom, Switzerland, Sweden, and the Netherlands granted most of the humanitarian status decisions made, in which a state decides that someone does not quite meet the requirements for refugee status but should be allowed to stay (UNHCR, 2001: 3). People are granted refugee status at different rates as well, despite the common international obligations. For example, in 2000 asylum applicants from Afghanistan gained either refugee or humanitarian status at a rate of 35 percent in all countries combined. Austria recognized 8 percent of people applying for refugee status from there, Germany recognized about 25 percent and the United Kingdom recognized about 40 percent (UNHCR, 2001). These vastly different recognition rates came at a time when Human Rights Watch and Amnesty International condemned the Taliban regime in Afghanistan for its persecution of the Afghan people. States have political reasons for recognizing problems in one country more than another, though international obligations are to recognize individuals at risk, not national states. Even so, the structure of support for claiming rights varies cross-nationally, and differences in support are a good place to look to explain differences in recognition (Epp, 1998; Conant, 2002: ch.2).

GETTING HELP: USING DOMESTIC SUPPORT

Domestic pressures shape the practice of immigration control. States depend on cooperation from nonstate actors. Employers and carriers have been drafted into the business of immigration control. European states and the United States have enacted carriers' liability laws, making airlines liable for those who land without proper documents. Airlines cooperate with immigration authorities in the United States to try to pre-empt demands for exclusion hearings, and to return people rapidly to their states of origin (Gilboy, 1997). Employers have also been drafted in the effort to police immigration; in the United States they are subject to sanctions for employing undocumented workers. The INS seldom implements sanctions, not least because it is both politically and legally difficult to do so. For example, they allow "good faith" exceptions for employers who try to check immigration status (Calavita, 1990). Political environments in the receiving country shape interpretation of rules: those already settled from a country press governments not to examine closely those entering from that country (Gilboy, 1991, 1992).

Class action suits, available only in the United States, challenge a policy rather than the decision to exclude or deport one person. In the United States, for example, the American Baptist Church, members of which gave sanctuary to people from El Salvador and Guatemala in the 1980s, sued the American government for discrimination against Salvadorans and Guatemalans in granting asylum. In a settlement they won a right to an asylum interview, under legal conditions that were made more difficult via statute (Coutin, 2000: 4–8). The asylum seekers did not win everything; administrative policy reinforced by legislation could and did still make it very difficult for any claimant to win asylum. Still, lawsuits were one avenue to challenge administrative practices as a whole. In Europe, individual cases determine that one person should not have been excluded. Officials can decide to read those cases as making a common claim and applicable beyond the instant case or not (Conant, 2002). Class action suits allow officials a little less room to limit a decision from a court.

Taking cases requires access to lawyers. Those settled in a country usually have the greatest ability to find help; they have settled friends and family and possibly an ethnic association that can help. Asylum seekers are usually in a much worse position. They arrive in a country in which they may not speak the language, and in which they do not understand the legal system. Many have left friends and family behind, and many have been subject to terrible acts at home, including torture and loss of their home. Yet with outreach by those who can help in the country of application, even those applying for asylum can muster a domestic application, appeal, and judicial review.

For example, some countries provide legal assistance to those who file claims for asylum. The United Kingdom funds the Refugee Legal Centre (www.refugee-legal-centre.org.uk), which provides advice to asylum seekers. It also represents asylum seekers who cannot afford private representation before the administrative authorities responsible for deciding claims. It has had a very good reputation among solicitors and barristers. For example, in 1995 the Refugee Legal Centre used information from similar organizations in other Western European countries concerning the treatment of asylum seekers to get United Kingdom officials to treat even Western European states as unsafe. That provided the factual basis to litigate safety in the domestic courts, gaining the ability to apply for asylum in the United Kingdom rather than elsewhere. Parliament responded by declaring through legislation that the member states of the European Union were safe, thereby cutting off an issue from adjudication (Blake, 2001: 103, 117). Since the courts in the United Kingdom are not generally well known for their willingness to read statutes in a way favorable to those challenging the central government (Sterett, 1997a), the victories in courts are testimony to the fact-gathering work of representatives and the lawyering required to ensure that nothing they request looks like innovative statutory interpretation.

NGOs that provide advice to those settled have also made rights more meaningful. NGOs in France pursue test cases to the European Court of Human Rights from the large numbers of expulsions the French authorities order (Groenendijk, Guild, and Dogan, 1998: 38–9). The disproportionate number of losses before the ECHR that France has had is as much a result of political organization as it is of distinctively French violations of rights to family life. People settled in the United Kingdom may avail themselves of the services of the Joint Council for the Welfare of Immigrants, a nongovernmental organization that provides advice and referrals to lawyers. The line between NGOs and government can be blurry; in Britain, for example, the government long financed one advisory service, and many advocates for immigrants mistrusted it, seeing it as papering over exclusionary policies (on NGOs, see Fisher, 1997). Finally, the government provides legal aid for those pursuing judicial review, or supervision of administrative decisions. Both solicitors and barristers have specialized in immigration law, and they have organized to improve practice. The Immigration Law Practitioners Association collects and disseminates knowledge to practitioners; it also responds to government policy proposals. One goal of leading practitioners is to improve the level of practice in immigration law, leading the organization to sponsor classes in focused areas of immigration practice. These seminars, the discussion of issues, and the publication of books on immigration practice by energetic practitioners all promote the availability of European legal rights. Not knowing the law is one practical limit on the reach of decisions from the European Court of Justice (Conant, 2002). Legal aid has also made it possible to vindicate claims in the courts, keeping up the pressure required to make European rights mean something. In the United States, NGOs help to fill out the government paperwork required for Salvadorans applying to stay in the United States (see e.g., Coutin, 2000).

Although decisions from the United States Supreme Court, the European Court of Justice, and the European Court of Human Rights declare rights that states are to follow, governments have to decide what to do with the decisions. They can use one to govern the instant case or treat it as though it states a general principle applicable in many cases. European approaches to law do not treat judicial decisions as binding precedents, allowing domestic courts and executive officials to limit the meaning of any decision to the case at hand (Conant, 2002). Without a number of suits brought following an initial decision from the ECHR or ECJ, domestic officials have no reason to pay any attention to the meaning of a case beyond the way it resolves the instant case. Even in common law systems such as the United States, governments distinguish cases from each other on the facts; repeat filings keep up the pressure.

The availability of people who care about immigrants' international rights shape the possibilities in deportation of people with family ties as well. The European Court of Human Rights has held repeatedly that expelling immigrants with long-standing ties in the signatory country in which they reside and few ties to their country of nationality violates the Article 8 right to a family life. Ongoing political pressure in the Netherlands ensured that immigration officials would take that ruling into account (Groenendijk, Guild, and Dogan, 1998: 54–5). Administrative officials in both France and the Netherlands refer to the relevant decisions from the Court, but in France local immigration authorities have substantial discretion and expel people despite the European Court decisions, leading to the NGOs taking test cases. The significance of these rights, then, depends on the existence of NGOs willing to follow through on implementation. In turn, dispersed state authority provides multiple places to challenge decisions, encouraging organizations to try (Conant, 2001: 99, 2002: ch. 2). Of course, dispersed authority also increases the number of people who can ignore decisions. Being able to challenge cases in domestic courts and international courts, and the provision in some countries of legal aid to pursue review in the courts, makes it more possible to challenge decisions.

Appeals to the public focus debate over exclusion on particular individuals, sometimes promoting discretionary permission to remain. "Campaigns against double punishment" in some European states accompany the case law that limits the discretion to exclude those with extensive ties in the European state in which they live. Those who participate in these campaigns argue that immigrants convicted of a crime pay not only the price of a criminal conviction and a prison sentence but also expulsion. To be expelled from the country in which one is living is to be subject to punishment twice for the same crime. Embedded in that claim is the claim that noncitizens are as entitled to live within a country as citizens are, erasing the legal significance of citizenship. Both the United Kingdom and the Netherlands have campaigns against double punishment (see e.g., http://www.ncadc.co.uk).

Each wave of asylum seekers provides new grist for the legal mill concerning definitions of all the terms in the intercountry agreements that have been interpreted domestically, from "safe third country" to "right to family life." One prominent London immigration solicitor in 1995 said sarcastically that he was grateful for the policies of the government that were hostile to asylum seekers because they made work for refugees' lawyers. Each level of victory in confounding whether a European country is safe – something government officials thought they could take for granted – or what constitutes a manifestly unfounded claim, can lead to legislative redefinition to try to cut off litigation. Lawyers, administrative officials, legislators, domestic courts, and international courts also constitute the fields of family and labor immigration.

Law in Envisioning Where We Belong

States exclude because they also include. Benedict Anderson has conceptualized nations as groups of people who imagine they belong together, and embody their imagination in histories and cultural practices; scholars have applied and extended his conceptualization to make sense of the ethnic admixtures that describe societies (Anderson, 1983; Tan, 2001). In making choices about whose cultural practices are acceptable or who can become a citizen and how, legal officials participate in imagining the community. Those communities are cultural mixes in part as a result of law: Bollywood movies from India find a large market in California's Silicon Valley because the United States government's H-1 visa program has drawn computer workers from India to the area.

Every state has had to confront diversity and what it means for citizenship, particularly in light of the horrors of "ethnic cleansing" that accompanied fragmentation in the late twentieth century. The basic frameworks of citizenship are *jus soli*, or citizenship by birth, and *jus sanguinis*, or citizenship by blood (Brubaker, 1992). Germany, which had represented *jus sanguinis* in its clearest form, excluded the children of immigrants born in Germany from citizenship. Even Germany has eased naturalization and allowed provisional citizenship to children of immigrants whose parents were legally resident for eight years (Brubaker, 2001: 538–9). States that allow citizenship by birth explain their cultures either as one in which immigrants must assimilate to the dominant culture, though even the most assimilationist states have recognized difference in public policy (Brubaker, 2001), or as one that is multicultural.

Recognizing difference seldom comes easily. In France threats from the right cut off the beginnings of what Americans would call bilingual education (Brubaker, 2001: 536). For nativists in Britain, integration into Europe and the ways that it makes identity as cultural homogeneity impossible to maintain has been experienced as an invasion (Darian-Smith, 1999).

Between a right to family life, chain migration settling family members of those already settled, and the granting of permits based on long-term residence, people emigrating experience belonging as living in between places. Furthermore, remittances back to the country of origin maintain material ties, and the Internet makes it easier to maintain personal ties (Anderson, 1994; Chander, 2001). Political theorists have tried to explain and advocate different models of belonging. Will Kymlicka and Bhikhu Parekh have argued that multicultural societies must respect cultural differences and practices. For Kymlicka, how that plays out depends on how a culture became part of a state – through subordination or through immigration (Kymlicka, 1996; Kymlicka and Norman, 2000, Parekh, 2000, Waldron, 1992). To say that a state is multicultural says little without attending to the details of practices. Who does a state take to be a spokesperson on what a culture requires? For example, to accept what men chosen as leaders say is to recognize cultural difference at the cost of subordinating women (Okin, Cohen, Howard, and Nussbaum, 1999; see also Sterett, 1997b). Doubts about what happens to individuals when we recognize cultures color critiques of Kymlicka's work (Okin et al., 1999; Barry, 2001).

Emphasizing the individual as the constitutive element of politics, however, can invite us to ignore the stories that brought people to where they are, stories that can best capture the intercultural space people make (Coutin, forthcoming; Yngvesson, 2002). That may or may not matter in law. For example, the United States has mass naturalization ceremonies to welcome new citizens. Naturalization frames the United States as the chosen country, the one to which people willingly move (Coutin, forthcoming). Relying upon choice strips away the political and historical context of that choosing: the dire trouble at home and the family members who are already in the United States (Coutin, forthcoming). Although the United States bases governance on consent, we have no formal ceremonies for acceding to citizenship upon adulthood for those born here. Without a ceremony of agreeing to citizenship, the contractarian element of American citizenship is rather abstract, learned in courses about the meaning of the Constitution or in debates about the obligation to work as an element of what it means to be American (Shklar, 1991). As Bonnie Honig has argued, mass naturalization ceremonies enact belonging publicly for us; they are as much for those who already belong as for those who are just joining. They tell citizens that the United States is a country worth choosing (Honig, 2001: ch. 4).

No matter how people experience belonging, states draw lines that include and exclude, shaped by international commitments. Drawing lines based on race or presumptions concerning which cultures most naturally belong fits badly with complex cultural and historical ties. In the early twentieth century, Asian people settled in the United States were denied citizenship. Long before anyone argued for multiculturalism, they could (and did) point out their assimilation, from having served in the military to having attended American universities, but they still could not become citizens because of their race (Haney-Lopez, 1996; Calavita, 2000). In the process of excluding, courts and immigration authorities moved uneasily between popular and scientific meanings of race, teaching us more about those doing the categorizing than those categorized.

NATIONAL SECURITY AND IMMIGRATION CONTROL

In the First World, the focus in public debate about immigration before September 11, 2001 concerned labor migrants and asylum seekers and under what conditions both should be allowed to stay in the country. After September 11, state officials around the world have discussed national security and the rights of both citizens and noncitizens. In Europe, very few people had been excluded at the borders or deported as a result of national security concerns before September 11 (Groenendijk, Guild, and Dogan: 1998: 45–6, 67). The European Court of Human Rights has held that a threat to national security cannot allow deportation to a country likely to torture the deportee (Goodwin-Gill, 2001: 150–1). Beyond the formal statement of rights, problems of coordination of policy plague expulsion orders: in Germany and Spain, for example, local authorities are responsible for determining who should be expelled, and the orders are not always enforced. In the United States, detaining people on immigration violations has permitted the national government to investigate them as public security threats, making visible the use of immigration law as a

364 SUSAN STERETT

disciplinary force. The policy in the United States to provide different trial procedures for those accused of terrorism and who are not citizens of the United States also makes it clear that declaring the death of the legal significance of citizenship is premature. Even the rights of citizens are uncertain, as they often are in wartime; the Bush administration has designated some citizens enemy combatants who are therefore not subjects of the civilian courts. International instruments form the context for the exercise of immigration control for reasons of national security as well: Spain declared that it would not allow extradition to the United States of those accused of terrorism because the United States allows the death penalty (Dillon with McNeil, 2001).

Migration has been a central topic of concern across disciplines; scholars often emphasize the significance of legal categories such as rights and sovereignty. Law and society scholars can analyze (and have analyzed) these broad categories, to see how participants make and unmake them in the routines of trying to control movement. Officials, political campaigners, and lawyers and immigrants themselves all have made immigration law, though not just as they would have chosen.

Note

I am grateful to Kitty Calavita, Lisa Conant, Susan Coutin, and Austin Sarat for comments on earlier drafts of this essay.

References

Aleinikoff, T.A (2000) "Between principles and politics: U.S. citizenship policy," in T.A. Aleinikoff and D. Klusmeyer (eds.), *From Migrants to Citizens: Membership in a Changing World*. Washington, DC: Brookings Institution, pp. 119–74.
Anderson, B. (1983) *Imagined Communities: Reflections on the Origin and Spread of Nationalism*. London: Verso Press.
Anderson, B. (1994) "Exodus," *Critical Inquiry* 20(2): 314–27.
Arendt, H. (1951) *The Origins of Totalitarianism*. New York: Harcourt, Brace, Jovanovich.
Barry, B. (2001) *Culture and Equality: An Egalitarian Critique of Multiculturalism*. Cambridge, MA: Harvard University Press.
Bhabha, J. (1998) "Enforcement of human rights of citizens and non-citizens in the era of Maastricht: Some reflections on the importance of states," *Development and Change* 29(4): 697–725.
Bhabha, J. (1999) "Belonging in Europe: Citizenship and post-national rights," *International Social Science Journal* 51: 11–24.
Blake, N. (2001) "The Dublin Convention and rights of asylum seekers in the European Union," in E. Guild and C. Harlow (eds.), *Implementing Amsterdam: Immigration and Asylum Rights in EC Law*. Oxford: Hart Publishing, pp. 95–120
Brubaker, R. (1992) *Citizenship and Nationhood in France and Germany*. Cambridge, MA: Harvard University Press.
Brubaker, R. (1994) "Are immigration control efforts really failing?" in W.A. Cornelius, P.L. Martin, and J. F. Hollifield (eds.), *Controlling Immigration: A Global Perspective*. Stanford, CA: Stanford University Press, pp. 227–32.
Brubaker, R. (2001) "The return of assimilation? Changing perspectives on immigration and its sequels in France, Germany, and the United States," *Ethnic and Racial Studies* 24(4): 531–48.

Calavita, K. (1990) "Employer sanctions violations: Toward a dialectical model of white collar crime," *Law and Society Review* 24(4): 1041–70.

Calavita, K. (1992) *Inside the State*. New York: Routledge.

Calavita, K. (1994) "Italy and the new immigration," in W.A. Cornelius, P. L. Martin and J. F. Hollifield (eds.), *Controlling Immigration: A Global Perspective*. Palo Alto, CA: Stanford University Press, pp. 52–82.

Calavita, K. (1998) "Immigration law and marginality in a global economy: Notes from Spain," *Law and Society Review* 32(3): 529–67.

Calavita, K. (2000) "The paradoxes of race, class, identity, and 'passing': Enforcing the Chinese Exclusion Acts, 1882–1910," *Law and Social Inquiry* 25(1): 1–40.

Chander, A. (2001) "Diaspora bonds," *New York University Law Review* 76: 1005–99.

Cohen, R. and Joly, D. (1989) "Introduction: the 'new refugees' of Europe," in D. Joly and R. Cohen (eds.), *Reluctant Hosts: Europe and Its Refugees*. Aldershot, UK: Avebury Press, pp. 5–18.

Conant, L. (2001) "Europeanization and the courts: Variable patterns of adaptation among national judiciaries," in M.G. Cowles, J. Caporaso, and T. Risse (eds.), *Transforming Europe: Europeanization and Domestic Change*. Ithaca, NY: Cornell University Press, pp. 97–115.

Conant, L. (2002) *Justice Contained: Law and Politics in the European Union*. Ithaca, NY: Cornell University Press.

Constable, M. (1993) "Sovereignty and governmentality in modern American immigration law," *Studies in Law, Politics, and Society* 13: 249–71.

Coutin, S.B. (2000) *Legalizing Moves*. Ann Arbor: University of Michigan Press.

Coutin, S.B. (forthcoming) "Cultural logics of belonging and movement: Transnationalism, naturalization, and U.S. immigration politics," *American Ethnologist* 30.

Darian-Smith, E. (1999) *Bridging Divides: The Channel Tunnel and English Legal Identity in the New Europe*. Berkeley: University of California Press.

Dillon, S. with McNeil, D.G., Jr. (2001) "Spain sets hurdle for extraditions," *The New York Times* November 23: 1.

Duncan, W. (2000) "The Hague convention on protection of children and co-operation in respect of intercountry adoption," in Peter Selman (ed.), *Intercountry Adoption: Developments, Trends and Perspectives*. London: British Agencies for Adoption and Fostering, pp. 40–52.

Epp, C. (1998) *The Rights Revolution*. Chicago: University of Chicago Press.

Ewick, P. and Silbey, S.S. (1998) *The Common Place of Law: Stories From Everyday Life*. Chicago: University of Chicago Press.

Fisher, W.F. (1997) "Doing good?: The politics and anti-politics of NGO practices," *Annual Review of Anthropology* 26(1): 439–65.

Gilboy, J. (1991) "Deciding who gets in: Decisionmaking by immigration inspectors," *Law and Society Review* 25(3): 571–600.

Gilboy, J. (1992) "Penetrability of administrative systems: Political 'casework' and immigration inspection," *Law and Society Review* 26(2): 273–314.

Gilboy, J. (1997) "Implications of 'third party' involvement in enforcement: The INS, illegal travellers and international airlines," *Law and Society Review*, 31(3): 505–30.

Goodwin-Gill, G.S. (2001) "The individual refugee, the 1951 convention and the treaty of Amsterdam," in E. Guild and C. Harlow (eds.), *Implementing Amsterdam: Immigration and Asylum Rights in EC Law*. Oxford: Hart Publishing, pp. 141–63.

Groenendijk, K. (2001) "Security of residence and access to free movement for settled third country nationals under Community law," in E. Guild and C. Harlow (eds.), *Implementing Amsterdam: Immigration and Asylum Rights in EC Law*. Oxford: Hart Publishing, pp. 225–40.

Groenendijk, K., Guild, E., and Dogan, H. (1998) *Security of Residence of Long Term Residents: A Comparative Study of Law and Practice in European Countries*. Strasbourg: Council of Europe.

Guild, E. (ed.) (1999) *The Legal Framework and Social Consequences of Free Movement of Persons in the European Union*. Cambridge, MA: Kluwer Law International.

Guild, E. (2001) "Primary immigration: The great myths," in E. Guild and C. Harlow (eds.), *Implementing Amsterdam: Immigration and Asylum Rights in EC Law*. Oxford: Hart Publishing, pp. 65–94.

Guild, E. and Harlow, C. (eds.) (2001) *Implementing Amsterdam: Immigration and Asylum Rights in EC Law*. Oxford: Hart Publishing.

Haney-Lopez, I. (1996) *White by Law*. New York: New York University Press.

Harlow, C. (1994) "The accidental loss of an asylum seeker," *Modern Law Review* 57(4): 620–6.

Honig, B. (2001) *Democracy and the Foreigner*. Princeton, NJ: Princeton University Press.

Ihenacho, J.M. (1991) *The Effect of the Introduction of DNA Testing on Immigration Control Procedures: Case Studies of Bangladeshi Families*, Working paper. Coventry, UK: Centre for Research on Ethnic Relations.

Jacobson, D. (1996) *Rights Across Borders: Immigration and the Decline of Citizenship*. Baltimore, MD: Johns Hopkins University Press.

Jencks, C. (2001) "Who should get in? Part I." *New York Review of Books* 48(19): 57–62.

Joly, D. (1996) *Haven or Hell? Asylum Policies and Refugees in Europe*. New York: St. Martin's Press.

Joppke, C. (1998) "Why liberal states accept unwanted immigration," *World Politics*, 50(2): 266–93.

Kymlicka, W. (1996) *Multicultural Citizenship: A Liberal Theory of Minority Rights*. New York: Oxford University Press.

Kymlicka, W. and Norman, W. (eds.) (2000) *Citizenship in Diverse Societies*. New York: Oxford University Press.

Lavery, B. (2001) "Irish police find 8 people dead and 5 sick in cargo container," *The New York Times* December 9: 5.

Lee, J. (2001) "The racial and ethnic meaning behind *Black*: Retailers' hiring practices in inner-city neighborhoods," in J. Skrentny (ed.), *Color Lines: Affirmative Action, Immigration and Civil Rights Options for America*. Chicago: University of Chicago Press, pp. 168–88.

Lichter, M. and Waldinger, R. (2001) "Producing conflict: Immigration and management of diversity in the multiethnic metropolis," in J. Skrentny (ed.), *Color Lines: Affirmative Action, Immigration and Civil Rights Options for America*. Chicago: University of Chicago Press, pp. 147–67.

Maurer, W. (1997) *Recharting the Caribbean: Land, Law and Citizenship in the British Virgin Islands*. Ann Arbor: University of Michigan Press.

Neuman, G. (1993) "Buffer zones against refugees: Dublin, Schengen, and the German asylum amendment," *Virginia Journal of International Law* 33: 503–26.

Okin, S.M., Cohen, J., Howard, M., and Nussbaum, M.C. (eds.) (1999) *Is Multiculturalism Bad for Women?* Princeton, NJ: Princeton University Press.

Parekh, B. (2000) *Rethinking Multiculturalism: Cultural Diversity and Political Theory*. Cambridge, MA: Harvard University Press.

Perea, J.F. (ed.) (1997) *Immigrants Out!: The New Nativism and the Anti-Immigrant Impulse in the United States*. New York: New York University Press.

Riles, A. (2000) *The Network Inside Out*. Ann Arbor: University of Michigan Press.

Roseberry, W. (1994) "Hegemony and the language of contention," in G.M. Joseph and D. Nugent (eds.), *Everyday Forms of State Formation: Revolution and the Negotiation of Rule in Modern Mexico*. Durham, NC: Duke University Press, pp. 71–84.

Salyer, L. (1994) *Laws Harsh as Tigers*. Chapel Hill: University of North Carolina Press.

Sassen, S. (1996) *Losing Control? Sovereignty in an Age of Globalization*. New York: Columbia University Press.

Sayer, D. (1994) "Everyday forms of state formation: Some dissident remarks on 'hegemony',"
    in G.M. Joseph and D. Nugent (eds.), *Everyday Forms of State Formation: Revolution
    and the Negotiation of Rule in Modern Mexico*. Durham, NC: Duke University Press,
    pp. 367–78.

Selman, P. (2000) "The demographic history of intercountry adoption," in P. Selman (ed.),
    Intercountry Adoption: Developments, Trends and Perspectives. London: British Agencies
    for Adoption and Fostering, pp. 15–39

Shklar, J. (1991) *American Citizenship: The Quest for Inclusion*. Cambridge, MA: Cambridge
    University Press.

Soysal, Y. (1994) *Limits of Citizenship: Migrants and Postnational Membership in Europe*.
    Chicago: University of Chicago Press.

Sterett, S. (1997a) *Creating Constitutionalism?* Ann Arbor: University of Michigan Press.

Sterett, S. (1997b) "Domestic violence and immigration in Britain," *PoLAR: Political and
    Legal Anthropology Review* 20(2): 63–9.

Sterett, S. (1999) "Intercultural citizenship: Statutory interpretation and belonging in Britain,"
    in S.J. Kenney, W.M. Reisinger, and J.C. Reitz (eds.), *Constitutional Dialogues in Compara-
    tive Perspective*. New York: Macmillan Press, pp. 119–42.

Tan, E.K.B. (2001) "From sojourners to citizens: Managing the ethnic Chinese in Indonesia
    and Malaysia," *Ethnic and Racial Studies* 24(6): 949–78.

Thompson, G. (2001) "La rumorosa journal: To risk death in the desert: An inalienable
    right?" *The New York Times* September 20: 4.

Torpey, J. (1999) *The Invention of the Passport: Surveillance, Citizenship and the State*. New
    York: Cambridge University Press.

United Nations High Commissioner for Refugees (2001) *Trends in Asylum Decisions in
    38 Countries, 1999–2000*, Population data unit, 22 June. Geneva: UNHCR. Available at:
    <http://www.unhcr.ch/cgi-bin/texis/vtx/home/++wwFqzvx8n+wwW6xFqzvx8n+wwW6h
    FqhT0NuItFqnp1xczFqn7uFPAFqwDzmwwwwwwww1Fqn7uFP>.

Waldron, J. (1992) "Minority cultures and the cosmopolitan alternative," *University of
    Michigan Journal of Law Reform* 25(3&4): 751–93.

Ward, I. (1994) "The story of M: A cautionary tale from the United Kingdom," *International
    Journal of Refugee Law* 6(2): 194–206.

Wayne, L. (2001) "Workers, and bosses, in a visa maze," *The New York Times* April 29: 1.

Yngvesson, B. (2002) "Placing the 'gift child' in transnational adoption," *Law and Society
    Review* 36(2): 227–56.

Further Reading

Aleinikoff, T.A. and Klusmeyer, D. (eds.) (2000) *From Migrants to Citizens: Membership in a
    Changing World*. Washington, DC: Brookings Institution.

Calavita, K. (1994) "U.S. immigration policy: Contradictions and projections for the future."
    Indiana Journal of Global Legal Studies 2: 143–52.

Coutin, S.B. (1993) *The Culture of Protest: Religious Activism and the U.S. Sanctuary
    Movement*. Boulder, CO: Westview Press.

Coutin, S.B. (2001a) "The oppressed, the suspect, and the citizen: Subjectivity in competing
    accounts of political violence," *Law and Social Inquiry* 26(1): 63–94.

Coutin, S.B (2001b) "Cause lawyering in the shadow of the state: A U.S. immigration
    example," in A. Sarat and S. Scheingold (eds), *Cause Lawyering and the State in a Global
    Era*. New York: Oxford University Press, pp. 87–103.

Coutin, S.B. and Chock, P.P. (1995) " 'Your friend, the illegal': Definition and paradox in
    newspaper accounts of immigration reform," *Identities* 2(1–2): 123–48.

Joppke, C. (1999) *Immigration and the Nation-State: The United States, Germany, and Great
    Britain*. New York: Oxford University Press.

Sassen, S. (2000) *Guests and Aliens*. New York: New Press.

Schuck, P.H. (1998) *Citizens, Strangers and In-Betweens: Essays on Immigration and Citizenship*. Boulder, CO: Westview Press.

Spencer, S. (ed.) (1994) *Strangers & Citizens: A Positive Approach to Migrants and Refugees*. London: Rivers Oram Publishing.

Sterett S. (1998) "Caring about individual cases: Immigration lawyering in Britain," in A. Sarat and S. Scheingold (eds.), *Cause Lawyering and the State in a Global Era*. New York: Oxford University Press, pp. 293–316.

Zolberg, A.R. (1994) "Changing sovereignty games and international migration," *Indiana Journal of Global Legal Studies*, 2: 152–63.

20

Commodity Culture, Private Censorship, Branded Environments, and Global Trade Politics: Intellectual Property as a Topic of Law and Society Research

Rosemary J. Coombe

Intellectual property has become a rich topic of interdisciplinary inquiry in the past 15 years, attracting the interest of anthropologists, communications and cultural studies scholars, economists, geographers, historians, traditional legal scholars, political scientists, sociologists, and philosophers. Not all of this scholarship addresses the role of intellectual property in actual social contexts, however, and a great deal of it is both hypothetical and abstract. Scholarship on intellectual property that represents a "law and society" approach is explored here through dominant themes in the literature. Briefly, these include the effect of intellectual property rights (IPRs) in shaping conditions of communication, the exercise of IPRs as a new form of social power, the spatial politics of branded environments, the cultural power of fame afforded to celebrities, global inequities occasioned by the emergence of trade-based intellectual property protection for informational goods, and a concern with the fate of the public domain in this new information economy.

THE COMMODIFICATION OF CULTURE: THE COMMUNICATIVE CONDITIONS OF INTELLECTUAL PROPERTY

One of the dominant themes in the interdisciplinary study of intellectual property concerns the ways copyright, trademark, and publicity rights (and to a lesser extent laws of unfair competition, design patent, and database protection) shape communications in capitalist societies by enabling the commodification of cultural texts. Most critical scholars of intellectual property agree that the law of copyright has expanded protections for owners of artistic, literary, and musical works to the detriment of the public domain by threatening freedom of expression, inhibiting creativity, and stifling democratic dialogue. Communications scholar Siva Vaidhyanathan (2001) makes a convincing case that the history of copyright in the twentieth century is one of continually expanding, lengthening, and strengthening protections and that American copyright policy has lost sight of its original goals: "to encourage creativity, science, and democracy. Instead, the law now protects the producers and taxes consumers. It rewards works already created and limits works yet to be created. The law has lost its mission and the American people have lost control of it" (Vaidhyanathan, 2001: 4). In this prognosis, Vaidhyanathan joins a large number of legal scholars such as Keith Aoki, Yochai Benkler, James Boyle, Julie Cohen, Niva Elkin-Koren, Wendy Gordon, Peter Jaszi, David Lange, Mark Lemley, Jessica Litman, Neil Netanel, Lyman Ray Patterson, and Pamela Samuelson. I summarize his work because it is comprehensive, current, and accessible, and because, in keeping with the emphasis here upon law and society scholarship, it engages in primary as well as secondary research.

The history of the US Constitution indicates that the copyright clause was not considered a property right but a policy that balanced the interests of authors, publishers, and readers so as to provide an incentive for the creation and distribution of new works. Its framers recognized that creativity itself depended upon the use, criticism, supplementation, and consideration of prior works. Authors' exclusive rights were a necessary evil in a market economy – a limited monopoly to encourage creation for the purpose of furthering progress in the arts and sciences, the learning essential to an enlightened citizenry, and the ongoing enrichment of the public domain. This was considered a "tax" on the public (Vaidhyanathan, 2001: 21) but one that was strictly limited in time so as to ensure that works became part of the common property of the reading public. The right was also limited in scope; it protected the work's expression but not the ideas it contained. Thomas Jefferson was ambivalent about the copyright (and patent) power (Chon, 1993). He was suspicious of concentrations of power afforded by artificial monopolies and was afraid that the protection of expressions would ultimately expand to attempts to control the use of ideas by creating artificial scarcity, limiting access, fixing prices, restricting licensing, intimidating potential competitors with threats of litigation, and misrepresentations of the law. Thus Jefferson forewarned us about the "negative externalities" that characterize copyright practice today (ibid.: 24).

The original constitutional mandate for US copyright has been abandoned in the twentieth century in favor of a neoliberal vision that locates and protects "property" at all costs and sees nothing desirable in any form of "public goods." The distinction between ideas and expressions is eroding, the "limited times" of these monopolies are ever longer, and the public's fair use privileges are diminishing through technological change and international pressures. Copyright is increasingly used as a form of corporate legal intimidation. In *Owning Culture* (2001) communications theorist Kembrew McLeod also makes this point and shows that ever more areas of social life are being transformed by the expansion of IPRs. Folk music, for instance:

> ... is based on the practice of drawing on existing melodic and textual elements and recombining those elements in ways that create a song that can range from a slightly

modified version of an older song to a wholly new piece that contains echoes of familiar melodic or lyrical themes. At the center of this mode of cultural production is intertextuality, in which texts are (re)made from other texts to create a "new" cultural text. (McLeod, 2001: 39)

These acts of production and performance are increasingly defined as copyright infringements. As a consequence, folk music itself is transformed. In attempting to avoid legal scrutiny, professional musicians produce music that has less and less relation with folk traditions. Others are deprived of rights to engage in many acts of musical creativity in performance. Historical links with culturally diverse oral traditions are thereby severed. Emphasis upon intellectual property tends to exalt originality rather than creative variation, singular authors rather than multiple interpreters, canonical works rather than social texts, and to privilege a moment of inscription over the process of ongoing appropriation even though the latter is actually the way most popular music is made.

Judges and lawyers, McLeod argues, have been predisposed to "freeze" or at least slow modes of intertextual cultural production. Certain appropriators (those with corporate backing and the power to engage lawyers) are permitted to control and contain the circulation of "their" copyright works, even when these have been taken from the public domain or from the folk traditions of peoples whose music has not been legally protected (African-American and indigenous peoples' traditions in particular). Other popular tunes – like "Happy Birthday to You" – have made their way into everyday life and ritual, after having evolved from a number of sources over the years. Nonetheless, the melody – composed by two school teachers borrowing from the public domain – was registered as a copyright in 1935. The lyrics, created by children in classrooms and parties, are nonproprietary, but every time the song is sung in public, a royalty is due to the copyright owner. The song's very popularity ensures that its value continues to grow. The copyright continues to change hands and to attract more powerful owners because managing these rights requires an ever larger and more aggressive team of lawyers. Not surprisingly, it is now controlled by AOL/Time-Warner (with the American Society of Composers, Authors, and Publishers who administers the performing rights) who ensure that restaurant owners, summer camps, daycare centers, and telegram delivery services pay the royalties due for the customary musical means of celebrating birthdays.

Copyright has become a means of rewarding the economically privileged with even further compensation and cultural control, Vaidhyanathan notes, while taxing and limiting the activities of the general public. Copyright policy, however, is not made in the public sphere but in highly specialized courts, tribunals, and hearings where those who might represent the public interest find themselves up against lawyers for Microsoft and Disney. These developments correspond to a:

> ... steady centralization and corporatization of information and access ... Occasionally, technological innovations such as the Internet threaten to democratize access to and use of information. However, governments and corporations – often through the expansion of copyright law – have quickly worked to correct such trends ... a healthy public sphere would depend on "thin" copyright policy. (Vaidhyanathan, 2001: 7)

This would entail protection "just strong enough to encourage and reward aspiring artists, writers, musicians, and entrepreneurs, yet porous enough to allow full and rich democratic speech and the free flow of information" (Vaidhyanathan, 2001: 5).

However, once all questions of authorship, originality, use, and access to ideas and expressions become framed in terms of property rights, discussion simply seems to end and maximum protection seems ordained; how can one argue in favor of theft (ibid: 12)? Thus, Vaidhyanathan suggests, we need to change the terms of the debate to invite the creation of an intellectual or information *policy* that takes into account the social need for expressive cultural activity and democratic dialogue.

Scholarship on trademarks illustrates similar tendencies. Legal scholars are concerned with the social and cultural implications of expanding trademark protections, the lack of a specific and certain "fair use" defense, and the widening doctrine of trademark "dilution" (liability for use of a trademark that "dilutes" its meaning or merely detracts from its positive connotations but does not confuse consumers) (Aoki, 1993, 1994, 1997; Coombe, 1991; Dreyfuss, 1990, 1996; Gordon, 1990; Lemley, 1999). The uncertain legal status of using IPR-protected texts in satires and parodies has long been an area of fascination for law students, scholars, and in the general press (Cordero, 1998; Klein, 2000; Kotler, 1999; Pearson, 1998) and it has become a new basis for corporate intimidation on the Internet (Schlosser, 2001).

In my legal ethnography *The Cultural Life of Intellectual Properties* (Coombe, 1998a) I show how intellectual properties shape and invite dialogic practices of making popular culture in which the signifying properties of intellectual property holders are reappropriated by others who simultaneously inscribe their own authorship of those works the law deems to be owned by their corporate disseminators (Coombe, 1998a: 23). With respect to trademarks the law clings to the ideological belief that "through investment, labor, and strategic dissemination the holder of a mark creates a set of unique meanings in the minds of consumers ... and that this value is produced solely by the owner's efforts" (ibid: 61). The "distinction" that accrues to a mark, in short, is legally treated as a capital asset (goodwill). "Sociolinguistics and anthropological scholarship would suggest, instead, that meanings are always created in social contexts, among social agents, in social practices of communication, reproduction, transformation and struggle: in short, that cultural distinction is socially produced"(ibid). Trademarks are potentially arenas of struggle that embody the dialectic of two tendencies: the monologic (linked with authority and officialdom) and the dialogic (tendencies of those who are other to authority to transgress and transform the forms they encounter). This movement of meaning between center and periphery is a dynamic and productive one. Conditions of cultural hegemony are always at risk because they must be continually articulated and are constantly rearticulated by the agencies of others. The law promotes and protects a monologic communicative environment in which those who hold intellectual capital are permitted to make signs uniaccentual rather than acknowledge the social struggles that are inherent in signs because meanings are contested and contingent. "Intellectual properties often operate to stifle dialogic practice in the public sphere, preventing people from using the most powerful, prevalent, and accessible cultural forms to express alternative visions of social worlds" (Coombe, 1998a: 42).

Laws of copyright and trademark also appear, however, to provoke those who have an affective relation to the forms that IPRs protect into forming communities dedicated to forging alternative moral economies of value to counter those of their corporate proprietors. This is illustrated by sociologist Andrew Herman and communications scholar John Sloop (1998) in a discussion of a copyright and trademark lawsuit against a group of performance artists called Negativland. This group created music by compiling samples taken from the media landscape "to produce what could best be described as parodic collages of various spectacles of contemporary culture" (Herman and Sloop, 1998: 4). In the "song" at issue, they pulled together samples from a single composed by the band U2, quotations from interviews with that band's members, and outakes from television shows to comment on the ways in which bands are marketed and achieve popularity in mass culture. The case generated a great deal of controversy and conversation amongst Negativland's fans. They used the Internet to comment on the propriety of using intellectual property in this fashion, the need to protect this kind of art and those who make it, and the necessity of freely appropriating cultural forms from the mass media to make authentic art in postmodern conditions. Digital communications were used to create communities of judgment upon the exercise of IPRs as a form of private censorship for corporate profit. Fans also created an alternative space for the music to be appreciated. As part of their legal settlement with the music publishers and the record company Negativland was prohibited from further distribution of the offending song, required to retrieve and to destroy all copies of it, and compelled to assign the copyright in the satire to the record company so that it could exercise control over its future use. Their satire was considered to dilute the value of the corporate investment in U2 (which the latter's lawyers argued, had acquired the status of a brand) and thus to pose a threat to consumer goodwill (a corporate asset). Nonetheless, proliferation of digital copies of the offending work among electronically linked fans made it impossible for the corporation to effectively police these demands, creating negative publicity for U2 that ironically worked to further dilute whatever goodwill the corporation felt they were protecting.

These studies are indebted to the groundbreaking book *Contested Culture* (Gaines, 1991), an early work addressing the emergence and impact of intellectual property law in contemporary consumer societies. Gaines considers intellectual property law as an object of culture and a discourse of power that restrains persons and regulates other cultural forms (1991: 4) by restricting the availability of popular signs and shaping the social production of meaning. Copyright, for example, interests her to the extent that it can "function in two opposite ways" (ibid: 9). To the extent that copyright is enforced, it puts limits around elements of culture and to the extent that copyright is not extended to a particular form, it can make those forms available to others. She refers to this as "the double movement of circulation and restriction" (ibid.). To the extent that forms are accessible, however, they are also available to be turned into new forms of intellectual property that will, at some point, return to the public domain. (Progressive extensions of the copyright term, however, make it less likely that cultural forms will return to the public sphere while they still have cultural value.)

Gaines limits her study of intellectual property, however, to its canonical texts; she examines appellate case law and legal treatises exclusively, and in this way reinforces the law's own understanding of itself as a body of authoritative texts. For most law and society scholars this is an inadequate understanding of where law exists and how it functions. Law and society scholarship is concerned with the ways in which law shapes consciousness, the ways in which it enables us to perceive the world in particular but limited ways, and the resources it provides for forging identities and communities. Nonetheless, given that Gaines's study is concerned with law as a form of ideology, the emphasis upon key appellate cases is not misplaced. These do provide important texts for exploring the categories, contradictions, and forms of argumentation characteristic to liberal legalism.

Trademark, copyright, unfair competition, patent, and publicity rights laws provide cogent instances of the ideology described as the commodity form of bourgeois law by jurist Evgeni Pashukanis in the 1920s. This law is structured around the individual (who in liberal legalism may well be a corporation) as the juridical holder of property rights including those over his or her own personality. The subject who holds rights is created by those rights. Individuated personality provides the ideological basis for this capacity for holding rights which is itself a fiction created by the needs of the commodity form; only when a subject is needed to engage in the sale of labor as an exchange value is it ideologically necessary to create the individual who has the freedom to contract. IPRs are an important area of bourgeois law in which the forms assumed by the legal subject are inscribed, as well as being the major legal site in which the extension of the commodity form to ever more areas of the social and natural world is both legitimated and contested.

Literary theorist John Frow (1995) and sociologist Celia Lury (1993) are drawn to issues of intellectual property precisely because they reveal just how fundamental this liberal category of the person is to capitalist accumulation. As Frow puts it, "the concept of the unique and self-determining person – precisely what seems most to *resist* the commodity form" (1995: 144) is used to legitimate – through such ideas as originality, invention, and the singularity of aesthetic labour – the commodification of ever more cultural forms. The application of measurable labor to raw materials to produce a work that expresses the unique character of each individual's personality and creativity – authorship – is fundamental to the means by which IPRs are justified, expanded, and denied (Boyle, 1996). The trope of authorship emerges in cases as diverse as the ownership of human cell lines, celebrity personas, plant genetic resources, folklore, and agricultural cultivation methods.

The study of celebrity provides a clear instance of the commodification of the human persona. Sociological studies address the social construction of the celebrity and the ways in which the famous become marketed as products and help to market products by investing goods with the symbolic values the public associates with the celebrity. The law enables the famous to protect their name, image, and other indicia that the public has come to associate with the celebrity persona. Law and society scholars are concerned that the enormous expansion of legal protections for publicity values, has enabled publicity rights to effect forms of private censorship, and question the ideological nature of the law's rationale for these protections (Coombe, 1994; Cordero, 1998; Frow, 1995, Gaines, 1991; Langvardt, 1997; Madow, 1993; McLeod, 2001). Many consider the peculiarities of the historical transmogrification of a right of privacy into a right of publicity in the United States. For years judges shared the public belief that the famous had chosen to live in the public eye and thus could not complain of any invasion of privacy when their image was publicly used. Eventually, the common law was "reconciled" with the advertising practice of paid use for celebrity names and imagery. The right to be left alone became a right to decide how and when to replace privacy with publicity by vesting the exclusive rights to authorize publicity. The right to assign and license rights of mass reproduction was vested in an individual whose persona was, in the process, commodified. Intellectual property law followed commercial practices by acknowledging a right to protect new areas of capital investment while claiming that the right it was protecting was based in property. As the legal realists noted, the law purported to base the protection on the economic value, when in fact the property would have no value unless it was legally protected (Gaines, 1995: 135).

As Frow (1995) and Coombe (1998a) demonstrate, the law does more than simply protect the celebrity's name and likeness. By encompassing ever more representations in the public sphere that are associated in any way with the celebrity, it encroaches upon the cultural activities of making social meaning. It enables celebrities to control social activities that draw upon their iconic status in society and places unnecessary restrictions upon cultural vocabularies available for expressive activities. Gaines, Madow, and Coombe all take note of cases in which those who controlled legal rights over popular cultural icons objected to subcultural usages of celebrity indicia; they insist upon the social significance of this work of reclaiming images in different registers of value. They argue that owners of celebrity texts can never wholly control this activity or the new contexts in which these images will circulate to accumulate new meanings. Informed by semiotic scholarship on the star image as a socially created phenomenon, these cultural analyses illustrate how social actors make meaning with the images mass culture provides them. Fans also forge identities and communities while creating new norms, values, and ethics of propriety with respect to the use of celebrity images (Coombe, 1994). In these social responses to the exercise of IPRs we see the creation of alternative moral economies of value.

Sociological studies of how intellectual property shapes communicative conditions now tend to consider particular social institutions and locations. The extension of copyright and patent appears to be transforming communicative exchange in digital environments (Lessig, 2001; Litman, 2001), in universities (McSherry, 2001; Polster, 2000), in scientific research generally (Reichman and Uhlir, 1999, 2003), and in biopharmaceutical research particularly (Rai and Eisenberg, 2003). These studies are critical of recent extensions of IPRs which appear to be inhibiting expression, research, development, and innovation.

CONTROLLING ACCESS: THE EXERCISE OF INTELLECTUAL PROPERTY AS SOCIAL CONTROL

In *The Age of Access* (2000), social critic Jeremy Rifkin makes global pronouncements on the social consequences of intellectual property. Although he rarely addresses the law as such, the "new economy" he explores is fundamentally dependent upon the strategic exercise of IPRs. Looking at changes in corporate investment and business strategies, he suggests that ownership and exchange of real and personal property is giving way to new relationships. "In the new era, markets are making way for networks, and ownership [of physical properties] is steadily being replaced by access [to suppliers of intangible goods]" (Rifkin, 2000: 4). IPRs become more significant as companies attempt to divest themselves of real estate, inventories, and equipment. "Concepts, ideas, images – not things – are the real items of value in the new economy... intellectual capital, it should be pointed out, is rarely exchanged. Instead, it is closely held by the suppliers and leased or licensed to other parties for their limited use" (ibid.: 5) in strategic networks that operate to concentrate power in fewer corporate hands. These relationships are dependent upon the strategic licensing and pooling of trade secrets, patents, trademarks, and copyright.

Rifkin estimates that a full 40 percent of the US economy is made up of new information-based industries and life sciences industries (2000: 52) whose major assets are intellectual properties. If Rifkin is correct in his prognosis that every industry is becoming more knowledge-intensive and that all corporations in this knowledge-intensive industry (from software to the automotive industry) aspire to rid themselves of physical assets and employees, then an economy based on the exercise of IPRs may also ensure greater concentrations of power. This new form of power appears to be less accountable to people and communities or for the conditions of human work and habitation it enables.

The concept of "informational capital" is important to an understanding of "knowledge-intensive" industries in the new economy. Briefly, goods are informational to the extent that their value lies predominantly in their symbolic or textual components rather than their physical substrate or medium of delivery. Things like literature, music, films, software, chemical compositions, methods of manufacture, screenplays, business formats, or furniture designs are fundamentally "public goods." This means that until they are made artificially scarce by the imposition of legal restrictions on their use, they could be easily copied and transposed to new mediums. It is through IPRs that capital in informational goods is created, and as a consequence of technological advances in genetic sequencing all flora, fauna, microbes, plant germplasm, cultural knowledge, and even human cells are now, potentially, informational goods (Coombe, 2003b).

Many product life cycles have become shorter as a consequence of technological innovations in computer memory and telecommunications speeds. As "products come alive with information and animated with continual feedback, the pressure to upgrade and innovate increases" (Rifkin, 2000: 20). More investment goes into the research and development of the information components while the costs of embedding it in its material form decline. Only to the extent that this informational core is protected by intellectual property (e.g., protected against the copy of its integrated circuit topography, the reverse engineering of its technology, or shielded from unauthorized appropriation of its software or its DNA sequence) will it yield profit. Ironically, Rifkin's research reveals that most products become obsolete very quickly and R&D costs must be recouped long before the underlying protection expires (current terms for IPRs are thus obviously too extensive). It also suggests that the new economy's reliance upon intellectual property is fostering relations of industry "cooperation" that in other eras might have been considered anticompetitive:

> Shorter process and product life cycles and the increasing costs of sophisticated high-tech research and development – as well as the additional marketing costs involved in the launch of new product lines – have led many firms to come together to share strategic information as well as to pool resources and share costs as a way both to stay ahead of the game and to ensure against losses in an increasingly mercurial, volatile, and fast-paced cyberspace economy. (Rifkin, 2000: 23)

This may have less than optimal consequences from the perspective of consumers. The pooling of patents, for instance, and the conditions corporations impose upon other corporations who need access to their intellectual properties may result in a decline of research, a slowing down of innovation, and fewer and more costly products in the market. The exercise of patent rights over simple gene sequences (objectionable even under traditional legal principles) has created new obstacles to biomedical research (Heller and Eisenberg, 2000). Holders of IPRs in the products of basic research may refuse to license their technology unless they retain a veto over all future uses of it and insist that licensees provide royalties from all products derived from the licensed use. Licensing costs may become so prohibitive that they function to limit innovation in the field. Difficulties in bargaining between "upstream" and "downstream" researchers become formidable (Rai, 1999).

Genes are the raw materials of biotechnology, one of the growth sectors of the new economy. Petrochemical industries have become life-science industries, shifting from chemical to genetic research and innovation. They have been immeasurably aided by recent changes in patent law:

> Like nonrenewables, genes exist in nature and must be extracted, distilled, purified, and processed.... When genes with potential commercial values are located, they are patented and become, in the eyes of the law, inventions. This critical distinction separates the way chemical resources were used in the industrial era from the ways genes are being used in the biotech century. When chemists discovered new chemical elements in nature in the last century, they were allowed to patent the processes they invented to extract and purify the substances, but were not allowed to patent the chemical elements themselves – patent laws in the United States and in other countries prohibit "discoveries of nature" from being considered inventions... In 1987, however, in apparent violation of its own statutes... the PTO issued a sweeping policy decree declaring that the components of living creatures – genes, chromosomes, cells and tissues – are patentable and can be treated as the intellectual property of whoever first isolates their properties, describes their functions, and finds useful applications for them in the marketplace. (Rifkin, 2000: 65–6)

Much of the world's gene pool is likely to be controlled by a handful of corporations unless other forces intervene. This will have significant implications for human well-being (Amani and Coombe, forthcoming). People's own cell lines may be owned by those medical authorities who isolate these from their tissues; those who require medical treatments based upon these lines will thus be dependent upon those authorities and the payments they demand. Research into the development of treatments that require access to several sequences may be deterred by the high transactions costs of obtaining multiple licenses. Genetic screening and diagnostic tests that use proprietary sequences are much more expensive to use and may be too costly for insurance companies to cover. Holders of these IPRs maintain close control over networks of licensees who are expected to share the profits of their own (more socially beneficial) research. Such practices operate to eliminate markets of buyers and sellers, and to restrict competition. As Seth Shulman notes, "we have yet to establish a clear sense of what anti-trust means in the knowledge economy" (1999: 190).

The "Hollywood Organizational Model" posed by Rifkin is an exemplary instance of such network-based approaches to organization (Rifkin, 2000: 24–9). Once again, the exercise of IPRs ensures its profitability. The early film industry relied upon "Fordist" mass production principles and vertical integration. The forced divesture of cinema chains under antitrust law pushed the industry to consider new methods of production that relied upon more customized production of fewer film products – the "blockbuster" whose value was built through advertising and the capitalization of merchandising rights. Such values required legal protection of ever more aspects of the expressive product (not only the film itself, but its characters, its footage, its memorable stills, its title, and other distinguishing features) as exclusive properties. Production companies realized that exercising these IPRs enabled them to control returns from a film's distribution and to "tie in" the film into other areas of popular consumption. Control over the full range of IPRs also makes it profitable to outsource film production. Groups of companies with particular expertise (scripting, casting, set design, cinematography, sound mixing, editing, film processing, etc) are brought together for the life of the film's production but the major players are primarily distribution firms who employ few people and own few resources. More companies may be involved in film-making but they are dependent upon a few major industrial players for investment capital and they realize none of the royalties from the film's distribution and merchandising. The burdens and obligations of owning assets or employing people can simply be avoided by maintaining control over intellectual property.

Comparing the balance sheets of Microsoft with IBM is illustrative; Rifkin shows that Microsoft owns virtually no fixed assets, while IBM's are considerable (over a fifth of its market capitalization compared to less than 2 percent of Microsoft's). Under traditional accounting practices, a large difference between market value and assets was treated as an indicator that a stock was overpriced. Today the world's best performing companies have extraordinarily high ratios "but are still considered good investments because of their intangible assets, which are immeasurable but are a more accurate gauge of the company's future performance"(Rifkin, 2000: 51). Philip Morris, for example, purchased RJR Nabisco for $12.6 billion in 1988 which was six times what the company was worth on paper, largely, it seems, because of the value of the brand names it held and the goodwill these were judged to represent.

THE SOCIAL LIFE OF THE TRADEMARK

The trademark is perhaps the most significant of the legal forms that underlie the profits to be made from informational goods. The Nike success story is a case in point. It is clearly a knowledge-intensive industry:

> Nike is, for all intents and purposes, a virtual company. While the public is likely to think of the company as a manufacturer of athletic footware, in point of fact, the company is really a research and design studio with a sophisticated marketing formula and distribution mechanism. Although it is the world's leading manufacturer of athletic shoes, Nike owns no factories, machines, equipment, or real estate to speak of. Instead, it has established an extensive network of suppliers – which it calls "production partners" – in Southeast Asia who produce its hundreds of designer shoes and other gear. Nike also outsources much of its advertising and marketing operations. (Rifkin, 2002: 47)

What Nike does own and control is intellectual property – a trademark and the goodwill that has accrued to it, patents on some design features, slogans associated with the company by virtue of its advertising campaigns, and copyright in those ads themselves. It is the company's success at trademark management and its flair for branding that distinguishes it. Nike doesn't sell products so much as it uses products as marketing vehicles for the building of brand value as it does in "Nike Town" – a chain of retail outlets that sell only the company's products. The logo has migrated into ever more areas of social life. It now marks sports teams, clothing, and athletic equipment, colonizing the gymnasiums, classrooms, and washrooms of our schools and is even cut into the designs of people's hair and voluntarily branded onto the flesh of many North Americans who have marked their own bodies with swoosh tattoos to proclaim their brand loyalty.

Journalist Naomi Klein (2000) has authored perhaps one of the most provocative and influential studies of how legal practices of protecting and promoting trademarks have shaped the social, cultural, and physical landscapes of contemporary capitalist societies. Her research investigates the phenomenal growth and extension of "branding" from the mid-1980s. Companies became convinced that success should be measured not by things owned or people employed, but by the strength of the positive images of their brands and their capacities to extend these images into new spaces. The brand is the core meaning, identity, and consciousness of the corporation (Klein, 2000: 5); advertising, sponsorship, logo licensing, and merchandising are merely vehicles for conveying that meaning. These are also activities of intellectual property management that are beginning to attract academic attention. Feminist sociologists, for example, describe how global brand management strategies "are explicitly constituted through familial, genealogical and sexual connections" (Franklin, Lury, and Stacey, 2000: 68) that naturalize culture and culturalize nature. A form of naturalized connection (family bonds) is transferred to produce an analogy for relations among products and between products and their consumers:

> Integral to the power of successful global brands, such as Ford, Nike, McDonalds and Benetton, is the creation of so-called family resemblances among products, through which commodities come to be seen as sharing essential character traits: the shared substance of their brand identities...brand work may be seen to produce a form of *commodity kinship*...producing a diacritical kinship of family resemblances through distinctive proprietary marks. (Franklin et al., 2001: 69)

These rhetorical forms of brand management, however, are fairly typical even within domestic markets; it is not clear what makes this a logic particular to globalization.

Klein, however, suggests that global branding's communicative conditions have generative social effects. Implicitly evoking the Nike swoosh, Klein has coined the term "the brand boomerang" to explain how the corporate trademark becomes a means of calling companies to account under conditions of globalization and how it has served to rally people around anticorporatism as a new brand of politics.

If logos have become the lingua franca of the global village, Klein suggests, "activists are now free to swing off this web of logos like spy/spiders – trading information about labor practices, chemical spills, animal cruelty and unethical marketing around the world...it is in these logo-forged global links that global citizens will eventually find sustainable solutions for this sold planet" (Klein, 2000: xx). As companies seek to brand more and more of our lives while censoring our communications and we feel more restrained by the lack of noncorporate space, social energies and longings become focused on the multinational brand itself as the source of restriction (ibid.: 130–1). Although such a movement is still in its infancy, Klein sees it as the beginnings of a battle to find new mechanisms to hold corporations accountable to a broader public. She provides detailed discussions of how mergers, franchising, brand synergy, corporate censorship, and employment practices have converged to create a massive assault on the social pillars of employment, civil liberties, and civic space, giving rise to an anticorporate activism that she calls "No Logo." These conditions are created by the power of corporations to employ the ever expanding protections afforded by IPRs. However, the vulnerability of corporations to having the publicity value of these properties tarnished provides leverage for new forms of resistance. Although the outsourcing of production, for instance, can and often does lend itself to the exploitation of workers, the capacity of corporations to obscure conditions of production is limited. The same communications technologies that enable such dispersed operations also permit activists to link consumers and workers. Digital communications are key to this politics.

In digital environments, opportunities for recontextualizing trademarks and calling corporations into account have expanded and multiplied. Coombe and Herman (2000, 2001a, 2001b) show how trademark management becomes more politicized in digital environments. The world-wide web, they argue,

> ...enable[s] practices that promise to transform the nature of corporate/consumer relations by undermining the traditional capacities of companies to manage their images and control their imagery...[and] create conditions in which consumers have the ability to challenge the very forms of commodity fetishism (erasures of both conditions of production and the conditions under which symbolic value is produced) that have enabled the development of goodwill on which the corporate persona as an asset has historically relied. (2000: 597)

If consumer culture to some degree always exists in a dialogical relationship with legal power and its popular interpretation, this process of dialogue appears to have become more explicit and to have intensified in scope as corporations attempt to control their intellectual properties in cyberspace. Exploring a number of disputes over trademarks and domain names, they suggest that a system of proprietary control, dominant under modern conditions of mass marketing, is being transformed into a more dynamic negotiation of the ethics of property and propriety in the digital public sphere. The means that enable corporations to disseminate and capitalize upon brand equity in cyberspace also provides opportunities for consumers, employees, and artists to intervene in these communications to ensure that goodwill bears some relationship to public evaluations of a more comprehensive range of corporate behavior (Coombe and Herman, 2001b).

Branding has extended beyond goods and services to mark spaces and experiences. Increasingly, sociologist Mark Gottdiener asserts that "our daily life occurs within a material environment that is dependent upon and organized around overarching symbols, many of which are clearly tied to commercial enterprises" (1997: 4). Today's environmental symbolism is derived from mass media – common themes found in films, popular music, and novels are deployed to ensure that we live in themed environments. Gottdiener discusses the "signature logos" of fast food and themed restaurant chains, the aggressive merchandising of professional sports teams, and the theming of shopping experiences, family vacations, casinos, and hotels. Sociologist John Hannigan (1998) updates Gottdiener's thesis to account for the emergence of urban entertainment destinations in the late 1990s that constitute "Fantasy Cities."Aggressively branded, they are designed not only to provide entertainment but to sell licensed merchandise in standardized architectural forms that stand in economic and cultural isolation from surrounding neighborhoods (and appear oblivious to local social problems). Neither author considers the legal infrastructure that makes this new form of spatial culture possible. The liberalization of trademark law has permitted owners of marks to engage in extended marketing in contexts increasingly distant from the goods in association with which they first acquired "secondary meaning" (associated by consumers with a singular source). The concept of "trade dress" evolved to permit rights of exclusivity over restaurant decor, store designs, and other distinctive organizations of space that had or might acquire symbolic meaning. IPRs expanded to provide greater protection for fictional characters, cartoon imagery, and logos. All of these legal developments provided new incentives for investing in the creation of distinctive environments to the degree that energies put into the creation of signifying environments produce "works" which can then be multiply licensed through franchising arrangements.

While these developments were viewed as keys to continued urban growth in the face of the limited tax base that most cities draw upon, they have encountered opposition from academics, neighborhood activists, and architectural critics on both political and aesthetic grounds. Decrying their lack of authenticity and the fact that they cater to desires for comfort, safety, and security entwined with fears of encountering social difference, critics like Hannigan fear that our urban centers are becoming "protected playgrounds for middle-class consumers" (1998: 7) without regard for issues of equity, civility, and social community needs.

Like most scholars of cultural studies, neither Gottdiener nor Hannigan recognize the power of the law in shaping the processes they explore (Coombe, 1999). IPRs are selectively deployed as a means of controlling how these mass cultural texts are appropriated in local lifeworlds, and whenever possible containing their polysemy for fear of trademark "dilution." The law enables, invites, and indeed, insists, that owners of these signs control and monitor their uses deploying a series of complex feints and fictions to legitimate what is essentially a form of corporate cultural power (Coombe, 1998a). A concern with law in society might encourage considerations of the use of intellectual property law in structuring commercial built environments, social practices of IPR management, and the law's role in regulating behavior in these spaces. To what extent, for example, do IPRs serve as a mechanism for risk management? Gottdiener sees themed environments as privatized spaces structured by practices of segregation and surveillance that have usurped the urban public sphere. I would suggest that the ways in which intellectual property laws protect investments in symbols allows those symbols to acquire meanings that shape activities within and exclusions from built environments. People may "self-segregate" in relation to particular symbolic environments; certain trademarks become signals of social safety while others may evoke forms of discomfort. Unbranded environments, like ethnic enclaves and city parks, are often considered unsafe; many municipalities have deliberately invited the presence of known coffee franchises into publicly owned spaces to make the middle classes feel more secure (and to make the homeless and the marginalized less comfortable?). Counterhegemonic spatial tactics in relation to trademark codes also need to be explored (should feminists nurse babies at Hooters franchises?). This has not been a subject of any sustained inquiry, to my knowledge, but it is one more way in which intellectual property could be addressed as law *in society*. We might think about the relationship between the globalized conditions of production for trademarked goods and their local use and interpretations in specific urban spaces, recognizing that they are encountered and engaged by peoples in different social positions, with different histories, who must interpret them with resources drawn from diverse lifeworlds (Coombe and Stoller, 1995).

Klein, for example, looks at practices in which brands are targeted in acts of resistance to these new urban landscapes. Her explanation of "brand bombing," the "superstore" phenomena, and the emergence of community protests against "big box" retailing traces precise business strategies and the social injuries they are perceived to inflict. Throughout the world, residents, workers, farmers, and environmental and labor activists are targeting the more prominent urban locations of corporate logos with protests against the practices their owners are deemed responsible for and the social injuries these effect.

Rifkin's discussion of business franchising illustrates that the management of IPRs has become a means of exercising control over the conditions of commerce, while controlling risk and limiting accountability. Exclusive rights over patents, copyrights, trademarks, trade secrets, and relationships of trust and confidentiality are being used to forge new concentrations of economic power. "Business format franchising" is a method of doing business in which parent companies license their intellectual properties and leave the burden of holding tangible assets to their franchisees. This has fundamentally changed the social role of small businesses.

No longer administrators of autonomous and independent operations, franchisees are merely functionaries and subcontractors for larger businesses who closely control their activities and put them under continuous scrutiny and surveillance. Although they bear the risk and burden of owning property and hiring workers, they have no capacity to earn any autonomous goodwill. One consequence of this, surely (although Rifkin does not address it), is that today's so-called small businesses may be less able to adapt to local circumstances, support local causes, or respond to local conditions. Those who hold the real power, by controlling the valuable IPRs, cannot be held to account by the communities in which their franchisees are located.

THE GLOBAL INFORMATION ECONOMY: THE POLITICS OF INCLUSION AND EXCLUSION

One of the myths of the "postindustrial" society is the perception that intellectual property norms are becoming internationalized. The Eurocentric premises that characterize the dominant ideologies of intellectual property have long been the subject of critical commentary (e.g., Amani, 1999a, 1999b; Jaszi and Woodmansee, 1996). The so-called "level playing field" for trade works ideologically to obscure fundamental inequalities of bargaining power in the global arena and to ignore significant forms of creative activity. These imbalances and exclusions are now sites of struggle in emerging social movements that promise to further politicize the field of intellectual property.

The hegemony of neoliberal logic in the global governance of intellectual property may be traced to the emergence of the Agreement on Trade-Related Aspects of Intellectual Property (TRIPs) which, as legal scholar Neil Netanel (1998) usefully summarizes:

> ...came into effect on January 1, 1995, as part of the agreement that established the WTO [World Trade Organization] and substantially revamped the General Agreement on Tariffs and Trade ("GATT"). TRIPs, which now binds some 130 countries, brings minimum standards of intellectual property protection into the WTO regime of trade liberalization. Its underlying premise is that a country's failure adequately to protect the intellectual property of foreign nationals effectively constitutes a nontariff barrier to trade. (Netanel, 1998: 308)

Legal theorist Peter Drahos views the emergence of the TRIPs Agreement as a remarkable achievement: "because one country, the US, was able to persuade more than 100 other countries that they, as net importers of technological and cultural information, should pay more for the importation of that information. Assuming rational self-interest on the part of these other states, their willingness to sign off on TRIPs constitutes a real world puzzle worth studying" (Drahos, 1995: 7). Taking issue with more complicated theories of hegemony and structural determination, he suggests that theories of global regulation still need to attend to the realities of coercion, institutional entrepreneurship, and inequalities of bargaining power. The incorporation of IPRs into the trade framework was a goal aspired to by US corporate interests who were able to capitalize upon widespread social fears over deindustrialization and loss of US competitiveness.

Under the international conventions administered by the World Intellectual Property Organization (WIPO) – the USA lacked leverage and clout: it could always be outvoted by developing countries and WIPO had no enforcement mechanisms. In the trade arena, the USA had substantial power because it was so significant a market for developing country exports. The US business sector, with direct input into trade policy, began agitating for IPR enforcement and advocated the use of all levers of US power (from foreign aid to loan restructuring) to achieve this goal.

While industry associations provided the US Trade Representative's office with all of the data on "estimated losses" due to "piracy," other business alliances pushed foreign business communities to pressure their own governments to place IPRs squarely in the next round of GATT. In these negotiations the US was in a position of advantage because it could send negotiators with strong IP expertise. The GATT framework allowed deals to be traded freely so that developing countries might secure gains in some areas (like favorable terms for textile and agricultural exports) if they gave up their resistance in others (like the extension of IPRs). Clearly, developing countries felt that the related trade advantages outweighed the costs of these new measures. Political scientist Susan Sell (2003) shows that two trends have become evident in the wake of the adoption of TRIPs. Industry representatives have kept states under strict surveillance to ensure TRIPs compliance while a global civil society movement has mobilized around opposition to TRIPs, focusing on access to drugs, patents on lifeforms, farmers rights, and food security. She describes this as a "tension between the commercial and social agendas for intellectual property" (2002) that has created an increasingly politicized global policy environment.

Struggles over the interpretation of key provisions of TRIPs are legion. Developing countries, civil society organizations, and other UN intergovernmental institutions have battled to ensure that TRIPs does not take precedence over international human rights norms, environmental commitments, or development objectives. There is as yet little scholarship on these new political activities (but see McAfee, 1999).

The trade regime however, has been subject to critical scrutiny. Communications theorist Shalini Venturelli suggests that critical policy issues pertaining to the emergence of a globalized information society have been elided due to the failure to consider the communicative ramifications of a policy that determines "the conditions for innovation, ownership, production, distribution, and exploitation of cultural expression"(1998: 48). Rights of cultural self-determination, the cultural rights of creators, and state rights to adopt alternative modes of cultural and political development have all been ignored, downgraded, or prohibited by international information liberalization policies such as the TRIPs Agreement. The emerging

384 ROSEMARY J. COOMBE

global information infrastructure, she believes, has a dire effect on the expressive conditions necessary to a democratic civil society. Despite increased technological capacities for democratic deliberation (through digital technology), information liberalization has actually decreased the prospects for democracy both by increasing proprietary concentration in the information sector and by transforming the state from the guarantor of public interests in conditions of expression to the guarantor of private proprietary claims. The new regimes governing IPRs may potentially limit the ability of states to determine public interests for their citizens in the arena most essential to the survival of democracy itself: namely, the structure, form, and accessibility of expression in the public sphere. Under the TRIPs framework, for example, the economic incentive model that favors expansive proprietary protections eclipses other dimensions of the copyright tradition, such as the US constitutional aim of enriching the public domain through the dissemination of knowledge and information, the public access rights of citizens, and the human rights of creative labor. New initiatives under way globally, such as the move to protect databases (and I would add, the move to increase protections for plant varieties and extend patent protections to new lifeforms) exacerbate this trend.

The adoption of copyright protections may be seen as a means of furthering democratic development (Netanel, 1998) and to advance democratic principles (particularly in the US constitutional context). Without countervailing international pressures and independent agency by individual states to tailor local regimes to enhance democratic objectives, however, the TRIPs regime will undermine the political potential that copyright might otherwise promise. John Frow, sees the TRIPs Agreement as a "planned attack on the key institutions of civil society" (2000: 176). The world market in information has been dramatically restructured by the abandonment of the New World Information and Communication Order (NWICO) – an information management model that emphasized information disclosure for development purposes – in favor of a model that puts the emphasis upon trade in informational goods as privately held commodities (ibid.: 178). Frow is ultimately equivocal about the likely social effects of the regime:

> Like any complex political formation, it has the potential for both negative and positive consequences. . . . the GATT protocols tend to favor universality and openness of access to information, and to work against both restricted cultures and cultures of secrecy. They enhance the often corrosive effects of the mass media on face-to-face cultures, and the universality they propound is, in one sense, no more than the universalized particularity of the wealthy nations. Yet, however contradictory this openness, it may serve to stimulate reactive cultural production, or cultural hybridization, or merely an uncontainable dissatisfaction with repressive political orders. At the same time, despite the rhetoric of the 'free flow of information' it is also the case that the strengthening of private property rights in information has potentially serious consequences for the protection of local cultures and for the further enclosure of the public domain. (Frow, 2000: 181)

Mary Footer and Christoph Graber (2000) believe that obligations under the new WTO regimes threaten national cultural policy objectives. Trade liberalization has created fears of cultural homogenization and desires for the protection of national identities. Conflicts between trade obligations and cultural policies are emerging. Europe and Canada, for example, have resisted the implication that film and television are the same as other marketable commodities because of their influence in shaping cultural identities. Under the WTO, all forms of cultural policies may be subject to dispute settlement procedures for a determination of whether these create illicit trade barriers. Aspects of IPRs that tend to reflect national cultural values (Samuelson, 1999) will be subject to scrutiny.

The variety of copyright regimes in the world illustrates that artistic, literary, dramatic, and musical works are never completely commodified. Many states entertain both inalienable moral rights and collective licensing regimes that restrict owners from exercising full control over all usages of their works. The collective administration of IPRs historically worked to promote and protect national cultural activities, although this tradition appears to be threatened by industry consolidation (Wallis et al., 1999). Copyright exemptions, clearly contemplated by TRIPs as a means of furthering national policy objectives, are increasingly the subject of dispute in the WTO. The nexus of trade obligations, intellectual property provisions, and cultural policy objectives will be a source of continuing international controversy. Canada and France have proposed and UNESCO has supported the creation of an independent multilateral legal instrument for the preservation and promotion of cultural diversity to counter the hegemony of the trade regime. Such an instrument seems unlikely to gain international acceptance, but the resurgence of issues of cultural identity in all areas of international law under conditions of informational capitalism (Coombe, 2003a) combined with the growing power of NGOs (who are best positioned to represent social interests in international law) suggests that these cannot be denied and evaded by trade regimes in perpetuity.

Some scholars may overstate the social and political impact of the TRIPs Agreement, key provisions of which remain without interpretation. Some argue (e.g., Reichman, 2000; Correa, 2000; Trebilcock and Howse, 1999) that TRIPs itself provides many potential opportunities for states to craft limitations and exemptions to IPRs for consumer welfare, and economic and social development objectives as well as possibilities for compulsory licenses. The need for copyright protections to be tailored to enable expressive diversity, transformative uses, free flows of information, participation in public discourse, and public access to existing works, is evident in the history of international conventions which must be interpreted to determine TRIP's meanings.

THE FATE OF THE COMMONS: THE POLITICS OF PROTECTING THE PUBLIC DOMAIN IN INFORMATIONAL ECONOMIES

Many critics' concerns with the GATT system governing intellectual property focus on its failure to ensure the continuing viability of the public domain. With respect to genetic resources in the natural world, information, facts, methods of operation, language, or ideas (all areas traditionally unprotected by intellectual property laws), we have witnessed an erosion of domains of public access by virtue of the hegemony of neoliberal philosophy (Amani and Coombe, forthcoming). To the extent that the new international intellectual property regimes are committed to the commodification of culture – and it should be added, the enculturation of nature (Coombe, 2003b) – important values are put at risk. These include the desirability of debate and critique in an open public sphere and the importance of the free sharing of knowledge to further progress in the arts and sciences (Frow, 2000: 184).

Concern with the status of the public domain and alarm about the implications of its enclosure is central to many critical studies of globalization and intellectual property, but the issue is certainly not limited to control over *textual* resources – *all* resources have the capacity to become informational and thus to be *textualized* under contemporary technological and legal conditions (Coombe, 2003b; Perry, 2000). Current debates about the scope and desirability of intellectual property protections focus upon the world's crop genetic resources, the rights of farmers (Cleveland and Murray, 1997), and the rights of the rural poor to the continuing use of seed from harvested crops for the maintenance of food security. Should traditional cultivators and medicinal practitioners have rights of recognition and compensation when their knowledge and skills are appropriated, and what are the rights of the poor to continue to create biological diversity as a form of risk insurance in conditions of insecurity (Brush, 2000)?

Unfortunately many scholars have addressed these issues in dichotomous terms – arguing against private rights in favor of an implicitly singular public domain, sometimes imposing an essentialist collective communitarianism on indigenous and rural peoples (Brush, 1999; Gari, 1999), posing stark contrasts between indigenous or traditional and modern or scientific knowledge (Dove, 1996), and romanticizing the sacred dimensions of other cultural worldviews by unwarranted generalizations from specific cases. Fortunately there are now correctives to these projections, including a greater understanding of the variations of both private rights and the multiplicity of public domains (Dutfield, 1999, 2000); the complexity of different cultural means of possessing, protecting, and conveying interests in intangible assets; and the inextricably hybridized forms that contemporary knowledges, both "traditional" and "modern," tend to assume (Agrawal, 1995; Gupta, 1998). Still, it is important to acknowledge the revival of the image of the "commons" in contemporary movements of social resistance (Barnes, 2001; Goldman, 1998; Rowe, 2002) and critical scholarly aspiration with respect to informational policy (Benkler, 2001; Boyle, 2003; Lange and Lange Anderson, 2001).

Nor is the significance of the commons acknowledged only in countercultures. Although the phenomenon has not been subject to sufficient academic attention, social networks insisting upon the virtues of respecting a permanent commons in human and plant genetic material are becoming more vocal (the "no patents on life" movement, for instance) and link together hitherto unimagined coalitions of environmentalists, feminists, farmers, food and health activists, indigenous peoples, and religious groups in the articulation of alternative moral economies of value. The recognized need for a viable public domain in the area of agricultural research also motivated the negotiation of the twenty-first century's first international treaty. The International Treaty on Plant Genetic Resources, adopted by 184 states in November 2001, creates an agricultural commons and a safeguarded public domain in 35 of the worlds most important crop and forage plants (representing 70% of human dietary energy needs) (CIPR, 2001). Significantly, the Treaty provides for mandatory sharing of profits from the use of included resources with the developing world's farmers, who are also recognized as having rights to have access to, exchange, and sell seed in the covered crops, as well as rights of participation in relevant decision-making fora. Developing countries also seek to have their TRIPs obligations narrowed to permit them to recognize these farmers' rights, but the USA continues to pressure states in the hopes of eliminating them.

Global movements to recognize and protect the activities and practices of those traditionally excluded from the purview of intellectual property regimes have put the issue of IPRs and the consequences of their exercise into a broader realm of international policy making and legal obligation (Correa, 2001). Debates about IPRs are now inextricably intertwined with international human rights norms (Amani and Coombe, forthcoming; Chapman, 1998; Coombe, 1998b, 2001), environmental politics (Martinez-Alier, 1997; McAfee, 1999), assertions of cultural and territorial rights (Escobar, 1998), rights to health (Sell, 2003), and international struggles over indigenous self-definition and self-determination. Given the growing politicization of IPRs, the study of intellectual property in society promises to be a rich field of inquiry for years to come.

Note

The author wishes to thank Graham Boswell, Moira Daly, Simon Proulx and Monique Twigg for their excellent research and editorial assistance.

References

Agrawal, A. (1995) "Dismantling the divide between indigenous and scientific knowledge," *Development and Change* 26: 413–39.

Amani, B. (1999a) "Fact, fiction or folklore? It's time the tale were told – Part I," *Intellectual Property Journal* 13: 237–73.

Amani, B. (1999b) "Copyright, cultural industries and folklore: A tall tale of legal fiction – Part II," *Intellectual Property Journal*, 13: 275–303.

Amani, B. and Coombe, R.J. (forthcoming) "The human genome diversity project: Politicizing patents at the intersection of race, religion, health and research ethics," *Law and Policy Review* 26.

Aoki, K. (1993) "Authors, inventors and trademark owners: Private intellectual property and the public domain. Part I," *Columbia-VLA Journal of Law and the Arts* 18: 1–73.

Aoki, K. (1994) "Authors, inventors and trademark owners: Private intellectual property and the public domain. Part II," *Columbia-VLA Journal of Law and the Arts* 18: 191–267.

Aoki, K. (1997) "How the world dreams itself to be American: Reflections on the relationship between the expanding scope of trademark protection and free speech norms," *Loyola of Los Angeles Entertainment Law Journal* 17: 523–47.

Barnes, P. (2001) *Who Owns the Sky?* Washington, DC: Island Press.

Benkler, Y. (2001) "Siren songs and Amish children: Autonomy, information, and law," *New York University Law Review* 76: 23–113.

Boyle, J. (1996) *Shamans, Software, and Spleens*. Cambridge, MA: Harvard University Press.

Boyle, J. (2003) "The second enclosure movement and the construction of the public domain," *Law and Contemporary Problems*, 66: 33–74 Available online at <http://www.law.duke.edu/journals/lcp/>.

Brush, S. (1999) "Bioprospecting the public domain," *Cultural Anthropology* 14: 535–55.

Brush, S. (2000) "The issues of in situ conservation of plant genetic resources," in S. Brush (ed.), *Genes in the Field: On Farm Conservation of Crop Diversity*. Rome: International Plant Genetic Resources Institute, pp. 3–36.

Brush, S. and Stabinsky, D. (eds.) (1996) *Valuing Local Knowledge*. Washington, DC: Island Press.

Chapman, A. (1998) "A human rights perspective on intellectual property, scientific progress, and access to the benefits of science," in WIPO/UNHCR *Intellectual Property and Human*

Rights: A Panel Discussion to Commemorate the 50ᵗʰ Anniversary of the Universal Declaration on Human Rights, Publication No. 762(E). Geneva: WIPO, pp. 128–62. Available online at <http:www.wipo.org/globalissues/events/1998/humanrights/papers/pdf/chapman.pdf>.

Chon, M. (1993) "Progress: Reconsidering the copyright and patent power," *De Paul Law Review* 43: 97.

CIPR (2001) "International Treaty on Plant Genetic Resources," available from <iprcommission@topica.com> November 8, 2001. For further details see <www.ukabc.org>.

Cleveland, D. and Murray, S. (1997) "The world's crop genetic resources and the rights of indigenous farmers," *Current Anthropology* 38: 477–515.

Coombe, R.J. (1991) "Objects of property and subjects of politics: Intellectual property laws and democratic dialogue," *Texas Law Review* 69: 1853–80.

Coombe, R.J. (1994) "Author/izing the celebrity: Publicity rights, postmodern politics, and unauthorized genders," in M. Woodmansee and P. Jaszi (eds.), *The Construction of Authorship: Textual Appropriations in Law and Literature*. Durham, NC: Duke University Press, pp. 101–131. Reprinted in Peter K. Yu (ed.), *The Marketplace of Ideas: Twenty Years of the Cardozo Arts and Entertainment Law Journal*, 2002, pp. 236–66.

Coombe, R.J. (1998a) *The Cultural Life of Intellectual Properties: Authorship, Appropriation, and the Law*. Durham, NC: Duke University Press.

Coombe, R.J. (1998b) "Intellectual property, human rights and sovereignty: New dilemmas in international law posed by the recognition of indigenous knowledge and the conservation of biodiversity," *Indiana Journal of Global Legal Studies* 6: 59–115.

Coombe, R.J. (1999) "Sports trademarks and somatic politics," in R. Martin and T. Miller (eds.), *Sportcult*. Minneapolis: University of Minnesota Press, pp. 262–88. Reprinted in D. Goldberg, M. Musheno, and L. Bower (eds.), (2001), *Between Law and Culture: Relocating Legal Studies*. Minneapolis: University of Minnesota Press, pp. 22–49.

Coombe, R.J. (2001) "The recognition of indigenous peoples' and community traditional knowledge in international law," *St. Thomas Law Review* 14: 275–85.

Coombe, R.J. (2003a) "Fear, hope, and longing for the future of authorship and a revitalized public domain in global regimes of intellectual property," *DePaul Law Review* 62: 1171–91.

Coombe, R.J. (2003b) "Works in progress: Traditional knowledge, biological diversity and intellectual property in a neoliberal era," in R.W. Perry and W. Maurer (eds.), *Globalization Under Construction: Governmentality, Law, and Identity*. Minneapolis: University of Minnesota Press, pp. 273–314.

Coombe, R.J. and Herman, A. (2000) "Trademarks, property, and propriety: The moral economy of consumer politics and corporate accountability on the World Wide Web," *De Paul Law Review* 50: 597–632.

Coombe, R.J. and Herman, A. (2001a) "Culture wars on the Net: Intellectual property and corporate propriety in digital environments," *South Atlantic Quarterly* 100: 919–47.

Coombe, R.J. and Herman, A. (2001b) "Defending toy dolls and maneuvering toy soldiers: Corporate-consumer wars of position on the World-Wide Web," Powerpoint presentation available at <http://www.mit.edu>.

Coombe, R.J. and Stoller, P. (1995) "X marks the spot: The ambiguities of African trading in the commerce of the black public sphere," *Public Culture: Society for Transnational Studies* 7: 249–74. Reprinted in The Public Sphere Collective (eds.) (1995), *The Black Public Sphere*. Chicago: University of Chicago Press, pp. 253–78.

Cordero, S. (1998) "Cocaine-Cola, the velvet Elvis, and anti-Barbie: Defending the trademark and publicity rights to cultural icons," *Fordham Intellectual Property, Media & Entertainment Law Journal* 8: 599–654.

Correa, C. (2000) *Intellectual Property Rights, the WTO and Developing Countries: The TRIPS Agreement and Policy Options*. London and New York: Zed Books.

Correa, C. (2001) "Traditional knowledge and intellectual property: Issues and options surrounding the protection of traditional knowledge: A discussion paper," Geneva: Quaker

United Nations Office, November. Available from <http://www.quno.org> (click on Geneva pages).

Dove, M. (1996) "Centre, periphery and biodiversity: A paradox of governance and a developmental challenge," in S. Brush and D. Stabinsky (eds.), *Valuing Local Knowledge: Indigenous People and Intellectual Property Rights.* Washington, DC: Island Press, pp. 41–67.

Drahos, P. (1995) "Global property rights in information: The story of TRIPS at the GATT," *Prometheus* 13: 6–19. Reprinted in P. Drahos (ed.) (1999), *Intellectual Property.* Aldershot, UK: Dartmouth Publications, pp. 419–32.

Dreyfuss, R. (1990) "Expressive genericity: Trademarks as language in the Pepsi generation," *Notre Dame Law Review* 65: 397–424.

Dreyfuss, R. (1996) "We are symbols and inhabit symbols, so should we be paying rent? Deconstructing the Lanham Act and rights of publicity," *Columbia-VLA Journal of Law and the Arts* 20: 123–56.

Dutfield, G. (1999) "Rights, resources and responses," in United Nations Environment Program, *Cultural and Spiritual Values of Biodiversity.* London: Intermediate Technology Publications, pp. 503–46.

Dutfield, G. (2000) "The public and private domains: Intellectual property rights in traditional knowledge," Science Communication 21: 274–95.

Escobar, A. (1998) "Whose knowledge, whose nature? Biodiversity conservation and the political ecology of social movements," *Journal of Political Ecology* 5: 53–82.

Footer, M. and Graber, C. (2000) "Trade liberalization and cultural policy," *Journal of International Economic Law* 3(1): 115–44.

Franklin, S., Lury, C., and Stacey, J. (eds.) (2000) *Global Nature, Global Culture.* Boulder, CO: Sage Publications.

Frow, J. (1995) "Elvis' fame: The commodity form and the form of the person," *Cardozo Studies in Law and Literature* 7(2): 131–71.

Frow, J. (2000) "Public domain and the new world order in knowledge," *Social Semiotics* 10(2): 173–85.

Gaines, J. (1991) *Contested Culture: The Image, the Voice, and the Law.* Chapel Hill, NC: University of North Carolina Press.

Gaines, J. (1995) "Reincarnation as the ring on Liz Taylor's finger: Andy Warhol and the right of publicity," in A. Sarat and T. Kearns (eds.), *Identities, Politics and Rights.* Ann Arbor, MI: University of Michigan Press, pp. 131–48.

Gari, J. (1999) "Biodiversity conservation and use: Local and global considerations," *Science, Technology and Development Discussion Paper No. 7.* Cambridge, MA: Harvard University Center for International Development and Belfer Center for Science and International Affairs.

Goldman, M. (ed.) (1998) *Privatizing Nature: Political Struggle for the Global Commons.* New Brunswick, NJ: Rutgers University Press.

Gordon, W. (1990) "Toward a jurisprudence of benefits: The norms of copyright and the problem of private censorship," *University of Chicago Law Review* 57: 1009–49.

Gottdiener, M. (1997) *The Theming of America: Dreams, Visions, and Commercial Spaces.* Boulder, CO: Westview Press.

Gupta, A. (1998) *Postcolonial Developments: Agriculture in the Making of Modern India.* Durham, NC: Duke University Press.

Hannigan, J. (1998) *Fantasy City: Pleasure and Profit in the Postmodern Metropolis.* London and New York: Routledge.

Heller, M. and Eisenberg, R. (2000) "Can patents deter innovation? The anticommons in biomedical research," *Science* 280: 698–702.

Herman, A. and Sloop, J. (1998) "The politics of authenticity in postmodern rock culture: The case of Negativland and *The Letter 'U' and the Numeral '2',*" *Critical Studies in Mass Communication* 15: 1–20.

Jaszi, P. and Woodmansee, M. (1996) "The ethical reaches of authorship," *South Atlantic Quarterly* 95: 947–78.

Klein, N. (2000) *No Logo: Taking Aim at the Brand Bullies*. Toronto: Knopf Canada.

Kotler, J.S.T. (1999) "Trade-mark parody, judicial confusion and the unlikelihood of fair use," *Intellectual Property Journal* 14: 219–40.

Lange, D. and Lange Anderson, J. (2001) "Copyright, fair use and transformative critical appropriation," in Duke Conference on the Public Domain (ed.), *Focus Paper, Discussion Drafts*, pp. 130–56. Available online at <http://james-boyle.com/papers.pdf>.

Langvardt, A. (1997) "The troubling implication of a right of publicity 'wheel' spun out of control," *Kansas Law Review* 45: 329–452.

Lemley, M. (1999) "The modern Lanham Act and the death of common sense," *Yale Law Journal* 108: 1687–715.

Lessig, L. (2001) *The Future Of Ideas: The Fate of the Commons in a Connected World*. New York: Random House.

Litman, J. (2001) *Digital Copyright*. New York: Prometheus Books.

Lury, C. (1993) *Cultural Rights: Technology, Legality, Personality*. London: Routledge.

Madow, M. (1993) "Private ownership of public image: Popular culture and publicity rights," *California Law Review* 81: 125–240.

Martinez-Alier, J. (1997) "The merchandising of biodiversity," in T. Hayward and J. O'Neill (eds.), *Justice, Property and the Environment: Social and Legal Perspectives*. Aldershot, UK: Ashgate, pp. 194–211.

McAfee, K. (1999) "Selling nature to save it? Biodiversity and green developmentalism," *Environment and Planning D; Society and Space* 17: 133–54.

McLeod, K. (2001) *Owning Culture: Authorship, Ownership, and Intellectual Property Law*. New York: Peter Lang.

McSherry, C. (2001) *Who Owns Academic Work? Battling for Control of Intellectual Property*. Cambridge, MA: Harvard University Press.

Netanel, N. (1998) "Asserting copyright's democratic principles in the global age," *Vanderbilt Law Review* 51: 217–349.

Pearson, A. (1998) "Commercial trademark parody, the Federal Dilution Act, and the First Amendment," *Valpariso University Law Review* 32: 973–1028.

Perry, B. (2000) "The fate of the collections: Social justice and the annexation of plant genetic resources," in C. Zerner (ed.), *Peoples, Plants and Justice*. New York: Columbia University Press, pp. 374–402.

Polster, C. (2000) "The future of the liberal university in the era of the global knowledge grab," *Higher Education* 39: 19–41.

Rai, A.K. (1999) "Regulating scientific research: Intellectual property rights and the norms of science," *Northwestern University Law Review* 94: 77–152.

Rai, A.K. and Eisenberg, R. (2003) "Bayh-Dole reform and the progress of biomedicine," *Law and Contemporary Problems*, 66: 289–314. Available online at <http://www.law.duke.edu/journals/ lcp/>.

Reichman, J.H. (2000) "The TRIPS Agreement comes of age: Conflict or cooperation with the developing countries?" *Case Western Reserve Journal of International Law* 32: 441–70.

Reichman, J.H. and Uhlir, P.F. (1999) "Database protection at the crossroads: Recent developments and their impact on science and technology," *Berkeley Technology Law Review* 14: 793–838.

Reichman, J.H. and Uhlir, P. (2003) "A contractually reconstructed research commons for scientific data in a highly protectionist intellectual property environment," *Law and Contemporary Problems* 66: 315–462. Available online at <http://www.law.duke.edu/journals/ lcp/>.

Rifkin, Jeremy. (2000) *The Age of Access: The New Culture of Hypercapitalism, Where All of Life is a Paid-For Experience*. New York: J.P. Tarcher.

Rowe, J. (2002) "Fanfare for the commons," *Utne Reader* January-February: 40–4.

Samuelson, P. (1999) "Implications of the agreement on trade related aspects of intellectual property rights for the cultural dimension of national copyright laws," *Journal of Cultural Economics* 23: 95–107.

Schlosser, S. (2001) "The high price of criticizing coffee: The chilling effect of the Federal Trademark Dilution Act on corporate parody," *Arizona Law Review* 43: 931–64.

Sell, S. (2002) "Post-TRIPS developments: The tension between commercial and social agendas in the context of intellectual property," *Florida Journal of International Law* 14: 193–216.

Sell, S. (2003) *Private Power, Public Law: The Globalization of Intellectual Property Rights.* Cambridge, UK: Cambridge University Press.

Shulman, S. (1999). *Owning the Future.* Boston: Houghton, Mifflen.

Trebilcock, M. and Howse, R. (1999) *International Trade Regulation*, 2nd edn. London and New York: Routledge.

Vaidhyanathan, S. (2001) *Copyrights and Copywrongs: The Rise Of Intellectual Property and How It Threatens Creativity.* New York: New York University Press.

Venturelli, S. (1998) "Cultural rights and world trade agreements in the information society," *Gazette: International Journal for Communication Studies* 60(1): 47–76.

Wallis, R. et al. (1999) "Contested collective administration of intellectual property rights in music: The challenges to the principles of reciprocity and solidarity," *European Journal of Communication* 14: 5–35.

Further Reading

Bettig, R.(1996) *Copyrighting Culture: The Political Economy of Intellectual Property.* Boulder, CO: Westview Press.

Blakeney, M. (ed.) (1999) *Perspectives on Intellectual Property: Intellectual Property Aspects of Ethnobiology.* London: Sweet and Maxwell.

Brown, M. (2003) *Who Owns Native Culture?* Cambridge, MA: Harvard University Press.

Buranen, L. and Roy, A. (eds.) (1999) *Perspectives on Plagiarism and Intellectual Property in a Postmodern World.* Albany: State University of New York Press.

Drahos P. with John Braithwaite (2002) *Information Feudalism: Who Owns the Knowledge Economy?* New York: New Press.

Frow, J. (1997) *Time and Commodity Culture: Essays in Cultural Theory and Postmodernity.* Oxford: Clarendon Press.

Gordon, W. (1993) "A property right in self-expression: Equality and individualism in the natural law of intellectual property,"*Yale Law Journal* 102: 1533–609.

Maskus, K. and Reichman, J. (eds.) *International Public Goods and Transfer of Technology Under a Globalized Intellectual Property Regime.* Cambridge, UK: Cambridge University Press.

May, C. (2000) *A Global Political Economy of Intellectual Property Rights: The New Enclosures.* New York: Routledge.

Netanel, N. and Elkin-Koren, N. (eds.) (2002) *The Commodification of Information.* The Hague: Kluwer Law International.

Stenson, A. and Gray, T. (1997) "Cultural communities and intellectual property rights in plant genetic resources," in T. Hayward and J. O'Neill (eds.), *Justice, Property and the Environment: Social and Legal Perspectives.* Aldershot, UK: Ashgate, pp. 178–93.

21

Legal Categorizations and Religion: On Politics of Modernity, Practices, Faith, and Power

GAD BARZILAI

INTRODUCTION

Western constitutionalism and modern liberalism have constructed and promoted the problematic hegemonic myth of separation of religion from state and politics in democracies (Carter, 1998). Yet a careful and critical analysis of modern politics, law, and society that deconstructs formal legal categorizations would point to the irreducible significant role of religion in modern states, laws, and legal ideologies. As this essay expounds, while institutional and cultural variances between and among political regimes and religions exist, religion in the midst of neoliberal transnational and international expansion ("globalization") is prominent as a sociopolitical and legal force. Religion is conspicuous in various states and societies despite – even in reaction to and as part of – the ethos and practices of secular rationality and teleological modernity at the outset of the third millenium.

Some studies in law and society have conceived religion in constitutional terms of freedom of religion, state neutrality concerning religious institutions and faith, and freedom from religion (Friedman, 1990). Other studies in law and society have looked at religion as a substantive component in tribal cultures that reflect premodern systems of law (Currie, 1968; Pospisil, 1973). Such an inclination to identify religion and religious law with premodern social phenomena, sometimes even with savage appearances, has characterized the significant bulk of law and society research until the beginning of the 1980s. Later, with the emergence of more sensitivity to the interplay between religious law and nationality, more emphasis was rendered to the analysis of the versatility of religious law, the plurality of religions, and their possible adaptations to and reconciliation with modernity (Rosen, 1980; Messick, 1988). Thus these studies have pointed to the flexibility of Islamic law (*Shari'a*) and its pragmatic features despite its theological narratives.

Max Weber's sociological skepticism concerning modernity, and his respect for religions as marginalized phenomena in the midst of regulated modern capitalism, has not attracted the scholarly attention it deserves among law and society students of religion. Max Weber was fascinated by religions all over the globe and he considered religions and religious laws as the basis for understanding evolvement of capitalist and noncapitalistic settings (Weber, 1964; Trubek, 1986). For almost 30 years after Weber's death in 1920, his studies of Buddhism, Christianity, Confucianism, Hinduism, Islam, Judaism, and Taoism (Weber, 1951, 1952, 1956, 1960) had remained unmatched and infrequently touched by law and society scholars. Only with the influence of anthropological studies of law and society, mainly by Adamson Hoebel and his students, the law and society movement has enriched our knowledge with insights into case studies of religions and religious laws (Hoebel, 1954; Pospisil, 1973). While religious law was comprehended outside the realm of state's legal ideology, its conjunction with and struggles against other legal traditions was largely neglected.

Legal pluralism that has unfolded since the end of the 1980s has called for the need to comprehend various legal traditions and practices in their interactive relations through unveiling state law and legal ideology. It has underscored special attentiveness to cultural disharmonies in law as empowering sources of a pluralistic, possibly ordered, social justice (Calavita, 2001: Merry, 1988; Sarat and Berkowitz, 1994; Twining, 1986, 2000; Santos, 1995). I am writing this essay within that tradition of legal pluralism, submitting a critical communitarian approach, which has been marginal in studies of legal pluralism heretofore. I suggest that a multiplicity of religious communal practices, even fundamentalist, can be seen as reconcilable with democratic order (Sarat and Berkowitz, 1994). This study conceives religion as a set of epistemological guides to view the world, and as a system of cultural communal practices, driven by beliefs in transcendental sacred forces. Religion constitutes and reflects meanings of existence in every domain of human life in modernity. Such a set of values, norms, and practices cannot be comprehended and judged based on criteria of "rational" and "irrational."

The perspective that this essay presents is different from the liberal explication of religion as a category of faith that is constitutionally separated from the state. Furthermore, it is different from viewing religion as purely primordial and even tribal. I share the criticism of Talal Asad (Asad, 1993) concerning Geertz's project (Geertz, 1973) that conceptualizes religion mainly as a distinct symbolic entity. As this essay submits, religion and law are inseparable and interchangeable within power and in conflict with power in various, sometimes contradictory, sociopolitical interactive spaces.

Accordingly, understanding religion becomes a challenge to students of law, society, and politics in multicultural settings. While fantasies of neoliberalism imagining a global Western-led society become more apparent, at the outset of the twenty-first century religions in diversity of localities do matter in most countries around the world as part of daily practices and states' practices. A neoliberal concept of teleological modernity presumes the cultural supremacy of rational secular legality, and it excludes the constructive significance of religions to plurality in democracies. Paradoxically, that concept has been strengthened in the American-led West after the September 11, 2001 terrorist attacks on the World Trade Center. Yet contrary to secular expectations surveys from the 1990s display high figures of religious practices in contemporary Western and central European democracies:

inter alia, 88% in Ireland, 69% in Northern Ireland, 51% in Italy, 43% in Switzerland, 41% in Portugal, 39% in Spain, 34% in Hungary, 34% in Germany (West), 20% in Germany (East), 19% in Britain, 17% in France, had attended church at least monthly (Bruce, 1999).

Conflicts between liberalism and nonliberal (nonruling) religious communities are common among many democracies. Since liberalism pretends to privatize religion, locating faith and religious practices in the individual sphere, and due to its fundamentalist claim for nonreligious virtues, it threatens to infringe upon rights of nonruling collectivities that aim to preserve and maintain nonhegemonic religious cultures. These minorities' religious cultures are perceived in modern liberal legality as confrontational to majoritarian cultures. Such a conflict between self-asserted liberal state law and nonruling religious collectivities is articulated through cultural legal conflicts in, inter alia, England, France, Germany, India, Israel, Netherlands, Turkey, and the USA. The conflicts are palpable even in states where a formal liberal separation between state and religion exists, like in France, Germany, and the USA. Whether the state should institutionally and financially assist nonruling religious communities is under public and legal contentions in these political regimes; the dominant constitutional stand of state courts is against such facilitation due to the principle of freedom of religion. Subsequently, an advantage is practically granted to the hegemonic religions and churches in these regimes.

Conflicts between liberalism and nonruling (nonliberal) religious communities exhibit the inability of Kantian categorizations to generate universal discourse of human rights that also addresses local predicaments of nonruling communities. Writings in law and society scholarship that point to the virtues of secularization do not expound the needs of those local communities and evade the dilemma of how to address them in an inclusive democratic setting (Starr, 1989).

This essay examines the knowledge in law and society scholarship and deconstructs the interactions between law and religion through and within a decentered law and society prism (Garth and Sterling, 1998). Following problematizations of the liberal dichotomy between state and religion, this essay criticizes the epistemological, logical, and theoretical deficiencies of liberalism that prevent it from addressing properly the significant role of religion in democratic politics. Liberalism has failed in comprehending the complex practices in which religion is part of state power foci and a component in modern legality. It has privatized religion as a matter of individual right and hence it has not offered constitutional and political avenues of including nonliberal religious minorities in contemporary multicultural societies. I critically explicate the escape of liberalism from the challenges of religion and law in a democratic context.

The essay also deals with and advocates the critical communitarian argument for inclusion of religious communities in democracies through evolvement of collective rights for protecting and empowering religious minorities that challenge hegemonic concepts of modernity, rationality, and secularism. I propose to view multiculturalism not as a liberal project, rather as an empowering political framework for cultivation of cultural and institutional tolerance toward religious minorities, including fundamentalist minorities, and nonliberal communities. In the context of multiculturalism, law should perceive liberalism with all its virtues and importance to democracy, as a relative tradition by itself, not as an absolute ordering criterion for legality. This essay offers to inject such cultural relativism into our future studies of religion and law. Deconstruction and reconstruction of law and religion through exploring their genealogical categorizations in society and politics may inspire reforms in contemporary political regimes and make them inclusive entities that constitutionally include, protect, and empower diversity of religious nonruling communities.

GENEALOGICAL INQUIRY OF RELIGIOUS CATEGORIES IN LAW AND LEGAL CATEGORIES IN RELIGION

Through a genealogical analysis of religion and law I explore below the interplay between law in religion, religion in law, and modern politics of law and religion. Natural religious law, namely a law driven from a faith in God or in divine forces, has used religion to construct given, sanctified, unchangeable, and universal legal categorizations as normative guidelines of a just behavior. Such a natural religious law is the absolute criterion for obedience and disobedience to human law, according to the principle of *lex iniusta non est lex* ("an unjust law is not law") (Bix, 1996).

That basic category of law as hermeneutics and practices derived from the will of God and its prophets has been a major characterization in the writings of Saint Augustine, Thomas Aquinas, Abu Alhasan Ali ibn Muhammad Almaourdi, Maimonides, and other theological thinkers in different religions. Accordingly, morality and legality are based on religion as a set of divine and transcendent ordering criteria. Law in that context is a universal, and not a contingent, category in religion that should generate obedience. Law is intended to formulate the space for human choices and for judicial discretion within the scope of a sacred normative order. Natural law has often been a source of dissent to state law in modern times, and a source of empowerment to democracy and multiculturalism. Natural religious law, however, in distinction from natural law in general, persisted primarily until the fourteenth century AD. From then on, natural law has remained a powerful concept, but it has experienced a process of secularization that was spurred by the gradual rise of postmedieval science, and rationalization of law as part of it.

The Copernican revolution and Kantian philosophy have constructed religious morality as a product of human consciousness. Whatever legal categories we construct, they are a matter of our own morality, and a generation of our own consciousness. Objectified categories exist, but as part of our own will and desire that we are framing and implementing as autonomous human beings. Religion is based on morality, and human law creates God; law might even be perceived as God. Hence, religion becomes a category in law. Kant himself knew and used biblical law, but in the more general framework of his own humanistic conceptions of universal laws as consciousness-driven objectified categories (Fletcher, 1996: 519).

The gradual secularization of law has centered it and constructed it as omnipotent. As evident from writings of Hugo Grotius in the sixteenth and seventeenth centuries, post-Kantian philosophers of the eighteenth century onwards, and English positivists (Horwitz, 1996), a concept of divine sovereignty was replaced by a concept of a secular one. The latter was imagined as the aggregation of individual wills and originated in contractual relations. While religious institutions could have been separated from the state, religious identities have remained part of state law and its legal ideology. Hence, any project of deconstruction of modern law should be a project of deconstructing the imagined separation between religion and state law.

I share the anthropological concept of Talal Asad (Asad, 1993) in his historical exploration of Islam and Christianity. Asad argues that religion is not a separated category, but a constitutive set of practices that cannot be understood unless within the broader notions of power, structures, agents, and historical circumstances.

Nationalism, mainly since the nineteenth century, has utilized religion for its own political purposes. From Hindu India and Muslim Pakistan to Jewish Israel and Catholic Ireland, from Protestant USA to Lutheran Germany, nationalism has used through legality religious categorizations for empowering some collective identities and marginalizing others. Religion – due to its perceived supranatural magic and transcendental myths – has the power to consolidate a communal ethos in ways that significantly affect the communal normative and practical "order" and its relations with its surroundings. Since religion, as Karl Marx has keenly observed, may be an epiphenomenon, it reflects discriminated ethnic identities, social stratification, and subjugation of minorities. As such it is a political mechanism to mobilize people with different sources of interests to what may wrongly be perceived as a common public goal.

Emile Durkheim argued that modern societies would necessarily experience intensive secularization. Therefore he was concerned with the question what would happen to modern societies without the effects of religion as a crucial republican consolidating force. Durkheim, one of the most influential founding fathers of modern sociology, alongside Karl Marx and Max Weber, had presumed – in a neo-Kantian way – that as a primordial social phenomenon religion is expected to be expelled by secularism as a unifying sociopolitical force (Pickering, 1984). Falsifying Durkheim's teleological argument, most probably made under a Kantian influence, religion has become a national civil force in many diverse and contingent facets of modernity.

Inter alia, one legalistic strategy of the nation-state was to exclude religion as a recognizable political force. Such legalistic attempts, as in modern Turkey during the 1920s and the 1960s and in some authoritarian regimes like China after 1949, have often resulted in resistance and aggravation of religious dissent and violence among minorities (Turkey) and in various localities (China). The other strategy has been to constitutionally privatize religion, as in France and the USA since the eighteenth century, and in Germany after World War II. Such a legalistic strategy has resulted in national attempts to ignore the religious collective demands and needs of nonliberal (nonruling) religious communities.

A third legalistic strategy has formally recognized the communal nature of religion, though it has used it for negating other collective identities of the very same nonruling community. Israeli law has to some extent followed the *Millet* (community) system of the Ottoman Empire. Israeli Arab-Palestinians were recognized in state law as religious minorities (Muslims, Christians, Bedouins, Druze), and then they were denied collective rights as a Palestinian (national) minority. Thus religion has largely become a means to procure national control and governance.

Following its consolidation in John Stuart Mill's writings in the mid-nineteenth century, liberalism has intruded in national politics and legal ideologies from the 1950s. Its conjunction with the nation-state has generated "liberal nationalism." Namely, it has privatized religion of nonruling communities through "freedom of religion" legalistic clauses, as one can find in two major liberal constitutional projects, the USA Constitution and the 1998 European Convention for the Protection of National Minorities. Liberal jurisprudence in the modern nation-state has

had the challenge to reconcile the state's (veiled) religious identities and its egalitarian asserted commitments to freedom of and from religion. Remarkably, this challenge has further been empowered by the spirit of neo-Kantian globalization that
since the 1990s has spurred liberalism (and its foes) in various localities.

Liberalism as a theory of justice has responded to that challenge by two arguments: (1) individual rights precede any other concrete and distinct definition of the
"common good"; (2) the state is neutral and can provide impartial procedural justice
(Rawls, 1973, 1993; Barry, 1995). In other words, the religious identities of the state
do not exist, and nevertheless cannot hamper the preference given to individuals'
freedoms over any republican religious good. These two fundamental liberal claims
are wrong.

Legal pluralists, feminists, critical legalists, and communitarians in law and society scholarship have argued that individual rights are a certain "good" that should be
referred to within a broader context of cultures, conflicts, plurality of orders,
possibilities, needs, and constraints (Crenshaw, Gotanda, Peller, and Thomas,
1995; Greenberg, Minow, and Roberts, 1998; Kairys, 1990; Sarat and Kearns,
1999; Selznick, 1992). Such a "good" is crucial to democracy. Notwithstanding,
giving absolute and exclusive preference to individual rights, under all possible
circumstances, in all imaginary contexts, and invariably, would repress nonliberal
cultures, and nonliberal communities in democracies, which have a different, not
indispensably contradictory, ontological conception of the "good" (MacIntyre,
1984, 1988; Sandel, 1982, 1996). To underscore individual rights as the absolute,
transcendental ordering criterion, makes any liberal deontological justice regretfully
disengaged from the variety of historicity, circumstances, social beings, structures,
and processes in human life.

The liberal discourse does not empower nonruling and nonliberal communities.
Their members – unless stripped of their embedded identities – cannot enjoy the
liberal discourse, which does not enable nonruling and nonliberal communities to
preserve their own cultures and to fulfill their distinct communal needs. Religious
nonliberal and nonruling communities do not necessarily negate human rights and
individual rights (Asad, 1993; Barzilai, 2003; Carter, 1998). However, they contemplate and demand more emphasize in public policy to their own minority's cultures.

Likewise, states and courts are not impartial since they maintain and generate
identities, ideologies, and interests (Benhabib, 1992; Epstein and Knight, 1998;
Feeley and Rubin, 1998; Horwitz, 1992; Jacob, Blankenburg, Kritzer, Provine, and
Sanders, 1996; Lahav, 1997; McCann, 1994; Migdal, 1988; Rosenberg, 1991; Sarat
and Kearns, 1999; Scheingold, 1974; Shamir, 1996). In more practical terms, liberal
states have had to face the reality of multicultural societies and religious fundamentalist communities, which do not have a preference of individual rights as the
exclusive, universal, and absolute good.

Can individual rights, alone, guarantee the freedoms and needs of nonliberal
religious communities in democracies? Generally, Western-led scholarship has
ignored that dilemma, partly due to the liberal vision as a meta-narrative, and partly
since in the American academic reality of the twentieth century religious minorities
have not been regarded as a severe problem for human rights activists, and much
more attention was devoted to the predicament of Afro-Americans and native
Americans. Moreover, with the exception of intellectuals such as Talal Asad and
Edward Said, Muslims in the USA and West Europe have suffered from intellectual
marginalization. The September 11, 2001 terrorist event has made things even

worse, and protecting the Muslim minority, let alone empowering its voice, has become an even more criticized concept.

The deficiencies in liberalism may be exemplified by referring to Joseph Raz, one of the most prominent liberal thinkers, who considers multiculturalism as an axiom of modern democracy. Communities should be respected, Raz contends, as long as they respect the individual freedom of their members. If communities are not liberal, Raz demands the enforcement of individual freedom in these communities (Raz, 1994). Thus, in that theory freedom should be imposed, and all choices are liberal choices. Four erroneous presumptions lead Raz, and liberalism in general, to that oxymoron of imposed freedom.

First, Raz presumes that most communities in democracies are liberal. That error articulates a Western epistemological bias. In many countries, however, communities are often not liberal. Inter alia, one may mention Brazil, India, Ireland, Israel, Peru, and (even) North America. Second, Raz believes that individual freedom and its absence can be objectively defined. Indeed, if people want to leave a community they should be entitled to exit, notably when the community condones violence against them. But these instances are rare. Often, members in communities, including in nonliberal communities, do not wish to leave their sources of identity and empowerment (Asad, 1993; Mautner, Sagie, and Shamir, 1998; Renteln and Dundes, 1994; Sheleff, 1996). How do liberals decide in which instances people do or do not have the freedom to chose their lifestyles in a nonliberal setting? In effect, Raz avoids this issue. As I show elsewhere (Barzilai, 2003), nonliberal religious communities do offer spaces of practices and choices to individuals. Individual freedom is a relative term, and it is culturally and contextually contingent on the specific community.

Third, Raz presumes, as do other neo-Rawlsian scholars, that individual freedom is an absolute value, superior to any other conceptions of "good" and justice. Let us suppose that we can arrive at an "objective" meaning of "individual freedom"; does this make it an absolute value? Do we know of any organization or political regime that has justified complete individual freedom, under all circumstances, and is it always desirable to maintain "individual freedom" as an absolute value at the expense of other values like communal faith and caring? If not, why presume that individual freedom is (always) superior to a communal right to preserve its non-liberal religious collective culture?

This argument leads us to the fourth error in the liberal endeavor. If we perceive a certain antinomy between the value of individual freedom (in its absolute liberal terms) and communal cultural preservation, how can we normatively endorse the liberal argument as appropriate for multiculturalism? To do so, we must presume – like Raz – that liberalism is superior to any other theory of justice. However, if we presume the superiority of the liberal theory of justice, which is one tradition among others, we are enforced to exclude the principle of cultural relativity that is the basis of multiculturalism. Hence, Raz's arguments do not respond to the needs of non-liberal religious communities of protection – let alone empowerment – in multicultural settings.

Historically, liberal legal culture has primarily been individualistic. As "associations," communities do not relish collective rights or systematic collective protection in public policy and law (Lomosky, 1987; Roberts, 1999). Liberals have emphasized the importance of groups to multicultural political articulation and to collective participation in decision-making processes. Yet they have avoided the logical consequences of this position and have continued to embrace the primacy of individual rights (Dahl, 1971; Kymlicka, 1995; Smith, 1997).

The facets of religion in law and law in religion that were expounded above are not progressively ordered in a linear clear historicity of teleological modernity. Rather, they are complementary in any historical period, despite some very significant distinctions in the intimacies of law, religion, and power in various historical periods, according to the genealogical analysis presented above. A genealogical analysis of law and religion in the midst of a neoliberal politics of globalization requires us to dwell upon the hermeneutics and practices of nonruling communities. The essay turns now to explicate some aspects in a critical communitarian concept of law and religion. Then it explores religion and law in contemporary intersections of globalization and nonruling communities.

LIBERALISM AS TRADITION, COMMUNITARIANISM AS CRITIC

As Robert Cover (Minow, Ryan, and Sarat, 1993) and Stephen Carter (1998) have expounded, state law has been violent toward nonruling religious hermeneutics. It has eliminated these hermeneutics as viable sources of lawmaking and policy making. The jurispathic essentialism of modern state law – that is, its paternalism, deference to violence of state officials, and coercion – is embedded in its intervention in the life of nonliberal (nonruling) communities. Cover has highlighted the collision between the *nomos* (i.e., basic worldview and normative aspirations) of nonruling religious communities that have challenged the state, and the interest of the state to subdue that *nomos* since nonruling communities could endanger dominant narratives and state hegemony. The conflict between state legal ideology and the nonruling religious communities reflects the proclivity of the state to veil its own religious partiality and to extinguish any alternative modes of faith and religious practices.

Cover has perceptively comprehended the prescriptive effects of religion on statehood and political power. Religion has accordingly been perceived as a constitutive force of normative order and civil obedience, but also as a source of oppression. Accordingly, Cover has invited the pluralistic interplay of all religious ontological conceptions of the "good" as part of lawmaking and legal interpretations, while being aware of the inability of the state to suggest an impartial justice. Cover points to the fact that in a ruling like *Wisconsin v. Yoder* in 1972 state law has acknowledged its limits of power in recognizing the Amish community's legal authority to remove its children from public schools after the eighth grade (Minow et al., 1993: 165). Yet, as Sarat and Berkowitz have shown (1994), in *Yoder*, state law was not conceived as being under threat, and hence multiplicity of religious practices was considered as reconcilable with order. *Yoder* has articulated the liberal concept that state law is the superior regulating order, while communal practices can be considered as legally valid only when they do not endanger the state's order.

Carter has primarily underscored the collision between liberal constitutionalism of separation of state from religion, and nonruling religious communities. Religion is perceived as a political redemptive force that renders criticism and dissent to state law and its ideology. Like Cover, Carter distrusts state law, but unlike Cover he is not only a legal pluralist. Carter is also a communitarian who puts much more trust than Cover in the internal normative order of nonliberal religious communities, while Cover admits cases in which state intervention is required for redemptive purposes as prevention of racial discrimination. Both Cover and Carter have seen state judges as the focus of the liberal erroneous project of constitutionalism. Cover as a legal pluralist has primarily underscored the exclusiveness of liberal constitutional language, which through adjudication "kills" alternative hermeneutics, while Carter as a communitarian has emphasized the blindness of liberalism to the virtues of nonruling religious communities. Both Carter and Cover have partly neglected to explicate the political power of liberalism as an anticommunitarian force, which is generated through state law and its ideology.

Liberalism, as Marxists have keenly noted, has been a political force of particularization that has advanced individualistic legalities concerning collectivities. The individualistic legalities – as reflected in Marx's criticism of contract law and property law – have deconstructed collective consciousness. While Marx has referred to the deprived social class, I underscore the communal aspect, since religion has been an important force in consolidating communal normative orders of nonruling communities that may resist state law and its ideology.

The attempts of states to subdue religious nonruling communities have had several facets. First, religious practices have been interpreted as irrational acts, especially under the effects of individual liberalism and later under the influence of rational choice conceptions. For example, adherents of rational choice theory condemn a usage of religious symbols during elections as irrational acts that affect voters' discretion (Barzilai, 2000; Bruce, 1999). It has followed a wrong concept of modernity, as if religion is an irrational setting that contradicts modern rational law (French, 2001; Likhovski, 1999). There are two types of accustomed mistakes concerning religion and rationality. It is mistaken to profess that religions are irrational. It is based on the evidently erroneous presumption that believing in anything is good, but believing in God/Goddess is evil. It is also erroneous to avow that liberalism offers a free choice between religions. In every political regime there is hegemonic religion; therefore people who have been born into religious minorities are often discriminated against because of their faith and practices.

Second, in countries where formal separation of religion from state exists, funds for education in religious communities have been conceived as encouragement for segregation (Carter, 1998). Furthermore, religious acts of nonruling communities that have been part of cultural preservation have often been conceived as coercive and jeopardizing the "rule of law" (Roberts, 1999). Third, religion of majoritarian groups and dominant groups has been conceived as part of nationality, while religion of minorities has been considered as part of primordial culture, which may endanger individuals and the modern state. Since a Western modernity has a narrative of secular progression, any religious resistance to it may be perceived as fundamentalism, even extremism, and may be criminalized in state law.

As Max Weber has suggested in his writings – published after his death as *The Sociology of Religion* ([1922] 1964) – any categorization of religion should be problematized. Furthermore, in Hegelian terms, secularism may be a religious faith if it renders the sense of "absolute being." Thus, Judaism, Christianity, Buddhism, and Islam are religions, but also scientology, psychotherapy, and nationalism itself may be considered as religions. Due to the empowerment of nationalism in modernity, states have categorized what is "religion" for political purposes of constitutionally recognizing communities and controlling them, or denying communities and marginalizing them. Consequently, religion has become a source of dissent if and to the extent that it has been marginalized and discriminated against. In countries that have aimed to suppress religion, like in Poland and Lithuania in Europe, and Turkey in Asia, religion has incited some collective resistance to the state.

Other examples in which oppressed and marginalized religions were a source of dissent are telling, as well. The Catholic Church in communist regimes, for example, used its power to unreservedly oppose the regimes and to significantly intervene in their internal affairs, as was the case with the Catholic Church in East Germany. This applies also to Islamic movements in India, Indonesia, and Israel. In Israel, nationalistic Jewish fundamentalists were inclined to severely criticize the state, which they had conceived as too secular and therefore too pro-Palestinian, especially after the conclusion of the Oslo Accord (1993–99). Eventually it led to the assassination of Prime Minister Yitzhak Rabin on November 4, 1995. The same phenomenon of religious dissent to state law has repeated itself in Egypt and Jordan, and in the West Bank and the Gaza Strip, where Muslim groups and factions have become major localities of dissent and violence against the political regimes and their ruling elite. Invariably, in democratic and nondemocratic regimes, in secular and nonsecular constitutional settings, religions do not only construct identities, and incite action in law, but they also constitute practices outside it, and toward it.

Correspondingly, the challenge is to understand what is happening beyond the veil of formal constitutional formulations of religion and state. Scholars of law and society have indeed looked at alternative legal texts to that of state law (Ewick and Silbey, 1998; Sarat and Kearns, 1996). Religions have rather been unique in the sense that they have offered to their believers a structured and sacred text that has embedded detailed normative guidelines of alternative order in all spheres of life. That normative order, based on a faith in a superior divine force, has frequently challenged the state. Furthermore, religions have offered absolute irreducible criteria for "good" and "evil." The more a religious community is fundamentalist, the more it may challenge the state through its legal religious texts. Efforts of states to quell religions have often resulted in religious resistance and violence.

How can we reconcile the totality of the domination of the state and the absolute desire of nonruling communities for their own religious communal hermeneutics and practices? Let us look at two possible categorizations. First, individual autonomy and identity, and second, dissent versus jurispathic law.

I borrow the logic of the first from Joseph Raz, the liberal intellectual, and the second from Robert Cover the legal pluralist, and Alasdair MacIntyre and Stephen Carter the communitarians. Personal autonomy and personal identity justify the legal protection of individual affiliations with religious communities. This is a concept emphasized by national liberals such as Joseph Raz, and analyzed by prominent liberal historians such as Rogers Smith (Smith, 1997). Yet the problem is that nonruling religious communities are not protected as collectivities in a liberal context.

In the case of *Board of Education of Kiryas Joel v. Grumet* (1994), for example, the US Federal Supreme Court refused to justify federal support for a religious community of ultra-Orthodox Jews. Similarly, for example, in the case of *Sharei Tzedeck*, the European Court of Human Rights has not granted recognition of nonruling religious communities as such (in France), veiling this under the argument for the need to respect national sovereignty even within the EU. That is the dilemma mainly recognized by Cover and Carter, and illuminated in philosophy by MacIntyre. State law – and liberal modern law promoted through the state – is jurispathic and therefore inclines to eliminate alternative types of hermeneutics and practices. Hence, this essay suggests seriously considering the collective rights of religious nonruling communities. This means autonomy in most spheres of life, like education, property, jurisdiction, and worship.

Possible conflicts between human rights and religious normative orders in non-ruling communities may exist. The predicament of women has been prominent in that context. Muslim women, for example, have suffered from killing for the family honor (*Katal al-Sharaf*). Amnesty International reported in 2001 about 5,000 such killings around the globe. The phenomenon of "honor" murders is particularly prominent in regions with large Muslim populations such as Nigeria, Sudan, Turkey, Egypt, the Gaza Strip, and the West Bank, and also exists among Muslim communities in Western Europe. Should the communitarian stand justify such killings or any other violence in communities, as part of an argument for maintaining communal nonliberal cultures of minorities? Obviously, it should not.

Two principles may be sources of solutions in cases of these conflicts. First, the right of exit; second, the redemptive principle suggested by Robert Cover (Minow et al., 1993). The first principle claims that potential victims deserve to leave their community, and that they deserve a state's protection against violence. The second principle is that if a state's interference in a specific sphere of communal life is necessary to abolish discrimination, the interest in social redemption should over-come the principle of communal singularity and autonomy. According to both principles, however, the internal normative order of the nonruling community should not be dissolved.

It is very doubtful whether religious communities are more violent than any other organization and collectivity that has some control over the means of ruling. The danger in secular fundamentalism is that due to lack of cultural relativism, religion is characterized as equivalent to violence, and religious fundamentalism is regarded as extremism and terrorism. Various studies elucidate that even fundamentalist religious interpretations of law might turn out to be constructive hermeneutics. They have enriched plurality in societies, and sometimes have led to reforms in state law in ways that have improved human rights (Barzilai, 2003; Likhovski, 1999; Theriault, 2000). In religions one can often find strong traditions that call for reforms within the religious community. Religions, even these that are characterized as fundamentalist, do have trends that call for constant reforms as part of lawmaking and law application within the community (Asad, 1993; French, 1998, 2001).

At the cultural level, religious texts and hermeneutics may contribute to the normative order through infusion of values, norms, and methodology of interpreting legal texts. At the institutional level, religions have sometimes democratized public life either through consolidating state power or through withdrawing from it. A good example of democratic consolidation is the action taken by the Catholic Church in East Germany, which had encouraged unification with West Germany in order to hold more public strongholds under the German Basic Law of 1949 (Theriault, 2000). In other instances, like in Nigeria, religion would impel women to withdraw to communal life since state law does not protect them (Ifeka, 2000). Palestinian Muslim women in Israel have applied for the state's protection against their husbands in cases of expected violence due to *Katal al-Sharaf*. They have done so despite their Palestinian national and Muslim religious consciousness, which challenges the Jewish state. Yet the state, despite its liberal egalitarian assertions, has not been inclined to intervene in communal life. Consequently, the Palestinian feminists are in a struggle against an unexpected coalition of Muslim male elite and state law of the Jewish state that has experienced since the beginning of the 1990s liberal legislation for protection and advancement of women. Hence, more efforts by Palestinian feminist organizations in Israel are focused on helping women to help themselves within their own community through creating feminist communal consciousness. In these instances, exemplified in Nigeria and Israel, withdrawal through religion is intended to practically form and enlarge a civic space within the community.

The contradictions between religious communities and modern state law may be imaginary, especially in non-Western political regimes. In practice, the relations between the sacred texts and the secular texts may be somewhat complementary. John Bowen, for example, describes how religious courts in Indonesia have interpreted religious and secular laws in complementary ways. That mode of interaction is explained, again, through power, since the state has increased its influence over the religious courts in different regions of the country (Bowen, 2000). In African countries – especially in Chad, Djibouti, Egypt, and Guinea – there is criminal legislation that prohibits the often-utilized genital cutting among women. Boyle and Preves demonstrate that due to transnational effects, African countries have followed the West in formally prohibiting genital cutting that prevails in Muslim societies (Boyle and Preves, 2000). However, that impressive legislation does not intrude in the religious communities but rather aims to change one value within a more comprehensive and diverse communal religious culture.

LIBERALISM AND RELIGIOUS COMMUNITIES – THE CHALLENGE OF GLOCALIZATION

Exploration of religion and law should be a focus of interest for students of law and society under conditions of *glocalization* (*glo*balization in various *local*ities). Globalization in its neoliberal sense may not supersede local religious practices. Studies point to the fact that religion in various nonruling communities is as vigorous as ever (Barzilai, 2003; Merry, 2001). Furthermore, the fear of and the uncertainty concerning the meaning of globalization may further incite religious beliefs and religious practices as significant sources of identities. Religious communities are important sources of constituting, articulating, and generating identities because the uncertainty facing the meaning of linear time and neoliberal progression generates religion as a source of circular time that empowers collective and individual identities through traditions and divine texts. Thus religious fundamentalist movements in Christianity, Islam, and Judaism have been generated as a resistance to modernity and to its exclusive secular conception of historicity and legality.

The collisions between globalization and religious fundamentalism may result in violence, as was horribly proven in the September 11, 2001, Al-Qaeda attack on the WTC and the Pentagon. It has followed a series of serious terrorist attacks against US and other Western targets all over the world. Religious terrorism has a lengthy experience. Religions may include subcultures of violence against "external enemies," such as state law and state legal institutions that symbolize secular depravity. Subcultures of violence have emerged in various religions, including Buddhism, Christianity, Islam, and Judaism (Juergensmeyer, 2000). Religious terrorism has been manifested in Western and non-Western political regimes including Algeria, Egypt, England, France, India, Indonesia, Israel, Japan, Northern Ireland, Lebanon, Philippines, Turkey, and the USA.

Indeed, not all terror incidents and terror organizations are religious. In fact, most terror incidents and terror organizations in Europe, heretofore, have been secular – ETA in Spain, Bader Meinhoff in Germany, and the Red Brigades in Italy, to name a few examples. In the context of this essay, however, I would like to briefly examine why religions may propose terrorism as a possible hermeneutics against state law and its ideology, in the midst of neoliberal globalization. It is an especially intriguing dilemma since religious fundamentalism is not necessarily violent.

Religious texts often ingrain a binary theological distinction between eternal redemptive good and irreducible evil. The cosmic and canonized struggle, including a violent clash, between good and evil is ahistorical and should end in apocalyptic warfare (Juergensmeyer, 2000). Believers symbolize the good, while the heretics and the seculars, the "others," represent the evil in that cosmic struggle. Notwithstanding, most religions condemn warfare in general (Weber, [1922]1964). Religious texts include legalistic categorization that makes it possible to determine whether a war is just or unjust. Hence religious texts as other legal texts are subjected to a variety of hermeneutics that constitute their practical application and reconstitution. When believers are convinced that they are under attack from secularism, the probability that they will use a religious text, as a manifesto of warfare against the perceived aggressor, is significantly higher due to the binary distinction between good and evil.

Liberal globalization has propelled the expansion of exhibitionist secularism, and has spurred a sense of siege mentality among religious fundamentalist (nonruling) communities. They have protested against prominent manifestations of liberal secularism such as pornography, homosexuality, abortion, free sex, and even personal computers connected to the Internet. Furthermore, perceptions of transcendental cosmic justice have legitimated violence as a means to revolutionize the praxis, and to impose religious law on earth. Instead of religious categorization in law, religious terrorism has aspired to see law as a categorization in a fundamentalist religion.

The question why a certain religious text would be subjected to hermeneutics of violence is outside the range of this essay. In general, the more a nonruling community perceives itself as discriminated against, the more it will be inclined to use religion as a source of violent resistance against hegemonic legal ideology. Invariably, a religious text cannot be isolated from the sociopolitical context that affects the utilization of religion to different public purposes. Islam, for example, may have very moderate hermeneutics toward non-Muslims, or a very violent hermeneutics, depending on the leadership that makes use of religion to various purposes and contingent on the sociopolitical context that frames the usage of the religious text.

In a context that pays a great deal of attention to nonruling religious communities, two processes may take place. I follow Santos's terms (Santos, 1995). The first process is globalization of local knowledge. Religion may become more transnational and its ability to influence and construct cross-national identities and practices may become broader through means such as the Internet and the international media. Thus a study among religious Indian and Pakistani communities in the USA explicates how these communities have maintained their fundamentalist beliefs and practices and have contributed to transnational networks between USA, India, and Pakistan (Williams, 1998).

The Internet constructs virtual transnational interactions, and in turn nonruling communities may better mobilize support and better control their members. The technological usage of the Internet in religious, even fundamentalist, nonruling communities has been multiplied as a prevailing phenomenon. Other aspects of transnational liberalism, such as the international media, make the dissemination of ideas an easier task for religious communities. Since the state's regulation of the virtual space and of the international media may be somewhat fragile, though still meaningful, the ability of religious nonruling communities to universalize their virtues and practices is growing fast. Transnational liberalism is becoming a major dialectical source of advancing, among other things, religious and even fundamentalist ideas and practices. Contrary to visions of universal self-celebrated secularism, the partial decline of the state, and its partial but significant sensitivity to virtual spaces may strengthen expansion of religious ideas and practices that challenge liberal secular globalization.

A second process is localization of globalization. Religious communities may adopt practices that are affected by increasing liberal values. Using (secular) technology and more litigation in courts for communal purposes are two examples of attempts to challenge state law, like immigration and education laws, in ways that may deregulate state supervision over religious nonruling communities. The legal setting in the USA has already been altered in that direction, while educational autonomy has increased and been legalized. Globalization in that sense generates more multiplicity of religious practices. A good example is feminism and its conjunction with religion. Thus feminism has gained in the last decade some empowerment through religion; an observation that demystifies the conventional claim that suggests that religion is an alternative to feminism. Religious women affected by the liberal mood would like to gain more equality in their community without secularizing it. Therefore they raise religious arguments for gender equality based on human dignity and preservation of the communal culture, despite its stigmatization as being violent against women in the midst of liberal globalization (Katz and Weissler, 1996; Reece, 1996).

Hence, I expect, religious categorizations may be more diverse but their importance will remain central in political power and law. Religious categorizations are to remain avenues in the twenty-first century of construction, generation, marginalization, and elimination of identities that build and challenge power. Religious categorizations will remain a source of coercion and resistance in and toward law. On the one hand, religion will continue to reflect ethnic and other social identities in law. On the other hand, religion will continue to be a source of reforms in the legalities of the global-local world.

CONCLUSION

This essay has embarked on deconstructing and conceptualizing the relations between law and religion, through a prism of legal pluralism in which power, state, and nonruling religious communities were the main focus of exploration. It has explicated to what degree power, state, and nonruling communities are crucial for understanding law and religion. Consequently, we may conclude that scholars of law and society should pursue the decentering critical approach of law and society studies to deconstruct the relations of law in religion and religion in law.

Religion is not autonomous from power, and the attempts to use it for political purposes have been reflected in various types of legalities. Especially after the September 11, 2001 terror events, we should not be misled by liberal expectations of separation of state from religion, nor should we be captives of illusions concerning globalization of secular values and the inevitable cultural war between them and religious fundamentalism.

Communities are crucial to the study of law and religion, since the conflict between nonruling religious communities and the state is a valuable source of legal practices and hermeneutics. It also points to the deficiencies of contemporary liberalism that is aloof to the predicaments of various religious localities. Accordingly, this essay encourages more emphasis in law and society scholarship on the importance of nonliberal and nonruling religious communities to the evolvement of just and democratic societies.

Can we reconcile the legal texts of nonliberal religious communities and the aspiration for a universal code of human rights? This is a challenge for law and society scholars that I would like to pursue. Since religions are not autonomous from other cultures and historicity, and they constitute parts of human experiences and practices, abstraction of basic human rights from diversity of religions should and can be a component in the aspiration for a universal minimal legal code. That code should admit cultural relativity. It should acknowledge the importance of political spaces in which various nonruling communities, nonliberal and religious, can be included as legitimate components in civilizations of legality.

References

Asad, T. (1993) *Genealogies of Religion: Discipline and Reasons of Power in Christianity and Islam*. Baltimore: Johns Hopkins University Press.

Barry, B. (1995) *Justice as Impartiality*. Oxford: Oxford University Press.

Barzilai, G. (2000) "On religion, rationality, and ethnicity: Legal culture of Oriental religiosity-shas in the legal field," Paper presented at the International Conference on Law and Religion, *Book of Abstracts*. Jerusalem: Hebrew University.

Barzilai, G. (2003) *Law and Communities. Politics and Cultures of Legal Identities*. Ann Arbor: University of Michigan Press.

Benhabib, S. (1992) *Situating the Self; Gender, Community and Postmodernism in Contemporary Ethics*. New York: Routledge.

Bix, B. (1996) "Natural law theory," in Patterson D. (ed.), *A Companion to Philosophy of Law and Legal Theory*. Oxford: Blackwell Publishers, pp. 223–40.

Board of Education of Kiryas Joel V. Grumet (1994) 512 U.S. 687.

Bowen, R.J. (2000) "Consensus and suspicion: Judicial reasoning and social change in an Indonesian society 1960–1994," *Law and Society Review* 34(1): 97–127.

Boyle, E.H. and Preves, E.S. (2000) "National politics as international process: The case of anti-female-genital-cutting laws," *Law and Society Review* 34(3): 703–37.

Bruce, S. (1999) *Choice and Religion: A Critique of Rational Choice*. Oxford: Oxford University Press.

Calavita, K. (2001) "Blue jeans, rape, and the 'de-constitutive' power of law," *Law and Society Review* 35(1): 89–115.

Carter, S.L. (1998) *The Dissent of the Governed. A Meditation on Law, Religion, and Loyalty*. Cambridge, MA: Harvard University Press.

Crenshaw, K., Gotanda, N., Peller, G., and Thomas, K. (eds.) (1995) *Critical Race Theory*. New York: The New Press.

Currie, P.E. (1968) "Crimes without criminals: Witchcraft and its control in Renaissance Europe," *Law and Society Review* 3(1): 7–32.

Dahl, R.A. (1971) *Polyarchy.* New Haven, CT: Yale University Press.

Epstein, L. and Knight, J. (1998) *The Choices Justices Make.* Washington, DC: Congressional Quarterly.

Ewick, P. and Silbey, S.S. (1998) *The Common Place of Law; Stories from Everyday Life.* Chicago: Chicago University Press.

Feeley, M.M. and Rubin, E.L. (1998) *Judicial Policy Making and the Modern State.* Cambridge and New York: Cambridge University Press.

Fletcher, P.G. (1996) "Punishment and responsibility," in Patterson R. (ed.), *A Companion to Philosophy of Law and Legal Theory.* Oxford: Blackwell Publishers, pp. 514–23.

French, R.R. (1998) "Lamas, oracles, channels and the law: Reconsidering religion and social theory," *Yale Law Journal and Humanities* 10: 505–36.

French, R.R. (2001) "Time in the law," *University of Colorado Law Review* 72(3): 663–748.

Friedman, L.M. (1990) *The Republic of Choice. Law, Authority, and Culture.* Cambridge, MA: Harvard University Press.

Garth, B. and Sterling, J. (1998) "From legal realism to law and society: Reshaping law for the last stages of the social activist state," *Law and Society Review* 32(2): 409–71.

Geertz, C. (1973) *The Interpretation of Cultures.* New York: Basic Books.

Greenberg, J.G, Minow, M.L., and Roberts, D.E (eds.), (1998) *Women and the Law.* New York: Foundation Press.

Hoebel, E.A. (1954) *The Law of Primitive Man: A Study in Comparative Legal Dynamics.* Cambridge, MA: Harvard University Press.

Horwitz, J.M. (1992) *Transformation of American Law 1870–1960.* Cambridge, MA: Harvard University Press, pp. 39–51.

Horwitz, J.M. (1996) "Natural law and natural rights," in A. Sarat and T. Kearns (eds.), *Legal Rights: Historical and Theoretical Perspectives.* Ann Arbor: University of Michigan Press.

Ifeka, C. (2000) "Ethnic 'nationalities,' God and the state: Whither the Federal Republic of Nigeria," *Review of African Political Economy* 27: 450–9.

Jacob, H., Blankenburg, E., Kritzer, H.M., Provine, M., and Sanders, J. (1996) *Courts, Law and Politics.* New Haven, CT: Yale University Press.

Juergensmeyer, J. (2000) *Terror in the Mind of God: The Global Rise of Religious Violence.* Berkeley: University of California Press.

Kairys, D. (ed.) (1990) *The Politics of Law.* New York: Pantheon Books.

Katz, J. and Weissler, C. (1996) "On law, spirituality, and society in Judaism," *Jewish Social Studies* 2(2): 87–115.

Kymlicka, W. (1995) *Multicultural Citizenship: A Liberal Theory of Minority Rights.* Oxford: Oxford University Press.

Lahav, P. (1997) *Judgement in Jerusalem.* Berkeley: University of California Press.

Likhovski, A. (1999) "Protestantism and the rationalization of English law: A variation on a theme by Weber," *Law and Society Review* 33(2): 365–91.

Lomosky, E.L. (1987) *Persons, Rights, and the Moral Community.* Oxford: Oxford University Press.

MacIntyre, A. (1984) *After Virtue: A Study in Moral Theory.* London: Duckworth.

MacIntyre, A. (1988) *Whose Justice? Which Rationality?* Notre Dame, IN: University of Notre Dame Press.

Mautner, M., Sagie, A., and Shamir, R. (eds.) (1998) *Multiculturalism in a Jewish and Democratic State – A Book in Memory of Ariel Rozen-Zvi.* Tel Aviv: Ramot (in Hebrew).

McCann, M.W. (1994) *Rights at Work.* Chicago: Chicago University Press.

Merry, S.E. (1988) "Legal pluralism," *Law and Society Review* 22(5): 869–96.

Merry, S.E (2001) "Rights, religion, and community: Approaches to violence against women in the context of globalization," *Law and Society Review* 35(1): 39–88.

Messick, B. (1988) "Kissing hands and knees: Hegemony and hierarchy in shari'a discourse," *Law and Society Review* 22(2): 637–59.

Migdal, S.J. (1988) *Strong Societies, Weak States*. Princeton, NJ: Princeton University Press.

Minow, M., Ryan, M., and Sarat, A. (eds.) (1993) *Narrative, Violence, and the Law: The Essays of Robert Cover*. Ann Arbor: University of Michigan Press.

Pickering, W.S.F. (1984) *Durkheim's Sociology of Religion*. London: Routledge & Kegan Paul.

Pospisil, L. (1973) "E. Adamson Hoebel and the anthropology of law," *Law and Society Review* 7(4): 537–9.

Rawls, J. (1973) *A Theory of Justice*. Oxford: Oxford University Press.

Rawls, J. (1993) *Political Liberalism*. New York: Columbia University Press.

Raz, J. (1994) *Ethics in the Public Domain*. Oxford: Oxford University Press.

Reece, D. (1996) "Covering and communication: The symbolism of dress among Muslim women," *Howard Journal of Communication* 7(1): 35–52.

Renteln, A.D. and Dundes, A. (eds.) (1994) *Folk Law*, 2 vols. Wisconsin: University of Wisconsin Press.

Roberts, E.D. (1999) "Why culture matters to law: The difference politics makes," in A. Sarat and T. Kearns (eds.), *Cultural Pluralism, Identity Politics, and the Law*. Ann Arbor: University of Michigan Press, pp. 85–110.

Rosen, L. (1980) "Equity and discretion in a modern Islamic legal system," *Law and Society Review* 15(2): 217–45.

Rosenberg, G. (1991) *The Hollow Hope: Can Courts Bring about Social Change*. Chicago: Chicago University Press.

Sandel, J.M. (1982) *Liberalism and the Limits of Justice*. Cambridge, UK: Cambridge University Press.

Sandel, J.M. (1996) *Democracy's Discontent*. Cambridge, MA: Harvard University Press.

Santos, D.S.B. (1995) *Towards a New Commonsense: Law, Science, and Politics in Paradigmatic Transition*. Routledge: New York.

Sarat, A. and Berkowitz, R. (1994) "Disorderly differences: Recognition, accommodation, and American law," *Yale Journal of Law and the Humanities* 6: 285–316.

Sarat, A. and Kearns, T.R. (1996) *Legal Rights: Historical and Theoretical Perspectives*. Ann Arbor: University of Michigan Press.

Sarat, A. and Kearns, T.R. (1999) *Cultural Pluralism, Identity Politics, and the Law*. Ann Arbor: University of Michigan Press.

Scheingold, S.A. (1974) *The Politics of Rights: Lawyers, Public Policy, and Political Change*. New Haven, CT and London: Yale University Press.

Selznick, P. (1992) *The Moral Commonwealth – Social Theory and the Promise of Community*. Berkeley: University of California Press.

Shamir, R. (1996) *Managing Legal Uncertainty*. Durham, NC: Duke University Press.

Sheleff, L. (1996) *Legal Authority and the Essence of the Regime: On the Rule of Law, The Approach of the State and Israeli Heritage*. Tel Aviv: Papyrus (in Hebrew).

Smith, R.M. (1997) *Civic Ideals – Conflicting Visions of Citizenship in U.S. History*. New Haven, CT and London: Yale University Press.

Starr, J. (1989) "The role of Turkish secular law in changing the lives of rural Muslim women, 1950–1970," *Law and Society Review* 23(3): 497–523.

Theriault, B. (2000) "The Catholic Church in Eastern Germany: Strategic and rhetoric of a changing minority," *Religion, State, and Society* 28(2): 163–73.

Trubek, D.M. (1986) "Max Weber's tragic modernism and the study of law in society," *Law and Society* 20(4): 573–98.

Twining, W.L (ed.) (1986) *Legal Theory and Common Law*. Oxford: Blackwell.

Twining, W.L. (2000) *Globalisation and Legal Theory*. Butterworths: London.

Weber, M. (1951) *The Religion of China – Confucianism and Taoism*. Glencoe, IL: The Free Press.

Weber, M. (1952) *Ancient Judaism*. Glencoe, IL: The Free Press.

Weber, M. (1956) *The Protestant Ethics and the Spirit of Capitalism*. New York: Charles Scribner's Sons.

Weber, M. (1960) *The Religion of India: The Sociology of Hinduism and Buddhism*. Glencoe, IL: The Free Press.

Weber, M. ([1922] 1964) *The Sociology of Religion*. Boston: Beacon Press.

Williams, R.B. (1998) "Asian Indian and Pakistani religions in the United States," *Annals of the American Academy of Political and Social Science* 58: 178–95.

Wisconsin v. Yoder (1972) 406 U.S. 205.

Further Reading

Barzilai, G. (2001) "Law is politics: Comments on 'Law or politics: Israeli constitutional adjudication as a case study'," *UCLA Journal of International Law and Foreign Affairs* 6(1): 207–13.

Brown, J. Nathan (1995) "Law and imperialism: Egypt in comparative perspective," *Law and Society Review*, 29(1): 103–25.

Dane, P. (1996) "Constitutional law and religion," in D. Patterson (ed.), *A Companion to Philosophy of Law and Legal Theory*. Oxford: Blackwell, pp. 113–25.

French, R.R. (2001) "A conversation with Tibetans? Reconsidering the relationship between religious beliefs and the secular legal discourse," *Law and Social Inquiry* 26(1): 95–112.

Hostetler, A.J. (1993) *Amish Society*. Baltimore: The Johns Hopkins University Press.

Kidder, L.R. and Hostetler, A.J. (1990) "Managing ideologies: Harmony as ideology in Amish and Japanese societies," *Law and Society Review* 24(4): 895–922.

Shamir, R. (2000) *The Colonies of Law – Colonialism, Zionism, and the Law in Early Palestine*. Cambridge, UK: Cambridge University Press.

Sierra, T.M. (1995) "Indian rights and customary law in Mexico: A study of the Nahuas in the Sierra de Puebla," *Law and Society Review* 29(2): 227–54.

22

The Role of Social Science in Legal Decisions

Jonathan Yovel and Elizabeth Mertz

In this chapter, we explore the problems and the potential involved in combining social science and legal decision making, drawing primarily on examples from the United States. We also briefly discuss the situation in Israel, which provides an interesting comparison. We suggest that a complex act of translation is needed in order for law to incorporate social science findings, particularly in light of the many differences between law and social science in terms of goals, methods, social roles, and epistemologies. On the one hand, social science has much to offer legal decision makers, both in terms of the information it provides about how society and law operate, and in terms of critical vantages on the law itself. On the other hand, there may be important limits to judges' comprehension of the social science arena, so that caution is necessary in attempting to bring the two fields together.

In scrutinizing the institutional dimensions of translation difficulties between social science and law, we can identify a number of core tensions associated with the fields' quite distinct approaches to the reconstruction of facticity. These tensions are not only abstract questions of epistemology; they speak to the core of law's claims to rationality, and thus are particularly significant for any theory of democracy. The first tension, most crucial to democracy discourse, can be termed *political* or *institutional*. Simply put, the tension is between the democratic reluctance to delegate adjudicative facticity to expert discourse, on the one hand – and on the other hand, society's interest in adjudication that is based on the "best available" knowledge rather than fragmentary "lay notions" (whose political or ideological character hides behind conceptions of "common sense" or "experience"). The second tension may be termed *metascientific* and involves the validity conditions of social scientific findings qua science: in other words, it is the concern that courts rely upon and apply valid rather than "junk" science. Here we must deal with the internal dynamics that yield legitimacy within the institution of social science itself. The third tension is both scientific and institutional, resulting from the intersection of social science and law, and emanates from the controversies between different legitimate scientific approaches and findings as they play out in court. As we will see below, the line between the second (*metascientific*) and third (*scientific–institutional*) tensions can at times be difficult to discern, when advocates of one competing scientific paradigm attempt to convince the court that their competitor is in fact "junk" rather than legitimate science. Finally, a fourth tension – not dealt with directly here – concerns situations where social science functions ideologically in the background of the case, and where portions of social science have infiltrated legal discourse. Economics is a case in point, as can be seen in the example of the relatively successful "Chicago School."

Our discussion begins with an overview of the distinct methods, goals, social roles, and epistemological positions of social science and law, outlining the scholarship discussing this divergence. This necessarily schematic presentation provides a general template for identifying some of the potential difficulties that legal decision makers might encounter in achieving a fruitful marriage of law and social science. We briefly compare the overt tensions that exist in the United States with the contrasting situation of law and social science in Israel today. The next section examines the ways in which social science has actually been used in US and Israeli courts to date. What role have social scientists played in mediating data and reconstructing facticity? How has the legal system translated the complex world of social science knowledge? After a brief survey of the wider terrain, in the third section we will focus in on a few "paradigmatic" examples for more in-depth discussion. The final section considers the critical promise of social science, suggesting that a "new legal realism" can emerge from more careful attention to the process of translation between social science and law.

TRANSLATING SOCIAL SCIENCE IN LEGAL ARENAS: SOME FUNDAMENTAL CHALLENGES

A number of authors have noted that fundamental differences exist between the way law approaches social problems and the way that social scientists operate. In an at times blistering critique of legal academics' attempts to perform empirical research, political scientists Lee Epstein and Gary King outline what they see as a key distinction:

> While a Ph.D. is taught to subject his or her favored hypothesis to every conceivable test and data source, seeking out all possible evidence against his or her theory, an attorney is taught to amass all the evidence for his or her hypothesis and distract attention away from anything that might be seen as contradictory information. An attorney who treats a client like a hypothesis would be disbarred; a Ph.D. who advocates a hypothesis like a client would be ignored. (Epstein and King, 2002: 9)

Epstein and King express concern that legal academics typically conduct empirical research with little awareness of the fundamental rules governing social scientific inquiry, nor of the considerable developments that have occurred in the social sciences for decades, so that law review readers "learn considerably less accurate information about the empirical world than the studies' stridently stated, but overly confident, conclusions suggest" (2002: 1). Research on law school teaching suggests that this perceived gulf between lawyers and social scientists begins with a divergence in training, where law students are encouraged to tackle just about any social problem presented in a legal text with the confidence given them by the strategies that accompany legal reading (Mertz, 2000). Legal epistemology centers on the textual structures that allow readers to ascertain whether a form of legal "truth" or at least authoritativeness has been established (Yovel, 2001a; Mertz, 2002). "Facts" are established when legal procedures are followed and authoritative decision makers decree the facts to be so. Social scientists, by contrast, are trained to approach "fact" claims with caution, and to scrutinize empirical claims and studies for limitations.

Ewick, Kagan, and Sarat note the problem that this creates for translation between social science and law: social scientists are increasingly pointing to the great complexity and nuance that characterize how law operates in society, while "[l]aw has to act in the world and act with whatever information it has, however partial, incomplete, or biased" (1999: 29). Legal decision makers can hardly be expected to delight in the "complexity and often increased uncertainty" that accompany attending to empirical research (ibid.). The aim of social science is increased understanding, which draws researchers into ever more circumscribed conclusions and a form of epistemological modesty (wherein knowledge is inevitably partial and hedged). The aim of legal knowledge is to provide a "good enough" foundation for acting in the world – for making decisions based in at least some pretense of certainty; social power and engagement are thus necessary concomitants of legal forms of knowing (resulting in the opposite of epistemological modesty). Numerous scholars have addressed the differences between law and social science, at times coming to pessimistic conclusions about the possibility of effective communication between the two fields (see, e.g., Tanford, 1990; see also Lindman,1989; Monahan and Walker, 1986; Sarat and Silbey, 1988).

This difference in methods, aims, and epistemologies is given institutional expression in the four core tensions outlined above. We see this perhaps most strongly in the *political–institutional* tension, where the important difference between social-scientific and legal aims and institutional mandates creates a difficult dilemma. Citizens in a democracy have a vested interest, indeed some would say a "right," to have their disputes adjudicated based on an understanding of social reality that is as free as possible of arbitrary assumptions or outright prejudice. Although, of course, social science itself is hardly devoid of the echoes of power and prejudice, the legal system has turned to social-scientific findings to assist in its efforts to achieve practical rationality (and this "rationality" carries a double meaning: overtly, the effort is to rise above the "impurities"of lay knowledge through the cleansing apparatus of social science method; while at the same time there is a "rationalizing" effect that helps to legitimate law and the legal use of power). However, the concern that adjudicative agents be presented with reliable knowledge about the social world by sound social science is met with the other, "jurisdictional" interest that fears the reduction of legal actors to the role of passive, lay consumers of scientific data – ill-equipped to critique expert evidence and influenced by "extra-scientific" factors such as the plausibility of expert witnesses.

Similarly, legal decision makers are unlikely to have a sophisticated grasp of the ideological, ontological, and psychological presuppositions revealed in some critiques of social science – which courts may uncritically and unconsciously adopt. We will examine some manifestations of this tension and its manipulations, from relatively authentic judicial concern to dogmatic rejection of social scientific findings.

We also see the institutional ramifications of the division between legal and social-scientific aims and methods in our second (metascientific) and third (scientific–institutional) tensions, which move beyond the strictly political dilemmas of the first tension to more epistemic domains. When reaching decisions in individual cases, courts often authoritatively decide the line demarcating "junk" from legitimate social science – a choice that is "ruled on" only incrementally by social science fields through acceptance of papers in peer-reviewed journals, presentations by scholars at professional meetings, and so forth. The history of social science abounds with examples of approaches, first deemed illegitimate, that later became accepted – and the reverse, "scientific" theories later debunked. Thus although the division between "junk" and legitimate science is a complex one, perhaps best described as a continuum rather than a dichotomy, courts must draw bright lines, at times adopting particular philosophical and metascientific criteria to deal with ambiguous or "protoscientific" knowledge. For example, as we will see, courts struggle with Popperian and Kuhnian theories of science in allowing or disallowing the introduction of social scientific evidence. In the process, they at times slide from decisions about the definition of "junk" science into adjudicating disputes among accepted schools of thought in social science fields. There is an inevitable political dimension to the delineation of "junk" from canonical science, even within the social science academy itself. This leads us to ask whether the courtroom is the correct institutional locus for resolving such scientific controversies. There are obvious concerns about allowing courts to make rulings in contests between behaviorist versus cognitive approaches, for example, or in arguments over competing methodologies. Apart from questions of expertise, one could also argue that the diversity of approaches found among the social science fields is one of their strengths – albeit one that creates great difficulties for legal actors bent on "yes/no" decision making. This points to the importance of field-specific metanorms in deciphering the "meaning" of particular social science studies. Arguably, their import relies on a complex social and linguistic matrix of settings that indicate the norms for understanding limits to epistemological claims, how to approach conflicting findings, and so forth. These metalinguistic norms are rarely made explicit, and are generally conveyed through professional socialization into the social sciences; thus they are most likely unavailable to most jurists.

The fourth tension described above also represents an institutional manifestation of the divide between law and social science; here the issue is the odd hybrid that results from an explicit marriage of legal and social scientific discourses such as was found in "Chicago School" law-and-economics. Characterized by relatively transparent discussions of the applicability of efficiency arguments to legal analysis, the law- and-economics movement became a vehicle for the assimilation of such arguments (and thus of the philosophical, psychological, social, and even ethical principles they presuppose) into legal argumentation and discourse generally. Legal discourse in such cases becomes an odd form of economic discourse – posing as expert but often lacking many of the usual indicia of economic expertise. Coase's theorem is by now as much a part of legal discourse as it is of economic theory. In contemporary American jurisprudence, the term "pragmatic" has at times become a stand-in for "economically justified" (and even that in the narrow sense of the Chicago School), in defiance and even abuse of the specifically American philosophical school going by that name, ranging from Dewey, James, and Peirce to Rorty and Bernstein (see Posner, 2001). We will discuss this "backdoor" application of economic models of behavior further below.

Interestingly, at this time there is not the same degree of tension between legal and social science scholarship in Israel as is found in the United States. Instead, we find a more welcoming attitude on the part of Israeli legal academics toward the use of social science, and a noticeable – though at times inconsistent – interest in benefitting from social science findings and approaches (Sebba, 2001). It may be that in time, conflict and boundary guarding may emerge as Israeli social scientists come to question the use to which their work is put, or to balk at any persistent status differentials. Or it may be that the difference between the USA and Israel in this regard reflects more profound distinctions between the two countries in terms of institutional, legal, and intellectual structures and cultures. We turn now to an examination of how social science has been appropriated in legal fora.

LAW'S APPROPRIATION OF SOCIAL SCIENCE: THE PROMISE AND THE PROBLEMS

We begin by tracing the relationship between law and social science in the United States, from the introduction of the "Brandeis brief," through the famous case of *Brown v. Board of Education*, to today's standard set by the case of *Daubert v. Merrell Dow*. The section concludes with a brief contrasting Israeli example.

Given the apparent gulf between law and social science in the United States, how have the two managed to meet? Despite admitted tensions, the US courts have for some time turned to social science, albeit in inconsistent and episodic ways. Indeed, there are numerous potential avenues through which social science information can affect legal developments. Expert witnesses testify at trials about relevant social science studies; social scientists contribute to amicus briefs to inform courts regarding the current state of knowledge in their fields; social science also enters the legal door during legislative hearings, and so forth. Legal historians typically point to the "Brandeis brief" as a watershed event in the introduction of social science to legal decision making in the USA (Rosen, 1972). This famous brief, over 100 pages in length, was filed by Louis Brandeis in the 1908 case of *Muller v. Oregon*. It drew upon social science of the time that purported to document inherent differences between men and women. Although the science cited therein was subsequently largely discredited, the brief itself has been hailed as a legal innovation that began a long-standing effort to marry law and social science.

Perhaps one of the most controversial uses of social science in adjudication concerns *Brown v. Board of Education*, a case of far-reaching significance. *Brown*, decided by the US Supreme Court in 1954, centered on a challenge to the constitutionality of state-mandated racial segregation in the public education system. This segregation had previously been approved under the infamous "separate but equal" doctrine enunciated in prior cases such as *Plessy v. Ferguson* – an 1896 case addressing a Louisiana law requiring separate railway carriages for "white and colored races." Instead of merely attacking the constitutionality of the "separate but equal" doctrine on purely legal grounds, the *Brown* appellants argued that segregated schools could be proven – on an empirical, social-scientific basis – to do prejudicial harm to African American students. The social scientific studies, which were subsequently relied upon by the court in its decision, have since been intensely criticized – as well as defended (Jackson, 2000). Criticism centered around the quality of the social science, and also around the perception that in *Brown* no line was respected between science and advocacy.

The social-science studies most generally associated with *Brown* were the project-ive "doll tests," whereby social scientists observed, among black schoolchildren in segregated southern schools, a manifest preference for and identification with white dolls, and apprehension regarding black dolls. This finding was interpreted as an indication of low self-esteem and a lack of an authentic sense of identity among the children, problems which were in turn attributed to segregation. Arguments based on inequality of educational resources and conditions might simply have resulted in a more egalitarian distribution of resources within the framework of segregation. However, these social-scientific findings permitted the court to make the much stronger assertion that "separate educational facilities are inherently unequal."

Almost 50 years later, many social scientists would take issue with the particular studies used in *Brown* and the inferences drawn from them (Jackson, 2000: 240), although there is also broad consensus about the overall harms caused by segregation – with school segregation high on the list of important loci (Erickson and Simon, 1998: 16). Critics such as Gregor (1963: 627) pointed out that the attitude studies did not isolate any critical variables among the numerous dependent ones, stressing that in a social reality of "segregation, prejudices, discrimination, as well as their 'social concomitants'," no study could causally ascribe the inferred attitudes to any one variable, such as school segregation. Additionally, the Clarks – who administered parallel studies among nonsegregated black schoolchildren in northern states – observed similar and even more pronounced preference patterns there (Clark and Clark, 1947; Clark, 1950; see also Kluger, 1976: 456). In light of such methodological critiques, Van den Haag, who was later to serve as an expert witness on behalf of apartheid (Jackson, 2000), essentially characterized *Brown* as a case in which an elitist court imposed a progressive agenda masked as scientific knowledge, based on the testimony of shady scholars which bordered on perjury (van den Haag, 1960). Clearly, there is an institutional and political component not only to how social science is generated, and how it is received by courts, but also to how it is subsequently critiqued.

Thus we see exemplified in *Brown* several of the major tensions outlined at the outset of this chapter. First, there is the issue of the legitimacy of social science, particularly when viewed over time. Clearly, just as in the case of natural science, social science that was once deemed acceptable will often be rejected as methods and understandings change through time. Using a "presentist" critique, one could easily argue on the basis of current social science information that many prior decisions were wrong. Historicism and justice maintain an uneasy relationship. Needless to say, adjudication and other legal-political processes produce not merely particular decisions but rules and doctrine; and just as law evolves in accordance with changed information from other sources, it will have to from time to time revisit doctrine (and even specific cases) in light of changed social science understandings. There are numerous examples of an ongoing dialectic, a dialogue, in which the courts slowly take in changed understandings from social science – shifting from the biologically based racist view of earlier cases to the social/environmentally based vision of *Brown*.

Nonetheless, the patent fallibility of dated social science leads to a different kind of tension, the first "democratic" tension outlined above. Edmond Cahn (1955) most fully expressed this democratic, rule-of-law, populist view in the context of *Brown*.

Cahn "would not have the constitutional rights of Negroes – or of any other Americans – rest on any such flimsy foundation as some of the scientific demonstrations in these records," nor

> ...have our rights rise, fall, or change along with the latest fashions of psychological literature. Today the social psychologists...are liberal and egalitarian in their basic approach; suppose, a generation hence, some of their successors were to...present us with a collection of racist notions and label them "science." What then would be the nature of our constitutional rights? (Cahn, 1955: 157–8)

This is a common critique of social science, for its "very young, imprecise, and changeful" findings and methodologies (id.). This criticism also highlights the important epistemological consequences of the distinct purposes for which law and social science seek out knowledge. A social scientist who is exploring new territory may feel free to experiment – to generate ideas and hypotheses that may later be proven wrong as part of a process that will also uncover new truths. This tentative or exploratory mode of knowledge production does not sit well with legal actors, who must reach decisions with important real-world consequences based on the knowledge they obtain. However, critics such as Cahn never satisfactorily answer the question of how the courts should know the social world: if not with the help of social science, however susceptible to errors, then what is left is "common sense," tradition, "accepted truths," prejudices, and other ideologically informed sources of knowledge. It is not clear that these are less susceptible to manipulative or "changeful" applications than are social scientific findings. Nonetheless, we can see here in sharp relief the ongoing tensions created by attempts to translate across two such different fields.

These tensions emerge again in the landmark case of *Daubert v. Merrell Dow*, in which the Supreme Court formulated the modern criteria for allowing introduction of scientific evidence into federal litigation. (Further cases broadened *Daubert*'s scope to nonscientific expert evidence and to numerous state laws as well – see Faigman, Kaye, Saks, and Sanders, 1997). *Daubert* generated massive progeny – over 300 articles and dozens of high court decisions dealing with the ruling – including a body of jurisprudential work concerning the metascientific questions upon which it touched.

The pre-*Daubert* rule regarding admissibility of scientific evidence, laid down in *Frye v. United States*, required that all such evidence be "generally accepted" as reliable in the relevant community (*Frye*, 1923: 1129–30). *Frye* was concerned with what later became known as "junk science" (in that case, a physiological "deception test" based on systolic blood pressure). At issue, then, are the second and third tensions outlined above – the metascientific question of delineating valid science, and the scientific-institutional problem of how courts are to enter the definitional fray. The *Frye* test was formulated before philosophers such as Popper, Lakatos, and Kuhn addressed the relationship between science and other ways of treating facticity, and when sociology of science was an undeveloped discipline; science was far from attaining its later prestige, when for many philosophers it became the model for rational activity generally. As the Court in *Daubert* suggests, the conservative *Frye* test excludes novel or simply new research, as well as any method that has not achieved consensus among scientists; it presupposes a monolithic, uniform, and homogenous image of "good" science that is a far cry from the creative diversity that describes actual social science. *Frye* does, however, make one point that *Daubert* retains: that when dealing with admissibility criteria for social science, it is the method or technique that generated the findings that must be scrutinized, rather than the findings themselves. The adoption of the Federal Rules of Evidence – and in particular Rule 702 dealing with expert testimony – effectively overruled prior precedents and called for a new interpretive approach to admissibility of "scientific...or other specialized knowledge [that] will assist the trier of fact to understand the evidence or to determine a fact in issue..." (Federal Rules of Civil Procedure 702), thereby prompting the courts to revisit the old *Frye* standard.

The lead metaphor in *Daubert* pertains to the courts themselves and, of all things, invokes Kafka: the court is to act as a "gatekeeper" (*Daubert*, 1993: 597) for scientific evidence. As such (and unlike the gatekeeper in Kafka's parable "Before the Law"), it must use two kinds of criteria for making up its lists of welcome guests and *personae non gratae*: criteria of scientific reliability for the court's purposes, and criteria of "fit" – namely, the relevance of the social data to the legal claim (relevance actually serves more complex, "metapragmatic" functions – see Yovel, 2003). In considering possible admissibility criteria for such "guests," the Court did not shy away from examining demarcation criteria developed by philosophers of science to distinguish between scientific and unscientific propositions. Yet at the same time, the Court in fact did not adopt nor formulate a unified or exclusive (perhaps not even a coherent) demarcation criterion for admissibility, a fact that has allowed wide variability in how courts in subsequent decisions have interpreted and applied the *Daubert* standard.

Reading the *Daubert* opinion feels somewhat like surfing an uneven doctrinal wave that constantly breaks to reveal the competing currents beneath it. In this case, those components are two approaches to the philosophy and sociology of science, both making themselves felt in *Daubert*. The first is an attempt to find a characteristic that is *essential* to genuine scientific propositions, one that separates them decisively from pseudoscientific assertions. Forming such a demarcation criterion was a major contribution of philosopher Karl Popper (1959, 1968) to the philosophy of science. In the first half of the twentieth century, a school of thought known as "logical positivism" (or the Vienna Circle) had promoted an empirically founded "principle of verifiability" as a linguistic condition of meaning (propositions are meaningful if and only if they are susceptible to truth functions; the truthfulness of some propositions is determined by their semantic content alone – "analytic" propositions, all others by empirical verifiability). By contrast, Popper, searching for a demarcation criterion to identify genuine scientific propositions, came up with the "falsifiability principle," according to which a proposition is scientific if and only if it is empirically falsifiable; science advances through "conjectures and refutations" (Popper, 1968). Whatever the merits of this principle, it has gained wide endorsement among scientists, who approved of a seemingly clear-cut distinction between scientific and other propositions, such as those of religion, aesthetics, and so forth.

It was not surprising, then, that *Daubert*'s primary concern was that "scientific knowledge can be (and has been) tested" and that by "tested" the Court meant "generating hypotheses and testing them to see if they can be falsified" (Green, 1992: 643). However, the Court already stumbles onto an interpretive bump – namely, the distinction between falsifiability as a matter of logical structure ("this proposition can be falsified") and falsification ("this proposition has in fact been tested"). Popper's business was to define what kind of things science may say, which of course includes new and untested propositions. Note that this does not necessarily even restrict the category of scientific propositions to those that actually can be tested given current technologies – although some would redefine "falsifiability" in this way, thereby providing a socially and historically contingent (rather than absolute) demarcation criterion. Here we see the tangle that is produced by a difference in metalinguistic norms and concomitant social-institutional needs; the philosopher of science is implicitly developing demarcation criteria suited to the discourse and institutional needs of science, while courts are operating under quite different discursive and social exigencies. That a proposition might in theory be testable, even though we do not currently possess the technology to do so, is hardly reassuring to the judge seeking "scientific" grounding for evidence in an actual court case. The resulting inconclusiveness of what the majority in *Daubert* means by "falsifiability" led the minority to admit being "at a loss to know what is meant when it is said that the scientific status of a theory depends on its 'falsifiability,' and I suspect some [federal judges] will be, too" (*Daubert* [Rehnquist dissent], 1993: 600). Indeed, numerous subsequent cases have simply ignored the falsifiability criterion. (It is thus a bit early to claim that in *Daubert*, "Popper's philosophy... became U.S. law," Edmond and Mercer, 2002: 309.)

In fact, having invoked falsifiability as an essential characteristic of scientific knowledge, *Daubert* then shifts to what can best be termed a Kuhnian model of science. According to Kuhn (1962), there is no essential characteristic that makes any proposition scientific or that *guarantees* it a higher level of rationality than other propositions. Rather, scientific propositions are those that conform to the prevailing paradigms of any given "scientific community" at any given time. Those paradigms – the accepted methodologies, techniques, and metaphysical frameworks that underlie "normal science" – are socially rather than philosophically determined, and by definition are historically transitory. If at a certain time scientists generally use a "falsifiability" criterion, that, too, is a paradigm – a conventional fact about the practices of scientific communities. Giving a pragmatist twist to positions expounded by Lakatos and Paterson, courts could approach science as what is justifiable to them as the relevant actor or audience. This point reminds us of the first tension delineated above: using social science need not (indeed, arguably, cannot) mean delegating facticity to "experts," but rather constitutes the mobilization of expertise generated in other institutional/discursive settings for the courts' institutional purpose – namely, justice.

Popperian and Kuhnian philosophies are thus at odds: while the former defines an analytical demarcation criterion for scientific propositions, the latter claims that any such criteria must have social rather than analytic roots. Having invoked falsifiability as the core attribute rendering a scientific proposition admissible into evidence, *Daubert* then seems to jump into the Kuhnian camp, looking to the scientific community for guidance: "Another pertinent consideration is whether the theory or technique has been subjected to peer review and publication... submission to the scrutiny of the scientific community is a component of 'good science'" (*Daubert*, 1993: 593). The Court does acknowledge that "in some instances well-grounded but innovative theories will not have been published" (id.). We see here the grounds for possible confusion regarding our second and third tensions – the "metascientific" and the "scientific-institutional": it is not clear how the courts are to exercise their "gatekeeping" function in a way that rises above the debates within scientific fields over preferred methodologies, rather than preferring one school of thought to another. A lower federal court judge, faced with the remanded *Daubert* case, laments the gatekeeping function as delineated by the Supreme Court's decision on precisely these grounds – because it requires him "to resolve disputes among respected, well-credentialed scientists about matters squarely within their expertise, in areas where there is no scientific consensus as to what is and what is not 'good science'" (*Daubert*, Kozinski opinion, 1995: 1316). The judge's hesitance is well taken in light of social science research indicating that judges fare no better than laypeople in distinguishing studies performed with scientifically accepted methodologies from those performed without (Kovera and McAuliff, 2000). Ironically, Kozinski says nothing of falsifiability in the Ninth Circuit opinion, but instead turns to a best-selling work of popular science (Huber, 1991) for his definition of what constitutes "good science" – that is, asking whether the scientific witnesses conducted their research "independent of the litigation... or expressly for the purposes of testifying" (*Daubert*, Kozinski opinion, 1995: 1317).

The second requirement put in place by *Daubert* is that the scientific evidence "fit" the issue at hand: does it contribute to a causal proof of a point in controversy? (Yovel, 2003). Do the "doll tests" presented in *Brown* measure low self-esteem, and is there a "fit" between low self-esteem and educational segregation? In our discussion of capital punishment below, we will discuss how courts have consistently rejected statistical evidence that imposition of the death sentence is affected by race – on the grounds that none of these studies could show that this *particular* defendant was discriminated against by the *particular* jury that sentenced him. In light of the kind of preference we saw above for studies conducted independent of litigation, it may be very difficult to meet both the "good science" and the "fit" requirements for social science data in the post-*Daubert* era. This double bind is yet another indication of the difficulties that emerge from unreflective translations between social science and law, without sufficient attention to the divergence in discursive and institutional norms. In the case of *Kumho Tire* (1999), the Supreme Court officially extended the *Daubert* gatekeeping function beyond the natural sciences to include other kinds of expert testimony, rendering *Daubert* fully applicable to social science testimony as well. As *Daubert* included such criteria as "the known or potential rate of error" and "the existence and maintenance of standards controlling the technique's operation" (Daubert, 1993: 594) in addition to the Popperian criterion discussed above, this creates a clear misfit between the courts' toolkit for assessing social science and qualitative, interpretive research such as ethnography or historiography. The third tension is evident here in a cultural bias toward quantitative methodologies.

Having traced the historical context of US courts' translations of social science, we turn now to a brief comparative example from Israel. In particular, we examine how liberal courts are in admitting social science evidence, and also the degree to which courts actually rely on social science – an aspect of which is judicial activism in either critiquing social science that has been admitted, or producing alternative interpretations to those proffered by experts.

Israeli law makes no formal distinction between "scientific" and "expert" evidence, and the former is taken as a subset of the latter. Consequently, witnesses are not generally required to prove the scientific status of their findings. Instead, courts look to the scientific status of the *witness*. In preliminary hearings, expert witnesses are expected to prove an expertise relevant to the factors at hand. (Framing facticity through relevance claims is a typical – and typically ideological – aspect of any litigation, see Yovel, 2003.) As the focus of the inspection is not the science but the scientist, such traditional metascientific questions as "what is a scientific proposition?" squarely dealt with in *Daubert* through the Popperian falsifiability criterion, do not surface. Witnesses' scientific status is established through more Kuhnian, conventional tests, namely their standing and reputation in the scientific community. In this regard, Israeli courts would look into "substantive" as well as "formal" expertise – that is, the witness's competence regarding the factual and interpretive question at hand, in addition to general institutional or academic distinction. Thus scientific witnesses may be required to submit condensed *vitae*, complete with lists of publications, to the court, in addition to undergoing cross-examination on their expertise – or, more precisely, on the image of their expertise as captured by reputation and other marks of "professional" competence.

By primarily focusing on social constructions of scientific authority, Israeli courts rarely need to deal with the metascientific tension that haunted *Daubert* and *Brown*. This, however, does not exempt such evidence from challenge. On the contrary, it still has to face two other obstacles. First, there is the tension created by counter-evidence introduced by other scientific witnesses – the problem of competing scientific paradigms bemoaned by Judge Kozinski. Second, there are challenges posed by Israeli judges themselves, delivered as "common sense" (Mautner, 1998, 2002), factual fictions and presumptions (Shamir, 1996), entrenched social and ethical notions (Barkai and Massas, 1998; Yovel, 2001b), and other ideologized forms of knowledge. These would also include entrenched narrative patterns employed by judges, which implicitly encode assumptions regarding social issues such as gender (Kamir, 1997), political conflict and violence (see Yovel, 2002a). Because Israel's prevailing jurisprudence is nonpositivistic (Barak, 2002, 2003) and its piecemeal constitution still partially unwritten, some judges are comfortable invoking constitutional "fundamental principles" and even "natural law" models that manifest cultural and ideological biases.

As explored below through the *Bank Leumi* case, an interesting contrast emerges between Israeli and American courts' approach to social science evidence. While American courts following *Daubert* emphasize admissibility, Israeli courts are relatively liberal in allowing introduction of social science evidence. However, they may subsequently prove more resistant to actually relying on it. Nor do Israeli courts shy from offering original interpretations and contributions that compete with social science, as opposed to merely assessing admissibility. Thus it is difficult to characterize Israeli courts as more receptive to social science than American courts: the resistance simply lies elsewhere, in the language-game of application – of weight and effect – rather than the formal language-game of admissibility. Additionally, pointing to a less creative, more conservative trend, commentators have shown Israeli courts to be resistant to social-scientific and other expert findings when those findings threatened courts' entrenched social notions of normativity and propriety. Examples include cases where courts refused to accept expert testimony that reconceptualized "parental competence" outside of the standard, bourgeois interpretation of the atomistic family (Massas and Barkai, 1998; Yovel, 2001b), or that questioned ideological, narrative, and indeed protomythological patterns regarding Israeli–Palestinian hostilities (Yovel, 2002a). In summation, Israeli courts may seem relatively relaxed in their openness to "external" knowledge, focusing their gatekeeping function on the expert rather than on the particular chunk of information offered to them. However, despite permitting novel social science to be heard, the courts then frequently rely on entrenched extrascientific notions, at times even producing original critiques of scientific findings. As we will see in the next section, despite apparent doctrinal guidelines to the contrary, judges in the USA also enter the fray in similar ways, taking sides with one social science school as against another, or inserting their own brand of judicial "nonpeer" review into their decisions.

TRANSLATING SOCIAL SCIENCE IN LAW: SPECIFIC CASE EXAMPLES

Having provided a broad historical and comparative outline, we turn now to examine some specific examples of the ways in which core tensions between law and social science have been played out in the courts. This will provide a more in-depth sense of the narrative structures through which translations – and translation misfires – occur.

"False memories" and scientific validity: Adjudicating psychology in court through the lens of *Daubert*

The field of psychology yields fertile ground for examining what happens when competing social science paradigms wind up in court. The differences among distinct schools of thought in psychology are dramatic, generating not only contrasting recommendations for treatment but also surprising diversity in theories of the basic constitution of the psyche and accepted methods for demonstrating psychological "truths." One division that has attracted much attention in the USA is that between more biologically oriented psychological models, which tend to prefer pharmaceutical solutions to psychological problems, and more psychodynamic models, which look more to the "talking" therapies for solutions. We should stress that there are many who argue for eclectic models that quite reasonably draw on multiple sources and solutions. There are also interesting distinctions by professional credentials; while some in the field have MDs (and thus are entitled to prescribe medication), others have PhDs, MSWs, and indeed other credentials as well. Another divide within the field of psychology is that between those with a clinical focus and those whose work lies exclusively within the laboratory – although it should be pointed out again that there are numerous researchers who bridge this divide. Nonetheless, the differences between these two groups actually led to an institutional splintering in the USA, in which some of the "laboratory" researchers formed their own group, the American Psychological Society (APS), in contradistinction to the larger American Psychological Association (APA), which has traditionally served as an umbrella organization for psychologists of all kinds. Although members of both groups conduct studies accepted as scientific by their relevant communities, which regularly pass peer review in approved journals, there have been attempts to characterize the APS as somehow more "scientific" – attempts which themselves have a sociology and a politics that merit analysis (see Garth and Dezalay, 2002; Garth and Sterling, 1998 for discussions of the sociological underpinnings of academic/professional struggles over legitimacy). In addition to these broader divisions within psychology, there are numerous debates over particular theories.

What happens, then, when these competing psychological theories wind up in court? In an earlier analysis of this question in the Dutch context, Renée Romkens contrasts traditional psychiatric approaches with newer paradigms based upon studies of trauma, noting "a difference between a powerful and established scientific community... and a less powerful, relatively young scientific community of experts in the field of... traumatology" (2000: 363). This same division can be found in a number of US cases dealing with the phenomenon of recovered abuse memories – that is, memories of traumatic events that did not surface until years after the abuse occurred. In the case we will discuss here, the Supreme Court of New Hampshire reviewed a lower court's decision to bar testimony based upon recovered memories, using *Daubert*-based criteria (*State of New Hampshire v. Hungerford*, 1997). This is an interesting extension of the logic of *Daubert*, for the witnesses who were barred from recounting their memories were not experts, but rather were the complainants in the case. However, under New Hampshire's version of the law, if the complainants' testimony could not be understood without the help of expert witnesses, it could be ruled inadmissible based on the status of the experts' theories. The court then embarked on an analysis of the social science debate at hand, reviewing a lower court hearing that had been a virtual showdown between leading experts on two sides of a hotly debated social science issue. Both sides presented experts with impressive credentials, and supported their arguments with findings from peer-reviewed articles.

The New Hampshire court's opinion makes fascinating reading, for faced with a competition between two social scientific schools of thought, it basically enters the fray and adopts the position of one of the competing schools. Its opinion relies heavily on the literature from one side, even when purporting to present the other side. Thus approximately 75 percent of the references are drawn from the experts contesting the validity of recovered memories, with many of the remaining citations referring to the other side only to dismiss it. When the court turns to a presentation of the scientific trauma literature supporting the phenomenon of delayed recall, it uses writing by a vocal opponent of that school as its main source. (So, for example, its exposition of the trauma literature that begins "According to the theory of repression..." was followed by a cite from an article coauthored by Elizabeth Loftus, a leading spokesperson for those contesting use of recovered memories in court. This pattern continued throughout the court's recitation of the "theory of repression." Indeed, approximately 30 percent of the references to social science literature in the opinion are to work by Loftus.) All peer-reviewed articles presented in support of recovered memory are subjected to methodological critiques of the kind one would expect from members of the opposing school of thought, whereas the literature disputing recovered memory is not similarly critiqued. Following a seemingly reluctant admission that there have been some corroborated cases of recovered memory, the court immediately cited an article that dismisses the "theory of repression," without mentioning that the article openly presents a "minority" position in an edited volume otherwise filled with work supporting that theory. In examining the *Daubert* criterion of empirical testability, the court dismissed all but one study and then proceeded to accept the methodological critique of that one study that had been proffered by members of the opposing school. (We will see this pattern of knocking out all but one study, which is then viewed as too flimsy a basis, again in our discussion of death penalty cases.) Whether the court was influenced by differences in the advocacy on one side or the other, or by other social factors (including well-documented tendencies to discredit women's claims of sexual abuse), we cannot say. Analysis of power dynamics in these cases has pointed to extremely effectual lobbying by those who oppose the concept of repression, reaching from the courts to the media (Stanton, 1997; Bowman and Mertz, 1996). In any case, the court's narrative in this case cannot be characterized as a balanced review of the literature.

Thus we see that, under the guise of *Daubert*-style hearings, US courts can be drawn into taking sides in academic debates between two legitimate schools of social science thought. This phenomenon takes on particular importance in areas of high social conflict, where social power tends to be wielded unevenly. These kinds of cases exemplify the blurring of boundaries between our second and third tensions, as courts become arbiters of arguments among social scientists – a role for which, as Judge Kozinski noted, they have no training. In our next subsection, we see the US Supreme Court take still further steps into this arena in which jurists have no expertise.

Metalinguistic deficits and the death penalty: The US Supreme Court's translation problem

Capital punishment litigation in the United States provides an especially interesting case study of the relationship between appellate adjudication and social science. An unusually high quantity of social science has been submitted to US courts during appellate review of capital punishment cases. As Ellsworth (1988) has shown, since the late 1960s, constitutional challenges to capital punishment have been grounded in a diverse array of social-scientific studies using a broad range of methods and paradigms, from econometric and statistical analysis (of actual case outcomes) to interviews and simulations (with jurors and mock jurors) to attitude surveys. And overwhelmingly, American courts have distinguished themselves by an all but total rejection of social scientific findings – despite tacitly accepting that social scientific data may be relevant to these cases. Ellsworth concludes that this rejection has little to do with genuine metascientific concerns, despite rhetoric to the contrary, and has everything to do with extrascientific ideological commitment to capital punishment. Baldus, Pulaski, and Woodworth suggest that the Court's resistance may also stem from apprehension that permitting such claims could undermine other areas of criminal justice as well (Baldus et al., 1983, 1990).

Death-row appellants in the United States typically challenge capital punishment verdicts on the basis of the practices, or patterns of practices, that led to their sentencing. These challenges generally involve one or more of the following claims: (1) violations of the Eighth Amendment's "cruel and unusual punishment" clause or the Fourteenth Amendment's "equal protection of the laws" clause, in that they were rendered on arbitrary or discriminatory bases (typically because of race); (2) violations of the Eighth Amendment by virtue of being excessive; and/or (3) violations of the Sixth Amendment guarantee of procedural justice in jury proceedings, generally by virtue of procedures that produce "death qualified juries." We shall briefly elaborate on the first and third types.

The question of arbitrariness in meting out capital punishment was one of the major concerns that persuaded the Supreme Court to decree what turned out to be a three-year hiatus to death sentencing and executions, the case of *Furman v. Georgia* (1972). Although none of the many separate opinions in *Furman* relied heavily on social science studies, subsequent cases saw an abundance of social science centered, for the most part, not on arbitrariness per se, but on the issue of racial discrimination. By and large, quantitative research using various methods has consistently shown capital punishment to be susceptible to racial bias. Earlier studies focused more on the race of the perpetrator, finding that blacks were more likely than whites to be indicted, convicted, sentenced to death, and executed for capital crimes than were white perpetrators in similar circumstances (Bowers, 1974; Dike, 1982). Wolfgang and Reidel (1973), who examined capital sentencing for rape in southern and border states, found that black men who raped white women were 18 times more likely to be sentenced to death than were white rapists.

Wolfgang and Reidel's study was one of the first to be presented in a constitutional challenge to capital punishment. In *Maxwell v. Bishop* (1970), the Eighth Circuit refused to consider its findings on several grounds, one of which was that it did not show that the defendant's particular jury had actually been racially biased against him, or that such bias influenced their sentence. This form of "critique from causation" results from courts' insistence on the kind of causation relations that underlie legal discourse rather than the kind of correspondence relations that quantitative social science generally establishes (see Hart and Honore, 1985, on causation). This is a manifestation of the first tension we discussed, the political or institutional tension – one between the conventions and norms underlying legal argumentation and logic, and those underlying social science. It is also an example of the translation problems posed by differences in metadiscursive norms. Ellsworth (1988) dismisses this gap in discursive approaches to probabilities as an ideologically motivated excuse. However, there does seem to be a genuine metadiscursive disagreement about how to perform inferences from general patterns to particular cases. On the other hand, courts did not resist adjudicating based on such patterns as long as they pointed to arbitrariness rather than to discrimination (see *Furman*, 1972; *Gregg v. Georgia*, 1976). And, clearly, there is a difference between convicting an individual based on a probabilistic argument and assessing the severity of problems in a system based upon statistical evidence.

By the time *McCleskey v. Kemp* (1987) came in front of the Supreme Court, an array of studies employing a variety of methods had shown a consistent pattern according to which the race of a murder victim corresponded to the likelihood of a perpetrator receiving the death sentence (Redelet and Peirce, 1985; Gross and Mauro, 1984). Black felons who murdered white victims were 13 times more likely to receive the death penalty than were black defendants who murdered black victims. Baldus et al. (1983), submitted to the court in this case, was an extremely comprehensive study, collecting data on over 200 variables in over 2,000 Georgia murder cases during the 1970s. Although the opinion mentioned the Baldus findings and did not challenge their statistical validity (the "scientific" tension), in the end the Court repeated its "argument from causation".

Quantitative studies were not the only ones to be rejected by the Supreme Court in capital punishment cases. The case of *Lockhart v. McCree* (1986) dealt with death-qualified juries; these juries are selected using procedures that allow prosecutors to screen out prospective jurors who are opposed in principle to capital punishment. Justice Rehnquist analyzed 15 different studies, ranging from attitude surveys to simulations to interviews with actual jurors, showing that death-qualified juries tend to find defendants in capital cases guilty more than do generally qualified juries (Ellsworth, 1988). Rehnquist examined each study separately, dismissing each as inconclusive, until one "lone study" remained and was deemed insufficient as such (*Lockhart*, 1986: 1764). However, as Ellsworth (1988: 195) points out, the study was never evaluated in the context of the other studies submitted; it was never intended to make a legal argument on its own. Here the Court is rejecting a common social scientific approach that bases conclusions on an aggregate of findings, each of which alone may be insufficient. The American Psychological Association argued this point in its amicus brief, noting that when such a diversity of methods and approaches all yield the same conclusion, the result is all the more powerful. Rehnquist is here essentially revealing a metalinguistic deficiency; he is not able to decode the social science according to the meta-level principles that govern the discourse when deciphered by experts.

Interestingly, as Ellsworth (1988) notes, the Supreme Court reverses itself in considering the value of social science submitted in support of capital punishment. In the case of *Barefoot v. Estelle* (1983), the Court reviewed a Texas statute which permitted imposition of the death penalty if and only if the convicted defendant was likely to pose a violent threat to society in the future. Texas courts use psychological and psychiatric testimony to help juries determine future dangerousness. In *Barefoot*, the American Psychiatric Association submitted a brief stating that such evaluations were impossible under contemporary scientific competence and knowledge. The Court, otherwise quite conservative when dealing with social scientific evidence, nevertheless determined that "[n]either the petitioner nor the Association suggest that psychiatrists are always wrong with respect to future dangerousness, only most of the time" (*Barefoot*, 1983: 901). This incongruity certainly lends support to those who suspect that ideology plays a large part in the Court's "meta-scientific" jurisprudence.

The "rhetorical sting" of economic translations in legal settings: An Israeli example

The case of *State of Israel v. Bank Leumi and others* provides a good context for exploring the role of economic models in adjudication rather than in rule forming. This was one of the longest and most costly criminal cases in Israel's history. The country's four largest commercial banks – as well as a slew of executives ranging from CEOs downward – were indicted on several fraud, accounting, and security regulations offenses. Since the early 1970s, and particularly during the early 1980s, the banks had used indirect means to "support" or "adjust" their common stock, which was traded on the Tel Aviv Stock Exchange. This meant that for virtually the entire period, some of which saw hyperinflation and negative national growth, the banks arranged for their shares to be purchased in such quantities that the shares' price rarely if ever dropped. While this was partially accomplished through commercial activities of subsidiaries, most of the investors in the banks' stock were the banks' own customers, as well as virtually every mutual fund in the entire country. By 1983 the financial burden that this created for the banks – financing huge daily purchases of their own stock on the open market – threatened to blow up and send the banks into bankruptcy, dragging with them not only their customers but also the largely overlapping investor group. When the financial bubble neared collapse, the country's central bank intervened and bailed out the banks to the tune of 8 billion US dollars (in 1983 terms). The losses to the public were enormous.

The banks and their executives were indicted on several counts of securities regulations violations, corporate fraud, and accounting felonies. The most interesting charge for our purposes was a charge for common-law fraud. Quite simply, the banks were charged with making a fraudulent promise to their customers and investors, upon which the latter relied, that the banks would ensure that their share price would never drop. This was fraudulent, the prosecution charged, because the banks could not actually perform the promise; at a certain point the self-perpetuating price "support" mechanism was bound to crash, taking share prices down with it. However, the prosecution could adduce very little evidence to demonstrate that bank employees made direct verbal commitments concerning the shares' future performance.

In the absence of such evidence, the prosecution based its fraud case on an economic model called "signaling theory" as applied to the so-called "efficient market" thesis. Under the "efficient market" thesis, financial markets are regarded as more or less efficient processors of information. The input is all the publicly available information about, for example, a company's financial condition and revenue predictions. This information is "processed" into a share price through investors' behavior. One way to conceive of information about a company's financial condition is through "signaling." A signal is any communicative act that might affect the price of the share. Signaling theory's main insight is that the market trusts – and thus acts on – signals that carry some cost in terms of risk. A CEO who publicly purchases the company's stock is assuming a risk that the market would interpret as a strong signal, as opposed to the weaker signal of the CEO simply commenting favorably on the company's performance. Institutionally, a corporation paying out cash dividends signals that its profits allow for sending a relatively costly signal, given to two levels of taxation – once at the corporate level and again at the capital gains level.

This was the foundation of the prosecution's case in *Bank Leumi*: that the banks' own consistent investment behavior sent a strong and clear signal to investors that the banks would continue to support the share price indefinitely. The so-called "signal" was clear due to its consistency and duration, and strong due to the undeniable cost each bank had incurred in generating it. The market efficiently processed this signal to a relatively stable stock price. Through their industrious efforts to hold the stock prices constant, the banks made a representation that the share price would continue to be "adjusted" indefinitely – a representation they knew to be fraudulent.

Predictably, both sides called upon economists to provide expert scientific evidence. These were all acclaimed, senior, tenured professors in top research universities in Israel and the United States. They were largely in agreement over authorities, methodologies, and worldview. The defense's main claim was that the prosecution failed to draw the correct conclusion from signaling theory. Its experts pointed to the apparent circular structure of the banks' "adjustments": everyone, economist or not, should (and thus does) understand that as a long-term strategy an "increase only" adjustment is impossible. Thus no one could reasonably interpret the banks' performance as an indefinite commitment. The economic model provided a social epistemology, a way of interpreting the social world. Under either the prosecution's or the defense's account, the court was asked to reconstruct facticity on the basis of a social-scientific model. In the end, Judge Naor did not accept the defense's notion that because it was irrational for lay investors to rely upon the "perpetual adjustment" representation, they in fact did not do so.

Interestingly, the court's analysis pointed out that the banks and their top executives wielded considerable *rhetorical* power, which the economic analysis of signaling wrongly discounted. Rhetoric is a stick in the wheels of signaling theory

(McCloskey, 1998), because signaling theory is rationalized on representational rather than on rhetorical or performative approaches to language and communication (Yovel, 2002b). It considers signals in terms of their locutionary content and how that is to be interpreted, based in part on the pragmatics surrounding the locution. It allocates much less significance to rhetoric and to context. The relative rhetorical and social power wielded by a "signaler" is discounted in favor of a rational evaluation of the risk the signaler's behavior carries. However, if a player carries significant social and/or rhetorical clout, what might be considered a "weak" signal under signaling theory may take on additional effect. Because of the considerable rhetorical and social power of the banking establishment and its ranking executives in Israeli society, uninformed investors (dazed during a period of hyperinflation) would be much more willing to succumb to the rhetorical temptations of the banks. The longer the banks kept the "adjustment" going, the more they seemed successful in making adjustments work. While the prolonged length of the "adjustment" might signal to expert observers a diminishing capacity to keep it going, it signaled just the opposite to the multitude of lay investors – a reality, the court notes, that is not accounted for by representational signaling theory.

The court, then, actually adduces its own brand of economic-social theory, nowhere presented to it by experts in the case. In essence, the court weighed the authority and rhetoric of the banks at the time, mingled with hyperinflation conditions, and concluded that under such circumstances regular investors will in fact rely on what the defense called "irrational" interpretations and beliefs – and that the banks should have taken this into account. Interestingly, the court here is taking it upon itself to develop an ad-hoc, elementary version of what is now considered cutting-edge social science to those familiar with the work of Tversky, Kahneman, and Slovik (1982; see also Kahneman and Riepe, 1998) – social science that did not make an appearance in court due to both sides' reliance on more standard neoclassical economic theory. In terms of our first tension, we see that the court was reluctant to delegate decision making to pure economic models that did not take account of the social and rhetorical aspects of power, status, roles, cultural pluralism, subjectivity, and other social parameters. Contrary to the US courts' approach described above, expert evidence was liberally admitted, and the court did not attempt to dismiss one side or the other as scientifically inadequate (our second and third tensions). However, as per our fourth tension above, the court proceeds to create its own brand of legal-economic discourse (albeit one with, it turns out, substantial support in other schools of thought not presented to the court). Although judicial prerogative enters in different forms and at different points in the proceedings, we see that judges in both the US and Israeli systems feel free to reject and critically assess the social science that is put before them. At times, this may lead to a more socially grounded understanding, as in the *Bank Leumi* case, but at others it may wind up closing the ears of the court to important information about the shortcomings of the legal system or the truths of those with less power.

CONCLUSION: CRITIQUE, CAREFUL TRANSLATION, AND A "NEW" LEGAL REALISM

In conclusion, we have seen that there are pervasive tensions impeding a direct translation between social science and law. The two fields have vastly different epistemologies, metadiscursive rules, and social purposes. On the one hand, social science stands poised to provide useful and incisive critiques of legal systems and assumptions. Social science is also a promising source of information and critical questioning when the law attempts to interpret and understand aspects of society that social scientists are trained to analyze.

On the first issue, social science as a source of critique, Sarat and Silbey (1988) issued a well-taken warning: that if social science is truly to provide trenchant criticism, it must stand outside the frames provided by law and policy discourses. There is a "pull" to these frames, and it is tempting to simply offer small amendments, or ways of tinkering with existing systems, rather than to stand outside and question the framework as a whole. At the same time, the risk of standing totally outside of existing frameworks is that the critique will not be heard; discourse from a completely different frame can be very difficult – if not impossible – to absorb (Mertz, 2000).

As to the second role for social science, that of providing information and analysis relevant to the social "facts" with which courts must of necessity deal, we have noted the pervasiveness of ongoing tensions. First, is the political issue of to what degree courts in a democratic state should delegate the construction of social facts, and the assessment thereof, to experts. Social science asks questions for different reasons than does law, and so it is not completely obvious that law should subject itself too completely to social science (Constable, 1994). Nonetheless, some kind of dialogue between the two seems to be not only desirable but inevitable, as agents of the law engage in at times clearly flawed, but nonetheless active, efforts to translate the knowledge of social science into legal discourse. In the process, tensions also emerge over the definition of valid science, the arbitration of disputes among "bona fide" social scientists, and the status of hybrid discourses created when law appropriates areas of social science.

Thus our review of the complex relationship between law and social science urges caution in attempting to translate between the two. In particular, we point to a meta-level of discourse and surrounding professional cultures as crucial. Lawyers are trained in advocacy and adversarial contest; the terms are painted in black and white and the point of discursive exchange is to win. Social scientists revel in hedging and probability, cushioning their claims to truth in layers of methodological and epistemological caution and nuance. It is not enough to teach lawyers the "content" of a social science translation; rather, the norms of social science discourse must also be conveyed as part of any effective translation. Recent research in linguistic anthropology has demonstrated the importance of metadiscursive structure in the unpacking of linguistic meaning (see Silverstein, 1992). Legal efforts to translate and appropriate social science have proceeded in persistent ignorance as to social science metalinguistic norms, leading to some serious misfires, as we have seen.

We suggest that efforts to build a "new legal realism," one that would put today's social science to effective use in legal settings, must begin by taking this aspect of translation much more seriously. As the anthropologist Renato Rosaldo observed, in the "contact zones" where different disciplines meet, "social relations are often unequal and people may speak different languages or the same language with different inflections, meanings, or purposes" (Rosaldo, 1994: 527; see also Dezalay and Garth, 2002). At times, those wielding power – such as courts – will not be willing to bend sufficiently to make the effort to understand other paradigms without pressure from outside of the legal system, as with the abolitionist movement surrounding the death penalty (Sarat, 2001). In their study of the use of social science data in US Supreme Court opinions, Erickson and Simon note that "[d]ata are used in the courtroom in a manner consistent with the standards of the legal community, not the social sciences community" (1998: 149). It is to be hoped that future progress in this dialogue will involve more of a compromise, enabling the legal system to bring to fuller fruition the promise of social science as a source of critique and information.

Note

The authors would like to thank Marianne Constable, Marc Galanter, Karl Shoemaker, Bryant Garth, and Dan Simon for helpful suggestions.

References

Baldus, D.C., Pulaski, C.A., and Woodworth, G. (1983) "Comparative review of death sentences: An empirical study of the Georgia experience," *Journal of Criminal Law and Criminology* 74: 661–753.

Baldus, D.C., Pulaski, C.A., and Woodworth, G. (1990) *Equal Justice and the Death Penalty: A Legal and Empirical Analysis*. Boston: Northeastern University Press.

Barak, A. (2002) "The Supreme Court 2001 term, Forward – A judge on judging: The role of a supreme court in a democracy," *Harvard Law Review* 116: 6–162.

Barak, A. (2003) *Purposive Interpretation in Law*. Tel Aviv: Nevo (in Hebrew).

Barefoot v. Estelle (1983) 463 U.S. 880.

Barkai, M. and Massas, M. (1998) *On the Meaning of the Terms "Parental Competence" and "Child Welfare" in Supreme-Court Verdicts Concerning the Adoption of Minors*. Jerusalem: Sacker Foundation for Statutory Research and Comparative Law.

Bowers, W.J. (1974) *Executions in America*. Lexington, MA: D.D. Heath.

Bowman, C.G. and Mertz, E. (1996) "A dangerous direction: Legal intervention in sexual abuse survivor therapy," *Harvard Law Review* 109: 549–639.

Brown v. Board of Education (1954) 347 U.S. 483.

Cahn, E. (1955) "Jurisprudence," *New York University Law Review* 30: 150–69.

Clark, K.B. (1950) *Effect of Prejudice and Discrimination on Personality Development: Fact-Finding Report Mid-Century White House Conference on Children and Youth*. Washington, DC: Children's Bureau, Federal Security Agency.

Clark, K.B. and Clark, M.P. (1947) "Racial identification and preference in negro children," in E. Hartley and T. Newcomb (eds.), *Readings in Social Psychology*. New York: Henry Holt and Co., pp. 169–83.

Constable, M. (1994) "Genealogy, jurisprudence, and the social scientification of law," *Law & Social Inquiry* 19: 551–90.

Daubert v. Merrell Dow Pharmaceuticals (1993) 509 U.S. 579.

Daubert v. Merrell Dow Pharmaceuticals (1995) 43 F.3d 1311, 1995 U.S. App. LEXIS 12 (9th Cir. Cal. 1995) (Kozinski opinion).

Dezalay, Y. and Garth, B. (2002) *The Internationalization of Palace Wars: Lawyers, Economists, and the Contest to Transform Latin America*. Chicago: University of Chicago Press.

Dike, S.T. (1982) *Capital Punishment in the United States*. New York: Council on Crime and Delinquency.

Edmond, G. and Mercer, D. (2002) "Conjectures and exhumations: Citations of history, philosophy, and sociology of science in U.S. federal courts," *Law and Literature* 14: 309–53.

Ellsworth, P.C. (1988) "Unpleasant facts: The Supreme Court's response to empirical research on capital punishment," in K.C. Haas and J.A. Iniardi (eds.), *Challenging Capital Punishment: Legal and Social Science Approaches*. London: Sage, pp. 177–211.

Epstein, L. and King, G. (2002) "Empirical research and the goals of scholarship: The rules of inference," *University of Chicago Law Review* 69: 1–132.

Erickson, R. and Simon, R. (1998) *The Use of Social Science Data in Supreme Court Decisions*. Urbana: University of Illinois Press.

Ewick, P., Kagan, R., and Sarat, A. (1999) "Legacies of legal realism: Social science, social policy, and the law," in P. Ewick, R. Kagan, and A. Sarat (eds.), *Social Science, Social Policy, and the Law*. New York: Russell Sage, pp. 1–38.

Faigman, D.D., Kaye, M., Saks, M., and Sanders, J. (1997) *Modern Scientific Evidence*, S1–3.0. St Paul, MN: West.

Frye v. United States (1923) 54 App.D.C. 46, 293 Fed. 1013.

Furman v. Georgia (1972) 408 U.S. 238.

Garth, B. and Sterling, J. (1998) "From legal realism to law and society: Reshaping law for the last stages of the social activist state," *Law & Society Review* 32: 409–72.

Green, M.D. (1992) "Expert witnesses and sufficiency of evidence in toxic substances litigation: The legacy of Agent Orange and Bendictine litigation," *Northwestern Law Review* 86: 643–99.

Gregg v. Georgia (1976) 428 U.S. 153.

Gregor, J.A. (1963) "The law, social science, and school segregation: An assessment," *Western Reserve Law Review* 14: 626–56.

Gross, S.R. and Mauro, R. (1984) "Patterns of death: An analysis of racial disparities in capital sentencing and homicide victimization," *Stanford Law Review* 37: 27–153.

Hart, H.L.A. and Honore, T. (1985) *Causation in the Law*, 2nd edn. Oxford: Oxford University Press.

Huber, P. (2000) *Galileo's Revenge: Junk Science in the Courtroom*. New York: Basic Books.

Jackson, J.P. (2000) "Triumph of the segregationists? A historiographical inquiry into psychology and the Brown litigation," *History of Psychology* 3: 239–61.

Kamir, O. (1997) "How reasonableness killed the woman: The 'boiling blood' of the 'reasonable person' and the 'typical Israeli woman' in the teasing doctrine of *Azualus*," *Plilim*, 6: 137–85 (in Hebrew).

Kovera, M. and McAuliff. B. (2000) "The effects of peer review and evidence quality on judge evaluations of psychological science: Are judges effective gatekeepers?" *Journal of Applied Pyschology* 84: 574–86.

Kluger, R. (1976) *Simple Justice*. New York: Alfred Knopf.

Kuhn, T.S. (1962) *The Structure of Scientific Revolutions*. Chicago: University of Chicago Press.

Kumho Tire Co. v. Carmichael (1999) 119 S.Ct. 1167.

Lindman, C. (1989) "Sources of judicial distrust of social science evidence: A comparison of social science and jurisprudence," *Indiana Law Journal* 64: 755–68.

Lockhart v. McCree (1986) 106 S.Ct. 1758.

Mautner, M. (1998) "Common sense, legitimization, coercion: On judges as storytellers," *Plilim* 7: 11–76.

Mautner, M. (2002) "Contract, culture, compulsion, or: What is so problematic in the application of objective standards in contract law?" *Theoretical Inquiries in Law* 3: 545–75.

Maxwell v. Bishop (1970) 398 U.S. 262.

McClesky v. Kemp (1987) 481 U.S. 279.

McCloskey, D. (1998) *The Rhetoric of Economics*. Madison: University of Wisconsin Press.

Mertz, E. (2000) "Teaching lawyers the language of law: Legal and anthropological translations," *The John Marshall Law Review* 34: 91–117.

Mertz, E. (2002) "Performing epistemology: Notes on language, law school, and Yovel's legal-linguistic culture," *Stanford Agora* 2, online at agora.stanford.edu.

Monahan, J. and Walker, L. (1986) "Social authority: Obtaining, evaluating and establishing social science in law," *University of Pennsylvania Law Review* 134: 477–517.

Muller v. Oregon (1908) 208 U.S. 412.

Plessy v. Ferguson (1896) 163 U.S. 537.

Popper, K. (1959) *The Logic of Scientific Discovery*. London: Harper & Row.

Popper, K. (1968) *Conjectures and Refutations*. London: Harper & Row.

Posner, R. (2001) *Frontiers of Legal Theory*. Cambridge, UK: Harvard University Press.

Redelet, M. and Peirce, G.L. (1985) "Race and prosecutorial discretion in homicide cases," *Law and Society Review* 19: 587–621.

Romkens, R. (2000) "Ambiguous responsibilities: Law and conflicting expert testimony on the abused woman who shot her sleeping husband," *Law & Social Inquiry* 25: 355– 91.

Rosaldo, R. (1994) "Whose cultural studies?" *American Anthropologist* 3: 524–9.

Rosen, P. (1972) *The Supreme Court and Social Science*. Urbana: University of Illinois Press.

Sebba, L. (2001) "Law and society in Israel: An emerging agenda," *Israel Studies Forum* 17: 83–110.

Sarat, A. (2001) *When the State Kills*. Princeton, NJ: Princeton University Press.

Sarat, A. and Silbey, S. (1988) "The pull of the policy audience," *Law and Policy* 10: 97–166.

Shamir, R. (1996) "Suspended in space: Bedouins under the law of Israel," *Law & Society Review* 30: 101–26.

Silverstein, M. (1992) "Metapragmatic discourse and metapragmatic function," in J. Lucy (ed.), *Reflexive Language*. Cambridge, UK: Cambridge University Press, pp. 33–58.

Stanton, M. (1997) "U-turn on Memory Lane," *Columbia Journalism Review*, July/August: 44–9.

State of Israel v. Bank Leumi and others (1994) Criminal Case 524/90, District Court of Jerusalem, unpublished.

State of New Hampshire v. Hungerford (1997) N.H.LEXIS 64.

Tanford, J.A. (1990) "The limits of a scientific jurisprudence: The Supreme Court and psychology," *Indiana Law Review* 66: 136–74.

Tversky, A., Kahneman, D., and Slovic, P. (eds.) (1982) *Judgment Under Uncertainty*. Cambridge, UK: Cambridge University Press.

Van den Haag, E. (1960) "Social science testimony in the desegregation cases – a reply to Kenneth Clark," *Villanova Law Review* 6: 69–79.

Wolfgang, M.E. and Reidel, M. (1973) "Rape, judicial discretion, and the death penalty," *Annals of the American Academy of Political and Social Science* 407: 119–33.

Yovel, J. (2001a) "Invisible precedents: On the many lives of legal stories through law and popular culture," *Emory Law Journal* 50: 1265–93.

Yovel, Y. (2001b) "Trigger-happy courts: Culture and ideology in coerced adoption cases," *Law and Government* 6: 259–68 (in Hebrew).

Yovel, Y. (2002a) "Narrative justice," *Bar-Ilan Law Review*, 16 (2002), 283–322 (in Hebrew).

Yovel, J. (2002b) "Rights and rites: Initiation, language, and performance in law and legal education," *Stanford Agora* 3, online at agora.stanford.edu.

Yovel, J. (2003) "Two conceptions of relevance," *Cybernetics and Systems* 34: 283–315.

Further Reading

Friedman, L. and Macaulay, S. (1977) *Law and the Behavioral Sciences*. Indianapolis: Bobbs-Merrill.

Monahan, J. and Walker, L. (1998) *Social Science in Law: Cases and Materials*. New York: Foundation Press.

Trubek, D. and Esser, J. (1987) "Critical empiricism," *Law & Social Inquiry* 14: 3–52.

Part V

How Does Law Matter?

23

Procedural Justice

Tom R. Tyler

My goal for this chapter is to review recent psychological research on social justice. This is a good time for such a review. I believe that recent research findings about social justice can truly make a contribution to our understanding of how to resolve conflicts and promote stable and harmonious relationships among individuals and groups. In this review I focus primarily upon issues of process and procedural justice, the area that research findings have suggested is most potentially useful in facilitating conflict resolution. I will both discuss this area of research and describe its implications.

In their classic book on procedural justice John Thibaut and Laurens Walker prefaced their research by commenting that:

> One prediction that can be advanced with sure confidence is that human life on this planet faces a steady increase in the potential for interpersonal and intergroup conflict. The rising expectations of a continuously more numerous population in competition for control over rapidly diminishing resources create the conditions for an increasingly dangerous existence. It seems clear that the quality of future human life is likely to be importantly determined by the effectiveness with which disputes can be managed, moderated, or resolved. Procedures or methods that may be put to this task of conflict resolution therefore claim our attention. (Thibaut and Walker, 1975: 1)

This comment is as relevant today as it was when it was made in 1975. The many interpersonal and intergroup conflicts that have long occurred within societies and organized groups continue, and people are increasingly turning to the law and to legal authorities to help them to resolve such conflicts. Now, as in the past, legal authorities need to seek ways to resolve conflicts and promote harmonious interpersonal and intergroup relationships. The authorities need to be able to effectively resolve disputes, in the sense that they make decisions that the parties accept, and they need to do so in ways that both lessen long-term animosity among the parties and minimize any feelings of hostility toward law and legal authorities. An ideally resolved conflict is one in which the parties involved accept the decisions made by the legal system; continue their relationship with each other; and feel good about the legal authorities with whom they dealt, as well as the law and legal authorities more generally.

One clear possible avenue for the peaceful resolution to conflicts is through an understanding of the psychology of social justice. People's views about what is just or fair are a social facilitator through which the interaction among people and groups is enabled. The value of justice lies in allowing people and groups to interact without conflict and societal breakdown. Social interactions can break down amid conflict and hostility, and when such breakdowns threaten, people turn to authorities for help. Procedural justice both minimizes such breakdowns and contributes to the continuation of productive long-term interactions among people – in the manner hoped for by Thibaut and Walker – by helping authorities to resolve conflicts when they occur. As a consequence, it is an important topic of concern to the legal authorities with the responsibility to prevent, contain, or end social conflicts.

The especially striking thing about justice is that it is a social concept that exists only in the minds of the members of an ongoing interaction, a group, an organization, or a society. Hence, justice is a socially created concept that exists and is useful to the degree that it is shared among a group of people. This shared idea facilitates the task of social coordination within the group that holds it or among groups with common conceptions of justice.

For justice to be effective, it is important that people's behavior actually be shaped by their judgments about what is right or wrong, ethical or unethical, just or unjust, separately from judgments about what is personally beneficial. Authorities must be able to gain acceptance of rules and decisions that depart from individual or group self-interest by acting fairly. If people are only motivated by issues of personal gain or loss, as is often suggested by rational models of the human actor, then justice will be of little value because it will not be an effective motivator of human behavior.

It is also important that people share a set of principles for defining justice. If one person regards a jury trial as the fair way to resolve a conflict, while another person thinks that trial by combat is the fair way to resolve the same dispute, both parties may be interested in having a fair procedure, but they will not be able to agree about what such a fair procedure would look like. Hence, even if people are motivated by the desire to be ethical, morality and justice are only socially useful concepts if people agree about what constitutes justice.

Studies suggest that, at least among Americans, there is widespread agreement concerning appropriate principles of both distributive and procedural justice (see Tyler, Boeckmann, Smith, and Huo, 1997). People generally regard equity as appropriate in work settings, equality in social and political settings, and need in family settings. So, when rewards are to be allocated, people have considerable agreement about what is the "just" or "ethical" way to make that allocation.

In the case of procedural justice, there is also widespread agreement about what constitutes a fair procedure for making allocations and resolving disputes. For example, Tyler (1988) found that judgments about the meaning of fair procedures to be used by the police and the courts were constant across age, gender, income, and ethnicity (also see Tyler, 1994, 2000a, 2000b).

Cross-cultural studies yield a more complex set of findings, and it is not clear whether there are universally shared views about fair principles of distributive justice or about what constitutes a fair procedure. Research to date suggests that there are widely differing views about fair principles of distributive justice within different cultures. Research on the universality of procedural fairness judgments is more unclear, with some studies suggesting that common principles underlie procedural justice judgments in different cultures (Thibaut and Walker, 1975), and other research suggesting that there may be important differences (Tyler, Lind, and Huo, 2000).

SOCIAL JUSTICE RESEARCH

The first wave of social justice research began with the development of the concept of relative deprivation during the period following World War II (Tyler, Boeckmann, Smith, and Huo, 1997; Tyler and Smith, 1997). The theory of relative deprivation argues that satisfaction/dissatisfaction in social situations is not a direct function of the objective quality of the rewards or resources that people receive from others. Instead, satisfaction is socially determined through comparisons between one's own outcomes and some type of standard. The same objective outcome can be satisfying or upsetting depending upon the standard to which it is compared. The nature of these standards is socially determined. As a consequence, people shape their subjective experience through their choice of comparison standards.

The theory of relative deprivation became important during the 1960s because of its ability to provide insights into the urban riots that occurred toward the end of the civil rights era (Gurr, 1970). The occurrence of the riots was difficult for many people to understand, since they came at the end of an historical period during which the objective situation of minority group members improved in both economic and social terms. Relative deprivation theory suggested, as subsequent research has shown to be the case, that whether people would be satisfied was more the result of their social comparison choices than their objective situation. After the civil rights era minority group members were more likely to compare themselves to whites and, hence, often felt more dissatisfied than they had during earlier eras. Further, it was the most advantaged members of minority groups that were most likely to make such comparisons, so the advantaged were found to feel more anger than the disadvantaged, and were also more likely to engage in acts of collective unrest. Hence the theory of relative deprivation provides important insights into the causes of unrest and is important in efforts to understand minority discontent.

The roots of subsequent justice theory lie in the insights of relative deprivation theory. Justice judgments involve comparisons, and the standards of comparison used are principles of deserving, entitlement, and justice. In the case of relative deprivation, for example, comparisons of one's own situation and outcomes to those of others can only be converted into feelings of injustice if one has a standard of what is an appropriate set of relative outcomes. Should one's outcomes, for example, be equal to those of others, or is equity the appropriate standard? Without such an underlying justice model, the feelings resulting from social comparisons cannot be understood.

There are two types of justice judgments that might potentially be of interest to sociolegal scholars. The first are judgments about distributive justice. Distributive justice examines people's views about what is a fair outcome or distribution of resources. Norms of distributive justice effectively resolve coordination problems when people accept them and defer to decisions that give them less than they want as long as they think that the outcomes they have received are fair. To the degree that people defer to allocation decisions because those allocation decisions are just or fair, judgments about distributive justice are an important factor in creating and maintaining peace.

Distributive justice research

The first important type of research developing from the idea of distributive justice focused upon the application of the distributive justice norm of equity. Equity theory argues that fairness means that people's rewards should be proportional to their contributions. Equity researchers hoped to be able to resolve conflicts by making outcome allocations in response to people's sense of what constitutes a fair outcome. It was hoped that people would be willing to accept fair outcomes, as opposed to being angry if they did not receive all of the resources or opportunities they wanted. This willingness to defer to justice was seen as one way of lessening conflicts over pay and promotion within work settings.

Although most equity-inspired research focuses on outcomes in work settings, it is important to emphasize the potential breadth of equity-inspired thinking. Studies of the disadvantaged in America, for example, typically find that dissatisfaction with the economic system is minimal among those who are the "losers" in the economic competition represented by the American free market system. Why? One reason is that most Americans believe that economic outcomes are distributed fairly, since those who work hardest or have the greatest intelligence or creativity are rewarded with the greatest incomes. Hence differences in outcomes are fair when evaluated against principles of equity (Hochschild, 1995; Kleugel and Smith, 1986).

While research on dissatisfaction in work settings has supported the importance of outcome fairness judgments in shaping people's satisfaction with pay and promotions, equity theory-based approaches have not been found to be as effective as researchers hoped they would be at resolving conflicts over pay and promotions. The problem with applying equity concepts comes out of people's tendency to exaggerate the importance or value of their contributions to groups. Because of this tendency, it has proved difficult to provide people with the level of rewards they regard as fair, relative to their subjective sense of their own contributions. Hence research on outcome fairness has not proved as useful in resolving social conflicts as its proponents originally thought was possible.

No doubt these difficulties would also apply to efforts by judges and mediators to resolve conflicts in legal settings, since exaggerated feelings of entitlement are typically central to the disputes that come before legal authorities. Studies of people who bring their cases before judges find that people usually feel that they are "in the right." In divorce cases, for example, both parties often bring unrealistic expectations into court, with neither receiving the level of outcomes that they feel their contribution to the marriage merits.

Further, equity studies have been ineffective in finding distributive mechanisms for resolving conflicts because it has been found that issues of outcomes, such as concerns about pay and promotion, are often not the key concerns driving unhappiness in interactions with others. For example, Messick, Bloom, Boldizar, and Samuelson (1985) asked people to list unfair behaviors others had enacted toward them. They found that respondents seldom mentioned unfair allocations. Instead, they focused upon issues such as being treated with consideration and politeness. Similarly, Mikula, Petri, and Tanzer (1990) found that "a considerable proportion of the injustices which are reported . . . refer to the manner in which people are treated in interpersonal interactions and encounters" (1990: 133). I will refer to these concerns about the quality of the treatment received from others, whether other people or third-party authorities, as elements of procedural justice.

The findings outlined suggest that outcomes are less central to the feelings and actions of the individuals who receive those outcomes than is supposed by theories of distributive justice. Recent distributive justice research suggests another import- ant area within which outcome fairness judgments may be important. This area involves people's willingness to help others. Here our concern is with whether people will find the outcomes received by others to be unfair and, if they do, whether they will be willing to take actions to help those who are receiving too little.

A key distributive justice question is when the advantaged are motivated by their distributive justice judgments to redistribute resources to the disadvantaged. The advantaged are particularly important because it is against their self-interest to give away resources or opportunities to the disadvantaged, and they often have the power to act on their self-interest if they choose to do so. Hence, we would be especially impressed by the power of justice motivations if they led the powerful to voluntarily give up their power and resources because they were motivated by justice.

Montada and Schneider (1989) found that evaluations of justice and deservedness were central to the emotional reactions of the advantaged to those who are less well off. Both moral outrage, in which society and social institutions are blamed for the situation of the disadvantaged, and existential guilt, in which people feel personal blame for the situation of the disadvantaged, led to a readiness on the part of the advantaged to perform prosocial actions. Interestingly, while both existential guilt and moral outrage led people to engage in actions, such as spending money, to help the disadvantaged, political actions were shaped only by moral outrage. That is, if people felt that the system was unjust, they wanted to change it. If they felt personal guilt about the disadvantaged, they wanted to help particular people who were viewed as in need.

As justice theory predicts, responses to the disadvantaged were not predicted by sympathy or by self-interest. That is, people are not motivated by sympathy or empathy; and they act even when it is not in their self-interest to do so. People were willing to engage in redistributive behaviors that were not in their self-interest when they felt that others were entitled to help, with judgments of entitlement or deservingness linked to justice judgments. So if people felt that an injustice was occurring they were willing to give up resources to help others. If they felt sympathy for the suffering of others, they did not support redistribution. So justice can and does promote willingness to allocate resources and opportunities to people who lack power and would have difficulty forcing such reallocations.

While the potential redistributive effects of injustice are clear, it is also important to note that the advantaged can, and do, justify their advantage psychologically as a way of avoiding their possible responsibilities to help others. In other words, they create explanations for the status quo in which their possession of resources and other advantages is reasonable and fair. One example is the belief that society rewards those who are smarter and work harder, so whatever they have, they have because they have "earned it."

Such justifications occur in individual relationships and on a societal level – through the construction of justifying ideologies (see Tyler, Boeckmann, Smith, and Huo, 1997). Justifications lessen the psychological pressure to redistribute resources and opportunities, since those who are advantaged feel less psychological pressure to redistribute resources to the disadvantaged if they feel that their own advantages are "deserved." The widespread acceptance of the principle of equity makes clear that inequality is not necessarily viewed by people as being inappropriate or unfair. The key issue is an understanding of why people have advantages, and it is here that there is considerable possibility of psychological justification.

The disadvantaged also engage in psychological justification processes that lead them to feel that their disadvantaged status is deserved. While it might seem to be in the self-interest of the disadvantaged to press for redistribution, and hence there would seem to be little motivation for the disadvantaged to justify their own disadvantage, the situation of the disadvantaged is found to be more complex. On one level, there are risks involved in pressing for redistribution, and powerful others often react punitively to being presented with accusations of injustice. In addition, viewing oneself as disadvantaged activates feelings of being a victim, which hurts self-esteem and lessens feelings of control. The disadvantaged, therefore, have complex motivations. They are motivated to some degree to recognize their disadvantage, and to some degree to deny or minimize acknowledging their disadvantaged status.

Procedural justice research

Thibaut and Walker's early work on procedural justice develops from a core issue in the law – the ability of legal authorities to be authoritative in resolving disputes and enforcing rules. Being authoritative involves the ability to issue directives that are adhered to by the parties involved (Tyler, 1990). Unless people are willing to accept the decisions of legal authorities, those authorities cannot effectively engage in their social regulatory roles.

During the period in which Thibaut and Walker conducted their studies there was a feeling within the legal system that better mechanisms needed to be found to gain acceptance among the parties to disputes, as well as among the public more generally. High profile cases, such as those involving child custody mediation, highlighted the difficulties of gaining compliance with judicial orders. The desire to heighten the acceptance of the decisions of legal authorities led to the general movement toward the use of mediation and other alternative dispute resolution procedures, procedures that were found to lead to greater satisfaction and higher levels of compliance with the decisions of third-party dispute resolvers (Kitzman and Emery, 1993; McEwen and Maiman, 1984).

Thibaut and Walker's research was based upon the hope that people would be willing to accept outcomes because those outcomes were fairly decided upon – that is, due to the justice of the decision-making procedures (procedural justice). Their work developed as a second wave of justice research, following the era of equity research. It focused on the manner in which authorities exercised their authority – on the fairness of processes rather than the fairness of outcomes.

I am pleased to say that more recent research on procedural justice suggests a much more optimistic conclusion about the utility of procedural justice as a mechanism for resolving social conflicts than did the results of early research on distributive justice.

The results of procedural justice research are optimistic about the ability of social authorities to bridge differences in interests and values and create agreements that the parties to a dispute will accept. Further, the findings of procedural justice research suggest some clear models concerning how authorities should act to pursue procedural justice strategies.

Thibaut and Walker (1975) performed the first systematic set of experiments designed to show the impact of procedural justice. Their laboratory studies demonstrate that people's assessments of the fairness of third-party decision-making procedures shape their satisfaction with their outcomes. The original hope of Thibaut and Walker was that the willingness of all the parties to a dispute to accept decisions that they view as fairly arrived at would provide a mechanism through which social conflicts could be resolved, and their work suggests that this basic argument is valid. This finding has now been widely confirmed in subsequent laboratory studies of procedural justice (Lind and Tyler, 1988).

Subsequent field studies have found that when third-party decisions are viewed by the disputants as being fairly made, people are more willing to voluntarily accept them (Kitzman and Emery, 1993; Lind, Kulik, Ambrose, and de Vera Park, 1993; MacCoun, Lind, Hensler, Bryant, and Ebener, 1988; Wissler, 1995). What is striking about these studies is that these procedural justice effects are found in studies of real disputes, in real settings, involving actual disputants. They confirm the earlier experimental findings of Thibaut and Walker.

Procedural justice judgments are found to have an especially important role in shaping adherence to agreements over time (Pruitt, Peirce, McGillicuddy, Welton, and Castrianno, 1993; Pruitt, Peirce, Zubek, Welton, and Nochajski, 1990). Pruitt and his colleagues studied the factors that lead those involved in disputes to adhere to mediation agreements that end those disputes. They found that the procedural fairness of the initial mediation session was a central determinant of whether people were adhering to the agreement six months later.

Beyond reactions to particular decisions, groups generally benefit when those within them engage in cooperative actions that help the group. As was true in the case of accepting the decisions of authorities, one way that groups can gain desired cooperative behaviors is through shaping the costs and benefits associated with cooperation. People can be made to accept decisions by threats of punishment or incentives for cooperation. However, groups benefit when the people within them voluntarily engage in actions that help their group out of internal feelings of identification with and commitment to the group. Within formal organizations such actions have been labeled "extrarole" behaviors, since they involve nonrequired actions that help the group. Research suggests that people voluntarily cooperate with groups when they judge that group decisions are being made fairly (Bies, Martin, and Brockner, 1993; Moorman, 1991; Moorman, Niehoff, and Organ, 1993; Niehoff and Moorman, 1993; Tyler, 2000a). Hence, the use of fair decision-making procedures has the general effect of encouraging people to voluntarily help the groups to which they belong.

A common response of the members of groups seeking to manage themselves is to organize their group by creating rules and establishing authorities and institutions. These authorities and institutions are then given the responsibility of facilitating social regulation. They seek to bring people's behavior into line with group rules.

Authorities can gain compliance with rules in a variety of ways. One is through the use of rewards or threats of punishment. However, such strategies are costly and unwieldly. As a consequence, authority structures based upon compliance are inefficient and ineffective. The efficiency and effectiveness of rules and authorities are enhanced when group members are willing to voluntarily support the empower-ment of authorities and to willingly defer to the decisions of those authorities and to follow social rules. The willingness to defer to social rules flows from judgments that authorities are legitimate and ought to be obeyed. Studies of the legitimacy of authority suggest that people decide how legitimate authorities are, and how much to defer to those authorities and to their decisions, primarily by assessing the fairness of their decision-making procedures. Hence, using fair decision-making procedures is the key to developing, maintaining, and enhancing the legitimacy of rules and authorities and gaining voluntary deference to social rules (Kim and Mauborgne, 1991, 1993; Sparks, Bottoms, and Hay, 1996; Tyler, 1990).

Again, procedural justice is especially important in gaining deference to rules over time. For example, Paternoster and his colleagues interviewed men who had dealt with police officers who were called to their homes because they were abusing their wives (i.e., due to domestic violence). They explored which aspects of police behav-ior during the initial call predicted subsequent compliance with the law against domestic violence among the men interviewed. It was found that those men who felt that they were fairly treated during their initial encounter with the police adhered to the law in the future. Interestingly, procedural justice judgments during this initial encounter with the police were more powerful predictors of subsequent law-abiding behavior than were factors such as whether the police arrested the man during the initial contact, fined them, and/or took them into the police station (Paternoster, Brame, Bachman, and Sherman, 1997).

Earlier it was noted that advantaged people will redistribute resources to achieve justice. As this research on deference to authorities suggests, procedural justice also shapes people's willingness to defer to policies that are designed to help others. For example, advantaged citizens are more likely to accept policies that redistribute resources and opportunities to disadvantaged citizens if they think that the govern-ment agencies making the policies make their policies fairly (Smith and Tyler, 1996). Citizens are generally more willing to accept policies that they disagree with when they feel that government policy-making processes are fair (Ebreo, Linn, and Vining, 1996; Tyler and Mitchell, 1994).

In other words, an alternative to seeking to encourage the advantaged to feel responsible for others is to create authorities who will use fair procedures to create policies that redistribute resources, policies such as affirmative action. To some degree such policies will be accepted and followed because of procedural justice, even if people do not see those policies as leading to distributive justice.

This approach focuses on understanding when people will accept the decisions of authorities that lead to social change, as opposed to when people will personally decide that social change is needed. It is based upon the belief that legal authorities may be more generally inclined to act as agents of social change than are people within the general population. Whether, in fact, this is a true depiction of legal authorities is a matter of contention (see Scheingold, 1974).

The research outlined above has primarily been conducted within the context of organized groups that are ongoing and have existing authority structures. These authorities are typically widely viewed as legitimate and hence as entitled to be obeyed. However, when people regard authorities as less legitimate, they are less willing to defer to their decisions because those decisions are fairly made. Instead, they focus upon the favorability of the decisions made (Tyler, 1997b). It is more difficult for authorities lacking legitimacy to bridge issues and problems and gain deference to common policies. When new authorities are created, for example the new parliament in Russia, or the European Union, a central problem for authorities is how to legitimize those new political authorities. Here procedural justice also plays a key role.

If people view or personally experience the authorities within their society, group, or organization as making decisions fairly, they increasingly view them as legitimate. Over time, this legitimacy shapes deference, which becomes increasingly independent of the favorability of policies and decisions. Similarly, studies of work organizations show that such organizations often adopt symbols and decision-making procedures associated with justice and fairness in an effort to legitimize their authority structures and encourage employees to defer to organizational authorities and to identify with the organization (Tyler and Blader, 2000).

Of course, procedural justice effects are not confined to hierarchical relationships or established groups. Studies suggest that people are influenced by issues of procedural justice across a variety of types of social settings. Barrett-Howard and Tyler (1986) systematically varied situations across the four basic dimensions that represent the fundamental dimensions of social situations. They found that procedural justice concerns generally dominated people's reactions to allocations in all situations. Similarly, Sondak and Sheppard (1995) utilized the situational typology created by Fiske (1992) as a basis for identifying possible types of authority structures. They found that procedural issues were important across all types of social situations.

JUSTICE AND INTERNALIZED VALUES

Fair decision-making procedures encourage voluntary cooperation with groups because they lead to identification with and loyalty and commitment toward groups (Folger and Konovsky, 1989; Korsgaard, Schweiger, and Sapienza, 1995; McFarlin and Sweeney, 1992; Schaubroeck, May, and Brown, 1994; Taylor, Tracy, Renard, Harrison, and Carroll, 1995). Similarly, procedural justice promotes deference to social rules because it promotes the belief that authorities are legitimate (Tyler, 1997b). This internal value is important because when people feel that authorities ought to be obeyed, they take the obligation to do so on themselves, and voluntarily defer to authorities and rules.

In both of these cases, procedural justice is central to creating and maintaining internal values that support voluntary cooperative behavior on the part of the members of groups. The importance of developing and maintaining such values is increasingly being emphasized, as social scientists recognize the limits of strategies of conflict resolution that are based upon seeking to shape the rewards and punishments received by the parties to a dispute. Recent social science thinking has been dominated by rational choice models of the person. As a consequence, command and control, deterrence, or social control strategies have dominated discussions about social regulation. These strategies focus upon the individual as a calculative actor, thinking, feeling, and behaving in terms of potential rewards and costs in their immediate environment.

Increasingly, social scientists have recognized the limits of command and control approaches to managing conflict. In political and legal settings, authorities have recognized that both social regulation (Tyler, 1990, 2001) and the encouragement of voluntary civic behavior (Green and Shapiro, 1994) are difficult when authorities can only rely upon their ability to reward and/or punish citizens. Similarly, organizational theorists are recognizing the difficulties of managing employees using command and control strategies (Pfeffer, 1994). The alternative to such strategies is to focus on approaches based upon appeals to internal values. If people have internal values that lead them to voluntarily defer to authorities and to act in prosocial ways that help the group, then authorities need not seek to compel such behavior through promises of reward or threats of punishment. They can instead rely upon people's willingness to engage in the behavior voluntarily.

Research suggests that using fair decision-making procedures is central to the development and maintenance of supportive internal values. Those authorities that use fair decision-making procedures are viewed as more legitimate, and people more willingly defer to their decisions. This produces uniformity of behavior in line with organizational rules and the decisions of organizational authorities. When authorities want people to defer their own desires in the interests of the group, they can obtain such behavior by calling upon people's views that they are legitimate.

In addition, organizations that use fair decision-making procedures encourage commitment and identification on the part of their members, which leads to voluntary cooperative behavior. People want the group to succeed and engage in behaviors to help achieve that objective. In other words, people willingly engage their own creative efforts and energies into efforts to advance the interests of the group. They might help others do their jobs during a crisis; help and encourage new group members; engage in activities that are nonobservable, and hence will not be rewarded, but that help the group.

In other words, the recognition of the importance of creating a "civic culture" or an "organizational culture" that supports the development and maintenance of internal values among group members is increasing as the limits of command and control approaches to managing conflict become clearer. Procedural justice is central to both developing and maintaining judgments that authorities are legitimate and feelings of commitment and identification with groups, organizations, and societies.

These findings demonstrate that providing people with procedural justice can be an important and viable mechanism for gaining deference to decisions. This effect occurs across a variety of settings, including both hierarchical and nonhierarchical situations, in political, legal, managerial, interpersonal, familial, and educational settings, and when important issues of outcomes and treatment are involved. Hence, conflict resolution efforts can gain viability through the use of fair decision-making procedures.

What is a Fair Procedure?

There are two levels upon which we can address the question of what type of procedures people think are fair. One is to focus upon possible legal procedures, and to discuss whether people view them as fair. When we do so, it becomes clear that informal legal procedures are viewed as particularly fair. In fact, in civil cases, defendants rate mediation to be fairer than a formal trial, and it is typically rated as more satisfactory (Tyler, 1997a). In criminal cases, defendants rate plea bargaining to be fairer than a formal trial (Tyler, 1997a). In terms of procedural fairness, giving people fair procedures means putting more emphasis upon informal dispute resolution.

What characteristics lead people to associate informal justice with procedural fairness? Studies typically find seven, eight, or even more elements that contribute to assessments of their fairness (Sheppard and Lewicki, 1987; Lissak and Sheppard, 1983; Tyler, 1988). However, four elements of procedures are the primary factors that contribute to judgments about their fairness: opportunities for participation (voice), the neutrality of the forum, the trustworthiness of the authorities, and the degree to which people receive treatment with dignity and respect.

Participation

People feel more fairly treated if they are allowed to participate in the resolution of their problems or conflicts by presenting their suggestions about what should be done. Such opportunities are referred to as process control or voice. The positive effects of participation have been widely found, beginning in the work of Thibaut and Walker (1975). These effects have been found in studies of plea bargaining (Houlden, 1980), sentencing hearings (Heinz and Kerstetter, 1979), and mediation (Kitzmann and Emery, 1993; MacCoun et al., 1988; Shapiro and Brett, 1993). In all of these diverse settings, people feel more fairly treated when they are given an opportunity to make arguments about what should be done to resolve a problem or conflict.

Participation effects have been found to be enhanced when people feel that the things they say are shaping the outcomes of the dispute – an instrumental influence (see Shapiro and Brett, 1993). However, voice effects have not been found to be dependent just upon having control over the actual outcomes of conflicts. People have also been found to value the opportunity to express their views to decision makers in situations in which they believe that what they are saying has little or no influence upon the decisions being made (Lind, Kanfer, and Earley, 1990; Tyler, 1987). For example, victims value the opportunity to speak at sentencing hearings irrespective of whether their arguments influence the sentences given to the criminals involved (Heinz and Kerstetter, 1979).

People are primarily interested in sharing the discussion over the issues involved in their problem or conflict, not in controlling decisions about how to handle it. In fact, people often look to societal authorities to make decisions about which legal or managerial principles ought to govern the resolution of their dispute. In other words, they expect societal authorities to make final decisions about how to act based upon what they have said.

The finding that people value the opportunity to participate by expressing their opinions and stating their case helps to explain why people like mediation. Mediation is typically rated as providing greater opportunities for participation than formal trials (McEwen and Maiman, 1984). Similarly, defendants involved in disposing of felony charges against themselves indicate that they have greater opportunities to participate in plea bargaining than in a formal trial (Casper, Tyler, and Fisher, 1988), and they rate plea bargaining to be a fairer procedure for resolving their case.

Neutrality

People are influenced by judgments about the honesty, impartiality, and objectivity of the authorities with whom they are dealing. They believe that authorities should not allow their personal values and biases to enter into their decisions, which should be made based upon rules and facts. Basically, people seek a "level playing field" in which no one is unfairly disadvantaged. If they believe that the authorities are following impartial rules and making factual, objective, decisions, they think procedures are fairer.

The trustworthiness of the authorities

Another factor shaping people's views about the fairness of a procedure is their assessment of the motives of the third-party authority responsible for resolving the case. People recognize that third parties typically have considerable discretion to implement formal procedures in varying ways, and they are concerned about the motivation underlying the decisions made by the authority with which they are dealing. They judge whether that person is benevolent and caring, is concerned about their situation and their concerns and needs, considers their arguments, tries to do what is right for them, and tries to be fair. All of these elements combine to shape a general assessment of the person's trustworthiness.

Interestingly, judgments about the trustworthiness of the authorities are the primary factors shaping evaluations of the fairness of the procedures used by those authorities (Tyler and Lind, 1992). The importance of trust is illustrated by a finding of the literature on participation. People only value the opportunity to speak to authorities if they believe that the authority is sincerely considering their arguments. They must trust that the authority sincerely considered their arguments, even if they were then rejected, before having had the chance to participate leads to the evaluation of procedures as fairer.

How can authorities communicate that they are trying to be fair? A key antecedent of trust is justification. When authorities are presenting their decisions to the people influenced by them, they need to make clear that they have listened to and considered the arguments made. They can do so by accounting for their decisions. Such accounts should clearly state the arguments made by the various parties to the dispute. They should also explain how those arguments have been considered and why they have been accepted or rejected.

I have already outlined the importance of neutrality to assessments of the fairness of procedures. There is considerable evidence that the basis of the authoritativeness – the ability of authorities to gain deference to their decisions – is shifting from a neutrality base to a trust base. That is, in the past authorities have often gained their authoritativeness through the neutral application of rules, that is, through the use of facts and formal decision-making procedures that are objective and factual in character. A person, for example, can go to any police officer or judge and receive more or less equivalent treatment and outcomes, since the particular authority with whom they are dealing will be following universal rules. Having personal knowledge about the specific authority involved in an interaction is not important. On the other hand, trust is linked to judgments about particular authorities. Hence, trust is linked to particularized personal connections between citizens and authorities. For example, people might get to know a beat cop because that person patrols their neighborhood. They might trust that person because they have dealt with them, know their motives and values, and, consequently feel that they can trust them.

An organization can gain deference by having formal rules that reflect neutrality. It can also gain deference through the personal relationships that exist between employees and their own particular supervisors. The former approach reflects a neutrality model of procedural fairness, the latter approach a trust-based model. Similarly, the police can gain deference because they are viewed as following professional rules of conduct and uniform procedures, or particular police officers can be respected and known in their communities and can, through these personalized connections, gain deference.

Treatment with dignity and respect

People value having respect shown for their rights and for their status within society by others. They are very concerned that, in the process of dealing with authorities, their dignity as people and as members of society is recognized and acknowledged. Since politeness and respect are essentially unrelated to the outcomes people receive when they deal with social authorities, the importance that people place upon this affirmation of their status is especially relevant to conflict resolution. More than any other issue, treatment with dignity and respect is something that authorities can give to everyone with whom they deal.

LIMITS TO THE EFFECTIVENESS OF PROCEDURAL JUSTICE MECHANISMS

I have presented a generally optimistic picture of the viability of procedural strategies for resolving conflicts. However, there may be limits to the range within which such strategies will be effective. I want to discuss one type of potential limit, the impact of the nature of the society within which conflicts are being resolved (also see Tyler, 2000b).

The first issue is that of *social consensus*. There have been widespread concerns about the potential of cultural backgrounds to disrupt the viability of procedures strategies. There are two ways that such disruption might occur. First, cultural background might change the degree to which people care about whether they receive procedural justice. Second, it might change the criteria by which people define the fairness of procedures. How important are such concerns?

As noted earlier, research among people of varying ethnicity in the United States suggests that authorities have considerable ability to manage diverse groups and communities. Little difference is found in the importance placed upon procedural justice by the members of varying ethnic groups. Both whites and minorities are more influenced by the fairness of the procedures they experience than they are by the fairness of the outcomes they receive through third-party conflict resolution decisions (Tyler and Huo, 2002). Further, studies consistently find that whites and minorities define the meaning of procedural fairness in the same way (Tyler and Huo, 2002; Tyler, 1988; Tyler, 1994). Hence these findings are fairly optimistic about the ability of procedures to be robust across differences in ethnicity.

Interestingly, research also finds that procedures are robust across ideologies. That is, people who differ in their fundamental social values or political ideologies are often found to agree about whether or not a particular procedure is fair (Bierbrauer, 1997; Peterson, 1994; Tyler, 1994). This is especially striking, since ideological differences have a strong impact upon views about what constitutes a fair outcome. In this respect, procedural justice may be a better bridge across social and ideological groups than is distributive justice.

These findings do not suggest that there is some type of universal fair procedure that is appropriate in all situations (Tyler, 1988). On the contrary, the same studies suggest that people view different procedural elements as key to defining procedural fairness within particular situations. For example, in a conflict between people, the opportunity to state one's views is central to procedures that are viewed as fair. However, in other situations opportunities to participate are less important to judgments about the fairness of procedures. People differentiate among situations and apply a different model of fairness to different situations. So we know that people are not thinking about procedural fairness in simple-minded terms. This makes it especially interesting that there is little evidence of differences linked to ethnicity or gender.

This research suggests an optimistic conclusion about the robustness of procedures. They seem to be viable mechanisms for bridging differences among people of varying ethnic and ideological backgrounds. However, it is important to note that not all research suggests that procedures are robust. For example, studies of decision making in political settings suggest that majority and minority factions often disagree about what constitutes a fair decision-making procedure for their organization (Azzi, 1993a, 1993b).

The second issue is *social categorization*. Basically, we find that people are less concerned about justice when they are dealing with people who are outside of their own ethnic or social group (Tyler, Lind, Ohbuchi, Sugawara, and Huo, 1998). For example, when people have a dispute with someone who is not a member of their own social group, they pay more attention to the personal favorability of a proposed dispute resolution when deciding whether to accept it. If the dispute is with someone who is a member of their own social group, they pay more attention to whether they have been treated fairly when deciding whether to accept a proposed dispute resolution. Hence group boundaries may pose a limit to the effective scope of justice.

This points to a strategy for dealing with conflict. We need to encourage people to frame their group memberships in terms of superordinate categorizations that build across subgroups. Instead of seeing two separate groups, we want people to see one common group. This suggestion develops from the prior recognition within social psychology that superordinate categorization encourages cooperation within the group (Gaertner, Dovidio, Anastasio, Bachman, and Rust, 1993). We need to focus on how people frame their group boundaries. After all, if we think of ourselves as members of the "human race" then everyone is a member of our group. Therefore, the question is how authorities can encourage such high order identifications, with people viewing the members of other groups as having some degree of joint membership in a larger group.

The third issue is *identification*. People are more likely to care about justice when they identify with the group within which their conflict is occurring, and with the authorities responsible for dealing with the conflict. Several studies support this argument by showing that people who identify more strongly with an organization or society rely more heavily on justice judgments when deciding whether to defer to the decisions of authorities (Huo, Smith, Tyler, and Lind, 1996; Smith and Tyler, 1996; Tyler and Degoey, 1995).

This also points to a strategy. We need to focus on building up people's identification with society and with social institutions. If people identify more strongly with the group that authorities represent, they are more concerned about whether or not they receive fair treatment, and less concerned about receiving favorable outcomes. How can we build positive identification? By treating those within groups in procedurally fair ways. Research suggests that procedural justice builds commitment to the group, identification with the group, and feelings of obligation to authorities and group rules.

CONCLUSIONS

As this review of justice research makes clear, there are important reasons for optimism concerning the viability of justice-based strategies for conflict resolution. In particular, approaches based upon an understanding of people's views about fair decision-making procedures have been very successful in gaining deference to decisions and to rules, authorities, and institutions more generally. This does not mean, of course, that people do not care about outcomes. They do. However, they do not care *only* about outcomes. On the contrary, their feelings and behaviors have an important ethical and moral component. This ethical/moral aspect to people's reactions to others in social settings provides an approach to the constructive resolution of social conflicts.

References

Azzi, A. (1993a) "Group representation and procedural justice in multigroup decision-making bodies," *Social Justice Research* 6: 195–217.

Azzi, A. (1993b) "Implicit and category-based allocations of decision-making power in majority–minority relations," *Journal of Experimental Social Psychology* 29: 203–28.

Barrett-Howard, E. and Tyler, T.R. (1986) "Procedural justice as a criterion in allocation decisions," *Journal of Personality and Social Psychology* 50: 296–304.

Bierbrauer, G. (July, 1997) *Political Ideology and Allocation Preferences: What do Turkish Immigrants in Germany Deserve?* Potsdam, Germany: International Network for Social Justice Research Conference.

Bies, R.J., Martin, C.L., and Brockner, J. (1993). "Just laid off, but still a 'good citizen': Only if the process is fair," *Employee Responsibilities and Rights Journal* 6: 227–48.

Casper, J.D., Tyler, T.R., and Fisher, B. (1988) "Procedural justice in felony cases," *Law and Society Review* 22: 483–507.

Ebreo, A., Linn, N., and Vining, J. (1996) "The impact of procedural justice on opinions of public policy: Solid waste management as an example," *Journal of Applied Social Psychology* 26: 1259–85.

Fiske, A.P. (1992) "The four elementary forms of sociality: Framework for a unified theory of social relations," *Psychological Review* 99: 689–723.

Folger, R. and Konovsky, M.A. (1989) "Effects of procedural and distributive justice on reactions to pay raise decisions," *Academy of Management Journal* 32: 115–30.

Gaertner, S.L., Dovidio, J.F., Anastasio, P.A., Bachman, B.A., and Rust, M.C. (1993) "The common ingroup identity model," *European Review of Social Psychology* 4: 1–26.

Green, Donald P. and Shapiro, Ian (1994) *Pathologies of Rational Choice Theory*. New Haven: Yale.

Gurr, T.R. (1970) *Why Men Rebel*. Princeton, NJ: Princeton University Press.

Heinz, A.M. and Kerstetter, W.A. (1979) "Pretrial settlement conference: Evaluation of a reform in plea bargaining," *Law and Society Review* 13: 349–66.

Hochschild, J.L. (1995) *Facing up to the American Dream: Race, Class, and the Soul of the Nation*. Princeton, NJ: Princeton University Press.

Houlden, P. (1980) "The impact of procedural modifications on evaluations of plea bargaining," *Law and Society Review* 15: 267–92.

Huo, Y.J., Smith, H.J., Tyler, T.R., and Lind, E.A. (1996) "Superordinate identification, subgroup identification, and justice concerns: Is separatism the problem, is assimilation the answer?" *Psychological Science* 7: 40–5.

Kim, W.C. and Mauborgne, R.A. (1991) "Implementing global strategies: The role of procedural justice," *Strategic Management Journal* 12: 125–43.

Kim, W.C. and Mauborgne, R.A. (1993) "Procedural justice, attitudes, and subsidiary top management compliance with multinationals' corporate strategic decisions," *Academy of Management Journal* 36: 502–26.

Kitzman, K.M. and Emery, R.E. (1993) "Procedural justice and parents' satisfaction in a field study of child custody dispute resolution," *Law and Human Behavior* 17: 553–67.

Kluegel, J.R. and Smith, E.R. (1986) *Beliefs About Inequality*. New York: Aldine-Gruyter.

Korsgaard, M.A., Schweiger, D.M., and Sapienza, H.J. (1995) "Building commitment, attachment, and trust in strategic decision-making teams: The role of procedural justice," *Academy of Management Journal* 38: 60–84.

Lind, E.A., Kanfer, R., and Earley, P.C. (1990) "Voice, control, and procedural justice," *Journal of Personality and Social Psychology* 59: 952–9.

Lind, E.A., Kulik, C.T., Ambrose, M., and de Vera Park, M. (1993) "Individual and corporate dispute resolution," *Administrative Science Quarterly* 38: 224–51.

Lind, E.A. and Tyler, T.R. (1988). *The Social Psychology of Procedural Justice*. New York: Plenum.

Lissak, R.I. and Sheppard, B.H. (1983) "Beyond fairness: The criterion problem in research on dispute resolution," *Journal of Applied Social Psychology* 13: 45–65.

MacCoun, R.J., Lind, E.A., Hensler, D.R., Bryant, D.L., and Ebener, P.A. (1988). *Alternative Adjudication: An Evaluation of the New Jersey Automobile Arbitration Program*. Santa Monica, CA: RAND.

McEwen, C. and Maiman, R.J. (1984) "Mediation in small claims court," *Law and Society Review* 18: 11–49.

McFarlin, D.B. and Sweeney, P.D. (1992) "Distributive and procedural justice as predictors of satisfaction with personal and organizational outcomes," *Academy of Management Journal* 35: 626–37.

Messick, D.M., Bloom, S., Boldizar, J.P., and Samuelson, C.D. (1985) "Why we are fairer than others," *Journal of Experimental Social Psychology* 21: 389–99.

Mikula, G., Petri, B., and Tanzer, N. (1990) "What people regard as unjust: Types and structures of everyday experiences of injustice," *European Journal of Social Psychology* 22: 133–49.

Montada, L. and Schneider, A. (1989) "Justice and emotional reactions to the disadvantaged," *Social Justice Research* 3: 313–344.

Moorman, R.H. (1991) "Relationship between organizational justice and organizational citizenship behaviors: Do fairness perceptions influence employee citizenship?" *Journal of Applied Psychology* 76: 845–55.

Moorman, R.H., Niehoff, B.P., and Organ, D.W. (1993) "Treating employees fairly and organizational citizenship behavior," *Employee Responsibilities and Rights Journal* 6: 209–25.

Niehoff, B.P. and Moorman, R.H. (1993) "Justice as a mediator of the relationship between methods of monitoring and organizational citizenship behavior," *Academy of Management Journal* 36: 527–56.

Paternoster, R., Brame, R., Bachman, R., and Sherman, L.W. (1997) "Do fair procedures matter?: The effect of procedural justice on spouse assault," *Law and Society Review* 31: 163–204.

Peterson, R. (1994) "The role of values in predicting fairness judgments and support of affirmative action," *Journal of Social Issues* 50: 95–116.

Pfeffer, J. (1994). *Competitive Advantage Through People*. Cambridge, MA: Harvard University Press.

Pruitt, D.G., Peirce, R.S., McGillicuddy, N.B., Welton, G.L., and Castrianno, L.M. (1993) "Long-term success in mediation," *Law and Human Behavior* 17: 313–30.

Pruitt, D.G., Peirce, R.S., Zubek, J.M., Welton, G.L., and Nochajski, T.H. (1990) "Goal achievement, procedural justice, and the success of mediation," *The International Journal of Conflict Management* 1: 33–45.

Schaubroeck, J., May, D.R., and Brown, F.W. (1994) "Procedural justice explanations and employee reactions to economic hardship," *Journal of Applied Psychology* 79: 455–60.

Scheingold, S.A. (1974) *The Politics of Rights*. New Haven, CT: Yale University Press.

Shapiro, D. and Brett, J. (1993) "Comparing three processes underlying judgments of procedural justice," *Journal of Personality and Social Psychology* 65: 1167–77.

Sheppard, B.H. and Lewicki, R.J. (1987) "Toward general principles of managerial fairness," *Social Justice Research* 1: 161–76.

Smith, H.J. and Tyler, T.R. (1996) "Justice and power," *European Journal of Social Psychology* 26: 171–200.

Sondak, H. and Sheppard, B. (1995) *Evaluating Alternative Models for Allocating Scarce Resources: A Relational Approach to Procedural Justice and Social Structure*. Vancouver: Academy of Management.

Sparks, R., Bottoms, A., and Hay, W. (1996) *Prisons and the Problem of Order*. Oxford: Clarendon Press.

Taylor, M.S., Tracy, K.B., Renard, M.K., Harrison, J.K., and Carroll, S.J. (1995) "Due process in performance appraisal: A quasi-experiment in procedural justice," *Administrative Science Quarterly* 40: 495–523.

Thibaut, J. and Walker, L. (1975) *Procedural Justice*. Hillsdale, NJ: Erlbaum.

Tyler, T.R. (1987) "Conditions leading to value-expressive effects in judgments of procedural justice: A test of four models," *Journal of Personality and Social Psychology* 52: 333–44.

Tyler, T.R. (1988) "What is procedural justice? Criteria used by citizens to assess the fairness of legal procedures," *Law and Society Review* 22: 301–55.

Tyler, T.R. (1990) *Why People Obey the Law*. New Haven, CT: Yale University Press.

Tyler, T.R. (1994) "Governing amid diversity: The effect of fair decision-making procedures on the legitimacy of government," *Law and Society Review* 28: 809–31.

Tyler, T.R. (1997a) "Citizen discontent with legal procedures: A social science perspective on civil procedure reform," *American Journal of Comparative Law* 45: 871–904.

Tyler, T.R. (1997b) "The psychology of legitimacy," *Personality and Social Psychology Review* 1: 323–45.

Tyler, T.R. (2000a) "Social justice: Outcome and procedure," *International Journal of Psychology* 35: 117–25.

Tyler, T.R. (2000b) "Multiculturalism and the willingness of citizens to defer to law and to legal authorities," *Law and Social Inquiry* 25: 983–1020.

Tyler, T.R. (2001) "Trust and law abidingness: A proactive model of social regulation," *Boston University Law Review* 81: 361–406.

Tyler, T.R. and Blader, S.L. (2000). *Cooperation in Groups*. Philadelphia: Psychology Press.

Tyler, T.R., Boeckmann, R., Smith, H.J., and Huo, Y.J. (1997) *Social Justice in a Diverse Society*. Boulder, CO: Westview.

Tyler, T.R. and Degoey, P. (1995) "Collective restraint in a social dilemma situation: The influence of procedural justice and community identification on the empowerment and legitimacy of authority," *Journal of Personality and Social Psychology* 69: 482–97.

Tyler, T.R. and Huo, Y.J. (2002). *Trust and the Rule of Law.* New York: Russell-Sage Foundation.

Tyler, T.R. and Lind, E.A. (1992) "A relational model of authority in groups," *Advances in Experimental Social Psychology* 25: 151–91.

Tyler, T.R., Lind, E.A., and Huo, Y.J. (2000) "Cultural values and authority relations," *Psychology, Public Policy, and Law* 6: 1138–63.

Tyler, T.R., Lind, E.A., Ohbuchi, K., Sugawara, I., and Huo, Y.J. (1998) "Conflict with outsiders: Disputing within and across cultural boundaries," *Personality and Social Psychology Bulletin* 24: 137–46.

Tyler, T.R. and Mitchell, G. (1994) "Legitimacy and the empowerment of discretionary legal authority: The United States Supreme Court and abortion rights," *Duke Law Journal* 43: 703–814.

Tyler, T.R. and Smith, H.J. (1997) "Social justice and social movements," in D. Gilbert, S. Fiske, and G. Lindzey (eds.), *Handbook of Social Psychology*, 4th edn, vol. 2. New York: Addison-Wesley, pp. 595–629.

Wissler, R.L. (1995) "Mediation and adjudication in small claims court," *Law and Society Review* 29: 323–58.

24

A Tale of Two Genres: On the Real and Ideal Links Between Law and Society and Critical Race Theory

Laura E. Gómez

Introduction

The point of departure for this essay is the claim that law and society scholars have not been sufficiently attentive to issues of racial inequality, racial ideology, and racial identity. Given their interest, as a group, in inequality and ideology more generally, it is surprising that sociolegal scholars have not paid more attention to racial inequality and racial ideology. What accounts for this? The short answer is that many, if not most, law and society scholars conceive of race as a readily measurable, dichotomous (black/white) variable that affects the law at various points. Even law and society scholars whose work is not positivist in style tend to view race as a concept that is relatively simple to map. But race *is* complicated, and the relationship between race and law is messy. Race does not exist outside of law; it is constituted by law. And, in the United States among other places, law does not exist apart from race; it is constituted by racial classification systems, racial ideology, and racial inequality.

These ideas are the starting point of a relatively new genre of legal scholarship known as critical race theory. By and large, law and society scholars have not engaged the claims put forward by critical race scholars over the past 15 years or so. And even when they do so, they have not taken the literature as seriously as they might. My hope is to persuade law and society scholars that our work would be improved by engaging critical race theory. (In a forthcoming project, I make a similar injunction to critical race scholars: that their work would be improved by more fully engaging the methodologies, theories, and findings in the law and society field.) To do so, I discuss some recent law and society scholarship and discuss how critical race theory has influenced and could have further enhanced their analyses.

Critical race theory emerged in the middle-to-late 1980s, concomitant with a critical mass of racial minorities (particularly African Americans) entering the legal professoriate. Today, more than 20 American law schools offer courses or seminars on critical race theory and one, UCLA, offers an advanced specialization in critical race studies (Harris, 2002; see http://www.law.ucla.edu/crs). Critical race scholars write not only in those doctrinal areas traditionally conceived of as relevant to civil rights and race relations (such as constitutional law, employment discrimination and civil rights generally), but also in an increasingly diverse array of doctrinal areas such as the following: criminal law and procedure (Austin, 1992; Carbado, 2002a; Butler, 1995; A. Harris, 2000; Lee, 1996; Meares, 1998; Alfieri, 1998, 1999, 2001; Johnson, 1993, 1998; Ammons, 1995); torts (Austin, 1988; Matsuda, 2000); property (C. Harris, 1993); family law (Moran, 2001; Banks, 1998; Perry, 1994, 1993; Roberts, 1997); civil procedure (Brooks, 1994); tax law (Moran and Whitford, 1996); and environmental law (Yamamoto and Lyman, 2001).

Critical race theory is one of the few genres of legal scholarship that has drawn widespread attention outside the legal academy, with departments of education, American studies, African American studies, and ethnic studies now posting course offerings in critical race theory (Harris, 2002). Professor Cornel West, a leading scholar of African American studies, has labeled critical race theory "the most exciting development in contemporary legal studies" (1995: iii). Given its positive reception by scholars in the humanities and social sciences, critical race theory would seem a good fit for law and society, given the latter's commitment to multidisciplinary and interdisciplinary scholarship. Critical race theory has even broken out of the academy altogether to capture a popular audience, with critical race scholar Patricia Williams writing a regular column for *The Nation* (entitled "Diary of a Mad Law Professor"; see also Williams, 1991; Rosen, 1996).

All of this is to say that critical race theory deserves to be read by scholars of law and society. But what is "critical race theory"? Three anthologies of critical race theory scholarship, all edited by law professors, provide a good starting point (Valdes, Culp, and Harris, 2002; Delgado, 1995; Crenshaw, Gotanda, Peller, and Thomas,1995). Three law school casebooks also draw heavily from the critical race literature (Bell, 1992; Perea, Delgado, Harris, and Wildman, 2000; Yamamoto, Chon, Izumi, Kang, and Wu, 2001). Crenshaw et al. characterize critical race theory as "a movement of left scholars, most of them scholars of color, situated in law schools, whose work challenges the ways in which race and racial power are constructed and represented in American legal culture and, more generally, in American society as a whole" (1995: xiii).

That said, neither what constitutes critical race theory nor which authors write from this perspective are self-evident; both questions are contested by people within the field and outside it (Carbado, 2002b). I take a broad view of the field by including those authors who expressly identify themselves with critical race theory as well as those who engage the scholarship of authors who so identify. I also include, within the critical race theory rubric, other literatures that I view as having their genesis in critical race scholarship, including legal scholarship focused more specifically on the Asian American and Latino/Latina (LatCrit) experiences, race-oriented queer legal theory, and feminist legal theory focused on women of color. Noted critical race scholars Francisco Valdes (see chapter 15 in this volume) and Cheryl Harris (2002) recently have taken a similarly broad view of the field.

Critical race scholars write about race and the law but do so from the perspective of writing against the antidiscrimination model that has been dominant in American jurisprudence and legal scholarship for the past 30 years. This literature has been written almost entirely by white men (Delgado, 1984, 1992). The antidiscrimination model essentially conceives of racism and racial discrimination as individualized, aberrational, and capable of remedy within the current jurisprudential framework, both constitutional (the equal protection clause of the Fourteenth Amendment) and legislative (Title VII of the Civil Rights Act of 1964). In contrast, critical race scholars view racism and racial discrimination as systemic (institutional) and endemic and, therefore, frequently as immune to antidiscrimination remedies (see, e.g., Bell, 1992; Lawrence, 1987; Haney-Lopez, 2000).

Critical race theory and law and society both share at least partial lineage in critical legal studies (CLS) – the leftist scholarly movement that rocked legal scholarship in the 1970s (for an introduction to critical legal studies, see Kairys, 1982). Critical race theory formed, in part, from a rupture within CLS, led by racial minority scholars who rejected the nihilism in the CLS claim that all law is ideology, in the service of dominant class interests (Crenshaw et al., 1995). Instead, critical race scholars continue to write scholarship that attempts to change American law, whether radically or via incremental reforms.

For law and society scholarship, one legacy from CLS has been the oft-noted centrality of research on inequality in the field (Abel, 1995a: 297–357; Sarat, Constable, Engel, Hans, and Lawrence, 1998: 4–6; Munger, 1998: 36). Law and society scholars have sought to document unequal results or outcomes of various legal processes, especially the criminal process. (The representative literature is too voluminous to cite here.) They have posited overarching theories of inequality in the legal system (Spitzer, 1983; Galanter, 1975; Bumiller, 1988; Fineman, 1995; Sarat, 1990). And they have studied social movements organized to promote equality (Handler, 1978; McCann, 1994; Abel, 1995b). While inequality has been a central theme in law and society scholarship, researchers in the field have been much more focused on class- and gender-based inequality than on racial inequality. (See Daly, 1987, 1994, 1998, for an example of a law and society scholar whose work has become increasingly attentive to race, within a central focus on gender inequality.)

When law and society researchers have taken up race, they have tended to treat race as an independent variable that influences the outcome of the legal phenomenon under study (the dependent variable). I am not suggesting that this approach is inherently flawed – it may make a great deal of sense in the context of a particular study. Moreover, law and society scholarship of this nature focused on criminal justice processes, and specifically on the administration of the death penalty, has played an important role in policy debates. Indeed, we might view the positivist approach to race, at its apex in law and society in the 1980s, as quite progressive in that political moment. These studies brought race into law and society research and they contributed to the critique of liberalism as well (by revealing large cracks in the law's veneer of neutrality and fairness).

Today, however, treating race as an easily measurable independent variable has led law and society researchers to have a kind of collective myopia when it comes to studying race. Rarely have they made racial inequality, racism, or racial identity the central focus of their inquiry (the dependent variable), and thus a certain lopsidedness characterizes law and society scholarship on race. In sharp contrast, critical race scholars often have made racial identity, racial ideology, or racism the focus of their inquiry, with law being the factor that explains race. Indeed, Crenshaw et al. describe the critical race theory endeavor "as uncovering how law was a constitutive element of race itself: in other words, how law constructed race" (Crenshaw et al., 1995: xxv). Critical race scholars, then, often flip the traditional approach of law and society scholars to race: for the latter, racial inequality makes law (or produces legal outcomes), whereas, for the former, law makes race.

RACE IN LAW AND SOCIETY SCHOLARSHIP

Ideally, then, sociolegal scholars would borrow this strategy from critical race scholars in order to see what shifting the emphasis might yield for what we know (and think we know) about law and society. To what extent has this occurred? In an attempt to provide one answer to this question, I surveyed articles published over a decade in the two leading law and society journals, *The Law & Society Review* and *Law and Social Inquiry*. Between 1990 and 2000, these two journals published, respectively, nine and 15 articles dealing with race, racial inequality, or legal doctrine in the civil rights arenas (excluding book reviews). (Seven of the 15 articles published in *Law and Social Inquiry* were published in 2000 for a symposium on affirmative action in legal education, vol. 25.)

Although most of these studies are not quantitative, the majority still reflect the tendency to operationalize race unproblematically as a dichotomous, black/white variable that helps predict the legal outcome that is at the center of the research. In most of these studies, racial inequality, racial classification, and/or racial ideology are, at best, peripheral to the analysis despite the fact that the articles explicitly or implicitly deal with legal or social phenomena closely associated with race or racial inequality (see Provine, 1998; Morrill, Yalda, Adelman, Musheno, and Bejarano, 2000; Romero, 2000; Bybee, 2000; Phillips and Grattet, 2000). Some noteworthy exceptions that place race at the center of the analysis and that consider it deeply and contextually are Nielsen (2000), Glenn (2000), Weitzer (2000) and Oberweis and Musheno (1999). By and large, the authors noted above fail to seriously engage the burgeoning critical race literature, despite its bearing on their inquiries and analyses. It is almost as if this genre of legal scholarship does not exist, despite these authors' engagement with a wide range of other subfields of legal scholarship that are quite separate from law and society.

An important exception is a subset of about one-third of these articles, historical in approach, that builds on insights from the critical race literature. Historical studies dealing with race, as a subset of articles on race published in the leading law and society journals between 1990 and 2000, numbered eight, as follows: Brandwein, 2000; Calavita, 2000; Elliott, 1999; Goluboff, 1999; Gómez, 2000; Mack, 1999; Plane, 1998; Polletta, 2000. Each of these articles engages critical race theory, though to differing degrees. Four of the authors expressly situate their work as joining a dialogue previously initiated by critical race theory scholars (Brandwein, 2000: 319; Calavita, 2000: 3; Elliott, 1999: 612; Mack, 1999: 380). Of the remaining four, two more cite authors affiliated with the field (Gómez, 2000; Polletta, 2000). While neither of the two remaining articles invoke critical race theory nor cite scholars identified with that scholarly movement, they nonetheless engage central debates within critical race theory and their work would have been strengthened by incorporating work in the field (Goluboff, 1999; Plane, 1998).

In a similar way, the articles fall along a continuum in terms of their engagement with empiricism – traditionally, one of the hallmarks of the law and society field. One of the authors conducted interviews to supplement archival research – Francesca Polletta, who interviewed more than 100 former southern civil rights workers about their experiences and attitudes. Three of the authors utilized a range of diverse primary sources including court or administrative records, newspapers, appellate decisions (Calavita, 2000; Gómez, 2000; Mack, 1999), with Calavita and Gómez involving analysis of hundreds of case files. Three of the studies focused exclusively on discourse or rhetoric in legislative debate and/or case law (Brandwein, 2000; Elliott, 1999; Plane, 1998), with Elliott and Plane consisting of a close reading of only one or two appellate cases. Thus, methodologically, the subset of historical articles is quite diverse.

Also, although each focuses on some period in the past, they foreground a range of different time periods, as far back as the US colonial period (Plane, 1998) and as recent as the 1960s (Polletta, 2000). Five authors' engagement with the late nineteenth century (Brandwein, 2000; Calavita, 2000; Elliott, 1999; Gómez, 2000; Mack, 1999) suggests the importance of that historic period for understanding the contemporary American racial hierarchy. Brandwein and Elliott concern themselves specifically with the repercussions of the Civil War, and how the ideology of white supremacy would come to be worked out and reproduced in legal discourse. Mack continues the interest in the south, focusing on the complexity of the links among race, gender, and social class in Tennessee in the last quarter of the nineteenth century and early twentieth century. Calavita and Gómez examine the same time period, but shift our gaze to the southwest and west and to nonblack racial minority groups. Four of the articles focus on nonblack groups: Calavita on the Chinese, Elliott on Indians and blacks, Gómez on Mexicans (and somewhat on Indians), and Plane on Indians, while the remaining authors focus exclusively on blacks and/or black/white relations (Brandwein, Goluboff, Mack, Polletta). In addition to explicit comparisons across racial groups, several of the articles in this subset consider how racial identity intersects with other bases of social status, namely, gender and sexuality (Mack, Plane) and social class (Calavita, Goluboff, Gómez, Mack, Polletta).

The resonance between this group of articles, as a subfield of law and society, and critical race theory and critical race theory is striking and evidenced by two common themes. The first theme involves the related claims that race is socially constructed and that law has played a major role in the construction of race. The second theme explores how race has shaped law, but race is operationalized in a more nuanced, complex way as *racial ideology* and *racial conflict*. In each section that follows, I first describe how critical race scholars have engaged these themes and then how this subset of law and society scholars has approached them.

LAW'S ROLE IN THE SOCIAL CONSTRUCTION OF RACE

It has become axiomatic that race is socially constructed, that racial classifications are historically contingent, the product of political contestation, and that, by definition, they are dynamic rather than fixed or essential. Yet this view of race has not been broadly accepted for long and, indeed, in law, race has been viewed at times in quite the opposite way. Supreme Court justices, taking a page from popular and scientific attitudes, often have viewed racial difference as rooted in essential and immutable characteristics, and this has had a profound and lasting affect on how lawyers, legal scholars, and others have viewed race. Only in recent decades and largely due to the pressure from both the more radical and mainstream elements of the mid-twentieth-century civil rights movement has there been a shift toward viewing racial categories as devoid of meaning and, as a result, recognizing that the intense meaning carried by those categories even today is the result of human interaction, politics, and social conflict (i.e., the result of social construction processes). And while the shift from viewing race as fixed and biological to viewing it as dynamic and historically contingent has been accomplished in the social sciences and, to an extent, in popular culture, mainstream legal scholarship and jurisprudence lag far behind.

Critical race scholars have been at the vanguard of legal scholars who have embraced the social constructionist perspective, even as they have emphasized that it does not lessen the historic or contemporary significance of race and racism (Alfieri, 1996; Calmore, 1992; Espinoza and Harris, 1997; Haney Lopez, 1994a, 1994b; Kang, 2000). In particular, critical race scholars have argued that law (in its varied forms as positive law, legal institutions, and law in action, to name just a few) has played a central role in the social construction of racial identity (Aoki, 1997; Carbado and Gulati, 2000, 2001a, 2001b; Gross, 1998; Montoya, 1998). Critical race scholars have documented the central role of law in shaping racial inequality (Johnson, 2000; Lee, 1996; Volpp, 2002). Others have emphasized law's role in the construction and reformulation of racial ideology, and vice versa (Gotanda, 1991; Harris, 1993).

Six of the eight law and society articles mentioned in the previous section expressly took up the theme of the social construction of race and law's role in the construction process (Calavita, 2000; Goluboff, 1999; Gómez, 2000; Mack, 1999; Plane, 1998; Poletta, 2000). Three of these authors (Calavita, Gómez, Mack) took this on as a central theme, and their focus on mid to late nineteenth-century law and society suggests the importance of this period's racial dynamics in shaping both historic and contemporary racial ideology in Supreme Court jurisprudence and in the USA generally.

In her essay on late nineteenth-century laws targeted at Chinese immigrants to the USA, sociologist Kitty Calavita begins with the premise that both race and social class are socially constructed and that they interact with each other in important, mutually constitutive ways (2000). "The most critical of these contradictions," she says, "involved paradoxical assumptions about race as a biological condition on one hand, but offset by class status on the other" (Calavita, 2000: 2). When Congress enacted a xenophobic ban on Chinese immigration in 1884, however, it targeted only Chinese laborers, leading those who applied the law to effectively carve out an exception for Chinese immigrants who could argue they were merchants rather than laborers. In this way, the administrative law in action created a space for Chinese immigrants to strategically construct their identities and to resist legislation widely acknowledged as racist in its orientation.

Calavita's dependent variable is the law in action or, specifically, how gatekeepers in the immigration service applied the Chinese exclusion law, given that the law on the books excluded only Chinese laborers. The inherent discretion delegated to immigration service workers may have softened the impact of the law, and such an outcome may or may not have been intended by members of Congress. (Calavita seems to take it for granted that Congress would not have wanted this loophole, but

I find it just as plausible to believe that some in Congress would have wanted immigration gatekeepers to broaden the exception, either to preserve the interests of American capitalists whose fortunes were linked to Chinese merchants or to soften the blow of the exclusion law for geopolitical reasons.) Thus the "paradox" to which Calavita refers in the title of her article arises because some Chinese immigrants successfully asserted membership in the merchant class despite being working class ("passing"), therefore circumventing the legislation's intent to exclude Chinese workers. She concludes that "the indeterminancy of law parallels and reflects (what is for all practical purposes) the indeterminancy of identity" (2000: 3).

Calavita builds upon critical race scholars' work on the social construction of race (whom she cites), but she ultimately does not sufficiently mine the critical race literature for its application to her work. For instance, she could have effectively drawn upon a growing literature within critical race scholarship that employs the notion of "performance" of race in a manner linked to her notion of "passing" (which was undertheorized in the article) and that takes seriously the intersection of racial, sexual, and class identities with which she is concerned (Carbado and Gulati, 2000, 2001a, 2001b; Gross, 1998, 2001).

Like Calavita, Mack (1999) takes seriously the ways in which racial identity was continually reconstituted based on intersections with other bases of identity (gender, social class). He is more explicit in building upon critical race theorists, whom he credits with two foundational insights: "that racially neutral laws and legal doctrines often perpetuate race and gender privilege, and that racial identity itself can be a creation of law" (Mack, 1999: 380). Mack uses railroad segregation practices as the context for studying the links between social mores, the law, and racial identity. He argues that the legally informal social practice of segregating public transportation (de facto segregation) that eventually led to a hardened segregation enshrined in state statutes (de jure segregation) both produced spaces for shaping black (and, less central in his analysis, white) identity.

Tennessee in the 1870s and 1880s, like most of the south, was characterized by a complex, sometimes contradictory, system of informal racial segregation in all walks of life, including the transportation sector. In this complexity, Mack identifies what amounted to flexibility for certain blacks to avoid some of the costs of segregation, often, according to him, by parlaying class and/or gender strategically. Prior to de jure segregation of common carriers, middle-class black men and, especially, black women sought to assert their rights to access to typically white-only "ladies' cars" on trains. But they faced a dilemma: "to gain access to ladies' cars and claim the mantle of respectability, they often had to appear subservient and deny that very respect-ability" (Mack, 1999: 390). After all, black women and men who accompanied white women as servants or employees had no problem gaining access to the ladies' cars; but middle-class blacks' respectability hinged in large part on their occupa-tional mobility away from precisely that kind of dependence on white employers (Mack, 1999: 390–3). Middle-class black women asserted their rights – and their respectability – by regularly bringing lawsuits against conductors and train com-panies for their exclusion from ladies' cars prior to the 1905 enactment of Tennes-see's first de jure segregation statute dealing with common carriers. Thus these women used legal strategies to affirm their identity as black and "respectable" (middle-class), and, in this way, law shaped racial identity.

One of the most fascinating aspects of Mack's analysis is the complexity of the interaction between class, race, gender, and sexuality. More specifically, sexual

stereotypes grounded in racist ideology very much shaped white demand for
segregation (*de facto* and *de jure*), as well as blacks' resistance to it. On the one
hand, both middle-class whites and blacks recognized the legitimacy of excluding
"jezebels" from the ladies' cars, though they disagreed mightily about which women
would fall into that category. "The image of the Jezebel, the sexually promiscuous
Black woman, helped solidify the identities of the white women riding in ladies' cars,
and possibly those of the white men as well . . . No ladylike treatment [by conduct-
ors] was necessary for presumed Jezebels" (Mack, 1999: 389). In bringing lawsuits
against their ejections from ladies' cars by conductors, black women fought against
this stereotype as applied to themselves, and in doing so may have solidified its
applicability to lower-class black women. Middle-class black men, too, faced sexual
stereotypes, as train employees and other whites often justified their exclusion from
ladies' cars by invoking the racist stereotype of the "black beast rapist" – "lustful,
predatory creatures who could not control their desire for white women" (Mack,
1999: 396).

In my article on territorial New Mexico (Gómez, 2000), I similarly explore the
role of law in the social construction of race and racial identity, but by situating the
analysis within the context of American colonization. The colonial transfer of power
from a Mexican sovereign to an American sovereign in mid-nineteenth-century New
Mexico provided the opportunity to explore the effects of the law in action in
constructing the numerically dominant group, Mexicans, in a number of contradictory ways: as both "native" and citizen, as both citizens and members of a racially
subordinate group (2000: 1140–4). The colonially imposed legal system provided
Mexican men with the incentive to claim whiteness and to disenfranchise Pueblo
Indian men, who, under Mexican positive law, had citizenship rights. In this sense,
the law shaped Mexicans' racial identity as legally "white," despite the social reality
of Mexicans' position as nonwhite in the larger American racial structure. (For
additional explorations of Mexicans' simultaneous claims of and distance from
whiteness, see Martinez, 1994, 1997, 1999). At the same time, other facets of the
colonial law in action shaped Mexicans' identity as racially subordinate to European
Americans who were both private citizens and appointees to the colonial government. I argue that a variety of criminal litigation processes spearheaded and, over
time, hardened Mexicans' collective identity as a group marked as "othered" and
racially inferior.

Michael Elliott expressly seeks to elaborate upon critical race theory insights and
to bring them into dialogue with the field of American studies (1999: 613). He
begins from the social constructionist position, contending that "those confronted
by issues of race and racial difference drew from a compendium of competing ideas,
ideas that were constantly being reshaped and redefined. Race, in other words, was
being continually reinvented – and some in the nineteenth century recognized this
process as surely as we do today" (Elliott, 1999: 614). Elliott uses a close reading of
two post-Civil War legal texts, published appellate decisions, to argue that judicial
opinions constituted an important source of construction and reformulation of
racial categories and racial identity.

Plane (1998) tells the story of a single legal struggle in early eighteenth-century
Massachusetts involving threats to an Indian leader's political authority for the
purposes of Anglo acquisition of grazing lands. The Indian leader, Jacob Seeknout,
appealed a county court's ruling that he return 420 sheep that he had impounded for
illegal grazing. In the process of the appeal, Seeknout's Anglo lawyer, Benjamin

Hawes, crafts a narrative in which he manipulates local Indian mating practices to conform to contemporary English norms and laws about paternity, legitimacy, and inheritance. Plane argues that, in so doing, the lawyers "managed to bring an order and a 'civility' to Indian practices of marriage in that century" that led both to his client's victory on appeal and the creation of "complementary racial identities" of some Indians as "civilized" and others as "savages" (1998: 58). Hawes's translation of Indian customs as "civilized," within the Anglo cultural and legal context, allowed for his client's legal victory, but ultimately functioned as a cultural straightjacket for Indians in the region who were not connected with the litigation. And, at the end of the day, Seeknout and his tribe lost the larger battle, since the Anglo lawyer took much of the disputed land as payment for his legal services.

Two additional law and society scholars (Goluboff, 1999; Polletta, 2000) explored how legal struggle shaped African Americans' racial identity, but they did so largely without drawing on the substantial, relevant literature produced by critical race theorists. Goluboff traces southern blacks' petitions, in the 1940s, to the federal government, claiming their children were being held as "peons" by Florida companies, in violation of the Thirteenth Amendment. Goluboff's agenda is an important one:

> [to] remind us that African Americans in World War II lived in a post-Plessy v. Ferguson, pre-Brown world in which the federal courts had not yet vindicated the rights of African Americans in any significant way, and the president had not yet dispatched troops on their behalf. In this pre-Brown world, claims to equality and federal protection against local injury were often emphatically denied. (1999: 781)

Thus, she argues, these unorganized efforts facilitated the emergence of rights-consciousness at the grass-roots level.

Goluboff's claim mirrors critical race scholars' responses to CLS claims about rights being illusory at best, and at worst contributing to the downfall of radical political movements. Crenshaw et al. (1995) recount this debate, in which critical race scholars parted ways with the CLS view of rights, rights discourse, and rights organizing as furthering a kind of false consciousness among people of color. According to crits, rights are problematic because they inherently are "indeterminate and capable of contradictory meanings" and, as a result, function to legitimize the status quo (Crenshaw et al., 1995: xxiii; see also Crenshaw, 1988). In sharp contrast, many scholars who attended the early critical race theory workshops believed that "the transformative dimension of African-Americans re-imagining themselves as full, rights-bearing citizens within the American political imagination" was a key part of a radical movement for social change (Crenshaw et al., 1995: xxiii–iv).

Goluboff's study essentially functions as an empirical test of that critical race claim, but it is weakened by her failure to expressly engage the critical race literature. In her study of black participants in the civil rights movement, Francesca Polletta (2000) takes up a similar project: to empirically test the critique of rights. Unlike Goluboff, Polletta squarely address the CLS claim that rights claiming and organizing around rights actually hurts radical politics. Unfortunately, she is not as comprehensive in drawing from critical race scholars: she cites an article by critical race scholar Patricia Williams, but she does not identify the critical race theory movement or cite the relevant work of other critical race scholars.

Despite this omission, Polletta's study is engaging and important. She isolates the CLS critique of rights around the idea that talk and organizing about rights essentially functions to deradicalize and coopt radical political movements. To test the claim, then, Polletta interviewed participants in the radical wing of the US civil rights movement, represented by organizations such as the Student Nonviolent Coordinating Committee (SNCC) and the Congress of Racial Equality (CORE). She explored how these activists understood the links between "rights, politics, and protest" (Polletta, 2000: 368), and she finds that rhetoric and activities centered around claims to be a "first class citizen" shaped black activists' racial identity and fueled (rather than inhibited) more radical political demands. Polletta identifies several conditions around rights claiming that were more likely to result in maintenance of a radical agenda: the relative autonomy of institutional arenas, organizers' distance from national centers of state and movement power, and interorganizational competition (2000: 380). But Polletta's seeming preoccupation with identifying only "color-blind" (or race-neutral) conditions ultimately leads her to overlook empirical exploration of how the race-based nature of these organizations' membership and goals might have blunted cooptation along the lines of the CLS critique.

How Race Shapes Law

I have argued that at least a subset of law and society scholars have begun to take seriously the insights of critical race theory as they relate to law's powerful role in constructing race, racial inequality, and racial identity. Yet for critical race scholars, this is only half of the equation; they are equally concerned with how race, in all its manifestations, has shaped the law. "Racial power, in our view, was not simply – or even primarily – a product of biased decision-making on the part of judges, but instead, the sum total of the pervasive ways in which *law shapes and is shaped by "race relations"* across the social plane" (Crenshaw et al., 1995: xxv). Thus, just as law and society scholars have argued that the dimensions of "law" and "society" are mutually constitutive (Munger, 1998), so too do critical race scholars take as axiomatic that race and law are mutually constitutive.

At one level, it might seem that this is quite similar to what I characterized as the traditional sociolegal studies approach to race: treat race as an independent variable that impacts law, as the dependent variable. But, as the quote above shows, thinking about how race shapes law involves more than simply analyzing judges' racial bias. Instead, critical race theory beckons a deeper, more complicated vision of "race." Rather than conceive of race – as quantitative social science studies often do, for instance – as an easily measurable, dichotomous independent variable, we should attempt, in terms of how we empirically operationalize race, to capture some of the complexity of race as a social reality that changes in different historical and social contexts.

One way in which critical race scholars have done this is to explore individual and group identity as multifaceted and, in so doing, view racial identity as intersecting with other identities, such as gender, sexual orientation, social class, and immigrant status (see Austin, 1989, 1992; Caldwell, 1991; Carbado, 2000, 2002b; Chang, 1993, 1999; Crenshaw 1989; Gross, 2001; Harris, 1990; Hutchinson, 1999, 2001, 2002; Iglesias and Valdes, 1998a, 1998b, 2000; Ikemoto, 1992, 1993; Johnson, 2002; Valdes, 1997a, 1997b, 2000; Volpp, 1994, 1996, 2001, 2002; Wing, 1997).

Another way to make race more complicated (and, hence, to more accurately map its impact in the real world) is to conceive of race as more than racial identity or racial categories, the ways in which social scientists typically operationalize race. For instance, critical race scholars have analyzed how race as *racial ideology* has shaped legal doctrine (Gotanda, 1991; Flagg, 1993; Harris, 1993; Lawrence, 1987, 1995).

In some respects, however, critical race scholars have not taken this approach to its logical conclusion and, in my view, this is due in part to a failure to engage methodologies common in law and society research. Thus law and society scholars who draw upon critical race insights are uniquely situated to carry this project forward. Judging by the articles in the historical subset of law and society work on race, the project is well under way.

Pamela Brandwein expressly incorporates insights from critical race theory into her work and cites contributing to critical race scholarship as one of the four benefits of her article (2000: 320). She documents the role of the ideology of white supremacy in shaping US Supreme Court doctrine on the Fourteenth Amendment and, specifically, in the Court's 1873 decision in the Slaughter-House Cases. Previous constitutional scholars and legal historians have emphasized these doctrinal developments as essentially stemming from conflicting interpretations of original intent, but, Brandwein argues, in so doing they have missed the most central influence on doctrine – that stemming from partisan conflict about race and African Americans' place in the nation. "The Northern Democratic narrative was shaped by a strong strain of white supremacy that denied black membership in "the people." Republican war narratives contained a weaker strain of white supremacy but also a commitment to black membership in the national collective" (Brandwein, 2000: 320). In the Slaughter-House Cases, the Supreme Court embraced the Democrats' narrative about the causes and effect of the Civil War and, in so doing, the "Northern Democrats' racial ideology was silently institutionalized in Reconstruction-era [Supreme] Court doctrine" (Brandwein, 2000: 316). Although the Republicans won the Civil War, Democrats espousing white supremacy won the war in the Supreme Court, which left its own powerful legacy in the form of a narrow and stilted equal protection doctrine that lingers today.

Michael Elliott (1999) also explores the role of racial ideology in the post-Civil War era, but with a focus on how white supremacy shaped the legal doctrine governing racial classification. The larger racial ideology of white supremacy was supported by "a single hypothesis necessary to the idea of race itself: that each individual belongs to a race and to only one race" (Elliott, 1999: 613). Whites could believe they were superior to blacks and other nonwhites only if they could be sure the demarcations between these groups had a hard meaning. And because a wide range of nineteenth-century laws were racially specific (e.g., miscegenation laws, voting law, citizenship requirements, etc.), "American judges throughout the nineteenth century were forced to tell narratives of racial taxonomy – legal opinions that set the boundaries marking particular bodies as white, black, Indian, and Asian" (Elliott, 1999: 614). In this way, the ideology of white supremacy (which was both a racial and a racist ideology) made law.

Three additional authors – Mack (1999), Calavita (2000) and Gómez (2000) – explore how race constitutes law by looking at the law in action rather than legal doctrine (for summaries of the articles, see above). In addition to revealing how law shaped African American identity in late nineteenth-century Tennessee, Mack's study is equally impressive in demonstrating that racial conflict and racialized social patterns over a 30-year period shaped the judicial and legislative responses that eventually culminated in state-mandated segregation of common carriers. Because of the US Supreme Court's 1896 holding that such statutes comported with the Fourteenth Amendment in *Plessy v. Ferguson*, we tend to see these processes as inevitable historical movements, but Mack's work shows that this is anything but true. Instead, racial identity and racial conflict evolved in complex and often contradictory ways, and how they affected the law must be explored in highly contextualized, locally situated sites of social action.

Calavita's study is similar to Mack's in foregrounding the complexities of the interaction between racial identity and the law. But her work differs from his in its emphasis on the agency of legal system actors – customs workers who functioned, literally, as gatekeepers to the nation. These legal workers' own racial reality (i.e., how they conceived of themselves racially and how they conceived of racial "others," especially potential Chinese immigrants to the USA) was a powerful force in how they implemented the Chinese Exclusion Act, given that they had great discretion to decide who fit the exception to being a Chinese "laborer." In this way, racial identity had a powerful impact on the law in action.

My study focuses a great deal on race as *racial conflict*, specifically, social conflict between European Americans and Mexicans, who were racialized as inferior to their American colonizers (Gómez, 2000; see also Gómez, 2002). New Mexico Territory's demographic character as majority Mexican, combined with the fact that Mexican men had citizenship rights, created a unique situation for colonizers bent on the consolidation of American political and legal authority in the region. The result, at least in one northeastern county, was the creation of what I term a racial power-sharing regime that governed the administration of the criminal justice system (2000: 1164–76). Racial conflict, then, shaped law by resulting in the institutional-ization of Mexican participation in a variety of ways, including as the majority of grand and petit jurors. One of the strongest symbols of Mexicans' major role in the criminal justice system was the prominence of the Spanish language in trials and in other legal proceedings. At the same time, the highest levels of the system were controlled exclusively by European American newcomers to the region, who held the appellate and trial judgeships (that were one and the same) and who made up the vast majority of the bar.

CONCLUSION

If the articles published in the field's two most important journals are representative, it appears that law and society scholars are lagging behind in their recognition of and engagement with the ideas of the emergent critical race literature. Although law and society has in some senses moved away from a staunch positivist tradition to embrace a set of more ecumenical methodologies (Handler, 1992), law and society scholarship on race seems not yet to have found a new course. My hope is that those of us writing about race from within the field will look carefully at critical race theory to see whether it provides new questions and new approaches.

I am encouraged that a subset of scholarship that is historical in its approach *is* engaging and building upon this literature. These works prove that at least some law and society scholars are taking critical race theory seriously, and I hope this analysis has persuaded the reader that their venturing into this legal genre has been intellectually profitable. In many respects, the much more pronounced engagement of critical race theory by sociolegal scholars doing historical research makes sense given the centrality of history within critical race theory. Explorations of history and historical methodologies have been deployed in a range of contexts by critical race scholars (Cho, 1998; Iijima, 1998; Gotanda, 1991; Harris, 1993; Martinez, 1994, 1999; Yamamoto, 1998). Crenshaw et al. argue that, for critical race scholars, historical inquiries have been a means of showing "that the contemporary structure of civil rights rhetoric is not the natural or inevitable meaning of racial justice but, instead, a collection of strategies and discourses born of and deployed in particular political, cultural, and institutional conflicts and negotiations" (Crenshaw et al., 1995: xvi).

Note

I am grateful to my colleagues Rick Abel and Devon Carbado for their feedback on this essay.

References

Abel, R (ed.) (1995a) *The Law & Society Reader.* New York and London: New York University Press.
Abel, R. (1995b) *Politics by Other Means: Law in the Struggle Against Apartheid, 1980–1994.* New York and London: Routledge.
Alfieri, A.V. (1996) "Race-ing legal ethics," *Columbia Law Review* 96: 800–7.
Alfieri, A.V. (1998) "Race trials," *Texas Law Review* 76: 1293–369.
Alfieri, A.V. (1999) "Prosecuting race," *Duke Law Journal* 48: 1157–253.
Alfieri, A.V. (2001) "Race prosecutors, race defenders," *Georgetown Law Journal* 89: 2227–77.
Ammons, L.L. (1995) "Mules, madonnas, babies, bath water, racial imagery and stereotypes: The African-American woman and the battered woman syndrome," *Wisconsin Law Review* 1995: 1003–80.
Aoki, K. (1997) "Critical legal studies movement, Asian Americans in U.S. law and culture, Neil Gotanda, and me," *Asian Law Journal* 4: 19–38.
Austin, R. (1988) "Employer abuse, worker resistance and the tort of intentional infliction of emotional distress," *Stanford Law Review* 41: 1–58.
Austin, R. (1989) "Sapphire bound!" *Wisconsin Law Review* 1989: 539–78.
Austin, R. (1992) "'The black community', its lawbreakers and a politics of identification," *Southern California Law Review* 65: 1769–817.
Banks, R.R. (1998) "The color of desire: Fulfilling adoptive parents' racial preferences through discriminatory station action," *Yale Law Journal* 107: 875–964.
Bell, D. (1992) *Race, Racism and American Law.* Boston, Toronto, and London: Little, Brown.
Brandwein, P. (2000) "Slavery as an interpretive issue in the reconstruction congresses," *Law & Society Review* 34: 315–66.
Brooks, R.L. (1994) "Critical race theory: A proposed structure and application to federal pleading," *Harvard Blackletter Journal* 11: 85–113.
Bumiller, K. (1988) *The Civil Rights Society: The Social Construction of Victims.* Baltimore: Johns Hopkins University Press.

Butler, P. (1995) "Racially based jury nullification: Black power in the criminal justice system," *Yale Law Journal* 105: 677–725.

Bybee, K.J. (2000) "The political significance of legal ambiguity: The case of affirmative action," *Law & Society Review* 34: 263–90.

Calavita, K. (2000) "The paradoxes of race, class, identity and 'passing': Enforcing the Chinese Exclusion Acts, 1882–1910," *Law and Social Inquiry* 25: 1–40.

Caldwell, P.M. (1991) "A hair piece: Perspectives on the intersection of race and gender," *Duke Law Journal* 1991: 365–96.

Calmore, J.O. (1992) "Critical race theory, Archie Shepp, and fire music: Securing an authentic intellectual life in a multicultural world," *Southern California Law Review* 65: 2129–229.

Carbado, D.W. (2000) "Black rights, gay rights, civil rights," *UCLA Law Review* 47: 1467–1519.

Carbado, D.W. (2002a) "(E)racing the Fourth Amendment," *Michigan Law Review* 100: 946–1044.

Carbado, D.W. (2002b) "Race to the bottom," *UCLA Law Review* 49: 1283–312.

Carbado, D.W. and Gulati, M. (2000) "Working identity," *Cornell Law Review* 85: 1259–308.

Carbado, D.W. and Gulati, M. (2001a) "Conversations at work," *Oregon Law Review* 79: 103–45.

Carbado, D.W. and Gulati, M. (2001b) "The fifth black woman," *Journal of Contemporary Legal Issues* 11: 701–29.

Chang, R.S. (1993) "Toward an Asian American legal scholarship: Critical race theory, poststructuralism, and narrative space," *California Law Review* 81: 1241–323

Chang, R.S. (1999) *Disoriented: Asian Americans, Law, and the Nation-State.* New York and London: New York University Press.

Cho, S. (1998) "Redeeming whiteness in the shadow of internment: Earl Warren, Brown, and a theory of racial redemption," *Boston College Third World Law Journal* 19: 73–170.

Crenshaw, K. (1988) "Race, reform, and retrenchment: Transformation and legitimation in antidiscrimination law," *Harvard Law Review* 101: 1331–87.

Crenshaw, K. (1989) "Demarginalizing the intersection of race and sex: A black feminist critique of antidiscrimination doctrine, feminist theory and antiracist politics," *University of Chicago Legal Forum* 1989: 139–87.

Crenshaw, K., Gotanda, N., Peller, G., and Thomas, K. (eds.) (1995) *Critical Race Theory: The Key Writings That Formed the Movement.* New York: The New Press.

Daly, K. (1987) "Structure and practice of familial-based justice in a criminal court," *Law & Society Review* 21: 267–89.

Daly, K. (1994) *Gender, Crime and Punishment.* New Haven, CT and London: Yale University Press.

Daly, K. (1998) "Black women, white justice," in A. Sarat, M. Constable, D. Engel, V. Hans, and S. Lawrence (eds.), *Crossing Boundaries: Traditions and Transformations in Law and Society Research.* Evanston, IL, Northwestern University Press and The American Bar Foundation, pp. 209–39.

Delgado, R. (1984) "The imperial scholar: Reflections on a review of civil rights literature," *University of Pennsylvania Law Review* 132: 561–78.

Delgado, R. (1992) " 'The imperial scholar' revisited: How to marginalize outsider writing, ten years later," *University of Pennsylvania Law Review* 140: 1349–72.

Delgado, R. (ed.) (1995) *Critical Race Theory: The Cutting Edge.* Philadelphia: Temple University Press.

Elliott, M. (1999) "Telling the difference: Nineteenth-century legal narrative of racial taxonomy," *Law and Social Inquiry* 24: 611–34.

Espinoza, L. and Harris, A.P. (1997) "Afterword: Embracing tar-baby – litcrit theory and the sticky mess of race," *California Law Review* 85: 1585.

Fineman, M.A. (1995) *The Neutered Mother, the Sexual Family, and Other Twentieth Century Tragedies*. New York and London: Routledge.

Flagg, B.J. (1993) "'Was blind but now I see': White race consciousness and the requirement of discriminatory intent," *Michigan Law Review* 91: 953–1017.

Galanter, M. (1975) "Why the 'haves' come out ahead: Speculations on the limits of legal change," *Law & Society Review* 9: 95–160.

Glenn, B.J. (2000) "The shifting rhetoric of insurance denial," *Law & Society Review* 34: 779–808.

Goluboff, R. (1999) " 'Won't you please help me get my son home': Peonage, patronage, and protest in the World War II urban south," *Law and Social Inquiry* 24: 777–802.

Gómez, L.E. (2000) "Race, colonialism and criminal law: Mexicans and the American criminal justice system in Territorial New Mexico," *Law & Society Review* 34: 1129–202.

Gómez, L.E. (2002) "Race mattered: Racial formation and the politics of crime in Territorial New Mexico," *UCLA Law Review* 49: 1395–416.

Gotanda, N. (1991) "A critique of 'Our constitution is color-blind'," *Stanford Law Review* 44: 1–68.

Gross, A.J. (1998) "Litigating whiteness: Trials of racial determination in the nineteenth-century south," *Yale Law Journal* 108: 109–86.

Gross, A.J. (2001) "Beyond black and white: Cultural approaches to race and slavery," *Columbia Law Review* 101: 640–89.

Handler, J.F. (1978) *Social Movements and the Legal System: A Theory of Law Reform and Social Change*. New York: Academic Press.

Handler, J.F. (1992) "Postmodernism, protest, and the new social movements," *Law and Society Review* 26: 697–730.

Haney-Lopez, I.F. (1994a) *White by Law: The Legal Construction of Race*. New York: New York University Press.

Haney-Lopez, I.F. (1994b) "The social construction of race: Some observations on illusion, fabrication, and choice," *Harvard Civil Rights-Civil Liberties Law Review* 29: 1–62.

Haney-Lopez, I.F. (2000) "Institutional racism: Judicial conduct and a new theory of racial discrimination," *Yale Law Journal* 109: 1717–883.

Harris, A.P. (1990) "Race and essentialism in feminist legal theory," *Stanford Law Review* 42: 581–616.

Harris, A.P. (2000) "Gender, violence, race, and criminal justice," *Stanford Law Review* 52: 777–807.

Harris, C.I. (1993) "Whiteness as property," *Harvard Law Review* 106: 1707–91.

Harris, C.I. (2002) "Critical race studies: An introduction," *UCLA Law Review* 49: 1215–36.

Hutchinson, D.L. (1999) "Ignoring the sexualization of race: Heteronormativity, critical race theory and anti-racist politics," *Buffalo Law Review* 47: 1–116.

Hutchinson, D.L. (2001) "Identity crisis: 'Intersectionality,' 'multidimensionality,' and the development of an adequate theory of subordination," *Michigan Journal of Race & Law* 6: 285–317.

Hutchinson, D.L. (2002) "Progressive race blindness?: Individual identity, group politics and reform," *UCLA Law Review* 49: 1455–80.

Iglesias, E.M. (1998) "Out of the shadow: Marking intersections in and between Asian Pacific American critical legal scholarship and latina/o critical legal theory," *Boston College Law Review* 40: 349–83.

Iglesias, E.M. and Valdes, F. (1998) "Religion, gender, sexuality, race and class in coalitional theory: A critical and self-critical analysis of Latcrit social justice agendas," *Chicano-Latino Law Review* 19: 503–88.

Iglesias, E.M. and Valdes, F. (2000) "Expanding directions, exploding parameters: Culture and nation in Latcrit coalitional imagination," *Michigan Journal of Race & Law* 5: 787–816.

Iijima, C.K. (1998) "Reparations and the 'model minority' ideology of acquiescence: The necessity to refuse the return to original humiliation," *Boston College Third World Law Journal* 19: 385–427.

Ikemoto, L.C. (1992) "The code of perfect pregnancy: At the intersection of motherhood, the practice of defaulting to science, and the intervention mindset of law," *Ohio State Law Journal* 53: 1205–306.

Ikemoto, L.C. (1993) "Furthering the inquiry: Race, class, and culture in the forced medical treatment of pregnant women," *Tennessee Law Review* 59: 487–517.

Johnson, K.R. (2000) "The case against race profiling in immigration enforcement," *Washington University Law Quarterly* 78: 675–736.

Johnson, K.R. (2002) "The end of 'civil rights' as we know it?: Immigration and civil rights in the new millennium," *UCLA Law Review* 49: 1481–511.

Johnson, S.L. (1993) "Racial imagery in criminal cases," *Tulane Law Review* 67: 1739–805.

Johnson, S.L. (1998) "Batson ethics for prosecutors and trial court judges," *Chicago-Kent Law Review* 73: 475–507.

Kairys, D. (1982) (ed.) *The Politics of Law: A Progressive Critique*. New York: Pantheon.

Kang, J. (2000) "Cyber-race," *Harvard Law Review* 113: 1130–208.

Lawrence, C.R. III (1987) "The id, the ego, and equal protection: Reckoning with unconscious racism," *Stanford Law Review* 39: 317–88.

Lawrence, C.R. III (1995) "Foreword: Race, multiculturalism, and the jurisprudence of transformation," *Stanford Law Review* 47: 819–47.

Lee, C.K.Y. (1996) "Race and self defense: Toward a normative conception of reasonableness," *Minnesota Law Review* 81: 367–500.

Mack, K.W. (1999) "Law, society, identity and the making of the Jim Crow south: Travel and segregation on Tennessee railroads, 1875–1905," *Law and Social Inquiry* 24: 377–409.

Martinez, G.A. (1994) "Legal indeterminacy, judicial discretion and the Mexican-American litigation experience: 1930–1980," *UC Davis Law Review* 27: 555–618.

Martinez, G.A. (1997) "The legal construction of race: Mexican-Americans and whiteness," *Harvard Latino Law Review* 2: 321–47.

Martinez, G.A. (1999) "Latinos, assimilation and the law: A philosophical perspective," *Chicano-Latino Law Review* 20: 1–34.

Matsuda, M.J. (2000) "On causation," *Columbia Law Review* 100: 2195–220.

McCann, M.W. (1994) *Rights at Work: Pay Equity Reform and the Politics of Legal Mobilization*. Chicago and London: University of Chicago Press.

Meares, Tracey L. (1998) "Social organization and drug law enforcement," *American Criminal Law Review* 35: 191–227.

Montoya, M.E. (1998) "Border/ed identities: Narrative and the social construction of legal and personal identities," in A. Sarat, M. Constable, D. Engel, V. Hans, and S. Lawrence (eds.), *Crossing Boundaries: Traditions and Transformations in Law and Society Research*. Evanston, IL, Northwestern University Press and The American Bar Foundation, pp. 129–59.

Moran, B.I. and Whitford, W. (1996) "A black critique of the Internal Revenue Service," *Wisconsin Law Review* 1996: 751–820.

Moran, R. (2001) *Interracial Intimacy: The Regulation of Race and Romance*. Chicago and London: University of Chicago Press.

Morrill, C., Yalda, C., Adelman, M., Musheno, M. and Bejarano, C. (2000) "Telling tales in school: Youth culture and conflict narratives," *Law & Society Review* 34: 521–65.

Munger, F. (1998) "Mapping law and society," in A. Sarat, M. Constable, D. Engel, V. Hans, and S. Lawrence (eds.), *Crossing Boundaries: Traditions and Transformations in Law and Society Research*. Evanston, IL, Northwestern University Press and The American Bar Foundation, pp. 21–80.

Nielsen, L.B. (2000) "Situating legal consciousness: Experiences and attitudes of ordinary citizens about law and street harassment," *Law & Society Review* 34: 1055–90.

Oberweis, T. and Musheno, M. (1999) "Policing identities: Cop decision making and the constitution of citizens," *Law and Social Inquiry* 24: 897–923.

Perea, J., Delgado, R., Harris, A.P., and Wildman, S. (eds.) (2000) *Race and Races: Cases and Resources for a Multiracial America*. St. Paul, MN: West Group.

Perry, T.L. (1993) "The transracial adoption controversy: An analysis of discourse and subordination," *New York University Review of Law & Social Change* 21: 33–108.

Perry, T.L. (1994) "Alimony, race, privilege, and dependency in the search for theory," *Georgetown Law Journal* 82: 2481–520.

Phillips, S. and Grattet, R. (2000) "Judical rhetoric, meaning-making, and the institutionalization of hate crime law," *Law & Society Review* 34: 567–606.

Plane, A.M. (1998) "Legitimacies, Indian identities and the law: The politics of sex and the creation of history in Colonial New England," *Law and Social Inquiry* 23: 55–77.

Plessy v. Ferguson (1896) 163 U.S. 537.

Polletta, F. (2000) "The structural context of novel rights claims: Southern civil rights organizing, 1961–1966," *Law & Society Review* 34: 367–406.

Provine, D.M. (1998) "Too many black men: The sentencing judge's dilemma," *Law and Social Inquiry* 23: 823–56.

Roberts, D. (1997) *Killing the Black Body: Race, Reproduction, and the Meaning of Liberty*. New York: Pantheon Books.

Romero, F.S. (2000) "The Supreme Court and the protection of minority rights: An empirical examination of racial discrimination cases," *Law & Society Review* 34: 291–313.

Rosen, J. (1996) "The bloods and the crits," *New Republic*, 9 December: 27.

Sarat, A. (1990) "The law is all over: Power, resistance and legal consciousness of the welfare poor," *Yale Journal of Law and the Humanities* 2: 343–79.

Sarat, A., Constable, C., Engel, D., Hans, V., and Lawrence, S. (eds.) (1998) *Crossing Boundaries: Traditions and Transformations in Law and Society Research*. Evanston, IL, Northwestern University Press and The American Bar Foundation.

Spitzer, S. (1983) "Marxist perspectives in the sociology of law," *Annual Review of Sociology* 9: 103–23.

Valdes, F. (1997a) "Foreword: Under construction – Latcrit consciousness, community, and theory," *California Law Review* 85: 1087–142.

Valdes, F. (1997b) "Queer margins, queer ethics: A call to account for race and ethnicity in the law, theory, and politics of 'sexual orientation'," *Hastings Law Journal* 48: 1293–341.

Valdes, F. (2000) "Race, ethnicity, and Hispanismo in a triangular perspective: The 'essential Latina/o' and Latcrit theory," *UCLA Law Review* 48: 305–52.

Valdes, F., Culp, J.M., and Harris, A.P. (eds.) (2002) *Crossroads, Directions and a New Critical Race Theory*. Philadelphia: Temple University Press.

Volpp, L. (1974) "(Mis)identifying culture: Asian women and the 'cultural defense'," *Harvard Women's Law Journal* 17: 57–101.

Volpp, L. (1996) "Talking 'culture': Gender, race, nation, and the politics of multiculturalism," *Columbia Law Review* 96: 1573–617.

Volpp, L. (2001) "Feminism vs. multiculturalism," *Columbia Law Review* 101: 1181–218.

Volpp, L. (2002) "The citizen and the terrorist," *UCLA Law Review* 49: 1575–99.

Weitzer, R. (2000) "Racialized policing: Residents' perceptions in three neighborhoods," *Law & Society Review* 34: 129–55.

West, C. (1995) "Introduction," in K. Crenshaw, N. Gotanda, G. Peller, and K. Thomas (eds.), *Critical Race Theory: The Key Writings That Formed the Movement*. New York: The New Press.

Williams, P.J. (1991) *The Alchemy of Race and Rights*. Cambridge, MA and London: Harvard University Press.

Wing, A.K. (1997) "Conceptualizing violence: Present and future developments in international law: Panel III," *Albany Law Review* 60: 943–76.

Yamamoto, E.K. (1998) "Racial reparations: Japanese American redress and African American claims," *Boston College Law Review* 40: 477–523.

Yamamoto, E.K., Chon, M., Izumi, C.L., Kang, J., Wu, F.H. (eds.) (2001) *Race, Rights and Reparation: Law and the Japanese American Internment*. Gaithersburg, NY: Aspen Publishers.

Yamamoto, E.K. and Lyman, J.W. (2001) "Racializing environmental justice," *University of Colorado Law Review* 72: 311–60.

25

The Constitution of Identity: Gender, Feminist Legal Theory, and the Law and Society Movement

Nicola Lacey

The antecedents of feminist legal scholarship are probably more diverse than those of any other significant theoretical paradigm in contemporary legal studies. Feminist legal theory has grown – albeit to different degrees in different parts of the world – out of relatively autonomous social and political movements as well as out of a range of intellectual movements in philosophy, in political and social theory, in sociology and anthropology, and in law. In Australian, European, and North American contexts, the genesis of feminist legal theory has been closely associated with that of a group of philosophically inspired approaches to legal scholarship which, though themselves diverse, may conveniently be identified as "critical legal studies." The political and policy-oriented commitments of feminist writers, however, have generally entailed a greater degree of engagement with empirical and material questions than has been the case within much nonfeminist critical legal theory. For this reason among others, feminist scholarship has had a central place not only within critical legal studies but also within the law and society or sociolegal movements of many countries (see, e.g., Bumiller, 1988; Daly, 1994; Fineman, 1991, 1994; Smart, 1995).

Over the last decade, however, a number of key theoretical and practical questions have arisen out of feminist scholarship's dual engagement with philosophical and with sociopolitical questions. A heightened (and generally welcome) sensitivity to questions of difference and identity has generated an important set of intellectual debates across the contested borderlines of feminist theory, critical race theory, queer theory, and postcolonialism, and feminist scholars have become important contributors to the debates about the politics of identity and about multiculturalism that have come to occupy such a central place in the academy in recent years. One important strand within this genre of feminist scholarship has drawn on the insights of post-structuralist philosophy to explore the ways in which embodied femininities are materialized and enacted within powerful social discourses such as law. Yet other feminists have begun to register signs of discomfort with the radically construction-ist approach to feminine (and other) identities, and to argue for a re-engagement with material questions such as the distribution of resources and the allocation of political and legal power. Within this dynamic tension, the international movement arguing for human rights for women – both as a matter of the interpretation of national constitutions and in the development of international standards in contexts such as war and enforced migration – has come to occupy a particularly significant place.

   In this essay, I shall set out and assess these contrasting dynamics within current feminist scholarship, examining in particular their implications for the potential contributions of feminist studies to law and society scholarship. Implicit in my argument is a view of feminist legal theory as a broad set of approaches identified not so much by an autonomous methodology as by the distinctive substantive questions that it places on the agenda of sociolegal scholarship.

FEMINIST LEGAL THEORY AND THE CONSTITUTION OF THE GENDERED LEGAL SUBJECT

The gradual development of feminist legal scholarship from its early project of placing issues of special concern to women on the scholarly, pedagogic, and reform agenda, through its concern to analyze more systematically the role of gender in shaping the form, content, and operation of legal rules and arrangements, has been much analyzed in published work. By the mid-1980s, it is generally accepted that feminist scholarship had become a well-established and self-confident field: a dis-tinctive though theoretically eclectic genre related to, yet in productive critical dialogue with, other radical and interdisciplinary movements such as critical legal studies and sociolegal scholarship. Its roots in a social movement and a set of political commitments lent it a particularly strong orientation to exploring the links between theory and practice. This feature strengthened the relationship be-tween feminist and law and society scholarship engaged in the analysis of not only legal doctrine but also the legal institutions and practices within which law is interpreted and enforced. On the other hand, feminist legal theory's institutional relationship, both in Europe and in North America, with the more philosophically oriented scholarship associated with critical legal theory, entailed a strong engage-ment with debates in philosophy, social theory, and psychoanalysis. It is this engagement that, arguably, has most decisively shaped feminist legal scholarship over the last 15 years, and that has been of particular importance in identifying the question of law's role in the constitution of gendered identities, and of the complex intersections between gender and factors such as race, culture, class, and sexual orientation. For this reason, and because this development has posed some interest-ing challenges to received ideas of the relationship between theory and practice in feminist scholarship, it merits close analysis.

   It is useful to distinguish between three somewhat different ways of thinking about law as a social site for the construction and enactment (in the broadest sense) of gendered identities. The first is *analytic*: an important stream in contem-porary feminist legal scholarship moves away from the simple idea that subjects arrive in the legal arena already constituted as women or men, as gay or straight within other social practices, with law merely confirming, overtly or covertly, the effects of these extralegal vectors of power. Rather, the argument is that law plays an active, dynamic role in shaping gendered (sexually oriented, raced, and so on) subjects: that its categories, rules, institutional arrangements, modes of reasoning and analysis, make a decisive and productive difference to the kinds of subjects we think of ourselves as being, and to the kinds of social subjects that we can be. There are therefore two distinctive, albeit related, aspects to the analytic claim about law's role in constituting gendered identity. On the one hand, law has a positive role in creating and authorizing sex/gender identity in the sense of the relatively stable ways in which we think of ourselves and our relations to others and to the social world. On the other, law plays a negative role in constraining the kinds of sexed social subjects which we can be.

On this view, gendered identities are, hence, in an important sense an *effect* of powerful social discourses such as law. To say, for example, that the law of rape discriminates against women, or perpetuates stereotypes of women, or fails to respect women's autonomy or rights, is to oversimplify. For, in a specific sense, the law of rape is also what makes women rapable: the way in which the definition of rape works – in particular the emphasis on consent and nonconsent, and the exclusions marked by the rules of evidence, which block the articulation of other narratives – constitutes a subject position into which the rape victim is inserted: the only "speakable" subjectivity is that endorsed by and enacted within prevailing legal arrangements (Lacey, 1998: ch 4). Much of this genre of analysis has been inspired by the post-structuralist philosophy of Michel Foucault (Foucault, 1981) and by its distinctive development in Judith Butler's work (Butler, 1993). A yet more structural line of analysis, also drawn upon by Butler and influential in the work of legal feminists such as Drucilla Cornell, is that flowing from Lacanian psychoanalysis (Cornell, 1995). On this approach, the sexually specific structure of the subject's entry into language is such as to silence women's distinctive *jouissance*: the acceptance of the "law of the father" entails women's position of abjection – a position radically realized, in the view of some theorists, within the law of the state.

This insight into the dynamic role of law in constituting gendered identities has combined, secondly, with feminism's political commitments to produce a flourishing genre of scholarship engaged in *critique* of the various aspects of current, gendered, legal subjectification. The shape of the female (or, in queer or critical race theory, gay or black) identities produced by legal discourse are elicited and analyzed and, within a feminist normative framework, their silencing, oppressive, constraining, dignity-denying, insulting, or otherwise unappealing features subjected to vigorous critique (Bumiller, 1997; Smart, 1995). Within this genre we find, for example, powerful analyses of the promiscuous, dangerous, gay sexual subjectivities; the eroticized passivity of female sexuality, and the possessive, imperative male sexual identity enacted in criminal law; the impoverished and dependent female and black social identities enacted in family and social welfare law; the victim-litigant of antidiscrimination law; the atomistic and proprietary legal subjectivity that infuses areas of law ranging from contract through property to human rights. As these examples suggest, both the analytic framework deployed and the normative commitments that inform this scholarship entail a broad set of interactions and alliances between feminist scholarship and scholarship focused on other axes of differentiation, domination, or injustice in social arrangements.

A further genre of feminist legal scholarship builds out from the normative commitments underpinning this critique to develop, thirdly, a *reconstructive* project. The radically constructive nature of legal discourses, rules, and institutional arrangements is, on this view, double-edged: the very institution that currently enacts oppressive gender identities can be reconstructed to enable and express different visions of gender, of sexuality, of human subjectivity. The subject that is, according to the first genre described above, an *effect* of legal discourse can, in a beautiful (but, as we shall see, not untroubling) paradox, turn the tables and deploy legal language, legal institutions, legal reforms to enact new (and more normatively satisfactory) gendered/sexed identities. Within the reconstructive genre, we also need to distinguish between what we might call *normative* or *conceptual* reconstruction and *institutional reconstruction* or *reform*. Normative reconstruction is oriented to the reinterpretation of the conceptual building blocks – rights, autonomy, sovereignty, harassment (Nedelsky, 1993; Knop, 1993; Schultz, 1998) out of which legal identities and classifications are constructed. Institutional reconstruction is oriented to the redesign of legal rules or institutions, based on normative principles and/or empirical insights. This distinction is, of course, not clear-cut; it is plausible to think that all instances of institutional reconstruction are in some sense premised on projects of normative reconstruction. Within feminist legal scholarship, however, there is an important difference in emphasis – and perhaps in principle (see Lacey, 1998: ch. 8) – between writers who regard the development of reformist policy blueprints as part of their project and those who confine themselves to normative reconstruction. In work that combines the analytic, critical, and reconstructive modes of analysis, feminist theory aspires to have it both ways: to assume the post-structuralist subject constituted as an effect of (inter alia) legal discourse, while prescribing a politics shaped in terms of a more assertive and perhaps liberal conception of subjective agency. This takes us to a later stage in the progression of my argument; before pursuing this point, it will be useful to sketch an analysis of the implications of the first, analytic, genre identified in this section for feminist legal praxis.

Sex/Gender as an Effect of Legal Discourse/ Language: Implications for Feminist Legal Praxis

In this section, I shall for the most part leave aside the Lacanian strand and focus on the more moderate and (to me at least) more persuasive version of the thesis which I take to be broadly Foucauldian. Notwithstanding its analytic power, and indeed its pervasive influence on feminist legal scholarship, the analysis of sex/gender as an effect of law or legal discourse has given rise to a significant set of theoretical and practical problems. Four may usefully be distinguished and considered. First, it has been argued that the effort to analyze the ways in which legal rules, categories, and arrangements constrain the articulation of social identities and produce authorized identities has left feminist legal theory without a conception of active and autonomous agency which is in fact crucial to the practice of feminist politics (Frazer and Lacey, 1993: chs. 4–6; Lacey, 1998: ch. 5; Benhabib, 1992). If the subject and her identity are so firmly embedded in, so comprehensively produced by, powerful social discourses such as law, how can oppositional subjectivities and identities be imagined, let alone acted upon? Is the constructed subject, in short, a passive, victimized, engulfed subject? The facts of feminist and other oppositional forms of consciousness over the centuries belie such a conclusion, but the question remains as to how the constructivist analysis can accommodate an adequate conception of subjectivity as in critical dialogue with the institutions that produce it. In philosophical terms, there is in other words an anxiety that post-structuralism shades into structuralism, with all its attendant difficulties.

Secondly, the insight that crucial features of identity such as sex/gender are produced within social practices such as law goes hand in hand with the insight that there are significant interaction effects between class, sex/gender, race/ethnicity, and so on in the production of social identities. While this clearly does nothing to undermine the importance of sex/gender as one line of analysis, it both opens up important questions about the nature of these various intersections, while also posing a difficulty for the political stance of feminism as devoted – simply put – to the analysis and dismantling of women's oppression. If women's oppression is not simply women's oppression, but relative to a cluster of other vectors, what happens, as it were, to the feminist subject (Harris, 1990; Kapur, 1999)? A problem of political fragmentation appears to sit alongside the first problem of political passivity. The seemingly interminable debate in feminist philosophy about the so-called problem of "essentialism" is testimony to the fact that this issue has theoretical as well as political ramifications (Fuss, 1989).

Thirdly, it has been argued that the focus in feminist theory on sex/gender as an effect of discourse has had a distorting effect on the balance of concerns within both feminist analysis and feminist politics. The distributive questions – questions about equality, about political voice, and about women's entitlements to access to and fair shares of the material conditions for fulfilling lives – which have long been central to the feminist cause, have arguably become somewhat eclipsed by a conception of the feminist ideal as a demand for cultural recognition comparable to the claims articulated by distinctive ethnic or religious groups. There has been a slippage, moreover, between the analytic claim that discourses such as law produce identities, and the claim that identity – in this case feminine identity – has a *value* (sometimes instrumental, sometimes intrinsic) that is not adequately captured by the analytic framework of preferences or interests and that merits independent recognition. The claim that feminine identity should be opened up, reconstructed, and empowered – that feminine values be respected (claims that, evidently, invoke once again the specter of essentialism) – may be seen to reconstitute feminism as one aspect of the politics of multiculturalism; the "essence" of the feminist complaint is the assertion that women's "authentic" identity has been repressed in the social practices that enact and authorize prevailing sex/gender norms (Fraser, 1997).

Finally, particularly among feminists strongly committed to the institutionally reconstructive project identified in the last section, there has been a widespread perception that the broader post-structuralist positions that feed productively into the analysis of sex/gender as constituted by social discourses and practices have nonetheless obstructed the full development of the normative, reconstructive, political aspects of feminism. The focus on the ways in which social discourses produce relatively autonomous systems of knowledge and authorize particular claims to truth, it is argued, have become associated with a form of cultural relativism or at least with a tentativeness about our own commitments as themselves potentially repressive, violent "regimes of truth" (Nussbaum, 1999: ch. 1). This in turn is argued to have led to a range of ills, spanning parochialism through political passivity to a wholesale rejection of the normative project itself in which the political space apparently opened up by feminism is blocked, and projects of institutional reform reconceived in terms of utopian (in the literal sense) fantasies that resemble a form of aesthetics (Barron, 2000).

These four objections are, evidently, not only distinct but also to some extent inconsistent with each other. For example, the idea that identity analysis has under-cut or fragmented the subject of feminist politics sits unhappily with the critique of feminist politics as unduly concerned with questions of recognition. I am distilling here what I see as the main themes within a diverse literature, and in the next section I shall try to separate out the various strands of objection in considering various responses in contemporary feminist theory and politics. But before moving on, I would like to mention a further concern about the focus on sex/gender as an effect of legal discourse, one which, when properly attended to, seems to me to unravel several of the theoretical knots considered in this section.

Within much scholarship dealing with the legal constitution of gender identity, the focus, obviously enough, is on linguistic forms of discourse, and hence, within legal materials, on legal rules and doctrines rather than on legal institutions. Indeed, it is perhaps this (deceptive) linguistic primacy of law – its superficial susceptibility to reform via conceptual reconstruction – that has made it such a popular object of prescription among social and political theorists. These scholars tend to take law as more readily reformable than other social and political institutions, and they often make what appear to sociolegal scholars to be exaggerated and simplistic assump-tions about the social efficacy of legal change. Within both philosophical appopria-tions of law and feminist-legal analyses of identity there often remains an important gap. This is the lack of any sustained attempt to deploy the tools of the social sciences to analyze, at a general level, the institutional form of law within which its discursive practices are enacted, or to analyze the interactions between law and other social, economic, and political institutions. Certainly, there is much valuable work that draws upon social science models to analyze the operation of particular areas of law (see, e.g., Freshman, 2000; Wax, 1998). But a more general mapping of the relationship between legal and extralegal institutions *other than prevailing discourses of sex/gender* has been curiously lacking in feminist legal scholarship. Relevant work within the sociology of law – systems theory, for example (Teubner, 1993) – is a significant absence from the debates about the contours of law's identity-constituting and identity-reshaping potential.

This absence is, I would argue, unfortunate: for only within an institutionally focused account – and within an account that explores the, often locally specific, relationships between legal and extralegal institutions – can we begin to resolve the problems canvassed in this section, and hope to draw on conceptual reconstruction in the service of institutional change. Excellent examples of the illuminating power of such integrated approaches include Sally Engle Merry's his-torical and anthropological analysis of the role of law in shaping Hawaiian social practices and gendered identities in the nineteenth century (Merry, 2000: chs. 8 and 9) and Kristin Bumiller's (1988) study of the disempowering effects of the attempt to empower women and others through antidiscrimination law. Bumiller's study is particularly instructive in undermining the assumption that a positive conception of agency (the empowered claimant) can unproblematically be delivered through legal enactment.

More generally, within an adequately complex, institutionally contextualized analysis, the post-structuralist subject is saved from the threat of structuralist passivity: subjectivities, being produced across a range of discourses and practices, are not unitary: and this diversity of experience, the movement of subjects across institutional and discursive spaces, is surely a key to understanding how the reflexive, dialogic, and potentially critical moment is opened up. Furthermore, an analysis of the construction of identity in legal discourse in isolation from the broader institutional context may help to explain the current focus on issues of recognition rather than distribution (to the extent that these can be adequately distinguished). For law and its reform is arguably more powerful in effecting recognition of identities than in determining distributive outcomes or in directly effecting material change. Furthermore, institutional legal changes often have unforeseen effects in relation to identities – as in the case of antidiscrimination law's effect in constructing a victim identity (Bumiller, 1988). It also seems clear that an adequate understanding of interaction effects between legal and other social – economic, political, ethical, traditional – arrangements, and of the specificity of such effects within different national or other systems, is a necessary condition for the effective pursuit of the institutionally reconstructive projects espoused by some feminists. I shall pursue these claims, and the further claim that feminist sociolegal scholars are well placed to meet them, in the concluding section of the chapter.

CRITICAL AND NORMATIVE ANALYSES OF THE LEGAL CONSTITUTION OF IDENTITY IN CONTEMPORARY FEMINIST THEORY

I want now briefly to examine four influential contributions to contemporary feminist thinking about the legal constitution of sex/gender identity, by way both of mapping the state of the discipline and of further considering how the problems set out in the previous section have been encountered and/or addressed in the field.

First, let us consider projects that argue for a radical reconstruction of law and legal categories as a basis for reconstructed gender identity. In a series of striking essays, Luce Irigaray has argued for the institution of a specific set of civil rights for women (Irigaray, 1994). These rights, which include rights to virginity and to guardianship of the home, as well as to equal recognition in political, civil, and religious spheres, are premised on the view that human identity is, inevitably (structurally?) dual: it spans the male and the female. Yet existing law reflects only the male aspect of this pair. The solution is therefore to reconstruct the law by adding to it a distinctive set of rights designed to reflect and – perhaps – to institutionalize female identity. In attempting to move away from a structural notion of legal rights as founded in property relations – in relations, as she puts it, of having rather than of being – Irigaray's program has much in common with Jennifer Nedelsky's powerful critique of the repression of the inevitably relational aspect of rights (Nedelsky, 1993) and of the embodied aspects of autonomy (Nedelsky, 1997). It also resonates with a large literature inspired by Carol Gilligan's identification of distinctive voices within moral reasoning – a literature that prescribes, in various ways, the infusion of the rights-dominated ethic of law with aspects of the "ethic of care" (Gilligan, 1982). Irigaray moves beyond Nedelsky, however, in advocating a distinctive set of substantive rights premised on a certain conception of identity that re-enacts, mimetically, many of the features generally associated with sexist, traditional (and culturally specific), or "essentialist" views of woman. In this sense, Irigaray's project certainly courts the essentialism objection considered in the last section. It also focuses primarily on questions of recognition. In its complete inattention to questions of institutional design beyond the legislative, it also constitutes the kind of utopian feminist thought that has been argued to be problematic from a political point of view (Lacey, 1998: chs. 7 and 8).

A very different response to the insight that law produces gendered identities can be seen in the recent work of Judith Butler (Butler, 1997, 2000) who, in ways that echo the work of Carol Smart (Smart, 1989), in effect argues for a decentering of law as a reconstructive strategy on the basis of a critique of the way in which even reformist projects tend to confirm law's violent fixing of its subjects within preformed identities and categories. For Butler, the radical possibilities inherent in the "performativity" of gender (Butler, 1990) are often better explored in less institutionally structured contexts: the strategies of parody and resistance that she favors sit uncomfortably with the constraining structure of legal discourse – though even here there is some scope for transcending the status quo through the adaptive reiteration of legally sanctioned identities. Butler's is a position that has been argued to be vulnerable to the objections both that it risks the fragmentation of subjects constituted, or perhaps constituting themselves, within multiple discursive sites, and that it is insufficiently attentive to the normative and redistributive aspects of the feminist political project.

A third way of pursuing the critical and normative projects arising from law's identity-producing power, and one that has assumed a fascinating salience in recent feminist legal and political theory, combines a focus on the radically constructionist analytic thesis (of whatever specific shape) with a return to aspects of the universalism, conceptions of agency, and normative commitments central to the liberal and Kantian traditions. In Drucilla Cornell's work, for example (Cornell, 1995, 1998), we find a juxtaposition of deconstruction, poststructuralist, and Lacanian analysis with the normative resources of Rawlsian liberalism (Rawls, 1971): the critique of law's enactment of gendered identity is informed by a Lacanian analysis of the subject's access to the imaginary, psychic domain as a precondition to the realization of liberal guarantees of dignity, equality, and respect. At the level of normative reconstruction, however, it is the liberal ideals that are dominant: as feminism moves into the political domain, it is assumed that it must use the dominant language of progressive reform.

Cornell's return to liberalism sits alongside other powerful feminist voices: Martha Nussbaum's defense of a social constructionist, internationalist, and humanist liberalism (Nussbaum, 1999: Part I); Seyla Benhabib's insistence, from within the critical theory tradition, on the importance of a certain understanding of universalism to feminist normative commitments (Benhabib, 1992); Susan Okin's immanent critique of Rawls, which points out that commitment to the public–private divide blocks the realization of justice in the public sphere (Okin, 1989); and Renata Salecl's claim, from within the Lacanian tradition, of the necessity to rights discourse of a certain commitment to universalism (Salecl, 1994: ch. 8; on the revival of liberal feminism, see Dailey, 1993).

Indeed, this combination of constructivist analysis and liberal strategy is a persuasive way of understanding Catharine Mackinnon's radical feminism (MacKinnon, 1989), which has often been criticized for combining a structuralist ontology in which women appear as the determined, victimized, passive products of a seamless system of male sexual violence with an optimistic, liberal reformist strategy premised on the idea that legal changes can effect real changes in the distribution of power. The great attraction of the combination, of course, is that it appears to offer a strong conception of agency and a confident conception of the basis for normative projects focused both on recognition and distribution. In this eclectic strategy, the question of how a focus upon women as a group can be justified – the problem of the feminist subject, as it were – is resolved either (less often) pragmatically in terms of the defensibility of interest group politics or (more usually) normatively in terms of the distinctive injustices, relative to liberal commitments, attaching to the treatment of women.

Inevitably, the genre of liberalism defended by these and other writers varies; while Nussbaum sees her position as, essentially, implicit in that of J.S. Mill (Mill, 1988) and Okin hers as a refinement of Rawls, Cornell would doubtless claim that the Lacanian analysis of the imaginary domain as a precondition for subjects' access to public justice effects a profound transformation in the structure of the theory. However, what each of these positions shares is a response to the powerful feminist critique of liberalism's abstract individualism; of its inattention to the social construction of gendered identity, its public–private distinction, its focus on formal rather than substantial equality, its pretension to sexual neutrality. A detailed analysis of the strategies adopted to meet this acknowledged critique is beyond the scope of this essay, but four points may usefully be made.

First, the shared assumption is that many of the feminist objections to liberalism have more to do with particular interpretations of the liberal tradition than with its formal structure: there is a possibility, in short, of constructing a radically feminist liberalism. Secondly, one crucial feature of such a reconstruction is that it places at center stage precisely the analysis of the social construction of gender and of gendered identity that we have considered; this is, one might say, not only a feminist but a postpost-structuralist liberalism. Thirdly, in its most persuasive forms, this is a liberalism whose values are taken, à la Zygmunt Bauman's "postmodern ethics" (Bauman, 1993) or Richard Rorty's "postmodern bourgeois liberalism" (Rorty, 1991), to be human commitments rather than transcendent goods: to argue in defense of these is not to adopt a "view from nowhere," but to argue, explicitly, from a position. And, related to this point, while the commitment to the possibility and propriety of (a degree of) universalism varies across writers, there is nonetheless a view that our value commitments are to some extent generalizable, albeit in an adequately contextualized way, across social and political spaces.

There is a significant overlap, finally, between this revival of a certain genre of liberal commitment within feminism, and indeed of alliances between neoliberal feminists such as Nussbaum and radical feminists like MacKinnon (Abrams, 1995: Part II) and what is one of the most politically significant feminist legal movements today in global terms. This is the cross-national and cross-institutional attempt to enact and realize human rights for women, both in international treaties and institutions, and in the interpretation of national constitutions and nonlegal regimes. This significant development merits further analysis.

CASE STUDY: THE CONSTITUTION OF WOMEN AS THE
BEARERS OF INTERNATIONAL HUMAN RIGHTS

The emergence over the last 15 years of a number of international campaigns framed within the discourse of human rights for women surely constitutes one of the most important legal/political developments since the inception of the "second wave" of the women's movement in the late 1960s (Charlesworth and Chinkin, 2000). The size and breadth of the international movement for women's rights (as well as the diversity of positions represented within it) was epitomized by the UN-sponsored Beijing Conference on Women in 1995; it has realized itself in campaigns to bring the use of rape and sexual torture as instruments of war to public attention and legal remedy; to publicize issues of violence against women in a vast range of contexts, notable among them being the slaughter or undernutrition of female children in societies in which gender identities constitute females as economically and culturally unproductive; to investigate and regulate international trafficking in women and children for the purposes of prostitution. In many of these campaigns, as will be immediately apparent, issues of recognition and of distribution are inextricably linked: where, for example, female identity is devalued culturally, this generally goes hand in hand with poverty and lack of political voice.

The movement for international women's human rights presents a fascinating case study for the state of contemporary scholarship on the legal constitution of gendered identities for a number of reasons. Some of the most intellectually powerful voices in feminist legal theory and feminist philosophy – Catharine MacKinnon and Martha Nussbaum to name just two – have been key actors in the movement itself. Of more theoretical interest, however, is the fact that, notwithstanding the vigor with which the movement is developing, the arena of human rights in the international context raises in vivid form many of the difficulties canvassed in the second section of this paper. Let us recapitulate on each of the four objections, within this specific context. First, the passive or engulfed subject of discourse: we find that one of the most pervasive criticisms, particularly from postcolonial scholarship, of many of the human rights campaigns is indeed that they tend to construct a victimized, passive subjectivity for women in developing countries (Kapur, 2001), an identity that does not encompass either agency or desire, pleasure or enjoyment. Secondly, the fragmentation of the feminist subject: given the vastly different contexts in which women across the globe live and interact with other human beings and social institutions, can a universal, postcolonial female subject of rights be posited or even imagined? Thirdly, does the institutional weakness of international legal structures entail that – international treaties, tribunals, and congresses notwithstanding – the movement amounts in effect to a form of discursive utopianism rather than a comprehensible political strategy, implying political action on redistribution but instead delivering a materially empty rhetoric of recognition? And finally, can the attempt to enact and enforce a common conception of human rights across the globe be realized in a sufficiently contextualized way not to reenact the violence of colonialism in the name of a universal set of norms: is international human rights, in short, the new imperialism?

An overview of the copious literature charting the rise and rise of this set of international social movements provides an illuminating insight into the ways in which these theoretical problems are managed within feminist praxis. It suggests, overall, that the problems are real and yet not paralyzing. Each of them gives rise to issues that are objects of fierce political controversy and contestation, and that find differently balanced solutions in different times and at different places; yet the movements continue to work within the various tensions that they encounter. They give evidence, therefore, of the possibility of living, politically, with theoretical eclecticism. The focus on women as a group is underpinned by a sometimes articulate, sometimes implicit, but nearly always cheerful "strategic essentialism" which may be justified by the empirical evidence that women, even across their many differences from one another, are often subject to rights abuses that relate specifically to un/authorized gender identities. It is further justified by the fact that the publicization of these abuses may act as a spur to that collection of more differentiated data that is so crucial to the construction of gender as an axis of social organization on a par with the (far better investigated) index of class or, in some societies, caste. At the level of feminist praxis, strategic essentialism is justified, in short, by both political commitment and the goals which that commitment entails. While the portrayal of women as victims of human rights abuses, particularly in situations of war or economic "underdevelopment," has been a matter of concern, most of those who have voiced this criticism would therefore like to address it not by rejecting the framework of human rights but rather by supplementing it with a focus on women as claimants, as subjects who can assert their rights, whose lives as desiring subjects are not inconsistent with their structural position in relation to justice and power (Cornell, 1998; Kapur, 1999). As Bumiller's study shows, however, legal claimant identities can all too easily shift to supplicant/victim identities (Bumiller, 1988). The patchy success of human rights for women in effecting material change highlights the need for systematic sociotheoretical understandings of the potential for law to effect real change in particular contexts.

It is the question about the "violence" of imposing a "neutral" or "universal" model of rights across the globe that has led to most intense disagreement and debate in the international human rights movement. This is particularly true in relation to issues such as clitoridectomy and access to education, where Western, liberal interpretations conflict with values strongly adhered to by well-established local conventions and institutions. While it would be wrong to underplay the passion of these debates or the depth of the relevant disagreements, they have generated some creative attempts at theoretical resolution. One of the most interesting combines a defense of a certain kind of universalism focused not (purportedly) on values but on resources and entitlements underpinning a set of basic capabilities for human living with an admission of the need for localism in the development of more textured values within that framework, as well as in the development of specific political strategies. Though at first sight the international arena may seem well suited for the articulation of the multiple voices celebrated by postmodernism, the question remains whether "universal" values sufficiently rich to generate concrete principles, let alone guidelines for their implementation, can ever be detached from their culturally specific origins. The appeal to the "universal" should rather be interpreted as the articulation of a set of political commitments to the application, universally, of particular values.

A further, striking feature of the international human rights literature is the tension between the appeal to the universal and the need to contextualize political strategies. Once again, the institutional, sociolegal lack in much feminist scholarship appears as a difficulty. Evidently, any attempt to institutionalize human rights will be dependent on an understanding of how institutions interlock, and hence on detailed empirical evidence of conditions in localities. Let us take the example of prostitution, trafficking in women and children, and sexual slavery (Chang, 1998; Fitzpatrick and Kelly, 1998). This is an especially vigorously contested campaign, with some (particularly those well informed on conditions in the relevant places) arguing that the convention against trafficking imposes an American radical feminist obsession with sexual violence (to the relative exclusion of poverty) onto the international agenda, with devastating effects upon the economic and political well-being of the very objects of the humanitarian intervention (Murray, 1998). For the immediate implication of such rights-oriented regulation may well be to intensify the vulnerability of migrant women sex workers, whether voluntary or involutary, to prosecution as illegal migrants or prostitutes.

PROSPECTS FOR THE FUTURE

How, then, is this field likely to progress over the next 15 years, and what would be the most productive intellectual developments and alliances that could be envisaged? Both the intersections between feminist legal theory and philosophy, and the international political movement for women's human rights, seem set to flourish: far from being intellectually or politically exhausted, it is reasonable to envisage a burgeoning of theoretical debate and political activism over the next decades. A more open question, however, is that of how intimate the relationship between these two areas of feminist activity is likely to be. Notwithstanding the feminist axiom of the links between theory and practice, it is instructive to reflect on the fact that the increasing institutional influence of feminism in the international scene has been informed most obviously by a resurgence of a liberal normative framework in feminist theory (Dailey, 1993). More work, evidently, needs to be done in thinking through what, if anything – trust, solidarity, a focus on collective goods? – is lost by this.

In particular, I would argue that three questions call for further analysis. First, that of universalism: has "postmodern bourgeois liberal feminism" really abandoned an implicit claim to the transcendent values that have long been an object of critique in feminist theory and, if it has not, how is this tension within feminist theoretical and political commitments to be resolved (Phillips, 2001)? Second, that of generalizablity: if feminism is inevitably identified in terms of a set of normative commitments – the dismantling of women's oppression, the pursuit of women's equality or autonomy – what does this imply about the generalizability of claims about the kinds of oppression or injustice that women suffer, and how is this to be handled in the context of the intersection of race, class, sexuality, and so on, particularly within an increasingly international political arena? A third, political and open question is how the tension between the liberal ideal of autonomy and of feminist visions of substantial equality will be resolved, both theoretically and amid the power relations shaping the international movements in its various arenas.

In the future pursuit of each of these questions, we must hope that two things will be borne in mind. First, while analytic, critical, and reconstructive projects must remain equally a part of the feminist project, the distinctions between them should always be respected. To understand that law genders its subjects, in both positive and constraining senses, is not to understand what is problematic about this; and to have a clear view of why we find law's gendering practices, as currently structured, problematic, is not yet to have a grasp of the possibilities for reconstructing them. The analytic and critical may be necessary conditions for both the conceptual and institutional reconstructive projects, but they do not accomplish them. At the level of institutionally reconstructive projects, we encounter perhaps the most intractable questions faced by feminist theory: philosophical and moral questions about the shape and genesis of the values involved, political questions about building necessary alliances, practical questions about the operation of interlocking social institutions in different parts of the world.

Furthermore, as we have seen, it is necessary to recognize that reconstructive projects themselves take different shapes – the most obvious being the distinction between primarily imaginative/utopian, rhetorical interventions or concrete/institutional interventions. Of course, this is not to imply that one project or campaign cannot take both shapes: the movement for human rights for women, for example, may not be so different from Irigaray's meditations on civil rights for women, even though it seeks to effect specific legal and institutional changes and thereby to produce certain effects. The distinction is, nonetheless, important: for the conditions for success of the two reconstructive projects are different. While the imaginative, conceptual project seeks to effect changes in social and political consciousness – to alter hearts and minds, and thereby to make new political alliances and forms of activism possible – the institutional project has the no less ambitious goal of material change. Though the former is almost invariably a condition of the latter, it is perhaps a less risky project: for, as much of the data on feminist law reform at both international and national levels shows, institutional reform constantly risks counterproductive effects (see, e.g., Bumiller, 1988; Fineman, 1991: chs. 7–8, 1994).

The problem of counterproductivity brings me to the second issue to which further attention needs to be paid in the development of this field – an issue that bears closely on the relationship between feminist and law and society movements in the academy. Probably the best – though an imperfect – way of minimizing the counterproductivity of feminist reformism is through a detailed knowledge of how particular institutions work in specific, local, contexts. How important are legal changes likely to be in particular contexts? How do gender-oriented reforms intersect with the constitution of other forms of identity in legal practice? How do legal institutions interact with political, economic, religious, cultural institutions in the field (see, in the international law context, Spahn, 1998)? This implies that feminist normative projects must proceed in the light of a great deal of data. Though this may seem obvious, it is in fact an enormous problem for political feminism: in all too many areas, the marginalization of women as a political group means that we still lack the basic data on which projects of reform need to be based. Countering this marginalization is just one way in which the imaginative reconstructive projects can play – indeed, have played – a vital role. But without textured understandings of the workings of law in its legal-institutional and extralegal institutional contexts, little progress can be made.

But it is not merely a matter of data collection. It is also a question of building intellectual alliances with a range of other disciplines, alliances that, unfortunately, continue to be blocked by contingent but powerful facts about the history of the disciplines and their attitude to questions of sex/gender. Sociology, anthropology, and, more recently, philosophy and law have been relatively responsive to feminist arguments; but reconstructive feminism cannot operate without the insights of

disciplines such as political science and economics, which have been far less receptive to the feminist agenda. Feminists working within the tradition of law and
society scholarship, who are often equipped with disciplinary skills across a range
of social sciences, are surely exceptionally well placed to begin to break down these
arbitrary and practically damaging obstructions. While critical doctrinal interpretation has been crucial to the development of feminist legal theory, it is sociolegal
scholarship that has provided the textured understanding of how legal doctrines and
arrangements work in practice: their symbolic and instrumental effects.

This is, of course, a field in which law and society scholarship has made a number
of crucially important contributions in fields such as family law (Fineman, 1991,
1994), criminal justice (Daly, 1994; Smart, 1995), and antidiscrimination law
(Bumiller, 1988). The task that all too often remains unfinished, I would argue, is
the drawing out of more general implications about the nature of sociolegal relations
from specific case studies. To take two contrasting examples, it might be expected
that systems theory – a paradigm little taken up in feminist scholarship – could
generate important insights into the limitations on law's capacity directly to shape
the other systems that constitute its environment; while organization theory and
comparative political science – equally little drawn upon in feminist scholarship –
may sharpen our view of the distinctive local possibilities for institutional reconstruction. While existing feminist law and society scholarship already does much to
illuminate the gendered dynamics of particular legal practices, I would argue that
there is room for greater theoretical boldness in building out from these local studies
toward the more general sociotheoretic and institutional understandings that are
spectacularly lacking in feminist theory of a philosophical flavor.

In short, I would argue that we need to build a feminist social theory informed not
only by legal analysis but also by what we might broadly call comparative institutional analysis. Only within such an alliance will gender come to occupy the
central place in political practice across the globe that class and its intellectual
descendants such as "social exclusion" have long enjoyed.

Note

My warm thanks are due to Hilary Charlesworth, Hugh Collins, Elizabeth Frazer, Emily
Jackson, Ratna Kapur, Martin Loughlin, Austin Sarat, and David Soskice for their helpful
comments on a draft of this paper, and to Shuping Wang for invaluable research assistance.
The essay also benefited greatly from discussion at seminar presentations at the LSE and at
Columbia and Harvard Law Schools.

References

Abrams, Kathryn (1995) "Sex wars redux: Agency and coercion in feminist legal theory,"
    Columbia Law Review 95: 304–76.
Barron, Anne (2000) "Feminism, aestheticism and the limits of law," Feminist Legal Studies 8:
    275–83.
Bauman, Zygmunt (1993) Postmodern Ethics. Oxford: Blackwell.
Benhabib, Seyla (1992) Situating the Self. Cambridge, UK: Polity.
Bumiller, Kristin (1987) "Rape as a legal symbol: An essay on sexual violence and racism,"
    Miami Law Review 42: 75–91.

Bumiller, Kristin (1988) *The Civil Rights Society: The Social Construction of Victims*. Baltimore: Johns Hopkins University Press.

Butler, Judith (1990) *Gender Trouble*. New York: Routledge.

Butler, Judith (1993) *Bodies that Matter*. New York: Routledge.

Butler, Judith (1997) *Excitable Speech*. New York: Routledge.

Butler, Judith (2000) *Antigone's Claim*. New York: Columbia University Press.

Chang, Jamie (1998) "Redirecting the debate over trafficking in women," *Harvard Human Rights Journal* 11: 65–107.

Charlesworth, Hilary and Chinkin, Christine (2000) *The Boundaries of International Law: A Feminist Analysis*. Manchester, UK: Manchester University Press.

Cornell, Drucilla (1995) *The Imaginary Domain*. London and New York: Routledge.

Cornell, Drucilla (1998) *At the Heart of Freedom: Feminism, Sex and Equality*. Princeton, NJ: Princeton University Press.

Dailey, Anne C. (1993) "Feminism's return to liberalism," *Yale Law Journal* 102: 1265–92.

Daly, Kathleen (1994) *Gender, Crime and Punishment*. New Haven, CT and London: Yale University Press.

Fineman, Martha (1991) *The Illusion of Equality: The Rhetoric and Reality of Divorce Reform*. Chicago: University of Chicago Press.

Fineman, Martha (1994) *The Neutered Mother, the Sexual Family and Other Twentieth Century Tragedies*. New York: Routledge.

Fitzpatrick, Joan and Kelly, Katrina R. (1998) "Gendered aspects of migration: Law and the female migrant," *Hastings International and Comparative Law Review* 22: 47–112.

Foucault, Michel (1981) *The History of Sexuality*, vol. 1. London: Penguin.

Fraser, Nancy (1997) *Justice Interruptus*. New York: Routledge.

Frazer, Elizabeth and Lacey, Nicola (1993) *The Politics of Community: A Feminist Analysis of the Liberal-Communitarian Debate*. Hemel Hempstead, UK: Harvester Wheatsheaf.

Freshman, Clark (2000) "Whatever happened to anti-semitism: How social science theories identify discrimination and promote coalitions between 'different' minorities," *Cornell Law Review* 85: 313–442.

Fuss, Diana (1989) *Essentially Speaking*. London and New York: Routledge.

Gilligan, Carol (1982) *In a Different Voice*. Cambridge, MA: Harvard University Press.

Harris, Angela (1990) "Race and essentialism in feminist legal theory," *Stanford Law Review* 42: 581–616.

Irigaray, Luce (1994) *Thinking the Difference*. London: Athlone Press.

Kapur, Ratna (1999) " 'A love song to our mongrel selves': Hybridity, sexuality and the law," *Social and Legal Studies* 8: 353–68.

Kapur, Ratna (2001) "Post-colonial economies of desire," *Denver University Law Review* 78: 855–85.

Knop, Karen (1993) "Re/statements: Feminism and state sovereignty in international law," *Transnational Law and Contemporary Problems* 3: 293–344.

Lacey, Nicola (1998) *Unspeakable Subjects*. Oxford: Hart Publishing.

MacKinnon, Catharine A. (1989) *Toward a Feminist Theory of the State*. Cambridge, MA: Harvard University Press.

Mill, John Stuart (1988) *The Subjection of Women*, ed. Susan M. Okin. Indianapolis, IN: Hackett.

Merry, Sally Engle (2000) *Colonizing Hawaii: The Cultural Power of Law*. Princeton, NJ: Princeton University Press.

Murray, Alison (1998) "Debt-bondage and trafficking: Don't believe the hype," in Kamala Kempadoo and Jo Doezema (eds.), *Global Sex Workers: Rights, Resistance and Redefinition*. New York: Routledge, pp. 51–64.

Nedelsky, Jennifer (1993) "Reconceiving rights as relationship," *Review of Constitutional Studies* 1: 1–26.

Nedelsky, Jennifer (1997) "Embodied diversity and the challenges to law," *McGill Law Journal* 42: 91–117.

Nussbaum, Martha C. (1999) *Sex and Social Justice*. New York: Oxford University Press.

Okin, Susan Moller (1989) *Justice, Gender and the Family*. New York: Basic Books.

Phillips, Anne (2001) "Nussbaum's "illiberal" liberalism," *Constellations* 8: 249–66.

Rawls, John (1971) *A Theory of Justice*. Cambridge, MA: Harvard University Press.

Rorty, Richard (1991) *Objectivity, Relativism and Truth*. Cambridge, UK: Cambridge University Press 1991)

Salecl, Renata (1994) *The Spoils of Freedom*. London and New York: Routledge.

Schultz, Vicki (1998) "Reconceptualizing sexual harassment," *Yale Law Journal* 107: 1683–805.

Smart, Carol (1989) *Feminism and the Power of Law*. London: Routledge.

Smart, Carol (1995) *Law, Crime and Sexuality*. London: Sage.

Spahn, Elizabeth K. (1998) "Difficult straits: Economic interdependence and women's labor in Taiwan," *New England Law Review* 32: 779–95.

Teubner, Gunther (1993) *Law as an Autopoietic System*. Oxford: Blackwell.

Wax, Amy (1998) "Bargaining in the shadow of marriage: Is there a future for egalitarian marriage," *Virginia Law Review* 84: 509–72.

Further Reading

Conaghan, Joanne (2000) "Reassessing the feminist theoretical project in law," *Journal of Law and Society* 27: 351–85.

Grant Bowman, Cynthia and Schneider, Elizabeth M. (1998) "Feminist legal theory, feminist lawmaking and the legal profession," *Fordham Law Review* 67: 249–71.

Kapur, Ratna and Cossman, Brenda (1996) *Subversive Sites: Feminist Engagements with Law in India*. London: Sage.

Naffine, Ngaire (2001) "In praise of legal feminism," *Legal Studies* 22: 71–101.

Nessiah, Vasuki (1993) "Toward a feminist internationality: A critique of U.S. feminist legal scholarship," *Harvard Women's Law Journal* 16: 189–210.

Schultz, Vicki (1990) "Telling stories about women and work: Judicial interpretations of sex segregation in the workplace in Title VII cases raising the lack of interest argument," *Harvard Law Review* 103: 1749–1843.

Schultz, Vicki (1992) "Race, gender, work and choice: An empirical study of the lack of interest defence in Title VII cases challenging job segregation," *University of Chicago Law Review* 59: 1073–1181.

26

Sexuality in Law and Society Scholarship

LESLIE J. MORAN

INTRODUCTION

Born in the late nineteenth century, sexuality is a relatively new category within the human sciences. Despite its novelty, as Eve Sedgwick (1990) has noted, sexuality is now a central category within Western societies in general and Western scholarship in particular. It is a key concept through which we make the sense and non sense of individual and collective human behavior. The objective of this chapter is to examine scholarship on sexuality in the field of law and society. Key themes, new developments, and the limits of this body of work will be explored. Reference will be made to diverse sources of work in a range of different legal jurisdictions.

I want to begin with an enigma that is at the core of work on sexuality. Heterosexuality, formally the dominant sexuality, is largely absent from law and society work. The field is dominated by work on gay and lesbian sexualities. How are we to make sense of the absence of the dominant heterosexuality? A key objective of this chapter is to explore and challenge this "absence." I begin to address this absence first by way of more general work on heterosexuality. I then turn to a small but important body of law and society scholarship on heterosexuality to explore the issues raised by way of attempts to engage directly with the heterosexual norm. I then return to law and society scholarship more generally to expose and explore the silences and evasions through which heterosexuality is produced as a pervasive but absent theme of law and society scholarship. My purpose here is to draw attention to the urgent need to challenge the largely unspoken heteronormative (Warner, 1993) frame of law and society scholarship.

The analysis will then turn to the rapidly growing body of work on gay and lesbian sexualities. In part the importance of this work lies in the fact that it offers the most sustained scholarship on heterosexuality in the field of law and society. In part its importance lies in the way it documents and analyzes the form and effects of the violent sexual hierarchy of hetero- and homo-sexualities, as a hierarchy of inclusion and exclusion, upon the lives of those who are perceived to be the sexual "other." While much of this work does not fall within any narrow definition of law and society scholarship, I argue that it has importance in that context. In the limited space available here I point to some of the key scholars writing in this area and offer a brief summary of some of the themes and preoccupations of this work. I want to focus rather more attention on a gap that is emerging within this scholarship. It is concerned with the relation between sexual identity and law's violence. Much of lesbian and gay work is dominated by a concern with the use of law's violence *against* lesbians and gay men. Little attention has yet been paid to lesbian and gay demands *for* law's violence. I want to explore this silence.

THE ENIGMA OF HETEROSEXUALITY

In his study *The Invention of Heterosexuality*, Jonathan Katz notes that, "...talk of heterosexuality so often and so easily glides off into talk of homosexuality, leaving heterosexuality – once again – forgotten" (Katz, 1995: 12). Here Katz points to the difficulties of making heterosexuality an object of critical inquiry. It has a tendency to disappear and to turn into a discussion about other sexualities. This echoes my own experiences of searching various scholarly indexes pertinent to the interdisciplinary and multidisciplinary basis of law and society work. In general, sexuality appears most persistently in association with "homosexuality," "lesbian," "gay," and more recently "queer." Heterosexuality remains largely absent. For example, a search of the *Sociological Abstracts Index 1986–2001* produced 2,792 records of work on homosexuality (similar figures and similar work appears by way of a search under "gay" and "lesbian"). In stark contrast a search by reference to "heterosexuality" produced 779 items. An examination of the abstracts falling under the category of "heterosexuality" quickly reveals that in this work "heterosexuality" focuses on same-sex not opposite-sex relations. Nor is this pattern peculiar to sociological work. A similar search in another domain of scholarship relevant to law and society scholarship – political science – produces a similar pattern. How are we to make sense of this state of affairs?

Katz points to a difficult and persistent problem that needs to be addressed in any attempt to review work on sexuality in general and work on sexuality in law and society scholarship in particular; the problem of representing the norm. The dominance of "homosexual," "gay," and "lesbian" draws attention to the fact that in Western societies to have sexuality is to be marked: to be marked as the "other," the "outsider" (Butler, 1990, 1993; Fuss, 1991; Foucault, 1980). The norm remains unrepresented and unrepresentable. The negative term (homosexual, lesbian, gay) plays a central role in defining the positive term which remains absent (Fuss, 1991). Heterosexual as an erotic/genital relation is represented only by way of the negative – homosexuality – that stands as the abnormal, the perverted, the deviation from that which remains unmarked: the norm.

If categories of sexual identity emerge by way of the figure of the "other," the "outsider," is the appearance of the term "heterosexual" a departure from this? Scholarship on heterosexuality suggests not (Weeks, 1981, 1986). It is used to define "an abnormal or perverted sexual appetite toward the opposite sex" (quoted in Penelope, 1993: 261). More specifically, heterosexual first names an aberration of opposite sex relations: as practices of pleasure in contrast to practices of reproduction.

The problem with heterosexuality that Katz (1995) points to is not so much a problem of the heterosexual as the other, but the problems and difficulties associated with attempts to use "heterosexuality" to bring the norm into the frame of representation in general and of critical inquiry in particular. As the unmarked, as many recent studies of heterosexuality have noted, "heterosexuality" is not so much absent as the unspoken, the unquestioned, the taken for granted, the natural, that which is in the background over against which everything else becomes the exception, an aberration, and problematic. It is both always present and that which most resists appearance (Kitzinger and Wilkinson, 1993 and see generally Wilkinson and Kitzinger, 1993; Richardson, 1996; Weeks, 1986). In its absence it offers a unity and a singularity over against an ever proliferating catalogue of perversity, of otherness that marks the impossibility of the norm. These opening observations draw attention to the need for a particular vigilance when thinking about sexuality. With this in mind I now want to turn to the scholarship that attempts to directly address the enigma of heterosexuality within law and society scholarship.

FINDING THE HETEROSEXUAL IN LAW AND SOCIETY SCHOLARSHIP

Work that formally addresses heterosexuality in law and society is rare. Two notable exceptions are to be found in the work of Alison Young and Richard Collier.

I want to consider two contexts in which heterosexuality appears in Alison Young's work. The first is in her monograph *Femininity in Dissent* (1990). Heterosexuality arises in the context of her reflections on press representations of lesbianism associated with a group of women engaging in antinuclear protests at Greenham Common airbase in the UK. She explains: "For me, practising a hetero rather than a homo sexuality, and therefore situated at present on that side of the boundary, I am trying to discover further meanings of the taboo [on lesbianism], its meanings for those like me on the authorized side, who have never yet crossed over" (1990: 78). Here heterosexuality comes into the frame of analysis by way of an examination of the meanings of its "other," lesbianism. What, Young asks, can the "other" tell us about the norm?

Heterosexuality is summoned a second time in Young's work by way of reflections provoked by a letter from lesbian scholars Celia Kitzinger and Sue Wilkinson. They invited Young (and a number of others identified as heterosexual feminists) to participate in a project about heterosexuality (Wilkinson and Kitzinger, 1993). In this context heterosexuality comes into the frame of critical reflection in a different way: not by way of "a self-naming" *through* the "other" of lesbian but as an experience of being named heterosexual *as* "other."

Young describes an experience of the norm being made "other" in the following terms. First it is experienced as being fixed. "[T]he name 'heterosexual'," she concludes, "seems far more permanent and concrete than in my own use of it" (1993: 37). She also describes the process of nomination as an experience of loss of control, "Now, my identity feels out of control" (ibid.).

Young's reflections are of interest in various ways. They report the experiences of occupying the place of the heterosexual as norm. She draws attention to the importance of the "other" in producing both the norm and critical reflections on the norm. That norm, she reveals, is produced through a fixing of the "other" and in the policing of the boundaries of the "other" to secure its name and the values associated with it. Of particular interest is the way the "othering" of heterosexuality may have strategic purchase. It might be used to disrupt the silences through which heteronormative power is (re)produced and enforced.

Heterosexuality, and more specifically male heterosexuality, are an important focus in Collier's work. Drawing upon lesbian, gay, and queer, as well as feminist scholarship, Collier explores the production of male heterosexuality by way of the violent hierarchies of hetero/homo and masculine/feminine. His work examines a range of institutional, organizational, and political sites of production of masculine subjectivities encoded as heterosexual (the family, Collier, 1992, 1996, and the law school, Collier, 1998). Of particular interest is his exploration of the multiple male heterosexualities represented in the constitution of the male heterosexual as norm. He offers an exploration of the various ways in which the male heterosexual is made "deviant," as other, in the constitution of that norm. Of particular interest is the way the hetero/homo binary works to produce a range of normative inclusions and exclusions: the distinction between the good hetero and bad hetero (cf. Phelan, 2001).

Collier's essay on male heterosexuality in the legal academy exploring the hetero-sexual encoding of masculine subjectivities also draws attention to the way sexuality is produced by way of the structural relation of gender, "nam[ing] men as men." The danger here is that through gender heterosexuality may slip out of the frame. The challenge, as Andrew Sharpe demonstrates in his pioneering monograph *Trans-gender Jurisprudence* (2002) is to keep both in the frame in order to expose and critique the (re)production of heterosexuality.

For both Young and Collier heterosexuality is produced *through and in relation to* the "other." The "other" may take various forms, lesbian or gay, the hetero in general or bad hetero in particular. Young's reflections on being named the heterosexual as "other" in relation to lesbian as norm inverts the structural relation, offering a rather different deployment of the hetero/other, this time in a homonormative context.

In the first instance their work appears to reproduce the violent binary normative structure of I/Other through which the heterosexual as norm is produced, rather than challenging it. In addition these attempts to focus on the norm appear to become work that reproduces the obsessive concern with the sexual "other" that is the hallmark of the (re)production of the hetero as the norm. How are we to make sense of the difficulties of keeping the norm of heterosexuality in view and of giving it substance beyond that which is displaced onto the other?

The reproduction of heterosexuality as a structural relation of I/Other needs to be taken seriously. Young and Collier's struggle to pin down the substance of the norm of heterosexuality is perhaps nothing more than a manifestation of a desire for substance, our search for an illusion, that is the effect of the structural relation of I/Other. Perhaps we need to read the difficulties they encounter in a different way. They may offer a major challenge to the way that we understand the norm of heterosexuality. Maybe the norm of heterosexuality has no essential substance? Maybe their research indicates that we need to take more seriously the idea of heterosexuality as a set of practices of exclusion that produce in many instances devastating and life-destroying effects.

The reflections on heterosexuality in the work of Young and Collier illustrate some of the difficulties of bringing heterosexuality into the frame of critical inquiry.

Particular attention needs to be paid to the uses of the rhetoric of that structural relation and its social and political effects. The challenge is to explore the minutiae of the struggle undertaken by Young and Collier, which reflects the minutiae of the politics of the hetero/homo binary in operation.

The work of Young and Collier remains exceptional within law and society scholarship. Where is the hetero in that great body of work that makes up the overwhelming majority of law and society scholarship? In an attempt to begin to answer that question I want to turn my attention to the flagship journal of the American Law and Society Association, *Law & Society Review*. I do this for various reasons. From time to time editors of the journal have noted that this journal seeks to reflect both the diversity of disciplines that make up law and society scholarship and acts as their point of connection; a "forum linking different research communities" (Galanter, 1973). As such it offers a mirror into the many disciplines that fill the frame of law and society scholarship. It is also a high profile indicator of the parameters of law and society scholarship.

The journal was founded in 1966, and it takes a survey of some 28 volumes of scholarship spanning a period of 18 years before we find the first explicit scholarship on sexuality. This takes the form of Lisa Bowers's article, "Queer acts and the politics of 'direct address': Rethinking law, culture and community" (1994), which deals with lesbian, gay, and queer sexualities. To date it would appear to be the *only* published article in that journal to directly address sexuality. But the argument already developed in this chapter suggests that this is hardly surprising. It also suggests a need for caution. The unmarked of heterosexuality should not be read as an absence. Heterosexuality is present and presented by way of a silence. With that in mind I want to return to the pages of *Law & Society Review* to search for the heterosexual in law and society scholarship.

Such a return holds many rewards. Heterosexuality makes its appearance in the very first volume of the journal. It appears on the inside of the front cover of the new journal facing the contents page. Its first appearance is under the directions to would-be subscribers. We are advised that the following categories of subscription were available: "Student (non-voting) $5.00; Regular $7.00, Joint (husband and wife) $8.00." "Joint" subscriptions provide the context in which heterosexuality silently appears. It is present in the gendered and sexualized (contingent) prerequirements of "husband and wife."

At the same time heterosexuality is formally absent. To my knowledge the American Law and Society Association has never officially declared itself to be an association of heterosexuals or an association that promotes heterosexuality as the preferred relationship of choice. "Joint subscriptions" suggests otherwise. By way of the category and practices of "subscriptions," heterosexuality is embedded within its modes of participation and inscribed in the flagship institution of law and society scholarship.

A second example of the absent heterosexuality of law and society scholarship is taken from the second edition of volume 1. In that edition several articles address issues relating to the family, marriage, and the institutions of divorce. The limits of space dictate that I can briefly consider the appearance of heterosexuality in only one of the articles.

In, "Institutions of divorce, family, and the law," Paul Bohannan and Karen Huckleberry (1967) examine divorce law and the practices of divorce lawyers. They characterize this area of law and legal practice as a "back up institution."

They explain that as a "backup" it is an institution that carries out the work of another institution when that institution fails. Their conclusion is that divorce law, and more specifically the practices of divorce lawyers, put law and lawyers in the position of a "backup" institution. But they only provide a partial "backup." The parameters of the institution are limited and lawyers, they conclude, have inadequate skills and resources to fully realize such a role. A wider range of services and providers is needed, as are new skills.

The married couple is variously described as "the core institution of American Society" and "the basic social unit" (1987: 81, 101). Throughout it is described in terms of the sexed and gendered distinctions of "husband" and "wife." The closest the authors get to an overt definition is in the context of their attempt to define "marriage." They conclude that "there is no generally agreed referents to what the word "marriage" means" (p. 92). One definition that is pervasive but never formally raised, is that marriage was an institution of heterosexuality. Margaret Thornton has described this operation of heterosexuality as "the normative sexual transparency which overlays the sexed pairing" (Thornton, 2002).

Heterosexuality is formally absent but a pervasive organizing theme. The challenge is to make the transparency of heterosexuality opaque. As a "backup" institution law and its practitioners are characterized as keepers and (re)producers of this institution of heterosexuality in a social medium outside the family. Paraphrasing the authors, and adding the missing term "heterosexual," this particular article argues that law, as a "backup," is an institution of heterosexuality that carries out the work of the heterosexual family when the heterosexual family fails in its tasks (Bohannan and Huckleberry, 1967: 81). The analysis of its limits and the suggestions for further review and change is an analysis of the expansion and improvement of this legal institution of heterosexuality.

Before I leave the pages of *Law & Society Review* I want to briefly explore another, and in some ways more surprising, silence. It occurs in the context of work that takes gender as its critical focus. My example comes again from the early volumes of *Law and Society Review*. Kirtine Olson Rogers's article, "'For her own protection...': Conditions of incarceration for female juvenile offenders in the State of Connecticut" (1972) compares two juvenile offender institutions, one for young men and the other for young women. She catalogs a series of distinctions between these institutions. In general she argues that the young women are subjected to harsher and more damaging regimes than are to be found in the institution dealing with young men. This takes various forms: lower and different thresholds of criminalization, longer periods of incarceration, more restrictive regimes, poorer facilities.

Gender is central to the examination of and understanding of these two institutional settings and key to the generation of Olson Rogers's critical analysis of them. My concern here is to focus on the silent operation of sexuality in that context. Gender appears to (re)produce silences around heterosexuality in the analysis. There is only one formal reference to sexuality: "Girls are then lined up in the doorways and 'excused' to go to the bathroom, one at a time, under close supervision, supposedly to cut down on 'chicking' behavior (an undeveloped form of adolescent homosexual activity)" (1972: 231). It is perhaps no surprise that sexuality makes its appearance by way of same-sex genital/erotic behavior. But a more careful examination reveals that this exceptional reference is not the only context in which heterosexuality appears. Heterosexuality is a pervasive organizing theme of the analysis of these juvenile institutions.

In the young women's institution it appears in the context of the heterosexual as other. The first point Olson Rogers makes is that young women are incarcerated for actions that in adults (and for the young men in the neighboring institution) would not be criminal. They are the main grounds for the incarceration of young women. "Sexual misconduct" and "pregnancy" lead the field. She reports that they account for over 30 percent of female incarcerations. Furthermore, she explains, there is a tendency for the other main rationales for incarceration (incorrigibility, neglect, and runaway) to "fuse together" with sexual misconduct and pregnancy. The policing of female sexuality thus appears to be a primary function of the institution.

What is the nature of this sexuality? The sex encounters are overwhelmingly heterosexual. Examples abound. The release of a "girl" may be delayed, even though behavior would warrant a release because of fear of "summer temptations." Once pregnant, inmates often had their release delayed for two months after the birth to ensure that they were "medically cleared." The quotation marks refer to the civil euphemisms through which heterosexual sex may be represented at this point in time.

The extract making reference to "chicking" demonstrates the way compulsory heterosexuality is institutionalized in the regimes of surveillance and in the circulation of women in the institutions by way of the lesbian "other." This is amplified in the reported contrast between the incarceration practices relating to the females, where the young women were kept separated in individual bedrooms, and the institution for the males, where the boys were housed in dormitories. Female heterosexuality as an unruly, disordered sexuality is a structuring principle of the institution for young women.

The hetero/homo and masculine/feminine that informs the two young offender institutions work to produce two very different institutions of heterosexuality. The institution for young men is described by Olson Rogers as being "in the throes of constant turmoil and consequently under severe public scrutiny." In contrast the institution for young women is "a very tight ship" that generates "pride in their undisputed tradition" (1972: 223). The "tight ship" is a form and an effect of a particular instance of the legal institutionalization of hetero femininity. So the "constant turmoil" is a legal institution of hetero masculinity.

But in producing this rereading of the article we should not forget the tenacious transparency of the rhetoric and politics of heterosexuality. Despite these many examples of heterosexuality, they *never* appear within the frame of critical contemplation or analysis in this article. Olson Rogers makes no overt reference to the heterosexuality of these institutions.

While I hesitate to reach sweeping generalizations based on these few examples from the early days of law and society scholarship, there are lessons to be drawn. The formal absence of a concern with heterosexuality from much law and society scholarship, these examples suggest, is far from an absence of any concern with heterosexuality. Nor is sexuality a recent preoccupation. My preliminary review suggests that it is a pervasive preoccupation of law and society scholarship from the very start of that scholarly enterprise. However, it is a largely silent and unreflexive preoccupation. One of the limits of law and society scholarship has been its failure to expose the ubiquitous operation of the violent hierarchies of hetero/homo sexualities within that scholarship. It has also failed to bring heterosexuality within the critical gaze of that scholarship as it explores the multiple interfaces of the relation between law and society. A look at other journals that make a formal nod toward the law and society canon may suggest that the *Law & Society Review* is a rather easy target in this context, being a more conservative example of that genre of law and society scholarship. In Canada, the *Canadian Journal of Law and Society*, in Australia, the *Australian Feminist Law Journal*, and in the UK, *The Journal of Law and Society* and *Social and Legal Studies*, offer a different window into the world of law and society scholarship on sexuality. Sexuality has been a more prominent feature of scholarship published in these journals. *Social and Legal Studies* is outstanding in this respect. It has published and continues to publish many pioneering works.

The Heterosexual in Lesbian and Gay Scholarship

There are also other reasons for some caution in reaching conclusions about the impoverished nature of scholarship on heterosexuality. If we return to the Sociological and Political Science Indexes we find a large and rapidly growing body of scholarship on heterosexuality. This takes the form of lesbian and gay scholarship. Likewise if we search an index of law scholarship in the various jurisdictions we will find thousands of references to work on heterosexuality under the banner of gay and lesbian sexuality. This work includes monographs and specialist legal journals dedicated to sexuality and the law such as the *Journal of Law and Sexuality* and the *Gay and Lesbian Law Journal* (previously the *Australasia Lesbian and Gay Law Journal*). Established mainstream journals have included special editions dedicated to lesbian and gay issues in law and various symposia on particular topics (see, e.g., Albany, 2001; Cleveland State, 2000; New York, 2000). Much of this work on sexuality and law focuses upon the United States and relates to the idiosyncrasies of that country's juridical landscapes but there are also many examples of this work concerned with other common law contexts (*Social and Legal Studies*, 1997).

However, only a limited amount of this work directly engages with the heterosexuality that is being produced in and through the sexual "other" of homosexuality, gay, or lesbian. This approach to sexuality is most apparent in the lesbian and gay work informed by post-structuralism and queer theory. It is in this context that there is most likely to be an explicit rejection of the idea of homo and hetero as separate unrelated spheres of either sexual identity in particular or the sexual social order more generally. The most interesting examples of work focusing on the homo/hetero relation includes Janet Halley's work on *Bowers v. Hardwick* (1993, 1994), Lisa Bowers's essay "Queer acts and the politics of 'direct address'" (1994), and Carl Stychin's *Law's Desire* (1995). Their work is more explicitly concerned with an examination of the deployment of homosexual as the sexual "other" in the constitution of heterosexuality as the norm. Other more recent work with a lesbian and gay focus explores the way in which the heterosexual assumption is also informed by way of gender (Eaton, 1994; Sharpe, 2002), race (Eaton, 1995; Hutchinson, 1999, 2000; Jefferson, 1998; Kwan, 1997), ethnicity (Valdes, 1995, 1997, 1998, 1999), and ability. One theme that remains underdeveloped in this context is work on the role of class in the production of the hetero/homo relation (see Moran, 1999).

The issues and work considered so far has been framed by way of the enigma of heterosexuality in law and society scholarship. I now want to reframe the analysis and to turn to explore and analyze that body of works on sexuality that is concerned directly with lesbian and gay experiences and encounters with law.

LESBIAN, GAY, AND ITS LIMITS

Gay and lesbian scholarship on law saw a massive expansion in the last decades of the twentieth century. Several factors fueled this rise: the growth of gay and lesbian identity politics, the political and social effects of the AIDS pandemic, and, particularly in the USA, the Supreme Court decision of *Bowers v. Hardwick* (1986) and the rise of the religious right (Herman, 1998). How much of this scholarship falls within a law and society frame?

Empirical work using quantitative (statistical) and qualitative (interviews, focus groups, ethnography) methods associated with scholarship on law as a more broadly based social science is not the dominant mode of this scholarship. Much of the work falls within a legal positivist approach. Another dominant approach has a jurisprudential focus. H.L.A. Hart's *Law, Liberty, Morality* (1963) and Lord Devlin's *The Enforcement of Morals* (1965) remain the canonical texts in this field of scholarship, offering respectively libertarian and utilitarian perspectives. More recently natural law has gained importance, being used as a philosophy and an epistemology that both legitimates lesbian and gay as the "other" (see Finnis, 1970, 1983, 1993, 2001) and challenges that heteronormative position (see Bamforth, 1997; Ball, 1997; Koppelman, 1997; Mohr, 1988).

In general neither the legal positivist nor philosophical bodies of scholarship fit within the frame of work on law and society (see Moran, 2002). Work that might be more readily characterized as law and society scholarship focuses upon a variety of issues in various disciplinary contexts. Herek and Berrill's work, *Hate Crime: Confronting Violence Against Lesbians and Gay Men* (1992) and Gary Comstock's 1991 study, *Violence Against Lesbians and Gay Men* raise new questions about the operation of criminal law and the process of criminal justice. Their work has played a key role in mapping forms of violence that were both promoted and condoned in and through the law and invisible within the institutions and practices of law. Work by Lobel (1986), Taylor and Chandler (1995), and Leventhal and Lundy (1999) has begun to explore violence within lesbian and gay domestic relationships and legal responses to it. Valerie Jenness, with colleagues Kendal Broad (1997) and Ryken Grattet (2001) have undertaken important work within sociology developing a social problems analysis on the rise of a lesbian and gay politics of violence and activism around the enactment of hate crime provisions. Work by Rosga (1999, 2000, 2001) develops a post-structuralist analysis of homophobic hate and legal and personal responses to it. Much of this work has a strong empirical focus, using questionnaires, surveys, statistical analysis, and drawing upon interview data to generate knowledge of those who are subjected to law and of those who function in the name of the law (cf. Moran and Skeggs, 2004).

Within political science, work can be organized around two themes: the critical analysis of key concepts and canonical texts of political science and sexual citizenship. Phelan (1997) and Kaplan (1997) provide examples of work that addresses themes of sexuality within the domain of political science. Phelan's collection contains essays on "rights talk," "equality," "justice," and "official recognition," analyzed through the lens of queer. Kaplan's study of sexual justice draws upon more traditional ideas of political science. Phelan's study, *Sexual Strangers* (2001) offers a critical reflection on sexual citizenship. Bowers's essay, "Queer acts and the politics of 'direct address'" (1994), sets the politics of sexual citizenship, which she describes in terms of strategies of "official recognition," within the context of wider landscapes of political action. She attempts to theorize "new" strategies of direct action and performance that characterized the heady moments of queer activism. In other social science fields associated with law and society scholarship, particularly criminology and criminal justice, lesbian and gay work is still exceptional. A small body of work studies gay and lesbian sexuality in the context of the institutions and practices of policing and more generally in the administration of law and order in Anglo-American contexts (Burke, 1993; Leinen, 1993; Buhrke, 1997). Recent work within criminology includes Groomridge's work on "Perverse criminologies" (1999), prisons (Alarid 2000), Dalton's study of homosexuality, criminality, and the media (2000) and Stanko and Curry's work on homophobia and policing (1997).

Law scholarship on lesbian and gay sexuality that is aligned more closely with the social sciences, directly incorporating and deploying its knowledge and methods and, more recently, that associated with the arts and humanities, is growing. This is work not only informed by lesbian, gay, and more recently queer scholarship and activism, but also by Marxist, post-Marxist/post-structuralist theory, and feminisms (Backer, 1998; Boyd, 1999; Cooper, 1994; Davies, 1999; Eaton, 1994, 1995; Halley, 1993, 1994; Herman, 1994; Herman and Stychin, 1995; Howe, 1998, 1999; Kapur, 1999; Mason, 1995, 1997, 2001; Mason and Tomsen, 1997; McGhee, 2001; Moran, 1996, Moran and McGhee, 1998; Moran, Monk, and Beresford, 1998; Morgan, 1994, 1997; Robson, 1992, 1998, 2001; Stychin, 1995, 1998, 2000; Stychin and Herman, 2000). Much of this work challenges assumptions about the essence, coherence, and fixity of identity and the totalizing characteristics of categories of identity. Particular attention has been paid to the ways in which sexualities are contested in and through legal categories. Their contingency and instability has also been emphasized in this work. It explores the way sexualized subjects are produced by way of violent hierarchies of hetero and homo, of masculine and feminine. In this work sexualities are relational, partial, subject to failure, never contained, always subject to a surplus.

In this section I want to briefly explore a problematic silence in lesbian and gay scholarship: the lesbian and gay demand for law. More specifically I want to put this demand in the context of the work of Robert Cover (1986) and others (Derrida, 1992; Sarat and Kearns, 1992) who suggest that the demand for law is a demand for law's violence. Cover's work highlights the relation between law and violence in various contexts. It is perhaps most apparent and extreme in the context of criminal law, which is intimately connected to the imposition of pain and in certain jurisdictions, death. But the law/violence relation is more general. Through the "interpretation" of the text of law, the rule (language and reason) is turned into an action. Lesbian and gay activism and scholarship has long worked to draw attention to law's violence and to document its operation in the (re)production of same-sex relations as "other" in both public and private law contexts, in civil and criminal law. In turn lesbian and gay politics has long been undertaken as a practice of resistance to this legal violence. Many of the demands of that politics have taken the form of a call for an end to and liberation from the violence of the law. The longstanding and continuing demand for the decriminalization of prohibited genital acts between persons of the same sex is perhaps the best example of this mode of engagement with law's violence.

In some instances these initiatives have also developed a different relation to law's violence to facilitate decriminalization (Heinze, 1995; Waaldijk and Clapham, 1993; Wintermute, 1995). An example of the changing relation between sexual politics and law's violence is to be found in lesbian and gay law and order politics that focus upon homophobic hate. This law and order politics is a call for access to law's violence. While on the one hand it seeks to challenge the use of law's violence for a heteronormative agenda, at the same time it is a demand for full access to law's violence for use against the heteronormative status quo (Jenness and Broad, 1997; Jenness and Grattet, 2001). Little activism or scholarship has addressed the question of the relationship between sexuality and violence that is being forged in the context of demands for law.

One context in which lesbian and gay scholars have engaged with problems arising out of law's violence is in their consideration of the effects of a politics of lesbian and gay "resistance through the law" (Merry, 1995). Various scholars have noted the way in which successful lesbian gay resort to "rights" (Stychin, 1995, 1998), "privacy" (Thomas, 1992), "equality" (Majury, 1994), and "sexual orienta-tion" as the basis for antidiscrimination initiatives in particular, and human rights more generally (Majury, 1994; Wintermute, 1995), has imposed new limits (new disadvantages) on social justice for lesbians and gay men. However, this body of criticism has rarely addressed these problems by way of an analysis of law as violence.

This is somewhat surprising as their work is about law's violence. The violence of law appears in two ways. First, and most explicitly, it appears in the analysis of the impact of law reform on the lives of lesbians and gay men. Second, it appears in an unarticulated form as the a priori of law. As such it is necessarily a theme of their work. At best, as an unarticulated assumption, these scholars give lesbian and gay license to law's violence. Their failure to make this assumption explicit makes them unthinking participants in the reproduction of an appeal to the "official" story of law as reason and rationality over against violence as that which is an always threatening presence outside the law (Sarat and Kearns, 1992). Their failure to engage with law's violence limits their capacity to engage with law in a critical way. The failure to address law's violence produces a paradox. The work of lesbian and gay scholars threatens to render the violence of law, that they have so persistently and diligently exposed, invisible one more time.

Ruthan Robson's (1998) work offers an exception to this. She offers a critique of lesbian and gay engagement with the law that pays particular attention to the complex relation between lesbian and gay identity politics and law's violence. There are two dimensions to her work. The first makes explicit the violence of legal categories, advocated to promote social justice for lesbians and gay men. Robson argues that by way of these reforms lesbian and gay demands for law connects identity politics with a violence that normalizes sexual (in this instance lesbian) identity (cf. Phelan, 2001).

One example she gives is the incorporation of sexual orientation into the US Hate Crimes Statistics Act 1990. The successful incorporation of "sexual orientation" as a category of "hate crime" provides a context for this "new" violence of law, which takes the form of qualifications added to the Act. "Sexual orientation," the Act declares, is not to be interpreted as a positive reference to lesbian or gay sexuality.

Nor is it to be taken as a legislative basis for new antidiscrimination claims. Robson suggests a second instance of law's violence against lesbians and gay men in the context of distinctions that are made in the legislation between various identities. The enactment of identity categories installs a logic of either/or (either lesbian or black, gay or latino) that does considerable violence to experiences of the injuries connected to identity. These categories fail to take the multiplicity and complexity of identity seriously. Identity categories offer a complex of criteria through which distinctions are generated to differentiate good lesbians from bad lesbians, deserving lesbians from undeserving lesbians (cf. Collier, 1998). As such they work to produce new exclusions at the same time as they produce new dimensions of social inclusion. Robson's analysis warns us that what might appear in the first instance to be lesbian and gay access to good violence, of turning the state against itself, may at the same time be an experience of another good violence where state violence is used against lesbians and gay men.

A strength of Robson's analysis is that it draws attention to the ambivalence of law's violence as a means to an end. Having exposed the contradictory and unstable relation of lesbian (and gay) politics to the violence of law, in the final instance much of her analysis emphasizes law's violence as bad violence. This does not exhaust her analysis of the relation between sexual identity and violence. The second and novel feature of her analysis is that her exposure of law's violence as "bad violence" does not lead her to abandon violence. She works to retrieve an idea of good violence for lesbian politics. It is to that part of her analysis that I now want to turn. She pursues this through an exploration of another violence.

Her point of departure is that, "violence mediates all relationships between lesbians and the law" (Robson 1998: 15). She declares, "I want to claim violence as an attribute of lesbianism" (p.16). It is in this context that her work offers a rare example of an attempt to address the question of the use of violence as a lesbian (or gay) resource (cf. Scalettar, 2000).

The first step in her attempt to forge a link between violence and sexual identity is to rename that violence as "fire." In part her resort to a different metaphor of violence is a response to the negative associations connected with violence: "To posit an identification between lesbianism and violence implies that lesbianism is bad (since violence is negative)" (Robson, 1998: 16). "Fire" is offered as an alternative metaphor in order to retrieve an idea of good violence. Her choice of metaphor is not arbitrary. "Fire," she argues, has strong historical and cultural associations with women in general and lesbians in particular. At the same time Robson notes the ambivalence of "fire" as violence: it connotes both "good" violence as well as "bad" violence.

She then proceeds to explore the terms of the lesbian/violence relation. Her point of departure is that lesbianism "is inherently violent" (1998: 26). This is explained in various ways. Lesbianism is violence over against the violence of the law, which is a violence of "heterosexual hegemony." Lesbian is a violence that not only challenges that law but a violence that offers resistance to it. It is also, she notes, a violence that is "non-negotiable." It is a challenge to law. It is, she suggests, a violence that provokes an "emancipatory change" in contrast with the violence of law that conserves and is conservative.

How are we to make sense of Robson's characterization of lesbianism as violence? Derrida's work on the force of law is useful here. Derrida suggests that: "The state is afraid of fundamental, founding violence, that is, violence able to justify, to legitimate or to transform the relations of law, and so to present itself as having a right to law. This violence thus belongs in advance to the order of a *droit* that remains to be transformed or founded . . . " (1992: 34–5).

Robson's lesbian violence is violence that challenges the status quo. It is a challenge that takes the form of protofounding violence and as such is always already of the order of a *droit*. The reference to its "emancipatory" potential gives it the attribute of a potential to "transform" and thereby to present itself as having a "right to law." As such it is a good violence that is always already in the image of the good violence of law.

Robson's analysis is important in various ways. It is exceptional in the way it points to lesbian (and gay) politics as violence and lesbian (and gay) politics as a demand for good violence. A second important insight is the recognition that violence is ambivalent, both good and bad. However, it is in this context that Robson's analysis begins to falter. Her, albeit preliminary, thoughts on lesbianism as violence give priority to that violence as a founding or originary violence. Little or no attention is given to the conservative aspect of that violence.

A second problem is in Robson's ability to sustain the ambivalence of violence, both good and bad. Ambivalence is difficult to sustain. There is a tendency to manage ambivalence by separating out the contradictory attributes that inhere in each particular instance in both time and space (cf. Freud, 1985; Bauman, 1991; Moran, 2002). This process of repression and displacement feeds a logic of either/or that further perpetuates the denial of ambivalence. In Robson's analysis the displacement and repression tends to take the form of lesbian violence as good violence in contrast to law's violence as bad violence. Perhaps the clearest example of this is the suggestion that lesbian violence may be emancipatory (good) over against the violence of law that conserves and is conservative (bad). It is important to remind ourselves of Derrida's insight that the two are intimately connected. Lesbianism as violence is both good violence (emancipatory) and bad violence (conservative) both before the law and as a challenge to law and as the law.

Conclusions

It has not always been possible to draw out the many themes that are being subject to interrogation in the lesbian and gay work that dominates sexuality studies in law and society. For example, within lesbian and gay scholarship there is much growing recognition that lesbian experiences of law are very different from that of gay men (Boyd, 1999; Chapman and Mason, 1999; Majury, 1994; Mason, 1995, 1997, 2001; Robson, 1992, 1998). As histories of the sexual relations between women in law emerge it becomes clear that same-sex sexual relations between women, rather than being absent from the field of criminal law, were policed in different ways (Doan, 2001; Duggan, 2000; Hart, 1994). There remains much work to be done to examine how different sexualities are produced in different legal categories in different spheres of law (Crompton, 1980; Faderman, 1981, 1983; Robson, 1992). The failure to take account of the different economic position of women, the different social status of women, the different priorities of women, and the different social experiences of women is also being challenged (Majury, 1994; Boyd, 1999). Much needs to be done to take seriously the interface between the global (totalizing) and local (individualizing) dimensions of the sexuality/law interface (Berger, 2000;

Kapur, 1999, 2001; Phillips, 1997; Stychin, 1998). Finally a small body of trans-gender scholarship has begun to challenge some of the assumptions about the nature of sexuality and the relations between sexuality and gender in law (Sharpe, 1997, 1998, 1999, 2002; Whittle, 1998, 2000).

Most of the work discussed here remains focused upon the "high culture" of law as represented in legislative literature and the reported decisions of its superior courts. Less common is work that focuses upon law as it figures in the "everyday" (Bowers, 1994; Moran and Skeggs, 2001). Little work has addressed sexuality in law and society scholarship by reference to "low" and "popular" culture (Loizidou, 1998; Moran, 1998). In 1994 Lisa Bowers pointed to the need to situate law within the context of wider cultural practices and to examine the connections and discon-nection between law and the multiple sites of practices of identity formation outside that domain. It is one of the many challenges that still needs to be addressed in studies of sexuality in law and society scholarship.

This review of work on sexuality in law and society scholarship is inevitably a partial and idiosyncratic overview. The more extended reflections on the enigma of heterosexuality in law and society scholarship and the silences relating to violence as a resource for lesbians and gay men point to some of the important limits of this work. A rereading of the canon of law and society scholarship as a heteronormative project is one major task that lies ahead. A critical reflection on the politics of violence being produced through identity politics is another.

These, I suggest, are urgent issues that need to be addressed by both current and future scholars. While I have presented them in discrete contexts in this essay they are problems and challenges that are intimately connected. Nor are they matters that are unique to scholarship on sexuality in the field of law and society. Sexuality provides a context in which these issues might be subject to rigorous interrogation. There are many contemporary challenges. Many lie ahead. Much work remains to be done.

Note

The chapter was written while I was joint visiting research fellow in the Fisher Center for the Study of Men and Women and the Department of Political Science, Hobart and William Smith Colleges, Geneva, NY. Special thanks to colleagues in the Fisher Center who provided an intellectual home during this period.

References

Alarid, L.F. (2000) "Sexual orientation perspectives on incarcerated bisexual and gay men: The county jail protective custody experience," *Prison Journal* 80(1): 80–95.
Albany Symposium (2001) "'Family' and the political landscape for lesbian, gay, bisexual and transgender people," *Albany Law Review* 64.
Backer, L.K. (1998) "Queering theory: An essay on the conceit of revolution in law," in L. Moran, D. Monk, and S. Beresford (eds), *Legal Queeries*. London: Cassell, pp 185–203.
Ball, C.A. (1997) "Moral foundations for a discourse on same-sex marriage: Looking beyond political liberalism," *Georgetown Law Journal* 85: 1872–1912.
Bamforth, N. (1997) *Sexuality, Morals and Justice*. London: Cassell.
Bauman, Z. (1991) *Modernity and Ambivalence*. Cambridge, UK: Polity.

Berger, N. (2000) "Queer readings of Europe: Gender, identity, sexual orientation and the (im)potency of rights politics at the European Court of Justice," *Social and Legal Studies* 9(2): 249–70.

Bohannan, P. and Huckleberry, K. (1967) "Institutions of divorce, family and the law," *Law and Society Review* 1(2): 81–102.

Bowers v. Hardwick (1986) 92 L Ed (1986), pp. 140–65.

Bowers, L. (1994) "Queer acts and the politics of 'direct address': Rethinking law, culture, and community," *Law & Society Review* 28(5): 1009–34.

Boyd, S. (1999) "Family law and sexuality: Feminist engagements," *Social and Legal Studies* 8(3): 369–90.

Buhrke, R.A. (1997) *A Matter of Justice*. London: Routledge.

Burke, M. (1993) *Coming Out of the Blue*. London: Cassell.

Butler, J. (1990) *Gender Trouble: Feminism and the Subversion of Identity*. London: Routledge.

Butler, J. (1993) *Bodies that Matter: On the Discursive Limits of "Sex."* New York: Routledge.

Chapman, A. and Mason, G. (1999) "Women, sexual preferenec and discrimination law: A case study of the NSW jurisdiction," *Sydney Law Review* 21: 525–66.

Cleveland State (2000) "Symposium: Re-orientating law and sexuality," *Cleveland State Law Review* 25.

Collier, R. (1992) "'The art of living the married life': Representations of male heterosexuality in law," *Social and Legal Studies* 1(4): 543–63.

Collier, R. (1996) "'Coming together?': Post-heterosexuality, masculine crisis, and the new men's movement," *Feminist Legal Studies* 4(1): 3–48.

Collier, R. (1998) "'Nutty professors,' 'men in suits' and 'new entrepreneurs': Corporeality, subjectivity and change in law school and legal practice," *Social and Legal Studies* 7(1): 27–53.

Comstock, G.D. (1991) *Violence Against Lesbians and Gay Men*. New York: Columbia University Press.

Cooper, D. (1994) *Sexing the City: Lesbian and Gay Politics Within the Activist State*. London: Rivers Oram Press.

Crompton, L. (1980) "The myth of lesbian impunity," *Journal of Homosexuality* 6(1–2): 11–32.

Cover, R. (1986) "Violence and the word," *Yale Law Review* 95: 1601–29.

Dalton D. (2000) "The deviant gaze: Imagining the homosexual as criminal through cinematic and legal discourses," in C. Stychin and D. Herman (eds.), *Sexuality in the Legal Arena*. London: Athlone, pp. 69–83.

Davies, M. (1999) "Queer property, queer persons: Self-ownership and beyond," *Social and Legal Studies* 8(3): 327–52.

Derrida, J. (1992) "Force of law: The mystical foundation of authority," in D. Cornell, M. Rosenfeld, and D.G. Carlson (eds.), *Deconstruction and the Possibility of Justice*. London: Routledge, pp. 3–67.

Devlin, P. (1965) *The Enforcement of Morals*. Oxford: Oxford University Press.

Doan, L. (2001) *Fashioning Sapphism*. New York: Columbia University Press.

Duggan L. (2000) *Sapphic Slashers*. Durham, NC: Duke University Press.

Eaton, M. (1994) "At the intersection of gender and sexual orientation: Towards a lesbian jurisprudence," *Southern California Review of Law and Women's Studies* 1994: 183–220.

Eaton, M. (1995) "Homosexual unmodified: Speculations on law's discourse, race and the construction of sexual identity," in D. Herman and C. Stychin (eds.), *Legal Inversions*. Philadelphia: Temple University Press, pp. 46–76.

Faderman, L. (1981) *Surpassing the Love of Men*. New York: William Morrow.

Faderman, L. (1983) *Scotch Verdict*. New York: William Morrow.

Finnis, J.M. (1970) "Natural law and unnatural acts," *Heythrop Journal* 11: 365–87.

Finnis, J.M. (1983) *Natural Law and Natural Rights*. Oxford: Clarendon Press.

Finnis, J.M. (1993) "Law, morality and 'sexual orientation'," *Notre Dame Law Review* 69: 1049–98.

Finnis, J. (2001) "Virtue and the Constitution of the United States," *Fordham Law Review* 69(5): 1595–1630.

Foucault, M. (1980) *The History of Sexuality, Volume 1: An Introduction*, trans. R. Hurley. New York: Vintage Books.

Freud, S. (1985) "The uncanny," in *The Pelican Freud Library, Vol. 14, Art and Literature*. London: Penguin Books, pp. 335–76.

Fuss, D. (1991) *Inside/Out*. London: Routledge.

Galanter, M. (1973) "From the new editor," *Law & Society Review* 8(1).

Groombridge, N. (1999) "Perverse criminologies: The closet door of Dr. Lombroso," *Social and Legal Studies* 8(4): 531–48.

Halley, J.E. (1993) "The construction of heterosexuality," in M. Warner (ed.), *Fear of a Queer Planet: Queer Politics and Social Theory*. Minneapolis: University of Minnesota Press, pp. 82–104.

Halley, J.E. (1994) "*Bowers v. Hardwick* in the Renaissance," in J. Goldberg (ed.), *Queering the Renaissance*. Durham, NC: Duke University Press, pp. 145–204.

Hart, H.L.A. (1963) *Law, Liberty and Morality*. Oxford: Oxford University Press.

Hart, L. (1994) *Fatal Women*. Princeton, NJ: Princeton University Press.

Heinze, E. (1995) *Sexual Orientation: A Human Right*. Dordrecht: Martiinus Nijhoff.

Herek, G.M. and Berill, K.T (1992) *Hate Crimes: Confronting Violence Against Lesbians and Gay Men*. London: Sage.

Herman, D. (1994) *Rights of Passage: Struggles for Lesbian and Gay Legal Equality*. Toronto: University of Toronto Press.

Herman, D. (1998) *The Antigay Agenda: Orthodox Vision and the Christian Right*. Chicago, Chicago University Press.

Herman, D and Stychin, C (eds.) (1995) *Legal Inversions*. Philadelphia: Temple University Press.

Howe, A. (1998) "Green v the Queen: The provocation defence finally provoking its own demise?" *Melbourne University Law Review* 22: 466–86.

Howe, A. (1999) "Reforming provocation (more of less)," *Australian Feminist Law Journal* 12: 127–40.

Hutchinson, D.L. (1999) "Ignoring the sexualization of race: Heternormativity, critical race theory and anti-racist politics," *Buffalo Law Review* 41 (Spring/Summer): 1–116.

Hutchinson, D.L. (2000) "'Gay rights' for 'gay whites'? Race, sexual identity and equal protection discourse," *Cornell Law Review* 85: 1358–91.

Jefferson, T.R. (1998) "Notes towards a black lesbian jurisprudence," *Boston College Third World Law Journal* 18 (Spring): 263–94.

Jenness, V. and Broad, K. (1997) *Hate Crimes: New Social Movements and the Politics of Violence*. Hawthorne NY: Aldine deGruyter.

Jenness, V and Grattet, R. (2001) *Building the Hate Crime Policy Domain: From Social Movement Concept to Law Enforcement Practice*. New York: Russell Sage Foundation.

Kaplan, M. (1997) *Sexual Justice*. New York: Routledge.

Kapur, R. (1999) "'A love song for our mongrel selves': Hybridity, sexuality and law," *Social and Legal Studies* 8(3): 353–68.

Kapur, R. (2001) "Postcolonial erotic disruptions: Legal narratives of culture, Sex and nation in India," *Columbia Journal of Gender and Law* 10: 333–84.

Katz, J.N. (1995) *The Invention of Heterosexuality*. New York: Penguin.

Kitzinger, C and Wilkinson, S. (1993) "Theorizing heterosexuality," in S. Wilkinson and C. Kitzinger (eds.), *Heterosexuality: A Feminist and Psychology Reader*. London, Sage, pp. 1–32.

Koppelman, A. (1997) "Is marriage inherently heterosexual?," *American Journal of Jurisprudence* 42: 51–74.

Kwan, P. (1997) "Jeffrey Dahmer and the cosynthesis of categories," *Hastings Law Journal* 48: 1257–92.

Leventhal, B. and Lundy, S.E. (eds.) (1999) *Same-Sex Domestic Violence.* Thousand Oaks, CA: Sage.

Leinen, S. (1993) *Gay Cops.* New Brunswick, NJ: Rutgers University Press.

Lobel, K. (ed) (1986) *Naming the Violence: Speaking Out About Lesbian Battering.* Boston: Seal Press.

Loizidou, E. (1998) "Intimate celluloid: *Heavenly Creatures* and criminal law," in L. Moran, D. Monk, and S. Beresford (eds.), *Legal Queeries.* London: Cassell, pp. 167–84.

Majury, D. (1994) "Refashioning the unfashionable: Claiming lesbian identities in the legal context," *Canadian Journal of Women and the Law* 7(2): 286–306.

Mason, G. (1995) "(Out)laws: Acts of proscription in the sexual order," in Margaret Thornton (ed.), *Public and Private: Feminist Legal Debates.* Oxford: Oxford University Press, pp. 66–88.

Mason G. (1997) "Boundaries of sexuality: Lesbian experience and feminist discourse on violence against women," *Australasian Gay and Lesbian Law Journal* 7: 40–56.

Mason, G. (2001) *The Spectacle of Violence.* London: Routledge.

Mason, G. and Tomsen S. (eds.) (1997) *Homophobic Violence.* Sydney: Hawkins Press.

McGhee, D. (2001) *Homosexuality, Law and Resistance.* London: Routledge.

Merry, S. (1995) "Resistance and the cultural power of law," *Law and Society Review* 29(1): 11–26.

Mohr, R.D. (1988) *Gays/Justice: A Study of Ethics, Society and Law.* New York: Columbia University Press.

Moran, L.J. (1996) *The Homosexual(ity) of Law.* London: Routledge.

Moran, L.J. (1998) "From part time hero to bent buddy: The male homosexual as lawyer in popular culture," *Studies in Law Politics and Society* 18: 3–28.

Moran L.J. (1999) "Homophobic violence: The hidden injuries of class," in Sally Munt (ed.), *Working Class and Cultural Studies.* London: Cassell, pp. 206–18.

Moran, L.J. (2002) "The poetics of safety: Lesbians, gay men and home," in A. Crawford (ed.), *Crime, Insecurity, Safety in the New Governance.* Cullompton, UK: Wilans Publishing, pp. 274–99.

Moran, L.J. and McGhee, D. (1998) "Perverting London: Cartographic practices of policing," *Law and Critique* IX(2): 207–24.

Moran, L.J., Monk, D., and Beresford, S. (eds.) (1998) *Legal Queeries.* London: Cassell.

Moran L.J. and Skeggs, B. (2001) "The property of safety," *Journal of Social Welfare and Family Law,* 23(4): 1–15.

Moran L.J. and Skeggs, B. (2004) *Sexuality and the Politics of Violence and Safety.* London, Routledge.

Morgan W. (1994) "Identifying evil for what it is: Tasmania, sexual perversity and the United Nations," *Melbourne University Law Review* 19: 740–70.

Morgan W. (1997) "A queer kind of law: The senate inquiries into sexuality," *International Journal of Discrimination and Law* 2: 317–32.

New York (2000) "Symposium: Queer law 2000," *New York University Law Review of Law and Social Change* 16.

Olson Rogers K. (1972) "'For her own protection...': Conditions of incarceration for female juvenile offenders in the State of Connecticut," *Law and Society Review* 7(2): 223–46.

Penelope, J. (1993) "Heterosexual identity: Out of the closets," in S. Wilkinson and C. Kitzinger (eds.), *Heterosexuality: A Feminist and Psychology Reader.* London: Sage, pp. 261–5.

Phelan, S. (ed.) (1997) *Playing with Fire: Queer Politics, Queer Theories.* New York: Routledge.

Phelan, S. (2001) *Sexual Strangers: Gays, Lesbians and the Dilemmas of Citizenship.* Philadelphia: Temple University Press.

Phillips, O. (1997) "Zimbabwean law and the production of a white man's disease," *Social and Legal Studies* 6(4): 471–93.

Richardson D. (ed) (1996) *Theorizing Heterosexuality.* Buckingham, UK: Open University Press.

Robson, R. (1992) *Lesbian (Out)law.* Ithaca, NY: Firebrand.

Robson, R. (1998) *Sappho Goes to Law School.* New York: Columbia University Press.

Robson, R. (2001) "Our children: Kids of queer parents and kids who are queer; looking at minority rights from a different perspective," *Albany Law Review* 64: 915–48.

Rosga, A. (1999) "Policing and the state," *Georgetown Journal of Gender and Law* 1 (Summer): 145–71.

Rosga, A. (2000) "Ritual killings: Anti-gay violence and reasonable justice" in J. James (ed.), *States of Confinement: Policing, Detention and Prisons.* New York, St. Martins Press, pp. 172–90.

Rosga, A. (2001) "Deadly words: State power and the entanglement of speech and violence in hate crime," *Law and Critique* 12(3): 223–52.

Sarat A. and Kearns, T.R. (eds.) (1992) *Law's Violence.* Ann Arbor: University of Michigan Press.

Scalettar, L. (2000) "Resistance, representation and the subject of violence: Reading 'Hothead Paisan',," in J.A. Boone and Queer Frontiers Editorial Collective (eds.), *Queer Frontiers: Millenial Geographies, Genders and Generations.* Madison: University of Wisconsin, pp. 261–78.

Sedgwick, E.K. (1990) *Epistemology of the Closet.* Hemel Hempstead, UK: Harvester Wheatsheaf.

Sharpe, A. (1997) "Anglo-Australian judicial approaches to transsexuality: Discontinuities, continuities, and wider issues at stake," *Social and Legal Studies* 6(1): 23–50.

Sharpe, A (1998) "Institutionalising heterosexuality: The legal exclusion of 'impossible' (trans)sexualities," in L. Moran, D. Monk, and S. Beresford (eds.), *Legal Queeries.* London: Cassell, pp. 26–43.

Sharpe, A. (1999) "Transgender performance and the discriminating gaze: A critique of antidiscrimination regulatory regimes," *Social and Legal Studies,* 8(1): 5–24.

Sharpe, A. (2002) *Transgender Jurisprudence: Dysphoric Bodies of Law.* London: Cavendish.

Social and Legal Studies (1997) Special issue on "Legal perversions," *Social and Legal Studies* 6(4).

Stanko B. and Curry P. (1997) "Homophobic violence and the self at risk," *Social and Legal Studies* 6(4): 513–32.

Stychin, C. (1995) *Law's Desire.* London: Routledge.

Stychin, C. (1998) *Nation by Rights.* Philadelphia: Temple University Press.

Stychin, C. (2000) "'A stranger to its laws': Sovereign bodies, global sexualities, and trans-national citizens," *Journal of Law and Society* 27(4): 601–28.

Stychin, C. and Herman, D. (2000) *Sexuality in the Legal Arena.* London: Athlone.

Taylor, J. and Chandler T. (1995) *Lesbians Talk Violent Relationships.* London: Scarlet Press.

Thomas, K. (1992) "Beyond the privacy principle," *Columbia Law Review* 92: 1431–516.

Thornton, M. (2002) "Foreword," in A. Sharpe, *Transgender Jurisprudence: Dysphoric Bodies of Law.* London: Cavendish, p. vii.

Valdes, F. (1995) "Sex and race in queer legal culture," *Review of Law and Women's Studies* 5: 25–71.

Valdes, F. (1997) "Queer margins, queer ethics: A call to account for race and ethnicity in the law, theory, and politics of 'sexual orientation,'" *Hastings Law Journal* 48: 1293–1341.

Valdes, F. (1998) "Beyond sexual orientation in queer legal theory: Majoritarianism, multidi-mensionality, and responsibility in social justice scholarship," *Denver University Law Review* 75(4): 1409–64.

Valdes, F. (1999) "Theorizing 'outcrit' theories: Coalitional method and comparative jurisprudential experience. Race crits, Queer crits, Lat crits," *University of Miami Law Review* 53: 1265–322.

Waaldijk, K. and Clapham, A. (1993) *Homosexuality: A European Community Issue*. Dordrecht: Nijhoff.

Warner, M. (ed.) (1993) *Fear of a Queer Planet*. Minneapolis: University of Minnesota.

Weeks, J. (1981) *Sex, Politics and Society: The Regulation of Sexuality Since 1800*. London: Longmans.

Weeks J. (1986) *Sexualities*. London, Routledge.

Whittle, S. (1998) "Gemeinschaftsfremden – or how to be shafted by your friends: Sterilization requirements and legal status recognition for the transsexual," in L. Moran, D. Monk, and S. Beresford (eds.), *Legal Queeries*. London: Cassell, pp. 42–56.

Whittle, S. (2000) *The Transgender Debate*. London: South Street Press.

Wilkinson S. and Kitzinger, C., (eds.) (1993) *Heterosexuality: A Feminist and Psychology Reader*. London, Sage.

Wintermute, R. (1995) *Sexual Orientation and Human Rights: The United States Constitution, the European Convention, and the Canadian Charter*. Oxford: Clarendon Press.

Young, A. (1990) *Femininity in Dissent*. London: Routledge.

Young, A. (1993) "The authority of the name," in S. Wilkinson and C. Kitzinger (eds.), *Heterosexuality: A Feminist and Psychology Reader*. London, Sage, pp. 37–9.

Further Reading

Binnie, J. and Bell, J. (2001) *Sexual Citizenship*. Cambridge, UK: Polity Press.

Bray, A. (1982) *Homosexuality in Renaissance England*. London: Gay Men's Press.

Chauncey, G. (1994) *Gay New York*. New York: Basic Books.

Goldberg, D.T., Musheno, M., and Bower, L. (eds) (2001). *Between Law and Culture: Relocating Legal Studies*. Minneapolis: University of Minnesota Press.

Goldberg Hiller, J. (2002) *The Limits to Union*. Ann Arbor: The University of Michigan Press.

Humphreys, L. (1970) *The Tearoom Trade*. London: Duckworth.

Keen, L. and Goldberg, S.G. (2000) *Strangers to the Law: Gay People on Trial*. Ann Arbor: The University of Michigan Press.

Munt, S. (1994) *Murder by the Book?* London: Routledge.

Stein, A. (2001) *The Stranger Next Door: The Story of a Small Community's Battle over Sex, Faith and Civil Rights*. Boston: Beacon Press.

Weeks, J. (1977) *Coming Out*. London: Quartet.

27

Law and Social Movements

MICHAEL McCANN

INTRODUCTION

Much recent scholarship has contributed to our understanding regarding how law matters for the political struggles of social movements. Two rather different intellectual traditions have proved most directly relevant to the topic. Sociolegal scholars have provided manifold insights about both the ways that prevailing legal norms tend to legitimate social hierarchy and the complex manifestations of legal claims and tactics aiming to challenge those hierarchies and injustices. Indeed, sociolegal scholars have contributed many types of studies – of judicial impact, interest group litigation, cause lawyering, the politics of rights, civil disputing, and everyday resistance, to name just a few – that are highly relevant to understanding the relationships of law and social movements. However, most of this scholarship grants at best passing notice to the extensive body of academic study focusing directly on social movement politics. In similar fashion, social movement specialists have documented many case studies where legal claims, tactics, and actors figured prominently, but these scholars have rarely provided direct conceptual analysis about how law does or does not matter for the struggles at stake, and generally have remained quite uninformed by sophisticated sociolegal analysis. Consequently, the extant scholarship that directly joins the rich literatures analyzing the two topics, law and social movements, is relatively scarce and specialized. This general disjuncture is as true for studies of the United States as it is for national-level and transnational activism around the world.

The following essay draws heavily on one synthetic approach – labeled "legal mobilization" theory – to analyzing law and social movements. Such an interpretive framework merges a dynamic dispute-oriented, interpretivist understanding of legal practice with insights from social movement theorizing about collective action based on "political process" (McCann, 1994; Silverstein, 1996; Keck and Sikkink, 1998).

This approach illustrates the benefits of joining these different academic traditions as well as providing a useful framework for mapping the many types of sociolegal study that directly or indirectly address social movement politics.

LAW AND SOCIAL MOVEMENTS: DEFINING CONCEPTS

Conceptualizing law

Much of the debate regarding how law matters for social movements derives from quite divergent ways of understanding and studying law itself. Most generally, when we refer to "the law," we imply different types of phenomena. We refer sometimes to official *legal institutions*, like courts or administrative bureaucracies; sometimes to *legal officials or elites*, such as judges, bureaucrats, or lawyers; and sometimes *to legal norms, rules, or discourses* that structure practices in and beyond official legal institutions (Thompson, 1975). Most recent studies grant attention to all three usages, although often in somewhat unclear or unsystematic ways. Legal realists and behavioralists, for example, tend to identify law in quite formal, determinate, positivist terms. Law, in this account, matters to the degree that official institutional actions cause direct, immediate, tangible effects on targeted behaviors (Rosenberg, 1991; Bogart, 2002). Measured by such a standard, legal institutions and officials often appear to provide powerful support for the status quo but feeble sources for challenging the prevailing order.

By contrast, interpretive, process-oriented legal mobilization approaches are typically much more expansive in conceptualizing law, especially regarding the legal norms and discursive logics at stake in many social struggles. The interpretive perspective begins by rejecting conventional positivist understandings of law largely limited to discrete, determinate rules or policy actions. Rather, law is understood as particular traditions of knowledge and communicative practice. As Galanter (1983: 127) has argued, law should be understood broadly "as a system of cultural and symbolic meanings [more] than as a set of operative controls. It affects us primarily through communication of symbols – by providing threats, promises, models, persuasion, legitimacy, stigma, and so on." The focus is not simply on behavior, but on the intersubjective power of law in constructing meaning. As such, legal discourses and symbols intersect with and are expressive of broader ideological formations within societies (Hunt, 1990; McCann, 1994; McCann and March, 1996).

Such an understanding of law as knowledge and linguistic practice calls attention to law's power as a *constitutive* convention of social life (Brigham, 1996). This constitutive power is ambiguous. On the one hand, legal knowledges to some degree shape, or prefigure, the identities and practical activities of subjects in society. Learned legal conventions mold the very terms of citizen understanding, expectation, and interaction with others. Law thus is a significant part of how we learn to live and act as citizens in society. Legal constructs shape our very imagination about social possibilities. Among the most important of liberal legal conventions constituting both national and transnational relations are what we call *rights* – those legal forms that designate the distribution of legitimate social entitlements and burdens among citizens.

On the other hand, law is also understood to be a resource that citizens utilize to structure relations with others, to advance goals in social life, to formulate rightful claims, and to negotiate disputes where interests, wants, or principles collide. Legal knowledges thus can matter as both an end and means of action; law provides both normative principles and strategic resources for the conduct of social struggle. Indeed, this is the core meaning of what many scholars label legal mobilization: *law is mobilized when a desire or want is translated into an assertion of right or lawful claim* (Zemans, 1983). Most such specific legal claims refer, of course, to settled, relatively uncontested entitlements. But at other times citizens often interpret laws in different ways, reshaping law in the process to fit shifting visions of need and circumstance; we reconstitute to some degree the law that constitutes us. In this sense, legal conventions are understood as a quite malleable medium, routinely employed to reconfigure relations, redefine entitlements, and formulate aspirations for collective living (Merry, 1985). As Professor Martha Minow (1987: 1867) puts it, legal "rights can give rise to a rights consciousness so that individuals and groups may imagine and act on rights than have not been formally recognized or enforced" by state officials. We soon shall see that this concept *of rights consciousness* – as a developing understanding of social relations in terms of rights – is a critical one for analysis of law and social movements throughout the world.

Of course, this indeterminacy or plasticity of legal conventions is limited. Legal practices carry with them their own inherent constraints on what is accepted as legally sensible or compelling, and governing authorities often back these constraints up with organized force. This is where the role of official legal institutions and state or transnational elites, such as judges, matter. Official institutions function to "police" the range of law's legitimate meanings, to enforce limits on those meanings, and to use selectively organized violence against those who violate official readings of law or who are outside law's inherent protections. But law also thrives outside of such direct police power intervention, and outside of courtrooms in particular, where official legal meanings rule only indirectly as a possibility of intervening force to settle disputes or enforce particular legal practices. Indeed, this possibility, either implicit or explicitly threatened, that official third parties (such as judges or police) might intervene tends to shape social interaction and bargaining relations far more than actual direct official interventions (Galanter, 1983).

It is law's complex life throughout society – within workplaces, corporate board rooms, families, neighborhoods, and communities as well as throughout public institutional spaces of national and transnational politics – under the "shadow" of official rule on which most conflict-based, process-oriented studies focus attention. Indeed, it is here that the primary project of legal mobilization analysis is aimed – that is, to analyze the constitutive role of legal rights both as a strategic resource *and* as a constraint, as a source of empowerment and disempowerment, for struggles to transform, or to reconstitute, the terms of social relations and power (see Scheingold, 1989; Silverstein, 1996). This understanding is especially important for appreciating the increasing power of human rights norms around the world, in polities and transnational or international arenas where authoritative legal institutions are often underdeveloped or contested.

One more aspect of law fills out the picture. In short, the process-oriented, constitutive approach presumes that law is a partial and contingent force in society. This calls attention, on the one hand, to the fact that legal tactics of social movements are most often coordinated with other political tactics such as legislative lobbying, partisan electoral advocacy, media campaigns, information disclosure, or public protest. Indeed, much study emphasizes that litigation and other official legal actions are most often and effectively utilized as a secondary or supplementary political strategy in social movement struggles. On the other hand, the legal mobilization approach recognizes as well that legal conventions constitute just one of the many variable types of norms that govern and give meaning to social life. This suggests that any assessment of specific legal mobilization practices by social movements must be undertaken with reference to the larger context of multiple legal and extralegal forces that structure social relations.

Social movements

The core term "social movements" is defined in quite variable ways by scholars, including by specialists on the topic. Political scientist Charles Tilly's definition in a 1984 book is as useful as any. A social movement is "a sustained series of interactions between powerholders and persons successfully claiming to speak on behalf of a constituency lacking formal representation, in the course of which those persons make publicly visible demands for changes in the distribution or exercise of power, and back those demands with public demonstrations of support" (Tilly, 1984: 306). The problem with this definition, of course, is that it does not clearly distinguish social movements from interest groups, minority political parties, protesting mobs, and other forms of collective action. Scholarly efforts have been made to differentiate social movements by what they want, whom they represent, and what tactics they use – but few such efforts are entirely successful at an abstract level. The dilemma is exacerbated, further, by the fact that the organization and activities of what we call social movements often overlap with, grow out of, or transform into other forms of organization over time in complex, elusive ways.

Despite these caveats, however, I will limit the range of activity referred to as "social movements" for the purposes of this paper. Social movement activity here is identified broadly with social struggles of a particular type. First, social movements aim for a broader scope of social and political transformation than do most more conventional political activities. While social movements may press for tangible short-term goals within the existing structure of relations, they are animated by more radical aspirational visions of a different, better society. Second, social movements often employ a wide range of tactics, as do parties and interest groups, but they are far more prone to rely on communicative strategies of information disclosure and media campaigns as well as disruptive "symbolic" tactics such as protests, marches, strikes, and the like that halt or upset ongoing social practices. One of the surprising findings of much research is that litigation and other seemingly conventional legal tactics sometimes can be fused with such disruptive forms of political expression. Law sometimes serves disorder as well as order (Lowi, 1971). Litigation can provide a form of, or forum for, "rebellion" (Meranto, 1998), a lethal "weapon" in social conflict (Turk, 1976).

Third, social movements tend to develop from core constituencies of nonelites whose social position reflects relatively low degrees of wealth, prestige, or political clout. While movements may find leadership or alliance among elites and powerful organizations, the core "indigenous population" of social movements tends to be "the nonpowerful, the nonwealthy and the nonfamous" (Zirakzadeh, 1997: 5). It is worth noting that this definition can include reactionary or highly conservative as well as "progressive" or left-leaning movements, although the overwhelming amount of academic study concerns only the latter groups. Fourth, the discussion below includes traditional modernist social movements focusing on class relations and material politics as well as new (or postmodern) social movements that emphasize a broad range of principled social justice commitments, including especially human rights (Buechler and Cylke, 1997). Lastly, this essay addresses social movements that develop *within* particular nations, generally focused on states as targets or means of transforming societies, as well as transnational movements for human rights, environmental change, peace, and the like. Studies of transnational activism have developed rapidly in recent years, and tend to rely on dynamic process-based approaches similar to those emphasized here (Keck and Sikkink, 1998). Indeed, cooperation among transnational and domestic national social movements on human rights issues is one of the most important manifestations of contemporary legal mobilization politics (Sarat and Scheingold, 2001).

LEGAL PRACTICES OF SOCIAL MOVEMENTS: A PROCESS-BASED OVERVIEW

With these general understandings in mind, we can now review some of the insights generated by scholars, especially those in the interpretive, process-based tradition, about law and social movements. The legal mobilization approach in particular envisions social disputing or struggles as processes that involve different moments or stages of development and conflict. This discussion of law's workings in various social movements will proceed by focusing on potential stages of conflict. At each stage, I will attempt to give examples where legal tactics and practices have proved empowering as well as disempowering for various movements.

It is important to emphasize at the outset, however, that legal practices or mobilization activities rarely are imposed as exogenous forces on nonlegalized social relations. Social terrains of struggle themselves are always constituted by a complex array of institutional norms, relations, and structures of power, including in most cases legally authorized norms backed up by the violence of individual states, coalitions of states, or transnational institutions like the United Nations. Hence, legal mobilization politics typically involves reconstructing legal dimensions of inherited social relations, either by turning official but ignored legal norms against existing practices, by reimagining shared norms in new transformative ways, or by importing legal norms from some other realm of social relations into the context of the dispute. In short, law often significantly supports prevailing social relations as well as provides resources for challenging those relationships. Social movement struggles often entail struggles over the very meaning of indeterminate, contradictory legal principles.

Law and the genesis of social movements

Perhaps the most significant point at which law matters for many social movements is during the earliest phases of organizational and agenda formation. The core insight has been expressed by Stuart Scheingold's (1974: 131) well-known argument regarding the "politics of rights." As he put it, it is possible for marginalized groups "to capitalize on the perceptions of entitlement associated with [legal] rights to initiate and to nurture political mobilization." This process of what is conventionally labeled "rights consciousness raising" can be understood to involve two separate, if often intimately related, processes of cognitive transformation in movement constituents.

The first of these entails the process of "agenda setting," by which movement actors *draw on legal discourses to "name" and to challenge* existing social wrongs or injustices. As such, legal norms and traditions can become important elements in the process of explaining how existing relationships are unjust, in defining collective group goals, and in constructing a common identity among diversely situated citizens (McCann, 1994; Schneider, 1986). "One of the main tasks that social movements undertake...is to make possible the previously unimaginable, by framing problems in such a way that their solution comes to appear inevitable," note two specialists (Keck and Sikkink, 1998: 40–1). Some scholars emphasize ways in which sense of injury and political challenge are formulated in legal terms from the outset, while yet others emphasize the process of "translation" from nonlegal grievances to legal claims (Paris, forthcoming). In either case, scholars emphasize how the very identities, interests, and ideals of movement activists can be constituted by, or even against, law (Brigham, 1996).

A second related way in which legal practices can contribute to movement building is by *defining the overall "opportunity structure"* within which movements develop. This insight draws on the common scholarly premise that movement formation and action is more likely in periods when dominant groups and state-authorized relationships are perceived as vulnerable to challenge (Piven and Cloward, 1979; McAdam, 1982). Advances through formal legal advocacy – and especially through high-profile litigation – many times have contributed to this sense of vulnerability among both state and nonstate authorities. In particular, judicial victories can impart salience or legitimacy to general categories of claims, such as equal rights, as well as to specific formulations of challenges within these broad legal traditions (Scheingold, 1974; Silverstein, 1996). Indeed, many scholars have noted a sort of "contagion effect" generated by rights litigation over the last 40 years in the United States (Tarrow, 1983; Epp, 1990), by legal rights mobilization increasingly in other regions such as the European Union (Cichowski, 2002), and by human rights advocacy around the world (Keck and Sikkink, 1998). There is some evidence that legal mobilization often succeeds in movement building because the mass media tend to be particularly responsive to rights claims and litigation campaigns for social justice, although this evidence is primarily limited to the US experience (McCann, 1994; Haltom, 1998) and is contested even there (Rosenberg, 1991). It is also worth noting that such opportunities for mobilization typically define just one of several potential venues for activity, each of which may vary widely in its promise. Moreover, opportunities often carry with them significant constraining or disciplining logics whereby legal action requires moderation of claims, narrowing of demands, or forfeiting of other tactics. The history of US labor activism exemplifies this point well (Forbath, 1991), as do the legacies of labor struggle and other modes of human rights advocacy (Dezalay and Garth, 2001) in various regions of the world.

These two dimensions of legal activism typically are interrelated in social movement development. For example, formal legal actions like litigation can work initially to expose systemic vulnerabilities and to render legal claims "sensible" or salient to aggrieved citizens. As marginalized groups act on these opportunities, they often gain sophistication and confidence in their capacity to mobilize legal conventions to "name" wrongs, to frame demands, and to advance their cause. Piven and

Cloward recognize this in their classic discussion of consciousness raising in protest politics. When citizens "begin to assert their 'rights' that imply demands for change," there often develops "a new sense of efficacy; people who ordinarily consider themselves helpless come to believe that they have some capacity to alter their lot" (1979: 4).

This complex process of legal catalysis was illustrated by the US civil rights movement in the 1950s. To begin with, a program of litigation leading up to the famous 1954 *Brown v. Board of Education* decision was vital to the evolving civil rights movement in two ways. First, it sparked southern blacks' hopes by demonstrating that the southern white power structure was vulnerable at some points and by providing scarce practical resources for defiant action. As historian Aldon Morris summarizes, "The winning of the 1954 decision was the kind of victory the organization needed to rally the black masses behind its program; by appealing to blacks' desire to enroll their children in the better equipped white schools it reached into black homes and had meaning for people's personal lives" (1984: 30).

Second, the increasing pressure on the southern white power structure to abolish racial domination led to a massive, highly visible attack – including legal assaults as well as physical violence – on the formal black leadership group, the National Association for the Advancement of Colored People. These reactions in turn forced a split between local, church-affiliated NAACP leaders urging more radical forms of protest action and the more bureaucratic, legally oriented leaders of the national organization. The result was a burst in both the momentum of the grassroots protest campaign among southern blacks generally and their frustration about the effectiveness of legal tactics alone. "The two approaches – legal action and mass protest – entered into a turbulent but workable marriage" (Morris, 1984: 39). Moreover, it was the resulting escalation of conflicts between whites and blacks on both fronts that "expanded the scope" of the dispute to include Washington officials, federal courts, the northern media, and national public opinion. Court decisions alone thus did not "cause," by moral inspiration, defiant black grassroots action or, by coercion, federal support for the civil rights agenda. Critics like Gerald Rosenberg (1991) are correct about this. But legal tactics pioneered by the NAACP figured very prominently in elevating civil "rights" claims and intensifying the initial terms of racial struggle in the south.

Similar dynamics have been evident in the movements for the rights of the disabled, gay rights, animal rights, and women's rights in the United States. These examples are especially interesting because they demonstrate that conclusive, far-reaching victories in courts or other official forums are not necessary to achieve this legal catalyzing effect. The wage equity issue in the United States, for example, largely developed in response to the limitations of traditional court-approved affirmative action policies for remedying discrimination against women workers locked into segregated jobs. After a string of defeats in the 1970s, the wage equity movement won a small victory in wage discrimination law at the Supreme Court level and one pathbreaking lower court ruling, which later was overturned on appeal. But in the five-year interim between the first and the last of these three rulings, movement leaders effectively used legal actions – despite doctrinal case law limitations – to organize women workers in hundreds of workplaces around the nation. A massive publicity campaign focusing on court victories initially put the issue on the national agenda and alerted leaders that wage equity was "the working women's issue of the 1980s." Lawsuits were then filed on behalf of working women as the centerpiece of a successful union and movement organizing strategy in scores of local venues around the nation. Again, the evidence suggests *not* that court decisions worked to "enlighten" working women about their subordination, as sometimes is claimed. Rather, sustained legal action over time worked to render employers vulnerable to challenge, to expand the resources available to working women, to provide them with a unifying claim of egalitarian rights, and to increase both their confidence and sophistication in advancing those claims (McCann, 1994).

These latter insights are particularly relevant to appreciating the considerable power of human rights advocacy in defining challenges to authoritarian regimes. Indeed, framing social issues as human rights issues has often been quite effective and empowering for movement mobilization. Rick Abel (1995) has shown how "speaking law to power" provided a powerful orienting frame for mobilizing challenges to apartheid in South Africa. The enterprise of renaming women's rights as human rights, and specifically of challenging female circumcision as violence against women, has redefined the symbolic terrain of struggle and mobilized nongovernmental organizations (NGOs) in support of women's issues around the globe in recent decades (Keck and Sikkink, 1998). There is also evidence that rights advocacy, often supplemented by litigation or other legal tactics, has generated considerable movement-building impetus in the European Union (Cichowski, 2002) and various parts of Latin America (Cleary, 1997; Meili, 2001).

Legal action often fails as a resource for expanding social movement activism, of course, largely due to the absence of favorable social conditions. This has been the case to some degree in various environmental justice campaigns and actions for the poor or homeless in the United States. Many labor rights campaigns against the sweatshop conditions of US-owned factories in developing countries and human rights campaigns against authoritarian violence, such as the massacre of protesting students in Mexico City's Tlatelolco Plaza and in Central Europe (Keck and Sikkink, 1998), have proved similarly limited in capacity to mobilize strong movement support and public attention. Feminists in Israel likewise were unable to use notable victories in the Israeli High Court of Justice as effective grassroots mobilizing resources. Moreover, legal tactics have arguably worked sometimes to discourage or thwart social movement development. One common critique is that legal tactics divert resources to lawyers who focus on litigation rather than on grassroots mobilization and other forms of arguably more effective political organizing (Scheingold, 1974; McCann and Silverstein, 1998). There is some limited evidence for this tendency in particular struggles within many countries (McCann, 1986; Rosenberg, 1991; Morag-Levine, 2001) as well as for the thesis that lawyers are often coopted or constrained by the elite institutional relations in which they are enmeshed (Dotan, 2001; Handler, 1978). Dezalay and Garth's (2001) argument about the containment of human rights lawyers' agendas in Latin America resulting from their dependence on US foundations and target states identifies an especially discouraging pattern of constraints in this regard.

Legal mobilization as political pressure

Other dimensions of social movement activity involve a common legal dynamic. In particular, legal advocacy often provides movement activists with a source of institutional and symbolic leverage against opponents. This leveraging activity is closely related to – indeed, it is the flip side of – law's generative contributions to movement building. Just as legal rights advocacy sometimes can "pull" in strong affirmative support for reform goals from various groups, so can it be employed as a weapon to "push" otherwise uncooperative foes into making concessions or compromises. As in movement-building efforts, this second dimension of legal mobilization usually entails some measure of litigation or other formal legal action. Nevertheless, we shall see that triumph in the courts is not always necessary to either short-term or long-term successful legal leveraging.

In some respects, this is hardly a pathbreaking insight. The uses of legal tactics and threats to compel informal resolution of everyday "private" disputes regarding divorce settlement, contractual obligations, liability for property damages, and the like are familiar to legal scholars (Galanter, 1983). However, the dialectical relationship between formal and informal legal action in social reform politics has generally received less scholarly attention (but see Handler, 1978; Olson, 1984; Silverstein, 1996).

There are several ways in which litigation often offers formidable tactical leverage for social policy advocates. For one thing, organizations targeted by reformers often are well aware that litigation can impose substantial costs in terms of both direct expenditures and long-term financial burdens. Indeed, court costs in major public disputes – over race and gender discrimination, unsafe workplaces, or environmental damage, for example – often run in the millions of dollars and can tie up economically vital operations for years. More important, powerful public and private interests typically fear losing control of decision-making autonomy – whether concerning capital investment, wage policy, externalized costs, or the like – to outside parties such as judges. Hence, they have a stake in cutting potential losses by negotiated settlements of conflicts directly with reform activists. Finally, the symbolic normative power of rights claims themselves should not be discounted. Because populations around the world increasingly are responsive to rights claims, defiant groups often can mobilize legal norms, conventions, and demands to compel concessions even in the absence of clear judicial or other official support (Scheingold, 1974, 1989; Handler, 1978). Again, media propensities to publicize legal rights claims, especially when taken to official tribunes and linked to dramatic information disclosure, often magnify the public power of legal mobilization pressure tactics in many settings (McCann, 1994; Keck and Sikkink, 1998).

The implicit promise at stake here is that political struggles may advance more quickly, cheaply, and effectively when conducted in the shadow of favorable legal norms and threats of judicial intervention. Such legal gambits are hardly costless guarantees of success for social reformers, of course. Initiating legal action often does not generate concessions from powerful opponents, and thus may commit movement supporters to long, costly, high-risk legal proceedings that they can afford far less than can their institutional foes. Even more important, eventual defeat in official forums can sap movement morale, undercut movement bargaining power, and exhaust movement resources. Consequently, legal leveraging is most successful when it works as an unfulfilled threat, but activists must be willing to follow through occasionally with action or lose considerable clout. In any case, the symbolic manifestations of law, as both a source of moral right and threat of potential outside intervention, invest rights discourse with its most fundamental social power.

It stands to reason that legal leveraging practices tend to depend on the existence of independent judiciaries or other official legal institutions, rules granting standing for legal action by relevant social movement groups, and a well-developed "support structure" of lawyers, organizations, and financial resources for legal advocacy (Epp, 1998; McCann, 1994). These conditions have long existed in the United States, especially with the proliferation of public interest law firms and cause lawyers in the post-World War II era. Many other nations have traditionally possessed some but not all of these elements. For example, many nations have national courts and constitutions, but those judiciaries often lack independence and, partially as a result, strong networks of legal advocates for opposition movements (Epp, 1998). However, formal institutional structures, access to rights advocates, and networks of support for legal mobilization have mushroomed across the globe at both national and transnational levels. The explosion of human rights, environmental, peace, and indigenous people's NGOs and cause lawyers, along with the growth of regional (European Court of Justice) and international (World Court, United Nations) adjudicatory institutions, has facilitated the rise of legal leveraging as a key tactic of social movement politics around the globe (Sarat and Scheingold, 2001). Most notably, as Keck and Sikkink (1998) demonstrate, transnational human rights organizations often ally with domestic groups to produce "boomerang" pressures for change that effectively bypass traditional forms of state resistance.

As noted earlier, the deployment of legal resources to pressure dominant groups takes place at different points of movement struggles. Two types of leverage are worth noting here.

Generating policy responsiveness

One phase of many struggles entails using legal tactics in an effort to generate responsiveness to basic policy demands, or at least some partial concessions, by the state or other authority. Political scientist Helena Silverstein (1996) has demonstrated how this tactic has generated some relatively important advances by the US animal rights movement in recent years. In a variety of instances, she illustrates, litigation has been used to dramatize abuses of animals, to embarrass particular institutional actors, and to win favorable media attention. When carefully coordinated with demonstrations and other media events, high-profile litigation worked as a double-barreled threat – at once mobilizing public opinion against targeted "abusers" and threatening costly legal proceedings and possible defeats in court. Overall, such legal tactics have proved to be one of the movement's most effective modes of forcing change by state and nonstate authorities alike. Michael Paris (forthcoming) and Douglas Reed (2001) have separately demonstrated a similar dynamic in the very different state-level campaign for egalitarian school finance reform in the United States.

Such examples confirm again some often overlooked aspects of legal leveraging tactics. For one thing, these cases illustrate that repeated clear victories in court or other official institutions are not necessary to effective legal mobilization. In many successful struggles lawsuits failed to generate appellate decisions directly authorizing many of the new rights and remedies that activists sought. The ability at least to win some small advances on related issues and to win standing in court for major claims often poses enough actual costs (such as bad publicity, legal fees) and potential risks (of judicially imposed policies) to pressure opponents into making significant concessions. Moreover, legal tactics again tend to be most useful in concert with other tactics, such as demonstrations, legislative lobbying, collective bargaining, electoral mobilization, and media publicity. The fact that legal norms and institutional maneuvers constitute only one dimension of movement strategy complicates evaluation of their independent contributions, to be sure. But, in each movement noted above, both activists and specific case histories confirmed the importance of such contingent, secondary legal actions. Other notable examples of such legal leveraging dynamics could be cited from the environmentalist, consumer, women's rights, wage equity rights, civil rights, and disability rights movements in the United States.

Legal leveraging is often different and difficult in nations with less independent and powerful courts than in the United States. However, such tactics have generated influence for women's rights movements in specific European nations (Epp, 1998), in the European Union (Cichowski, 2002), in Latin America, and in Israel, Egypt, and other Middle Eastern nations. Human rights activity and litigation have provided a notable force for challenging authoritarian rule in Latin America, South Africa, Egypt, and other nations as well. Indeed, groups like Amnesty International and broader networks of rights activists have changed the whole calculus of politics within and between nations. Eric Feldman (2000) has demonstrated in similar fashion how both rights and legal mobilization efforts have had far greater impact even in Japan, a nation where independent courts and cause lawyers traditionally have not played a major role in public policy.

Important examples where legal tactics either have failed to generate, or even have impeded, progressive change are notable as well, however. The abortion case arguably offers a revealing legacy. While US feminists won support for women's "right to choose" in *Roe v. Wade*, the provision of both medical services and financial aid to pay for exercising those rights did not materialize to any great degree. What is more, *Roe* generated a significant conservative countermovement bent on denying, or at least substantially restricting, the capacity of women to choose the abortion option (Rosenberg, 1991). In short, legal tactics not only failed to leverage real change; they arguably undermined the potential for change that alternative tactics might have produced. Similar patterns of failed campaigns can be seen in response to legal mobilization efforts around the globe, again especially in places lacking in strong legal traditions, institutions, and support structures of organized activists. Noga Morag-Levine (2001) has shown how litigation-focused, rights-oriented approaches "imported" from the United States fail, and actually divert effective politics, in more corporatist structures such as in Israel. Finally, legal mobilization efforts have generated backlashes in virtually every part of the world where social movements have attempted to challenge hierarchical social power and authoritarian state rule.

Policy implementation and enforcement

Legal leveraging often figures prominently at the policy implementation stage of political struggles as well. This is important, for gaining acceptance of new laws or policies "on the books" without effective policy implementation processes accomplishes little. And it is at this stage that many scholars, with some justification, have contended that legal tactics are relatively limited in significance. The most common explanation for this tendency is that both national and transnational courts generally lack the independence and resources to enforce their decisions against recalcitrant groups in government and society alike (Rosenberg, 1991; Handler, 1978; McCann, 1986; Scheingold, 1974).

Nevertheless, legal mobilization studies have provided some useful insights into how law can and does matter sometimes for struggles over policy implementation. In particular, a host of empirical inquiries have documented how legal tactics – and especially actual or threatened litigation – can help movement activists to win voice, position, and influence in the process of reform policy implementation, whether sanctioned by state or nonstate authorities. These include policy areas regarding the environment, gender and race discrimination, and the rights of the disabled, among others in the United States. There is evidence for similar dynamics in the European Union and in various nations around the world, but the politics of legal leveraging at implementation has been studied rather less than other stages of social movement activity.

Law is often especially important to one specific aim of many "outsider" groups – that of "formalizing" policy formulation and implementation processes. Formality, as understood here, refers to the degree to which relations are conducted according to procedures and standards that are public, general, explicit, and uniform (Lowi, 1979). The basic supposition here is that dominant groups tend to prefer relatively insular (autonomous or hidden) modes of highly discretionary policy implementation unhampered by standardized procedures, substantive guidelines, high visibility, and outside supervision. In such informal settings, established prerogatives of prevailing elites can more easily prevail to minimize costs, maintain control, and protect their own privileges while granting empty symbolic gestures to challengers. By contrast, marginalized groups usually benefit from more formalized processes where specified procedural rights and substantive standards can be employed to render accountable dominant interests who control the bulk of material and organizational resources (Delgado et al., 1985).

Social movement groups often use litigation specifically to create such formal institutional access to state power as well as to apply pressure to make that access consequential. In this way, legal resources often provide a series of more refined tools – basic procedures, standards, and practices – along with blunt leveraging tactics for shaping the "structure" of ongoing administrative relations at the "remedial" stage of struggles over policy (Galanter, 1983). For example, sociologist Lauren Edelman (1990) has demonstrated how employers routinely established in-house offices to avoid litigation and maintain an appearance of good faith compliance with race-based affirmative action principles in the United States during the 1970s. While initially established for largely deceptive or defensive purposes, such offices often mobilized antidiscrimination norms and the specter of litigation to force "real" changes from within many corporate and state institutions. In many nations, this concern for formality likewise has led human rights and other activists to work for increased independence of courts, of judicial appointments, of the legal profession, and of procedures identified with the "rule of law" in an effort to provide leverage against recalcitrant state and social interests. Indeed, transnational NGOs, local opposition groups, and judges often form alliances that strengthen courts and groups alike against authoritarian or undemocratic rule. This process can be seen in Egypt, Israel, various Latin American nations, and the European Union since the 1980s, and even to some degree in various historical moments of American politics.

Of course, as judicial impact studies suggest, legal leveraging often offers as little to reformers in policy implementation battles as at other stages of struggle (Handler, 1978). The fact that judges and other legal officials shrink from cases requiring great technical knowledge and experience may make leveraging tactics less effective generally at the policy implementation stage. Moreover, openly hostile courts again often greatly undercut opportunities and deny resources in ways that actually disempower movement actors in the policy process. And, again, even where courts act favorably for disadvantaged groups, injustice in most institutional settings will go unchallenged in the absence of well-organized constituencies willing to mobilize legal resources for change. Indeed, apparent advances in official law may even add insult to injury for marginalized citizens lacking organizational resources. In short, law's relative formality often does not help reformers, and may constitute a considerable constraint on action. Again, understanding these variations requires analysis of law's workings within the larger web of social relations where struggle occurs.

The legacy of law in/for struggle

A final phase or dimension of movement activity requires the most complex, subtle, and unique reflections both about law and about social change. This is often labeled the "legacy" phase. It concerns the aftermath of movement struggles for people, relationships, and institutions throughout society. Legacies surely include movement agents and targets of specified policy reform actions, but also include far more general, often unintended implications as well. These latter sorts of implications are the least studied aspect of law and change, so I will rely heavily on my own research to very briefly illustrate the point.

In my own studies of wage equity in over a dozen organizational settings in the United States, I found that the direct and tangible policy accomplishments were modest but important (McCann, 1994). While women's jobs were accorded rather less than full equity, women often received raises of 10 to 25 percent in their wages. But my interviews with women revealed that was not the only, or even the most important, gain. Rather, women workers repeatedly talked to me about matters of what we might call workplace empowerment. They told me about how their sense of efficacy as citizens was greatly enhanced, and even more how their identification with other women workers had been increased markedly. This was related to a growth in the organizational power of women within their unions, and of their unions relative to their employers. Many women specifically talked about the significance of increased "rights consciousness" that resulted from the legal mobilization efforts around wage equity. The result is that, in most workplaces, the pay equity struggle quickly gave rise to new issue demands for maternity leave, fringe benefits, job mobility opportunities, better work conditions, and the like.

Such evidence makes it hard to deny that law and legal mobilization activity made a difference in many people's lives and institutional situations. At the same time, my study did not find this same outcome everywhere. In some venues, there was little clear trace of positive change; in some workplaces, conditions had even deteriorated and women involved in the earlier struggle had largely given up or left. Similarly mixed legacies can be traced in the aftermath of the black civil rights movement, the second wave of women's rights activism, environmental legal advocacy, prisoner rights advocacy, animal rights movements, and other movements in the United States. Yet other movements – including gay and lesbian rights advocacy, welfare rights, advocacy for the homeless – have found very little at all to cheer about in the records of legal action. Indeed, legal rights claiming and appeals to official legal institutions in many cases have generated far more "backlash" or countermobilization from reactionary political forces in the United States (Rosenberg, 1991;

Goldberg-Hiller, 2002). It is more daunting to assess the legacies of legal mobilization by social movements in other parts of the world, but evidence likewise suggests a wide range of implications. Specific human rights struggles have often generated considerable drama and transformed the terms of political struggles, but patterns of significant change in social relations, state power, and material welfare have been more variable. As noted above, legal mobilization efforts have generated the full gambit of short-term impacts on social relations, and the longer term implications – from transformative legacies to backlash – are only to be expected.

That brings us back to the starting point on which most analysts agree: legal mobilization does not inherently disempower or empower citizens. How law matters depends on the complex, often changing dynamics of context in which struggles occur. Legal relations, institutions, and norms tend to be double-edged, at once upholding the larger infrastructure of the status quo while providing many opportunities for episodic challenges and transformations in that ruling order (Scheingold, 1974).

New Directions in Research

Given the emphasis on the inherent indeterminacy of law and politics that informs this essay, it should not be surprising that I conclude by emphasizing both the vast opportunities and great need for new research on the topic of law and social movements. Limited space permits only brief suggestions about further directions for study.

1   Sociolegal theory and social movement theory, I noted at the outset, have been joined relatively infrequently in scholarly study. One goal of this essay has been to demonstrate the value of much more empirical and theoretical inquiry that connects these two traditions.
2   Legal mobilization politics has very rapidly become a familiar activity of social movements around the world. More comparative cross-national and transnational study is needed on the topic. In particular, studies that engage with, build on, transcend, and challenge existing theorizing developed largely out of the American experience are necessary.
3   This essay has noted several times how legal mobilization politics seems both to depend on and to contribute to robust, independent courts, judges, and legal professions. This relationship deserves considerable empirical and theoretical exploration in a variety of national, subnational, and transnational contexts.
4   Much critical literature has suggested not only that legal mobilization produces a relatively feeble form of politics, but that it tends to generate countermobilizations of unique scale and success. These questions about the efficacy and legacy of legal mobilization deserve study in a variety of institutional and cultural contexts.

References

Abel, R. (1995) *Politics by Other Means: Law in the Struggle Against Apartheid, 1980–1994.* New York: Routledge.

Bogart, W.A. (2002) *Consequences: The Impact of Law and its Complexity.* Toronto: University of Toronto Press.

Brigham, J. (1996) *The Constitution of Interests: Beyond the Politics of Rights.* New York: New York University Press.

Brown v. Board of Education (1954) 347 U.S. 483

Buechler, S.M. and Cylke, F.K., Jr. (eds.) (1997) *Social Movements: Perspectives and Issues.* Mountain View, CA: Mayfield Publishing Co.

Cichowski, R.I. (2002) " 'No discrimination whatsoever': Women's transnational activism and the evolution of European sex equality policy," in N. Naples and M. Desai (eds.), *Women's Community Activism and Globalization.* New York: Routledge, pp. 220–38.

Cleary, E.L. (1997) *The Struggle for Human Rights in Latin America.* Westport, CT: Praeger.

Delgado, R., Dunn, C., and Hubbert, D. (1985) "Fairness and formality: Minimizing the risk of prejudice in alternative dispute resolution," *Wisconsin Law Review* 85: 1359–405.

Dezalay, Y. and Garth, B.G. (2001) "Constructing law out of power: Investing in human rights as an alternative political strategy," in A. Sarat and S. Scheingold (eds.), *Cause Lawyering and the State in the Global Era.* Oxford: Oxford University Press, pp. 354–81.

Dotan, Y. (2001) "The global language of human rights: Patterns of cooperation between state and civil rights lawyers in Israel," in A. Sarat and S. Scheingold (eds.), *Cause Lawyering and the State in a Global Era.* Oxford: Oxford University Press, pp. 244–63.

Edelman, L. (1990) "Legal environments and organizational governance: The expansion of due process in the American workplace," *American Journal of Sociology* 97: 1531–76.

Epp, C. (1990) "Connecting litigation levels and legal mobilization: Explaining interstate variation in employment civil rights litigation," *Law and Society Review* 18: 551–82.

Epp, C. (1998) *The Rights Revolution: Lawyers, Activists, and Supreme Courts in Comparative Perspective.* Chicago: University of Chicago Press.

Feldman, E.A. (2000) *The Ritual of Rights in Japan: Law, Society, and Health Policy.* Cambridge, UK: Cambridge University Press.

Forbath, W.E. (1991) *Law and the Shaping of the American Labor Movement.* Cambridge, MA: Harvard University Press.

Galanter, M. (1983) "The radiating effects of courts," in K.D. Boyum and L. Mather (eds.), *Empirical Theories of Courts.* New York: Longman, pp. 117–42.

Goldberg-Hiller, J. (2002) *The Limits to Union: Same-Sex Marriage and the Politics of Civil Rights.* Ann Arbor: University of Michigan Press.

Haltom, W. (1998) *Reporting on Courts: How the Mass Media Cover Judicial Actions.* New York: Wadsworth.

Handler, J.F. (1978) *Social Movements and the Legal System: A Theory of Law Reform and Social Change.* New York: Academic Press.

Hunt, A. (1990) "Rights and social movements: Counter-hegemonic strategies," *Journal of Law and Society* 17: 309–28.

Keck, M.E. and Sikkink, K. (1998) *Activists Beyond Borders: Advocacy Networks in International Politics.* Ithaca, NY: Cornell University Press.

Lowi, T.J. (1971) *The Politics of Disorder.* New York: Basic Books.

Lowi, T.J. (1979) *The End of Liberalism: The Second Republic of the United States.* New York: Norton.

McAdam, D. (1982) *Political Process and the Development of Black Insurgency, 1930–1970.* Chicago: University of Chicago Press.

McCann, M.W. (1986) *Taking Reform Seriously: Critical Perspectives on Public Interest Liberalism.* Ithaca, NY: Cornell University Press.

McCann, M.W. (1994) *Rights at Work: Pay Equity Reform and the Politics of Legal Mobilization.* Chicago: University of Chicago Press.

McCann, M. and March, T. (1996), "Legal tactics and everyday resistance: A political science assessment," *Studies in Law, Politics, and Society* 15(Winter): 207–36.

McCann, M.W. and Silverstein, H. (1998) "The 'lure of litigation' and other myths about cause lawyers," in A. Sarat and S. Scheingold (eds.), *The Politics and Practice of Cause Lawyering*. New York: Oxford University Press, pp. 261–92.

Meili, S. (2001) "Latin American cause-lawyering networks," in A. Sarat and S. Scheingold (eds.), *Cause Lawyering and the State in the Global Era*. Oxford: Oxford University Press, pp. 307–33.

Meranto, O. (1998) "Litigation as rebellion," in A. Costain and A. McFarland (eds.), *Social Movements and American Political Institutions*. Lanham: Rowman and Littlefield, pp. 216–32.

Merry, S.E. (1985) "Concepts of law and justice among working-class Americans: Ideology as culture," *Legal Studies Forum* 9: 59–70.

Minow, M. (1987) "Interpreting rights: An essay for Robert Cover," *Yale Law Journal* 96: 1860–915.

Morag-Levine, N. (2001) "The politics of imported rights: Transplantation and transformation in an Israeli environmental cause-lawyering organization," in A. Sarat and S. Scheingold (eds.), *Cause Lawyering and the State in the Global Era*. Oxford: Oxford University Press, pp. 334–53.

Morris, A. (1984) *The Origins of the Civil Rights Movement*. New York: Free Press.

Olson, S.M. (1984) *Clients and Lawyers: Securing the Rights of Disabled Persons*. Westport, CT: Greenwood Press.

Paris, M. (forthcoming) *Educational Inequality on Trial: Legal Mobilization and the Politics of School Finance Reform*. Cambridge, UK: Cambridge University Press.

Piven, F.F., and Cloward, R.A. (1979) *Poor People's Movements: Why They Succeed, How They Fail*. New York: Vintage.

Reed, Douglas (2001) *On Equal Terms: The Constitutional Politics of Educational Opportunity*. Princeton, NJ: Princeton University Press.

Roe v. Wade (1973) 410 U.S. 113.

Rosenberg, G. (1991) *The Hollow Hope: Can Courts Bring About Social Change?* Chicago: Chicago University Press.

Sarat, A. and Scheingold, S. (eds.) (2001) *Cause Lawyering and the State in the Global Era*. Oxford: Oxford University Press.

Scheingold, S.A. (1974) *The Politics of Rights: Lawyers, Public Policy, and Political Change*. New Haven, CT: Yale University Press.

Scheingold, S.A. (1989) "Constitutional rights and social change," in M.W. McCann and G.L. Houseman (eds.), *Judging the Constitution*. Glenview, IL: Scott, Foresman and Little, Brown, pp. 73–91.

Schneider, Elizabeth M. (1986) "The dialectic of rights and politics: Perspectives from the women's movement," *New York University Law Review* 61: 589–652.

Silverstein, H. (1996) *Unleashing Rights: Law, Meaning, and the Animal Rights Movement*. Ann Arbor: University of Michigan Press.

Tarrow, S. (1983) *Struggling to Reform: Social Movements and Policy Change During Cycles of Protest*, Occasional Paper #15. Center for International Studies, Cornell University.

Thompson, E.P. (1975) *Whigs and Hunters: The Origin of the Black Act*. New York: Pantheon.

Tilly, C. (1984) "Social movements and national politics," in C. Bright and S. Harding (eds.), *Statemaking and Social Movements*. Ann Arbor: University of Michigan Press.

Turk, A. (1976) "Law as a weapon in social conflict," *Social Problems* 23: 276–91.

Zemans, F.K. (1983) "Legal mobilization: The neglected role of law in the political system," *American Political Science Review* 77: 690–703.

Zirakzadeh, C.E. (1997) *Social Movements in Politics: A Comparative Study*. London: Longman.

Further Reading

Guidry, J.A., Kennedy, M.D., and Zald, M.N. (eds.) (2000) *Globalizations and Social Movements: Culture, Power, and the Transnational Public Sphere.* Ann Arbor: University of Michigan Press.
Santos, B.S. (1995) *Toward a New Common Sense: Law, Science, and Politics in the Paradigmatic Transition.* New York: Routledge.
Stychin, C.F. (1998) *A Nation by Rights: National Politics, Sexual Identity Politics, and the Discourse of Rights.* Philadelphia: Temple University Press.
Trubeck, D.M., Dezalay, Y., Buchanan, R., and Davis, J.R. (1994) "Global restructuring and the law: Studies of the internationalization of legal fields and the creation of transnational arenas," *Case Western Law Review* 44: 407–98.

28

"The Dog that Didn't Bark": A Sociolegal Tale of Law, Democracy, and Elections

STUART A. SCHEINGOLD

It was not necessary to believe that elections and the first government in which everyone would have a vote would stop the AK-47s and petrol bombs, defeat the swastika wearers, accommodate the kinglets clinging to the knobkerries of ethnic power, master the company at the Drommedaris; no purpose in giving satisfaction to prophets of doom by discussing with them the failure of mechanisms of democracy "free and fair", in other countries of the continent.

– At last – a year, a month, an actual day! – our people are coming to what we've fought for. They can't be cheated! It can't happen! Not to us. We can't let it! What a catastrophe if people started thinking it's not worthwhile voting because whatever they do the old regime will rig the thing.

(Gordimer, 1995: 294–5)

Lawyers are attached to public order beyond every other consideration, and the best security of public order is authority. It must not be forgotten, also, that if they prize freedom much, they generally value legality still more: they are less afraid of tyranny than of arbitrary power; and provided the legislature undertakes of itself to deprive men of their independence, they are not dissatisfied.

(Tocqueville, 1959: vol. 1: 285)

At least at first glance, the primary contribution of law to democracy might seem obvious and directly related to protecting *electoral accountability*. There is scholarly research on how to ensure fair and free elections and on the democratic implications of different kinds of electoral systems – one person one vote, proportional representation, single-member districts, gerrymandering, and the like (Grofman and Lijphart, 1986). Sociolegal scholars, however, have not investigated these matters. Instead, their efforts to understand how law, elections, and democracy contribute to one another have focused on *legal accountability* and largely ignored *electoral accountability*.

Sociolegal scholarship has largely neglected the study of elections, because, I will argue, of a belief that legal accountability, or the rule of law, makes a unique and elemental contribution to democracy. According to this distinctively legal way of thinking, electoral accountability, though a necessary condition of democracy, becomes a sufficient condition only in combination with legal accountability. Without legal accountability, electoral accountability is deemed incomplete, unreliable, and self-destructive.

While intrinsic to sociolegal studies, this approach has its origins in a longstanding canon generated within classical political theory and jurisprudence – what I will henceforth refer to as the classical canon. Sociolegal studies borrows from, adapts, and, to some extent, challenges this classical canon. According to the classical canon, legal accountability protects against too much democracy by way of rights, which insulate civil society from unwarranted intrusions by a state in the grip of intemperate egalitarian objectives. In contrast, sociolegal scholarship sees legal rights as weapons against inequality and too little democracy – a means of correcting injuries done to democracy by a state working in league with, and at the behest of, powerful interests. Despite dramatically different diagnoses of the problem, then, legal accountability emerges as a necessary corrective to shortcomings that are inherent in the electoral process, irrespective of how fairly it is organized and administered.

This is complex and contested intellectual terrain in which competing premises about both democracy and law yield multiple narratives. My goal in this essay is not to choose among these narratives. Instead, I want to indicate how the intellectual community comprising sociolegal scholars has used social theory and empirical research to destabilize the classical canon and to enhance and enrich our understanding of the relationships among law, elections, and democracy.

- Sociolegal research began by revealing gaps between the law on the books and the law in action. This mostly positivistic social science research often generated quantitative data and subjected it to tests of statistical significance. Sociolegal theorists used the resultant findings to explain and to remedy the classical understanding of law and democracy, without rejecting it.
- More recently, sociolegal theorists have made a sharp break with the classical canon, seeking to replace it with a radically reformulated understanding of both democratic aspirations and legal accountability. At the same time, sociolegal researchers have deployed interpretive research methods borrowed from cultural anthropology to analyze culture and consciousness among individuals and within primary groups. The findings from this research, I will argue, feed into the search for a more robust democracy and for a suitably reformulated legality.

In sum, sociolegal scholarship both builds on and questions the classically derived affinities between legality and democracy. Accordingly, it is necessary to begin with the classical canon before considering the challenges to it posed by sociolegal theory and empirical research.

THE CLASSICAL CANON

According to classical political theory and jurisprudence, law and democracy have developed in tandem and are interdependent. Political theorists see order as a precursor to, and a necessary but an insufficient condition of, democracy. This view builds from the Hobbesian insight that without law, there can be no order and without order, there can be no freedom. Subsequently, democratic theorists adapted Hobbes's *un*democratic insight by incorporating expanded conceptions of political freedom and political accountability – thus creating *liberal* democracy.

Liberal democratic political theory

Hobbesian conceptions of order and freedom are widely regarded in modernist accounts as a kind of prelude to democracy. Bridging the gap between Hobbesian order and liberal democratic order are constitutionalism and individual rights, two quintessentially legal phenomena associated with John Locke and, thus, with liberal democracy.

Constitutionalism, rather like Hobbesian order, is more about peace than democracy. Constitutionalism does, however, impose non-Hobbesian accountability on the ruler – thus creating a distinctively legalized vision of political authority. Constitutionalism, according to David Held, leads to a state that is "restricted in scope and constrained in practice in order to ensure the maximum possible freedom of every citizen" (1995: 50). The result is both a more expansive notion of freedom and the seeds of popular sovereignty. It is in this sense that Locke declared "Wherever Law ends Tyranny begins" (quoted by Held, 1995: 44).

If, however, constitutionalism takes a step toward popular sovereignty and democracy, their realization requires much more. Accordingly, Held goes on to distinguish between two kinds of modern states:

- a constitutional "modern state which circumscribes power and provides a regulatory mechanism and checks on rulers and ruled alike" (ibid.: 49),
- a *democratic* modern state "in which 'rulers' are representatives of, and accountable to, citizens" (ibid.).

The latter required the introduction of individual rights constituting citizens and citizenship within a political community. The liberal democratic state that emerged rested on a combination of civil rights among citizens and political rights that invested citizens in, and protected them from, the state. The former rights were to maintain the integrity of civil society and the latter to assure democratic accountability and the autonomy of individual citizens (Held, 1995: 50).

For the purposes of this essay, it will be important to distinguish this liberal vision of democracy from the social democratic and the emancipatory (or postmodern) versions associated with sociolegal scholarship. Whereas liberal democracy aspires primarily to freeing individuals and civil society from an abusive and nonaccountable state, the core aspiration of social democracy is to redress material privation. As Held puts it, social democratic rights are directed at incorporating "redistributive welfare measures – including measures introducing social security, public health provision and new forms of progressive taxation" (1995: 69). More broadly, the distinctions among the liberal, social democratic, and emancipatory iterations of democracy emerge, respectively, from the three so-called generations of rights.

- First-generation rights are associated with the rule of law and social contract theory. They tend to be negative – limiting interference by the state and other social actors and protecting liberty, privacy, due process, and the like. However, first-generation rights also include positive rights to *political participation* like free speech, franchise, running for office, and so forth.

- Second-generation rights have to do with economic and social well-being. They include, for example, education, health care, minimum income, secure employment, workplace organization, food, housing, social security. These second-generation rights were first articulated in social democratic theory.
- Third-generation rights include sweeping and controversial claims to communal goods. These include peace, security, a healthy environment, safe natural resources, and group self-determination. In this essay, these third-generation rights are identified with emancipatory democracy.

The progression among rights' generations introduces tensions into democratic theory. The democratic claim of first-generation rights is that it is necessary to protect citizens and civil society from the power of the state. Conversely, in the name of social democracy, second-generation rights invoke the state's power to intrude into civil society in order to protect the haves from the have-nots. Third-generation rights muddy the water still further, because they do not identify the institutions that are responsible for their realization. Second- and third-generation rights also challenge classical legality, to which we now turn.

Liberal democratic legality

According to *classical political theory*, constitutionalism represented the first step from a rudimentary Hobbesian conception of law as command to legality as a precondition of democracy.

> Constitutionalism defines the proper forms and limits of state action, and its elaboration over time as a set of doctrines and practices helped inaugurate one of the central tenets of European liberalism: that the state must be restricted in scope and constrained in practice in order to ensure the maximum possible freedom of every citizen. (Held, 1995: 50)

From this perspective, the transition to democracy occurs when constitutionalism and accountability are combined.

Classical legal theory contributes to this progression:

- the rule of law: a more fully realized iteration of the connections among legality, constitutionalism, and legitimate authority;
- enforceable individual rights as the agent of liberal democratic legal accountability.

The former derives from legal positivism and the latter from neonatural law theory. Neonatural law's contribution to democratic accountability is, we will see, emphatically liberal – enabling *liberal* democracy while obstructing the realization of social democratic and emancipatory democracy.

Among contemporary legal positivist theorists of the common law world H.L.A. Hart is the most widely recognized and eloquent voice. His contribution to a full-blown legal theory of legitimate political authority is, as I see it, direct and relatively straightforward. Hart's comprehensive and coherent legality is anchored in a rule of recognition from which flows an integrated system of secondary and primary rules. This legality is comprehensive in that it covers a multiplicity of relationships – with primary rules imposing behavioral obligations and secondary rules conferring power to make and alter primary rules (Hart, 1961: 77–96). It is coherent in that the rules are consistent with one another, according to principles set forth in the rule of recognition – the *constituent act*. As such, Hart, takes us from the nonaccountability of John Austin's conception of law as coercive commands of the sovereign (ibid.: 18–25) to the brink of a theory of liberal democratic legality.

Neonatural theorists then take us over the brink to liberal democratic legality. They link legality as a guarantor of legitimate political authority to legality as an agent of individual rights, and thus of democratic accountability. Lon L. Fuller begins from the premise that the essence of law is "subjecting human conduct to the governance of rules" (1964: 162). But this is possible, he argues, only insofar as law sticks to certain standards. Thus, for example, people can conduct themselves according to rules only if these rules are clear enough to be understood, only if they are not retroactive, and so forth. When taken together, according to Fuller, the standards that must be met if human conduct is to be truly subjected to the governance rules add up to a kind of moral code – what he refers to as the "inner morality of law." It is moral, according to Philip Selznick, in identifying a distinctively legal ideal (1962: 177) and internal because it has "to do with the way rules are made and with how they are applied" (ibid: 173). As such, it is both an agent of legitimate authority and an agent of public accountability. "The essential element of legality...is the governance of official power by rational principles of civic order" (pp. 171–2). While neither Selznick nor Fuller offers a fully realized theory of individual rights, much less a catalog of first-generation liberal democratic rights, they do identify legality with the right to have rights.

From a slightly different perspective, the internal morality of law requires a coherent complex of rules that specify legal obligations in a timely, clear, and noncontradictory manner. It follows that coherence is dependent on a well-developed system of legal reasoning, which articulates rules, structures, and the relationships among them. While it is intricate, and thus difficult to master, legal reasoning nevertheless constitutes a public language that is universally accessible – albeit only indirectly through the intervention of those with legal training. As such, legality empowers individuals to act on their own behalf as well as to call the state to account.

With all of that said, it remains true that two prominent and widely accepted distinctions in classical legal theory strongly suggest that legality's affinities to democracy begin and end with liberal democracy. On the one hand, this *liberal–legal* connection can be traced to the distinction drawn within classical legality between law and politics. Thus, in the United States, the judicial activism associated with the civil rights movement and thus with opening American political and social institutions to African Americans was regularly denounced by those with commitments to classical legality. According to Alexander Bickel and others, the Constitution vests the resolution of such disputes in the duly elected representatives of the American people and not the "countermajoritarian" federal courts (Bickel, 1962: 16–23). There is a double irony to this affirmation of majoritarianism. Legality was traditionally viewed as a protection against majoritarian rights abuses. Secondly, redressing the denial of the rights of African Americans constituted American democracy's major move forward.

Similarly, Fuller's distinction between law and economics rooted in his conception of classical legality renders law largely incompatible with the mission of administrative agencies, and thus with social democracy. Administrative agencies are at the core of the welfare state, because they are its primary instruments for addressing problems of poverty and material inequality. According to Fuller, legality serves settled expectations by the dependable enforcement of established rights and rules. Conversely, administrative agencies are supposed to maximize outcomes and thus rely on marginal utility calculations, which put settled rules at risk. For example, consider the choice between enforcing a rule against anticompetitive practices and overlooking those violations in response to an economic calculation concerning the health and vitality of the market (Weaver, 1977). For Fuller, this is not about democracy but simply about acknowledging the distinctive and mutually exclusive terrain of law and economics. Still the implications are clear. To pursue social democracy is, *ipso facto*, to jeopardize legal accountability, which is, according to the classical canon, essential to democracy.

In sum, classical legality, which puts first-generation political and civil rights beyond the reach of electoral accountability, is not only compatible with, but constitutive of, liberal democracy. Conversely, the protections of classical legal accountability do not extend to the second-generation rights associated with social democracy nor to the third-generation rights, which define emancipatory democracy. Indeed, with respect to these second- and third-generation rights classical legal accountability is more enemy than ally.

REFORMIST SOCIOLEGAL STUDIES: FROM THE CLASSICAL CANON TO SOCIAL DEMOCRACY

Beginning in the late 1950s, deviant American social scientists challenged the liberal democratic paradigm – in particular consensus pluralism and the halfhearted interventions of the US welfare state. At its inception in the 1960s, sociolegal studies joined this challenge by contributing supportive empirical research and by reworking classical legal theory. Empirical sociolegal research revealed evidence of the shortcomings of classical legal accountability. In addition, sociolegal theorists revised classical legality to better protect first-generation rights and to validate second-generation rights associated with social democracy.

This is not the place to detail the disenchantment with liberal democracy among social scientists. Three related lines of argument and research are, however, especially relevant to sociolegal inquiry.

- C. Wright Mills and others challenged the assumption of a relatively even distribution of political power. Mills identified an interdependent "power elite" whose "unity rests upon the corresponding developments and the coincidence of interests among economic, political, and military organizations" (1957: 292).
- E. E. Schattschneider (1960) and Peter Bachrach and Morton Baratz (1970) went on to analyze the unobtrusive process – "the mobilization of bias" – through which those with disproportionate power exercised it less to suppress opposition than to deny it voice.

- Frances Piven and Richard Cloward (1971) charged that welfare benefits were not only inadequate but were used to regulate the poor rather than to reduce inequality and poverty.

Viewed from these new perspectives, liberal democracy was doubly problematic. The unequal distribution of political power meant that pluralist bargains were regularly struck at the expense of society's most vulnerable groups – providing them with inadequate resources and treating them more as serfs than as citizens.

Sociolegal studies began to flourish in this intellectual climate and in rough parallel with the civil rights, antiwar, antipoverty, and environmental movements of the 1960s and 1970s. On the one hand, sociolegal research documented how the broader context of social, economic, and political inequality compromised equality before the law. On the other hand, sociolegal theorists, drawing inspiration from "movement" politics, reimagined legal accountability to increase its contribution to the reduction of inequality.

Events in the United States – like the "massive resistance" to civil rights in the South and the repression of the antiwar movement – were widely read as a measure of the gap between what classical legality promised and what it delivered. Yet it seemed equally clear in the heady days of Lyndon Johnson's war on poverty and the Kerner Commission's report on violence, that delivery was tantalizingly close and that legality could contribute to it. In short, both rights-based activism and the sociolegal research that analyzed and charted its progress rested on faith in the underlying, but insufficiently realized, structural affinities between legality and democracy.

More recently, sociolegal researchers working in settings where neither the rule of law nor liberal democracy can be taken for granted have, however, developed a renewed and less jaundiced interest in liberal democracy and liberal legality. These inquiries highlight efforts to mobilize liberal legality against the repressive practices of autocratic regimes *and* on behalf of groups who because of their outsider status are denied basic rights in otherwise democratic states. In these precarious circumstances, legal accountability serves its classic compensatory role as a counterweight to the shortcomings of electoral accountability.

The limits of classical legal accountability: Inequality before the law

Sociolegal scholarship got underway largely through a comprehensive inquiry into the divergence between law in action and law on the books. Among other things revealed by this inquiry were the hollowness of formal equality and the limited efficacy of constitutional constraints on governmental power. Insofar as the hallmarks of classical legality were often no more than empty promises, so too was legal accountability's putative contribution to liberal democracy.

The emblematic, and indeed the seminal, work here was Marc Galanter's (1974) analysis of "Why the 'haves' come out ahead." Galanter's central thesis was that beneath the appearance of equal justice under law, "repeat players" in the legal process had a decisive advantage over "one shotters." These repeat players were, moreover, overwhelmingly drawn from among the privileged and powerful, while one-shotters were just as overwhelmingly numbered among the inefficacious and dispossessed. Both Galanter's findings and his mode of inquiry – looking beneath the reassuring surface of formal equality – became defining elements of sociolegal scholarship. Similarly, Joel Handler (1966) led the way in exposing the inadequacy of the due process protections afforded welfare recipients against the mean-spirited and abusive procedures of the state agencies on which they depended. This work, as well as other research on welfare dependency, demonstrated legality's complicity in welfare's regulating rather than liberating the poor, as Piven and Cloward charged.

This scholarship led inescapably to the conclusion that law and courts were more likely to ignore than to embrace egalitarian values. Moreover, sociolegal research by political scientists demonstrated the disappointing policy consequences of those relatively rare instances when courts embraced egalitarian values. "Compliance" and "impact" research documented how, why, and to what extent judicial decisions failed to become operative public policy. The controversial matters that were explored in this research included educational and social desegregation, school prayer, and defendants' rights. Virtually everywhere they looked – at administrative agencies, political leadership, and the public – researchers uncovered widespread resistance to, and neglect of, judicial decrees (Canon and Johnson, 1999). Absent the political will to enforce judicial decisions, the courts could do little to redress the unequal distribution of resources within the polity.

Most fundamentally, sociolegal research cast doubt on one of the mainstays of the classical canon, the much vaunted autonomy of the law:

- if in matters of public policy the courts cannot assure remedies for the rights that they articulate the political dependence of the courts is undeniable;
- if the "haves" do reliably come out ahead, law, like politics, is responsive to differentials in status and material resources.

In sum, the initial thrust of sociolegal research was to call into question the underlying integrity of constitutional legality, while at the same time casting seemingly decisive doubt on legal accountability as a guardian of liberal democracy.

Two bodies of subsequent sociolegal research have significantly qualified this negative reading of legal accountability. Research conducted mostly outside the United States suggests that a reassessment of the democratic potential of liberal legality is in order. Research in the United States reveals that the politicization of legal accountability can redress the shortcomings of liberal legality.

Rethinking liberal legality

The political and intellectual ferment of the 1960s and 1970s, as well as their own research findings, led US sociolegal scholars to look beyond the liberal legal paradigm. In their quest for more robust forms of democracy, they tended to take for granted and even to denigrate what liberal legality has to offer. However, in settings where liberal legal protections are altogether out of reach, they attracted much more interest. There, political activists and sociolegal scholars alike have rediscovered, so to speak, the imperfect virtues of liberal legalism.

In authoritarian regimes, the rule of law and minimal human rights are the best case scenario. Research in Indonesia and Malaysia traces the uphill struggle of lawyers to give the rule of law a meaningful presence (Lev, 1998). Much the same is true of the efforts of lawyers working on behalf of Palestinians in the occupied territories (Bisharat, 1998) or on behalf of opponents of the former apartheid regime in South Africa (Abel, 1995). In thus "talking law to power" (Abel, 1998), legal advocacy is ordinarily limited to waging defensive struggles against repressive practices. The international human rights movement sometimes aids these struggles, as do global capital's efforts on behalf of the rule of law – even though their primary purpose is to facilitate commercial activity.

Classical legal accountability also enhances democracy in nonauthoritarian settings. Consider neocorporatist democratic regimes like those in Israel and Japan, where neocorporatist solidarity tends to be privileged and where adversarial legalism is suspect (Morag-Levine, 2001; Dotan, 2001; Kidder and Miyazawa, 1993; Miyazawa, 1996). Neocorporatist accommodation is, of course, particularly costly to those outside the corporatist compact – Israeli Arabs and Bedouins, for example. Even where liberal democracy and liberal legality are otherwise well entrenched, as in the United States and the United Kingdom, outsiders are often deprived of legal protections. These "outlaws" include resident immigrants, refugees, asylum seekers, those deemed political enemies, and other marginalized groups. Sociolegal research reveals a mixed record for legal advocacy on their behalf (Coutin, 2001) – effectively abetted by extranational legal accountability within the European Union (Sterett, 1998).

To varying degrees, all of these experiences suggest that liberal legal accountability can make vital, if undependable, contributions to democracy. Still, both liberal democracy and liberal legality are afflicted by major shortcomings – all amply documented in research discussed above. Accordingly, there is reason to be encouraged by sociolegal research indicating that the politicization of legal accountability can make legal advocacy into a useful tool of democracy.

Politicizing legal accountability: A politics of rights

Whereas classical legality celebrated the separation of law from politics, the politics of rights renews the vigor of legal accountability by embracing, rather than evading, the inextricable connections between law and politics. Specifically, sociolegal scholarship has demonstrated that a politics of rights can help defeat the mobilization of bias, which subverts electoral accountability.

A politically inflected account of rights and legality treats rights and judicial decisions neither as legal entitlements nor as moral imperatives, but as discursive political resources. They offer access to the symbols of legitimacy and, as such, have been shown to serve redistributive objectives. The symbolic currency of rights has proven effective in mobilizing and organizing inchoate interests that are ordinarily excluded from pluralist bargaining. In so doing, the politics of rights also enhances the likelihood that rights proclaimed will be realized.

Consider, for example, the course of desegregation in the United States. The record indicates that the constitutional entitlements affirmed by the Supreme Court were in themselves largely ineffectual and that desegregation proceeded only after the civil rights movement gathered momentum (Rosenberg, 1991). There is, however, also reason to believe that constitutional litigation did, by way of a politics of rights, contribute *indirectly* to the emergence and success of the civil rights movement (Scheingold, 1988). On the one hand, the judicial validation of civil rights claims generated hopes that fed the organizing efforts of African Americans and their supporters. On the other hand, the "massive" legal resistance to judicial decrees – not to mention the TV-documented spectacle of extralegal resistance – sparked the support of northern liberals. Taken together, these *unintended* consequences of constitutional litigation helped to destabilize the political stalemate that had protected segregation since the end of the Reconstruction.

Sociolegal research on rights-based campaigns for people with disabilities (Olson, 1984), pay equity (McCann, 1994), and animals (Silverstein, 1996) has revealed how, why, and to what extent a politics of rights can be successful. One message of this research is that judicial *defeats* can be leveraged by political activists for movement-building purposes (McCann, 1994). The companion message is that the democratic opportunities provided by the politics of rights are indirect and contingent – working best as a prelude to, and in combination with, complementary political strategies.

In recent years, cause lawyering research has revealed multiple instances around the globe in which politicized strategies of legal accountability have served democratic aspirations. Lawyers in the United States engaged in movement building among Central American immigrants (Coutin, 2001), and Latin American cause lawyers have worked at the grassroots to organize opposition to authoritarian state structures (Meili, 1998). Similarly, cause lawyers in Japan enter the political arena to mobilize support, because they doubt that judges will recognize rights claims (Kidder and Miyazawa, 1993). A somewhat different kind of politicization entails use of the law in order to subvert it. This strategy was uncovered among American lawyers working against capital punishment (Sarat, 1998) and among Israeli lawyers trying to desegregate housing (Shamir and Ziv, 2001).

Clearly, the politicization of legal accountability is rooted in an altered conception of legality in which law and politics merge inextricably into one another. Thought of as entitlements, legality and rights are direct, absolute, and conclusive. Thought of in political terms, they are indirect, contingent, and dependent on strategic choices. The politics of rights, thus, transforms rights from ends in themselves to a means of political action. Legality, with its locus in social and cultural practice, becomes a terrain of political struggle.

The sociolegal documentation of, and explanation for, legal inequalities amounted to a sea change in the study of legality. This research refocused legal scholarship from the normative and doctrinal concerns of the classical canon to social science and social theory. Moreover, the research findings made clear the shortcomings of classical legal accountability as a sustaining element of liberal democracy – demonstrating that the realization of constitutional rights was more the exception than the rule. On the other hand, sociolegal scholarship also revealed the democratizing capabilities of a politicized legality – providing, in the politics of rights, a revisionist model of legal accountability.

THEORIZING A POSTLIBERAL LEGALITY

A politics of rights provides political leverage for those effectively disenfranchised by the inequities of consensus pluralism. In so doing, the politics of rights reinvigorate the democratic potential of legal accountability while also serving liberal legality by helping to assure that rights declared will become rights realized. From this perspective, the politics of rights, liberal democracy, and liberal legality emerge as an interdependent triad.

From another perspective, the politics of rights appear doubly subversive of the classical canon. To establish that the strategic politicization of legal accountability works is one thing. To reconcile it with the classical canon is another. The boundary between law and politics has been a foundational element of classical legal theory. Moreover, the open-ended reach of the politics of rights can, in principle, transcend and challenge first-generation liberal democratic legality by recognizing second- and third-generation rights. So is it possible to both politicize legality and preserve it?

Sociolegal studies have responded with two versions of a postliberal legality – each of which is meant to validate a mutually constitutive relationship between a politicized legality and more ambitious democratic aspirations. The first of these is reformist in spirit – formulating an expanded, but still traditional, legality, which accommodates sufficient politicization to serve social democracy's second-generation rights and redistributive objectives. Secondly, there is transformative postliberal legality, which expressly repudiates the classical canon – creating in its place emancipatory conceptions of legality and democracy.

Social democratic legality

Phillipe Nonet and Philip Selznick (1978) have proposed an instrumental conception of legality that goes at least part of the way towards reconciling political legality and a social democratic agenda with classical legality. They do so by shifting the locus of legality from its classical base in political theory and jurisprudence to social theory and sociolegal studies.

Nonet and Selznick offer a developmental account of law, which identifies a three-stage legal progression from "repressive law" through "autonomous law" towards "responsive law." The first two stages are, in effect, drawn from the historical record and, as Nonet and Selznick point out, "evoke, and with some fidelity, the classic paradigms of legal theory" (1978: 17).

> The repressive law recalls the imagery of Thomas Hobbes, John Austin, and Karl Marx. In this model law is the command of a sovereign who possesses, in principle, unlimited discretion; law and the state are inseparable. Autonomous law is the form of govern-ance conceived and celebrated as the "rule of law" in the jurisprudence of A.V. Dicey. The writings of legal positivists, such as Hans Kelsen and H.L.A. Hart, as well as their natural-law critics, especially Lon L. Fuller in *The Morality of Law*, also speak to the subordination of official decisions to law, the distinctiveness of autonomous legal institutions and modes of thought and the integrity of legal judgment. (Nonet and Selznick, 1978: 18)

While Nonet and Selznick's autonomous law is, thus, equivalent to the legality of the classical canon, their third – and as yet unrealized – responsive stage of law provides sociolegal studies with an egalitarian democratic legal paradigm.

As they put it, responsive law envisages "a legal order that would undertake affirmative responsibility for the problems of society" (1978: 115) – while somehow retaining its distinctive identity as law. To do so, legality must, they claim, become more regulatory and less judicial – "that is, capable of reaching beyond formal regularity and procedural fairness to substantive justice" (ibid.: 108). In their analy-sis, regulation is a metaphor for privileging purpose over procedure and for acknow-ledging the inevitable expansion of the bureaucratic state. Because the bureaucratic state is intrinsically discretionary and subject to capture by the politically powerful, it is necessary to control discretionary abuse. Thus Nonet and Selznick associate themselves with the critique of consensus pluralism and with Handler's findings concerning the inadequacies of the procedural remedies of classical legal accountability (ibid.: 105).

In their judgment, responsive law serves both accountability and democracy by providing a forum for social advocacy by interests that tend to be excluded from pluralist bargaining. They build their case on the familiar ground of the civil rights litigation conducted in the United States by the National Association for the Advancement of Colored People's Legal Defense Fund and the antipoverty campaigns of the Office of Economic Opportunity's legal services program. They view all of this approvingly as a "deliberate effort to make the legal process an alternative mode of political process" (1978: 96). It follows that judges and other legal professionals are to welcome and encourage opportunities for "participatory decision making as a source of knowledge, a vehicle of communication and a foundation for consent" (ibid.: 97). Responsive law is, however, about purpose as well as consent. To this end Nonet and Selznick call upon the legal order "to lend affirmative authority to purpose . . . The focus of legal analysis must be the social patterns and constitutional arrangements that frustrate legal ends . . . In the context of responsive law, claims of right are understood as opportunities for uncovering disorder or malfunction, and hence may be valued administrative resources" (ibid.: 106).

While Nonet and Selznick take major steps toward a politicization of legal authority, they are determined to preserve the core of classical legality. The result is an unwillingness to face up to the full implications of politicization. This is clearest with respect to politicization because they stop well short of embracing the lessons of a politics of rights: "Social advocacy invokes legal authority and uses forums that can be held accountable to legal rules and principles. Hence, the characteristic locale of such advocacy is the court or the administrative agency rather than legislative bodies. *The appeal is to legal entitlement, not to political will*" (1978: 97; my italics). In contrast, the politics of rights, as was noted earlier, is about taking law outside of legal forums and even using it to subvert the law.

It also seems clear that Nonet and Selznick's vision stops well short of facing up to the implications of incorporating purpose into legality. They fail to acknowledge, much less to address, the extent to which their effort to assimilate law to regulation is in conflict with the requisites of classical legality. They explicitly associate Fuller with purposive law. They do so, however, without addressing the contradiction that Fuller, as noted earlier, articulates between law and regulation – between subjecting human conduct to the governance of rules and basing decisions on the fluid terrain of marginal utility calculations.

Even with these caveats, Nonet and Selznick emerge as both the first theorists of sociolegal scholarship and as influential transitional figures in the emergence of an emancipatory democratic legality.

Emancipatory democratic legality

The pursuit of an emancipatory democratic legality moves sociolegal research into postmodern theory and still further from the classical canon and electoral accountability. In the spirit of postmodernism, Boaventura de Sousa Santos, the preeminent voice of postmodern sociolegal scholarship, embraces as virtues what the modern project tends to regard as vices. Thus he constructs visions of democracy and law that celebrate dispersion, subversion, indeterminacy, and codependence, while being deeply distrustful of order, regularity, coherence, and coordination. Accordingly, the state and its law emerge as enemies of emancipation.

Santos's conception of emancipatory democracy is complex, elaborate, and elusive, and I am able to do it cursory justice, at best. At the heart of the matter, is a rejection of *power* – in all of its settings, all of its forms, and no matter how well intended its objectives – as inimical to emancipatory democracy. This is because Santos, taking his cues from Steven Lukes, identifies power with inequality – or more specifically with "any social relation ruled by an unequal exchange" (Santos, 1995: 407).

It follows then that both the liberal state and the welfare state work at cross purposes to emancipation. Santos acknowledges that liberal democracy is the best that the modern project has to offer and, indeed, has given birth to the "pillar of emancipation" (1995: 2). However, the fatal flaw of the liberal state and political democracy is that it is both too weak and too little disposed to reach out beyond the political order to curb power within the social and economic orders. As for the social democratic state, while it is attentive to social and economic power, its remedy is the blunt instrument of regulation. In effect, social democracy calls upon the state to use its sovereign power to redress imbalances of power within the social and economic orders. Because of this reliance on regulatory means, the social democratic state is too strong and indeed too much of a menace to serve as an agent of emancipatory democracy. In sum, for Santos the problem with the liberal democracy is its incapacitating preoccupation with the power of the state, while the problem with social democracy is an inherently self-defeating reliance on state power.

Accordingly, if emancipation is to succeed, it must effectively neutralize all forms and constellations of power, and must eschew the vertical impositions intrinsic to regulation. To these ends, Santos turns, in the spirit of the dialectic, knowledge, one of the tools of unequal exchange, against itself. Drawing on Gramsci, Santos notes that each site of unequal exchange produces its own hegemonic local knowledge – a specific common sense, a local hegemony. From this perspective, knowledge provides discursive reinforcement for unequal exchange and is, thus, inimical to emancipation. On the other hand, because knowledge is permeable it can also serve emancipation. "Emancipatory relations develop, then, inside power relations, not as the automatic outcome of any essential contradiction, but rather as created and creative outcomes of created and creative contradictions" (Santos, 1995: 409). For emancipation to proceed, it is therefore necessary "to promote, through dialogic rhetoric...in each of the...clusters of social relations, the emergence of emancipatory topoi and arguments or counterhegemonic common senses... eventually to become knowledges-as-emancipation" (ibid.: 441).

In terms of this essay, two elements of Santos's formulation emerge as crucial. On the one hand, emancipation works not through regulation but through dialogue and persuasion – thus purging power from emancipatory democracy. Secondly, there is a need for multiple versions of emancipatory knowledge suitable, respectively, to the hegemonic common sense prevailing at each site of power. In short, emancipatory democracy embraces fragmentation and persuasion – thus largely banishing the state from the core and relegating it to the periphery of democracy.

Santos calls for parallel transformations of legality in order for it to become a partner in building and sustaining emancipatory democracy. Predictably, he targets the privileging of state law, the search for coherence, and the reliance on regulation. In their place, he proposes a decentered legality, which substitutes mediation for regulation and nurtures reciprocity and mutual dependence.

Thus he uncouples law from the state, because state law is directly at odds with his emancipatory objectives. To begin with, state law has a unique potential for colonizing other legal sites.

> On the one hand, it tends to be more spread out across social fields than any other legal form ... On the other hand, since it is the only self-reflexive legal form, that is, the only legal form that thinks of itself as law, territorial state law tends to conceive of the legal field as exclusively its own, thus refusing to recognize its operations as integrating broader constellations of laws. (Santos, 1995: 429)

What makes the imperialism of state law so dangerously problematic to Santos is that, although the rights embedded in state law promote democratic values, state law is compromised beyond redemption by its inevitable reliance on regulation and thus on power.

Above all, Santos's postmodern legality is protean and centrifugal. Put another way, he wants to move from a single legality to multiple, concurrent, and heterogeneous legalities intermingling with one another. Santos argues that such multiple legalities can be, if properly constructed, "constitutive of an emancipatory legal practice in a radically democratic, socialist society" (1995: 240). However, the emancipatory potential of multiple legalities will be realized only if legality is:

- nonprofessional, so that "the relationship between power and knowledge is strikingly transparent" (Santos, 1995: 242);
- accessible, "both in terms of its costs in money and time, and in terms of the general pattern of social interaction" (ibid.: 242);
- participatory, which means "parties present their own cases" (ibid: 244);
- consensual, meaning that conflict resolution is through "mediation" rather than through the intervention of regulatory authority (ibid.).

With all these elements in place, postmodern legality can and should "organize autonomous social action by the popular classes against the conditions of reproduction imposed by capitalism" (ibid.: 238).

The radical decentering of emancipatory legality further attenuates the link between legal and electoral accountability. The object of emancipatory legality is not to compensate for the inadequacy of electoral accountability. Instead, the mission of emancipatory legality is to facilitate nonelectoral forms of counterhegemonic participation and consent. All of this may sound abstract, elusive, and without any real world referents. There is, however, interpretive sociolegal research on legal consciousness that provides suggestive empirical confirmation of Santos's prescription for an emancipatory legality.

Interpretive sociolegal research

Santos tells us that emancipatory democracy and legality are dependent on nurturing genuine reciprocity at the microsites of power. Accordingly, it follows that research on legal consciousness would be one way to discover whether, and under what circumstances, legality could be emancipatory. Sociolegal research on community dispute resolution has pursued this path. Initially, the focus was on *state-based* dispute resolution and revealed, as Santos might have predicted, the prevalence of a hegemonic legal consciousness (Greenhouse, Ynvgvesson, and Engel, 1994). However, there is also research suggesting, again in accord with Santos's vision, that an emancipatory legal consciousness may emerge in nonstate settings.

Consider Ewick and Silbey's discovery of "polyvocality" in the stories they collected about the infusion of the law into everyday life: "The polyvocality of legality, that is, the varieties of legal consciousness and multiple schemas of and by which it is constituted, permit individuals wide latitude in interpreting social phenomena, while at the same time still deploying signs of legality" (1998: 52). Thus *legal* consciousness varies from individual to individual, group to group, time to time, and so forth – meaning that a melange of different and contradictory strains of legal consciousness regularly coexist. Specifically, Ewick and Silbey identify three competing patterns with varying implications for hegemonic, counterhegemonic, and emancipatory legal consciousness.

The first two patterns and their immediate implications are relatively straightforward. *Before-the-law* narratives are unequivocally hegemonic. These narratives emphasize the preeminence of the law and the inappropriateness of questioning it. *Against-the-law* narratives are just as unequivocally counterhegemonic. The law emerges from these stories as an instrument of domination, an enemy of justice and, accordingly, deserving resistance and subversion. However, while counterhegemonic, these *against-the-law* narratives do not necessarily lead to either a counterhegemonic or an emancipatory *legal* consciousness. Instead they convey an irreconcilable conflict between legality and emancipation (Gilliom, 2001).

The opportunities for an emancipatory legal consciousness emerge from Ewick and Silbey's discussion of *with-the-law* narratives, which recognize that law is not "discontinuous from everyday life and its concerns [but] enframed by everyday life" (1998: 48). Legality emerges as inextricable from strategic action. Its efficacy rests on being "played like a game, to draw from and contribute to everyday life, and yet exist as a realm removed and distant from the commonplace affairs of particular lives" (ibid.: 234). This demystification of legality is, however, only the first step toward an emancipatory legal consciousness. *With-the-law* awareness can simply result in efforts by those able to do so to manipulate legality in the manner attributed, with resentment, to savvy lawyers.

However, Ewick and Silbey argue that as "people tell stories that make visible and explicit the connections between particular lives and social organization, they may be liberatory" (1998: 244). Lucie White's research on "Mrs. G's" battle with welfare officials leads her to similar conclusions. She emphasizes the importance of reversing the way that "cultural images and long-established legal norms construct the subjectivity and speech of socially subordinated persons as inherently inferior to the speech and personhood of dominant groups" (White, 1990: 4). She calls instead for a legal process that provides space for the defiant articulation of "emancipatory language practice" (ibid.: 50). Neither Ewick and Silbey nor White specifically address Santos's emancipatory legality. Their findings do provide, however, a glimpse of what an emancipatory legal consciousness would look like and how to construct it – namely within a Santos-like legality, which is nonprofessional, accessible, participatory, and consensual.

CONCLUSIONS

This paper began with a paradox. Although sociolegal scholarship has been much concerned with the relationship between law and democracy, there has been virtually no research on elections – the lifeblood of democracy. The explanation is rooted in classical political and legal theory. According to the classical canon, electoral accountability and legal accountability are mutually constitutive elements of democracy. While democracy without law and law without democracy are conceivable, only in combination are they sufficient in democratic terms. Thus there is a long-standing tradition in legal scholarship of distinguishing electoral accountability from legal accountability and focusing on the former to the exclusion of the latter.

Sociolegal scholarship builds on this foundation – albeit in revisionist ways that conflict with much of the classical canon. While there is general agreement that structural affinities link legality to democracy, classic and sociolegal scholarship rest on contested conceptions of legality, democracy, and modes of scholarly inquiry. Classical scholarship celebrates an autonomous, top-down conception of law for its capacity to protect electoral accountability, to insulate individuals from the unmediated power of the state and, in general, to keep liberal democracy within its proper boundaries. In contrast, sociolegal scholars explore the ways in which a politically, socially, and culturally engaged legality can serve more robust forms of democracy. Moreover, whereas classical legal scholarship focuses on rules, doctrine, legal reasoning, and jurisprudence, sociolegal scholarship introduces social theory and empirical social science into the study of legality.

There are, however, divisions within sociolegal scholarship itself – thus resulting in two challenges to the classical canon. The more cautious challenge emerged from conventional social science research revealing that legal outcomes reflected and reinforced social, economic, and political inequality. These findings cast disabling doubt on the classical vision of an autonomous law as a guarantor of political democracy – suggesting instead that legality and politics were intertwined and interdependent. In the legal process, as elsewhere, the "haves" regularly come out ahead (Galanter, 1974).

By revealing the regular transgression of the boundary between law and politics, this research suggested that an adequate account of law must incorporate, rather than exclude, politics. Sociolegal scholars went on to document efforts to deploy legality politically. This research on class-action litigation revealed something of a mixed picture. Under some circumstances, a politicized legality made meaningful contributions to both liberal and social democracy. These achievements were, however, more likely to stem from political action ancillary to, facilitated by, but potentially subversive of classical legality. Reform-minded sociolegal theorists have been only partially successful in reconciling a politicized legality with the core of classical legality, which they wish to preserve.

The second and distinctly more radical challenge of sociolegal scholarship grows out of aspirations for emancipatory democracy. Emancipatory sociolegal theory abandons efforts to preserve the core elements of classical legality. Instead, the goal of emancipatory legality is a counterhegemonic, noncoercive, and deprofessionalized legality of "different legal spaces superimposed, interpenetrated and mixed in our minds, as much as in our actions" (Santos, 1995: 473). This emancipatory vision rejects state law and electoral democracy, thus definitively severing legal accountability from electoral accountability and linking legality instead to partici-patory, grassroots democracy. Interpretive sociolegal research into the workings of legality in everyday lives suggests that an emancipatory legal consciousness can be generated in settings that conform to the theoretical prescriptions of emancipatory theory.

In sum, sociolegal research has provided evidence for a greatly expanded concep-tion of legality. Both of the sociolegal critiques of the classical canon shift the discursive terrain from state law and legal forms to the political, the social, and the cultural milieus, which shape, and are shaped by, legality. In so doing, sociolegal scholarship has provided new, contested, and nonelectoral understandings of the relationship between legality and democracy.

References

Abel, R. (1995) *Politics by Other Means: Law in the Struggle Against Apartheid, 1980–1994.* New York: Routledge.

Abel, R.L. (1998) "Speaking law to power: Occasions for cause lawyering," in A. Sarat and S. Scheingold (eds.), *Cause Lawyering: Political Commitments and Professional Responsi-bilities.* Oxford: Oxford University Press, pp. 69–117.

Bachrach, Peter and Baratz, Morton (1970) *Power and Poverty.* New York: Oxford University Press.

Bickel, Alexander M. (1962) *The Least Dangerous Branch: The Supreme Court at the Bar of Politics.* Indianapolis, IN: Bobbs-Merrill.

Bisharat, George (1998) "Attorneys for the people, attorneys for the land: The emergence of cause lawyering in the Israeli-occupied territories," in A. Sarat and S. Scheingold (eds.), *Cause Lawyering: Political Commitments and Professional Responsibilities.* Oxford: Oxford University Press, pp. 453–86.

Canon, Bradley C. and Johnson, Charles A. (1999) *Judicial Policies: Implementation and Impact,* 2nd edn. Washington, DC: Congressional Quarterly Press.

Coutin, Susan Bibler (2001) "Cause lawyering in the shadow of the state: A U.S. immigration example," in A. Sarat and S. Scheingold (eds.), *Cause Lawyering and the State in the Global Era.* New York: Oxford University Press, pp. 117–40.

Dotan, Yoav (2001) "The global language of human rights: Patterns of cooperation between state and civil rights lawyers in Israel," in A. Sarat and S. Scheingold (eds.), *Cause Lawyering and the State in the Global Era.* New York: Oxford University Press, pp. 244–63.

Ewick, Patricia and Silbey, Susan S. (1998) *The Common Place of Law: Stories From Everyday Life.* Chicago: University of Chicago Press.

Fuller, Lon L. (1964) *The Morality of Law.* New Haven, CT: Yale University Press.

Galanter, Marc (1974) "Why the 'haves' come out ahead: Speculations on the limits of legal change," *Law & Society Review* 9: 95–160.

Gilliom, John (2001) *Overseers of the Poor: Surveillance, Resistance, and the Limits of Privacy.* Chicago: The University of Chicago Press.

Gordimer, Nadine (1995) *None to Accompany Me.* New York: Penguin.

Greenhouse, Carol J., Yngvesson, Barbara, and Engel, David M. (1994) *Law and Community in Three American Towns.* Ithaca, NY: Cornell University Press.

Grofman, Bernard and Lijphart, Arend (eds.) (1986) *Electoral Laws and their Political Consequences.* New York: Agathon Press.

Handler, Joel (1996) "Controlling official discretion in welfare administration," *California Law Review* 54: 479–510.

Hart, H.L.A. (1961) *The Concept Of Law.* London: Oxford University Press.

Held, David (1995) *Democracy and the Global Order: From the Modern State to Cosmopolitan Governance*. Cambridge, UK: Polity Press.

Kidder, Robert and Miyazawa, Setsuo (1993) "Long-term strategies in Japanese environmental litigation," *Law and Social Inquiry* 18: 605–27.

Lev, Daniel S. (1998) "Lawyers' causes in Indonesia and Maylaysia," in A. Sarat and S. Scheingold (eds.), *Cause Lawyering: Political Commitments and Professional Responsibilities*. Oxford: Oxford University Press, pp. 431–52.

McCann, Michael (1994) *Rights at Work: Pay Equity Reform and the Politics of Legal Mobilization*. Chicago: University of Chicago Press.

Meili, Stephen (1998) "Cause lawyers and social movements: A comparative perspective on democratic change in Argentina and Brazil," in A. Sarat and S. Scheingold (eds.), *Cause Lawyering: Political Commitments and Professional Responsibilities*. Oxford: Oxford University Press, pp. 487–522.

Mills, C. Wright (1957) *The Power Elite*. New York: Oxford University Press.

Miyazawa, Setsuo (1996) "Cause lawyering by a cartelized legal profession: Profiles in cause lawyering in Japan," Paper presented to the Joint Annual Meeting of the Law and Society Association and the International Sociological Association's Research Committee on the Sociology of Law, July 10–13, 1996, University of Strathclyde, Glasgow.

Morag-Levine, Noga (2001) "The politics of imported rights: Transplantation and transformation in an Israeli environmental cause-lawyering organization," in A. Sarat and S. Scheingold (eds.), *Cause Lawyering and the State in the Global Era*. New York: Oxford University Press, pp. 334–53.

Nonet, Phillipe and Selznick, Philip (1978) *Law and Society in Transition: Toward Responsive Law*. New York: Harper.

Olson, Susan (1984) *Clients and Lawyers: Securing the Rights of Disabled Persons*. Westport, CT: Greenwood Press.

Piven, Frances Fox and Cloward, Richard (1971) *Regulating the Poor: The Functions of Public Welfare*. New York: Vintage.

Rosenberg, Gerald N. (1991) *The Hollow Hope: Can Courts Bring About Social Change?* Chicago: University of Chicago Press.

Santos, Boaventura de Sousa (1995) *Toward a New Common Sense: Law, Science and Politics in the Paradigmatic Transition*. New York: Routledge.

Sarat, Austin (1998) "Between (the presence of) violence and (the possibility of) justice: Lawyering against capital punishment," in A. Sarat and S. Scheingold (eds.), *Cause Lawyering: Political Commitments and Professional Responsibilities*. Oxford: Oxford University Press, pp. 317–46.

Schattschneider, E.E. (1960) *The Semi-Sovereign People*. New York: Holt, Rinehard and Winston.

Scheingold, Stuart A. (1988) "Constitutional rights and social change: Civil rights in perspective," in Michael W. McCann and Gerald L. Houseman (eds.), *Critical Perspectives on the Constitution*. Boston: Little, Brown, pp. 73–91.

Selznick, Philip (1962) "Natural law and sociology," in *Natural Law and Modern Society*. Cleveland, OH: World Publishing, pp. 54–93.

Shamir, Ronen and Ziv, Neta (2001) "State-oriented and community oriented lawyering for a cause: A tale of two strategies," in A. Sarat and S. Scheingold (eds.), *Cause Lawyering and the State in the Global Era*. New York: Oxford University Press, pp. 287–304.

Silverstein, Helena (1996) *Unleashing Rights: Law, Meaning, and the Animal Rights Movement*. Ann Arbor: University of Michigan Press.

Sterett, Susan (1998) "Caring about individual cases: Immigration lawyering in Britain," in A. Sarat and S. Scheingold (eds.), *Cause Lawyering: Political Commitments and Professional Responsibilities*. Oxford: Oxford University Press, pp. 293–316.

Tocqueville, Alexis de (1959) *Democracy in America*. New York: Vintage.

Weaver, Suzanne (1977) *The Decision to Prosecute: Organization and Public Policy in the Antitrust Division*. Cambridge, MA: MIT Press.

White, Lucie (1990) "Subordination, rhetorical survival skills, and Sunday shoes: Notes on the hearing of Mrs. G.," *Buffalo Law Review* 38: 1–58.

Further Reading

Bakan, Joel (1997) *Just Words: Constitutional Rights and Social Wrongs*. Toronto, University of Toronto Press.

Bumiller, Kristin (1988) *The Civil Rights Society: The Social Construction of Victims*. Baltimore: Johns Hopkins Press.

Cahn, Edgar S. and Cahn, Jean C. (1964) "The war on poverty: A civilian perspective," *Yale Law Journal* 73: 1317–52.

Hajjar, Lisa (1997) "Cause lawyering in transnational perspective: National conflict and human rights in Israel/Palestine," *Law & Society Review* 31: 473–504.

Herman, Didi (1996) *Rights of Passage: Struggles for Lesbian and Gay Legal Equality*. Toronto: University of Toronto Press.

Hunt, Alan (1993) *Explorations in Law and Society: Towards a Constitutive Theory of Law*. New York: Routledge.

Katz, Jack (1982) *Poor People's Lawyers in Transition*. New Brunswick, NJ: Rutgers University Press.

Keck, Margaret and Sikkink, Kathryn (1998) *Activists Without Borders: Transnational Advocacy Networks in International Politics*. Ithaca, NY: Cornell University Press.

Lowi, Theodore J. (1979) *The End of Liberalism: The Second Republic of the United States*, 2nd edn. New York: W.W. Norton.

McCann, Michael and Scheingold, Stuart (2001) "Rights in law," in N.J. Smelser and Paul B. Baltes (eds.), *International Encyclopedia of the Social and Behavioral Sciences*. Pergamon, Oxford, pp. 1339–44.

Mouffe, Chantal (ed.) *Dimensions of Radical Democracy: Pluralism, Citizenship, Community*. London: Verso.

Rose, Nikolas (1999) *Powers of Freedom: Reframing Political Thought*. Cambridge, UK: Cambridge University Press.

Scheingold, Stuart A. (1974) *The Politics of Rights: Lawyers, Public Policy and Political Change*. New Haven, CT: Yale University Press.

Shamir, Ronen and Chinsky, Sara (1998) "Destruction of house and the construction of a cause: Lawyers and Bedouins in the Israeli courts," in A. Sarat and S. Scheingold (eds.), *Cause Lawyering: Political Commitments and Professional Responsibilities*. Oxford: Oxford University Press, pp. 227–57.

Unger, Roberto Mangabeira (1976) *Law in Modern Society: Toward a Criticism of Social Theory*. New York: Free Press.

Part VI
Studying Globalization:
Past, Present, Future

29

Ethnographies of Law

Eve Darian-Smith

Introduction

From the time of Montesquieu in the first half of the eighteenth century, ethnographies, and specifically ethnographic studies of law, have been an emblematic feature of anthropological inquiry. The underlying rationale for these ethnographies was that by studying laws and customs in foreign lands, one could better analyze and understand one's own legal system and its taken-for-granted assumptions. While Montesquieu erroneously argued in *The Spirit of the Laws* that the natural environment helped to explain why some people were enslaved and some people were free, his intentions are familiar to contemporary ethnographers in that he was trying to analyze different laws by studying the terrain, climate, and overall social context of a specific legal system and legal culture (Montesquieu, [1748] 1989).

The writing of ethnography as a genre and method materialized in a time of great political upheaval and social unrest in Europe with the rise of nationalism and the building of modern nation-states throughout the seventeenth and eighteenth centuries. Ethnographies emerged as descriptive case studies of exotic peoples and their peculiar customs, norms, and behaviors. Wonder at and awe of other cultures by early explorers, missionaries, and military men gradually gave way to superiority and derision.[1] By the mid-nineteenth century, there was open contempt by Europeans for the lack of law, justice, and discipline among peoples from other parts of the world. Initially however, Western intellectual curiosity in the other was fueled by a desire to understand, and originally imitate, alternative forms of custom, government, and law. China, for instance, while openly despised by Europeans as "barbarous" and "uncivilized" in the nineteenth century, was centuries earlier considered by legal philosophers such as Hobbes, Locke, and Leibniz as a sophisticated legal model and bureaucratic state system (see Locke, 1988; Leibniz, 1994; Darian-Smith, 2002). The point I want to stress is that one of the central reasons that early ethnographers found studying people in far-away places so fascinating was that they were grappling in their own lives with questions that revolved around how to best distinguish and govern themselves (Baudet, 1976; Lach, 1965, 1968).

Today, ethnography is no longer confined to the discipline of anthropology, and as a methodology and genre of writing is receiving much interest across the social sciences and humanities. But the premises and assumptions of ethnography that emerged in the nineteenth and twentieth centuries with the professionalism of the discipline have in recent years been very much transformed to reflect new productions of knowledge and new questions of interest. Legal ethnography, which up until the 1970s mapped small-scale societies along a continuum that ended with large-scale industrial nations, has had to dramatically alter its conceptual – and evolutionary – frames (see Collier, 1997; Merry, 2000a; Moore, 2001). This change reflects current political challenges to the stability of state systems through subnational and transnational social movements, and the forces and flows of a global economy and its new sites and types of labor and commodities (see Merry, 1992). With respect to ethnography, no longer can myths of center and periphery, of exoticized "savages" and autonomous state actors, be sustained and granted credibility.

In this chapter I analyze contemporary studies in legal ethnography that typically adopt a range of interdisciplinary perspectives (Riles, 1994). However, before examining specific studies, I first explore what ethnography is, as well as the problems and crises associated with ethnographic analyses in general. These problems plague anthropology departments across the United States and other parts of the world. They stem from an increasing recognition that the conventional subjects of ethnographic inquiry – closed and singular cultural groups living in such places as villages, reservations, or ghettos – do not exist. Today's ethnographic studies, in short, have to deal with the shattering of modernist myths through which ethnography as a methodology and genre initially emerged.

I should be clear from the outset that I am not writing a survey of the literature of law and ethnography. Moreover, the scholars I discuss tend to be anthropologists living in the Anglo-American world, and I apologize for not being able to adequately represent trends in legal ethnographies that are being written in other disciplines, countries, and places (see Snyder, 1996, for comments on some European developments). Despite this limitation, what unites authors of contemporary legal ethnography is that each seeks, in different ways, to engage with the everyday complexities of law facing ordinary people situated within a global political economy. In an attempt to transcend the artificiality of a global/local divide and the opening up of legal spaces previously unrecognized, new legal ethnographies suggest that the impact and production of globalization – however defined – occur within and without the formal boundaries of nation-states. Moreover, these studies indicate that in any examination of law and its relationship to globalization, analysis must take into account a range of theoretical perspectives and subject positions.

I conclude the chapter with a point that is neither new nor revolutionary, yet seems to demand constant reiteration. No matter how stable or dominant a legal system appears (e.g., that of the United States), it is constantly having to accommodate, and in certain cases appropriate, a vast array of legal meanings, logics, values, identities, and cultural contexts emerging inside and outside established jurisdictional lines. What we are experiencing with the current political economy is an acceleration of these accommodations, borrowings, and challenges. With the current pace of legal exchange kept firmly in mind, contemporary developments in legal ethnography offer a unique opportunity to ground legal studies in the dynamic experiences of people without having to take as a given the "state" as the unit of analysis, and so without having to avoid or obscure macro institutional change at local, regional, state, and transnational levels. Through innovative and exploratory examinations of others' concepts of legal processes, and in turn an examination of how our own are constantly being modified in response to exposure to alternatives, it is becoming more and more possible, and indeed necessary, to rethink the assumptions underlying what we in developed countries continue to call modern "Western" law. Now more than ever before "Western law" is associated with a "civilized" and "free" world, and the "East" is again being construed – as it was in the nineteenth century – as a monolithic, barbaric, and uncivilized counterpart to a superior West. Ethnographic inquiry that seeks to explore alternative interpretations of law is valuable since it forces us to recognize the constant need to ask ourselves not only what constitutes "law" and "legality" in particular political and cultural contexts, but also who does a particular law represent and whose interests does it serve.

LEGAL ETHNOGRAPHY – PAST AND PRESENT

The history of legal ethnography is fascinating and complex. It is a history entrenched in shifting social attitudes by Europeans about foreign peoples, which is integrally related to the moving agendas throughout the nineteenth and twentieth centuries of imperial regimes and their relative power in particular colonial contexts. It is a history that is in part shaped by the emerging disciplines of anthropology and sociology and their respective disciplinary intellectual theories and methods. In short, it is a history deserving considerable attention, which I cannot give it here (see Moore, 2001; Snyder, 1996; Sack and Aleck, 1992; Nader, 2002; Starr and Goodale, 2002; Darian-Smith, forthcoming; Just, 1992). That being said, one can only appreciate how innovative and exciting contemporary legal ethnography is by knowing a little about what it has left behind.

Classic texts in legal ethnography, such as Karl Llewellyn and Edward Hoebel's *The Cheyenne Way* (1941), Max Gluckman's *The Judicial Process Among the Barotse of Northern Rhodesia* (1955), and Paul Bohannan's *Justice and Judgement Among the Tiv* (1957), were all concerned in varying ways to highlight the logic and rationale in the so-called "customary" law of indigenous peoples. While some argued that indigenous law was comparable with Western law, others argued against universal assumptions and claimed that law could only be understood in the unique contexts of particular cultures (see Moore, 2001).

Today, legal anthropologists are no longer fixated with defining "law" in other cultural settings. Gone is the need to either reinforce or belie a social evolutionary scale mapping the most sophisticated legal cultures through to those who have no identifiable legal system at all (Maine, 1861; Hoebel, 1954). Gone too are scholars centered solely on the functional strategies adopted by people to regulate dispute resolution and conflict control (Gluckman, 1955, 1969; Bohannan, 1957, 1969; Moore, 1969). Moving beyond the obvious sites of legal process in the courtroom, police station, and regulatory institutions, contemporary legal anthropologist are exploring how law features in the richly textured arenas of social relationships that frame forms of legal consciousness and understanding (Comaroff and Roberts, 1981; Moore, 1978). Not bound to studying cultural interactions in faraway lands, legal ethnographers are more and more studying complex developed "Western" societies, including their own (Borneman, 1992; Darian-Smith, 1999; Greenhouse, 1986; Greenhouse, Yngvesson, and Engel, 1994). Importantly, these ethnographers are contextualizing their subjects within a global political economy and are highly sensitive to issues of power in their studying up as well as down (Starr and Collier, 1989; Moore, 1993; Greenhouse, Warren, and Mertz, 2002). As stated succinctly by two legal anthropologists, power in law rests in "the authority to legitimate certain visions of the social order, to determine relations between persons and groups, and to manipulate cultural understandings and discourses" (Hirsch and Lazarus-Black, 1994: 1). In this way, writes Susan Coutin, legal ethnography "provides insights into phenomenon that are not, on the surface, legal" (Coutin, 2000: 10).

WHAT IS ETHNOGRAPHY?

In order to appreciate shifts in legal ethnography, it is first important to turn to changing concepts about what constitutes ethnography that have emerged over the past 20 years. All anthropologists, including legal anthropologists, tend to assume that everyone knows what ethnography is, and that sociolegal scholarship in other disciplines will benefit from its methodological contributions (see Merry, 2000a). However, as others have noted, such as Paul Willis on the use and abuse of ethnography in cultural studies (Willis, 1997), the lack of understanding about what actually constitutes ethnography has led some scholars outside anthropology to mistakenly believe that what they do amounts to ethnographic analysis. Before making the case for legal ethnography and engaging with its specific value, I believe it is first necessary to explore what constitutes contemporary ethnography. Moreover, it is important to ask how should one go about it so that it remains both a relevant and appropriate methodology and genre in the examination of increasingly complex and globalized societies.

Questions as to what constitutes ethnography have attracted serious reflection by leading anthropologists in recent years, and relate to anxieties about the enduring credibility of a discipline founded upon assumptions of "primitive," colonized subjects and easily accountable small-scale communities (see Gupta and Ferguson, 1997; Augé, 1994; Ahmed and Shore, 1995; Herzfeld, 2001; Marcus, 1999). As has been so aptly demonstrated by Napoleon Chagnon's (1968) study of so-called "fierce people" – one of the latest scandals to rock the anthropology discipline in the United States – there no longer exists, if there ever has, pristine, unblemished societies or tribes. Everyone, even those living in supposedly remote areas of the world, are connected and affected to various degrees and in a variety of ways by a global political economy and the modern technologies of information exchange. Moreover, since the 1960s, the rise of interpretive anthropology has highlighted the theoretical limitations of conventional ethnography as descriptive case study, in turn creating a surge of interest in reassessing and revitalizing anthropology's significance and methods. This interest exploded in the mid-1980s with books such as George Marcus and Michael Fisher's *Anthropology as Cultural Critique* (1986) and James Clifford and Goerge Marcus's *Writing Culture: The Poetics and Politics of Ethnography* (1986). These texts forced many anthropologists to seriously reflect upon the epistemological and disciplinary productions of certain types of knowledge.

As all the standard textbooks in sociocultural anthropology reiterate, ethnography is an in-depth study of one culture involving "firsthand, detailed, description of a living culture based on personal observation," and "experiences gained by going to the place of study and living there for an extended period" (Miller, 2002: 5). As Michael Herzfeld has succinctly put it, ethnography refers to "fieldwork and to writing, to a practice and a genre" (Herzfeld, 2001: 25). Through field research and face-to-face communications with the other, anthropologists attempt to expose the commonsense assumptions behind a localized exotic social world and make it sensible to people back home. The underlying rationale for this kind of investigation is that by understanding other peoples we will be better equipped to understand ourselves. Ethnography depends upon "participant observation," or what others have more casually called "hanging out" with people from a different culture from one's own. This often suggests that ethnographers are limited to bounded cultural units or groups with whom they can build relationships and establish rapport. Conventionally, anthropologists live for some years with the group of people they are studying, becoming fully integrated in their way of life, speaking their language, participating in their rituals, and so forth, in an attempt to understand "the native's point of view." Ideally, anthropologists return to their original fieldsite periodically throughout their professional career, building on an in-depth understanding over time of other people's way of life and experience. In this way, the anthropologist becomes an "expert," gaining status and credibility through length of exposure to, and presumably acceptance by, the subjects of a particular study.

Yet ethnography is more than a means of obtaining information about others. As Daniel Miller writes:

> It is also a series of commitments that together constitute a particular perspective. The first commitment is to be in the presence of the people one is studying, and not merely of the texts or objects they produce. The second is a commitment to evaluate people in terms of what they actually do. i.e. as material agents working with a material world, and not merely of what they say they do. The third is a long-term commitment to an investigation that allows people to return to a daily life that one hopes goes beyond what is performed for the ethnographer. This reflects a commitment to the refinement of an act of observation that is essential to the plausibility of anthropological scholarship outside a context of naturalistic science. All of these are tempered by a fourth commitment, which is a holistic analysis, which insists that such behaviours be considered within the larger framework of people's lives and cosmologies, and thereby is to include the speculative construction of much that is not observed, but conjectured on the basis of what can be observed. This last commitment explains why a study that relies so much on observation lies quite outside the normal form of positivistic enquiry. (Miller, 1997:17)

Ethnography, then, refers to a methodology and a perspective. Yet it also refers to the type of writing that has, over the course of the twentieth century, become emblematic of British and American sociocultural anthropology (see Stocking, 1983). Conventionally, the form of writing is a substantial monograph, filled with a bevy of facts, data, descriptions, and insights about exotic others. Early ethnographers, in their attempt to present a holistic description of another way of life, followed a standardized list of chapter headings covering topics such as religion, law, family, rituals, and food production. Unlike travel diaries, with which ethnographies have many similarities, ethnographies were presented as scientific evidence, in turn claiming to be objective, value-free, replicable, and authoritatively reliable.

SHIFTS AND CHANGES IN CONTEMPORARY
ETHNOGRAPHY

As George Marcus and others have noted, throughout the 1980s and 1990s conventional anthropological inquiry has been seriously challenged. Innovative graduate students, as well as anthropologists with job security embarking on "second projects" beyond their dissertation, have begun to question the notion of a fieldsite and hence traditional methods of data collection (Gupta and Ferguson, 1997; see also Willis, 1997). Some anthropologists have also seriously reconfigured what constitutes ethnography and the acceptable forms of representing constructions of cultural difference. The "thick description" called for by Geertz in the early 1970s has helped generate new forms of textual presentation that no longer adhere to standardized topics and conventional investigative frames (Geertz, 1973). Bounded cultural groups are now generally treated as embedded in regional and global forces, with longstanding historical contexts. Moreover, the ambitions of early ethnographers to create a holistic description of another's culture have been largely abandoned as "an important but impossible ideal. You cannot see everywhere or think everything. You must select and emphasize" (Peacock, 1986: 19; see also Friedman, 2000). Perhaps most significantly of all, the notion that anthropologists only study exotic peoples has been dismantled, and increasing numbers of students, albeit still limited in number, are now studying industrialized countries and Western centers of power such as the ownership of transnational media (for examples see Marcus, 1999).

Importantly, these new ways of doing and writing ethnography are evolving on the margins of the discipline, often through collaborative experimentation, and are largely the result of an engagement with interdisciplinary scholarship and new sets of ideas, theories, and ethics.[2] Marcus notes:

> There are many specialized discussions and debates within the discipline arising from the multiplicity of subfields and specialties, but no longer any discourse at the center that self-consciously engages the identity of the discipline as such.... Rather, the core debates that now define anthropology are on its boundaries and peripheries as it diversely revises and re-creates effective forms of authority in its participation in various interdisciplinary spheres such as science and media studies.... Anthropology, then, is perhaps unique in drawing on interdisciplinary participations to continue to define a distinctly disciplinary authority for itself. (Marcus, 1998: 249)

New ways of doing and writing ethnography have shattered forever the myth that ethnography is "science" in the sense that as a body of evidence about a particular "case" it can be empirically replicated, experimentally predicted, and legitimized as a singular truth, history, or reality (Grimshaw and Hart, 1995; see also White, 1999).[3] Also shattered is the idea that ethnography is neutral and objective. Writing ethnography is implicitly, and increasingly for many anthropologists explicitly, a political and ideological practice and form of engagement with a variety of human experiences and social arrangements.

This shattering of foundational myths means that ethnography is now more widely appreciated as a process, both in the collecting of information, and in the practice of writing up. There is an emerging realization that the voice of the ethnographer, and the multiple voices of those he or she studies, are increasingly bound together in an overall process of exchange and dialogue (Comaroff and Comaroff, 1992: 3–48). No longer can an ethnographer assume the safe perspective of a superior West examining the rest, as more and more diversity within the discipline grant peoples traditionally studied opportunities to authoritatively critique the "experts." The distance between "us" and "them" is closing (for a wonderful ethnography on the use of the exotic in the USA see Di Leonardo, 1998). For some anthropologists this is profoundly disturbing, for others a welcome and exciting prospect. Studying complex societies, and perhaps even one's own, necessitates accommodating new sources of criticism, and hence opens up the discipline to new forms of critique as well as new contexts and sites through which any particular ethnography must now be legitimated.

Above all, then, contemporary ethnographers realize that the work they produce is limited in the sense that they are not producing grand theories of sweeping application. Ethnography represents only one of many possible interpretations. Ethnography thus has to be considered open-ended, always open to revision and re-examination, not reproducible, or reducible to quantifiable data. As the legal anthropologist Paul Bohannan has noted:

> We are forced to realize that facts in ethnography are far more complex than facts in physical sciences such as chemistry. Neither chemical or ethnographic facts can be separated from the observer, but laboratory experiments allow a chemist to minimize context by controlling every variable except the ones chosen for observation. For ethnographers, however, part of the task is to determine what is context and what is subject, and how subject and context influence each other. Precisely because context is always part of ethnographic observation, it can never be totally controlled for; ethnographers consequently have far more trouble agreeing on what they see than chemists do, and replicability – the *sine qua non* of natural science – can only be approximated, never achieved. You really cannot step into the same river of evolving culture twice. Chemists would never put up with such ambiguity, but for the study of culture, a tolerance for ambiguity is a primary prerequisite. (Bohannan and van der Elst, 1998: 29)

The last two sentences of the above quotation raise a crucial point. For despite the continuation of area studies in most anthropology departments (see Gupta and Ferguson, 1997; Fardon, 1990), and despite the need for scholars to present the subjects of their research in some delimited form to satisfy granting agencies and book publishers, anthropologists now generally agree that talking about "culture" does not assume cultural groups are in some manner static or in some way reducible to a statistical variable (which is quite common in statistical projects in sociology and political science). For anthropologists, the concept of culture is only useful as an analytical category since the defining of cultural difference in actual lived experiences and daily events points to dynamic and ongoing political, social, and economic practices. As Sally Falk Moore notes, "culture has lost its political innocence" (Moore, 2001: 96). In sum, the boundaries of cultural identities – the sites ethnographers study – are fluid and porous. There are no continuous cultures or traditions, and no authentic cultures from which origins are drawn and people supposedly descend (Clifford, 1988: 10). To talk about cultures as fixed entities, bound by language, law, religion, custom, ethnic identification, or more commonly state borders, buys into, among other things, a political discourse of multiculturalism that ultimately seeks to delineate and perpetuate cultural differences and discriminations (see Herzfeld, 2001: 47; see Abu-Lughod, 1991; Turner, 1994; Goldberg, 1994).

METHODOLOGICAL DILEMMAS IN CONTEMPORARY ETHNOGRAPHY

If cultural affiliation is seen as a fluid and dynamic process, and discreet cultural groupings can only be analyzed in contexts of individuals interacting with others, how does one do ethnography? How and where do you "hang out" if you are studying, for instance, immigration law and the impact of international treaties on the Afghanistan diasporic communities driven from their homes by civil war and religious persecution? What constitutes the fieldsite and face-to-face communications for a project examining the impact of antitrust legislation on white-collar professionals involved in the international stock exchange, or a project exploring perceptions of censorship in international media? How is it possible to study people's constructions of lifeworld and everyday meanings in contexts that explode the concept of the "local" by connecting it to macroeconomic, social, and political processes? Can the views of the individual ever be extrapolated to speak for or represent larger social collectivities that are not bounded by geographical territories or any obvious institutional limitations? What would the ethnographic methods be in a study of globalizations, postcolonialisms, and/or capitalisms?[4]

I make no claims to knowing answers to these questions, which I have grappled with in my own work and writing (Darian-Smith, 1999: xiv). Despite many scholars feeling that anthropology has profited by the reflexive rethinking of the discipline in recent years, there are very few concrete suggestions about what methods would be appropriate to deal with the range of new interests, sites, cultural affiliations and technologies of power now bearing on any research agenda. George Marcus has called for a multisited imaginary. By this he means that we need to move beyond the naturalized sites of bounded ethnographic research, which embody the idea of community and its assumptions of shared values, shared identities and shared culture, by juxtaposing new sites and new fields. This could entail actually doing ethnography in a variety of sites and places (see, e.g., Marcus 1998: 21–5). But it could also include a less literal approach, simply meaning that as investigators we have to begin "developing knowledge of the relationships and connections that extend beyond the frames that have held the traditional act of fieldwork in place" (Marcus, 1998: 14, 21).

I agree with Marcus that the contexts of significance for ethnography in general, and ethnographies of law in particular, require a multisited research imaginary that intrinsically depends upon the notion of social and cultural fluidity and ambiguity. In order to be open to new relationships and connections, we have to forever give up the claim for bounded and static units of cultural differentiation. As Gupta and Ferguson have argued, there is a need for "attentiveness to different forms of knowledge available from different social and political locations" (Gupta and Ferguson, 1997: 39). These new locations, or new sites of ethnographic fieldwork, open up new spaces to explore questions of power and its practice, be they in the form of institutionalized laws or the more abstract concept of "social justice" (see Harvey, 1996). Toward the end of this chapter I return to the topic of legal space, time, and aesthetics which adds depth to the multisited imaginary called for by Marcus. The point I stress is that fieldsites are not longer restricted to geographical places. Rather, in an effort to rehumanize law we have to pay attention to the myriad of in-between legal spaces through which people create meaning, such as website

Illustration 29.1   Graffiti, Las Ramblas, Barcelona 1999

chatrooms, legal symbols like the flag, visual media in films and television, archival documentation that substantiates nationalist myths, as well as judicial rhetoric reinforcing particular codes of morality and ethics.

Recording on-the-ground personalized experiences of the law, and abstracting from these memories and narrations of identity and collectivity in order to better grasp historical contexts of struggles over power is the job of the ethnographer. It is what makes the contribution of ethnography so important to an understanding of the world – a commitment to exploding ethnocentrism, defamiliarizing common sense, and, in the practice of exploring alternative voices and realities across a range of socioeconomic and political levels, a willingness to listen and take seriously critiques of one's own perspective on the world. This need to analyze alternative points of view, be these at the level of impoverished minorities or state policy makers, is an increasing imperative. National legal systems are being pushed and pulled in new and unforeseen directions, being forced to govern new spaces of regulation such as the Internet, and new subjects of control such as cloned fetuses or cyber-terrorists. We are experiencing a period of great legal transition and transformation as nation-states creak and strain under the transnational forces of a global political economy and the implicit challenges to conventional centers of international authority (see Illustration 29:1). If possible, we need to return to the intellectual curiosity in other peoples that motivated early European philosophers and ethnographers of the seventeenth and eighteenth centuries. We are currently living in a period of transition. This transition is not one of new state building such as occurred over 200 years ago, but of state deconstruction and reconfiguration along new axes of power, national interests, and international relations. A search for alternative methods of law and governance, and an examination of how legal differences may coexist and be mutually transformed by each other, is just as pertinent as it was at the time of Montesquieu. But in our seeking knowledge we must appreciate (which Montesquieu did not) that our very questions and conceptual frames embody particular worldviews that are not of universal application. This appreciation is more relevant to analyzing law and legal processes than ever before. Despite the last decade's rousing rhetoric by politicians, lawyers, economists, and theorists espousing the taken-for-granted compatibility of capitalism and democracy, and the supposed inevitability of victorious neoliberalism, there is no hegemonic world legal system and no such thing as global law (see Jensen and Santos, 2000). Again, in the words of Herzfeld who makes the point more elegantly than most:

> [G]lobalization has reduced, or at least threatens to reduce, the arenas of choice for all societies. Anthropology thus becomes a precious resource, not only because of the esoteric knowledge of strangely different cultures that it can offer (although this is not trivial in itself), but also because its characteristic techniques of defamiliarization can be made to question the globalizing assumptions that increasingly dominate political decision-making. It is abundantly clear that the vast increase in available topics, scale of perception, and sheer complexity of subject-matter do not seem to be compelling the discipline to early retirement. On the contrary it is precisely at such a moment that the more intensive focus of anthropology becomes especially valuable. The amplification of symbolic actions on a global scale gives such actions a resonance that perhaps we can sense only through the intimacy – now defined in a host of new ways – of ethnographic research. (Herzfeld, 2001: 15, 19–20)

THE RESISTANCE OF LAW TO ETHNOGRAPHIC INQUIRY

Modern law – at least what we characterize as law – is resistant to ethnographic inquiry and its finely textured, grounded interpretations of people's perception of law through numerous subject positions ranging from those on the periphery of society to those at elite centers of control. This is because modern law, which over the past 200 years has evolved in contexts of imperialism and colonialism, and has been sustained by ideologies of progress and a quasi-religious objectification, is widely assumed to be a body of autonomous and sovereign rules not subject to "context, experience and intuition" (Flyvbjerg, 2001: 24). This helps to explain why academic legal scholars and lawyers tend to quickly dismiss the relevance of legal ethnography, which, implicitly and explicitly, challenges the very legitimacy of their reified legal world (Snyder, 1996; see also French, 1996: 432).

As argued powerfully by Peter Fitzpatrick, law does not open itself up to inquiry about its ambiguities and limitations precisely because it depends on sustaining myths of its supreme sovereignty and all-encompassing authority (Fitzpatrick, 1992; see also Bourdieu, 1987). As a strategy of power, the universalist assumptions in Western law allowed nation-states to transport their legal system across the globe, where it was assumed to apply to all subjects of empire, be these Australian Aborigines, African communities or Indians (Fitzpatrick, 1992; Cohn, 1996). Of course, in practice European law did not operate uniformly or neutrally and was to varying degrees effective in specific places (Stoler, 1992: 322).[5] Moreover, European law was not immune from local political and legal practices and was often forced to accommodate new rationales and new norms in order to maintain its presence (see Moore, 1986).[6] Yet despite of, and because of, the realities of colonialism in practice, there prevailed a widespread belief that law was objective, impersonal, universal, and indeed necessary as part of the "civilizing" process of other peoples.

In a different form, this attitude about the superiority of Western law exists today in the rhetoric of democracy, and the call for countries around the world to install constitutional systems of governance modeled on the United States. There remains a sense that law is transportable and transferable across the world to a wide range of cultural and historical sites. The rationale for an international human rights regime relies upon this assumption (see Lisa Hajjar's chapter on human rights in this volume). Law, as a mechanism of power and a subject of study, claims to be immune from ethnographic inquiry precisely because it appears to float above the melee of ordinary experience and context. Legal practitioners, policy makers, and those in power cannot afford for law to be seen as ambiguous or open to question. Hovering between the sacred and profane, law functions as a secularized religion, demarcating true believers from those who continue to uphold "customs" or "rituals" (Fitzpatrick, 1992: 51–5; Kahn, 1999: 46).

Fortunately, in recent years increasing numbers of legal theorists and philosophers are recognizing that law must first and foremost be understood as a form of cultural experience. Responding to the realities of a transnational world and new cleavages of conflict, tension, and power in the ongoing formations of cultural identity, socio-legal scholars are taking on board a cultural approach to law and legal meaning (see Sarat and Kearns, 1998; Goldberg, Musheno, and Bower, 2001; Danielsen and Engle, 1995). As the legal anthropologist Rosemary Coombe has suggested, we should "see law as providing the very signifying forms that constitute socially salient distinctions, adjudicating their meanings, and provoking the shape of those practices through which meanings are disrupted" (Coombe, 1998a: 36). Paul Kahn puts this point another way.

> If we approach law's rule as the imaginative construction of a complete worldview, we need to bring to its study those techniques that take as their object the experience of meaning. Inquiry must begin a thick description of the legal event as it appears to a subject already prepared to recognize the authority of law. That subject brings to the event a unique understanding of time, space, community and authority. He or she also brings an understanding of the self as a legal subject. These are the constitutive elements of that form of political experience we describe as the rule of law. A cultural study of law advances from thick description to the interpretative elaboration of each of these imaginative structures, all of which together make possible the experience of law's rule. All questions of reform – the traditional end of legal study – are bracketed. They are not abandoned forever, but they are left aside as long as this form of inquiry continues. The object here is not to make us – personally or communally – better, but to understand who we already are. (Kahn, 1999: 2)

Taking seriously the need for a cultural study of law underscores the value of an ethnographic approach, which, as discussed above, embodies commitments to "be in the presence of the people one is studying, and not merely of the texts or objects they produce," to "evaluate people in terms of what they actually do. i.e. as material agents working with a material world, and not merely of what they say they do," and to produce a "holistic analysis, which insists that such behaviours be considered within the larger framework of people's lives and cosmologies" (Miller, 1997: 17). Ethnography helps us to overcome the resistance of law to more nuanced analysis on the ground, among real people. It allows us to begin to explore how law features in different ways for individuals from different ethnic and socioeconomic backgrounds.

Ethnography enables us to appreciate first-hand that law is not monolithic and universalistic in its practice, that it does not correlate to any one culturally discreet unit, and that it is not devoid of sites of resistance, challenge, and modification. Perhaps most importantly of all, ethnography lets us "approach law's rule from the perspective of the subject who finds herself already within the practice, rather than from the perspective of rules operating on a collection of individuals" (Kahn, 1999: 45).

Four recent legal ethnographies written by sociocultural anthropologists highlight a range of subjects and types of questions that characterize what I believe are innovative and exemplary ethnographies of law. These are Dara Culhane (1998) *The Pleasure of the Crown: Anthropology, Law and First Nations*, Erin Moore (1998) *Gender, Law and Resistance in India*, Susan Coutin (2000) *Legalizing Moves: Salvadoran Immigrants' Struggle for U.S. Residency*, and Rosemary Coombe (1998) *The Cultural Life of Intellectual Properties*. Following this, I turn to innovative directions in legal ethnography by anthropologists as well as scholars from a range of other disciplines interested in questions revolving around space, time, and aesthetic dimensions of legal interaction and legal meaning.

Dara Culhane's book *The Pleasure of the Crown* represents one of the finest historical and contemporary analyses of aboriginal claims to land title. Focusing on the Gitksan and Wet'suwet'en case and trial of *Delgamuukw v. Regina* (1987–91), she charts the arguments and practices of legal practitioners that led to a landmark ruling in 1997 by the Supreme Court of Canada granting First Nations rights to territory. Culhane's sweeping historical narrative complements the work of other legal anthropologists concerned with the historical contexts of colonial and postcolonial injustices that shape the contours of legal consciousness in particular ways and settings (Merry, 2000b; Maurer, 1997; Comaroff and Comaroff, 1993, 1997; Moore, 1986). Rejecting conventional anthropological approaches which treat indigenous peoples as discrete entities, with unique authentic customs and traditions subject to close analysis and description, Culhane considers processes of cultural differentiation between aboriginal and nonaboriginal peoples as dynamic and contested. The British legal assumptions that prevailed throughout the nineteenth century stating First Nations people did not legally exist, or in some profound way were inferior to nonaboriginal people, remain a legacy with political and cultural ramifications playing out in today's legal articulation of cultural difference (Culhane, 1998: 96; see also Darian-Smith, 1996).

A social evolutionary scale whereby some people are deemed more "civilized" and so more capable of governing themselves is also the historical backdrop to Erin Moore's book *Gender, Law and Resistance in India*. Drawing on theorists such as Patha Chatterjee and Edward Said, she argues that the British empire throughout the nineteenth century and first half of the twentieth century "feminized" the Indian population, construing people through an orientalist discourse as passive, submissive, and morally bankrupt (Moore, 1998: 27).

Moore's book focuses on a traditional legal ethnographic subject – dispute processing and a "series of related conflicts in multiple legal forums" (Moore 1998: 36). But her approach differs greatly from conventional ethnographies of India, which typically pivot on issues of caste, religion, and the male-centered arenas of private and public life (see Fardon, 1990). Through finely textured descriptions and interviews, Moore presents her analysis of the current plight of Indian women by focusing in particular on one woman's experiences and decision making occurring within local symbolic and ideological frames of meaning. These frames are integrally shaped by the woman's understanding of the law and her ability to periodically manipulate the legal system, at local, regional, and state levels, to her advantage despite the overriding power inequities that continue to exist between the sexes.[7]

Throughout *Gender, Law and Resistance in India*, Moore shows that law can be interpreted as both a weapon against discrimination and a form of oppression, depending upon the specifics of political and social conditions. The law is "Janus-faced," at times aiding resistance, at other times legitimizing existing power structures of domination (Moore, 1998: 35; Comaroff, 1994). Recognizing the contradictions and ambiguities in legal practice, and that legal meanings and strategies are entirely contingent upon localized context, is a central message of the book. And, as Moore notes in her chapter on legal pluralism in north India, these legal ambiguities and uncertainties are further complicated by the layered conflicts between competing legal jurisdictions.

Law as Janus-faced, operating as both a tool of resistance and oppression, is also a backdrop to Susan Coutin's work on El Salvadoran immigrants attempting to enter the Untied States and obtain permanent residency status from the early 1980s up to 1997. *Legalizing Moves* is first and foremost an exemplary ethnography in its sensitive and powerful presentation of observations and personal narratives that often involve harrowing topics of death and torture, and people's search to reinstate a sense of stability and cultural identity amidst immense suffering (Coutin, 2000: 24, 27–48). One of the most powerful messages that emerges in *Legalizing Moves* is that debates and conflicts over immigration law, and the determining of who qualifies at any particular time to legally reside in the United States, necessarily raise much bigger issues that center on what it means to be American (see also Calavita, 1992 for a compelling ethnography on the INS) (see Illustration 29.2). So while the plight

Illustration 29.2 Interstate 5 driving south toward the San Diego Border–roadsign warning motorists of fleeing illegal immigrants

of Salvadoran refugees may seem remote and peripheral to mainstream society, the very presence of these people affects in a multiplicity of ways the assumptions on which modern Western law and national identity are based: that is, stable territorial jurisdiction, enforced border controls, unambiguous concepts of citizenship, and the overriding power of the state (see Darian-Smith, 1999). Unauthorized immigrants – illegal aliens – occupy an in-between space similar to "criminals" and "savages." They become "beings on whom the differences between law and illegality, merit and undeservingness, citizenship and alienation, are inscribed" (Coutin, 2000: 174).

Coutin's concern to engage with competing legal ideologies and jurisdictions, and connecting these tensions to identity politics and the constant rearticulation of the state, nationalism, and images of otherness, is excitingly illustrated in Rosemary Coombe's *The Cultural Life of Intellectual Properties*. This legal ethnography is a very different enterprise from the other works discussed above. There is no specific group or cultural affiliation that provides the central focus of her examination, such as aboriginal peoples, north Indian women, or Salvadoran immigrants. Rather, Coombe's study is a *tour de force* in its ranging across a myriad of topics and themes in her examination of how intellectual property laws figure in the constant remaking of cultural difference and cultural relations. In this way, Coombe's study represents a new form of legal ethnography, not bound by geographical place or culturally identifiable group, but intensely interested in how intellectual properties are indices of shifting codes of legal meaning that mark the constant redefinitions of people's relations with each other and with themselves (Coombe, 1998: 27).

On the surface, the legal ethnographies by Culhane, Moore, Coutin, and Coombe are quite different and engage with a wide range of subject positions across conventional fieldsites as well as more radical terrains of legal investigation such as Coombe's exploration of intellectual property. However, what ties together the four legal ethnographers are their interdisciplinary approaches that draw upon cultural studies, literature, sociology, history, as well as a range of sociolegal scholarship and legal theory. Each scholar is concerned with positionality and reflexivity vis-à-vis their subjects of study, and presents individuals' narratives in an effort to understand how people make meanings out of personal experiences, strategies, and opportunities.[8] Each author writes "against culture," which means that each is interested not in a predetermined essentialist idea of a particular culture, but rather in the shifts in relations between people, spaces, and identities that inform the dynamic social contours of their fields of study and their methods of investigation (Abu-Lughod, 1991, 1993). Each is adamantly engaged in rethinking modernist myths, often articulated through legal categories such as "indigenous rights," "wife," "refugee," "proprietor," and "property," that are used to legitimate asymmetrical power relations between peoples and things. And each author is engaging with an exploration of localized legal tensions within complex modern societies, set against a backdrop of macro political and economic processes. Interestingly, in all four works multisited ethnographic approaches dominate, both literally in the sense of living, interviewing, and observing from a number of sites and places, and metaphorically in terms of employing what Marcus calls "a multi-sited research imaginary" that traces and describes connections and relationships among sites previously thought incommensurate (Marcus, 1998: 14).

Thinking About the Space, Time, and Aesthetic of Legal Meanings

In this final section I want to return to the idea of a multisited research imaginary and further explore its applicability given new theoretical and empirical studies on shifting representations of legal space, time, and aesthetics. According to Richard Ford: "law is defined and constituted by its borders, and borders are defined and created by law" (Ford, 1996: 1173). There is an emerging acknowledgement among sociolegal scholars that law is, in the words of David Engel, "self-consciously spatial in orientation, and its first concern is to define the boundaries within which it operates" (Engel 1993: 130; see Blomley, 1994; Darian-Smith, 1999; Cooper, 1998; Milner and Goldberg-Hiller, 2002). This interest in the spatial dimensions of law is most obviously celebrated by the recent publication of *The Legal Geographies Reader* (2001). The volume, edited by Nicholas Blomley and David Delaney (both geographers) and Richard Ford (legal scholar), brings together a variety of people from various fields and disciplines to analyze articulations of space and their impact on legal processes and practices. As a whole, the volume seeks to examine such things as racial segregation, environmental activism, public space, national identity, as well as transnational border crossings as new sites of governance and legalization. Together the essays underscore that articulated divisions and scales between local and global arenas are artificial, fluid, and porous (Blomley, Delaney, and Ford, 2001: xx, fn 11; see also Santos and his concept of "interlegalites," 1995: 473).[9]

The editors of *The Legal Geographies Reader* claim three significant consequences to a convergence of legal and geographical perspectives. First, "by reading the legal in terms of the spatial and the spatial in terms of the legal, our understandings of both 'space' and 'law' may be changed. Old stabilities begin to reveal gaps and tensions." Second, our very experiences and imaginations are "profoundly molded by inherited legal notions such as 'rights,' 'ownership' and 'sovereignty'... Social space is saturated with legal meanings, but these meanings are always multiple and usually open to a range of divergent interpretations." Third, and most importantly, "the legal and the spatial are, in significant ways, aspects of each other and as such, they are fundamental and irreducible aspects of a more holistically conceived social-material reality." This social-material reality involves inequalities of power and access to opportunities and experiences (Blomley et al., 2001: xvii–iii).

Of course, constructions of space cannot be divorced from representations of time. While anthropologists have long been interested in cross-cultural understandings of time (see Greenhouse, 1996: Part 1), to date there has been little research on time in the law except by a few innovative legal ethnographers anxious to highlight how modern Western law embraces particular representations of time that are not universal and not value-free (see French, 2001; Greenhouse, 1996, 1989; Engel, 1987; Wilkinson, 1987). A culturally diverse approach to time in the law is provided by Carol Greenhouse's *A Moment's Notice: Time Politics Across Cultures*. Here the author offers an exciting exploration of how ethnographic study of cultural understandings of time relate to forms of social order. According to Greenhouse, "other kinds of time are actually other formulations of agency, as represented by particular people under particular circumstances" (Greenhouse, 1996: 5). Drawing on three case studies including battles over Supreme Court nominees in the United States, Greenhouse documents how different representations of time open up new ways to conceptualize normative behaviors and legal experiences.

Space and time are two important arenas of emerging sociolegal inquiry that put a slightly different spin on the multisited research imaginary proposed by Marcus, discussed above. New ethnographic studies strongly argue that not all fieldsites are equivalent, and as an analyst one has to be attendant to the spatial relations and networks of power from which subject positions are formed and articulated. Similarly, sensitivity to competing and often conflicting time representations opens up new ways of conceiving agency and strategies for legal action. Attention to space and time moves ethnographic inquiry away from conceiving law, and people's understandings of law, as primarily narrative-based. This move can be more broadly characterized as an increasing concern by sociolegal scholars in examining in tandem with institutional structures the power of legal aesthetics. By legal aesthetics, I mean "the ways in which law is intimately connected to visual, sensual, and textural phenomena, and hence the need to explore how an aesthetic redefinition of people's views of their material, symbolic, and metaphoric landscapes influence how they experience the powers that order specific territories and shaped related forms of morality" (Darian-Smith, 1999: 14). The anthropologist Edmund Leach argued in the 1950s that "[l]ogically, aesthetics and ethics are identical. If we are to understand the ethical rules of a society, it is aesthetics that we must study" (Leach, 1954:12). More recently, Peter Goodrich has noted, "A reading of the legal text which ignores the power of its imagery or the aesthetics of its reception is a reading which is in many senses beside the point in that it ignores precisely that dimension of the text and its contents which performs the labor of signification and so gives text its effect" (Goodrich, 1991: 236–8)

Historically modern Western law has differentiated between art, imagination, creativity, and subjective interpretation on the one hand, and rational, controlled, objective reasoning on the other. However, distinctions between these two arenas of intellectual activity are based on modernist assumptions of rationality and objectivity, and are in fact highly artificial. People's senses, which are themselves culturally informed – sight is privileged over all other sensory factors in European societies – inform an individual's legal understandings and representations (Darian-Smith, 1999: 54–62; Bently and Flynn, 1996). According to Costas Douzinas and Lynda Nead in *Law and the Image*:

> Legal discourse in modernity has become, according to conventional jurisprudence, a literature that represses its literary quality, a rhetoric that forgets its textual organization and aesthetic arrangement.... Despite the musing of judges and planners to the contrary, the law has always had an aesthetic policy, an attitude of policing images and licensing pleasures... Indeed, in modernity, law has become a literature that represses its literariness and an aesthetic practice that denies its art.... The law arranges, distributes, and polices its own image through icons of authority and sovereignty, traditional and fidelity. (Douzinas and Nead, 1999: 5, 9)

Space, time, imagery, rhetoric, metaphor and sensory perception – together these lines of investigation suggest new sites for grounded and detailed inquiry (see, e.g., Hyde, 1997; Hibbits, 1994, 1992; Costonis, 1989; Abramson and Theodossopoulos, 2000).

Thinking about the value of legal aesthetics, or forms of cultural difference as played out in a multitude of social relations, daily practices, as well as individual and collective experiences, points to innovative and exciting ways to approaching legal ethnography. Just as early legal ethnographers of the nineteenth century were interested in the legal aesthetics of "primitive cultures," as represented through religious icons, art, symbols, spirituality, language, movement, dance, household organization, and so on, we need to refocus our attention on the basics of social and cultural interaction in our own highly complex societies. However, unlike nineteenth-century legal ethnographers, today we are in a better position to analyze alternative and unfamiliar legal processes, since we are at least theoretically capable of acknowledging our ethnocentric biases, even if not yet getting past them. Ambiguity, context, intuition, and careful attention to the shifting "grounds of law," to borrow from Peter Fitzpatrick, or "the revolving door of rationality," to borrow from Michel Foucault, is what legal ethnography can help us reveal (Fitzpatrick, 2001; Rabinow, 1984: 249). These concerns are ever more pertinent to a world now constituted through new forms of visual stimulation and imagery brought about by electronic technologies, as well as new aesthetic experiences of law connected with such things as biological and terrorist violence, new modes of surveillance and control, new codes of morality, and an ever growing number of propertyless individuals with no home or homeland, and no obvious claims to a singular ethnic or legal identity. Who knows what will transpire over the next 30 years that will challenge our conceptions of law and perceptions of legal meaning, as well as challenge our understanding of cultural difference and how individuals operate within and in between changing frames of social order, cultural place, and ideas of personal and national sovereignty. Increasing anxieties about the future underscores the value of legal ethnography for sociolegal scholars of all disciplines and all theoretical positions, precisely because, as I have tried to argue above, legal ethnography "provides insights into phenomenon that are not, on the surface, legal" (Coutin, 2000: 10).

Notes

1   Out of the enlightenment obsession with custom, a different and degraded form emerges. Custom becomes reduced to a peripheral category set in opposition to law through its association with the savage and with those small-scaled remnants of a recalcitrant past yet to be transformed by modernity. It is produced by implacable habit and is everything that reasoned will is not. It is, said Bentham, "for brutes – written law [being] the law for civilized nations." (Fitzpatrick, 1992: 60)

2   However, as Nugent notes, the relationship between anthropologist and cultural study scholars has not been without tension and resentment (Nugent and Shore, 1997). Paul Willis, a cultural studies scholar renowned for his use of ethnography, has observed that there is a great discrepancy between claims by cultural studies scholars and the reality of their research. Despite cultural study scholars arguing " . . . for the centrality of ethnography, very little has actually been done" (Nugent, 1997, fn. 5). Willis has called for theoretically informed ethnography, arguing that both anthropology and cultural studies have a lot to still learn from each other. For anthropologists, Willis states that they are trapped

   . . . in an imperial past, and specifically, by a too bounded notion of "the field". It's something you "do" virtually for itself. It's your institutional and professional rite of passage. If you haven't been through that rite of passage you're not really an anthropologist, and no matter what the sophistication with which you describe and analyze the baggage you seem obliged to take with you, your main orientation and set of definitions still revolve around the "field".

With respect to cultural studies scholars, Willis argues "The lack of a really genuine ethnographic root in cultural studies, I think, has allowed it to drift into a theoreticism which has removed it from the engagement [with contemporary reality] from which it originally grew" (Willis 1997: 186–8).

3   A fascinating book that seeks to get beyond the "science wars" that have plagued anthropologists and most social scientists is that by Bent Flyvbjerg (2001) *Making Social Science Matter: Why Social Inquiry Fails and How It Can Succeed Again.* Flyvbjerg argues that the world cannot be reduced to abstract, rule-based, universalistic, and predictive epistemic theories. Therefore, when the social sciences seek to emulate the natural sciences and create general theories of context and reasoning, they inevitably fail (Flyvbjerg 2001: 3). Importantly, Flyvbjerg does not claim that natural science is less relevant than social science or that one deserves more attention than the other. Rather,

> the rule-based, rational mode of thinking generally constitutes an obstacle to good results, not because rules and rationality are problematic in themselves, but because the rational perspective has been elevated from being necessary to being sufficient, even exclusive. This has caused people and entire scholarly disciplines to become blind to context, experience, and intuition, even though these phenomena and ways of being are at least as important and necessary for good results as are analysis, rationality, and rules. (Flyvbjerg, 2001: 24; see also Knorr Cetina, 1999)

4   I take seriously the argument that there is no singular notion of globalization (Jensen and Santos, 2000: 10). Global forces are plural and multidimensional, and deeply embedded in unequal power relations. Moreover, global forces incorporate economic change as well as a wide range of cultural, social, and political transformations. I would add that thinking about globalization in the plural suggest the need to stress the plurality of postcolonialism and capitalism as well (see Darian-Smith and Fitzpatrick, 1999). Sociologists working on this issue, and the differences perceived between a sociological and anthropological perspective in current ethnography, are interestingly presented by Burawoy et al. (2000) *Global Ethnography: Forces, Connections, and Imaginations in a Postmodern World.*

5   Moreover, as Ann Stoler has pointed out:

> Colonial cultures were never direct translations of European society planted in the colonies, but unique cultural configurations, homespun creations in which European food, dress, housing, and morality were given new political meanings in the particular social order of colonial rule. Formal dress codes, sumptuary laws, and military display did more than reiterate middle-class European visions and values.... The point is that colonial projects and the European populations to which they gave rise were based on new constructions of Europeaness: they were artificial groupings – demographically, occupationally, and politically distinct. Not only white settlers but the more transient European residents in the colonies were occupied with social and political concerns that often pitted them against policy-makers in the metropole as much as against the colonized. (Stoler, 1992: 321)

6   Foucault has called this *effet de retour,* a "return-effect," whereby "colonialization had a return effect on the mechanisms of power in the Occident, on the institutional apparatuses and techniques of power. There has been a whole series of colonial models that have been

brought back to the Occident and that made it so that the Occident could traffic in something like a colonialization, an internal colonialism" (cited in Stoler, 1995: 75).

7 Taking seriously women's perspectives is a relatively recent phenomenon in anthropological circles, and legal anthropologists writing about women and their relationship to prevailing power structures at local, regional, national, and transnational levels are making important contributions in this regard (see Griffiths, 2001 for an important summary of this field). Two outstanding examples of this kind of contribution come to mind, but there are many more that are worthy of attention. The first is Susan Hirsch's book *Pronouncing and Perservering: Gender and the Discourses of Disputing in an African Islamic Court* (1998). Here the author explores how Muslim women are in particular circumstances able to use the legal system to advance their own domestic interests, while appearing to remain subordinate to their husbands. The second book of note is Annelise Riles's work on the Beijing Conference, or United Nations Fourth World Conference on Women in 1994. She analyzes the global networks established through women participants in the conference and in particular the local responses of indigenous Fijian and part-European women to this network process (Riles, 2000, 1995).

8 See French (1996) on narrative in law and anthropology, and Sarat (1990) and Ewick and Silbey (1998) for exemplary uses of narrative in the understanding of legal consciousness in modern American culture.

9 Besides a brief comment about law and the Internet in the Introduction to the volume, there is a noted absence of any substantive discussion about whether ideas about space provoked by the Internet play out in attempts to govern it and related information technologies (Blomley et al., 2001: xii–iv; see Katsh, 1989; Boyle, 1996; Sunstein, 2001). This somewhat surprising absence, however, by no means detracts from the volume's challenging agenda.

References

Abramson, Allen and Thedossopoulos, Dimitrios (2000) *Land, Law and Environment: Mythical Land, Legal Boundaries*. London: Pluto.

Abu-Lughod, Lila (1991) "Writing against culture," in R.G. Fox (ed.), *Recapturing Anthropology: Working in the Present*. Santa Fe, NM: School of American Research Press, pp. 137–62.

Abu-Lughod, Lila (1993) *Writing Women's Worlds: Bedouin Stories*. Berkeley: University of California Press.

Ahmed, Akbar and Shore, Cris (eds.) (1995) *The Future of Anthropology: Its Relevance to the Contemporary World*. London and Atlantic Highlands, NJ: Athlone.

Augé, Marc (1994) *An Anthropology for Contemporary Worlds*, trans. Amy Jacobs. Stanford, CA: Stanford University Press.

Baudet, Henri (1976) *Paradise on Earth: Some Thoughts on European Images of Non-European Man*, trans. Elizabeth Wentholt. Westport, CT: Greenwood Press.

Bently, Lionel and Flynn, Leo (eds.) (1996) *Law and the Senses: Sensational Jurisprudence*. London and Chicago: Pluto Press.

Blomley, Nicholas K. (1994) *Law, Space, and the Geographies of Power*. New York and London: The Guildford Press.

Blomley, Nicholas, Delaney, David, and Ford, Richard T. (eds) (2001) *The Legal Geographies Reader*. Oxford: Blackwell.

Bohannan, Paul (1957) *Justice and Judgement Among the Tiv*. London: Oxford University Press.

Bohannan, Paul (1969) "Ethnography and comparison in legal anthropology," in Laura Nader (ed.), *Law in Culture and Society*. Chicago: Aldine, pp. 401–18.

Bohannan, Paul and van der Elst, Dirk (1998) *Asking and Listening: Ethnography as Personal Adaptation*. Propsect Hills, IL: Waveland Press.

Borneman, John (1992) *Belonging in the Two Berlins: Kin, State, Nation*. Cambridge, UK: Cambridge University Press.

Bourdieu, Pierre (1987) "The force of law: Toward a sociology of the juridical field," *Hastings Law Journal* 38(July): 805–53.

Boyle, James (1996) *Shamans, Software and Spleens: Law and the Construction of the Information Society*. Cambridge, MA: Harvard University Press.

Burawoy, Michael et al. (2000) *Global Ethnography: Forces, Connections, and Imaginations in a Postmodern World*. Berkeley: University of California Press.

Calavita, Kitty (1992) *Inside the State: The Bracero Program, Immigration, and the INS*. New York: Routledge.

Chagnon, Napoleon (1968) *Yanomamö: The Fierce People*. New York: Holt, Rinehart & Winston.

Clifford, James (1988) *The Predicament of Culture: Twentieth-Century Ethnography, Literature, and Art*. Cambridge, MA: Harvard University Press.

Clifford, James and Marcus, George E. (eds) (1986) *Writing Culture: The Poetics and Politics of Ethnography*. Berkeley: University of California Press.

Cohn, Bernard S. (1996) *Colonialism and Its Forms of Knowledge: The British in India*. Princeton, NJ: Princeton University Press.

Collier, Jane (1997) "The waxing and waning of 'subfields' in North American sociocultural anthropology," in Akhil Gupta and James Ferguson (eds.), *Anthropological Foundations*. Berkeley: University of California Press, pp. 117–30.

Comaroff, John (1994) "Foreword," in Susan Hirsch and Mindie Lazarus-Black (eds.), *Contested States: Law, Hegemony and Resistance*. New York: Routledge, pp. ix–xiii.

Comaroff, John L. and Comaroff, Jean (1992) *Ethnography and the Historical Imagination: The Cultural Logic of Dispute in an African Context*. Chicago: University of Chicago Press.

Comaroff, John L. and Comaroff, Jean (1993) *Modernity and Its Malcontents: Ritual and Power in Postcolonial Africa*. Chicago: University of Chicago Press.

Comaroff, John L. and Comaroff, Jean (1997) *Of Revelation and Revolution: The Dialectics of Modernity on a South African Frontier*. Chicago: University of Chicago Press.

Comaroff, John and Roberts, Simon (1981) *Rules and Processes: The Cultural Logic of Dispute in an African Context*. Chicago: University of Chicago Press.

Coombe, Rosemary J. (1998a) "Contingent articulations: A critical cultural studies of law," in Austin Sarat and Thomas R. Kearns (eds.), *Law in the Domains of Culture*. Ann Arbor: University of Michigan Press, pp. 21–64.

Coombe, Rosemary J. (1998b) *The Cultural Life of Intellectual Properties*. Durham, NC and London: Duke University Press.

Cooper, Davina (1998) *Governing Out of Order: Space, Law, and the Politics of Belonging*. New York: New York University Press.

Costonis, John L. (1989) *Icons and Aliens: Law, Aesthetics, and Environmental Change*. Urbana and Chicago: University of Illinois.

Coutin, Susan Bibler (2000) *Legalizing Moves: Salvadoran Immigrants' Struggle for U.S. Residency*. Ann Arbor: University of Michigan Press.

Culhane, Dara (1998) *The Pleasure of the Crown: Anthropology, Law and First Nations*. Burnaby, British Colombia: Talon.

Danielsen, Dan and Engle, Karen (eds.) (1995) *After Identity: A Reader in Law and Culture*. New York: Routledge.

Darian-Smith, Eve (1999) *Bridging Divides: The Channel Tunnel and English Legal Identity in the New Europe*. Berkeley: California University Press.

Darian-Smith, Eve (2002) "Myths of 'East' and 'West': Intellectual property law in postcolonial Hong Kong," in David Goldberg and Ato Quayson (eds.), *Re-Thinking Postcolonialism*. Oxford: Blackwell, pp. 294–319.

Darian-Smith, Eve (forthcoming) *Culture, Custom, Power, Law: Implications of Legal Anthropology for the Study of Law.* Oxford and Malden, MA: Blackwell.

Darian-Smith, Eve and Fitzpatrick, Peter (eds.) (1996) Special issue on law and postcolonialism. *Social and Legal Studies* 5(3): 291–427.

Darian-Smith, Eve and Fitzpatrick, Peter (eds.) (1999) *The Laws of the Postcolonial.* Ann Arbor: University of Michigan Press.

Di Leonardo, Micaela (1998) *Exotics at Home: Anthropologies, Others, American Modernity.* Chicago: University of Chicago Press.

Douzinas, Costas and Nead, Lynda (eds.) (1999) *Law and the Image: The Authority of Art and the Aesthetics of Law.* Chicago: University of Chicago Press.

Engel, David M. (1987) "Law, time, and community," *Law & Society Review* 21: 605–38.

Engel, David M. (1993) "Law in the domains of everyday life: The construction of community and difference," in A. Sarat and T.M. Kearns (eds.), *Law in Everyday Life.* Ann Arbor: University of Michigan Press, pp. 123–70.

Ewick, Patricia and Silbey, Susan (1998) *The Common Place of Law: Stories from Everyday Life.* Chicago: University of Chicago Press.

Fardon, Richard (ed.) (1990) *Localizing Strategies: The Regionalization of Ethnographic Accounts.* Washington DC: Smithsonian Institute Press.

Fitzpatrick, Peter (1992) *The Mythology of Modern Law.* London: Routledge.

Fitzpatrick, Peter (2001) *Modernism and the Grounds of Law.* Cambridge, UK: Cambridge University Press.

Flyvbjerg, Bent (2001) *Making Social Science Matter: Why Social Inquiry Fails and How It Can Succeed Again.* Cambridge, UK: Cambridge University Press.

Ford, Richard Thompson (1996) "Beyond borders: A partial response to Richard Briffault. Symposium "Surveying Law and Borders," *Stanford Law Review* 48(5): 1173–96.

French, Rebecca R. (1996) "Of narrative in law and anthropology," *Law & Society Review* 30(2): 417–35.

French, Rebecca R. (2001) "Time in the law," *University of Colorado Law Review* 72(3): 663–748.

Friedman, Jonathan (2000) "Ethnography as a social system: Parts, wholes, and holes," in Sjoerd R. Jaarsma and Marta A. Rohatynskyj (eds.), *Ethnographic Artifacts: Challenges to a Reflexive Anthropology.* Honolulu: University of Hawai'i Press, pp. 195–209.

Geertz, C. (1973) "Thick description: Towards an interpretive theory of culture," in C. Geertz, *The Interpretation of Culture.* London: Fontana, pp. 3–32.

Gluckman, Max (1955) *The Judicial Process Among the Barotse of Northern Rhodesia.* Manchester, UK: University of Manchester Press.

Gluckman, Max (1969) "Concepts in the comparative study of tribal law," in Laura Nader (ed.), *Law in Culture and Society.* Chicago: Aldine, pp. 349–73.

Goldberg, D.T. (ed) (1994) *Multiculturalism: A Critical Reader.* Oxford: Blackwell.

Goldberg, David T., Musheno, Michael, and Bower, Lisa C. (2001) *Between Law and Culture: Relocating Legal Studies.* Minneapolis: University of Minnesota Press.

Goodrich, Peter (1991) "Specula laws: Image, aesthetic and common law," *Law and Critique* 2(2): 233–54.

Greenhouse, Carol J. (1986) *Praying for Justice: Faith, Order, and Community in an American Town.* Ithaca, NY: Cornell University Press.

Greenhouse, Carol J. (1989) "Just in time: Temporality and the cultural legitimation of law," *Yale Law Journal* 98: 1631.

Greenhouse, Carol J. (1996) *A Moment's Notice: Time Politics Across Cultures.* Ithaca, NY: Cornell University Press.

Greenhouse, Carol J., Yngvesson, Barbara, and Engel, David M. (1994) *Law and Community in Three American Towns.* Ithaca, NY: Cornell University Press.

Greenhouse, Carol J., Warren, Kay, and Mertz, Elizabeth (eds.) (2002) *Ethnography in Unstable Places.* Durham, NC: Duke University Press, pp. 249–75.

Griffiths, Anne (2001) "Remaking law: Gender, ethnography, and legal discourse," *Law & Society Review* 35(2): 495–509.

Grimshaw, Anna and Hart, Keith (1995) "The rise and fall of scientific ethnography," in Akbar Ahmed and Cris Shore (eds.), *The Future of Anthropology: Its Relevance to the Contemporary World*. London: Athlone, pp. 46–64.

Gupta, Akhil and Ferguson, James (eds.) (1997) *Anthropological Foundations*. Berkeley: University of California Press.

Harvey, David (1996) *Justice, Nature & the Geography of Difference*. Malden, MA and Oxford: Blackwell.

Herzfeld, Michael (2001) *Anthropology: Theoretical Practice in Culture and Society*. Malden, MA: Blackwell.

Hibbitts, Bernard (1992) "Coming to our senses: Communication and legal expression in performance cultures," *Emory Law Journal* 41(4): 873–960.

Hibbitts, Bernard (1994) "Making sense of metaphors: Visuality, aurality, and the reconfiguration of American legal discourse," *Cardozo Law Review* 16: 229–356.

Hirsch, Susan (1998) *Pronouncing and Perservering: Gender and the Discourses of Disputing in an African Islamic Court*. Chicago: University of Chicago Press.

Hirsch, Susan and Lazarus-Black, Mindie (1994) "Introduction: Performance and paradox. Exploring law's role in hegemony and resistance," in Susan Hirsch and Mindie Lazarus-Black (eds.), *Contested States: Law, Hegemony and Resistance*. New York: Routledge, pp. 1–31.

Hoebel, E. Adamson (1954) *The Law of Primitive Man: A Study in Comparative Legal Dynamics*. Cambridge, MA: Harvard University Press.

Hyde, Allan (1997) *Bodies of Law*. Princeton, NJ: Princeton University Press.

Jensen, Jane and Santos, Boaventura de Sousa (eds.) (2000) *Globalizing Institutions: Case Studies in Regulation and Innovation*. Aldershot, UK: Ashgate.

Just, Peter (1992) "History, power, ideology, and culture: Current directions in the anthropology of law," *Law & Society Review* 26: 373–412.

Kahn, Paul W. (1999) *The Cultural Study of Law: Reconstructing Legal Scholarship*. Chicago and London: University of Chicago Press.

Katsh, M. Ethan (1989) *The Electronic Media and the Transformation of Law*. New York and Oxford: Oxford University Press.

Knorr Cetina, Karin (1999) *Epistemic Cultures: How the Sciences Make Knowledge*. Cambridge, MA: Harvard University Press.

Lach, Donald F. (1965) *Asia in the Making of Europe*. Chicago: University of Chicago Library.

Lach, Donald F. (1968) *China in the Eyes of Europe: The Sixteenth Century*. Chicago: University of Chicago Library.

Leach, Edmund (1954) *Political Systems of Highland Burma*. Cambridge, MA: Harvard University Press.

Leibniz, Gottfried Wilhelm ([1697–1716]1994) *Writings on China*. Chicago and La Salle, IL: Open Court.

Llewellyn, Karl and Hoebel, E. Adamson (1941) *The Cheyenne Way*. Norman: University of Oklahoma Press.

Locke, John ([1690]1988) *Two Treaties of Government*, ed. Peter Laslett. Cambridge, UK: Cambridge University Press.

Maine, Sir Henry (1861) *Ancient Law*. New York: Dutton.

Marcus, George R. (1998) *Ethnography Through Thick and Thin*. Princeton, NJ: Princeton University Press.

Marcus, George (ed.) (1999) *Critical Anthropology Now: Unexpected Contexts, Shifting Constituencies, Changing Agendas*. Santa Fe, New Mexico: School of American Research Press.

Marcus, George E. and Fischer, Michael M.J. (1986) *Anthropology as Cultural Critique: An Experimental Moment in the Human Sciences*. Chicago: University of Chicago Press.

Maurer, Bill (1997) *Recharting the Caribbean: Land, Law, and Citizenship in the British Virgin Islands*. Ann Arbor: University of Michigan Press

Merry, Sally E. (1992) "Anthropology, law, and transnational processes," *Annual Review of Anthropology* 21: 357–79.

Merry, Sally E. (2000a) "Crossing boundaries: Ethnography in the twenty-first century," *Political and Legal Anthropology Review* 23(2): 127–33.

Merry, Sally Engle (2000b) *Colonizing Hawai'i: The Cultural Power of Law*. Princeton, NJ: Princeton University Press.

Miller, Barbara (2002) *Cultural Anthropology*. Boston: Allyn & Bacon.

Miller, Daniel (1997) *Capitalism: An Ethnographic Approach*. Oxford and New York: Berg.

Milner, Neal and Goldberg-Hiller, Jonathan (2002) "Reimagining rights: Tunnels, nations, spaces," *Law and Social Inquiry* 27(2): 339–68.

Montesquieu ([1748]1989) *The Spirit of the Laws*, trans. and ed. A. Cohler, B. C. Miller, and H. S. Stone. Cambridge, UK: Cambridge University Press.

Moore, Erin P. (1998) *Gender, Law, and Resistance in India*. Tucson: University of Arizona Press.

Moore, Sally Falk (1969) "Introduction," in Laura Nader (ed.), *Law in Culture and Society*. Berkeley: University of California Press, pp. 337–48.

Moore, Sally Falk (1978) *Law as Process: An Anthropological Approach*. London: Routledge & Kegan Paul.

Moore, Sally Falk (1986) *Social Facts and Fabrications: "Customary Law" on Kilimanjaro, 1880–1980*. Cambridge, UK: Cambridge University Press.

Moore, Sally Falk (1993) "Introduction: Moralizing states and the ethnography of the present," *American Ethnological Society Monograph Series* 5: 1–16.

Moore, Sally Falk (2001) "Certainties undone: Fifty turbulent years of legal anthropology, 1949–1999," *Journal of the Royal Anthropological Institute* 7: 95–116.

Nader, Laura (2002) *The Life of the Law: Anthropological Projects*. Berkeley: University of California Press.

Nugent, Stephen (1997) "Introduction: Brother, can you spare a paradigm?" in Stephen Nugent and Shore, Cris (eds.), *Anthropology and Cultural Studies*. London and Chicago: Pluto Press, pp. 1–10.

Nugent, Stephen and Shore, Cris (eds.) (1997) *Anthropology and Cultural Studies*. London and Chicago: Pluto Press.

Peacock, James L. (1986) *The Anthropological Lens: Harsh Light, Soft Focus*. New York: Cambridge University Press.

Rabinow, Paul (ed.) (1984) *Foucault Reader*. New York: Pantheon Books.

Riles, Annelise (1994) "Representing in-between: Law, anthropology, and the rhetoric of interdisciplinary," *University of Illinois Law Review*: 597–650.

Riles, Annelise (1995) "The view from the international plane: Perspective and scale in the architecture of colonial international law," *Law and Critique* 6: 39–54.

Riles, Annelise (2000) *The Network Inside Out*. Ann Arbor: University of Michigan Press.

Sack, Peter and Aleck, Johnathon (eds.) (1992) *Law and Anthropology*. New York: New York University Press.

Santos, Boa Ventura (1995) *Toward a New Common Sense: Law, Science and Politics in a Paradigmatic Transition*. New York: Routledge.

Sarat, Austin (1990) "The law is all over: Power, resistance and the legal consciousness of the welfare poor," *Yale Journal of Law and the Humanities* 2: 343–79.

Sarat, Austin and Kearns, Thomas R. (eds.) (1998) *Law in the Domains of Culture*. Ann Arbor: University of Michigan Press.

Snyder, Francis (1996) "Law and anthropology," in Philip Thomas (ed.), *Legal Frontiers*. Aldershot, UK: Dartmouth, pp. 135–79.

Starr, June and Collier, Jane F. (1989) *History and Power in the Study of Law: New Directions in Legal Anthropology*. Ithaca, NY: Cornell University Press.

Starr, June and Goodale, Mark (2002) *Practicing Ethnography in Law: New Dialogues, Enduring Practices.* New York: Palgrave/St. Martin's.

Stocking, George (ed.) (1983) *Observers Observed: Essays on Ethnographic Fieldwork.* Madison: University of Wisconsin Press.

Stoler, Ann Laura (1992) "Rethinking colonial categories: European communities and the boundaries of rule," in Nicholas B. Dirks (ed.), *Colonialism and Culture.* Ann Arbor: University of Michigan Press, pp. 319–52.

Stoler, Ann Laura (1995) *Race and the Education of Desire: Foucault's History of Sexuality and the Colonial Order of Things.* Durham, NC: Duke University Press.

Sunstein, Cass (2001) *Republic.com.* Princeton, NJ: Princeton University Press.

Turner, T. (1994) "Anthropology and multiculturalism: What is anthropology that multiculturalists should be mindful of it?" in D.T. Goldberg (ed.), *Multiculturalism: A Critical Reader.* Oxford: Blackwell, pp. 406–25.

White, Hayden (1999) "Afterword," in Victoria E. Bonnel and Lynn Hunt (eds.), *Beyond the Cultural Turn. New Directions in the Study of Society and Culture.* Berkeley: University of California Press, pp. 315–24.

Wilkinson, Charles F. (1987) *American Indians, Time and the Law.* New Haven, CT: Yale University Press.

Willis, Paul (1997) "TIES: Theoretically informed ethnographic study," in Stephen Nugent and Cris Shore (eds.), *Anthropology and Cultural Studies.* London and Chicago: Pluto Press, pp. 182–92.

30

Colonial and Postcolonial Law

SALLY ENGLE MERRY

The law of contemporary societies was forged in the colonial era. Although there were significant transplants and transnational adoptions of law in the period before 1500, the imperial era from the sixteenth to the twentieth centuries saw an unprecedented transplanting of legal systems. Colonialism almost always involved the transfer of legal codes and institutions from one society to another. Law moved from Europe and North America to Latin America, Asia, and Africa. The colonial encounter not only defined relations of land, labor, and family in the colonies, but also reshaped the law of the metropoles. The challenges of colonial governance spawned new technologies of governance and rule, some of which were applied at home as well as in the colonies (Fitzpatrick, 1992; Comaroff, 2001). One legacy of this history is a racialized system of law, in which different legal systems are used for racially distinguished populations. Fitzpatrick shows how modern law itself is defined in opposition to an allegedly savage "other" which it excludes (Fitzpatrick, 1992; Darian-Smith and Fitzpatrick, 1999).

Postcolonial states now confront highly complex systems of plural law within their territories. Much of the early anthropological theory about colonial law comes from the analysis of British Africa. This region had separate legal systems targeted to racially distinct populations. This ultimately led to the extreme of apartheid in South Africa, but institutional segregation was common throughout colonized Africa (Mamdani, 1996). During the colonial era, separate legal systems for racially or religiously distinct populations were widespread. Often, European courts served Europeans while "natives" took their conflicts to customary law courts (Roberts and Mann, 1991). Postcolonial states contain remnants of these dual legal systems and often incorporate old European regulations in their law codes, particularly concerning marriage, family, and divorce.

The legacy of this historical process is a complex legal pluralism in which countries have overlapping and contradictory legal systems of unequal powers and distinct jurisdictions. A fundamental feature of sociolegal research is recognizing that more than one legal system frequently exists in the same social space, each with different rules and procedures. Understanding the dynamic interactions among these separate systems of ordering is a central problem for law and society research (see Merry, 1988, 2000). The analysis of colonial and postcolonial law requires examining the intersections among these legal spheres and the implications of their unequal authority and power. This means an archeology of law: an historical analysis of layers of legality and the historical contexts of their deposition. The archeology metaphor suggests simple contiguity in chronological order, but in practice each system affects the operation of the others, either through appeals or through multiple jurisdictions leading to forum shopping or because of inconsistencies among them (see Benda-Beckmann, 1981). As the systems interact with one another, they redefine each other's concepts and practices, although not with equal power and influence. Legal innovations, legal transplants, and changing legal consciousness among ordinary people produce changes in the relations between these multiple legal systems over time. Imposed or introduced systems are not adopted in whole cloth but are appropriated and adjusted to fit new contexts. The important questions for sociolegal scholarship concern the nature of the relationships among the constituent layers.

Although the prevailing view assumes that European systems of law were imposed on recalcitrant and resistant colonized peoples by an energetic imperial power, recent research draws a more complicated picture. Colonized local elites were often active in constructing new legal systems and appropriating European/American ones. Some did so to consolidate their power as well as to reform their legal systems along the lines of liberal legality. They sometimes did so even if that meant limiting their power. For example, Nathan Brown's study of the process of legal reform in Egypt in the late nineteenth century shows the critical role of national elites in importing law and emphasizes the importance of domestic considerations over the pressures of imperialism. Egyptian elites were attracted to adopting liberal legality as long as it also supported local political authority (Brown, 1995, 1997: 18). Even outside the circle of European colonial control, some states adopted European law by choice, primarily as a strategy to defend themselves against imperial takeovers. States that independently constituted themselves as civilized nations under the rule of law include Thailand (Engel, 1978), the Kingdom of Hawai'i (Merry, 2000), Japan, Ethiopia, and Turkey.

Even in noncolonized states, law is deeply pluralized. Pluralities are common in states that incorporate indigenous peoples or immigrant communities with separate legal systems. Indigenous peoples often struggle to retain separate legal orders (e.g., Biolsi, 2001; Coulter, 1994; Anaya, 1994, 2000). Privatization has increased reliance on nonstate forms of governance ranging from internal judicial procedures within organizations to private policing and surveillance systems (e.g., Macaulay, 1963, 1986; Galanter, 1981). The spread of alternative dispute resolution mechanisms to many aspects of legal regulation has diversified the procedures of law and its outcomes (e.g., Merry and Milner, 1993). Ironically, many of the pluralizing influences are postcolonial imports. In the United States, for example, the movement to adopt alternatives to formal law drew heavily on examples of conciliatory justice described in China, Ghana, and Mexico (Merry and Milner, 1993). All these nonstate forms of law interact with state law, reshaping the nature of state law itself.

The dramatic social transformations of the last two decades that are generally grouped under the term globalization have spawned new systems of legal regulation and new relations among legal orders. Legal borrowing has continued apace in the postcolonial era, as transitional states such as those in Eastern Europe borrow legal codes and procedures from elsewhere, primarily the United States and Western Europe. There has been extensive adoption of constitutions, commercial codes, and discrete legal systems from one country to another (e.g., Chanock, 2001; Klug, 2000). Legal transfers and transplants are rapidly Americanizing law in many parts of the world, particularly commercial law (Dezalay and Garth, 1996; Sassen, 1994, 1996). The modern development agenda promotes reforms of courts and the expansion of the rule of law in Latin America and Africa (see Dezalay and Garth, 2002a: 220). The European Union has superimposed a regional legal system over existing national ones (Peterson and Zahle, 1995). Movements of illegal immigrants and refugees create pockets of alternative legalities among groups denied full citizenship in the states they inhabit (see Coutin, 2001). The global legal system is also expanding in scope. International law has stretched from regulating commerce and relations between states to regulating the legal relations between citizens and their states, economic relationships, the environment, the cultural integrity of indigenous peoples, and the status of vulnerable populations such as racial minorities, women, and children. A burgeoning human rights system located in transnational organizations such as the United Nations and nongovermental organizations (NGOs) augments nation-state systems of rights and protections for citizens. As the human rights system has expanded in the postwar period, it has reached into new domains of social life such as violence against women and rights to food, housing, and development. Globalization has fostered a new level of legal pluralism.

Thus the contemporary postcolonial world holds a rich diversity of overlapping, contradictory, and complementary systems of law at the local, national, and international level. It includes global regulation of trade, commerce, and labor rights as well as legal regimes protecting human rights. There are new globally based judicial institutions designed to regulate commercial relationships, enforce human rights, and most recently, to punish individuals for war crimes, crimes against humanity, and genocide. Many have been established since 1990, such as the International Criminal Court for the Former Yugoslavia, created 1994/5 and the International Criminal Court, formed in 2002. This situation is the legacy of colonialism, decolonization, and globalization.

A focus on the dialectic, mutually constitutive relations among global law, nation-state law, customary law, and other normative orders emphasizes the interconnectedness of social orders and the vulnerability of local places to structures of domination far outside their immediate worlds. For such a postmodern view of law, legal pluralism is a key concept (Santos, 1995). Santos uses the metaphor of the map to suggest that law is a system of signs which, like maps, represents/distorts reality through the mechanisms of scale, projection, and symbolization (Santos, 1987: 297). Different legal orders, like maps, have different scales, different forms of projection and centering, different systems of symbolization.

A theory of unequal but mutually constitutive legal orders leads to new questions: how do these systems interact and reshape one another? To what extent is the dominant system able to control the subordinate? How do subordinate systems subvert or evade the dominant system? Are there ways in which the disputing strategies of subordinate users reshape the dominant system? To what extent do contests among plural legal systems explain historical change?

This review examines theoretical developments in the analysis of colonial law and the legacy of this history for the postcolonial present. It then looks at new forms of global law such as international human rights law and commercial law and considers the complex and fraught relationships between international legal orders and state and local law.

COLONIAL LAW

Law was one of the major institutional systems used in the nineteenth-century expansion of capitalism and Euro-American political control over Africa, Asia, and the Pacific. Laws against deserting labor contracts, drinking, holding festivals, and vagrancy were fundamental to creating a docile, disciplined labor force in colonized countries as they were earlier in the European transition to capitalism (Thompson, 1967; Cooper, 1987, 1989; Fitzpatrick, 1987). The transition from communal ownership to the private land tenure demanded for capital investment in plantations and mines depended on law. Law helped to inculcate European ideas of work, time, property, debt, individualism, rights, personal discipline, and sexuality (Comaroff and Comaroff, 1991, 1997).

In Anglo-American colonialism, law was a central legitimating narrative, one of the ways in which conquest and appropriation were reinterpreted as the expansion of civilization (see Fitzpatrick, 1992). The rule of law was viewed as a "gift" to people who were typically envisioned by nineteenth-century European imperialists in the eloquent metaphors of *The Heart of Darkness*: chaotic and bestial, wholly unregulated, and without morals or rules. Law contributed to the construction of the great oppositional metaphors by which Europeans and Americans made sense of colonial conquest and its drive to transform the culture of the colonized to that of the master. The oppositions were painted in images of family and moral order: the "mother country" and "young nations";[1] the colonized as "half-devil, half-child" in contrast to the dutiful but unappreciated white adult male colonizer in Kipling's famous poem, "The White Man's Burden." The colonized were depicted as "superstitious," lazy, and morally degenerate in contrast to European rationality and efficiency (Said, 1978; Mitchell, 1988); their cities disorderly and educational systems chaotic in contrast to the broad boulevards and neatly graded and orderly schools of the Europeans (Mitchell, 1988). These images are gendered and raced, based on metaphors of parents and children, giver and receiver, superior and inferior race. Ideas of white racial supremacy developed out of these same oppositions. As considerable anthropological work has demonstrated, Europeans and Americans defined themselves in opposition to the imagined "others" they created (Fabian, 1983; Todorov, [1984] 1999; Comaroff and Comaroff, 1991). Fitzpatrick (1992) finds the same oppositions and exclusions in the mythology of modern law, forged during the colonial encounter.

This cultural map of oppositions existed in legal institutions as well as in missions, schools, plantations, and mines. Law itself became part of the set of cultural oppositions through which colonialism was understood and legitimated to European actors. Colonial legal officials saw themselves as bringing civilization and the rule of law to peoples whose customs (since they were typically seen to lack law) were arbitrary, capricious, and irrational. They distinguished between "law" and "custom," the one rational and just, the other irrational and situational.[2]

Race identities acquired meaning and form out of the encounters accompanying capitalist expansion and colonialism. In the period from the sixteenth to the nineteenth century, identities of difference depended largely on religious faith and customs. Terms such as heathen, infidel, kaffir, savage, and barbarian point to this kind of distinction in the mind of the labeler. But, at various points in various ways during the nineteenth century, identities based on cultural and religious difference were gradually displaced by identities based on physical characteristics. In other words, dominant groups defined the identities of the subjugated in terms of appearance rather than belief. The site of difference was now the body, not the soul. It was signaled by skin shade rather than religious practices. Thus difference shifted from mutable to immutable characteristics, a change with vast consequences for human society today. Race and gender identities and the more subtle but deeply embedded connection to class are fundamental to modern processes of power. Incorporated into legal regulations and the structure of the colonial legal system itself, often divided into racially coded distinct systems of "native law" and European law, the law served to fix and to legitimate the new racialized society it produced. Martin Chanock's (2001) study of South African law shows how this racialization of law was fundamental to its operation in that country.

Research on law in colonial situations has produced several important insights about the nature of the process and the legacy it has left. One involves challenging overly simple ideas of imposition. Early studies focused on the imposition of colonial law, although even at this time there were questions about the adequacy of the framework (see Burman and Harrell-Bond, 1979). Over the last two decades, studies have shown that new legal regimes were not simply imposed but were introduced through processes of accommodation and appropriation. Colonial rulers struggled to establish control at minimal cost, while the elites in colonized societies sought to use the new legal resources introduced by colonial governments in their own struggles for power (Chanock, 1985, 2001; Brown, 1997). Peoples in some colonized countries resisted the ideology of the colonizers (Guha, 1997) while in others, as Laura Nader (1990) demonstrates, they closed themselves off from intervention by an ideology of harmony.

A second major insight is that customary law is not the remnant of a pristine, unchanged past, as it was often imagined by colonial administrators, but the product of interactions between colonial powers and various groups within the colonial state (Chanock, 1985). An extensive body of scholarship has explored the origins of so-called customary law, a regime of law still widely used in many postcolonial countries. Francis Snyder did one of the earliest studies showing that this law was formed in the colonial context, often constructed by advice given colonial administrators by the new elites conversant in the colonial language and its economic and political relationships (Snyder, 1981; see also Chanock, 1985; Moore, 1986). It reflected the power relations within colonial spaces and the capacity of some to articulate for colonial officials the nature of "traditional" law (Chanock, 1985). These rules were invented and redefined to accommodate the new circumstances of colonialism (Comaroff and Comaroff, 1991, 1997). In India, British colonial scholars worked with religious legal texts from Hinduism and Islam to produce a localized, religiously based system of law (Galanter, 1989; Cohn, 1996; Strawson, 1999). However, as Cohn (1996) points out, in the processes of translation, interpretation, and codification, Hindu law became something quite different; something more like British law in form despite its Hindu derivation.

A third set of insights concerns the scope of control established in the colonies through law. Although early studies focused on land and labor, subsequent research shows that law and associated forms of discipline reached deeply into family and community life, regulating even dress, drink, and ritual life. Analysis of law's colonial intervention moved from a Marxist focus on the contribution of law to changing material relationships to a more Foucauldian concern with systems of discipline and knowledge and regulation of the body and sexuality. Capitalism's demands for land and labor clearly drove the expansion of European systems of law to the colonies. Law redefined land to make it available for capitalist development and constructed notions of contract and wages that converted subsistence farmers into wage laborers.

But the law regulated other spheres of social life as well: marriage and the family, sexuality, festivals, drinking, and even dress, comportment, and forms of habitation (Comaroff and Comaroff, 1991, 1997; Stoler, 1989, 1991, 1995, 1997; Cooper and Stoler, 1997). Colonial law criminalized practices of everyday social life that had been to varying degrees acceptable under earlier legal regimes. Colonial officials in Papua New Guinea endeavored to prohibit tribal fighting (Gordon and Meggitt, 1985). The Americans and the Canadians energetically sought to suppress the religious and ritual practices of native peoples during the colonial era (e.g., Cole and Chaikin, 1990). Egypt tried to make festivals illegal (Mitchell, 1988). The colonial law of South Africa joined with other kinds of disciplinary regulation located in the workplace, the school, the hospital, and even the design of houses to produce not only wage laborers but also new selves, engaging in the forms of bodily comportment and management seen as signs of civilization in Europe (Comaroff and Comaroff, 1991, 1997). In nineteenth-century Hawai'i, the courts actively regulated sexuality, labor contracts, alcohol, drugs, and violence against superiors (Merry, 2000). In colonial Zanzibar of the early twentieth century, Africans were often arrested for drinking, dancing, and assaults: events associated with idleness and the absence of labor discipline (Cooper, 1987: 240). Cooper quotes contemporary officials who were concerned that the "childish savages" would dissipate their "very small stock of energy in a demoralizing dance" and would reach a "dangerous state of sexual excitement" (1987: 240).

While some of the new regulations facilitated a steady and punctual labor supply, others were related only indirectly to labor force participation. Efforts to control sexual practices, drinking, and festivals, in particular, were typically framed in a discourse of disorder and immorality rather than indolence and the virtues of work. Their prohibition was designed to engender a new kind of person managed by self-restraint and internal control. It was not simply the demand for laborers that fueled the criminalization of everyday life. Instead, a distinctive theory of the potential social disorder of subordinate groups released from the control of masters, owners, or chiefs drove government officials to define as crimes some of the everyday practices of these subordinate groups. The authority of masters and chiefs was, of course, being undermined by capitalist labor and land relations. Officials feared that, absent the control of slave owners, chiefs, or colonial authorities, these groups would become cauldrons of immorality and chaos. Their fears grew out of conceptions that the subordinated peoples were more passionate, unrestrained, and intractable than those attempting to rule them (see Collier, Maurer, and Suarez-Navaz, 1995). Conceptions of "dangerous classes" fused with emerging notions of race and gender difference. Whites defined their racial supremacy by contrasting themselves to people of color envisioned as animalistic, bestial, and lustful (Comaroff and Comaroff, 1991, 1997; Merry, 2000). Discourses of labor control paralleled those of social disorder, but each provided its distinctive justification for the extension of criminal prosecution. Fears of social disruption flowed alongside complaints about unreliable and erratic laborers. The desire for reforming social life frequently joined with demands for social order and labor control. Subjugated peoples developed strategies for hiding, for reinterpreting their marriage practices, for fooling judges and courts. Masell (1968) described this form of resistance in Soviet Central Asia and Lazarus-Black (1994) has documented similar patterns in the colonial and contemporary Caribbean. Nader (1990) documents similar forms of resistance in Mexico. As Hirsch and Lazarus-Black (1994) show, law has a cultural capacity to construct categories, rules, and modes of understanding that shape the way people see the world and the ways they think they should behave within it, so that its power lies in the realm of culture and consciousness as well as in the imposition of force. But this form of power is never complete, and always subject to forms of contestation and revision.

A fourth set of insights concerns the agency of the colonized in the introduction of colonial law. Much research focuses on law as a mode of control deployed by colonial authorities. However, the process was more complicated. The colonial state clearly used law to appropriate land and labor, but the law also limited the extent of this appropriation. In some areas, such as South Africa, imperial authority served as a check on the white settlers and their expropriation of land and labor (Comaroff, 1989). In many parts of the British Empire, such as New Zealand, land alienation proceeded by sale rather than conquest. Although this appears to place the colonized in a more powerful position than direct appropriation by conquest, Banner's study of New Zealand shows how the legal regulations of the market weakened the position of Maori land sellers and facilitated extensive land acquisition by white settlers (Banner, 2000; see also Ward, 1973). Similarly, labor regulations served, at least in theory, to constrain the power of employers over laborers. However, the constraint depended a great deal on the laborer's access to the law and ability to use it. But it did offer an alternative to forms of coerced labor such as slavery or unregulated market forces that might produce permanent and inheritable debt peonage (Cooper, 1980, 1987, 1989).

In this sense, law played a curiously ambiguous role in the colonial project. Law was of course the handmaiden of colonialism, facilitating conquest and control, but it also retained a discourse of resistance in its emphasis on rights. It was a means of regulating the market to dull its effects on the subjects of colonial rule (Hirsch and Lazarus-Black, 1994. It was a prominent part of the legitimating narrative of colonial takeover, justifying the conquest and subjugation of previously autonomous peoples. It established new relationships and new categories of persons, restructured community and family life, and enforced new modes of discipline. At the same time, the law provided a language and a forum to challenge colonial and village authority. It enabled women to escape the control of fathers and husbands and servants and to protect themselves against the demands of masters (Chanock, 1985; Moore, 1986). Subjugated groups could use the law to challenge the colonial rulers, the settlers, the mine owners, and even the owners of slaves (Lazarus-Black, 1994). In many colonial areas, there was a curious conundrum: colonial courts served to implement oppressive new laws concerning land, labor, and taxation, yet colonized peoples nevertheless used the new local courts with some enthusiasm (e.g., Chanock, 1985; Matsuda,

1988; see also Fitzpatrick, 1987; Hayden, 1984). They saw the courts as a form of domination by colonial elites, but at the same time absorbed the legal consciousness of the colonial legal system and took advantage of its services.[3]

Rather than seeing the imposition of colonial law as a straightforward act of domination, it is more accurate to see an ongoing contest between dominant groups attempting to use the courts to introduce new forms of family and community life and subjugated groups. They sought to employ ideologies of equality before the law and individual rights to resist these new definitions of family and community life and new ideas of work in their roles as police, magistrates, and plaintiffs in the lower courts. The legal system was simultaneously a mode of control and a place of resistance; an ideology that justified domination and offered modes of resistance to domination. It created new cultural categories of persons and duties, but within local communities, the new legal systems were seized upon and deployed in ways not intended by the colonial officials. What kinds of spaces it created and how they were used remains a critically important area for future research.

As the study of law and colonialism matures, scholars have turned to an increasingly diverse set of historical situations. Lauren Benton's (2002) ambitious comparative historical study of the spread of legal regimes accompanying colonialism over a period of five hundred years demonstrates the variety of intersections this produced. Benton shows that even in the absence of an overarching legal order, actors within different legal traditions are able to work together to arrange exchanges of goods and information (2002: 5). Her work is framed by the theory of legal pluralism, but she emphasizes the fluid and shifting nature of the legal entities and the porosity of their borders. Ronen Shamir (2001) applies the colonial framework to his analysis of law in Palestine. He notes the centrality of law in the way nations tell stories about who they are and how their national identities have been forged. He asks why in Israeli histories, the Zionist settlers of the 1910s and 1920s are portrayed as acting alone, as forging their own society and institutions, when in fact the British government was very important in creating the conditions for Zionist settlement and land acquisition. Thus the story of autonomous self-creation by intrepid Zionist settlers has effaced the extent to which Zionism was actually facilitated by British colonialism. Shamir shows that the way we understand – or deny – colonialism forms the postcolonial present. The colonial framework has been productive for questions concerning the legal situation of indigenous peoples in North America as well (e.g., Asch, 1988). Thomas Biolsi's (2001) study of the legal struggles around sovereignty on the Sioux reservation shows vividly how the historical legal legacy of Indian policy has created a contemporary morass of conflicting and contradictory laws. Nevertheless, Native Americans turn to the law repeatedly to defend their sovereignty and community. These are all examples of how colonial legal relations have persisted into the current era of postcolonialism and globalization.

POSTCOLONIAL LAW AND GLOBALIZATION

What are the legacies of colonialism for contemporary societies and for modern law? The existence of a pervasive pluralism is one consequence, a pluralism often conceived as that of common law and customary law. These boundaries incorporate notions of race and difference, and have often been subject to efforts at unification by postcolonial states. Careful ethnographic research suggests that even where they remain, however, in practice, the lines are far from sharp. In Anne Griffiths' (1997) study of disputing and family conflict in a Botswana town, she finds that despite the conventional distinction of the postcolonial state between a common law system and a customary law system, a distinction that essentializes these social categories, the boundary is porous and negotiable. Focusing on conflicts surrounding marriage and support, Griffiths demonstrates that women's use of the law depends both on the resources the legal system offers them and on their social position in kinship and economic patterns. Although the educated elites in Botswana are dismissive of customary law, seeing it as irrelevant, she finds that ordinary people move easily between these apparently distinct systems. Customary law provides important resources to women seeking support from husbands and partners (1997: 103). Similarly, Susan Hirsch's (1998) study of a Swahili Muslim court in Kenya shows that the court offers women a site where they can exercise some agency in negotiating their marriage and family relationships.

Another way of thinking about the legacies of colonial law for postcolonial law is to consider the way the colonial encounter has reshaped European law itself. Fitzpatrick and Darian-Smith argue that one legacy is the law's incorporation of Orientalism (1999; see also Bhabha, 1997, 1998). The oppositions and racial codings of colonial law are fundamental to the nature of modern law (Fitzpatrick, 2001; Darian-Smith and Fitzpatrick, 1999). Antony Anghie (1999) describes the origin of international law in the colonizing moment of the sixteenth-century encounter between the Spanish and the Indians. He shows how the theories of Francisco de Vitoria, seen as the originator of international law, substituted a secular and universalizing basis for legal authority for the notion of a religious papal authority. He did so because he determined that the Indians had a capacity for reason. This allowed the Spanish to incorporate the Indians under the same system of natural law as the Spanish. However, this natural law system also allowed the Spanish to travel and sojourn in the Indians' territory and to respond to any Indian attempt at resistance as an act of war that justified retaliation. Thus, under this theory, the Spanish gained the right to "defend" themselves against Indian resistance defined as aggression (Anghie, 1999: 95). Thus, rather than seeing international law as a preexisting system brought to the colonial encounter, Anghie shows how the encounter and the new problems it posed formed international law.

Along with the globalization of labor and capital in the postcolonial era has come a new level of legal pluralism: a series of legal technologies, institutions, and laws located in global space as well as an extensive process of legal transplanting (Dezalay and Garth, 2002a, 2002b). Building on the long-established system of international law, new regional and global legal orders have emerged such as forms of commercial law, humanitarian law, and human rights law (e.g., Hannerz, 1992; Shapiro, 1993; Aman, 1995; Dezalay and Garth, 2002a). Institutions for resolving international conflicts such as the International Court of Justice, the dispute resolution system of GATT, or mechanisms for arbitrating international commercial disputes (Dezalay and Garth, 1996) have developed since World War II, along with a system of treaties, conventions, and declarations that form the basis of international human rights law. The Bretton Woods institutions such as the World Bank, the International Monetary Fund, and the General Agreement on Tariffs and Trade formed in the late 1940s are fundamental to the new legal order of global capitalism. Some human rights conventions, such as the Universal Declaration of Human Rights, from the same era, are so widely accepted as to constitute international customary law (see

Donnelly, 1995). Along with the emergence of transnational legal regulations has come some fracturing of the nation-state and demands for autonomous local legalities and self-determination by subgroups of nation-states, sometimes framed in the language of human rights. Some postcolonial states respond by seeking to unify their legal systems and crush localisms.

This new pluralism represents a shift from the centrality of the state as the source of legal ordering. The creation of the modern state involved efforts to capture and control disputing processes, to extinguish local forms, and develop uniformity (e.g., Bossy, 1983). There was always a tension, a resistance to this capture, however, in the form of legalities that escape or deny state control. The more contested dominance of state law contributes to the appearance of the state as weakening although, as Santos (1995) points out, states may be choosing to be weaker.

In some ways, the current situation can be seen as a new imperialism, only now it is based on a regime of sovereign nations rather than the political control of empire. Nations are treated as formally equal within the new international organizations such as the United Nations, despite their sharp informal inequalities (Fitzpatrick, 2001). The shape of the international legal order is a contractual arrangement of formally equal and sovereign states that are deeply unequal. This system operates through institutions that claim to embody the community of nations, especially the International Monetary Fund and the World Bank. Otto (1999) points out that these institutions were formed soon after World War II by predominantly European countries and still retain the original European basis of control. In contrast, developing countries have been numerically dominant in the General Assembly of the United Nations since decolonization. Thus, despite the formal equality among nations, they are unequal in the ability to govern the key financial institutions of the international community.

Fitzpatrick argues that the new imperialism is neoliberal in that the market is supreme internationally and domestically while the role of the nation-state is managerial and supplementary. It should not impose barriers to the economy such as tariffs, import controls, or restraints on foreign investment. Internally, it should promote liberalization, deregulation, and privatization. The political principles of this new order are democracy, human rights, and the rule of law. This includes transplanting or adopting occidental laws, especially commercial ones, and reforming the legal system to make it more like that in core countries. The sanctions supporting the system are national and international laws enabling seizure of the assets of a recalcitrant nation and its citizens or the threat of withdrawing reciprocity or recognition. Withdrawing reciprocity means denial of access to further loans and aid, leading to economic collapse for some countries (Fitzpatrick, 2001: 212–15).

Christopher Arup's (2000) study of the texts and impacts of the World Trade Organization, especially two of its new multilateral agreements – General Agreement on Trade and Services (GATS) and the Agreement on Trade-Related Aspects of Intellectual Property Rights (TRIPs) – examines how these new forms of global legal regulation operate. He analyzes them as examples of legal pluralism, or interlegality, to use Santos's term (1995). This term emphasizes how legalities clash, mingle, hybridize, and interact with one another. This takes place at several levels: between national legalities, and among legalities not necessarily centered on any nation state (Arup, 2001: 5). These legalities include the reemergence of a supranational *lex mercatoria* based on transnational contracts, model codes, and private arbitration.

Arup does not anticipate increasing homogeneity or convergence in law but instead a continuing diversity. Global suppliers will still have to negotiate across differences and will continue to call on the legal support of the nation state (2001: 7).

The expansion of transnational corporations and transnational economic activity in the absence of the political structure of colonialism has, over the last two decades, produced an enormous expansion of international mechanisms of managing disputes and negotiating rules. Although international mercantile law has existed since at least the medieval period, its expansion in recent years has taken new forms. As Sassen (1996) notes, with the expansion of the global production system and the global market for financial services there has also been a global expansion of legal regulation, particularly commercial arbitration. New legal regimes to guarantee property rights and contracts for firms doing transnational business are increasingly important (Sassen, 1996: 12–20). Dezalay and Garth describe the emergence of an international private justice system for commercial arbitration in this space (1995: 33, 1996). Between 1970 and 1990 there has been a transformation from relatively informal arbitration based on European scholars and the International Chamber of Commerce in Paris to "offshore litigation" with greater emphasis on Anglo-American law firms for resources, clients, emphasis on fact finding, and adversarial lawyering (Dezalay and Garth, 1995: 34–6). In their more recent study, they examine the circulation of elite lawyers and economists between the major academic institutions of the United States and Europe and positions in Latin American countries, human rights organizations, and UN bodies (Dezalay and Garth, 2002a). They trace a shift from European gentleman lawyers to US-trained economists as the leading policy makers in Brazil, Argentina, Chile, and Mexico. By focusing on the careers of particular individuals, they are able to show how legal technologies and expertise developed in one arena are transferred to another. They show the increasing importance of international spaces such as UN bodies in the career paths of leading policy makers in Latin America. And they demonstrate how legal reforms in Latin America are typically promoted by these cosmopolitan elites but subverted by local notables as they confront deeply ingrained practices and ways of negotiating power carried out under the legitimacy of existing legal arrangements (Dezalay and Garth, 2002a: 248–50).

The rapid development of offshore financial systems and tax havens provide ways to evade state control of financial transactions for taxation purposes. Carried out under the aegis of the free market, such systems build on discourses of unique and distinctive places within a global market and the celebration of flexible persons who can readily move from one place to another (Maurer, 1997, 1998, 2001). They provide places for escaping state regulation of financial transactions and tax payments while the digitalizing of financial transactions makes them more difficult to trace and police. Although such changes are typically seen as an assault on state sovereignty, they may represent more fundamental shifts in the location of regulation. Investors still need to operate with high levels of trust and to have some guarantees of security of ownership and guarantees of contracts in offshore locations. The rapid proliferation of offshore financial systems raises new questions about the location and institutionalization of the regulatory systems that enable them to function (see Maurer, 1997).

The international human rights system and its legal instruments provide another form of legal regulation that crosses national boundaries. Since World War II, an elaborate system of human rights documents and institutions for implementing these documents has developed internationally, focused largely on the United Nations and its subsidiary organizations (see Merry, 2003). This system is also built on a formal structure of autonomous, sovereign states tied through contracts. Local, national, and transnational NGOs have become increasingly important actors in this system, contributing in significant ways to the drafting of documents and also shouldering a significant portion of the burden of implementing human rights declarations (Keck and Sikkink, 1998). The expansion of a rights discourse and enthusiasm for the rule of law was greatly facilitated by the 1990 collapse of the USSR and the establishment of liberal political orders in parts of Eastern Europe, against the backdrop of destructive ethnonationalism in the former Yugoslavia (see Wilson, 1997: 2).

Donnelly noted in 1995 that despite worries that the human rights system is fundamentally European in origin, it has not resulted in interventions to protect human rights. However, violations of human rights principles are increasingly being used as justifications for various forms of international military action, as in Kosovo. At the same time, pressure to protect the human rights of vulnerable populations by international NGOs as well as other states has circumscribed sovereignty in some ways (see Foot, 2000). Within the new global order, sovereignty is increasingly dependent on compliance with a minimum of human rights principles. South Africa represented an example of a country whose systematic violations of human rights principles under the apartheid system led it to be seen as an international pariah state. However, it appears that it is primarily powerful countries that are successful in putting pressure on less powerful ones, while some of the most powerful, such as the United States, refuse to be bound by some human rights conventions (see Ignatieff, 2001).

Thus, the human rights system represents a new international legal regime, although it is an edifice constructed on the international order of sovereignty. Human rights discourse is a powerful part of contemporary global cultural flows. As it expands from its initial preoccupation with civil and political rights of the 1940s and 1950s to social and economic rights, and more recently to rights of vulnerable groups such as women, children, and racial minorities, as it has in the 1980s and 1990s, it has taken on increasing ideological significance as a mode of regulating global society. Unlike nation-state law, individuals are endowed with human rights on the basis of their human dignity rather than on the basis of their membership in a nation. No one stands outside the system, as an alien stands outside the regime of citizenship in a state. Population movements such as illegal immigration and refugee flights are generating increasingly large pockets of peoples living in states in which they must hide from systems of law (see Coutin, 2001). These are groups excluded from citizenship but still endowed with human rights (see Sarat and Kearns, 2001).

The concept of rights itself has been dramatically transformed over the past 50 years as activists have deployed it in a variety of innovative contexts. The major expansion is from an individually based conception of civil and political rights adhering to individual rights with relationship to the state, such as rights to freedom from torture, to a collective set of rights to food, housing, and cultural practices (see Messer, 1993; Sarat and Kearns, 1995). With this transformation, human rights no longer focuses entirely on individual entitlements.

The development of human rights documents dealing with indigenous peoples raised issues of group or community rights with particular force. Indigenous peoples incorporated into settler states such as the United States, Canada, Australia, and New Zealand draw on the language of self-determination developed in the late 1940s and 1950s to fight colonialism (see Trask, 1993). Beginning from a movement by leaders of indigenous groups in the Americas, an initial declaration on principles for the defense of indigenous nations was formulated and presented at a UN conference in 1977. The UN Sub-Commission on Prevention of Discrimination and Protection of Minorities, part of the UN Human Rights Commission, created a Working Group on Indigenous Populations in 1982. This soon became the leading international forum for hundreds of indigenous peoples' leaders and representatives as they met each year in July at the Working Group meetings in Geneva (Coulter, 1994: 37; see also Anaya, 1994, 2000). Although indigenous groups sought self-determination under international law, they were not generally seeking statehood or independence but survival of their cultural communities. They were searching for cultural identity rather than an autonomous state (Lam, 1992). This has been a fundamentally legal struggle, using the language and institutions of the law rather than other forms of political contestation. One of the major objectives has been some degree of legal autonomy and self-governance. The Draft Declaration on the Rights of Indigenous Peoples, finalized in 1994 after years of discussion among indigenous groups and UN representatives, includes the right to create and maintain indigenous peoples' own governments and their own laws and legal systems (Coulter, 1994: 40).

One of the emerging forms of global law is some form of tribunal that will hold governments or leaders of various kinds accountable for their offenses such as war crimes, genocide, or abuses connected with war such as rape or sexual slavery (see Teitel, 2000). There are currently tribunals convened for the war crimes in Rwanda and in the former Yugoslavia, with others under discussion. In 2002, the International Criminal Court came into existence to try war crimes, crimes against humanity, and genocide. These innovations suggest the creation of a new global legality focused on charging individuals with criminal violations and punishing them across national borders. At the same time, a second type of transitional justice focuses on tribunals for truth telling and reconciliation, although not necessarily for dispensing justice in the sense of holding offenders accountable. In Richard Wilson's (2001) study of the most famous of the latter form of tribunal, the South African Truth and Reconciliation Commission, he describes how its message of redemption and reconciliation incorporated some groups but failed to resonate with ideas of popular justice among urban African neighborhoods in Johannesburg.

As both of these approaches to restoring justice after conflict expand, there will be continuing questions about the relative merits of criminal trials, with their delay and expense and small defendant rolls, and the more open, conciliatory, and amnesty-focused proceedings of truth commissions. Examining when and why one or the other of these models emerges or what kinds of hybrids are possible will be an important question for the future, both in understanding how societies overcome intense and brutal internal conflict and how this can be done most effectively. There are also ongoing questions about the role of the international community and the judiciary of the postconflict society in such processes. Nevertheless, the gradual emergence of these new global legal institutions for commercial law, humanitarian law, human rights law, and more recently international criminal law, is another indication of a developing global legal system. The relationship between these relatively weak international systems and nation-state law remains complex and uncertain.

COMPARING COLONIAL AND POSTCOLONIAL LEGALITY

The focus on global legality raises new questions. As new forms of transnational legality emerge, is this a new colonialism? Or is it an entirely new legal regime? Is it rooted in nation states or does it challenge and weaken those states? As the human rights system expands, along with commercial legal transplants and the strength of global financial institutions, does this lead to homogeneity? Or does it foster new negotiations and diversities? Are the fundamental cultural categories of colonialism still implicit, although not often articulated, such as images of civilization and the savage? What is the future for the current interest in what is called transitional justice – the move to incorporate a criminal law system as well as a commercial one into the global network?

To what extent can we see human rights as a form of global law? Do they have any force? How has the expansion of these forms of global legality redefined sovereignty? Despite some talk about the erosion of sovereignty, it is not clear that the nation-state is weakening; instead it seems to be changing in form (see Sassen, 1996, 1998). Indeed, Ignatieff (2001) points out that the focus of human rights activism continues to be the state; the international arena is mobilized in order to put pressure on states.

And what can we learn about globalization from considering the role of law in the colonial era? Although there are great differences between the historical conditions of pluralization accompanying colonialism and those associated with globalization, both made legal systems more diverse and contradictory. In both historical processes, existing systems merged with imports developed under quite different social conditions. The ideological justifications of the imports are similar: nineteenth century colonialism focused on civilization and reform; twentieth century globalization emphasizes democracy, development, and the rule of law. There is still a center and an "other," subject to reform and absorption, although then it was the heathen savage and now it is the diseased, corrupt society riven by ancient hatreds. In both situations, some countries are vastly richer and more powerful than others, a fault line that roughly parallels the distinction between colonizer and colonized. And in the present, as in the colonial era, new legal technologies and laws have enormous consequences only dimly anticipated by those engaged in adopting them or imposing them.

But the power dynamics within which the legal transplants of the imperial era took place are quite different from those under contemporary globalization. A political takeover often came first, although the exigencies of commerce meant that some changes occurred before overrule. In contrast, it is economic forces that are driving the spread of Anglo-European law in the period of globalization. Adopting countries wish to seem modern in order to attract foreign investment. Foreign investment requires some kinds of legal guarantees and dispute settlement mechanisms. International institutions such as the United Nations and its human rights instruments are gradually constructing a global jurisprudence of human rights while the creation of international courts is forming a set of institutions to enforce both civil and criminal law, although this is only at the beginning stages. Under this system, nations do not sacrifice sovereignty but sovereignty becomes redefined depending on compliance with international human rights standards. Nations ratify human rights conventions to demonstrate to the world that they are modern, developed states and to gain admission into the international community as formal equals.

Thus the new international legal order is ideologically and politically the descendant of the colonial order of empire. The same economic and political inequalities of that era pervade the present, despite its apparently different legal organization. The pervasive legal pluralism of the colonial past, rooted in racialized conceptions of difference, continues to have an influence. Contemporary legal technologies and ideas have been forged in the interactions among these legal systems. Legal transplants and appropriations still take place within an intransigent structure of unequal power on the global terrain.

Notes

1 In one of many examples of this genre of colonial discourse, Ranger cites the address of the King of England to the Sotho in 1910:

> When a child is in trouble he will go to his father, and his father after hearing all about the matter will decide what must be done. Then the child must trust and obey his father, for he is but one of a large family and his father has had great experience in settling the troubles of his older children and is able to judge what is best not only for the young child but for the peace and advantage of the while family... The Basuto nation is as a very young child among the many peoples of the British Empire. (quoted in Ranger and Hobsbawm, 1983: 231)

2 A significant body of scholarship in the anthropology of law has challenged this distinction, arguing both for the legal, rational characteristics of "custom" (Gluckman, 1955) and that societies that lack law, as it was defined by the colonial authorities, have social order (Evans-Pritchard, 1940; Gulliver, 1963). While accepting the division between law and custom, Diamond (1973) challenged the negative evaluation placed on "custom" in comparison to "law." More recent work indicates that the "customary law," which colonial officials conceptualized as deriving from a timeless and unchanging past, was itself a construct of the colonial period, very much shaped by the activities of new elites in colonized populations actively reformulating the law in their own interests (Chanock, 1985; Snyder, 1981; Moore, 1986). The "customary law" of colonized peoples developed through political struggles over leadership and power within local communities as well as from the effects of global economic and political pressures (Moore, 1986).

3 One example from the Hawaiian Monarchy period concerns the effort to introduce rape laws that embodied American rather than Hawaiian conceptions of the crime (Nelligan, 1983). These laws were sometimes used by Hawaiian women and local judges to raise funds. The woman would accuse a foreign seaman of rape, and, as the law required, the fine was divided between the woman as compensation and the judge who decided the case.

References

Aman, Alfred C., Jr. (1995) "A global perspective on current regulatory reform: Rejection, relocation, or reinvention?" *Indiana Journal of Global Legal Studies* 2: 429–64.

Anaya, S. James (1994) "International law and indigenous peoples," *Cultural Survival Quarterly* Spring: 42–4.

Anaya, S. James (2000) *Indigenous Peoples in International Law.* Oxford: Oxford University Press.

Anghie, Antony (1999) "Francisco de Vitoria and the colonial origins of international law," in Eve Darian-Smith and Peter Fitzpatrick (eds.), *Laws of the Postcolonial*. Ann Arbor: University of Michigan Press, pp. 89–109.

Arup, Christopher (2000) *The New World Trade Organization Agreements: Globalizing Law through Services and Intellectual Property*. Cambridge, UK: Cambridge University Press.

Asch, Michael (1988) *Home and Native Land: Aboriginal Rights and the Canadian Constitution*. Toronto: Methuen.

Banner, Stuart (2000) "Conquest by contract: Wealth transfer and land market structure in colonial New Zealand," *Law and Society Review* 34: 47–96.

Benda-Beckmann, Keebet von (1981) "Forum shopping and shopping forums – dispute settlement in a Minangkabau village in West Sumatra," *Journal of Legal Pluralism* 19: 117–61.

Benton, Lauren (2002) *Law and Colonial Cultures: Legal Regimes in World History 1400–1900*. Cambridge, UK: Cambridge University Press.

Bhabha, Homi (1997) "Of mimicry and man: The ambivalence of colonial discourse," in Frederick Cooper and Ann Laura Stoler (eds.), *Tensions of Empire: Colonial Cultures in a Bourgeois World*, Berkeley: University of California Press, pp. 152–62.

Bhabha, Homi (1998) "Anxiety in the midst of difference," *Polar: Political and Legal Anthropology Review* 21(1): 123–37.

Biolsi, Thomas (2001) *Deadliest Enemies: Law and the Making of Race Relations On and Off Rosebud Reservation*. Berkeley and Los Angeles: University of California Press.

Bossy, John (ed.) (1983) *Disputes and Settlements: Law and Human Relations in the West*. Cambridge, UK: Cambridge University Press.

Brown, Nathan (1995) "Law and imperialism: Egypt in comparative perspective," *Law and Society Review* 29: 103–27.

Brown, Nathan J. (1997) *The Rule of Law in the Arab World: Courts in Egypt and the Gulf*. Cambridge, UK: Cambridge University Press.

Burman, Sandra B. and Harrell-Bond, Barbara E. (eds.) (1979) *The Imposition of Law*. New York: Academic Press.

Chanock, Martin (1985) *Law, Custom, and Social Order: The Colonial Experience in Malawi and Zambia*. Cambridge, UK: Cambridge University Press.

Chanock, Martin (2001) *The Making of South African Legal Culture 1902–1936: Fear, Favour, and Prejudice*. Cambridge, UK: Cambridge University Press.

Cohn, Bernard S. 1996. *Colonialism and its Forms of Knowledge: The British in India*. Princeton, NJ: Princeton University Press.

Cole, Douglas and Chaikin, Ira (1990) *An Iron Hand Upon the People: The Law against the Potlatch on the Northwest Coast*. Vancouver and Toronto: Douglas & McIntyre; Seattle: University of Washington Press.

Collier, Jane, Maurer, William, and Suarez-Navaz, S. (1995) "Introduction," Special Issue on Sanctioned Identities, *Identities: Global Studies in Culture and Power* 2: 1.

Comaroff, Jean and Comaroff, John L. (1991) *Of Revelation and Revolution: Christianity, Colonialism, and Consciousness in South Africa*, vol. I. Chicago: University of Chicago Press.

Comaroff, John L. (1989) "Images of empire, contests of conscience: Models of colonial domination in South Africa," *American Ethnologist* 16: 661–85.

Comaroff, John L. (2001) "Colonialism, culture, and the law: A foreword," *Law and Social Inquiry* 26 (2): 305–14.

Comaroff, John L. and Comaroff, Jean (1997) *Of Revelation and Revolution: The Dialectics of Modernity on a South African Frontier*, vol. II. Chicago: University of Chicago Press.

Cooper, Frederick (1980) *From Slaves to Squatters: Plantation Labor and Agriculture in Zanzibar and Coastal Kenya, 1890–1925*. New Haven, CT: Yale University Press.

COLONIAL AND POSTCOLONIAL LAW 585

Cooper, Frederick (1987) "Contracts, crime, and agrarian conflict: From slave to wage labour on the East African coast," in Francis Snyder and Douglas Hay (eds.), *Law, Labour, and Crime: An Historical Perspective*. London and New York: Tavistock, pp. 228–53.

Cooper, Frederick (1989) "From free labor to family allowances: Labor and African Society in colonial discourse," *American Ethnologist* 16: 745–65.

Cooper, Frederick and Stoler, Ann Laura (eds.) (1997) *Tensions of Empire: Colonial Cultures in a Bourgeois World*. Berkeley: University of California Press.

Coulter, Robert T. (1994) "Commentary on the UN Draft Declaration on the Rights of Indigenous Peoples," *Cultural Survival Quarterly* Spring: 37–41.

Coutin, Susan Bibler (2001) *Legalizing Moves: Salvadoran Immigrants' Struggle for U.S. Residency*. Ann Arbor: University of Michigan Press.

Darian-Smith, Eve and Fitzpatrick, Peter (1999) *Laws of the Postcolonial*. Ann Arbor: Univeristy of Michigan Press

Dezalay, Yves and Garth, Bryant (1995) "Merchants of law as moral entrepreneurs: Constructing international justice from the competition for transnational business disputes," *Law and Society Review* 29: 27–65.

Dezalay, Yves and Garth, Bryant (1996) *Dealing in Virtue: International Commercial Arbitration and the Internationalization of Legal Practice*. Chicago: University of Chicago Press.

Dezalay, Yves and Garth, Bryant (2002a) *The Internationalization of Palace Wars: Lawyers, Economists, and the Contest to Transform Latin American States*. Chicago: University of Chicago Press.

Dezalay, Yves and Garth, Bryant (eds.) (2002b) *Global Prescriptions: The Production, Exportation, and Importation of a New Legal Orthodoxy*. Ann Arbor: University of Michigan Press.

Diamond, Stanley (1973) "The rule of law versus the order of custom," in Donald Black and Maureen Mileski (eds.), *The Social Organization of Law*, New York: Seminar Press, pp. 318–44. Reprinted from *Social Research* (1971) 42.

Donnelly, Jack (1995) "State sovereignty and international intervention: The case of human rights," in Gene M. Lyons and Michael Mastanduno (eds.), *Beyond Westphalia: State Sovereignty and International Intervention*. Baltimore: Johns Hopkins University Press, pp. 115–47.

Engel, David (1978) *Code and Custom in a Thai Provincial Court*. Tuscon: University of Arizona Press.

Evans-Pritchard, E.E. (1940) *The Nuer*. Oxford: Oxford University Press.

Fabian, Johannes (1983) *Time and the Other: How Anthropology Makes its Object*. New York: Columbia University Press.

Fitzpatrick, Peter (1987) "Transformations of law and labour in Papua New Guinea," in Francis Snyder and Douglas Hay (eds.), *Law, Labour, and Crime: An Historical Perspective*. London and New York: Tavistock, pp. 253–98.

Fitzpatrick, Peter (1992) *The Mythology of Modern Law*. London: Routledge.

Fitzpatrick, Peter (2001) *Modernism and the Grounds of Law*. Cambridge, UK: Cambridge University Press.

Fitzpatrick, Peter and Darian-Smith, Eve (1999) "Laws of the postcolonial: An insistent introduction," in Eve Darian-Smith and Peter Fitzpatrick (eds.), *Laws of the Postcolonial*. Ann Arbor: University of Michigan Press, pp. 1–19.

Foot, Rosemary (2000) *Rights Beyond Borders: The Global Community and the Struggle Over Human Rights in China*. Oxford: Oxford University Press.

Galanter, Marc (1981) "Justice in many rooms: Courts, private ordering, and indigenous law," *Journal of Legal Pluralism and Unofficial Law* 19: 1.

Galanter, Marc (1989) *Law and Society in Modern India*. Delhi: Oxford University Press.

Gluckman, Max (1955) *The Judicial Process Among the Barotse of Northern Rhodesia*. Manchester, UK: Manchester University Press.

Gordon, Robert J. and Meggitt, Mervyn J. (1985) *Law and Order in the New Guinea Highlands: Encounters with Enga*. Hanover, NH: University Press of New England (for University of Vermont).

Griffiths, Anne (1997) *In the Shadow of Marriage*. Chicago: University of Chicago Press.

Guha, Ranajit (1997) *Dominance Without Hegemony: History and Power in Colonial India*. Cambridge, MA: Harvard University Press.

Gulliver, P.H. (1963) *Social Control in an African Society*. London: Routledge and Kegan Paul.

Hannerz, Ulf (1992) *Cultural Complexity: Studies in the Social Organization of Meaning*. New York: Columbia University Press.

Hayden, Robert M. (1984) "A note on caste panchayats and government courts in India: Different kinds of stages for different kinds of performances," *Journal of Legal Pluralism* 22: 43–53.

Hirsch, Susan F. (1998) *Pronouncing and Persevering: Gender and the Discourses of Disputing in an African Islamic Court*. Chicago: University of Chicago Press.

Hirsch, Susan and Lazarus-Black, Mindie (eds.) (1994) *Contested States: Law, Hegemony, and Resistance*. New York: Routledge.

Ignatieff, Michael (2001) *Human Rights as Politics and Idolatry*. Princeton, NJ: Princeton University Press.

Keck, Margaret E. and Sikkink, Kathryn (1998) *Activists Beyond Borders: Advocacy Networks in International Politics*. Ithaca, NY: Cornell University Press.

Klug, Heinz (2000) *Constituting Democracy: Law, Globalism, and South Africa's Political Reconstruction* (Cambridge Series in Law and Society). Cambridge, UK: Cambridge University Press.

Lam, Maivan Clech (1992) "Making room for peoples at the United Nations: Thoughts provoked by indigenous claims to self-determination," *Cornell International Law Journal* 25: 603–22.

Lazarus-Black, Mindie (1994) *Legitimate Acts and Illegal Encounters: Law and Society in Antigua and Barbuda*. Washington, DC: Smithsonian Institution Press.

Macaulay, Stewart (1986) "Private government," Disputes Processing Research Program Working Paper 1983–6, Madison: University of Wisconsin Law School. Reprinted in Leon Lipson and Stanton Wheeler (eds.) (1986) *Law and the Social Sciences*. New York: Russell Sage Foundation, pp. 445–518.

Macaulay, Stuart (1963) "Non-contractual relations in business: A preliminary study," *American Sociological Review* 28: 55–67.

Mamdani, Mahmood (1996) *Citizen and Subject: Contemporary Africa and the Legacy of Late Colonialism*. Princeton, NJ: Princeton University Press.

Masell, Gregory (1968) "Law as an instrument of revolutionary change in a traditional milieu: The case of Soviet Central Asia," *Law & Society Review* 2: 179.

Matsuda, Mari J. (1988) "Law and culture in the District Court of Honolulu, 1844–1845: A case study of the rise of legal consciousness," *The American Journal of Legal History* 32: 16–41.

Maurer, Bill (1997) *Recharting the Caribbean: Land, Law, and Citizenship in the British Virgin Islands*. Ann Arbor: University of Michigan Press.

Maurer, Bill (1998) "Cyberspatial sovereignties: Offshore finance, digital cash and the limits of liberalism," *Indiana Journal of Global Legal Studies* 5: 493–519.

Maurer, Bill (2001) "Rewiring technological and financial circuits in the 'offshore' Caribbean," *Comparative Studies in Society and History* 43(3): 467–501.

Merry, Sally Engle (1988) "Legal pluralism," *Law and Society Review*: 22: 869–96.

Merry, Sally Engle (2000) *Colonizing Hawai'i: The Cultural Power of Law*. Princeton, NJ: Princeton University Press.

Merry, Sally Engle (2003) "Constructing a global law? Violence against women and the human rights system," *Law and Social Inquiry* 28(4): 913–50.

Merry, Sally Engle and Milner, Neal (eds.) (1993) *The Possibility of Popular Justice: A Case Study of American Community Mediation*. Ann Arbor: University of Michigan Press.

Messer, Ellen (1993) "Anthropology and human rights," *Annual Review of Anthropology* 22: 221–49.

Mitchell, Timothy (1988) *Colonising Egypt*. Cambridge, UK: Cambridge University Press.

Moore, Sally Falk (1986) *Social Facts and Fabrications: Customary Law on Kilimanjaro, 1880–1980*. Cambridge, UK: Cambridge University Press.

Nader, Laura (1990) *Harmony Ideology: Justice and Control in a Zapotec Mountain Village*. Stanford, CA: Stanford University Press.

Nelligan, P.J. (1983) "Social change and rape law in Hawaii," Unpublished PhD dissertation, Dept. of Sociology, University of Hawaii.

Otto, Diane (1999) "Subalternity and international law: The problems of global community and the incommensurability of difference," in Eve Darian-Smith and Peter Fitzpatrick (eds.), *Laws of the Postcolonial*. Ann Arbor: University of Michigan Press, pp. 145–80.

Petersen, Hanne and Zahle, Henrik (eds.) (1995) *Legal Polycentricity: Consequences of Pluralism in Law*. Aldershot, UK: Dartmouth.

Ranger, Terence and Hobsbawm, Eric (eds.) (1983) *The Invention of Tradition*. Cambridge, UK: Cambridge University Press.

Roberts, Richard and Mann, Kristin (1991) "Law in colonial Africa," in Kristin Mann and Richard Roberts (eds.), *Law in Colonial Africa*. Portsmouth, NH: Heinemann, pp. 3–61.

Said, Edward (1978) *Orientalism*. New York: Vintage.

Santos, Boaventura de Sousa (1987) "Law: A map of misreading. Toward a postmodern conception of law, *Journal of Law and Society* 14: 279–302.

Santos, Boaventura de Sousa (1995) *Toward a New Common Sense*. New York: Routledge.

Sarat, Austin and Kearns, Thomas R. (eds.) (1995) *Identities, Politics, and Rights*. Ann Arbor, MI: University of Michigan Press.

Sarat, Austin and Kearns, Thomas R. (eds.) (2001) *Human Rights: Concepts, Contests, Contingencies*. Ann Arbor: University of Michigan Press.

Sassen, Saskia (1994) *Cities in a World Economy*. Thousand Oaks, CA: Pine Forge Press/Sage.

Sassen, Saskia (1996) *Losing Control: Sovereignty in an Age of Globalization*. New York: Columbia University Press.

Sassen, Saskia (1998) *Globalization and its Discontents*. New York: The New Press.

Shamir, Ronen (2000) *The Colonies of Law: Colonialism, Zionism, and Law in Early Mandate Palestine*. Cambridge, UK: Cambridge University Press.

Shapiro, Martin (1993) "The globalization of law," *Indiana Journal of Global Legal Studies* 1: 37–64.

Snyder, Francis G. (1981) *Capitalism and Legal Change: An African Transformation*. London: Academic Press.

Stoler, Ann Laura (1989) "Making empire respectable: The politics of race and sexual morality in 20th century colonial cultures," *American Ethnologist* 16: 634–61.

Stoler, Ann (1991) "Carnal knowledge and imperial power: Gender, race, and morality in colonial Asia," in Micaela di Leonardo (ed.), *Gender at the Crossroads of Knowledge: Feminism in Anthropology in the Postmodern Era*. Berkeley: University of California Press, pp. 55–101.

Stoler, Ann Laura (1995) *Race and the Education of Desire: Foucault's History of Sexuality and the Colonial Order of Things*. Durham, NC: Duke University Press.

Stoler, Ann Laura (1997) "Sexual affronts and racial frontiers: European identities and the cultural politics of exclusion in colonial Southeast Asia," in Frederick Cooper and Ann Laura Stoler (eds.), *Tensions of Empire: Colonial Cultures in a Bourgeois World*. Berkeley, CA: University of California Press, pp. 198–237.

Strawson, John (1999) "Islamic law and English texts," in Eve Darian-Smith and Peter Fitzpatrick (eds.), *Laws of the Postcolonial*. Ann Arbor: University of Michigan Press, pp. 109–27.

Teitel, Ruti (2000) *Transitional Justice*. Oxford: Oxford University Press.

Thompson, E.P. (1967) "Time, work discipline, and industrial capitalism," *Past and Present* 38: 56–97.

Todarov, Tzetevan ([1984]1999) *The Conquest of America: The Question of the Other*. Norman: University of Oklahoma Press.

Trask, Haunani-Kay (1993) *From a Native Daughter: Colonialism and Sovereignty in Hawai'i*. Monroe, ME: Common Courage Press.

Ward, Alan (1973) *A Show of Justice: Racial "Amalgamation" in Nineteenth Century New Zealand*. Auckland: Auckland University Press.

Wilson, Richard A. (1997) "Human rights, culture and context: An introduction," in Richard A. Wilson (ed.), *Human Rights, Culture and Context: Anthropological Perspectives*. London: Pluto Press, pp. 1–27.

Wilson, Richard A. (2001) *The Politics of Truth and Reconciliation in South Africa: Legitimizing the Post-Apartheid State*. Cambridge, UK: Cambridge University Press.

31

Human Rights

LISA HAJJAR

Toward the end of *Calling the Ghosts*, a documentary film about the war in Bosnia, there is a scene in which the two central characters are looking through a rack of postcards. Jadranka Cigelj and Nusreta Sivac, Bosnian Muslim women who survived the Serbian concentration camp of Omarska, had come to the Netherlands to testify about their experiences before the International Tribunal for the Former Yugoslavia. The voiceover is Cigelj, reading the card they sent to their former Serbian colleagues in their former hometown, the ethnically cleansed city of Prijedor: "Greetings from The Hague. Hope to see you here soon." Those two short sentences speak volumes about modern ethnic hatred, genocidal violence, and torture, as well as the survivor spirit and demands for justice.

When the women were incarcerated and repeatedly raped by Serbian soldiers, the possibility of legal retribution was virtually unthinkable. The *illegality* of Omarska was obvious, as evidenced by the precautions taken by the commanders of the camp prior to a visit by foreign journalists to obscure the harms being perpetrated there. But they had little reason to imagine, let alone fear, that they could be held accountable. At that time, there was no institutional mechanism to enforce the international laws being violated in Omarska. But the fact that there *were* laws "in the books" inspired the women, when they were released, to document their own and fellow prisoners' suffering. Although the initial purpose of their documentation project was to facilitate recovery, it also constituted evidence of crime.

In 1993, when the United Nations created an ad hoc tribunal for the former Yugoslavia, the testimony of survivors was instrumental in preparing indictments. The postcard scene in *Calling the Ghosts* portrays this transitional phase in international law enforcement and institution building. It also provides a vivid, ethnographic image of "law in action." For Cigelj and Sivac, their transformation from "victims" to "witnesses" is an empowering rejoinder to the violence that unmade their world.

HUMAN RIGHTS IN THE FIELD OF LAW AND SOCIETY

Studying the power of law to make and to change social relations is a cornerstone of law and society scholarship. It is a shared interest in law as a social phenomenon and force that brings scholars from across the disciplinary spectrum to this interdisciplinary field. However, until the 1980s, little attention was devoted to international law or law in the international arena. Rather, the field was dominated by the study of law in a particular country or community, or comparative analysis of law in select countries. Research on globalization and international law has picked up over the last two decades. Commenting on this trend, Silbey writes:

> [S]tudying the social organization of law is a particularly good way to study the exercise of power under globalization: first, because so many of these new forms of interaction and exchange are organized through law; and, second, because to some extent, we have already been there. . . . Not only is there a noticeable structural homology between the narratives of globalization and liberal legalism, but the gap between law in the books and law in action revealed in much sociolegal scholarship can also be observed in the accounts and practices of globalization. Not only do we observe a consistent contradiction – the gap between ideal and reality – but the same gap is produced: abstract formal equality and substantive concrete/experiential inequality. (Silbey, 1997: 230)

Human rights are a creation of international law, and therefore a manifestation of the globalization of law. As such, they constitute a rich and relevant vein of inquiry for law and society scholars. Moreover, like human rights discourse, much of law and society scholarship tends to embody a commitment to justice, empowerment, and rights.

In the Anglo-American academy, the field of law and society has been enriched by research on human rights and related topics. Indeed, this has contributed to the internationalization of the field itself. Conversely, the interdisciplinarity of the field can enrich scholarship on human rights. For example, the burgeoning interest in cause lawyering illuminates connections among legal activism, international laws, and social movements mobilized in struggles for rights. The field's venerable tradition of applying sociopolitical analysis to legal texts and institutions is inspiring work on these topics at the international level. Enduring concerns about legal pluralism and legal consciousness lend themselves readily to investigations of human rights organizations and activism.

In this chapter, I provide a brief (and admittedly selective) history of human rights, highlighting some of the concerns that resonate in the field of law and society. I am particularly interested in one of the abiding concerns of the field: the "gap" between "law in the books" and "law in action." I would also note at the outset that the concept of "human rights" has multiple meanings and interpretations; in my analysis, I emphasize the centrality of violence.

VIOLENCE, JUSTICE AND SOCIAL CHANGE

In the twentieth century, planned and organized violence to achieve political ends reached unprecedented levels. But also unprecedented in this era were efforts to construct a global regime of law to regulate and restrict violence. The relationship between these two phenomena, violence and law, is dialectical. As Austin Sarat and Thomas Kearns point out:

> [V]iolence . . . is integral to the constitution of modern law, and . . . law is a creature of both literal violence, and of imaginings and threats of force, disorder and pain. . . . Violence thus constitutes law in three senses: it provides the occasion and method for founding legal orders, it gives law (as the regulator of force and coercion) a reason for being, and it provides a means through which the law acts. (Sarat and Kearns, 1993: 1, 3–4)

These three dimensions of the relationship between violence and law are useful for understanding developments in international law. The violence of two world wars was a constitutive factor in strengthening humanitarian law (otherwise known as the laws of war), and international shock and revulsion at the Nazi Holocaust provided a crucial negative inspiration leading to the creation of a new body of international law to establish human rights. The third dimension, the violence *of* law, features in this account, too, but until quite recently it remained a promise (or threat) unfulfilled.

Until the end of World War II, international laws were oriented almost entirely to relations among states, excluding, for the most part, matters concerning the relations between states and their own subjects. Sovereign states comprised a "community of equals," and sovereignty constituted a form of supreme authority, based on principles of independence, domestic jurisdiction, and noninterference. Most human beings had no claim to international rights because they had (virtually) no standing in international law. But World War II took a toll on the legitimacy of this Westphalian order. The grimmest lesson of the war was that the most egregious atrocities were not *illegal* because there were no laws to prohibit them and no authority to prevent them.

At the end of the war, new legal ground was broken when tribunals were established in Nuremberg and Tokyo to try Axis leaders. The process of establishing the tribunals and the proceedings that took place therein clarified the content and extended the parameters of "war crimes," articulated a new category of crimes ("crimes against humanity"), and established the basis for a new form of rights ("human rights"). Criminalizing and prosecuting state violence was a radical legal innovation because it eroded states' sovereign prerogatives to use violence with impunity. Indeed, Hermann Goering, one of the architects of the Nazi "Final Solution," used this transgression of legal precedent to challenge the prosecution: "But that was our right! We were a sovereign state and that was strictly our business."

Even some legal experts who condemned the violence were concerned about the legitimacy of prosecuting its authors. While law can be (and often is) used to innovate changes, the legitimacy of law depends on an appearance of stability and predictability. Legal reasoning appeals to precedent, to pre-existing principles, to prevailing views about order, justice, and rights. Thus these tribunals defied legal convention: they were created and used to hold individuals legally accountable for violence they undertook as agents of their states, actions that were not, at the time they were perpetrated, recognized as crimes. As Aryeh Neier explains the legalistic critique of the tribunals:

> Adherents of positive law – that is, those who reject the application of natural law or higher law principles and who believe that only laws enacted by appropriate authorities

are valid – argued that trying Germans and Japanese for crimes against humanity violated the fundamental principles of legality: *nullum crimen sine lege* (no crime without law) and *nulla poena sine crimine* (no penalty without crime). (Neier, 1998: 16)

But the heinousness of the violence overwhelmed legal conservatism in that transitional moment. According to Robert Cover, "The defense of the Nuremberg trials…was sounded at the outset in terms of the capacity of the event to project a new legal meaning into the future" (Minow, Ryan, and Sarat, 1995: 196). In his opening statement as lead prosecutor at the Nuremberg tribunal, US Supreme Court Justice Robert Jackson justified the undertaking as commensurate with the rule of law:

> If these men are the first war leaders of a defeated nation to be prosecuted in the name of the law, they are also the first to be given a chance to plead for their lives in the name of the law [and given] a fair opportunity to defend themselves – a favor which these men, when in power, rarely extended to their fellow countrymen. Despite the fact that public opinion already condemns their acts, we agree that here they must be given a presumption of innocence, and we accept the burden of proving criminal acts and the responsibility of these defendants for their commission. (cited in Minow, 1998: 31–2)

The principles justifying the prosecution of Axis leaders were as lofty as they were radical. In principle, individuals were being tried for crimes against "humanity" and "peace," not against the particular victims of their regimes. In principle, the authority of the tribunals derived from the "international community," not the victorious nations. In principle, the indefensibility of superior orders would serve as a deterrent against future atrocities, a ringing warning of "never again." And in principle, the precedents established through the tribunals would enable the pursuit and prosecution of other individuals suspected of engaging in similarly heinous acts. According to Neier, "The tribunals advanced the idea that law generally, and international law in particular, can deal with great matters and that legal process may be relied upon to deal appropriately with the most grievous offenses by human beings against other human beings" (1998: 18).

Along with the tribunals, in the immediate postwar period, two of the most significant initiatives to build an international legal regime were the creation of the United Nations (UN) in 1946 and the passage of the Universal Declaration of Human Rights (UDHR) in 1948. The mandate of the UN, enshrined in its Charter, made human rights a prominent theme, albeit conceiving such rights not as an end unto themselves but rather as a means to ensure global peace and security. The UDHR was more high-minded, declaring human rights to be "inalienable" – an end in themselves. Although the UDHR was a nonbinding agreement, it laid out a framework for a common set of rights that all humans could claim, and served as a reference for subsequent promulgation of laws to codify those rights.

The postwar tribunals had operationalized the violence of law. But stripping state agents of "sovereign immunity" and prosecuting them for political crimes had a chilling effect on international law enforcement in their aftermath. Early efforts to build on the Nuremberg precedent by instituting an international criminal justice system were thwarted because, as Louis Henkin explains, "the principal powers [i.e., the permanent members of the new UN Security Council] were not prepared to derogate from the established character of the international system by establishing law and legal obligation that would penetrate Statehood in that radical way: clearly they themselves were not ready to submit to such law" (cited in Steiner and Alston, 1996: 123).

Ironically, as the rhetorical influence of human rights was gaining ground, the ground itself was eroding. In the postwar era and for decades thereafter, political exigencies, notably states' defense of their sovereign prerogatives and Cold War polarizations, subverted the enforceability of human rights and humanitarian laws.

HUMAN RIGHTS AS UTOPIA

The concept of utopia, once defined as imagined perfection, has expanded to include cures for imperfection. By this definition, any struggle or movement for rights could be conceived as utopian to the extent that it represents a desire to make the world a "better place" for the (would-be) beneficiaries. The utopianism of rights, and the vision of human dignity (and vulnerability) upon which rights strategies are based, is grounded in modern legal liberalism: rule of law, equality among the subjects of law, and universalized application and enforcement within the jurisdiction of law (see Dworkin, 1977; Donnelly, 1998; for skeptical assessments, see Fitzpatrick, 1992; Scheingold, 1974).

The *idea* of human rights is undisputedly utopian because it assumes and asserts that all human beings are equal in their humanity. But since humans do not actually live as equals, the idea is also revolutionary because it challenges hierarchies of power and privilege upon which political, economic, and social orders around the world are based.

Louis Henkin (1990) has described the twentieth century as the "age of rights." His intention was not to proclaim a victory for rights, but rather to acknowledge the influence of the idea of rights on the expectations and struggles of people around the world. Indeed, the *right to rights* has become an internationalized – if far from universalized – norm. Abdullahi An-Na'im defines the "human rights paradigm" as "the idea that the protection of certain individual and collective/group rights...is a matter of international concern, rather than the exclusive internal affair of states" (2001a: 87). According to Richard Wilson: "Notwithstanding disputes over their conceptualization and application, human rights are among the few utopian ideals left, and there is still a remarkable degree of consensus by governments on the principle at least that certain rights be protected under international law" (Wilson, 1997: 1).

Human rights are legal entitlements. To understand what human rights "do" or can do, it is necessary to appreciate what rights are. Rights can be defined as *practices that are required, prohibited, or otherwise regulated within the context of relationships governed by law.* To create new rights requires the creation of new laws, or reinterpretation of existing laws in new ways, or extension of the jurisdiction of laws to new subjects. The process of creating new rights emerges and proceeds in response to changing perceptions about social needs and problems, which, in turn, mobilizes a swell or shift in the balance of politicolegal forces to act. The products of that process, new laws that establish new rights (or revise or extend existing rights), impose changes by legally regulating relationships and practices in new ways. In short, rights are both markers and means of social change.

The idea of international human rights had been in circulation for decades prior to the first substantive steps to institutionalize it (see Keck and Sikkink, 1998; Lauren,

1998). One of the leading crusaders for human rights was the prominent British utopian writer, H.G. Wells. At the beginning of World War II, Wells wrote:

> At various crises in the history of our communities, beginning with the Magna Carta, and going through various Bills of Rights, Declarations of the Rights of Man and so forth, it has been our custom to produce a specific declaration of the broad principles on which our public and social life is based. . . . The present time seems particularly suitable for such a restatement of the spirit in which we face life in general and the present combat in particular. (cited in Lauren, 1998: 52)

In true utopian fashion, Wells and the many other individuals and groups who mobilized and collaborated during the war years strived both to enunciate principles of human rights and to advocate their incorporation into the postwar international order. While this mobilization replicated and built upon similar activities during World War I, the failures of those earlier efforts to prevent a second global conflagration fortified the movement and legitimized their demands for change. For example, whereas in World War I nine out of ten of the millions of casualties were soldiers, in World War II the proportions of soldier and civilian casualties were roughly even (Gutman and Rieff, 1999: 10). In addition to concerns about the harms wrought by the war, rights activists like Mohandas Gandhi and W.E.B. DuBois were animated by the injustices of colonialism and racism. World War II highlighted the linkages among these concerns; the politics of race (racial superiority and extermination), and the conquest and control of foreign lands were central to Axis war aims, and thus became central to the discourse and aims of the Allies' campaign as well. The war against fascism was pitched to the public as a fight for "freedom" (e.g., see US President Franklin D. Roosevelt's "Four Freedoms" speech), and the Allies' victory seemed to offer an opening to connect anticolonialism and antiracism to the postwar agenda for international legal reform.

But in the process that ensued, the utopian vision prioritizing the interests and needs of human beings was overwhelmed by realpolitik. The changes in international law after World War II that created human rights did not undermine the centrality of states to political life around the world. Nor did the new international institutions replace or diminish the authority and power of states over their subjects. Rather, the creation of human rights entailed the elaboration of new *internationalized norms of government* to which all states would be expected to adhere, while preserving the general principle of states' rights as sovereign entities. Consequently, while states' rights were revised (e.g., they could no longer claim the "right" to exterminate civilians), states retained their status as the premier *subjects* of international law. Put simply, human rights obtain their "universalizing" character from the fact that people are subjects of states, and states are subjects of international law. Thus the establishment of human rights simultaneously revised and reinforced the state-centrism of the international order.

The most obvious problem with this arrangement was the lack of effective means of global governance to ensure law enforcement. Under the state-centric structure of the UN, states were both the governors and the governed – the makers, the enforcers, and the subjects of these laws. This meant, for the most part, that the protection and promotion of human rights depended on self-enforcement by states. Thus the *availability* of human rights was contingent on the willingness of individual states to behave and conform, and dependent on the system of states to act against those that did not (see Falk, 1985).

While some states willingly instituted domestic reforms in keeping with their international obligations, most refused to regard human rights law as binding and enforceable, especially if the implications would compromise vested interests. Obvious examples were resistance by imperial states to relinquish colonial possessions, or to dismantle racial or ethnic hierarchies. Unenforceability of international law was compounded by the dynamics of Cold War rivalries between "East" and "West," and superpower competitions for power and influence across the global "South." Certainly, the rights of "self-determination" and "equality" enshrined in the UN Charter and the UDHR informed anticolonial and antiracist struggles, but these moral-legal imperatives did not mitigate the difficult and often violent processes of decolonization and desegregation.

The human rights idea was further compromised by sharp ideological disagreements over the nature of rights and the contested legitimacy of universalism. In the UDHR, political and civil rights and social and economic rights were conceived as "indivisible." However, Western leaders and leading human rights scholars tended to argue that political and civil rights were the priority, or even the only kind of "real" rights, since social and economic rights could not be guaranteed or enforced without violating the "freedom" of the market and the rights to profit and property. Leaders of socialist and developing states and scholars committed to those goals tended to argue that social and economic rights had to be prioritized to create conditions of equality. This would inevitably entail limitations on political and civil rights, and justify the use of force in putting down resistance. Socialists challenged the liberal legal emphasis on individual autonomy and freedom, emphasizing alternatively the need for a strong state with a centralized economy capable and committed to pursuing an agenda to remake the social order by redistributing goods.

The other major debate about human rights arose over the meaning and legitimacy of "universalism." Specifically, the debate circulates around the changes envisioned and imposed through the establishment of international legal norms. Critics of universalism assumed or were given the title of "cultural relativists." Their arguments were twofold: that human rights enshrined Western values of individualism (since individuals were constructed as the "beneficiaries" of human rights law) which contradicted social arrangements and values emphasizing collective relations and mutual duties, and that the imposition of universal standards was a new form of imperialism over non-Western societies (see Pollis and Schwab, 1979; Renteln, 1990).

THE "GAP" PROBLEM

The paramount "problem" of human rights has always been the gap between codified principles of rights ("law in the books"), and the enforcement or enforceability of law ("law in action"). To illustrate these gaps and their ramifications, we can consider three bodies of law: the Genocide Convention, the four Geneva Conventions, and the Torture Convention.

The Genocide Convention, promulgated in 1948, was a clear rejoinder to the Holocaust. Its aim was to prohibit and thus deter mass killing. But the Convention reflected a very particular – and limited – understanding of prohibited violence. While genocide was categorized as an international crime whether it occurred in war or peace, prohibited practices are defined as those intended "to destroy, in whole or in part, a national, ethnical, racial or religious group, as such." The exclusion of "political groups" and the insertion of the phrase "as such" during negotiations over the language of the Convention were insisted upon by the major powers as means of preserving their own prerogatives to act – including violently – against *"political enemies"* (Kuper, 1994: 32). As Diane Orentlicher notes,

> What was left out of the convention is as important as what was included. Although earlier drafts... listed political groups among those covered by the intent requirement, this category was omitted during final drafting stages. Too many governments, it seemed, would be vulnerable to the charge of genocide if deliberate destruction of political groups fell within the crime's compass. (Orentlicher, 1999: 154)

The omissions in the Genocide Convention's wording, as well as the lack of political authority to enforce the prohibition preserved the very vulnerability that the Convention was intended to rectify. Since 1948, millions of people have been systematically slaughtered by their governments, and until 1993 there was not a single effort by signatories to fulfill their own obligations to "prevent and punish" this crime. Moreover, even military responses to thwart genocide have been protested and resisted by the UN as illegitimate interference in sovereign states' "internal affairs" (see Finnemore, 1996).

Unlike the Genocide Convention, which was part of the "new" body of international human rights law born in the aftermath of World War II, the four Geneva Conventions (1949) fall within the domain of international humanitarian law, which has a longer and more established pedigree. These Conventions address the legal conduct of war, armed conflict, and military occupation, identifying and prohibiting actions against civilians or combatants that would constitute "war crimes." Prohibited practices include forced relocations and deportations, torture, collective punishment, hostage taking, extrajudicial killings, and the deliberate targeting of civilians during military operations (see ICRC, 1989).

The Geneva Conventions have status as "customary law," which means that they are binding on all states. (The alternative, "conventional law," is binding only on signatory states.) As customary law, "grave breaches" of the Geneva Conventions carry universal jurisdiction, meaning that violators can be prosecuted in any competent legal system (i.e., a national legal regime). But despite this provision, violations of the Geneva Conventions were rampant and unpunished. As Lawrence Weschler opines,

> [I]nternational humanitarian law has stood largely mute, palsied in part by the fear of most national governing elites – and in particular the successive leaderships of the five permanent Security Council members most in a position to invoke those norms – that the glare of such attention might one day be turned on their own actions. (In the United States this tenor of concern often took the form of the anxious assertion that "by that logic Henry Kissinger could have been held liable for the Christmas bombing of Hanoi" – as well he might have been.) (Weschler, 1999: 21)

Like the Genocide and the Geneva Conventions, the Torture Convention outlaws particular forms of violence. However, the former were immediate responses to World War II whereas the latter was promulgated in 1984. Another difference was that the Torture Convention came into being as a result of pressure and advocacy by nongovernmental organizations (NGOs) rather than an initiative of government representatives. Indeed, torture was the breakout issue for the development of an international human rights movement, led by Amnesty International (AI). AI, which was formed in 1961 in response to concern about the arrest of people because of their political ideas and activities, and concern about the torture and ill-treatment of prisoners, led the campaign for a UN convention prohibiting torture (see Rodney, 1996).

The Torture Convention differs from the Genocide Convention in certain crucial ways. First, the prohibition of torture and ill-treatment extends to every human being regardless of any aspect of his or her identity. Second, the prohibition is absolutely nonderogable (although the definition of torture does exclude coverage of "pain and suffering arising only from, inherent in or incidental to lawful sanctions"). Nonderogability means that there is no basis upon which any state can *legally* claim a "right" to torture, as the practice is defined under the convention. Third, the Convention criminalizes the use of violence by public agents against people *in custody*, which distinguishes torture empirically and legally from other forms of violence, such as those arising in the context of warfare or conflict (see Hajjar, 2000; Scarry, 1985). Fourth, the Convention explicitly recognizes universal jurisdiction for the prosecution of perpetrators.

The Genocide, Geneva and Torture Conventions were created to redress problems of violence. Did these laws make the world a "better place"? If assessment depends on whether these laws have been enforced, then the answer would be no. However, the creation of these laws did articulate principles and outlaw practices that would constitute violations, and this provided a "standard against which the conduct of governments is measured – an indirect yet still important contribution to human rights" (Neier, 1998: 21).

ACTING ON PRINCIPLE

The history of human rights encompasses not only the creation of laws but failures to adhere to and enforce those laws. Human rights activism is the organized response to this failure. Because of the institutional weaknesses of law enforcement mechanisms at the interstate level, NGOs with human rights mandates were established to operate in the breach. The various strategies deployed for such purposes include monitoring and reporting on violations to foster awareness (see Cohen, 1995), advocacy work to encourage actions or interventions to curb or stop violations, and litigation to adjudicate the applicability of international laws.

Over the last 30 years, the human rights movement has become truly globalized, evident in the mushrooming of organizations around the world and the strengthening of transnational and international networks. Notwithstanding disagreements over priorities and strategies, this movement is united by a common mandate to improve adherence and enforcement of international laws. Human rights activism and networking developed to fulfill a panoptic function of international surveillance by documenting and protesting violations. In so doing, the harms and injustices to which people around the world are subjected have been brought into the public domain where they demand and command an audience. While human rights activism rarely has been sufficient to end violations, it certainly has contributed to the influence of law in the international arena, and the influence of international law in domestic arenas.

WOMEN'S RIGHTS AS HUMAN RIGHTS

In many ways, the kinds of activities to achieve and protect women's rights replicate initiatives to secure other types of human rights. Violence and vulnerability have been abiding concerns in the construction and promotion of women's rights. However, women's rights pose the quintessential challenge to the "universality" of human rights, which is premised on the principle of human equality. In societies around the world, sexual and other differences between men and women lend themselves to understandings of gender inequalities as both derivative of and conforming to "nature." Moreover, gender inequalities and hierarchies have been justified as crucial to social order and cohesion, and staunchly defended as an aspect of a given culture.

Initially, the means of establishing women's human rights hinged on the principle of nondiscrimination. Thus any rights enshrined in the UDHR and other international legal instruments would, in principle, apply to women. However, reliance on nondiscrimination made international law a weak resource for women because the primary danger was envisaged as an invasive and repressive state. Consequently, forms of violence and harm to which were women were subjected *as women* were ignored by international lawmakers and thus remained immune to prohibition. For example, violence perpetrated between family members was (until recently) regarded as beyond the scope of international intervention.

The process of making women's issues, needs, and vulnerabilities "visible" entailed the extension of the human rights paradigm to previously excluded areas, including the so-called "private sphere" of the family. The Convention on the Elimination of All Forms of Discrimination Against Women (CEDAW), which came into force in 1981, established the "indivisibility" of women's rights in public and private life (see Fried, 1994). While CEDAW recognizes the importance of culture and tradition, it imposes on signatory states an obligation to take "all appropriate measures" to modify social and cultural patterns of conduct that are discriminatory or harmful toward women.

But CEDAW failed to identify violence against women as a human rights violation. Responding to this lacuna, in the 1980s, women's organizations around the world began campaigning for international recognition and prohibition of domestic violence as a human rights violation. In the 1990s, domestic violence became a major issue in a worldwide campaign to end violence against women. In 1993, women's groups presented a petition with almost 500,000 signatures from 128 countries to delegates at the World Conference on Human Rights (held in Vienna, Austria), demanding recognition of violence against women as a violation of their rights. In response, the UN adopted the Declaration on the Elimination of Violence against Women, defining it as "any act of gender-based violence that results in, or is likely to result in, physical, sexual or mental harm or suffering to women, including threats of such acts, coercion or arbitrary deprivation of liberty, whether occurring in public or private life." In 1994, the UN appointed the first Special Rapporteur on Violence against Women. In 1995, the Beijing Platform of Action (issued at the conclusion of the UN Fourth World Conference on Women held in Beijing, China) included an affirmation of the need to combat domestic violence and outlined specific measures to combat it (United Nations, 1996).

These initiatives have extended the reach of international law into the "private sphere," while seeking to "mainstream" women's rights by holding states accountable for their enforcement. But the successes of this campaign also sparked criticism and reprisals by social conservatives around the world, who have responded negatively to efforts to empower women and endow them with enforceable rights, *especially* within the context of the family. In many societies, official and popular aversion to enforcing international standards for domestic relationships has proven far more powerful and influential than the forces seeking to promote and protect the rights and well-being of women.

Debates over women's rights have been particularly rancorous in many developing countries (see Hajjar, forthcoming; Merry, 2001; Riles, 2000). Indeed, women's rights, and the issue of gender relations more generally, have become the primary redoubts of anxieties about the (putative) Western imperialism of human rights. Ongoing struggles over women's rights exemplify enduring disputes over legal jurisdiction and authority, namely whether international standards will prevail, or whether other bodies of law (constitutional, religious, customary) are accorded precedence when there is a contradiction.

TRANSITIONS TO JUSTICE

One of the necessary characteristics of law is the realistic threat of "legitimate violence." Indeed, while human rights often are spoken about and championed in idealistic terms as a means of helping people, *harming* people – perpetrators of violations – by prosecuting and punishing them for their illegal actions is an integral, if long unfulfilled, dimension of the human rights enterprise.

In the 1990s, the enforceability of international law entered a new phase, often designated as a "transition to justice" (see Kritz, 1995a, 1995b, 1995c; Teitel, 2000). This phase is marked by a broadening of human rights activism and strategies from *struggles for rights* to include *struggles against violators*. It began with the creation of UN ad hoc tribunals to prosecute the perpetrators of gross violence in the former Yugoslavia (1993) and in Rwanda (1994). Since then, tribunals have been established or planned in other places, including Sierra Leone, Cambodia, and East Timor (see Bass, 2001; Robertson, 2000). A "nonjudicial" alternative to dealing with past atrocities is truth commissions, to date established in over 23 countries (see Hayner, 2001).

Another major development was the indictment in 1998 of former Chilean dictator Augusto Pinochet, who was arrested in London on a warrant by a Spanish judge, charging torture, genocide, and other gross violations. The Pinochet case became a precedent because of his political status as a former head of state, and because of the willingness of a foreign national court to regard that status as irrelevant, albeit the charges that held up in Britain were restricted to torture and he was released because of "ill health" (see Sugarman, 2002). The "Pinochet precedent" was heralded as a recuperation of the Nuremberg legacy by depriving leaders of the protection of "sovereign immunity" for certain classes of crimes. But also like the Nuremberg legacy, the enforceability of international law has had a chilling effect to restrict or thwart the use of universal jurisdiction to prosecute officials accused of perpetrating or abetting gross violations (see Hajjar, 2003).

A third development was the passage in 1998 of the Rome Treaty to establish a permanent International Criminal Court. The treaty obtained the needed number of ratifications in July 2002. The ICC is intended for the prosecution of individuals

charged with the most serious human rights violations when national courts fail or are
unable to bring them to trial. But the ICC will have jurisdiction only over crimes
committed after its creation (i.e., no retroactive jurisdiction), and it remains a matter of
debate whether perpetrators from countries that have not signed the ICC treaty can be
prosecuted in this venue. Of particular concern to ICC supporters is the US government's adamant opposition, including the passage of national legislation that would
punish (non-NATO) foreign countries for cooperating with the ICC, and dozens of
bilateral "immunity agreements" the US has pressured other countries to sign.

These recent developments have had substantial impact on international law, but
also reveal the durability of the "gap problem." The laws in the books have been
changing under the auspices of the UN tribunals and the ICC, and in response to the
"Pinochet precedent." One significant aspect of these changes is a burgeoning merger
of humanitarian and human rights law. Ruti Teitel refers to this amalgamation as
"humanity's law."

> In the emerging regime, the scope of the humanitarian law system is expanded dramat-
> ically, and merged with the international law of human rights. In the new humanitarian-
> ism, the normative apparatus of the law of war, particularly its criminal justice
> dimension, is expanded way beyond its historic role. This move ... shifts the law of
> war ... from the periphery of international law to its core ... The new legal humanitar-
> ianism emerges to address the pervasive political violence of recent years, [and] in so
> doing, it restructures the reigning international value system, and redefines global rule
> of law. (Teitel, 2001: 5–6)

For the international human rights community and scholars and commentators
concerned about human rights, the "new legal humanitarianism" is being lauded as a
breakthrough in the decades-long efforts to close the gap between the principles and
practice of human rights. Martha Minow expresses the kind of cautious optimism
that has become a common theme:

> Perhaps more unusual than the facts of genocide and regimes of torture marking this era
> is the invention of new and distinctive legal forms of response. The capacity and
> limitations of these legal responses illuminate hopes and commitments of individuals
> and societies seeking, above all, some rejoinder to the unspeakable destruction and
> degradation of human beings. (Minow, 1998: 1)

But the new legal humanitarianism is also spurring resistance. "Political realists,"
who champion state sovereignty and geopolitical stability through balance-of-power
politics, are opposed to strengthening international law enforcement because it
necessarily comes at the expense of state power and discretion. Moreover, realists
argue, legal humanitarianism is a slippery slope that threatens the stability of the
international order and risks overextension (or misuse) of resources (i.e., military
and intelligence) needed for domestic/national security. The US government is at the
forefront of resistance, selectively utilizing the discourse of human rights to justify
the "war on terrorism" launched in response to the September 11, 2001, attacks,
while rebuffing the applicability of international law to its own practices in waging
that war, and actively undermining the goals and efforts of other states to strengthen
law enforcement mechanisms.

Critics of the new legal humanitarianism also include some political and intellectual progressives, who see a connection between the expansion of "global law" and

other deleterious forms of globalization. Tony Evans argues that the current era of unbridled free-market capitalism and US global hegemony is just as inimical to human rights, if differently so, as polarizing Cold War politics of previous decades. He writes, "Since the structures and practices of globalization are the cause of most violations of human rights, reliance on a legal system that seeks to apportion blame and punish individuals seems misplaced" (Evans, 1998: 17).

In response to this line of criticism, Michael Ignatieff rebuts the conflation of international law and economics: "[T]he moral globalization does not go hand in hand with economic globalization. On the contrary, human rights activism is working to mitigate globalization's effects" (2001: 16). In a similar vein, Abdullahi An-Na'im argues that

> the modern concept of human rights is the product of a long history of struggle for social justice and resistance to oppression that is constantly adapting to changing conditions in order to better achieve its objectives . . . [A]s local particularities diminish under the force of globalization, the push for universal human rights becomes more common. But since globalization reflects the unequal power relations between developed and developing countries, the tension between the relative and the universal will remain. To keep this unavoidable tension from repudiating the concept of human rights and frustrating its purpose in different societies, there must be a deliberate effort to build an overlapping consensus around the normative content and implementation mechanisms of human rights. (An-Na'im, 2001b: 95)

An-Na'im urges a balance between the emphasis on protection of political and civil rights through prosecution and other legalistic strategies with a wider set of nonlegal strategies in order to strengthen "nonjusticiable" claims and entitlements, namely those relating to social, economic, and cultural rights (see An-Na'im, 2001b).

Admittedly, the new legal humanitarianism is only one dimension of contemporary human rights discourse and practice. But its importance lies in its potential to change the content and uses of international law, and to create new goals and consequences of legal action and activism. Equally important are the measures and pressures mounted to inhibit law enforcement in the twenty-first century.

New Directions for Law and Society Research

At this juncture, the interpenetrations and overlapping interests of human rights scholarship and the field of law and society are increasingly evident. In particular, the new legal humanitarianism raises questions that beg for the kinds of theoretically informed analysis of the organization and power of law that characterize scholarship in this field.

Rapidly changing circumstances in the international legal arena have inspired calls for more theoretical clarity for its own sake as well as to ground and guide empirical investigations. According to Adamantia Pollis, "At present human rights scholarship is in what Thomas Kuhn calls a preparadigmatic state, a condition that characterizes social science theory as a whole" (Pollis, 2000: 22). While there could be no unifying "theory of human rights" any more than there could be a "theory of law," there is a compelling need to develop and refine intellectual resources to understand and explain, to support and/or to criticize the transforming impact of international law on the global order. According to Ruti Teitel,

The core predicates of the [post-World War II] regime are now undergoing substantial transformation that goes to the basic structure and core values of the international legal system; but these changes are not necessarily self-evident, and do not easily comport with our intuitions about the direction of international law. Therefore, we need to better understand the constitutive interaction of law with historical experiences. This necessitates interpretative principles regarding the development of the international legal domain. (Teitel, 2001: 15)

Among many scholars working in the field of law and society, there is a sense that we are "here together" to contribute substantively to progressive social change. The prevailing assumption that the field is comprised of "engaged intellectuals" is often a starting point for suggestions about the direction our scholarship should take. For example, Boaventura de Sousa Santos encourages engaged academics to devote more concerted attention to the relationship between law and emancipatory projects, which would include human rights.

[W]e must reinvent the future by opening up a new horizon of possibilities mapped out by new radical alternatives... We must also define the emergent paradigm, this being the really important and difficult task.... Utopian thinking has thus a double purpose: to reinvent maps of social emancipation and subjectivities with the capacity and desire for using them. No paradigmatic transformation of modern law would be possible without an utopian legal subjectivity: from the law-abiding citizen to the law-influencing citizen. (Santos, 1995: 572, 573)

Scholars can play a role in influencing the development and uses of international law by weighing in on debates over interpretations and applications of law, and evaluating the impact of legal initiatives to promote human rights and punish violators. The field of law and society is well positioned to respond to calls for paradigmatic work and political engagement to service the visions of justice, empowerment, and rights that underlie demands for human rights.

References

An-Na'im, Abdullahi (2001a) "Human rights," in Judith R. Blau (ed.), *The Blackwell Companion to Sociology.* New York: Blackwell, pp. 86–99.
An-Na'im, Abdullahi (2001b) "The legal protection of human rights in Africa: How to do more with less," in Austin Sarat and Thomas Kearns (eds.), *Human Rights: Concepts, Contests, Contingencies.* Ann Arbor: University of Michigan Press, pp. 89–115.
Bass, Gary Jonathan (2001) *Stay the Hand of Vengeance: The Politics of War Crimes Tribunals.* Princeton, NJ: Princeton University Press.
Cohen, Stanley (1995) *Denial and Acknowledgement: The Impact of Information about Human Rights Violations.* Jerusalem: Center for Human Rights, The Hebrew University.
Donnelly, Jack (1998) *International Human Rights.* Boulder, CO: Westview Press.
Dworkin, Ronald (1977) *Taking Rights Seriously.* Cambridge, MA: Harvard University Press.
Evans, Tony (1998) "Introduction: Power, hegemony and the universalization of human rights," in Tony Evans (ed.), *Human Rights Fifty Years On: A Reappraisal.* Manchester, UK and New York: Manchester University Press, pp. 2–23.
Falk, Richard (1985) *Human Rights and State Sovereignty.* New York: Holmes & Meier Publishers.

Finnemore, Martha (1996) "Constructing norms of humanitarian intervention," in Peter
    J. Katzenstein (ed.), *The Culture of National Security: Norms and Identity in World
    Politics*. New York: Columbia University Press, pp. 153–85.
Fitzpatrick, Peter (1992) *The Mythology of Modern Law*. London: Routledge.
Fried, Susana (1994) *The Indivisibility of Women's Human Rights: A Continuing Dialogue*.
    New Brunswick, NJ: Center for Women's Global Leadership.
Gutman, Roy and Rieff, David (1992) "Preface," in Roy Gutman and David Rieff (eds.),
    Crimes of War: What the Public Should Know. New York: W.W. Norton & Company,
    pp. 8–12.
Hajjar, Lisa (2000) "Sovereign bodies, sovereign states and the problem of torture," *Studies in
    Law, Politics and Society* 21: 101–34.
Hajjar, Lisa (2003) "Chaos as utopia: International criminal prosecution as a challenge to
    state power," *Studies in Law, Politics and Society* 30.
Hajjar, Lisa (forthcoming) "Religion, state power and domestic violence in Muslim societies:
    A framework for comparative analysis," *Law and Social Inquiry* 29(1).
Hayner, Priscilla (2001) *Unspeakable Truths: Confronting State Terror and Atrocity*. New
    York: Routledge.
Henkin, Louis (1990) *The Age of Rights*. New York: Columbia University Press.
Ignatieff, Michael (2001) "Human rights as moral imperialism," Paper presented at a confer-
    ence on The Politics and Political Uses of Human Rights Discourse, Columbia University,
    November 8–9, 2001.
International Committee of the Red Cross (ICRC) (1989) *The Geneva Conventions of August
    12, 1949*. Geneva: ICRC Publications.
Keck, Margaret and Sikkink, Kathryn (1998) *Activists beyond Borders: Advocacy Networks
    in International Politics*. Ithaca, NY: Cornell University Press.
Kritz, Neil (ed.) (1995a) *Transitional Justice: How Emerging Democracies Reckon with
    Former Regimes: General Considerations*, vol. 1. Washington, DC: United States Institute
    of Peace.
Kritz, Neil (ed.) (1995b) *Transitional Justice: How Emerging Democracies Reckon with
    Former Regimes: Country Studies*, vol. 2. Washington, DC: United States Institute of
    Peace.
Kritz, Neil (ed.) (1995c) *Transitional Justice: How Emerging Democracies Reckon with
    Former Regimes: Laws, Rulings, and Reports*, vol. 3. Washington, DC: United States
    Institute of Peace.
Kuper, Leo (1994) "Theoretical issues relating to genocide: Uses and abuses," in George
    Andreopoulos (ed.), *Genocide: Conceptual and Historical Dimensions*. Philadelphia:
    University of Pennsylvania Press, pp. 31–46.
Lauren, Paul Gordon (1998) *The Evolution of International Human Rights: Visions Seen*.
    Philadelphia: University of Pennsylvania Press.
Merry, Sally Engle (2001) "Women violence and the human rights system," in Marjorie
    Agosin (ed.) *Women, Gender and Human Rights: A Global Perspective*. New Brunswick,
    NJ: Rutgers University Press.
Minow, Martha (1998) *Between Vengeance and Forgiveness: Facing History after Genocide
    and Mass Violence*. Boston: Beacon Press.
Minow, Martha, Ryan, Michael and Sarat, Austin (eds.) (1995) *Narrative, Violence, and the
    Law: The Essays of Robert Cover*. Ann Arbor, MI: University of Michigan Press.
Neier, Aryeh (1998) *War Crimes: Brutality, Genocide, Terror, and the Struggle for Justice*.
    New York: Times Books, Random House.
Orentlicher, Diane (1999) "Genocide," in Roy Gutman and David Rieff (eds.), *Crimes of War:
    What the Public Should Know*. New York: W.W. Norton & Company, pp. 153–7.
Pollis, Adamantia (2000) "A new universalism," in Adamantia Pollis and Peter Schwab (eds.),
    Human Rights: New Perspectives, New Realities. Boulder, CO: Lynne Rienner Publishers,
    pp. 9–30.

Pollis, Adamantia and Schwab, Peter (1979) "Human rights: A western construct with limited applicability," in A. Pollis and P. Schwab (eds.), *Human Rights: Cultural and Ideological Perspectives*. New York: Praeger Publishers, pp. 1–17.

Renteln, Allison Dundes (1990) *Human Rights: Universalism versus Relativism*. Newbury Park, CA: Sage Publications.

Riles, Annelies (2000) *The Network Inside Out*. Ann Arbor, MI: University of Michigan Press.

Robertson, Geoffrey (2000) *Crimes against Humanity: The Struggle for Global Justice*. New York: New Press.

Rodney, Nigel (1996) "Preface," in Duncan Forrest (ed.), *A Glimpse of Hell: Reports on Torture Worldwide*. New York: Amnesty International and New York University Press, pp. vi–vii.

Santos, Boaventura de Sousa (1995) "Three metaphors for a new conception of law: The frontier, the baroque, and the south," *Law and Society Review* 29: 569–84.

Sarat, Austin and Kearns, Thomas R. (1993) "Introduction," in Austin Sarat and Thomas Kearns (eds.), *Law's Violence*. Ann Arbor, MI: University of Michigan Press, pp. 1–21.

Scarry, Elaine (1985) *The Body in Pain: The Making and Unmaking of the World*. New York: Oxford University Press.

Scheingold, Stuart (1974) *The Politics of Rights: Lawyers, Public Policy and Political Change*. New Haven, CT: Yale University Press.

Silbey, Susan (1997) "'Let them eat cake': Globalization, postmodern colonialism, and the possibilities of justice," *Law and Society Review* 31: 207–35.

Steiner, Henry and Alston, Philip (eds.) (1996) *International Human Rights in Context*. Oxford: Clarendon Press.

Sugarman, David (2002) "From unimaginable to possible: Spain, Pinochet and the judicialization of power," *Journal of Spanish Cultural Studies* 3(1): 107–24.

Teitel, Ruti (2000) *Transitional Justice*. New York: Oxford University Press.

Teitel, Ruti (2001) "Humanity's law: Rule of law for the new global politics," Paper presented at a conference on The Politics and Political Uses of Human Rights Discourse, Columbia University, November 8–9, 2001.

United Nations (1996) *Platform for Action and the Beijing Declaration*. New York: United Nations.

Weschler, Lawrence (1999) "International humanitarian law: An overview," in Roy Gutman and David Rieff (eds.), *Crimes of War: What the Public Should Know*. New York: W.W. Norton & Company, pp. 18–22.

Wilson, Richard (1997) "Human rights, culture, and context: An introduction," in Richard Wilson (ed.), *Human Rights, Culture, and Context: Anthropological Perspectives*. New York: Pluto Press, pp. 1–27.

32

The Rule of Law and Economic Development in a Global Era

Kathryn Hendley

Events over the past few decades have revolutionized how we interact with one another, whether as individuals, corporations, or countries. The source of these changes is a combination of technological innovation and political transformation. The sheer speed at which information travels and the comprehensive global reach of the Internet has had a profound impact on economic relationships (e.g., Helleiner, 2001; Gilpin and Gilpin, 2000). In seeking trading partners, businesspeople now routinely look beyond their national borders. Absent personal knowledge of one another, or even a shared history in which their expectations could be grounded, law has emerged as a means of protecting themselves. Ideally, law provides a common language that is impersonal and universal that helps to even the stakes between more and less economically powerful actors (e.g., Coase, 1988; North, 1990; Olson, 2000). As state socialism has been rejected by more and more countries in favor of the market, domestic policy makers in these countries have come to appreciate the extent to which a functional legal system can facilitate mundane business transactions and the development of capitalism over the long haul. Likewise, the increasingly interconnected nature of the global economy has provided a strong incentive for Western governments and multilateral funding agencies to encourage transition countries to embrace legal development as part of broader programs aimed at facilitating transitions to the market.

The end of the Cold War and the collapse of state socialism as a feasible alternative to neoliberal market democracy as a model for organizing states has also contributed to the renewal of interest in law as a way of spurring economic development. No other viable options exist for countries that want to participate in the global economy. As the countries of the former Soviet bloc cast off the machinery of state planning, they have uniformly looked to a variety of market institutions as a means of rebuilding their economies. China's leadership has taken a different and less precipitous path away from state socialism. While opening the door to some types of market transactions, the Communist Party in China has tried to maintain its monopoly on political power. The resulting differences in the scope and sequencing of reform are reflected in the legal realm, making it more confusing than helpful to consider the two seemingly similar regions together. (On the legal reform process in China, see Turner, Feinerman, and Guy, 2000; Murray, 1999.) Yet in both regions, the move toward the market is grounded in law (e.g., Posner, 1998) and has been accompanied by large-scale projects to pass along the experience and expertise of the advanced industrialized countries in building institutions and drafting legislation.

The effort to remake the legal systems of transition countries has been framed by the goal of moving toward the "rule of law." This phrase, once the province of legal philosophers, has become a trendy political slogan around the world. Virtually everyone on the world stage, from George W. Bush to Boris Yeltsin to James Wolfensen, has espoused the "rule of law" as a goal. With its popularization has come a disintegration in the clarity of the concept. To be sure, the objective of attaining the "rule of law" enjoys a consensus (if not unanimity) among world leaders and multilateral lending organizations. Indeed, they generally agree that the "rule of law" is positively correlated (if not causally related) to what are often seen as the more important goals of democracy and the market. What is less clear is the precise content of this goal, and almost entirely obscure is how it is to be achieved. What would a legal system imbued with the "rule of law" look like, and how do countries go about achieving that end? Should the form and content of the "rule of law" be determined by local needs (including cultural norms) or should there be some model set of laws and institutions that need only be emulated? Would the images of the desired end as sketched out by the leaders of transition countries and by policy makers at multilateral lending institutions be the same? These are not easy questions. Indeed, they are questions that have perplexed both legal scholars and policy makers for decades (e.g., Weber, 1967; Unger, 1976; Nonet and Selznick, 1978). It is far simpler to support a vague idea that seems to promise justice for all than to delineate the specifics. The chorus would undoubtedly break down if its members were forced to articulate the substance of the concept. The inherent amorphousness of the "rule of law" in the contemporary setting has facilitated its universal acceptance.

Although I recognize that the "rule of law" serves as the political justification for undertaking legal reform, it is not my purpose in this essay to detail the evolution of the concept, either generally or in terms of its use by various players in the transition from state socialism (see generally Krygier, 1990; Carothers, 1999). My purpose is to reflect on the nature of contemporary efforts at legal development in the realm of the economy in the context of the transition from state socialism. This is not the first time legal reform has been pursued on a global scale. (For a critical analysis of the legal development movement of the 1960s, see Gardner, 1980; Carty, 1992; Adelman and Paliwala, 1993.) How is this iteration of the process different? I pursue this question by inquiring into the reasons why legal reform and economic development have become intertwined, and how this set of issues has come onto the political agenda of transition countries. I then turn to an analysis of the scholarly literature. I describe the basic trends in how social scientists have chosen to study this reform process, comparing it to the literature generated by previous reform campaigns and identifying the persistent gaps.

THE CONTEXT OF THE CONTEMPORARY TRANSITION

What distinguishes the current effort at legal development from previous efforts? With its focus on countries making the transition from state socialism to some form of market economy in the wake of the Cold War, the current effort might seem to be a complete departure from anything witnessed in the past. Yet the basic goal differs little from that of previous efforts dating back centuries. Stated simply, the goal is to move away from a concept of law as a pliable tool used by the powerful to exert their will over the powerless to one of law as a relatively stable set of rules that can be used by all to protect or advance their interests vis-à-vis other private actors or the state.

Notwithstanding the common goal, this iteration of legal development has several distinctive characteristics in addition to its unprecedented geopolitical context. First, it focuses on countries with highly developed formal legal systems, distinguishing it from earlier efforts which often focused on countries emerging from colonialism (e.g., Merry, 1996). These former colonies typically had a rich tradition of customary law that had been suppressed, and the debate centered on how (or whether) to integrate this customary law with the formal institutions imposed by the colonizer. Although the Soviet Union's imposition of its legal system on the vast territory of the former Russian Empire following the 1917 Revolution and on Eastern Europe and the Baltic states in the 1940s might suggest certain parallels, most of these countries had formal legal systems that were "Sovietized" and which could be "de-Sovietized." Second, the current round of legal development arises in countries that for much of the twentieth century marginalized law, especially in economic transactions. Third, it is taking place in concert with profound political and economic reforms and, as a result, legal reform is often seen as a means to an end rather than as the end itself. Finally, it coincides with (and perhaps has played a role in triggering) the increased interest of multilateral funding organizations and development agencies of individual Western democracies in the outcome of the legal development process and an unwillingness on the part of these groups to sit by silently.

Like other authoritarian countries that came before and after them, the Soviet Union and the Soviet bloc countries have often been described as "lawless" in the popular media. Taken literally, they were not. As scholars have documented, these countries had all the accouterments of a legal system: courts, legislation, regulations (e.g., Barry, Ginsburgs, and Maggs, 1977–9; Lasok, 1973–5). But how meaningful were they? Was the law on the books enforced? The familiar stereotype of judges willfully ignoring law at the behest of their political patrons turns out to be only part of the story. To be sure, when Communist Party officials took an interest in a case, they were likely to try to influence the outcome by putting pressure on the judge (e.g., Shelley, 1986). This happened not only in the so-called "show trials" (Litvinov, 1972; Katkov, 1969) but also in less high-profile cases that came to the attention of those with political influence (Kaminskaya, 1982). This "telephone law" rarely mirrored the written law. As the utopian goals of socialism faded and material interests replaced ideal interests, corruption became a problem (e.g., Feofanov and Barry, 1996; Simis, 1982). Yet the vast majority of cases passed with little fanfare and were decided in accordance with the written law (Solomon, 1996; Hendley,

1996; Ulc, 1972; Feifer, 1964). The result has been described as a "dual system of law and terror" in which there was a "surprising degree of compartmentalization of the legal and extralegal" (Sharlet, 1977: 155, with reference to Fraenkel, 1941; see also Markovits, 1995). This ability on the part of the political elite to penetrate the legal system and to use law in a crudely instrumental fashion to achieve their short-term goals was a persistent feature of legal systems under state socialism. Over time, the chilling effect of self-censorship motivated by self-preservation can be observed as judges strived to please their political patrons by anticipating their desires and ruling accordingly (Markovits, 1995; Kaminskaya, 1982; Ulc, 1972). Thus, while the formal structures built up during the years of state socialism could, with some reworking, serve as a foundation for market-driven transactions, the uneven enforcement of law constituted a more substantial obstacle. A successful transition toward market capitalism requires some degree of acceptance of universality in the application of legal norms. Indeed, predictability provides law with much of its value among economic actors. Absent predictability, the efficiency of law is undermined in that there can be no assurance that the relevant law will be applied as written or even as it was to others in analogous circumstances. As a result, law does not have the desired effect of reducing transaction costs.

The dual nature of the legal tradition under state socialism left an equivocal legacy. On the one hand, formal legal systems existed and, to a considerable extent, were functional. On the other hand, the political elite were able to orchestrate outcomes of specific cases or rule changes when their interests were threatened. Equally problematic was the predilection of these regimes for mounting campaigns to address social problems through the use of law (e.g., Smith, 1979). Typically a flurry of new laws (often a combination of executive decrees and legislation) would be announced with great fanfare, only to recede into the background when the regime's attention turned elsewhere. This illustrates a tendency not only to churn out new laws rather than figure out how to make those already on the books work more effectively, but also to create the appearance of activity with these new laws. As a result, ordinary citizens understood law as a tool available to the state and the political elite, but not to them. For them, law was something to be gotten around, not something that could be relied upon. The idea of law as a set of fixed rules that bound both state and society would have been regarded as absurd. This skepticism toward law is not necessarily a permanent feature and may gradually diminish of its own accord under market democracy, but was a reality that ought to have been taken into account by those bent on reforming the legal system. Legal development programs that focused on institutional reforms at the expense of attitudinal factors were seen by ordinary citizens as a continuation of the old campaign approach. Due to the historical legacy, such reforms have enjoyed only limited success in encouraging people to use (rather than avoid) law in ordering their economic transactions.

Further complicating legal reform in the postsocialist world is the fact that it is occurring simultaneously with an unprecedented transformation of the political and economic systems. At least initially, policy makers focused primarily on these other aspects. Changes in the legal system were made in order to facilitate the transition toward democracy and/or the market. This reinforced the technocratic approach to legal development that international lenders have traditionally favored. The emphasis on finding just the right legislative and institutional infrastructure to accommodate the broader transition pushed concerns with societal attitudes toward law off the agenda. The assumption of the reformers – both domestic policy makers and their international advisors – was that when the "right" institutions and laws were put into place, people would respond. In the realm of the economy, this often boiled down to initiatives to introduce private property rights. Making assumptions about how people will react to legal reform is hazardous at best, but was particularly problematic in light of the legacy of distrust that came in the wake of state socialism. As the first round of reforms foundered, often as a result of well-intentioned laws lying dormant, policy makers began to pay more attention to legal reform as an independent goal (rather than merely as a means of achieving the desired end of establishing a market democracy). But the devotion to the technocratic approach rarely waned.

The enhanced role of international actors in this most recent effort at legal development no doubt contributed to the appeal of this approach. In prior efforts, international agencies had concentrated more on building democratic political orders, but the transition from state socialism brought the economy to the forefront. The perceived need to introduce market institutions attracted the attention of the World Bank and similar institutions that are interested in ensuring a stable and efficient economic order throughout the world. These institutions have a fairly rigid template for how reform is supposed to work, and for what the final outcome should look like (e.g., World Bank, 1996, 1997, 2001). The expectation is that countries desirous of assistance will adapt themselves to the standard format, rather than adapting the format to the specific conditions of a given country. Law has only gradually become part of the story. As the former general counsel of the World Bank wrote, "until recently, few outside the legal profession saw the direct relevance of law to development or appreciated its importance" (Shihata, 1995: 127). Now that legal reform is on the agenda, the task is seen as reordering incentives in order to encourage greater reliance on law. There is little recognition of the importance of societal attitudes toward law or legal culture more generally. The timing of the transition gave international actors unprecedented influence. It came at a moment in world history at which the market had effectively displaced all other theories for how to organize economic systems, and at which the countries seeking to make the transition had few resources, either financial or intellectual. Decades of state social-ism (along with the arms race) had drained the coffers and had left them with cadres well-versed in Marxism–Leninism, but woefully unversed in the theory of the market. Into this void came armies of experts brimming over with confidence as to how to reinvent the now-discredited planned economies as markets (e.g., Privatiza-tion, 1992; Kornai, 1990).

Legal Reform – Moving From Plan to Market

The effort at reforming the legal systems of formerly socialist countries to facilitate market transactions has been underway for more than a decade. Assessing the results is tricky. If institutional snapshots of each of the legal systems were taken at the outset of the transition and then again in 2003, the occurrence of profound changes would be indisputable. Across the region, the stranglehold of the state planning agencies on the economy has been broken. Indeed, these agencies have been dis-banded (though many of their top officials successfully translated their connections into wealth during the transition). In place of the dismantled machinery of the planned economy are the institutions generally regarded as necessary for the market to operate. Private property has been legalized and, at least on paper, ownership of the means of production has been shifted from the state to private hands. Certain pre-existing institutions have been reinvented and others have been constructed from scratch. In the former category, the now democratically elected legislatures have enacted a plethora of legislation, some of which is completely new but much of which reworks pre-existing codes, stripping them of their socialist veneer. These statutes have effectively eliminated the state controls on enterprise management and have freed them to engage in profit-driven market-based transactions. Along similar lines, changes have been made to the judicial systems that eradicate the formal mechanisms used by Communist Party officials to exert control over case outcomes.

These reforms, while undoubtedly a necessary first step, have not been sufficient on their own to revitalize law in postsocialist societies. The lesson of the legal development movement of the 1960s that legal reform takes hold only when both well-designed and appropriate given the institutional and cultural heritage of the country in question has been disregarded or perhaps was never known by this new generation of reformers. The technocratic approach to reform places great weight on getting the design right, guided by the belief that economic actors will embrace law if motivated by the proper incentives (e.g., Braguinsky and Yavlinsky, 2000). It is an argument that is almost impossible to disprove. If the new laws and institutions fail to produce the desired outcome, then its adherents can always claim that they are not yet quite perfected or that some other piece of the institutional puzzle is still missing (e.g., Hay and Shleifer, 1998). But no legal system operates in an idealized form; they all exist in the real world and are populated by flawed actors who respond to domestic political pressure and/or act in accordance with historical tradition. Such behavior can appear to the outsider to be unpredictable or even irrational, but could easily have been predicted had the empirical reality of the legal system been investigated and factored into the reforms.

Privatization is a good example. It is aimed at accomplishing a basic economic goal, yet requires fundamental legal modifications as a prerequisite and, therefore, stands at the crossroads of economic and legal reform. All agreed that getting industrial capital out of the hands of the state was essential. The details of the privatization programs differed (see Frydman, Rapaczynski, and Earle, 1993a, 1993b; Stark and Bruszt, 1998: 80–105), but the goal was uniform as were the intended consequences. Putting the means of production into private hands was intended to engender capitalism. More specifically, it was intended to create a class of new owners that would be committed to the enforcement of property rights. Along with the shift in ownership typically came a legislative package that included a reworked set of rules for businesses that encompassed both intrafirm and interfirm matters. The rules endeavored to scale back, if not entirely eliminate, the role of the state in the economy. When these new owners took advantage of the absence of the state to exert dominance over both their competitors and their shareholders, the reformers professed great surprise and laid much of the blame at the door of the law. The culprit was the inadequacy of the rules for corporate governance or their enforcement or other violations of the newly established regime for property rights (e.g., Coffee, 1999; Estrin and Wright, 1999; Lumelsky, 1997; Black, Kraakman, and Hay, 1996; Kuznetsov and Kuznetsova, 1996) or the absence of the much-vaunted "rule of law" (e.g., Miller and Petranov, 2000; Banaian, 1999; Åslund, 1995). No doubt the laws on the books were imperfect and the legal institutions were flawed, but perfection is rarely encountered in the realm of law. What was noticeably missing from the discussion was an exploration of why the prevailing informal norms within the nascent business community in postsocialist countries allowed and even rewarded blatantly predatory behavior (e.g., Black, Kraakman, and Tarassova, 2000). For the most part, the now-disparaged laws had been drafted with the assistance of foreign experts without much interaction with local business-people. This sort of technocratic approach produced laws that appeared on the surface to meet the coming needs, but missed the mark because the empirical reality of how law works was never explored. Interestingly, in the parts of Eastern Europe where economic growth has taken off, commentators attribute the success to other incentives, making little mention of law (e.g., Stephan, 1999, on success in Hungary due to monetary stabilization; Johnson and Loveman, 1995, on success in Poland due to start-up small businesses).

So long as legal development remains mired in the search for the "silver bullet," that is, the ideal set of institutional incentives that will produce entrepreneurs who respect the behavioral boudaries established by law, the process seems doomed to repeated failure. A variant on the same pattern can be seen as the Soviet bloc countries work to gain entry to assorted regional economic, political, and military alliances (e.g., Broadbent and McMillian, 1998; Alexandrov and Petkov, 1998; Fox, 1997; Sewerynski, 1997; Steinberg, 1997). The prerequisites for membership typically include the harmonization of certain laws that are of particular interest to the members of the alliance. For the most part, changing the letter of the law has proven to be a fairly low hurdle. Had more attention been paid to demonstrating that the new laws had actually been put into effect, the outcome of these application processes might have been dramatically different.

The upshot of the legal reform efforts has been tremendous progress in expunging the institutional manifestations of state socialism. Without minimizing the signifi-cance of this accomplishment, it is not necessarily accompanied by the increase in trust for law on the part of economic actors that is essential for the "rule of law" to become embedded in these postsocialist societies. Indeed, the rigid assumptions about cause and effect that are inherent in the present-day technocratic approach harken back to the Soviet-era legal campaigns, in which new laws or decrees were marketed as having transformative effects on society. Both claim to be able to recognize and solve problems in the legal system without any empirical investiga-tion. The arrogance and determinism at the core of both approaches carry with them a danger of misdiagnosis and of making things worse, especially in terms of people's attitudes toward law.

The technocratic approach to legal development adopted by domestic policy makers in countries making the transition from state socialism can be explained in terms of learned behavior. Although the nature of the political economy is changing, the methods of problem solving learned in earlier life persist. Under state socialism, asking too many questions about how things actually worked was perilous. Policy makers became accustomed to making decisions based on their perceptions rather than empirical data (whether quantitative or qualitative). Whether this will change as social scientists begin to fill in the gaps in knowledge with gritty details of how law works in these countries remains to be seen.

The rigidity exhibited by their counterparts in multilateral lending organizations and development agencies of foreign governments provides little reason for opti-mism. In spite of the documented futility of the "fix now – ask questions later" approach, it endures. The reasons can be traced back to a combination of ideological and practical factors. Although not in the sway of Marxism–Leninism, the reformers retained by these international organizations come with their own set of beliefs about what a legal system that facilitates the market ought to look like, and how to achieve it. These beliefs are naturally shaped by their educational training and experiences in their home countries. In the current transition, this amounts to a commitment to principles of free market capitalism. The predominance of economists in the legal reform efforts aimed at the economy makes efficiency the most prized quality to be achieved in the reformed systems. This desire for efficiency is not limited to outcomes, but permeates the entire process. The pressure to move quickly is overwhelming. Often funding is contingent on quick turnarounds. Speed can be a double-edged sword in this context. On the positive side, it discourages malingering and minimizes the danger that a specific reform project will become anyone's life work. In a part of the world where the practice of dragging out construction projects for decades was a notorious tactic for squeezing funds out of the state into perpetuity, it is perhaps wise to send a signal that reform is a time-bounded process. But this may give too much credit to the reformers in that the emphasis on speed is not specific to the transition from state socialism, but has long been a way of life in the legal development world. The negative side is that it encourages (sometimes forces) reform projects into the field before they are ready. The intense time pressure results in a de-emphasis on the sort of thorough research required to diagnose the problem and propose appropriate solutions. As a result, much as armies seem always to be fighting the last war, development agencies tend to solve old problems rather than those currently plaguing the legal system being reformed.

STUDYING LEGAL REFORM

The process of reforming legal systems in order to make them amendable to market transactions has attracted a considerable amount of scholarly attention in recent years. In contrast to earlier large-scale legal development efforts, interest is not limited to a narrow group of legal researchers. This flows from a combination of the resurgence of interest in the operation of institutions among social scientists and the unprecedented geopolitical significance of the region under transition. Scholars from other disciplines, notably economics and political science, have entered the field and have brought new theoretical insights and methodologies to the enterprise. The questions posed and the methods employed in studying the legal transition reflect broader trends within the respective disciplines. Interdisciplinary work has also flourished. The result is a richer and more diverse body of literature than was produced in response to earlier efforts at legal development. At the same time, certain aspects of the process remain stubbornly enigmatic.

The interest of legal scholars in the operation and evolution of foreign legal systems is not new, though it remains peripheral to their concern with domestic law. Research on the countries emerging from state socialism as conducted by legal scholars tends to be narrowly drawn, often taking the form of single-country case studies of a set of laws or institutions (e.g., Solomon and Foglesong, 2000; Los and Zybertowicz, 2000; Cole, 1995). The body of work produced by legal scholars can be further separated into a few basic categories. Whether or not the author participated in the reform process is a useful dividing line, as is the extent to which the analysis is limited to the law on the books.

Studies written by participants – typically foreign advisors – can provide information that is elsewhere unavailable. At their best, they untangle the rationale behind reform programs and provide a glimpse into a process that usually eludes uninvolved researchers due to problems with access, trust, and memory (e.g., Palvolgyi and Herbai, 1997). This sort of insight is particularly valuable in the context of postsocialist states where the positivism prevailing among domestic policy makers leads them to believe that law becomes interesting and worthy of study only in its final form. Merely opening up the process as a legitimate arena for investigation is an accomplishment. Unfortunately, a review of the writings of participant-advisors reveals it to be the exception rather than the rule. More often these studies amount to little more than translations of the law with a thin gloss of commentary (e.g., Jersild, 2001; Bush, 1999; Boner and Kovacic, 1997; Brown, 1995). Rarely is the approach critical. The reluctance of advisors to criticize their former colleagues or to contemplate what might have happened if a different road had been taken is understandable. But it limits the scholarly value of the work. For those not fluent in the relevant language and unable to read the text or the scholarly commentary in its original form, such articles may be helpful. They provide information to the Western scholarly and policy-making community about the formal structure of foreign legal systems. But because they stop short of analyzing the actual day-to-day operations of the law or of specific institutions, they do little to advance the understanding of how these legal systems work.

Much of the legal scholarship by nonparticipants – by both Western and local scholars – reflects a similar approach. Relying on textual analyses of the law on the books, the authors are content with description and/or formalistic comparisons between the system in transition and other legal systems (usually the US legal system). This represents a continuation of the type of research undertaken in the past. The objectivity of the nonparticipant scholars brings greater rigor to this work and their deep knowledge of how the legislation and legal institutions within a country have changed over time bring a historical depth to the analysis. The luxury of political and ideological neutrality marks a shift for regional scholars. Under state socialism, scholars were expected to toe the line in both their underlying assumptions and their findings. The broader spectrum of opinion now found in regional law journals is like a breath of fresh air. Yet certain predilections endure. While religiously documenting the outcomes of the legal development process, such as changes in the substance of basic codes, regional legal scholars have shown almost no interest in the process itself. In this, they are joined by most of their Western colleagues. The sorts of questions deemed worthy of analysis by most Western and regional scholars rarely take them out of the library (e.g., Blumenfeld, 1996; Rudnick, 1995; Biernat, 1994; Maggs, 1992). The results are edifying for specialists, but rarely advance the understanding of the reform process and its consequences.

A smaller body of work by legal scholars digs into the reality of how specific laws have evolved and the extent to which law works in a given society. The collapse of state socialism and the attendant controls on social science have opened up avenues of research that were previously closed. Based on this research, scholars have begun to question the prevailing common wisdom about the role of law in these societies and to fill in the gaping holes in knowledge about how law is understood and used. Some of these studies seek to establish base lines in terms of attitudes and usage rates that will facilitate ongoing comparisons. The methods used are not groundbreaking, but are novel for the region. There is a mix of case studies (e.g., Hendley, 2001;

Hayden, 1990), analysis grounded in official statistical data (e.g., Hendley, 2002; Raiser, 1994), and survey-based studies (e.g., Frye, 2001; Earle and Estrin, 2001; Korlaska-Bobinska, 1994). The access needed to carry out this research made it impracticable, even unthinkable, under state socialism. At the outset of the transition, studying "law in action" was mostly the province of foreign scholars. The tradition of using sociological methods to study law had stronger roots in Eastern Europe than in the territory of the former Soviet Union. Even under state socialism, some East European scholars preserved this tradition (e.g., Kurczewski and Frieske, 1977), and it has reclaimed a more central role with the loosening of state controls on the academy (e.g., Alexander and Skąpska, 1994). But the collapse of state socialism to the east, in the former Soviet Union, has not produced similar changes. Although legal scholarship in this region has lost much of the ideological fervor that previously pervaded it, the attachment to doctrinal analysis persists. Whether this will change in the near future is unclear. As sociological methods became better known through exchanges with Western universities and interactions with Western scholars, legal scholars in the former Soviet Union have begun to ask different questions. Rather than limiting themselves to textual analysis, they have begun to probe how law works and why.

The deep involvement of foreign advisors of all stripes with reforms across the region resulted in a considerable amount of borrowing from other countries' legislation. But the sort of borrowing that went on was different than what went on in earlier transitions. This time, because of the pre-existing legal structure, the wholesale adoption of codes rarely occurred. Instead, bits and pieces of legal machinery from other countries were incorporated into the codes of the transition countries as they were reworked in pursuit of the market. Sometimes the results were schizophrenic as the cadging of what was perceived as potentially helpful from divergent foreign systems failed to gel coherently but produced mishmashes. Perhaps for this reason, those who have reflected on the legal aspects of the transition from state socialism have not been much attracted to "transplant theory" (Ewald, 1995; Watson, 1991), with certain exceptions (e.g., Nichols, 1997; Ajani, 1995).

The study of the legal aspects of the transition from state socialism is not the exclusive province of legal scholars. This distinguishes it from most previous efforts at legal development. At the same time, the interest of nonlegal scholars should not be overstated. The vast majority of political science scholarship on the transition either ignores the legal dimension or treats it merely as one of a number of technical problems to be solved in service of the bigger goals of creating a democracy and/or building a market. For example, the primers on the transition from authoritarianism to democracy relegated legal reform to secondary status, limiting their discussions of law to constitutions and electoral laws (e.g., Diamond and Plattner, 1996; O'Donnell and Schmitter, 1986). Missing was a recognition of the potential importance of law in building legitimacy for the system as a whole and otherwise facilitating democracy. More recently, political scientists have begun to include the "rule of law" in their short list of prerequisites for democracy, but precisely what they mean by this term remains obscure (e.g., Linz and Stepan, 1996; Lijphart and Waisman, 1996). The literature focusing on the transition from the state socialist variant of authoritarianism to some form of democracy follows this same pattern (e.g., Bunce, 2000; Eckstein, Fleron, Hoffmann, and Reisinger, 1998). Oddly enough the studies of the economic transition by political scientists have been slower to integrate legal variables into the analysis (e.g., Johnson, 2001; Appel, 2000). Along similar lines, assessments of the linkages between the political and economic transition have become popular, but rarely integrate the legal transition (e.g., Roland, 2002; Melich, 2000; Przeworski, 1991). For political scientists, the dualistic (rather than triadic) nature of the transition from state socialism seems immutable (e.g., Kubicek, 1999; Bartlett, 1997).

Spurred by the growing disciplinary fascination with institutions, economists have been quicker to embrace the study of law as a means of understanding the transition. But like political scientists, legal reform is not their primary concern (e.g., Kornai, 2000). Law is deemed worthy of study because it has the potential to lower transaction costs and thereby facilitate the transition to capitalism. The initial optimism that legalizing private property would lead economic actors to embrace law has been tempered by the postprivatization reality in the postsocialist world. But the search for the institutional change or constellation of changes that will trigger the desired result continues. Economists have tested a wide range of hypotheses in an effort to find the key to the puzzle. Recognizing that having property rights on the books is not enough, they have explored the potential role of corporate governance regimes (e.g., Pistor 2001; LaPorta, Lopez-de-Silanes, and Shleifer, 1999; LaPorta, Lopez-de-Silanes, Shleifer, and Vishny, 1997) and cadastres (DeSoto, 2000), the level of corruption (e.g., Treisman, 2000; Kaufmann and Siegelbaum, 1997), and the impact of centuries-old choices of legal structure (i.e., the division between civil law and common law traditions). For the most part, they eschew cultural explanations and seek answers in the structure of institutions and the content of laws. Their desire to compare large numbers of cases and to explore a variety of explanatory variables mandates the use of statistical methods. Even causal variables that have traditionally resisted quantification, such as legal custom and levels of equality under the law, have been subjected to this method (e.g., Berkowitz, Pistor, and Richard, 2003; Glaeser and Shleifer, 2002; World Bank, 2001). By coding the experiences of a large number of countries and using statistical methods to analyze the results, these scholars have generated a series of intriguing models of how legal systems work and what sorts of small changes might give rise to profound alterations in behavior. What has unfortunately been lost in the mix is the descriptive detail of individual countries. This approach leaves no room for idiosyncracies within legal systems that can arise as the result of factors such as political pressure and/or ethnic conflict.

Indexes that attempt to measure the level of such elusive qualities in the legal system as the "rule of law," "judicial independence," and "transparency" have blossomed and are regularly integrated into analyses of the transition. The use of indexes is most prevalent among economists (e.g., World Bank, 2001: 117–32; Johnson, Kaufmann, and Shleifer, 1997), but has also grown popular among political scientists (e.g., Fish, 1998; Hellman, 1997) and legal scholars (e.g., Pistor, 2001; Buscaglia and Dakolias, 1999). Nongovernmental organizations have been instrumental in the creation of several of them, albeit with heavy funding from institutional and/or country-based development agencies (e.g., Freedom House, 2002; Transparency International, 2001; American Bar Association, 2001). The penchant for quantitative indicators of success (or at least demonstrable progress) is not new. Indeed, it is driven by the need of domestic governments and international funding agencies to justify their expenditures. Prior efforts at standardized measures, such as the number of laws passed or the number of lawyers or judges trained, were crude and unsatisfying. The current generation of scales is a major step forward in their use of econometric methods that allow for the inclusion of many contributory factors in assigning a single grade. As with any scale of this sort, their value depends on the accuracy of the country-specific information and the validity of the choices made when coding this information.

Economists have also made good use of surveys. Typically, their surveys are targeted at the behavior and attitudes of economic actors, rather than at general public opinion. There is, of course, nothing inherently innovative in this methodology. The originality lies in its application to settings that had previously been off-limits due to the fear on the part of the regimes in question of exposing the dysfunctional side of state socialism. Under state socialism, the access of Western social scientists to industrial enterprises was almost nonexistent. An effort was made to piece together a picture of how they operated through surveys of emigrés (e.g., Berliner, 1957; Granick, 1954). This path-breaking work allowed for some understanding of how the official economy (as laid out by the national economic plan) operated in an uneasy partnership with the so-called "second" economy, and how these unofficial and illegal transactions actually lubricated the system (e.g., Grossman, 1977). Probing more deeply and systematically into the relational side of state socialism was simply impossible as long as the system itself endured. Its collapse opened up the opportunity to study the role of law in the economy in new ways and a number of economists have risen to the challenge. Some have focused on specific countries (e.g., Hendley, Murrell, and Ryterman, 2000; Gray and Holle, 1998), while others have fielded surveys across Eastern Europe and the former Soviet Union (e.g., Johnson, McMillan, and Woodruff, 2000). These snapshots of behavior and attitudes at a given point in time provide valuable information, yet there are certain sacrifices of depth in the pursuit of breadth. Designers of multicountry surveys often have to raise the level of generality of their questions in order to make them work across a set of diverse legal systems and, as a result, forego the detail that single-country surveys generate (e.g., Lee and Meagher, 2001; Hellman, Jones, Kaufmann, and Shankerman, 2000). Thanks to this survey work, a more complete and in-focus picture has emerged of the extent to which law meets the needs of, and is used by, economic actors. It suggests that law is not nearly as marginalized as had previously been believed. Some resistance to this view is apparent within the scholarly community. The reasons why are less apparent. Perhaps they stem from a reluctance to abandon long-held beliefs and to abandon a convenient scapegoat for economic failures.

The creation of, and increased reliance on, quantitative indicators of legal development by social scientists of all stripes allows hypotheses to be generated and tested in the abstract. Although appealing in terms of speed, the validity of these rapid responses deserve to be questioned. Transition is an inherently unstable process and would seem ill-suited to being captured in one or two statistically generated scores. At a minimum, the conclusions ought to be verified (at least occasionally) through ethnographic methods. But the disenchantment with "area studies" within the academy has devalued this style of research and has discouraged young scholars from gaining the skills and knowledge necessary to carry it out. The time required and the lack of appreciation of the value added has led policy makers and funders to spurn qualitative approaches. Yet the price paid for this disdain may be high. Policy makers rely on the diagnoses produced in reliance on the indexes and similar indicators in designing legislative and institutional change. If the assessment is not on target, then the solution may end up doing more harm than good or, at best, lying dormant.

Next Steps?

The logic of the argument that policy solutions should be preceded by careful research to establish the existence and parameters of the problems seems compelling. Yet time and time again, this simple prescription is ignored. The need to investigate how economic actors actually used (or ignored) law was particularly pressing in this latest iteration of legal development. Thanks to the penchant for secrecy and the incentives to sugarcoat the truth that were embedded into state socialism, the level of knowledge about law in action was low and unreliable. These gaps deserve to be filled. Research is needed that looks back to the era of state socialism and tries to make sense of the conflicting versions of the role of law. Likewise, the present-day status of law and the extent to which that is changing in transition countries are questions that could easily occupy a small army of researchers for many years. Particularly lacking are studies of the process of change.

Such empirical work could serve as the foundation for theory building. The question of how and why societies embrace or reject law as a mechanism of ordering economic life is one that has vexed legal scholars for centuries. Much of the theoretical work is grounded in the experience of the Middle Ages, during which a transition to the market was experienced in many parts of the world (e.g., Greif, 1992; Milgrom, North, and Weingast, 1990; Weber, 1967). Some of the insights gleaned from this earlier sea change can be put to good use in making sense of present-day changes. But the profound differences between the two periods complicate matters. A rich body of empirical studies from across the region would allow scholars to isolate the similarities and, by raising the level of abstraction, to put forward hypotheses as to the catalysts for making law meaningful for economic actors in the aftermath of state socialism. Ideally, once proven, this theory could then be tested in other postauthoritarian settings.

The first decade of legal reform efforts on the part of foreign governments and multilateral agencies aimed at the former communist world cries out for a sober assessment. Why were the tactics that had been shown to be ineffective decades earlier brought out of mothballs? Why were the agencies pushing legal reform so insistent on doing it at breakneck speed? The critiques that have been written do not address these fundamental questions. Instead, they rarely rise above finger-pointing (e.g., Cohen, 2000; Weidel, 1998). They tend to focus more on personalities and scandal than on whether the basic approach was misguided. Scholars of international organizations have begun to explore whether the culture of multilateral lending agencies dictates a repetition of past patterns of behavior. But these studies remain mostly at the level of theory, rarely venturing into detailed examinations of how reforms were carried out and whether they have had any positive impact (e.g., Barnett and Finnemore, 1999).

References

Adelman, Sammy and Paliwala, Abdul (eds.) (1993) *Law and Crisis in the Third World*. New York: H. Zill.

Ajani, Gianmaria (1995) "By chance and prestige: Legal transplants in Russia and Eastern Europe," *American Journal of Comparative Law* 43: 93–117.

Alexander, Gregory S. and Skąpska, Grażyna (eds.) (1994) *A Fourth Way? Privatization, Property, and the Emergence of New Market Economies*. New York: Routledge.

Alexandrov, Stanimir and Petkov, Latchezar (1998) "Paving the way for Bulgaria's accession to the European Union," *Fordham International Law Journal* 21: 587–601.

American Bar Association (2001) *Judicial Reform Index for Bosnia and Herzegovina*. Washington, DC: American Bar Association and Central and East European Law Initiative.

Appel, Hilary (2000) "The ideological determinants of liberal economic reform: The case of privatization," *World Politics* 52: 520–49.

Åslund, Anders (1995) *How Russia Became a Market Economy*. Washington, DC: The Brookings Institution.

Banaian, King (1999) *The Ukrainian Economy since Independence*. Northampton, MA: Edward Elgar Publishing.

Barnett, Michael N. and Finnemore, Martha (1999) "The politics, power, and pathologies of international organizations," *International Organization* 53: 699–723.

Barry, Donald D., Ginsburgs, George, and Maggs, Peter B. (eds.) (1977–9) *Soviet Law After Stalin: Parts I–III*. Leyden: A.W. Sijthoff.

Bartlett, David L. (1997) *The Political Economy of Dual Transformations: Market Reform and Democratization in Hungary*. Ann Arbor: University of Michigan Press.

Berkowitz, Daniel, Pistor, Katharina, and Richard, Jean-Francois (2003) "Economic development, legality, and the transplant effect," *European Economic Review* 47: 165–95.

Berliner, Joseph S. (1957) *Factory and Manager in the USSR*. Cambridge, MA: Harvard University Press.

Biernat, Stanisław (1994) "The uneasy breach with socialized ownership: Legal aspects of privatization of state-owned enterprises in Poland," in Gregory S. Alexander and Grażyna Skąpska (eds.), *A Fourth Way? Privatization, Property, and the Emergence of New Market Economies*. New York: Routledge, pp. 19–32.

Black, Bernard, Kraakman, Reinier, and Hay, Jonathon (1996) "Corporate law from scratch," in Roman Frydman, Cheryl W. Gray, and Andrzej Rapaczynski (eds.), *Corporate Governance in Central Europe and Russia: Insiders and the State*, vol. 2. Budapest: Central European University Press, pp. 245–302.

Black, Bernard, Kraakman, Reinier, and Tarassova, Anna (2000) "Russian privatization and corporate governance: What went wrong?" *Stanford Law Review* 52: 1731–808.

Blumenfeld, Lane (1996) "Russia's new civil code: The legal foundation for Russia's emerging market economy," *The International Lawyer* 30: 471–515.

Boner, Roger Alan and Kovacic, William E. (1997) "Antitrust policy in Ukraine," *George Washington Journal of International Law and Economics* 31: 1–48.

Braguinsky, Serguey and Yavlinsky, Grigory (2000) *Incentives and Institutions: The Transition to a Market Economy in Russia*. Princeton, NJ: Princeton University Press.

Broadent, Christian L. and McMillian, Amanda M. (1998) "Russia and the World Trade Organization: Will TRIPS be a stumbling block to accession?" *Duke Journal of Comparative & International Law* 8: 519–62.

Brown, J. Robert (1995) "Order from disorder: The development of the Russian securities market," *University of Pennsylvania Journal of International Business Law* 15: 49–71.

Bunce, Valerie (2000) "Comparative democratization: Big and bounded generalizations," *Comparative Political Studies* 33: 703–34.

Buscaglia, Edgardo and Dakolias, Maria (1999) *Comparative International Study of Court Performance Indicators: A Descriptive and Analytical Account*. Washington, DC: World Bank.

Bush, Larry S. (1999) "Romanian regulation of trade unions and collective bargaining," *Cornell International Law Journal* 32: 319–66.

Carothers, Thomas (1999) *Aiding Democracy Abroad: The Learning Curve*. Washington, DC: Carnegie Endowment for International Peace.

Carty, Anthony (ed.) (1992) *Law and Development*. New York: New York University Press.

Coase, R.H. (1988) *The Firm the Market and the Law*. Chicago: University of Chicago Press.

Coffee, John C., Jr. (1999) "Privatization and corporate governance: The lessons from securities market failure," *Iowa Journal of Corporate Law* 25: 1–39.

Cohen, Stephen F. (2000) *Failed Crusade: America and the Tragedy of Post-Communist Russia*. New York: Norton.

Cole, Daniel H. (1995) "Poland's progress: Environmental protection in a period of transition," *Parker School Journal of East European Law* 2: 279–319.

DeSoto, Hernando (2000) *The Mystery of Capital: Why Capitalism Triumphs in the West and Fails Everywhere Else*. New York: Basic Books.

Diamond, Larry and Plattner, Marc F. (eds.) (1996) *The Global Resurgence of Democracy*, 2nd edn. Baltimore: Johns Hopkins University Press.

Earle, John S. and Saul Estrin (2001) "Privatization and the structure of enterprise ownership," in Brigitte Granville and Peter Oppenheimer (eds.), *Russia's Post-Communist Economy*. Oxford: Oxford University Press, pp. 173–212.

Eckstein, Harry, Fleron, Frederic J. Jr., Hoffmann, Erik P., and Reisinger, William M. (1998) *Can Democracy Take Root in Post-Soviet Russia? Explorations in State-Society Relations*. Lanham, MD: Rowan & Littlefield.

Estrin, Saul and Wright, Mike (1999) "Corporate governance in the former Soviet Union: An overview," *Journal of Comparative Economics* 27: 398–421.

Ewald, William (1995) "Comparative jurisprudence (II): The logic of legal transplants," *American Journal of Comparative Law* 43: 319–66.

Feifer, George (1964) *Justice in Moscow*. New York: Simon and Schuster.

Feofanov, Yuri and Barry, Donald D. (1996) *Politics and Justice in Russia: Major Trials of the Post-Stalin Era*. Armonk, NY: M.E. Sharpe.

Fish, M. Steven (1998) "The determinants of economic reform in the post-communist world," *East European Politics and Societies* 12: 31–78.

Fox, Eleanor M. (1997) "The Central European nations and the EU waiting room: Why must the Central European nations adopt the competition law of the European Union?" *Brooklyn Journal of International Law* 23: 351–63.

Fraenkel, Ernst (1941) *The Dual State: A Contribution to the Theory of Dictatorship*, trans. E.A. Shils. London: Oxford University Press.

Freedom House (2002) "The world's most repressive regimes 2002," Special Report to the 58th Session of the United Nations Commission on Human Rights, Geneva. Available online at <www.freedomhouse.org>.

Frydman, Roman, Rapaczynski, Andrzej, and Earle, John S. (1993a) *The Privatization Process in Central Europe*. Budapest: Central European University Press.

Frydman, Roman, Rapaczynski, Andrzej, and Earle, John S. (1993b) *The Privatization Process in Russia, Ukraine, and the Baltic States*. Budapest: Central European University Press.

Frye, Timothy (2001) "Keeping shop: The value of the rule of law in Warsaw and Moscow," in Peter Murrell (ed.), *Assessing the Value of Law in Transition Economies*. Ann Arbor: University of Michigan Press, pp. 211–28.

Gardner, James A. (1980) *Legal Imperialism: American Lawyer and Foreign Aid in Latin America*. Madison: University of Wisconsin Press.

Glaeser, Edward L. and Shleifer, Andrei (2002) "Legal origins," *Quarterly Journal of Economics* 117: 1193–229.

Gilpin, Robert and Gilpin, Jean M. (2000) *The Challenge of Global Capitalism*. Princeton, NJ: Princeton University Press.

Granick, David (1954) *Management of the Industrial Firm in the USSR*. New York: Columbia University Press.

Gray, Cheryl W. and Holle, Arnold (1998) "Classical exit processes in Poland: Court conciliation, bankruptcy, and state enterprise liquidation," in Leszek Balcerowicz, Cheryl W. Gray, and Iraj Hoshi (eds.), *Enterprise Exit Processes in Transition Economies: Downsizing, Workouts, and Liquidation*. Budapest: Central European University Press, pp. 207–48.

Greif, Avner (1992) "Institutions and international trade: Lessons from the commercial revolution," *American Economic Review* 82: 128–33.

Grossman, Gregory (1997) "The 'second economy' in the USSR," *Problems of Communism* 26: 25–40.

Hay, Jonathon R. and Shleifer, Andrei (1998) "Private enforcement of public laws: A theory of legal reform," *American Economic Review* 88: 398–403.

Hayden, Robert M. (1990) *Social Courts in Theory and Practice: Yugoslav Workers' Courts in Comparative Perspective*. Philadelphia: University of Pennsylvania Press.

Helleiner, Gerald K. (2001) "Markets, politics, and globalization: Can the global market be civilized?" *Global Governance* 7: 243–63.

Hellman, Joel (1997) "Constitutions and economic reform in the post-communist transitions," in Jeffrey D. Sachs and Katharina Pistor (eds.), *The Rule of Law and Economic Reform in Russia*. Boulder, CO: Westview Press, pp. 55–78.

Hellman, Joel, Jones, Geraint, Kaufmann, Daniel, and Shankerman, Mark (2000) "Measuring governance and state capture: The role of bureaucrats and firms in shaping the business environment: Results of a firm-level study across 20 transition economies," EBRD Working Paper No. 51. London: European Bank for Reconstruction and Development.

Hendley, Kathryn (1996) *Trying to Make Law Matter: Legal Reform and Labor Law in the Soviet Union*. Ann Arbor: University of Michigan Press.

Hendley, Kathryn (2001) "Beyond the tip of the iceberg: Business disputes in Russia," in Peter Murrell (ed.), *Assessing the Value of Law in Transition Economies*. Ann Arbor: University of Michigan Press, pp. 29–55.

Hendley, Kathryn (2002) "Suing the state in Russia," *Post-Soviet Affairs* 18: 122–47.

Hendley, Kathryn, Murrell, Peter, and Ryterman, Randi (2002) "Law, relationships, and private enforcement: Transactional strategies of Russian enterprises," *Europe-Asia Studies* 52: 627–56.

Jersild, Thomas M. (2001) "Duties of company directors: The developing law in Macedonia," *Review of Central & East European Law* 27: 71–91.

Johnson, Juliet (2001) "Path contingency in postcommunist transformations," *Comparative Politics* 33: 253–74.

Johnson, Simon, Kaufmann, Daniel, and Shleifer, Andrei (1997) "The unofficial economy in transition," *Brookings Papers on Economic Activity* 2: 159–239.

Johnson, Simon and Loveman, Gary (1995) *Starting Over in Eastern Europe: Entrepreneurship and Economic Renewal*. Boston: Harvard Business School Press.

Johnson, Simon, McMillan, John, and Woodruff, Christopher (2000) "Entrepreneurs and the ordering of institutional reform: Poland, Slovakia, Romania, Russia, and Ukraine compared," *Economics of Transition* 8: 1–36.

Kaminskaya, Dina (1982) *Final Judgment: My Life as a Soviet Defense Attorney*; trans. Michael Glenny. New York: Simon and Schuster.

Katkov, George (1969) *The Trial of Bukharin*. New York: Stein and Day.

Kaufmann, Daniel and Siegelbaum, Paul (1997) "Privatization and corruption in transition economies," *Journal of International Affairs* 50: 419–58.

Kolarska-Bobinska, Lena (1994) "Privatization in Poland: The evolution of opinions and interests 1988–1998," in Gregory S. Alexander and Grażyna Skąpska (eds.), *A Fourth Way? Privatization, Property, and the Emergence of New Market Economies*. New York: Routledge, pp. 119–37.

Kornai, Jànos (1990) *The Road to a Free Economy: Shifting from a Socialist System: The Example of Hungary*. New York: W.W. Norton.

Kornai, Jànos (2000) "What the change of system from socialism to capitalism does and does not mean," *Journal of Economic Perspectives* 14: 27–42.

Krygier, Martin (1990) "Marxism and the rule of law: reflections after the collapse of communism," *Law & Social Inquiry* 15: 633–63.

Kubicek, Paul (1999) *Unbroken Ties: The State, Interest Associations, and Corporatism in Post-Soviet Ukraine*. Ann Arbor: University of Michigan Press.

Kurczewski, Jacek and Frieske, Kazimierz (1977) "Some problems in the legal regulation of the activities of economic institutions," *Law & Society Review* 11: 489–505.

Kuznetsov, Andrei and Kuznetsova, Olga (1996) "Privatisation, shareholding and the efficiency argument: Russian experience," *Europe–Asia Studies* 48: 1173–85.

LaPorta, Rafael, Lopez-de-Silanes, Florencio, Shleifer, Andrei, and Vishny, Robert (1997) "Legal determinants of external finance," *Journal of Finance* 52: 1131–50.

LaPorta, Rafael, Lopez-de-Silanes, Florencio, and Shleifer, Andrei (1999) "Corporate ownership around the world," *Journal of Finance* 54: 471–517.

Lasok, Dominik (ed.) (1973–5) *Polish Civil Law*, vols. 1–4. Leyden, The Netherlands: A.W. Sijthoff.

Lee, Young and Meagher, Patrick (2001) "Misgovernance or misperception? Law and finance in Central Asia," in Peter Murrell (ed.), *Assessing the Value of Law in Transition Economies*. Ann Arbor: University of Michigan Press, pp. 133–79.

Lijphart, Arend, and Waisman, Carlos H. (1996) *Institutional Design in New Democracies: Eastern Europe and Latin America*. Boulder, CO: Westview Press.

Linz, Juan J. and Stepan, Alfred (1996) *Problems of Democratic Transition and Consolidation: Southern Europe, South America, and Post-Communist Europe*. Baltimore: Johns Hopkins University Press.

Litvinov, Pavel (1972) *The Trial of the Four; A Collection of Materials on the Case of Galanskov, Ginzburg, Dobrovolsky & Lashkova 1967–68*, trans. Janis Sapiets, Hilary Sternberg, and Daniel Weissbort. London: Longman.

Los, Maria and Zybertowicz, Andrzej (2000) *Privatizing the Police State: The Case of Poland*. New York: St. Martin's Press.

Lumelsky, Grey (1997) "Does Russia need a securities law?" *Journal of International Law & Business* 18: 111–64.

Maggs, Peter B. (1992) "Legal forms of doing business in Russia," *North Carolina Journal of International Law and Commercial Regulation* 18: 173–92.

Markovits, Inga (1995) *Imperfect Justice: An East–West German Diary*. New York: Oxford University Press.

Melich, Jiri S. (2000) "The relationship between the political and the economic in the transformations in Eastern Europe: Continuity and discontinuity and the problem of models," *East European Quarterly* 34: 131–57.

Merry, Sally Engle (1991) "Law and colonialism," *Law & Society Review* 25: 890–922.

Milgrom, Paul R., North, Douglass C. and Weingast, Barry R. (1990) "The role of institutions in the revival of trade: The law merchant, private judges, and the Champagne fairs," *Economics and Politics* 2: 1–23.

Miller, Jeffrey B. and Petranov, Stefan (2000) "The first wave of mass privatization in Bulgaria and its immediate aftermath," *Economics of Transition* 8: 225–50.

Murray, Scott Tanner (1999) *The Politics of Lawmaking in Post-Mao China: Institutions, Processes and Democratic Prospects*. Oxford: Clarendon Press.

Nichols, Philip M. (1997) "The viability of transplanted law: Kazakhstani reception of a transplanted foreign investment code," *University of Pennsylvania Journal of International Economic Law* 18: 1235–79.

Nonet, Philippe and Selznick, Philip (1978) *Law and Society in Transition: Toward Responsive Law*. New York: Octagon Books.

North, Douglass C. (1990) *Institutions, Institutional Change and Economic Performance*. Cambridge, UK: Cambridge University Press.

O'Donnell, Guillermo and Schmitter, Philippe C. (1986) *Transitions from Authoritarian Rule: Tentative Conclusions about Uncertain Democracies*. Baltimore: Johns Hopkins University Press.

Olson, Mancur (2000) *Power and Prosperity: Outgrowing Communist and Capitalist Dictatorships*. New York: Basic Books.

Palvolgyi, Rita, and Herbai, Istvan (1997) "Public participation in cooperative planning: A local tax issue in Nagykanizsa, Hungary," *Annals of the American Academy of Political and Social Science* 552: 75–85.

Pistor, Katharina (2001) "Law as a determinant for equity market development – the experience of transition economies," in Peter Murrell (ed.), *Assessing the Value of Law in Transition Economies*. Ann Arbor: University of Michigan Press, pp. 249–87.

Posner, Richard A. (1998) "Creating a legal framework for economic development," *The World Bank Research Observer* 13: 1–11.

"Privatization in Poland: An interview with Jeffrey Sachs" (1992) *Suffolk Transnational Law Journal* 15: 441–67.

Przeworski, Adam (1991) *Democracy and the Market: Political and Economic Reforms in Eastern Europe and Latin America*. Cambridge, UK: Cambridge University Press.

Raiser, Thomas (1994) "The challenge of privatization in the former East Germany: reconciling the conflict between individual rights and social needs," in Gregory S. Alexander and Grażyna Skąpska (eds.), *A Fourth Way? Privatization, Property, and the Emergence of New Market Economies*. New York: Routledge, pp. 3–18.

Roland, Gérard (2002) "The political economy of transition," *Journal of Economic Perspectives* 16: 29–50.

Sewerynski, Michal (1997) "Prospects for the development of labor law and social security law in Central and Eastern Europe in the twenty-first century," *Comparative Labor Law Journal* 18: 182–203.

Sharlet, Robert (1977) "Stalinism and Soviet legal culture," in Robert C. Tucker (ed.), *Stalinism: Essays in Historical Interpretation*. New York: W.W. Norton, pp. 155–79.

Shelley, Louise I. (1986) "Soviet courts as vehicles for political maneuver," *Soviet Union* 13: 163–86.

Shihata, Ibrahim F.I. (1995) *The World Bank in a Changing World: Selected Essays and Lectures*, vol. II. The Hague: Martinus Nijhoff Publishers.

Simis, Konstantin M. (1982) *USSR: The Corrupt Society*, trans. Jacqueline Edwards and Mitchell Schneider. New York: Simon and Schuster.

Smith, Gordon B. (1979) "Procuratorial campaigns," in Donald D. Barry, George Ginsburgs, and Peter B. Maggs (eds.), *Soviet Law After Stalin: Part III: Soviet Institutions and the Administration of Laws*. Leyden, The Netherlands: A.W. Sijthoff, pp. 143–67.

Solomon, Peter H., Jr. (1996) *Soviet Criminal Justice Under Stalin*. Cambridge, UK: Cambridge University Press.

Solomon, Peter H., Jr. and Foglesong, Todd S. (2000) *Courts and Transition in Russia: The Challenge of Judicial Reform*. Boulder, CO: Westview Press.

Stark, David, and Bruszt, Laszlo (1998) *Postsocialist Pathways: Transforming Politics and Property in East Central Europe*. Cambridge, UK: Cambridge University Press.

Steinberg, Richard H. (1997) "Trade-environment negotiations in the EU, NAFTA, and WTO: Regional trajectories of rule development," *American Journal of International Law* 91: 231–80.

Stephan, Johannes (1999) *Economic Transition in Hungary and East Germany: Gradualism and Shock Therapy in Catch-up Development*. New York: St. Martin's Press.

Transparency International (2001) *Global Corruption Report* (2001). Available online at <www.globalcorruptionreport.org>.

Treisman, Daniel (2000) "The causes of corruption: A cross-national survey," *Journal of Public Economics* 76: 399–457.

Turner, Karen G., Feinerman, James V., and Guy, R. Kent (eds.) (2000) *The Limits of the Rule of Law in China*. Seattle: University of Washington Press.

Ulc, Otto (1972) *The Judge in a Communist State: A View From Within*. Columbus: Ohio University Press.

Unger, Roberto Mangabeira (1976) *Law in Modern Society: Toward a Criticism of Social Theory*. New York: Free Press.

Watson, Alan (1991) *Legal Origins and Legal Change*. London: The Hambledon Press.

Weber, Max (1967) *Max Weber on Law in Economy and Society*, ed. Max Rheinstein. Cambridge, MA: Harvard University Press.

Weidel, Janine R. (1998) *Collision and Collusion: The Strange Case of Western Aid to Eastern Europe 1989–1998*. New York: St. Martin's Press.

World Bank (1996) *World Development Report: From Plan to Market*. New York: Oxford University Press.

World Bank (1997) *World Development Report: The State in a Changing World*. New York: Oxford University Press.

World Bank (2001) *World Development Report: Building Institutions for Markets*. New York: Oxford University Press.

33

Economic Globalization and the Law in the Twenty-first Century

Francis Snyder

Economic Globalization and Law

Globalization and the development of new legal forms and regimes during the past half century have gone hand-in-hand. The term "globalization," and even its existence, are contested (cf. Robertson, 1992; Hirst and Thompson, 1996; Giddens, 1990; Sassen, 1996; T. L. Friedman, 1999). However, globalization is not new, it cannot be reduced merely to market integration, still less to the neoliberal political and economic project of free trade and open markets, and its ultimate destination is unknown, depending as much on politics and power as economics. Here, it is taken to mean "a process (or set of processes) which embodies a transformation in the spatial organization of social relations and transactions – assessed in terms of their extensity, intensity, velocity and impact – generating transcontinental or interregional flows and networks of activity, interaction, and the exercise of power" (Held, McGrew, Goldblatt, and Perraton, 1999: 16).

Among the main shaping factors have been the tremendous growth of multinational companies and international production networks, new technology, changes in the nature and form of work, and the rise of new actors on the international scene. Associated with this transformation have been numerous legal changes, both on a transnational scale and within countries (Blomley, Delaney, and Ford, 2001). The early years of the twenty-first century witness a startling variety of new legal forms and regimes which sometimes differ substantially in nature, content, scale, and operation from the largely state-based system of governance of the past several centuries. A multiplicity of other sites of governance complement, supplement, or compete with the state, hence the term "governance" instead of "government." While sometimes eroded or even reconfigured, the state remains powerful, if not predominant, with the relative strength of different institutions, norms, and dispute resolution processes depending frequently on the specific context (Jayasuriya, 2001).

While globalization thus raises a number of challenges for thinking about law (Arnaud, 1998; Twining, 2000; Delmas-Marty, 1998; Chemillier-Gendreau and Moulier Boutang, 2001), the sheer volume of published work makes a comprehensive survey impossible here. This chapter aims instead to provide a retrospective and prospective assessment of the field, a brief guide to the literature which at the same time seeks to set the agenda for the future. It deals mainly with the legal effects of economic globalization, while recognizing that globalization is not simply economic, and that many aspects of globalization have implications for law. It focuses primarily on work within the broad fields of sociology of law, international relations, and political economy of law, as these are the main disciplinary touchstones of writing on law and globalization, It focuses mainly on literature in English, partly because this represents most published work so far, since many scholars regardless of mother tongue publish in English, and partly because English-language work has tended to establish and define the field. In the long run, however, it is necessary to transcend this parochial view, and the article provides a stepping-stone for doing so. Human rights or law and development are not discussed in detail, because they are dealt with in other chapters.

INTERNATIONALIZATION OF LEGAL FIELDS

During the past several decades globalization has affected many if not all areas of law to a striking extent. The first substantial treatment of law and globalization (Trubek, Dezalay, Buchanan, and Davis, 1994) used Bourdieu's concept of social fields (e.g., Bourdieu, 1987) to show how new transnational and global economic and political processes and political trends changed the role of lawyers, the logic of legal practices, and the nature of the legal field. National legal fields became more "internationalized," in two senses. First, legal and political arenas that had previously been mainly national in terms of background assumptions, actors, and orientation were increasingly influenced by "external" factors. Second, purportedly "domestic" decisions were conditioned, shaped, or even actually made elsewhere as transnational legal regimes penetrated national legal fields. These changes enhanced the status and role of actors with international linkages and expertise, as well as the power of certain states relative to others.

More recent research by Sassen (2002: 195) refers to the "denationalization" of much of contemporary rule making. It addresses the question of the relationship of "international" norms to "domestic" norms in a situation in which the two are so intertwined that it is no longer possible to assert that that one set of norms are international and another set are national. Many so-called "national" norms have in effect been "denationalized," since their source, content, logic, and even interpretation or application owes much if not everything to international, transnational, or intergovernmental institutions, norms, and dispute resolution processes. This is not a question of extraterritoriality, but rather of the extent to which the norms of nation-states, or of regional organizations such as the European Union (EU), are based on or impregnated by "international" norms, including World Trade Organization (WTO) international trade rules, codes of conduct, standards, or the results of international dispute settlement processes. Formally speaking, the sources of "international" and "national" norms are different, and this difference has its legal doctrinal importance in each of the two institutional and normative settings.

However, the traditional distinction between "domestic" and "foreign," or between "national" and "international," often does not adequately capture the political origins, legal content, cultural understandings, economic assumptions, and social practices of contemporary law, for example, the need for certain types of specialized legal professionals.

Nevertheless, some legal fields have always been more internationalized than others. Areas of law most closely connected with international trade and multinational companies, such as international business contracts (Bonell, 1994), antitrust law and competition policy (Graham and Richardson, 1997), high finance, intellectual property (Symposium Issue, 1996–7), the Internet and new technology (Lessig, 1999), cybercrime (Capeller, 2001), labor and social law (Sengenberger and Campbell, 1994; Drummonds, 2000), and now environmental law have been affected more than family law and property law. But even discounting for our lack of empirical knowledge of the effects of globalization on many areas of law, it is clear that the internationalized sector has tended to grow, despite national and local diversity (L.M. Friedman, 2001).

In understanding the implications of this trend, however, it is useful to bear in mind Krasner's (1999) distinction between four concepts of sovereignty: international legal sovereignty, Westphalian sovereignty, interdependence sovereignty, and domestic sovereignty. Quiggin (2001), for example, has contended that the loss of interdependence sovereignty does not necessary mean the erosion of Westphalian sovereignty: a decline in a state's capacity to control flows of people and goods across its frontiers does not inevitably lead to the adoption of neoliberal economic policies.

The internationalization of legal fields is often viewed as being more or less equivalent to Americanization (Hardt and Negri, 2000). The American way of law, embedded in a particular variety of capitalism (Hall and Soskice, 2001), has been exported by multinational business, large law firms, international organizations, development programs, cultural archetypes, and reception or imposition of US law in many other countries. Often this amounts merely to "thin globalization," in the sense of a thin veneer covering an often quite different social, cultural, and legal reality, so that the future social practices, normative content, and legal culture of globalized law remain contested (see Appelbaum, Felstiner, and Gessner, 2001). Nevertheless, Shapiro's (1993: 38) remark that "much of the time, the globe will turn out to be the U.S. and Western Europe with shadowy addenda" reflects the fact that the center of gravity of the global economy lies in the transatlantic relations between the United States and the EU, notably in foreign direct investment and capital market relations (Sassen, 2000); this is unfortunate because it testifies to the extremely unequal distribution of wealth in the world today. A similar view is captured in more theoretical terms by Santos's distinction between globalized localism and localized globalism: the former refers to the process by which local phenomena are successfully globalized, while the latter denotes the impact of transnational practices on local conditions (Santos, 1995; see also Darian-Smith, 1998). In the legal world, given the fact of US hegemony in the international political economy, the localisms that have been most frequently globalized are American. A striking example is intellectual property protection through the WTO Agreement on Trade-Related Aspects of Intellectual Property (TRIPS) (Sell, 1999), even though, as Shaffer (2000) shows, the United States itself is deeply affected by external pressures and international networks.

GOVERNANCE OF GLOBALIZATION

Different empirical views and normative assessments of this imbalance of power are reflected, directly or indirectly, in ideas about how globalization is governed. Five main conceptions have emerged so far: (1) contract, (2) hierarchy, (3) networks, (4) *lex mercatoria*, and (5) sites of global legal pluralism. To some extent these perspectives overlap, but they differ fundamentally in their starting points, conceptual frameworks, and the importance they accord to different factors. Each provides only a partial view, and further work is needed to explore their points of convergence or divergence, as well as possible synergies.

Contract

In this view, globalization is governed essentially by contracts between nominally equal parties, such as states, companies, or individuals, whose agreement is consecrated either in bilateral or multilateral form. An example is the 1997 OECD Convention on Combatting Bribery (Bontrager Unzicker, 2000). This view is usually associated with an emphasis on strong state sovereignty in external political and economic relations. It also frequently underpins the law of international business transactions. In the first case the main actors are states, while in the second they are businesses, usually multinational firms or partners in international production networks.

Hierarchy

A second perspective, which emerged partly from studies of European integration, focuses on multilevel governance, according to which different levels of governance interact, sometimes with regard to the same subject matter, sometimes with regard to different areas of social life (Marks, 2001). Coordination is required to ensure the coherence of the system. Federal systems, such as the United States, Canada, Australia, or Germany illustrate this scenario. So too, on an international plane, do the North American Free Trade Association (NAFTA), the EU, and relations between the WTO and its members, which of course include federal states and regional organizations as well as unitary states. The Massachusetts "Burma" law illustrates the complexities of multilevel governance (Hellwig, 2000).

Networks

A third perspective focuses on transnational networks, which may be public, private, or a hybrid of the two. Transnational public networks, according to Slaughter (1997: 197), "offer the world a blueprint for the international architecture of the 21st century." Transgovernmental cooperation among judges or national regulators, for example, helps to strengthen the state through external cooperation and allows governments to benefit from the expertise of nonstate actors. However, executive agreements and transgovernmental networks involve substantial problems of democracy and accountability (see Picciotto, 2000; Slaughter, 2000). There also remains a fundamental contradiction between the power of the nation-state and further international integration (Picciotto, 1996–7).

Private networks usually include production alliances, cartels, business associations, and the use of coordination service firms, involving private regimes and informal industry norms and practices. In contrast to intergovernmental and transgovernmental networks, they rely primarily upon multinational corporations (Cutler, Haufler, and Porter, 1999). But private networks are not always based on business organizations. An example is the International Social and Environmental Accreditation and Labelling Alliance, which embraces seven international environmental networks, thus enlisting civil society in the formulation and enforcement of international private standards (Meidinger, 2001). Such arrangements raise equally serious problems of transparency, participation, and accountability. These issues require more research in the future.

While studies of private governance often draw substantially upon previous work on corporate governance (Hopt, Kanda, Roe, Wymeersch, and Prigge, 1998), they have gone further to focus on corporate control and accountability (McCahery, Picciotto, and Scott, 1993) and also to analyze new hybrid forms of international regulation, such as international business taxation (Picciotto, 1992). Hybrid networks play an important role in the governance of transatlantic relations between the United States and the EU (Bermann, Herdegen, and Lindseth, 2000; Pollack and Shaffer, 2001), even though the primary architects of these relations appear to have high-level intergovernmental (public) networks (see Pollack and Shaffer, 2001: 293). They are also significant in other types of international business regulation. In their important study of the globalization of regulation, as distinct from the globalization of firms or the globalization of markets, Braithwaite and Drahos (2000: 9) argue that "regulatory globalization is a process in which different types of actors use various mechanisms to push for or against principles." They analyze a wide variety of sectors, such as the environment, food, telecommunications, labor standards, and trade and competition.

Some scholars have argued that global regulation consists mainly in competitive interaction among different national legal systems, in other words, regulatory competition among public authorities (Bratton, McCahery, Picciotto, and Scott, 1996). However, others suggest that, in many fields, the legal framework of regulation takes the form of networks of regulatory agencies, often working together with private actors, thus relying on decentralized enforcement, for example through national agencies, rather than international or transnational enforcement (Jayasuriya, 1999). In either situation, transparency, dispute settlement, and capacity building may be more effective than coercion in inducing compliance (Chayes and Chayes, 1995). Such processes deserve more attention in the future.

Lex mercatoria

A fourth, related perspective concentrates on the *lex mercatoria*, the contemporary analog of the medieval law merchant which private actors used to organize trade and settle business disputes. Drawing on a longstanding tradition in comparative law (De Ly, 1992), modern writers have focused on the development of a private international trade law, notably contract law, and the growth of international commercial arbitration. The modern law merchant is a complex mix of public and private authority, which though designated as "private" plays an important role in allocating risks, regulating market access, and linking local and global domains (Cutler, 2001).

Recent research owes much to Teubner's (1983, 1993) concept of reflexive law, a self-governing system or form of regulated self-regulation. From this standpoint, *lex mercatoria* is a paradigm of the new global law. It consists less of detailed rules than of broad principles, such as good faith. Its boundaries are markets, professional communities, or social networks, not territories. Instead of being relatively autonomous from political institutions, it depends heavily on other social fields, being especially subject to economic pressures. It is not unified but decentered and non-hierarchical (see Teubner, 1997a, 1997c). Stimulated by globalization, it constantly breaks the hierarchical frame of the national constitution within which private rule making takes place, resulting in a new heterarchical frame, a characteristic of this new global nonstate law (Teubner, 1997b).

Its main institutional locus is international commercial arbitration (e.g., Kahn, 1989; CREDIMI, 2000). Resulting from international coalitions of private agents, it influences the size of markets just as the evolution of markets shapes legal doctrine and recourse to arbitration itself (Casella, 1996). Garth and Dezalay's important study (1996) shows empirically how international commercial arbitration has been socially constructed and how it contributes to the reorganization of hierarchies, modes of authority, and structures of power.

However, international commercial arbitration is not entirely independent of the nation-state, either in legal terms or in terms of the questions it raises about the role of law in society. Many of the same political and normative questions that have been posed within the framework of domestic constitutions gain in importance when raised at the international level. An example is the formation of a constitution, not necessarily in the sense of a written document, but rather in the sense of continuing processes of constitutionalization or, in Zumbansen's terms, of "precipitates of constitutional law" (2002: 431). Another is provided by empirical studies showing that local institutions, interest-specific institutions or even personal relationships may be more effective than universalistic norms in providing legal certainty for cross-border or international transactions (Gessner and Budak, 1998).

Sites of global legal pluralism

A fifth perspective combines public, private, and hybrid forms of governance with an emphasis on strategic action: the theory of sites of governance as part of global legal pluralism. Snyder (1999) argues that globalization is governed by the totality of strategically determined, situationally specific, and often episodic conjunctions of a multiplicity of sites throughout the world. Sites may be public, private, or mixed. Some are market-based, while others are polity-based. Each site has structural aspects and relational aspects. Structural aspects include institutions, norms, and dispute resolution processes. Relational aspects refer to the relations that a site has with other sites. For instance, sites may be hierarchically organized, autonomous, or even independent; competing or overlapping; part of the same or different regimes; or converging or diverging in terms of institutions, norms, or processes of dispute resolution. The totality of sites represents a new form of global legal pluralism.

Strategic actors, such as companies, governments, nongovernmental organizations (NGOs), and others, use the law and are shaped by it (Mytelka and Delapierre, 1999). In addition, they are fundamental in determining which sites are created, which survive, and how. They influence the development of sites, so that some take on more or less judicial and legal characteristics, and some do not. For example, the dramatic growth of global economic networks has had contradictory effects on recent attempts to develop constitutional systems based on regional integration. In the EU, globalization sustains and creates interests and relationships which tend to undercut traditional constitutionalism as mode of regional governance (see Snyder, 2000). Not surprising, it has provoked not only demands for the constitutionalization of global governance but also debates about its feasibility and desirability.

Research so far has focused mainly on the structural aspects of sites, and more work is needed on relations between sites. However, two examples can be given of research already done on intersite relations. Perhaps the most well-known illustration of the convergence of norms among several sites is the internationalization of human rights (Risse, Roppe, and Sikkink, 1999; Scott, 2001; Riles 2002). Another example is the social construction of the concept of "nonmarket economy" in the antidumping law of the United States, the EU, and the WTO (Snyder, 2001). It formed part of a specific legal discourse, which emerged from the gradual elaboration of a handful of basic principles and concepts into an international antidumping law repertoire during the Cold War. The relations between sites involved asymmetrical power relations, with the most importance influence being the United States.

New Norms and Institutions

Among the most striking developments in recent years is increased attention to norms (Haufler, 1999), in particular the emergence of "soft law" or rules of conduct that in principle are not legally binding but that nevertheless have practical and even legal effects (Snyder, 1993). Long familiar to international lawyers (see Shelton, 2000), it gained prominence during the 1970s in the form of international codes of conduct to govern the activities of multinational corporations (see, e.g., Nixon, 1987). During the 1990s, codes of conduct were elaborated increasingly by private actors, not by international organizations, both as codes among private actors and codes internal to private actors (Hepple, 1999), to the extent that Sobczak (2001) argues that they represent a new generation of codes of conduct as part of a transformation of global and corporate governance. These so-called "informal agreements" are often used because the obligations they embody are more equivocal and less visible than those contained in legally binding agreements (Lipson, 1991). Compared to hard law, soft law has the advantages of lower contracting costs and lower sovereignty costs, and is often better adapted to conditions of uncertainty or those requiring compromise (Abbott and Snidal, 2000).

To what extent does soft law actually work? This is a question, not about the boundaries between politics and law, but rather about the social effectiveness of different types of norms. The basic issue is whether soft law can provide the optimum institutional design for governing sensitive issues, on which companies, unions, NGOs, or governments do not initially agree, such as international standards concerning working conditions, human rights, or protection of the environment. This question is sometimes interpreted as seeking to reconcile economic interests and ethical considerations, but it is more properly read as referring to a balance between different kinds of economic interests and different kinds of ethical considerations.

Though focused initially on codes of conduct for multinational corporations, the debate about the legitimacy and efficacy of these norms is relevant also to the wide range of standards being produced by international standards organizations and other institutions (Salter, 1999). The best known are probably those of the International Standards Organization (ISO), the International Accounting Standards Committee (IASC), and debt security rating agencies such as Moody's and S&P. For example, IASC currently includes 153 professional accounting bodies in 112 countries and is responsible for developing and approving international accounting standards. IASC standards are not legally binding, so the IASC acts as a "strategic networker" (Braithwaite and Drahos, 2000: 121) to convince governmental actors to adopt and give legal force to its voluntary standards. Debt security rating agencies, such as Moody's and S&P, exercise significant powers of "governance without government": these nonstate institutions derive their international leverage from their gate-keeping role concerning investment funds sought by companies and governments (Sinclair, 1994).

Recently, Abbott and colleagues (Abbott, Keohane, Moravcsik, Slaughter, and Snidal, 2000) have proposed the concept of legalization as a systematic framework for analyzing these (and other) new norms and procedures. Legalization has three dimensions: the existence of legal obligations, the precision with which these obligations are defined, and the extent to which responsibility for dispute resolution is delegated to third parties. Each dimension is a continuum, composed of differences of degree, and each can vary independently of the others. Specific norms or specific procedures may be more or less legalized. Applying these ideas, Keohane, Moravcsik, and Slaughter (2000) define interstate dispute resolution and transnational dispute resolution as two ideal types, differing in independence from concrete state interests, access by parties other than states, and embeddedness in the sense that decisions can be implemented without governmental action. They argue that the transnational dispute resolution is more successful than interstate dispute resolution in controlling case loads and ensuring compliance, hence it limits the behavior of states to a greater extent.

In principle at least, the analytical framework does not assume that greater legalization is inherently superior to less legalization. Yet it is difficult to escape the conclusion that the concept of legalization is based implicitly on a dichotomous distinction between legal and nonlegal. The concept thus resembles earlier social theories of law based on an implicit teleology, such as modernization theory. This is despite the authors' effort to define the concept in terms of three dimensions and to articulate each dimension as a continuum. Indeed, the three dimensions themselves suggest that the authors prefer more legalization, not less. This is reinforced by the remark that "When future international legal scholars look back at . . . the end of the twentieth century, they probably will refer to the enormous expansion of the international judiciary as the single most important development of the post-Cold War age" (Romano, 1999: 709, quoted in Keohane et al., 2000: 457). Kahler (2000: 671) notes that the demand and supply of legalization depends heavily on the preferences of powerful states. Unfortunately, the analytical framework gives little weight to the role of power in determining the extent of delegation to third party dispute mechanisms (see Keohane et al, 2000: 459, n. 7). Hence it needs to be tempered by more attention to power and the political context in which law operates. In sum, further research is required in order to assess this general analytical framework.

DEMOCRATIZING GLOBAL GOVERNANCE

Globalization and its legal implications have provoked a vigorous, often acrimonious, and sometimes violent debate about the democratization of global governance (Klein, 2000). Among the many reasons for this are that globalization has made substantial demands on traditional international institutions and has also been embodied in new legal forms, regimes, and institutions, which to the average person seem (and frequently are) remote, fundamentally different from general rules of law made by public authorities, lacking in transparency, and unaccountable. The creation of the WTO, with a wide mandate, based on the "single undertaking principle," and characterized by binding dispute resolution, has extended international trade law forcefully into areas that previously were solely under national jurisdiction, thus blurring the traditional distinction between the "international" and the "domestic" (Trebilcock and House, 1999). Partly as a consequence, and partly as a result of other aspects of globalization, areas such as the environment (Shaffer, 2001; Wiener, 2001), public health (Fidler, 1999; Jost, 2000), food safety, and social welfare systems no longer fall within the province of a single nation-state alone and can no longer be dealt with adequately on this basis. Together with the rise of new international or transnational institutions and norms, the partial reconfiguration of the state means that norms "created somewhere else" affect daily life in ways that were previously inconceivable.

In addition, as a result of the blurring of the public–private distinction, and the use of the private sector to carry out what previously were public functions, it is more difficult to discern a public interest, to identify any specific institutions that should represent it, and to decide how decisions about the production and allocation of public goods should be made. Globalization produces winners and losers, in rich countries (Thomas, 2000) as well as poor countries (Darian-Smith, 2000); and losers, rejecting loyalty and denied exit, may voice their views in a variety of ways, often conditioned but not necessarily constrained by their national political systems. Indeed, globalization itself has provided some of the means for the creation of new transnational social movements, for example through the Internet, and these movements themselves, regardless of their politics, foster increased globalization (Keck and Sikkink, 1998; O'Brien, Goetz, Scholte, and Williams, 2000).

The intensity of the discourse about democracy seems to be correlated with the degree of institutional, normative, and social integration of international institutions: in the context of economic globalization, the key triggering element was the strengthening of the WTO, notably its judicial function (Stein, 2001). The Washington Consensus of the 1980s and 1990s, based on liberalization, deregulation, and privatization, has collapsed, at least to the extent that the current Post-Washington Consensus "has added civil society, social capital, capacity building, governance, transparency, a new international economic architecture, institution building, and safety nets" (Higgott, 2000: 139–40). As Higgott (2000: 152) notes, however, the Post-Washington Consensus remains sadly deficient. First, it does not have a sufficient theory of politics, and second it is not underpinned by any ethical theory of justice. Management, not legitimate (and legitimacy) political contest, remains the predominant vision of global governance. This perspective is totally inadequate to address the questions in the current debate. More broadly, especially among people who never accepted the Washington Consensus in the first place, this has given rise to a fierce debate about the emergence and role of global civil society (Anheier, Glasius, and Kaldor, 2001). The collapse of the WTO ministerial conference in Seattle in 1999 was followed by a series of parallel summits. The best known was the first World Social Forum (WSF) in January 2001 in Porto Alegre, Brazil, followed by a second WSF the following year, a third in 2003 and a fourth planned for Mumbai, India, in January 2004.

What does democracy mean in the context of the legal forms, regimes, and institutions of today? Who should participate in decision making, and how? How should decision making be structured? A crucial issue is the disparities of political power that inform and shape legal relationships (see Likosky, 2002). Arguing that global social exchanges should be named "postmodern colonialism," Silbey (1997) urges further efforts to identify connections between law and power and thus make justice more probable. The current system is unbalanced in favor of countries, organizations, and individuals who can afford technical and in particular legal expertise, even though, as Dezalay and Garth (2002) show, imported expertise is profoundly shaped by local power struggles.

Aman (1998) argues that, confronted with a globalizing state, courts and lawmakers need to recognize the continuing delegation of power to the private sector, and develop new forms of accountability to preserve a public voice. In this respect, "public" international law needs serious rethinking. In addition, an important role will be played by NGOs. Often described as the emergence of global civil society, NGOs play such an important role in fields such as development aid, sports, human rights, and the environment that they have become a competitor of the state in legal as well as factual terms, and such nonstate interests should be recognized in international law (Hobe, 1997). They should be granted an international legal status, while at the same time there should be a global legal framework to structure their participation and make them accountable (Nowrot, 1999). They should also be given an increased role in the legislative, executive, and judicial branches of the WTO (Charnowitz, 2000). What is important is to establish basic principles to ensure effective participation in the new global public sphere: they include transparency, accountability, responsibility, and participation and empowerment (Picciotto, 2001).

How should global governance be organized? Reforms of global governance must go further than simply rebalancing access to expertise and structuring NGO participation in decision making (see Charnowitz, 2002). The "insider" culture of international organizations, including the WTO, remains a major obstacle (Howse, 2002). One necessary step forward is a continuing debate on global equity, ethics, and justice, for example regarding the global distribution of food. Another is serious research on the role of law in achieving the necessary reforms of global governance. Unfortunately the WTO does not participate in the Global Compact, proposed by UN Secretary-General Kofi Annan and launched in July 2000 to disseminate best practices on human rights, labor, and the environment. In addition, internal administrative and procedural reforms of the WTO, and perhaps other international institutions, are required (Stein, 2001: 531–4). Whether such forms of global governance should be "constitutionalized," and indeed what "constitutionalization" means in this context, remain highly controversial (see Petersmann, 1998; Howse and Nicolaidis, 2001). Global constitution making is a highly political and risky exercise in a pluralistic world, not just because it might fail but because, as articulated so far, it tends to assume incorrectly that "the best comes from the West."

A better way forward is to build on the existing diversity of legal forms, institutions, expertise, different forms of participation, and legal cultures, but also to strengthen coordination among international institutions, institutionally, normatively, and in terms of dispute resolution processes. In a world of increasing legal pluralism, this could link together a plurality of sites of a soft web of global governance.

Note

I am grateful to the following for their contributions to this chapter: Stéphane Arnaud, Laurence Henry, Frédérique Pellaton-Capitani, Austin Sarat, Anne-Lise Strahtmann, Magda Tovar-Gomis, Eve Truilhé, Lina Tzankova, and the staff of the libraries at the Centre de Recherches Internationales et Communautaires (CERIC), the London School of Economics, and the Wissenschaftskolleg zu Berlin (Institute for Advanced Study). I wish also to thank the Globalization Working Group at the Wissenschaftskolleg zu Berlin, (Institute for Advanced Study), where I was a Fellow during the 2000–1 academic year.

References

Abbott, K.W. and Snidal, D. (2000) "Hard law and soft law in international governance," *International Organization* 54: 421–56.

Abbott, K.W., Keohane, R.O., Moravcsik, A., Slaughter, A.-M., and Snidal, D. (2000) "The concept of legalization," *International Organization* 54: 401–19.

Aman, A.C., Jr., (1998) "The globalizing state: A future-oriented perspective on the public/private distinction, federalism, and democracy," *Vanderbilt Journal of Transnational Law* 31: 769–870.

Anheier, H., Glasius, M., and Kaldor, M. (eds.) (2001) *Global Civil Society 2001*. Oxford: Oxford University Press.

Appelbaum, R.P., Felstiner, W., and Gessner, V. (eds) (2001) *Rules and Networks: The Legal Culture of Global Business Transactions*. Oxford: Hart Publishing.

Arnaud, A.-J. (1998) *Entre modernité et mondialisation: Cinq leçons d'histoire de la philosophie du droit et de l'Etat*. Paris: L.G.D.J.

Bermann, G.A., Herdegen, M., and Lindseth, P.L. (eds.) (2000) *Transatlantic Regulatory Cooperation: Legal Problems and Political Prospects*. Oxford: Oxford University Press.

Blomley, N., Delaney, D., and Ford, R.T. (2001) *The Legal Geographies Reader*. Oxford: Blackwell.

Bonell, M.J. (1994) *An International Restatement of Contract Law: The UNIDROIT Principles of International Commercial Contracts*. New York: Transnational Juris Publications, Inc.

Bontrager Unzicker, A.D. (2000) "From corruption to cooperation: Globalization brings a multilateral agreement against foreign bribery," *Indiana Journal of Global Legal Studies* 7: 655–86.

Bourdieu, P. (1987) "The force of law: Toward a sociology of the juridical field," *The Hastings Law Journal* 38: 814–53.

Braithwaite, J. and Drahos, P. (2000) *Global Business Regulation*. Cambridge, UK: Cambridge University Press.

Bratton, W, McCahery, J., Picciotto, S., and Scott, C. (eds.) (1996) *International Regulatory Competition and Coordination: Perspectives on Economic Regulation in Europe and the United States*. Oxford: Clarendon Press.

Capeller, W. (2001) "Not such a neat net: Some comments on virtual criminality," *Social & Legal Studies* 10: 229–42.

Casella, A. (1996) "On market integration and the development of institutions: The case of international commercial arbitration," *European Economic Review* 40: 155–86.

Charnowitz, S. (2000) "Opening the WTO to nongovernmental interests," *Fordham International Law Journal* 24: 173–216.

Charnowiz, S. (2002) *Trade Law and Global Governance*. London: Cameron May Ltd.

Chayes, A. and Chayes, A.H. (1995) *The New Sovereignty: Compliance with International Regulatory Agreements*. Cambridge, MA: Harvard University Press.

Chemillier-Gendreau, M. and Moulier Boutang, Y. (eds.) (2001) *Le droit dans la mondialisation (Actes du congrès Marx International II)*. Paris: Presses Universitaires de France.

CREDIMI (Centre de Recherche sur le Droit des Marchés et des Investissements Internationaux, Université de Grenoble, France) (2000) *Soveraineté étatique et marches internationaux à la fin du XXè siècle, A propos de 30 ans de recherché du CREDIMI, Mélanges offerts à Philippe Kahn*. Paris: Litec.

Cutler, A.C. (2001) "Globalization, the rule of law, and the modern law merchant: Medieval or late capitalist associations?" *Constellations* 8: 480–502.

Cutler, A.C., Haufler, V., and Porter, T. (eds.) (1999) *Private Authority and International Affairs*. Albany: State University of New York Press.

Darian-Smith, E. (1998) "Power in paradise: The political implications of Santos's utopia," *Law & Social Enquiry* 23(Winter): 81–120.

Darian-Smith, E. (2000) "Structural inequalities in the global legal system," *Law & Society Review* 34: 809–28.

De Ly, F. (1992) *International Business Law and Lex Mercatoria*. Dordrecht: North Holland.

Delmas-Marty, M. (1998) *Trois defis pour un droit mondial*. Paris: Editions du Seuil.

Dezalay, Y. and Garth, B.G. (2002) *The Internationalization of Palace Wars: Lawyers, Economists, and the Contest to Tranform Latin America*. Chicago: University of Chicago Press.

Drummonds, H.H. (2000) "Transnational small and emerging business in a world of Nikes and Microsofts," *Journal of Small and Emerging Business Law* 4: 249–306.

Fidler, D.P. (1999) "Neither science nor shamans: Globalization of markets and health in the developing world," *Indiana Journal of Global Legal Studies* 7: 191–224.

Friedman, L.M. (2001) "Erewhon: The coming global legal order," *Stanford Journal of International Law* 37: 347–64.

Friedman, T.L. (1999) *The Lexus and the Olive Tree*. New York: Farrar, Strauss, and Griroux.

Garth, B. and Dezalay, Y. (1996) *Dealing in Virtue: International Commercial Arbitration and the Construction of a Transnational Legal Order*. Chicago: University of Chicago Press.

Gessner, V. and Budak, A.C. (1998) *Emerging Legal Certainty: Empirical Studies on the Globalization of Law*. Aldershot, UK: Dartmouth, for the Oñati International Institute for the Sociology of Law, 1998).

Giddens, A. (1990) *The Consequences of Modernity*. Cambridge, UK: Polity Press.

Graham, E.M. and Richardson, J.D. (eds.) (1997) *Global Competition Policy*. Washington, DC: Institute for International Economics.

Hall, P.A. and Soskice, D. (2001) *Varieties of Capitalism: The Institutional Foundations of Comparative Advantage*. Oxford: Oxford University Press.

Hardt, M. and Negri, A. (2000) *Empire*. Cambridge, MA: Harvard University Press.

Haufler, V. (1999) "Self-regulation and business norms: Political risk, political activism," in A.C. Cutler, V. Haufler, and T. Porter (eds.), *Private Authority and International Affairs*. Buffalo: State University of New York Press, pp. 199–222.

Held, D., McGrew, A., Goldblatt, D., and Perraton, J. (1999) *Global Transformations: Politics, Economics and Culture*. Cambridge, UK: Polity Press.

Hellwig, J.F. (2000) "The retreat of the state? The Massachusetts Burma Law and local empowerment in the context of globalization(s)," *Wisconsin International Law Journal* 18: 477–510.

Hepple, B. (1999) "A race to the top? International investment guidelines and corporate codes of conduct," *Comparative Labor Law and Policy Journal* 20: 347–63.

Higgott, R. (2000) "Contested globalization: The changing context and normative challenges," *Review of International Studies* 26: 131–53.

Hirst, P. and Thompson, G. (1996) *Globalization in Question: The International Economy and the Possibilities of Governance*. Cambridge, UK: Polity Press.

Hobe, S. (1997) "Global challenges to statehood: The increasing important role of non-governmental organizations," *Indiana Journal of Global Legal Studies* 5: 191–209.

Hopt, K.J., Kanda, H., Roe, M., Wymeersch, E., and Prigge, S. (eds.) (1998) *Comparative Corporate Governance: The State of the Art and Emerging Research*. Oxford: Clarendon Press.

Howse, R. (2002) "From politics to technocracy – and back again: The fate of the multilateral trading regime," *American Journal of Comparative Law* 96: 94–117.

Howse, R. and Nicolaidis, K. (2001) "Legitimacy and global governance: Why constitutionalizing the WTO is a step too far," in R.B. Porter, P. Sauvé, A. Subramanian, and A. Beviglia-Zampetti (eds.), *Efficiency, Equity, and Legitimacy: The Multilateral Trading System at the Millennium*. Washington, DC: Brookings Institution Press, pp. 227–52.

Jayasuriya, K. (1999) "Globalization, law and the transformation of sovereignty: The emergence of global regulatory governance," *Indiana Journal of Global Legal Studies* 6: 425–55.

Jayasuriya, K. (2001) "Globalization, sovereignty, and the rule of law: From political to economic constitutionalism?" *Constellations* 8: 442–60.

Jost, T.S. (2000) "The globalization of health law: The case of permissibility of placebo-based research," *American Journal of Law and Medicine* 26: 175–86.

Kahler, M. (2000) "Conclusion: The causes and consequences of legalization," *International Organization* 54: 661–83.

Kahn, P. (1989) "Les principes généraux de droit devant les arbitres du commerce international," *Journal du droit international* 1989: 305–27.

Keck, M.E. and Sikkink, K. (1998) *Activists Beyond Borders: Advocacy Networks in International Politics*. Ithaca, NY: Cornell University Press.

Klein, N. (2000) *No Logo: Taking Aim at the Brand Bullies*. London: Flamingo.

Keohane, R.O., Moravcsik, A., and Slaughter, A.-M. (2000) "Legalized dispute resolution: Interstate and transnational," *International Organization* 54: 457–88.

Krasner, S. (1999) *Sovereignty: Organized Hypocrisy*. Princeton, NJ: Princeton University Press.

Lessig, L. (1999) *Code and Other Laws of Cyberspace*. New York: Basic Books.

Likosky, M. (ed.) (2002) *Transnational Legal Processes: Globalisation and Power Disparities*. London: Butterworths LexisNexis.

Lipson, C. (1991) "Why are some international agreements informal?," *International Organization* 45: 495–538.

Marks, G. (2001) *Multi-level Governance and European Integration*. Boulder, CO: Rowman & Littlefield.

McCahery, J., Picciotto, S., and Scott, C. (1993) *Corporate Control and Accountability: Changing Structures and the Dynamics of Regulation*. Oxford: Clarendon Press.

Meidinger, E. (2001) "Emerging trans-sectoral regulatory structures in global civil society: The case of ISEAL (the International Social and Environmental Accreditation and Labelling Alliance)," Paper prepared for the "Tools for Regulation" Panel, Joint Annual Meetings of the Law and Society Association and the Research Committee for the Sociology of Law, July 4–7 2001, Budapest, Hungary; revised Draft 1.2 available at <http://law.buffalo.edu/homepage/eemeid/scholarship/ISEAL.pdf>.

Mytelka, L.K. and Delapierre, M. (1999) "Strategic partnerships, knowledge-based network oligopolies, and the state," in A.C. Cutler, V. Haufler and T. Porter (eds.) *Private Authority and International Affairs*. Buffalo: State University of New York Press, pp. 129–49.

Nixon, F. (1987) "Controlling the transnationals? The UN code of conduct," in Y. Ghai, R. Luckham, and F. Snyder (eds.), *The Political Economy of Law: A Third World Reader*. Delhi: Oxford University Press, pp. 416–24.

Nowrot, K. (1999) "Legal consequences of globalization: The status of non-governmental organizations under international law," *Indiana Journal of Global Legal Studies* 6: 579–645.

O'Brien, R., Goetz, A.M., Scholte, J.A., and Williams, M. (2000) *Contesting Global Governance: Multilateral Economic Institutions and Global Social Movements*. Cambridge, UK: Cambridge University Press.

Petersmann, E.-U. (1998) "How to constitutionalize international law and foreign policy for the benefit of civil society?" *Michigan Journal of International Law* 20: 1–30.

Picciotto, S. (1992) *International Business Taxation: A Study in the Internationalization of Business Regulation*. London: Weidenfeld & Nicolson.

Picciotto, S. (1996–7) "Networks in international economic integration: Fragmented states and the dilemmas of neo-liberalism," *Northwestern Journal of International Law & Business* 17: 1014–56.

Picciotto, S. (2000) "North Atlantic cooperation and democratizing globalism," in G.A. Bermann, M. Herdegen, and P.L. Lindseth (eds.), *Transatlantic Regulatory Cooperation: Legal Problems and Political Prospects*. Oxford: Oxford University Press, pp. 495–519.

Picciotto, S. (2001) "Democratizing globalism," in D. Drache (ed.), *The Market or the Public Domain: Global Governance and the Asymmetry of Power*. London: Routledge, pp. 335–59.

Pollack, M.A. and Shaffer, G. (ed.) (2001) *Transatlantic Governance in the Global Economy*. Lanham, MD: Rowman & Littlefield.

Quiggin, J. (2001) "Globalization and economic sovereignty," *The Journal of Political Philosophy* 9: 56–80.

Riles, A. (2002) "The virtual sociality of rights: The case of 'women's rights are human rights'," in M. Likosky (ed.), *Transnational Legal Processes: Globalisation and Power Disparities*. London: Butterworths LexisNexis, pp. 420–39.

Risse, T., Ropp, S., and Sikkink, K. (eds.) (1999) *The Power of Human Rights: International Norms and Domestic Change*. Cambridge, UK: Cambridge University Press.

Robertson, R. (1992) *Globalization: Social Theory and Global Culture*. London: Sage.

Romano, C. (1999) "The proliferation of international judicial bodies: The pieces of the puzzle," *New York University Journal of International Law and Politics* 31(4): 709–51.

Salter, L. (1999) "The standards regime for communication and information technologies," in A.C. Cutler, V. Haufler, and T. Porter (eds.), *Private Authority and International Affairs*. Buffalo: State University of New York Press, pp. 97–127.

Santos, B. de Sousa (1995) *Toward a New Common Sense: Law, Science and Politics in the Paradigmatic Transition*. New York: Routledge.

Sassen, S. (1996) *Losing Control? Sovereignty in an Age of Globalization*. New York: Columbia University Press.

Sassen, S. (2000) "The locational and institutional embeddedness of the global economy," in G.A. Bermann, M. Herdegen, and P.L. Lindseth (eds.), *Transatlantic Regulatory Cooperation: Legal Problems and Political Prospects*. New York: Oxford University Press, pp. 47–97.

Sassen, S. (2002) "Opening remarks: Producing the transnational inside the national," in M. Likosky (ed.), *Transnational Legal Processes: Globalisation and Power Disparities*. London: Butterworths LexisNexis, pp. 189–96.

Scott, C. (ed.) (2001) *Torture as Tort: Comparative Perspectives on the Development of Transnational Human Rights Litigation*. Oxford: Hart Publishing.

Sell, S.K. (1999) "Multinational corporations as agents of change: The globalization of intellectual property rights," in A.C. Cutler, V. Haufler, and T. Porter (eds.), *Private*

Authority and International Affairs. Buffalo: State University of New York Press, pp. 169–97.

Sengenberger, W. and Campbell, D. (1994) *International Labour Standards and Economic Interdependence (Essays in commemoration of the 75th anniversary of the International Labour Organisation and the 50th anniversary of the Declaration of Philadelphia)*. Geneva: International Labour Organisation.

Shaffer, G. (2000) "Globalization and social protection: The impact of EU and international rules in the ratcheting up of U.S. privacy standards," *Yale Journal of International Law* 25: 1–88.

Shaffer, G. (2001) "The World Trade Organization under challenge: Democracy and the law and politics of the WTO's treatment of trade and environmental matters," *Harvard Environmental Law Review* 25: 1–93.

Shapiro, M. (1993) "The globalization of law," *Indiana Journal of Global Legal Studies* 37: 37–64.

Shelton, D. (ed.) (2000) *Commitment and Compliance – The Role of Non-Binding Norms in the International Legal System*. Oxford: Oxford University Press.

Silbey, S.S. (1997) " 'Let them eat cake': Globalization, postmodern colonialism, and the possibilities of justice," *Law and Society Review* 31: 207–36.

Sinclair, T.J. (1994) "Passing judgment: Credit rating processes as regulatory mechanisms of governance in the emerging world order," *Review of International Political Economy* 1: 133–59.

Slaughter, A.-M. (1997) "The real new world order," *Foreign Affairs* 75(5): 183–97.

Slaughter, A.-M. (2000) "Agencies on the loose? Holding government networks accountable," in G.A. Bermann, M. Herdegen, and P.L. Lindseth (eds.), *Transatlantic Regulatory Cooperation: Legal Problems and Political Prospects*. New York: Oxford University Press, pp. 521–46.

Snyder, F. (1993) "The effectiveness of European Community law: Institutions, processes, tools and techniques," *Modern Law Review* 56: 19–54.

Snyder, F. (1999) "Governing economic globalisation: Global legal pluralism and European law," *European Law Journal* 5: 334–74; slightly shorter version published in M. Likosky (ed.), *Transnational Legal Processes: Globalisation and Power Disparities*. London: Butterworths LexisNexis, 2002, pp. 65–97.

Snyder, F. (2000) "Europeanisation and globalisation as friends and rivals: European Union law in global economic networks," in F. Snyder, *The Europeanisation of Law: The Legal Effects of European Intergration*. Oxford: Hart Publishing, pp. 294–320.

Snyder, F. (2001) "The origins of the 'nonmarket economy': Ideas, pluralism and power in EC antidumping law about China," *European Law Journal* 7: 369–424.

Sobczak, A. (2001) "Réseaux de sociétés et codes de conduite: Un nouveau modèle de regulation des relations de travail pour les entreprises européennes," PhD thesis, European University Institute, Florence.

Stein, E. (2001) "International integration and democracy: No love at first sight," *American Journal of International Law* 95: 489–534.

Symposium Issue (1996–7) "The inaugural Engelberg conference on the culture and economics of participation in an international intellectual property regime," *New York University Journal of International Law and Economics* 29.

Teubner, G. (1983) "Substantive and reflexive elements in modern law," *Law & Society Review* 17: 239–85.

Teubner, G. (1993) *Law as an Autopoietic System*. Oxford: Blackwell. (Originally published as *Recht als autopoietisches System*, Frankfurt, 1989.)

Teubner, G. (1997a) "Global Bukowina: Legal pluralism in the world society," in G. Teubner (ed.), *Global Law Without a State*. Aldershot, UK: Dartmouth, pp. 3–28.

Teubner, G. (1997b) "Breaking frames: The global interplay of legal and social systems," *American Journal of Comparative Law* 45: 149–69.

Teubner, G. (ed.) (1997c) *Global Law Without a State*. Aldershot, UK: Dartmouth.

Thomas, C. (2000) "Globalization and the reproduction of hierarchy," *University of California at Davis Law Review* 33: 1451–501.

Trebilcock, M.J. and Howse, R. (1999) *The Regulation of International Trade*, 2nd edn. New York: Routledge.

Trubek, D.M., Dezalay, Y., Buchanan, R., and Davis, J.R. (1994) "Global restructuring and the law: Studies of the internationalization of legal fields and the creation of transnational arenas," *Case Western Reserve Law Review* 44: 407–98

Twining, W. (2000) *Globalalisation and Legal Theory*. London: Butterworths.

Wiener, J.B. (2001) "Something borrowed or something blue: Legal transplants and the evolution of global environmental law," *Ecology Law Quarterly* 27: 1295–371.

Zumbansen, P. (2002) "Piercing the legal veil: Commercial arbitration and transnational law," *European Law Journal* 8: 400–32.

Further Reading

Abel, R.L. (1994) "Transnational legal practice," *Case Western Research Law Review* 44: 737–870.

Appelbaum, R.P. (1998) "The future of law in a global economy," *Social & Legal Studies* 7: 171–92.

Cioffi, J.W. (2000) "State of the art: A review essay on comparative corporate governance: The state of the art and emerging research," *American Journal of Comparative Law* 48: 501–34.

Diller, J.M. and Levy, D.A. (1997) "Child labor, trade and investment: Toward the harmonization of international law" *American Journal of Comparative Law* 94: 663–96.

Dinwoodie, G.B. (2000) "A new copyright order: Why national courts should create global norms," *University of Pennsylvania Law Review* 149: 469–580.

Fidler, D.P. (1997) "The globalization of public health: Emerging infectious diseases and international relations," *Indiana Journal of Global Legal Studies* 5: 11–51.

Gilson, R. (2001) "Globalizing corporate governance: Convergence of form or function," *American Journal of Comparative Law* 49: 329–57.

Goldmann, B. (1979) "La lex mercatoria dans les contrats et l'arbitrage internationaux: réalité et perspectives," *Journal du Droit International*, Juillet-Août-Septembre: 475–505.

Jones, C.A.G. (1994) "Capitalism, globalization and rule of law: An alternative trajectory of legal change in China," *Social & Legal Studies* 3: 195–221.

Marsden, C.T. (2001) "Cyberlaw and international political economy: Towards regulation of the global information society," *Law Review of Michigan State University Detroit College of Law*, Summer: 355–414

Mazlish, B. (1999) "A tour of globalization," *Indiana Journal of Global Legal Studies* 7: 5–16.

Ohmae, K. (1995) *The End of the Nation State*. New York: Free Press.

Pape, W. (1999) "Socio-cultural differences and international competition law," *European Law Journal* 5: 438–60.

Peng, S.Y. (2000) "The WTO legalistic approach and East Asia: From the legal culture perspective," *Asian-Pacific Law & Policy Journal* 1: 13–35.

Petito, D.S. (20001) "Sovereignty and globalization: Fallacies, truth, and perception," *New York Law School Journal of Human Rights* 17: 1139–72.

Rotman, E. (2000) "The globalization of criminal violence," *Cornell Journal of Law and Public Policy* 10: 1–43.

Sattar, I.M. (1997) "The UNIDROIT principles of international commercial contracts and the WTO: Between an 'international restatement' and a 'globalization' of contract law" [review article on Bonell, 1994 above], *Indiana Journal of Global Legal Studies* 5: 375–88.

Slaughter, A.-M. (1995) "International law in a world of liberal states," *European Journal of International Law* 6: 503–38.

Slaughter-Burley, A.-M. (1993) "International law and international relations theory: A dual agenda," *American Journal of International Law* 87: 205–39.

Steiner, H. and Alston, P. (2000) *International Human Rights in Context – Law, Politics, Morals*, 2nd edn. Oxford: Oxford University Press.

Upham, F. (1994) "Speculations on legal informality: On Winn's 'Relational practices and the marginalization of law'," *Law & Society Review* 28: 233–41.

von Struensee, V. (2002) "Sex trafficking: A plea for action," *European Law Journal* 6: 379–407.

Winn, J.K. (1994) "Relational practices and the marginalization of law: A study of the informal financial practices of small businesses in Taiwan," *Law & Society Review* 28: 193–232.

Index

and bail system 313–14
comparative studies 171, 177–9
and decision making 34, 36–7, 96, 171, 177, 184–7, 275, 311
and juries 43–4, 196, 200
and law and politics 274–6, 280
lay 197
limitations on judicial power 183–4
and mass media 100
methodology 174–5
research issues 36–7, 171–2
selection and retention 171, 175–9, *178*, 297, 517
and social science role 410–29
theory 173–4
see also courts
juries 97, 195–208
  and attitudes 203
  and bias 195–6, 198–9, 207, 423–4
  civil 197, 198, 199, 200, 203, 205, 206–7
  criminal 197–8, 199, 200, 207
  in current debate 198–9
  de mediatate linguae 196
  and death penalty 199, 202, 203, 206, 423–4
  in early studies 33, 200–1
  future research 207–8
  and group decision processes 43–4, 204–5
  historical and comparative study 196–9
  and judges 43–4, 196, 200
  reform 205–7
  research findings 43–5, 202–4, 206, 207–8
  selection 199, 203–4, 205–6
  simulation methodology 201–2, 204–5
  size 202, 205
  women and minorities on 199, 203, 206
jurisprudence
  backlash 271–5, 278, 279–82, 283–6, 334–5, 516
  liberal 271–6
  outsider 271–3, 274, 276–9, 280–1, 287
jurors *see* juries
justice
  actuarial 296–7
  conciliatory 570
  and critical lawyers 161
  distributive 65, 436, 437–40
  and human rights 590–3
  and poverty 330–47
  procedural 87, 397, 435–49
  and relative deprivation 437
  research 437–43

as socially constructed 436
substantive 32, 38, 65, 69, 76, 533
transitional 581, 582, 599–601
see also criminal justice; inequality

Kagan, Robert A. 49
Kahn, Alfred 224
Kahn, Paul W. 555–6
Kahn, Ronald 185
Kalven, Harry Jr. and Zeisel, Hans 44, 45, 117, 200, 202, 204–5
Kant, Immanuel 395
Kaplan, M. 495–6
Katsh, Ethan M. 91
Katz, Jonathan N. 488–9
Katz, M.B. 338, 345
Katzenbach v. McClung 282
Keck, M.E. and Sikkink, K. 73, 511, 515
Kelsen, Hans 533
Kennedy, Anthony 176
Kennedy, J.F. 316, 332
Kennedy, Robert 323 n.5
Keohane, R.O., Moravcsik, A., and Slaughter, A.-M. 631
Kerner Commission (US) 332, 529
Kieslowski, Krzysztof 103
King, Gary, Keohane, Robert O., and Verba, Sidney 173
King, Rodney 99, 142
Kitzinger, Carol 489
Klein, Naomi 379, 381
Knight, Jack and Epstein, Lee 187
knowledge
  and ideology 81, 86
  local 19, 118, 315, 404
  and power 20, 147, 317, 376, 412, 535–6, 548
Korean Republic, and selection of judges 177
Kozinski, Judge 419, 420, 423
Krasner, S. 626
Kritzer, H.M. 159–60
Kuhn, Thomas 418, 601
kulturkampf 272, 283
Kumho Tire 419
Kymlicka, Will 65, 362–3

labor market, and inequality 330, 338–40, 341, 343, 345
LaFave, Wayne 312, 323 n.4
Landy, David and Aronson, Ellott 201–2
Langdell, Christopher 151
Lange, David 370